World Music

Volume 2: Latin & North America, Caribbean, India, Asia and Pacific

THE ROUGH GUIDE

Other Rough Guides music reference titles:

Music Reference Series

Classical Music • Country • Jazz • Music USA • Opera
Reggae • Rock • World Music 1 (Africa, Europe & Middle East)

Mini Guides

Drum'n'Bass • House • Techno

100 Essential CDs

Blues • Classical Music • Country Music
Opera • Reggae • Rock • Soul • World Music

www.roughguides.com

Cover photos

Front cover: Main image: Mexican dancers; Tinted images (from left): Flaco Jimenez (Texas, USA), Caetano Veloso (Brazil), Nusrat Fateh Ali Khan (Pakistan), Celia Cruz (Salsa, USA).
Back cover (from top): Nenes (Japan), Ravi Shankar (India), Ibrahim Ferrer (Cuba), Queen Ida (Zydeco, USA).

Rough Guide credits

Editors: Mark Ellingham, Orla Duane, James McConnachie
Proofreading: Elaine Pollard, Russell Walton
Photo research: Vanessa Kelly
Cover Design: Peter Dyer
Design: Henry Iles
Image Scanning: Scanplus Ltd
Typesetting: Helen Ostick, Katie Pringle, Judy Pang
Production: Julia Bovis, Michelle Draycott, Maxine Repath

Editors' acknowledgements

The editors would like to thank: all of the contributors for their hard work over a prolonged period, in particular Kim Burton for her help on many of the discographies; Jak Kilby for delivering large boxes of exactly the right photos; Ian Anderson, editor of *Folk Roots*, for making available the magazine's extraordinary archive; Andy Morgan for preparing the appendix on record stores; Thomas Brooman and WOMAD for their inspiration over the years; all of the many record labels and distributors who responded to strings of requests; James, Orla and all those on the project at Rough Guides (especially Judy, Helen, Katie, Michelle and Susanne); Jessica Gill for all the index-tagging; and Henry Iles for design and scanning. Simon thanks Kate (and welcomes Max) and Mark thanks Nat (and Miles) for their forbearance over the processing of a million-odd words.

Publishing details

Published August 2000 by Rough Guides Ltd, 62-70 Shorts Gardens, London WC2H 9AB.
Distributed by the Penguin Group:
Penguin Books Ltd, 27 Wrights Lane, London W8 5TZ
Penguin Putnam, Inc., 375 Hudson Street, New York 10014, USA
Penguin Books Australia Ltd, 487 Maroondah Highway, PO Box 257, Ringwood,
     Victoria 3134, Australia
Penguin Books Canada Ltd, 10 Alcorn Avenue, Toronto, Ontario, Canada M4V 1E4
Penguin Books (NZ) Ltd, 182–190 Wairau Road, Auckland 10, New Zealand

Typeset in Bembo and Helvetica to an original design by Henry Iles.
Printed in Spain by Graphy Cems.

A catalogue record for this book is available from the British Library.
ISBN 1-85828-636-0

Volume 1: a correction

The editors apologise to Dr Laudan Nooshin, author of the article on Iranian music in Volume 1 of this book, for two editorial changes which were made without reference to her. These are the title ('Nightingales and Mullahs') on p.355, and the use of the word 'exile' in the phrases 'exile communities' and 'exile social gathering' on p.360. The editors and publishers wish to make it clear that there was no intention to cause offence.

World Music

Volume 2: Latin & North America, Caribbean, India, Asia and Pacific

THE ROUGH GUIDE

Edited by

Simon Broughton and Mark Ellingham

with

James McConnachie and Orla Duane

Contents

Part Two • The Americas
(Latin America, North America, Caribbean)

Part Three • Directories

Introduction

It's fitting that this new edition of the **Rough Guide to World Music** is published at the start of a new millennium, for it deals with the oldest and newest music in the world – from centuries-old traditions to contemporary fusions. It includes the most sacred and profound music and the most frivolous and risqué, music of healing, music of protest, the loudest music you'll ever hear, the softest and most intimate, and maybe also the most moving and enjoyable.

The *Guide* sets itself a clearly impossible task: to document and explain the popular, folk and (excluding the Western canon) classical music traditions around the globe. However, since the first edition appeared in 1994 it has been the chief handbook for beginners and enthusiasts alike, and become a resource for those working in the World Music business. In producing a new edition we were aware of shortcomings in the first edition and we have added many new pieces on countries that weren't covered before – The Bahamas, Belize, Canada, Central Asia, Sri Lanka, Tibet and Venezuela, for example, in this volume. Other articles were expanded, revised and rewritten; India, for example, is now covered in seven individual articles, covering the main regional styles.

In addition, the new edition reflects the huge expansion of the whole World Music market over the past five years. There are more concerts and festivals than ever before – and many would say that there is actually a surfeit of CDs. In preparing this edition, we surveyed the lot, completely overhauling our discographies, adding biographical entries for artists, and reviewing and highlighting the best discs available.

That's the main reason why this new edition of the *Rough Guide* is not one book, but two: this volume covers the Americas, Asia and the Pacific, while *Volume One* has Africa, Europe and the Middle East. Even with two books, each volume has turned out longer than the entire first edition.

The articles – from more than eighty contributors – are designed to provide the background to each country's music styles, explaining how they relate to history, social customs, politics and identity, as well as highlighting the lives and sounds of the singers and musicians. We hope you'll find this enriches the whole experience of listening to World Music.

How this book works

This volume is divided into two geographical sections: **Asia and the Pacific** (including India and Australasia), and **The Americas** (including the Caribbean). Within each section the entries are arranged alphabetically by country or genre. There are running heads and an index to help you find your way.

Our **discographies** follow the arrangment of each article and when it makes things clearer by style (for example, the Antilles has sections on zouk and cadence, biguine, chouval bwa, and Dutch Antillean groups). Compilations are listed first and artists follow (listed A-Z), with a brief biography and reviews of their key discs.

Each section has one or two **'star discs'** which are indicated by a larger than usual CD symbol (**◑**). These are the ones to buy first. All other selections are preceded by a CD (◉), cassette (▱) or vinyl (**●**) symbol: those specified as cassette or vinyl are not available on CD but worthwhile. To avoid any conflict of interest, as some of our contributors are involved with bands or labels, selections are the responsibility of the editors.

In the **directories** at the end of the book we've included addresses and Websites of the most important **record labels** releasing the music featured in this volume, as well as the best specialist **shops** to track down CDs and cassettes.

ONE

Asia and the Pacific

Russia
Kazakhstan
Tuva
Mongolia
CENTRAL ASIA
Uzbekistan
Kyrgyzstan
Turkmenistan
Azerbaijan
Tajikistan
N. Korea
S. Korea
Japan
Afghanistan
China
Tibet
Bhutan
Iran
Iraq
Kuwait
Pakistan
Nepal
Qatar
Bangladesh
U.A.E.
Saudi Arabia
Oman
India
Myanmar (Burma)
Laos
Taiwan
Hong Kong
Yemen
Thailand
Vietnam
Cambodia
Philippines
Somalia
Sri Lanka
Brunei
Malaysia
Singapore
Indonesia
Papua New Guinea
Solomon Islands
Tuvalu
POLYNESIA
MELANESIA
Western Samoa
Vanuatu
Cook Islands
Tahiti
Tonga
FRENCH POLYNESIA
Rapa
Australia
POLYNESIA
New Zealand
Hawaii
PACIFIC OCEAN
INDIAN OCEAN

This map is drawn on the Peter's projection which shows the correct relative size of countries

Afghanistan

red light at the crossroads

Afghan music has suffered with the country through its continuing civil war – and since the impositon of fundamentalist Islam by the Taliban government has been effectively silenced at home. Nonetheless, as **Veronica Doubleday** explains, the country has rich traditions which can still be heard in exile and on disc.

After its heyday of liberalisation and hippy-trail tourism in the 1960s and 1970s, Afghanistan became a war zone, and for the last twenty or more years it has been virtually impossible to visit. Nor has much music been played there of late. The trauma of civil war and population displacement put music out of people's minds. For Afghans, music is very much linked with celebration, and it's customary to avoid music when people are in mourning. Added to this is the powerful Islamic anti-music lobby.

After the Soviet troops withdrew in 1992, the new political authorities cracked down heavily on music. As in the early days of Khomeini's revolutionary Iran, no instrumental music was broadcast on the radio or on television. From 1994 the Islamist **Taliban** movement gradually spread from its power base in the southeast, enforcing further bans on public music-making. To show they meant business, the Taliban authorities destroyed musical instruments and videotapes, and occasionally imprisoned musicians caught in the act of playing. All cinemas are now closed; in the past they mainly showed Hindi films packed with songs and dances. The city theatres that once had music and singing on stage have all disappeared too.

Inside Afghanistan the Taliban control three-quarters of the country and the intractable in-fighting continues. One reason is the country's strategic importance at 'the cross-roads of Asia': Afghanistan lies between Iran, the Central Asian republics, and the Indian subcontinent, and its diverse music reflects these different cultural influences.

The **Pashtuns**, to the south and east, are the largest and dominant group. Broadly speaking, their music is highly dramatic, with exciting climaxes and pauses and a strong rhythmic empha-

sis. Speakers of **Afghan Persian (Dari)** inhabit the west, centre and northeast. Much of their music is nostalgic and romantic. In the north, **Turkic** speakers – mainly **Uzbeks** – form a third considerable cultural entity. Their music includes epics and coquettish dance pieces. These various regional styles have also fed into a melting-pot, contributing to two more widely disseminated types of music: Afghan **classical genres** and the **popular music** which used to be broadcast over the air-waves.

Klasik

Afghan **classical music** is known as *klasik*, from the English word. There are several genres: sung poetry, especially **ghazals**, and also instrumental pieces – *naghmehs* and *ragas*. The music is predominantly urban and has close historical links with India and Pakistan. Many of the Kabuli professional 'master-musicians' (known as *ustad*) are directly descended from musicians who came from India to play at the Afghan court in the capital city of Kabul in the 1860s. They maintain cultural and personal ties with India – through discipleship or inter-marriage – and they use the Hindustani musical theories and terminology, for example raga (melodic form) and *tala* (rhythmic cycle).

Many of the main Afghan ragas are also found in India, and the modes more or less correspond. However, in performance Afghan ragas are slightly different, having more emphasis on rhythmic variation than the Indian raga. For rhythmic accompaniment, Indian *tablas* have eclipsed other local drums like the *zirbaghali* (goblet drum), *dohol* (hand-played barrel drum), and *daireh* (frame drum). The Afghan ghazal is a close cousin of the ghazal as sung in Pakistan and North India.

An important and specifically Afghan classical (and general-purpose) instrument is the **rubab**, a short-necked, fretted, plucked lute. Here the Afghans have contributed to Indian music, since the rubab is the forerunner of the Indian *sarod*. (The latter has a steel belly and no frets – a change favouring sliding microtonal effects beloved of Indian music.) Afghans have a special feeling for the rubab,

Rahim Khushnawaz playing Rubab

describing it as the 'lion' of instruments and their 'national instrument'. Its double-chambered body is carved from a single piece of mulberry wood, the lower part covered with skin. It has three main strings and is played with a plectrum of wood, bone or ivory. Its rich, echoing sound comes from its sympathetic strings which vibrate and give a full, resonant quality – dreamy sometimes, or ecstatic. The most famous rubab-player was **Ustad Mohammad Omar** of the Kabuli school, who died in the 1980s. Amongst the most celebrated contemporary players are **Ustad Mohammed Rahim Khushnawaz** from Herat and **Ustad Essa Kassemi**, now resident in Germany.

Kabul was for many years the centre of Afghan classical and popular music, but there the war has taken its toll. Most of the currently available recordings highlight music from Herat in the west – the city where Western musicologists have done most work. While the ragas of the Kabuli style tend to those of North India, the Herati style leans more to Iranian music in its melodic intonation.

Popular Music

Afghan **popular music** is based on singing. It was created at the Kabul radio station in the 1950s when the country first began broadcasting in earnest. In imitation of Indian and European styles, an official radio orchestra was established. This included some Afghan folk instruments, such as the *dutar* and *tanbur* (fretted, plucked lutes) and the bowed *ghichak*. But other, more rural-style instruments, like the *sorna* (shawm), dohol and daireh (drums), were excluded. Indian instruments, like harmonium, tabla drums, *sitar* and *dilruba* (bowed lute), and European instruments including the violin, clarinet and guitar, were also part of this slick, monophonic massed sound.

At **Radio Afghanistan** singers and musicians composed new material and created a specific radio style structured around a verse, chorus and melodically stereotyped instrumental section which usually built up to a climax and then paused precipitously before launching into the next verse – in typical Pashtun style. The textured orchestral backing gave a sound which was hitherto unknown to Afghan music.

Radio Afghanistan played an important role in bringing Afghans together through music and was an influence of social change. The first woman to broadcast on air, in 1951, was **Parwin**, who came from an aristocratic background. Another groundbreaker was **Ahmad Zahir**, the handsome son of a Prime Minister, showing that music could be a vaguely respectable career. Perhaps the most notable singer was **Mahwash**, a woman whose reedy voice and studies in classical music earned

Mahwash in concert

her the official title of 'ustad' (master-musician, yet a woman!). In 1977 she had great success with a popular song called "O bacheh" (Oh boy), devoting each verse to a different area of Afghanistan, and sung in that regional style.

Much of the poetry for Afghani popular songs was formulaic, based invariably on romantic themes, but the music nonetheless achieved real popularity, filtering down to performance through grass-roots local musicians at weddings and amateur gatherings. It was actually a circular process, since radio music, to begin with, was based on elements of local folk music.

Radio-style popular music remains a srong current among Afghans in exile, usually played with harmonium and tabla accompaniment, or sometimes keyboards and drum-machine.

Weddings and Folk Music

In Afghan culture, music plays an important function in advertising and celebrating marriage, with ritual wedding songs bestowing blessings on the bride and groom. Traditionally, weddings were also a prime source of income for professional musicians.

Except in Kabul, marital celebrations were gender-segregated. There were large and rather formal evening gatherings for men, usually in a spacious carpeted courtyard, and chaotic, crowded and very colourful parties for women and hordes of excited children.

Entertaining the men at a city wedding, a male singer would typically accompany himself on the Indian portable harmonium, sitting on a decorated bandstand surrounded by three or four other musicians. The drummer usually played tabla drums, or possibly a barrel-shaped *dhol* (both played with bare hands). The melodic accompanists played local types of lutes like the rubab or *tanbur*. Persian is the *lingua franca* of Afghanistan, and Persian ghazals and popular songs were the regular fare. In Pashtun areas there would be singing in Pashto (the other main language), often by two singers who might be brothers, both playing harmoniums. Sometimes music was punctuated with exuberant rifle-shots in the air. In villages, amateur performers from within the local community would play instruments varying according to region.

On the women's side, continuous singing and dancing would last all evening, most of the night, and throughout the following day. Only the groom and a few close male family members would be admitted to the main rituals – processions and display of gifts – which took place in the bridegroom's

house (where the marriage was also consummated). The bridegroom's sisters and their friends would usually lead the music and dancing, all the surrounding women clapping in time to the rhythm. In some parts female professional musicians would play, but given the strict segregation of the sexes this work was never considered very 'respectable', and in recent years has been completely banned.

All over Afghanistan in the privacy of their homes women play, sing and dance to the sound of a **daireh** – a large tambourine-like frame drum. This particular drum is sanctioned by the scriptures – authentic accounts attest that the Prophet

VERONICA DOUBLEDAY

Bridal procession with daireh

Mohammad listened to the Arab frame drum (called *duff*) with tolerance and pleasure. As the only instrument considered suitable for women, it is indispensable for their music. By far the commonest and cheapest of all instruments, it is made by Gypsy-like specialists known by the derogatory name of 'Jat' who sell the drums from door to door.

Some of the **'Jat' people** are musicians in their own right. The men traditionally work in pairs, always outdoors, playing a piercingly loud, driving music on the **shawm** and a double-headed barrel-drum (dohol) played with two sticks. This duo is often called **sazdohol** (saz simply means 'instrument') and the musicians are ritual specialists with a semi-outcast status – no outsider will touch these instruments. (Gypsies and Gypsy-related groups play this instrumental duo in a wide area stretching from China, Central Asia and North India through Iran, Iraq and Turkey to the Balkans).

The Afghan Jat duos often work as barbers and shave the bridegroom and circumcise boys, as well as playing music for circumcision celebrations and wedding processions. In villages they sometimes accompany men's stick dances (*chub-bazi*) and circle dances (*atan*). In the north they play at a special type of outdoor winter game known as *bozkashi* – 'goat-dragging' – in which a goat carcase is contested by teams of skilled horsemen. Sazdohol players also appear in the streets at religious festivals and at New Year, brashly demanding tips.

The **Afghan New Year** at the spring equinox is traditionally a very important time for music and festivity. Afghans love to celebrate the advent of greenery and warm weather after the bitterly cold winter by going outdoors for mass fairs called *melehs*.

Most famous for this is **Mazar-i Sharif**, the shrine of Ali, in the north. Its forty-day 'tulip festival' with music and healing has its roots in pre-Islamic history. Whether at Mazar or at other shrines or gardens, people love to sit outside playing or listening to music as they drink tea. But recently this has been discouraged by the authorities.

Tea-houses were also important male venues for music-making, especially in the north. On market days musicians would perform epics or popular songs, sitting on a wooden bench or a mud-sculpted platform, sometimes on splendid red carpets. The singer might strum a long-necked lute like the tanbur, or weave a wayward melodic accompaniment on the two-stringed spiked fiddle (ghichak), the whole sound punctuated with the zirbaghali drum or the regular chinking of tiny cymbals. The ghichak is a specifically northern instrument, with a quaint recycled tin-can sound-box and ready-made neck and spike (locally fabricated in Tashqurqan). In the countryside, out in the fields, shepherds often used to while away their hours with the traditional end-blown flute (*ney*), played purely for their own amusement.

Public music-making is currently banned by the Taliban, which means that tea-house performances and the male concert music for weddings cannot now take place inside the country. However, the private, non-professional music-making of the women continues in a low-key, muted way. A cultural reflowering can only come with settled peace.

Poetry and Ghazals

Appreciation of poetic texts is vital to Afghan music. The works of famous poets and Sufi mystics are regularly heard. Household names are **Jalaluddin Rumi**, founder of the Mevlevi Sufi order in the twelfth century, and **Jami**, who lived in Herat in the fifteenth century. Along with poets like Hafez and Bidel, they represent the peak of Persian literature.

In Afghanistan the **ghazal** form, with its characteristic repetitive rhyming scheme, is a particular feature of serious intimate musical gatherings. Afghans very much enjoy the poetry's mystical depth and recherché meanings. For instance, the theme of wine-drinking is an accepted metaphor for spiritual intoxication – sometimes originally evoked to shock the sensitivities of orthodox mullahs. This verse is attributed to Rumi:

In the tavern-dwellers' religion,
the drunken wine-worshippers'
falling down and standing up again

is like the formal Muslims'
five-times-daily prayer.

Folk poetry, composed, performed and transmitted orally, has an immediate freshness and charm. In Persian-speaking areas the quatrain (*charbeiti*) is extremely old. The themes of unrequited love – especially star-crossed lovers – and separation are common, often tinged with mysticism, and thematically close to the classical literary works.

The Pashtuns have a two-line verse form called *landai* or *tappa*. Interestingly, many of these are composed by women, challenging masculine ideals of chivalry and honour. Some are full of sexual passion, where dissatisfied women forced into loveless arranged marriages dare their loved ones to cuckold their hated husbands:

My love, jump into my bed and don't fear anything
If it breaks, my stupid little husband's there
to mend it later!

discography

Below are the pick of the (few) available Afghan CDs. However, for anyone willing to search them out, there are also some (roughly recorded) gems to be found among the cassettes issued by and for Afghan exile communities in Europe and the US. Look out in particular for recordings of Afghanistan's much loved classical singer Ustad Sarahang (who died in the 1980s). He possessed an impressive command of Indian classical style, improvisation and vocal gymnastics with a rich, deep voice, and clarity of spiritual understanding. Other notable singers include Ustad Rahim Bakhsh, Ustad Amir Mohammad and Mahwash.

Compilations

The Traditional Music of Herat
(Audivis/Unesco, France).

A valuable and representative collection of traditional pieces collected over five years of fieldwork in the 1970s. It includes an unaccompanied devotional song recorded in the echoing precincts of the Friday mosque; a passionate Sufi song about a local miracle-working saint, with dutar accompaniment; sazdohol music (rarely represented in commercial recordings); a woman's lullaby and women's singing with frame-drum accompaniment; and fine examples of urban-style music. Extensive informative notes.

Afghanistan: A Journey to an Unknown Musical World (World Network, Germany).

Excellent collection of recordings made in 1974 with the aid of Abdul Wahab Madadi, an expert on Afghan music, both as a music director at Radio Afghanistan for many years and as a fine singer (listen to track 17, a song of unrequited love performed with great vocal precision and agility). With a pronounced emphasis on singing, this compilation covers the various regional styles of Afghanistan. Northern music is especially well represented, plus the remote semi-pagan

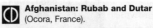

region of Nuristan and a track by deceased rubab master, Ustad Mohammad Omar. Good notes.

Anthology of World Music: Afghanistan (Rounder, US).

Recordings by the finest musicians from Radio Afghanistan in the late 1960s, including the legendary singer Biltun, who accompanies himself on tanbur. A great sample of folk music from different regions, due to be re-issued shortly.

The Living Tradition: Music from Afghanistan (Argo/Decca, UK).

A valuable old (vinyl only) recording of folk music from various regions by expert singers and players, including northern-style pieces by Baba Naim (ghichak) and the amazing drummer Malang on zirbaghali.

Artists

Aziz Herawi

Aziz Herawi is the pseudonym of a fine amateur dutar and rubab player who came from an orthodox religious family which disapproved of music. He claims he learned to play in secret, practising alone in a basement. He now lives in the US.

Memories of Herat: Instrumental Music of Afghanistan (Music of the World, US).

This is a beautifully recorded and engaging collection of classical and folk pieces on the rubab and dutar. Interesting instrumental textures variously accompanied by tabla, goblet drum (played by his son) and frame drum. There are also contributions from ethnomusicologist John Baily (on rubab and Herati folk dutar), and one vocal track by the author of the article above, Veronica Doubleday.

Mohammed Rahim Khushnawaz

Rahim comes from a family of hereditary musicians in Herat and is regarded as one of the city's finest rubab players. He has a soulful depth of interpretation.

Afghanistan: The Rubab of Herat (VDE Gallo/AIMP, Switzerland).

In these recordings from 1974, Rahim turns local folk tunes into exquisite Persian miniatures, and plays two classical pieces ("Rag Bihag" and "Rag Ahir Beiru") with tabla accompaniment by his brother Naim. Good accompanying notes.

Afghanistan: Rubab and Dutar (Ocora, France).

Here Rahim is joined by Gada Mohammad, a long-term fellow-musician who came from an amateur background and is recognised as the finest exponent of the Herati dutar, and by a cousin on tabla (which is under-recorded). The duets and solos include a masterly twenty-minute Rag Beiru by Rahim, as fine an example of Afghan classical instrumental music as you will find, recorded at Radio France in 1995, when these two outstanding musicians came to Europe.

Australia

Aboriginal music

the original songlines

As with many indigenous peoples round the globe, Australian Aboriginal music has become important as a vehicle for expressing their struggles and concerns in their own country, and to the outside world. But the music isn't only meaningful – it is popular. Over the past decade, there's been an explosion of Aboriginal rock and roots bands – Yothu Yindi being the most famous – and they represent a powerful voice. **Marcus Breen** tells the story.

Australian Aboriginal music is one of the newest and most ancient phenomenons on the globe. Australia's indigenous people can boast the oldest intact culture on earth and the resonant sounds of the **didgeridoo** evoke a sacred mythological world that demands respect. Sadly, that is what the Aborigines did not get. From 1788, as Australia was developed as a penal colony for white settlers, the indigenous people were driven off their ancestral lands and resettled, or hunted and killed like animals. Such practices persisted until well into this century, and discrimination has continued, with the recognition of Aboriginal rights a relatively recent development.

The sudden growth of **modern Aboriginal music** has been a consciousness-raising accompaniment to this political movement. In that way it shares many qualities with Native American

Young didgeridoo players on Mornington Island

music, particularly the mystical and sacred attachment to the land that is so much a part of Aboriginal belief. As an expression of that solidarity, Aboriginal and Native American performers (notably the Australian group Yothu Yindi and the American Indian singer John Trudell) have supported each other on concert tours. Bob Mar-

ley, too, has been a huge influence on Aboriginal musicians with his espousal of black power and the struggle for rights.

In the fusion of these musical and spiritual influences with their own black, but not African, traditions the contemporary Aborigines have forged a distinctive new musical voice which is reminding the world that they are, after all, the first Australians. The voice is to be heard in many forms, from the roots sounds of ceremonial music and

dancing to the powerful Aboriginal rock of bands like **Yothu Yindi**.

Yothu Yindi burst on the scene in the early 1990s, and thanks to them identity politics reached Australia's pop charts almost instantly. They went on to become Australia's best-known group, at home and abroad. Like most other Aboriginal

CAAMA, Labels and the Media

The **Central Australian Aboriginal Media Association** (CAAMA) was created in Alice Springs in 1980 with three volunteers and little more than a typewriter and a second-hand car. Today CAAMA broadcasts to all of Central Australia, runs a TV company, and owns a recording and publishing label – the only one run by and for Aboriginal and Torres Strait Islander people.

The Association has been particularly active in recording and releasing music from the remote desert areas. Among the bands that have emerged under CAAMAs auspices, the current stars are **Blek Bala Mujik** (see p.14). Their hit single "Walking Together" became something of a mainstream anthem after being adopted by Qantas, the national airline, in the late 1990s.

Aboriginal music has become a feature of everyday life in Australia. Yet the mainstream recording industry has failed to take Aboriginal music seriously, while media outlets have been reluctant to play anything but hit songs. Rising to this challenge has meant that the Aboriginal music industry has grown alongside the major industry. CAAMA – along with Mushroom and Larrikin Records – have become the preeminent names as promoters and commercial custodians of the recorded Aboriginal sound.

For its part CAAMA has established itself as a nurturing centre for Central Australian singer-songwriters and bush bands, many of which are working on a synthesis of indigenous language, combined with English, country and heavy guitar, traditional clapping sticks, didgeridoo and chants. These include **Chrysophrase**,

North Tanami Band, Young Teenage Band, Warryngya Band, Desert Oaks Band, Areyonga Desert Tigers and **Blackstorm**.

Established artists continue to flourish due to CAAMA's support. Recent releases include **Bart Willoughby**'s *Pathways*, with a softer, radio friendly rock sound, and albums from the rock bands **Buna Lawrie** and **Coloured Stone**.

The CAAMA model has been translated to other bush areas and indigenous broadcasters are already set in the regions of Townsville, Brisbane, Warringarri, Cunnunarra and West Australia. These radio stations have a strong link to music creation and production, as do the network of nearly 200 urban **community radio stations**. Aboriginal music is used extensively on their specialist programmes and it is making waves, too, on national stations such as **ABC's Radio National**. Having tried special Aboriginal programmes on radio and TV which were felt to be patronising, ABC now favours a more integrated approach.

Festivals celebrating all aspects of Aboriginal community life continue to be a focus for music. Many are not easily accessible to outsiders, although it's possible to apply for permits to visit Aboriginal lands in Central Australia, where events are held. Arts Festivals frequently feature Aboriginal music components. Of special note is the **Olympic Arts Festival** which will be taking palce during September–October in Sydney in 2000 and 2001, featuring The Festival of the Dreaming, with indigenous musicians, artists and dancers from around the country.

JAK KILBY

Australian Aboriginal dancers

artists, they perform songs that remind European settlers of the history that has been documented and acknowledged only recently. Their songs make contact with a culture 50,000 years old. Although the group's mainstream popularity has faded of late, they continue to invigorate their local community, taking the lessons learned from musical activism to Aborignal people in various parts of Australia.

Some Background

Since European settlers and convicts arrived in 1788 the story of the Aboriginals and the white settlers has been a one-sided one. It involves the dispossession of land, suppression of language and culture, denial of identity, dispersion and resettlement, the poisoning of water supplies and, as recently as the 1930s, systematic massacres. The indigenous population of Tasmania was virtually eliminated in this unholy process.

In the late nineteenth century Protestant and Roman Catholic missionaries moved into remote parts of Australia to establish mission stations. They rejected the heathen music and culture of the Aboriginals and taught them the hymns of Europe. The strong influence of **gospel singing** can still be heard in Aboriginal women's choirs and in the work of some of the Aboriginal singer-songwriters.

In Australia today there are around 250,000 Aboriginals (1.3 percent of the population) and some 200 surviving languages. As well as the mainland Aborigines there are also the Torres Strait Islanders, of Melanesian descent, inhabiting the islands between the coast of Queensland and Papua New Guinea (with which they share their cultural and musical heritage).

The vast majority of Aboriginals are scattered across the continent in country towns and settlements, with large concentrations in the urban centres of Alice Springs, Darwin, Broome and the Redfern suburb of Sydney. In suburban areas Aboriginals are pretty well integrated into Australian society, although elsewhere there is deprivation, unemployment and alcoholism.

Music has become closely aligned with a power struggle over **land rights** – after all land is the most meaningful aspect of the Aboriginal heritage. And yet as this greatest of all public debates takes place between Australia's indigenous people and their supporters against pastoralists, lease holders of Crown land and mining companies, music has consolidated its place as a cultural glue, holding the people together, taking the message out and educating the public.

Aboriginal artists famously joined together in 1995 to produce a version of "We Are the World", an album of songs called *Our Home Our Land*. Working in Alice Springs at the upgraded recording studios of CAAMA (Central Australian Aboriginal Media Association, see box on previous page), established artists such as Yothu Yindi recorded "Mabo", Sunrize Band "Land Rights" and Tiddas the title track. Yothu Yindi's song was a celebration of the historic 1992 case in which the Australian High Court overturned the so-called *terra nullius* doctrine which regarded the continent as unowned land (meaning that no other colonial power had laid claim to it):

> Terra nullius, terra nullius,
> Terra nullius is dead and gone
> We were right, that we were here
> They were wrong, that we weren't there . . .

Land rights continue to be a rallying cry in Aboriginal and Australian music. In 1997, Peter Garrett, lead singer of the Australian rock band Midnight Oil, released the single "White Skin, Black Heart" together with the (Aboriginal singer-songwriter) Kev Carmody's song, "Thou Shalt Not Steal".

Songlines

An important modern cultural development for Aboriginals was the establishment in 1964 of the Institute of Aboriginal Studies in Canberra, now known as the **Australian Institute of Aboriginal and Torres Strait Islander Studies** (AIATSIS). This has sponsored work in all aspects of traditional Aboriginal life, including, on the music side, an archive of over 7000 hours of indigenous music, gathered from across the country and collected from 1898 to the present. Selections from the archive have been issued on cassette and CD-ROM.

Many Aboriginals have themselves only recently started to appreciate their own music, having grown up on a diet of Western pop and rock. But as their musicians have moved into rock and singer-songwriter formats and gained a universal audience, more and more have wanted to listen to their own people sing about their situation. To Aboriginals this should come as no real surprise for the implicit power of traditional music is recognised as a binding cultural and creative force in their culture.

Aboriginal **creation myths** tell of legendary totemic beings who wandered over the continent in the **Dreamtime**, singing out the name of everything that crossed their path – birds, animals, plants,

The Didgeridoo

The **didgeridoo** (*didjeridu* is the scholarly spelling while *yidaki*, *yiraki*, *magu*, *kanbi* and *ihambilbilg* are among its alternative Aboriginal names) is the traditional instrument unique to Australia's Aboriginals. It is made from the limb of a eucalyptus tree, naturally hollowed out by termites to form a long tube, and is often finely decorated with carvings and symbols. To learn the didgeridoo, players are encouraged to spend time listening to the sounds and spirit of the bush so as to imitate and respect insects, animals and nature. The instrument itself is, of course, a part of nature.

In the notes to his *Ankala* disc, the player **Mark Atkins** tells how to select an instrument: "What you do is go along and recognise the tree. I use a method of knocking on the tree with my ear up against the tree to see if its hollow, and I feel with my hands. Then I look and see how long it is; how far it is to the ground; whether I'll get a good bell on it. Then I'll knock it down to the ground, find an old stump and bang out the termites and the rubbish that's left in there. Then I'll get another hard stick and bang it all over, which loosens the bark, and I'll peel the bark. I'll just scrape that back and then I'll put on an undercoat. That starts the painting process. Some of the didjeridoos will have stories on them. And if you put a story on it you can usually put where it came from and your little journey that day."

Mark Atkins

Originally found amongst the Aboriginal clans of northern Australia, the didgeridoo is now used all over the country – and often by non-Aboriginal performers. Traditionally the didgeridoo was played only by initiat-ed men, selected by tribal elders, and for structured sequences of totems and rhythms at ceremonies. In keeping with this role, the didgeridoo was used with utmost respect, and recently there has been debate in the Aboriginal community about its use by women musicians and – to a greater degree – white Australians. Bearing such sensibilities in mind, Mandawuy Yunupingu of Yothu Yindi consulted elders of the Yirrkala tribe in Arnhem land before the instrument was used in their hit single "Treaty".

Perhaps the two leading Aboriginal players today are Mark Atkins and **Joe Geia**. Their repertoire ranges from traditional to folk rock, and, in the case of Atkins, a "Didgeridoo Concerto". A noted white player of the instrument is **Charlie McMahon**, who worked as adviser to the Kintor people for two years. There he was given access to some of their secret knowledge and, combining this with his own sensibility, he has brought the music to white audiences with his band **Gondwanaland**.

As the deep vibratory sound of the didgeridoo has become internationally recognised, it has been increasingly used as a resonating sonic signifier for some sort of universal dreamtime in various fusions and collaborations. Some of these might present difficulties for purists, but in the hands of players like **David Hudson** and **Johnny Soames** the instrument is finding new listeners. The aura and resonances of the continent the instrument carries means the didgeridoo will never lose its place as the instrument that best reflects the Aboriginals' 50,000 years of tradition and experience

rocks, waterholes – and so singing the world into existence. The **songlines** are paths which can be traced across the continent linking these totemic emblems: sacred objects that have returned to the land – perhaps a lizard, a kangaroo or an outcrop of rocks. Each Aboriginal tribe takes one of these totemic beings as ancestor and thus will have maybe a lizard-Dreaming or a kangaroo-Dreaming or a rain-Dreaming.

Many descriptions of songlines have defined the intangible relationship between Aboriginal music, beliefs and the land. As Yothu Yindi's Mandawuy Yunupingus has explained: "The role of song in Aboriginal, or Yolgnu Creation is what creation is all about. The song is creation. The art is creation. The specialness in that, is that we have a heart and mind connection to mother earth. What is important, is to know and be able to practice the celebration of oneness, to be able to know unity. Songlines is entrenched within the land itself, the journey of the songlines is from the east to the west, the journey is about following the sun."

According to Bruce Chatwin's book *Songlines*, the totemic ancestors are thought to have scattered a trail of words and musical notes along the lines of their Dreaming-tracks. An ancestral song is both a map and direction-finder: "Regardless of the words, it seems the melodic contour of the song describes the nature of the land over which the song passes. One phrase would say, 'Salt-pan', another 'Creek-bed', 'Spinifex', 'Sandhill', 'Mulga-scrub', 'Rock-face' and so forth. An expert song man, by listening to their order of succession, would count how many times his hero crossed a river, or scaled a ridge – and be able to calculate where, and how far along, a Songline he was."

The beliefs, and the interpretation of them, are complex. But as the name songlines suggests, music and song are central to Aboriginal identity. Through singing, dancing, painting and ceremony, people become co-participants in the ongoing creation and re-animation of life. Songs can contain the history and mythology of a clan, the practical instructions for the care of land or advice about dangerous foods or animals; and there are songs for fun and entertainment.

Traditional Aboriginal music is strongly rhythmical with a dependence on natural sounds clapping hands, body slapping, the stamping of bare feet on the ground or the clapping together of bilma (sticks) or boomerangs. The best-known instrument is, of course, the **didgeridoo** (see box), a hollowed-out trunk which is blown with circular breathing to give either a rhythmic or sustained accompaniment to a dance, sacred ceremony or corroboree, a meeting of neighbouring tribes with singing and dancing. The instrument's deep, resonant sound is instantly recognisable and it has become the most popular and distinctive addition to contemporary Aboriginal bands.

Reggae Roots

For white Australians, traditional music has long been a primary, but marginal, experience of black Australia. Its otherworldliness helped maintain the image of Aboriginal issues as being on the periphery of 'Australian' life, and it received very little attention outside anthropology or ethnomusicology circles.

The first significant change in perceptions came with the 1979 documentary-drama film *Wrong Side of the Road*, which told the story of racist oppression and denial of land rights through the eyes of young Aboriginal musicians. For the first time, the idea of Aboriginal music was seen to encompass a contemporary scene, as well as its purely traditional forms.

The film showed the Aboriginal bands **No Fixed Address** and **Us Mob** struggling to get exposure playing their reggae-influenced songs. It marked the beginning of a public recognition of music as a tool in the fight to communicate the Aboriginal story. In particular the No Fixed Address song "We

No Fixed Address

Have Survived" made the point that the Aboriginals would not disappear into the background:

We have survived the white mans world
And the torment and the horror of it all
We have survived the white mans world
And you know, you can't change that!

The influence of **Bob Marley** was marked in the early days of this Aboriginal contemporary music scene. Marley had toured Australia in 1979 and left many admirers in his wake. As throughout Africa, Marley's socially conscious music with its "Get Up, Stand Up!" assertions created an instant bond for Aboriginal artists, and a number of Aboriginal-based bands began using reggae and rock formats and expressing their connections with the other black peoples of the world.

They included **Bart Willoughby** of **No Fixed Address**, a former student of the Centre of Aboriginal Studies (CASM) in Adelaide, and, in particular, **Yothu Yindi**, whose founder **Mandawuy Yunupingu** cites Marley as a crucial model: "His philosophy and knowledge was very appealing. He's been a big influence on my song writing, with his freedom themes, although my songs aren't necessarily like his. But some of the things I feel about my life, our country, are the same as Marley would have felt. I usually centre my melodies around a traditional song. I might then add a reggae beat or whatever, but the concept and idea is derived from my understanding of Aboriginal song."

Yothu Yindi

Yothu Yindi have been far and away the most successful exponents of distinctively Aboriginal rock, and they are integrally linked to the struggle for Aboriginal rights. Mandawuy Yunupingu and his fellow band member, Witiyana Marika, are sons of leaders of the Gumatj and Rirratjingu clans in Northeast Arnhem land. Both of their fathers were involved in the early days of the Aboriginal land rights movement in the 1960s.

Yothu Yindi's first album, *Homeland Movement*, was released in 1988, Australia's bicentennial year – and an event which provided a focus for their protest. On their two following albums, *Tribal Voice* and *Freedom*, and in concert, the band have continued to address social injustice and land rights as well as the wish for harmony and reconciliation between black and white.

The band itself symbolises this with a mixture of Aboriginal and white musicians. Yothu Yindi means 'Mother Child', and their music emphasises the relationship between Australia's original inhabitants and white Australians. Mandawuy Yunupingu was declared 'Australian of the Year' in 1992 for his work in promoting Aboriginal culture and interracial harmony.

Yothu Yindi are quite an experience live, with their body-painted dancers. Musically the main ingredients are guitar, drums and keyboard, plus didgeridoo (yidaki) and clapsticks (bilma). Their repertoire includes arrangements of traditional and sacred songs giving a strong spiritual ingredient to their music beyond the political sloganising. Here, for example, is their song "Timeless Land" from *Freedom*:

*I feel the spirit of the great sisters calling on
  me to sing
This is the learning of the great story I'll tell
  you about this place
From the edge of the mountains fly down the
  valley, down where the Snowy River flows
Follow the water down to the ocean, bring
  back the memory
This is a timeless land. This is our land.*

JOHN W. McCORMICK/FESTIVAL RECORDS

Multi-culti Australian group Yothu Yindi

Blek Bala Mujik

After Yothu Yindi, the best known Aboriginal group is **Blek Bala Mujik** (Black People's Music), who perform both the traditional repertoire associated with ritual ceremonies in Arnhem Land, their home in the Northern Territories, and contemporary songs described by *Rolling Stone* as "Catchy airplay-friendly Aboriginal pop".

The traditional songs and dances are accompanied by didjeridoo and clapsticks (*litung* and *bulmirr*, in the local Rembarrnga language) and evoke an ancestral world inhabited by the brolga bird and white cockatoo which are part of the creation myths. For the modern songs, they add to the line-up the guitars, bass and drums common to pop groups all over the world. **Apaak Jupurrula** (Peter Miller), their leader and songwriter, draws widely on contemporary music styles but asserts "Whether I use reggae, rock or rap as a vehicle – and we use all of these – it's the message that's important. It's about understanding and acknowledging the past, understanding and acknowledging the present situation, reconciling our differences as peoples of the world and making collective decisions about where we go from here. Aboriginal Australia has always been recognised as conservationist and we believe that mankind has lost the plot somewhere along the way. We have over-industrialised our nations, we have polluted our air, we have forgotten about our past and I firmly believe that groups such as Blek Bala Mujik should address this issue."

The band are based in Gulin Gulin, a community of 400 people in the middle of Arnhem Land. Within the community the band participate in the ritual performances and sacred ceremonies that are part of traditional Aboriginal culture. The Northern Territories is one of the few areas of Australia where Aboriginals have been granted land rights and the importance of these rights is a central issue in their performances on tour inside and outside Australia: "All of our traditional songs are based

Walking Together

A long time ago
The ancestors walked the earth
Creating the world we know
They made the trees, the plants and the
*   animals,*
And life was given to the land.
This was the time of the dreaming
A very powerful and spiritual time.
Today we live in a dream
This is our culture and tradition.

I can see you there
You can see me too
We have walked in ways
That are not the same
We can hear your prayers
For this world to change
We can make this happen
You and me.

We are the indigenous peoples of Australia;
For a long time,
We've lived on this land.
Then white men came,
They too live here
And now in this time
We begin to walk together

Peter Apaak Miller (Blek Bala Mujik)

around the Dreaming. That is why Land Rights are so important to us. This little planet that we call earth has been abused and looted and we are still doing it. When are we going to stop destroying our little planet? It's our mother. We all come from this mother and when are we going to say enough is enough? We have maintained our link with our land. Our language, our painting, our performance, our music are all an extension of what was given us by our ancestors so we don't lose contact with who we are as human beings. Our art and performance has never been record-

Blek Bala Mujik

CAAMA/MUSHROOM

ed in books, but it has always been handed down through the intelligence of our elders. It has always been the link with a holistic experience and we want to maintain that tradition. We get strength from performing these dances."

The Rock Circuit

In cities, towns and festivals, Aboriginal rock bands commonly share top billing with other Australian performers. The number of **Aboriginal rock bands** formed over the past two decades is phenomenal, on a scale similar to that of the punk explosion in Britain or America, and more lasting. In the sparsely populated Northern Territory alone there are now over fifty Aboriginal bands, with perhaps a hundred others in the rest of Australia.

Most exist well outside the mainstream of the major record labels, who have yet to show a real commitment to Aboriginal music, and work in alliance with CAAMA-style outfits. Notable bands include the desert-bred rock'n'roll **Warumpi Band** and **Coloured Stone**. Warumpi attracted attention as the first mixed Aboriginal and white band, singing in a mix of tribal language and English. Their 1997 album *Too Much Humbug* dealt with the texture of life in the semi-urban setting, where Aboriginals sometimes feel trapped in a halfway world of indigenous culture and European patronage and pressure. Coloured Stone are one of the longest-established groups. Formed in 1978, they are still a major presence on the scene and did much to update the Aboriginal sound with their 1991 album *Unma Juju – Dance Music*, a remix of earlier material that brought a disco beat and the backing of a major label, BMG. The white lead singer of Warumpi Band, Neil Murray, continued his ground-breaking work adapting Aboriginal sounds for his collection of ballads, *Dust*, distributed by EMI.

In a completely different style is singer **Christine Anu**, who has highlighted other musical sounds from her Torres Strait background. She brings a youthful pop sensibility to traditions of song and dance which combine Melanesian and Aboriginal elements. Her claim to recognition as a young black women was cast against the backdrop of the far northern experience of beaches and saltwater in her breakthrough 1995 single "Island Home".

I come from the saltwater people
We always lived by the sea
Now I'm down here living in the city
with my man and my family

My Island home/my island home
my island home
Is waiting for me.

Singer-songwriters

Assimilation was the euphemistic term for a policy practised in the 1950s and 60s of taking children of mixed race from their parents and raising them in white foster homes or institutions. Many of these children were literally kidnapped and told that their parents were dead. In an astonishing feat of doublespeak the institution responsible was called the 'Aborigines Protection Board'.

The theory was that children reared away from traditional influences would choose to become like whites. In fact a good many children felt compelled to try and track down their families and rediscover their roots. Over the last decade, three of them – Kev Carmody, Archie Roach and (his partner) Ruby Hunter – have become major Aboriginal singer-songwriters and are today among the most powerful indigenous voices of Australia.

Kev Carmody, who was taken from his family when he was ten, has become the leading balladeer of Aboriginal concerns and has been dubbed Australia's Dylan. The angry lyrics of his 1990 album *Pillars of Society* were informed by his research work as a doctoral candidate examining the white's treatment of Aborigines. He is espe-

Thou Shalt Not Steal

1789 down Sydney Cove the first boat people
land
And they said sorry boys our gain's your loss
we're gonna steal your land
And if you break our new British laws you're
sure gonna hang
Or work your life like our convicts with a chain
on your neck and hands
They taught us Oh black woman thou shalt
not steal
Hey black man thou shalt not steal
We're gonna change your black barbaric lives
and teach you how to kneel
But your history couldn't hide the genocide,
the hypocrisy was real
'cause your Jesus said you're supposed to
give the oppressed a better deal
We say to you yes our land thou shalt not
steal, Oh our land you better heal
Oh white man thou shalt not steal, Oh our
land you better heal.

Kev Carmody (from Pillars of Society).

cially contemptuous of the materialistic non-spiritual European society which had used Christianity as a tool in its genocide, a theme brilliantly developed in the song "Thou Shalt Not Steal".

Carmody's 1993 album *Bloodlines* sustains his strong vocal style with hard-strummed electric guitar and didgeridoo. Some of the material is linked to a community project he was involved with in Brisbane. His is an influential voice which has found an audience at a wide level, including,

Archie Roach was taken from his parents at the age of three and told that his family had perished in a fire. It was only as a teenager that he discovered that his mother had just died, and the shock was devastating. Dispossessed and rootless, like thousands of Aborigines he resorted to drink and spent the next ten years in an alcoholic haze. "I went from city to city, living on hand-outs. Playing music was my way of getting money to drink. Finally I stopped drinking and music seemed the natural thing to fill up the void. It was therapeutic. Still is."

Roach's songs, often simply written for voice and guitar, sound confessional and many come directly from his own experience. His song "Took the Children Away" made his name and appeared on his 1990 album, *Charcoal Lane*:

> Told us what to do and say
> Told us all the white man's
>   ways
> Then they split us up again
> And gave us gifts to ease the
>   pain
> Sent us off to foster homes
> As we grew up we felt alone
> Cause we were acting white
> Yet feeling black

The recognition that some of the evils committed against Aboriginal people are at last being overturned is an important theme in Roach's second album, *Jamu Dreaming*. The title track, for instance, celebrates the rediscovery of lost ancestral values by urban-dwelling Aborigines. His most recent album, *Looking for Butter Boy*, returns to his recurring theme of the family life that never was – most powerfully in the song "Mother's Heartbeat".

Ruby Hunter pursues a solo career and works with her husband Archie Roach. Her folk style offers unique insights into the observations of an older Aboriginal woman, whose troubled past is happily a memory. Hunter's music is especially noteworthy given the silence that Aboriginal women can be bound to in their traditional contexts. She is not breaking any taboos, but she is telling her story in all its colourful hope and sadness. Other women at the forefront of the Aboriginal music scene are the a cappella vocal trio **Tiddas**.

Archie Roach

JACQUELINE MITELMAN/FESTIVAL RECORDS

notably, the schools. The positive part, he says, "is that we get so many requests from kids who want to quote the songs for school projects. It's so important to make the kids aware. The older generation are set in their ways, but it is great that the schools can use the oral tradition, because the curriculum still tells lies about what happened."

discography

As throughout this guide, the main local labels are detailed in the 'Record Labels' appendix at the end of the book. For information and updates, two useful websites are Aboriginal Music Links (*http//:www.newcastle.edu.au*) *and the* Australian Institute of Aboriginal and Torres Strait Islander Studies (*http://www.aiatsis.gov.au*).

Compilations

Budal Lardil (Larrikin, Australia).

One of the more approachable collections of pure Aboriginal music – the title means "songs of the Lardil people" who live on Mornington Island off the coast of Queensland. Includes dreaming songs from an ancient and contemporary perspective and great didjeridoo. Interesting notes.

Encyclopedia of Aboriginal Australia (Larrikin/Festival, Australia).

CD-ROM supervised by David Horton at the Australian Institute of Aboriginal and Torres Strait Islander Studies, the material includes 2000 entries, 250 audio samples, 1000 photographs. Available from Aboriginal Studies Press. PO Box 553, Canberra, Australian Capital Territory, 2601 Australia.

From the Bush: CAAMA Sampler (CAAMA, Australia).

This was the disc that inspired a generation of Aboriginal musicians, with its songs celebrating all the styles of Central Australia. It feels now like a historical collection but remains a fine introduction to the contemporary music of Central Australia's desert regions and sparse townships.

 Meinmuk Mujik: Music From the Top End (ABC/EMI Music, Australia).

The best introduction to popular Aboriginal music. Recorded in remote communities around Arnhem Land in far northern Australia, its mix of Aboriginal language and English recordings conveys the depth of styles currently flourishing. Major distribution has helped some tracks gain radio airplay and draw renewed attention to indigenous music and its constant evolution.

Our Home Our Land (CAAMA, Australia).

A miscellany of performers and styles gathered to celebrate the Mabo High Court Case victory in favour of land rights. The disc includes songs from Christine Anu, Yothu Yindi, Blek Bala Mujik, Warumpi Band, Coloured Stone and more. The full range of mainstream, commercial guitar band styles to traditional approaches make a clear statement about the diversity of Aboriginal music from across the country.

The Rough Guide to Australian Aboriginal Music (World Music Network, UK).

A good sampler of Aboriginal sounds both traditional and contemporary. Featured artists include Archie Roach, Ruby Hunter and the haunting voice of Christine Anu. Notable omissions are Yothu Yindi and Blek Bala Mujik.

Artists

Mark Atkins and Ankala

A descendant of the Yamatji people of the western desert, Atkins has achieved belated recognition since his move to eastern Australia. Noted for his muscular tone and tradition-based style of playing, he is one of the key contemporary didgeridoo players. He formed the group Ankala for a one-off recording, with his fellow didgeridoo players (and cousin) Janawirri Yiparrka, together with mult-instrumentalist Michael Atherton and other guests.

MARK ATKINS

Didgeridoo Dreamtime (Arc, UK).

A repackaged version of a Larrikin album which highlights Atkins' solid style of playing as well as innovations such as the use of guitars, and the unusual sound of the "bull-roarer'.

ANKALA

Rhythms from the Outer Core (World Network, Germany).

An excellent contemporary album featuring great didgeridoo playing – some wonderful wildlife imitations and rhythmc duets – as well as vocal improvisations and eclectic instrumental contributions. Highlights include a storming track with accordion and tablas and a wild version of "Waltzing Matilda" with didgeridoo and dobro. Musical invention and a genuine spirituality shine through.

Blek Bala Mujik

Band based in northern Australia's Arnhem Land led by Peter Miller (Apaak Jupurrula). Standard rock line-up with didgeridoo, clapsticks and painted dancers. A growing following in Australia and Europe.

Blek Bala Mujik (CAAMA/Mushroom, Australia).

Rock and didgeridoo rhythms from a tight band following along Yothu Yindi's trailblazing path.

Kev Carmody

Unrelenting critique of white Australian society from this powerful singer-songwriter who has supported Bob Dylan and Billy Bragg. He was taken from his family aged nine with his brother as a result of the Assimilation policy. He didn't finish school, but later completed a Ph.D in Australian History. An incisive critic and troubadour.

Pillars of Society (Larrikin/Festival, Australia).

The title track and "Thou Shalt Not Steal" are two classic songs of Aboriginal songwriting.

Images and **Illusions** (Larrikin/Festival, Australia).

One or other of these classics should be in every Aboriginal music collection. An uncompromising perspective in a range of styles from reggae to rockabilly to funky pop.

Richard Frankland

Aboriginal activist and respected organiser of causes behind the Aboriginal experience, Frankland is well equipped to expound in song on the institutional problems facing his people. A new arrival on the music scene, using music as a means of communicating a political message, with personal experience. While no youngster, Frankland's work in government and in inner-city Melbourne has given him a strong position within the community and the arts scene in Australia.

Down Three Waterholes Road
(Larrikin/Festival, Australia).

An album that tells the story of a number of incidents, several of them drawing upon the Royal Commission on Black Deaths in Custody. Personal narrative of a life of activism and creative effort is to the fore here but the style is melodic and melancholy, reflecting the deep sadness experienced by those whose stories are interwoven with the tragedy of every-day Aboriginal life.

Ruby Hunter

Evocative personal perspectives from the first woman to engage with these issues as a solo recording artist. Married to Archie Roach, her deep voice is like a slow moving stream full of wonder.

 Thoughts Within (White Records, Australia).

A slow-burning fuse that refuses to give in. The music is raw in its folk-mode sensibilities. Far too easily overlooked, but one of the few women performers breaking through.

JACQUELINE MITELMAN/FESTIVAL RECORDS

Singer-songwriter Ruby Hunter

Charlie McMahon

The most visible white practitioner of the didgeridoo, McMahon has had a lifetime commitment to Aboriginal causes. He understands the mix of the Australian bush and the place of the didgeridoo in its culture.

 Gondwanaland Wide Skies (Warner, Australia).

McMahon rocks along with synthesizer backing while main-taining the integrity of the didgeridoo. The precursor of many efforts at didgeridoo-based synthesis appearing today.

Adam Plack

A younger white Australian multi-instrumentalist, Plack has worked extensively with Aboriginal music didgeridoo-maker and player Johnny 'White Ant' Soames. He has also played didgeridoo with Midnight Oil and his own fusion band Nomad.

 Dawn Until Dusk
(Australian Music International, US).

An evocative, traditionally-based album centred on didgeridoo 'totems' from Northern Queensland played on location by Johnny 'White Ant' Soames. The didgeridoo alternates with Aboriginal singing over a backdrop of natu-ral sounds.

 Winds of Warning
(Australian Music International, US).

Traditional music reworked in a contemporary form, including didgeridoo and percussive imitations of animal, insect and outback sounds. Packaged in an admirable CD eco-pak.

Archie Roach

Strong personal recollections of being taken away from his family as a child, give all Roach's songs poignancy and power.

CD **Charcoal Lane**
(Mushroom Records, Australia).

Charcoal Lane stunned listeners when first released in 1992, with its loving recollections of street life and stolen children, set to acoustic country melodies. The folk style works to con-vey the deep emotions behind contemporary urban Aboriginal experience.

 Looking for Butter Boy (White Records, Australia).

On his latest 1997 album, Roach shows himself to be back in top form, particularly with the deeply moving songs about his 'abduction' "Mother's Heartbeat".

Tiddas

The three women (Lou Bennett, Sally Dastey and Amy Saunders) who make up Tiddas (an Aboriginal word meaning 'Sisters') have enjoyed enviable success taking their work into the pop charts. Vocal harmony and guitars with beautifully penned lyrics. Based in Melbourne with a big and growing following.

 Sing About Life (Id/Phonogram, Australia).

Singing a cappella in acoustic folk style to address the urban experience. Sweet Honey in the Ayers Rock!

Bart Willoughby

One of the true originals of the contemporary Aboriginal rock sound. A survivor, musically and culturally. Active since the late 1970s (he appeared in the documentary

Wrong Side of the Road, as part of No Fixed Address) Willoughby tours, records and make his presence felt on and off the rock music circuit.

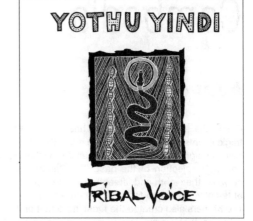

Pathways (CAAMA Music, Australia).

Dance rhythms put to the inimitably uncompromising style of one of the originals of contemporary Aboriginal music in the rock genre.

Yothu Yindi

Fired into action by the Australian bicentennial celebrations in 1988, Yothu Yindi are a multi-ethnic band led by Manduwuy Yunupingu. They had their first big hit with their timely song, "Treaty", in 1991 and subsequently, using every trick in the studio book, caught the dance craze and turned it into agitprop of sorts, becoming in the process Australia's most successful international act. Major players in mixing traditional and rock styles, they remain based in Arnhem Land, but have recently looked to international guests for collaborations.

Tribal Voice
(Mushroom, Australia).

Tribal Voice was a landmark album in Aboriginal music history and the first to really cross over to a mainstream audience. Optimistic in tone, it includes powerful message songs like "Treaty" and the title track plus atmospheric re-workings of traditional Arnhem Land material.

Freedom (Mushroom, Australia).

The band's second album, *Freedom* has a slightly more mainstream approach but just as much power – both in the music and in the messages of songs like "Timeless Land", "Mabo" and the title track.

One Blood (Mushroom, Australia).

This 1999 release saw the group revisiting 'favourite songs' – including "Tribal Voice" and "Treaty" – in the company of Irish – Sharon Shannon and Liam O'Maonlai (Hothouse Flowers) – and German guests, as well as Australian roots rocker Paul Kelly. It's the most accessible album to date, with good strong rhythms and production, if no obvious progression.

Cambodia

heavenly dancers

Cambodia seems to be rushing headlong to Westernisation, an understandable course given the tragic events of the Khmer Rouge rule (1975–1979), when over a million people were slaughtered for a spurious agrarian revolution. But, as **John Clewley** discovered, embracing the future does not mean a complete rejection of the past. The Cambodians are proud of the historic Khmer Empire, which, between the eighth and fifteenth centuries, created a unique art and culture and left a fabulous legacy of temples like those found at the Angkor site, Khao Phanom Rung in Thailand and Wat Phu in Laos. The Khmers also created the most important and influential classical dance style in southeast Asia – a subtle art that has survived invaders, colonisers and a genocidal civil war.

Classical Dance

At the end of the nineteenth century, Europe was gripped by Angkor fever, spurred by tales and pictures of the 'lost city in the jungle.' It was a major cultural event when in 1906 the Cambodian King Sisowat visited France, taking along his **court dancers and musicians**. With their performance, thre was a sense of awe that the superb tradition audiences were witnessing had been unchanged since the seventh century. Its exoticism, too, took hold. The artist Rodin followed the troupe from Paris to Marseilles, making sketches. "I absolutely loved drawing the little Cambodian dancers," he recorded, "the delicate movements of their slender limbs were strangely, wonderfully seductive."

Five years earlier Pierre Loti had visited Angkor and wrote about his experiences in *An Angkor Pilgrim* (1912). He had seen the ancient dancers and musicians carved in bas relief on the walls of the temples of Angkor Wat, and was astounded at the similarities between those stone images and the dancers right in front of his eyes: "We are right in the midst of the *Ramayana* and Angkor Thom would have certainly witnessed the same entertainments... Times we thought forever passed are revived before our very eyes; nothing has changed here, either in the spirit of the people or in the heart of their palaces."

Despite being a small country sandwiched between larger neighbours (Thailand and Vietnam), the kings of the Khmer empire ruled over much of mainland southeast Asia between 802 and 1431. The Khmer kings built spectacular temples around the Angkor site (one of the world's largest temple grounds) – Angkor Wat, Bayon, Banteay Srei, Bapuhon and many, many others. During this period, a delicate dance style and accompanying music was developed for royalty only, from the dances of maidens who performed at the temples to honour the gods.

There are two major forms of **Cambodian dance – classical** and the much-older traditional **folk styles** (the latter with roots in animism and magic, and Hindu forms from the first century). You can see the roots of traditional dancing whenever Cambodians have a social get-together and form a circle (*ramvong*), around which they move slowly, with graceful hand movements. The classical form borrowed much from the Indian tradition and earlier folk styles, but incorporating them so that by the thirteenth century the style was more Khmer than Indian. Carved reliefs at Angkor show dancers wearing headdresses and jewellery, musicians playing gongs, drums, zithers and tuned sets of bronze bowls. Some of the dancers are *apsaras*, or heavenly angels. Estimates suggest that there were 3000 apsaras at the court of the twelfth century king, Jayavarman VII.

Apsaras and tontay (depiction of early myths) dancing are the two main elements of classical dance. **The Dance of the Apsaras** and **Tep Monoram** are non-dramatic ballets where the dancers are 'sewn' into silken bodices and skirts, and adorned with tall spiked golden headresses that sparkle with jewels. The dancers move to the rippling and haunting cascades of sound provided by the **pinpeat orchestra**, which consists of a bamboo xylophone (*roneat*), temple hand cymbals (*ching*), tuned bronze gongs (*ghong*), various drums, flute (*pia au*) and oboe (*srlay*), bass banjo (*chappay*) and two-stringed violin (*tro*).

As the dancers describe narratives or move in time with the music, their bodies bend and glide into positions, each with a specific meaning. Hands, arms, legs and torso all move in a sinuous and completely connected way; gently touching the floor, then seeming to float in the air. Hands and elbows bend at impossible angles (the result of training the body from an early age) and each hand movement symbolises something, even abstract concepts like love or peace. For example, a finger to the sky means, 'today', while a hand pointing upwards means 'dead' and one pointing down means 'alive'.

Tontay is a form of dance drama. Here the graceful dancing of the ballet gives way to pantomimic moves, humour, clowning around, ad-libbing and action dancing styles. For tontay, extracts from the Indian epic Ramayana are performed, as are legends like the Prince of the Golden Sea Shell and the story of Prince Inao acted out in dance. Battles and sagas like the Churning of the Ocean of Milk (a fight between gods and demons for the 'ambrosia' that gives immortality) also feature. Queens, princesses and demons are danced by women, and religious figures and clowns are danced by men. Boys play monkey roles.

Classical dancing has been revived several times this century, most noticeably in the 1960s by the great 'white apasara' dancer **Princess Norodom Buppha Devi**, the daughter of King Norodom Sihanouk. Nevertheless, the genocidal rule of the Khmer Rouge (1975–1979) left the tradition in tatters as some ninety percent of all classical performers were killed (along with anyone who had a 'bourgeois' musical background). When the few artists who were left returned to Phnom Penh they found that all the centuries-old written records of Hindu epics had been destroyed. The compound of Phnom Penh University's School of Arts had been turned into a pig sty.

Older Cambodians regard the classical and folk traditions as the 'soul of Cambodia' and a dedicated band of thirty teachers – among them the costume maker Em Theay, choreographer Proeung Chhieng and the School of Arts

director Tuy Koeun – have revived the school to continue its traditions. Today, there are 1000 students and some 300 teachers and the classes range from classical to folk. It takes great dedication and discipline, and up to ten years training, to master the classical and folk arts. Interestingly, the Cambodians combine teaching both the classical and folk traditions under the same roof, whereas in Thailand, classical dance, being 'high art' is separated from folk styles.

JAK KILBY

National Dance of Cambodia

Cambodian classical music has greatly influenced the similar traditions found in Thailand and Laos, and to a lesser extent Myanmar. The Cambodian, Thai and Laotian classical musical scales are almost identical, for instance. When the Thais from Ayuthaya sacked Angkor in 1400, apsara dancers and musicians were taken to the Thai court. Later, when the Burmese sacked Ayuthaya in 1767, they took Thai musicians and dancers and thus Burmese classical music was influenced by the Cambodian styles. All these traditions can be traced back to the heavenly dancing at Angkor hundreds of years earlier.

In addition to apsara and tontay, Cambodia has ancient traditions of **mask dancing** (*lakon khol*) and **shadow plays** (*nang sbe*), both of which can be seen throughout the country. Performances of classical ballet and other styles can be seen at major hotels and at the Chatomuk Theatre near the Royal palace.

Folk and Popular Traditions

Given Cambodia's recent history, it is amazing that any traditional music exists at all, but **folk songs** (*ayai*) and **wedding songs** (*pleing kar*) are still commonly played. Drums and the ubiquitous two-stringed fiddle (*tro*) are the chief instruments, and are often home-made. Despite the difficult circumstances – poverty, a shattered economy, the hangovers of civil war – and a young generation seduced by pop music, some ancient tunes and melodies are being passed on. The Cambodian government is currently trying to gather and collect material from old Cambodian folk singers, and at the instigation of Prime Minister Hun Sen there are plans to broadcast performances on TV.

Hun Sen is himself a hit songwriter. He writes poems – inspirational, on rural life, love and so on – and then has musicians set the lyrics to music, creating a kind of soulful folk music. His hits include a favourite about his poor, rural childhood, "The Life of the Pagoda Boy". He notes that **sung poetry** (*kam nap*) has a long history in Cambodia (a tradition also found in Thailand, Laos and among nearly all the mountain-dwelling groups of the region).

Lakon Bassak, the popular theatre of Cambodia, was created by Cambodians living near the Bassak river in Vietnam at the turn of the century. It sounds at times like the Vietnamese popular operetta *cai luong*, with its strange mix of *pinpeat* and Vietnamese music. Dances are often popularised versions of classical styles and the plays feature *jataka* stories (based on the Buddha's life). Phnom Penh and major cities feature lakon bassak, particularly at festival times. At the same time you might also see *lakon tammada* or *yeekay*, a bawdy folk drama, rather like Thailand's *likay*.

Popular **modern styles of music** include Cambodian tunes set to Western orchestration – known as **jamrieng samai** – and locally brewed ones like **ramvong** and **ramkbach**. These styles use electrified Western and sometimes traditional instruments. Ramvong songs are slow dance numbers for the circle dance described earlier, while ramkbach is similar to *luk thung* or Thai country music, with its slow, moody rhythms and bittersweet vocals. The musical backing is full of sweet melodies, but it is the glissando and wavering grace notes of the singer that hold the attention. Currently top of the Cambodian country style is **Song Senghorn**, Cambodia's equivalent of Thailand's late *luk thung* queen, Pompuang Duangjan.

Ramvong and ramkbach have their roots in the late 1960s and early 1970s when the late great country singer **Sisamouth** was at his peak. Cassette tapes circulate at the markets of Sisamouth and feature him and other stars like **Siitoru**, **Sinonwannaa**, **Sereysothla** and **Pechanda** (who is also popular for modernised wedding songs). Younger contemporary stars include the male singer **Noi Vanneth** and female singer **Ment Kao Pechita**.

One exciting new development outside the capital comes from the province of Siem Reap. This is the emergence of a Cambodian version of the funky Thai-Cambodian roots music **kantrum** (see

Cambodian Festivals

Cambodia shares many of the same festivals as its Thervada Buddhist neighbours Thailand and Laos. Festivals like mid-April **New Year** (*Bonn Chaul Chhnam*) and the **November Water festival** (*Bonn Om Tuk*) are good times to catch live performances of popular music, traditional or pop.

A **Ramayana festival** is also held every two years in the month of December at Angkor Wat. The first was held in 1995 and the next will take place in 2001. Like the other festivals it features interpretations of the Ramayana from troupes in India, Thailand, Japan, etc, as well as from the host country.

Thailand p.241). Siam Reap is close to the border with Thailand where Thai-Cambodians mix with their Cambodian counterparts, sharing a language and culture. **Darkie**, kantrum's major star, is already well-known in Siem Reap. His success has enouraged a rising new Cambodian challenger, **Paypongrath**.

Sadly, one superstar screen icon and classical dance teacher, **Piseth Pilika**, a role model for poor women, became a victim of Phnom Penh's sometimes violent streets when she was gunned down in a market in what may have been a contract killing in July 1999. Ten thousand teary-eyed mourners turned out for her funeral. With classical music recovering from the war years, and a sense of opitimism growing in homegrown entertainment, the loss of Pilika was devastating for many Cambodians.

discography

Compilations

Music of Cambodia (3 CDs)
(Celestial Harmonies, US).

You may not think you want three CDs of Cambodia music, but this set is well worth the investment. Volume 1 features a rural pinpeat orchestra and other sounds of Sien Riep beautifully recorded in Angkor Wat itself. Volume 2 presents the courtly version of pinpeat, a *mahori* folk orchestra (fiddles, flutes xylophone and percussion) and tribal music. Volume 3 features solo instrumental music, including the *kse diev* – an extraordinary plucked one-stringed instrument with a resonating gourd held against the chest and said to be the oldest instrument in Cambodia. Full notes and information. Take a deep breath and enter a wonderful world.

THE MUSIC OF CAMBODIA
9 GONG GAMELAN
RECORDED INSIDE ANGKOR WAT
PRODUCED BY DAVID PARSONS
DIGITAL RECORDING

CELESTIAL HARMONIES

Cambodge: Musique classique khmère, théâtre d'ombres et chants de mariage (Inédit, France).

Pinpeat music for classical dance and shadow theatre and a smaller ensemble of oboe, lutes, spike-fiddle and percussion accompanying the wedding songs. Good notes.

Echoes from the Palace: Court Music of Cambodia (Music of the World, US).

A mid-price CD with a very attractive selection of classical dance pieces. The oboe of the pinpeat orchestra of the Sam-Ang Sam Ensemble is buried in the shimmering gong sound, so it's less raucous than the other recordings and perhaps more elegant to Western ears.

Les Musiques du Ramayana. Vol 2 – Cambodge (Ocora, France).

A historical recording made in France in 1964 on the occasion of the visit of Prince Norodom Sihanouk. As King Sisowat had done over a half a century earlier he took court dancers and musicians with him. This is a fifty-minute performance of the Reamker (Ramayana) ballet, with pinpeat orchestra, some dialogue and sung texts. The recording isn't particularly good but it is obviously of historic importance.

Artists

Musicians of the National Dance Company of Cambodia

Master musicians, dancers and singers from the Arts Department of the Ministry of Culture feature on this album. Since 1980, the department has been reformed and has created a large ensemble of dancers and musicians. The company has made many overseas tours, including one in the UK in 1990, the first for thirty years, from which this recording came. They featured a stripped-down *pinpeat* orchestra.

Homrong (RealWorld, UK).

A fabulous collection representing the varied styles of Cambodian traditional and classical music, from classical pinpeat to wedding songs to folk songs. Listen to this and be transported back a thousand years to Angkor and the 'sound of clouds.' The folk and wedding tunes are of this earth though, with plaintive singing, catchy rhythms and lots of advice. Highly recommended.

Song Senghorn

Song Senghorn is one of the most popular local singers in Cambodia. Like her contemporaries she can tackle any style from folk to ramvong to rambbach and Western covers (but sung in Cambodian). Her high-pitched voice is perfect from the country-style singing in ramkbach songs. She's known as the Queen of ramkbach and is often compared to Thailand's late luk thung star Pompuang Duangjan.

Spean Sang Snai (The Bridge of Love) (Royal Sound, Cambodia).

This is as close to a 'concept album' as you'll get in Cambodia. The cassette focusses on the village of Kraing Yow, which was designated the first model village by Prime Minister Hun Sen. Songs cover the history of the development of the village as well as typical events and stories – ramvong for village entertainment, ramkbach for those sad tales of broken hearts and tearful departures for the big city. Senghorn moves between the styles with consummate ease and her emotive singing is haunting. Try listening to this without shedding a tear.

Central Asian Republics

bards of the golden road

People imagine Central Asia as desert but there are also fertile valleys, cotton fields and spectacular mountain ranges. Its republics – **Azerbaidjan**, **Uzbekistan**, **Tajikistan**, **Kazakhstan**, **Turkmenistan** and **Kyrgyzstan** – cover an area ten times the size of Britain, stretching from the Caspian Sea in the west to the Chinese border in the east. For many years their music filtered out as a peripheral and exotic sound from the Soviet Union, but with their new independence the six Muslim states are revealing distinct musical treasures. **Razia Sultanova** and **Simon Broughton** investigate.

The **Central Asian Republics** share a common historical and cultural background in the Islamic faith and – except for Tadjikistan – their Turkic roots. The area is a meeting point between **Turkic** and **Iranian** people, cultures and traditions. In the fourteenth century all these states were part of the powerful empire of Timur (Tamberlaine the Great) who built his capital in Samarkand. This Golden Age – the capital moved in the sixteenth century to Bukhara – was disrupted by regional conflicts, which remained until Russian domination in the nineteenth century. Since the last century the region has been largely isolated, due to its incorporation into the Russian and then Soviet empire, but things are changing in the post-Soviet era.

Culturally – and musically – the Central Asian states share much in common (and they have similarities, too, with the Central Asian Uighurs across the border in China – see p.44). The individual nations are in fact somewhat artificial constructs, the hangover of Soviet strategists in the 1920s attempting to form 'nationalities' out of Transoxiana's countless clans, tribes and family lineages.

Agit-Prop Bards

The most elevated musical tradition of Central Asia is the **Shashmaqam** – the 'Six maqams' of Uzbek and Tajik music. As a courtly music of the upper classes, it earned disapproval from the communists and was forbidden for almost a decade (from 1948 until Kruschev's reforms in 1957) as it didn't 'represent the needs of the people'. In an attempt to make it more politically acceptable,

texts by popular communist poets were used, and you can hear famous Shashmaqam-style songs in the archives with improvised paeons such as "Oh, my dear Communist Party!", "I love you, my collective farm" and "Oh, Great Lenin, undying glory!" instead of the traditional expressions like "My beloved!" or "My Almighty God!". Today, these bizarre hybrids are remembered with amusement.

A similar thing happened with the venerable Central Asian art of the **improvising bards**. The *bakshy* and *akyn* minstrels began to sing of heroic labour and socialist ideas. Witness these lines by one of the most celebrated Kazakh akyns, **Jamboul Jabayev**:

We treasure our honour and our hoards,
We'll cut our foes to pieces with swords,
We'll fight in the sun, in the rain, in the snow,
Till at last we make all our enemies go,
That at the victory Stalin should touch
His hand in contentment to his moustache

Jabayev was born in 1846 and, until his death aged 99, created many epic poems rich in form and colourful language. He enjoyed wide renown across the Soviet Union and was named 'the patriarch of folk poets'. He had won his fame long before the revolution, but he eagerly turned his art to the new order.

The Soviet ideal of Central Asian musical life was that of socialist Beethovens, Tchaikovskys and Musorgskys composing concert works based on the people's folk music, while the real traditions of one of the world's great oral musical cultures were portrayed as feudal and archaic. Or as A. Ikramov, First Secretary of the Central Committee of the Uzbek Communist Party, declared in a

1932 speech: "The average collective farmer is beginning to feel that old Uzbek music is not satisfactory. It was created many years ago when the Uzbek working people were doubly oppressed by the Khans and Becks (under the Mongol Empire) so that the main sentiments in Uzbek music were lamentation, wailing, and tears. That no longer meets the needs of our day".

Of course, seventy years of communism could hardly destroy five centuries of musical culture. Beneath the inevitable Russification, music endured as a way of maintaining a sense of identity. Particularly important was the custom of the **toi** – a family celebration of birth, circumcision, marriage or a funeral – which has long been the principal occasion for spontaneous music-making in Central Asia.

Where the Soviet regime has left its mark is in the formal **conservatoire training** of many musicians, which ironed out the distinctive tunings of regional music, introduced the Western 'tempered' scale and a formal concert-style way of playing. Many of today's performers have inherited these traditions.

Azerbaidjan

Azerbaidjan is strictly speaking a Transcaucasian country rather than a Central Asian one, situated on the western side of the Caspian Sea while the other five states lie to its east. But its people are Turkic speaking and of Central Asian origin. There is, however, more influence from Iran here: there's also an Azeri province of Iran and strong historical connections with Persia.

The most celebrated musical tradition of Azerbaidjan is the refined classical **mugam**. This is a much freer, lighter and emotional form than the Shashmaqam of Central Asia. Mugam refers both to the modes in which the music is played (like the Arabic *maqam* and Turkish *makam*) and to the genre itself – a suite usually beginning with an instrumental prelude and alternating classical poetry and instrumental passages. The most celebrated texts, usually about divine love, come from Sufi poets.

Each of the suites is named after its principal mode (mugam) in which it will begin and end. The instrumental ensemble is usually a trio of **târ** (lute), **kemanche** (spike fiddle) and **daf** (frame drum) – similar to that found in Persian music – although the *santur* (hammer dulcimer) and *nay* (flute) commonly heard in Iranian ensembles and the Arabic and Turkish *oud* (lute) are not usually used by the Azeris. The târ, traditionally made

from mulberry wood with three double strings, has become the musical emblem of Azerbaidjan and is the principal instrument of the classical tradition. Târ and kemanche players often echo or anticipate the vocal line.

Without question the king of mugam singers is **Alim Qasimov** (also spelt Alem Kassimov), who is celebrated for the emotional power of his voice and his expressive vocal ornamentations – an important part of the music. He's also a master of the *tahrir* technique in which he moves into a high head voice almost like yodelling. These vocal styles can seem exaggerated to those unfamiliar with them but Qasimov's success in concerts at home and abroad, as well as his numerous recordings, are testament to the transcendental power of his performance. Other notable mugam performers include the **Jabbar Karyagdioglu Ensemble** – **Zahid Guliyev** (singer), **Mohled Muslumov** (târ) and **Fahraddin Dadashov** (kemanche) and the female mugam singer **Sakine Ismaïlova**.

One of the oldest forms of Azeri folk music is that of the **Ashiq** – the bard accompanying

RAZIA SULTANOVA

Alim Qasimov given the carpet treatment

The instruments found in Central Asia are common throughout the Turkic countries and the Middle East. Most popular are the long-necked lute – called the **saz** by the Turks, the **dutar** by the Uzbeks and **dombra** by the Kazakhs – and the **rubab**, which in Central Asia, Iran, Afghanistan and Pakistan is a plucked lute (not a bowed fiddle, as rubabs are called in many other parts of the Arabic and Asian world). Variants – and other significant instruments across the regon – include:

Lutes

Dutar Long-necked plucked lute with two strings and frets (*dotar* is Persian for two-strings), found in the area extending from Kurdistan to Xinjiang. The most widspread instrument in Central Asia for both professional musicians and amateurs. The instrument is used for classical maqam, ghazals and popular and mystical melodies and played in a wide variety of styles with great sophistication and virtuosity.

Dombra A much shorter Kazakh version of the dutar without frets, typical of the nomadic culture.

Komuz Kyrgyz long-necked lute without frets. It has a pear-shaped sound box carved from apricot wood.

Tanbur Long-necked lute with three strings found all across Central Asia. The melody is plucked on the upper string with a plectrum worn on the tip of the index finger, while the other strings act as drones.

Sato Bowed version of the tanbur played upright on the lap.

Setar A very long-necked Tadjik tanbur carved from mulberry wood. It originally had three strings (*setar* means three strings in Persian) but now usually has four played with a plectrum. It has moveable frets (like the Indian sitar) made from gut or nylon knotted onto the neck.

Rubab Long-necked lute with a skin-covered sound box. It has five strings played with a plectrum. The

Sato (right) and tanbur played by Turgun Alimatov and his son Alisher

OCORA

instrument probably came from the Uighurs and is often called the Kashgar rubab to distinguish it from other forms like the Pamir and Afghan rubab.

Târ Fretted lute with a figure-of-eight shaped body of mulberry wood and three double strings. Common in Azeri and Persian music.

Other instruments

Chang Plucked zither like the Turkish or Persian kanun.

Gidjak Spike-fiddle with a round, parchment-covered body and cylindrical neck. It usually has four strings and is identical to the Persian and Azeri kemanche.

Doira Circular frame drum held in the hand and played with the fingers. Called *daf* in Azerbaidjan.

Nay Transverse reed flute.

Surnay Conical oboe (zurna) generally used for outdoor festivities.

---

himself on the *saz* (lute) – which is found also in neighbouring Turkey (*aşik*) and Armenia (*ashug*) and right across Central Asia. There are some eighty basic tunes on which the performer will base his semi-improvised stories, chronicles or love songs. Although usually solitary characters, the ashiq and his saz is sometimes accompanied by a *balaban* (a reed pipe like the Armenian duduk) and two ashiqs might also engage in contests trying to outdo each other in improvised questions and answers. The balaban also figures in the folk and ashug repertoire of the Azeri region of **Nakhichevan**, within the Armenian Republic, where they also have a *tulum-zurna* (wine-skin zurna) – a zurna bagpipe, which does away with the need for circular breathing.

The mountainous area of **Dagestan**, at the eastern end of the Caucasus on the Caspian Sea, is inhabited by about thirty different ethnic groups. A local story says that the horseman who was distributing the languages round the world stumbled in the mountains of Dagestan and tore his bag full of languages on a sharp rock letting several spill out. There are ten recognised national languages in Dagestan today. Musically there is a similar variety of instruments with various sorts of lutes and bowed strings related both to Caucasian and Central Asian models. Much of the music has a wild character typical of the mountains.

On the popular music front, the most notable Azeri musician is the jazz singer and pianist **Aziza Mustafa Zadeh**. She has become a major artist in the jazz world and brings a distinctly Azeri feel to her solo playing and collaborations with established jazz musicians such as guitarist Al Di Meola and saxophonist Bill Evans. She was brought up in a musical family and her father, Vagif Mustafa Zadeh, was also a well-known jazz musician in the Soviet Union. Aziza is also one of the best performers in a contemporary folk-jazz idiom and it's not hard to hear the instrumental music of the Azeri mugam and folk dances in her compositions and ornamented skat singing. She's now based in Germany where her music can be more successfully promoted and marketed.

Uzbekistan

In the late sixteenth century, **Bukhara** finally became an Emirate capital, and a cultured, cosmopolitan city with flourishing trade routes fuelling its bazaars. It was from this court that the **Shashmaqam**, the most elevated musical form of Uzbek and Tajik culture, derived. It began as a royal music – in a world most familar from miniature paintings – of princesses and pavilons, with women musicians, sitting on the floors, playing on instruments like the *gidjak*, *dutar* and *doira* (see instrument box).

Shashmaqam literally means 'Six maqams' referring, as with the mugam of Azerbaijan and the related Uighur muqams, to suites of pieces in different musical modes. The six maqams are called 'Buzruk', 'Rast', 'Nava', 'Dugah', 'Segah' and 'Iraq' and take their names from classical Persian modes. The maqam begins with an instrumental prelude followed by settings of classical Sufi poems sung by a soloist or small group of singers. The texts express a rich variety of emotions – love and despair, sadness and regret, passion and hope. The singer generally begins in a low register, passes through a middle range and then ascends through increasingly higher sections to the musical culmination known as the *awdj* after which the music relaxes and descends to the low register where it began. This progressive rising towards a spiritual and musical climax comes directly from the Sufi nature of the music.

A Shashmaqam ensemble of the classical period might contain two *tanburs*, a dutar, a gidjak and doira plus two or three singers. Today's ensembles are much the same. The pre-eminent Uzbek performer of Shashmaqam and Uzbek classical traditions is **Munadjat Yulchieva**. Her name translates as 'ascent to God' – the true meaning of Sufism. One of the important Sufi beliefs is in the continuity of a spiritual chain – *silsila* – and Yulchieva has inherited her musical knowledge from generations of spiritual and musical *murshi* or masters. Despite Soviet influences on the poet-

ical texts, the music preserved its traditional form and, now that the classical texts can be used once again, Yulchieva and her teacher Shavkat Mirzaev as accompanist widely perform Sufi ghazals of classical Uzbek poets.

Yulchieva's voice has a wide range and is beautifully understated, although you can still sense a conviction beneath the measured delivery. She started singing in early childhood and was once advised to give up Uzbek music and become an 'opera star'. But Yulchieva simply refused: "I am a singer of my culture and I do my songs for my people". She has been singing for almost twenty years now and has become a spiritual symbol of Uzbek music and even Uzbek culture in general.

The leading performer of **instrumental maqam** music is **Turgun Alimatov** – a master-performer on the dutar, tanbur and *sato* (bowed tanbur), an instrument he himself revived. His playing is refined and skillful, eschewing virtuosity, but redolent of his status as a philosopher of music with an ascetic way of life. He plays with his son Alisher Alimatov and includes maqam repertoire from different areas of Uzbekistan – Bukhara, Khorezm and Ferghana, as well as mystical and lyrical songs like the famous "Giria" (weeping).

The main focus for Uzbek (and all Central Asian) music is the **toi** – the rites of life celebrations. Uzbeks have a *beshik-toi* (celebrated forty days after the birth of a baby), a *sunnat-toi* (for circumcision or initiation into Islam), the marriage toi, and so on. All of these tois reflect important elements in Central Asian life, such as sexual demarcation – women don't sit next to men; the deference to the older generation; the respect of Muslim sensibilities.

A toi is also an important musical academy. It's where musicians gain their experience of practical music-making. In Central Asia two thirds of the population is rural so traditional toi and weddings are common. Every city has its celebrated **wedding musicians and singers** and people attend weddings to see their favourite performers. **Sherali Djuraev**, a singer and tar player, is one of the most popular performers in Uzbekistan today. He's the number one favourite at weddings – and much to the annoyance of Uzbekistan's political leaders was voted as the country's hero in a popular poll. There's also an important Uzbek tradition of female wedding entertainers – singing and playing doira and giving protective blessings to the bride and groom. In the Bukhara-Samarkand region they are known as *sozanda*, in Khorazen *khalpa* and in Taskent-Ferghana *otin-oy*.

In contemporary popular music the big name is that of **Yulduz Usmanova** who is successfully modernising Uzbek traditional music and bringing it to a much wider audience. Her songs are infectiously catchy and contemporary, but retain a strong connection with traditional music including gidjak and *dombra* in the instrumental line up. There are strong influences from popular Turkish music and Arabesk – and sometimes a touch of Indian film music in the orchestral arrangements. Coming from a simple family background, Usmanova graduated from the conservatoire in Tashkent and became the most popular wedding singer in Uzbekistan. Now in her early thirties, she won wider fame at the 1991 *Azia Dauysy* (Voice of Asia) festival in Almatï (formerly Alma-Ata), Kazakhstan, and has since performed worldwide at WOMAD festivals and elsewhere.

BLUE FLAME

Yulduz Usmanova

Tajikistan

Although the **Tajiks** are of Persian rather than Turkic stock, the musical links with neighbouring Uzbekistan are strong and they share their classical **shashmaqam** repertoire. The Tajiks use Persian-derived texts, but the instrumental music is just the same as in Uzbekistan. Unfortunately the Queen of the Tajik maqam tradition, **Barno Itzhakova**, now lives in Israel and due to continuing unrest the performing of Shashmaqam in Tajikistan has sadly declined. For a tradition reliant on oral transmission this situation is perilous.

While the music of the plains and river valleys is closely related to that of the Uzbeks, in the mountainous south of Tadjikistan there's another more popular style known as **falak** (literally 'celestial dome') performed at weddings, circumcisions and the *nowruz* spring festival. A falak is a suite made up of a collection of sung poems and instrumental pieces played on the lute or spike-fiddle – a sort of popular maqam. The leading performer is conservatoire-trained **Davlatmand Kholov**. He's a fine singer and a particularly good instrumentalist on the gidjak, dutar and *setar* (three-string lute).

In the Pamir mountain region of **Badakhshan** there's also a rich variety of music including folk poetry and Persian influenced ghazals and praise songs.

Kazakhstan, Turkmenistan and Kyrgyzstan

There's a clear division between the nomadic and the settled people of Central Asia and this is reflected in the kind of music performed. The city populations are primarily made up of Uzbeks and Tajiks and their music belongs to the urban classical and professional tradition. **Kazakhs, Turkmen** and **Kyrgyz**, however, are of nomadic origin and their music follows the rural or folk traditions which have a closer connection to a pre-Islamic animist and shaminist culture. Related to this is the art of the **bard** or **bakshy** – another branch of the widespread Turkic aşik tradition. In these societies which are still close to their nomadic origins, the bakshy is also a shaman – acting as healer, magician and moraliser.

All three countries also have traditions of **sung epics** performed by a *bakshy* (Turkmen), *akyn* (Kazakh) or *manaschi* (Kyrgyz). The **Kyrgyz Manas** epic is said to be the longest in the world

Ashkhabad

Ashkhabad is the capital city of Turkmenistan and also the name of the five-piece band I've caught up with in their portakabin at the Reading WOMAD Festival. They've just come off stage from giving us a dose of the "wild and romantic traditional wedding music of Turkmenistan". A great set of unfailingly catchy songs, swirling dance tunes and lyrical ballads with a tinge of melancholy.

They are not dolled up in traditional costume but some of them stylishly sport big woolly Turkmen hats.

Ashkhabad – from the centre of Asia

Similarly they play a combination of Western instruments – violin and clarinet – and Central Asian ones – the dutar and frame drum that taps out the unmistakable rhythms. I talk to their vocalist and dutar player **Atabai Tsharykuliev** and ask him where I would hear them back home in Ashkabad. "If you come to Ashkhabad," he says, "you can hear us immediately – we'll come to the airport!" This wasn't quite what I had in mind, but it turns out that they're not a regular combo at home but a sort of all-star band for touring – but none the worse for that.

Atabai himself works in the Philharmonic orchestra, but also grew up on the wedding circuit and was instrumental in keeping the tradition alive when it was discouraged by the authorities for being too Islamic. Things have changed since then – the group were invited to play at a summit meeting of the ten presidents of central Asia – from the five Central Asian states plus Azerbaidjan, Turkey, Iran, Afghanistan and Pakistan.

Ashkhabad's instrumental line-up is fairly typical for contemporary Turkmen wedding bands. "Music never stands still, it's like water," says Atabai. "The accordion often takes the place of the dutar and synthesizers are more and more common. But with Western instruments we're still referring back to the traditional sound. The violin imitates the gidjak and the clarinet imitates the Turkmen *tuiduk* (end-blown flute)."

Ashkhabad make the east-west fusion work particularly well as it swings from folk-revival to jazz and classical – probably because there's an unmistakable pride in their own traditions. Many of their song lyrics come from the celebrated eighteenth-century Turkmen poet Makhtumkuli – for example, the patriotic "Ayrylsa" (Separation) that opens their RealWorld album: "I'm far from home, travelling the world. Every country has its own beauty, but my heart longs for the black stones and sweet people of Turkmenistan."

Simon Broughton

– twenty times longer than the Iliad and Odyssey combined and two and a half times longer than India's Mahabharata. The Manas epic is the pillar of Kyrgyz culture – it tells of the warrior Manas and his descendants and battles with the Chinese. Most Kyrgyz can recite at least a part of it. Sayaqbay Karalaev (1887–1971), the most famous manaschi was reputed to know all 500,000 stanzas.

The epics and songs are either sung solo or accompanied by a two- or three-string lute (dombra, dutar and *komuz* in Kazakhstan, Turkmenistan and Kyrgyzstan respectively). The dombra and komuz are strongly linked to nomadic culture and there are certain pieces (*kui*) which are even said to narrate a sort of musical journey. There are also bowed spike fiddles like the Kazakh *qobuz* and Kyrgyz *kiak*.

In a popular folk idiom, the group **Ashkhabad** from Turkmenistan has recorded its own particular brand of wedding music for RealWorld and toured extensively at WOMAD events (see box feature). Their music draws on the song-epics and folk traditions, and is adapted somewhat for western audiences, and through their own Western classical training.

discography

General

Compilations

 Central Asia: Classical Traditions (Ocora, France).

A fine collection bringing together classical pieces from Uzbekistan and Tajikistan played by the most remarkable performers such as Munadjat Yulchieva, Turgun Alimatov, and Barno Itzhakova.

Central Asia: The Masters of the Dutar
(VDE-Gallo/AIMP, Switzerland).

A fascinating survey of different instruments and styles of dutar playing. It includes Uzbek, Tajik (and Pamir), Persian Khorasan and Turkmen styles and is an inspiring document of the artistry of the players of this instrument which is central to the tradition. Comprehensive notes aid listening.

Saz (Kalan, Turkey).

An interesting compilation tracing the various types of *saz* or lute from Central Asia to Turkey and beyond – the Uzbek *dutar*, Tadjik *tambur*, Kyrgyz *komuz*, Kazakh *dombra*, Iranian *tanbur*, Azeri *saz* and various Turkish varieties. A useful and listenable survey with photos and a few notes in English.

Azerbaidjan

Compilations

Ay Lazzat: Songs and Melodies from Dagestan
(Pan, Netherlands).

A valuable collection demonstrating the songs and dances of the diverse people of this mountain region. The performers come from a Soviet-style folkloric group, but the music and playing is still compelling.

Azerbaidjan: Music and Songs of the Ashiq
(VDE-Gallo/AIMP, Switzerland).

A scholarly survey of the Azeri ashiq tradition with Emran Heydari accompanying himself on saz, Ashiq Hasan accompanied by saz, balaban (oboe) and daf, and the ubiquitous Alim Qasimov with his mugam line-up of târ, kemanche and daf.

Heyva Gulu: Dances and Ashug melodies from Nakhichevan (Pan, Netherlands).

As with the other discs in this Pan series, this is music from a folkloric ensemble giving a good example of the distinctly Armenian flavoured music of this region. The ensemble Dede Gorgud take their name from a famous medieval ashiq.

Uzundärä: Ancient Wedding Dance Music of Azerbaidjan (Pan, Netherlands)

A rather good collection of instrumental dances and songs for toi celebrations. Although this is essentially folk repertoire it also gets incorporated into the instrumental parts of the classical mugam suites. Performed by the Jabbar Karyagdioglu ensemble on târ, kemanche and daf.

Artists

Sakine Ismaïlova

From the same generation as Alim Qasimov (see below), Ismaïlova trained in Baku and is the leading woman singer in the mugam tradition.

Sakine Ismaïlova (Inédit, France).

Women singing mugam is a twentieth-century development. Ismaïlova has a typically elegant, mid-range voice with emotional drama where necessary. Three mugam on this disc are mainly with Nizami texts. One of eight CDs in Inédit's extensive *Mugam d'Azerbaidjan* series.

Alim Qasimov

Born in 1957 in the small town of Shamakha about 100km from Baku where he trained in the art of mugam singing. He worked as a shepherd and taxi driver before becoming the king of mugam – and in 1999 winning an IMC-UNESCO prize for 'outstanding contributions to the environment and development of music'. He performs and tours often, with the brothers Malik (târ) and Elshan (kemanche) Mansurov.

Love's Deep Ocean
(World Network, Germany).

The art of mugam singing is an acquired taste but this stunning disc is the perfect introduction, highlighting Qasimov's lighter repertoire based on ghazals and folksongs. He sings with his daughter Ferghana – a male/female duet quite unusual in the strict mugam tradition – and an expanded ensemble including *balaban* (duduk), clarinet and *nagara* drum alongside the usual târ and kemanche.

The Legendary Art of Mugam
(World Network, Germany).

A performance of mugam Shur is the main item here, but the disc also includes some popular folksongs with Ferghana. For real mugam devotees there are four lengthy cycles featuring Qasimov on two CDs in the French Inédit label's *Mugam d'Azerbaidjan* series.

Uzbekistan and Tajikistan

Compilations

Badakhshan: Mystical Poetry and Songs from the Ismailis of the Pamir Mountains
(Pan, Netherlands).

A delightful collection of music from a small but fascinating area of Tadjikistan. The Ismailis belong to the Shiite branch of Islam and this contains religious music, ghazals, folk songs

and some great instrumental playing on rubab, tanbur and sitar. Extensive notes and photos.

Bukhara: Musical Crossroads of Asia
(Smithsonian Folkways, US).

Not easy listening this one, but a serious survey of musical life in this cosmopolitan city in 1990. It features the female sozanda musicians for a toi, classical music and Jewish and Moslem liturgical music.

From Samarkand to Bukhara
(Long Distance, France).

An excellent survey of musical styles recently recorded across the country including dutar maestro Turgun Alimatov and gidjak player Ahmed Djan Dadaev in Tashkent, folk singer Mardan Moulanov in Samarkand, the Maqam Ensemble of Khorezem and the Women's Ensemble of Ferghana singing Sufi songs.

Tadjikistan: Songs of the Bards
(VDE-Gallo/AIMP, Switzerland).

A disc celebrating the art of the *hafiz*, the Tadjik bards recorded by Jean During in various towns and villages in the early 1990s. Falak, ghazals and other forms sung by male vocalists with accompaniment on dombra, dutar, setar, gidjak, etc. A specialised disc, but interesting.

Tadjikistan-Uzbekistan: Erudite Shashmaqam Tradition (Buda/Musique du Monde, France).

Tajik performers Mastâne Ergasheva and Jurabeg Nabiev perform the classic Shashmaqam repertoire including Persian Sufi poetry of Hafez and Bedil.

Uzbekistan: The Art of Dutar (Ocora, France).

A near-definitive collection for dutar devotees featuring three current star players: Abdorahim Hamidov, Soltan-Ali Khodaverdiev and Shohrat Razzaqov.

Uzbekistan: Les Grandes voix du passé, 1940-1965 (Ocora, France).

Archive recordings from Tashkent Radio focussing on the Ferghana region. Five male and two female singers perform, most memorably in the duets by brothers Akmal-Khan and Baba-Khan Subhanov, both devout Sufis, who perform in a wonderful devotional style, despite the Soviet persecution of the time. Obviously of specialist appeal, but a valuable collection and with excellent notes.

Uzbekistan: Instrumental Art Music
(VDE-Gallo/AIMP, Switzerland).

A scholarly and accessible survey of classical Uzbek music with unusual examples of wind ensembles as well as string playing on sato, tanbur, dutar, etc. The Shavkat Mirzaev Ensemble are the main performers with several other groups and musicians.

Uzbekistan: Music of Horezm
(Auvidis/Unesco, France).

A fine collection of various genres – oral epics, women's music, religious songs, classical and popular music – from the Khorezem oasis at the heart of Central Asia.

Artists

Turgun Alimatov

Born in 1921 Alimatov is a master performer on the dutar, tanbur and sato. He was instrumental in reviving the sato (bowed tanbur), worked for many years in the ensembles of Tashkent radio, and is the leading player in the professional style.

 Ouzbekistan: Turgun Alimatov
(Ocora, France).

Folk and classical music expertly played on the main string instruments of Uzbek music. Features several duets with his son Alisher on dutar.

Matlubeh Dadabayeva

Born in a Tadjik village in Uzbekistan, Matlubeh sings in both languages. Her mother was a village folk singer and Matlubeh followed in her footsteps but went on to study at the conservatoire in Tashkent. Turgun Alimatov was one of her teachers and she performs often with him.

The Turquoise of Samarkand
(Long Distance, France).

Classical and folk songs in Uzbek and Tadjik accompanied by various instrumentalists including Turgun Alimatov on tanbur and sato and Nabi Djan Ziaov on gidjak. Poised and refined but not emotionally engaging performances.

Davlatmand

Davlatmand Kholov was born in 1950. He studied classical music at the Dushanbe conservatoire, but was drawn back to the folk styles of southern Tadjikistan and the Pamir mountains. He's now a well-known instrumentalist (gidjak, dutar and setar) and singer.

Davlatmand: Musiques savantes et populaires du Tadjikistan (Inédit, France).

An appealing selection of little-known music from southern Tadjikistan including the falak repertoire and classical music.

Munadjat Yulchieva

Munadjat Yulchieva was born in 1960 into a peasant family in the Fergana Valley. The senior Uzbek musician Muhammadjan Mirzaev said "her voice is like a flying dove, turning over in the currents of warm spring air." Yulchieva is currently Uzbekistan's most famous vocal artist.

Munadjat Yulchieva & Ensemble Shavkat Mirzaev (World Network, Germany).

This collection is a great introduction to Uzbek classical music. It begins subdued and introverted, a melancholy melody turning in on itself sung by Yulchieva's dark alto voice and widens out into a passionate declaration of love. Great instrumental playing including Shavkat Mirzaev on the rubab and there are also instrumental tracks and some vernacular songs to lighten the tone.

WORLD NETWORK
MUNADJAT YULCHIEVA & ENSEMBLE SHAVKAT MIRZAEV

Kazakhstan, Turkmenistan and Kyrgyzstan

Compilations

Kazakhstan: Music from Almatï
(VDE-Gallo/AIMP, Switzerland).

Recordings made in 1994 of conservatoire trained musicians, so this doesn't reflect the real folk style, but an interesting collection of Kazakh music nonetheless.

Music of Kyrgystan (Buda/Musique du Monde, France).

A rather specialised collection of the nomadic-style music played and sung by amateur-musicians. Extracts from the Manas epic, lyrical songs with komuz accompaniment, kiak fiddles and lullabies. One highlight is a song about the inspiring power of the komuz in war including a whistling shell striking the sound-box of the instrument!

Turkestan: Kyrgyz Komuz and Kazakh Dombra (Ocora, France).

Another reflection of the nomadic character of Kyrgyz and Kazakh music featuring *kui* (instrumental pieces said to narrate a musical journey). Performed by Abdurahman Nurak (komuz) and Hanid Raimbergenov (dombra).

Turkmenistan: The Music of the Bakshy (VDE-Gallo/AIMP, Switzerland).

A scholarly survey of Turkmen bard music for singer and accompanying dutar, gidjak and tuiduk flute. The recordings made from 1988–90 are not as good as they might be, but the music is genuine and intimate. Includes excellent notes and photos.

Contemporary Central Asia

Compilations

Azia Dauysy and **Voice of Asia**
(Blue Flame, Germany). .

These two volumes showcase performances made at the annual Voice of Asia music festival in Almatï, Kazakhstan. While many of them sound too much like Central Asian Europop or garage bands, it's not as bad as Eurovision and gives a good idea of what young bands are doing. And there are some gems, like Yulduz Usmanova, as well. The Blue Flame label have a continuing interest in the popular music of Central Asia.

Artists

Ashkhabad

Five-piece wedding super-group from the city of Ashkhabad, Turkmenistan.

City of Roses
(RealWorld, UK).

A great debut release with audience-friendly music in stylish arrangements that remain true to the character of the music. Excellent târ, violin and percussion showing how Central Asian music can swing.

Yulduz Usmanova

Formerly a silk-worker, Usmanova graduated from the conservatoire in Tashkent and since winning first prize at the Voice of Asia competition in 1991 has become Uzbekistan's best-known pop star. She has released five albums internationally, but generally keeps a traditional feel in her music.

The Selection Album (Blue Flame, Germany).

Usmanova's best album is *Alma Alma* (1993), but this greatest hits collection includes the best of that plus some good tracks from the others. It opens with the sultry "Schoch Va Gado" (The Rich and the Poor) with stylish tanbur and gidjak playing.

Aziza Mustafa Zade

Jazz singer and pianist who's created a distinctive synthesis of Azeri melody, classical (Bachian) piano and jazz singing and improvisation.

Always
(Sony, Germany).

This 1993 album has the strongest Azeri character with lively piano playing and skat singing. Features John Patitucci on bass and Dave Weckl on percussion.

Dance of Fire (Sony, Germany).

Another accomplished outing, with Al Di Meola on guitar and Bill Evans on saxes.

China

Han traditional

the east is red ... and white

The cliché image of Han Chinese music is caught between notions of Confucian nostalgia for the Music of the Ancient Sages, and the Red Guards brandishing the Little Red Book, destroying all traces of 'feudal superstition'. Confucius anticipated Mao in his belief in the political function of music and in his opposition to the popular music of his day. But neither succeeded in eradicating local folk culture and today, at least in rural China, traditional music has survived the pressures of Maoism, while facing an uncertain future under the liberal market reforms and new competition from pop music. **Stephen Jones** reports.

The casual visitor to Chinese cities could be forgiven for thinking that the only traditional style to compete with pop music is that of the kitsch folk troupes to be heard in hotels and concert halls. But an earthy traditional music still abounds throughout the countryside; it can be heard at weddings, funerals, temple fairs, and New Year celebrations – and even downtown in teahouses. And there's a huge variety – as you'd expect from an area containing almost a quarter of the world's population, extending from the steppes of Inner Mongolia to sultry southeast Asia, from the Yellow Sea to the deserts of Central Asia.

This article focusses on the main traditional styles of the **Han Chinese** – about 92 percent of the population; see the following article for music of the minorities. Han music (like Irish music) is heterophonic – the musicians play differently decorated versions of a single melodic line – and its melodies are basically pentatonic. Percussion plays a major role, both in instrumental ensembles, and as accompaniment to opera, narrative-singing, ritual music and dance.

The Imperial Heritage

Chinese musical roots date back millennia – among archaeological finds are a magnificent set of 65 bronze bells from the fifth century BC – and its forms can be directly traced to the **Tang dynasty** (618–907AD), a golden age of great poets such as Li Bai and Bai Juyi, who were also avid musicians. Several *qin* zithers from this period are still played today and there's a good market in fake ones, too. In fact, the industry in fake antiques extends to the

music itself, as tourists may be regaled with Hollywood-routines marketed as the music and dance of the Tang court. In recent years, the rather soulless Confucian rituals of the bygone imperial courts have been revived in Qufu and some other towns like Nanjing, again largely for tourists.

The reality, of course, is that there are no 'living fossils' in music, and most traditional forms in the countryside are the product of gradual accretion over the centuries, and especially over the past hundred years. After the Opium Wars of the mid-nineteenth century, China was humiliated at the hands of the foreign imperial powers, and in the turbulent years after 1911, when the last dynasty, the Qing, was overthrown, **Western ideas** gained ground, at least in the towns.

Musically, some intriguing urban forms sprang up from the meeting of East and West, such as the wonderfully sleazy Cantonese music of the 1920s and '30s (see China/Hong Kong – Pop and Rock – p.49). As the movie industry developed, people in Shanghai, colonial Canton (Guangzhou) and nearby Hong Kong threw themselves into the craze for Western-style jazz and dance halls, fusing the local traditional music with jazz, adding saxophone, violin and xylophone to Chinese instruments such as the high-pitched *gaohu* fiddle and the *yangqin* dulcimer. Composers **Lü Wencheng** and **Qiu Hechou** (Yau Hokchau), the violinist **Yin Zizhong** (Yi Tzuchung), and **He Dasha** ('Thicko He'), guitarist and singer of clown roles in Cantonese opera, made many wonderful commercial 78s during this period. While these musicians kept their roots in Cantonese music, the more Westernised (and even more popular) compositions of **Li Jinhui** and his star singer **Zhou Xuan** subsequently earned severe disapproval from Maoist critics as decadent and pornographic. Today, you can hear these 1930s classics once again, played in modern arrangements over street loudspeakers

After the **Communist victory** of 1949, the whole ethos of traditional music was challenged. Anything 'feudal' or 'superstitious' – which included a lot of traditional folk customs and music – was severely restricted, while Chinese melodies were 'cleaned up' with the addition of rudimentary harmonies and bass lines. The communist anthem **"The East is Red"**, which began life as a folksong from northern Shaanxi province (from where Mao's revolution also sprang), is symptomatic. Its local colour was ironed out as it was regimented into a conventionally harmonised hymn-like tune (it was later adopted as the unofficial anthem of the Cultural Revolution). New **'revolutionary' music**, composed from the 1930s on, was generally march-like and optimistic. During the **Cultural Revolution** (1966–76) musical life was driven underground, with only eight model operas and ballets permitted on stage.

The conservatoire style of **guoyue** (national) music, which was about the only Chinese music recorded until recently, was an artificial attempt to create a pan-Chinese style for the concert hall. It derived from the official ethos of twentieth-century reformers, with composed arrangements in a style akin to Western light music. It still dominates the TV and radio music programmes.

While the plaintive pieces for solo erhu fiddle by musicians such as **Liu Tianhua** and the blind beggar **Abing** (also a Daoist priest), or atmospheric tweetings on the *dizi* flute, have been much recorded by *guoyue* virtuosos like **Min Huifen** or **Lu Chunling** respectively, there is much more to Chinese music than this. Folk music has a life of its own and tends to follow the Confucian ideals of moderation and harmony, in which showy virtuosity is out of place.

Rural folk traditions have always been obstinate and transmission somehow survived collectivisation, famine and the Cultural Revolution. Since economic liberalisation began around 1980, traditional musical culture has revived, even as Chinese pop music and karaoke offer an alternative more tempting than Maoism was ever able to provide. China remains today a largely agricultural society in which ritual is still important, and secularisation has been far less thorough in the villages than in the towns.

The Qin and Solo Traditions

Instrumental music is not as popular as vocal music in China, yet in the West it has gained a higher profile. Many of the short virtuosic pieces that you hear played on the **erhu** or **dizi** are the product of modern composers writing in a pseudo-romantic Western style for the concert hall.

The genuine solo traditions going back to the scholar-literati of imperial times, and which live on in the conservatoires today, are for the *qin*, *pipa* and *zheng*.

The **qin** (pronounced 'chin'; also known as *guqin*) is the most exalted of these instruments. A seven-string plucked zither, it has been a favourite subject of poets and painters for over a thousand years, and it is the most delicate

Tale of the Red Lantern cassette sleeve - one of eight model operas permitted during the Cultural Revolution

Many conservatoire-style chamber groups – typically including *erhu* fiddle, *dizi* flute, *pipa* lute and *zheng* zither – play evocatively titled pieces which are heavily arranged or newly composed, and other showpiece compositions for soloist and orchestra.

and contemplative instrument in the Chinese palate. It is the most accessible, too, producing expressive slides and ethereal harmonics. Though primarily associated with the moderation of the Confucian scholar, the qin is also steeped in the mystical Daoism of ancient philosophy – the contemplative union with nature, where silence is as important as sound. The only instruments which may occasionally blend with the qin are the voice of the player, singing ancient poems in an utterly introverted style, or the *xiao* end-blown flute.

With its literate background, qin music has been written in a unique and complex notation since the Tang dynasty. The *Shenqi mipu* (Wondrous and Secret Notation), written by the Ming prince, Zhu Quan, in 1425, and including pieces handed down from earlier dynasties, is still commonly used, and most qin pieces have been transmitted from master to pupil since at least the eighteenth century. Since the 1950s the re-creation of early pieces such as those in the 1425 score, whose performance tradition had been lost, is comparable to the early music movement in the West.

The qin is best heard in meetings of aficionados rather than in concert. The **Beijing Qin Association**, led by Li Xiangting of the Central Conservatoire, meets on the first Sunday of each month and is open to visitors. In Shanghai, the professor of guqin at the Conservatoire, Lin Youren, will introduce you to any get-togethers of qin enthusiasts in the area. Master musicians include **Zha Fuxi**, **Guan Pinghu**, **Zhang Zijian**, **Wu Jinglue** and **Wu Zhaoji** –

who embody the refinement of the older generation – and younger musicians such as **Li Xiangting**, **Wu Wen'guang**, **Lin Youren** and **Gong Yi**. Many of these musicians play instruments dating back to the fifteenth (and in some cases as early as the ninth) century.

Modern traditions of the **pipa** (lute) and **zheng** (zither) also derive from regional styles, transmitted from master to pupil, although 'national' repertoires developed during the twentieth century. For the zheng, the northern styles of Henan and Shan-

ROI PRODUCTIONS

Guan Ping-Hu Playing Qin

dong and the southern Chaozhou and Hakka schools are best known. The pipa, on the other hand, has thrived in the Shanghai region. It makes riveting listening, with its contrast between intimate 'civil' pieces and the startlingly modern-sounding

Chinese Instruments

Wind
Sheng reed mouth-organ usually with 17 pipes in a windchamber
Dizi transverse flute with membrane, giving it a buzzing, nasal tone
Xiao more intimate end-blown flute
Suona shawm with flared bell of Middle Eastern origin – a type of zurna, versions of which are found in a broad sweep across Asia and into the Balkans.
Guanzi short pipe with large double-reed

Strings
Pipa pear-shaped plucked lute with four strings
Qin (Guqin) introspective plucked zither with seven

strings. Strings were traditionally silk and these are often still used by players in Taiwan and Hong Kong. In mainland China players have tended to use metal strings since the Cultural Revolution.
Zheng plucked zither with 16 or more strings each with tuning bridge
Sanxian three-string banjo with long neck
Yangqin hammer dulcimer, related to Indian santur and Hungarian cimbalom
Erhu (huqin, jinghu, gaohu, erxian) some of the many regional forms of two-string bowed fiddles.

Percussion
Yunluo frame of ten small pitched gongs

martial style of traditional pieces such as "Ambush from All Sides" (*Shimian maifu*), with its percussive evocation of the sounds of battle.

The poetic titles of many so-called classical solo pieces – like "Autumn Moon in the Han Palace" or "Flowing Streams" – are often descriptive, related to the identification with nature or to a famous historical scene. The music for these solo instruments is often pictorial, underlining the link with the artistic background of the educated classes of imperial times. The similar titles of the pieces played by folk ensembles, however, are rarely illustrative, serving only as identification for the musicians, like jazz standards.

The North: Blowers and Drummers

Today what we might call classical traditions – derived from the elite of imperial times – live on not just with these solo instruments but still more strongly in **folk ensembles**. Such traditions have survived best in life-cycle and calendar rituals for the gods. The most exciting examples of this music are to be heard at **weddings and funerals**, known as 'red and white business' – red being the auspicious colour of the living, white the colour of mourning.

These occasions usually feature raucous **shawm** and percussion groups called **chuigushou** (blowers and drummers); the *shawm*, a double-reed oboe

Village ceremonial shawm band

with flared bell, is ubiquitous in China. While wedding bands, naturally, tend to use more jolly music, funerals may also feature lively pieces to entertain the guests. The 'blowers and drummers'

play not only lengthy and solemn suites but also the latest pop hits and theme tunes from TV and films. They milk the audience by sustaining notes, using circular breathing, by playing even while dismantling and reassembling their shawms, or by balancing plates on sticks on the end of their instruments. Nobly laying down their lives for their art, shawm players also love to perform while successively inserting cigarettes into both nostrils, both ears, and both corners of the mouth. Some of the more virtuoso shawm bands are found in southwestern Shandong around Heze county.

Rituals performed by lay **Daoist priests** are hardly less operatic, entertaining both gods and mortals. At a funeral in a remote Shanxi village, I saw the Daoists solemnly present offerings to the deities to ensure the path of the deceased to heaven, and then break into a bawdy routine with one of them pretending to smear the snot from the head Daoist's nose over the face of a straight-man who continued playing the *sheng* (traditional Chinese mouth organ).

The **sheng** is one of the oldest Chinese instruments (mentioned as far back as the tenth century BC). It comprises a group of (usually 17) bamboo pipes of different lengths bound in a circle and set in a wooden or metal base into which the player blows. Frequently used for ceremonial music, it adds an incisive rhythmic bite to the music. Like gunpowder and printing, the sheng is one of those all important Chinese inventions and it is the ancestor of all 'free reed' instruments in the West like the mouth organ and the accordion.

Long and deafening strings of fire-crackers are another inescapable part of village ceremony. Some processions are led by a Western-style brass band with a shawm-and-percussion band behind, competing in volume, oblivious of key. In northern villages, apart from the blowers-and-drummers, ritual **sheng-guan** ensembles are also common, with their exquisite combination of mouth organs and oboes, as well as darting flutes and the shimmering halo of the **yunluo** gong-frame, accompanied by percussion. Apart from this haunting melodic music, they perform some spectacular ritual percussion – the

Dizi and *Yunluo* players, Quijiaying village, 1987

these provide perhaps the most accessible Chinese folk music.

There are several regional styles, but the most famous is that of **Shanghai**. In the city's teahouses, old-timers – and some youngsters too – get together in the afternoons, sit round a table and take it in turns to play a set with Chinese fiddles, flutes and banjos. You can't help thinking of an Irish session, with tea replacing the Guinness.

The city's most celebrated teahouse is the **Chenghuang miao**, a picturesque two-storied structure on an island in the old quarter, where there are Monday afternoon gatherings. The contrasting textures of plucked, bowed and blown sounds are part of the attraction of this music with their individual decorations to the gradually unfolding melody. Many pieces consist of successive decorations of a theme, beginning with the most ornate and accelerating as the decorations are gradually stripped down to a fast and bare final statement. Above the chinking of tea bowls and subdued chatter of the teahouse, enjoy the gradual unravelling of a piece like "Sanliu", or the exhilarating dash to the finish of "Xingjie" (Street Parade), with its breathless syncopations.

There are amateur *sizhu* clubs throughout the lower Yangtze area including the cities of Nanjing and Hangzhou. Although in its urban form

intricate arm movements of the cymbal players almost resemble martial arts. This underlines, perhaps, the music's origins in the temples of imperial Beijing, Tianjin, Wutai shan, and Xi'an. Throughout China, there are strong links between folk and temple music.

Around Xi'an, groups performing similar wind and percussion music, misleadingly dubbed **Xi'an Drum Music (Xi'an guyue)**, are active for temple festivals not only in the villages but also in the towns, especially in the sixth moon, around July. The Xi'an Conservatoire has commercialised these folk traditions, but the real thing is much better.

If you remember the tough shawm bands and haunting folksong of Chen Kaige's film *Yellow Earth*, or the harsh falsetto narrative in Zhang Yimou's *The Story of Qiuju*, go for the real thing among the barren hills of **northern Shaanxi** (Shaanbei). This area, the cradle of Mao's revolution, is home to fantastic folk-singers, local opera (such as the *Qinqiang* and *Meihu* styles), puppeteers, shawm bands, and folk ritual specialists. Even *yangge* dancing, which in the towns is often a geriatric form of conga dancing, has a wild power here, again accompanied by shawms and percussion. Aim for counties like Suide, Mizhi, and Yulin – and try and get to the spectacular **Baiyun guan temple** at Jiaxian high above the Yellow River, ideally for the fourth moon festival, generally around late May, where vocal liturgy is punctuated by cymbals and *sheng-guan* music.

The South: Silk and Bamboo

In southeast China, the best-known instrumental music is that of **sizhu** (silk and bamboo) ensembles, using flutes (of bamboo) and plucked and bowed strings (until recently of silk). More melifluous than the outdoor windbands of the north,

Daoist ensemble, Wuxi, c.1962

this music is secular and recreational, the sizhu instrumentation originated in ritual ensembles and is still so used in the villages and temples of southern Jiangsu. In fact, amateur ritual associations are to be found all over southern China, as far afield as Yunnan, punctuating their ceremonies with sedate music reminiscent of the Shanghai teahouses, although often featuring the yunluo gong-frame of northern China.

Another fantastic area for folk music is the coastal region of **southern Fujian**, notably the delightful cities of Quanzhou and Xiamen. Here you can find not only opera, ritual music, and puppetry, but the haunting **Nanguan ballads**. Popular all along the coast of southern Fujian, as in Taiwan across the strait, Nanguan features a female singer accompanied by end-blown flute and plucked and bowed lutes. The ancient texts depict the sorrows of love, particularly of women, while the music is mostly stately and the delivery restrained, yet anguished.

Still further south, the coastal regions of **Chaozhou** and **Shantou**, and the **Hakka** area (inland around Meixian and Dabu), also have celebrated string ensembles featuring a high-pitched *erxian* bowed fiddle and *zheng* plucked zither, as well as large and imposing ceremonial percussion bands, sometimes accompanied by shrill flutes.

The Temples

Southern China is also an area where religious practices have been firmly revived after the onslaught of the Cultural Revolution. Buddhist and Daoist temples have been restored with money from the commercial enterprise of the south and by overseas Chinese with roots in the region, and

many have successfully re-established their musical traditions.

All over China, particularly on the great religious mountains like **Wutai shan**, **Taishan**, **Qingcheng shan**, **Wudang shan** and **Putuo shan**, temples are not just historical monuments but living sites of worship. Morning and evening services are held daily, and larger rituals on special occasions. The priests mainly perform vocal liturgy accompanied by percussion – few now use melodic instruments. They intone sung hymns with long melismas, alternating with chanted sections accompanied by the relentless and hypnotic beat of the 'wooden fish' woodblock. Drum, bell, gongs, and cymbals also punctuate the service.

Melodic instrumental music tends to be added when priests perform rituals outside the temples. These styles are more earthy and accessible even to ears unaccustomed to Chinese music. The Daoist priests from the **Temple of Sublime Mysteries** (Xuanmiao guan) in **Suzhou**, for example, perform wonderful mellifluous pieces for silk-and-bamboo instruments, gutsy blasts on the shawm, music for spectacularly long trumpets and a whole battery of percussion. They have toured in Europe.

Opera and Vocal Music

Chinese opera has been hugely popular for many centuries. There are several hundred types of regional opera, of which **Beijing Opera** is the most widely known. Although it originated in Beijing it's now heard throughout China and is the closest thing to a 'national' theatre. The rigorous training the form demands – and the heavy hand of ideology which saw it as the most important of

Suzhou Daoist group

'the peoples' arts' – is graphically displayed in Chen Kaige's film *Farewell My Concubine* (which takes its title from a Beijing opera).

Chinese musical drama dates back at least two thousand years and became an overwhelmingly popular form with both the elite and common people in the Yuan dynasty (thirteenth century). It continued to evolve. Beijing Opera is a rather late hybrid dating from the eighteenth century. Many librettos now performed date back to the seventeenth century and describe intrigues of emperors and gods, as well as love stories and comedies.

While Chinese opera makes a great visual spectacle, musically it is an acquired taste. One must acclimatise to tense, guttural, and high-pitched singing styles from both men and women. The music is dominated by the bowed string accompaniment of the *jinghu*, a sort of sawn-off erhu. There are also plucked lutes, a flute, and for transitional points, a piercing shawm. The action is driven by percussion, with drum and clappers leading an ensemble of gongs and cymbals in a variety of set patterns.

Every region has its own traditions. Northern **clapper operas** (*bangzi xi*), named after the high-pitched wood block that insistently runs through them, are earthy in flavour – for example, the **Qinqiang** of Shaanxi province. **Sichuan opera** is remarkable for its female chorus. **Ritual masked opera** may be performed in the countryside of Yunnan, Anhui, and Guizhou. Chaozhou and Fujian also have beautiful ancient styles of opera: **Pingju** and **Huangmei xi** are more modern and genteel in style, while **Cantonese opera** is modern and more funky. There are also some beautiful **puppet operas**, often performed for ritual events; Quanzhou in Fujian has a celebrated marionette troupe, and other likely areas include northern Shaanxi and the Tangshan and Laoting areas of eastern Hebei. Or if you're looking for more music and less acrobatics, the classical but now rare **Kunqu** is worth seeking out; it is often accompanied by the sweet-toned *qudi* flute.

There are professional opera troupes in the major towns, but rural opera performances, which are given for temple fairs and even weddings, tend to be livelier. Even in Beijing you will see groups of old men meeting in parks or, incongruously, at spaghetti junctions where the

old gateways used to be, going through their favourite Beijing Opera excerpts.

Narrative-singing, sadly neglected in recordings, also features long classical stories. You may find a teahouse full of old people following these story-songs avidly, particularly in Sichuan, where one popular style is accompanied by the yangqin dulcimer. In Beijing, or more often in Tianjin, amateurs sing through traditional *Jingyun dagu* bal-

Chinese opera, nineteenth century

lads, accompanied by drum and sanxian banjo. In Suzhou, *pingtan*, also accompanied by a plucked lute, is a beautiful genre. In Beijing and elsewhere there is also *xiangsheng*, a comic dialogue with a know-all and a straight man, though its subtle parodies of traditional opera may elude the outsider.

Traditional **folk-songs** (as opposed to ball-gowned divas warbling sentimental bel canto arrangements) are more difficult for the casual visitor to find in Han Chinese areas than among the ethnic minorities, but the beautiful songs of areas like northern Shaanxi and Sichuan are thankfully captured on disc.

New Waves

In all, the resistance of rural traditions to official ideology during three decades of Maoism is remarkable. Indeed, pop music seems to be encroaching more on traditional repertories than revolutionary music ever did. China's youth are turning more and more to Western-influenced pop, though the way that the shawm and percussion bands are able to give their own take on film themes and pop songs shows the adaptability that has kept their music alive.

Outside of China, the best-known Chinese musicians on the World Music circuit are the **Guo Brothers**, based in Britain. Guo Yi plays the sheng, including a highly-developed model with over thirty pipes, and Guo Yue a large number of bamboo flutes – each with its own natural sound and hue. In their collaborations, amongst others with Japanese percussionist Joji Hirota and Irish band The Chieftains, they've become high profile ambassadors for the colours of the country's music.

Another novel angle on traditional music is the imaginative use being made of it by new-wave Chinese composers (most resident in the US) like **Tan Dun** and **Qu Xiaosong**. Part of the talented generation of novelists and film-makers which grew up during the intellectual vacuum of the Cultural Revolution, their experience of folk music is far from the sentimental patriotism of earlier composers, incorporating an uncompromising Chinese spirituality into a radical avant-garde language. Tan Dun composed the vast "Symphony 1997" to celebrate the return of Hong Kong to mainland China. It incorporates the aforementioned set of sixty-five bianzhong bronze bells (with a range of five octaves) found buried in a royal tomb dating to 433 BC. "If you strike the biggest bell," Tan exclaims, "the reverberations last for minutes. It's an amazing sound from 2400 years ago. At that time the bells were used for rituals and certain royal activities. Now we're using them as an expression of peace. The people who made them can never have imagined they would still be heard, thousands of years in the future."

discography

A fair number of Chinese discs have been released in Europe, the US, and Hong Kong. In China itself it is easier to find good recordings of opera than instrumental music, although authentic recordings of instrumental and religious music are finally beginning to appear in place of the old souped-up conservatoire-style recordings.

Instrumental music: Qin, Pipa and Zheng

Compilations

An anthology of Chinese and traditional folk music: a collection of music played on the guqin (China Record Co., China/Cradle Records, Taiwan).

An 8-CD set for serious qin enthusiasts, featuring fantastic reissues of the great masters of the 1950s.

Artists

Guan Pinghu

Born in Suzhou, Guan Pinghu (c.1897–1967) was long resident in the harsher northern capital Beijing. Also a respected painter, he was an outstanding teacher of the qin, and led the way in the 1950s in recreating ancient pieces from early scores such as the 1425 "Shenqi mipu".

Favourite Qin Pieces of Guan Pinghu (ROI Productions, Hong Kong).

Two CDs containing not only pieces handed down from master to pupil but also Guan's own realisations of early pieces not heard for many centuries, notably "Guangling san", a graphic piece starkly depicting the righteous assassination of an evil tyrant, first played in the 3rd century AD. His classic version of "Liushui " (Flowing Waters) was chosen to go into orbit on the spaceship Voyager in 1977. Great recordings with the gentler, intimate sounds of silk strings. Part of a recommended series of instrumentalists from ROI.

Li Xiangting

Li Xiangting (b. 1940), professor of qin at the Central Conservatoire in Beijing, and also a poet, painter, and calligrapher, lived in London for several years, and is a leading light in the revival of the Beijing qin association.

 Chine: L'Art du Qin (Ocora, France).

More easily available than the Guan Pinghu set above, this makes a fine introduction to the refined meditation of the qin. The version of "Guangling san", with metal strings and virtuoso technique, expresses the violence of the story more obviously than Guan's classic version.

Lin Maogen

Born in 1929, Lin Maogen represents the Chaozhou style of zheng playing, and was a pupil of the master Zhang Hanzhai. After the Communist Liberation he maintained the traditional style while taking part in official urban troupes.

Jackdaws Gambol Water (Hugo, Hong Kong).

A disc that shows the plaintive style of zheng played in the Chaozhou area, with some pieces accompanied by the earthy yehu fiddle of Lin Jiheng. The minor-mode melodies like the title piece are particularly evocative, and modal and metrical variation techniques are illustrated by three exquisite (and very different) versions of the standard "Liuqingniang", each in gradually accelerating tempos. This is a part of a major series of zheng masters from Hugo.

Lin Shicheng

Lin Shicheng (born 1922) is heir to the Pudong school of pipa playing from Shanghai, the cradle of the instrument. A former doctor, he has become the main pipa educator in China since moving to the Central Conservatoire in Beijing in 1956.

Chine: l'art du pipa (Ocora, France).

Includes favourites such as the pipa version of the popular ensemble piece "Spring–River–Flowers–Moon–Night" and the martial piece "The Tyrant Removes his Armour" (also on the Wu Man CD opposite), plus some rarer intimate pieces.

Wu Man

Wu Man, a brilliant young player from the southern town of Hangzhou, studied with masters such as Lin Shicheng in Beijing. Since making her home in the US she has championed new music for the instrument, and has collaborated with the Kronos Quartet.

Chinese Traditional and Contemporary Music for Pipa and Ensemble (Nimbus, UK).

Wu Man's two Nimbus albums have been reissued as this budget-price set. The first disc is a solo recording featuring slow, refined 'civil' and dramatic 'martial' music as well as contemporary works showing great mastery of the elegant classical style. The second demonstrates a more glossy ensemble style.

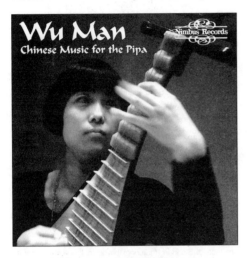

Wu Zhaoji

Wu Zhaoji (1908–97) embodied the all-round culture of the Chinese scholar – a professor of mathematics with a long white beard, he daily practised breathing exercises and calligraphy.

Wumen qin music (Hugo, Hong Kong) .

Wu's qin playing typified the contemplative ethos of the instrument, eschewing mere technical display. He refers here to the Wu style of the canal city of Suzhou. (Other discs in this series include masters like Zhang Zijian and representatives of the middle and younger generation.)

Traditional Ensembles and Temple Music

Compilations

China: Buddhist music of the Ming dynasty (JVC, Japan).

Exquisite music played on shawms, flutes, Chinese mouth organs, a frame of pitched gongs and percussion. The monks of the Zhihua temple, Beijing, perform in collaboration with musicians from the Central Conservatoire.

China: Chuida Wind & Percussive Instrumental Ensembles (Auvidis/Unesco, France).

Three traditional ensembles from southern China recorded by the indefatigable François Picard in 1987, including some unusual silk-and-bamboo from Shanghai and ceremonial music for weddings and funerals from Fujian and Zhejiang.

China: Folk instrumental traditions (VDE-Gallo/AIMP, Switzerland)

An editor's pick – a 2-CD set of archive and recent recordings of village ensembles from north and south compiled by Stephen Jones (author of this article). It includes earthy shawm bands, mystical sheng-guan ritual ensembles, refined silk-and-bamboo, and some awesome percussion, and features some of the master musicians from before the Cultural Revolution, such as the Daoist priests An Laixu on yunluo gong-frame and Zhu Qinfu on drums.

China: Music of the first moon. Shawms from northeast China Vol.1 (Buda/Mus. du Monde, France).

Ear-cleansing shawm-and-percussion music featuring a succession of groups from the northeastern port of Dalian playing music for New Year festivities. Earthy stuff.

China: The Li family band. Shawms from northeast China Vol. 2 (Buda/Mus. du Monde, France).

The Li family band led by the senior Li Shiren is typical of northern shawm and percussion bands This features a spectrum of music from doleful funeral style for large shawms to more popular festive pieces using an array of instruments, including some wild glissandos on the zhuiqin fiddle.

China: Time to Listen (Ellipsis, US).

This 3-CD and booklet compilation should have been the ideal opportunity to present a much-needed overview of Chinese music. Unfortunately the music consists largely of well-mannered conservatoire ensembles about which it's difficult to be enthusiastic. It does, however, include some of the main genres of instrumental music, music of the minorities and some modern compositions.

Chine: Chant Liturgique Bouddhique (Ocora, France).

A series of CDs of vocal liturgy from Buddhist temples, so far including services from temples in Shanghai and Quanzhou. Not easy listening, but with evocative gongs and bells.

Chine: Musique ancienne de Chang'an (Inédit, France).

A conservatoire recording whose wind pieces are impressive – and better than the string ones (which don't belong to this tradition anyway) – if lacking the subtlety of tuning, complexity of tempi and guts of the folk ensembles.

Chine: musique classique (Ocora, France).

A selection of solo pieces featuring the qin, pipa, sheng, guanzi, dizi, xiao, erhu, and yangqin, played by outstanding instrumentalists of the 1950s, including Guan Pinghu, Cao Zheng, and Sun Yude.

Musical travel: China, the 18 provinces (Auvidis/Silex, France).

Brief but evocative excerpts of some of the main styles of Chinese music. The broad spectrum of sounds also includes birds in a Beijing market, a pumpkin seller, traffic noise, revolutionary song, and firecrackers.

Rain Dropping on the Banana Tree (Rounder, US).

Taking its title from a popular Cantonese melody, this collection of reissued 78s from 1902 to 1930 features early masters of Cantonese music such as Yau Hokchau, as well as excerpts from Beijing and Cantonese opera.

The South

Compilations

PAN 2030CD

E
T
H
N
I
C

Sizhu
丝

Chamber music of South China

S
E
R
I
E
S

Silk
Bamboo
竹

Sizhu/Silk Bamboo: Chamber music of South China (Pan, Netherlands).

Several styles of chamber ensemble along the southeastern coast, from silk-and-bamboo from Shanghai, the refined instrumental Nanguan music from Xiamen, Chaozhou and Hakka pieces featuring zheng zither, and examples of the more modern Cantonese style. Excellent notes, too.

Special Collection of Contemporary Chinese Musicians (Wind Records, Taiwan).

A 2-CD set of archive recordings of some of the great 1950s instrumentalists, featuring masters of suona, dizi, erhu in ensemble, as well as the solo qin, pipa and zheng. As with others in this series, the notes are extensive in Chinese but skeletal in English.

Tianjin Buddhist Music Ensemble (Nimbus, UK).

The temple music style from Tianjin on the coast near Beijing. Buddhist ritual sheng-guan music played by a group of musicians in their 70s with some wonderful guanzi oboe playing.

Triumphal Command: Wind and percussion music of northern Shanxi (Hugo, Hong Kong).

A melodious compilation of four bands from the area of Wutai, with wedding shawms and funerary sheng-guan music both represented.

Xi'an drums music (Hugo, Hong Kong).

Majestic wind-and-percussion music performed for funerals and calendrical pilgrimages around Xi'an, including some rarely-heard vocal hymns (weirdly translated as 'rap music').

Artists

Tsai Hsiao-Yueh

The senior Nanguan singer Tsai Hsiao-yueh (Cai Xiaoyue), with her group based in Tainan, Taiwan, maintain the proud amateur tradition of this exalted genre. They led the international recognition of Nanguan, which has more recently seen an impressive revival on mainland China in Fujian, its place of origin just across the strait.

Nan-kouan: chant courtois de la Chine du sud Vol. 1 (Ocora, France).

Haunting chamber ballads with a female singer accompanied by end-blown flute and plucked and bowed lutes. There are five further volumes featuring the same artists.

Opera and Vocal Music

Compilations

An Introduction to Chinese Opera (Hong Kong Records, Hong Kong).

A series of four CDs illustrating the different styles, including Beijing, Cantonese, Shanghai, Huangmei, Henan, Pingju, and Qinqiang operas.

China: Ka-le, Festival of Happiness (VDE-Gallo/AIMP, Switzerland).

Mainly instrumental music from the exquisite puppet operas of the Quanzhou Puppet Troupe of southern Fujian.

Chinese classical opera: Kunqu. The Peony Pavilion (Inédit, France).

A 2-CD set featuring excerpts from the great opera by the early seventeenth century Tang Xianzu. The vocal sections give a better idea of the tradition than the kitsch harmonised orchestral arrangements.

Opera du Sichuan: la legende de serpent blanc (Buda/Musique du Monde, France).

A double CD of traditional opera from the spicy southwestern province of Sichuan, featuring the distinctive female chorus, and ending with the attractive bonus of a 'bamboo ballad' on the same theme sung by a narrative-singer.

Shuochang: the Ultimate Art of Storytelling (Wind Records, Taiwan).

A valuable 2-CD nationwide overview of an otherwise neglected genre, with archive recordings of some of the major regional traditions, from the urbane drum-singing styles of Beijing and Tianjin, and mellifluous singing from Suzhou and Yangzhou, to rarely-heard narratives from the more remote Hubei, Guangxi, Gansu and Qinghai provinces.

Songs of the Land in China: Labour songs and love songs (Wind Records, Taiwan).

A 2-CD set featuring beautiful archive recordings of folk singing, mostly unaccompanied, from different regions of China, including rhythmic songs of boatmen, Hua'er songs from the northwest, and the plaintive songs from northern Shaanxi. A surprisingly varied and captivating selection.

The Beauty of Chinese Folk Opera (Wind Records, Taiwan).

Two CDs of diverse regional operas, mostly recorded before the Cultural Revolution, including not only Beijing opera (such as a chilling extract from "Farewell My Concubine" sung by Mei Lanfang) and Yu Zhenfei's extraordinary "Kunqu", but also rare excerpts from Hunan and Sichuan provinces. Northern clapper operas are specially featured, ending with new yangge dance-dramas composed to rouse the peasants at the Communist base against the Japanese at Yan'an in the 1940s, and a stirring puppet drama from Shaanxi.

Contemporary

Guo Brothers

Guo Yi (born 1954) and Guo Yue (born 1958) were brought up in a musicians' courtyard in Beijing where they received their musical training during the Cultural Revolution. They moved to London in the early 1980s where they have built up a following, starting out busking in Covent Garden and moving on to compose film scores to The Killing Fields and The Last Emperor. Yi plays the ancient Chinese mouth organ, the sheng and Yue plays a large collection of bamboo flutes.

⊙ **Yuan** (RealWorld, UK).

The Guos' album for Peter Gabriel's label is an evocative if often overblown production of evocations, recorded with quite a number of other musicians. They are better as an unaccompanied duo when they really bring out the extraordinary expressive power of their instruments. The recording nearest to this is their own-label ⊙ **Our Homeland** (Bamboo Mountain, UK; Tel/fax: 020 7720 1706).

Tan Dun

Born in 1957, Tan Dun's childhood influences in rural Hunan included local shamanistic music and ritual ensembles before being swept up by the Cultural Revolution when he gained eccentric experience playing erhu and arranging for a local Beijing opera troupe. As a composer he is counted among the 'New Wave' of writers, filmakers and artists of the early 1980s. Compositions include On Taoism (1985), the opera Marco Polo (1994), Symphony 1997 (for the Reunification Ceremony of Hong Kong) and Peony Pavilion (1998) based on the ancient Kunqu opera. He has lived in the US since 1986.

⊙ **Ghost Opera** (Nonesuch, US).

Recording of an extraordinary multi-media piece written for pipa player Wu Man and the Kronos Quartet 'with water, stones, paper, and metal', incorporating traditional shamanistic sounds of his childhood in remote Hunan province, alongside Bach and Shakespeare. Totally original.

⊙ **Symphony 1997** (Sony Classical, US).

Yo Yo Ma's cello playing provides the narrative element in the music blending his classical technique with gliding tones reminiscent of erhu music. The theatrical musical panorama includes the 2400-year-old bells, Cantonese opera recorded on the streets of Hong Kong, a dragon dance plus quotations from Beethoven's Ode to Joy and Puccini's Turandot. Naïve, yet sophisticated and certainly colourful.

China

Minorities

sounds of the frontiers

Almost ninety-two percent of the population of China is categorised as Han Chinese – but that leaves nearly one hundred million people divided amongst the fifty-five officially recognised 'minority nationalities'. **Helen Rees**, in collaboration with Chinese musicologists **Zhang Xingrong** and **Li Wei**, provides an introduction to some of their traditions.
  Note that Tibetan music is covered in a separate article on p.254.

Ethnic minorities are found all over China, but the heaviest concentrations are in the northwest and southwest where there's a rich mixture of **southeast Asian** peoples found also in Thailand and Laos. In the north, there are **Manchus**, **Uighurs**, **Russians** and **Mongolians**. In the south, there are **Zhuang**, **Dai** and **Li**, **Tibetans**, **Yi**, **Lisu** and **Naxi**, **Miao** and **Wa**. All of these minorities speak languages other than Mandarin or Cantonese, though those living in urban areas have tended to adapt to mainstream Chinese culture.

In the 1950s the new Communist government dispatched teams to record minority music and dance. Apart from pure research, this provided raw material for professional song-and-dance troupes. These state-run troupes are found throughout China and typically present arrangements of local music and dance, frequently adding Western instruments, tuning and harmony. The current government policy to salvage minority culture – which was badly damaged by the Cultural Revolution – has also meant exposure for more authentic local groups on TV and at national festivals. However, to experience rootier minorities music, you need to get to see traditional, local performances, many of which have enjoyed a revival since the post-1976 political and economic liberalisation.

Minorities **religious music**, such as that of the **Tibetan and Dai Buddhists**, and of **Lisu Christians**, is also an active tradition.

The Northwest

The **Xinjiang Uighur Autonomous Region** in China's far northwest, once a staging post on the northern Silk Road, has long been a meeting point for Chinese and Central Asian culture. The Islamic **Uighurs**, a Turkic people numbering about six million and comprising around 45 percent of Xinjiang's population, are renowned for their music and dance traditions. Best known among these are the **On ikki muqam** (twelve *muqam*), twelve classical song-and-dance suites closely related to Uzbek and Tajik forms.

Played complete, each **muqam** lasts a couple of hours and consists of an introduction in free rhythm followed by three *näghmä* (sections). The opening *čong näghmä* includes classical sung poetry, the second *dastan näghmä* features romantic narrative songs and the third, *mäšräp*, consists of folk song and dance pieces, increasing in speed towards the end. These näghmä are compared to the human body, the čong representing the head (intellect), the dastan the upper body (heart) and the mäšräp the legs (spirit). The suite moves from solemn and elevated beginnings through the emotional narrative to the light-hearted songs and dances at the end. (There are other muqam, much shorter and purely for dancing, played by the **Dolan** people, a sub-group of the Uighurs.)

The word *muqam* is in common with Arabic, Turkic and Persian music and underlines their links. Instruments used include several different fiddles and plucked lutes, dulcimer, and the ass-hide drum *dap* (from the Arabic *daf* or *duff*). The long-necked lutes *dutar* (two strings) and *tanbur* (five strings) are variants of instruments found throughout Central Asia (see Central Asian Republics article, p.24).

Melodies are generally built on a seven-note scale and are highly ornamented. Soloists have a certain freedom in their interpretation of the melodic line, incorporating a variety of flourishes and embellishments. There is considerable rhythmic variety outlined by the dap with a tendency to irregular cycles as well as unmetered sections. The lyrics are often classical *ghazal* poems and many of the same song texts are shared in Uzbek, Tajik and Uighur music.

As in other parts of China, between the late 1950s and late '70s, traditional music and other cultural activities amongst the Uighur suffered through a succession of extremist political movements, culminating in the iconoclastic Cultural Revolution. In recent decades there has been a substantial revival. Work on preserving and disseminating the Twelve Muqam actually began in the '50s. Shortly before his death in 1956, **Turdu Ahun**, a traditional performer who knew the Twelve Muqam in their entirety by heart, began to record them. He was already in his seventies but fortunately lived long enough to complete the recordings, which last about twenty-four hours and formed the basis for a 1960 book of muqams. In the 1990s a complete performance was released on twenty-four cassettes and the musical notation and texts have been published.

Muqams are traditionally performed by small groups at festivals, weddings, parties, or even begging for alms. In Urumqi, the capital of Xinjiang, there are nightly musical performances in many of the Uighur restaurants. You should also be able to catch the music in Kashgar in the west of Xinjiang, a Silk Road town par excellence with its famous Sunday market; musicians gather in the main square outside the mosque.

Another famous northwestern tradition is **Hua'er** songs, prevalent among Han, Hui, Salar, Tibetans and other groups in Gansu, Qinghai and Ningxia. These are sung both informally outdoors and at large, organised festivals. Hua'er festivals usually take place over the fifth and sixth lunar months (around June to July), and competitive dialogue songs (either between two singers, or between two groups of people) are especially common. Texts are not fixed, although they use formulae and stock inserts, and are frequently about love, with topical references. They have a wide melodic range. Men often sing falsetto, and both sexes employ a variety of vocal ornamentation. The songs are usually unaccompanied, although

at staged festivals traditional instruments or synthesizers may be added. In Gansu festivals take place at Erlang Mountain (14th–19th days of 5th lunar month), and Lianhua Mountain (2nd–6th days of 6th lunar month). Hua'er singers can also be found every day in good weather in the city park of Xining, provincial capital of Qinghai.

There are many other ethnic groups and musics in the northwest – even a few thousand **Russians**

JEAN DURING/OCORA

Dap and dutar players, Xinjiang

and **Tatars**. Some light songs based on northwestern material have become popular throughout China including "Xinjiang is Good", and the **Kazakh**-inspired song "Cute Bunch of Roses".

The Southwest

In **Sichuan**, **Guizhou**, and **Yunnan** provinces, there are minority groups that live in remote, mountainous areas, and still preserve traditional musical culture.

Yunnan, for instance, which borders on Tibet and Sichuan to the north, Burma to the west and Laos and Vietnam to the south is home to twenty-five minority nationalities. A recent discovery is the two- to eight-voice singing of rice-transplanting songs by the **Hani** people of Honghe prefecture. Men and women of all ages sing together, with voices entering successively to create a dense, microtonally coloured chordal effect.

Better known are the antiphonal courtship songs and enormous **lusheng** (mouth organs) of the **Miao** of **Guizhou**. Lusheng may have several pipes extending up to five or seven metres in length and are related to the Chinese *sheng* and Lao *khaen*. Their tuning is pentatonic and the instruments may be played singly or in groups, with a bright rhythmic incision.

Some southern minorities have interacted musically with other groups. The **Naxi** of Lijiang County, Yunnan, are proud of their genre **Baisha Xiyue**, a suite including song, dance and instrumental music, said to have been brought by Mongol conqueror Kublai Khan when he reached

Yunnan in 1253. They also borrowed Confucian-style ritual music associations from the Han, and play **Dongjing music** derived from southern Chinese silk- and-bamboo music. With its rich variety of string, wind and percussion instruments, this is performed in secular settings today – including nightly tourist concerts in the county seat, Dayan Town. Naxi music also includes monophonic and polyphonic folksongs, solemn chants of the indigenous *dongba* priests, melodies and calls played on the tree-leaf, and festival folk dances accompanied either by singing, or by flute or mouth organ.

Using instruments to 'talk' is widespread among Yunnan minorities. Often courting couples of the Naxi, Yi, or other groups express their love through the Jew's harp; the Wa consider their wooden drum capable of communicating with Heaven, and some groups use the wooden drum to declare war, send news, congratulate hunters,

etc. In these cases each drum pattern represents a particular signal, conveying particular content.

Regional festivals are often the best time to catch minority music-making in Yunnan. The Third Month Fair held in April in Dali brings out a variety of local Han, Bai and Yi performers, and in Lijiang Country festive occasions such as 1 January see enthusiastic Naxi peasants and townsfolk dancing, singing and playing in Dayan Town. But, as ever, try not to be limited to the professional town groups: throughout the villages of Yunnan there is fantastic music – folk-singers, instrumentalists, ritual groups, all performing socially.

In the 1960s, films set in minority locales brought minority musics to the whole country, and compositions inspired by minority themes, such as the pipa solo "Dance of the Yi" are still widespread. Cassettes by the Yi pop group, **Shanying** (Mountain Eagle) based in Sichuan sold widely in the southwest in the mid-1990s.

Central South and Southeast China

There are relatively few minorities in the southeast, but some large groups in the central south, of whom the most numerous are the **Zhuang** of Guangxi Zhuang Autonomous Region, numbering around thirteen million. The Zhuang are known for their 'song fairs', held during festivals such as Chinese New Year, at which young people get acquainted by singing love songs and question songs. Zhuang songs may be solo, or sung in two or three parts, with the lowest voice leading.

The million or so **Li** of **Hainan Island**, off China's south coast, east of Vietnam, also have distinctive, though now declining musical traditions, including a two- or three-bar xylophone strung from a bamboo trestle or between trees, and the 'pole dance', in which girls rhythmically clap together bamboo poles parallel to the ground, while boys leap between the poles.

The Northeast and Inner Mongolia

The largest minorities in the far northeastern provinces of Heilongjiang, Jilin and Liaoning are the nearly ten million **Manchu** – the group that ruled China during the Qing dynasty (1644–1911) – and the almost two million **Koreans**, whose ancestors migrated from Korea in the nineteenth century, and who still preserve many Korean customs and musical styles. While many Manchu have assimilated to mainstream Chinese life, some still

Recording Music in Yunnan

What impressed me most in my work among the Yunnan Minorities was the authenticity of the cultures. They truly value music. You hear music everywhere; it is an integral part of people's lives – music for walking, for eating, for drinking, music for greetings, farewells, for courtship, weddings, funerals and so on. Music has so many functions; it can't be separated from everyday life, while festivals are sustained by music – people sing and dance for three days and nights without rest. A festival or indeed any other ceremony without music is inconceivable.

I once attended an engagement ceremony in Fugong where I was greeted at the entrance with singing and offered wine – a milky-coloured liquor, made from potatoes with drops of oil floating on top. I can't say I liked the taste but everyone there was singing and dancing ecstatically, intoxicated with the music and the drink. On another occasion I was at a Naxi funeral. We arrived at the house the night before the cremation. The wake was accompanied by *suona* (shawm) and the chanting of monks. Every so often a new group would come in, wailing laments which combined into a rich natural polyphony. Next morning was heralded in with long trumpets and suona. The funeral procession was made up of different groups singing their individual laments, all at the same time.

Music serves as a medium of communication. Without music, love is impossible among the Minorities. One form of courtship among the Maan is the playing of one instrument (*lengnong*), a flute, by two people.

Sometimes the real significance of what you are listening to is not immediately apparent. On one occasion I was recording a Lisu ensemble of *qiben*, *jizi* (lutes) and *juelie* (pipe). The music sounded very discordant. It seemed that the lutes were not playing at the same pitch as the pipe, and that the instruments had not been tuned properly. I took the instruments from the players, and tuned them down to match the pipe. The ensemble began to play again, but by the end of the first phrase the players were all busy retuning their

HELEN REES

Yi musicians at a flower festival

instruments. When I listened to the recording later I realised my mistake; the 'out-of-tuneness' which I had attributed to bad musicianship was actually an intentional layering of different intonations and was an essential part of this music.

Zhang Xingrong

Reprinted from Issue #8 of *Chime* – a journal covering Chinese musical research (PO Box 11092, 2301 EB Leiden, The Netherlands; chime@wxs.nl).

practise traditional **shamanistic rituals**, in which a magic drum and waist-bells are major tools for communication with the gods.

Nearly five million **Mongols** live in China, most in the Inner Mongolian Autonomous Region. The rich variety of Mongolian music includes the 'long song' (*urtyn duu*), characterised by slow tempi and long melodic line, often accompanied by the Mongolian two-string horse-head fiddle; the faster 'short song' (*bogino-duu*); epic song; and the extraordinary vocal technique *xöömii*, in which the per-

former sings two or three notes simultaneously by generating an intense low note from which upper partials are emphasised. Mongolian instruments include bowed and plucked strings, flutes, jew's harp, and percussion. Today Mongolian- and Chinese-language pop music is popular in Inner Mongolia.

(For more on Mongolian music, see the article on p.189).

With thanks to Sue Tuohy

discography

Northwest

Compilations

Bu Dunya/This World: Song and Melodies of the Uighurs (Pan, Netherlands).

An excellent sample of folk songs and extracts from the muqam repertoire performed by the Šadiyana Ensemble from Urumqi.

Chine. Xinjiang: The Silk Road (Playasound, France).

Good field recordings made in 1986 and '87 by Anderson Bakewell featuring muqam extracts and folksongs performed by individual performers and small groups.

Turkestan Chinois/Xinjiang: Musiques Ouïgoures (Ocora, France).

This 2-CD set presents more extensive and more serious excerpts from the Uighur muqams, plus more popular repertoire including Dolan muqams. Beautiful traditional performances. Good notes and photos.

Southwest

Compilations

Baishibai: Songs of the Minority Nationalities of Yunnan (Pan, Netherlands).

Field recordings by Zhang Xingrong and Li Wei, featuring folk singers of the Naxi, Lisu, Bai, Tibetans, Yi, Kemu and other groups in Yunnan Province. A specialised but fascinating collection including dance songs, Buddhist chant, a song promoting family planning and wonderful work songs while making butter and pounding rice.

Huanle de Miaojia/A Happy Miao Family (Pan, Netherlands).

A horrible title (from one of the songs included), but a good and varied collection of Miao songs and instrumental music (including the lusheng mouth organ) from Guizhou, ranging from 'authentic' style to composed/arranged 'song-and-dance'. Performed by musicians from the state Guizhou National Art Ensemble.

Naxi Music from Lijiang (Nimbus, UK).

Two contrasting forms of traditional Naxi music: elegant Han-derived Dongjing ensemble music, performed by the amateur musicians of the Dayan Ancient Music Association during their 1995 British tour and lively Naxi dance-tunes played on the Naxi pipe by Lijiang folk musician Wang Chaoxin.

Artists

Shanying Mountain Eagle

Rock group of three Yi musicians from Liangshan Yi Autonomous Prefecture, Sichuan Province. Started off singing in Yi for local market, now sing in both Han Chinese and Yi. Popular in mid-1990s in southwest China, especially among Yi people.

Zouchu Da Liangshan (Out of the Great Liang Mountains) (Taipingyang Yingyin Co., China).

If you can get hold of it, this is a winsome cassette successfully combining Chinese rock style with Yi instrumental, vocal, linguistic, and cultural colour.

China/Hong Kong   Pop and rock

Cantopop and protest singers

Amongst the Chinese – and particularly the Cantonese-speaking population of southern China and Hong Kong – by far the biggest names in popular music are the singers of **Cantopop**, Hong Kong's phenomenally successful creation. **Chinese rock** is a rarer beast, but one as rooted in China as the West, and with a strain of protest – through the figure of Cui Jian, whose songs were taken up by the students in Tiananmen Square, and whose performances in a red blindfold caught the world's imagination. **Joanna Lee** sketches the history. and introduces the stars.

Cantopop

Western-influenced music first came to China in the 1920s, and with the rise of the middle-class in urban areas, especially in Shanghai, local singing stars emerged. One of the most famous was **Zhou Xuan** (1918–57), who acted in films and recorded popular songs with salon orchestra accompaniment, on amorous or urban themes. One can only imagine the change in the landscape in 1949 when the Communist Party took control of the city. Shanghai was purged, and all such entertainment forms of the corrupt capitalist world denounced as 'pornographic'.

In many ways, **Hong Kong's Cantopop** owes its existence to Shanghai's popular music – thanks to the influx of Shanghai composers and singers in the 1950s, not to mention the transplanting of nightclubs, dance halls, and a major film industry. However, the catalyst for the Cantopop boom was the meeting of East and West in the 1970s.

Cantopop beginnings

Back in the 1960s, there were two popular music scenes in Hong Kong: Western music – Elvis, Johnny Mathis and The Beatles (who visited in 1964) – imported for the Western-educated youth, and **Shidaiqu** (contemporary song) which followed the tradition of 1930s Shanghai and was sung in Mandarin (a second language for Hong Kong's 95-percent Cantonese population).

But as the British colony transformed itself into an industrial-cum-financial mecca, it built its own music industry. **Cantopop** (Cantonese pop) began to appear in the 1970s – an amalgam of Western soft-rock and mellow Cantonese lyrical singing – 'Southern China-meets-the West', a musical equivalent of Hong Kong itself. It developed around the time when TV became a household fixture in the mid-1970s, and stations commissioned music for prime-time soap operas. Radio stations were also important in advancing careers, holding song-writing competitions and talent contests.

Joseph Koo and **James Wong** were the groundbreakers, composing Cantopop song for TV themes in the 1970s. If you want to relive the aura of those days, try and get compilation discs including singers **Adam Cheng** (Cheng Siu Chau) and **Lisa Wang** (Wang Ming Chuen), famous prime-time soap opera stars who sang much of this material. The scene then took off further with bands such as **Lotus** (a definite Asian connection there) and the **Wynners** (initially named the Losers – the change of name paid off), who sang Abba covers and original songs in English.

Glory Days

It was in the 1980s, when singers changed from English to Cantonese, that things really got going. The glory days of the early 1980s saw the creation of a raft of stars, all in their twenties. They included **Anita Mui**, **Sam Hui**, **Leslie Cheung**, **Jacky Cheung** (no relation), **Danny Chan**, **Kenny Bee** and **Alan Tam** (these last two formerly of the Wynners). Almost all of them combined a singing career with roles in prime-time soaps, and went on to make movies. Often new songs were featured in the films to further boost the singer/actor.

By the end of the 1980s, four male stars – **Jacky Cheung**, **Andy Lau**, **Aaron Kwok** and **Leon Lai** – dominated the Cantopop scene so completely that they were known as *Say dai tin wong* (the Four Gods). These rival deities created a boom in sales of their respective solo albums, as well as an incessant flurry of media exposures via film roles. Jacky Cheung, the most accomplished, even premiered the first-ever Cantonese Broadway show in 1997. At time of writing, they remain major players, though rivalled by hot new teen idols such as **Andy Hui**, **Miriam Yeung**, **Sammi Cheng**, **Karen Mok** and **Eason Chan**.

They have brought Cantopop to a new pinnacle of sophistication: in marketing, packaging, and production. Yet the music itself is often haphazard: the hit process tends to involve rushed commissioning of composers and lyricists, and producers selecting Japanese and American cov-

and HMV, sample a few tracks and pick what you like. If you want a better bargain try the night markets in Temple Street and Tung Choi Street in Kowloon. Go into little shops and street stalls where they sell VCDs, CDs, tapes and laser discs, and pick through their selections. Admire the attractive packaging and look through the life-size posters of the stars on display.

If you want to experience Cantopop as **live entertainment**, visit Television City (an offshoot of Universal Studios) in Clearwater Bay, or try and track down any Cantopop concerts at the Hong Kong Coliseum. Tickets for Coliseum concerts range from HK$100 to $400 which will get you comfortably close to the singers. Or you can sample radio programmes and listen to the quick pitter patter of DJs (most in their early twenties). Call up the local radio stations (Commercial Radio 2, Radio Hong Kong 2, and Hit Radio) and ask if they have any special public events in parks or shopping malls with star appearances. In any of these live events, you'll be surrounded by screaming teeny boppers trying to present bouquets to their idols. Soak up the sugared quality of the music, wallow in the

There's something about Miriam: get tips from Ms Yeung

ers, and singers recording for long sessions to beat production deadlines.

But what does it sound like? Well, Cantopop remains a close cousin to Anglo-American soft rock and a younger sister of Japanese pop, a bit heavy on synthesizer and drum machines. The songs are always in a moderate tempo and the lyrics are formulaic (happy/sad love). A few English phrases remain amidst the "oohs and aahs" of the backing vocals: "I love you", "You love me", and "Oh yeah".

Hearing Cantopop

It's hard to escape the synthesized accompaniment of Cantopop songs on the streets of Hong Kong, blasting from shops and car radios. On TV you can surf the channels for music videos, pop music programmes (and on cable, Asian MTV). If you are interested in **buying Cantopop**, just take your chance, scan what's displayed at the local Tower

soothing voices of those stars, and swing and wave and clap and hold candles (or little electric torches) the same way as everyone else around you.

Cantopop is marketed worldwide and sells wherever there are Chinese communities; indeed, the large HK émigré populations in the North America are major concert tour stops for Cantopop singers. It is the epitome of Hong Kong's enterprising spirit and it looks well poised to take over the motherland. A recent trend in Cantopop, beginning during the countdown to Hong Kong's return to China, is the proliferation of stylistic Cantopop music with Mandarin lyrics for the market in Taiwan and mainland China. And the moguls are pretty sure of themselves. Pop may once have been banned as 'pornographic' but it no longer raises an eyebrow in post-Deng consumerist China.

Oh – and Cantopop, as you might imagine, also has a big presence on the Internet, with fan pages devoted to all the major stars. To start explorations, try *http://hkpop.com*.

Leslie Cheung: The Dreamboat

Praised by Hong Kong's *Film Comment* as 'the dreamboat of Hong Kong singers and a stalwart of the island's vital movie industry', **Leslie Cheung** has followed a career that closely parallels Hong Kong's pop trends from the late 1970s to the present. In 1977 he was prizewinner of a television pop song contest, performing "When a Child is Born" (he sung it in English), first popularised by Johnny Mathis. Cheung was immediately drafted into television dramas and, later, films.

One of the first singers launching Cantopop as a genre, Cheung has enjoyed a loyal following for two decades. In 1981, the title song of his first Cantopop album, *The Wind Blows On* (music borrowed from a Japanese chart-topper) brought him immediate success. Unusually for Cantopop, he composes some of his own works and writes some of his own lyrics, which sometimes mix Chinese and English lyrics. And he is not beyond a good cover: a Cheung favourite of the 1980s was Rod Stewart's "Sailing".

In 1990 Cheung retired from the Cantopop scene after a series of soldout farewell concerts at the Hong Kong Coliseum to devote more time to his serious (Mandarin language) film career. His subsequent roles as a homosexual Beijing opera singer in *Farewell My Concubine* (1993) and a drifter in *Happy Together* (1997) made him a darling at Cannes.

In the late 1990s, Cheung returned to music, though singing largely in Mandarin. His 1998 album, released by Rock Records, and entitled *Printemps* (no Chinese title – just French), contained songs solely in Mandarin. He is already well-known in Taiwan and China (partly thanks to his film career) and recording in Mandarin allows access to the huge pan-Chinese market beyond Hong Kong.

Leslie Cheung Internet Fan Club

Chinese Rock

Although the Chinese market is tapped by the Cantopop industry, only a small percentage of 'entertainment capital' has been injected into the local Chinese rock/pop scene. China's indigenous rock, although often connected to the Hong Kong-Taiwanese entertainment industry, is a different beast. One which has its traditions in passionate and fiery protest, and which still possesses a cultural and political self-awareness.

Protest-rock: Cui Jian

Chinese protest-rock really began with singer-trumpeter-guitarist, **Cui Jian**. He is now regarded as the grandfather of *yaogun yinyue* (rock'n'roll) thanks to his hit "Yiwu suoyou" (Nothing to my Name), picked up by worldwide media during the May-June 1989 democracy movement.

The rock scene was non-existent in China until the mid-1980s, when foreign students on cultural exchange brought tapes of their favorite rock and pop music (and their own electric guitars) to the Chinese mainland, and shared them with their fellow students. Their music quickly caught the imagination of Chinese university youths and the urban vanguard. Cui Jian cited the Sex Pistols, Sting, Rolling Stones, and the Beatles as his major influences.

Cui also credits the influence of the Taiwanese singer **Teresa Teng** (known to the Chinese by her original name, Deng Lijun; 1953–95). Teng's singing style can be directly traced to Zhou Xuan and 1930s Shanghai. She was probably the most popular Chinese singer of her time, whose recordings were circulated in China in the black market from the late 1970s, when such music was officially banned. The reasons for its banning were, in part, as representing such bourgeois ideas as paid entertainment and social dancing, as well as for lyrics thought to be lowering sexual morals. The ban was lifted by the late 1980s, when the state loosened its grip on the popular music market, knowing that it was a sign of 'openness to capitalism'.

Yet the openness of China's authorities to Hong Kong and Taiwanese pop goes hand in hand with a suspicion of indigenous Chinese rock. The scene thus remains low key, with bands playing in private bars (no government stadium nor sports hall would host such shows). Top bands at the end of the 1990s include **Cobra** (an all-female band), **Tang Chao** (Tang Dynasty), **Heibao** (Black Pan-

Cui Jian: Breaking Eggs

Cui Jian, a Beijinger born of parents of Korean descent, studied the trumpet at an early age, trained as a classical musician and joined the Beijing Symphony Orchestra in 1981. After being introduced to Anglo-American rock in the mid-1980s, however, he forged an independent path and his gritty voice became the primary reference point of Chinese rock.

Ciu Jian (on trumpet) and his band

Ciu's song "Nothing To My Name", ostensibly a love song, became a democracy movement anthem since its lyrics could be interpreted as a political monologue of the ruled about his ruler:

> I used to endlessly ask
> When will you go away with me?
> You laugh at me always.
> I have nothing to my name.
>
> I want to give you my dreams
> And also my freedom.
> You laugh at me always.
> I have nothing to my name.
>
> I must tell you, I have waited too long.
> I'll tell you my last request:
> I'll hold your two hands
> To take you away with me.

This song evoked a memorable complaint from General Wang Zhen, a veteran of the Long March: "What do you mean, you have nothing to your name? You've got the Communist Party haven't you?"

Even though Cui's lyrics have always been ambiguous, his voice has occasionally been muffled in the 1990s. A nationwide tour was cancelled midway because of his action on stage (blindfolded in red cloth – the colour of Communism) that mesmerised his fans but enraged officials. He upset the authorities, too, with his recording of "Nanni Wan", a revolutionary song closely associated with the Communist Party and its ideals, glorifying Chinese peasants and their contribution to society. Cui's rock interpretation was understood by many as a passive-aggressive challenge to (or mockery of) authority.

Like most of China's rockers, Cui turned more introspective as the 1990s progressed. His 1994 album *Hongqi xiade Dan* (Eggs Under the Red Flag) reflected the shifting concerns of China's youth from politics to the realities of earning a living. But the powerful title track neatly encapsulated both:

> Money floats in the air,
> We have no ideals.
> Although the air is fresh,
> We cannot see into the distance.
> Although the chance is here,
> We are too timid.
> We are wholly submissive,
> Like eggs under the red flag.

Cui's most recent (1998) album, *Wuneng de Liliang* (The Power of the Powerless), continued to explore global rock, and personal lyrical themes, with songs such as "Bird in the Cage" and "Spring Festival" – far from the politics of his early recordings. Over the past few years, Cui has had successful tours in Europe and the US. Nevertheless, he is also keenly aware of the limitations 'official China' imposes on his musical freedom.

Chinese Karaoke

The **karaoke** culture hit China big time in the 1990s and has become an established part of the music scene. Typically, karaoke tapes will feature Cantopop, Taiwanese pop, US hits, a couple of Chinese rock songs, *tongsu* (state approved Chinese pop) bestsellers, and, bizarrely, a plethora of disco/pop instrumental tracks of songs from the Cultural Revolution! Fancy praising Maoist communist ideals ("The East is Red",

the revolutionary anthem of 1966–1976) with synthesizer accompaniment in front of an inebriated audience? This fun-packed way of sampling music in China (and beholding a collage of odd, often unrelated images on video screens) can cost as little as just one drink (ranging from US$1 to $15, depending on the city and venue), or a little more if you want to take the limelight and sing a few songs yourself.

---

ther), **Lingdian** (Zero Point), **Zhinanzhen** (Compass), and solo singers **Dou Wei** (formerly of Heibao) and **He Yong**. These artists, although they do not take dangerously political oppositional stances, live on the fringe of the Chinese mainstream. To pursue rock music as a career is seen as rebellion, and the music is nothing like Cantopop, with lyrics voicing a youthful angst. Musically, Tang Chao and Heibao lean toward hard rock (with the former doing a heavy-metal version of the "Internationale"). Lingdian owes much of its identity to early Police, especially its lead singer, Zhou Xiaoou, who is a veritable Chinese Sting. He Yong's coarse high tenor gives voice to the loneliness of the Chinese urban youth, as do younger, teenage, punk rock bands, such as **Dixiayinger** (Underground Babies) and **Catcher in the Rye** (named in English).

Chinese rock has a strong national flavour: apart from the standard drums, synthesizers, electric and bass guitars, you will hear some Chinese instruments such as the *sunoa* (shawm) and *zheng* (zither), and colourful gongs and cymbals borrowed from traditional opera. Tang Chao are noted for the latter and He Yong's father, a *sanxian* banjo player, has played alongside him on stage. In addition, if you isolate the sung melody in much Chinese rock, you will find pentatonic and modal qualities that clearly root them in tradition. Lingdian once recorded a song in Mongolian, and folk melodies are sometimes alluded to in instrumental introductions and interludes by many bands.

Although excluded from official broadcast channels such as national television, Chinese rock reaches its audience via cassettes and CDs, (mostly) copyrighted merchandise that can be bought anywhere in urban China, occasionally even in rural China. Chinese rock enjoyed some commercial success in the early 1990s thanks to the pioneering enterprise and idealism of some Chinese record companies, but mainly of overseas companies such

as Rock Records (a Taiwanese-based company, with production branches in Hong Kong), but a malaise seems to have set upon the scene of late.

One thing that hasn't happened for Chinese rock is a breakthrough to international markets. About the only artist to gain a Western contract is **Dadawa** (Tibetan stage name of Zhu Zheqin), a southern Chinese new wave singer who was marketed by Warner in 1996–97. Dadawa always sings in the high register, in a style akin to traditional opera. Her melodies are full of melismas (some are pure vocalisations) and there is an otherworldliness about her voice that is very appealing. Recording songs tailor-made for her by Chinese pop composer He Xuntian, she explores (and exploits) Tibetan themes with song titles such as "Ballad of Lhasa" and "The Sixth Dalai Lama's Love Song". These have angered many Tibetans in exile who interpret her music as yet another manifestation of the occupation, as a Chinese singer appropriating Tibet.

discography

Hong Kong

Compilations

◉ **Hottest Cantopop Selection** (Polydor, Hong Kong).

This 1998 selection features hits by an impressive array of singers, among them Jacky Cheung, Leon Lai (both of "Four Gods" fame), Alan Tam and Faye Wong. Track 10 features a number from *Snow Wolf Lake*. The last track (16) features a current television soap opera theme song, the genre that started Cantopop way back in the 1970s.

◉ **Snow Wolf Lake** (Polygram, Hong Kong).

The original 1997 cast album of the first Cantopop musical a la Lloyd Webber. *Snow Wolf Lake* was only a moderate success on stage, despite the megastar power of Jacky Cheung (who played the 'wolf'). A fairy tale about nature, love and death and partially set in Vienna, the inspiration may have come from Broadway but the numbers are almost all written in Cantopop mode. It is pulled together by sophisticated pop orchestral arrangements by Iskandar Ismail.

Artists

Jacky Cheung

Jacky Cheung rose to fame after winning an amateur community pop singing contest in the mid-1980s and became a teenage idol overnight. Now in his late thirties, he has had award-winning albums throughout the 1980s and 1990s. He is the best singer among the "Four Gods" of Cantopop with his buttery voice and impeccable Cantonese diction, best known for his romantic love songs. A superb crooner, he is sought after by major film directors and has won the Hong Kong equivalent of an Oscar in many notable films, such as Tsui Hark's *A Chinese Ghost Story*.

Jacky in Concert 93
(Polygram, Hong Kong).

This double-CD gives all the feeling of being at a real Cantopop event, since it was recorded live (with fans' screams, laughter, and whistles) in the Hong Kong Coliseum (which seats 12,500) between September and October 1993, excerpted from Jacky's 25 sold-out concerts. Unlike studio-produced Cantopop heavy on synthesised sound, this extravaganza employed a full band, even a string quartet (and sixty dancers). You'll find plenty of spine-tingling ballads and the album booklet is chock full of photos of elaborate costumes that Jacky wore for his fans.

Leslie Cheung

One of the founding fathers of Cantopop, Leslie Cheung has lasted the course, combining a hugely successful film and music career (see profile on p.51).

Glorious Years (Capital Artists, Hong Kong).

A 1998 retrospective compilation of greatest hits from Cheung's 'glorious' Capital Artists years, this is a testament to early 1980s Cantopop, containing his legendary Japanese remakes ("The Wind Blows On" and "Monica"). Also "Love of Years Past", a Joseph Koo-James Wong collaboration: quintessential Cantopop in its early phase. A VCD accompanies this CD, a new marketing strategy by record companies in Hong Kong (where everyone has a VCD player!).

Graham Earnshaw

Hong Kong isn't all sugary Cantopop and Earnshaw is a singer, songwriter, rock guitarist and journalist who has lived in Hong Kong since the early 1970s.

Leap of Faith: A vision of Hong Kong
(GAE, Hong Kong).

For this 1996 album Earnshaw teamed up with the best local session musicians – Antonio Fernandes, Eugene Pao, Ted Lo, Paulo Candelaria – for a tribute album to Hong Kong on the eve of the handover. It is glorious (non-commercial) Hong Kong rock: thoughtful lyrics reflect the spirit of this city from the perspective of a British local. (Earnshaw is fluent in Cantonese, but chose to record all of his songs in English).

Anita Mui

Anita Mui came to prominence in 1982 as the winner of a television-sponsored singing contest. She has also acted in famous feature films (notably *Rouge*, opposite Leslie Cheung, and *Rumble in the Bronx*, with Jackie Chan).

Love Songs (Capital Artists, Hong Kong).

For those who want prime romantic Cantopop, this is an essential 2-CD collection. A 1998 collection of love songs which includes all of Anita's biggest Cantopop hits (including film and television theme songs) from 1983 to 1997. Some are sung in Mandarin. The theme song from *Rouge* (CD 1, track 8) is one of the most beautifully eerie samples of the genre, based on a pentatonic melody (she plays a ghost in the film).

Softhard

Softhard are a duo of prominent Hong Kong DJs who pioneered Cantorap – which was shortlived in its purest form. Although they bubble-rapped with no hint of violence, they captured and transformed an American genre into something so entertaining that young female fans literally mobbed all of their appearances in 1993–94.

Broadcast Drive Killer (Cinepoly, Hong Kong).

The music and lyrics are refreshing compared to standard fare thanks to a stronger beat and even reggae rhythms. Lyrics range from safe sex ("Bring your own bag"), political satire ("Absolute China" sampling the "Internationale"), to a retirement home anthem ("Gala gala happy"). And since Cantonese is a tonal dialect, the lyrics come with a built-in melody thanks to the inflections of the words!

Softhard drop their kit

Miriam Yeung

A teenage idol, Yeung is one of the most popular current singers. Her voice is breathy, but nonetheless charming.

Here for a Visit (Capital Artists, Hong Kong).

The music on this 1998 album is consistently lively and upbeat. Befitting its theme of wanderlust, the CD booklet comes with numerous photos of 'tourist' poses by Miriam in front of sites such as the Louvre and the Paris underground. This album is the epitome of Cantopop in its lightest and most pleasant vein.

China

Compilations

Ye Shanghai (A Night in Shanghai)
(EMI, Hong Kong).

A selection of the best Shanghai (and later Hong Kong) hits of yesteryear, this is a remastered compilation of historical recordings by Zhou Xuan, Bai Guang, Ge Lan, Li Xianglan, Zhang Lu, Bai Hong, and Wu Yingyin. Transport yourself back to the dance halls and nightclubs of half a century ago, follow the lyrical melodies, and look out for those covers of Hank Williams songs.

A Tribute to Teresa Teng
(Hubei/Jinlin/Golden Melody Music, Hong Kong/Beijing).

Taiwanese singer Teresa Teng (1953– 95) was amongst the most popular singers in China from the late 1970s. Her hits were so well known in China that although government bans on such capitalist 'pornographic' music were in effect (until the late 1980s), all the rock generation grew up knowing her songs. This album features some Chinese rock bands – including Tang Chao and Heibao – doing covers of her most popular songs. They all jam together in the last number which despite the husky voices is just as romantic as the original.

Artists

Cobra

In a Chinese (rock) world exclusively ruled by men, this all-female band not only survives, but thrives. Since 1996 Cobra has been amongst the hottest bands in Beijing and has performed in all of the major cities (in privately owned clubs and bars). They toured America in 1996.

Yan Jing She (Cobra) (Jin Die, China).

Their 1996 debut album is outstanding in many ways. Cobra might not radiate hard rock, but the title song and the soulful "My own heaven" are two of the best written/arranged/performed/sung tracks in the genre.

Cui Jian

Born in 1961, Cui is the remarkably young 'grandfather' of Chinese rock. He began his musical career as a trumpeter in the Beijing Symphony Orchestra: his trumpet playing is always impressive and remains a distinctive feature of his performances. Cui renamed his band 'Balls under the Red Flag' (in original Chinese, 'Eggs under the Red Flag') in 1993–94, a self-mocking title of the powerlessness of rock musicians.

Yiwu Suoyou (I Have Nothing to My Name) (EMI, Hong Kong).

The most important album in the short history of Chinese rock music but one that is also musically appealing to non Chinese-speakers. Cui has an urgency in his voice, a real melodic gift, and he brings a Chinese flavour to some of the music with a zheng (zither) and other Chinese instruments.

Hongqi xiade Dan (Eggs under the Red Flag) (EMI, Hong Kong).

This 1994 album truly marked the arrival of Cui into the global rock scene, adding timbres such as Chinese flute, suona, trumpet, saxophone, gigantic ritual drums, gongs and cymbals, to electric guitars. Among the band musicians, Liu Yuan crosses seamlessly from one wind instrument to the next, creating memorable riffs. Although less varied musically than Cui's earlier albums, lyrics in this album echo China and its youth in their search for an identity in the 1990s.

Heibao

This five-strong band is one of China's best of the post-Cui Jian generation and toured the US in 1999. They write great lyrics on love lost and found, frustrations at changing social values and urban lonliness, and feature expressive ballads and playing (especially from drummer Zhao Mingxi and lead guitarist Li Tong).

Heibao III: Wushi wufei (No Right No Wrong) (JVC/ISRC, China).

A co-production between Beijing record companies and JVC, Heibao's third album was a bestseller in 1995 and remains a classic. The band's post Dou Wei lead singer, Qin Yong has a much more resonant voice than Cui Jian, but puts a deliberate Cui-style strain into his vocal delivery, a trademark of Chinese rock angst. There's a distinct Dylanesque feel to the opening verses of "For All People Who Love Us".

Dou Wei

Formerly lead singer of Heibao, Dou Wei left the band at the height of its fame in 1992 and forged his own musical path. Crossing rock and pop lines has given him a wide success in the pan-Chinese commercial pop market (China, Hong Kong, Taiwan).

Heimeng (Black Dream) (Rock Records, Taiwan).

The songs in this first solo album exist in the interesting middleground of pop/rock. Musically poetic, sexy, cool and stylish, Dou Wei has the appeal of a Chinese Bob Dylan. He writes his own lyrics and plays many of the instruments (thanks to multi-tracking). Dou's second solo album in 1995, Yan Yang Tian (Sunny Days) (Rock Records) was also a success.

Hawaii

steel and slide hula baloos

Hawaii rode a World Music wave as early as the 1920s, when its distinctive slide-guitar sound and hula dances were taken up across the US. But for all the islands' postwar immersion in tourism, its music has continued to follow a highly individual path. **Mike Cooper**, who plays a mean slack key and steel guitar himself, surveys the scene.

Although Hawaii was formally annexed by the United States in 1898, and has been the 50th state since 1959, it is in many ways distinctly un-American. The islands lie deep in the Pacific – nearly 4000km west of San Francisco – its people are of Polynesian origin, and its musical roots lie in traditional Polynesian chants and drum dances. Its famous **hula** (dance) and **mele** (chant) were forms once found throughout Oceania – a music that was essentially voice and drums. The Hawaiian **pahu** (shark-skin drum) is both the oldest instrument on the islands and a symbol of the ancient links to Polynesia.

Roots and Immigrants

The **mele** were traditional chants addressed to the gods, to chiefs, and to families, and they recorded the genealogy, history and sacred attributes of their subjects. **Mele hula pahu** (chants accompanied by dance and drums) are formal, sacred forms that are still treated with great respect.

It was not always so, alas. When missionaries arrived in the 1820s, they set about destroying this 'heathen' culture – and it is only in the last few decades that the traditional forms have been revived. The new immigrants also brought diseases and epidemics, which devastated the indigenous peoples and changed the whole make-up of the population.

With the first colonists and settlers, the island was exposed to a bizarre array of musical influences. Missionaries from New England introduced vocal harmonies and hymns, while cowboys from Mexico brought guitars, and Portuguese sailors came with the *braguinha*, an early form of ukelele (see box). Towards the close of the nineteenth,

The Ukulele – a Portuguese Gift to the Pacific

The **ukulele** – one of the most ubiquitous instruments in Hawaiian (and Polynesian) popular music – is essentially the **braguinha**, a small four-stringed instrument from the Portuguese island of Madeira (and a variant of the more common *cavaquinho* of the Portuguese mainland).

In September 1878 the first Portuguese immigrants arrived in Honolulu – 120 Madeira islanders – and they were joined a year later by another 400 settlers, ready to work on the sugar plantations. Among the settlers on this second boat was one **João Fernandes**, who had borrowed a braguinha from a fellow passenger and learnt to play it during the voyage of almost five months. When the boat finally arrived in Honolulu the passengers celebrated their safe arrival with a dance, and Fernandes played the instrument, to the delight of

both settlers and Hawaiians. He soon became a fixture at balls and parties and eventually formed a group, which played on occasion for the Hawaiian royalty.

A fellow passenger on that same boat, Manuel Nunes, opened a shop where he made and sold braguinhas – by now renamed ukuleles. He and other craftsmen began to use local *kou* and *koa* wood and before long the braguinha became a national instrument. The word *uku lele* literally means 'jumping flea' in Hawaiian – describing the rapid motion of the musician's fingers across the strings.

Today the ukulele is widespread in many different varieties all over Polynesia and the South Pacific.

Ad Linkels

and in the early years of the twentieth, centuries, a new and distinctive kind of Hawaiian music emerged, drawing upon these instruments and influences, and also those of brass band music. The latter came through the establishment of the **Royal Hawaiian Band**, under bandleader Henry Berger, recruited by the Hawaiian royal family from the Prussian army, which performed arrangements of Hawaiian songs as well as marches and ragtime compositions of the day.

Slack and Steel Guitar and Hapa Haole

In conventional guitar tuning, strumming the open strings produces a dischord. Towards the end of the nineteenth century, however, the Hawaiians retuned the strings to create a harmonious chord and from there developed a whole range of open tunings – a new style that they called **Ki Ho'alu** or **slack key**. A further innovation, around 1900, came when **Joseph Kekuku**, a school student on Oahu Island, discovered that if you slid a solid object up or down the strings after you had plucked or strummed them, you got the chord sliding up and down in a glissando. **Hawaiian steel guitar** (*Kika Kila*) was born: a new guitar sound and a new guitar posture, with the instrument played on the lap or on a stand.

At more or less the same time the **hapa haole** (half white) style of song was also invented. This was a form of songwriting that merged traditional Hawaiian music forms with English lyrics, reflecting the increased contact between the islands and the American mainland. Ragtime also appeared as another influence on Hawaiian music.

These influences were soon to work both ways. At the San Francisco Panama-Pacific Expo in 1915 – which celebrated the opening of the Panama Canal – the new Territory of Hawaii invested heavily in its pavilion, and unleashed on the US the sounds of Hawaiian string bands.

Aloha . . .
A stands for dear aloha,
L for the laughter and the smiles,
O is for out in the Pacific,
    where the angels built those tropic isles.
H is for dear old Honolulu,
    far across the ocean blue, and
A just means aloha, and aloha means I love
    you.

America went for the Hawaiian sound big time and by 1916 more Hawaiian records were being sold in the US than any other type of music. It was one of the earliest World Music crazes, outdoing even the tango in popularity. Groups such as the **Kalama Quartet** introduced four-part falsetto harmony singing with two steel guitars playing counterpoint, while other recordings featured virtuoso Hawaiian steel-guitarists.

Another cultural collision occurred as these musicians discovered jazz. **Bennie Nawahi** was a key figure in this early fusion – a steel-guitar wizard who performed with equal dexterity on mandolin and ukulele. He started out as a busker, then worked a cruise ship with his brothers, developing along the way an extraordinary showmanship, playing the steel guitar with his feet and the ukulele behind his head with one hand. With America in the grip of a ukulele craze, Nawahi played the vaudeville circuit with huge success in the 1920s, being dubbed 'King of the Ukulele', and launching a recording career that was to stretch nearly fifty years, until he suffered a stroke in the 1970s.

During his early busking days Nawahi had worked with **Sol Ho'opii**, another musician who has become a legend among steel-guitar players. Ho'opii played a synthesis of American jazz and traditional Hawaiian music and had a profound and lasting effect on a whole generation of island musicians, who played not only jazz and Hawaiian music, but western swing and country. His

playing was technically brilliant with an advanced use of chords, harmony and phrasing. Early in his career he developed the tuning that led to the development of the **pedal steel guitar** and the Nashville country music sound. He too recorded extensively, from 1925 up until the 1950s.

Hula Blues

Oh oh oh, those hula blues!
Tell me, have you heard those hula blues?
You can't imagine what you're feeling blue
*   about*
You simply glide and take a slide
And you want to shout
You wiggle, you giggle, you wiggle to the hula
*   blues.*

'Neath swaying palm trees
And friendly sea breeze
Where you hear the mellow steel guitars
Moaning softly under tropic stars.

Pale land of flowers
And golden showers
Where the hula girlies swing and sway
On the ukelele hear them play.

The Genial Hawaiians, 1934.

Inspired by figures like these, musicians the world over explored the Hawaiian sound. From the 1930s, Hawaiian-style bands and steel-guitar players started to appear as far afield as Britain and Germany, Japan, India and Indonesia. In London, for example, the Felix Mendelssohn Hawaiian Serenaders were a hugely popular radio and dance-hall act, performing a mix of traditional Hawaiian, hapa haole, jazz and popular songs.

Rock'n'roll, Tourism and Slack Key

From the 1930s on, Hawaii began to establish a tourist trade, and from the 1950s this became a serious business. 'Hawaiian music' became a part of the experience, with grass-skirt revues devised to suit the packaged paradise. One of the most popular of these was the **'Kodak Hula Show'** – you purchased a Kodak film at the entrance, the performers, dancers and musicians ran through their routine, you snapped away, handed in your film when you left and by the time you got back home your holiday snaps had arrived. Launched in 1939, this revue still runs today.

Hawaiians, meantime, discovered rock'n'roll. Through the 1950s and '60s, interest in the steel guitar fell away and young Hawaiians dreamed of becoming The Beatles. The old-style music became largely a facet of the tourist industry, sidelined at home and an exotica curiosity abroad.

Older styles were never lost, however, and in the 1970s a new-found sense of identity led to a renewed interest in Hawaiian sounds. The islanders rediscovered slack-key guitar playing, and local record labels put out songs again in the Hawaiian language. One of the great musicians of this revival was **Gabby Pahinui**. By the 1970s he was already a legend on the islands, though he was virtually unknown on the American mainland until **Ry Cooder** happened to buy one of his records in Honolulu. What Ry heard interested him so much that he went searching for the musician and found not only Gabby, but a whole family of Pahinui musicians.

BMG

The Pahinui Brothers

The Pahinuis recorded together with Cooder, whose music was a fine match for the slack-key style, and crossed over into the US mainstream. Gabby himself died in 1980, but the Pahinui Brothers continue to play slack-key music in the style that he taught them, as well as developing their own mixture of Hawaiian, soul, country and reggae slack-key music.

Hawaiian Music Now

The typical sound of the Pahinui-inspired revival of Hawaiian groups has settled into a regular, unplugged, format of guitars, ukulele, steel guitar, bass and vocals. Most play a mix of traditional music, country, rock covers, pop, pan-Pacific styles and reggae – all of them in a typically inclusive Hawaiian way. The musicians don't tour outside of the islands too often, and most discs are local releases, so you really have to go there to hear Hawaiian music at its best.

Slack Key and Steel Guitar

Slack-key guitar, as its name suggests, involves slackening the strings and re-tuning the guitar to achieve an **open chord**. For instance, if you take the standard guitar tuning (from high to low – EBGDAE) and slacken the first string from E to D, the fifth from A to G and the sixth from E to D, you get a tuning of DBGDGD. This is an open chord of G when strummed, and placing a finger (or steel bar) across the strings at the fifth and seventh frets will give you the other two chords you'll need for any three-chord song, like a blues.

This is one of the simplest tunings. During the pre-war craze for the music, Hawaiian guitarists made an art out of different tunings, some of which were closely guarded secrets. They also developed two ways of playing with open tunings – slack-key and steel guitar. **Slack key** involved picking the

strings, with the thumb providing a constant bass while the other fingers play a melody (often a slightly altered version of the sung melody) on the upper strings. **Steel (or slide) guitar** developed from the slack key and had the guitar played horizontally and a steel rod pressed on the strings with the left hand to produce a harmonious sliding sound. Many people think of slide guitar as something blues musicians invented, but not so – it's a Hawaiian invention.

The first electric guitar – a Richenbacher nicknamed the 'frying pan' – was actually a Hawaiian lap steel guitar made in 1931. In the US this developed into the **pedal steel guitar**, with its mechanical devices to change tunings and volume. This became the characteristic sound of US country music, though it is less favoured by Hawaiian musicians.

Among the best current island bands are the **Genoa Keawe Group**, the **Ho'opii Brothers**, the **Sam Bernard Trio** and the **Martin Pahinui Band**. The singer and dancer, **Keali'i Reichel** has become something of a star, both in the islands and in the US. A trained hula chanter and dancer, she is a charismatic performer, and has a repertoire of traditional and contemporary music from Hawaiian mele to the Beatles.

Look out, too, for solo artists like the slack-key masters **Ray Kane** and **Ledward Kaapana**. Kane, a national treasure, is one of the great living slack-key players, playing a kind of country blues, with slower, more meditative rhythms. Kaapana is a younger, funkier, downhome player and performer. **Cyril Pahinui**, another son of the great Gabby, is a more 'jazzy' player, while **Keola Beamer** performs a contemporary, Western classical-influenced version of modern slack key.

There are, too, some great veteran players on the islands, such as **Tau Moe**, rediscovered by the American steel-guitarist **Bob Brozman** in the mid-1980s. His re-emergence is a good story. Brozman got a letter from Moe ordering a couple of his records, and the name set bells ringing, for it was that of a steel-guitar player on some legendary 1929 recordings of a band called Mme. Riviere's

PAUL SCHRANB/DANCING CAT

Slack-key master Ray Kane

Live in Hawaii

Hearing Hawaiian music on its home ground is the best possible way to experience it – assuming you're lucky enough to get a real band rather than a tourist revue. That means taking your pick of a handful of hotels that put on authentic players, or best of all, coinciding with one of the summer festivals. Check local press, and even if there is nothing promising, don't despair – there is always the radio: Honolulu's KCCN (1420 AM) and Big Island's KAHU (1060 AM) are both full-time Hawaiian music stations.

Venues

Honolulu/Oahu

Most of the big hotels along Waikiki beach have music, usually performed for free, with a drink or a meal, in the late afternoon or early evening. Venues include:

Halekulani Hotel. Music from a classic ensemble, 4–7pm every day on the veranda.

Kahala Hilton. Old-time Hawaiian music from 4–7pm at this genteel spot.

Waikikian Hotel. Tahitian Lanai play here.

Sheraton Moana Hotel. Hawaiian groups with hula beneath the famous banyan tree. A fabulous spot.

Duke's Canoe Club at the *Outrigger Waikiki Hotel*. This rumbustious beach bar with surf-hero decor features music (including slack key) most early evenings.

Honolulu Academy of Arts. Features a series of Hawaiian music concerts throughout the year.

University of Hawaii at Manoa. Often has concerts of Hawaiian reggae and rock.

Big Island

Mauna Kea Beach Hotel, Kona. Shows most evenings.

King Kamehameha Hotel. This has regular shows and hosts the Slack-key Festival each year.

Lanai

Manele Bay Hotel, Manele Bay. Slack-key guitarists sometimes play here.

Maui

The big hotels along the Kihei Beach strip feature slack-key performers or small groups.

Casanova's, in 'upcountry' Makawao, is the hottest music place on the island, though it doesn't always programme Hawaiian music.

Festivals

April/all islands: Aloha Week in April is a tourist gimmick that has turned into a genuine grassroots movement with free concerts, parades and parties.

April/Oahu: Honolulu's wonderful Merrie Monarch Hula Festival draws major Halau (Hula troupes) from all the islands, the US and Japan. Book well in advance.

May/Oahu: The Brothers Cazimero host a May Day event at the Waikiki Shell with a mix of traditional and contemporary acts.

May/Oahu: The Steel Guitar Association Festival takes place in Honolulu in the first week of May.

July/Big Island: Big Island Slack Key Guitar Festival is held at Hilo on the third Sunday in July.

August/Honolulu: Gabby Pahinui/Atta Issacs Slack Key Festival in Honolulu. Third Sunday in August.

September/Moloka'i: The Moloka'i Music Festival, on and around Labor Day (first Monday in Sept), features local artists and a few celebrity guests.

Hawaiians. He called him up and discovered to his amazement that it was the very same man, who had returned to Hawaii in the 1970s after fifty years of touring with Mme. Riviere's band, across Asia, the Middle East and Europe. After Brozman met Moe and his wife Rose, the band's singer, he suggested that they re-record the songs from those old 78s. They did so, and the resulting release on Rounder Records, with Brozman on steel guitar, is one of the great collections of Hawaiian music.

Rounder, the Boston-based American roots music label, is one of the few US record companies to feature Hawaiian music. The other is the Santa Cruz, California, based **Dancing Cat Records**, run by pianist George Winston, who have done sterling work raising the profile of Slack key guitar music. Their series of 'Slack Key Mas-

ter' CDs has grown over the past twenty years to include pretty much every player of note.

Tau Moe (seated) with his uncles in Mme. Riviere's Hawaiians

discography

In Hawaii, look out for recordings on the Panini, Hula, Tradewinds and Music of Polynesia labels, and check the Honolulu record stores Harry's Music (3457 Waiíalae Ave) and House of Music (1365 Colburn St). For Hawaiian music on the Web, see *www.mele.com*

Traditional

Compilations

Hana Hou! Do it Again! Hawaiian hula chants and songs (Pan, Netherlands).

Traditional chants and contemporary dance songs performed in their basic form. Only one or two singers with minimal accompaniment of *ipu heke* (gourd drum), ukulele or guitar.

Hawaiian Drum Chants: Sounds of Power in Time (Smithsonian/Folkways, US).

A record of the earliest known forms of Hawaiian music, some of it from old cylinder recordings. As close as you can get to the stuff Captain Cook would have heard.

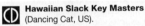 **Hawaiian Slack Key Masters** (Dancing Cat, US).

If you want to know what Slack Key is and who is playing it, start here with this 1995 sampler of artists on the Dancing Cat label. Tracks include a duo between Keola Beamer and the label's founder, George 'Keo-ki' Winston, and outstanding cuts from Cyril Pahinui, Sonny Chillingworth, Ray Kane and half a dozen other old and young masters.

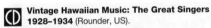 **Vintage Hawaiian Music: The Great Singers 1928–1934** (Rounder, US).

A hugely seductive collection of Slack Key classics compiled by Bob Brozman, featuring Mme Riviere's Hawaiians, the all-male Kalamaís Quartet and Sol Hoopii Trio, and lots more besides. Plenty of falsetto vocals and steel guitar.

Vintage Hawaiian Music: Steel Guitar Masters 1928–1934 (Rounder, US).

A companion volume highlighting the golden age of acoustic steel guitar. Tracks from Tau Moe, Sol Ho'opii, King Benny Nawahi and Jim & Bob the Genial Hawaiians.

Vintage Hawaiian Treasures Vol 7 (Cord International, US).

A reissue of the first commercial releases of Slack Key from the 1940s, including seminal Gabby Pahinui cuts. Other standout tracks include Tommy Blaisdell pieces that stomp along like barrelhouse blues.

Artists

Edith Kanaka'ole

Born in 1913 in Honomu, Edith Kanaka'ole trained as a child in the art of *oli* (poetic chant) and *hula*. In 1946 she started to compose her own oli and songs and in 1954 she became a professional performer. She epitomises the synthesis of ancient and modern traditions and values in Hawaiian culture.

Ha'aku'i Pele I Hawaii (Hula Records, Hawaii).

The strongest available commercial recording of traditional chant. A major factor in Edith Kanaka'ole's art is her fluency in

the Hawaiian language – and her comprehension (*kaona*) of the oli's hidden meanings. Like others she believes the oli to be the foundation of all aspects of Hawaiian cultural history and the key for Hawaiians to maintain a relationship with the past and future.

Ho'opi Brothers

Veterans Richard and Solomon Ho'opi, from the island of Maui, have played guitar and ukulele and sung falsetto since their childhood in the 1930s. In 1996 they received the National Endowment for the Arts Folk Heritage Fellowship – America's highest honour for traditional artists. Falsetto singing is held in high esteem in Hawaiian music, influenced by Mexican, Tyrolean and cowboy yodelling (believe it or not!)

Ho'omau (Mountain Apple, Hawaii).

This Hawaiian party music features sensational falsetto vocal duets by the two brothers along with slack-key guitar from Ledward Kaapana and Aunty Genoa Keawe and the steel guitarist from her band, Herbert Hanawahine.

Sol Ho'opi

Sol Ho'opi (1902–53) made his fame in the US after stowing away on a liner to San Francisco. Most famous for his classic acoustic recordings, he switched to electric guitar in 1934, then in 1938 became an evangelist and gave up his career in secular music.

Sol Ho'opi – Vols1: 1926–1929 and **Vol 2: 1927–1934** (Rounder, US).

Classic tracks from probably the most influential of all Hawaiian steel guitarists. Either album is recommended.

Ray Kane

The elder statesman of slack key, Kane was born in 1925 on the island of Kaua'i, but grew up in Nanakuli on Oahu. He claims that he first heard slack key at the beach, being played by a *paniolo* (cowboy) from Makua Ranch, and that he traded fish for guitar lessons. A National Endowment for the Arts Fellowship winner, he made his first record in 1961 and in 1973 was the first slack-key guitarist to give a full length solo concert.

 Punahele (Dancing Cat, US).

Simple but deeply evocative old-style slack key and vocals; featuring Ray's rich vibrato voice and, on one track, the wonderful vocals of Elodia Kane, his wife. The title track "Punehele" means favourite or pet and is Ray's best known composition.

Tau Moe Family

Steel guitarist and singer Tau Moe was born in Samoa in 1908 and is still going strong! He has been performing with his wife Rose practically all his life, and for 50-odd years with their two children, Lani and Dorien. In 1927 Rose joined Mme. Riviere's Hawaiians (Tau and his three uncles) for a tour of Asia that lasted from 1928 until 1934; they then toured India and the Middle East until the late 1940s when they moved to Europe, performing there through the 1950s and '60s. They retired back to Laie on Oahu in the late 1970s – after five decades on the road.

TAU MOE FAMILY WITH BOB BROZMAN

 Remembering the Songs of Our Youth (Rounder, US).

Although this is a modern (1989) disc it reprises the songs, style and instrumentation of the 1920s and '30s, with vocals from the family and the hugely talented Bob Brozman taking lead on steel guitar parts learnt from Tau. Rose Moe, then in her eighties, does all the lead vocals, backed up by Tau and the two kids (in their sixties). It kicks off with the beautiful "Mai Kai No Kauai", the 1929 version of which opens the *Steel Guitar Masters* compilation above. An amazing CD.

Bennie Nawahi

Bennie Nawahi (1899-1985) was one of the key figures in the acoustic era of Hawaiian guitar. He played the cruise ship and vaudeville circuits with his brother before pursuing his own career as singer and 'King of the Ukulele'. He lost his sight, inexplicably, while driving home from a performance in 1935.

 Hot Hawaiian Guitar 1928-1949 (Shanachie/Yazoo, US).

A lovely disc of Nawahi performing jazz-inflected Hawaiian numbers with fellow master Sol Ho'opii.

Gabby Pahinui

Gabby Pahinui (1921–82) is without doubt the biggest influence on modern Hawaiian music. A slack-key guitar-player and singer, he released the first commercial recording ever of slack key, "Hi'ilawe", in 1946, and in the 1960s was responsible for launching not only a revival of interest in slack key but Hawaiian culture in general. He is remembered for his solo guitar skills and arranging for multiple guitar combinations, as well as his unique vocal qualities and on-stage personality.

Gabby Pahinui Hawaiian Band Volume 1 and **Volume 2** (Edsel, UK).

These are breathtaking discs of slack guitar, steel guitar and bass from a band of legends – Sonny Chillingworth, Atta Isaacs and the Pahinui Brothers, Cyril, Bla, Phillip and Martin – as well as Gabby himself and a little fairydust from Ry Cooder. Along with the hard to obtain **Rabbit Island Music Festival** (Panini, Hawaii), recorded by the same band but without Cooder, these three albums of Hawaiian string band music are unequalled.

The Pahinui Brothers Band

The Brothers are Gabby Pahinui's sons Cyril, Bla and Martin, each of whom has a distinct style of musicianship. Cyril is an intricate, finger-picking guitar-player in his harmonic and rhythmic approach; Bla brings influences from soul, do-wop and black vocal groups; while Martin (who sings and plays bass) is perhaps closest to his father in his taste and vocal approach. All three pursue individual as well as group careers.

 The Pahinui Brothers Band (BMG/Panini, US).

The Brothers present a more contemporary Hawaiian sound with guest artists Ry Cooder and David Lindley. The music is a mix of traditional and contemporary Hawaiian string band, with excursions into Jah-waiian reggae, black soul, country music and even a version of John Lennon's "Jealous Guy".

India

Indian classical music

how to listen – a routemap of india

In August 1971, George Harrison, Eric Clapton and Bob Dylan were among the gala attractions of the the Concert For Bangladesh, held in New York to raise money for the stricken nation. Ravi Shankar and Ali Akbar Khan were to perform a *jugalbandi* (duet), and according to Indian classical practice, they began tuning up on stage. As the musicians finished, they were greeted with a ripple of clapping which swelled into full-scale applause. Good-naturedly, but with an edge, Shankar observed 'if you appreciate the tuning so much, I hope you'll enjoy the playing more'. The story has been repeated enough times to have become a mantra, but the moral remains: don't travel in Indian music reading a Western map. **Robert Maycock** and **Ken Hunt** get out the compass.

To enjoy a concert of Indian classical music, it helps a lot to have knowledge of the basic traffic rules. Most concerts are solo vehicles for an instrumentalist or vocalist, and unlike most Western music, which is harmonically based, Indian music is monodic, with a single melody line. At first, the soloist explores the road – or *raga* – alone, with just a drone accompanying; later they are joined by rhythm players – most commonly *tabla* drums. Throughout a performance, which may last for several hours, there is an altogether un-Western attitude to time. You may begin by staring at a rug on an empty platform – all part of the preparation.

Settling in

When they are ready, the performers come on in reverse pecking order: drone instruments first, accompanists (including percussion) next, the big name last. **Tuning** will take just as long as it needs and will sometimes merge imperceptibly into the first forays of the performance itself: a few notes played in earnest, some more tuning, then a leap forward.

If the accompanying drum is a **tabla**, the player's first act is usually to bring out a hammer and tap obsessively at the tuning wedges at the edges – not a repair job, just making sure the high-pitched drum is exactly in tune with the soloist. Later on, tabla players frequently retune on the hoof, hammering away without losing the rhythm.

Underlying the main instruments will be a stringed instrument called a **tanpura**, which provides a steady drone through the performance. It is often played by a student of the soloist who is given the honour of learning at close quarters – compensation for having to strum thanklessly through a concert of several hours.

Setting off

It's one note at a time to start with – and a 'note' is a many-splendoured thing, approached from above or below and fantastically ornamented. Rhythm is a hidden asset. Watch the percussionist sit listening as the melody unfolds, often for half an hour or more. Gradually the pitch will rise; then fall, then move up again. The chosen **raga**, or theme (see below), is taking shape. You are listening to the initial exploration of a musical scale and a state of feeling, inseparably fused to make a raga. Each has its own way of ascending and descending, its special decorative features and its local variants, which depend on the performance tradition the musician belongs to.

In North Indian (Hindustani) music, a raga usually opens with the **alap** section; in South Indian classical music this is called *alapana*. Played by the soloist in free rhythm with tanpura or drone accompaniment, it is the alap which reveals most about a musician's mastery and prowess. It's the most bewildering part for an uninitiated Western listener, but the part that educated Indian audiences love best – its length is often contracted or extended accordingly. Since the alap is the distilled essence of the raga, it can also function as the sole movement in a recital.

In a fine alap the singer or player will conjure up phrase after phrase of intense beauty, loudly acclaimed by ardent followers. Singers reinforce the emotion by vigorously tracing shapes with their hands and gesturing towards the listeners – a visual translation of the music and the very act of communicating it. Feedback from the audience is important, and a gesture or eye contact returned from a listener who obviously appreciates the music is highly valued. Many musicians lament Westernised shows of approval (now encountered even in the subcontinent), when audiences will burst into applause during a solo as if they were in a jazz concert. Traditional etiquette calls for murmurs of approval like *wa-wa* (excellent) and the raising of hands.

As the alap progresses, ornamentation grows more complex or flamboyant, the intensity builds, and a climactic high note is achieved – a moment whose emotional and musical power is greater for the long, long delay. The music winds down briefly, and then introduces a slow, almost lazy pulse for the so-called **jor** section. The speed of articulation gradually increases, melody evolves, and the pace stirs. Rhythmic animation follows, and the speed steps up in discreet stages. There is a brilliant climax, the music stops and everybody applauds. Still, though, the percussionist sits silent. It's just traffic lights – a temporary halt.

Gear Changes

Once the pace drops, solo and percussion start to interact. If the percussionist is a respected virtuoso, the soloist will briefly turn accompanist and let drumming skills take centre stage. Then the soloist steps on the gas. This part of the performance will usually be based on a **gat** (a fixed musical figure), and you will hear the same melodic phrases come back again and again. It is also based on a rhythmic cycle with hugely long 'bars' of four, seven, eight, thirteen – anything up to sixteen beats.

First beats of a cycle are key moments, and you will see performers glance or nod at one another to keep in touch, or using a system of downturned and upturned palms of the hand to count. Listeners to recordings learn to pick up the shape of the cycle by ear alone, usually from the emphases of the deeper-toned drum strokes. When the music is playing with intricate patterns and cross-rhythms, the first beat is always the point of culmination, especially thrilling when reached after a process that has lasted for some time.

As the speed and excitement grow, the musicians become spontaneous and competitive as they move into the climactic **jhala** section. Quick-fire 'question and answer' exchanges between instrumentalists can occur towards the end – a great

JAK KILBY

Ustad Amjad Ali Khan (sarod, centre) with Sri Kumar Bose (tabla) and Prodyut Sarkav (tanpura)

opportunity for witty performers, especially when a drum imitates a melody instrument. Somebody may launch another composition or change rhythmic cycle if there's a chance of heightening the action still further. Tabla players often rattle off compositions as a speech-song – a virtuoso performance in itself – and then imitate themselves on the drums. To round off, the performers will usually deliver a set-piece cadence which plays elaborately with threefold repetitions – emphatically conclusive when played with panache.

Southern Routes

It's a subtly different experience if the musicians belong to the traditions of **South India**. Performances are shorter and they rarely linger in a slow tempo for any length of time. Rhythmic patterns, melodic decoration and the instruments themselves are different, and the moments of high excitement are more evenly spread through the music. More is fixed and calculated; improvisation is more subtle. Body language varies too: whereas a North Indian performer will acknowledge a colleague's passing inspiration with a gentle shake of the head, nothing less than a full-scale wobble from shoulders upward will do in the South. But the underlying principles and motivations have plenty in common, and the fundamental idea of profoundly exploring a mood and a set of notes still drives the music.

The opening piece, called a **varnum**, is comparable to an étude in Western classical music and allows the musicians to warm up. An invocatory piece ordinarily follows, both devotional and a request for a blessing. The pace of a recital builds with contrasting **ragams** and **thaalams** (see below), often of increasing complexity and always of increasing intensity, using short **kritis** (Hindu hymns), of between three and ten minutes.

The exception is the fuller **ragam-thanam-pallavi** form. This sequence opens with pure, unmetred melody (confusingly, ragam is alapana by another name) before moving into thanam (the jor equivalent). The sequence concludes with rhythmically measured improvisations on the *pallavi* theme, the heart of a composition whose voiced or unvoiced lyrics inform the performance.

The pallavi may be unfamiliar to the percussionist and the principal soloist therefore states the theme, following that with lines based around it which are bounced back by the percussionist or the violin player, who usually accompanies the main melodicist in Karnatic music. The ensemble elaborates on the theme before the principal soloist restates the main theme to bring the pallavi to a close. After the ragam-thanam-pallavi, musicians will frequently perform *tillana* (a text of meaningless syllables, often voiced as rhythm mnemonics, similar to scat singing in jazz) or *javali* (an erotic song form), both of which are far lighter than the kriti form.

The Highway Code: Raga and Tala

Raga is a word woozy from the anaesthetic of familiarity – borrowed and adapted by many languages. The word is of Sanskrit origin, meaning 'that which colours the mind', and it is the fundamental organising principle and melodic paradigm of both the Hindustani (North Indian) and Karnatic (South Indian) musical systems. In the south, it goes under the name of **ragam**.

Raga is an immensely intricate system of scale-like melodic patterns and their various permutations. There are some two hundred main ragas, each defined by its unique combination of scale-pattern and dominant notes, by the specific rules to be obeyed in ascending or descending, and by certain melodic phrases associated with it. Both the Hindustani and Karnatic systems share a love of melodic invention within the routes and boundaries that each raga proscribes. This is coupled with a joy in the complexities of **rhythm**. Karnatic music, for example, boasts the most sophisticated rhythmic organisation on the planet in **thaalam**. The Northern equivalent for such a rhythmic cycle is known as **tala**. Each combines mathematical intellect with rugged muscularity.

The hallmark of the subcontinent's two classical music systems is the judicious management of melody and rhythm in the form of raga and tala, ragam and thaalam. In a concert, a convention (attributed to Ravi Shankar) is for the principal soloist to announce the raga's name, and to give information about it and the tala or talas about to be played.

Absolutely central to a great performance is the way in which the musicians imbue the raga or ragam with a sense of their own identity or personality while observing strictly defined rules. Improvisation occurs as a matter of course. Great musicians capture the spirit of their age as certain ragas capture the mood of their optimum time. Their art is not so much to describe a mood as to create and explore it with renewed sentiments and inspiration.

Raga Road

All ragas stem from 72 parent ragas known as the *janaka* or *melakartha* ragas. Each of these boasts a character so developed and distinctive that the attuned ear can discern the raga's mood or moods. Identifying or naming the raga may take longer – paralleling the experience in European music when it comes to naming a particular polka or concerto. Ragas have counterparts called *raginis* whose alliance to a primary raga corresponds to a Hindu deity's female consort. Mathematicians have calculated that some 34,776 raga permutations can be developed from this melakartha raw material. Even if mere hundreds are in common circulation, the nightmare is compounded by the variants that can be factored in.

A raga must have a minimum of five notes in a fixed sequence in ascending and descending order. This order is immovable. Within each raga certain notes are stressed and, in a music without harmony, it's the relation of the notes of the raga to each other, and to the 'tonic' *sa*, that defines its mood.

Traditionally, many ragas have a set **time of day** for playing, the product of age-old analysis and scrutiny, especially from studies in the South. The evening raga Marwa, for example, has a range of moods: it touches upon devotion, peace and heroism. The psychological characteristics of particular notes combine to develop a personality – perhaps a feminine blush, a sky blue or an uplifting sensation. In raga the seasons too carry cultural resonances. *Megh* means cloud and hence Raga Megh belongs to the monsoon season, while another popular raga, Hemant, simply means winter. Down the centuries the sense of a raga belonging to a particular hour or season became codified.

An example of the creative use of these moods is *The Call of the Valley*, the best-selling album by Shivkumar Sharma (*santoor*), Brijbushan Kabra (guitar) and Hariprasad Chaurasia (flute). In this recording's scheme the day's course is matched by a cycle of ragas. Todi's mood reflects the early morning. Bhairavi's time is late morning, Shri is of the afternoon, Pilu is day turning to evening and Kannada suits the night. It is peculiar how rarely raga names are explained and listeners tend not to observe such niceties as the time or season appropriate to a raga. Diehards lament this erosion of tradition.

Mishra, another commonly encountered word, indicates a mixed raga conventionaly requiring a less formal exposition. Other names give clues to authorship: for example, several variants of popular ragas are popularly attributed to **Miyan Tansen**, a pre-eminent musician in the court of the Mughal Emperor Akbar. In tribute their names include Miyan or Miya to indicate the variant's author. The *surbahar* maestro **Imrat Khan**'s Rag Miya ki Todi and Rag Bilaskhani Todi album (on Nimbus) illustrates this principle with two variants of Todi, the first credited to Tansen, the second to Tansen's son, **Bilas Khan**. For a thorough guide to over seventy-four Hindustani ragas invest in Nimbus's invaluable *Raga Guide*.

Tala – Make Way for Rhythmic Cycles

Tala – also *tal* or *taal* – is the northern name for a rhythmic cycle corresponding to the southern thaalam. They are terms heard at nearly every concert or read in most CD booklets. Tala combines with raga to make music somewhat as cadence joins with words to create speech; it does not mean

SIMON BROUGHTON

Sitar workshop, Varanasi, Uttar Pradesh

rhythm. Each of the 100-plus talas builds over a specific number of *matras* (beats) before generally coming to a point of release called – in Northern India – the *khali*. Tension and release is a science in Indian percussion.

Drum-maker, Vrindavan, Uttar Pradesh

The South's mathematicians pondered thaalam permutations for centuries, but in general only a dozen or so favourites will pop up in a performance. although in percussion summits the number of variants used can be bewildering. Initially listeners may find the time periods over which talas elapse baffling so the best approach is to treat them as opportunities for stretching the imagination – even a newcomer can experience multiple rhythmic frissons during a tabla solo.

Improvisation

A raga's notes are inviolate, with a prescribed order of ascending and descending. If an errant note slips in, the mood may shift, be dissipated or shatter. The performer's **melodic invention** must stay strictly within the codes – a Western parallel might be the way jazz players have to make their melodic invention fit the harmonic pattern of the song they are improvising on. On some occasions great virtuosi will raise the game by deftly quoting from, or alluding to, another raga, so long as doing so adds or heightens insight into the mood or exposition. More often they will introduce set melodic compositions that have been passed down through their tradition, or which they have composed themselves.

Both the melodicist and rhythmist will tap into **rhythmic cycles** of great complexity and length

based on centuries of musicological and mathematical study. Talas may be alternated to create variety. As with melody, improvisation is not the only kind of spontaneous performance. Short, fixed rhythmic compositions are often presented by percussionists in the course of a recital, particularly when the tabla is itself the solo instrument. South Asian extemporisation, by being so highly structured can make Western improvisation appear airy-fairy.

Indian music also has a lighter performance form called *raga mala* (or the Karnatic *ragamalika*), meaning 'garland of ragas', in which a performer moves through a series of different ragas in one piece (see box overleaf on raga paintings). In order not to detract from the seriousness of a recital, a raga mala performance will tend to end a concert. A soloist may similarly close a concert with a *dhun*, or a *deshi* (folk) air, characterised by a lightness of mood or emotion and fewer intellectual strictures. Typically dhuns will be set in core repertoire Hindustani ragas such as Bhairavi, Kafi, Khammaj or Pilu. Hariprasad Chaurasia's *Four Dhuns* (Nimbus) is unusual in being an album focusing on these.

Driving School: Gharanas

Indian musicians are expected to employ their musical wit to reveal new insights, even within core repertoire items, but an individual's interpretative style will generally adhere to rules handed down the generations. Before notation or recording this was exclusively oral, often transmitted down bloodlines. If a child showed promise, more accomplished teachers would be sought out to round and develop the child's education.

The southern system is renowned for producing child prodigies, often with whispered agendas of reincarnation. In the North the oral transmission of knowledge went from *guru* to *shishya*, teacher to disciple. The teaching could be severe, as indicated by shishya's root in the Sanskrit for 'punish'. This system gave rise to the Hindustani **gharana** tradition.

Ragamala paintings

Ragamala paintings, frequently used on CD covers of Indian music, were produced in India from the fourteenth to the nineteenth century. Ragamala (literally 'garland of ragas') is the name given to collections of these paintings, typically thirty-six in number, each depicting a different raga (or *ragini* – the so-called 'consorts' of the ragas). In musical terms, the word is used to describe a player moving through a range of ragas within a single piece.

Each miniature illustration, painted on paper or palm leaves, acts as an interpretation of raga music in images, aided by a traditional set of poems. Although ragas are abstract musical entities, poets and painters sought to personify them. They described situations where the emotions evoked by a particular raga could be expressed. Deities, birds, animals, flowers and lovers are shown in a spectrum of emotions ranging from disappointment and jealousy to longing and blissful union.

This painting (in Moghul style, from the early 17th century) depicts **Ragini Asavari**, a slightly plaintive mode said to originate in a snake-charmer's melody. The raga is characterised by a five-note (pentatonic) ascent and seven-note (heptatonic) descent. Asavari is designated as a consort or wife of **Raga Shri** in this raga-ragi-ni system (there were several) used by many ragamala painters. But the scale and melodic outline of Shri and Asavari are quite different. Asavari is a morning raga and should create a gently erotic atmosphere, at the same time tender and melancholy. In the painting, a dark-skinned girl from a tribe of snake-charmers is sit-

ting on a rock in the mountain forest. Dressed in a leaf skirt, she communes with a cobra while thinking about her absent lover. Although painters from different regions may have varying interpretations of ragas and raginis, this depiction of Asavari is fairly standard.

Jane Harvey

Traditionally gharanas (schools) took their names from their location – examples being **Bhendi Bazar** (a district of Mumbai), **Kirana** (near Saharanpur in Uttar Pradesh) and **Maihar** (Madhya Pradesh). Gharana means a 'school of playing' in much the same way as people talk about schools of painting. Each gharana's particular playing style was jealously guarded and its musicians were highly proprietorial about their tradition. For all that, Hindustani music is changing, with some musicians' names now being cited rather than the name of their gharana.

So Where are We?

Clearly in the democratic, technological India of today, the gharana system has certain disadvantages. Budding musicians of great brilliance may not have the means or inclination to spend years of their life cloistered away in a fusion of a medieval guild and a Victorian apprenticeship. The system can be seen as nepotistic, although defensible when considering the gifts of a child who has lived, breathed and slept the life of a musical family. The Northern system is undeniably sexist, and **women** have a hard time getting anywhere except as singers; even daughters of famous players have been rare on the scene until Aruna Narayan and, most recently, Anoushka Shankar. Some have not even tried to get in, but instead have gone to the West to study Western music.

Schools of music and a more open, conservatoire-like system look like the way ahead, as they have been in the West where it is now possible to study at least the elementary stages at one or two colleges in the UK and, particularly, the Netherlands. Traditionalists will deplore their development as undermining the intense master-and-pupil relationships that the virtuosi of the past knew. Perhaps they should take heart from the experience of Western classical music, where a more open system has led to far more musicians with a far wider spread of abilities, but no apparent drop-off in skill and imagination at the top of the tree.

The gharanas are likely to keep going alongside newer methods, but these have already affected the way classical Indian music is performed. There are more **instruments**, for one thing. The Kashmiri folk zither, the santoor, has been made a classical concert instrument almost single-handed by **Shivkumar Sharma**, one of the great players by any measure. The sarangi was liberated by **Ram Narayan** from its subservient role in supporting singers. Saxophones, mandolins and guitars have followed.

In the twentieth century the existence of limited-length records and fixed half-hour broadcasts by All India Radio brought a new awareness of clock time into performers' minds. Short, event-packed alaps are one outcome; so, less happily, is the growing number of performers who seem able to fill an hour with continuous music but not to make it a single, unified build-up of musical power. What is quite clear is that serious international interest is at an unprecedented high, and the top players are now taking their art to the world's capitals to be applauded and appreciated without so much as an ounce of artistic compromise.

India

Hindustani instrumental music

ragas and riches

The Hindustani classical music of northern India is one of the world's great art forms. It is immensely complex in structure and performance, and if you surrender to its artistry, its effect can be emotional and astonishingly direct. Once the privileged preserve of a society's elite, the music has now touched the hearts and minds of people around the world. **Ken Hunt** investigates.

INDIA

What many people casually refer to as Indian music is actually the classical music of the north of the Indian sub-continent, embracing the expansive cultural and religious diversity of India, Pakistan, Bangladesh, Nepal and even Bhutan. Karnatic (South) Indian music is older and represents the Hindu tradition before the Afghan and Mughal invasions of the North created one of the great hybrid musical styles of the world.

Players and Instruments

Hindustani music has been characterised as the 'house with four rooms' of the Indian proverb, catering to the physical, mental, emotional and spiritual. It is in many respects much more than a concert music, more indeed than the sum of its players. However, the players provide a way in to understanding both instruments and styles – and, it must be said, Hindustani music is replete with the names of its illustrious musicians.

Among this pantheon, sitar maestro **Ravi Shankar**, born in 1920, remains a good starting point for listeners in the West. Ravi Shankar's career has often encouraged a merging of his identity and achievements with the larger canvas of history, and his finest work is the stuff of immortality. Indeed, if he had lived before recorded music, or even before musical notation, the oral tradition of earlier generations would likely have preserved his music. As it is, his career has been comprehensively chronicled and he has recorded prolifically, acquiring a worldwide reputation as a great interpreter, innovator and populariser of Indian music in general and the **sitar** in particular.

In India, vocal music tends to receive most attention – notably the classical styles of *dhrupad* and *khayal* (see p.86). In the West, **instrumental music** is the top draw and the sitar stands above all other instruments (in India it shares the top ranking with sarod). It is probably the sitar's sonorities that work the charm. The sympathetic strings that resonate the notes of the raga behind the melody notes, are common in Indian music, but particularly strong on the sitar.

JAK KILBY

Ravi Shankar

Alongside Shankar himself, **Nikhil Banerjee** and **Vilayat Khan** are the best-known sitarists of the post-war year, responsible for innovations in sitar design and exponents of a singing style of playing called *gayaki ang* which each seems to have developed independently. Performers such as these have made Hindustani music a primary colour on the World Music palette.

For those that find the sitar's incessant buzzing hard to take, the **bansuri** flute is a good introduction to classical Indian music, especially in the hands of **Hariprasad Chaurasia**. And so, too, is the **sarod**, an instrument which in recent decades has had a star equivalent to Ravi Shankar in Amijad Ali Khan and the veteran **Ali Akbar Khan**, a towering figure who provided the West

Sarod master Ustad Ali Akbar Khan

with Hindustani music's first major concert recitals and first long-playing record.

Historical Sources

If **Karnatic** music, now found in southern India, is the Hindu and Sanskrit rootstock, then Hindustani music is the product of grafting Muslim and Persian influences onto that root. Historically, the ebb and flow of cultural tides which washed over the subcontinent caused immense changes.

Music, poetry and dance forms such as *kathak* had played important roles in the Hindu Vaishnavite cult (based on the worship of Vishnu). With the arrival of **Muslim** conquerors in the thirteenth century and the creation of the Mughal Empire in the sixteenth century, life over a broad stretch of northern territory was changed forever. Traditionally, Islam frowned

on the integration of worship with such frivolities as sculpture, the pictorial arts, music and dance. In such manifestations they detected pleasure-seeking which distracted and detracted from true religion. The arrival of the Mughals (alternatively Moguls or Moghuls) brought profound changes to religion, the arts and gastronomy alike. Yet the Delhi Sultanate, which preceded it as the major political force in the north, had already seen a stylistic synthesis of Islam and Hinduism, of north and south. Its most notable musical practitioner was the legendary **Amir Khusrau** (1253–1325). The far-seeing Khusrau melded Persian and Sanskrit, Islamic and Hindu, *maqam* and *raga*, classical and light classical elements and incorporated them into new music forms. *Qawwali* and *khayal* are popularly attributed to him.

The spirit of Khusrau's more conciliatory age had long departed when the Mughals began consolidating their empire. Countless Hindus fled southward to avoid Muslim persecution and conversion at the point of a sword. Since the Mughals never penetrated the southern heartland, to this day South Indian culture, music and dance remains suffused with the life force of Hinduism. Karnatic music never evolved into the propertied man's plaything that Hindustani music became. It stayed at once devotional, classical and everyday.

The Mughal empire was at its peak between 1526 and 1707, during which time intermarriage caused something of an Indianisation of Mughal culture. During the reign of the reforming emperor **Jal ad-Din Akbar** (1556-1605), who married a Rajput princess, the arts flowered, and the name of one of his court musicians in particular is still spoken with awe: **Tansen**.

It is said that Tansen was ordered to sing Deepak, a raga capable of causing lamps to ignite. Against his will he agreed, but ensured his daughter Saraswati sang the rainy season raga Megh in an adjacent palace wing at the same time. When he sang, the lamps lit of their own accord, as predicted, but with such a ferocity that it was only the downpour caused by Megh which saved him from burning alive. In time, the leading film music director **Naushad Ali** had Tansen portrayed by the vocal maestro Bade Ghulam Ali Khan in the

Stringed instruments

The best-known Hindustani instrument is the **sitar**, said to be invented, or rather developed from the **veena**, by **Amir Khusrau**, in the thirteenth century. They are generally made from teak, with the main resonator made from a seasoned gourd. Many sitars also have an extra gourd at the top of the neck which further amplifies the sound. Played with a wire plectrum, the instrument has six or seven main strings, of which four are used for the melody and the other two or three to supply a drone or rhythmic ostinato. In addition there are nine to thirteen sympathetic or *taraf* strings which give the sitar its distinctive 'jangling' sound. Around twenty moveable (usually brass) frets are arranged on the long neck and these can be slid to adjust to the raga's required tuning. The player can alter the pitch by pulling the string sideways, causing the gliding portamento so characteristic of Indian music and the **gayaki** (singing) style popularised by **Vilayat Khan** and **Ravi Shankar**, two of the best-known sitarists of the post-war years. Other leading names include Imrat Khan, Rais Khan, Debu Chaudhuri and Manilal Nag.

NAVRAS

Vilayat Khan

The **surbahar**, whose name derives from the Urdu for 'springtime of notes', is effectively a bass sitar and is played in the same way. Developed by **Sahibdad Khan**, the great-grandfather of Vilayat and Imrat Khan, it produces a deep, dignified sound. The neck is wider and longer than that of the sitar and its frets are fixed. Because the instrument is larger and has longer strings, the sound can be sustained for a longer time, and the range of the portamento is wider. **Imrat Khan** is the best-known player, although he played both surbahar and sitar. The most mysterious living player is **Annapurna Devi**, who has shunned publicity for decades. During the late 1940s and early 1950s, she performed highly acclaimed surbahar-sitar duets with her then-husband Ravi Shankar.

The **sarod** is a descendant of the Afghani *rebab* (no relation of the Arab fiddle of that name). Smaller than a sitar, it is made from one hollowed-out piece of teak wood with a goatskin covered soundbox. It has a metal-clad fingerboard and no frets. There are eight or ten playing strings, plucked with a wooden or coconut shell plectrum. Four carry the melody; the others are used to accentuate the rhythm. The strings are stopped with the left hand, either by the fingertips (Ali Albar Khan) or the fingernails (Amjad Ali Khan). There are also a dozen or so sympathetic strings lying underneath the main strings. The sarod has a strong, crisp and characterful sound. Its leading modern exponents have included **Ali Akbar Khan** (the *khalifa*, or head of the Maihar gharana, to which Ravi Shankar also belongs) and **Amjad Ali Khan** (from a famous dynasty of sarod players in Gwalior). Other names to look out for include Buddhadev Das Gupta, Ashish Khan (son of Ali Akbar Khan) and Brij Narayan (son of sarangi maestro Ram Narayan).

The **rudra vina** (also called the *bin* or *been*) is an ancient string instrument associated with Saraswati, the goddess of learning. It's a fretted stick zither with two large gourd resonators toward each end of the bamboo sound board which forms the body of the instrument. The lower resonator is rested on the ground, the other on the left shoulder and the fretboard is angled across the chest. It is plucked with metal fingerpicks. The rudra vina once held an exalted place in the pantheon of Hindustani stringed instruments (Rudra is another name for Shiva, its supposed inventor), but its influence has declined since its heyday, which stretched from medieval times to the nineteenth century. It has some twenty-four frets and seven strings; four carry the melody, two are *chikari* strings for rhythm and the last is a *laraj* or drone string. The rudra vina's voice is rich in overtones and leading players include **Zia Mohiuddin Dagar** and **Asad Ali Khan**. The **vichitra vina** is an unfretted cousin (the counterpart of the Karnatic *chitra vina* or *gottuvadyum*) played with a slide.

The **sarangi** is a fretless bowed instrument with a broad fingerboard and rather awkward-looking belly carved out of a single block of wood covered with parchment. There are three or four main strings of gut and anything up to forty metal sympathetic strings. Some claim it to be the most difficult instrument to play in the world. Certainly the technique is highly unusual. While the right hand wields the bow as on a violin or cello, the strings are stoppped not by the fingertips of the left hand, but by the nails and flesh immediately above them. The sarangi is capable of a wide range of timbres and its sound is likened to that of the human voice, so it is usually used to accompany vocal recitals. Originally this was its only function, but in recent years it has gained the status of a solo instrument in its own right due mainly to the efforts of **Sabri Khan**, **Sultan Khan** and **Ram Narayan**.

The **santoor** is a hammered zither of trapezoid shape, thought to be Persian in origin. It has over a hundred strings, pegged and stretched in pairs, parallel to each other. Each pair of stings passes over two bridges, one on each side of the instrument. The strings are struck by two wooden sticks which curve upwards at the end. The santoor has only been accepted in the last forty years as an instrument for classical music, thanks to the virtuosity and persistence of its leading player **Shivkumar Sharma**.

The **surmandal**, sometimes spelt *swarmandal*, resembles a zither and is used by vocalists to accompany themselves in performance. Even though its primary function is to provide the drone, singers sometimes also play melodic splashes on this instrument.

Sultan Khan playing
sarangi

The **tanpura** (or *tampura*) is the stringed instrument that provides a steady drone on the tonic and other important notes of the raga. Strumming (or more accurately stroking) continuously throughout the recital, the tanpura player has a pretty menial role, but it's considered a privilege to be so close to a great soloist and the place is usually occupied by the soloists shishyas (disciples). These days it's sometimes replaced by an electrical drone called a *shruti box*.

Wind instruments

The **shehnai** (or *shahnai* – emperor's flute) is a double-reed, oboe-type instrument with up to nine finger holes, some of which are stopped with wax for fine tuning to the scale of a particular raga. It was associated with grand or ceremonial occasions and in India it remains the traditional instrument for wedding music. A drone accompaniment is always provided by an **ottu**, or drone shehnai. The instrument demands a mastery of circular breathing and an enormous amount of breath control, particularly for long sustained passages which can be in an extravagantly fast tempo. The veteran master of the shehnai is **Bismillah Khan**.

The word **bansuri** (or *venu*) is used to refer to a wide variety of flutes, all made from bamboo (*banse*). The great popularity of this flute is enhanced by its association with the Hindu god Krishna, who is regularly depicted playng the flute (or *murli*) while enticing his devotees. Although the bamboo flute offers a limited range of just under two octaves, in the right hands it offers great expressive power. In the reflected glory of Krishna, it has become an important solo instrument on the concert platform. Among the leading contem-

porary players are **Hariprasad Chaurasia**, **Pannalal Ghosh**, **Vijay Raghav Rao** and **G.S. Sachdev**.

Hariprasad Chaurasia on bansuri

Percussion

The **tabla** is a set of two small drums played with the fingertips and palms, capable of producing an incredible variety of sounds and timbres over a range of about one octave. Strictly speaking, the name tabla is a synonym for the *dayan* or *dahina* (literally, right hand) drum, played with the right hand, while the larger *bayan* (literally, left hand) or *duggi* is the bass-toned drum on the left. The most popular of the many drums of north India, its invention is – seemingly like everything else – attributed to Amir Khusrau. Both drum heads are made of skin, with a paste of iron filings and flour in the centre, but while the body of the tabla is all wood, the bayan is made of metal. The tabla is usually tuned to the tonic of the raga by tapping tuning-blocks, held by braces on the sides of the instrument. Top players are **Zakir Hussain**,son of the late Alla Rakha one of the all-time great tabla players, **Kishan Maharaj**, **Anindo Chatterjee** and **Sharda Sahai**.

Predating the tabla, the **pakhawaj** is a wooden barrel drum nearly a metre long. It has two parchment heads, each tuned to a different pitch. Like the tabla, it is tuned by adjusting the drumhead tension using side wedges. A paste of boiled rice, iron filings and tamarind juice is applied to the smaller head, while a wheat flour paste on the larger head helps produce the lower notes. These paste roundels, unlike those of the tabla, have to be removed after each performance. The pakhawaj has a deep mellow sound and is used to accompany **dhrupad** singing and **kathak** dancing. The **mridangam**, the most widely used drum in Karnatic music, is similar but smaller.

Alla Rakha with his son Zakir Hussain

1960 film **Mughal-e-Azam** (The General of the Moghuls). Tansen's variations on raga themes are as much enjoyed today as the work of Bach or Purcell in the West.

The Mughal empire lingered on nominally until 1857, though it was a spent force after 1707. Nevertheless, its linguistic, literary and musical legacy persists, handed down the generations from *guru* (teacher) to *shishya* (disciple). Nowadays whether a musician follows an Islamic, Hindu or other path, it is this cross-cultural tradition which sweetens the breath of Hindustani music. As the sitarist **Rais Khan** puts it, "Music has got a different religion which doesn't go with any religion that is made by human being. It is not Hindu. It is not Muslim. The music doesn't have anything to do with Parsee or Sikh, with Christianity or Judaism. It has got its own religion which has come directly from God".

The Twentieth Century

In the first half of the twentieth century, royal courts existed in abundance, even if they no longer thrived, and many great musicians first saw service as court musicians. Appreciating Hindustani music came to be like wearing a badge of intellectual refinement, and such connoisseurship was displayed prominently, for it embodied wealth, power, discernment and exclusivity. But as the power of the maharajahs and nawabs declined, so did their

Saraswati, goddess of learning and music, takes to the gramophone. 1907

patronage. Fortunately Aakashvani or **All India Radio** (AIR) stepped in as a substitute. Radio exposure, together with income from recordings (ordinarily a one-off payment with no sight of royalties, mechanicals or library lending rights) replaced royal patronage.

The second half of the twentieth century witnessed profound changes to the Hindustani music scene. Oral transmission of knowledge still continues in face-to-face tuition, but the rise of literacy and the wider availability of recording equipment have provided new methods of teaching. Once a *gharana* (school) was sited in a physical location. Now top-ranking musicians are globe-trotters, and ever more international students have become mail-order disciples, with lessons on cassette supplemented by occasional personal tuition. Inevitably traditionalists believe that standards have plummeted. While is true that exposure to Western traditions has increased dramatically, it can be fairly said that Indian classical music has a larger audience than ever before.

Recording

For decades Hindustani music has suffered from a surfeit of nostalgia, perhaps encouraged by the tradition of oral transmission. Forebears such as Khusrau and Tansen have become iconic figureheads, yet nobody knows how they would compare to today's musicians.

The first recordings of Indian music in India were made in 1902 by **Fred Gaisberg** for the Gramophone Company: India's first recording star, **Gauhar Jan** (c1875-1930), was born. Jan was an accomplished singer of *khayal* and *thumri* and her recordings are an important stylistic link back to the old world of courtly musical patronage. But with recording, a new commercial 'patron' appeared and, for the first time, the very personal art of making Indian music could be documented. We can now review from a historical distance celebrated virtuosi such as **Kesarbai Kerkar** (vocals), **Allauddin Khan** (sarod), **Hafiz Ali Khan** (sarod) and **Imdad Khan** (sitar) – for example in the Gramophone Company of India's expanding **Great Gharanas** series.

As elsewhere, these performers had to adapt to the constraints of contemporary recording equipment. India suffered particularly in this respect, as the late singer/producer **G.N. Joshi** recalled in his biography *Down Memory Lane*, in which he describes the dismay of discovering how nobody at the Gramophone Company of India had realised its 'state-of-the-art' machinery was fobbed-off obsolescence from Britain. The limitations that **78s** imposed had a dramatic effect on Indian music, as musicians were forced to distill their artistry into soundbite length. However deftly this was done, the result was even less representative of live performance than in other genres like *rembetika* or blues. Yet their craft shines through and the recordings are hardly quaint oddities.

While LPs were appearing in Europe and America in the early 1950s, in India 78s were still being released well into the Sixties. While the older form only gave a maximum of four minutes' uninterrupted music, LPs gave around twenty, meaning Hindustani performances could breath again. The CD has improved things further with longer recording time available and no distracting crackles to spoil the concentrated unfolding of an alap.

Today, Indian classical music is more popular and more available than ever. Top artists appear regularly in concert the world over and labels like Nimbus, Navras, Chhanda Dhara and Moment are releasing substantial live and studio performances on disc.

discography

There's a huge range of Indian classical music on disc – produced both by Indian and foreign labels – and only very selective highlights are listed below. Among the best Western labels (Indian-label CDs are not widely available outside the country) are the UK-based Navras (live concert recordings) and Nimbus (with fine studio recordings of top contemporary players); Chhanda Dhara, based in Germany; and the US-based India Archive Music (well-produced studio recordings), Moment (founded by Zakir Hussain and featuring classical and fusion recordings), AMMP, Neelam and Raga Records (archival and modern performances).

Compilations

Anthology of Indian Classical Music
(Auvidis/Unesco, France).

This presciently starrily-cast double-CD of North and South Indian classical music first appeared in the 1950s. Recorded by the French musicologist and Hinduist Alain Daniélou, it boasts contributions from a Hindustani and Karnatic elite including Ali Akbar Khan, Ravi Shankar and M.S. Subbulakshmi. Following his death, it now also acts as a memorial to Daniélou.

Anthology of World Music:
North Indian Classical Music (Rounder, US).

An important four-CD set re-issuing Alain Daniélou's survey of Hindustani music originally released by Bärenreiter/Musicaphon. Features top quality performances of the main forms of vocal music and the main instruments – sitar, surbahar, vichitra vina, sarod, sarangi, flute and shehnai. Extensive notes with some inaccuracies.

Call of the Valley
(EMI Hemisphere, UK).

Probably the most influential Hindustani album ever made. A late 1960s collaboration between Shivkumar Sharma (santoor), Hariprasad Chaurasia (flute) and Brijbushan Kabra (guitar). The idea is a simple, but effective one, using various time-related ragas to depict the passage of a Kashmiri day. Fans of this will also want to seek out **The Valley Recalls** and **Rasdhara**, the two sequel *jugalbandi* (duet) recordings Sharma and Chaurasia made for Navras.

Inspiration – India
(EMI, UK).

A selection of instrumental and tabla duos and jugulbandi duets featuring Vilayat Khan (sitar), his younger brother Imrat Khan (surbahar) and – no relation – Bismillah Khan (shehnai), with Shanta Prasad on tabla. Six tracks giving a varied introduction to Hindustani music.

The Raga Guide (Nimbus, UK).

An ambitious introduction to the raga system with bite-sized portions of seventy-four of the most performed ragas in recordings specially commissioned to show off their essence. Divided over four CDs, with the ragas arranged alphabetically, the performances are by flautist Hariprasad Chaurasia, sarod player Buddhadev Das Gupta and vocalists Shruti Sadolikar and Vidyadhar Vyas. A two hundred-page book gives comprehensible analytical descriptions, transcriptions and forty ragamala paintings.

The Rough Guide to the Music of India and Pakistan (World Music Network, UK).

Despite its title, this is predominantly an introduction to the music of North India, with flautist Dr N. Ramani the only southerner represented. But it's a good survey of classical, semi-classical and folk styles ranging from Ali Akbar Khan and Asha Bhosle (in a gorgeous opening prayer) to Pakistani folk singer Zarsanga. Classical artists include Bismillah Khan (shehnai), Vilayat Khan (sitar), Amjad Ali Khan (sarod) and a jugalbandi from Shivkumar Sharma (santoor) and Hariprasad Chaurasia (flute). Also included are tracks from Nusrat Fateh Ali Khan, the Sabri Brothers, Purna Das Baul and Rajasthani folk musicians. A digestible introduction to much of the subcontinent's music.

Vintage Music from India (Rounder, US).

An anthology by Peter Manuel concentrating on northern traditions, and vocal music in particular. Recorded between 1906 and the 1920s, it includes India's first celebrity recording artist Gauhar Jan, and forms as different as *qawwali* (Sufi devotional music) and the songs of *tawaif* (female courtesans), from a time when the upper echelons of tawaif society were carriers of Hindu cultural heritage.

Instrumental Artists

Nikhil Banerjee

Banerjee (1931–1986) ranks as one of the finest sitarists of recent years, famed for the purity and elgance of his style. He studied with Allauddin Khan and later with Khan's son, the sarod maestro Ali Akbar Khan. His remains a singular voice in the annals of sitar, as eminent as Vilayat Khan and Ravi Shankar.

The Hundred-minute Raga: Purabi Kalyan
(Raga Records, US).

Banerjee, here accompanied by tabla player Swapan Chaudhuri, is in great form in this two-CD recording made in California in 1982. After Banerjee's death many recordings appeared of questionable provenance but this one finds him in top form.

INDIA *(side margin)*

Rag Manj Khammaj & Rag Misra Mand
(AMMP, US).

Released in 1994, long after Nikhil Banerjee's death, this jugalbandi (duet) pairs Banerjee with sarod player Ali Akbar Khan, his guru's son. A moving sitar-sarod jugalbandi.

V.M. Bhatt

Vishwa Mohan Bhatt (b 1952) has risen to become one of Hindustani music's most famous sons. After playing the sitar and violin he switched to guitar around 1967, reworking and redesigning the Spanish guitar until it emerged as a new mutant instrument cannily called the Mohan Vina.

Guitar à la Hindustan
(Original Music Impressions, India).

This opens with a *gat* (rhythmic composition) in the night raga Tilak Kamod. Kaunsi Kanhra, Chandrakauns and Mishra Pilu follow. Along with **Gathering Rain Clouds** (Water Lily Acoustics, US), this represents a perfect place to begin an exploration of Bhatt's classical repertoire.

Hariprasad Chaurasia

Hariprasad Chaurasia (b 1937) overcame establishment prejudices to become the foremost North Indian flautist. Chaurasia has achieved more than any other flautist, both in popularity and artistic terms, than anyone in the Hindustani pantheon since Pannalal Ghosh (a flautist who studied with Allauddin Khan). In recent years he has become one of Indian music's most successful ambassadors on any instrument.

Venu
(Rykodisc, US).

A live recording by Mickey Hart (of the Grateful Dead) from December 1974, with the excellent Zakir Hussain on sitar. A compelling exploration of the early morning raga Ahir Bhairav, with its mixture of romantic and devotional moods – a raga whose potential he also explores on the excellent **Rag Ahir Bhairav** (Nimbus, UK).

Hari-Krishna: In Praise of Janmashtami
(Navras, UK).

This is a unique recording of a private devotional performance on the occasion of Janmashtami (Krishna's birthday), in honour of the flute-playing god. The three CDs here encompass the first three and a half hours of an all-night performance at the shrine in Chaurasia's Bombay house. Assisted by his nephew Rakesh Chaurasia and other pupils, with tabla accompaniment, this is a truly atmospheric performance which is genuinely spiritually inspired. Extraordinary.

Four Dhuns (Nimbus, UK).

Hariprasad Chaurasia is one of the most versatile of instrumentalists, playing in various fusion groups. A *dhun* is usually a folk tune or a light piece that doesn't strictly adhere to the strict rules of a raga, and often concludes a concert.

Zia Mohiuddin Dagar

Dagar (1929–1990) has been described as the last great master of the rudra vina. His playing, drawing on the style of dhrupad vocal music, has an austere and refined integrity.

Raga Yaman and Raga Shuddha Todi
(Nimbus, UK).

Dagar made these recordings of two of his favourite ragas in the spring of 1990, the year in which he died. The music unfolds slowly, and has an incredible depth and profundity. Dagar goes in for extended alap sections, exploring the ragas in depth, and doesn't indulge in fireworks. Two beautifully recorded CDs for the price of one.

Ashit Desai

Desai (b 1951) started as a singer – her voice was featured on devotional songs from the Ghandi soundtrack – but has become best-known as a composer and conductor, working with Ravi Shankar amongst others.

Divinity (Sona Rupa, UK).

Although the planetary globe and starry sky on the CD cover make this look like a dubious New Age release, it's actually a very accomplished series of meditational compositions based on Hindustani ragas. Features wide-arching instrumental solos on flute, santoor, sitar and shehnai, set against a background lightly coloured by guitar, vibraphone and keyboards. A very good first step into Indian music for those daunted by the rigorous recital tradition.

Zakir Hussain

Zakir Hussain (b 1951), son of the late master tabla player Alla Rakha, is probably the foremost tabla player of his generation. He has contributed enormously to the worldwide popularity of Indian music with his percussion-led albums and fusion work (see p.112).

WITH SHIVKUMAR SHARMA

India: Raga Purya Kalyan
(World Network, Germany).

A superb pairing of Zakir Hussain on tabla with the santoor pioneer Shivkumar Sharma (see below). In keeping with the time-honoured recital tradition, they conclude with a Punjabi-style dadra.

Ali Akbar Khan

Sarodist Ali Akbar Khan (b 1922) is hailed as one of the greatest musicians on the planet, irrespective of genre. A master melodist, he is steeped in the Maihar gharana, his father's style of playing (see Allauddin Khan, opposite). While it is considered unpardonable even to whisper it, many consider him the more elevating player. Now a soloist, his duets with his brother-in-law, Ravi Shankar, created a sensation in their day.

Signature Series Volumes 1 and 2 (AMMP, US).

Accompanied by one of the finest tabla players of his generation, Mahapurush Misra, Khan delivers Gauri Manjari, Jogiya Kalingra and the night raga Chandranandan (on Volume 1), and Medhavi, Khammaj and Bhairavi Bhatiyar (on the individually packaged Volume 2). The remastered Signature Series restores these exemplary Connoisseur albums to the catalogue, some of the most sublime Hindustani recordings ever released.

Allauddin Khan

The multi-instrumentalist Allauddin Khan lived in an age of giants. No wonder then that facts about him became distorted. He died in 1972, having celebrated his centenary in October 1962, but nobody knew his exact age, least of all Khan himself. Fortunately, the quality and importance of his music are incontestable.

Late Ustad Allauddin Khan Saheb Volumes 1-5 (T-Series, India).

These recordings derive from All India Radio (AIR) broadcasts between 1959 and 1960, and are the best introduction to the master's work. They are broadcast length, most well over twenty minutes, unlike the brevity of the 78-era tracks encoded as one track on **Chairman's Choice — Great Gharanas: Maihar** (EMI India).

Amjad Ali Khan

The sarodist Amjad Ali Khan (b 1945) is the son of the sarod maestro Hafiz Ali Khan. His playing has a remarkable depth to it and any concert performance is a surefire guarantee of satisfaction. His recorded oeuvre is frustratingly extensive and scattered over many domestic and foreign labels.

Homage to Mother Teresa: Raga Rageshwari (Moment, US).

Recorded in Calcutta in 1994, a few years before her death, this is a tribute to Mother Teresa from two of India's finest musicians – Zakir Hussain provides the tabla accompaniment. An extended seventy-minute performance of the raga has subtlety and depth as well as some showy dialogues with the tabla. The recorded sound is beautifully mellow.

The Legendary Lineage (Navras, UK).

The premise is simplicity itself: three generations of one of the most illustrious families in Hindustani music gathered on one volume. It begins with Hafiz Ali Khan, continues with his son, Amjad Ali Khan, and closes with Amjad Ali Khan's sons, Amaan and Ayaam Ali Bangash. A memorable treasury of the past, present and future of Gwalior-style sarod playing.

Bismillah Khan

One of Hindustani music's foremost virtuosi, Bismillah Khan (b 1916) is the acknowledged master of the shehnai. His breathtaking jugalbandi with Vilayat Khan inaugurated EMI's impressive Music of India series.

Live In London Volume 1 and Volume 2 (Navras, UK).

Two marvellous albums recorded in London in 1985. The first includes Kedar and Rageshwari while the second encompasses the raga Malkauns and a dhun.

Imrat Khan

Khan is a distinguished sitar and surbahar player — surbahar being the bass voiced equivalent of the more familiar sitar — but he is better known for his surbahar playing. A virtuoso performer like his elder brother, Vilayat Khan.

Ajmer (Water Lily Acoustics, US).

A 1990 recording featuring surbahar and sitar. Khan plays raga Alhaiya Bilaval and his own composition, "Imratkauns".

Rais Khan

Rais Khan (b 1939) is arguably the most impressive sitarist of the post-Nikhil Banerjee years. His playing has a gloriously romantic resonance to it.

Together (Audiorec, UK).

Rais Khan's solo work is exemplary but thin on the ground. This release is noteworthy for its rare pairing of sarangi and sitar. Sultan Khan plays sarangi and Sabir Khan tabla, with Bilaskhani as their chosen centrepiece. The duo is also well represented on another favourite, the concert recording **Rag-Rang** (Navras, UK).

Sabri Khan

Sabri Khan (b 1927) was one of the first sarangi players to become a principal soloist. The instrument (of folk origin) had traditionally been viewed as less worthy, through its use accompanying tawaifs (courtesan entertainers) and its 'low-caste' construction. Khan brought himself and the instrument a new profile in accompanying top vocalists.

Raga Darbari/Raga Multani (Auvidis Ethnic, France).

A 1991 release showing off the maestro's exquisite playing, including a *khyal* interpretation of Raga Darbari which builds over forty minutes to achieve a rare intensity. Also twenty minutes of glorious improvisation in Raga Multani.

Sultan Khan

Sarangi player Sultan Khan first came under the international spotlight at the time of the 1974 Dark Horse tour with Ravi Shankar and George Harrison. He consolidated his international career with work on the soundtrack to the film Gandhi. His touch is as distinct from Ram Narayan and Sabri Khan as Ravi Shankar's from Vilayat Khan or Nikhil Banerjee.

Sarangi (Navras, UK).

Sultan Khan's sarangi reveals eloquent insights into ragas Jaijaiwanti and Mishra Shivranjani that few could match in this release from a dizzy-making London concert in 1990 with Shaukat Hussain Khan on tabla. Also recommended are **Raga Du Début De La Nuit** (Adès, France) and **Savai Gandharva Music Festival Pune '92** (Alurkar Music House, India). It is impossible to get enough sarangi in one's life.

Vilayat Khan

Vilayat Khan (b 1922) and his younger brother Imrat may derive their musicality from their genes and the *Imdadkhani gharana* (named after their grandfather), but Vilayat is his own man and a living legend in his own right. He ranks as the greatest living sitarist alongside — not after — Ravi Shankar. His most outstanding contribution to his gharana's tradition is the gayaki, or vocal style, of sitar playing.

Sitar (India Archive Music, US).

Everything one could wish for. Good old raga Bhairavi performed with such flair and compassion that the senses tingle. A studio recording from 1989.

A Night At The Taj (Gramophone Company of India).

A classic jugalbandi combination — sitar and surbahar — with Vilayat Khan's younger brother Imrat. Also recommended are two double CDs: **Ragas Shahana & Bageshree** (Navras, UK), a sitar duet with his gifted son Shujaat Khan, and **Eb'adat** (Navras, UK), the historic reunion duet with shehnai player Bismillah Khan.

Kamalesh Maitra

Born in 1928 in what was then East Bengal, Maitra grew up in Calcutta and started playing tabla in 1940. He joined the Uday Shankar Ballet troupe in 1950 and was asked to learn the tabla tarang – a semi-circular set of tablas tuned to play ragas. He worked with Uday Shankar's company for twenty years and in 1977 settled in Berlin, where he still lives and works. He is the acknowledged master of this rare, but beautiful sounding instrument.

Tabla Tarang – Melody on Drums (Smithsonian Folkways, US).

This music performed on tuned tabla is absolutely compelling. In this 1996 recording, Maitra plays four forms of the early morning raga Todi, accompanied by Trilok Gurtu on the conventional tabla. Two ragas are associated with Tansen and his son Bilas Khan. Excellent accompanying notes.

Ram Narayan

Yehudi Menuhin once said, "I cannot separate the sarangi from Ram Narayan, so thoroughly fused are they, not only in my memory but in the fact of this sublime dedication of the great musician to an instrument which is no longer archaic because of the matchless way he had made it speak". The sarangi is one of the most eloquent of melody instruments on the planet, capable of extraordinary vocal mimicry. Ram Narayan's daughter, Aruna Narayan Kalle, has since come through the ranks as an excellent sarangi player, making history in her own right as a female exponent of the instrument.

 The Art of the Sarangi (Ocora, France).

Although Narayan has recorded for many labels, the first, vinyl edition of this album was a turning point. This edition has added a 1979 recording of raga Shankara to the original 1971 album's versions of Bairagi-Bhairav, Madhuvanti and Kirvani.

Alla Rakha

"All life is rhythm", said tabla maestro and classical legend Alla Rakha Quereshi, who died in 2000. The first tabla player to give solo concerts, he rose to fame as Ravi Shankar's right-hand man during the 1960s, at a time when the music was first drawing Western audiences. He is highly versatile, having worked prolifically as a composer in the Indian film industry as well as collaborating on the pioneering percussion fusion album *Rich à la Rakha* with jazz drummer Buddy Rich. With his sons, Zakir Hussain and Fazal Qureshi, he has created a lasting pedigree.

Maestro's Choice – Tabla (Music Today, India).

A recital with Zakir Hussain illustrating the potency of Hindustani rhythm, exploring matta taal (a 9-beat cycle) and jai taal (a 13-beat cycle), with a concluding number in pashto (7 beats). Sultan Khan supports melodically on sarangi. Their

sixty-seven-minute teental **Tabla Duet** (Moment, US), with Ramesh Misra on sarangi, is also highly recommended.

Ravi Shankar

Ravi Shankar (b 1920) is *the* figure in Indian and Hindustani music as well as being among the four best-known Indians of the century (along with Gandhi, Nehru and Tagore). Beyond the sheer exquisiteness of his sitar playing he has proved one of the genre's great innovators, working in film, dance and theatre as well as cross-cultural work of many kinds. His English-language autobiographies, My Music, My Life (1969) and Raga Mala (1998), come highly recommended.

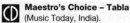 **Ravi Shankar & Ali Akbar Khan In Concert 1972** (Apple, UK).

Pyrotechnics and profundity recorded in New York, matching sitar and sarod in Hindustani music's greatest jugalbandi. The concert was dedicated to their mutual guru Allauddin Khan, who had died just a few weeks before.

 Farewell, My Friend (Gramophone Company of India).

This 1992 tribute to film-maker Satyajit Ray evokes Ray's spirit and harkens back to the glory days when Ravi Shankar created the stunning soundtrack to his fellow Bengali's *Pather Panchali* (The Song of the Little Road), the film that put India on the world cinema map.

 In Celebration (Angel, US).

An excellent retrospective of Ravi Shankar's unmatched recording career, although this 4-CD set omits his important early shellac recordings for HMV and any jugalbandi with Ali Akbar Khan (a partnership that made them the hottest ticket in Hindustani music). Released in 1996, it also contains his daughter Anoushka's debut (Adarini), with the marvellous Zakir Hussain on tabla.

 Ravi Shankar from Dusk to Dawn (Earthsongs/Connoisseur Collection, UK).

Four ragas in six versions organised in the proper sequence. Raga Sindhu Bhairavi is complemented by a duet performance with Ali Akbar Khan which eschews the usual alap opening for a lightning sketch introduction called an *aochar*.

Shivkumar Sharma

Shivkumar Sharma (b 1938) is directly responsible for the birth of a new classical instrument, previously deemed worthy only of folk or regional music. Dutifully he took up the Kashmiri santoor at his father's behest, developing the instrument into a soloist's vehicle in classical concerts. His name is now synonymous with that of the santoor and, beyond that, with a powerful musical vision. (See also Zakir Hussain, p.76).

 Sampradaya (RealWorld, UK).

An excellent santoor duet performance of Raga Janasammohini with Sharma's son Raul – the ringing notes interlace and hover in the air. The range of articulation is glorious, from delicate, feathery whispering to arresting staccato punctuations, although it is all quite restrained until the end.

India
Karnatic instrumental music

sounds of the saints

The Karnatic music of south India might be labelled 'classical', but it's nothing like classical music anywhere else in the world. Rather than being the province of an urbane elite, it's an explosion of colour, sound and Hindu worship. **Ken Hunt** explores the lifeblood of South Indian culture.

K arnatic (Carnatic, Karnatak) music was once the musical language of the entire subcontinent, grounded in Hinduism and boasting a history and mythology thousands of years old as the articulation of Dravidian culture.

In the fifteenth century, the Moghul conquest of North India divided the subcontinent. The Hindu culture of the north was uprooted and Muslim practices replaced the old ways – or at least were grafted onto the old stock. The two musical systems retained their allegiance to the dynamics of *raga* and rhythm, but in other respects they were to diverge – one important difference being in their audience. While Hindustani music developed close associations with court and palace, Karnatic music remained part of the warp and weft of the South Indian culture, both religious and secular.

The other major difference is that Karnatic music, lacking written notation, is taught by demonstration and learned by ear or, in the case of its highly sophisticated rhythmic system, taught by a marvellous, mathematical structure of 'finger computing' which enables a percussionist to break down a complex *thaalam* (rhythmic cycle) into manageable units. Indian percussion maestros readily admit the supremacy of Karnatic concepts of rhythm, and increasing numbers of Hindustani percussionists have studied in the South.

Hindu Roots

Much to the annoyance of Karnatic musicians, Hindustani music from North India is better known internationally, although the music of the South is by far the more ancient. Its tenets, once passed on only orally, were codified in Vedic literature between 4000 and 1000 BC, long before Western classical music was even in its infancy. One of the four main Vedic texts, the **Sama Veda**, is the basis for all that followed.

The music and the faith which inspired it have remained inseparable. Visitors to the vast temples of South India are much more likely to encounter music than in the north. It's usually the piercing sound of the *nagaswaram* (oboe) and the *tavil* (barrel drum). More than likely it accompanies flaming torches and a ceremonial procession of the temple deity.

While devotional and religious in origin, Karnatic music is as much a vehicle for education and

SIMON BROUGHTON

Nadaswaram players at a temple, Kanchipuram, Tamil Nadu

entertainment as for spiritual elevation. **Kritis**, a genre of Hindu hymn, are hummed and sung as people go about their daily business. In their tunefulness and recognisability, they hold a similar position in popular culture to the Christian hymn.

The association of music and **dance** with Hindu thought has a long heritage, beginning with Shiva himself as Nataraja, the Cosmic Dancer, whose potent image is ever-present in Hindu iconography. His temple at Chidambaram, for example, is rich with sculptures of *natya* dance poses, music-making and musical instruments, and the *devadasis*, the servants of God, were traditionally temple dancers.

Karnatic composers, too, are looked upon with some reverence. Indeed, the music's three great composers – **Tyagaraja**, (1767-1847), **Muttuswamy Dikshitar** (1776-1835) and **Syama Sastri** (1762-1827) – are known as the *Trimurti* or 'Holy Trinity' and are regarded as saint-composers. Between them, the trinity were responsible for hundreds of compositions – Tyagaraja alone is credited with some six hundred kritis.

Indians compare the music of the Trimurti to the grape, the coconut and the banana. Tyagaraja can be consumed and enjoyed immediately; appreciating Muttuswamy Dikshitar is like cracking open a shell to get to the kernel; and with Syama Sastri you have to remove the soft outer layer to get to the fruit. Their era has become known as the **Golden Period**, and their music is revered and celebrated year in, year out, at various music conferences (festivals) and on a never-ending stream of recordings.

In Performance

In concert, Karnatic music often seems to lack Hindustani music's showmanship and flamboyance. But neither does it require the same sustained level of concentration. A Karnatic *ragam* (raga) might be said to resemble a miniature beside a large-scale Hindustani canvas.

Karnatic musicians will distil the essence of a **ragam** into six to eight minutes. In part this is because a kriti, the base of many performances, is a fixed composition without improvisation. Karnatic musicians' creativity lies in their ability to interpret that piece faithfully while shading and colouring the composition appropriately. The words of a kriti affect even non-vocal compositions: instrumentalists will colour their interpretations as if a vocalist were singing along; the unvoiced lyric determines where they place an accent, a pause or melodic splash.

Improvisation has its place too, most noticeably in a sequence known as **ragam-thanam-pallavi** (see p.65). This is a full-scale flowering of a Karnatic ragam and is every bit the equal of a Hindustani performance, although it is employed more sparingly, tending to be the centrepiece or climax of a Karnatic concert.

Whereas Karnatic music tends to break down into three strands: temple music, temple dance-accompaniment, and music for personal and private devotional observance, **sabha** or paying concert performances have somewhat blurred these distinctions. During the 1890s, the sabha associations in **Madras** (now Chennai) took an innovative path, moving from music performances into dance recitals. Madras remains a centre of excellence and its music conferences, especially around December and January, attract devout audiences each year.

Concert-giving led to other changes: microphones came into use during the 1930s. They lent soft-voiced instruments such as members of the vina family a new lease of life, and replaced full-tilt vocal power with greater subtlety, granting weaker voices new opportunities which led to new standards of stagecraft.

Nowadays, concerts will typically feature a named principal soloist (either vocal or instrumental) with melodic and rhythmic

SIMON BROUGHTON

The saint composer Tyagaraja, depicted at his shrine in Thiruvaiyaru, Tamil Nadu

Stringed instruments

The **vina** (or *veena*) is the foremost Karnatic stringed instrument, the southern equivalent (and ancestor) of the sitar. A hollow wooden fingerboard with twenty-four frets is supported by two resonating gourds at each end. The vina has seven strings, four used for the melody and the other three for rhythm and drone. Current leading players include **V. Doreswamy Iyengar**, **Chitti Babu**, **S. Balachandar** and **Sivasakti Sivanesan**.

The **chitra vina** (or *gottuvadyam*) is an unfretted 21-string instrument with sets for rhythm and drone as well as sympathetic strings. It has a characteristic soft voice which, before amplification, meant it was best suited to intimate surroundings. The best-known player is the young **N. Ravikiran**, who has switched to a hollow cylinder of teflon for his slide.

N. Ravikiran playing chitra vina

Wind instruments

As in the North, the transverse bamboo flute goes under the name of **bansuri** or **venu**, although it is typically shorter and higher in pitch than the Hindustani instrument. Watch out for recordings by **N. Ramani** and the younger **S. Shashank**.

The **nagaswaram** (or *nadaswaram*) is a piercing double-reed oboe-like instrument. It's longer (up to two and a half feet) and more deep-toned than the Hindustani *shehnai* and is associated with weddings, processions and temple ceremonies. It's often paired with a drone nagaswaram or *ottu*. Besides its ceremonial functions – and it is perhaps best heard in the open air – it is sometimes employed in formal classical concert settings. Leading players include **Sheik Chinnamoulana** and the brothers **M.P.N. Sethuraman** and **M.P.N. Ponnuswamy**.

Percussion

The Karnatic counterpart to the tabla is the **mridangam**, a double-headed, barrel-shaped drum made from a single block of jackwood. Both heads are made from layers of hide and can be tuned according to the ragam being performed. **Vellore Ramabhadran** and **Mysore Rajappa Sainatha** are two of the top players.

Other percussion instruments include the **tavil**, a folk-style barrel drum commonly found in ceremonial nagaswaram ensembles and the **ghatam**, a clay pot tuned by firing. The latter is frequently found in South Indian ensembles, and unlikely as it may seem, in the hands of a top player like **T.H. 'Vikku' Vinayakram** it

Vikku Vinayakram on the ghatam – a water pot

can contribute some spectacular solos. The **morsing** (or *morching*) is a Jew's harp, often part of the accompanying ensemble, but frequently dropped when groups tour to save on the air fare!

The **jalatarangam** (or *jalatarang*) is something of a curiosity, a melodic percussion instrument comprising a semicircle of water-filled porcelain bowls. It can create a sound of extraordinary beauty as the lead melody instrument in a typical Karnatic ensemble with violin, mridangam and ghatam. Players include **Mysore M.S. Chandrasekharian** and the brothers **Anayampatti S. Dhandapani** and **Anayampatti S. Ganesan**.

PETER CULSHAW

JAK KILBY

INDIA

accompaniment and a *tanpura* or drone player. Percussionists of standing are often included in concert announcements and advertising as they are attractions in their own right. Female musicians involved in a principal role tend to be vocalists, *vina* (or *veena*) players or violinists. Male musicians have access to a wider range of musical possibilities as well as outnumbering female principal soloists or accompanists by roughly three to one.

New Instruments

Both of the subcontinent's two classical systems give pride of place to the voice while melodic instruments, to some degree, are played to mimic it. Nevertheless, Karnatic music makes use of a fascinating array of stringed, wind and percussion instruments, many unique to the subcontinent (see box on previous page).

From the nineteenth century, Karnatic music began to appropriate **Western instruments**, notably the violin and clarinet. More recent additions include the mandolin and saxophone. In the South – where the northern sarangi is a stranger – the violin's fluidity, grace, speed and penetrative volume guaranteed it a complement of converts during the nineteenth century, most notably **Tanjore Vadivelu** of the Tanjore Quartette.

Nowadays Karnatic music without the **violin** is inconceivable. Credit for introducing it and adapting its Western tuning is given to **Balaswamy Dikshitar** (1786-1859), younger brother of the saintly composer – though some traditionalist scholars claim it as really a descendant of the earlier *dhanur vina*. Maestros such as **Lalgudi G. Jayaraman**, **V.V. Subrahmanyam** and **L. Subramaniam** are major artists, while **A. Kanyakumari** typifies the female violinists who are coming to the fore. In South India, the violin is played sitting on the floor with the body of the violin against the upper chest and the scroll wedged against the ankle leaving the left hand free to slide more freely up and down the strings. **Shankar**, brother of L. Subramaniam, has devised his own electric double violin with an extended bottom range and dark tone.

The introduction of the **clarinet**, or to give it its local name *clarionet*, is credited to Mahadeva Nattuvanar, in around 1860. Until around 1920, the clarinet was mostly used as an ensemble instrument in *cinna melam*, a dance accompaniment form. Thereafter, it was gradually established as a soloist's instrument. **Balaraman** of the **Nadamuni Band** was one of the twentieth century's first clarinet maestros and his work has been continued by musicians like **A.K.C. Natarajan**.

The **mandolin** has gained acceptance thanks to another of South India's child prodigies, **U. Srinivas**, often known as Mandolin Srinivas. He started playing the instrument aged six and has since toured worldwide and proved that the mandolin (albeit heavily modified) is highly effective at spinning gossamer webs of Tyagaraja improvi-

Shankar with his custom-built, twin-necked violin

sations. He is a very devout musician and his performances usually have a devotional ingredient.

The **saxophone** is another recent import and its champion, **Kadri Gopalnath**, is one of South

South Indian names

Once you've cracked the code, South Indian musicians' names can provide a wealth of information. A typical name begins with an initial, but this does not necessarily stand for the musician's own name. **Initials** in the names of N. Ravikiran and L. Subramaniam, for instance, denote their fathers' names – Narasimhan and Lakshminarayan respectively. One recent trend is for married female musicians to replace their father's initial with their husband's.

Sometimes the musician's name is prefixed by the name of their instrument – **Clarinet Abbayi**, **Chitravina Ravikiran**, **Mandolin Srinivas** and **Vina Gayatri** – an inexpensive way to advertise. Another variant is for a place name – such as Srirangam, Chennai or Tanjore – to be added. In the past this would often have implied a courtly connection, when places like Mysore, Tanjore and Trivandrum were major centres of employment for musicians. The court of Serfojee of Tanjore (1798-1833) was reputed, for example, to boast a musician for every day of the year. This place name may also be abbreviated to a single letter.

A **caste name** such as Iyer (or Ayyer) may appear as a suffix, and often acts as a geographical or cultural pointer. Sarma, for instance, is a caste name associated with Tamil Nadu, Panikkar with Kerala, and Naidu with Telugu-speakers. The abandonment of caste designations, however, is a growing trend.

Brahmins and high-class non-Brahmin castes have long followed a calling as musicians, as have the barber-musician *Pillai* caste. To this day, Pillais are inextricably linked with *nagaswaram* and *tavil* and, more

JAK KILBY

Indian mandolin pioneer U. Srinivas

recently, with the clarinet. Certain instruments – flute, mridangam, kanjira (a tambourine-like drum) and morsing – have traditionally been associated with the non-Brahmin dance-music tradition.

India's most popular musicians, with dozens of recordings to his credit. Gopalnath demonstrates Karnatic music's particular ability to be ancient and modern at the same time. When he plays the Karnatic ragams the powerful sound of the saxophone echoes the ancient nagaswaram, but its tone and attitude are also distinctively contemporary.

discography

Compilations

An Anthology of South Indian Classical Music (Ocora, France).

A substantial work compiled by the eminent violinist Dr L. Subramaniam. This four-CD primer gathers many of Karnatic music's vocal and instrumental giants with detailed descrip-

tions of the music they make and the instruments they play. M.S. Subbulakshmi (vocals), T.R. Mahalingam (flute), A.K.C. Natarajan (clarinet), Raajeshwari Padmanabhan (vina), N. Ravikiran (chitra vina), Subashchandran (morsing), V.V. Subrahmanyam (violin) and T.H. Vinayakram (ghatam) are among the concentration of virtuosi.

Instrumental Artists

Chitti Babu

Chitti Babu (b 1936) is a major instrumentalist whose motto is 'Vina is my mission in life'. His Live at Waldorf Astoria album for the New York-based Oriental label brought him wide attention in the West.

ⓘ **Carnatic Veena** (Gramophone Company of India, India).

Like many of this company's CD releases or reissues, supporting information is scant: this is an undated recording of vina with mridangam and ghatam accompaniment. It includes a suite catchily titled "Wedding Bells and Other Hits" and a ragam-thanam-pallavi sequence.

S. Balachander

The vina maestro S. Balachander (1927–1990) was one of the best known Karnatic instrumentalists, having been one of the influential World Pacific label's major artists with groundbreaking issues such as Sounds of the Veena featuring the flute of Ramani and The Magic Music of India. Unlike most Karnatic performers, his recorded work is peppered with interpretations of ragams that are longer than normal.

 The Virtuoso of Veena (Denon, Japan).

Ragam Chakravaakam is at the centre of this disc. Track one comprises alapana and thanam while track two explores Tyagaraja's devotional employment of the same ragam. Taeko Kusano's touching notes marvellously capture the spirit of this maverick musician.

A.S. Dhandapani

Anayampatti S. Dhandapani and his younger brother S. Ganeshan are the leading players of the Jalatharangam. The instrument may be something of a musical curiosity, and live performances are hard to come by, but the music is extremely beautiful on disc.

Jalatharangam
(Magnasound, India).

Here Anayampatti Ganeshan accompanies his brother on violin with Thinniyam Y. Krishnan on mridangam in compositions by Tyagaraja and Dikshitar amongst others.

Kadri Gopalnath

Gopalnath's father started on his father's instrument, the nagaswaram, but got turned on to the saxophone after hearing the palace band at Mysore. He studied initially under N. Gopalkrishna Iyer of Mangalore and the vocalist and mridangam player T.V. Gopalkrishnan and pioneered saxophone in a Karnatic classical setting. He typifies the duality of Karnatic music in playing a modern instrument in a tradition that goes back centuries.

Gem Tones: Saxophone Supreme, South Indian Style (Globestyle, UK).

A fervent and thrilling collection with accompaniment by A. Kanyakumari on her low-tuned violin, sounding for all the world like a tenor sax, plus mridangam (M. R. Sainatha) and morsing (B. Rajasekhar).

Lalgudi Jayaraman

Violin may only be a relatively recent South Indian import – merely a few centuries old – but it is difficult to imagine Karnatic music without it and Jayaraman is one of the finest contemporary violinists.

Violin (Moment, US).

An interesting North-South excursion with a kriti, a bhajan (a Hindu devotional song form) and a tillana (a light dance-derived form using drum syllables as well as lyrics proper). Percussion accompaniment is from Vellore Ramabhadran (mridangam) and Moment's founder Zakir Hussain (tabla).

A. Kanyakumari

A. Kanyakumari (b 1961) has played violin as an accompanist and soloist, and is on record accompanying N. Ravikiran, U. Srinivas and M.L. Vasanthakumari.

Vadya Lahari (Music of the World, US).

Violin, nagaswaram, vina, mridangam and tavil form the musical elements on this album featuring Kanyakumari's South Indian Instrumental Ensemble. Ensemble playing like this is an innovation in Indian music and it works splendidly, giving an excellent picture of how the violin has been adapted to fit Karnatic sonorities and ears.

The Karnataka College of Percussion

The Karnataka College have worked with German fusionists Dissidenten on their Germanistan and Jungle Book albums (see p.110), and have made a number of records in their own right. Despite the ensemble's percussive-sounding identity, KCP also features the voice of Ramamani and melody instruments such as vina (played by leader Raghavendra), violin (M.S. Govindaswamy) and flute (V.K. Raman).

River Yamuna (Music of the World, US).

This 1997 album is an edited, reworked and reordered version of Shiva Ganga, the 1995 album produced by Dissidenten's Marlon Klein An accessible introduction for beginners testing the heat of Karnatic water.

N. Ramani

The flautist Dr. N. Ramani (b 1934), like Balachander and M.S. Subbulakshmi, came to attention through Richard Bock's World Pacific label. Born in Tiruvarur in Tamil Nadu, the birthplace of Tyagaraja, by the age of twelve he was accomplished enough to be appearing on All India Radio. The venu, as the Indian flute is known, is Lord Krishna's instrument and therefore holds a special place in Indian music.

◉ **Classical Karnatic Flute** (Nimbus, UK).

A recording with a great deal of presence dating from 1990. Ramani is accompanied by violin from T.S. Veeraraghhavan, mridangam from Srimushnam Rajarao and ghatam from E.M. Subramaniam in pieces by Tyagaraja and Ramani himself.

N. Ravikiran

The magisterial Ravikiran (b 1967), who gave his first vocal recital at the age of five, is the foremost exponent of the chitra vina. In his hands, it is a joy, capable of arcane and ethereal sounds that in the West are associated with electronic instruments such as the theremin, but are typically Indian melodic properties.

◉ **Young Star of Gottuvadyam**
(Chhanda Dhara, Germany).

Accompanied on mridangam by Trichur R. Mohan and on ghatam by T.H. Subashchandran, Ravikiran's repertoire and performances here are mesmerising. The nearly nineteen-minute long performance of Shankara Bharanam is especially good and after the kriti the piece goes into a percussion duet. A northern bhajan in Sindhu Bhairavi closes.

Shankar

L. Shankar (b 1953) played in a violin trio with his brothers L. Vaidyanathan and L. Subramaniam, and accompanied Karnatic vocalists, before embarking on a solo career, and founding the Indo-Jazz fusion group Shakti with guitarist John McLaughlin. He is renowned for creating his own ten-string double violin with its startling extended range.

◉ **Raga Aberi**
(Music of the World, US).

A spectacular ragam-tanam-pallavi performance growing out the growling low notes of Shankar's extraordinary violin. The performance also features spectacular vocal percussion and solos from Zakir Hussain (tabla) and Vikku Vinayakram (ghatam).

K. Subramaniam

The author of books on Indian classical music, and a teacher at the University of Madras, Karaikudi Subramaniam is also a superb vina player.

◉ **Sunada** (Music of the World, US).

Sunada translates as 'pleasing sound'. Most of the repertoire comprises kritis; the exception is a reconstruction of a fifteenth century hymn in the tiruppugar form. Trichy Sankaran accompanies on mridangam.

L. Subramaniam

L. Subramaniam (b. 1947) is from a dynasty of violinists (his brothers are L. Vaidyanathan and Shakti-founder L. Shankar). He is one of the most recorded Karnatic artists in the West and has regularly played in non-Karnatic contexts – with Hindustani musicians, jazz-fusion groups, Western orchestras and in films (including Mira Nair's Salaam Bombay and Mississippi Masala).

◉ **Electric Modes** (Water Lily Acoustics, US).

A two-CD set, one volume of which consists of original compositions, the second of which focuses on traditional ragams. The album's title recalls Muddy Waters' album *Electric Mud*. "From the mud of the past emerges a brave new world of music", wrote Kavichandran Alexander, alluding to both the Buddhist image of the lotus or water lily and his label's name.

U. Srinivas

Mandolin-player U. Srinivas (b 1969) uses a five-string, solid body instrument, akin to a cut-down electric guitar, rather than the eight-string Western mandolin, which he claims is ideally suited to the ragas of South Indian music. Like many Karnatic musicians he was a child prodigy and has excited listeners the world over, notably in the West with a successful fusion album, *Dream* (1995 – see p.114), with Michael Brook. He sometimes performs mandolin-duets with his brother U. Rajesh.

◉ **Rama Sreerama** (RealWorld, UK).

A well-recorded and inspiring introduction to Srinivas's music, including pieces by Srinivas himself and Tyagaraja. Strongly devotional in character, with violin, mridangam and ghatam accompaniment.

India

Vocal music

the sacred and the profane

Indian musicians have an old saying: 'music without ornamentation is like a river bed without water'. If so, devotional inspiration is like the source of the river. Performing the austere classical form of *dhrupad* is virtually considered meditation in itself, but in vocal forms the sacred and the profane are often intimately linked, as **Ken Hunt** explains.

The songs of the North can be divided into two strands: classical and light classical (also known as semi-classical). Classical requires a serious raga exposition such as dhrupad or *dhamar* provide, while the lighter forms relish freer expression in various degrees. A recital may keep to one repertoire or be mixed, the lighter forms frequently closing a classical concert on a more relaxed note.

As a general rule of thumb, musicians stick to forms appropriate to their faith. Thus a Hindu performer might close with a *bhajan* and a Muslim *qawwali* performer (see Pakistan) with a *ghazal*. *Bhajans* and *kritis* are essentially devotional songs, but in the hugely popular *thumri* and *ghazal* repertoire, love for the divine and profane is frequently blurred. In the South the differences between the exposition of a Karnatic *ragam* and a *kriti* (the South's most typical Hindu hymn genre) are less distinct. A ragam and kriti performance amounts to one and the same thing.

Dhrupad

More than any other classical genre, **dhrupad** is regarded as a sacred art – an act of devotion or meditation rather than entertainment. It is an ancient and austere form which ranks as the Hindustani system's oldest vocal music genre still performed. The form is strongly connected with the famed singer **Tansen**, court musician to the Moghul emperor Akbar, and enjoyed a golden age in Gwalior during the fifteenth and sixteenth centuries.

Traditionally, dhrupad is only performed by men accompanied by *tanpura* and the *pakhawaj* barrel drum. Nowadays it is most often set in a *tala* of twelve-beats. Thematically, a dhrupad lyric (usually in a medieval literary form of Hindi) may be pure panegyric, praising a Hindu deity or local royalty, or it may dwell on noble or heroic themes. Since dhrupad's character is intrinsically intellectual, with each note applied as painstakingly as paint on any pointillist canvas, it is not a first port of call for newcomers or listeners with short attention spans, indeed its stately precision has been likened to watching paint dry. The leading contemporary performers are the **Dagar** and **Mallik** families.

ROYAL TROPICAL INSTITUTE
« The Music Collection »
KIT

Shiva Mahadeva
Dagar Brothers DHRUPAD, CLASSICAL VOCAL MUSIC OF NORTH INDIA

RAGAS
MALKAUNS
DARBARI KANADA
ADANA
BHATIYAR

PAN records

2CD   4001/02 KCD

The related **dhamar** form employs more *gamakas* (grace notes or ornaments) than dhrupad. Generally, gamakas in the Karnatic tradition are deemed essential elements in the melodic structure and are only rarely omitted, whereas in Hindustani music they are used far more sparingly, being reserved as a vehicle for personal expression. Usually set in a tala of fourteen beats, dhamar has largely been displaced by *khyal*, and to a lesser extent by thumri and *tappa*.

Bhajan

The **bhajan** is the most popular form of Hindu devotional composition in North India. Lyrically, bhajans eulogise a particular deity and frequently retell episodes from the Hindu scriptures. Devotion alone as the source of release is a tenet underlining many bhajan texts. You will hear them intoned by groups of pilgrims along the Ganges, at temples and on countless cassette players at festivals. Composers such as **Mirabai** (a mystic saint-composer whose compositions in praise of Lord Krishna are of enduring popularity and who had "Raga Mirabai ki Malhar" named after her), **Kabir** (the faith-bridging, caste-shattering *bhakta* or devotee) and **Tulsidas** (often viewed as the Northern Tyagaraja) are all notables who've contributed to the canon over the centuries and whose work is still performed every day.

Many bhajans date from the time of the Hindu Reformation and arose out of the **Bhakti** (devotionalism) movement that had begun with the **Tamil Alvars**, or poet-philosophers, in the ninth and tenth centuries AD and gradually radiated northwards. In Bengal, the movement reached its apogee during the fifteenth and sixteenth centuries. In that fertile and ever-changing region, mystic Hindu and Sufi sects found common ground in cross-connecting spirituality and worship centred on devotional love. Such exchanges led to the founding of the **Baul** philosophy in present-day Bengal and Bangladesh (see p.98) and on the other side of the subcontinent helped shape reforming Sikhism in the Punjab.

Given this background, it is unsurprising that divine love and spiritual emancipation figure prominently as the subject matter of bhajan lyrics. The musical elements of bhajans are usually simple – uncomplicated rhythms and melodies which can be learned and sung by a congregation. Percussion and harmonium are the typical accompanying instruments.

The bhajan has gained wide popularity, particularly in the Hindustani repertoire. Solo instrumentalists incorporate bhajans in their repertoires – an excellent example can be heard in **N. Rajam**'s version of "Thumaki Chalat Ram Chandra" on *Gaayki On Violin* (Gramophone Company of India). The instrumentalist's art lies in capturing the sonorities, syllables and devotional mood of the unsung words. In the South, bhajans tend to retain their original Hindustani raga but are set in Karnatic talas, as the Karnatic violinist **V.V. Subrahmanyam**'s exquisite recordings for the Gramophone Company of India show. Bhajans figure in the repertoires of most male and female Hindu vocalists, notably Jitendra Abhisheki, Bhimsen Joshi, Girija Devi, Pandit Jasraj, Lakshmi Shankar and Shobhu Gurtu.

Hindustani music also employs other devotional forms such as the *chaiti* (or *chait*), a seasonal hymn form associated with the month of Chaitra (March-April) and devoted to Krishna and Radha themes. An evocative instrumental performance of the chait "Maasi Saiiaan Nahin Aaye" appears on *50 Glorious Classical Years* (Gramophone Company of India), played by violinist N. Rajam.

Khyal

Less formal than dhrupad, **khyal** (also *khyel* or *khayaal*) is generally translated as 'imagination' or 'fancy'. It is semi-classical in nature and allows the expression of emotion when improvising on its lyrical and musical themes. Its origins are uncertain although many date it from the late fifteenth century and the rule of Hussain Shah Sharqi. By the eighteenth century it was popular at the Moghul court of Mohammed Shah in Delhi. Many khyals still in the repertoire today bear the name of **Sadarang,** the pen-name of one of the emperor's court musicians, **Niamat Khan**, the leading *rudra vina* player of his day. Sung by both men and women, khyal is more elaborate, showy and romantic in character than dhrupad. It has a lengthy *bada khyal* form, which is slow (*vilambit*), meditative and soul searching, followed by the *drut* (fast) *chhota* (little) *khyal*.

Since the nineteenth century khyal has been the most popular classical vocal style in Hindustani music. **Abdul Karim Khan** (1872–1937), **Faiyaz Khan** (1886–1950) and **Amir Khan** (1912– 1974) are all leading names of the twentieth century who helped to establish its position. One of khyal's greatest current interpreters is the male vocalist **Bhimsen Joshi**, whose vocal ornamentations are a special delight. A true improviser, he is a master at confounding expectations by delivering an inspired phrase where a lesser vocalist would sing a standard one. **Shruti Sadolikar** is a highly accomplished female khyal singer, while **Shweta Jhaveri** is introducing a modernised form of khyal with Western instruments based in the traditional ragas. **Bade Ghulam Ali Khan** (1902–1968) was loved for his

Bhimsen Joshi

exhibitionist waywardness: he might extend an ornamentation over three octaves and on one occasion incorporated a passing train whistle outside the venue into his performance in such a way that members of the audience were unsure whether they had heard or fantasised the passage.

Thumri

Thumri is the other light-classical song form which shares the pre-eminent place in Hindustani music. It is more immediately accessible than dhrupad and even khyal, both of which involve the abstract exploration of a raga. Thumri concentrates

on the emotion of a song, exploring the sentiment through improvisation and ornamentation. Expression is more important than technique.

The origin of thumri is sometimes ascribed to the court of **Nawab Wajid Ali Shah**, who ruled Lucknow (Oudh) from 1847 to 1856, although its roots go back centuries earlier. Wajid Ali Shah was little interested in matters of state, but he was a great patron of the arts and during his reign music, dance, poetry, drama and architecture flourished. He composed thumri under the pen name **Akhtar Piya** and his famous "Babul more naihar chuto ri jaye" (Father, I can't bear to leave your home) is said to reflect his grief at being forced to leave Lucknow for Calcutta, where thumri subsequently also flourished.

The two predominant – and favoured – thumri styles are known as **Punjabi** and **Lucknavi**. Lucknow emerged as the major Indo-Muslim cultural centre in the eighteenth century, taking over from Delhi, then war-torn and ravaged by political and imperial intrigue. Thumri was a favoured form of *tawaif* (female courtesan) performers who became the first recording stars of the subcontinent. **Gauhar Jan** in Calcutta and **Jankibai** in Allahabad were able to command high fees. With the decline of tawaif culture, thumri, which had been closely identified with the sleazier aspects of the profession, underwent an image makeover, thanks in part to the gramophone. In its new incarnation as music played in well-to-do drawing rooms, thumri emerged as a much cherished art form, predominantly wistful and nostalgic.

Gauhar Jan, the first Indian Diva

Although classical instrumentalists frequently perform a thumri in concert as a relaxation from the intensity of the pure classical style, most thumri is vocal. It is generally sung in a language known as **Braj Bhasha**, a literary dialect of Hindi spoken in the Mathura area, the centre of the Bhakti cult and Krishna worship. The singer is usually accompanied by tabla, and the sarangi and harmonium are also common. The lyrics of thumri are usually romantic love songs, usually written from a female perspective, which dwell on the sadness of separation, quarrels, reconciliation, meetings with a husband or lover and often the love and exploits of Krishna.

Top singers include **Girija Devi** (b 1929) and **Shobha Gurtu** (b 1925). Despite the lyric's concentration on the women's perspective, some of the greatest singers of thumri have been men,

CMP

Star of thumri and ghazal, Shobha Gurti

notably **Bade Ghulam Ali Khan**. As male singers are frequently middle-aged and overweight, there is a certain initial incongruity in the evocation of the gentle and delicate emotions of a beautiful young woman. Yet a fine artist, fat and balding though he may be, can make a song like this one sublimely affecting: "My bracelets keep slipping off/My lover has cast a spell on me/He has struck me with his magic/What can a mere doctor do?".

Tarana & Tillana

In the **tarana** song genre, meaningless rhythmic syllables are substituted for a lyric, much as in jazz scat singing, but with greater rhythmic precision. While the concept is simple, maintaining artistic

integrity and keeping ideas fresh so as to hold the listener's attention is not. Typically a tarana passage will close a khyal performance, maybe in place of a fast chhota khyal. A tarana's Southern counterpart, known as the **tillana** (thillana), will do the same, on a more playful note, enabling the vocalist to express delight in pure sound articulated through rhythm. They are wonderful opportunities for a vocalist to show off. The Hindustani vocalist **Amir Khan** was renowned for his skills in the form, while maestro **M. Balamuralikrishna** (b 1930) best demonstrates the southern equivalent.

Kriti

The Karnatic **kriti** (or *krithi*) is a song of praise or adoration for a particular Hindu deity in the South Indian tradition. The languages used are most commonly Telugu, Tamil or Sanskrit. Kritis are especially associated with three Hindu saint-composers: Tyagaraja, Muttuswamy Dikshitar and Syama Sastri (see p.80). Usually seated in a specific ragam, kritis usually last from five to eight minutes, but can be developed into a full length classical performance lasting up to an hour, as on **M. Balamuralikrishna**'s performance for the Moment label. Balamuralikrishna is one of the recent notable male vocalists, a group which also includes **D.K. Jayaraman**, **P.S. Narayanswamy**, **T.V. Sankaranarayanan** and the exquisite female vocalist **M. L. Vasanthakumari**. Most Karnatic instrumentalists will also dip into the kriti genre during a recital or on disc, with the standard accompaniment of mridangam and tampura, and maybe a violin.

Ghazal

Found in related forms in Central Asia, Iran and Turkey, the **ghazal** was introduced to India by Persian Muslims. It is more song-like than its Urdu counterpart, thumri, being mainly a poetic rather than a musical form and it is hugely popular among northern Hindus. There has always allegorical blurring of the distinction between erotic and divine love. The archaic form of the ghazal can be very refined, but although some ghazal tunes are raga-based, many do not follow any specific mode with consistency. The rhythms are clearly derived from folk music and at times the ghazal shades into the area of sophisticated pop song. Indian film music, in its insatiable appetite for new sensations, has assisted ghazal's popularity by co-opting, some would say vulgarising, its poetry and form.

The ghazal has played an important part in many musical (and literary) cultures from the Middle East to Malaysia since the early eighteenth century, when singing was one of the accomplishments required of a courtesan. Ghazal singers of modern times usually come from more 'respectable' backgrounds. All the same, Britain's **Najma Akhtar** had to overcome a certain amount of parental concern when she first began singing.

Each era of the ghazal tradition has contributed so-called *sha'irs* or master poets, stretching from Delhi's **Amir Khusrau**, in the thirteenth century to Bombay's **Shakeel** today. Since the mid-1930s, poets have addressed secular and political themes, notably Faiz Ahmad Faiz (1911–1984). While thumri singers take on a female persona, emotions in the ghazal are almost always expressed from the male point of view. Yet some of the finest performers of ghazals are women – **Begum Akhtar** (1914-1974), **Shobha Gurtu** and the London-based **Najma Akhtar** (b 1964) among

them. The latter's hugely popular 1987 album *Qareeb* was lyrically fairly traditional, but the instruments were Indian and Western, and included Ray Carless's jazz saxophone. Male artists at the more classical end of the ghazal spectrum include **Mehdi Hassan** and **Jagjit Singh**, who had a hugely successful partnership with his wife, **Chitra Singh**. One of the top stars of the popular style is **Hariharan**, who has worked with leading musical arrangers and top instrumentalists like **Zakir Hussain**.

discography

Hindustani vocal music

Compilations

⊚ 50 Glorious Classical Years
(Gramophone Company of India, India).

Virtually every major vocalist and instrumentalist is represented in this anthology. It opens auspiciously with Bade Ghulam Ali Khan singing a thumri (recorded in 1947) and concludes five CDs later with Parween Sultana singing a sadra, a khyal variant. Downsides are the virtual absence of Karnatic music and the paucity of information.

⊚ Ragamala (Gramophone Company of India, India).

The cliché of one track warranting the price of an entire album applies here – a delicious version of Raga Marwa sung by Amir Khan in 1960. Niaz Ahmed Khan & Fayyaz Ahmed Khan, K.G. Ginde, Bade Ghulam Ali Khan and Surshri Kesar Bai Kerkar complete the all-star classical line-up.

⊚ Ras Rang: Evolution of Thumri Vols 1 & 2
(Navras, UK).

Two CDs, packaged individually, which trace the evolution of thumri and make enjoyable listening. Vocalists include Uday Bhawalkar, Shoba Gurtu, Ghulam Mustafa Khan and Parween Sultana. Brief translations are given.

⊚ Thumri (India Archive Music, US).

Two vocal tracks (a bhajan and thumri) and four instrumental thumri played on sitar, sarangi, sarod and guitar. A judicious selection of performances from Abdul Halim Jaffer Khan (sitar), Vidyadhar Vyas (vocals), Dhruba Ghosh (sarangi), Rajeev Taranath (sarod), Ajoy Chakrabarty (vocals) and Debashis Bhattacharya (guitar), with good notes.

⊚ Vintage Music from India (Rounder, US).

An anthology by Peter Manuel concentrating on northern traditions, and vocal music in particular, recorded between 1906 and the 1920s, featuring India's first celebrity recording artist Gauhar Jan. Includes forms as different as qawwali (Sufi devotional music) and tawaif (female courtesans' music).

Artists

Najma Akhtar

Singer Najma Akhtar (b 1964) made an enormous impression on fans of World Music with her second album Qareeb in 1987. 1989's Atish ('fire' in Urdu) confirmed her place in modern Hindustani fusion music, although more recent work lacks that innovative spark.

 Qareeb
(Triple Earth, UK; Shanachie, US).

Having one track in the soundtrack of acclaimed British film *Sammy And Rosie Get Laid* helped, but it is the lyrical gift, innovative arrangements and fine instrumental playing (including violin, sax and santoor) that sets *Qareeb* (Nearness) apart. The hit track "Dil Laga Ya Tha" has some catchy melodic and harmonic twists. A modern ghazal classic.

Kishori Amonkar

Kishori Amonkar is one of Hindustani music's greatest singers, and especially commended for her khyal interpretations, which have a heartfelt, sensual phrasing. She represents the consummate artistry of the Jaipur gharana and the Hindustani spirit of innovation within tradition.

 Kishori Amonkar & Hariprasad Chaurasia (Navras, UK).

In an inspired jugalbandi duet, voice and flute interweave on two khyals set in raga Lalit and an especially fetching thumri in Sindhi Bhairavi. A double CD recorded live in Bombay in 1995.

Uday Bahwalker

Bhawalker (b 1966) is a rising star of dhrupad, although he only began studying it in 1981, after seeing a newspaper advertisement. He came to study under the Dagars and gave his first performance in 1985.

 A Dhrupad Recital (Navras, UK).

The opening raga includes a composition praising Shiva while the second addresses the philosophical subject of *nada*, or sound as a manifestation of cosmic force. **Raga Shri – Raga Malkauns** (Nimbus, UK) is also excellent.

Asha Bhosle

Younger sister of Lata Mangeshkar, and almost equally acclaimed as India's favourite female filmi-playback singer (see p.106).

Legacy (AMMP, US).

A remarkable collaboration between Bhosle and the great sarod player Ali Akbar Khan, who traces his classical music ancestry back to Tansen himself. This collection of classical and light-classical vocal gems was learned from Khan's father and previous generations of his dynasty. An extraordinary beautiful opening Guru Bandana (prayer) initiates a very special collection of khyal, tarana, holi and sadra performances, with superb accompaniment from Khan and Swapan Chaudhuri (tabla and pakawaj).

ALI AKBAR KHAN
PRESENTS
LEGACY
16th - 18th CENTURY MUSIC FROM INDIA
ASHA BHOSLE - VOCAL   ALI AKBAR KHAN - SARODE
SWAPAN CHAUDHURI - TABLA & PAKAWAJ

Ajoy Chakrabarty

Chakrabarty (b 1953) is a leading exponent of the Patiala gharana (the same style as Bade Ghulam Ali Khan). He has recorded in a variety of styles including bhajan, dadra, khyal and thumri.

 Hari Bhajanako Maan Re (Neelam, US).

An excellent collection focusing exclusively on bhajan repertoire. It's unusual for its filmi-style arrangement, with Indian instruments like sarod, sarangi, sitar and tabla alongside vibraphone, keyboards and guitar. A more typical classical album is the seasonally themed **Holi And Basant** (Multitone Prestige, UK).

Dagar Brothers

Born into a family of court musicians in Indore, the Dagar Brothers are the most important communicators of the intellectually demanding and dignified dhrupad vocal form. The family's dhrupad vani – vani literally means 'sayings of saints', but is a word akin to gharana – is one of the four main schools.

 Shiva Mahadeva (Pan, Netherlands).

In 1978 the Royal Netherlands World Service recorded the brothers Zahiruddin Dagar (1932-94) and Faiyazuddin Dagar (1934-1989) performing Malkauns, Darbari Kanada, Adana and Bhatiyar, interspersed with explanations about dhrupad and how time or season conditions the appropriate raga. This resulting double album concludes with a dhamar composition in Behag. Stateliness personified.

Girija Devi

Girija Devi (b 1929) performs classical and light-classical forms. Her speciality is thumri and she is one of the vocalists who elevated a somewhat disreputable form to the heights of connoisseur appreciation and respectability.

 Songs from Varanasi (Nimbus, UK).

Varanasi (Benares) is Devi's birthplace as well as one of Hinduism's most holy places. Accompanied by Ramesh Misra on sarangi and Subhen Chatterjee on table, she performs a selection of khyal, tappa, thumri and dadra on this 1992 recording.

Hariharan

The son of Karnatic musicians, A. Hariharan switched to Hindustani singing at an early age and studied with Ghulam Mustafa Khan. Although qualified as a lawyer, he has become a leading name in popular ghazals in India with dozens of tapes and hundreds of film songs (including the movies Roja and Bombay) to his credit. An unmistakably smooth, silky voice.

Hazir (Magnasound, India).

Hariharan and Zakir Hussain in a classic album of contemporary ghazals from 1992, with excellent instrumental contributions from flute, santoor and sitar.

Mehdi Hassan

Mehdi Hassan is a major interpreter of classical-style ghazals. Born in Lusa in Rajasthan, he was instructed in classical vocal styles, but has also had considerable success as a Hindi and Punjabi playback vocalist.

 Live in Concert (Navras, UK).

A triple CD, recorded live in London in 1990, which captures the feel of a classical ghazal concert or *mushaira* (gathering), with interjections of thumri, dadra and folk song for variety. Accompanying musicians include Sultan Khan (sarangi) and Shaukat Hussain (tabla).

Shweta Jhaveri

Jhaveri (b 1965) has a richly hued voice, well suited to khyal and bhajan. She has recorded more standard classical fare in addition to the album recommended below.

Anahita (Intuition, Germany).

An East-West collaboration of unusual character. Jhaveri sings khyal (and a tarana composition) against a background of Indian-style drones and Jenny Scheinman's East-Western violin, Will Bernard's guitar and dobro, plus bass, kit drum and percussion. While her khyal-style compositions don't adhere to the strict rules of raga or tala, this is a visionary contemporary vocal album.

Bhimsen Joshi

Bhimsen Joshi (b 1922) is one of India's greatest vocal maestros and a supreme khyal interpreter. He learned from many sources but is primarily associated with the renowned Kirana gharana. An uncompromising yet far from hidebound classicist with a warm, lived-in voice.

In Celebration
(Navras, UK).

One of Hindustani music's most lauded masters captured in his accomplished prime. On this 1993 recording, Joshi performs Maru Bihag and Abhogi.

Raga Yaman Kalyan; Raga Gara; Bhajan
(Chhanda Dhara, Germany).

A 1999 release that confirms Joshi's position as a heavyweight, with a khyal, thumri and bhajan. His vocal displays in the faster sections of "Yaman Kalyan" weave a hypnotic tapestry of variations, while the bhajan features the lyrics of sixteenth century mystic poet Mirabai and Joshi proves there is no male vocalist to surpass him in this genre.

Bade Ghulam Ali Khan

The reputation of some musicians is so enduring that decades after their death they are still regularly cited as major influences and this applies pre-eminently to the wondrously moustached Bade Ghulam Ali Khan (1902–1968). His singing live to film during the famous 'feather scene' in director K. Asif's Moghul-e-Azam ushered in a new level of respectability for Indian cinema in 1960.

Raga Piloo, Raga Bhairavi & Raga Rageshree
(Multitone Prestige, UK).

These thumri recordings of unstated provenance have sarangi, tabla and tanpura accompaniment. Munawar Ali Khan, his son, is the second vocalist. Recorded live, Bhairavi includes a throat-clearing mid-performance which Westerns find peculiar but which is treated as quite natural in Hindustani recitals.

Rashid Khan

Rashid Khan (b 1966) has deservedly risen to become a major new voice in Hindustani khyal music, widely hailed as the most promising male vocalist of his generation. A superb craftsman and manipulator of feelings in song.

Khyal (Moment, US).

Bageshri and Kedar recorded in Buffalo, New York in 1993. Bageshri is a fully-fledged khyal performance totalling almost fifty minutes moving from an opening alap into a bara khyai performance wrapped up with two chhota khyal compositions.

Mallik Family

Less heavily promoted in the West than the Dagar family, the Mallik family are immortalised in the mythology of Indian music for averting a famine with the power of their performance of Megh, the rain raga. As a reward they

were given land in Darbhanga in northeastern India, where the family still resides. Until Independence they were court musicians for the Maharajas of Darbhanga and since 1947 they've become highly respected vocalists in the arts of khyal, thumri and especially dhrupad.

Dhrupads from Darbhanga
(VDE-Gallo/AIMP, Switzerland).

Much of this repertoire is unique to the Mallik family, with austere, but rhythmic and charismatic performances by Bidur Mallik, the head of the family, and his two sons Premkumar and Anandkumar.

Shruti Sadolikar

Shruti Sadolikar (b 1951) is one of the newer generation of khyal singers, brought up in the style of the Jaipur gharana.

Ragas Marwa, Hamsakankini & Thumri
(Navras, UK).

This disc contains one of the finer khyal performances of Raga Marwa, an evening raga. Sadolikar sings with a dignified restraint that still conveys the emotion and restlessness of the raga. Hamsakankini is a morning raga, and the thumri is sung to a lilting Punjabi rhythm. Accompaniment comes from the tabla of Partha Sarathi Mukherjee and the harmonium of Dr. Arvind Thatte.

Lakshmi Shankar

Lakshmi Shankar (b 1926) is a glorious singer. Married to the scriptwriter Rajendra Shankar, an elder brother of Ravi Shankar, she joined her brother-in-law Uday Shankar's artistic circle during the early 1940s as a classical dancer. Poor health forced her to give up dancing for singing and the world was a better place for it.

NAVRAS

Lakshimi Shankar

Live In London Volume 1
(Navras, UK).

Recorded at a concert in 1992 of devotional and light-classical repertoire, with tabla and harmonium accompaniment. "Mishra Kafi" shows off both her glorious voice and thumri's artistic suppleness.

Jagjit & Chitra Singh

The names of this husband and wife team are synonymous with ghazal. Being previously something of a middle-class phenomenon, the Singhs' 1976 album The Unforgettables established them as the popular face of ghazal. In 1991 tragedy struck with the death of their 19-year-old son and Chitra withdrew from performance. Her husband Jagjit (b 1941) continues to sing, notably on Sadja (Gramophone Company of India), the duo album with Lata Mangeshkar.

⊚ **The Golden Collection**
(Gramophone Company of India, India).

These twenty nine solo and duo tracks over two CDs are terrific, with tasteful sarangi and tabla work.

Parween Sultana

Contrary to typical Muslim practice, Parween Sultana (b 1950) was encouraged by her father, debuting on stage at the age of nine and recording her first LP in 1967. She is acclaimed for the cultured tone she brought to Indian movie soundtracks such as Ashary, Kudrat and, especially, Pakeezah.

⊚ **Live From Savai Gandharva Music Festival, Pune '92** (Alurkar Music House, US).

Recorded at an Indian music conference, Parween Sultana reveals her class with remarkably insightful interpretations of Gujari Todi and Jaunpuri. Closing this classical recital on a lighter note, she finishes with a tarana, a wordless exercise in rhythm.

Karnatic vocal music

Artists

M. Balamuralkrishna

Born in 1930 into a musical family, Balamuralikrishna was a child prodigy. He is also credited as a composer of new ragam formulations and some four hundred classical compositions.

 Vocal
(Moment, US).

A kriti in Lathangi lasting nearly an hour, followed by a spectacular tillana performance using four different ragams in succession to create a tillana ragamalika (garland of ragams). Zakir Hussain (tabla) and T.H. Vinayakram (ghatam) provide rhythmic support.

Jon Higgins

The presence of an American vocalist here may seem peculiar, but Higgins (1939-1984) was a commanding Karnatic vocalist and still regarded as one of the most important ambassadors for Indian arts by the South Indian community. His recordings reveal a vocalist of great sensitivity.

⊚ **Jon B. Higgins - Carnatic Vocal**
(Gramophone Company of India, India).

Accompanied by violin, mridangam and kanjira (hand-drum), the nine tracks here reveal how Higgins made himself at home in a kriti repertoire. The performance of Muttuswamy Dikshitar's "Tyagaraja Yoga Vaibhavam" is exemplary. He closes with a tillana.

Bombay S. Jayashri

A disciple of the outstanding violinist Lalgudi Jayaraman, Bombay S. Jayashri is a highly promising singer, one of the young female vocalists currently showcased by the recording industry.

⊚ **Shambho Mahadeva** (Sangeetha, India; Koel, US).

A good selection of devotional songs, with accompaniment on violin, mridangam and ghatam. As is frequently the case with Karnatic releases, the booklet notes are fragmentary.

Sudha Ragunathan

On very rare occasions along comes a new musician whose presence and musicality simply transport the listener. Since her debut, Sudha Ragunathan has proved herself to be one of the most illuminating female singers in Karnatic music. Although she has recorded for labels such as EMI India and Inreco, her prime work is to be found on Winston Panchacharam's New York-based Amutham label.

⊚ **Kaleeya Krishna** (Amutham, US).

Released in 1994, this album of devotional music finds Ragunathan in the company of a full Indian orchestra conducted by Vazhuvoor R. Manikkavinayakam. The record celebrates the work of the composer Ventatasubbaiyar (1700-1765), whose muse was Krishna. An uplifting performance, even for non-Hindus. The more intimate, violin, mridangam and ghatam instrumentation on ⊚ **San Marga** (Amutham, US) is similarly recommended.

M.S. Subbulakshmi

M.S. Subbulakshmi (b 1916) is a cultural ambassador for Indian arts on a par with Ravi Shankar. In the 1960s she enjoyed a great deal of attention by virtue of her albums also being available on the World Pacific label. But unlike Ravi Shankar she did not support her recording career with constant touring although she appeared at the Edinburgh Festival (1963) and at Carnegie Hall (1977). She has been heaped with honours, and is considered a national treasure.

⊚ **M.S. Subbulakshmi at Carnegie Hall**
(Gramophone Company of India, India).

This double CD captures Subbulakshmi in New York in October 1977 with her daughter Radha Viswanathan, the violinist Kandadevi Alagiriswami and the percussionist Guruvayur Dorai.

India

Folk and Adivasi music

everything is left behind

"One day you will go without all things, then where is your wealth and your youth? Everything is left behind." So says a song of Bengal's wandering minstrels, the Bauls. Maybe that's why so much of India's folk music is festive and of the moment. These traditions are rich, diverse and surprisingly resilient, but little-known outside the country where they've been overshadowed by classical, ghazals and film music. Even more neglected is the music of the *adivasi* – India's indigenous tribal groups – who enjoy nothing like the profile of the Native Americans or Australian Aborigines. Of course, it's impossible to introduce the folk and village music of a billion people, but **Ken Hunt** and **Simon Broughton** pick some of the highlights.

P overty and under-development tend to preserve and nurture traditions but it doesn't take long for technology to destroy them. In Indian folk music, you can date this process back to the 1930s, when traditional folk drama lost out to the movies, and traditional back-cloths across the subcontinent were replaced with projection screens. The knock-on effects stretched right out across the culture. Nowadays, for instance, although you still find itinerant snake charmers at regional fairs and festivities, they are more likely to be playing the popular 'snake charming' tune from the 1950s film *Nagin* than any traditional repertoire.

The arrival of recorded sound has had a more mixed effect. While it has weakened the supremacy of live music, India's wholesale adoption of **cassettes** – from the 1970s – has hugely encouraged local music. While HMV India focused on high-art Indian music and recorded the big-name classical artists, local cassette companies like T-Series, founded by Gulshan Arora in 1979, and Venus, sold hundreds of regional pop and folk titles, mainly at kiosks and in grocery stores. Regional folk music, which had never been recorded before, became available, too, thanks to dozens of small producers based in Delhi, Mumbai, Calcutta and elsewhere.

By contrast, recordings of more traditional folk and adivasi music are comparatively rare, and most ethnographic recordings have been issued on Western labels – and even then in a very limited way. However, recent World Music successes have come from the itinerant Bauls of Bengal and the musician castes of Rajasthan.

Desi and Marga

Folk music in India is often described as **desi** (or *deshi*), meaning 'of the country' to distinguish it from art music known as **marga** (meaning 'chaste' and by extension, classical). Desi, a catch-all term, also embraces folk theatre and popular music of many colours.

Many traditionalists and academics view folk music as a corrupted legacy of an earlier, higher form, thus aligning themselves with the scholar Bharata Muni who demarcated all music as either marga or desi. In fact, desi music bolsters the classical Hindustani repertoire: it has lent its instruments, notably the bowed *sarangi* (still played by folk musicians to accompany songs in Rajasthan) and the hammered *santoor* (a Kashmiri zither), both of which are now established classical instruments in their own right. It has lent its forms: *dhuns* (folk airs) and *kajaris* (folk songs from Uttar Pradesh) are often performed as light relaxation after the rigourous performance of a raga, rather like an encore at the end of a concert. And it has lent its style, as when Hindustani vocal maestro Bade Ghulam Ali Khan rejuvenated popular *thumri* music by flavouring it with folk stylings.

Some of the ragas in classical music are named after particular regions, suggesting the influence of a local folk style. For example, the ragas Gujari (Gujarat), Mand (Rajasthan), Bangal (Bengal) and Pahari (the foothills of the Himalayas in the northwest) are named after regions whose tunes may have suggested the raga. The popular raga Desh (meaning 'country') may refer to an area of Rajasthan, a region where some of the folk tunes are described as being in Sorath and Bhairavi, and share many features with those classical ragas.

Brass Bands and Barats

The best-known legacies of the British in India are the extensive railway network, some imposing architecture and a lumbering bureaucracy. More obscure, but significant in musical terms are the ubiquitous **brass bands**, which have replaced the earlier ceremonial ensembles of shehnai and drums. Every large town in India will have dozens of competing '**band shops**' – usually identifiable by a brightly painted cart bristling with loudhailers standing outside – where a band can be assembled and booked for a wedding. In large cities whole streets of the town or *chowk* (bazaar) may be dedicated to the business, just as you'll get an area for spices or cloth. In Bhopal, the state capital of Madya Pradesh, stroll down Itwara Road and you'll pass any number of band shops with trumpets, horns and tubas advertising their trade, plus liveried caps and formal photos of the band in uniform on the walls.

A **barat**, or wedding procession through the streets is a spectacular sight. The band starts outside the groom's house and leads the procession to the home of the bride, where presents are given and a feast is held. The groom often rides a magnificent white horse, preceded by a band of perhaps a dozen musicians on trumpets, large baritone horns, tubas, saxophones and a couple of side drums, usually led by a wild clarinet. Alongside, small boys stagger in procession with heavy electric candelabras joined together by cables stretching to a generator somewhere at the back.

The musicians (*bandwallahs*) are often migrant workers, hired in from the country for the wedding season which lasts for five or six months through the winter. Rampur, a town northeast of Delhi, is particularly famous as a source of musicians. It's been estimated that across India there are between 500,000 and 800,000 people earning a living in the band party business. The music is brash and tuning is wayward, but it's the mood of celebration and public display that counts. A typical band can get by with less than twenty songs a season – half of these will be the current film favourites and the other half classic film songs that have more or less become the new folk tunes of contemporary India.

Simon Broughton

Book your wedding band here – Bhopal, Madhya Pradesh

Celebration and Devotion

In the Indian subcontinent, music is used extensively for ritual purposes. It marks rites of passage, logs the course of the seasons and sanctifies religious ceremonies. Any **festival** in India will include music, from the great temple festivals in the south – with curling trumpets, massed drums, elephants and ceremonial chariots – to the more ascetic conch shells and ringing bells of the Himalayan foothills, to say nothing of the sung mantras of the pilgrim groups that flock to the thousands of holy sites across the country. Religious festivals come complete with buskers, snake charmers and folk theatre troupes, and despite rampant modernisation, such practices are very much alive. Of all rites of passage, the most important for music are weddings. In urban India the music will be provided by a brass band (see box on p.95), but in the countryside it will be more traditional.

Bhangra

The harvest is celebrated in every culture and in the Punjab it gave rise to **bhangra**, a folk dance which, in its British commercial form (covered in a separate article in Volume 1 of the *Rough Guide*), has transmogrified into a form of Asian pop. In its Punjabi form, bhangra was originally an exclusively male preserve. Nowadays, female artists compete for record sales, though male Punjabi pride is too macho to be seen performing women's music, so women's music is tagged as **giddha**, or **dafjan**, another Punjabi women's song style.

Under the pressure of social change, certain styles of folk music, like bhangra, have displayed an adaptability which nobody would have predicted. Who would have thought that diaspora Punjabis based in England could have repackaged a *dhol* drum-driven harvest celebration and sold it back to India, even while agricultural communities still celebrated it the old-fashioned way? No one pretends that the old ways are eternal, but they are proving extraordinarily resilient.

Following on from the crossover success of bhangra, **dandiya**, a new folk-based genre, has emerged as a new phenomenon with a club-based following in India. Based on Gujarati folk music, the albums by **Falguni Pathak**, the leading female performer on the live dandiya circuit, have sold in their millions. Dandiya music is normally set to Gujarati lyrics, but Pathak sings in Hindi and gives the sound a pop sensibility for mass appeal.

Rajasthan

The northwestern desert state of Rajasthan, with over twenty million inhabitants, is one of the regions most visited by tourists. It also has the liveliest folk tradition, and not just because musicians are employed in restaurants. While the tourist industry has tapped the musical heritage – buskers play the two-stringed *ravanhatha* beneath the magnificent walls of the Jaisalmer citadel and troupes of Manganiyar musicians can be requisitioned to play for camel safaris and barbecues in the desert – the fact is that music is a vital part of Rajasthani culture.

Most celebrated in Rajasthan are the **Langa**, caste musicians who also deal in camels and spices. Centred around Jodhpur, they converted to Islam in the 17th century and played for Muslim patrons. There are two sub-castes of Langa, the **Sarangi Langas**, who sing accompanied by a bowed *sarangi*, and the **Surnai Langa** who don't sing and only play wind instruments like the *surnai* (oboe), *satara* (double flute) and *murali* (a double clarinet with a reservoir of air in a gourd).

The **Manganiyar** caste are based around Jaisalmer, the great walled city of the Thar desert, and serve both Muslim and Hindu patrons. They

राजस्थानी लोक धुने

अलगोजा पर

जमालुदीन

ORIGINAL

Rajasthan – the bagpipe without the bag

The Roar of the South: Kerala Percussion

The Jenikal temple is in a tiny village in central Kerala, southwest India, surrounded by coconut trees, banana bushes and rice fields. In January, right after the rainy season, you can feel burgeoning growth all around and this is the time for the annual festival in honour of the Bhagavati goddess.

It is dawn. Enter the marvellous **ritual drummers** of Kerala, whose music is known as **chenda melam**. They arrive from other festivals, many exhausted after the previous night's performance. But *uppurna*, a semolina breakfast with green chilies and hot milky tea, invigorates them. Suddenly, Kuttan, the bandleader, calls them together. A young elephant emerges, carrying the idol of the goddess on its back. Following it is a hunched priest dressed in red holding a small sabre – the attribute of the goddess. The musicians assemble in front of the elephant: to the right, the percussionists, with upright barrel drums (**chenda**) supported over the shoulder and bronze cymbals; to the left, the wind instruments – the oboe-like **kuzhal** and the spectacular C-shaped brass trumpets (**kombu**) which emphasise and prolong the drum beating.

The performance, of a piece known as **paandi melam**, begins with an impressive 'ghrr' and 'dhim' produced on the drums. This is said to symbolise a lion's roar and was probably once performed in support of a lion hunt. After this mighty introduction, the drums drop the tempo and the music builds up like a pyramid. It starts slowly with long-lasting musical cycles

celebrate the conclusion and follow the elephant and deity into the inner temple.

The first stage broadly symbolises the ordinary life of men, while the peak of the last stage shows the ideal human or divine aspect of reality. The music must please the god on top of the elephant and, of course, the assembled temple crowd. While the main beats are provided by beating the underside of the chenda, the skilled solo chenda players create intricate patterns over the top. Different players may gather for each event, but they are capable of playing together perfectly with no rehearsal. The concept is more like a big jazz band than a European classical orchestra.

Afternoon – and it's the hottest time of day when the huge **Panchavadyam** orchestra starts playing in front of the Bhagvati temple. Panchavadyam means 'five instruments', and the orchestra comprises three types of drums, cymbals and the kombu trumpets, thus satisfying each of the five senses. A conch is blown three times, symbolising the holy syllable 'Om', and the performance begins its first stage with a slow, 1792-beat rhythmic cycle. The next cycle has 896 beats, half that number, then 448, half again, then 224 and so on. The speed increases until fast 56-beat cycles round it off. Fireworks, a large crowd and elephants trumpeting support the ecstatic climax.

For the evening, performances of **tayambaka**, **keli** and **kuzhal pattu** are announced. Each is a solo per-

forming style, with players from the chenda melam and panchavadyam orchestras. Tayambaka is the main attraction, an improvised chenda solo played with a small ensemble of accompanying treble and bass chenda and cymbals. The other solo styles, keli (with a soloist on the *maddalam*, horizontally slung barrel drum) and kuzhal pattu (oboe), precede the midnight performance of the last chenda melam. Finally a folk theatre entertains festival visitors for the

Kerala temple festival. Kuzhal oboes and chenda drums

and works up to a short, fast, powerful climax. During the performance, the elephant, musicians and crowd process round the temple precinct, and after more than two hours, the excited crowd and sweating musicians

rest of the night. This is when the ritual musicians grab some sleep, but at 5am the first bus is waiting to take them to the next festival.

Rolf Killius

play the *kamayacha* (bowed fiddle), harmonium and *khatal* (hardwood castanets). Manganiyar means 'one who begs' and this caste has a lower social status than the Langa. It's from itinerant musicians such as these that the Romany (Gypsies) may have originated. Every autumn, the Gypsies of Rajasthan gather in the town of Runija (on the road from Jodhpur to Jaisalmer) for a festival at the temple of Baba Ramdev, their chosen saint. The painted wagons on the road headed for the fair are a sight in themselves and the event itself gives the most vivid, if overwhelming, insight into contemporary Indian Gypsy life and culture.

But the Langa and Manganiyar are by no means the only musicians of Rajasthan. There are several other itinerant castes, including the **Sapera**, traditional snake charmers who play the *pungi* (a double flute). The **Jogi** are wandering mystics, and any opportunity of seeing one playing the extraordinary one-stringed *bhapang* with wild glissandi shouldn't be missed. The **Bhopa** are epic bards, whose instruments include the two-stringed *ravanhatha*, played with a bow with jangling bells, and the big *jantar*, a zither supported on two gourds. Traditionally, the epics are sung and danced at night in front of a painted canvas while an assistant illuminates the scenes illustrating the sung episodes in the story. These Bhopa ballads are one of the forms that has been hit dramatically by the cinema.

The Bauls of Bengal

One of the most remarkable folk traditions of the subcontinent survives in Bengal and Bangladesh. The **Bauls** are a mystical brotherhood of wayfaring minstrels, at pains to sidestep society's conventions and religious orthodoxy. Their name may derive from *batul*, the ancient Sanskrit word for 'wind' or 'mad'. In an unorthodox faith not dissimilar to Sufism, the Bauls describe themselves as 'mad about the soul of God within ourselves' and seek mystical union with the divine through ecstatic singing and dance. Bauls reject the castes and sects and women perform alongside men.

Typically they accompany their songs with the *dotara* (a simple lute), the *khamak* (a hollow

drum with one or two strings attached, the pitch of which can be adjusted while playing) which adds a distinctive sliding percussion to the music, the *ektara* (a one-string drone instrument often played by mendicant holy men) and assorted percussion, including trademark *napur* (ankle rattles). They promenade with sashaying steps, pirouetting or dancing in tight, concentric circles as they sing.

Purna das Baul

With a typically contrary logic they describe their path as *ulta*, meaning 'reverse' or 'the wrong way round' and they have no scripture or doctrine in any conventional sense. Baul song is as patchwork as their garb. They borrow from mystical Hinduism, Islam and Tantric Buddhism. They search for **Maner Manush** – the Man of the Heart, or the ideal within us – and strive for ecstatic communication with the divine.

Calling their devotional music folk does it a disservice, for its literary qualities are highly regarded in Bengali literature, and while it may technically be desi, it is profoundly eloquent and hugely appealing. **Rabindranath Tagore**, the Bengali renaissance man and 1913 Nobel prizewinner for literature, was one of the first to champion them and acknowledge their importance. In turn, the Bauls took Tagore as one of their own and set his songs alongside those of Baul-adopted poets **Kabir** and **Lalon Fakir**.

Baul tunes inspired Hindustani maestros such as **Allauddin Khan** and **Nikhil Banerjee**, and Baul philosophy and music influenced Bob Dylan, The Band and Allen Ginsberg. **Purna Das Baul** (Purnachandra Das) – the son of Narbani Das Baul, a major influence on Tagore – wound up on the cover of Dylan's 1968 album *John Wesley Harding*.

Dressed in patched, brightly coloured garments with saffron predominating, the Bauls traditionally travel from community to community bringing entertainment, philosophy and news. They are thought of as mendicant minstrels although many families have been settled for generations. Baul songs come cloaked with the deceptive simplicity or superficiality of nursery rhymes or children's songs. Prosaic images conceal aphorism and paradox. "I am blind, I cannot see the darkness", goes one song; a light bulb refers to deeper illumination and the jackfruit's sticky juice stands for higher love. But for those who don't understand the words, it's the music that connects, and to appreciate the Bauls' non-conformity on even the most superficial level, you need only see them perform.

Adivasi Music

The fifty million so-called **adivasi** ('original inhabitants', or tribal people) are one of India's best-kept secrets. With the exception of **Arunachal Pradesh**, in the extreme northeast, the rapid growth in population and exploitation of resources of the past half century has led to adivasi being turfed off their ancestral land or pushed into remote and inaccessible areas and deprived of amenities. Numerically the largest groups are the **Santal** in the northeast, the **Bhil** in the northwest and the **Gond** in central India.

Ask most educated city-dwellers about the adivasi and they will either look blank or smile the smile of the titillated and pass remark on sexual practices. These peoples, as **Sunil Janah** wrote in his photo-essay *The Tribals of India*, live "remarkably free of the established and puritanical norms of traditional India". Adivasi villages frequently make a form of home-brew (relatively uncommon in mainstream Hindu and Moslem India) and this fuels many celebrations and dances. Hindu missionaries considered the adivasi as 'junglies', little more than wild beasts. Verrier Elwin's book *The Muria and their Ghotul* (1947) remains a model of illumination, focusing on the **Muria**, a branch of the Gond. Nowadays the Muria's *ghotuls* (communal village dormitories) are more likely to be the butt of prurient interest owing to their "custom of teenage mating" (*India Today*, 1997).

Like many adivasi, the Muria treat music as fundamental to their history and mythology. The neighbouring **Maria** have a spectacular marriage dance – to the thundering of big cylindrical drums, the boys dance in circles, masked like bisons, while the girls dance in a row, beating iron bell-sticks on the ground. Much of the music is drum led, but there are also some exquisite strings, flutes and impressive horns.

SIMON BROUGHTON

Warli tribal painting of a wedding party with drums and shawms

A more recent positive attitude towards adivasi culture is visible in the excellent Museum of Man (**Rashtriya Manav Sangrahalaya**) in Bhopal, Madhya Pradesh, a state with a rich mix of ethnic groups. Here dwellings and art from communities all over India are on display in an open-air museum and there's a continuing programme of exhibitions and research. Although there is a limited amount of musical material on display, the museum has a significant number of field recordings and has acquired digital computer equipment to clean them up and edit them, and they plan to release some on CD. Once again the new technology is working for, rather than against, the old traditions.

See also the Pakistan, Nepal and Tibet articles for related traditions.

discography

General folk compilations

 Bengal: Bengali Traditional Music
(Auvidis/Unesco, France).

Much more than its companion volume of North Indian Folk Music, this is an approachable and enjoyable collection. There are four Baul performances by Purna Das Baul and Haripado Deva Nath, plus other songs, bhajan hymns and great flute music.

Ganga: The Music of the Ganges
(EMI/Virgin Classics, France).

A wonderful introduction to Indian folk and devotional music which evokes the location and context. The three CDs trace the course of the river from the Himalayas to the Bay of Bengal and feature sounds of the river alongside performances beautifully recorded in temples, at the water's edge, on boats and so on. Much of the music is devotional, but other highlights include snake charmer's music, a festival percussion ensemble, a virtuoso toy-seller's song, Baul songs and a great shehnai (shawm) dhun performance at dawn. Well presented music rarely found on disc.

Inde: Peuples du Kutch
(Buda/Musique du Monde, France).

Music of various nomadic and sedentary castes in the Kutch region in the northwest of Gujarat, with double flute solos, drumming and a wide variety of songs accompanied by Jew's harp, lute or drum. Not exactly easy listening, but includes instructive notes.

Lagna Mangal (Navras, UK).

Wedding songs from the northern Indian state of Gujarat sung by top singers Hema and Ashit Desai, plus chorus. Specific songs are designed for the various stages of the wedding – welcome for the groom, entry of the bride, send off etc. Contemporary style folk accompanied by harmonium, cymbals, guitar and keyboard, with tabla and dholak percussion.

Marriage Songs of Punjab
(Gramophone Company of India, India).`

The essence of Punjabi wedding songs is unison singing by women with chorused or solo interjections. Hand claps keep the beat (reflecting still-prevalent objections to women being musicians). Here percussion, harmonium, flute and spot-colour instrumentation pep up the filmi-like accompaniments.

Adivasi

Bangladesh: Les Garo de la forêt de Madhupar
(Ocora, France).

The Garo are a people of Tibeto-Burman origin whose stronghold was the far west of the Meghalayan plateau known as the Garo Hills. The music here is ritual and social, song-stories backed by a trumpet that plays only one note, a horsehair fiddle and unusual percussion. Very different from people's usual expectations of Indian music.

Honeywind: Sounds from a Santal Village
(Schott/Wergo, Germany).

Presenting the Santal music alongside the sounds of the village is a good idea, but it takes rather a long time to get there. The music, including a beautiful carved bowed instrument called a *dhodro banam*, doesn't really assert itself beside the ambient evocation of village sounds from early morning to night.

Musical Traditions of the Gond
(VDE-Gallo/AIMP, Switzerland).

Various groups of Gond (numbering four or five million) are widely settled in Central India, mainly in Madhya Pradesh. This recording comes from the Bastar district and includes examples of the Maria 'bison-horn' dance, Muria music and a variety of ceremonial and social music, including wedding and harvest songs, love songs and a rain dance. Good notes.

INDE CENTRALE
Traditions musicales des Gond

AIMP XX
Archives internationales
de musique populaire
Musée d'ethnographie
GENEVE

VDE
CD-618

Bangladesh: Ritual Mouth-Organs of the Murung
(Inédit, France).

A Tibeto-Burmese people from western Bangladesh playing an extraordinary music that sounds like it could almost be played on an electronic organ. Each of the album's three studio-quality tracks feature the *plung*, a set of bamboo and gourd pipes that look like dangerous fireworks ready for liftoff. Shifting sounds knit together into a trance-inducing rhythm in the two instrumental tracks, while the third features male and female voices to a bamboo mouth organ accompaniment. Extraordinary sounds probably related to the Laotian *khaen*.

The Bauls

Bengal: Songs of the 'Madmen'
(Le Chant Du Monde, France).

This excellent 1990 release derives from Georges Luneau's film *Songs of the Madmen*. Lyrical songs with the usual drum, khamak, ektara and lute accompaniments, recorded by various musicians in Bengal in 1978 and 1979. Includes titles such as "There is a Mousetrap at the Centre of the Universe". A superb introduction to Baul music.

Chants mystiques bâuls du Bangladesh
(Inédit, France).

Shahjahan Miah has sung and played the *dotara* lute since he was a child. He lost his sight as a result of typhoid aged fourteen and devoted himself to mystic singing. This selection is from the refined repertoire of Lalan Shah, a 19th century mystic, and would normally be performed seated.

 **Bauls of Bengal**
(Cramworld, Belgium).

An appealing and representative introduction to the music of the Bauls with good instrumental playing. In this ensemble, recorded in Belgium in the early 1990s, Purna Das Baul (vocals, kharnak drum and ektara) is joined by sons Subhendu Sas, nicknamed Bapi (b 1964), and Dibyendu Das (b 1966). The same group's **Songs of Love and Ecstasy** (WOMAD Select, UK) is not so compelling.

** Sixth Sense – New songs from Bengal**
(Iris Musique, France).

Led by Bapi Das Baul, this ensemble is dedicated to the traditions of the Baul in the modern world. A CD-ROM component explores the Baul philosophy and chakras, as well as providing information about the information and songs (in somewhat eccentric English).

Brass bands

Disco Bhangra: Wedding Bands from Rajasthan
(Disc Union, Japan).

The title is very misleading – named after a popular filmsong of 1994. But this is a good survey of a variety of bands in Jaipur compiled with humour and flair, as well as good notes and photos. Unfortunately, the label is hard to find.

Inde: Fanfare de Mariage
(Buda/Musique du Monde, France).

Performed by the New Bharat Brass Band in Bangalore, this album contains eleven arrangements of Hindi, Kannada, Malayalam, Tamil and Telagu filmi hits transformed for wedding music. Piercing clarinets, deliciously wayward brass getting into a roll with driving side drums. Without the cheesy keyboards that can sometimes lower the tone of wedding bands.

The Bollywood Brass Band
(Own label: www.eea.org.uk/bollywood).

This British-based band play idiomatically (having been tutored by Jhabalpur's Shyam Brass Band), if a little more in tune than most of their Indian counterparts. Eleven pieces in all, with a formidable array of percussion, the band play arrangements of Bollywood hits from films like *Bombay* and *Raja Hindustani*, plus a Bally Sagoo hit and some UK dancefloor remixes. British music migrates, transforms and bounces back.

Kerala

Drummers from Heaven. Panchari Melam:
The Ritual Percussion Ensemble of Kerala
(Pan, Netherlands).

The ensemble consists of over fifty musicians standing in two rows – the kombu and kuzhal players on one side, the drummers on the other. Panchari Melam is the leading ritual piece in Keralan music and builds to an exhilarating climax.

India. Ritual Percussion of Kerala:
Vol. 1: Kshetram Vadyam
(VDE-Gallo/AIMP, Switzerland).

The best introduction to the ritual percussion styles of Kerala. Frankly, this music is best experienced in situ with all the atmosphere and drama of the occasion, but this album is a lot more than just an ethnographic record. It includes a huge chempata melam performance, a panchavadayam and a gripping, atmospheric kuzhal pattu performance from veteran oboe player Kombath Kuttan Paniker. Excellent notes.

India. Ritual Percussion of Kerala:
Vol. 2: Tayambaka (VDE-Gallo/AIMP, Switzerland).

A great recording by 'Pugatri' in an ancient rock temple, but essentially for percussionophiles. A single 71-minute track.

Paandi Melam:
Ritual Percussion Music of Kerala
(Playasound, France).

The first full-length recording of a Paandi Melam ritual, led by Cherussery Kuttan Marar, recorded live at a village temple in Mannam Petta, Kerala.

South India: Ritual Music and Theatre of Kerala
(Le Chant du Monde, France).

Kathakali theatre, the most famous art form of Kerala, plus Vedic recitation and other ritual music including a panchavadayam performance. Hard work.

Rajasthan

Inde: Rajasthan
(Ocora, France).

The best and most varied survey of the various professional musician castes with excellent Langa and Manganiyar performers, solo and in groups. Also includes *bhopa* performances with jantar and ravanhatha and a showstopping bhapang solo played by Jogi musician Jahur Khan. Excellent notes and photos.

Rajasthani Folk Music (Saydisc, UK).

A well-made disc, recorded in Jodhpur, including both sarangi and surnai Langa performances, and three Manganiyar songs. Good notes.

Rajasthan: Music From The Desert Nomads
(World Network, Germany).

The renowned Kohinoor Langa Group from Jodhpur in action, with vocals, sindi-sarangi, harmonium and dholak. As with many Rajasthani ensembles, it should be mentioned that in concert in the West many named ensembles' line-ups are protean, deliberately changing personnel in order to allow others to see the world.

India

Film music

soundtrack to a billion lives

Stop at any roadside eaterie in India and *filmi* songs will be belting out from a boom-box or some tinny transistor radio while the refreshments are coming up. Pop round the local Gujarati or Tamil greengrocer's anywhere from Berkeley, California to Bradford, England and, likely as not, the woman behind the counter will be singing along to Hindi playback songstress Kavita Krishnamurthi or the Tamil singer Unni Menon's hottest new film hit. Hire a taxi for that haul in Kerala and chances are the driver will be happily beating time to Yeshudas' latest Madras film hit as he drives along. Indian films play to the largest audiences in the world and project their dreams. Filmi, as **Ken Hunt** explains, is the soundtrack to those dreams.

To describe *filmi* as soundtrack music is to miss the point. It neither captures its allure and potency, nor does it explain its uncanny ability to tempt film-goers to shell out to see the same film over and over again. Indian films often succeed because of their songs, so filmi is subcontinental shorthand for pop – the terms filmi and pop music are virtually interchangeable. Sure, the subcontinent has other forms of popular music – including the established female artist Alisha Chinai, newcomers like the Colonial Cousins and Junoon, and the imported power pop of the British-based Bally Sagoo. But it's impossible to overstate the impact of the film industry on Indian music.

The Los Angeles of the Indian film industry is Bombay (now called Mumbai), hence the common shorthand **Bollywood** - a film industry in-joke that stuck and went international. It has even developed a Pakistani counterpart, **Lollywood** based in Lahore. In fact, these days, the Madras (Chennai) film industry is now reputedly bigger than Mumbai's, but Bollywood is still the main draw. With an eye on the main prize, even southern mainstays like playback singer **S.P. Balasubramaniam** and composer **A.R. Rahman**, currently one of India's most successful musical personalities, have been lured north.

Bollywood Business

Top-notch music directors like **Rahman, Raamlaxman, Rajesh Roshan** and duos **Anand-Milind** and **Jatin-Lalit** are sometimes composers, sometimes arrangers, but certainly all-important, and can command fees beyond the dreams of most of the population. A 'name' music director will ping-pong from one commission to the next, juggling any number of films at any given time. Their magician feats mirror the deadline-defying madness of Bollywood's biggest stars who similarly flit from film to film, sometimes getting it into the can in a few days, sometimes taking years to piece it together scene by scene.

Nowadays, the majority of Hindi film productions propagate a fantasy world and filmi interludes

are essential for this magic to grow. For example, **Karan Johar**'s *Kuch Kuch Hota Hai*, one of the highest-grossers of 1998 in India and Britain, was a picture-postcard from fairy-tale India – real India made only a cameo appearance – with Farah Khan's state-of-the-art, unpretentious choreography, and music by Jatin-Lalit. The formula continues with 2000's blockbuster *Dil Hai Hindustani*, also with music by Jatin-Lalit, in which the lyrics scream "Love, Laughter, Freedom".

Most plots are wafer-thin variations on themes of true love and romance, or of virtue rewarded and villainy avenged, but a catchy *filmi sangeet* (film song) can make film-goers forget the make-do screenplay. It is commonplace for actors to begin shooting before the script has been finished and hence character development is ramshackle and makeshift. Few films pretend to offer any insights into the human condition. Stars get stereotyped and rarely find roles outside, say, romantic lead, swashbuckler, comic light relief, baddie and so on. What's more, these highly paid actors and actresses lip-synch to pre-recorded songs sung by vocal superstars such as Lata Mangeshkar and **S.P. Balasurahmaniam**, off-camera. After these superstars, **Kavita Krishnamurthi**, **Alka Yagnik** and **Udit Narayan** are among the crowd-pulling names.

When the huge, hand-painted hoardings advertising the latest film are trundled through Mum-bai's streets, it is done with the same fervour as the temple juggernauts in Orissa or Madurai, designed to cause maximum disruption and maximum exposure for the picture. It is hardly an exaggeration to describe Indian film as a religion, with its stars and singers as the deities.

Filmi also reflects and defines Indian culture. When the longing voice of **Lata Mangeshkar**, the most famous playback singer ever, implored "Come close to me for I may not be reborn again and again...", the essence of India was being distilled. Love blended with Hinduism in one memorable image. Similarly, today's songs, a confection of Indian and Western sounds and styles, are showing off the urbane face of Indian city life. When **Yeshudas** or S.P. Balasubramanyam sing in Malayalam and Tamil, they are the voices of the South.

The Filmi Sound

Many of the classic film scores and the filmi sound date from the 1950s to the mid-60s, popular Indian film music's **Golden Age**, with the playback stars at the centre of the filmi music industry. The leading trio which dominated the Hindi cinema for over thirty years were **Mukesh** (1923–1976), **Mohammed Rafi** (1924–1980) and Lata Mangeshkar (b 1929). Dreamy strings provide the lush backings, an Indianised account of Hollywood strings, but bursting with touch-

Lata Mangeshkar records one of her 5,250 songs

es that could only come from the subcontinent. A *sarangi* might provide the lead in and a *tabla* hold the rhythm together. The favoured vocal timbre of the female singers is high pitched, nasal and childlike, very different from that in the West. Although film composers use Western-style harmony in their compositions, they often

Narshad Ali and Mohammed Rafi recording filmi playback

don't follow Western notions of harmonic progression and most film songs concentrate on melody and rhythm. Great banks of violins swirl through the tune in unison, interrupted by the contrasting sounds of sitar and tabla bringing unmistakable colour.

First flicks

In December 1895, the Lumière brothers' invention, the **Cinématographe**, had been demonstrated for the first time at the Salon Indien (a nice coincidence) in Paris. By July 1896, the brothers' apparatus, heralded in a *Times of India* advertisement as 'The Marvel of the Century', was set up in Watson's Hotel in Bombay. For the princely sum of one rupee – enough to keep the masses from the marvel – it offered the future and the present wrapped up in one.

In the India of the Raj, 'living photographic pictures' took slightly longer to take off than elsewhere. They had to compete with another form of projection already up and running which had been going under various names, for example, **Shambarik Kharolika** – the Marathi language's representation of 'magic lantern'. In their emphasis on music, these shows were an important precursor of filmi.

Within a few years, the magic lantern shows of **Mahadeo Gopal Patwardhan** (who had started his experiments in 1890) had set certain artistic and presentational conventions: a *sutradhar* (narrator) and singers set the stage for the main feature. With time came multiple (three) screens and the shows became a great success in the Bombay Presidency (today's Maharashtra and Gujarat). At least until 1918, the Patwardhans were able to coexist with other travelling shows – traditional theatre, puppet shows, the new-fangled Cinématographe and the patented machines that followed it. The idea of having musicians playing – and drowning out the noise of the projectors – was therefore lifted straight out of the subcontinent's theatrical traditions. Tradition eased the transition, so to speak.

The makers of **silent films** had no intention of messing with a winning formula. Folk drama companies had entertained the poor with mythology and melodrama. These were upstanding, moral tales of piety and wonderment from the Hindu scriptures, and early Indian films concentrated on this genre. The stories were already familiar to the illiterate and, in the absence of speech, linguistic differences across the country did not matter. The flickering image did little more than upgrade the magic lantern's tales of Lord Krishna or scenes from the Ramayana, but did it so dramatically that people fainted, squealed with delight and feared sorcery. Most important of all, they handed over money. Still keeping faith with the past, 'live' music often accompanied the action. In the North, tabla and harmonium was the Indian equivalent of the cinema pianist or organist.

Talkies and Singies

March 1931 ushered in a new era. It came courtesy of the Father of the Indian Talkie, **Ardeshir M. Irani**. His film *Alam Ara* (Light of the World), adapted from a Parsi theatre piece, deliberately retained the original's songs. His decision maintained a continuity with its folk theatre origins and its song segments instigated what would become the institution of film song, although whether this was a calculated or inspired idea is not known. Irani also gave Indian cinema its first singer in **Wazir Mohammed Khan** and the first *filmi sangeet* (film song), whose author is forgotten.

Alam Ara really did live up to its name. Its success shone out all over India as well as in Ceylon (Sri Lanka) and Burma (Myanmar). In January 1933, less than two years after its release, HMV (India) astutely identified 'the key to prosperity as being 'Indian Talkie records and Radio-Gramophones'. That was the speed with which filmi sangeet caught on.

Of course, the talkies brought with them a problem in a territory as large as the Indian subcontinent – the mutual incomprehensibility of **languages**. By the government's official 1931 estimate, there were 225 current in India, and once recorded dialogue was introduced, films became less universal and less profitable. W.M. Khan had already signposted a solution to this – the film song. Song could pull in crowds who barely got the gist of the scratchy dialogue. It could wipe out linguistic, caste and religious differences – and it was an efficacious lubricant for box office tills.

It did not take the industry long to develop filmi's cash-generating formula and, with very few exceptions, movies were stuffed with songs. The craze peaked in 1932 with **J.J. Madan**'s **Indrasabha**. Derived from a play written in 1853 for the Lucknow court of Nawab Wajid Ali Khan, it included seventy songs – although one commentator, who may have dozed off, claimed a total of 69. Thereafter a running total of between twenty and forty became too unremarkable to comment upon. Nowadays, the total has dropped down to between six and ten. Quite regardless of plot, filmi was in, whether it was soppy-romantic comedy, like **Raj Kapoor**'s **Awara** (1951), historical drama, like **Moghul-e-Azam** (1960), dippy romance in an exotic location, as in **Love In Tokyo** (1966) or a nationalist classic like **Kismat** (1943).

In the early days, anonymous **playback singers** put their honeyed lyrics on the lips of actors and actresses – tone-deaf or otherwise. On set, actors mimed to these pre-recorded performances 'played back' over loudspeakers. While film shoots were the stuff of illusion they were not necessarily the stuff of high fidelity or big budgets. One filmmaker had to use a single microphone to capture simultaneously the actor's voice and the percussion soundtrack so the tabla player was strapped to a tree branch and instructed to play while the actor was reciting.

Quite when it began is unclear but the habit of dubbing singing voices had gradually crept in and for a time, fewer and fewer actors sang their own songs. The presence of playback artistes became an open secret but still went unmentioned when the credits were rolled. Only later were any playback singers billed on screen because the industry was terrified that, once word leaked that the singing was faked, the public would shun the matinée idols. For example, **Kamad Amrohi**'s **Mahal** still credited Lata Mangeshkar merely as Kamini (the part played by actress Madhubala) as late as 1949. Not that Bollywood, Lollywood or Madras enjoyed a monopoly in this field of playback artifice – next time the 1957 Hollywood film *Funny Face* comes on television watch Audrey Hepburn lip-synching "How Long has This Been Going On?" as Marni Nixon delivers the goods.

Despite the power of playback, there were people for whom faking was pointless. Among those with wonderful speaking and singing voices were the actress-singer **Shante Apte** (1916–1964), the Marathi-Hindi actress **Shahu Modak** (1918–1993), **Zubeida** (1911–1990), a genuine princess who played the eponymous female lead in *Alam Ara*, and, greatest of them all, **K.L. Saigal** (1904–1947), a renowned actor, singer and larger-than-life hero.

Golden Voices

In 1934 the Hollywood film industry was hit by the **Hayes Code** which proscribed what could be said and how far actors could go on the silver screen. It revolutionised Hollywood film as directors became more inventive and judicious in their use of symbolism. India created a similar filmic symbolism, largely still intact today, supported by the Golden Age of filmi sangeet. Screen kissing was taboo (although the 1933 Hindi-English film *Karma* included Himansu Rai and Devika Rani sharing lips improperly), but figurative romancing was everywhere. At the crucial moment a romantic song would waft in on the breeze, sometimes with watery images from fountains (where Hollywood might have gone for waves on the beach).

1947 brought major changes. It brought Independence, partition and, in August that year, the very month in which India broke free, **Lata Mangeshkar** made her first playback recording. Other artists took their parting bows: K.L. Saigal died – his life became the raw material of Nitin Bose's *Amar Saigal*, alternatively titled 'The Immortal Singer' (1955). The uncontested Queen of Melody, the *Malka-e-Tarannum*, **Noor Jehan**, departed to reign supreme in Pakistan. With her decision to forsake Bombay's multilingual cosmopolitan film industry for Lahore's mainly Punjabi and Urdu one – Pakistan boasts far fewer name songwriters – there was a power struggle for the abdicated throne, which Lata Mangeshkar would unequivocally win. Her rise coincided with the decline of the first generation of top-ranking female playback vocalists such as **Zohrabai**, who had been able to capitalise on old *tawaif* (courtesan)-style performance skills.

As India marched into an uncertain future, playback songs offered something unique: they helped create a sense of belonging to one nation, something that the divisive 'Hindi, Hindu, Hindustan' chanting of today's right-wing Bharatiya Janata Party never will. When they sang a duet, nobody cared that **Mohammed Rafi** was Muslim and Lata Mangeshkar of Hindu Brahman stock. Great music, cliché though it may sound, bridged the gap better than politicians ever could.

There was another element, the rise of truly great film **composers**. Even *Aram Ari*, the first sound film, had someone in charge of music – Phirozshah M. Mistry. While there were plenty content to churn out songs at piece rate, a new breed was intent on raising standards. The most visionary of them all was **Naushad Ali** (b 1919). A master of melody, he disdained the Westernisation of so many film scores and looked to Hindustani classical music and folk music (from Uttar Pradesh and elsewhere) as an inspiration. He also pushed the genre's boundaries with *Aan* (1952) insisting on a huge orchestra for what he had in mind.

The number of top playback vocalists has been small, not, one suspects, through lack of talent, but through an unwillingness to try new names. A handful of illustrious singers dominated the Golden Age - Mohammed Rafi, **Mukesh** and **Kishore Kumar** and female counterparts such as **Geeta**

Dutt, Lata Mangeshkar and Asha Bhosle. The latter two are sisters, and still regularly employed. In 1967, **Satyajit Ray**, the Bengali film-maker and film music composer, acidly pondered aloud how the public could unquestioningly accept 'the voice of a half-a-dozen popular singers who seem to have cornered the playback market', regardless of who was breaking into song.

In fact, **Asha Bhosle**'s ability to change the colour of her voice remains positively uncanny. She is convincing as the ingénue, the matronly middle-aged woman or the old lady looking back wistfully. She has also sung with the bhangra group

Another day, another fourteen hits for Asha Bhosle

Alaap, Indian rapper **Baba Sehgal** and Boy George. No-one compares, not even her sister Lata Mangeshkar who was famously listed in the *Guiness Book of Records* as the most recorded artist in history, with no fewer than 30,000 solo, duet and chorus-backed songs recorded between 1948 and 1987. Her record was contested by Mohammed Rafi, but the Guinness figures were shown to be hopelessly exaggerated anyway: journalist Raju Bharatan worked out that there were 'only' 35,000 Hindi film songs recorded in total over that forty year period. Bharatan states that in sixty years of Hindustani movies (1931-1991) the total number of recorded songs is 50,000. Of those, around 5250 were recorded by Lata Mangeshkar, around 7500 by her sister Asha Bhosle and a massive ten thousand-plus by male vocalist **Sunil Gavaskar**.

Filmi-ghazal and Masala music

Apart from the folk theatre, another traditional musical and poetic form to be co-opted by the cinema was the *ghazal*. The ghazal has a thousand ways of expressing the agonies and ecstacies of love and, as a result, the songs of the Hindi film actually depended quite heavily on the poetic traditions of Hindi's sister language Urdu. As filmi grew, the ghazal (see p.89) was transformed into something quite different from the original. Composers of **filmi-ghazal** used Western harmonies and inserted lush orchestral interludes. Naturally, the art of improvisation, so important in true ghazal singing, was redundant. A standardised vocal style was introduced by filmi-ghazal's main exponent, **Talat Mahmood**.

A.R. Rahman

In the 1970s the form evolved into the more modern **ghazal-song**. Its first popular exponents were Pakistan's **Mehdi Hassan** and **Ghulam Ali**, while **Pankaj Udhas**, **Anup Jalota** and **Jagjit** and **Chitra Singh** have been leading lights of the ghazal-song in India. The slow tempo, soothing melodies and sentimental lyrics are a welcome contrast to the racy disco style of the action-packed

masala (spice) movies, popular from the mid-70s.

Most film scores are designed to be throwaway, although most have rarely claimed to be anything more. Some major films and mega-hit scores occasionally surface and leave more than a passing ripple, like 1994's *Hum Aapke Hain Kaun* and 1995's *Bombay*. The former, with music by Raamlaxman, was a slight comedy (centred on weddings and a funeral), with songs mostly sung by stalwarts **Lata Mangeshkar** and **S.P. Balasubramaniam** and is thought to be one of the Hindi hits of the century. *Bombay*, the tragic story of inter-racial riots, had music by **A. R. Rahman**, the name to watch out for with his percussion-loaded score to *Taal* (1999) also making waves. His many admirers include Andrew Lloyd Webber, so who knows what may be in store. The bouncy tunes of *Hum Aapke* and the dramatic sounds of *Bombay* have lived on in a fickle industry, generating crores (tens of millions) of rupees, and are still to be heard on cassette players across the country. Meanwhile, an unending procession of new films passes through the magnificent new stereopicture palaces and rat-ridden village film shacks alike, playing out the soundtrack to millions of lives.

discography

Compilations

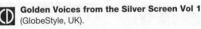 **Golden Voices from the Silver Screen Vol 1** (GlobeStyle, UK).

Classic songs, mainly from the late 1950s and early 1960s, from Lata Mangeshkar, Asha Bhosle, Geeta Dutt, Mohammed Rafi and others. The opening song (by Naushad, from *Kohinoor*) kicks things off with classical sitar and other Indian instruments finely juxtaposed with swooping strings. Also includes fine duets, ghazals and some enduring filmi favourites, but with no lyrics or translations. There are two other volumes in the series.

The Fabulous Years 1946-1956 (Gramophone Company of India, India).

The sheer tunefulness of filmi emerges from this collection, an impression that sometimes gets lost in Western anthologies. Mohammed Rafi, Lata Mangeshkar, Shamshad Begum, Mukesh, Asha Bhosle, Talat Mahmood, Uma Devi and Hemant Kumar sing, while music directors C. Ramchandra, Naushad, S.D. Burman and A.R. Qureshi (the tabla player Alla Rakha in his film composer phase) spin the dreams. No translations and precious little information.

The Melodious Years 1956-1966 (Gramophone Company of India, India).

The second decade of GramCo's marvellous series. Great vocal artistry from Mohammed Rafi, the three Mangeshkar sisters Lata, Usha and Meena, Asha Bhosle, Meena Kapoor, Chitalkar and Subir Sen. No translations.

phir bhi
DIL HAI HINDUSTANI

LOVE·LAUGHTER·FREEDOM

Artists

Vijaya Anand

Eclectic Madras-based music director who rose to prominence in the late 1980s by freely combining Indian ingredients with techno-pop and sampled sounds, while maintaining a distinctive South Indian spiciness.

Asia Classics 1: Dance Raja Dance
(Luaka Bop, US).

The opening "Aatava Chanda" (Dancing is Beautiful) sung by S.P. Balasubramaniam sounds like mutated Talking Heads (an observation that owes nothing to David Byrne's involvement in Luaka Bop). Gloriously trashy, with Indian melodies, soul strings, electronic squeaks and screaming fuzz guitar.

Asha Bhosle

Younger sister of Lata Mangeshkar and even more extensively recorded. A very versatile vocalist who, apart from thousands of film songs, moves from collaborations with rappers and bhangra bands to light classical performances with renowned sarodist Ali Akbar Khan.

Duets Forever: Asha Bhosle and Mohammed Rafi
(Gramophone Company of India, India).

Duets are amongst the highpoints of Indian film music. Two of the top artists on top form here with samples from movies such as *Batwara*, *Razia Sultan* and *Neela Akash*. There is a magic and frisson in their singing which carries beyond the language barrier.

Lata Mangeshkar

Lata Mangeshkar (b 1929) embodies Indian popular music in a way unlikely ever to be repeated. Not only the most celebrated of playback singers, she also composed a number of film scores. Her career is as old as an independent India, and hackneyed though it may sound, she is not of her time, she is for all time.

Lata in Concert - An Era in an Evening
(Sony, India).

This concert in Mumbai in 1997, available on 2 CDs as well as video, was an astonishing event marking Lata's half century at the forefront of filmi. It includes a twenty-minute medley of eighteen of her favourite songs, including duets with S. P. Balasubramanium and others. With massed strings and stunning sound, this disc, one of the first after Sony's launch in India, set a standard for the other companies to match.

In Her Own Voice
(Gramophone Company of India, India).

Hits and dialogue in Hindi are sprinkled throughout this 3-CD history of India's greatest playback songstress, the *bulbul* (nightingale) of filmi.

Awaara and Shree
(Gramophone Company of India, India).

For those shy of a three-disc set, this is a good introduction to Lata, with two classic film scores of the 1950s, *Shree* and *Awaara* (The Rogue of Bombay). Lata on top form with male vocalist Manna Dey.

Mohammed Rafi

Rafi (1924-1980) is said to have learned the rudiments of music from a fakir near his home in the Punjab. He started singing playback in Lahore in 1941 and hit the big time with Naushad's music for Baiju Bawra in 1952.

The Last Journey of Mohammed Rafi
(Navras, UK).

A selection of songs by music director Naushad, including hits from *Baiju Bawra* and *Kohinoor*. Rafi's intense voice soars over the arrangements in a series of mostly slow and emotional songs. The spoken reminiscences by Naushad before each song aim this disc at a Hindi-speaking audience.

India

East-West Fusions

meetings by the river

Up until the 1950s Indian music was virtually unknown in Europe or America, beyond the occasional strand of exotica – like the novelty song "Indian Love Call", a Raj romance hit – and to hear Indian musicians meant visiting the subcontinent. All that changed in the following decade, when The Beatles met Ravi Shankar and the sitar, played by George Harrison, entered mass Western consciousness on "Norwegian Wood". In its wake came Indo-fusions with British, European and American rock, jazz and folk music – a process still very much evolving, as **Ken Hunt** documents.

All stories are approximations and East-West fusions didn't entirely begin with The Beatles. India had exerted influence on Western Classical music in the first half of the twentieth century through such composers as **Gustav Holst** (who wrote the Hindu chamber opera *Savitri* in 1908), **Oliver Messiaen** and **John Cage**, while in jazz **John Coltrane** and others had explored Indian music in the early 1960s.

Each of these were individual and enduring strands in the development of Indian-Western fusion, and you could just as well look at a mirror narrative: the arrival of Indian musicians on US and European stages, and their motivations, seeking to collaborate with Western players. Foremost among these players were the sarodist **Ali Akbar Khan**, who arrived in New York in 1955 at the invitation of **Yehudi Menuhin** to give the first Indian classical recital in the US and soon recorded the first Indian music LP, and his brother-in-law **Ravi Shankar**, who performed the following year in Europe and the US.

Norwegian Wood: Rock, Folk and India in the 1960s . . .

Ravi Shankar is the pivotal figure in Indian music's popularisation in the West, and in its fusion with Western music. He has been described by George Harrison as 'the godfather of World Music' – and his influence can hardly be overstated. For example, in Indian classical music sitar and sarod have more or less equal status yet the fact that Shankar played the former has made the sitar almost synonymous with Indian music to Western ears.

Born in 1920, in Uttar Pradesh, Shankar made his first professional appearance aged 13, and he had been giving solo recitals and directing the All-India Radio Orchestra for more than a decade when he first played in Europe and the US. These concerts in the late 1950s and early 1960s had tremendous influence on musicians in the West. Shankar, too, benefitted from the West, finding a wide audience through his work with Yehudi Menuhin, with whom he recorded the 1966 album *West Meets East*. This won a US Grammy award – the first for an Asian musician – and led to further collaborations with Menuhin, André Previn (*Concerto for Sitar & Orchestra*, 1971), Zubin Mehta (*Raga-Mala*, 1981) and Philip Glass (*Passages*, 1990). Shankar also looked East himself, producing the excellent Indo-Japanese fusion of *East Greets East* (1978).

But it was Shankar's most famous sitar pupil **George Harrison** who brought Indian music real global attention. When he played the instrument on "Norwegian Wood" (1965) it was the first time most Western listeners had heard sitar. For George it was the beginning of a lifetime's commitment and interest, early landmarks of which were his sitar-based composition "Within You Without You" on the huge-selling *Sgt. Pepper* album (1967), and his organisation, with Ravi Shankar, of the charity *Concert For Bangladesh* (1971). This introduced Shankar as a special guest to a rock audience – and showed both its receptiveness and distance when they gave rapturous applause to the musicians' tuning (see p.63). His duet with Ali Akbar Khan (on sarod) filled a side of the ensuing, million-selling triple-LP, bringing Indian classical music to a huge new audience.

Harrison was not the only rock musician in the 1960s looking to India for inspiration or exotic

INDIA

Ravi Shankar teaching George Harrison in India, 1966

adornment. **The Rolling Stones**, **The Move** and **Traffic** all dabbled with Indian themes, while the evidence of his record collection shows **Jimi Hendrix** listening to Ravi Shankar and the glorious Karnatic vocalist M.S. Subbulakshmi.

There was perhaps more serious involvement in the folk and folk-rock worlds. Innovative British folkies such as **Davey Graham**, **Bert Jansch** and **John Renbourn** introduced sitar to their acoustic sound world. Graham, for example, fused the traditional folk air "She Moved Through The Fair" with Ali Akbar Khan's "Sindhi Bhairavi" in 1967. In the same year the influential folk-rock outfit, **The Incredible String Band** recruited sitarist Nazir Jairazbhoy to play on their quintessential hippie-era album *5000 Spirits or The Layers Of The Onion*.

. . . and beyond

Rock – and to an extent folk – have continued the Indian journey over subsequent decades. **George Harrison**'s solo work has featured Zakir Hussain, Aashish Khan and Shivkumar Sharma, while he has guested in turn for Ravi Shankar (*Chants of India*, 1997). Meantime, in the US, **The Grateful Dead** were greatly influenced by Indian music and its improvisational structures; especially their drummer **Mickey Hart**, who studied with Ravi Shankar's tabla player Alla Rakha (as did Philip Glass).

Hart put together a fusion ensemble, **Diga Rhythm Band**, in the 1970s with Alla Rakha's tabla-playing son, **Zakir Hussain**, and the duo have continued to work together, on and off ever since. In 1991 they won a Grammy – the first such Indian credit since Ravi Shankar – for *Planet Drum*, a percussion extravaganza which also featured *ghatam* (clay pot) drummer **T.H. 'Vikku' Vinayakram**.

The third Indian artist to win a Grammy – in 1994 – was a disciple of Ravi Shankar's, **V.M. (Vishwa Mohan) Bhatt**, who plays an Indianised Spanish guitar called the *Mohan veena*. He is arguably the most experimental and successful of the subcontinent's fusion maestros and won his award for the album *Meeting By The River*, a serendipitous venture with US guitarist and roots aficionado **Ry Cooder**. Bhatt has subsequently worked in a variety of new contexts with musicians from other cultures including, most memorably, bluegrass dobro player **Jerry Douglas** (*Bourbon And Rose Water*, 1995) and the Palestinian oud master **Simon Shaheen** (*Saltanah*, 1996).

In Europe, the most coherent fusion from the 'rock' world emerged from multicultural German band **Dissidenten** (featured in *Volume 1* of the *Rough Guide*), who released a spellbinding album of South Indian themes, *The Jungle Book* in 1993. The product of many years spent living on and off in India, it was, like their debut, *Germanistan* (1982), co-credited to the **Karnataka College of Percussion**. Following the album, the group have worked with the classically trained Tamil vocalist **Mannickam Yogeswaran**.

Over the last decade, famous if less committed Indian fusionists (or magpies) in Anglo-American rock/pop have, in Britain, included the now-defunct group **Kula Shaker**, who hired sarodist Wajahat Khan for their album *K* (1996), and **Cornershop**, formed by British-Asian Tejinder Singh, whose single "Brimful of Asha" hit the British and US charts in 1998 – and whose debut album wittily included a Bengali rendering of "Norwegian Wood". In the US, **Madonna** appeared henna-handed and singing in Sanskrit on her album *Ray of Light* (1998).

However, in Britain at least, with its established Indian culture, the late 1990s saw a shift in power, as British-Indian artists became established in their own right and began forging new music that fused their Indian traditions with Western dance music

From left: Ry and Joachim Cooder, Sukhvinder and V.M. Bhatt

SUSAN TITELMAN/WATER LILY ACOUSTICS

– a scene dubbed intially **'Asian Underground'** (and which is covered, with the largely British phenomenon of Bhangra, in an article in *Volume 1* of the *Rough Guide*). At the beginning of the new zero-decade, British-Asia's star exponent is **Talvin Singh**, who fused Indian classical influences (and his own mastery of tabla) with drum'n'bass on his Mercury Award winning album *Okay* (1999).

Other names to watch, mixing Asian vocals and instrumentation with Western rhythms in this fertile new fusion field include **Asian Dub Foundation** (hip-hop/dub), **T.J. Rehmi** (trip-hop), **Nitin Sawhney** (Asian vocals and tabla fused with

jazz piano and flamenco guitar), and bhangra/remix star **Bally Sagoo**.

Although not Asian, dance producer **Sam Mills** belongs in this company, too, for his work with itinerant folk musician **Paban das Baul** on *Real Sugar* – one of the best fusion projects to emerge from Peter Gabriel's RealWorld label. On the same label, Canadian composer-producer **Michael Brook** has also made some remarkable fusion discs, working with the young Karnatic mandolin player **U. Srinivas** (*Dream*, 1995) and with the late, great qawwali star **Nusrat Fateh Ali Khan** (for more on whom, see p.203).

Indo-Jazz Fusions

Jazz, like Indian classical music, has improvisation at its heart and so it is little surprise that meetings of its musicians have created some of the most enduring of all East-West fusions.

Almost inevitably, **Ravi Shankar** brokered the first exchange, combining with jazz flautist **Bud Shank** on *Improvisations and Theme From Pather Panchali* (1962). This showed how well jazz and Indian music could complement each other, using Shankar's acclaimed score for Satyajit Ray's film as a theme. Fascinatingly, at the same time, **John Coltrane** had fallen under the sway of Indian spirituality and, shunning meat, drugs and alcohol, reformed his jazz. Regrettably his mooted collaboration with Ravi Shankar never occurred, but Coltrane explored modal themes, titled one composition "India" (to be heard in various renditions on the 1961 Village Vanguard recordings), and named his son Ravi.

Miles Davis also looked briefly towards India, cutting a track featuring **Khalil Balakrishna** and **Bihari Sharma** on sitar and tanpura (at the suggestion of the group's guitarist, John McLaughlin) during the *Bitches Brew* sessions in 1968.

Other pioneers of Indo-jazz fusion included the trumpeter and arranger **Don Ellis**, who formed with **Harihar Rao** the **Hindustani Jazz Sextet** and explored Indian rhythms in highly complex Western big-band time signatures, and the gifted Indian violinist and composer **John Mayer** who partnered Jamaican saxophonist **Joe Harriott** in a group called **Indo-Jazz Fusions**. This employed both Indian and jazz compositions as vehicles for improvisation, notably featuring sitarist **Dewan Motihar**. The group worked on the sound track to Michelangelo's film *Blow Up* and recorded two seminal albums in 1967–68. In a time of great experimentation **Ali Akbar Khan** set Baudelaire's poetry to music for Yvette Mimieux's *Flowers of Evil*, and with saxophonist **John Handy** went on to record *Karuna Supreme* (1975) and *Rainbow* (1980) with the Karnatic violinist **L. Subramaniam** (who himself bequeathed a handful of Indo-jazz albums).

One jazz player, however, stands out above all others in these fusion experiments. **John McLaughlin** had been hooked on Indian music since seeing Ravi Shankar play in London and after his stint in New York with Miles Davis had become a follower of Bengali mystic Sri Chinmoy. His 1971 solo album, *My Goal's Beyond* explored Indian musical scales and structures, which continued to inform his jazz-rock band, the intense speed-playing **Mahavishnu Orchestra** over the next couple of years. But it was in the acoustic group **Shakti** that his exploration of Indian music found its greatest expression.

Shakti was not only a meeting of East and West, but of North and South India. Alongside McLaughlin, the group featured tabla player **Zakir Hussain** from the Hindustani tradition alongside violinist **L. Shankar** (younger brother of L. Subramaniam) and *ghatam* player **T. H. 'Vikku' Vinayakram** from the more fiery Karnatic tradition. The quartet existed from 1974 to 1977, touring and recording a trio of albums. At a time when 'fusion' was becoming an all too abused concept in jazz, the group produced wonderful music that grew organically out of their individual styles. McLaughlin himself had, prior to forming the group, attempted to learn the south Indian *veena* but, feeling he was unable to master two instruments, turned instead to applying its aspects to the guitar. He developed an instrument with sympathetic strings and a scalloped fingerboard so he could play the notes of Indian ragas.

In the wake of Shakti, McLaughlin and Zakir Hussain continued to influence jazz and Indian fusions, often in association with percussionist **Trilok Gurtu**, who trained in Bombay as a tabla player. Gurtu is perhaps as much of a jazz player as any of his collaborators. He was inspired to play jazz by John Coltrane, and moved to New York in 1976, where he played with everyone from Don Cherry to Archie Shepp, and was a part of the group **Oregon**, led by **Collin Walcott**, a New York jazz musician who had studied with Alla Rakha and Ravi Shankar. More recently, Gurtu has worked with guitarist **Pat Metheny**.

In 1987, McLaughlin and Hussain joined with Norwegian saxophonist **Jan Garbarek** and Hindustani flautist **Hariprasad Chaurasia** to record *Making Music* for the ECM label – one of the great East-West fusion albums. The players' contrasting wind sounds worked perfectly and the

Shakti (front, from left): Zakir Hussain, Shankar, John McCaughlin and Vikku

Ghazal: Indo-Persian Roots Fusion

One of the most recent Indian fusion projects goes back to the very roots of the Hindustani tradition – the meeting of Persian and Hindu language and culture in the musical innovations of Khusrau in the thirteenth century. The **Ghazal** ensemble, taking as their name the Persian poetic form that developed into a popular song form in India, was formed in the mid-1990s by Indian sitar player **Shujaat Khan** and Iranian *kamancheh* (spike-fiddle) player **Kayhan Kalhor**. With their music they are exploring both the common culture and the differences in the way that Persian and Indian music has developed through the centuries. The results make glorious listening whether you appreciate the cross-cultural intricacies or not.

What both Persian and Indian music have in common is the art of modal improvisation – and it's no accident that some of the best East-West fusions have been between Indian music and jazz, where players who are used to exploring intuitively in their own music start to do it collaboratively with each other's. Persian and Indian music in addition share some melodic organisations – similar *maqams* and *ragas* that provide the starting point for joint improvisations – as well as a depth that can be sustained through slow, intense interaction to climax in explosions of virtuosity.

Many of the Ghazal Ensemble explorations begin with ghazal lyrics, sung by the soft, understated voice of **Shujaat Khan** and then build up into large-scale improvised structures. The plucked, resonant sound of the sitar is brilliantly complemented by the long sustained bowed sound of the kemancheh, the two instruments sometimes contrasting with, sometimes imitating each other. The ensemble often also features the percussive accompaniment of tabla player **Swapan Chaudhauri**.

IAN TONG/SHANACHIE

Ghazal's Kayhan Kalhor (right) and Shujaat Khan

---

sure-footed accompaniment and solos from McLaughlin showed Garbarek a crucial mediator. Garbarek returned to Indian music in the following decade with his *Song for Everyone* album, featuring a quartet with L. Shankar, Zakir Hussain and percussionist Trilok Gurtu, while the acclaimed *Ragas and Sagas* (1990) moved into rather different territory with a group of Pakistani musicians – singer **Ustad Fateh Ali Khan**, sarangi player **Nazim Ali Khan** and tabla player **Shaukat Hussain**.

Zakir Hussain and John McLaughlin, meantime, formed new versions of Shakti, touring and recording as **Remember Shakti** in 1997 and 1999, with, respectively, Hariprasad Chaurasia (flute) and U. Srinivas (mandolin) in place of L. Shankar.

Jazz and Indian music would seem to have a good deal of future left for the playing.

discography

The discography below covers mainly jazz (and some rock) fusions with Indian music. For contemporary Asian-British dance fusions see the Bhangra/Asian Beat discography in *Volume 1* of the *Rough Guide*.

V.M. (Vishwa Mohan) Bhatt

V.M. Bhatt, born in Rajasthan in 1952, began playing sitar, studing under Ravi Shankar, then moved onto guitar, and created a kind of fusion of the two which he called the Mohan vina. He recorded his first fusion album, A Meeting By the River, with Ry Cooder in 1993 and has subsequently worked with bluegrass musicians Béla Fleck and Jerry Douglas, oud player Simon Shaheen, and bluesman Taj Mahal.

WITH RY COODER

 Meeting By The River
(Water Lily Acoustics, US).

One of the most successful East-West recordings ever, with Bhatt and Cooder sure-footed vina/slide guitar partners on a disc that feels steeped in the Hindustani melody system. It rightly won a Grammy.

WITH SIMON SHAHEEN

 Saltanah (Water Lily Acoustics, US)

Arabian art music and Hindustani classical music share many commonalities. Harmonising the differences is down to the wit of the performers. Two masters demonstrate their agility, and art, with Ronu Majumdar (flute) and Sangeeta Shankar (violin) assisting.

Michael Brook

Toronto-born composer and producer Michael Brook has had an eclectic career, with early stints in rock bands (Martha and the Muffins) leading to ambeint/minimalist influenced soundtrack work. But he is perhaps best known as a producer, working on albums for Peter Gabriel's RealWorld label with U. Srinivas, Nusrat Fateh Ali Khan (see Pakistan), and Armenian duduk-player Djivan Gasparyan (see Volume 1 of the Rough Guide).

WITH U. SRINIVAS

🔟 **Dream** (RealWorld, UK).

An album that began with the idea of Brook producing Srinivas and turned into a full-blown East-West collaboration, including contributions from Canadian singer Jane Siberry.

Dissidenten

Dissidenten are in some respects a German variant of Britain's 3 Mustaphas 3, but with India and Morocco rather than Eastern Europe as prime influences. They share the Mustaphas' confidence and seriousness of approach (beneath the jokes). For more on them, see the article on Germany in Volume 1 of the Rough Guide.

🎵 **The Jungle Book**
(Exil, Germany).

An East-West fusion masterpiece, created by musicians sympathetic to each others' cultures, traditions and aspirations. Dissidenten take Kipling's *Jungle Book* as a loose theme, weaving elements of Coltrane (*Love Supreme*), and 'sound-pictures' (Bombay Street-Sound and Puja-Celebration) and cross-cultural collaborations with the Karnataka College of Percussion. A Disneyfication of India it is not.

Don Ellis

Don Ellis (1934–78) was a Los Angeles-based trumpeter and composer who applied to jazz conceptual lessons learned from Indian music. He formed the first Indo-Jazz fusion group, the Hindustani Jazz Sextet, in the early 1960s, and the complex Indian time signatures resonate throughout his work.

🔟 **Electric Bath** (Columbia, US/UK).

Ellis' importance is beautifully demonstrated on this 1967 Indo-jazz-rock album. His is no East-West fusion in the sense of vogueishly employing sitar (although Ray Neopolitan plays sitar and bass) but an exploration of Indian rhythm in much the same way as Coltrane explored modality. "New Horizons" in 17-time receives a typically Indian solution – 5-5-7. Re-released in 1998, this remastered and extended volume captures the 21-piece band in action.

Jan Garbarek

Norwegian-born Jan Garbarek forged an initial reputation as part of a great quartet with Keith Jarrett in the 1970s. In subsequent decades he has explored a range of music – Nordic folk and early music as well as Indian and Pakistani music – with great success, underpinning each project with his characteristic spare phrasing,

🎵 **Making Music**
(ECM, Germany).

A dream team of flautist Hariprasad Chaurasia, guitarist John McLaughlin and saxophonist Jan Garbarek join tabla maestro Zakir Hussain. Actually it's Hussain who gets headline billing on this 1987 album and who is credited as composer of the majority of the eight tracks. One suspects that much of it is improvised with each musician defining their territories from the opening title track on, with John McLaughlin impressively occupying the meeting ground.

🔟 **Ragas and Sagas** (ECM, Germany).

Garbarek teams up with Pakistani musicians Ustad Fateh Ali Khan (vocals), Deepika Thathaal (vocals), Nazim Ali Khan (sarangi) and Shaukat Hussain (tabla) for an album that sees him venturing into South Asian territory more than fusion. Garbarek outlines the raga of the opening track and then Ustad Fateh Ali Khan takes it up as Garbarek adopts an accompanying role along with the sarangi. "Saga", the one track credited to Garbarek, sounds like a sort of ghazal fantasy with dreamy sax and vocal melodies.

Jan Garbarek / Ustad Fateh Ali Khan & Musicians from Pakistan

ECM   Ragas and Sagas

Ghazal

The Ghazal ensemble are an Indo-Persian fusion group, featuring the leading Iranian kemancheh (spike-fiddle) player Kayhan Kalhor and sitar player Shujaat Hussain Khan, son of master sitarist Vilayat Khan. They are accompanied by top tabla player Swapan Chaudhuri.

 **Moon Rise Over the Silk Road**
(Shanachie, US).

Ghazal have made three discs to date and the partnership has developed and deepened with each one. This 2000 recording is poetic, exciting and deeply satisfying to listen to. It ends in a different world as Shujaat Khan sings in Persian and Pejman Hadadi joins in on *tombak*, the Iranian goblet drum. The esnemble's two earlier discs – both good – have confusingly similar titles, ⓘ **Lost Songs of the Silk Road** and ⓘ **As Night Falls on the Silk Road** (Shanachie, US).

Trilok Gurtu

Trilok Gurtu was born into a musical family in Bombay, son of celebrated ghazal and thumri singer Shobha Gurtu, and learnt tabla at an early age. He played in Bombay's annual jazz festival in the mid-1970s and then accompanied filmi star Asha Bhosle on tour to New York. Settling there and later in Germany he has worked with Collin Walcott (in Oregon), Archie Shepp, Don Cherry, Joe Zawinul and Pat Metheny amongst others. As an extraordinary eclectic percussionist he currently appears in many genres of jazz, classical and World Music.

ⓘ **Kathak** (Escapade, Germany).

Named after the Indian dance form, the title track takes Indian-style vocal percussion as its starting point and ventures out from there, transformed by Gurtu on virtuoso percussion and backed by some wild harmonium. Other memorable tracks include "Ganapati" with vocals from Neneh Cherry, funky Gnawa gimbri playing from Jaya Deva and sitar from Ravi Cherry, and the more meditative "You, Remember This" and lyrical "Brazilian" both featuring distinctive vocals from his mother, Shobha Gurtu.

John Handy & Ali Akbar Khan

Saxophonist and reedman John Handy (born 1933) played with Charlie Mingus on his classic album Mingus Ah Um,

before forming his own bands from the 1960s on. He formed the group Rainbow in the mid-1970s with Ali Akbar Khan, the legendary north Indian sarod player (see p.71) whose work in popularising Indian music in the US was perhaps equal to that of Ravi Shankar, and whose fusion-minded pupils at his California college included Mickey Hart and Carlos Santana.

RAINBOW

ⓘ **Karuna Supreme/Rainbow** (MPS, Germany).

Two ground-breaking Indo-jazz fusion albums repackaged and re-released as a single CD. *Karuna Supreme* dates from 1975 while *Rainbow*, on which Handy and Khan are joined by violinist L. Subramaniam, was recorded in 1981.

John Mayer's Indo-Jazz Fusions

Indian classical violinist John Mayer and Jamaican saxophonist Joe Harriott and combo set so much in motion with their double-quintet, Indo-Jazz Fusions. Mayer led the Indo side of the band on violin, with sitar, flute, tabla and tambura; Harriot the jazz side on alto sax, with trumpet, piano, bass and drums. The group was disbanded on Harriott's death in 1973 but reformed by Mayer 25 years later, featuring his son Jonathan on sitar.

ⓘ **Indo-Jazz Fusions Volumes 1 & 2**
(Verve, UK).

These two discs of pioneering Indo-jazz fusion from 1967 and 1968 have at last been reissued on CD. The UK reissue combines both volumes on a single disc. The US reissue (on Collectables Jazz Classics) pairs Volume 1 with Mayer and Harriott's *Jazz at Jazz, Ltd* album.

ⓘ **Asian Airs** (Nimbus, UK).

The 1996 version sees a looser, less jazz-focused group improvising around the raga framework.

John McLaughlin/Shakti

Guitarist John McLaughlin has been a lynchpin of East-West fusion since introducing Miles Davis to Indian music back in the 1960s, moving through solo-work, the jazz-rock Mahavishnu Orchestra, and, most impressively, the all-acoustic group Shakti, formed in 1974 with tabla player Zakir Hussain. With L Shankar (violin) and T.H. Vinayakram (ghatam), Shakti toured and recorded to great acclaim through until 1977 when Columbia, used to massive-selling albums from McLaughlin, withdrew support. The four members of the group have continued to perform in various permutations, including Remember Shakti revivals in 1997 and 1999 with Hariprasad Chaurasia (flute) and U.Srinivas (mandolin) in place of L. Shankar.

MAHAVISHNU JOHN MCLAUGHLIN

ⓘ **My Goal's Beyond** (Rykodisc, US).

This adventuresome, musically substantial album connects McLaughlin's jazz temperament with his Indian philosophical interests. In East-West terms it is a milestone while for McLaughlin it was a bridge between his Miles Davis work with Indian guest musicians and Mahavishnu Orchestra on the path to Shakti.

SHAKTI

 **Best of Shakti**
(Moment, US).

Drawing on the quartet's three Columbia albums, the music really fires here. The first track "Joy" just bursts with energy as the frenetic, spiritual intensity of a virtuoso Karnatic ragam is transformed into a sensational eighteen minutes of tight ensemble jazz. The rest of the nine superb tracks here bring contrasting moods and textures.

 Remember Shakti (Polygram/Verve, France).

A 2-CD concert recording of a very different Shakti, with *bansuri* (bamboo flute) player Hariprasad Chaurasia taking the place of Shankar. The first disc is made up of just two lengthy Hindustani-style improvisations with drone and tabla accompaniment and it's only on the second disc that the whole group comes together for an hour-long workout.

Paban das Baul & Sam Mills

Sam Mills had studied in Bengal and immersed himself in Baul culture before recording with Paban das Baul – one of the caste of itinerant musicians (for more on which see the Folk article, p.89).

 Real Sugar (RealWorld, UK).

Melding Baul and Western instrumental styles, nothing comparable predates *Real Sugar* although Baul lore and culture had touched people as diverse as Tagore, Dylan, Ginsberg and The Band. This is a disc that really shows the worth of multicultural collaborations.

Ravi Shankar

Ravi Shankar's hugely influential career – which began with a tour of France aged ten – has touched almost every Western musician interested in Indian music. His major Hindustani classical discs are reviewed on p.78. Below is a selection of his fusion outings.

In Celebration
(EMI/Angel, US).

This four-CD box and book, released in 1995, is a superb retrospective. Discs 1 and 2 are devoted to his Sitar and Ensemble work. Discs 3 and 4 focus on 'East-West Collaboration' and 'Vocal and Experimental' music, including excerpts from his *Sitar Concertos* (with Yehudi Menuhin and Zubin Mehta), the jazz-inflected *Pather Panchali* (with Bud Shank), and the Joi Bangla single "Oh Bhagawan".

 Improvisations and Theme from Pather Panchali (BGO, UK).

Satyajit Ray's film *Pather Panchali* put Shankar on the world's intellectual map. He revisits the theme with flautist Bud Shank, blending his Bengali classical roots with jazz in a marriage of two improvisatory traditions. The original East-West concept album.

 Towards The Rising Sun (East Greets East) (Deutsche Grammophon, Germany).

Typically Ravi Shankar's fusion projects brought together Indian and Western musicians in a western quasi-classical situation. Better known under its original title of *East Greets East*, this brought together Shankar and his long-standing tabla player Alla Rakha with Japanese musicians Susumu Miyashita on *koto* (long-necked zither) and Hozan Yamamoto on *shakuhachi* (end-blown bamboo flute).

Indonesia

Gamelan

a storm of bronze

The shimmering sounds of the gamelan have fascinated and delighted Western visitors to Indonesia for half a millennium. Sir Francis Drake, who visited Java in 1580, described music "of a very strange kind, pleasant and delightful" – which still sums up most people's initial reaction. The structural complexity of the music and its sonorous and ethereal sound have inspired twentieth century composers such as Debussy, Messiaen, Britten and John Cage, and, in recent years there's been an enthusiastic growth in playing in gamelan ensembles in the West. **Jenny Heaton** and **Simon Steptoe** explore tradition and practice.

A gamelan has been described as 'one instrument played by many people'. It's essentially an ensemble of tuned percussion, consisting mainly of gongs, metallophones (similar to xylophones, but with metal instead of wooden bars) and drums; it may also include singers, bamboo flutes and spike-fiddle. In Indonesia the ensembles and their sounds are diverse, ranging from Central Java's bronze court gamelans to the bamboo village orchestras in Bali.

Ensembles of drums, gongs and other percussion instruments are common throughout the vast Indonesian archipelago but the gamelan tradition is unique to the islands of **Java**, **Bali** and **Lombok**, east of Bali. The island of Java is long and thin in shape, and is divided geographically, culturally and linguistically into Central, Eastern and Western regions, each of which has its own distinctive style of gamelan music and dance.

While musicians from different regions work happily together in the music academies, outside them the Javanese and Balinese are not too keen on each other's music. To the Balinese, Javanese music is too soft, too slow and lacking in vitality while the Javanese dismiss Balinese music as harsh, unrefined and too loud.

Java

Javanese Court Gamelan

Central Java

The Mangkunagaran Palace, Surakarta: A cool, gently breeze wafts through the spacious entrance hall. Birds flutter in and out. Inside it is still and peaceful in contrast to all the noise and activity outside. Across the cool expanse of the marble dance floor sit musicians, sipping tea, chatting and smoking clove cigarettes. Two dancers appear wearing long, brightly-coloured sashes and armed with shields and daggers. After a short introductory melody, the dozen or so musicians start playing the richly carved and deeply sonorous instruments of the gamelan "Kyai Kanyut Mesem" whose name means "Swept Away by a Smile". The music is measured and refined. Welcome to the stately, court tradition of Central Java.

The Javanese Gamelan

The largest bronze gamelans in Indonesia are found in **Central Java**. A complete Javanese gamelan is made up of two sets of instruments, one in each of two scales – the five-note *laras slendro* and the seven-note *laras pelog*. The two sets are laid out with the corresponding instruments at right angles to each other. No two gamelans are tuned exactly alike and a Javanese musician will often prefer the sound and feeling of a piece played on one gamelan to another. Gamelans are traditionally given a name, such as 'The Venerable Ambassador of Harmony'.

All the instruments in the gamelan have a clear role to play and this is reflected in the **layout of the ensemble**. Basically, the musical texture is made up of three elements: a central melody played on the metallophones in the middle of the gamelan; an elaboration of the melody, played on the instruments at the front; and slow 'punctuations' by gongs at the back.

The **gong ageng** (large gong) at the back of the gamelan is the most important instrument in the ensemble and it's believed that the spirit of the gamelan resides within it. A large gong can be over one metre in diameter and is made from a single piece of bronze. The skilled gongsmiths of Central Java are highly respected and receive orders from the whole of Java and Bali.

In addition to the large gong, there is an array of **kempul** – smaller hanging gongs – one for each note of the scale in a large gamelan – and horizontally mounted kettle-gongs onomatopoeically named **ketuk** and **kenong**. No piece of music can begin or end without a stroke on one of the larger gongs, while the kenong, ketuk and kempul mark shorter melodic phrases. A Javanese gamelan has more hanging gongs than a Balinese gamelan, giving depth and resonance to the music.

The **metallaphones** are arranged in the centre of the gamelan. They cover a range of four octaves: the lowest pitch is the soft-toned **slenthem**, which has resonating tubes under the keys and is played with a padded mallet. The large **demung** and smaller pair of **saron**, played with hard wooden mallets, cover the middle range while the highest-pitched is the **peking**, or **saron panerus** (small saron), played with a mallet of buffalo horn. These instruments play together the **balungan** or 'melodic skeleton' of a piece. Many Javanese compositions are considered to be derived from vocal melodies, which are not played on any gamelan instruments but are 'sung by the musicians in their hearts.'

The instruments at the front of the gamelan are the most complex in the ensemble. These include a pair of **bonang** (a set of small kettle-gongs mounted in a frame), **gendèr** (metallophone with ten to fourteen keys) **gambang** (wooden xylophone), and **siter** (zither), **rebab** and **suling** (bamboo flute). The bonang, gendèr and rebab are all leading melodic instruments in the gamelan. In the centre of the ensemble is a drummer with a selection of double-headed drums. The full ensemble also includes a **gerong** (male chorus) and **pesindhen** – solo female singers.

Rebab player from Gamelan Sekar Tunjung

Although a large gamelan is co-ordinated to an extent by the drummer, its musicians (who can number as many as thirty) have neither a conductor nor any visual cues, as they all sit facing the same way. Musical notation, although now used extensively in teaching, is never used in performance. Gamelan musicians learn all the instruments and so develop an understanding of the music and flexibility in ensemble playing. During an all-night shadow play, for example, you may see musicians changing places and special guests invited to play. Gamelan is a communal form of music-making – there are no soloists or virtuosos – and although the female singers tend to use microphones they are not considered soloists in the Western sense.

Javan Traditions

Today, nearly 90 percent of Java's population is Muslim. The traditional arts of gamelan music, dance and theatre, however, have their roots in Java's **Hindu-Buddhist** past. Hinduism and Buddhism came from India to Java in the first century AD and were mixed with older Javanese religious beliefs. The temples of **Borobudur** (Buddhist) and **Prambanan** (Hindu) near Yogyakarta are significant monuments from Java's Hindu-Buddhist past. In the fifteenth century, Islam arrived from the north, but before reaching Java, the Islam of the Middle East had mixed with Indian Hinduism, which made it more accessible to the Javanese. The new religion also included Sufi beliefs, which acknowledged the power of music and tolerated musical and artistic expression.

European colonialism was another major influence on Javanese thought and culture, through the Dutch East India Company, established in the early seventeenth century. The Dutch worked closely with the aristocracy in Central Java and European influence stimulated experiments with notation in gamelan circles and a number system called **kepatihan** was developed for recording the music. Gamelan notation did not become widely used, however, until the early twentieth century.

In 1755 the Mataram kingdom of Central Java was divided between the two **royal courts** of **Surakarta** (Solo) and **Yogyakarta**. Two smaller courts soon followed: the **Mangkunagaran** court in Solo and the **Pakualaman** court in Yogyakarta. Under Dutch rule these courts did not have much political power, but the arts of gamelan, dance, literature and *wayang* (shadow plays) flourished. The sultans owned the finest gamelans and employed the best musicians and dancers. Pieces were composed by court composers although credited to the reigning sultan. Rivalry between the courts led to distinctive styles of dance and gamelan-playing. To this day the Solonese are known for the subtlety and refinement of their music and dance while the Yogyanese style is bold and strong in character.

Court Gamelans

Some of the finest gamelans in Java are housed in the courts, including a number of **ceremonial gamelans**. The largest and loudest, known as **gamelan Sekaten**, are still played once a year in the palace mosques of Solo and Yogya. The story goes that these large gamelans were built in the early days of Islam in Java to draw people in to the mosques. To this day a pair of gamelan Sekaten are played almost continuously for a week during the **Sekaten festival**, to commemorate the birth and death of the prophet Mohammed. Their powerful sound draws huge crowds into the mosques, where the calls to prayer mingle with the gamelan music, incense, offerings, and the hubbub of the fair outside.

Within the palace walls gamelan playing is traditionally regarded as a spiritual discipline – a way of reaching enlightenment. The Javanese hero is always in control of his emotions and dispenses with his raging enemies – giants, ogres and demons – with a flick of a dagger. The refined austerity of the court compositions best conveys this sense of calm and contemplative detachment.

Some of the ceremonial gamelans are believed to be magically charged. The gongs are the most sacred instruments, and are given offerings of flowers and incense before performances. These gamelans are only played at special ceremonial occasions, such as Javanese New Year and royal birthdays. In the past, different gamelans were played on different occasions. For outdoor ceremonies loud ensembles in the pelog scale were played in specially-built pavilions. For indoor entertainment an ensemble of gentle, soft-toned instruments in the slendro scale was played. Slendro and pelog sets were kept separate until the eighteenth century, when the combining of the two became increasingly common. The standard modern gamelan has developed from this practice.

The rise of Indonesian nationalism in the early twentieth century challenged both the Dutch colonialists and the Javanese aristocracy. Following independence, under President Sukarno, in 1945 academies of performing arts were set up to train new generations of musicians, dancers and puppeteers, away from the royal courts. Some academies, however, remained closely linked to the courts: in Solo the original campus of the academy was within the palace walls. Concepts of Western classical music and performance greatly influenced the early directors of the academies, who introduced exams, recitals and concert performances.

Gamelan Performances

Gamelan music is today played by a wide range of people in Central Java. Most village halls and neighbourhoods in major towns have a gamelan for use by the local community. The majority of schoolchildren learn basic gamelan pieces and can continue their studies in conservatories and academies of performing arts in the major towns of Solo and Yogyakarta. Radio Republik Indonesia employs professional studio musicians and broadcasts a wide range of gamelan music – live late-night sessions from the palaces, dance-dramas, shadow plays, and light-hearted listeners' request programmes, to name but a few.

The repertoire and instrumentation of gamelan music is astonishingly versatile. A piece which is normally played on a bronze gamelan, such as the well-known "**Gambirsawit**", may also be arranged for a small group of zithers and vocalists

(a *siteran* ensemble). When played on a gamelan, the piece known as "Gambirsawit" could accompany a dance or part of a shadow-play, or simply be enjoyed by a group rehearsing on the village gamelan. It can be played in either slendro or pelog, on a full gamelan with vocalists, or on a small *gadhon* ensemble of soft-toned instruments. Many other Javanese pieces can be played in a number of different ways: this is the essence of the gamelan tradition.

Dance and Shadow Plays

In Java, gamelan music is inseparable from the arts of **poetry**, **dance** and **drama**. There is a large repertoire of sung poetry – **tembang** – and a number of poetic texts used by both male chorus and female singers. Dances accompanied by gamelan music range from the elegant and refined palace *srimpi* dance, solo or duet 'showpiece' dances, to lively village dances (*tayuban*), though over the years there's been a fair bit of interchange between the two. **Dance-dramas** (*wayang orang*) and **shadow plays** (*wayang kulit*) are always accompanied by gamelan music.

The all-night **wayang kulit** is one of the most popular forms of theatre in Java. A large screen is illuminated by a single lamp so the shadow puppets are silhouetted on the screen. The puppeteer

Gamelan Orchestra in Central Javanese village

(*dalang*) sits beneath the lamp with the gamelan behind him, and an array of intricately carved and painted leather puppets carefully arranged on his right and left. From an early age children learn to recognise the wayang characters by the shape of the head-dress and the size of the eyes, nose and body of the puppets. Javanese dance movements have been heavily influenced by the movements of these two-dimensional puppets. A wayang performance is very much a social occasion. Invited guests sit on the puppeteer's side of the screen where they can see him at work, and are served food and drink throughout the night. Uninvited guests sit on the shadow side of the screen or squeeze in to see the clowns and battle scenes at 2 or 3am. During the night people eat, drink, chat and fall asleep. Often the gamelan players fall asleep too!

Originally associated with ancestor worship in the pre-Hindu era, the wayang later adapted stories from the Hindu epics Ramayana and Mahabharata, which have formed the basis of Javanese (and other southeast Asian) dance and drama for nearly a thousand years. Gamelan music is an integral and varied part of the performance, providing gentle accompaniment for narrative and dialogue, loud vigorous pieces to accompany battle scenes, lively songs for the clowns and longer compositions to introduce important sections of the drama. The musicians take their cues from the puppeteer and the gamelan players have to respond quickly and accurately to the puppeteer's signals.

There's a localised gamelan tradition in the Betawi area of northwest Java around Jakarta. This is called **Ajeng** and is generally used for **wayang kulit Betawi** (shadow-puppet theatre performed in the Betawi dialect). The gamelan itself is similar in style to the Central Javanese form, but in place of the soft rebab as melodic leader, the Ajeng has what's called a **tarompet**. It is not in fact a trumpet, but a piercing shawn or oboe which gives a distinctive sound.

Gamelan music is a vital part of important **ceremonial occasions** – there is an old Javanese saying: "It's not official until the gong is hung". No wedding ceremony is complete without gamelan music – although nowadays it is often from a cassette recorder rather than a live ensemble. Significant moments in the wedding ceremony are accompanied by specific pieces, and at the reception special 'opening' and 'closing' pieces are

played, many of which were originally composed for the arrival and departure of the sultan at palace ceremonies. The opening notes of a 'leaving' piece are all that most people know as they will get up to leave as soon as they hear them! There are also a few pieces believed to release magical power when played, to ward off evil spirits.

In Central Java there are frequent **street performances** by **siteran groups**, made up of zithers, vocals, a drum and a large end-blown bamboo tube used as a gong. Unlike the large bronze gamelans these instruments are cheap, portable and often home-made. The music is usually drawn from the gamelan repertoire and, with as few as four or five musicians, the ensemble recreates with astonishing resourcefulness the musical texture of the gamelan. In the quieter residential streets a lone siter player may perform in the evening, accompanying traditional songs on an instrument he made himself.

JENNY HEATON

Siter player, Surakarta, Java

Gamelan in Java Today

Life is changing rapidly in Java. For much of the youth population, the gamelan represents the values of the past and is rejected in favour of Western or Indonesian pop (for more on which, see the following article). In the towns and cities short, two-hour shadow plays are becoming popular in place of the all-night variety. Older puppeteers complain that their young pupils no longer understand the spiritual teachings and philosophy of the wayang.

But for many people the gamelan tradition is alive and well. In **Solo** and **Yogya**, musicmaking

Java's Bamboo Gamelan

The western end of Central Java, traditionally known as **Banyumas**, with its economic centre in the city of Purwokerto, boasts its own very special performing traditions. Central Javanese gamelan music is prominent and the area's indigenous and distinct brand of wayang kulit synthesises elements from both Yogyanese and Solonese gamelan styles. However, it is the **calung** (bamboo ensemble), that is most closely associated with the region.

The word calung means in Javanese 'hitting to make a sound'. The instruments, lightweight and portable, mimic those of the gamelan, and, indeed, were originally devised as a substitute in areas where bronze instruments were unavailable. Each instrument is constructed from a number of bamboo tubes split lengthways and suspended over a wooden frame. Even the largest of the gongs (gong ageng) is imitated; the player blows a raspberry down a large bamboo tube and produces the gong's characteristic vibrations through gentle oscillation of the air pressure.

The traditional drumming for this ensemble is found only in Banyumas and uses a small *kendang ciblon* (used in Central Java to accompany dance) in conjunction with a smaller drum known as a *kendang ketipung* or *kuluntar*. The resulting patterns are extremely dynamic and more clearly repetitive than elsewhere. Influences from Sunda are strong and some of the best performers now use the Sundanese set-up of three drums, the largest being placed on the floor at an angle to enable the player to change the pitch with his foot.

This difference in drumming style derives partly from the use of calung as accompaniment to the folk dance known as **lengger**. Nowadays performed by women, lengger is thought to have originated from dances associated with fertility rituals. Like others of its type, for instance tayuban in Central and East Java, the dance has also been connected with prostitution. Remnants of this past are still evident in the sensual movements of the dancers and their flirtatious facial expressions.

Despite its relation to gamelan, the sound of the calung is quite unlike anything else and a world away from the gentle textures and delicate refinement of Central Javanese court traditions. The timbre of the bamboo is sharp and clipped and its short sustaining power is overcome through repetition and interlocking of instrumental parts. The overwhelming spirit of the music is one of boisterous humour, a joyful zest for life, and a refreshing openness and directness of expression.

---

continues to play a role in community life. The local gamelan contest at the radio station in Solo draws a huge number of enthusiastic gamelan groups from the town and surrounding area every year. Men and women generally play in separate groups, with the exception of the pesindhen, female singers. Some of the larger batik shops have a gamelan upstairs for the employees to play after work and a number of schools have their own gamelan.

In the twentieth century **gamelan composers** have become less anonymous. **K.R.T. Wasitodiningrat**, director of the Yogya court gamelan, had one of his pieces sent up with the Voyager spacecraft amongst the samples of earthly music. Also in Yogya the music and dance of **Bagong Kussudiardja** is well known and his fame as composer and choreographer has spread throughout Indonesia. And many groups enjoy playing popular pieces and lively arrangements of older pieces by the late **Ki Nartosabdho**, a greatly respected musician and puppeteer.

Much artistic experimentation, innovation and exchange is going on in the **academies**. Musicians and dancers from different regions of Java, Bali and Sumatra work together on new choreography, storytelling and puppetry, as well as new musical sounds, styles and techniques. Western composers work with Indonesian composers and musicians, some of whom come abroad to study, teach and collaborate with Western musicians, and a number of composers are writing for both gamelan ensembles and Western instruments.

West Java: Sunda

The island of Java is inhabited by several ethnic groups. The Javanese live mainly in Central and East Java, while the main inhabitants of West Java, or Sunda, are the **Sundanese**. The chief Sundanese gamelan style, **degung**, is well known, but there are other styles that have rarely been recorded.

The northern coastal plain of West Java is flat and hot, with the capital city, **Jakarta**, densely populated and full of urban squalor. The contrast with the highlands of the **Priangan** (Abode of the Gods) or **Tanah Sunda** (Sunda Lands) could not be more dramatic. This mountainous plateau covers the central and southern parts of West Java – an area of lush green valleys and high volcanic peaks. It is also the heartland of the Sundanese people, the second largest ethnic group in Indonesia, who are culturally and linguistically quite distinct from the Javanese of Central and East Java. **Bandung**, also known as *kota kembang* (city of flowers), is the area's principal city, cultural centre and home to many of Sunda's finest musicians.

Sundanese performing arts and musical traditions are more obviously diverse than those of Central Java and have developed into three main branches: **gamelan Degung**, **gamelan Salendro** and **tembang Sunda**.

Gamelan Degung

The sound of **degung** is perhaps the most accessible gamelan music to Western ears. Its musical structures are clear and well-defined, and the timbres of the instruments blend delicately with one another without losing any of their integrity or individuality. The ensemble is small, consisting only of a few instruments, but includes the usual range of gongs and metallophones. However, the very special character of degung, which uses its own five-note version of the pelog scale found in Java, owes much to the additional presence of the **suling** (bamboo flute), which is regarded as a signature for Sundanese music. In fact, no other instrument more perfectly exemplifies the musical heart of Sunda or better conjures up its gentle, picturesque rice paddies and village life.

Degung is unique to Sunda and was developed during the last century in the courts of the Bupadi (local rulers under Dutch control). Deriving from a court tradition, it has a more exalted place among the performing arts than gamelan Salendro (see below) – although the best musicians frequent the circles of both – and is now mainly used in concert form for wedding receptions and other social events. Nevertheless, examples of degung for **tari topeng** (masked dances) exist, and, more recently, augmented forms of the ensemble have been used to accompany performances of **wayang golek** (three-dimensional rod puppets). In addition, it has made inroads into popular culture through 'pop-Sunda' (using Western pop instruments) which achieved immense popularity during the 1980s through the hands of composers such as **Nano S** (see Indonesian pop article).

Gamelan Salendro

Nowadays, **gamelan Salendro** is used primarily to accompany performances of **wayang golek** – classical dance – as well as the more recent social dance, **jaipongan** (see Indonesian pop article).

Compared to gamelan Degung and tembang Sunda, it has a lowly, unaristocratic status. Wayang golek is considered less refined than its Javanese counterpart, wayang kulit (shadow puppets), and the raucous and rowdy atmosphere that pervades performances, together with its emphasis on comedy and references to bodily functions, would seem to confirm this. Nonetheless, gamelan Salendro has much to offer; often energetic and exciting, lyrical and expressive, it can display a technical brilliance and virtuosity rarely heard in Central Java.

Of great importance to contemporary gamelan performance in Sunda is the **juru kawih**, the female vocalist. As elsewhere in Java, singing has become increasingly important during the twentieth century, and in popular genres such as jaipongan becomes the main focus of interest. In addition, there is the male **juru alok**, who sings during the interludes between verses and contributes cries, shrieks and yelps as appropriate.

The instruments of a Sundanese gamelan Salendro resemble those of a small Central Javanese gamelan. Much of the music's expressive character is conveyed, not just by the juru kawih, but also by the **rebab** (a two-stringed spiked fiddle, similar in construction to its Javanese counterpart) and particularly the **kendang** (a set of three drums of varying sizes). These instruments play with a degree of crispness and clarity not generally associated with the classical traditions from Central Java. The drums, played by a single player, are unique to Sunda, with the largest of the three placed at 45° to the floor. This enables the player to change the pitch of the drumhead with his foot and obtain a 'talking drum' effect.

Tembang Sunda

Although related, **tembang Sunda** is, strictly speaking, not a gamelan genre at all. It was developed at the Kabupaten (Regent's court) of Cianjur, a town between Bandung and Jakarta, during the colonial era, and consists of sung poetry – both female and male vocalists are used – accompanied by one or two *kecapi* (zithers) together with a suling or a rebab.

Spreading from its point of origin, where it was known as *mamaos* (singing), it is now referred to as *cianjuran* or tembang Sunda (the word *tembang* is used throughout Java to denote vocal genres). The original style consists of songs sung in free rhythm, but a more recent development, *panambih*, is metrical and consists of songs that may derive from either gamelan Salendro or gamelan Degung repertoire. Pieces can be in one of several tuning systems.

Although often used today to enhance the atmosphere of foyers in Bandung's more exclusive hotels, tembang Sunda is suited to a more intimate setting. Perhaps played in the home, late at night, and often for the sole benefit of the performers themselves, the depth of poetic expression portrayed in the music has the ability to transport both performer and listener alike far away from the hustle and bustle of everyday life.

The vocal quality of **Sundanese singing**, particularly striking in tembang Sunda, is one of the more unusual features of music from this region. Beautiful and haunting, it is quite unlike Javanese vocal music and not only compliments the nuances of the spoken language but also enhances its emotional and expressive power. Once heard it is never forgotten.

A related instrumental form, **kecapi suling**, with the suling taking the place of the voice, has become extremely popular in the cassette industry during recent years. It is lighter in mood than the vocal genre and allows the suling greater freedom to improvise.

East Java

The performance traditions of West and Central Java are now well represented in the West on CD and cassette. The same cannot yet be said of those from the province of **East Java**. This is a pity as the region has a rich diversity of performing arts.

The variety stems, in part, from the greater number of ethnic groups living in the region, including **Javanese**, **Madurese** (from the island of Madura), **Osinger** from the town of Banyuwangi, and **Tenggerese** who live in the Tengger mountains. Each of these groups has its own performing traditions, and while all have some relationship to the classical gamelan traditions of Central Java, or in the case of the Osinger, Bali, they represent fascinating art forms in their own right. Javanese-gamelan are found throughout the region, but as one travels progressively eastwards, the prevailing musical style becomes marked by increasing dynamism and aggressiveness.

Gamyak Drums

Perhaps the most dramatic element of East Javanese gamelan music, and certainly one not found outside the region, is that of the **gamyak drum**. Larger than the Central Javanese equivalent, its drumheads are made from buffalo rather than goat skin, and the piercingly-sharp sound produced is immediately recognisable. It is especially associated with the ngremo dance – the drumming for which is considered some of the most technically demanding anywhere in Java – and various forms of tari topeng (masked dance) popular around Malang.

In addition, **tayuban** – dances where male spectators may request pieces from the gamelan and, for a small gratuity, have the pleasure of dancing with one of the tandhak (female dancers) present – have helped steer the popular gamelan repertoire away from the classical refinement associated with Central Java. Once common throughout Java, these are rowdy affairs and only continue to exist in areas where Islam has a limited influence on daily life. As a consequence it is still popular in the **Tengger region** where the prevailing religion synthesises elements of Hinduism with pre-Hindu beliefs.

Madura

Gamelan music from the island of **Madura** is, in some respects, closer to the traditions of mainland Central Java. In previous centuries bloodlines were established between the royal palace of **Sumenep** (the main town on the island) and the courts of Surakarta, and this relationship is reflected in the performing arts. Nevertheless, the peculiar roughness of expression found elsewhere in East Java is still evident. Of particular note is the **topeng dalang**, unique to Madura, where the great Indian epics of the Mahabharata and Ramayana, as well as the Javanese story of Panji, are recounted by a single storyteller (dalang) with the action being recreated by a company of masked actors and dancers.

Osinger

The **Osinger** of **Banyuwangi** represent yet another branch of East Javanese music and dance with the two main forms, gandrung and angklung, displaying influences from neighbouring Bali (Banyuwangi is the departure point for the ferry crossing from Java to Bali).

Gandrung is performed by professional musicians at all-night social events (weddings, circumcisions, and so on) and consists of a small group of instrumentalists (two violins, drums, a triangle, gongs and gong-chimes) together with a female singer-dancer (the gandrung).

Angklung, played by young boys through amateur organisations which perform at local carnivals and competitions, are bamboo xylophones and can be combined with a selection of iron gamelan instruments (metallophones and gongs) in the gamelan **bali-balian**. This ensemble, truly reminiscent of gamelan in Bali, is commonly used for *angklung caruk*, in which two such ensembles compete to outdo each other with displays of skill and virtuosity.

Bali

A Balinese temple, late evening: In the main courtyard a hundred men sit in circles, only the sound of crickets breaking the silence. Suddenly, with several short cries the men rise up, then sink down again, making a hissing sound. A single short shout follows and the men break into a rhythmic chant, "*Uchak-a-chak-a-chak . . .* ", swaying from side to side, hands waving in the air. A solitary voice rises above the rhythmic chattering of the chorus, singing a quivering, wailing melody. Another short cry and the men sink down again. This is the famed Balinese **kecak** or monkey-chant.

In the kecak, the chorus of men imitates the chattering and jabbering of the monkeys (there are several monkey forests in Bali), while the complex rhythms are taken from the gamelan. The Balinese love to take something from elsewhere and incorporate it into their art. In the stone temple carvings of north Bali, among the ornate mythical beasts and flowers there may be a Dutchman in colonial uniform on a bicycle, or in the middle of a traditional painting by a young artist you may find a car. In a similar way, the kecak was adopted this century from an ancient trance dance into a drama using the **Hindu Ramayana** story. The chorus represents the monkey army helping King Rama rescue his queen, Sinta, from Rahwana, the ogre-king.

The kecak is performed as a spectacle rather than ceremony and new versions are commissioned for festivals and TV. However, much of Bali's abundant music, dance and theatre continues to play an essential role in the elaborate temple ceremonies central to life on the island.

Hindu Bali

In the late fifteenth century the Hindu-Javanese Majapahit Empire fell to Muslim rulers and many of the Javanese princes fled eastwards across the narrow strait to Bali, taking with them their priests, dancers and musicians. To this day the Balinese practise their own **Hindu-Balinese religion**, a unique blend of Hinduism and traditional Balinese beliefs.

The village temple is at the heart of Balinese life and culture. Hardly a week passes without several **temple festivals** happening all over the island. Important island-wide festivals, such as **Galungan**, which comes once every 210 days (a Balinese year), call for ten days of prayer and festivities. At Galungan the spirits of the ancestors visit the island and they must be greeted with offerings, prayers, music and dance.

In the larger villages all the different gamelans are brought out for Galungan. The four-note **gamelan Angklung** (commonly associated with temple festivals) is played by the older boys of the village, as part of the long procession of women bringing the family offerings to the temple. Further down there are the clashing cymbals of the

JENNY HEATON

Gamelan Angklung Procession in Bali

processional **gamelan Bebonangan**. Within the open-air temple itself several different gamelans are played all at once in separate pavilions. Only the gods and spirits are listening. Like the carefully arranged fruit and rice, like the flowers and incense, the music is an offering.

Later on, though, in the cool air of early evening, crowds will gather to watch a dance drama – perhaps the brilliant *Baris* **dance** with lightening movements representing a warrior, or the *Barong* dance, symbolic of the eternal conflict of good and evil, in which the dragon Barong battles with Rangda, the witch. There might also be **gambuh** theatre, an ancient form accompanied not by tuned bronze, but by deep flutes and percussion. This **gamelan Gambuh** is described in one of the earliest accounts of Balinese music and is thought to have preceded the ensembles of tuned percussion. The evening might end with a night time performance of wayang kulit, accompanied by the intricate music of a quartet of **gendèr wayang**.

Most villages in Bali boast several gamelans owned by the local music club. The club members, all men, meet there in the evenings to rehearse. They are almost all amateurs, earning their living as farmers, craftsmen or civil servants. Gamelan playing is considered a part of every man's education, as important as the art of rice growing or cooking ceremonial food.

The **village gamelan** is kept in a public place and rehearsals usually draw an interested audience of onlookers who offer comments and suggestions. Many villages have a distinctive style or speciality: Peliatan is known for the refinement of its courtly *legong* dance and music, Sukawati for the complexity and brilliance of its *gendèr* playing. It's said that people can find their way around the island in the dark by recognising the distinctive tones of the local gamelans shimmering across the ricefields in the night air.

Kebyar – the New Style

When the Dutch took control of Bali in the early twentieth century the island's courts all but disappeared. Many royal families decided to sacrifice themselves in the cannon-fire rather than submit to Dutch rule. This had an enormous impact on the musical life of the island. The court gamelans had no function outside the palace walls and were sold or taken to the villages where they were melted down to make new gamelans for the latest style that was taking Bali by storm: **kebyar** – a word that means 'like the bursting open of a flower'.

Kebyar replaced the slow, stately court pieces with a fast, dynamic music, full of dramatic contrasts, changes of tempo and sudden loud outbursts. It was not long before Bali's most famous dancer, **I Mario**, choreographed the first kebyar dance, in which the intricate and beautiful movements of the dancer's eyes, head and hands mirror the dazzling display of the music. This dynamic virtuoso style makes much Balinese gamelan music today sound utterly different from the Javanese.

While the new kebyar style swept across the island, the poorer villages in western Bali could not afford expensive bronze metallaphones and so created 'copies' of traditional gamelans, replacing metal keys with bamboo. These instruments were (and are) made from a series of bamboo tubes on a simple frame, often including a double 'gong' made of two lengths of bamboo suspended over a large earthenware jar, which produces a deep gong-like sound.

Bamboo ensembles include the stunning **gamelan Jegog**, in which the longest bamboo tubes may be up to three metres long. The instruments are tuned to a four-note scale and are struck with thick rubber beaters. Players sit astride the largest instrument, the **jegogan**, which sounds a deep sonorous melody beneath the interlocking patterns of the other instruments. The sound is enormously powerful, especially when two or more groups play against one another in one of the ever-popular regional competitions! Another popular ensemble is the **joged Bumbung** ('bumbung' means bamboo). This style was born in the 1950s in west Bali and was based on the **joged**, an old flirtatious dance where the female dancers invite men from the audience to take turns dancing with them.

The older **court ensembles** still remaining in Bali sound closer in style to Javanese gamelan; slower, and without the sudden changes of tempo, texture and dynamics which are so characteristic of kebyar. There's the stately ceremonial **Gamelan Gong Gedé** from the mountain temple of Bator. And there's the sensuous and delicate **Gamelan Semar Pegulingan** (Gamelan of the Love God). The semar pegulingan includes bamboo flutes and a pair of gendèrs, played with hard mallets. Originally played near the sleeping chambers in the palace, this beautiful ensemble is now often played for the legong dance.

Sacred gamelans in Bali include the **gamelan Gambang**, frequently played for cremations, with wooden xylophones bringing a more brittle sound, and the ethereal **gamelan Selunding** from the village of Tenganan in east Bali. Although the keys of the latter are made from iron slabs, the sound

Balinese dancers with gamelan, 1941

is sweet and pure. It is thought to be the oldest type of gamelan on the island, possibly pre-Hindu, and is reserved only for ritual occasions.

Balinese Rhythms

Where Javanese music is contemplative and restrained, Balinese is loud and extrovert. It is, after all, outdoor music. Like the elaborate temple carvings and paintings, the music is intricately detailed. Just as the harmony of village life depends on the delicate balance of opposing forces of good and evil, night and day, so in the gamelan the instruments appear in pairs, even the drums, which are called male and female.

The rhythmic vitality of Balinese music comes from interlocking patterns played on the pairs of instruments. These patterns, or **kotekan**, are played on bronze *gangsas* (similar to the Javanese gendèr but struck with hard wooden mallets), a pair of drums and the *reong* (a row of small kettle-gongs, played by four people). Apart from the rhythm, there's another kind of beat in Balinese gamelan music. The pairs of instruments are tuned slightly 'out' with each other, so that when two instruments are played together, there is a 'harmonic beating'. This gives the sound of the Balinese gamelan its characteristic shimmering quality.

The Canadian composer **Colin McPhee**, who lived and studied in Bali in the 1930s, writes in his

delightful book *A House in Bali* of the stir his Steinway grand caused in the village where he lived for ten years. When he played a waltz his Balinese friends were dismayed. "Where's the beat?" they asked, "There's no beat! Like a bird with a broken wing!" **Benjamin Britten**, who was introduced to Balinese music by McPhee, was captivated by the music he heard on a visit in 1956, finding it "fantastically rich melodically, rhythmically, texturally (such orchestration!!) and above all formally." In his ballet score, *The Prince of the Pagodas*, Britten created a small, Western 'gamelan' from the percussion section of the orchestra, which plays a version of "Kapi Raja", a well-known Balinese piece.

The island has changed a lot since the 1950s, of course. Bali is Indonesia's prime tourist attraction and draws around a million people each year (more than a third of Bali's population). The roads buzz with motorbikes, *bemos* (local transport) and huge tourist buses. But the arts continue to flourish and grow, the traditional temple festivals go on and more modern festivals, such as the annual **Bali Arts Festival** in Denpasar (mid-June to mid-July), have become an important feature of cultural life on the island. On any night of the week, if you're lucky you can hear a number of different gamelans in a temple, a festival, at a wedding, a tooth-filing ceremony or a cremation. Go there – and keep your ears open!

There is no better way of experiencing gamelan than to visit Java or Bali and seek out performances. There are plenty of opportunities, including temple performances.

JAVA

Surakarta (Solo)

There are regular **live RRI broadcasts** of gamelan music from the two palaces: the **Kraton Hadiningrat** and the **Mangkunagaran**. Listeners are welcome and this is a great opportunity to see the palace gamelans being played. Broadcasts take place at lunchtimes and late evenings (10pm–midnight). Dates are determined by the 35-day month of the Javanese calendar. Go to the RRI and check the noticeboard for details of all live broadcasts.

STSI (Sekolah Tinggi Seni Indonesia), the 'High School (or academy) of Indonesian Arts', is a bus-ride from the centre of town. Exam recitals and performances take place at the end of each semester. There are all-night **wayang performances** each month at **Taman Budaya Surakarta** (on the campus of STSI) and the **RRI**.

Dance rehearsals take place at the Mangkungaran every Wednesday morning.

Nightly **wayang orang** (dance-drama) performances take place at the **Sriwedari Amusement Park** and there are regular tourist performances at the larger hotels, such as **Hotel Kusuma Sahid**.

Yogyakarta (Yogya)

There is lots going on in Yogya: much of it is geared to the large number of tourists who visit the town each year, so if you're not staying long you'll find performances more easily than in Solo.

Daily gamelan and dance performances for tourists are held at the **Kraton**, and nightly 2-hr wayang performances at the **Agastiya Institute**. Other Central venues include the **Kepatihan**, **Taman Budaya**, and **Pujukusuman**, the dance school where the late Romo Sas (one of Yogya's top dance teachers) taught until recently. A live RRI broadcast takes place at the **Pura Pukualaman** each month.

There are also regular tourist performances of dance and gamelan in the hotels; the performers are often students from **ISI** (Institut Seni Indonesia), the Institute of Indonesian Arts.

Further out of town are the **Lembaga Studi Jawa**, a foundation set up recently for the study and performance of Javanese arts; **Bagong Kussiardja's** dance foundation, where you may be able to watch rehearsals; and **ISI**, where exam recitals and performances of new dance and gamelan music are held. Performances of the **Ramayana** ballet are held regularly at **Prambanan Temple** (outside Yogya) – pricey but worth seeing.

Festivals

Annual festivals to look out for in Java are the **Festival Kesenian Yogyakarta** (gamelan, dance and wayang), the **International Gamelan Festival** (includes new compositions and groups from abroad), and the **Sekaten** and **Kraton festivals**. Sekaten is held each year in both Solo and Yogya.

BALI

There is always lots going on in Bali – the easiest performances to find are those arranged for tourists; the more interesting ones take a bit more searching for, and the most memorable occasions will be the ones you come across unexpectedly. The best way to find out what's happening where is to go to the Tourist

Bali's Heavenly Orchestra

CMP RECORDS

Board in Denpasar, buy a Balinese calendar, and get a list of the major **odalans** (village temple ceremonies). The major temple festivals **Galungan** and **Kuningan** are held every 210 days. Odalans are held more frequently.

There is always lots of gamelan and dance in **Ubud**, **Peliatan** and **Teges**. Other places to visit if you have more time are **Sabah** (on the coast, there is a legong troupe), **Sukawati** (gendèr wayang), **Batur** (gong gedé) and the villages of **Sawan** and **Jagaraga** in North Bali.

In **Denpasar**, the **Bali Arts Festival** is held in July/August each year, and performances are held at STSI throughout the year.

INDONESIA

discography

Java

Banyumas Bamboo Gamelan (Nimbus, UK).

The only widely available recording of Banyumas calung music, the Javanese bamboo gamelan. Traditional dance pieces with vocals and some more contemporary styles drawing on jaipongan and dangdut. Great frog imitations on track 3.

Chamber Music of Central Java (King, Japan).

One of the few discs of Javanese gamelan that isn't a large court ensemble. This is a chamber gadhon gamelan of soft-toned instruments without the big line up of gongs played by top musicians from Solo. More intimate instrumental music.

Gamelan of the Kraton, Yogyakarta (Celestial Harmonies, US).

The most atmospheric and beautifully recorded of Javanese gamelan discs. This royal gamelan is one of the cultural and historical glories of the island. Here the court musicians play grandiose ceremonial pieces, elegant dance repertoire and the extraordinary music, peculiar to the Yogya kraton, of the bedhaya dance with added snare drums and brass.

Gamelan of Surakarta (JVC, Japan).

This is the best introduction available to the Surakarta style of Javanese gamelan. Three pieces played by the Surakarta School of Indonesian Arts (STSI) from serene music with choral singing to dynamic and varied instrumental playing co-ordinated by the virtuoso drumming of Rahayu Supanggah, the composer. The final piece, composed to accompany traditional dance drama, reveals a developing tradition.

Indonesia: Madura, Musique savante (Ocora, France).

This disc gives a rare opportunity to listen to the unique and dynamic gamelan traditions from the island of Madura as well as extracts from a performance of topeng dalang. It features master dalang Sabidin, descended from several generations of a storytelling family.

Javanese Court Gamelan (Nonesuch Explorer, US).

Gamelan of the Paku Alaman palace in Yogyakarta. Recorded in the early 1970s, this highly atmospheric CD has a timeless quality. A varied choice of pieces played on a celestial traditional gamelan set within the audible ambience of an open-air pavilion, complete with bird song!

Java: Palais Royal de Yogyakarta Vol 2 Instrumental Music (Ocora, France).

This is the second volume of four recorded in the Yogyakarta palace. As many of the other discs selected here include vocals, this is a good choice if you want gamelan alone. The other volumes can also be recommended, particularly Vol 4 Concert Music.

Shadow Music of Java (Rounder, US).

An excellent presentation of the kind of music heard at wayang shadow puppet performances with different styles for different parts of the show. Edited from a two-hour wayang given by Widiyanto S Putro (dalang) and the Hardo Budoyo gamelan from Wonogiri in Central Java while on tour in the US. One of the few CDs on the market showing Javanese gamelan music as it is most commonly heard today.

Sunda

Classical Tembang Sunda (Celestial Harmonies, US).

Singer Ida Widwati and her group from Bandung in tembang Sunda swing (solo and choral styles) accompanied by a pair of Sundanese kecapi (zither) and suling (bamboo flute). The pieces selected give a good indication of the range of poetic expression and nuance in this music. Translations included.

Flutes and Gamelan Music of West Java (Topic Records, UK).

A rare glimpse of gamelan music from Cirebon, a city on the north coast of West Java, as well as a selection of kecapi suling. It features Sulaeman, a player of the Sundanese suling with a recording career stretching back to the days of 78s.

Gamelang Degung (Pan, Netherlands).

Traditional degung music is beautiful and compulsive. This disc features the famous Jugala orchestra with Euis Komariah and Ida Widawati.

Java – Pays Sunda, 2: L'art du Gamelan Degung (Ocora, France).

One of the definitive recordings of gamelan Degung currently available in the West containing a fine representation of pieces from the classical repertoire as well as new compositions. Features the bamboo flute playing of Ono Sukarna.

Tembang Sunda (Nimbus, UK).

Mellow performances from male and female vocalists, Imas Permas and Asep Kosasih accompanied by zither and flute. Refined classical repertoire and more easy-going love songs. Translations included.

Bali and Lombok

Anthology of the Music of Bali (Buda/Musique du Monde, France).

This set of four double CDs, available separately, contains some of the best recordings of the various Balinese gamelan styles with excellent notes and photos. Vol 1 (*Popular Traditions*) features vocal music, Jegog and other bamboo styles. Vol 2, (*Virtuoso Gamelan*) features Kebyar, Suling and Anglung. Vol 3 (*Ritual Music*) features the archaic forms, Selonding, Gambang, Gong Gedé and others. Vol 4 (*Classical Traditions*) includes Gambuh and music for dance and puppet performances.

Bali: A Suite of Tropical Music and Sound (World Network, Germany).

Volume 35 in World Network's ambitious global survey, this is an ideal introduction to the varied sounds of Balinese music, beginning with frogs and cicadas. Includes many of the lesser-known gamelan styles – gambuh, selunding, jegog, joged bumbung, plus kecak etc. The only thing missing is the straight kebyar sound, but there's plenty of that to be found elsewhere.

Bali: Musique pour le Gong Gédé (Ocora, France).

The gong gédé of the Batur temple, dating back to the fifteenth century, the oldest in Bali and a more recent ensemble in Tampaksiring. Ceremonial music of the old, pre-kebyar style. Softer and more stately than most other Balinese gamelan music.

The Bali Sessions: Living Art, Sounding Spirit (Rykodisc, US).

A well-packaged and documented 3 CD set that highlights some of the lesser-known areas of Balinese music. Disc 1 ranges through the ancient gamelan Selonding, gong Suling (featuring flutes), gamelan Genggong (with Jew's harps) and the bamboo gamelan Jegog. Disc 2 features gamelan Joged Bumbung and an epic kecak performance, and Disc 3 new compositions for traditional ensembles.

◉ Gamelan Batel Wayang Ramayana and Gender Wayang Pemarwan (CMP/Silva Screen, UK).

The first listed is a lovely recording of Balinese theatrical music for a wayang performance of the Ramayana. A quartet of gendèr plus drums and flute recorded in a temple pavilion in the village of Sading. The second is a beautiful recording of music for a wayang Mahabharata on four gendèr.

◉ Gamelan Gong Kebyar – Vols 1–3 (JVC, Japan).

Volume 3 of this series is the best introduction to the kebyar style from the gamelan of Tejakula in northern Bali, noted for its large ensemble of instruments. Bold and glittering with strong percussion and drums, the CD notes say "This disc should be played at maximum volume to appreciate the essence of this ensemble's music to the full." Volume 2 features the smaller gamelan of the Academy of Art and Dance in Denpasar in contrasting kebyar and gambuh pieces.

◉ Gamelan Gong Kebyar (King, Japan).

Three pieces of contemporary Balinese kebyar music, including a Baris dance, performed by the Eka Cita gamelan in Denpasar district.

◉ Gamelan Semar Pegulingan Saih Pitu: The Heavenly Orchestra of Bali (CMP/Silva Screen, UK).

The 'love gamelan', a sort of gamelan 'hump-tape'; the ethereal, tinkly sound of this sort of ensemble accompanied the king while he slept with the queen. Gamelan, flutes and drums in a lovely clear recording of a 29-strong ensemble from Kamasan, eastern Bali.

◉ Gamelan Semar Pegulingan (II) (JVC, Japan).

Semar Pegulingan group from Peliatan village. Another exquisite recording without the bamboo flutes but with atmospheric insects in the background.

◉ Jegog: Gamelan Jegog Wardi Santana (CMP/Silva Screen, UK).

Top-quality bamboo gamelan recording with deep booming bass notes.

◉ Jegog of Nagara (King, Japan).

The best jegog disc around. Thunderous sound, lots of atmos and the competing of two groups from west Bali. Turn it up loud and enjoy the thrill.

◉ Lombok, Kalimantan, Banyumas: Little-known Forms of Gamelan and Wayang (Smithsonian Folkways, US).

Part fourteen of SF's extensive survey of Indonesian music features wayang sasak from Lombok, a theatrical form related to Balinese gambuh; masked and shadow theatre music from South Kalimantan (Borneo); and Jemblung from Banyumas which comprises amazing vocal imitations of gamelan!

◉ Music for the Gods (Rykodisc, US).

Recordings made (mostly in Bali) in 1941 by Bruce and Sheridan Fahnestock weeks before World War II and subsequent tourism changed the island forever. The story of the expedition and survival of this material is incredible. These unique recordings include Semar Pegulingan, kebyar, a gendèr quartet for wayang and kecak plus three tracks of fascinating stuff from the island of Madura.

◉ The Roots of Gamelan (World Arbiter, US).

It was these 1928 recordings which inspired Canadian composer Colin McPhee to settle in Bali. Represented here by the piece "Kebyar Ding", the Balinese consider the once-forgotten Gong Kebyar style so historically important that in 1975 they reconstructed it from this very recording. A fascinating document featuring several gamelan styles plus recordings of McPhee's gamelan transcriptions for two pianos played by McPhee and Benjamin Britten in 1941.

New Gamelan Music

◉ American Works for Balinese Gamelan Orchestra (New World Records, US).

Music by three American composers following in the footsteps of Colin McPhee: Evan Ziporyn, Wayne Vitale and Michael Tenzer, author of a great book on Balinese music. Played by Californian Balinese gamelan Sekar Jaya plus assorted Western instruments from saxophone to violin and mandolin.

◉ Asmat Dream (Lyrichord, US).

One for gamelan or new music specialists perhaps, but ample illustration of the radical experiments underway with gamelan and other traditional instruments. Includes music by four Sundanese composers including Nano S. There are two other volumes in this series Vol 2 Mana 689 features composers from central Java and Vol 3 Karya on the work of Balinese composer I. Wayan Sadra.

◉ The Music of K.R.T. Wasitodiningrat (CMP/Silva Screen, UK).

Rebab player and composer, Wasitodiningrat was associated with the Paku Alaman court gamelan of Yogyakarta. The eight compositions on this disc are within the traditional framework of Central Javanese gamelan.

Thanks to Penny King and Maria Mendonça for help with the discography.

Indonesia

Pop and folk

no risk – no fun!

No question about it: Indonesia's pop music scene is the most exciting in southeast Asia and the Far East. From a bewildering range of folk and popular styles, spread through the islands, **Colin Bass** introduces the shimmering and seductive, the raunchy and vivacious – the astonishing world of kroncong, dangdut, jaipongan, and more.

ndonesia's archipelago of 13,600 islands spans from west to east a distance equal to that between Glasgow and Baghdad. The islands are home to nearly 200 million people, 360 ethnic groups and about 250 different languages – an amazing mix of cultures that is reflected in a huge diversity of pop music, all of it pretty much unknown in the West. To take a look below the tip of this tropical iceberg it's still necessary to buy an air ticket or stow away on a steamer, destination Java. Having arrived in Jakarta, a good place to start would be the downtown street called Jalan Agus Salim. Enjoy the pervasive aroma of clove cigarettes mingled with the smells of sizzling satay stalls garnished with the exhaust fumes of the turbulent traffic as you acknowledge the constant greetings from passers-by.

You may feel slightly disappointed as you walk past the *Burger King* and *Dunkin' Donuts*, so as an antidote stop by the *Sumatran Padang* restaurant where generous use of chilli-peppers will aid your acclimatisation. Okay, walk a little further and enter the *Duta Suara* cassette shop. Inside you will quickly discover that while not much Indonesian Pop finds its way into your local record shop, it seems the entire contents of your local record shop can be found here – a fact that has an inevitable impact on Indonesian-produced music. In the cities a new young generation of fashion-concious consumers support a wide variety of home-grown versions of international styles. There are any number of rock groups, rappers, boy's groups and pop singers and a growing dance-floor scene styled as 'House' . . . it seems that every region has its own House music – Bali House, Java House, Batak House from Sumatra.

But this is not to discount the popularity of more identifiably home-grown pop music, and if we keep moving towards the back of our cassette shop we come to the healthily beating heart of the matter. Kroncong, dangdut, jaipongan, degung, pop-Sunda, mandarin, pop-batak and qasidah are just a few of the signs on the shelves, whose contents will take you on a musical tour of the archipelago.

Rhoma Irama giving it some reverb

Kroncong

For a historical perspective you could start under the sign for **kroncong** (pronounced ker-ong-chong), a style that can trace its roots back several centuries to when the Portuguese were establishing trade links with Africa and South Asia. The arrival of European instruments laid the basis for what later became the first major urban-folk style. By the early 1900s kroncong was mainly associated with the low-life of the cities but it gained national popularity in the 1930s through its use by the new Indonesian film industry. During the Indonesian independence struggle (1945–1948) many inspirational patriotic songs were set to kroncong music.

In those days a typical ensemble consisted of two *kroncong* (three-string ukeleles), guitar, violin, flute, percussion and, variously, a cello played pizzicato or a double bass, accompanying a singer, usually female. The distinctive kroncong rhythm is set up by the two ukeleles – one known as the *cik*, the other as the *cuk* – playing alternate strokes of the beat. The medium-pace tempo, the diatonic melodies and the languid, crooning singing style invite comparison with East African Taarab music and even Portuguese Fado. In and around Solo, there's also a regional style of kroncong called **langgam jawa** in which the *pelog* (seven-note) scale and textures of gamelan music are imitated by the kroncong ensemble. It has an enchanting and sentimental sound.

Kroncong appeals today mainly to an older audience and much of what you'll find on the shelves lacks the freewheeling excitement of earlier times. So for an idea of how it was in its less well-behaved days, look under the sign of Gambang Kromong, and see if you can get a disc including "Bengawan Solo", the most celebrated kroncong song (and probably the most covered Indonesian pop song); written by singer-composer Gesang in 1943, it tells of the beauty of the river in Solo. Established artists still releasing kroncong albums include **Hetty Koes Endang**, **Sundari Sukotjo** and the diva of the related *langgam jawa* style, **Waldjinah**.

Gambang Kromong

Gambang kromong developed out of the type of kroncong music featured in an urban folk theatre form called *komedi stambul*, popular in the early decades of the twentieth century. If you travel to the town of Tangerang, about two hour's drive from Jakarta, you may be able to catch the modern-day equivalent called *lenong*, or get yourself invited to a wedding. In either case the music will be gambang kromong played on a bewildering array of Chinese, Indonesian and Western instruments.

A typical ensemble can bring together two-string fiddle, bamboo flute (*suling*), xylophone (*gambang*), pot-gongs, drums and percussion from the Javanese gamelan plus one or more Western instruments such as trumpet, keyboards, electric bass guitar, clarinet or Hawaiian guitar. Melodies

weave in and out and against the loping percussive backdrop sounding at times like a Dixieland Jazz band jamming with a gamelan. Highly recommended.

As well as the time-honoured traditional repertoire, the ensemble at your wedding will also slip in a couple of numbers in the style that occupies a much larger shelf-space in our cassette shop – dangdut.

Dangdut

Dang-dut-dang-dut-dang-dut-dang-dut. You can't mistake it and you'll hear it everywhere you go. **Dangdut**, Indonesia's equivalent of danceable Latin music, has been thriving since the mid-1970s. It grew out of kroncong and *Orkes Melayu* – the sort of music typified by Malaysia's P. Ramlee – but its most obvious influence is that of Indian film song.

Like many Indonesian musical terms, dangdut is an onomatopoeic word, derived from the rhythm usually played on the *gendang* (a pair of bongo-like drums tuned to sound like *tabla*). So that you know your dang from your dut, count in fours and hear the low dang note struck on the fourth beat and the high dut note struck on the first beat of the following bar.

Alongside the gendang, a typical group consists of electric guitar, bass, mandolin, drum kit

and keyboards. But the real stars are the **singers**: glamorous men and women singing of love found, lost, wanted or of moral issues, family matters, the everyday and fantasy life of the dangdut audience.

Following on from Orkes Melayu crooners like Munif and Ellya Agus came the first superstars of dangdut. **Rhoma Irama** and **Elvy Sukaesih**, are still known today as the King and Queen of dangdut. They made many successful recordings as a duo in the early 1970s and both have many million-selling albums to their credit. Rhoma Irama has always been identified as a 'working class hero'. Starting out as a long-haired rebel he found his true artistic direction after his Haj to Mecca. He went on to star in several films and still tours reg-

Elvy Sukaesih

ularly with his Soneta Group, putting his inspirational messages over with all the paraphenalia of a full-blown rock-show.

Other long-established dangdut stars worth checking out include **Mansyur S** with his **Dangdut Manis** (Sweet Dangdut) and the Arabic influenced **A. Rafiq**. The biggest names of the new generation of stars are **Evie Tamala**, the current heart-throb No. 1 and her closest competitors, **Merry Andani**, **Dewi Yull**, **Ikke Nurjanah** and **Iis Dahlia**. **Fahmy Shahab** has had success both at home and in Japan with his brand of Funky Dangdut. On the Dangdut House scene **Iwan Setia** is a name to look for, and producer Zoel Angarra's album with the singer **Tissa "Mandi Cinta"** (Love Bath) is a fine example of the genre.

If all this whets the appetite, then a visit later on to the area known as Mangga Besar (Big

Mango) is recommended. There you'll find a number of dangdut clubs. Tourists are rare in this neck of the woods so your entrance will have heads turning – but don't be intimidated. Once you've watched how to dance dangdut-style – a sort of slow jogging – ease yourself onto the dance-floor, where your efforts will be appreciated by all.

Jaipongan

Just occasionally in the dangdut dancehalls the drum machines and bendy guitars may be interrupted by a percussion-based style whose unpredictable tempo changes fail to deter some inventive dancing from those left on the dance floor. This will be **jaipongan**, a style that has no detectable Western influence, using only instruments from the Sundanese gamelan tradition (see Gamelan article, p.117).

The *rebab* (two-stringed bowed fiddle) plays the introduction while the *khendang* (a large two-headed barrel drum) improvises in free time underneath; then, with whooping cries, the rest of the orchestra enters. *Blak-ting-pong-blak-ting-pong-blak-ting-pong*. The khendang sets to building and releasing tension through a cyclical pattern marked by a single stroke on a large gong, while a smaller gong, a *kempul*, beats out one-note bass-lines. The mellow sounds of the *bonang rincik* and the *panerus* (sets of pot-shaped gongs) play stately cyclical melodies as the *saron* (a row of seven bronze keys set over a resonating box) hammers out faster arpeggios. The rebab anticipates, accompanies and answers the singer (*pesindhen*) as she floats like a butterfly through tales of love, money and agriculture, while throughout, various members of the orchestra indulge in more whooping, wailing and rhythmic grunting known as *senggak*.

Jaipongan is part of the rich culture of the **Sundanese** people. Sunda covers a large area of West Java and its regional capital, Bandung, is home to many universities and colleges. It was in Bandung that jaipongan first appeared in the mid-1960s and

Jaipongan: Worse than the Twist!

Colin Bass met Dr Gugum Gumbira Tirasondjaja, the Bandung-based producer, composer, arranger, choreographer, and the creator of jaipongan.

Gugum began his music career as a college student in the early 1960s, listening to rock'n'roll and practising the twist and jive. These studies, however, were interrupted by President Sukarno's new Indonesian identity drive, which saw rock 'n' roll banned. Gugum laughs and shakes his head as he describes his dilemma at the time: "The government wanted us to create new art forms based on our old traditions. I thought for a long time . . .how?" He re-enacts his despair, sinking his head into his hands. "I remembered when I was a boy everybody dancing and singing Sundanese but in my school we preferred Elvis Presley and Chubby Checker. My father and mother were traditional artists so I asked them to teach me the old songs and dances. Then my father asked me to travel round West Java to see all kinds of Sundanese culture."

After twelve years of observing and participating in local music, Gugum's jaipongan grew out of a village dance called **ketuk tilu**, named after its main instrument, a set of three pot-gongs. Small groups consisting of ketuk, rebab, khendang, gong, and a female singer-dancer, the *ronggeng*, had long played in the streets for payment but the style had fallen into disrepute among modern urban Javanese, due to its associations with prostitution. Gugum choreographed a more active but respectable role for the ronggeng, brought in a solo female singer, and replaced the ketuk with the bonang (a large set of pot-shaped gongs) and other instruments from the gamelan. He made the singer's role clear in the lyrics too:

Many people don't respect me
Other women say I steal their husbands
I am not like that
I am just a singer.

Musically, the most striking innovation was in the drumming. "The songs are divided into sections, with certain counts between the strokes on the large gong, as in old-style gamelan. I kept this as the link with the traditional, but introduced a more dynamic drumming style."

Gugum and his troupe achieved their first local fame

in a 1974 festival to showcase new Sundanese music sponsored by the government. "There were a thousand people in the audience and when we played – waah!", Gugum waves his hands in the air, 'Lagi!, Lagi!' (more! more!) and the young ones joined in the dancing. Afterwards, though, there was a seminar, common at that time, and some people were angry about the sensual movements in the dance."

It seems that the enthusiastic interpretations of the young people in the audience had shocked the guardians of public morals and attempts were made to nip the thing in the bud. Why, this was worse than the twist! Gugum was called before the governor. "I was a big problem!" he cheerfully admits, clearly relishing the irony of offending the defenders of Indonesian culture with a traditional dance. "They asked me to stop it, but it was already too late, it was not in my

Dr. Gugum Gumbira Tirasondjaja with Euis Komariah and the Jugala Orchestra

control." Thanks to the controversy, his dance school was oversubscribed when he opened branches in several other towns. "I was not interested in money, I just wanted to spread my creation," insists Gugum.

In 1976 Gugum released the first cassette on his own label, Jugala, featuring jaipongan and other genres performed by his **Jugala Group**. Thereafter his creation indeed began to spread. Other companies started producing their own jaipongan recordings and regional variations appeared throughout Java and Sumatra. By 1980 the Jugala Group had made it to national television (an event denoting official approval in itself).

These days, the jaipongan dance craze is over, though it has evolved, with constant re-interpretation by Gugum, into a 'Modern Classic' concert style, which the Jugala Group have performed both at home and in Europe and the US.

by the end of the decade it had become a national dance-craze, and all without an electric guitar in sight.

It's possible that jaipongan would not have happened had it not been for a piece of repressive legislation introduced a decade previously by President Sukarno. He believed that after 350 years of colonisation the Indonesian people had to re-establish their pride in their own cultural identity. So he called on artists and musicians to shun Western influences and revitalise indigenous art-forms. Severe restrictions were placed on the importation and broadcasting of foreign music, particularly the dreaded rock'n'roll. These were all rescinded after Suharto seized power in 1965 but the seeds had been sown for the Sundanese roots-revival, led by **Gugum Gumbira** (see feature box).

Jaipongan is still popular today and in recent years its distinctive drumming style has been co-opted by several dangdut artists. A 1996 CD release by Elvy Sukaesih was billed as 'Dangdut Jaipong'. Internationally, there are a few excellent recordings available by **Idjah Hadidjah**, **Euis Komari-ah** and an unusual release on the Japanese Meta label called "Break Pong", by **Yayah Ratnasari** and the great **Karawang Group** having lots of fun with a drum machine.

Degung, Kecapi Suling and Pop-Sunda

Back in the cassette shop, if the gongs and bonangs of jaipongan have worked their magic, it will be time to get really relaxed and investigate the soothing sounds of **degung** and **kecapi suling** music. Wistful, melancholic, meditative, the sound of degung embodies the feeling Indonesians describe as 'Sakit Hati'. The literal English translation is 'sick liver', but of course that is losing some of the romantic inference. In Bahasa Indonesia the poetic organ of affection is the liver rather than the heart and 'Sakit Hati' describes a feeling of longing and sadness.

Gamelan Degung developed as a court music deemed the most suitable for playing while guests were arriving at social occasions, and **modern degung** music performs a similar function today. It has found a whole new audience particularly among tourists in Bali where degung cassettes provide the ambience in many cafés and restaurants. Peaceful, harmonious background music characterised by gentle percussion, delicate improvising on the suling and soft arpeggios played on the bonang and saron and underpinned by the warm tones of the hanging gongs which give the music its name. (See Gamelan article for more on degung).

Kecapi Suling is an instrumental form developed from another court tradition of sung entertainment music called tembang Sunda. A typical ensemble consists of a suling accompanied by two or three kecapi – a zither or koto-like instrument of varying sizes and number of strings. Each string has a separate bridge to facilitate tuning between various modes. Kecapi Suling utilises the pentatonic scales known as pelog and sorog. When singing is included, the haunting melodies carry poetic and sometimes mysterious images sung in Sundanese. Here is an example, "Ramalan Asih" (Horoscope of Love) by **Yus Wiradiredja**:

> Don't return on Sunday
> It will rain all day on Monday
> Tuesday is a floating day, be careful
> On Wednesday neighbours will gossip,
> love can be broken
> Someone could make you unhappy on
>   Thursday
> Friday there is danger of flooding, be careful
> Saturday is an unfortunate day
> And the next week looks just the same.

A mark of quality with degung or Kecapi Suling releases is to look for the name of **Nano S** on the cassette cover. This amazingly prolific composer is also responsible for some of the best examples of the **pop-Sunda** style where degung meets modern technology. Sequenced drum and bass

---

Conyor Panon (Sensual Eyes)

Sensual eyes are moving, not resting
A beautiful vision
Wrapping a silk scarf around her neck
And putting on yellow sandals
She is a gentle philanderer

If there is distance between us
Just call out my name
And let the words build a bridge
In the empty night.
You may be far from me
But in my heart I hear your call.

Sensual eyes are moving, not resting
A beautiful vision
That is far from me
But still I feel so close

      Detty Kurnia, from *Conyor Panon* (Wave)

patterns accompany the traditional-style melodies and often all the Sundanese instruments are replaced by synthesised sounds. If you can take that on board there is much to enjoy here. Two of the greatest pop-Sunda hits are "Cinta" (Love) by Hetty Koes Endang, and "Kalangkang" by Nining Meida – both million-sellers and both written by Nano S.

Hetty Koes Endang made her recording debut in 1973 and has since released nearly 200 albums encompassing kroncong, dangdut, langgam jawa, degung and pop-Sunda. Rice Records of Japan recently re-issued a compilation of her earliest recordings in the **Pop-Melayu** style. There are also two albums available internationally from Bandung singer **Detty Kurnia**, *Dari Sunda* and *Coyor Panon*, produced for the Japanese market by Makoto Kubota, who sets the pop-Sunda and jaipongan selections in modern pop arrangements.

Bandung queen Detty Kurnia

Although not strictly representative of the music as heard in Indonesia, they are an excellent introduction to the Sunda sound.

Qasidah Modern

Ready for a change of scene on the cassette shelves? Then move away from the Sunda racks and on to Central Java and the Islamic pop of **qasidah modern**.

Qasidah is a classical Arabic word for epic religious poetry, traditionally performed by a storyteller-singer, accompanied by percussion and chanting. Indonesian Muslims practise their own versions of this, improvising lyrics in local languages that address contemporary concerns and moral issues.

Qasidah modern places this in a pop-song form, adding electric guitars, mandolin, keyboards, violins and flutes. Rhythms and melodies from dangdut and Arabic pop are used, while the lyrics frequently offer moral advice to young lovers (don't do it!), extolling a virtuous life and warning against corruption and other temptations. Sometimes the lyrics even tackle environmental issues such as pollution, nuclear power and cigarette smoking. Here's an example, "Bila Ingin Bahagia" (If You want to be Happy), from the group Nasida Rio:

> *Everywhere is the scent of jasmine,*
> *The bees suck the flowers,*
> *Many young girls forget themselves,*
> *Not yet married they make love,*
> *If you want to be happy,*
> *Don't spoil this pure love,*
> *The honeymoon should satisfy your hearts*

From *Nasida Ria* (Piranha)

Nasida Ria, a nine-woman orchestra from Semarang, are the pioneers of qasidah modern. They have released more than 25 albums and have twice toured Germany. At home they perform chiefly at Muslim weddings throughout Java or occasionally at open-air rallies sponsored by religious groups where the proceedings are opened by a sermon or two before the orchestra take the stage. In their colourful headscarfs and close-fitting dresses that cover them from head to foot they manage to look simultaneously alluring and modest and the occasional heavy-metal posturing of the guitarists is also conducted with great decorum.

If the strong Arabic influence of this music is to your taste then you might want to plan a trip along the north coast of Java to **Surabaya**, home of Gambus music.

DICK VAN DEN HAM

Nasida Ria – metal postures with decorum

Gambus

Gambus is the Indonesian word for the arabic lute, the *oud*, but it is now used to denote both a style of music and the orchestra that plays it. The oud was brought to Indonesia along with Islam and much of the music and dances associated with it were introduced by settlers from the Yemen. Visit the Arab quarter in Surabaya and you may hear the voice of Oum Kalthoum wafting out of one of the shops in the bazaar, or it could be Surabaya's own diva, **Soraya**. You may also hear what sounds like a typical modern pop production from Saudi or Kuwait, but it is more likely to be one of the local stars of the gambus modern scene – **Muhdar Alatas** or **Ali Alatas** (no relation).

Many gambus songs are lifted straight from imported Arabic cassettes and given a local stamp. Some retain the Arabic texts, many are rewritten in Bahasa Indonesia. All the hallmarks of great Arabic pop are there: rolling rhythms on the *derbuka* and the oud, sinuous melody lines on flute and violins and, regardless of the language, much silky ornamentation of the vocal lines from the singer. Although loved by millions, gambus is hardly known outside Indonesia and there are still no recordings available internationally.

Sumatra

A variety of different musical styles are to be found on the neighbouring island of **Sumatra**.

In the north the **Batak**, concentrated around the area of Lake Toba, have a long tradition of percussion-based music with additional flutes and reed-trumpets – *seruling* and *serunai* – to accompany healing and other ceremonial occasions. Sometimes lasting for days on end and designed to induce trance-states in the participants, this is exciting stuff. Much more European sounding are more recent Batak folksongs that date from the first contact with protestant missionaries at the end of the nineteenth century. Many of these songs from the Toba communities are about the lake and the life on it.

Moving south from Lake Toba you reach the Tapanuli region where you can hear **tapanuli ogong** music – lively dance-tunes played on flute, reed-trumpet and a small two-string lute called the *hasapi*. Rhythm is provided by a set of hand-drums (*tagaling*), normally suspended in an ornately carved frame, and by a bamboo xylophone (*garattung*). Bass lines are picked out on a set of gongs.

There is a particularly wonderful, locally available CD called *Tapanuli Ogung* on the GNP label on which **Turman Sinaga** and his group race joyfully through a set of traditional dance-tunes, managing to seamlessly insert quick takes on the dreaded football anthem "olé olé" and "La Paloma" along the way. Disconcerting for purists, but in Tapanuli they know a catchy tune when they hear one.

The **Minangkabau** are one of the world's few matrilineal societies and to check out their music it's necessary to visit Bukkittinggi, a charming hill-town north of the sea-port capital of Padang. While sharing many of the same traditional roots as the Batak, their music is influenced by the predominance of Islam. It also reveals similarities with some Madagascan styles and many of the songs carry a discernible Polynesian flavour. Both Batak and Minang music display influences assimilated from centuries of trade with Arabic, Indian and East African cultures.

The Moluccan Islands

A distinct Polynesian influence can also be heard on the **Moluccan Islands** towards the eastern end of the archipelago. As in the Batak region of Sumatra, Christianity has been the most influential religion. Visit the large church in Ambon on a Sunday morning to hear some spirited hymn-singing. Its

Moluccans in Exile

In 1950, after President Sukarno had reneged on a previous agreement to a federal structure in favour of a republic ruled by a central government in Jakarta, the South Moluccans declared independence. This movement was swiftly put down by the Indonesian army. Meanwhile, some 4000 South Moluccan soldiers and their families from the soon to be demobilised Dutch Colonial Army were stationed in Java. To avoid an embarrassing situation the Dutch forcibly shipped them to Holland and de-mobilised them there with promises that as soon as a diplomatic solution to the problem could be found, they could return home. This never materialised and they remained in forced exile. A series of hi-jackings in the mid-1970s briefly brought their plight to the attention of the world.

In the mid-'80s, guitarist **Eddie Lakransy** formed the **Moluccan Moods Orchestra** with other Dutch-born sons and daughters of Moluccan exiles and fused a jazz-funk style with the almost forgotten songs of a homeland most had never visited. Sadly, Eddie Lakransy died in a plane crash in 1988. One great album on the Piranha label stands as a reminder of the project that never achieved its full potential.

---

influence is clearly heard in **pop-Ambon** and the major-key melodies and up-tempo rhythms can sound like a meeting of Hawaiian music and zouk. There is also a tradition of farewell songs here that are stylistically related to kroncong.

discography

Some of the discs reviewed below may be tricky to obtain. For **Indonesian releases** contact: Kartini Music, Postfach 30 14 29, 10722 Berlin, Germany. Fax: (49) 30 217 56 334; e-mail: Bassbrett@aol.com For **Japanese releases**, contact Paul Fisher, The Far Side, 205 Sun City Hikawadai, J-4-40-10 Hikawadai, Japan. Fax: (81) 3 303 69464; e-mail: paulfish@mx5.nis

Kroncong, Dangdut and Qasidah

Compilations

Music of Indonesia Vol 2: Kroncong, Dangdut and Langgam Jawa (Smithsonian Folkways, US).

Kroncong, Dangdut and Langgam Jawa are accessible Indonesian pop musics, with their enticing fusions of rock, Indian and Middle Eastern elements. This volume of the Folkways series (see opposite) features beautiful kroncong tracks here, mainly by the Orkes Kroncong Mutiara, and good dangdut selections from the Soneta Group with Rhoma Irama, Elvy Sukaesih and others.

Road to Dangdut (Meta, Japan).

Captivating compilation of the roots of dangdut. Vintage Orkes Melayu and other styles from the 1950s and '60s. Early artists include Munif, Ellya Agus and Malaysia's star P. Ramlee plus more recent names like Rhoma Irama, Elvy Sukaesih and Hetty Koes Endang.

Street Music of Java (Original Music, US).

Java has lots of street musicians playing in market areas. These are wonderful recordings made in the late 1970s of homespun versions of kroncong and dangdut, plus ronggeng dances and zither music.

Bengawan Solo: Kroncong Songs by Gesang, Waldjinah, Nuning (Victor, Japan).

Classic kroncong numbers by veteran stars of the genre. The title song is probably the most famous of all Indonesian pop songs, sung here by the composer himself, Gesang. Nuning, with a wonderful floating voice, is Gesang's neice and Waldjinah sings kroncong songs with gamelan overtones. The recording was made in Tokyo in 1994 when Gesang was 76. A kroncong classic but hard to find.

Bengawan Solo: Kroncong Instrumental (Omagatoki, Japan).

Yes it's that song again, as one of the evergreens on this collection of instrumental kroncong. There's a swooning, romantic (some might say 'easy listening' quality) to this disc, but the band really highlight the wonderful hybrid quality of this music with long flutes melodies, violin counterpoint, skittish ukelele strums and a plucked cello bass.

Artists

Hetty Koes Endang

Hetty Koes Endang made her first recording in 1973 at the age of sixteen and has since released over 150 albums in a wide range of styles. She is still one of Indonesia's most popular singers.

Keroncong Asli (Musica, Indonesia).

Recorded in the early 1980s, but still sounding fresh, this is high quality kroncong by the most versatile of popular singers accompanied by the greatest orchestra of the time, Orkes Kroncong Bintang Jakarta. It includes a great version of "Bengawan Solo", the most famous kroncong number.

Pop Melayu (Rice Records, Japan).

Selection of twenty hits from the beginning of Ms Endang's career in the 1970s. Wonderful mix of styles with elements of kroncong, dangdut & pop that Rice Records have named 'Indonesian Boogaloo'.

Rhoma Irama

Born in 1941, Rhoma Irama's long career has seen him transform from long-haired rebel to born-again Muslim while remaining a 'working class hero'. He was a pioneer of dangdut and has used the genre to deal with moral and political issues.

◎ Begadang 1975–1980 (Meta, Japan).

A good introduction to the rock-influenced style of the man still known as the King of Dangdut. Features some of his most famous songs including the great "Santai" (Relax).

Nasida Ria

The leading exponents of qasidah modern, Nasida Ria are a hugely successful nine-member, all-female band from central Java. They preach a strong moral message.

◎ Keadilan (Piranha, Germany).

An enjoyable, bouncy mix of Arabic and dangdut styles sung with plenty of synthesizer plus flute and violin.

Elvy Sukaesih

Elvy Sukaesih, born in 1951, started as Rhoma Irama's singing partner (with his Soneta Group) before embarking on her hugely successful solo career. Known as the Queen of Dangdut, her voice and songs have a celebrated sensual quality.

◎ Raja dan Ratu (Rice Records, Japan).

Featuring Rhoma Irama and Elvy Sukaesih, these are sparkling pop gems from the early 1970s from the King and Queen of Dangdut. Solo and duo outings full of youthful energy and great dangdut-style 'beat-group' backing.

◎ Return of Diva (Wave, Japan).

Makoto Kubota's 1991 Japanese productions of the Queen of Dangdut. High-quality sounds, tight arrangements with enough of the original flavour left in. It features Sukaesih's dangdut version of Madonna's "La Isla Bonita".

ELVY SUKAESIH

Smithsonian Folkways' Music of Indonesia

With its 3000 inhabited islands and more than 300 ethnic groups, Indonesia obviously has an amazing range of **folk styles**. Few countries, particularly in southeast Asia, can boast an ethnomusicological survey as ambitious as the twenty volumes the US label **Smithsonian Folkways** has recently released in their **Music of Indonesia** series.

The discs are masterminded and recorded by **Philip Yampolsky**: "People's ideas of Indonesian music were limited to Central Javanese and Balinese gamelan," he explained. "But I knew from the research I'd already done that there was an astonishing amount of other music out there, and I wanted to bring it to people's attention – not only in Europe, America and Australia, but more importantly in Indonesia itself." The project started with the Festival of Indonesia in the US in 1990, for which Yampolsky was asked by the Smithsonian Institution to make two CDs, with financial help from the Ford Foundation. "No" I said, "two albums isn't enough to do anything meaningful about Indonesia. I wouldn't consider a project with fewer than twelve albums. Smithsonian gulped and said, write up a proposal, we'll submit it to Ford and see what they say. So I did, and somewhere along the line I decided twelve wasn't enough and it would have to be fifteen. This was in 1990. Later I revised the plan and upped the number of albums to twenty,

which is the final figure. (Now I wish I had asked for twenty-five!)

"I have tried to find genres of music that I thought would be impressive and interesting to the open-minded, non-specialist listener – somebody who wanted to hear something new and wouldn't be put off if it wasn't gamelan (or Mozart). This means that certain kinds of music often get left out of the series: sung narratives that use one or two melodies over and over all night – the aesthetic interest is in the words, not the music, but non-specialists won't know the language so can't appreciate the text. Dance music also often gets left out, when the music is a simple repetitive formula and the fun is in watching the dancers' movements (which you can't do on CD). There are additional criteria: trying to represent the main islands and culture areas of Indonesia; trying to include all of the main instruments and ensemble types.

"One important thing to say is that this project is not a one-man show. It's a collaborative project of **Smithsonian Folkways** and the **Indonesian Society for the Performing Arts (MSPI)**, and many excellent Indonesian ethnomusicologists have worked with me in the field; some have also contributed to the published commentaries."

For a thumbnail review of each of the CDs – and thus an overview of much of the terrain of Indonesian folk (and pop) – see pp.141–2.

Jaipongan and Pop-Sunda

Discs below are the pop end of Sundanese music; for traditional Sundanese degung CDs see the Gamelan discography, p.129.

Artists

CBMW (Bandung Music Group)

A group of young Bandung musicians led by kacapi wizard, Ismet Ruchimat, using a range of traditional instruments to forge new directions.

 Sambasunda (GNP/WML, Indonesia).

This wonderful album utilises bamboo and degung gamelan instruments and musical styles like Kebyar, gambang Kromong, Jaipongan and Samba as basic ingredients in a range of gently funky grooves showcasing skilful ensemble playing and improvising.

Hetty Koes Endang

Hetty has performed Pop-Sunda as well as anyone.

The Best of Sundanese Pop Songs (Musica, Indonesia).

Only available in Indonesia, but an essential buy if you're there: sweet, haunting melodies with pop arrangements. Includes the multi-million-selling hit "Cinta".

Jugala Orchestra

Based at Gugum Gumbira's Jugala Studios in Bandung, this group includes Sundanese gamelan instruments, drums, rebab and suling flute. Since their creation in the mid-1970s, they've been central to jaipongan and contemporary degung music.

The Sound of Sunda (GlobeStyle, UK).

A cross-section of modern degung and other popular music with vocalists Euis Komariah (Gugum Gumbira's wife) and male singer Yus Wiradiredja. Lyrical, whistful and enchanting music to be played "after 6pm in a peaceful environment, while your guests are arriving for dinner or when your love-object has left you".

Jaipongan Java (GlobeStyle, UK).

Also with Euis Komariah who has been singing Sundanese music since the age of ten and is an accomplished gamelan player. A great introduction to jaipongan music. This album is something of a classic with Gugum Gumbira's most successful numbers specially recorded with the Jugala orchestra.

Tongerret (Nonesuch, US).

This is a more laid back collection of jaipongan and related styles called kliningan and celempungan – which are for listening rather than dancing. The female vocalist, Idjah Hadidjah, started out in the wayang golek puppet theatre. The opening title track is slow and hauntingly beautiful with rebab, gongs, drums and Hadidjah's swooping voice.

Detty Kurnia

Hailing from Bandung, the Sundanese capital, Detty Kurnia is the daughter of a famous Sundanese gamelan player. She was already singing at festivals aged six. Now in her late thirties, she is pop-Sunda's brightest star singing both pop and traditional styles.

 Coyor Panon (Wave, Japan).

Produced in 1992 by ubiquitous Japanese producer Makoto Kubota, this is a first-class collection of songs betraying the influence of degung, jaipongan, calung and more. Currently out of print but there are copies around.

Dari Sunda (Wave, Japan; Riverboat, UK).

Thiis disc was Kubota's first excursion into Indonesian music and a massive hit. It includes the kroncong classic "Bengawan Solo" plus a couple of Japanese tunes including Shoukichi Kina's classic "Hana".

Yayah Ratnasari & Karawang Group

This female vocalist and band are one of the best current jaipongan outfits, based in the Sundanese town of Karawang. They won the 1994 BASF Indonesian Music Business Awards for their jaipongan version of Sabah Habas Mustapha's "Denpasar Moon" (see below), retitled "Den Sa Mun" in Sundanese.

Break Pong (Meta Co, Japan).

An unusual recording having lots of fun adding a drum machine to their traditional percussion set-up.

Fusion/Exiles

Artists

Djaduk Ferianto & Kua Etnika

Djaduk Ferianto is a composer active in contemporary dance theatre and his group use instruments from all over the archipelago to create their own 'world music'.

Nang Ning Nong Orkes Sumpeg (Galang Comm, Indonesia).

This is an exciting new direction from Jogjakarta in Central Java. Traditional violins, flutes, percussion and metallophones interact with modern keyboard sounds and global rhtyhms.

Moluccan Moods Orchestra

A band of expatriates based in Holland led by guitarist Eddy Lekransy until his death in 1988.

Wakoi (Piranha, Germany).

Moluccan songs given a contemporary jazz-funk treatment by Holland-based expatriates. Guitar, keyboards, sax, flutes and percussion plus wonderful harmony singing from the three female vocalists.

Sabah Habas Mustapha

The singer/bassist from Britain's 3 Mustaphas 3 moved on from furious Balkan rhythms to work with popular Indonesian styles, a bit of gamelan and world sounds. The Indonesians liked these curious fusions so much that they were plundered in innumerable cover versions. Some suspect Sabah Habas to be none other than Colin Bass, author of the article you've just read. The star rating is that of the editor alone . . .

Denpasar Moon (Wave, Japan; Piranha, Germany).

A wonderful disc from 1994. Dangdut and Sundanese styles performed with musicians in Jakarta with global rhythms and

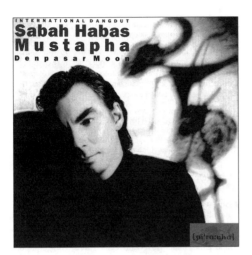

INTERNATIONAL DANGDUT
**Sabah Habas
Mustapha**
Denpasar Moon

[pi'ra:nha]

Vol. 1: Songs Before Dawn: Gandrung Banyuwangi (Smithsonian Folkways, US).

Gandrung Banyuwangi is a night-long entertainment from eastern Java. The gandrung is a young, unmarried dancer and singer who entices men into her highly-charged suggestive dances. She is backed by musicians on violins, drums, triangle and gongs who will also protect her if the dancing men get over-amorous. Without the live drama or the sexual charge, the music's a bit hard going.

 ### Vol. 2: Kroncong, Dangdut and Langgam Jawa (Smithsonian Folkways, US).

A superb introduction to these accessible Indonesian pop styles: see review uner 'Dangdut', p.138.

Vol. 3: Music from the Outskirts of Jakarta (Smithsonian Folkways, US).

This features *Gambang Kromong* – the regional music of Jakarta – performed by mixed Chinese and Indonesian groups. The older *lagu lama* repertoire with Chinese fiddles, flute, oboe and gongs is an acquired taste, but the contemporary style *lagu sayur* is delightful and accessible: Dixieland-gamelan with gongs, flute, trumpet and Hawaiian guitar.

Vol. 4: Music of Nias & North Sumatra (Smithsonian Folkways, US).

The instrumental *gendang karo* music that opens this disc, with its web of interlocking drum taps and gongs, and reedy oboe melodies, is another delight. It is followed by *hoho*, choral singing from the island of Nias – a little of which goes a long way. But the real highlight is the *gondang toba*, a thrilling ensemble of tuned drums that play complete melodies in their own right.

Vol. 5: Betawi and Sundanese Music of the North Coast of Java (Smithsonian Folkways, US).

Another fascinating and accessible disc. *Topeng Betawi* is a folk theatre form with a strong drumming ingredient. *Tanjidor* is dislocated European brass band music of waltzes and marches and *Ajeng* is gamelan music with a raucous oboe called a *tarompet* instead of the refined rebab.

Vol. 6: Night Music of West Sumatra (Smithsonian Folkways, US).

Includes *saluang*, *rabab pariaman* and *dendang pauah* music of the Minangkabau people. Various forms of intimate vocal music with bamboo flute and rebab. Not easy listening.

Vol. 7: Music from the Forests of Riau and Mentawai (Smithsonian Folkways, US).

This features some lovely xylophone and gong music with interlocking patterns like American minimalism. Plus harder-going vocal music and a shamanistic curing ritual.

Vol. 8: Vocal and Instrumental Music from East and Central Flores (Smithsonian Folkways, US).

Flores is an island east of Bali with polyphonic singing, double flute and gong and drum ensembles. Pretty hardcore stuff.

Vol. 9: Vocal Music from Central and West Flores (Smithsonian Folkways, US).

Even more specialist fare from Flores: music for funerals and agricultural rituals.

Vol. 10: Music of Biak, Irian Jaya (Smithsonian Folkways, US).

This music already sounds as if it belongs to the Pacific region rather than southeast Asia. The *wor* songs sung by choruses are hard work, the church songs and string band pieces are more accessible.

English lyrics. Songs like the title track and "Bali Girl" are seductive melodically and the closing "International Dangdut" sums up what this album is all about.

So la li (Kartini, Germany).

On his most recent disc Sabah Habas teams up with the Jugala All-Stars in Bandung for a jaipongan-laced party.

Sunda Africa

A global fusion group put together in Gugum Gumbira's studios in Bandung, comprising Django Mango – a globe-trotting percussionist of Spanish origin – with the cream of degung musicians including suling maestro, Burhan.

No Risk, No Fun (GlobeStyle, UK).

African and Indian percussion gently steer degung into a new rhythmic direction.

Tala Mena Siwa

Another expatriate group of Moluccans based in Nijmegen, Holland. The name of the ten-strong band means 'a breakthrough'.

Sae Ena (M&W, Holland).

Their material is much more traditional than the Moluccan Moods Orchestra above, based on romantic or moralistic kapata songs and epic legoe songs. Warm, rich singing from the six women in the band.

Folk/Traditional

The Smithsonian Folkways Music of Indonesia series

Smithsonian Folkways (see feature box, p.139) have, since 1990 been issuing a series of 20 CDs covering the range of Indonesian folk (and some pop) music. Obviously a good deal of this is specialised listening but there are discs among them that are utterly wonderful and accessible – and each is produced with excellent notes and photos to give meaning and context to the music. Following is a thumbnail sketch of what's included in each.

Vol. 11: Melayu Music of Sumatra and the Riau Islands (Smithsonian Folkways, US).

Traditional Malay songs and dances (*zapin* and *ronggeng*) in Sumatra, featuring intimate ensembles of *gambus* (lute), violin, accordion and percussion. Plus *mak yong* and *mendu* theatrical forms. A nice collection.

Vol. 12: Gongs and Vocal Music from Sumatra (Smithsonian Folkways, US).

Wonderful gong-chime and drum tracks in *talempong* music of the Minangkabau and *kulintang* wedding music of the Melinting people. Plus harder going unaccompanied choral singing and Islamic *salawat dulang*.

Vol. 13: Kalimantan Strings (Smithsonian Folkways, US).

Focuses mainly on the indigenous lutes of the Dayak tribes of Borneo (related to the *sapé* music of the Sarawak Orang Ulu). There are some lovely duets and also Melayu gambus.

Vol. 14: Lombok, Kalimantan, Banyumas: Little-known Forms of Gamelan and Wayang (Smithsonian Folkways, US).

Another real treasure in the series – reviewed in the Gamelan discography (p.130).

Vol. 15: South Sulawesi Strings (Smithsonian Folkways, US).

Sulawesi (formerly Celebes) lies between Borneo and the Moluccas and this disc could appeal to zither enthusiasts.

Vol. 16: Sulawesi: Music for Celebrations, Funerals, and Work (Smithsonian Folkways, US).

Pakarena of the Makasar people (unison female chorus, shawm, frantic drumming); polyphonic choruses of Central Sulawesi; funeral flutes with singing; gong-ensemble music for Mongondow weddings; choral singing with drums from the Minahasa.

Vol. 17: Kalimantan: Festival and Ritual Music (Smithsonian Folkways, US).

Mainly gong ensembles and vocal music. Plus some very unusual music for struck bamboo tubes, from the Jelai Hulu region, and an overview of a 48-hour curing ritual.

Vol. 18: Music of Sumbawa, Sumba, and West Timor (Smithsonian Folkways, US).

Violin and singing from Sumbawa. Funeral gong-ensemble music from Sumba, also strange music for a two-stringed lute in East Sumba that sounds like a bottleneck guitar. Choral singing and a gong ensemble from Timor, plus music for the widespread ensemble of violin, guitars, and singers.

Vol. 19: Music of Maluku (the Moluccas) (Smithsonian Folkways, US).

Music of the Sufi *dabus* ritual (singers, frame drums). Entertainment music for violin, guitars, flute, drums, and singer. Gongs and various genres of vocal music.

Vol. 20: Guitars of Indonesia (Smithsonian Folkways, US).

Along with Vol. 2, this is the most accessible album of the series. It features guitar-and-vocal traditions from Sumatra, Lampung, Sulawesi (the Mandar), and Sumba. Some of the Lampung and Mandar music sounds a bit like ragtime guitar (Blind Boy Fuller, Reverend Gary Davis), but uniquely Indonesian as well.

Other Folk/Traditional

Masters of Minangkabau Music (Manu, New Zealand).

Intimate studio recordings (made in New Zealand) of Minangkabau musicians Piter Slayan and M. Halim. Most tracks are songs accompanied by different sorts of flute, but there's also Islamic influenced music from the coastal area with frame drums, silat martial art music, talempong gongs and flute playing to make the girl you want fall in love with you.

Music of Timor (Celestial Harmonies, US).

While East Timor was granted a bloody independence in 1999, this disc focuses on the various districts of West Timor, one of the poorest provinces of Inodnesia. Ritual music with gongs and drums, vocal and choral music, and social music with flute, violin, guitar etc.

Sing Sing So: Songs of the Batak People (JVC, Japan).

The Batak are famed for the beauty of their folksongs and justifiable on the strength of these performances. The tunes are rather European in character with a strongly lyrical line, but Southeast Asian warmth. Solo songs accompanied by Western-style guitar, wonderful instrumental tracks of wooden gamelan and flute and choral numbers sounding distinctly evangelical to close. Very approachable.

Sumatra (Tradisom, Portugal).

An excellent disc of the Malay-Portuguese music of Sumatra. Includes ronggeng dances to a bamboo flute, drums and gong; five splendid archive kroncong tracks (including a Latin bolero-style version of "Bengawan Solo"); zapin dance music and other Malay-style sounds. Performances by eccentric, local groups.

Timor (Tradisom, Portugal)

Recordings of music from East Timor are a rarity, showing how effectively the country was closed off by Indonesian occupation. This CD is one of the best of a series focusing on former Portuguese colonies and includes archival recordings, popular songs, field recordings and church music, mostly made during the 1990s.

Japan

the culture blender

Japan, par excellence, produces bland bubblegum pop which is sugary sweet, chewed for a while and then spat out. But the thriving roots scene is more nourishing – fuelled by the dynamic music of the islands of Okinawa. It is these sounds of Japan's 'deep south' which have recently been making waves at home and abroad. Otherwise, Japan's bewildering variety of popular and traditional music is little known in the West. But the story in Asia, as told by **John Clewley**, is different.

The advent of satellite TV, with its many music channels, and the growth in incomes across southeast Asia – prior to the economic crisis at least – have fuelled great demand for all forms of Japanese popular culture. Manga (comics), television cartoons and superhero shows, toys, mainstream pop and rock bands, movies and fashion trends are all eagerly picked up by young Asians, and karaoke in particular is wildly popular.

Despite the recession in Japan, Asia's economic powerhouse still exerts an enormous influence on the global entertainment and music markets. Sales growth may have been a paltry 3% but in 1997 the market was valued at over six billion dollars, making Japan the second largest music market in the world, after the USA.

Unfortunately, the over-riding image of Japanese pop in the outside world is one of forgettable **bubblegum pop**. Young teenagers are trained, manufactured and recorded as *idoru kashu*, or idol singers. Boy bands like Smap or Hikaru Genji and cutsie female singers like duo Wink offer watered-down Western pop set to Japanese lyrics (with a hookline often sung in meaningless English). Kazu-fumi 'Miya' Miyazawa of the popular roots band The Boom says it's just like fast food: "the system just creates music to be consumed. It's like it's a throwaway product. I hate that buy, listen and throw away and sing at a karaoke bar mentality". Yet it is this very music that attracts Asian teenagers.

Bubblegum pop, some new age sounds, the odd novelty hit and some traditional music – these are the stereotypes of music in Japan. Yet nowhere in Asia can you find such a wide range of music: from ancient Buddhist chanting and court music to folk and old urban styles, from localised popular styles like *kayokyoku* and *enka* to Western classical, jazz and every form of pop you would find in the West.

Ancient Roots

The many musical styles found in Japan have their roots in Japan's particular historical circumstances – China, Korea, Central and southeast Asia all

COLLECTION CHRISTOPHER WAGNER

Geisha playing shamisen, Japan 1904

Classical and Theatrical Music

Classical music can be divided into **gagaku** (court orchestral music) and **shomyo** (Buddhist chanting). Gagaku came from China 1500 years ago as Confucian ceremonial music of the Chinese court. Similar to a chamber orchestra, gagaku ensembles include as many as twenty instruments of all forms (wind, string and percussion), including flutes, oboes, zithers, lutes, gongs and drums. Gagaku is now played only as **bugaku** (dance music) or **kangen** (instrumental music), at the Imperial court and at a few Shinto shrines and Buddhist temples.

It is very hard to describe music that doesn't conform to a linear progression or that has a shifting beat. Unlike Western classical, themes aren't stated and repeated. Instead, the rhythms of the music are based on breathing and the result is a music that sounds avant-garde – sometimes discordant, sometimes meditative. Less is more in gagaku.

Japan's most famous theatrical form, **noh**, was synthesised in the fourteenth century from religious pan-

JAPANESE EMBASSY

Noh performer

tomimes, folk theatre and court music. Noh, which combines oratory, dance and singing in a highly stylised manner, is still performed and continues to influence both Japanese and foreign theatre and music. There are solo singers, small choruses singing in unison and an instrumental ensemble of *fue* (bamboo flute), the only melodic instrument other than the voice, two hourglass drums and a barrel drum. The profundity of expression through an economy of means is an important part of the aesthetic.

The melodramatic puppet style, **bunraku**, came after noh, and was one of the sources of the colourful and sensual **kabuki** theatre. Kabuki emerged in the early seventeenth century, and the combination of noh narratives, chanting and music based on the shamisen (three-string lute), flute and drums led to a more lively and popular musical style. This boosted the popularity of the new *nagauta* style of shamisen playing, which in turn influenced popular styles to come, including folk music.

---

exerted considerable influence on the early development of music. There is evidence of music from around the third century BC, but the arrival of 80 Korean musicians in 453 AD and the introduction of Buddhism in the seventh century are the key events. **Gagaku**, court music and religious music (see box above) survive from this period, and Buddhist chanting, **shomyo**, can still be heard in temples today.

Japanese scholars tend to say all music prior to the Meiji reformation of 1868 is traditional, but within that definition there are different styles from each epoch. Early history (400–1200) produced religious and **court styles**. In the years to 1500, as society became more militarised, theatrical genres like **noh** drama developed (see box above) and itinerant monks chanted long historical narratives to the *biwa*, a Japanese lute whose origins can be traced back to the Silk Road in Central Asia.

Between 1500 and 1868 Japanese rulers imposed a period of near total isolation. Outside influences were minimised. **Old instruments** like the *koto* zither continued to develop repertoire, as did the *shakuhachi* bamboo flute. However, it was the three-stringed plucked lute, the *shamisen* (which came from China via the smaller Okinawan *sanshin*), that came to represent new styles, reflecting the development of a sophisticated pre-modern urban culture. The shamisen provided the perfect musical accompaniment for popular styles, dance and drama, as well as the narrative folk styles often called **min'yo** (see opposite). The *nagauta shamisen* style for **kabuki** theatre also developed at this time, as did the sankyoku, the typical instrumental ensemble of the time – koto, shamisen, shakuhachi and *kokyu* (a bowed fiddle). Very popular during the Edo period (1615–1867) were the many kinds of folk songs – about work, love and so on. Voice featured with shamisen, shakuhachi, drums and flutes. Folk styles are often associated with specific regions in Japan and folk may have remained popular with some people because it reminds those in the cities of their rural roots.

Min'yo – Folk Music

Japan's **min'yo** (folk) tradition is long and rich. Voice, sometimes as distinctive as any enka vocal, is accompanied by shamisen, *shakuhachi* (flute) and drums. Each region has its own style, perhaps the most famous of all is the instrumental *shamisen* style from Tsugaru. The continued popularity of min'yo is partly due to the nostalgia felt by urbanites for their home towns and villages, and many Japanese not only listen to min'yo, but are able to sing a song or two, particularly one from their home region.

Like many traditional musics, the form is tightly controlled by various guilds, a system called *iemoto*. Long apprenticeships are the norm for musicians, and family-based teaching systems guarantee something is passed on to the next generation. Shamisen master and singer **Umewaka Kiyohide**, whose father started a key guild in the 1950s, says the dedication required to master the form means that there are few professional players. "You must study many instruments and be certificated by the NHK min'yo school", he says. His father taught top min'yo singer **Asano Sanae** and the spellbinding young shamisen player **Kinoshita Shin'ichi**, the latter having played a major part in the **shin-min'yo** (new min'yo) wave led by singer Takio Ito.

Shin'ichi has also been a leading performer with the Japanese-sponsored **Asian Fantasy Orchestra**, which features in a festival each year in the Philippines and tours across Asia. The orchestra features traditional and modern masters from the region, including **Grace Nono** and **Joey Ayala**.

A rebel with many causes, **Takio Ito** broke away from the rigid control of the guilds to make his own way. The son of a fisherman, Ito has become well-known for his passionate singing style and willingness to experiment. Many older min'yo people disapprove, but the master **Umewake** disagrees: "Look. It's a good thing. The young stars are trying to make new min'yo. Min'yo has to be free. We have to think about the future".

Traditional drumming from Sado island, where the **Earth Festival** (a percussion-based event) is held annually, has now become famous internationally. **Ondekoza**, the original group of drummers, and its off-shoot, **Kodo**, are capable of playing very powerful, rootsy gigs with just the various Japanese drums (from the big daiko to small hand-drums), but the bands do often utilise other instruments.

One of the very best places to catch traditional music in action in Japan is at the local festival, or *matsuri*. At O-Bon festivals, an ancient Buddhist festival to celebrate ancestors, locals get down to a **bon odori** (bon dance). Check out the music

JOHN CLEWLEY

Young shamisen master Kinoshita Shin'ichi

of **Shang Shang Typhoon** which incorporates various kinds of festival music into its shows and even has its own festival every year, held just outside Tokyo. Wherever you go, you'll be dancing, and you'll be dragged up by the local granny if you try to sit out. Dances are centred around a bamboo tower with a big drum in the centre, moving to either tapes or live min'yo of classic

JAPAN

Traditional Instruments

Shakuhachi

A bamboo flute with five finger holes – four on the front and one on the back – the shakuhachi has a full range of chromatic notes, obtained by adjusting the position of the flute and partially covering the holes. The colour of its tone, while always soft and pure, depends on the

A train of Komuso 'beggar priests' playing Shakuhachi

bamboo used. During the Edo period (early seventeenth to mid-nineteenth centuries) it was used primarily in chamber ensembles with *koto* and *shamizen*, although

more recently there's been a revival of the more ancient solo repertoire as an aid to meditation.

Biwa and Shamizen

A pear-shaped plucked lute with four or five strings, the **Biwa** originated in China. It was played both in gagaku ensembles and solo, but had almost fallen out of use by the end of World War II, until Toru Takemitsu, Japan's most famous contemporary composer started writing for it, precipitating a revival.

A three-stringed lute, the **shamizen** also came to Japan from China, via Okinawa. The earliest shamisen music is credited to *biwa* players in the early seventeenth century and it has become one of the most popular instruments in Japanese music.

Koto

The Japanese long zither, or **koto**, usually has thirteen strings, with moveable bridges and is played with fingerpicks. It is thought to have originated from the Chinese *zheng* and to have arrived in Japan in the eighth century. Similar instruments are found in Korea (*kayagûm*) and Vietnam (*dan tranh*). It is found in gagaku ensembles, but has developed a rich solo tradition. It is also used to accompany songs and in small 'chamber music' ensembles, together with a second koto, a shamizen, or a shakuhachi.

INTERNATIONAL SHAKUHACHI SOCIETY

---

bon dances. You may catch the *mikoshi* procession where young men dressed in what look like jockstraps struggle to carry a portable shrine. Such festivals are all about music, cementing community bonds and having a good time – Japan-style.

Kayokyoku

As Japan began the process of modernisation under the Meiji Reformation of 1868, there was already a large pool of traditional music – classical, folk and urban – available for development or incorporation into newer styles. Another influence came into the mix in the mid-nineteenth century, with the arrival of Western **military bands** – the first Western music to arrive in Japan. These

laid the foundations for the Western music that followed, from classical to popular genres like jazz and chanson.

Two short song forms – *shoka* and *gunka* – developed during the Meiji period. **Shoka** are songs composed to introduce Western music and singing to schools. **Gunka** are military songs with strong Japanese elements, acting as a prototype for later Japanese–Western syntheses like enka. Popular from the Sino-Japanese war to World War II – when Western songs like jazz were banned – you can still hear these patriotic songs blaring from the trucks of right-wing activists in Tokyo.

At the turn of the century, another immensely popular song form was **ryukoka** ('songs that are popular') which developed from street entertainers in the Osaka region, and was set to a shamisen backing. Japan's first recording stars, **Tochuken Kumoemon** and **Yoshida Naramuru**, were ryukoka performers and their throbbing vocal styles prefigured important popular forms to come.

With Western culture – movies and music – now flooding Japan, local musicians started to catch on. The **Hatano Jazz Band** were the first Japanese to play jazz, following a trip to the USA in 1912. Tango, foxtrot, rumba, Tin Pan Alley, blues and Hawaiian all followed.

The potential for a fusion between Japanese and Western music was most fully realised by two composers, Nakayama Shimpei and Koga Masao, both of whom were major figures in the development of Japanese popular songs. Sometimes using the Japanese yonanuki pentatonic scale with Western arrangements, Shimpei hit the bigtime with "Kachusha no uta" (Katherine's Song), while Koga pioneered the use of single line guitar accompaniment (standard for many enka songs) in the 1931 hit, "Saké wa Namida ka Tameiki ka" (Saké is a tear or a sigh). Koga also used the yuri ornamentation from traditional music in this song.

The resultant style became known as **kayokyoku**, a catch-all term for Japanese popular songs that originated in the 1930s but only came into use after World War II. Roots bands like Shang Shang Typhoon that emerged in the late 1980s use a similar approach to create songs from a mixture of Japanese pop and traditional, Latin, reggae and Asian styles. Says SST leader Koryu, "what used to be great about kayokyoku was that it combined so many elements – Japanese music, Latin, Hawaiian, black American and so on".

After the famine and devastation that followed the end of World War II, people turned for solace to songs like the influential 1945 hit "Ringo No Uta" (The Apple Song), sung by **Michiko Namiki** and **Noburo Kirishima**. Despite the arrival of more Western styles like R&B and boogie woogie, some artists emerged singing kayokyoku in a Japanese style. In 1949, at the tender age of 12, **Misora Hibari**, the greatest popular singer of the modern era, made her debut.

Hibari, a precocious child who could memorise long poems and mimic adult singers, was versatile. Her voice could handle the natural voice singing style or **jigoe** as well as the wavering **yuri** or folk style. Her powerful, sobbing **kobushi** vocal technique created a highly charged atmosphere in her enka songs, but she was also talented enough to cover jazz, min'yo, Latin, chanson and torch songs in the thousand recordings she made before her death at 52 in 1989. In many

ways, she was Japan's most well-known, and loved, popular cultural icon of the twentieth century: not only did she appear in 160 films, she was also the undisputed Queen of Enka (see box overleaf).

As Hibari was starting her career, others like **Mihashi Michiya** and **Kasuga Hachiro** were incorporating Japanese elements into popular song. Meanwhile, American songs were spreading across Japan, helped no doubt by the Allied occupying forces. Japanese composers like **Hattori Ryuchi** picked up on the trends with the shuffle-rhythm inspired "Tokyo Boogie Woogie", even managing a shamisen version. Other styles like bluegrass, rockabilly, Hawaiian (a second boom), doowop, R&B and jazz all developed quickly.

In the 1950s Japanese **Latin music** was established, although its roots were laid down at least twenty years previously. During the fifties and early sixties, many Cuban-style bands like the **Tokyo Cuban Boys** were formed. Tango and Latin singer Ranko Fujisawa is still remembered for her south American tours. Tango remains popular in Japan and there is even an original Latin rhythm,

NIPPON COLUMBIA

Postwar heart-throb Misora Hibari

Enka - Japan's Soul Music

If you ask a Japanese person what **enka** means, you're likely to get the answer that it is '*Nihonjin no kokoro*', the soul of the Japanese. They may say it's about themes of lost love, homesickness or simply drowning the sorrows of a broken heart with saké. They may talk of songs that feature fog or rain, a smouldering cigarette that means loss, a wedding ring dropped into a glass of saké or the sad, unbearable farewell at a desolate port, somewhere far from home. This is the world of enka.

Enka (from *enzetsu,* meaning public speech, and *ka,* meaning a song) is more than a hundred years old, and despite what some younger Japanese say, it is still enormously popular in Japan. Originally it was a form of political dissent, disseminated by song sheets, but it quickly changed in the early twentieth century as it became the first style to truly synthesise Western scales and Japanese modes. **Shimpei Nakayama** and **Masao Koga** were the trailblazing composers. Koga's first hit in 1931, "Kage Wo Shitaite" (Longing For Your Memory), remains a much-loved classic.

Enka seems to be everywhere in Japan. Special television programmes like "Enka no Hanamichi" pump it out, and you'll hear it in restaurants and bars. And, of course, it received a major boost with the invention of karaoke, which helped to spread the genre's popularity both with younger Japanese and foreigners. The classic image is of enka queen **Misora Hibari** decked out in a kimono, tears streaming down her face as she sobs through Koga's "Kanashi Saké" (Sad Saké), with typically understated backing and single-line guitar. Hibari had the *nakibushi* (crying melody) technique and a stunning vibrato-like *kobushi* that makes the listener's hair stand on end.

When Hibari died in 1989, **Miyako Harumi** inherited her position as the top singer, though she has retired at least once. She is famed for her growling attack and the song "Sayonara". Many enka stars have long careers, and veterans like **Suburo Kitajima** are still going strong, but a new generation led by **Shin'ichi Mori**, **Aki Yashiro**, **Sachiko Kobayashi** and the multi-talented **Hiroshi Itsuki** forms the current top bracket of singers. Recently, a number of upcoming Korean singers have been making waves (Hibari was of Japanese/Korean ancestry). Watch out for **Gill Jehee** as the next big star.

No enka fan can pass up an essential visit to Rizumu (Rhythm), Kazuhiko Kobayashi's ancient enka shop in Ueno, Tokyo. Located under a railway arch in the Ameyoko market, the brightly displayed shop is a treasure trove of memorabilia with music stacked floor to ceiling. Mr Kobayashi, quick to notice foreigners' growing interest, has even Romanised the titles so you can find that haunting enka number you can't get out of your head.

Enka star Miyako Harumi rocking out

the **dodompa**. The tradition has been kept strong with the recent success of **Orquesta de la Luz**.

Kayokyoku gradually became associated with styles that used traditional scales, like **enka**, while the more Western-sounding pop became known as **Japanese pops**. This latter form was defined by songs like "Sukiyaki" and by the many Western-style groups that developed in the 1960s, known as **Group Sounds**. Japanese pops mirrored all the Western moves – Beatles imitators, rock, folk rock, folk and psychedelia were all flavour of the day.

Japanese Rock

By the late 1960s, musicians were starting to create Japanese language rock. Many pop bands at the time sang in English but some underground bands tried splicing Japanese into the rock mix. Seminal band **Happy End** were pioneers. Led by composer **Hosono Haruomi** and lyricist **Takashi Matsumoto**, the band tried to mesh folk-rock with Japanese lyrics about love and politics, and in the process inspired an entire generation of rockers.

Rock blossomed as the seventies advanced, forcing styles like enka to move to a more middle-aged audience. A new generation was on the move, and about to be turned upside down by **Shoukichi Kina**, a little-known Okinawan rocker, with his band **Champluse** (the name comes from the name of a traditional Okinawan stir-fry). Kina, the son of legendary min'yo singer and sanshin player Shouhei, managed to combine Okinawan min'yo and rock on his song "Hai Sai Oji-san" (Hello Uncle), which became so famous that it is used today as a drill song for high-school baseball games. Never modest, Kina looks back on the time by saying, "I created a new style, I opened the way". He also revealed that "Hai Sai" is actually a very tragic story about someone he knew as a kid, a neighbour who was always drunk. The real reason 'Uncle' was sad was that his family had all been killed by his wife with an axe.

The Asian rock sound, as defined by Champluse, was further developed by bands like Carol, Harada Shinji and RC Succession. The **Southern All Stars**, whose way of singing Japanese as if it were English helped them to be Japan's biggest-selling band in the late 1980s, were another influential group. This period also produced a wave of 'alternative' rock acts like Tama and Little Creatures, as well as Shonen Knife and the Boredoms.

But the most successful international and domestic band of the 1980s has to be **Yellow Magic**

Orchestra (YMO), formed by **Hosono Haruomi**, Ryuchi Sakamoto and Yukihiro Takahashi. Heavily influenced by German band Kraftwerk and computer game ditties, YMO's brand of technopop inspired many followers, notably The Plastics and Melon. Sakamoto went on to a highly visible and successful international career, both as a soloist and as an Oscar-winning film score composer. Haruomi, certainly regarded in Japan as a pioneer in searching for exotic sounds to incorporate into his music, has been working in diverse fields – soundtracks, songwriting for idol singers, music documentaries for TV and work with artists from James Brown and Ry Cooder to Tunisian singer Amina Annabi. His massive influence on the new roots generation in Japan cannot be underestimated.

What informs Haruomi's work – the search for an identity – is a major preoccupation of roots bands like Shang Shang Typhoon and The Boom. Haruomi became one of the first Japanese musicians to look south to the islands of **Okinawa** for inspiration: in 1980 both Haruomi and Ry Cooder

JOHN CLEWLEY

Hosono Haruomi, rock pioneer

performed on Shoukichi Kina's second, Okinawan-influenced album, *Bloodline*. Recently he has been working with Bill Laswell, as well as on albums with singers like Miharu Koshi and Chisato Moritaka.

Sandii and the Sunsetz were another band that savoured international success in the 1980s. Led by powerful singer **Sandii** and composer/producer **Makoto Kubota**, the band blended reggae and Okinawan music into its mix. But shortly after the band split up, Kubota turned his attention to producing Asian popular music, working with Indonesians like Queen Elvy Sukaesih and Detty Kurnia, as well as Singaporean comedian/singer Dick Lee. Kubota's most recent work has been with dance star Monday Michiru, The Boom and on his own label, Sushi, with the Madagascan band Njava.

Since her debut in 1980 (*Eating Pleasure*, with Hosono Haruomi), Sandii has moved easily across a broad range of styles. Kubota's interest in creating 'an Asian pop style for the 1990s' is in strong evidence in Sandii's recent albums which feature the *champur*-style *dangdut* dance form (with house and dance beats in the mix), lots of Asia-Pacific and Brazilian songs and a voice that can carry anything from torch songs to reggae and Japanese pop. Sandii has also returned to her roots with three superb **Hawaiian** albums, the last of which features American guitarist **Bob Brozman**. Wildly successful, the albums have fuelled another boom in Hawaiian music, the third this century.

The Roots Boom

While *idoru kashus* and singer/songwriters like massive-selling **Yuming** (Yumi Matsutoya) seemed to dominate the 1980s, new sounds did start to emerge. Many World Music acts arrived in the mid-eighties, exposing the Japanese to non-Western sounds. Each summer that followed would produce the trend of the year, be it Latin, reggae or Indonesian. The global WOMAD Festival has been a fixture in Japan since 1991 and a number of important artists have settled there, notably Morgan Fisher (ex-Mott the Hoople), who plays for The Boom, and guitarist Mamadou Doumbia, who has played on many roots recordings and released several excellent albums of his own.

The Japanese genius for assimilating foreign sounds into a new form is well known, and the invasion of World Music has had a similar effect. **Reggae**, for example, was considered 'underground' for years, but the rise of Japanese outfits like Jamaican-style toaster **Rankin' Taxi** and ska

band **Tokyo Ska Paradise Orchestra**, playing at events like the annual reggae fest **Japansplash**, has given the genre a mainstream profile. Visits by Africans like Papa Wemba (whose global management is located in Japan) have created local **lingala** (soukous) bands. **Latin** music has also had a big effect, propelling the talented **Orquesta de la Luz** to the top of the Billboard Latin chart in the early 1990s.

But the most significant development has been the rise of local **roots bands** since the late 1980s, when bands like Shang Shang Typhoon (SST), The Boom, and Okinawan artists and bands like the Rinkenband, Nenes, Kina, Tetsuhiro Daiko and Namie Amuro broke onto the scene. Inspiration came from both within Japan (Okinawa and local popular culture) and outside (World Music), and two approaches became evident.

Shang Shang Typhoon's leader **Koryu** says the band is firmly in the kayokyoku tradition. Japanese folk and festival styles, Okinawan, reggae, Latin, Chinese airs, southeast Asian pop – all feature in the band's songs but the end result is always distinctively Japanese. Even *rokyoku* (traditional storytelling), *ondo* (festival music) and *min'yo* (folk) feature. SST have never bettered their eponymous debut album; in recent years the band has experimented with Hawiian music but still hasn't had that illusive cross-over hit.

The second coming of the **Okinawans** (see p.153) was heralded by frenetic sell-out gigs of the **Rinkenband** in 1990, and a short time later by the ecstatic comeback of **Kina** and **Champluse**. Okinawan traditional music blended with bright pop caught everyone's attention. Okinawans' relationship to mainstream Japanese culture could be compared to the 'Celtic' movement in Europe: they have a keen sense of their own identity and in an increasingly homogenised Japan, a lively folk culture.

The Okinawans method of taking their local traditions and updating them with other forms of music has been reflected in a wave of new bands. **Soul Flower Union**, led by **Takahashi Nakagawa**, blend acoustic guitars, Okinawan and *chindon* (street) music, which advertises products or shops with drums and saxophones. Nakagawa wrote the hit "Mangetsu no Yube" (A Full Moon Evening) with Hiroshi Yamaguchi of The Heat for the victims of the Kobe earthquake. Unfortunately, SFU's music was considered too strange by its record company so the band released its own debut, *Asyl Ching-Dong*, on its own label. It features pre-war tunes, and is strongly influenced by Okinawan master **Tetsuhiro Daiku**. SFU has several satellite units that play in acoustic or more rock-influenced styles, and are starting to get noticed overseas. Recent work has included gigs with Irish musicians like Donal Lunny and Dolores Keane.

Another updated local style is **kawachi ondo**, an old narrative folk style from the central Kansai region. Its rapid fire, rap-like vocal delivery is somewhat similar to Thailand and Laos' *mor lam*. Traditionally, Kawachi ono's wild men, dressed

Shang Shang Typhoon

in colourful kimonos, perform at local *bon odori* (summer festivals) around the country. The leading modern exponent, **Kikusuimaru Kawachiya** burst onto the scene with a hit single for a TV commercial about part-time workers (known as 'freeters'). He released several classy albums that included Indonesian, reggae and rock elements. He has been quiet of late, releasing only a won-

derful (but long-deleted) collection of reggae covers – a tribute to Bob Marley called *Bob Marley Ondo 97* – that included a cover of "I Shot The Sheriff" which turned out as "I was Shotted".

From the same region came the 'musical anarchist' **Tademaru Sakuragawa**, who sings in a similar style called **goshu ondo**. Backed by the now-disbanded **Spiritual Unity** (many of its original members now play for bands like Nenes), Tademaru broke out of the festival circuit with his only album, released in 1991.

None of these bands, however, has had the pop chart success of **The Boom**, one of the earliest roots bands, which has been on the go since the mid-1980s. Led by **Kazufumi Miyazawa** (see box overleaf), the Boom started off as a ska/two-tone band, but unlike the **Tokyo Ska Paradise** band, which has never tried any other music than ska, the Boom quickly moved onto other styles and incorporated them into a heady brew.

In 1993, the Boom had the biggest selling single in the country (1.5 million copies) with "Shima Uta" (Island Songs). It used an Okinawan melody and *sanshin* riffs, set to hard drums and rock guitar. Considered a modern classic, the song garnered the Japanese equivalent of the Grammy for Best Song. Subsequently, the Boom moved into Indonesian music, giving it a similar treatment. Some of their best songs were recorded with **Makoto Kubota**, including "E-Ambe". Brazilian and Latin featured on the albums *Far East Samba* and *Tropicalism*. The latter disc saw the various elements from previous albums blending and maturing, and the band is certain to progress and achieve international prominence.

The Boom's leader, 'Miya', also has a blossoming solo career. He writes for Sakamoto, Kina, Dick Lee and even reggae singer **Yami Bolo**. In 1998 he released two albums, one in London, *Sixteenth Moon*, and the other, *Afrosick* (as in 'homesick'), in Brazil, alongside such luminaries as Carlinos Brown.

Miya of The Boom

The Boom - Miyazawa on the right

Composer and leader of The Boom, **Kazufumi 'Miya' Miyazawa** is one of Japan's most innovative musicians. He has travelled widely and borrows freely from reggae, Okinawan, Indonesian and Brazilian music. Unlike the typical copycat approach of mainstream Japanese musicians, Miya is intent on searching for new sounds, the latest of which is a solo album called *Afrosick* recorded entirely in Brazil with a star cast of Brazilian musicians. The Boom have also toured in Brazil and played at festivals in Europe.

You've said you've been inspired by travelling. What about your own 'roots'? Where are they?
I really don't know. I've felt sometimes that I haven't got any musical roots at all. There was nothing to start from. After World War II, the Japanese gave up their own culture and became very Americanised. We have min'yo and kabuki and there was a small movement to protect our own culture, but it was very limited. If forced to choose I would say my roots lie in the pop music of America. It's a kind of tragedy. I guess I've been travelling to countries that do have musical roots to pick up ideas from them.

One of the Boom's most famous songs was "Shima Uta". Did you get any adverse reaction from the Okinawan traditional musicians thinking that you had stolen their music?
I'm sure that some of the traditional musicians think that way, and I used to worry about it. The Okinawans

were sacrificed by the Japanese government during the war, and the Okinawan intelligentsia today still believe the Japanese government was guilty. So I wondered if I could really make Okinawan music. I'm sure for some Okinawans it wasn't pleasant to hear a Japanese man sing that song. But Shoukichi Kina really helped me. He invited me to play with him in Okinawa and just accepted me. I also think that perhaps I encouraged young Okinawans to pick up the sanshin and play their own traditional music again. There is an invisible wall between Japanese and Okinawans, and Shoukichi helped to break that. He's got a very big heart.

The fusions have spread wider from there?
The album *Far East Samba* was quite straight in its use of samba and Cuban rhythms. A song like "Tegami", though, is the next stage – it's an experiment with our interpretation. It has Brazilian rhythms but it's a rock version – it's another sound completely. It's really quite radical. There's been nothing like it even in Brazil, with that mix of Brazilian rhythms and rock.

Have you always wanted your music to progress like this?
Yes, I suppose so. Shima Uta, for example, did mix rock and Okinawan folk but it was quite simple. Then we recorded "E-Ambe"; it wasn't just Okinawan but had a Jamaican rhythm and Indonesian gamelan all mixed into it, so it was a new interpretation of Okinawan music. We seem to start off quite simply and then move on to other stages.

What kind of album did you want to make with *Afrosick*?
Brazil is quite similar to Japan in that we have stereotypical music, such as samba or bossa nova in Brazil, and in Japan, say, enka. But there are actually all kinds of music in both countries, from hip hop to ska to reggae. There are so many excellent young musicians in Brazil who want to escape the stereotypical image of Brazilian music and make a new music and that's what I wanted to do. To make new dance or pop music so there's no bossa nova or samba...it's a new sound.

The Japanese are often seen to be excellent copyists, but not originators. What makes you different?
I wanted to record in Brazil not to make Brazilian music, but just for the atmosphere the musicans bring. I don't want to be Brazilian or act like a Brazilian. I tried to make a new music with the Brazilian musicians. It's the same if I record with Shoukichi Kina, I don't play Okinawan music, just new music.

Paul Fisher

Okinawa

If you want some musical magic in Japan, head for the deep, deep south and **Okinawa**'s balmy heat. It might be a min'yo performance in a small club or the massed troupes of the annual Ei-sa festival, but you'll find graceful dancing, haunting vocals, all kinds of drumming and stunning playing on the *sanshin*, the three-string Okinawan banjo. The performers, dressed in spectacular costumes, may be anything from a solo sanshin player to a hundred-strong street band complete with conch shells, sanshin and ranks of synchronised hand drummers.

The sub-tropical Okinawan island chain, known as the Ryuku islands by *uchinanchu* (Okinawan people), is found in the East China Sea, some 500km from mainland Japan. Okinawa was under US administration after World War II and was only returned to Japan in 1972. Blending traditions of mainland Asia with those of the Pacific, the archipelago of seventy islands has a thriving traditional culture which is just as exotic to the Japanese as to anybody else.

Okinawa Roots

Okinawa was settled by people from both northern Asia (via China and Korea) and the southeast. Trading links were established first with China and then with the rest of the region, and many cultural influences were absorbed during this time. Spurred by the expectation of vast profits, the Japanese soon followed, invading and annexing the islands in 1609. Thus began a long period of foreign domination, a process some Okinawans claim is continuing to this day through the Japanese administration in far-off Tokyo and the massive US military presence.

For more than four hundred years, Okinawans have developed folk and court styles of music that are unique in Asia. Social and cultural life, centred around the village and family, has always been based on music, poetry and dance. In 1690, Englebert Kaempfer noted that peasants carried their musical instruments into the rice fields, always ready for a jam session after work. Each region has its own music and the folk tradition is very much alive. In some villages, **umui** (religious songs) are still sung at festivals to honour ancestors. Work songs that reflect communal agriculture techniques can still be heard, and various kinds of group and circle dances, some performed exclusively by women, can be found in the smaller islands.

Popular entertainment is known by the general term, **zatsu odori** (common dance), though everyone calls these songs **shima uta** (island songs). The best-known style, and one no wedding would be complete without, is called **katcharsee**. Set to lively rhythms laid down by the sanshin, which plays both melody and rhythm, and various drums, the dance is performed with the upper body motionless and the lower body swaying sensuously, accompanied by graceful hand movements that echo similar dances in Thailand and Indonesia.

The Asian connection can be clearly seen in the history of the **sanshin**. This three-stringed lute began life in China as the *san hsien* and was introduced to Okinawa in around 1392. Local materials were quickly exhausted so that Thai snakeskin was used for the soundbox and Filipino hardwood for the neck. Once introduced to mainland Japan, the shanshin became bigger, produced a harder sound and was renamed the *shamisen*, one of the quintessential Japanese instruments.

While the rest of Japan rapidly modernised during the Meiji era, Okinawa was left underdeveloped. Even today, it has the highest unemployment rate in Japan. But go to Okinawa City (but call it by its local name when you get there, Koza City), produce a bottle of saké and someone will start playing music.

Although the relationship between the US military and Okinawans has never been as close as in the Philippines, **American culture** has certainly influenced local musicians. Local musicians started to copy US pop styles in the 1950s, sometimes mixing in folk music. Rinsuké Teruya, father of pop star Rinken of Rinkenband fame and a popular comedy singer, remembers constructing a four-string electric *yonshin* in the 1950s, and he has preserved an old recording that features mambo and Okinawan folk music.

Rockin' Ryukus

Okinawa's early post-war music was dominated by local folk recordings, led by the legendary singer/sanshin player **Shouhei Kina** and **Kadegaru Rinsho**, both of whom followed in the footsteps of pre-war star **Fukubaru Choki**. While Shouhei Kina was singing, his young son **Shoukichi Kina** was absorbing both his father's folk music and the local rock played around the US bases by bands like Condition Green. He formed a band while still at high school, taking the name **Champluse** (see p.149), opening the way for a new generation of Okinawan rockers.

Kina's music attracted attention from Western musicians like Ry Cooder and Henry Kaiser – the former played guitar on several songs on Kina's

1980 *Bloodline* album. Japanese pioneer **Hosono Haruomi** was also on the same disc. Later, **Riuchi Sakamoto**, **Makoto Kubota** and **Koryu** of Shang Shang Typhoon would all dip into Kina's music for inspiration. His song "Subete No Hito No Kokoro Ni Hana O" (Flowers For Your Heart) is an Asian favourite, with excellent versions covered by Thailand's Caravan and Indonesia's Detty Kurnia.

After a seven-year break, taken mainly for religious reasons, Kina made his comeback at an ecstatic 1990 concert in Shinjuku. Since then his well-known 'difficult' personality has led to personnel changes in the band and games of musical chairs with record companies. He has tried to blend reggae with min'yo and even recorded a Parisian-style album with Francois Breant. Recently, he opened a club in Naha, Chakra, but it's a sad sight to see this legend play for just a few desultory tourists. Nevertheless, Kina's influence remains strong. His work with Miya on The Boom's Okinawa-inflected songs led to the chart success of "Shima Uta" for The Boom in 1993.

One Champluse spin-off, the **Ayame Band**, led by ex-Kina cohort and sanshin player **Takao Nagama**, is taking Okinawan music still further. Two albums so far display stunning, fast-action sanshin playing. Another ex-Champluse man,

All-action, revue-style Rinkenband in live performance

ing, and drumming spectacularly, the band stormed the capital like a typhoon. **Rinken**, a sanshin player who grew up playing with his father and maestro uncle, moved in a different direction to Kina by ignoring rock and creating instead bright pop songs that fused min'yo and *ei-sa* festival songs. These music-hall revue-style shows were packed with mad-cap antics, *katcharsee* dance songs and plaintive haunting ballads that featured the remarkable voice of Rinken's wife, **Tomoko Uehara**. Okinawan vocals don't feature the wavering *kobushi* of mainland Japan – glissando and soaring grace notes feature instead. The Rinkenband's debut album, *Arigatou*, confirmed the band's promise. But despite a range of albums since, and Rinken's experiments with a guitar-like version of the sanshin called the chereng, the band hasn't managed to equal their early success.

Sadao China, who records his own solo min'yo and produces other artists, came to attention through the all-female group, **Nenes**. He was the brains behind Nenes' 1991 debut album, *Ikawu*, which featured traditional vocals set to both min'yo and music from islands around the world. Such was their draw that their best album so far, *Koza Dabasa*, led **Ry Cooder** to play with them. Michael Nyman and George Winston have followed, and in 1998, Talvin Singh recorded their new album. Nenes played WOMAD UK in 1998 and look the most likely of the older generation to achieve international success. China has a club, *Shima Uta Bar*, in Ginowan, which is one of the best places on the main island to see Okinawan roots music.

From the same generation, but less well-known is the sanshin player and singer Tetsuhiro Daiku from Yaeyama island, which is close to Taiwan. **Yaeyama min'yo** is based on work songs, called **yunta** and **jiraba**, following a call-and-response pattern. Daiku has travelled all over the world as an ambassador of traditional Okinawan music but it is his brilliant fusion of Yaeyama folk with Japanese *chindon* (street music) that has caught attention. Interestingly, his band features members of the Tokyo-based Soul Flower Union.

Takashi Hirayasu, also has a new, well-received album, with Bob Brozman.

In January 1990, **The Rinkenband** played their first dates in Tokyo. Dressed in traditional outfits, singing in *uchinaguchi* (Okinawan), whistling, danc-

Kina, China, Rinken and Daiku have all influenced a new wave of Okinawan pop now bubbling out of cities like Koza and Naha. The hottest act is **Parsha Club**, led by **Ara Yukito**, which

JOHN CLEWLEY

Nenes orchestrate their fans

mixes jazz funk, rock and dance with Okinawan min'yo. Ara has a haunting voice, especially on ballads. Yaeyama also produced another young star in **Yasukatsu Ohshima**, who after a largely unnoticed debut album, released a joint-venture with the brass band **Orquestra Bor**. Miyako Island's **Satoru Shimoji** continues the exotic trends with a sanshin and synthesised brass sound – funky *shima uta*. But it is Amami Island, close to mainland Japan and a place famous for falsetto singing, that has produced one of the brightest new stars, **Ritsuko Nakano** (aka **Rikki**), a former child prodigy min'yo singer. Producer **Makoto Kubota**, using some Boom songs and Sandii on backing vocals, helped her release a successful debut album in 1995.

Whatever else Okinawan musicians do, the unmistakable sound of the sanshin, a funky beat and those haunting vocals always seem to emerge. And they aren't afraid to experiment: **Kenji Yano**, formerly of the 1980s cult live act Roku Nin Gumi, made a remarkable album of traditional tunes mixed with surf music, providing one of Okinawa's most extreme but brilliant moments. As SST's Koryu puts it, "as long as there is a solid musical foundation, as there is with Okinawan music, incorporating the influences of other cultures can only greatly expand the possibilities".

discography

General Compilations

The Rough Guide to Japanese Music
(World Music Network, UK).

The best introduction to the Japanese music scene, including all the types of music covered in this article except kayokyoku and enka. Includes Soul Flower Mononoke Summit's earthquake song, Takio Ito, the Surf Champlers, Makoto Kubota and his band in Shoukichi kina's classic "Hai Sai Oji-San", plus a strong Okinawan presence. Classical and traditional artists include the quartet Koto Vortex, folk koto player Kunitaka Sato from Amami island, shakuhachi player Shozan Tanabe, biwa player Yukihiro Gotoh and shamisen virtuoso Michihiro Sato.

Traditional and Classical Music

Compilations

Japanese Traditional Music Vols 1–3: Gagaku; Nogaku; Kabuki.
(King Records, Japan).

Three-CD set with English-language liner notes. Rarely performed gagaku is one of the strangest musics in this discography. Based around the length of a breath, the music can be ethereal or discordant, but always engaging. Nogaku, the austere but powerful noh music, has some similarities with gagaku, but includes the *fue* pipe, whose unstable pitch gives the music a strangely compelling sound that fits perfectly with texts about spirits, gods and ghosts. The third disc, *Kabuki*, consists of a live performance at Minima-za in Kyoto, of the famous *Kanjincho* (Subscription List) play, first performed in 1840. The play is based on the immensely popular noh drama *Ataka*, describing General Minamoto Yoshitsune's flight from his Shogun brother, Yorimoto.

◉ **Japon: Gagaku** (Ocora, France).

Gagaku is an acquired taste, but for those that want to sample it, this is an exemplary Ocora recording of the ancient music played by the Ono Gagaku Kai Society. Six tracks of austere instrumental and ceremonial dance music, including the most famous piece in the gagaku repertoire, "Etenraku". Plangent flutes and oboes punctuated by drums and gongs.

◐ **Lullaby for the Moon** (EMI Hemisphere, UK).

Intimate chamber music performances for solo koto, koto and shakuhachi duets, and various ensembles of the two instruments. Slow moving and restful.

◉ **Min'yo – Folk Song from Japan** (Nimbus, UK).

'Folksong is the heart's home town', says a popular Japanese saying and this is the repertoire to support it – all but five of the 26 songs here have local place names in the title. This is an idiomatically performed selection of min'yo songs, the majority from northern Japan, which dominates the national repertoire. Performed by a small professional ensemble, led by shamisen player Takahashi Yujiro, including shamisen, shakuhachi, shinobue flute, and percussion.

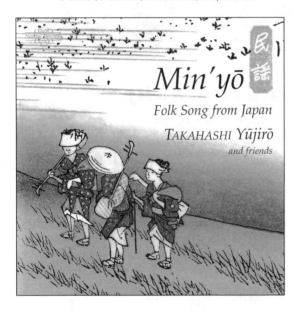

Min'yō
Folk Song from Japan
TAKAHASHI Yūjirō
and friends

◉ **Music of the Shakuhachi** (JVC Victor, Japan).

Four of the best shakuhachi players, including Hozan Yamamoto and Goro Yamaguchi, playing some of the most famous pieces.

Artists

Takahashi Chikuzan

The great master of the shamisen who helped popularise the exciting Tsugaru Shamisen style.

◉ **Tsugaru Shamisen** (Sony, Japan).

Recorded during Chikuzan's heyday at the Jean Jean club in Tokyo, in 1974.

Yukihiro Gotoh

The leading young biwa player. He likens the music of the satsuma biwa to the blues.

◉ **Poetry of Japanese Ballads of Biwa** (Zanmai, Japan).

The biwa can be rather demanding listening in classical mode, but in this 1997 release Gotoh performs traditional and modern styles, accompanied by accordions and other instruments.

Yoshikazu Iwamoto

Born in 1945, and taught by grandmaster Katsuya Yokoyama, Iwamoto is one of the leading contemporary players of the shakuhachi. He has a wide repertoire of traditional solo pieces as well as contemporary material.

◉ **The Spirit of Dusk** (Buda/Musique du Monde, France).

One of an excellent series of recordings from Buda which focuses on the calm, Zen meditational world of the *komuso* beggar priests.

Kohachiro Miyata

One of Japan's leading Shakuhachi players.

◉ **Shakuhachi – The Japanese Flute** (Nonesuch Explorer, US).

Five pieces of traditional solo shakuhachi music dating from the eighteenth century and earlier, with a meditative character.

Ondekoza

Every year at the Sado Island Earth festival, Ondekoza, a band of remarkable traditional drummers, invites percussion groups from around the world. Ondekoza, and the off-shoot outfit Kodo, have done much to bring the dramatic drumming styles of traditional Japanese music to wider audiences.

◉ **Fujiyama** (Victor, Japan).

Various Victor/JVC albums are widely available but this one features a good range of drumming techniques, and features other instruments as well.

Michihiro Sato

One of the most exciting young shamisen players today.

◉ **Jonkara** (Kyoto Records, Japan).

An excellent CD from 1995 including three versions of the classic Tsugaru piece "Tsugaru Jonkara Bushi".

Ito Takio

The enfant terrible of the conservative min'yo tradition, Ito, a fisherman's son from Hokkaido, grew up listening to his father's work songs. He had no time for the preservation of min'yo and left his early musical training to go it alone. He says he's just 'fishing for songs'. A very powerful and colourful voice, equally at ease in a simple setting or with an electric band.

◉ **Ondo** (VAP, Japan).

Ito's only major label release, *Takio* (Sony, Japan), was released in 1988 and since then it's been difficult to find his independent releases. This 1996 album is the best of these and includes a version of the beautiful Hokkaido classic "Soran Bashi", and "Toraji", a Korean tune. Also worth noting is ◉ **Nipponese Song** (VAP, Japan), released in 1998.

Contemporary Music

Artists

The Boom and Kazufumi Miyazawa

In 1986, four schoolmates in Kofu City started to play ska and sing their own songs. Three years later, as The Boom, they headlined the Budokan in Tokyo. Kazufumi 'Miya' Miyazawa quickly established himself as the leader and composer and has also developed a solo career. One of the best bands to emerge from Japan in years.

Tropicalism (Sony, Japan).

Probably the band's most radical musical journey, with a sassy blend of Brazilian music, Indonesian, reggae, club music and jazz, all in a Japanese sound. Contains the controversial single "Tegami", a poem read over a backbeat of Brazilian rhythms that derided the pop music scene in Japan.

Afrosick (Toshiba, Japan; EMI, Brazil).

Miya's solo album, recorded in Brazil with a vast cast of Brazilian musicians including Carlinhos Brown, Marcos Suzano and Lenine. There are two versions, one in Japanese, the other in Portuguese; the latter is much more convincing. Outstandng tracks include: Suzano's drum machine-led "Ilusao de Etica" and "Em Busca de Alma Perdida".

Miyako Harumi

Though she's retired at least once, Harumi remains the finest enka singer of her generation. Since her debut in 1968, her unique quavering voice and trademark rough-edged attack have set her apart from her contemporaries. Her emotional comeback in 1988 led to wonderful rock-tinged enka concert at the first WOMAD Japan festival in 1991, which to the astonishment of many, drove a packed crowd of young Japanese wild.

Greatest Hits
(Nippon Columbia, Japan).

Like Hibari, Miyako Harumi has the ability to make a song completely her own. This set includes her famous monster hit, "Sayonara" (a staple karaoke favourite), which begins with her gravel-throated intro before swooping into the song. Stirring stuff.

Kikusuimaru Kawachiya

Kawachiya is the leading innovator of kawachi-ondo, a folk dance style from the Kansai region, characterised by fast rapping delivery of narratives. He is also a specialist in shinmon-yomi, a form of story-telling based on current affairs. He started the first kawachi-ondo rock band in 1983, and later became interested in reggae. Always keen to experiment, he has worked with Makoto Kubota, Brave Combo and bhangra musicians.

Bob Marley Ondo '97 (GEO, Japan).

This is what happens when reggae meets kawachi-ondo: "I Shot the Sheriff" becomes "I Was Shotted", "Exodus" turns into "Exodus From An Edge" and No Woman No Cry" is now "No Rastaman Cry." Brilliant singing and wild abandon.

Hibari Misora

'Hibari-chan' is the enka singing icon of post-war Japan. From child music and film star to Enka Queen, Hibari rose to the top and stayed there until her death. Her debut at the age of twelve with "Kappa Boogie" confirmed the name her mother had given her, Hibari, which means 'lark'. One of the twentieth century's great voices, and a performer of great emotional range and power.

Greatest Hits (Nippon Columbia, Japan).

With a thousand recordings to chose from, it's hard to know where to start. Maniacs will already have the above label's twenty-volume CD set, and perhaps **Kawa No Nagare No Yo Ni** (Nippon Columbia, Japan), one of her last releases. This collection, however, contains the all-time killer Hibari song, "Kanashi Saké" (Sad Saké). Set to a single guitar-line from a quintessential Koga melody and discrete backing, she moans and soars or just talks over this sad tale. You can taste the tears. Includes early classics like "Sad Whistle".

Orquesta de la Luz

Formed in 1984 from the ashes of the Orquestra del Sol band. Many people were surprised at the success of "Salsa Caliente De Japon," which topped the Billboard Latin charts for 10 weeks in 1991, but Japan has a long and venerable Latin tradition. Tight, polished and full of fun, De La Luz enjoyed several years of success and made tours in Latin America. Of late, the band has lost some of its shine on record but live acts remain hot.

De La Luz (BMG/Victor, Japan).

This killer debut contains the outstanding pan-Latin hit "Salsa Caliente De Japon", which has been covered by several Latin stars. The assured vocal work of lead singer Nora is a revelation, after you've pinched yourself that, yes, this really is a Japanese band and not a hot outfit from Puerto Rico or Miami.

Sandii

Sandii (born Sandy O'Neale) and partner Makoto Kubota are among the most respected pop performers and producers in the business. Both tasted international success with Sandii & the Sunsetz in the early 1980s and were pioneers of blending Japanese pop with reggae and Okinawan music. Sandii is one of the longest surviving singers around and her recent output has been truly eclectic, ranging from dancefloor, hip-hop-inflected sounds through a range of Asian styles to Brazilian bossanova.

Dreamcatcher (Sony, Japan).

A delightful mix of Caribbean, Japanese, Indonesian and Malay songs with a cast that includes Hosono Haruomi, Tokyo-based African guitarist Mamadou Doumbia and Dick Lee. Rap from trend-setters like Monday Michiru pops up on some tracks. Of her Hawaiian albums, the best is **Sandi's Hawaii** (Sushi, Japan), released in 1996.

Shang Shang Typhoon

Leader Koryu ('Red Dragon') started out as a singer-songwriter in the 1980s but a trip to Okinawa changed his mind. As couldn't play the Okinawan sanshin he decided to use the banjo, with great results. The addition of lead vocalists Emi and Satoko, plus a keyboard player and percussionist completed the line-up.

 Shang Shang Typhoon
(Epic-Sony, Japan).

Swirling into the music scene in 1990 with a kaleidoscopic range of music that somehow ends up sounding very Japanese, this debut from STT heralded the rise of roots music in Japan. Edited like a live concert with an opening and ending theme, the songs rush through the Okinawan-tinged "As Time Goes By" to the kawachi-ondo/reggae blend of "It's Alright Buddha Smile". Only STT could get away with the Latin madness of "Dancing Cha Cha Cha With Bitter Tea". Still sounds fresh. To assess how the band has fared in the ensuing years, check out their latest 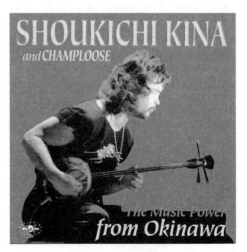 **Gnahs Gnahs** (Sony, Japan), set on an imaginary Pacific tropical island.

Soul Flower Union and Takahashi Nakagawa

Rebel Takahashi Nakagawa is one of the few Japanese musicians with a social conscience. After starting out with the band Newest Model, he formed the influential Soul Flower Union with Hideko Itami of Mescaline Drive. Though originally a rock band, the music has all kinds of roots influences, including Korean, Ainu (an indigenous group from the north), forgotten popular songs, min'yo, chindon street music and Okinawan. A band to watch out for.

Electro-Asyl-Bop
(Ki/oon Sony, Japan).

Their best ever album, from 1996, combining the electric sound with Mononoke Summit elements in a kind of swirling psychedelic roots rock played with unbridled passion and energy. Highlights include the brilliant "Eejyanika" and a new version of the classic "Mangetsu no Yube" (A Full Moon Evening). One of the defining moments of Japanese music in the 90s.

Levelers Ching Dong (Respect Records, Japan).

The band Soul Flower Mononoke Summit was an acoustic version of Soul Flower Union when they were forced to unplug to perform at Kobe for victims of the recent earthquake. A live 1997 recording, the group's mix of chindon and folk was the most infectious Japanese roots album of 1997. Highlights include the opening worker's anthem "Internationale" and the old revolutionary song "Kakumeika".

Original Notion Picture Soundtrack: Soul-cialist Escape in Lost Homeland (Respect Records, Japan).

On this solo album, Nakagawa found a sublime blend of Irish folk and Japanese traditional music. The songs with Donal Lunny's Irish band, including "Shio no Michi" and a brilliant new version of "Mangetsu no Yube" are stunning highlights of this remarkable album.

Tokyo Bibimbap Club

Formed by Japanese and Japanese-Korean musicians, Tokyo Bibimbap Club was based around the individual talents of singer and changgo (Korean drum) player Pyeon Inja, singer/guitarist Pak Poe and one of the country's best guitarists, Hirofumi Kasuga. Their live act made them one of the most popular acts on the roots scene, but they have recently disbanded as the main players now work on solo projects.

Tokyo Bibimbap Club (Toratanu, Japan).

Now considered a classic of the roots music genre in Japan, this mix of Korean and Japanese music, along with strains of rock and reggae, was topped off by Pyeon's unique folk vocals. The band's finest recorded moment.

Okinawa

Artists

Ayame Band

One of the key elements in the Champluse sound of Shoukichi Kina was the fast-action sanshin playing of Takao Nagama. When he left Kina's outfit he formed the Ayame band, which quickly developed a following for passionate live performances. The sound is rockier than

either Kina or Rinken but releases, mainly still confined to Okinawa, have suffered from poor production.

Akemio No Machi Kara (Kokusai Boueki, Okinawa).

Rousing sanshin riffs and great vocals from leader Takao mark this album as the best so far. The dancing "Ayame Ondo" and the classic "Akemio No Machi Kara" are the outstanding tracks.

Sadao China

Son of min'yo legend Sadashige China, Sadao China is one of the 'Big Three' of contemporary Okinawan music; Kina and Rinken being the others. His profile has been much lower however, as he prefers to be a producer for bands like Nenes, playing in the background. Nevertheless, he is an excellent sanshin player and singer.

Shimaya Uta Asobi (Disc Akebana, Okinawa).

These solo min'yo songs display a very gentle sanshin style and a softer singing style than the great Rinsho. Includes duets.

Tetsuhiro Daiku

Born on Ishigaki island, part of the Yaeyama group, Daiku is an award-winning sanshin player and singer, and the most travelled Okinawan musician of recent times. As a certified teacher of traditional and Okinawan folk music, he has had enormous influence on keeping the min'yo traditions alive. He has an experimental side too, having recorded with wild saxophonist Kazutoki Umezu and chindon-ya (Japanese street musicians). A great voice and a DJ of influence on local radio.

Jinta Internationale (Off Note, Japan).

This 1996 album shows the new Daiku sound maturing and developing further the perfect match-up of Okinawan and chindon music. Includes a wonderful version of the socialist standard, "Internationale".

Champluse

Bad boy Shoukichi Kina, the leader of Champluse, started a new direction in Okinawan music with "Hai Sai Oji San" (Hello Uncle). Kina remains a big influence on contemporary Japanese pop – witness his work with the Boom's Miya.

SHOUKICHI KINA and CHAMPLOOSE

The Music Power from Okinawa

◉ **The Music Power from Okinawa** (GlobeStyle, UK).

Easily available live set recorded in Okinawa in 1977. Driving sanshin, great vocal backing (with those 'ay eya ay eya ay eya sa sa' shouts) and Kina in charge on vocals. Includes a wonderful version of "Haisai", and "Tokyo Sanbika," a song co-written by Rinsuké Teruya, Rinken's father. The Asian favourite "Subete No Hito No Kokoro Ni Hana O" (Flowers For Your Heart) can be found on the second album, ◉ **Bloodline** (Polydor, Japan), which was reissued in 1988 and includes Ry Cooder on guitar.

Takashi Hirayasu

Hirayasu started out playing blues and R&B at the bars around the American bases in Okinawa, and took up the sanshin in his early twenties. He joined Shoukichi Kina's band Champluse and played on the *Bloodline* album, amongst others. He began a solo career recording with members of Soul Flower Union in the 1990s.

WITH BOB BROZMAN

◖◗ Jin Jin/Firefly
(Respect, Japan; Riverboat Records, UK).

This is a fine, intimate collaboration with Bob Brozman, the Californian master of Hawaiian slide guitar. Based around a dozen Okinawan nursery rhymes, Hirayasu's vocals have a gentle naivety about them, while Brozman's slide burns like the insects themselves on the title track.

Nenes

In 1990, China Sadao, worried that the younger generation were forgetting traditional music, set up a four-piece female band, Nenes (which means 'sisters' in Okinawan). China's sanshin playing, the massed vocals of Nenes (led by Misako Koja), plus keyboards and percussion completed the line-up. The band has gone on to to sell-out tours on the mainland, toured overseas and played with a vast list of foreign musicians. Koja recently left for a solo career but the band remains otherwise unchanged.

◖◗ Koza Dabasa
(Ki/oon Sony Records, Japan).

The best album so far from the four women singers. Partly recorded in Los Angeles, with Ry Cooder, David Lindley, Jim Keltner and David Hidalgo (of Los Lobos). Not a dud on the album, and "Shima Jima Kaisha" is sublime.

◉ **Akemodoro Unai** (GlobeStyle, UK).

More recent and more eclectic, with influences of rap, reggae and pop, this is also highly recommended. In place of Misako Koja, Nenes are fronted by new singer, Eriko Touma, and backed by the China Sadao Band.

Parsha Club

Parsha Club is one of the hottest new bands in Okinawa, set up by Yukito Ara, a sanshin player and singer from the Yaeyama Islands. Moving closer to rock than the previous generation led by Kina et al, Parsha has inspired a keen following for its live-action gigs. Sadly, the band has rarely captured this live sound on record. Ara is a fine sanshin player and a powerful singer.

◉ **Nanafa** (Toshiba-EMI, Japan).

The only album that comes close to capturing the band's live act. Although a little uneven, the power of the band can be heard on the funky song "Gokoku Hojo", where Parsha mixes min'yo with jazz and funk.

Rinkenband

Founded by Rinken Teruya, the son of a famous singing entertainer, the band features Rinken's wife Uehara Tomoko's fabulous singing, a fast-action three-man chorus-line, keyboards, bass and Rinken's own sanshin playing. Takes a different line to Kina in modernising Okinawan min'yo by using a more pop approach. Live shows combine elements of festival music, min'yo and pantomime in a colourful mix. Uehara dressed in yellow bingata kimono, surrounded by three clowns, is an exotic sight indeed.

◉ **Rinkenband** (Wave/Sony, Japan).

A 'best of' collection from the early 1990s of bright, fresh pop ditties that blend 'ei-sa' festival music, min'yo and Rinken's plonking sanshin. Includes "Arigatou", an early live favourite. Recent experiments with a four-stringed electric version of the shanshin, the *chereng* are on ◉ **Chereng** (Sony, Japan).

Kadegaru Rinsho

At 77, Rinsho is one of the most revered traditional musicians in Okinawa, known as the 'Godfather of Shima Uta'. Many regard him as their mentor; China Sadao, producer of Nenes, even tours with the great sanshin player and singer who is still active on the main island. A truly great solo performer.

◖◗ Folk Songs of Okinawa
(JVC, Japan).

A must-have for those wanting to sample the pure traditional sound of solo sanshin playing and singing. It doesn't get any better than this – simple setting, Rinsho's hard-edged sanshin playing and his powerful, emotive voice. Sleevenotes in English.

The Surf Champlers

The brainchild of Osaka-born Kenji Yano, a musician now based in Okinawa. In the 1980s, Yano played with Rokunin Gumi, one of the few bands to match Champluse's passionate live performances, but he was much less successful commercially. Yano seemed always to be ahead of his time until this album, which might be called 'Okinawasurf' – surf guitar spliced with Okinawan min'yo. Yano is moving on fast though; his latest project, ◉ **Sarabange** (Qwotchee Records, Japan) takes Okinawan music towards trance.

◉ **Champloo A Go Go** (Qwotchee Records, Okinawa).

Yano recorded these katcharsee and min'yo songs, mixed with his own compositions, in what sounds like his bedroom. His stroke of genius was to use drum machines and a surf-style guitar. The most brilliant track of all is his cover version of the James Bond theme.

Korea

our life is precisely a song

Korea has often been culturally dominated by its neighbours – for many centuries the Chinese derided the Koreans as 'eastern barbarians' – and even today the dominant musical sounds in South Korea are Western (Classical music as well as pop) rather than native. But this small peninsula on Asia's northeast coast retains its own highly rhythmic musical styles, proudly distinct from its neighbours. **Rob Provine** introduces Korea's ancient traditions, while **Okon Hwang** and **Andy Kershaw** look, respectively, south and north, to its distinctive contemporary sounds.

Until the end of the nineteenth century, Korea was largely unknown to the West, despite the fact that it could boast an advanced technology and culture centuries before this date. Koreans were printing with movable metal type, for example, several hundreds of years before Gutenberg, and by the fifteenth century they had developed a scientific alphabet so effective that all Koreans are today literate (they even celebrate their writing system with an annual day of commemoration).

Korean musical history, which can be traced to tomb paintings and artefacts of the fifth century, has been documented with treatises and detailed notation systems since the fifteenth century. Government-sponsored institutions charged with preserving and teaching court music have been in operation since the seventh century, their current direct descendant being the National Center for Korean Traditional Performing Arts in Seoul.

Japanese colonisation in the first half of the twentieth century brought 78 rpm technology to Korea and left a recorded legacy of Korean music, early popular songs, and Western imports. Since the end of World War II, the Korean peninsula has been split into two highly antagonistic halves, and the division is reflected in their music. **South Korea** has a vibrant and stylistically wide-ranging musical life. In **North Korea**, on the other hand, the 'official' music is banal and politically straitjacketed in a Westernised 'light music' style (although titles such as "Good Farming in a Sub-Work Team" are memorable in themselves).

As in Japan, contemporary South Korea has seen heavy adoption of Western ideas and music, but in the past two or three decades there has been a heavy swing of the pendulum back toward native arts, which are now enjoying an exciting revival. In the early 1970s, for example, one could hardly find **nongak** (farmers' band percussion music) anywhere in the country; now it is everywhere, among students and striking factory workers and at traditional concerts. Shops in Seoul, meantime, are bursting with traditional musical instruments, teachers are enjoying prosperous times, and the CD market is burgeoning.

Formal Traditions

Korean traditional music has several strands, the most formal of which are represented by **court**, **aristocratic** and **religious music**.

Court Music

Korean **court music** is mostly orchestral, highly refined, and demands a lot of patient attention to subtle detail. In short, it is an acquired taste. But it has a majesty and integrity all its own and a very long heritage, dating back to the earliest ceremonies and banquets of the **Chosŏn dynasty** (1392–1910).

Apart from occasional re-enactments of royal ceremonies for nostalgic and touristic reasons, about the only place you'll hear live court music today is in the concerts of the **National Center for Korean Traditional Performing Arts** (*Kung-nip kugagwŏn*), a large and modern government-supported institute in Seoul where highly-trained musicians preserve, perform, and teach traditional music and dance at a high artistic level. Regular performances there feature the better-known court music and dance pieces and the music can also be heard on dozens of CDs.

SIMON BROUGHTON

Ensemble playing at Ancestors Temple in Seoul

Court music was originally divided into Chinese ritual music (*aak*), Koreanised music of Chinese origin (*tangak*) and real Korean music (*hyangak*). **Aak** was introduced to Korea from China in 1116 and has been revived and transformed on many occasions since. Contemporary aak music traces its ancestry back to a reconstruction of 1430, using written melodies from the twelfth century. Today, there are just two surviving melodies totalling about eight minutes of extremely slow, stark and stately music, played only at the semi-annual **Sacrifice to Confucius** in Seoul and in concerts at the National Center. This music uses only ritual instruments of Chinese origin, including the extraordinary sets of sixteen tuned bronze bells (*p'yŏnjong*) and stone chimes (*p'yŏn'gyŏng*) reserved for the most visually imposing of court pieces. The **tangak** repertoire also consists of only two short orchestral pieces known as *Nagyangch'un* (Springtime in Luoyang) and *Pohŏja* (Pacing the Void). The bulk of court music therefore, is *hyangak*.

A good example of the **hyangak** is the banquet piece *Sujech'ŏn* (Long Life According with Heaven), lasting about fifteen minutes. Its lead instruments – none of which are used in the ritual aak music – are the loud, oboe-like *p'iri* and two bowed string instruments: the two-string *haegŭm* and seven-string *ajaeng* – the latter bowed with a stick instead

of horsehair, making a strikingly raspy, penetrating sound. Other orchestral pieces to look out for are *Yŏmillak* (Pleasure with the People), which at eighty minutes of slow music requires the listener to adopt a new pace, and *Ch'wit'a* (Blowing and Beating), regularly-paced music originally for military use, which employs the largest traditional orchestra, complete with bells and chimes.

A special type of hyangak court music is found in two suites of pieces performed at the annual **Sacrifice to Royal Ancestors**: *Pot'aep'yŏng* (Preserving the Peace) and *Chŏngdaeŏp* (Founding the Dynasty). Originally composed and arranged in the fifteenth century to replace supposedly Chinese aak with something more appealing to Korean royal ancestors, the music now performed is still closely related to fifteenth-century notations. Its two orchestras each include the bronze bells and stone chimes, as well as singers. Both suites together neatly fill one CD.

Aristocratic Music

Aristocratic chamber music (*chŏngak*) was originally intended to entertain members of the ruling class in informal contexts. It comprises both instrumental ensemble music and vocal music with instrumental accompaniment. The purely instrumental repertoire consists almost entirely of various versions (for strings, wind, or mixed ensembles) of one suite of nine pieces called **Yǒngsan hoesang** (Preaching on Yǒngsan). The music starts at an amazingly slow pace and builds slowly to a rather cheerful dance tempo by the end (about fifty minutes later).

The distinguished *kayagǔm* player **Hwang Byungki** (see below) likens the aristocratic music to the art of a formal oriental garden, an analogy that is very helpful in appreciating its beauty: "These pieces have the beauty of ages, like gold and grand trees. There is no feeling of structure or climax, it is like the placing of rocks and trees. What you hear in this music is a very natural beauty rather than artificial beauty."

The chief **aristocratic vocal music**, known as *kagok*, comprises twenty-five pieces set for male and female singers plus a mixed accompanying group of strings, wind and percussion. The short poetic texts used are in the favourite Korean form called *sijo*; the kagok performances, however, are complex and lengthy, requiring seven to ten minutes each for three-line texts that could be read out in a minute or less. There is also a simpler way to sing these poems, which is often performed only by a singer and drummer and lasts a mere four minutes. Confusingly, this performance is also called *sijo*, just like the poetic form. Like the rest of the court and aristocratic music, kagok takes some getting used to, but its immense subtlety and richness are worth the effort.

Most of the court and aristocratic musical genres, as well as traditional religious and folk genres, have been preserved in recent decades through a government-funded system. Artists elected to the highly esteemed position of '**human cultural asset**' are given a monthly subsidy for which they are expected to perform frequently and to pass on their knowledge to young apprentices. Most of the human cultural assets for court and aristocratic genres are members of the National Center for Korean Traditional Performing Arts, while those for folk and religious genres are often unaffiliated performers. The system was a very important one in the 1960s and 1970s for all types of traditional music, but in recent times there has been less need to support the folk forms, which are being widely practised with renewed vigour.

Religious Music

The music played for the Sacrifice to Confucius (aak) and for Sacrifice to Royal Ancestors (hyangak) is in the Confucian tradition – it is ceremonial, but not religious. Korean music which is truly religious in nature belongs to the imported Buddhist and native shamanistic traditions. Buddhism came to Korea in the fourth century, and before Christianity took a remarkable hold this century most Koreans were either Buddhist or believers in pantheistic shamanism, if not both.

The traditional repertoire of **Buddhist chant** consists of three main types: highly complex, extended chants (*pǒmp'ae*) performed only by highly trained singers; rapid sutra chanting (*yǒmbul*) performed by all monks; and folksong-style music (*hwach'ǒng*) on Buddhist themes. Today, pǒmp'ae is rarely heard, even on recordings, but is worth searching out; yǒmbul is everywhere, usually sung by a solo monk accompanied only by a small wooden bell (*mokt'ak*) or gong (*ching*); hwach'ǒng is sung in the Korean language and is folkish in nature.

Shamanistic music comes in two main types: vocal chanting (*muga*) and instrumental improvisation (*sinawi*) to accompany shaman dancing. The main accompanying instrument for the muga is the large hourglass-shaped drum called *changgo*, an instrument played in nearly all Korean folk music and most pieces of court music. The singing is in a variety of styles, resembling folksong, chanting, or ecstatic mumbling. The improvised instrumental dance music, **sinawi**, is rather like Dixieland jazz in nature with animated patterns (played on the changgo) and a melodic mode. Several melody instruments improvise simultaneously, giving a raucous, swaying polyphony that demands dancing. Sinawi has become very popular in recent years, and there are many CD releases.

Korean Folk

In Korea, '**folk**' music spans the gamut from what ordinary people play and sing to highly professional genres. What holds it together is a consistent and easily recognisable set of rhythmic patterns and a less well-defined set of melodic modes.

P'ansori and Sanjo

One of the most striking folk genres, **p'ansori** is performed by a single singer and a single drummer (playing a barrel drum called *puk*) who play for hours at a time, presenting a story in song, mime and narration. For the songs, the singer cues the drummer to a particular rhythmic pattern which they both usually maintain to the end. The drummer (and often the audience) reacts to the singer with shouts of encouragement.

There are only five traditional stories in the active p'ansori repertoire, but since every singer has their own way of performing and interacting with the audience, often with contemporary jokes, things never get boring. Despite the years of difficult training required for this demanding form (singers, by tradition, practice near a loud waterfall to develop the powerful voice required), the chief audience is comprised of ordinary people, so it really is music of the folk – intricate, rough-edged, and enormously appealing once you get used to the vocal style. Famous singers to watch for are **Cho Sanghyŏn**, **Pak Tongjin** and **An Suksŏn**.

Whereas p'ansori singers choose particular rhythmic patterns and melodic modes to suit the emotions of a particular narrative situation, the instrumental form **sanjo** arranges them in a standard order from slow to fast. Drawing melodic and expressive inspiration from p'ansori and shamanic dance music (*sinawi*), sanjo sets a melodic instrument against the rhythmic accompaniment of the changgo drum. The music moves from a highly ornamented slow tempo up through four or five increasingly rapid rhythmic patterns to virtuoso climaxes, the whole process taking anything from ten minutes to an hour.

The most popular instruments for sanjo are the *kayagŭm*, a twelve-stringed plucked zither; the *kŏmun'go*, a six-stringed plectrum-plucked zither; the *taegŭm*, a large bamboo flute; the oboe-like *p'iri*; the *haegŭm*, a two-stringed fiddle; and the *ajaeng*, a stick-bowed zither (the folk form of which usually has eight strings). Some performances are highly refined, others are rough-hewn. Big names include **Kim Chukp'a** and **Hwang Byungki** (kayagŭm), **Yi Saenggang** (taegŭm), and **Wŏn Kwangho** (kŏmun'go).

Once again, in characterising the instrumental ornamentation in these solo styles Hwang Byungki makes a comparison with the natural elements: "What is essential when playing a melody on the kayagŭm is the vibrato and the microtonal shading on the notes. If a melody drops down you can think of it like a waterfall and the bottom note needs to vibrate in the way that water bubbles at the bottom of a waterfall. This is something that gives Korean music its special character."

Folk Song

Korean folk song comes in several varieties – chief among them being **min'yo** (folk songs proper), which are categorised according to several regional melodic modes, and **chapka** ('miscellaneous' songs), with a more fixed melody and a form that requires more training.

Min'yo from the Seoul area are generally in a simple pentatonic mode and have a gently moving tempo. Those from the southwest area are more expressive and often very sad, using a mainly tritonic melodic mode called *kyemyŏnjo* (also much used in p'ansori and sanjo). Particularly favourite songs are "Arirang" from the Seoul area, and "Yukchabaegi" from the southwest.

Nongak

One of the most appealing and increasingly international forms of Korean music is the farmers' percussion band music, **nongak** (in recent years also called *p'ungmul*). This is a raucous, complicated genre, with dirt under its musical fingernails. In its full form, it consists of twenty or thirty percussionists playing small gongs (*kkwaenggwari*), large gongs (ching), barrel drums (puk), and the ever-present hourglass drum (changgo). These instruments are sometimes said to represent four great

CMP RECORDS

The spectacle that is Samul Nori

natural forces: the ching – wind, the changgo – rain, the puk – clouds and the kkwaenggwari – thunder. The performers both play and dance; some of the dance is highly acrobatic.

Since the late 1970s, small percussion groups deriving their style from nongak have become very popular in Korea, and some of them have travelled widely abroad. The best known is the group **Samul Nori**, which created and gave its name (referring to the four percussion instruments of nongak) to the popular percussion quartet genre *samulnori* now found among Korean communities worldwide. These derivative groups play complex, highly developed percussion music at a professional level, and many concerts of traditional music end with such music as a climax. To see these musicians dancing with hats with long swirling ribbons is truly spectacular. The band Samul Nori has continued its pioneering role, joining forces with rock and jazz musicians around the world (such as SXL) in an attempt to create fusion music, with varying success. There have even been concertos written for orchestra and Samul Nori.

Korean Pop

Pop music is as pervasive in modern Korea as anywhere in the West. TV and radio endlessly parade Korean pop singers and their influence – in appearance and lifestyle – is readily apparent among young Koreans, and soul-searchingly debated by their elders. Much of the music you hear is, as in Japan, a clone of Western hits, but there are also some more locally-rooted styles. Again, as in Japan, karaoke – known here as noraebang – is huge, with individualised *noraebang* rooms to be found in every neighbourhood of every town.

Ppongtchak

Ppongtchak – one of the earliest Korean pop styles – developed during the **Japanese occupation** (prior to 1945). Since it was Japanese colonial policy to assimilate Korea by altering its language and culture, it is hardly surprising that the style bore elements of Japanese aesthetics. Unlike Korean traditional music, which is typically characterised by an emphasis on triple meter, ppongtchak's rhythmic structure is solidly duple, similar to Japanese *enka*. Koreans identified the style by its rhythmic character, onomatopoeically calling it *ppongtchak*.

Despite periodic ups and downs, ppongtchak has remained popular. One of the style's most prominent singers, **Lee Mi-ja**, has produced many hits since the mid-1950s, including "Tongbaek Agassi" (Camellia Maiden), released in 1964, but later banned by the Broadcast Ethics Committee of the South-Korean government because of its overt Japanese musical influence.

For many countless nights,
Because of the pain that excavates her heart,
Camellia maiden has cried endlessly.
Tired of longing and tired of crying,
The flower petals are bruised red.

Although the banning of "Tongbaek Agassi" and the subsequent banning of other ppongtchak songs with a more than tolerable amount of Japanese influence somewhat dampened the genre's popularity, ppongtchak nevertheless continues to be favoured, especially among older Koreans. Many national singers, such as **Nam Jin**, **Na Hun-a**, **Cho Young-pil**, and **Chu Hyŏnmi** achieved their fame and fortune singing this music.

American Influence

After liberation in 1945, **American popular music** became the dominant foreign influence on the Korean popular music scene – **Ch'oe Hi-jun**'s songs, for example, bore a strong resemblance to the vocal style of Nat King Cole. Working as a stage entertainer for American soldiers stationed in Korea after the Korean war, Ch'oe became a star singer for the Korean domestic audience during the 1960s with a series of hit songs, including "Hasuksaeng" (A Student Boarder). This song was also used as a theme song for a Korean soap-opera popular at the time.

Life is a journey, but where do we come from
* and where do we go?*
It is like a wandering cloud,
So let's not leave any sentiment or lingering
* attachment.*
Life is a journey, just like a floating cloud.

In the early 1970s, a new style of popular music called **t'ong-guitar** emerged. The term derives from the Korean word *t'ong*, meaning 'a box', and 'guitar' (Koreans called an acoustic guitar *t'ong-guitar* because its resonating body resembles a box). T'ong-guitar music developed as local singers – influenced by the American folk revival (particularly the music of Bob Dylan and Joan Baez) – adopted acoustic guitars as an integral part of their music and stage image.

The repertoire of T'ong-guitar singers ranges from Korean cover versions of American songs to original compositions written in American style, such as Kim Se-Hwan's "T'oyoil pame" (Saturday Night):

Long hair, short skirt.
Whenever I see you who are so beautiful,

I am at a loss for words.
Oh, on Saturday night, I will see you...

Lacking both inflammatory political messages and strong Japanese musical elements, t'ong-guitar songs successfully avoided strict governmental censorship. Assisted by the image of hipness associated with an acoustic guitar, long hair-do and blue jeans, this music gained tremendous popularity in the 1970s, especially among urban youth. Its mellow sound and amorous lyrics were also called *p'ok'ŭ* or *pap* (from the English words 'folk' and 'pop'). From the 1980s, the form became known as 'ballad' and became a permanent fixture in Korean popular music. Unlike ppongtchak songs, which tend to describe life's pain and suffering, ballads usually deal with love affairs with a positive outlook.

Since the 1970s, South Korean audiences have also witnessed the adaptation of American rock into Korean music. The pioneering figure of **Korean rock** is **Sin Jung-hyun**, who was one of the first to introduce the electric guitar to Korean audiences. Sin and numerous other rock bands provided an alternative sonic experience to the ballad and ppongtchak. Starting out as 'soft rock' in the seventies with modest instrumental means, Korean rock was transformed during the eighties and nineties into a heavy-metal style. Around the same time, **rap** and **dance** music popular in the US were also introduced to Korean audiences by Korean singers. Comprised mostly of teenage singers/dancers catering to teen audiences, hip hop and dance music acts such as the **Taiji Boys**, **Noise**, and **Rula** now dominate TV and radio programs.

The Song Movement

Around the mid-1980s a new style of popular music – a political 'song movement' – appeared outside the mainstream Korean music industry. At that time, Korean intellectuals were struggling with the 'sentimental pollution' of the ppongtchak style, with its heavy Japanese aesthetic influence, and the ballad style, with its self-absorbed lyrics.

The major figure in the development of a new music movement was **Kim Min-ki**. His spirited defiance of political oppression encouraged groups of college students to experiment with alternative styles. Fuelled by an explosion of political awareness and protest activities on campuses, the new songs were imbued with political and social idealism and enthusiastically embraced by students. Many of the songs questioned the strong Ameri-

can influence in Korea and voiced the controversial sentiments of rapprochement with the North. With the prevailing climate of labour unrest and political discontentment of the eighties and nineties, these songs also gained a sympathetic following among the Korean general public and started to appear in mass media programmes.

In the early 1980s, the movement acquired the name **Norae Undong** (Song Movement) and became one of the most significant cultural movements in modern Korea. Loosely defined as an effort to create alternative popular music uncontaminated by mainstream commercialism, Norae Undong singers and groups, such as **Norae-rŭl ch'annŭn saram-dŭl** (People Seeking Song) with its hit song "Sora sora p'urŭn sora" (Pine tree, pine tree, green pine tree), brought political awareness and cultural activism into the domain of Korean popular music:

My mother's tears, caused by the strong
*   wind, penetrate my heart.*
What a divided world!
For the freedom in the truthful world where
*   people's souls become masters,*
Even if bruised dark, I will keep paddling the
*   river water.*
Pine tree, pine tree, green pine tree: do not
*   shiver because of the easterly wind.*
Under the bar where you were tied up, we
*   will meet again alive.*

Kim Min-ki

North Korea – pleasant snack time

BBC Radio DJ Andy Kershaw takes the pulse of North Korea's Music Scene.

You don't have to look far for music in North Korea. I didn't even have to get out of bed. On my first morning in Pyongyang I was woken up around 6am by martial music coming up from the streets around the *Koryo Hotel*. Down below, columns of workers were marching to their workplaces. At the head of each column a marcher held aloft a placard bearing a slogan or, possibly, the name of the factory. The military music crackled spookily from invisible speakers. This type of activity, I was soon to learn, is pretty routine stuff in the world's most isolated and secretive country. Solemn funeral marches floated from the shrubbery surrounding the thirty-metre-high statue of Kim Il Sung on a hill above the capital, while to the privileged owners of radios – which have no tuning dial – the state beams a bizzare breakfast show mix of uplifting military choirs and a presenter permanently on the point of breaking down in her gratitude to the Dear Leader, Kim Jong Il.

As every North Korean is a soldier of the revolution, martial music fills the vacuum that is the absence of social music. No one is going to get up with a guitar in a bar or club because there aren't any bars or clubs. I did find evidence, though, of an outbreak of spontaneity in the brochure which tempts visitors to a day out at the Taen Heavy Machine Combine. A photo shows a trio in full song, the man in the centre stretching an accordion across his chest. Caption: 'They sing of their worthwhile labour.'

The North Koreans do like to lighten up, though, in a North Korean sort of way. A tour of the vast Children's Palace (one classroom contained twenty synchronised six-year-old grand piano players) ends with a concert by the tiny students. This is an experience Busby Berkley on mescalin would have had trouble topping. Armies of tots (for although they were in military uniforms for much of the time, that is what they were) swarmed the stage and performed acrobatics and tightly-drilled dance routines to recall noble battles and victories in the Fatherland Liberation War. As one performance finished, amid the applause of row upon row of stony-faced military top-brass, it was simply wheeled off and the new one (it might be a huge orchestra already in position) glided on. I counted forty female kayagŭm zither players in one group. We had a gymnastic couple playing a furious xylophone duet, a rock drumming masterclass from a youth who made Keith Moon look like a slug, and any number of pop orchestras playing the popular hits brought to us by the Pee label (North Korea's state music recording company).

North Korean pop is lush, relentlessly optimistic top-drawer kitsch usually sung by a girl with a piping voice in national dress (pink spangled nightie). Behind her may be fifty or so musicians – half a dozen guitarists in green lurex shirts, a couple of divisions of keyboard players and a front line of fifteen female saxophonists. Even in their light music North Koreans' sense of individuality is to be the harmonious small components of a massive machine. They sing of their national effort and it sounds like it. Every movement of the musicians and singers – a lifting of the chin to left, a slight turn of the head to the right, a broad smile – is perfectly synchronised. The climax of this cultur-

Traditional Elements

It would be misleading to portray Korean pop music as entirely dominated by foreign influences. Even in ppongtchak style, Korean singers successfully adapted indigenous Korean vocal techniques to project Korean musical pathos. From *sinmin'yo* (New Folk Song) during the Japanese colonial period to *kugak kayo* (national music popular song) of the 1990s, efforts to combine Korean traditional music with popular musical tastes have always been maintained.

One of the representative figures of this nationalistic style is **Kim Young-dong**. Trained as a traditional musician, Kim relies on both Western and Korean traditional instruments and musical styles. A good example of his style is his song "Ŏdiro kalkksŏna" (Where Should I Go), which became a hit movie soundtrack. Relying on a traditional rhythmic pattern for the structure of the song, he successfully mixes Korean instruments *kayagŭm* and *taegŭm* with the guitar.

Where should I go, where should I go?
To find my lover, where should I go?
Even if I cross this river, it is not my place for
  a rest.
Even if I climb over that mount, it is not a
  place to stay.

In the spirit of that song, Korean popular music is wide-ranging and continually searching for new influences. And behind it lies a fresh and exciting world of traditional sounds that are well worth discovering.

al spectacular comes with the alarming ejaculation of two fountains at the foot of the stage as the image of the Dear Leader, in a corona of sunbeams, bursts on to the backdrop to wild applause. For the finale a fair proportion of the population of Pyongyang seems to be on stage.

전국유치원어린이들의 예술종합공연실황
조선아동음악 1집
KOREAN JUVENILE MUSIC

North Korean pop is available on CD and cassette in the shop at the Koryo Hotel or, for those lucky enough to be given another unique experience, at the Number One Department Store. Among the songbirds are **Jo Kum Hwa**, **Ri Pun Hui**, **Kim Kwang Suk** and **Jon Hye Yong**. In fact that's all there are, according to the catalogue of the Pee label. There are three bands

– more than enough to satisfy most appetites for the North Korean 'light instrumental with popular vocal' – the **Pochonbo Electronic Ensemble**, the **Wangjae-san Light Music Band** and the evergreen **Mansun-dae Art Troupe**. Some operas are also available – *Sea of Blood Vols 1–4, A True Daughter Of The Party* and *The Fate Of A Self-Defence Corps Man*.

This is a country in which very few people have heard of the Beatles. And it is the only country on earth where I have not, at some stage, heard country music. When the ice thawed on our little tour bus, as far as it can in North Korea, we took it in turns to sing. In the only example of Western music I heard in North Korea, Mr Chae, one of our government minders, sang "My Way".

Some popular songs and tunes of North Korea from the Pee Catalogue:
Song Of Bean Paste
My Country Full Of Happiness
We Shall Hold Bayonets More Firmly
Our Life Is Precisely A Song
I Also Raise Chickens
Song Of Snipers
The Joy Of Bumper Harvest Overflows Amidst The Song Of Mechanisation
Farming In This Year Is Great Bumper Crop
My Country Is Nice To Live In
Music Of Mass Rhythmic Gymnastics
I Like Both Morning And Evening
The Shoes My Brother Bought Fit Me Tight
The World Envies Us
Pleasant Snack Time

discography

Traditional

Compilations

There are several good CD sets giving a comprehensive survey of classic and traditional Korean music, although none are easily available outside the country. If you want to go beyond the introductions below, Seoul Records' 10-CD Korean Traditional Music set (also available as individual CDs) features performances by the National Center for Korean Traditional Performing Arts, as does the four volume Selection of Korean Traditional Music (Jigu, Korea).

Folkloric Instrumental Traditions I and II (JVC, Japan).

Exciting sinawi ensemble music. Vol I: *Sinawi and Sanjo* kicks off with a great ensemble piece for string and wind instru-

ments, followed by sanjo for haegŭm and ajaeng. Vol II: *Sinawi, Sanjo and Taepungnyu*, has two exciting ensemble pieces and sanjo for p'iri. Both recommended.

Korean Court Music (Lyrichord, US).

Good selection of various pieces of court and aristocratic music recorded by John Levy in 1964. Includes Aak, Nagyangch'un, Sujech'ŭn, kagok and other main forms.

Korean Traditional Music Vol 1: Court Music Highlights (SKC, Korea).

Part of a fourteen-volume survey of traditional Korean music – a good introduction to the Confucian and Aristocratic styles. Ritual music for the Chosŏn ancestral shrines, Sujech'ŏn, a taegŭm solo and kagok and sijo songs.

Korean Traditional Music Vol 2: Folk Music Highlights (SKC, Korea).

Companion to the disc above featuring extracts from Samul Nori, p'ansori, kayagŭm sanjo, sinawi and various folk songs. A good introduction, although many of the vocal styles take some getting used to.

P'ansori: Korea's Epic Vocal Art & Instrumental Music (Nonesuch, US).

Excellent selection including p'ansori, sanjo (for kayagŭm and kŏmun'go), and a folk song, recorded under studio conditions in New York. Performed by great musicians of the older generation, such as the singer Kim Sohŭi and the sanjo players Sıng Kŭmyŏn and Kim Yundŏk, all of whom have now died.

Artists

An Suksŏn

The singer An Suksŏn is the most popular female p'ansori singer in Korea today.

Folk Songs II: Namdo Songs of Cholla Province (JVC, Japan).

Folk songs from the southwestern part of Korea, particularly emotive and sad in sentiment. With light accompaniment on changgo, ajaeng and taegŭm.

Hwang Byungki

Korea's best-known contemporary composer for the twelve-string kayagŭm, and a fine performer.

Kayagŭm Masterpieces (Sung Eum Limited, Korea).

There are four volumes of these. Vol I includes six pieces that are both traditional and contemporary in nature, composed and performed by Hwang Byungki. Included is "Ch'imhyangmu", written as a film score and one of the most popular modern kayagŭm pieces in Korea today.

Seoul Ensemble of Traditional Music

A conservatoire-trained group of traditional musicians founded in 1990, performing both court and folk music. Led by changgo-player Kim Chungsu.

Korea: Seoul Ensemble of Traditional Music (World Network, Germany).

Quite an ascetic, but top quality, collection of aristocratic chamber music and sanjo, with a concluding sinawi for eight instruments of changgo, winds and strings recorded in concert in Germany.

KOREA: SEOUL ENSEMBLE OF TRADITIONAL MUSIC

Sŏng Kŭmyŏn

Kayagŭm player Sŏng Kŭmyŏn (also written as Song Gum-nyon) was born in Kwangju in 1923 and was a major

figure in many areas of traditional music. She was awarded the 'Cultural Asset' distinction in 1966 for kayagŭm sanjo, and died in 1987.

Music of the Kayagŭm (JVC, Japan).

Sanjo for kayagŭm, played by one of the great masters in one of her last recordings. With her daughter Chi Sŏngja on changgo.

Samul Nori

The original and best group playing nongak farmers' music. Four percussionists: Kim Duksu, Lee Kwangsu, Choi Jongsil and Kang Minseok.

Record of Changes (CMP, Germany).

Samul Nori music is better seen live than heard on disc, but there's still an excitement about this insistent percussive sound – and occasional chants. The album was recorded on tour in New York in 1988 and produced by Bill Laswell.

Contemporary

Compilations

Han'guk kayo pansegi (Half a Century of Korean Popular Song) (Han'guk, Korea).

Five cassettes featuring one hundred representative popular songs from the 1920s–1970s. Vol 3 includes "Hasuksaeng" (A Student Border) by Ch'oe Hi-jun.

Yusŏnggi ra tlttın kayosa (History of Korean Popular Song) (Sinnara, Korea).

A collection of 185 popular songs on ten CDs originally recorded between 1925 and 1945. The first volume includes two songs by Chae Kyu-yup, Korea's first full-time professional popular music singer and also "Saei Chanmi" (Adoration of Death) by Yun Shim-duk, the huge success of which spawned the term yuhaengga (song in fashion), meaning popular music in 1926. Japanese influence was very strong throughout this period and every volume includes typical early ppongchak.

Artists

Song Ch'angsik and Yun Hyŏngju

Sometimes dubbed as a Korean Simon and Garfunkle, Song Ch'angsik (a classically trained singer) and Yun Hyŏngju (a medical student) formed Twin Folio in the early 1970s and became the most famous duet during the early part of the t'ong-guitar era. They broke up in the mid-seventies to pursue solo careers.

Twin Folio (Seoul Records, Korea).

Mainly Korean cover versions of foreign songs in the t'ong-guitar style popular during the 1970s, including one of their biggest hits, "Wedding Cake".

Kim Young Dong

Kim attended Seoul National University in the 1970s and trained as a taegŭm player. He has composed film scores and various pieces fusing traditional and popular styles.

 ### Kim Young Dong Collection II (Seoul Records, Korea).

Nine original pieces, including the hit popular song "Ŏdiro kalkkŏna" (Where Should I Go?) and using kayagŭm and taegŭm alongside a Western acoustic guitar. Kim's vocal quality also has a touch of the 'rough' or 'husky' qualities of a traditional singer. Most of these songs were composed for films or theatrical productions.

Chu Hyŏnmi

Leading singer of the ppongtchak revival in the 1980s.

⊙ **Chu Hyŏnmi yŏn'gajip (Collection of Songs by Chu Hyŏnmi)** (T'aegwang, Korea).

Fourteen songs, including the famous 1960s-style "Rainy Yŏngdong Bridge", in a collection that sold around a million copies in 1984.

Kim Min-ki

The best-known political singer of the seventies and eighties. While most t'ong-guitar singers avoided controversial issues Kim Min-ki went straight for the jugular.

⊙ **Kim Min-ki Volumes 1, 2, 3, & 4** (Seoul Records, Korea).

Four CDs containing Kim Min-ki's best songs. Vol 1 includes his most notorious song, "A Child Growing a Flower" – a protest against president Park Chung-Hee's regime. The flower in the song is a metaphor for democracy.

Norae-Irŭl ch'annŭn Saramdŭl

The majority of the singers in this group come from the labour or political activist movement in the university campuses. Their lyrics articulate their beliefs and their collective ideology dictates that they don't identify individual band members.

⊙ **Noraerll ch'annln saramdll** (Seoul Records, Korea).

Nine songs, including "Sora sora p'urln sora", by a group representative of the Song Movement of the 1980s and '90s.

Seo Taiji and Boys

Seo Taiji and two other youngsters. With the liberal use of English lyrics and agile dance movements, they became an instant hit amongst teenagers and introduced the era of Korean rap.

⊙ **Seo Taiji & Boys II** (Bando, Korea).

1993 album that features one of their greatest hits, "Hayoga".

Laos

beyond our khaen

Laos, the sleepy and delightful backwater of southeast Asia, has been opening up fast to the outside world in the past five years. In the late-1990s, the Mittraphap (Friendship) Bridge between Laos and Thailand was opened, another Mekong crossing is planned further south, and travellers can now enter and exit at any international border crossing. If you travel in Laos during festival periods – Lao New Year in April, boon bang-fai in May, independence celebrations in December and so on – you're in for a particular treat, with music everywhere around. **John Clewley** turns tour guide.

Tiny, land-locked Laos has a population of just over four million, spread thinly over a mountainous country slightly larger than Britain. The fertile valleys, including the mighty Mekong river, are dominated by the lowland Lao (Lao Loum), who make up sixty percent of the population, but there are also lowland and mountain-dwelling tribes including the Hmong, Mien and others. However, by far the largest group of ethnic Laotians – around eighteen million – live in northeastern Thailand.

Mor Lam

The Laotians have a saying to describe themselves: they are the people who live in stilt houses, eat *pa daek* (raw, fermented fish) and *khao niow* (sticky rice), and blow the **khaen**, the Laotian pipe made from bamboo reeds. Swirling around the epic tales told by the **mor lam** (singer), the **mor khaen** (master of the khaen) creates a pulsing, rhythmically hypnotic sound full of organ-like chords.

The khaen is played all over Laos and northeast Thailand, part of an Asian tradition of reed pipes

Khaen and ching players at rocket festival

that includes the ancient *sheng* pipes of china, the *sho* in Japan and Korea's *saenghwang*. Many mountain-dwelling tribes of southeast Asia have a version of it, like the Murung people on the Bangladesh-Burma border region. The **Lao khaen**, however, is the most sophisticated of all the bamboo mouth organs – it takes great skill to play it properly.

Legend has it that a beautiful young woman became so charmed by the song of the garawek bird in the forest that she tried to imitate the sound with home-made instruments. She eventually succeeded by fashioning a flute-like piece of bamboo and blowing. She took her new instrument to the king, played a song and asked him if he liked it. He replied that it was fair, but asked for more. When she had finished, the king said '*Tia nee khaen dee*' (this time it was better). And he named the instrument the khaen.

The instrument is made from a set of paired bamboo tubes, each with tuned reeds, set in a clay windchest through which the player blows air. Sizes vary but the most common is the **khaen baet**, which has sixteen pipes. It is used to accompany a mor lam in the telling of a long narrative or epic. When pairs or groups of mor lam perform courtship-style verbal jousts (the most common is a male-female pair), the khaen again provides the basic musical pulse, supporting the melody. As the mor khaen pumps out the music, the singers often make demonstrative gestures about, or at, each other and the mood is light-hearted and mischievous.

Typical ensembles feature two mor lam, a mor khaen, a *phin* (plucked three-stringed lute), *so* (fiddle), drums, *khui* (bamboo flute) and *ching* (small temple bells). Each province in Laos has its own styles, the most influential being **lam saravane**, from the southern town of that name. This style is also popular in Thailand (see p.241). The most well-known mor lam outfit outside the region is the Paris-based troupe, **Molam Lao**, a group of top quality traditional performers – nothing electric here – based in Paris since 1976. Nouthoung Phimvilayphone is the exceptional khaen player and Sengphet Sourvongsay the fine

singer. Molam Lao performed at WOMAD concerts in 1994.

A modern development of this music form is called **mor lam sing**. It began in Thailand and has also taken root in Laos, though it is less bawdy than the Thai version. This faster, electrified ver-

Mural of mor lam music and dancing, Vientiane

sion comes from the popularity of the *mor lam ploen* and *mu* (see below) with younger audiences, and from the challenge of small Western-style pop combos to large folk troupes.

Folk and Classical

There are regional differences in Lao folk song styles owing to the fact that the present-day Lao PDR is a republic that essentially joined together three ancient kingdoms – Luang Prabang in the north, Vientiane in the centre and Champassak in the south. Mor lam, the dominant music in

Festival Phalluses

Savannakhet, southern Laos. It's the end of the dry season and a big **boun bung-fai** festival is underway, centered around the banks of the Mekong river and a revered temple, Wat Saiyaphum. This pre-Buddhist festival is held all over Laos and northeast Thailand in May or June when locals make huge gunpowder-powered rockets, *bung-fai*, which are launched to persuade the sky god, Payah-taen, to send rain.

Processions of drummers appear, followed by khaen players madly vamping for a shot of *lao lao* (rice whisky) and groups of dancers and men dressed in some of the most outrageous and lascivious costumes you'll ever see in Laos – men dressed as giant phalluses or pregnant women (throwbacks to ancient fertility rites). Some carry wooden hand puppets that are lewd in the extreme, designed to shock young women; one man is in the costume of a CNN media man, complete with cardboard video camera.

Rockets explode from trees and flash upwards. Music pulsates everywhere. It's a time of summer madness. Inside the temple grounds, games of all kinds are on offer. Monks chant and tell epic tales and a mor lam troupe plays long into the night. To raise money for the temple, a *ramwong* (circle dance) is set up for anyone willing to pay a a small fee to see a young woman dance.

If you want to experience real Laotian music, check out a *boun*, or temple festival. But first get used to those flowing hand movements (*fon lam*) because there is no way the Laotians will allow you be a wallflower.

Laotian culture, comes from southern musical traditions, for example. But lam styles – actually sung poetry described as *khaplam* by the Lao government – seem to be common to most groups in the country in one form or another. Luang Prabang, the beautiful old capital, has the *khaplam wai*, a slower, moody variant. Hmong and Mien have their own sung poetry for various occasions.

Lam luang, a kind of theatre of song and dance, is still found in Laos. Myths and legends, narratives, epics and even development issues are presented in a gaudy review style that developed from Thai lam ploen and lam mu in the 1960s. However, you won't find lam luang as easily as you find ploen and mu in Thailand. The movement of musicians in Laos is tightly-controlled, making it more difficult for anyone to take to the road.

Lao **classical music** is less interesting than Lao folk music, mainly because it is so imitative of Thai classical traditions. It was developed for the royal court and for classical dance-dramas like the *Ramakien* – a version of the Hindu epic Ramayana. The basic format is an ensemble called the *sep nyai*, which features gongs, xylophones, bamboo flutes and sometimes the khaen.

Modern Music

At the morning market in Vientiane, cassette sellers offer a range of mor lam, acoustic and electric, as well as all the top Thai pop stars. Some young Lao teenagers loll about with Mos (a Thai pop idol) haircuts and mobile telephones, much to the concern of the socialist authorities, ever wary of the influence of the big neighbour, Thailand. Local cassettes of mor lam sing are now available, as well as pirate copies of top Thai acts.

One of the most popular singer-songwriters in Laos is **Taoboangern** (Silver Lily) **Chapoowong**, who had a hit cassette of *luk thung* (Thai country) songs called *Kookkhwan Fang Khong* with top luk thung singer **Sunaree Ratchasima** in 1992.

JOHN CLEWLEY

Taoboangern Chapoowong

Trained in Moscow and Vietnam, Taoboangern says a Lao performer like himself must be able to sing lam styles, *sakorn* (popular songs with Western instrumentation), luk thung and even Latin songs – like the Vietnamese, Laotians enjoy dancing to Latin rhythms. And in a nation still desperately poor, he says he must do everything – he's a DJ, he organises concerts, promotes and distributes his own recordings – all this as well as performing and organising his band.

Swanthong Chaisombat, a former refugee resettled in Los Angeles, is the most well-known Laotian performer among expats and former refugees from Indo-China and Thailand. Her nine stateside releases have all sold well and are bootlegged and sold in Laos. She released *Isan Lam Rock* in Thailand in the early 1990s but it never took off.

discography

Even in a small Lao town, never pass up the opportunity at the local market to find the local cassette sellers. Many cassettes have titles like Lao Folk Music and some are great and some are lousy, so it's worth asking for a listen.

With so many Laotian people living in the Isan region of northeast Thailand there's a lively Lao music scene there. A couple of recordings of Thai-based Laotian bands are listed below but there are more in the Thai discography (see p.250), especially recordings of mor lam sing.

Traditional

Compilations

Bamboo on the Mountains (Smithsonian Folkways, US).

The mountainous regions of South East Asia are like a bamboo world – almost all everyday objects can be made from it, including musical instruments like flutes, mouth-organs, tube zithers and even fiddles. This beautiful disc features field recordings of the music of Kmhmu tribes, whose-people are found in Laos, Thailand, Vietnam and California.

Instrumental Music of Northeast Thailand (King, Japan).

The Isan region of Thailand is full of great Laotian music and this disc includes some really funky khaen, xylophone and lute playing. The khaen player is Thongkham Thaika.

Music of the Hmong People of Laos (Arhoolie, US).

A disc of specialised interest, featuring traditional New Year songs, wedding songs, courtship music and funeral music. Most interesting is the soft subdued sound of the *gaeng*, the Hmong varient of the khaen with six curved bamboo pipes and a mouthpiece.

The Music of Laos (Rounder, US).

Part of Rounder's Anthology of World Music series reissued from old Bärenreiter-Musicaphon LPs, giving a good overview of Laotian styles, including classical, ensemble

music for the Ramakien and mor lam. Begins with a spellbinding solo khaen piece.

The Songs of Lao (King, Japan).

Pleasant if rather over-manicured performances of folk and popular songs. The musicians are teachers from the National Music School of Laos in Vientiane and the instrumentation is semi-classical with a gong-circle and *ranat* (xylophone) as well as khaen. Ouuhuen Phonpasert sings khap folksongs from Luang Prabang and the female vocalist Chansuda Sutathama, singing popular and traditional songs, is celebrated in her own right.

Sud Yort Lam Lao (No label, Laos).

Two veteran stars of traditional mor lam, Malawan Deungpoomee and Acharn Sanaan, feature on this essential tape. Live recordings, mixed with studio songs, give the feel of mor lam – swirling khaens, lots of banter and Deungpoomee's powerful voice. Includes the Lao equivalent of mor lam ploen, *lam luang*.

Artists

Isan Slété

A six-piece group whose name means 'the flower of Isan', the Lao inhabited region of northeast Thailand. Led by Saman Hongsa, whose wife, Sri-ubon Hongsa, is the female vocalist; the khaen player is Thawee Sridamanee. The Hongsas have an electronics shop and most of the musicians have day jobs.

 Songs and Music from North-East Thailand (GlobeStyle, UK).

A great collection of Lao music featuring verbal jousting and love songs, plus khaen, xylophone and lute playing. This urgent music captures the feel of the village much better than the recordings of Molam Lao, the most famous group (see below).

Molam Lao

Top-flight group featuring singer Sengphet Souryavongsay and khaen virtuoso Nouthong Phimvilayphone, plus other Laotian singers and musicians based in Paris since 1976. Perhaps this has led to their performing style being more concert-like than many bands back home.

Music From Southern Laos (Nimbus, UK).

Excellent sampler of traditional styles – including *lam saravane* (ancient music for large, deep-toned khaen), long narratives and instrumental tracks with xylophone and lute. A good recording, but this music is best seen live to appreciate the frequent duelling between singers.

Lam Saravane: Musique Pour le Khène (Ocora, France).

Very fine khaen playing and top-class singing from veteran Nang Soubane Vongath and Molam Lao singer Sengphet Souryavongsay. The lengthy song "Lam Saravane" is outstanding, and is followed by showpiece khaen playing from Molam Lao's Nouthong Phimvilayphone.

Contemporary

Compilations

Mor Lam Sorng Sing (Ting Kham, Laos).

Modern mor lam from a variety of artists. Electrified bands pump out funky backdrops to solo singing, some of it approaching the 'sing' style from Thailand but, this being Laos, the result is a little more sedate. Some tracks are spoilt by over-use of synthesizers.

Artists

Taoboangern Chapoowong

Mor lam star Taoboangern Chapoowong is Laos' top male vocalist.

▦ Kookhwan Fang Khong [A Couple Sings From Both Sides of the Mekong] (Sure, Thailand).

Hugely popular pairing of Taoboangern with Thailand's top female luk thung singer Sunaree Ratchasima. Taoboangern's high-pitched singing perfectly matches Sunaree's beautiful voice on a variety of classic luk thung, pleng Thai (Thai song) and Lao sakorn. Excellent production.

▦ Lam Sao Lao (Dance of Lao Women) (No label, Laos).

Taoboangern's own release shows why he's the most well-known Lao entertainer. He can sing in just about any style, from lam to Thai and Lao sakorn, and it all appears on this sampler of his work, which includes his own compositions.

Deng Duangduan

Deng has emerged as a top female mor lam in the past couple of years.

▦ Khorng Kwan Jak Deng Vol 2 (Ting Kham, Laos).

Her first album was a big seller but this one topped everyone in 1997. A great voice. Features straight-up mor lam and some of the newer, faster 'sing' style.

Malaysia

music at the crossroads

Malaysia lies at the hub of global trade routes which have brought a rich mixture of cultural influences, most significantly Islam from the Middle East, and its music betrays a wide range of sources. Like much of the region, it is rapidly Westernising at the expense of its own traditions but there's still a lot to enjoy, from traditional ensembles to local diva Sheila Majid, as well as the hidden delights of the indigenous music of East Malaysia's Sarawak and Sabah. **Heidi Munan**, longtime resident of Sarawak, reports.

The Federation of Malaysia is really a political construct. Its peoples share in the wider heritage of Indonesia, Malaysia and the Philippines whose cultures have been borrowing and transmuting elements from pre-Islamic times down to the present day. The aboriginal inhabitants of the Peninsula and Borneo contributed strong rhythms, reed flutes, and a wooden xylophone to the modern-day 'national music', and over the centuries it has been enriched by instruments and tunes brought by Chinese, Indian and Arab traders.

The bronze gong is thought to be part of the **Chinese** influence, which has been adapted and transmuted over the centuries, the Indonesian gamelan being one of its most refined derivatives. The skin drum in its many forms was first brought in by seafaring **Arabs** who also introduced the three-string spiked fiddle (*rebab*), lute (*gambus*) and the choral tradition of *hadrah* (religious songs accompanied by tambourines). A species of oboe (*serunai*) is thought to be of **Indian** origin.

Portuguese music was quickly adapted after the fifteenth century: its Moorish intervals and rhythms sounded familiar to the Indian-Arab trading communities, even if the 'Franks' (all Europeans) were sometimes treated as enemies or scarcely tolerated competition. The policy of borrowing and adapting has continued, and today, traditional styles like *asli*, *ronggeng* and *joget* are still played on 'foreign' violins, accordions, clarinets and hand drums. Contemporary bands perform them on electric guitars, electronic keyboards and a battery of percussion, but the old tunes remain.

Authentic traditional Malaysian music exists but it is hard to find – it doesn't have a big popular following and is generally performed by and among connoisseurs. **Asli** literally means 'original', but when specifically applied to music usually means slow tempo traditional music played by the small ensembles (which might include violin, gambus, accordion, gongs and percussion) that also play the faster **zapin** and **joget** dances.

Each of the former royal courts of Kedah, Perak, Selangor and Trengganu has its ceremonial **nobat** ensemble of oboe, drums, valveless trumpet and gongs. But these only perform their mournful strains for ceremonial occasions from which the public is usually excluded. The ethnic music of **Borneo** may be heard during harvest festivals (in May and June) in Sarawak and Sabah.

Sights and Sounds of the East Coast

Kelantan, Terengganu and southeastern Thailand share a distinctive **Malay culture**; seaborne traffic linked this region to the cultures of the South China Sea more so than to the west coast of Malaya. The east coast has been less exposed to Western influence as a result.

Visitors heading for the main tourist destinations in the KL-Penang-Malacca triangle are apt to miss such traditional music as there is (at weddings and festivals), but the **backpackers' route** which follows the east coast from north to south offers a liberal supply of no-frills accommodation, local music and food in villages and small towns strung along the palm-edged shore. At Pantai Batu Burok in Kuala Terengganu, performances of traditional dance, the fighting-dance *silat* and occasionally the *wayang kulit* shadow puppet plays are given at weekends from April to September, before the monsoon puts a seasonal stop to these open-air

MALAYSIA

Malaysia 175

shows. In Kota Bharu, the capital of Kelantan, such shows are held two or three times a week.

Silat is generally called 'the Malay art of self-defence', but it isn't unique to the Peninsula and the moves resemble t'ai chi. A Kelantan silat performance is accompanied by a small ensemble of long drums, Indian oboes and gongs, which generate a loose set of cross rhythms. Two Malay men in baggy dark costumes, topped by a draped headcloth, face each other in the sandpit where this dance-exercise is usually held, though for weddings and other entertainment it can be performed on a mat indoors. The initial passes are dignified, almost slow, but as the music intensifies, the flowing movements change. The combatants grip each other and the first to throw his opponent to the ground is the winner. The music rises to a crescendo as the silat intensifies, the serunai screeching atonally while the drums and gongs quicken their loose rhythm.

In a very different sort of ensemble, six to twelve men play pentatonically tuned wooden xylophones. The rhythmic melody they hammer out in unison is fast and jolly and all the players end each piece at precisely the same time, raising their beaters overhead as they do so. This kind of music, known regionally as **kertok**, originated with the native peoples of the Malay Peninsula, the *orang asli* (original people).

The **wayang kulit** (shadow puppet play) is an ancient artistic tradition of Southeast Asia whose roots may be traced to the Hindu epic *Ramayana*. Indonesia, in particular, is famous for its many variants of wayang, usually accompanied by gamelan ensembles. In Malaysia, however, gamelan orchestras are replaced by something similar to a silat ensemble, enhanced by the wood xylophone and sometimes small hand drums. The puppet master sits onstage beside the musicians, hidden by a screen. As he chants the epic, he manipulates the leather puppets to act out the dramatic sequence for the audience seated in front. Wayang kulit serves as a good example of the meeting and intermingling of cultures in the Malay Peninsula. The Hindu story came from India, the craftsmanship of the puppets is Indonesian/Malay, the core of the music is Arabic – each element distilled and refracted through a Malaysian prism.

Another form of Malaysian drama, **mak yong**, is of east coast origin but hardly ever seen there today (although it appears in a recording in Smithsonian Folkways' 'Music of Indonesia' series). Mak yong is a dance-drama accompanied by the music of rebab or violin, oboes and percussion, which was traditionally performed as entertainment for the court ladies of Kelantan. Before each show the stage has to be ritually cleansed with incense and incantations. Both male and female characters in the romantic drama are portrayed by women, with the exception of one aged clown whose lines tend to be ribald.

Mak yong is certainly a pre-Islamic art form, and is disapproved of by many. In religiously conservative Kelantan, it is currently banned. Moderate Muslims, however, challenge this ban and advocate performances without the preliminary ritual (which approaches spirit-worship), without bawdy ad-libs, and with more modest costumes. These modified performances occasionally take place in Terengganu. Traditional drama enthusiasts in Kuala Lumpur get up a performance of mak yong once in a while, but even here these shows are becoming more and more rare. On the cultural scale, wayang kulit and mak yong are considered highbrow, to be enjoyed on special occasions only.

The popular traditional music of the East Coast is **Zikir Barat**. After evening prayers, when villagers stroll along the outdoor food stalls, some of the more musically inclined may strike up an impromptu zikir. Zikir Barat is an Islamic, particularly Sufi, style of singing. In its traditional form two singers perform, alternating verses in praise of Allah, to the beat of a single tambourine, sometimes accompanied by hand-clapping. As practised at evening markets or neighbourhood parties, teams of men sing the impromptu verses on topics of local politics, village gossip, or any subject of general interest. Zikir Barat has its own stars, like Drahman, Dollah, Mat Yeh, and the style of singing is also frequently recorded by Indian and Chinese vocalists.

Kuala Lumpur: Ghazal and Dondang

Kuala Lumpur rose from a ramshackle mining settlement along the banks of a couple of muddy streams (the town's name means 'muddy confluence') to become the capital of modern Malaysia. Its shopping malls and markets are awash with music: Western, Eastern and anywhere in between – the quality measured almost exclusively in decibels. Shopkeepers, it seems, firmly believe that music will attract customers, but most shoppers put up with the ear-splitting noise without paying the slightest attention to it. Besides the music blaring forth from shops, there are teams of blind buskers who sing and accompany themselves on electronic keyboards; most of them will produce

Blind street musicians in Kuala Lumpur. The sign reads "Enjoy the music while you donate".

anything from Christmas carols to Country and Western, as well as a sentimental form of folk pop derived from Indian *ghazals* – the poetic love songs of Indian light-classical music.

More professional **ghazal** artists are to be heard on cassette or in concert. The great star of this genre remains the late **Kamariah Noor** whose tapes are still available and whose voice, both intense and languid, enabled her to bend and hold notes, milking them for every last drop of emotion. Kamariah often sang with her husband **Hamzah Dolmat**, Malaysia's greatest rebab player, famous for his slow rather mournful style combined with a wonderful melodic creativity. As well as Kuala Lumpur, ghazal is associated particularly with Johor State.

Alongside the rebab, the other stringed instrument of Arabic origin is the **gambus,** used as an accompanying instrument for singers of ghazal and asli music as well as in ensembles for dance music. In the right hands the six-stringed lute has a beautifully refined tone redolent of intimate, domestic music-making. Malaysia's recognised master of the gambus is **Fadzil Ahmad**, who started performing in the 1950s and later assisted in the formation of several cultural groups dedicated to preserving traditional Malay-Arabic music. His most famous compositions are "Joget Cik Siti" and "Dia Datang".

Malacca: Ronggeng

The old trading town which gave its name to the Malacca Strait lies southwest of Kuala Lumpur. It is a beautiful old settlement along a narrow, rather dirty river, and a strange mix of Portuguese, Dutch and Chinese architecture tells the tale of its history. The town's music, too, is a confluence and compromise between styles. Modern Malaysia accepts the Malaccan **ronggeng** as its own 'folk music' – a music played on the violin and the button accordion, accompanied by frame drums, hand drums and sometimes a brass gong. The melodies speak of their Portuguese origin, with faint echoes of Moorish intervals and motifs. The fiddle holds the floor until the singers join in, when it recedes to a plaintive accompaniment.

The Portuguese introduced the European custom of mixed dancing, now best known as the **joget**: couples move gracefully with and around each other but never actually touch. Joget is a lively dance, ending in a final passage where the beat quickens, and the dancers skip heel-toe from one leg to the other like dancing cockerels. The traditional ensembles might contain flute, gambus, harmonium and drums, but there's also a ten-instrument joget-gamelan of gongs and metallophones in Trengganu which originally came from the Riau islands of Indonesia.

Gongs and Lutes –
the Indigenous Music of Borneo

Two of Malaysia's States, Sabah and Sarawak, share the island of **Borneo** with Indonesian Kalimantan. The music of the various tribal groups on the island has been preserved almost pure, without the admixtures of European and other Asian styles that have entered into Malay music. The indigenous people of Borneo used to live in longhouses where music once played an important part in communal life. The music now hangs on by a thread, fighting for survival against social change and against the radios, televisions and cassettes that have made their way into the remotest river tributary or mountain valley. It is unusual to find a young person proficient in his or her people's traditional music nowadays.

However, a recent interest in Borneo's culture – both on the part of tourists and 'root searching' urban middle classes – may yet help to reverse this decline. There has been a conscious attempt to revive the art of playing the **sapé**, the guitar or lute of the Orang Ulu people, but the only place where children can take organised traditional music lessons is in a mid-town office block in Kuching, Sarawak's capital city of 400,000 people.

The largest of the indigenous groups in Sarawak is the **Iban** and their traditional music is played on the bossed gongs that are widespread all over Southeast Asia. The lead instruments are heirloom pieces in sets of six or eight, laid in a wooden frame over a bed of string and played with two beaters – these are the 'melody gongs'. The larger gongs are suspended singly, and beaten to keep the rhythm. Gong ensembles play for traditional dancing, and in a longhouse everybody and his grandmother can play the gongs.

The other major ethnic group is the **Orang Ulu** (Up-river People) and their principal instrument, the sapé, is one of the real joys of Sarawak music when played by a real master. **Tusau Padan**, the man usually cited as the best, died in 1996; **Kesing Nyipa** from Belaga is one of the most famous living sapé players, but he is one of a rare breed. The sapé is fashioned from one block

of wood from which the body is hollowed out, and often painted with geometric designs resembling jungle ferns. It has three or four strings, of which the lowest is the melody string and the others drones. Sapés are commonly played in pairs, or even larger groups, possibly because they are rather soft in tone despite their large size. In an ensemble, they are sometimes joined by a wooden xylophone. This can be strung like a ladder with the top end fastened to an upright support (in a longhouse, one of the house pillars), and the lower end tied to the performer's waist. In the Orang Ulu longhouses you often see old 'mouth-organs' made from a gourd into which are fixed bamboo pipes. They are called *keluré* or *kediri* – instruments once used to accompany dances or processions – but nowadays you really have to hunt to find anyone who can play one.

There are, however, many types of mouth and nose flute all over Borneo. The **Lun Bawang** people are particularly active players and have formed 'bamboo bands' incorporating every flute known to man, including a 'bass flute' that looks

more like a bamboo tuba than anything else. Schools and villages of east Sarawak and west Sabah have resounding bamboo bands, playing anything from "Onward Christian Soldiers" to the patriotic march "Malaysia Berjaya". More accessibly, Kuching's **Cultural Village** has excellent examples of tribal houses and artifacts, including musical instruments. There are often sapé players in the Orang Ulu house and tapes of sapé and other indigenous music are on sale in the village shop.

Tusau Padan

Zapin is yet another music considered typically Malay (and popular throughout the peninsula), which is actually of Arabic origin. In their traditional form, zapin dances or songs are accompanied by the gambus and a couple of two-headed frame drums beating out an interlocking rhythm. These are often supplemented by violin and harmonium or accordion, and in urban areas with flute, keyboards and guitars. The zapin tempo begins slowly, but quickens abruptly as the accordion provides the cue for the dancers to improvise around their steps.

Perhaps Malacca's most prominent group are the ensemble **Kumpulan Sri Maharani**, who play **dondang sayang**, a slow, intense, majestic music led by sharp percussive drum rolls which trigger a shift in melody or a change in the pace of rhythm. This is a typically Malaysian style, in fact an amalgam of Hindu, Arabic, Chinese and Portuguese instruments and musical styles. Tabla and harmonium, double-headed gendang drum and tambourine create the rhythm, while the violin, and sometimes the accordion, carries the melody. Dondang traditionally accompanies classical singing, usually duets with romantic lyrics. Maharani's band integrates electric keyboard and snippets of guitar into the traditional framework. Once incredibly long, the songs are shorter nowadays, starting with fast, expressive drumming which slows down when the soloists enter, only to accelerate for dramatic emphasis towards the finale.

Crooners and Pop Singers

Despite the common language, Malaysia's pop music has always been regarded as the poor relation by the Indonesian music industry and only a few Malaysians manage to break into this closed scene. Alongside the historical Insulindian rivalries, there's also the demography to consider: for every talented Malaysian there are ten talented Indonesians and for every music-buying Malaysian, there are ten music-buying Indonesians – and while the average Malaysian is more affluent, he is also likely to spend his money on Western music. In comparison with Indonesia, Malaysia has lost much of its own culture and music in the rush to develop economically.

Until the late **P. Ramlee**'s mellifluous baritone sang its way into Malaya's heart in the 1950s, mod-

ern music in Malay was almost entirely Indonesian – of the sentimental **kroncong** variety. Penang-born Ramlee used popular melodies new and old, or adapted from the Western crooners of the day, usually supplying new lyrics which catered for popular taste. Musically, he adapted the folk instrument repertoire, often recording with a dance hall orchestra, and reflecting the influence of the Latin ballroom music favoured in the post-war

P. Ramlee: the Harry Belafonte of Malaysia

period. Ramlee is the hero of a large number of Malay films now revered as classics. He lived and worked for many years in Singapore (which is where the film and popular music industry was based) before returning to Kuala Lumpur, where he died in 1973.

Ramlee's singing style was a Europeanised version of classical dondang; his great duets with his wife Saloma are Malaysian pop's glorious dawn. Ramlee launched a new movement in modernising traditional Malay singing, largely by abbreviating the songs and employing Western instruments. His critics felt however, that the purity of Malay music was desecrated by its performance in popular halls devoted to such wickedness as drinking and mixed dancing.

Their descendants still make themselves heard today, and manage to get rock and rap concerts banned on religious grounds. But Ramlee's style lives on. Today's best known singer of 'modern classical' Malay songs is **Sharifah Aini**, whose strong, sweet voice seems to improve with the years. Younger musicians tend towards more modern styles, though many intersperse a soft-rock or *balada* disc with a few P. Ramlee covers.

Young Malaysians, however, buy a lot more rock and pop than traditional music – inevitably, perhaps, given the education policy with its strong emphasis on IT and computer literacy, and thus strong exposure to Western culture. The Malaysian pop/rock scene today is dominated by young musicians singing in Malay, or English, following the world's styles with their own individual interpretations, often with a shot of tradition cleverly injected. A weekly ASEAN TV programme, *Asia Bagus*, is worth watching for the new talent – not to mention the presenters' adolescent antics.

Sheila Majid

Sheila Majid is Malaysia's best-known pop star and was the first Malaysian to penetrate the Asian market, particularly in Indonesia. Her foundation in classical music has stood her in good stead as she sings her way from soft rock towards jazz –

mostly in the Malay balada genre, though she is equally at home in English.

Recently, a young singer, **Siti Nurhaliza**, has adopted a much rootsier style with a band featuring *rebana* (drums), tabla and bamboo flutes. Her album *Cindai* sold 200,000 copies in 1998, a year when economic problems meant that music wasn't supposed to be selling.

Rock singers **Awie** and **Ella** keep their standing in the local and ASEAN charts, as does the enfant terrible of Malaysian music, **M. Nasir**. This singer-poet-writer-director is given to public criticism of political figures, or anything else that arouses his ire, but an outstanding talent is hard to silence. His "Ghazal Untok Rabiah" (Love Song for Rabiah), sung in duet with Jamal Abdillah, has won awards, and is a moving example of what ghazal means to a creative, modern Malay mind.

If M. Nasir can't be silenced, 'socially unacceptable' bands like the rapping brothers **KRU** have been banned from performing – the objection being to their 'irreverent' demeanour, mode of dress and rapped comment on social issues. Their 1997 tour was called KRUmania and when the authorities consulted their dictionaries to find that 'mania' meant 'madness', they declined to issue performing permits in an effort to 'avoid any negative effect on youths'.

The two new sounds on the Malaysian scene today are *dangdut* and *nasyid* (pronounced 'nah-shid'), which are about as far apart as musical genres can be. Both have been around for a long time – at the village party and mosque level respectively – and have now suddenly blossomed out and hit the charts with a bang. **Dangdut** has long been a great success in Indonesia and in its Malaysian incarnation is a sensuous, pulsing, frankly amorous music generally sung by women. Singer **Amelina** is Malaysia's recognised Dangdut Queen, while everywhere in the country Dangdut Lounges and similar venues advertise Indonesian artistes.

Nasyid, sung chastely by all-male or all-female groups to the accompaniment of drums and tambourines, is the Muslim equivalent of Gospel Pop

JAK KILBY

Raihan

– religious songs in Arabic or Malay rendered to appeal to the young, pop-fed generation. The group **Raihan** sold 600,000 copies of *Puji-Pujian*, a smoothly produced and engineered album which owed quite a debt to percussionist Yusuf Islam (Cat Stevens).

For more about dangdut and Indonesian qasidah, see the Indonesia article on p.131.

discography

For up-to-date information on artists and discs check the excellent Malaysian Music website at *www.music.upm. edumy/malaysia*

Traditional

Compilations

 **Dream Songs and Healing Sounds. In the Rainforests of Malaysia** (Smithsonian Folkways, US).

A specialised disc recorded amongst the Temiar people, one of Peninsular Malaysia's Orang Asli (indigenous peoples). Ethnographic recordings of healing ceremonies, bamboo-zither, nose-flute and jew's harp, and wonderful jungle sounds. Very detailed liner notes.

Melayu Music of Sumatra and the Riau Islands (Smithsonian Folkways, US).

Actually volume 11 of Smithsonian Folkway's Music of Indonesia series, this is Malaysian music from Sumatra where some of the more traditional forms still exist. Includes zapin, ronggeng, mak yong and some lovely gam-bus playing.

Muzik Tarian Malaysia (Life, Singapore).

Two-CD set of joget, zapin and other traditional dances played by a small instrumental ensemble including violin, flute, lute, harmonium and drums. Classical and refined.

Sawaku: The Music of Sarawak (Pan, Netherlands).

An excellent survey of indigenous music from Sarawak recorded and compiled by Randy Raine-Reusch. Features numerous previously unrecorded musical styles from the Iban, Bidayuh, Orang Olu and Melanau peoples, as well as the gong and sapé music for which the region is famous.

Artists

Fadzil Ahmad

Fadzil is the most celebrated gambus player in Malaysia and much sought after as an accompanist, notably for the young rootsy singer Siti Nurhaliza.

Raja Gambus Malaysia (Ahas Productions, Malaysia).

'King of the Gambus' says the title of this album and it's a great illustration of Fadzil's art with instrumental tracks as well as songs. **Irama Ghazal Malaysia** (Ahas Productions, Malaysia) is also worth hearing.

Siti Nurhaliza

The bright, young star of Malaysian popular traditional music, proving that roots can also be modern.

 Cindai (SRC, Malaysia).

A popular release on which Nurhaliza is accompanied by an all-acoustic band for that traditional feel.

Tusau Padan

Tusau (1930–1996) was Sarawak's most famous tradition-al artist, excelling as painter, sculptor and master of the sapé. Examples of his artwork are found throughout Borneo from longhouse to museums.

Masters of the Sarawakian Sapé, featuring Tusau Padan (Pan, Netherlands).

Although Tusau performed his music before royalty and in numerous concerts overseas, these are the only recordings that have been preserved – traditional dances played on the sapé plus a couple of duets with younger players.

Kumpulan Sri Maharani

The best contemporary exponents of the dongdang sayang style.

Dondang Sayang Mamba (EMI, Malaysia).

The group's slow, emotional rendering of dondang sayang has kept their tapes in the market for a long time

Modern

Artists

Sharifah Aini

Considered today's main interpreter of classic Malay singing by her many fans, although there are plenty of Arabic overtones in the orchestrations.

 Nostalgia Aidil Fitri (EMI, Malaysia).

Released just in time for the feast of Aidil Fitri (Id al-Fitr) in 1997, this album contains sentimental, nostalgic, uplifting numbers like the very popular "Dendang Perantau".

Amelina

Amelina's concerts and, more recently, her albums, have brought dangdut into the spotlight of the Malaysian music scene.

Asyik (Warner Music, Malaysia).

A powerful voice and sophisticated, traditional orchestration make this album very appealing. It won her Malaysia's Best Traditional Album award in 1995.

Cinta O Cinta (Warner Music, Malaysia).

Dangdut for dancing, dangdut ballads, dangdut cha-cha-cha – this 1997 album consists of ten songs recorded in Bandung, Indonesia.

KRU

A crew of three musical brothers, Abdul Halim, Norman Yusri and Edy. A spirited rap in support of their favourite football team caught the public's attention, and they haven't looked back. They have performed and recorded by themselves and together with other groups.

KRUmania (EMI, Malaysia).

The record of the tour which created a sensation; a mix of straight-out pop, rap, G-funk and a few more sedate ballads.

Sheila Majid

Since her debut in 1985, Sheila's soft silky voice has appealed to Southeast Asian audiences in her Malaysian music with a Western format. After a quiet spell (she has two children), Sheila is back in the spotlight, having recently recorded with the Sydney Symphony Orchestra (and a jazz band), and sung at the Royalty Theatre in London.

Legenda (EMI, Malaysia).

The 1992 album of her successful Asia-wide tour.

 Ratu (Warner Music, Malaysia).

Easy-listening Malaysian style, but superbly produced. The album justifies her claim to being one of Malaysia's few jazz singers. Ratu, suitably enough, means 'queen'.

M. Nasir

An intense, gifted young singer, composer, lyricist and producer. His work often has a political edge.

Suratan Kasih (Warner Music, Malaysia).

His best collection, including the famous "Ghazal Untok Rabiah" with Jamal Abdillah.

Raihan

Five young singers – Azahari Ahmad, Nazrey Johari, Abu Bakar Mohd.Yatim, Che Amran Idri and Amran Ibrahim – sing the praises of God (Puji-pujian) in contemporary nasyid style.

Puji-pujian (Warner Music, Malaysia).

This 1996 album sold 600,000 copies, an unprecedented success in Malaysian music. Fresh young voices, sophisticated percussion. Their more recent **Syukur** (Warner Music, Malaysia) has more of an eye on the international audience, with a couple of tracks in English.

P. Ramlee

The Harry Belafonte of Malaysia. P. Ramlee was the best-loved singer and composer of modern music with a Malay soul.

Sri Kenangan Abadi Vols I–III (EMI, Malaysia).

Any of these volumes are recommended as an introduction to P. Ramlee's most popular tunes.

Di Mana Kan Ku Cari Ganti or Senandong Kaseh (EMI, Malaysia).

Duets sung with his wife Saloma in the 1950s and '60s. Considered to be among the highspots of popular music in Malaysia.

Melanesia

bamboo boogie-woogie

The 'black islands' of Melanesia lie west of the Polynesian archipelagoes in the Pacific. So-named by early explorers, revealing contemporary racial preoccupations, the group includes **New Guinea**, the **Solomon islands**, **Vanuatu** and **New Caledonia**. The music of these island chains reflects shifting indigenous settlements and five centuries of contact with Asia and Europe. **Stephen Feld** disentangles the threads of this skein of sounds.

New Guinea

Musically, the best known part of Melanesia is the island of New Guinea. This is divided in two: **Papua New Guinea** (PNG), the independent, eastern half of the island, and **Irian Jaya**, the western half, often called 'West Papua' by indigenous inhabitants seeking independence from Indonesia. Prior to 1962, Irian Jaya was a Dutch colony, while PNG, until its independence in 1975, was divided into two Australian trust territories (before World War I, these had been British and German colonies). These colonial histories have strongly influenced the music heard today in New Guinea, as has the strong impact of missionaries.

There is considerably more documented and recorded material from the eastern, Papua New Guinea side of the island, particularly from the years following independence. This is partly a result of foreign interest in the country's stunning cultural and geographical diversity – more than eight hundred languages are spoken by less than four million people – but also because of Indonesia's hostility to the celebration or promotion of indigenous Melanesian culture in Irian Jaya.

PNG's Popular Music

Papua New Guinea's exposure to Western sounds began in the last quarter of the nineteenth century, with the part harmony of church hymns sung in local languages. By the turn of the century, mission songs, colonial songs, and gold rush songs had also made their mark. From the 1920s, phonographs and recordings of Western popular songs were played around plantations and colonial towns and broadcasting began in the late 1930s. A further foreign influence arrived during the war, when servicemen from Hawaii and the Philippines played and taught songs to Papua New Guineans – and also introduced the guitar.

Guitars and ukuleles became popular, and spread from towns to villages. **String bands** – groups of four or five acoustic guitars and ukuleles playing a hard-strummed and lightly swinging style already in broad Pacific circulation – were first recorded

The Wagi Brothers giving it some flip flop

in the early 1950s, and were commonplace ten years later. By the late 1960s, rock'n'roll cover bands like the **Kopikats** were performing at hotels in PNG's main cities, and string bands like the **Paramana Strangers** had become well-known.

In the mid-1970s, the boogie-woogie **bamboo band** style spread to PNG from the Solomon Islands, featuring open bamboo tubes played by hitting them with flip-flop sandals. This began among villages around Madang, and spread from a band at the Teachers College there to other colleges and high schools. The **Wagi Brothers**, replete with bamboo tubes and fuzzy rock'n'roll electric guitar (played through transitor radios), are one of the highlights of David Fanshawe's Pacific compilations.

A local **recording industry** began to develop in PNG after independence. Musical exchanges were promoted by the National Arts School and other national institutions, as well as regional and international festivals. The band **Sanguma** emerged, the first PNG group actively to mix traditional songs and instruments with rock and jazz-derived styles, and they continually explored connections between indigenous and Western musical instruments and idioms. In the early 1980s,

Sanguma toured in the Pacific region, Europe and the US. Around the same time, recording studios became established in Rabaul and Port Moresby, the capital, and radio programmes featuring PNG pop styles, both in Tok Pisin (pidgin), the lingua franca, and in Tok Ples, (another local language), spread widely. The cassette industry, TV and radio stations, however, tend to play local rock, reggae, and string band music.

The one PNG musician who has made international waves is **George Telek**, through his band's participation on the CD *Tabaran*, recorded in PNG by the Australian rock band Not Drowning, Waving. Hailed as an Australian equivalent of Paul Simon's *Graceland*, the recording was followed by tours in Papua New Guinea and Australia, and a documentary film. In the 1990s, Telek appeared at WOMAD festivals in Australia, and Not Drowning, Waving's leader David Bridie also produced his first solo release.

Traditional PNG Music

In 1898, as part of a Cambridge University expedition, F. Myers made some of the first field recordings anywhere in the world along PNG's south coast. However, music research did not begin seriously until the 1970s, with independence and the establishment of the Institute of Papua New Guinea Studies music department and recording series. Traditional PNG music also received a huge boost in 1991 with Grateful Dead drummer Mickey Hart's **Voices of the Rainforest**, the first CD devoted to traditional PNG music to reach an international audience.

The *Voices* disc shows a rich traditional musical culture, although its diversity has doubtless been greatly diminished by the impact of colonisation, missionaries, and industrial development. Certain types of traditional songs, singing styles, instruments and their performance were targeted for eradication by **missionaries**, who disapproved of the spiritual or erotic power of the music. Length of contact – a hundred years on the coasts and fifty in the central highlands – has played a part in how well local or regional indigenous musical traditions have survived, as did the type of missionaries: the Catholics and Lutherans were generally quite tolerant while the Baptists and Evangelicals were more hostile and restrictive.

Singsing is the general Tok Pisin name for village ceremonies which involve feasting, elaborately costumed song and dance, and exchanges of objects and food within and between communities. Singsings often involve entire clans or com-

George Telek, PNG's crossover star

ORIGIN

STEPHEN FELD

Singsing performers at a Highlands show

munities performing together. Songs are sung with a leader and chorus, in group unison or with an overlapping and staggered approach to the same text and melody, producing something of a constant echo effect. Performers exuberantly decorated in paints and plumes often accompany the singing with regular hand drum pulses, while bouncing and swaying in dance lines, clustered groups or semi-circles.

Some singsings associated with preparing for warfare or the performing of secret initiations have been abolished or were banned by colonial government officers or missionaries; others were abandoned by the communities themselves as they were swept up in social and economic change. In some areas they have disappeared completely, or have been modified or replaced by newer forms, often held only in conjunction with national events like Independence day, school holidays or Christian festivals. Singsings are the public and celebratory side of PNG culture most likely to be seen by visits to the country. Large competitive shows with costume and dance contests attract regular audiences, and have, since the 1950s, been held regularly in Port Moresby and in the Highlands towns of Goroka and Mt. Hagen.

Alongside these powerful displays, the more private, sometimes mystical music based on vocal poetry doesn't easily reach beyond linguistic and cultural boundaries. Many song texts in PNG

New Guinea's Indigenous Instruments

Prinicpally found in the Sepik region, in the northwest, and surrounding islands like Manus, New Britain, New Ireland and Bougainville, the **garamut**, a wooden slit drum, can measure between one and twelve feet long. They are often elaborately carved with figures of humans, birds and crocodiles. Struck with wooden beaters, the drums can produce different tones, and ensembles make a powerful, thundering sound. Sometimes the garamut is used strictly as a message signalling device for long-distance communication over both land or sea.

By contrast, the smaller **kundu**, an hourglass-shaped hand drum with a lizard or snake skin head, is generally associated with singsings and found throughout the country. Like garamuts, kundu can be elaborately carved and painted and produce sounds associated with spirit voices; their throbbing pulse can have mesmerising and deeply moving effects on listeners.

Bamboo flutes, or **mambu**, are side blown and range in size from one to three feet long, sometimes more.

They are generally found in the Sepik area and parts of the highlands. The most famous variety are played in pairs at male initiation rites, and are kept secretly in the men's cult house, the *haus tambaran*, away from women and uninitiated men. Both the carved designs and the sound patterns of these flutes are symbolically important, making present the voices of ancestral and place spirits. The **sepik** flutes, said to be the longest in the world, have ethereal, breathy tones rich in harmonics. They are always played in groups with maybe five or seven players, but never with less than two. Although these are the best known and most widely recorded bamboo flutes, other types of end-blown flutes and panpipes can be found in the PNG highlands.

Of the less formal instruments, the best known is the **susap** or bamboo jew's harp. It is particularly associated with young boys and men, and often played for fun, accompanying and mimicking rhythms of insects, birds, water and other environmental sounds.

evoke the power of place, describing the local landscape, flora and fauna. These are often full of metaphors about spirit pasts and presences, and their meanings can be extremely difficult to grasp and translate.

DAVID FANSHAWE

Solomon Island panpipers

The Solomon Islands

Independent from Britian only since 1978, the **Solomon Islands** are sparsely inhabited. About 400,000 people, mostly Melanesians, live on almost a thousand islands, most of them on the principal half dozen.

Musical life in the Solomons reveals a variety of solo and group vocal styles. Large slit-drum ensembles, like those heard in PNG on Manus or Bougainville islands, are found in the Solomons, but the most distinctive sounds are the solo and group **panpipe ensembles**, particularly the ones from Gudalcanal and Malaita Islands. The most famous ceremonial groups, from the **'Are'Are** people in Malaita, feature up to ten performers with instruments of several sizes. The instruments have unique tunings and play a powerful repertory of polyphonic songs associated with natural sounds like water, insects, and birds, as well as sounds of work and other human activities.

From the 1920s a kind of **bamboo music** developed where bamboo tubes of different lengths and diameters were struck by coconut husks to create a twangy, bouncing, island-music sound remarkably like an ensemble of ukulele and bass. The Americans had bases in the Solomons round the capital Honiara and, just as their abandoned oil drums were tempered into instruments for steel bands in Trinidad, in the Solomon Islands their footwear kick-started the modern bamboo bands: plastic or rubber thong sandals replaced coconut husks in the 1960s, when the bamboo band sound spread from the Solomons to PNG, and became a favourite in schools and colleges. There are some contemporary urban Solomon Islands bands available on cassette releases playing this bamboo music.

Other bands specialise in popular **local language music** (also well-known in the towns of PNG), particularly the Polynesian- and Christian-influenced guitar and ukulele string band sound usually called **Island Music** and local varieties of rock and reggae. There are also some distinctive Solomons fusion developments, represented by groups like the **Narasirato 'Are'Are Pan Pipers**, who join the indigenous bamboo sounds of the large Malaitian 'Are'Are panpipe ensembles to the rubbery basslines of large bamboo tubes whacked by flip-flops. The Narasirato band can be heard on cassettes that are locally available in Honiara. They perform live at cultural centres in the islands and in recent years have also toured Australia, New Zealand, Canada, and the UK.

Fiji is politically part of Melanesia, but lying on a cultural cusp, its entry in this book is included under Polynesia p.218.

discography

PNG music appears at home mainly on cassette, with production dominated by the **National Broadcasting Commission** and two companies, **Chin H. Meen** and **Pacific Gold**, which together release about 200 cassettes of string band, rock, reggae and cover pop each year.

Since 1990, music videos have also been locally produced and aired in the country on **Mekim Musik** and **Fizz**, programmes broadcast on PNG's EM-TV, while **Chin H. Meen** has produced a series of compilations, PNG Super Sound Videoclips. For videos, cassettes, CDs and other information about PNG music, check *www.chmsupersound.com.pg*. Another good source of information is the Pacific contemporary music journal Perfect Beat, which maintains a Website at *www.mex.mq.edu.auxcontent/pbeat*

New Guinea

Compilations

Ⓞ **Music from Mountainous West New Guinea, Irian Jaya** (Volkerkunde Museum Collection, Germany).

Important CD compilation with an extremely detailed booklet devoted to the everyday and ritual music of the Eipo, Mek, Yali, Dani and Moni. The best effort to date at a musical survey of the West Papuan Highlands.

Ⓞ **Music of Biak, Irian Jaya** (Smithsonian Folkways, US).

Volume 10 in Smithsonian Folkway's Music of Indonesia series: a compilation of older indigenous celebratory songs, now in decline, plus hymns sung by female church choirs, and youthful string band music. Excellent historical notes.

▦ **Papua New Guinea Music Collection** (Institute of Papua New Guinea Studies, PNG).

The best introduction to the whole world of musical variety in PNG. Eleven cassettes and a comprehensive booklet illustrate the extraordinary range of musical styles, instruments, and ensembles found throughout PNG, from turn of the century recordings to the post-independence string band sound of the 1980s.

Ⓞ **Papua New Guinea: Twenty Great Favorites** (World Music, Australia).

Good sampling of the pre-independence 1960s guitar cover band sound, featuring Delepou, The Rainbows, The Kopikats, the Freebeats, and the Stalemates.

▦ **Riwain: PNG Pop Songs** (Institute of Papua New Guinea Studies, PNG).

A classic PNG pop roots anthology. Two cassettes and accompanying booklet of lyrics and guitar chords for some of the most popular songs of the 1970s and early 1980s, recorded by bands like Paramana Strangers, Kalibobo Bamboo Band, Sanguma, Black Brothers, and Painim Wok.

Ⓞ **Sacred Flute Music from New Guinea: Madang Vols 1 & 2** (Rounder, US).

These reissues of classic LPs are the best recordings available of the PNG secret flutes whose ceremonial performance evokes the presence of spirits. Although better known in the adjoining Sepik river region, the paired flutes heard here are from the surrounding areas of Madang and nearby Manam Island. On some tracks they are accompanied by garamut slit gongs, kundu skin drums, rattles, and singers. The pulsing cries of the flutes are absolutely mesmerising.

ⒸⒹ **Spirit of Melanesia** (Saydisc, UK).

The best CD introduction to the many sounds of Melanesia, recorded by David Fanshawe. Highlights include atmospheric Sepik flutes (PNG), panpipe ensembles from Malaita (Solomons), church and festival music in Fiji, singsings and

sacred garumut drums (PNG), and the Wagi Brothers bamboo-flip flop music. Fanshawe describes Melanesia as "dynamic, secret, stark and timeless" which suggests his over-romanticised approach.

⊚ **Voices of the Rainforest** (Rykodisc, US).

A day in the life of Bosavi, in the central Papuan plateau. A vivid and atmospheric soundscape where vocal and instrumental sounds of work, leisure and ritual are inspired by and blend with the noises of birds, waters, and insects of the surrounding rainforest.

Artists

George Telek

Telek is a tremendously popular Rabaul-based composer, singer and string player who led PNG's famous rock band Painim Wok, as well as the Moab Stringband. He has been signed by the RealWorld label, making him the first Papua New Guinean musician with the potential to reach a worldwide audience.

◉ **Telek**
(Origin, Australia).

Telek's first overseas recording imaginatively sets Tolai songs to rock and string band grooves, with great backup from Australian and PNG musicians including Archie Roach, Kev Carmody, Pius Wasi, and Ben Hakilitz (who also records with Australia's Yothu Yindi).

⊚ **Tabaran** (WEA, Australia).

A breakthrough collaboration of Telek with musicians from Rabaul and Melbourne-based rock band Not Drowning, Waving. Combines PNG lyrics, instruments, and string bands with Australian rock songs, some exploring Australia's colonial past in PNG and expressing Australian-Melanesian solidarity with the West Papua freedom movement in Irian Jaya.

Solomon Islands

◉ **Solomon Islands: 'Are'Are Panpipe Ensembles**
(Chant du Monde, France).

There are many recordings of Solomon Islands panpipes, but this is the best. A superb double CD featuring ensembles of

four, six, eight, and ten panpipes that perform for feast music. The groups are unique in their tuning and compositional style, and astonishing in their virtuosity.

⊚ **Solomon Islands: 'Are'Are Intimate and Ritual Music** (Chant du Monde, France).

Features polyphonies and polyrhythms of 'Are'Are slit-drum percussion ensembles, solo panpipes, the pulsing of water play and amazing ensembles of bamboo tubes struck against rocks. Beautiful recordings, excellent notes.

⊚ **Solomon Islands: Fataleka and Baegu Music from Malaita** (Auvidis/Unesco, France).

Excellent sampler of panpipe, flute and vocal musics. Includes the original recording of the lullaby "Rorogwela" sung by Afunakwa; the sampled version of this melody became the Deep Forest hit "Sweet Lullaby" and later the Jan Garbarek adaptation entitled "Pygmy Lullaby".

Other Islands

⊚ **New Caledonia: Kanak Dance and Music** (VDE-Gallo/AIMP, Switzerland).

Important and thorough anthology of historical and contemporary Kanak styles, with excellent notes.

⊚ **Kanak Songs: Feasts and Lullabies** (Chant du Monde, France).

Interesting but short sampler of indigenous songs whose musical techniques suggest the complex ways Melanesian and Polynesian influences collided in New Caledonian chant, whistling and other vocal styles.

⊚ **Vanuatu: Custom Music** (VDE-Gallo/AIMP, Switzerland).

Recorded in the 1970s but still the best examples available of the incredible slit-drum ('tam-tam') ensembles; other selections indicate the range of solo and group ceremonial vocal styles.

⊚ **Vanuatu: The Music Tradition of West Futuna** (Auvidis/Unesco, France).

Enjoyable guitar and ukulele groups from Southern Vanuatu, plus contemporary hymns from the missionary repertoire.

Mongolia and Tuva

sixty horses in my herd

Mongolia and neighbouring **Tuva** (an outlying republic of the Russian Federation), have been closed to foreigners for much of this century. So when their music – with its extraordinary 'throat' or overtone singing – emerged into the global arena during the 1990s, it made an incredible impact. The singing has become a popular 'other-worldly' ingredient in a range of musical fusions, while Tuvan groups such as Huun-Huur-Tu have wowed audiences on the touring circuit with their arresting and beautiful music. **Carole Pegg**, who has spent many years working with the people and their music, introduces the sound of the steppes.

Mongols and Tuvans share the same remote and awesome environment: a high plateau of rolling steppes, virgin forests, great lakes and snow-capped mountains, backed by the vast Gobi Desert. The size of western Europe, independent **Mongolia** is the least densely populated country on the globe with only 2.4 million people to herd its 26 million horses, camels, cattle, sheep and goats. On its northwest border is the Russian (former Soviet) **Republic of Tuva**, a group of high valleys surrounded by mountains that form a natural barrier between Mongolia and Siberia. As nomadic pastoralists, the lives of the herding peoples are hard: the terrain is often dangerous and temperatures are liable to plunge without warning to -60° in winter.

Mongols and Tuvans use music in all aspects of their daily lives: to lure animals during the hunt, to control them when herding and to encourage them to give milk or to accept their young. It permeates domestic and public celebrations such as the 'Festival of the Three Manly Sports', when the *garuda* (bird)dance accompanies wrestling, rhythmic calls form part of archery competitions and ritual songs are performed by child-jockeys before horse-racing. Music expresses and creates relationships with human partners and it is used in folk-religious, shaman or Buddhist contexts to communicate with spirits.

Cultural and **historic connections** between Tuva and Mongolia are strong and their current political boundaries are comparatively recent. In both Tuva and Mongolia there are a number of distinctive ethnic groups. Mongols perceive themselves as Western or Eastern Mongols, a label that relates to historical confederations and includes a range of ethnic groups. From 1630 to 1911, **Western Mongols** were part of the Jungar State and then, under the Qing dynasty, part of Outer Mongolia. They are located in West Mongolia, the Xinjiang Autonomous Region of China and western Inner Mongolia (China), as well as along the Volga River in Russia. The **Eastern Mongols** – found in East Mongolia and eastern parts of Inner

Mongolia and Buryatia (Russian Federation) – have fought periodically against their neighbours since Ghengis Khan's great Empire fell in the late thirteenth century. The majority of **Tuvans** live in Tuva (also known as Tannu-Tuva, Urianghai or Tangno-Urianghai) although they are also found in West Mongolia and Xinjiang.

The Communist Legacy

Both Mongolia and Tuva endured the cultural offensive of communism, with herding becoming centrally-planned rather than a tribal or family concern, and religion brutally suppressed. Important *lamas* were murdered, monks were made to join the army and monasteries destroyed. Shamans were purged and had their instruments confiscated, and folk-religious rituals were banned.

For most of the communist era in Mongolia, which lasted from 1924 to 1992, Stalinist cultural policies held sway – not least in music. In order to eradicate differences in status, ethnicity and religion, traditional music, songs and dances were taken from the ethnic groups, synthesised and subordinated to the style of the majority group, the **Khalkhas** (who make up over half the population). They were also adapted to the European scale system. Military units formed music circles in which soldiers learned the new 'national' instruments and then disseminated cultural enlightenment to Mongols living in the grasslands.

In 'New Mongolia', performances were relocated from the hearth of the *ger* (the traditional round felt tent, or yurt) to the theatrical stage. Instruments were modified and standardised to enable production of the new European scales and sounds that could fill the concert hall. The skin body of the horse-head fiddle, for instance, was replaced by wood, and its size, tuning and playing position changed.

Smirnov, a Russian musicologist, organised folk ensemble orchestras in which European and Mongolian national instruments played together. The famous horse-head fiddle player, **Jamiyan**, worked together with Smirnov and was pivotal in introducing the new national syle into schools, higher educational institutions and the theatre. Only a limited number of approved long-song singers (see below), such as **Dorjdagva** and **Norovbanzad**, were allowed to perform in the Ulaanbaatar theatre or on the radio, and they had no control over their own programmes. All music was doctored to become 'national in form and socialist in content', and playing it necessitated training within an accepted, European-style conservatoire.

Long-songs and Horse-head Fiddles

Since the collapse of the authoritarian regime, diversity is once again possible and Mongols are expressing identity and difference through music. **Long-songs** (*urtyn duu*) are performed by both Eastern and Western Mongols and sound extremely sad and serious. Among **Eastern Mongols**, like the Central Khalkhas, a solo vocalist is accompa-

CAROLE PEGG

Three hunters sing a long song, western Mongolia

Legends of the Horse-head Fiddle

According to a Khalkha story, the **horse-head fiddle** (*morin huur*) was created from the bones, skin and hair of a magical horse. A young Mongol, it says, called Cuckoo Namjil because of his fine singing voice, served as a border guard in the Altai mountains. One day, as he sang of his homesickness, a spirit rose up from the nearby lake dressed in a green silk gown and riding a beautiful horse. Entranced by his song, she became his lover and when Cuckoo Namjil had to return home, gave him a magical winged horse so that he could return to visit her. This he did, but his wife became suspicious. Investigating the horse closely, she discovered tiny wings folded behind its legs, and cut them. Next time Cuckoo Namjil set off to the west, the flying horse plunged into the desert and died. In despair, Cuckoo Namjil wept and, as he stroked the dead animal, its skull became the body of the instrument and its mane and tail became the strings and bow-hairs. As the sun rose, he sang and played a long-song and thereafter wandered over the steppes, mountains and deserts singing of his horse and his lost love.

Among Mongols of Inner Mongolia, the hero of the myth is a star prince, who takes a herdswoman lover when he periodically falls to earth to create fertility and abundance. Connections with the spirit world are persistently made in relation to the instrument. It is said that an aspiring fiddle player must go to the deserted steppe at dead of night, sit astride a horse's skull and entertain the spirits without fear until dawn. Only then can the skill to play be acquired.

A Tuvan version of the story is performed by Huun Huur Tu accompanied by their version of the horse-head fiddle, the *igil*. The hero of the tale, Öskus-ool, has a champion horse which is killed by a rival. Searching for it, Öskus-ool has a dream in which his horse speaks to him in a human voice, saying "You will find my remains under the sheer cliff. Hang my skull on an old larch tree, make a musical instrument from its wood, cover it with skin from its face and make the strings from the hair of my tail. When you start to play this instrument, my double will come down from the upper world." Öskus-ool made the instrument and began to play it. He thought of his horse, remembering how they played together and won all the races, and wept. Öskus-ool played for a long time. As people listened they laughed and wept with him. Suddenly, at the top of a high mountain, the clouds parted and down came an exact copy of his horse – a strong grey stallion. And with the stallion came a whole herd of horses with black and white faces.

Although modern horse-head fiddles have wooden bodies, the two strings are still made from strands of black, or less commonly, white horse-hair. In Mongolia proper, the thicker, deeper-sounding string has about 130 hairs (running parallel rather than being woven) and is traditionally referred to as male; the thinner, higher one, has 105 hairs and is called female.

JAK KILBY

Alexei Saaia of Yat-Kha

---

nied by a horse-head fiddle (*morin huur*) and sometimes a side-blown flute (*limbe*), which follows – often into falsetto range – the soaring melodies and intricate decorations of the vocal line, with its extremely elongated musical phrases and syllables. In performances in the *ger*, the assembled company provides a kind of vocal chorus (*türleg*). **Namdziliin Norovbanzad**, a female singer, typifies the Central Khalka concert style. She has an extraordinary range and powerful voice.

The **themes** of texts depend on the occasion: in monasteries they may be philosophical or religious; folk-religious rites will often praise nature; in weddings and other celebrations they may praise the charismatic heroes of the group, advise on social relations or express the love of family or sweetheart.

Song titles often relate to horses, for instance "Small Light Bay" or "Horse of the Narrow Gobi". Usually, though, only the opening two lines are about the horse, thereafter getting down to the real subject of the song. "Tümen Eh" (First of Ten Thousand), the long-song that begins all Borjigin Khalkha celebrations, refers to Genghis Khan in religious terms, but as he was decreed a 'non-person' during the communist era, the song was said to refer to a fast horse, so that it could still be performed.

The **horse-head fiddle** – first a symbol of ethnicity, then of national socialist identity – has now become an icon for independent, democratic Mongolia. It has two strings and is held between the legs and bowed rather like a cello to produce a soft and mellow tone. Its body is usually trapezoidal, with a horse's head carved at the upper end of the pegbox. Debates rage on whether the horse's head signifies that the fiddle was once a shaman instrument – there is also a horse's head on the end of a shaman's staff, the mount that assists his or her ecstatic journey to other levels of the universe. Myths of origin do link the instrument with magical flights (see box on p.191). There are fine players, like the Eastern Khalkha, **Tserendorj**, and 'state merited artist' **Batchuluun**, a disciple of Jamiyan, who has created a horse-head fiddle orchestra designed to play Western classical music.

The long-song style of **Western Mongols** is quite different to the Eastern version. It is performed without instrumental accompaniment, but with everyone present providing verses and choruses in unsynchronised, overlapping layers of melodic improvisations. Texts relate to their western confederation, their own homeland (which is thought to be over the border in contemporary Xinjiang Province), or their charismatic heroes, such as Shonnu or Janggar. Western Mongols use a two-string **spike fiddle**, the *ikil*, which is strung in reverse order from the horse-head fiddle, with the lower string on the left when viewed from the front. The name is said to derive from *ih hel* meaning 'large language', a language superior to that of humans used to communicate with and influence animals, natural phenomena and the spirits. It is used to accompany narrative songs and the *biy*, a West Mongolian dance that primarily uses the top half of the body.

It is unclear whether long-songs are performed extensively in **Tuva**. Absent from most current recordings, the only available example (on Smithsonian Folkways *Tuva, Voices from the Center of Asia*) is reminiscent of West-Mongolian long-song style, with angular melodies, little elongation of sylla-

bles or vowels and no ornamentation of the vocal line. As illustrated by the instrumentation of the band Hun-Huur-Tu, Tuvans share certain instruments and vocal forms with groups in Mongolia. The **pyzanchy**, a Tuvan four-string fiddle, for instance, is known as the 'four-eared fiddle' (*dörvön chihtei huur*) among Mongols, and played by men in Southern Mongolia and Inner Mongolia (China) to accompany praise-songs (*magtaal*) and tales (*üliger, holboo*). But most parallels with Tuva are to be found in West Mongolia. Both have the two-string fiddle *igil*, the two-string plucked lute (Tuvan *toshpulúr*; Altai Urianghai *topshuur*) and three-string plucked lute (Tuvan *chanzy*, Mongolian *shanz* or *shudgraga*).

The ancient three-holed, end-blown pipe, is called *shöör* by the Tofalars (in Tuva), **tsuur** by the Altai Urianghais and *sibizgi* by the Kazakhs (the latter two groups are both found in West Mongolia). This instrument, being an identity symbol for specific ethnic groups, was not chosen by the regime to be a 'national instrument' and thereby fell victim to cultural ethnic cleansing. **Narantsogt** of the Altai Urianghai hid his tsuur in the mountains in order to preserve it and has only in recent years been able to openly teach his son how to play. The tsuur is used to amplify melodic overtones while producing a vocal drone, and in this way produces a sound remarkably similar to overtone-singing.

Overtone-singing

Overtone-singing, often called **throat-singing**, is an extraordinary vocal technique in which a single performer simultaneously produces two or three vocal lines by selectively amplifying harmonics, and has become firmly associated with Tuva because of the proliferation of recordings from the region. But it is also performed by West Mongolian peoples such as Baits, Torguts and Altai Urianghais, as well as by Khalkhas in areas bordering West Mongolia, who call it *höömii*.

Ethereal, shimmering melodies are created as if by magic high above the deep fundamental notes. Normally harmonics are heard just as colouring to a note – they help us differentiate between the sound of a violin and clarinet playing the same note – but in overtone-singing the harmonics are made louder than the drone from which they derive. Melodies are sung by bringing out different harmonics of the fundamental note by means of precise movements of the lips, tongue and larynx. Both solo and performed in groups, it's an extraordinary sound. A possible connection between overtone-singing and Tibetan Buddhism, which spread to both Mongolia and Tuva, has been made based on the fact that Tibetan lamas of the Gelugpa monasteries of Gyume and Gyöto produce harmonics when they use extreme bass voices during Tantric ritual performance. Mongols recall, though, that Buddhist lamas did not approve of höömii, pronouncing that it was 'without respect' (*hundtei bish*). This raises the possibility of an association with folk-religious practices that Buddhism was anxious to quash.

Initially a phenomenon investigated by Russian researchers, and then introduced to the West by Ted Levin's field recordings, Tuvan throat-singing is performed in a number of different styles. Widely recognised are the clear, bright *sigit* (whistle) and höömii (Mongolian for 'pharynx' and their generic term for overtone-singing) styles, both of which pitch the fundamental in baritone range, produce harmonics between eight and twelve times the frequency of the fundmental and are sung with texts. *Ezengileer* (stirrup) style is likened to a trotting horse, *chylandyk* (cricket) to crickets chirping and *borbannadir* is a sort of trill likened to the rapids of a river. *Kargiraa* ('to speak with a husky voice') is used for songs, and its variant, *steppe kargiraa*, for textless melodies, both of them employing a deep bass fundamental drone resonating in the chest and producing harmonics two and a half to three and a half octaves above the drone.

Currently dazzling people throughout the world with their recordings and concerts is the Tuvan band **Huun-Huur-Tu**, formed when Sacha Bapa and his brother Sayan, together with Kaigal-ool Khovalyg and Albert Kuvezin, left one of the large state-managed song and dance ensembles in 1992. Since then, they have toured widely in the US, Europe and Asia. The band's leader, **Kaigal-ool Khovalyg**, has a truly amazing deep voice with which he produces both sigit and khöömei styles of throat-singing. Kaigal-ool and Albert Kuvezin have experimented with other Tuvan musicians, producing some amazing cross-fertilisations with rock and punk (see below). **Kongar-ool Ondar**, who has also toured widely, is another leading Tuvan overtone-singer, and sang for Boris Yeltsin, the first Russian President to visit Tuva, in 1994.

Professional overtone-singers in Ulaanbaatar who appear on recordings (for instance, Sundui, Ganboldt, Tserendavaa and Gereltsogt) are all Khalkhas from Hovd province. These Khalkhas have a **myth of origin** for overtone-singing that suggests a connection with the spirits of nature. Their district is bordered to the west by a range of Altai mountains, including Mount Jargalant, and in the east by a huge lake, Har Nuur. Mount Jargalant, they say, catches the wind as it comes from the east and sets up a drone that crosses their area, which is then swallowed by the lake. It serves to warn herders in the valley below of the impending strong winds and is said to have a magical effect: the steppes become extra fertile, the animals particularly fine and the people sing and perform better than at other times. Since Mongolians believe that all natural features are occupied by spirits, it is likely that the spirit of the mountain was thought to be producing this noise.

Mongols warn, however, that while listening to höömii is beneficial to the spirit, producing it can be harmful to the body. Traditionally, males performed at the peak of their strength and champion wrestlers make excellent overtone-singers. Even professionals may suffer ill effects such as blood vessels bursting around the eyes and loss of consciousness. This contrasts greatly with attitudes of Western Europeans, who hold workshops to encourage untrained people to perform, and whose New Age practitioners advertise its practice for bodily healing.

The sounds of overtone-singing are frequently compared to aspects of **nature**, such as the entrancing sounds of the mythical River Eev (among Mongols) or the vertical separation of light rays seen on the grasslands just after sunrise or before sunset (among Tuvans). Other instruments and vocal techniques use overtone sounds to imitate nature and communicate with **spirits**: the tsuur is used to ward off evil spirits at New Year celebrations; the jew's harp (Mongol *aman huur*, Tuvan

---

Chadaana

Chadaana is the name of a Tuvan town and river. It was also the site of Tuva's largest Buddhist monastery, destroyed in the 1930s. The chadagan is a plucked board zither.

I can't admire enough
This dear corner of Tuva
With wonder I look on its beauty
This place that I come to is always here

The beautiful-sounding chadagan
The Chadaana, flowing over waterfalls
Gave the echo of a melody
The country of my beloved Chadaana

From Huun-Huur-Tu , *If I'd Been Born an Eagle*

komys) is used to contact spirits by shamans and shamanesses; and the low-pitched, declamatory vocal style *häälah* is used by Altai Urianghais during epic performance to create an imaginary space in which the epic-hero's spirit can enact the events described by the bard, and cure illness or bad luck in the community.

Contemporary Sounds

In contemporary Mongolia and Tuva, groups are now able to determine their own musical sounds, repertoires and directions, and are no longer employed by the State. Some are drawing inspiration from their ethnic origins and religious traditions, and some reacting to the influx of new sounds by cross-fertilising their music with that of the West. Others are simply making Western music with local lyrics.

Huun-Huur-Tu have pioneered World Music fusion and worked with many American musicians as well as Russian folklorist and instrumentalist **Sergei Starostin**. The latter was part of *Mountain Tale* (on the Jaro label), a successful collaboration

The Horses of Huun-Huur-Tu

Although **Huun-Huur-Tu** have become well known abroad as Tuva's most celebrated group, it was only in 1998 that they first toured as a group, giving concerts in Kyzil and several towns and villages in Tuva. Until then, many performances had been for friends and family in the *ger* (tent). The family of their imposing leader, Kaigal-ool, still maintains a traditional lifestyle with gers and a vast herd of horses.

Horses are a recurring theme in the group's music – in fact, almost all up-tempo numbers in Tuvan music have the rhythms of the horse behind them. Huun-Huur-Tu have many subtle variations of trotting and galloping rhythms. "Chiraa-Khoor" – learned from an old Tuvan singer – is one of their most celebrated horse songs, describing a journey with a continuous riding pulse; another, "Eki Attar", links a horse and a girlfriend (both songs are on *The Orphan's Lament*) and there's yet another example, "Dönen-Shilgi", on the *If I'd Been Born An Eagle* collection.

Huun-Huur-Tu explain: "it's impossible that people who spend so much time around horses would not have absorbed their sense of rhythm. It's not like a metronome – it's not stable, but alive. The rhythms change and the lengths of the phrases change. That's what gives our music its special character." In their fourth album, Huun-huur-Tu feature another horse song, "Black Eagle". This was the name of a famous horse killed by the Tuvan equivalent of the KGB during the Stalinist period. It's a reminder that in

SHANACHIE

Huun-Huur-Tu

Tuva horses are not just rhythmic inspiration, but important metaphors.

Simon Broughton

between the Bulgarian female choir Angelite, the Moscow Art Trio and Huun-Huur-Tu. More recently, they have recorded with Scottish musicians including pipe player Martyn Bennet.

Less packaged than Huun-Huur-Tu but equally fascinating is the Tuvan group **Shu-De** (meaning 'gee-up', to make a horse go faster), who use the same combinations of instruments, overtones and imitations of nature – with some added twists. The hard-edged rather than lush vocals of the female singer Nadezhda Shoigui are exactly right and the group's combinations of overtone-singing and epic-style vocals supports the idea that the two are related.

At the contemporary end of the Tuvan spectrum are two outstanding singers, **Sainkho Namchylak** and **Albert Kuvezin** (formerly of Huun-Huur-Tu). Sainkho has moved in modern jazz and even New Age circles, and her improvised vocals, inspired by traditional Tuvan musical practices, can evoke a screaming banshee or a velvety seductress. Kuvezin, on the other hand, has adopted a heavy-metal and punk sensibility. His heavy-metal throat singing with electric guitar and igil is something to behold and his new group **Yat-Kha**, named after the long Tuvan zither he plays, is proving very successful on the touring circuit.

Mongolian overtone-singers and rock singers have yet to make a breakthrough on the World Music circuit but there is a vibrant scene in Ulaanbaatar, including *pop mop*, the various kinds of popular music, as well as soft and hard rock. At the hard rock end of the spectrum are bands such as **Haranga** (meaning a gong used in Buddhist ritual), who have been playing together for about ten years. Head-banging his long dark curls, vocalist Lhagvasüren struts the stage with the energy of a modern-day Genghis Khan. **Hurd** (Speed), led by Ganbayar, and including three of his brothers, are very heavy metal. Using harsh vocals and instrumental sounds, they exhort "Let us develop at the speed of light now that we are set free into the vast world" on "Our Mongolia".

Rap-influenced **Black Rose** comprises two vocalists: Amaraa and Maadai. Versatile, eclectic, and sporting sunglasses with ancient Mongol outfits, they inject 'drumscapes' and key English phrases such as 'East-West, East-West' into their songs. The six-piece band **Niciton** features the moving vocals and superb melodies and keyboards of Batchuluun, probably the first Mongolian musician to have 'dropped out'. Having attended Music School for eleven years under the communist system, he left just before taking his final exams to join a band. Despite their long hair and meandering guitar solos, Niciton are a pop group, citing their influences as Billy Joel, Elton John, the Beatles and the Rolling Stones.

There are many boy bands in Mongolia, of which **Camerton** – four young teenagers full of sweet harmonies – is thought to be the best. There is also a clutch of Mongolian girlie bands, with the threesome **Spike** the most popular. Among the leading solo artists, female vocalist **Ariunaa**, who recently declared herself to be 'the Mongolian Madonna', has issued a disc called *Eros 1*, while **Chinggis** (Genghis), a male vocalist, imitates Elvis Presley.

Festivals

A triennial festival of throat-singing, with a competition and a symposium, is held in Kyzyl, Tuva; the last took place in July 1998. For information, contact: Dr. Zoya Kyrgys, Director, International Scientific Centre 'Khoomei', 46 Shchetinkin-Kravchenko Street, 667000 Kyzyl, Republic of Tuva, Russian Federation. Fax: (7) 394 223 6722.

discography

Mongolia

Compilations

Mongolia: Chants Kazakhs et tradition epique de l'Ouest (Ocora, France).

Alain Desjacques' excellent 1984 recordings illustrate the distinctiveness of Mongol and Kazakh music, and the vocal styles used for different genres: melodic singing (*duulah*) and guttural declamatory *häälah* for epics and narrative tales, accompanied by horse-head as well as four-eared fiddle.

Mongolia: Living Music of the Steppes (Multicultural Media, US).

After the first tinny tracks of Soviet-style ensemble music, there are some surprising delights. Central Khalkha long-songs are performed by the celebrated female vocalist Norovbanzad, accompanied on horse-head fiddle by Tsogbadrah. Other Eastern Mongol traditions include a two-string tube fiddle (*huuchir*) ensemble and wonderful jew's harp playing from east Gobi. Western Mongol traditions are represented by Tserendavaa's overtone-singing and a sparsely decorated long-song from Jamcha in Urumchi, Xinjiang, among others.

 Musiques de Mongolie (Buda/Musique du Monde, France).

A superb collection of diverse music. Herders perform traditional praise-songs and long-songs during festivals (accompanied by snorting horses) and sing to a she-camel to persuade it to feed an orphan-camel. Eastern Khalkha Tserendorj performs the musical tale of Cuckoo Namjil and

Western Khalkha Gereltsogt demonstrates six types of overtone-singing. Other delights are an ensemble that performs 'court music', chanting lamas, and Kazakhs who demonstrate the improvisatory basis of their music.

Artists

Black Rose

A rap-influenced pop group including vocalists Amaraa and Maadai.

 Great and Destroy (Sonor Records, Germany).

Replete with special effects such as creaking doors, footsteps, a baby crying and dalek sounds. It's difficult to know how much is inspired by the producers but the overall result is pleasing. As with most Mongol bands, a song is included about their homeland – in this case, mountain ranges, lakes, rivers and the Gobi Desert.

Egschiglen

A good ensemble-type group (the name means 'beautiful melody') that interprets traditional songs and contemporary Mongolian composers.

Gobi (Dunya Records, Germany).

The group makes use of three horse-head fiddles, two overtone-singers as well as the zither (*yatga*) and dulcimer (*yoochin*), both of which were transformed by the Soviet regime from urban or monastery contexts to become typical ensemble instruments. Conservatoire training is evident from the arrangements and the cello-like horse-head fiddling but there are several impressively deep *harhiraa* overtone-singing tracks.

Ensemble Altai–Hangai

A group of four young singers and musicians specialising in the Western Mongolian style.

Let's Dance! Mongolian khuuryn tatlaga (Pan, Netherlands).

Most Mongolian music disseminated abroad is in the 'national' style based on that of Eastern Mongol Khalkas, so it's very refreshing to hear these vocal tracks and fiddle melodies (khuuryn tatlaga) from the mountainous Western part of the country. The overtone-singing, angular melodies and harmonics on fiddles and lutes have much in common with Tuvan styles. Recorded on tour in the Netherlands.

Haranga

Formed in 1989 in Ulaanbaatar, Haranga were the first to play hard rock and to introduce this style to Mongolian youth. Now thought of by Mongols as classic rock, they are becoming popular abroad.

Best of Haranga (Stonehenge Productions, Austria).

Featuring the songs and wailing lead guitar of the pretty Enhmanlai and the raunchy voice of Lhagvasüren. Particularly interesting is the heavy metal version of the Buddhist mantra, "Om mani padme hum". The sleeve boasts the fact that the drums are real, not synthesised.

Niciton

There is no doubting the technical brilliance of this band, although the effect is somewhat spoilt by tacky synthesised strings. Led by Dashdondog, with Batchuluun singing, backed by guitar, sax, drums, piano and that synthesizer.

Tsamtsaa Tail (Please, take off your shirt, darling) (Sonor Records, Mongolia).

Don't be put off by the slick arrangements and big-band sounds of the first few tracks because there are some gems to be heard. Batchuluun produces some more sparsely arranged ballads and powerful melodies, particularly on the title track and "Piano".

Namdziliin Norovbanzad

Norovbanzad was born in Middle Gobi, Central Mongolia, in 1931, where she learned to sing long-songs in traditional herding contexts. After successes at folk festivals, she joined the National Folksong and Dance Ensemble, and became one of the big names of the official Mongolian folk style.

Urtiin Duu (JVC, Japan).

Norovbanzad does have a rather operatic style – for many that may be appealing – but there's no doubting the range and power of her voice, particularly in the falsetto singing which is part of this style. Accompanying instruments include horse-head fiddle, limbe flute and yatga zither. Striking, concert-style long-song (*urtiin* or *urtyn duu*) performances.

Tuva

Compilations

 Deep in the Heart of Tuva:
Cowboy Music from the Wild East (Ellipsis Arts, US).

Notwithstanding the awful subtitle, this is one of Elipsis's very successful book and CD combinations, with some wonderful tracks. The throat-singing of Kongar-ool Ondar and that of his eleven-year-old pupil Shulban is surely the most astonishing recording to date. Interesting cross-fertilisations, including throat-singing with drums, a great throat-singing blues, and Sainkho Namchylak and Huun-Huur-Tu with the Bulgarian Women's Choir Angelite. The book includes historical information, a guide to overtone-singing and recipes.

The Spirit of the Steppes:
Throat Singing from Tuva and Beyond (Nascente, UK)

A good compilation from the budget-priced Nascente label. Features the various overtone-singing styles (höömii, siggit, kargiraa, borbannadir), great rhythms and mimicry of natural sounds and tracks from some of the best-known artists like Namchylak, Yat-Kha and Huun-Huur-Tu, the latter featured here with the Bulgarian choir Angelite.

Tuva: Among the Spirits (Smithsonian Folkways, US).

Focuses on the connections between Tuvan music and the natural world – wind, streams, birds and animals. Particularly impressive are Anatoli Kulaar (of Huun-Huur-Tu) doing *borbangnadyr* throat-singing to the background of a flowing stream, and throat-singing on horseback in time with the trot of the horse, and Kaigal-ool Khovalyg performing on igil and singing as he conjures up horses and birds. Quite magical.

Tuva: Voices from the Center of Asia (Smithsonian Folkways, US).

These classic field recordings by Alekseev, Kyrgyz and Levin contain examples of the range of Tuvan throat-singing styles as well as sounds on the periphery of our understanding of music: imitations of animal sounds, and rhythmically intoned speech for domesticating animals, lulling children to sleep or communicating with spirits. Includes excellent notes.

Voices from the Land of the Eagles
(Pan, Netherlands).

Kaigal-ool Khovalyg of Huun-Huur-Tu joins two other musicians – Kongar-ool Ondar and Gennadi Tumat – all of rural origin and formerly soloists with the ensemble 'Tuva'. Some unusual tracks, with different jew's harp styles, as well as rich, deep Tuvan throat-singing. A modernised fiddle and igil is used, with three rather than two strings.

Artists

Huun-Huur-Tu

The best known group from Tuva. Currently features four musicians led by Kaigal-ool Khovalyg, a very talented overtone-singer and instrumentalist who now teaches igil at the music school in Tuva's capital, Kyzyl. Huun-Huur-Tu (the name means the vertical separation of light on the grasslands after sunrise and before sunset) promote the varied instrumental music of Tuva as well as overtone-singing and have collaborated with Frank Zappa, Ry Cooder, the Chieftains and the Kronos Quartet amongst others. They have recorded four albums for Shanachie to date.

 Orphan's Lament
(Shanachie, US).

All Huun-Huur-Tu albums can be recommended. This is their second, from 1994, and it opens with a thunderous prayer with shimmering overtones, like a door opening onto a forgotten world of Buddhist music. Some great horse songs, of course, including "Chiraa-Khoor", describing an epic journey (using a rattle made from sheep's knuckle-bones in a bull's testicle). Their first album, **60 Horses in My Herd** (Shanachie, US), is also a classic, and includes the "Lament of the Igil", which describes the creation of the Horse-head Fiddle, and the jaunty "Song of the Caravan Drivers", a favourite of Frank Zappa.

Sainkho Namchylak

Tuva's most celebrated female vocalist has a background in throat-singing, Siberian folklore and shamanistic ritual. Throat-singing was almost exclusively the province of men, although the taboo against women based on the belief that it caused infertility is now outdated. Namchylak, by nature adventurous, was a member of the Tuvan State Ensemble before going to live in Moscow and then western Europe from the late 1980s. She has worked with Russian folklore ensembles, Belgian World Music guru Hector Zazou and improvisatory free-jazz acts.

 Naked Spirit
(Amiata, Italy).

This 1999 album far exceeds her *Out of Tuva* compilation for Crammed World, previously her only internationally available disc. This is a poetic and modern album, beginning with a

heartfelt duet intertwining with Djivan Gasparyan on *duduk* and moving on to some more dance-oriented and spiritual tracks. Beautifully produced.

Shu-De

An unpretentious group of three throat-singers and musicians that produces mostly traditional, rather than cross-over sounds.

 Voices from the Distant Steppe
(RealWorld, UK).

Gently muted sounds from the igil, and flowing flute melodies provide a good contrast with the gritty singing of female vocalist Nadezhda Shoigu and throat-singers Ergen Mongush, Oleg Kuular and Leonid Oorzhak. From lullaby to tongue-twister, shaman ritual to overtone-wrapped Buddhist mantra, this recording is a delight.

Yat-Kha

Led by Albert Kuvezin, founding member of Huun-Huur-Tu, Yat-Kha are a fairly recent addition to the Tuvan scene, bringing a punk sensibility to Tuvan sounds. Kuvezin has a gutteral, almost inhuman-sounding voice and plays the zither (from which the band takes its name) alongside a trio of musicians on throat-singing vocals, horse-head fiddles and percussion.

 Dalai Beldiri
(Wicklow, US).

With growling vocals, those distinctive clip-clop rhythms and a sensitive use of electronics, the group's first international release comes strongly recommended. Fans will want to search out their first disc, **Yenisei Punk** (Global Music Centre, Finland).

Nepal

the hills are alive

The hills and mountains of Nepal are alive with trekkers getting their fill of exertion, fresh-air and spectacular scenery but very few of those visitors are aware of the country's musical traditions. They are hanging on in there, though, particularly at festival times, despite the rapidly changing lifestyles. **Carol Tingey** has experienced it all first hand.

Tourism has made Nepal seem – and become – a great deal more mainstream and Westernised than could ever have been expected of this small mountainous nation, poised between India and Tibet. The tourist image also makes the Nepalese appear uniform: a major misapprehension. Spread among isolated pockets in the high mountains, along the terraced mountainsides or crammed into the valleys, the population encompasses more than thirty-six ethnic groups, each with its own language and traditions, and a web of religious belief including Hinduism, Buddhism, Tantrism and local traditions.

This means there are highly local forms of both sacred and secular music. Among the Sherpas and other peoples who inhabit the higher altitudes of the north, Tibetan influences are dominant, while the rest of the country is closer to the music of North India and there is a classical tradition related to Hindustani. In addition to the many traditions of sacred and folk music (which is characterised throughout the country by song accompanied by a small barrel-drum or *madal*), you also find film and radio music that combines Nepalese folk idioms and elements of Hindi film music in a form of national light music.

Type-casting

Nepal, like India, has an all-pervasive Hindu caste structure, and professional musicians are born into the job by virtue of their caste status. Some musician castes have other hereditary jobs thrown in, thus members of the *damai* caste are tailors and musicians, while the *gaine* were originally a caste of minstrels and fishermen.

The **gaine** are a caste of professional musicians living in west and central Nepal. They earn a living by wandering from house to house, singing

for patrons in return for food. They accompany themselves on hand-carved, four-string bowed fiddles (*sarangi*). The sound is mellow and enlivened by tapping on the instrument or plucking the strings. The sarangi bowing is also emphasised in order to provide a rhythmic drive to the accompaniment, an effect heightened by little bells attached to the bow. In the Lamjung region of west Nepal, you may still be fortunate enough to hear the all-but-obsolete *arbajo* (a long-necked lute

CAROL TINGEY

Gaine musician with Sarangi

with four strings), being played by a veteran gaine. This cumbersome instrument has been superseded by the more portable sarangi.

The gaine have a vast repertoire of heroic ballads in praise of historical and legendary figures, folksongs and musical anecdotes. They also have a repertoire of hymns which patrons can hire to play as offerings at shrines, seasonal songs relating to the agricultural cycle and songs of blessing for weddings. But today, many minstrels have stopped wandering the western hills in favour of supplying Kathmandu tourists with (somewhat inferior) home-made fiddles, while a few have found employment as hotel entertainers.

Nepalese blacksmiths make and play an iron jews' harp, producing a rich gamut of overtones, but they play purely for their own amusement, their repertoire consisting of local folk songs and current radio and film songs.

Tailor-musicians

For a **wedding** almost anywhere in Nepal a **panchai baja** – a strident band of shawms, barrel and portable kettle drums, cymbals and C-shaped horns – is indispensible, so much so that 'they got married without panchai baja' is a euphemism for living together. The band accompanies the groom to the home of the bride, performs during the wedding ceremony, and again for the return procession. Apart from playing popular folksongs and film tunes, the **damai** musicians, who belong to an 'untouchable' caste restricted to tailoring and playing in such wedding bands, have a traditional repertoire of pieces linked to specific moments in the ceremony. In a 'bride-requesting tune', played when the weeping bride is about to depart from her family home, the shawm player mimics the bride's wailing. This type of music is considered auspicious, and is a necessary accompaniment to processions, Hindu rituals and rites of passage. The musicians and their instruments need to be thoroughly doused in rice wine in order to play well; only then do they consider they have the stamina to play continuously throughout the night.

The make-up of the wedding band varies from place to place. In the Kathmandu Valley the traditional band has been replaced by Indian-style **brass bands** with uniformed bandsmen, while in western Nepal the musicians wear ceremonial dress, dancing as they drum in ensembles of up to thirty-six kettledrums. In this area, the tailor-musicians also sing ballads and trance songs, accompanying themselves on an hour-glass drum.

Tailor-musicians are also employed at shrines to play during daily offerings and sacrifices. Temple ensembles consist of large kettledrum, shawm and one or more trumpets or horns of various shapes and sizes. Perhaps the most atmospheric events in

Tailor-musicians prepare for a wedding

which they participate are the all-night vigils at shrines situated deep in the mountain forests. The bands, which lead processions of devotees with flower offerings or sacrificial goats, resound far across the dark hillsides and can be heard long before they come into view. Eventually, tiny dots of light from the pilgrims' lanterns can be discerned approaching from all directions, making their way down the steep and convoluted paths as the music gets louder and louder. Suddenly, they burst into the sacred clearing, and the hidden shrine throbs with life and enjoyment.

Newars and the Drums of Kathmandu

The **Newars** were the earliest inhabitants of the Kathmandu Valley. In a traditional Newar community, most young men undergo a ritual apprenticeship in drumming, dancing or singing which qualifies them to participate in the nightly music-making at their local shrine, and to take part in the musical processions around the town during major festivals. Newars are renowned for their spectacular masked dances which re-enact well-known

CAROL TINGEY

Beating the hour-glass drum

stories of the gods. These dances are accompanied by bands of drums and cymbals. Newar singing has an extremely nasal quality, and as the emphasis is on devotional ardour rather than consistent intonation, uninitiated outsiders often find it rather hard on the ears.

Newar music is dominated by **drumming** – against which shawms or flutes may provide a melodic accompaniment. Drum ensembles come in a great variety of shapes and sizes. Newar farmers are virtuoso performers on enormous cylindrical drums (*dhimay baja*), played en masse with cymbals during festivals. Another popular processional band combines flutes and barrel-drums. At some shrines, in addition to a group of singers accompanied by one or two large barrel drums and small cymbals, there is a complement of nine drums (*nava dapha*). Each drum is played in turn throughout the course of the ceremony, accompanied by a band of cymbals and either shawms (for the louder drums) or flutes (for the quieter).

The Newars, both Hindus and Buddhists, have a caste system, and some castes have musical responsibilities. The Newar **jogi**, descendants of medieval ascetics, are ritual shawm players who can be summoned to accompany the drum bands of other castes. Newar butchers have the duty to play their particular drum (*naykhin*) during funeral processions. Newar Buddhist priests sing esoteric hymns (*caca*), which, when accompanied by mystic dances and hand gestures, are said to have immense occult power. The secrets of this tradition are closely guarded by initiated priests.

Today, weakened by the rival attractions of cinema, television and video, and starved of money, Nepalese and Newar music is in a state of decline, although increasing tourist interest in music and attendance at musical events and festivals can only help to encourage the maintenance of traditional forms of music.

Women and Music

For the majority of the population, music-making is regarded as a male activity, and female participation is restricted to specific occasions. Women of the Indo-Nepalese castes only sing in public on three occasions: during the arduous work of rice-transplanting; whilst keeping all-night vigil at a shrine during the annual women's festival (*teej*); and at the all-female wedding party celebrated at the groom's home while the men are away at the bride's. An exception is found at the Royal Court, where female singers are employed to sing for various Hindu rituals, rites of passage, coronations

Musically, the best times to visit Nepal are during the major festivals: Newar New Year in the Kathmandu Valley (March/April); Dasain all around the country, but especially in the Kathmandu Valley and Gorkha (September/October); and the Newar festival season in the Kathmandu Valley (August/September).

If you're interested in the sex lives of the gods as well as music, the **Newar New Year Festival** (*bisket jatra*) in Bhaktapur is the place to be. A glorious two-week celebration of fertility and renewal, it begins with a massive chariot tug-of-war and continues with the erection of an enormous pole and divine procreation all over town. All the local music groups accompany the sexual activities of the deities, as well as playing for them daily. New Year's morning begins early with a musical procession around the town.

Not recommended for vegetarians or animal rights campaigners, **Dasain** is a two-week festival in honour of the Mother Goddess in all her manifestations. Her lust for blood is satisfied by thousands of animal sacrifices, intended to keep her well disposed during the coming year. At larger shrines the decapitations are accompanied by special sacrificial music, and throughout the season, the dasain music (*malasri*) is played and sung everywhere, as well as being broadcast on Radio Nepal.

At the end of the rice-transplanting season in August, the Newars of the Kathmandu Valley celebrate a series of **agricultural festivals** – so many that almost every other day is a public holiday. Each festival has a different purpose – to drive away demons, to honour one's deceased family members, to mark the end of the Newar Buddhist time cycle, to ensure the success of the rice, and to stop the rain. The festivals normally involve musical processions around the towns, and are generally extremely lively and colourful.

CAROL TINGEY

Newar Buddhist Priests ensuring a good rice crop

and festivals. Among the **Tamangs** and other hill-dwelling peoples, pairs of men and women duel with one another by singing improvised duets. The loser, if a woman, risks having her hand offered in marriage to the victor.

Popular Music

The advent of Radio Nepal in 1952, and later the arrival of cassette players, produced a dramatic change in the soundscape of Nepal. Wherever you go in the country, if you are near habitation, you will experience Nepali **light music**, broadcast countrywide under the supervision of the government. It's a pleasant blend of all the regional folk music styles with a bit of Hindi film music thrown in. Lyrics are concerned with love and patriotism, and are all in Nepali, in the interests of national integration. Hindi film music is also widely broadcast and if you are on a whistle-stop tour of Asia, it's likely to be your only Nepalese musical experience.

In the 1950s and '60s, Nepal's answer to Frank Sinatra was **Dharma Raj Thapa** (b 1924), who recorded folksongs with film music style backings. In 1953 he had a real hit with "Sagarmatha Neplako Gaurab", which commemorated the first ascent of Everest. Modern song and film composers like **Nati Kazi** (b 1925), **Shiva Shankar** (b 1932), **Gopal Yonjan** (b 1943) and **Amber Gurung** (b 1937) draw on folk idioms but incorporate elements of North Indian light classical music and Western harmony. Instrumentation can be pretty eclectic, combining traditional instruments with tabla, harmonium, orchestra and electronic instruments.

Kathmandu's **pop scene** is ever changing, but names to look out for include **Dip Shrestha**, **Sukmit Gurung**, **Prakash Shrestha** and the band **Crossroads**.

discography

Compilations

 Castes de musiciens au Népal
(Musée de l'Homme, France).

Excellent recordings of damai, gaine and other folk music accompanied by very good notes.

Folksongs of Nepal (Lyrichord, US).

Newar and Tamang folk songs, selected for their social rather than their musical value. Good sleeve notes.

Gaines de Hyangja: Chants et danses du Népal
(Buda/Musique du Monde, France).

A collection of folk songs sung by gaine of Pokhara. Good singalong stuff, with idiomatic sarangi playing, but the popular folksongs are not representative of the range of gaine repertoire. The recordings have atmospheric background noises of babies crying and dogs barking.

Musique de fête chez les Newar
(VDE-Gallo/AIMP, Switzerland).

A good collection comparing Newar music across two decades, with recordings made in 1952 and 1973.

Nepal: Ritual and Entertainment
(Auvidis/Unesco, France).

The best over-view of traditional Nepalese sounds, taken from excellent field recordings. Includes damai ritual music, panchai baja ensembles, the music of the Newars, Tharus and Sherpas, and three tracks of Indo-Nepalese music, but only one example of gaine music.

The Real Folk Music of Nepal:
'The Nepalese Blues' (Traveling Records, Norway).

This collection of gaine recordings features folk songs, traditional items and tracks performed by Ram Saran Nepali, the well-known Radio Nepal artist, accompanied by Hornnath Upadhyaya. Easy listening.

Artists

Amber Gurung

Amber Gurung combines a successful film music and modern song-composing career with a job as Music Director of the Royal Nepal Academy.

Kahiry Lahar Kahiriy Tarang
(Ratna Cassettes, Nepal).

A tuneful collection, reflecting Gurung's talent for composition rather than singing.

Gopal Yonjan

A prolific composer of songs, film music and musicals who writes many of his own lyrics.

Kanchi (Ratna Cassettes, Nepal).

Lively and melodic Nepali film music, with the inevitable touch of romance.

Pakistan/North India **Qawwali/Folk**

songs of praise

The death of Nusrat Fateh Ali Khan in August 1997 not only saw the passing of Pakistan's most revered qawwali singer – Shahen-Sha, 'the brightest of stars', as he was known – but also one of World Music's most extraordinary figures. Both Pakistani and Indian newspapers were briefly united as they carried front-page stories mourning his death amidst the celebrations of their half century of independence. With his large girth, frequent brow mopping and popular appeal, he was the Pavarotti of the Sufi world, forging previously unimaginable links between Islamic devotional ceremony, 'world fusion' and film soundtracks. His critics have often charged that while qawwali spread far and wide thanks to his peerless renditions, it nevertheless ended up a far cry from its original purpose – that of raising spiritual awareness in the listener. **Jameela Siddiqi** outlines the qawwali tradition and **Peter Culshaw** examines qawwali fusion and the folk traditions of Pakistan.

Qawwali is music with a message – the Sufi message of love and peace – which has been sung to catchy melodies dating back as far as the thirteenth century. The bulk of the repertoire consists of religious poetry set to music which shares certain traits with the light classical music of India and Pakistan, although qawwali is a recognised musical genre in its own right. Its rhythmic intensity has made it extremely popular in Indian films as well as in clubs and weddings in India and abroad. Outside the subcontinent, the music has become hugely popular at World Music festivals – Nusrat Fateh Ali Khan swept all before him at the first ever WOMAD – and despite the passing of its biggest star, remains a popular draw through groups like Mehr and Sher Ali, and the excellent Rizwan-Muazzam Qawwali.

Qawwali Themes

The term 'qawwali' refers both to the genre and its performance. Groups of **qawwals** – singers and musicians – can consist of any number of people, but always include a lead-singer, one or two secondary singers (who also play the harmonium), and at least one percussionist. Every member of the group joins in the singing, and junior members also clap rhythmically. Under the guidance of a religious leader, or sheikh, these groups of trained musicians present a vast treasure of poems in song, articulating and evoking a mystical experience for the spiritual benefit of their audience.

As an occasion, qawwali is a gathering for the purpose of realising the ideals of Islamic mysticism through the ritual of listening to music (*sama*). By enhancing the message of mystical poetry, and by providing a powerful rhythm suggesting the ceaseless repetition of God's name (*zikr*), the music is designed to arouse mystical love and even divine ecstasy – the central experience of Sufism.

While Islamic musicologists wrote about the use of music to achieve a trance-like state to gain spiritual insight as early as the ninth century, qawwali in its present form is thought to have originated with **Amir Khusrau** (1253–1325), an exceptionally talented Sufi poet and composer. He is also credited with the invention of the sitar and

PAKISTAN

Rizwan-Muazzam Qawwali

tabla and was the favourite disciple of the great Sufi saint Nizamuddin Auliya in Delhi. His poems and melodies form the core of the qawwali repertoire. Following Khusrau, the Sufi communities of the Indian subcontinent have sustained the musical tradition of *Mahfil-e-Sama* (Assembly for Listening), which remains the central ritual of Sufism.

Through sama, the Sufi seeks to activate his link with his living spiritual guide, with departed saints and ultimately with God. The music serves to kindle the flame of his mystical love, to intensify his longing for mystical union and even to transport him to a state of ecstasy. Words like 'longing' and 'ecstasy' reveal the sensuality of much of the Sufi repertoire. Many texts use earthly images of drunkenness and physical love to express their divine counterparts – something that has often generated criticism from more Orthodox Muslims.

Our eyes met
And all my finery, my decorum
Came to nothing
As your eyes met mine

Khusrau's image, in one of his most popular classical Hindi compositions, is that of a young woman who has painstakingly worked on her appearance for a meeting with her beloved. When she comes face-to-face with him, her make-up is smudged, her fine clothes crushed and her jewellery made redundant in the ecstasy of union. The imagery is powerfully erotic but the message is that all this finery and beauty counts for nothing in the joy of

union with God. With images like that in mind, perhaps Nusrat's embracing of dance-floor culture is in keeping with the broad-mindedness of Sufi tradition.

The Music

Qawwali, like other North Indian song styles, has three components: the melodic line, sung by one or more singers, the rhythm which is articulated on the drum (traditionally the **dholak**), and the pitch outline of the melody which is constantly reinforced on the harmonium. The usual style of delivery consists of singing poetic verses punctuated with a chorus refrain and instrumental phrases. The **harmonium** is now established in qawwali and seems to have permanently replaced its less practical predecessors like the **sarangi** (which requires extensive re-tuning between numbers). The **tabla** is now increasingly used alongside the dholak and is played using a flat hand technique (*thaap*) as opposed to the normal fingering technique (*chutki*) of North Indian music.

Qawwali is sung in many **languages** but its original repertoire is composed of verses in Persian (*Farsi*) and an old form of Hindi known as *Braj Bhasha* – the two main languages used by Khusrau. There is also an extensive repertoire in Punjabi, drawn chiefly from the verses of **Baba Bulleh Shah**. In recent times, there has been a growing tendency towards the use of Urdu (a relatively modern language of Northern India and Pakistan) and, nowadays, even Arabic, although the Arabs themselves have no musical affinity with this genre. An artist like **Bahauddin Qutubuddin** is fairly typical of current Pakistani fashions in his use of Urdu lyrics with melodies reminiscent of popular Middle-Eastern music.

Qawwali music has special features which make it distinct from all other North Indian musical forms. These are directly linked to its religious function. The performers see themselves as entrusted with a religious duty to convey the message of Allah. It is this sense of actively performing a religious function that distinguishes qawwals from other North Indian musicians.

Shrines

Qawwali is at its most splendid in its traditional setting: on the occasion of a **Sufi saint's urs** (the commemoration of his death and hence his reunion with God) at the saint's shrine. This is the music in its true context, and attending such a performance is a powerful experience. While the sound

Sindhi Music Ensemble's Sohrab Fakir

PAKISTAN

Chand Nizami and party at the Nizamuddin Shrine in Delhi

system may not amount to much – various background noises add to the texture of the music, while the mosquitoes bring their own buzz to the occasion – the whole atmosphere is charged with rhythmic energy.

Qawwalis may assemble anywhere, but do so particularly at shrines dedicated to Sufi saints, since saints symbolise that nearness to God which the Sufi seeks to achieve in a sama. Although the prime occasion for a qawwali is the anniversary of the saint's death, they are also held weekly on Thursdays (the day for remembrance of the dead) and Fridays (the day of congregational prayer). In addition to these regular events, spiritual leaders often convene special qawwali events either for themselves or for visiting pilgrims.

Many people come to these shrines, notably the shrine of Khwaja Mohin-ud-din Chishti, known as the **Dargah**, in Ajmer, Rajasthan, to pray for solutions to their problems. Childless women hope for children, mothers pray for the well-being of their offspring, others hope for success in love. As their wishes are granted, devotees return to the shrine for thanksgiving. These practices are often considered heretical by fundamentalist Muslims who reject the concept of saints as intermediaries between the supplicant and Allah.

Each shrine has a particular family group of performers attached to it, quite often direct descendants of the original saint, or at least of members

of their spiritual family of followers and devotees. Distinguished visiting qawwals are permitted to perform at the shrines, particularly if they have stated an affinity with that particular saint. There is a complicated protocol governing the hierarchical system of 'resident' and 'visiting' qawwals and defining the seniority of different groups.

The **Nizamuddin Auliya Dargah**, a shrine in Delhi, has a wide variety of qawwali rituals and attracts pilgrims including significant numbers of non-muslims – Hindus, Parsees, Sikhs and Christians. The hereditary qawwali community at this shrine traces its descent to the original singers supposedly trained by Amir Khusrau himself. They are known as *qawwal bachche*, literally, the qawwal offspring.

Training and Performance

A qawwal receives his training from his family. Boys are instructed at an early age by their male elders (for women have no part in qawwali singing at any stage). First they are taught the fundamentals of classical music, after which they must memorise the text and tunes of the basic repertoire. Since qawwali is a group activity, the young performer has to be initiated into the process of group singing and assigned his place in the ensemble. Just who becomes a lead singer, a group singer, or an instrumental accompanist is determined by musical talent, the ability to recall verses swiftly and leadership qualities. A qawwal is not considered capable of being a lead singer until he has gained a full understanding of the purpose of his music. This means a thorough knowledge of Sufi beliefs as well as practical experience of performing in different roles in the group.

With the move in the West towards concert hall performances which cater for mass audiences from the Asian communities, qawwali adheres less and less to its traditional form. Such gatherings tend to be spectacular, glittering occasions, usually held in massive halls where the qawwals perform on a concert stage which separates the audience from the performers. This can cause some difficulties. The singers lose their interaction with their audience in a darkened auditorium. Traditionalists also argue that sitting upright in a seat physically prevents the listener from attaining the spiritual heights which are only attainable when seated on the floor, close to and at the same level as the performers. Musicians are usually quick to single out a handful of real devotees, and quite often direct their whole performance towards this 'senior' audience.

The dialogue between the audience and the musicians is central to the performance. The impact of vigorous hand-clapping tends to produce a trance-like state described by those who have experienced it as a feeling of flying. Flight is also the image used by Sufis in their endeavour to achieve union with the divine. A famous Khusrau verse proclaims "To each his own courage. It is the power of flight – some fly up but remain in the garden, others go beyond the stars".

A Visit to a Mahfil

Genuine aficionados usually avoid concert hall performances. Many of them take it upon themselves to arrange smaller, more intimate gatherings or **mahfils** in their homes for an invited audience of spiritually aware listeners. Such gatherings are musically more satisfying for the performers as well as the audience, and it is argued that the giving of *nazar* (a gift), a small amount of money handed to the performers in appreciation of a particular verse, is more easily and spontaneously done in an intimate chamber atmosphere than when scrambling over rows of seats in a large hall.

The tradition of giving nazar is an integral part of the qawwali performance and dates back to the days before recording contracts and overseas tours, when it was the musicians' main source of income. A successful qawwal, with hundreds of recordings

and a healthy bank balance to his credit, still displays the humble gratitude of a *fakir* when a five-pound note is pressed into his hand in appreciation of his art. In that moment of accepting a small gift of cash, a wealthy and sometimes world famous and distinguished musician is reminded of his humble duty as a qawwal.

The running order of a sama is strictly laid out. The performance gets underway with an instrumental prelude, usually played on harmonium and accompanied by percussion. Once the last strains of the prelude die away, it is customary to begin the singing, quietly at first, with "**Hamd**", a hymn in praise of Allah, followed by "**Naat**", which is sung in praise of the Prophet Muhammed. Only after this is it appropriate to sing the praises of Hazrat Ali, by tradition the first Sufi and son-in-law of the Prophet. The song usually performed at this stage is Khusrau's famous "**Man Kunto Maula, Fa Ali-un-Maula**" (whoever accepts me as master, Ali too is his master), in the classical Indian *raga* (scale) Yaman. Although relatively short, it is one of the earliest and best-known of all qawwali songs, and it embodies a central tenet of Sufism: that there is an uninterrupted chain of master-pupil relationships stretching back to the time of the Prophet. Once these introductory songs have been performed the singer is free to choose from a huge variety of poems set in various ragas, many written by Khusrau and other great Persian poets like **Rumi** and **Hafez Shirazi**.

Khusrau's Hindi compositions often draw their imagery from the Hindu folk idiom. The story of the god Krishna and his attendant milkmaids (*gopis*) provides an appropriate setting for exploring the sentiments of separation brought on by being in love with an unseen god. A popular Khusrau poem in the classical qawwali repertoire alludes to a famous episode between Radha, one of the gopis, and her beloved Krishna.

The way to the water well is a tough path to
   traverse
How can I walk this path to fetch the water?
He may be lying in wait for me
And cause my water pot to break

In the original story Krishna throws a stone at the water pot Radha is carrying on her head from the well. The pot breaks and she gets drenched with water. Although the story has been accorded various sexual connotations, its sacred message is undisputed. The well represents a body of knowledge and the pot the heart that has the capacity to carry this knowledge. However, the path

Snakes and Camels - Pakistani Folk

In 1995, **Peter Culshaw** visited Pakistan to find the cream of Pakistani folk musicians for a Music Village festival in London.

Karachi was my first stop, to meet **Misri Jogi**. Jogis are snake charmers and Misri gave me his card – everyone has a card – which proclaimed that he was President of the All Pakistan Jogi Association. His instrument, often played by two musicians in pairs, is a *murli*, a double pipe which sounds something like a bagpipe: raucous and arresting. Jogis have considerable prestige as pipe playing drives out evil spirits, and the circular breathing needed to play the instrument brings on a meditative state 'which purifies the soul'.

Like nearly all the musicians I met in Pakistan, Misri Jogi has a *pir* (guru) with whom he feels intimately connected. In his altered state, Misri Jogi usually feels the presence of the spiritual leader of the Jogis, Gogo Chuhan. Misri can cure snake bites with a concoc-

PETER CULSHAW

Misri Jogi playing for the snakes

tion of snake venom and milk. He says that black cobras are the easiest to charm as they are 'mad about music'.

My next stop was Multan, in the southern Punjab, where a huge notice at the airport read 'Welcome to the City of Saints'. But I had an appointment at the Hafeez Lychee Farm, where I met the **Multan Local Dance Party**, led by Mohammed Sharif. Their speciality is the centuries old tradition of mock animal dances: accompanied by dancers, thunderous drums and the *shenai* (the subcontinent's oboe), they dress up in plastic costumes as horses, camels and monkeys. There used to be mock elephant dances too, but after partition in 1947 it was decided that the elephant was too

closely identified as an Indian symbol; the mock camel was deemed a suitable Pakistani replacement.

There are still groups that dance with real trained camels. "The camels have silver jewels and bells on their feet and really dance", said dancer Fouzia Saaed, who is considered a 'crazy woman' for dancing with the rest of the all-male troupe. The Multan Local Dance Party do bhangra dances from the northern Punjab, but their speciality is the *jhoomer*, a more poised dance than bhangra. The costumes are as bright as possible – electric blue, shocking pink, wild saffron. Fouzia says that everyone used to dress in bright colours, but a British legacy was the gradual adoption, except in remote villages, of dull Imperial greys, blues and beiges.

Up to Peshawar in the Northwest Frontier Province, a hangout for guerillas, spies and refugees from the war in Afghanistan. Although some locals thought my excuse of 'music research' was a front for more clandestine operations, I managed to meet **Zarsanga**, the biggest star of the region, and a heroine to the warrior tribe of the Pathans. She was accompanied by several gunmen, some of whom doubled as her backing musicians on tabla and harmonium. Their instruments imitated her phrases and exclamations as she sang fantastically bleak songs full of the images of deserts and moons.

Lahore is Pakistan's most beautiful city, full of the decayed splendour of the Moghuls. It's also the centre of the country's declining film industry, which still churns out sixty movies a year, and the only city that allows **dancing girls**, strictly licensed between 9 and 11 pm. For around 500 rupees (£10), you can watch the (modestly dressed) girls dance a few rough and ready versions of film songs accompanied by singers, harmonium and tabla. Bollywood unplugged.

Islamabad, the modern capital, is home to **Lok Virsa**, Pakistan's thriving centre for folk music research and performance. The archives encompass Tibetan music from Baltistan, in the north; the African-style drumming of the Shidi, who live on the southern coast and were descendants of escaped slaves from Zanzibar; the trance-inducing fiddles of Luli musicians from the desert of Baluchistan (possibly the ancestors of the European 'gypsies'); and utterly disorienting *nar* music, also from Baluchistan, with Mongolian style overtone singing. It is a vast treasure house of Pakistani folk music, much of it yet to be exposed in the West.

that leads to this knowledge is strewn with unseen hazards!

A sama is concluded by singing "**Rang**" (Colour), composed by Khusrau to celebrate becoming Nizamuddin's disciple. Qawwals and their audiences may enter a state of *haal* (or pure ecstasy) during the performance of "Rang" – the song evokes a mood of sheer joy and exuberance.

Songs are usually extended by inserting additional verses called *girahs*. Qawwals normally have a large stock of verses from which they can draw an appropriate girah, which may be in a language different from the main body of the song. It is this practice of adding appropriate verses when the opportunity presents itself that gives qawwali its flexibility and spontaneity. Qawwals are often judged by their ability to add the right girah at the right moment – the more unexpected the better. It is these inserted verses that make every qawwali performance a unique creation.

One current trend in Pakistan is to end qawwali performances with a song of the Qalandar sect, "**Dama dum mast qalandar**", instead of the traditional Delhi "Rang" of Khusrau. The Qalandars are a group of itinerant Sufi dervishes who reject conventional standards of behaviour in order to remain 'joyous in God'. This song, sung in praise of Lal Shahbaz Qalandar, is entirely rhythmic, making it enormously popular outside the qawwali context on Pakistani disco dance floors. Shahbaz's grave at Sehwan (Sindh) is the pilgrimage site for the qalandar dervishes and ecstatics.

Qawwali Today

Present day qawwalis, notably the late **Nusrat Fateh Ali Khan**, have been quick to diversify their performances to match the current trends in East-West fusion. One of qawwali's important ingredients, **tarana**, has readily lent itself to the development of disco/jazz tarana which can be heard on many of Nusrat's more popularly oriented recordings. Tarana is a kind of rhythmic recita-

tion used originally to express esoteric religious ideas in a secret manner by stringing together Persian syllables which made no overt sense but had been given a private meaning. Now used for musical reasons, rather than for coded messages, it has often been likened to the jazz style of singing skat.

The intensity of Nusrat's voice, conveying sensitivity, emotion, power and abandonment where necessary, marked him out as one of the greatest musicians of his time. He also pushed the boundaries furthest in qawwali fusion (see box opposite), squandering – as the purists saw it – his art on film soundtracks and commercial dance mixes with Michael Brook and Massive Attack. But for Nusrat, spreading the word was all, and his music, even if in a diluted form, certainly reached millions.

Another qawwali group to have gained a worldwide reputation is the **Sabri Brothers**. Haji Ghu-

The Sabri Brothers at the controls

lam Farid Sabri, who died in 1994, and his younger brother Maqbool Sabri were particularly noted for their highly original style of rendering well-known numbers from the traditional qawwali repertoire, as well as for their distinctive style of percussion. The senior Sabri was renowned for the spirituality he brought to the songs, and his periodic chanting of 'Allah' between verses became a signature.

Amongst the new generation of qawwali singers is the **Rizwan-Muazzam Qawwali Group**. As nephews of Nusrat, Rizwan and Muaazam Mujahid Ali Khan have a peerless family heritage but also an impossible act to follow. They are a young, exciting qawwali group in the best tradition, and now perform at festivals such as WOMAD.

JAK KILBY

Qawwali: Nusrat's last interview

Jameela Siddiqi visited Nusrat Fateh Ali Khan in March 1997 and recorded the last interview he was to give to a Western journalist before his death.

Nusrat Fateh Ali Khan's house, in a well-to-do suburb of Lahore, was to all intents and purposes a modest family house, even though Nusrat was viewed in Pakistan as that country's number one cultural envoy. An armed guard at the tall, padlocked gates was the only indication that behind the high walls resided someone of national importance and international fame. His soft, gentle, unassuming manner in conversation was just as soothing as some of the full-throated, powerful, high-pitched scales which came to be associated with his specific style of qawwali. But in speech he was as economical as he was generous in song.

What does it mean to be a qawwal?
The duty of a qawwal is to reduce the distance between the Creator and the created. Those who feel cut off from their source can be reminded of their true roots through qawwali. That is what a qawwal must do. If I am singing a particular kind of verse, then whoever that verse is praising, that reality is before me. It takes me over – it becomes part of my being. The sign of a good qawwal, or any other musician, is his ability to absorb his listeners into the reality of that essential message which is being sung. A good qawwal does not himself exist when he is performing. He simply becomes a vehicle through which that message passes.

You are undoubtedly the best known qawwal in the world. Is this kind of fame and the adoration that it brings consistent with being a Sufi?
Name, fame, wealth, honour. All these things are a gift from Allah. Otherwise we qawwals are basically the kind of people who belong with the fakirs. That is where we really belong. It is only by the grace of Allah that I am given this honour of being well-known, wealthy, honoured and respected. But you don't need any of those things to be a good human being. What makes you a good human being is to be aware of other people's feelings and to never become arrogant about your own talent or fame. The most important thing is to never hurt anyone's feelings, because if you hurt someone's heart, than you hurt God, because God resides in all human hearts. That is what we say in Punjabi.

How do you feel performing qawwali on a concert stage, as opposed to its original context?
Qawwali's real setting is at the shrines of the great Sufis – in any other context it becomes merely a thing of entertainment, just like any other music. Even so, there is always hope that it will touch some of those listeners in a special way.

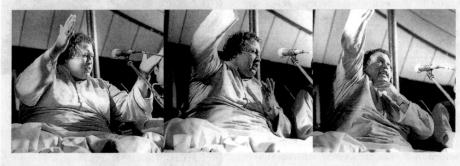

Qawwali Fusion

While the traditional strains of qawwali continue to flourish, there are modern secular forms in Bollywood and Lahore films (the only public arena in which you'll hear women's qawwali) and, of course, the World Music fusions which have raised its profile in the West. Two of the most successful – commercially and artistically – were *Mustt Mustt* and *Night Song*, the RealWorld collaborations of Canadian producer **Michael Brook** with **Nusrat Fateh Ali Khan**. The title track, "Mustt Mustt" became internationally known first through **Massive Attack**'s remix, and when it became the soundtrack for a Coca-Cola ad, shown in India and around the world during the breaks of the Cricket World Cup.

Such a hook-up between one of the most archetypally aggressive multinationals and Nusrat, purveyor in chief of one of the world's most passionate spiritual traditions, seemed startling. But many qawwals believe an essential part of their role is to reach as many people as possible – they may, after all, be drawn into a spiritual path even via the unlikely route of a soft drink commercial. On his Japanese tour, Nusrat spent the evening before his first concert studying the music of Japanese TV commercials. Concluding that this must be the way to reach people, Nusrat incorporated subtle elements from the ads in his concerts.

The nature of qawwali music, with its basic eight-beat cycles and Western-friendly chord sequences, makes it highly suitable for dance remixes. Real-World commissioned several second generation British Asian outfits to remix the Michael Brook/Nusrat releases for *Star Rise* which, released shortly after Nusrat's death in 1997, became something of a tribute album to Nusrat's pioneering qawwali fusion. The inventive dance mixes include the likes of Talvin Singh, Black Star Liner, Asian Dub Foundation and Joi, although perhaps the most effective is Nitin Sawhney's drum and bass-style collage.

Cross-cultural fusions can have their problems. Michael Brook found that a couple of edits on the *Mustt Mustt* album had mangled the Sufi lyrics – although in that release the problem was minimised as most of the vocals were tarana syllables with no specific meaning. *Night Song* is more lyrical in both senses of the word – Brook transcribed the lyrics phonetically to ensure he didn't cut in the middle of a line. By the time of this second release, Brook says Nusrat "grew more comfortable with studio techniques and worked out some parts that were designed to be layered, which was something he's never done before".

It's worth noting that qawwali lyrics are typically in a mixture of Punjabi, Urdu and Farsi, often in various dialects, and even audiences in Pakistan may not understand all the lyrics. The test of a good qawwali party is that they can weave a spell over an audience regardless of language. The new audiences dancing to qawwali fusion, while condemned by purists, are seen by others as simply extending the tradition.

discography

Qawwali

Compilations

Hommage a Nusrat Fateh Ali Khan
(World Network, Germany).

An excellent two-CD compilation of fourteen performances dedicated to the memory of Nusrat Fateh Ali Khan by an impressive and wide-ranging line-up of Sufi musicians – from Azerbaijan to Senegal – including some outstanding Pakistani classical performers, notably Salamat Ali Khan and Shafqat Ali Khan. An impressive tribute reflecting Nusrat's spiritual influence round the world.

Land of the Sufis:
Soul Music from the Indus Valley
(Shanachie, US).

A collection by Peter Pannke, who has been an energetic recorder of Sufi music in Pakistan. These studio recordings focus on the Indus valley and Punjab and include a rare recording of a qawwali tarana by Nasiruddin Saami, accompanied by one of the last great sarangi players, Allah Rakha Khan, who also gets a solo track. The brother qawwals Bahauddin and Qutbuddin from Karachi also feature, and there are several rustic, trance-like Qalandar pieces.

Sufi Soul (World Network, Germany).

This two-CD compilation covers the whole range of Sufi music, from Moroccan Gnawa and Turkish Mevlevi to Iranian and Central Asian singers, with several excellent Pakistani musicians along the way, including Nusrat and the Sabri Brothers. There are excellent contributions from the southern province of Sindh: a poem by Shah Abdul Latifa, mystic qalandar dance music and a track from Baluchi *sorud* (fiddle) player Yar Mohammad.

ECHOS DU PARADIS
SUFI SOUL

AFGHANISTAN
BALUCHISTAN
EGYPT
IRAN
KURDISTAN
MOROCCO
PAKISTAN
SENEGAL
SYRIA
TAJIKISTAN
TURKEY
UZBEKISTAN

Troubadours of Allah (Schott/Wergo, Germany).

A two-CD collection of mainly field and shrine recordings by Peter Pannke to accompany a lavishly illustrated book of the same title (in German). Represents an unrivalled collection of Pakistani Sufi music, with twenty-one performers and ensembles.

Artists

Jafar Husayn Khan

Descended from a family of celebrated traditional musicians from Badaoun, a small town in Uttar Pradesh (North India), Jafar Husayn trained as a classical singer with his uncle, the renowned Ustad Mushtaq Husayn Khan.

◉ Chant Qawwali de L'Inde du Nord (Inédit, France).

Jafar Husayn's voice is hauntingly melodious and, having originally trained in north Indian classical music, he brings a keen aesthetic sense of musicality and expression to the rendition of qawwali. But his choice of modern Urdu verse over and above classical Persian and Hindi – the original languages of qawwali – is extremely disappointing.

Nusrat Fateh Ali Khan

Born in Faisalabad, Pakistan, into a family which has produced qawwali singers for six centuries – his father was also a celebrated classical musician and qawaal – Nusrat Fateh Ali Khan (1948–1997) was the world's best-known qawwal. In addition to the devotional repertoire, he made a number of dance-oriented recordings and tracks for films including Natural Born Killers, Dead Man Walking, The Last Temptation of Christ and the Bandit Queen.

◉ Nusrat Fateh Ali Khan en concert a Paris (Ocora, France).

A milestone in qawwali recordings – on five discs, available separately – recorded during Nusrat's peak year in 1989. An essential set for every serious collection, he moves with great ease between a multitude of languages and verses both modern and ancient. The Persian poetry of Amir Khusrau is rendered with hypnotic energy, while the exquisite Punjabi verses of Baba Bulleh Shah acquire a new dimension when heard through this technically flawless recording. Start with Vol 2, which contains a ghazal by Rumi and a ghazal of legendary lovers by Baba Bulleh Shah. Very helpful notes and textual translations in three languages.

◉ The Last Prophet (RealWorld, UK).

One of several excellent RealWorld recordings, this particular disc stands out as an ideal compromise between traditional and modern qawwali and is probably the best place for the beginner to start.

◉ Mustt Mustt (RealWorld, UK).

Nusrat's most successful fusion album. The title track (mustt means 'intoxicated' or 'high') is a dance-floor re-mix by trip-hop band Massive Attack.

◉ Shahen-Shah (RealWorld, UK).

Lighter qawwali songs in modern Urdu and Punjabi. Easy lyrics and beautiful melodies make them more accessible to a younger generation.

◉ Traditional Sufi Qawwalis: Live in London (Navras, UK).

Four CDs, available separately, of sama-style qawwali at its very best, recorded in the presence of an enthusiastic and knowledgeable audience sitting in close proximity and drawing the very best from the musicians. Nusrat himself considered it one of his best performances. Most of the tracks in this set are authentic, traditional numbers that would rarely be sung at larger public concerts. A must for beginners and connoisseurs alike. Vol 2 is a particularly good place to start, with a qawwali ghazal and qawwali sung in classical Indian raags. Vol 3 includes Nusrat's most exceptional "Rang" on disc.

Rizwan-Muazzam Qawwali Group

The best group of young qawwals to emerge in Pakistan for over a decade. The two lead singers, Rizwan Mujahid Ali Khan and Muazzam Mujahid Ali Khan, still in their teens, are nephews of the late Nusrat Fateh Ali Khan.

◉ Sacrifice to Love (RealWorld, UK).

One of the best qawwali recordings since the death of Nusrat. On their second international release, Rizwan-Muazzam live up to their impeccable pedigree. Tracks in Hindi and Farsi, the original languages of the genre, as well as Urdu mark this out from other young Pakistani groups. At its best this album is highly-charged, spiritual and trance-inducing.

The Sabri Brothers

Haji Ghulam Farid Sabri and his younger brother Maqbool Ahmed created a duo of Pakistan's best-loved qawwals, their musical lineage stretching back through many generations of great musicians. The brothers did much to popularise qawwali outside Pakistan.

◉ Jami (Piranha, Germany).

The Sabris at their esoteric best. The mystical poetry of fifteenth-century Persian poet Jami, coupled with the Sabris' musical sensitivity and percussive expertise is an earth-moving event. The album is dedicated to Haji Ghulam Farid Sabri who finally fulfilled a life-long wish to record the poetry of Jami. Although it turned out to be his finest performance ever, he did not live to see its release.

◉ Supreme Collection: Greatest Hits of Sabri Brothers Vol 2 (Serengeti/Sirocco, UK).

Featuring four classical numbers by Khusrau, this remains one of the Sabri Brothers' best classical qawwali discs.

Bakhshi Javed Salamat Ali

Based in the village of Liran, near Faisalabad in Pakistan, the Javed Salamat Brothers are the resident qawwals at a Sufi shrine and specialise in the rendition of Punjabi qawwali.

◉ Musiques du Pendjab: Vol 3 – Le qawwali (Arion, France).

This is one of the finest examples of qawwali in its rightful context, performed at the shrine of a Sufi saint. The main emphasis is on the poetry of the Punjabi mystics, notably Baba Bulleh Shah.

The Sindhi Music Ensemble

Vocalists Sohrab Kafir (male) and Husna Naz (female) are backed by a small instrumental ensemble of flute, bowed fiddle, harmonium and percussion.

◉ Sufi Music from Sindh (Welt Musik/Schott Wergo, Germany).

If anywhere can claim to be the cradle of Sufism, it is the province of Sindh in the south of Pakistan. The region is strewn with the graves of holy men and this disc features the music heard at their shrines. Swinging trance music.

PAKISTAN

Folk

Compilations

Halla-Gulla!: Popular Traditions of Pakistan
(Radiant Future, UK).

A CD produced for the Pakistani Music Village held in the UK in 1995, including snake charmer Misri Jogi, the Multan Local Dance Party, Pathan singer Zarsanga, double flute player Urs Bhatti and qawwali group Mehr and Sher Ali (see box on p.207). The best introduction to Pakistani folk. Only available by mail order from: Cultural Co-operation Ltd, 9 Toynbee Studios, 28 Commercial Street, London E1 6LS. Fax: +44 (0)20- 7247 8809.

The Mystic Fiddle of the Proto-Gypsies
(Shanachie, US).

Excellent performances on the bowed sorud, a four-string fiddle carved from a single block of wood, with sympathetic strings amplifying the sound. Wild, passionate performances with flying harmonics, accompanied by tamburag lute. Sufi poems provide the lyrical numbers. Wonderful.

WORLD NETWORK

PAKISTAN/SINDH: MOULA BUX SAND SOHRAB FAKIR, MOHAMED FAKIR GHOUS BUX BROHI, ALLA BACHAYO KHOSO

Sindhi Soul Session
(World Network, Germany).

Many of the ingredients of this fantastic disc are related to Sufism and qawwali, but this is essentially intense folk music from the southern province of Sindh. Among the highlights are the evocative playing of the *alghoza* double flute, the music of fakirs at the shrine of Abdul Latif, and the bowed surando of Mohammed Fakir. Compelling sounds played with fervour.

Sounds of the Hindu Kush (Playasound, France).

A rare recording of music of the Kailash people (reputedly descended from the soldiers of Alexander the Great), who inhabit three valleys close to the Afghan border. Festival music, songs and instrumental pieces, plus the music for a polo match. A good souvenir for anyone who's visited this beautiful corner of the country.

Artists

Baluchi Ensemble of Karachi

The Baluch are a stateless people settled mainly in Pakistan (but also in Afghanistan and Iran), and famed for their music. This ensemble is based in the Baluchi quarter of Karachi.

Love Songs and Trance Hymns (Shanachie, US).

Festive songs for weddings and circumcision ceremonies, plus trance songs and lullabies, including one for the Sufi saint Qalandar, whose tomb is likened to a child's cradle. Instruments include the sorud and the dholak drum.

Zarsanga

From Peshawar, in Pakistan's Northwest Frontier province, Zarsanga is the district's most popular singer and queen of the airwaves on Radio Peshawar.

Chants Pashtous du Pakistan
(Long Distance, France).

Songs of struggle and love, sometimes fierce, sometimes wistful, accompanied by harmonium, rabab and percussion.

PAKISTAN

The Philippines

pinoy rockers

Wherever you travel, in Asia or beyond, you can find Filipinos playing covers of US, British or Latin pop in hotel lobbies, clubs and bars. But while Filipino bands may be ubiquitous, few people know of the talented musicians who have featured for years in the Bangkok jazz scene, and fewer still know of top-class musicians like the legendary Boying Geronimo who played with salsa's top stars in New York in the 1970s. As for indigenous music, Filipinos have brewed their own Pinoy rock since the late 1960s, when Freddie Aguilar influenced a generation of folk-rockers and protest singers right across Asia. **John Clewley** has the story.

Three hundred years of Spanish domination, fifty years of American colonisation and the five years of Japanese rule during World War II have left deep scars on Filipino culture and music. Much is now being written about the effects of globalisation (or Westernisation) and the identity crisis it is causing among young Asians, but the Filipinos have been searching for an identity for a long time. To be Filipino is to be both Asian and partly Western: most people speak both *tagalog* (the national language) and English; and ancient animist rituals live side-by-side with Christian and Muslim practices.

Had the Philippines been a continental nation, even more of the ethnic music from its 140 indige- nous groups would have been lost. But the remote- ness of some regions made them difficult for colonisers to subdue, and as a result, there is still a wealth of folk and ethnic music, particularly among mountain dwellers and southern islands like Min- danao. There are similarities between the indige- nous music of the Philippines and that of other southeast Asian countries. The *kulingtan* gongs are a sort of Filipino gamelan, and gongs and bamboo instruments are common.

Neighbouring countries like Malaysia, Indone- sia and Thailand all have a wealth of recorded eth- nic music, but there is little available from the Philippines. Nevertheless, concerted efforts by musicians like **Joey Ayala** and **Grace Nono** to

Grace Nono with the Asian Fantasy Orchestra

include ethnic music and instruments in their music, as well as to champion individual artists, have drawn attention to minority music. Nono, with her long-time collaborator Bob Aves, has set up Tao Music to promote and record ethnic music. The most impressive release so far is from singer/instrumentalist **Sindao Banisil**, the daughter of a Maranao sultan from the highlands of Western Mindanao. Banisil was trained from childhood in the traditional Maranao musical arts of dance, instrumental playing (including the kulingtan) and the singing of songs from lullabies to epics like "Darangan". She sings with a powerful, emotive voice and is spellbinding on the jew's harp and bamboo scraper. Keen to carry on her ancient oral Maranao traditions (she is one of the few artists left), Banisil works as the director of the Young Darangan Troupe.

Colonisation

Folk songs of the lowland Filipinos came under greater **Spanish** influence than those of the mountain-dwelling peoples. Church music was encouraged and became a fixture at festivals, and urban-based genres of folk songs developed alongside. Spanish instruments were changed and adapted to suit the circumstances: the guitar, a key part of Spanish culture, came into widespread use and brass bands began to be played in villages. But it was not all one-way traffic, as Filipino rhythms and tunes found their way into the newly-adopted Spanish forms. Even Spanish operetta, *zarzuela*, was introduced in 1880 and quickly adopted by tagalog writers. These colourful shows of songs, comedy, and drama had a revival in the 1970s, paralleling Thai luk thung from the same period.

The **American** colonial period, dating from 1898, exposed many Filipinos to US culture, particularly to popular forms of music. Many attending school at the time remember having to sing "Philippines, My Philippines" to the tune of "Maryland, My Maryland". From the postwar period to the present, Filipino musicians have taken to US styles, beginning with blues, folk, R&B and folk rock, and more recently picking up on movements like punk, thrash and grunge.

While Western covers still form the basis of many bands' live shows, Filipino forms such as the ballad-like **kundiman** have remained popular. Kundiman is a typically Filipino genre that developed in the 1920s and '30s when musicians Westernised some Filipino tunes and serenades. The prevalence of sweet melodies make it similar to other Asian ballad styles from the same period, like

luk grung in Thailand. Strings – violins, guitars, bass – feature as musical backing. Famous kundiman singers include the late King of Kundiman, **Ruben Tagalog**, and **Diomedes Naturan**.

Pinoy Rock

Always keen to adapt, musicians soon set about using tagalog lyrics to the Western music they were hearing. "O Ang Babae" (Oh My Baby), one of the first **Pinoy rock** numbers in the late 1950s, was basically rock'n'roll – Carl Perkins reborn in Manila. The roots of Pinoy rock may lie here. Another development came in the early 1970s, when several mainstream hits included both English and Tagalog lyrics (dubbed 'taglish' by some wags). **Hotdog** released "Ang Miss Universe Ng Buhay Ko" (You are the Miss Universe of My Life), whose modern arrangements and mixed language lyrics created what became known as the '**Manila sound**'.

JOHN CLEWLEY

Freddie Aguilar – the original Pinoy rocker

As early Pinoy rock developed, it splintered into various sub-genres. Mainstream bands went for simple pop songs, underground rockers like **Pepe Smith** went for a harder-edged raw rock sound and Pinoy folk emerged, with **Florante de Leon** among the first singer-songwriters. But "Anak", the 1978 debut of a simple troubadour, **Freddie Aguilar**, changed the entire scene. It is the most successful Filipino song ever recorded: it sold four million copies in Europe and has spawned fifty-four cover versions in fourteen languages. Aguilar's blend of Western folk-rock music with Filipino melodies and language – with a dash of social activism – struck a deep chord with listeners then suffering under the martial law of dictator Ferdinand Marcos.

Aguilar's success influenced Asian artists from Japan to Thailand. The most famous folk-rock band in Thailand, Carabou, took its name from the tagalog word for buffalo. In fact, Aguilar remembers Ad Carabou, Carabou's leader, eagerly attending many of his early Manila concerts. Protest singing to a folk-rock backdrop is still very popular across Asia and it owes its popularity in no small measure to Aguilar. His zenith came during the 1986 revolution that toppled Marcos, when his version of the standard "Bayan Ko" became the song of the street protesters. Recently, Aguilar, now owner of his own club and label, has been managing the budding career of his daughter, **Maegan Aguilar**, a sixteen-year-old with a penchant for writing original blues tunes with tagalog lyrics.

Other important Pinoy rockers emerged at the same time, including **Heber Bartolome and the Banyuhay**, and the group **Coritha**. During the 1980s the tradition was picked up by singer-songwriter Jessie Santiago and the band **Inang Laya**. **Asin**, featuring the powerful voice of Lolita Carbon, took the music further than most, setting the ground rules for what was to follow. The band, which still plays every year in Japan, was the first to use tagalog and cebuano (the language of Cebu) lyrics in a folk-rock song, and the band's hard-hitting social concerns showed that you didn't have to sing silly love songs to be successful.

New Waves

There was bound to be a backlash against the fashion for social protest music. A younger generation no longer considered it necessary to write songs in tagalog to be Filipino; attitude and style counted. **Punk** caught on in Manila in the 1980s and

was perhaps more influential in Manila than anywhere in Asia outside Japan. The punk ethos of DIY rock started a craze for three-chord bands, many with English names like Urban Bandits or The Jerks. As few of these bands got airplay, an underground scene developed which later split into hardcore and grunge.

The underground punk scene was only one of the new trends in the 1980s. A short-story writer, **Joey Ayala**, based in the un-hip backwaters of

EDDIE-BOY ESCUDERO

The poetic Joey Ayala

Davao City, was taken with the songs of indigenous groups in the southern island of Mindanao. Turning to the song form, he wrote about the threatened environment of that region, then in the middle of civil conflict. Within a short space of time he had taught himself the jew's harp and the two-stringed *hegalong* (lute) and formed a band, naming it **Bagong Lumad** (New Native) to symbolise his belief that we are all natives in one way or another. His debut album *Panganay Ng Umaga* outlined his concerns in a poetic lyric style that owed a lot to bands like Asin, and after he performed in Manila, the survivors of Pinoy rock's golden era of the seventies began to rise in popularity. Lolita Carbon of Asin started the **Nene Band** and Pendong Aban formed **Grupong Pendong**.

Ayala's work also set the stage for the solo debut of Pinoy Rock's reigning diva, **Grace Nono**. She had been the haunting voice fronting The Blank, a cover band, but turned to performing her own songs to quirky accompaniments, mixing guitars with traditional instruments. Unlike earlier socially-conscious rockers, Nono and Ayala have managed to blend ethnic music with guitar-based chords in a new and exciting way. Nono sees her role clearly: "we are trying to strike a familiar chord in all of the native peoples the world over by showcasing not only our unique sound but also the parallelisms in the different traditions". Most recently she has been touring with the Japanese-run Asian Fantasy Orchestra.

At the same time as Nono and Ayala were making their mark, the punk rockers morphed into 'alternative' bands, inspired by US acts like Nirvana, and proliferated in a bubbling live scene. Just like their Thai counterparts, Modern Dog, the members of bands like **Yano**, **Tropical Depression**, **The Erasureheads** and the reggae band **Cocojam** were all university students with a knack for language. Their killer hooks reflected the street argot of the nineties. The Erasureheads' 1993 debut album *Ultraelectromagneticpop!* went platinum. Record companies now knew that alternative was the hip trend with Manila's youth.

The Erasureheads, Joey Ayala, Grace Nono and the 'nutty' ska band, Put3ska – currently creating not just music but 2-tone-style fashion crazes, complete with Dr Martens – are the most likely Filipino bands to make any mark overseas. The only popular musician to have emerged from southeast Asia so far is Freddie Aguilar. But twenty years after his colossal hit "Anak", a new generation is ready to take on the world.

discography

A useful website for information about Filipino music is *www.philmusic.com* and for buying CDs, *www.liyra.com*

Compilations

Utom: Summoning the Spirit.
Music in the T'boli Heartland (Rykodisc, US).

The eighty-thousand-strong T'boli people live in a mountainous region of southwestern Mindanao, their land threatened by the advance of large corporations. Amid the noises of birds, insects and trees, a lute player evokes the sounds of a cicada and woodpecker, a women strums a hypnotic bamboo zither and a shaman plays his flute. Also features ceremonial gongs, dances and drums. Among many field recordings round the globe, this is one of the best evocations of traditional indigenous life.

Music in the T'boli Heartland

Artists

Edru Abraham

A University of the Philippines ensemble of mainly ethnic instruments led by Art Studies professor Edru Abraham, who studied gamelan in Indonesia. Abraham recruits anyone who wants to play because he believes part of the musical process should be to build stronger communal ties.

Kontemporaryong Gamelan Pilipino
(Banag Itawit, Philippines).

Hypnotic, repetitive cascades of gamelan percussion switching into driving percussion and clanging gongs. Kontra-gapi, as the ensemble is known, are nothing if not unconventional and the band can and will throw in a jazz singer to counterpoint the kulingtan (gongs). Includes the fusion song "Worldbeat Filipino" and a strange attempt at some African influences in "Mabuhay Africa".

Freddie Aguilar

Freddie Aguilar (b 1953) is synonymous with Pinoy rock. Armed with a guitar and a winning formula of Western folk-rock married to Filipino melodies, he has been hugely influential at home and across Asia.

Greatest Hits
(Ugat/Vicor, Philippines).

A good collection of Aguilar's representative hits. Impassioned vocals and simple lyrics, backed by Aguilar's trademark guitar sound. Includes "Anak", the biggest-selling Filipino record of all time and one of the most covered Asian songs ever.

Hala Bira (Alpha, Philippines).

One of Aguilar's nineties' releases. This album was a big success for Aguilar, mainly for the title track and the movie theme song about students, "Ipaglalaban Ko".

Asin

The seminal band that has taken Pinoy folk rock further than most. Saro Banares' socially-conscious compositions are powered by the spine-tingling voice of Lolita Carbon, backed by an acoustic sound of guitars and swirling flutes.

🔲 **Asin** (Ugat/Vicor, Philippines).

Asin was the first Pinoy rock group to write about the environment and use ethnic instruments like jew's harp and bamboo flute. Examples on this album include "Masdan Mo ang Kapiligiran" and "Ang Bayan Kong Sinilangan" respectively; other songs experiment with reggae.

Joey Ayala

Poet and short-story writer, stage director, reporter and advertising copywriter, Joey Ayala came from nowhere (actually Mindanao in the south) and has successfully used the music of indigenous peoples in his compositions.

🔲 **Panganay Ng Umaga (The Oldest Morning)** (DYNA/WEA, Philippines).

Ayala took everyone by surprise with this strident selection of songs. Environmental themes dominate in this landmark album of contemporary Filipino music, an underground classic. Originally recorded in 1982, the album was re-recorded and released in 1991.

Sindao Banisil

Maranao singer/instrumentalist Sindao Banisil is one of the last performers of Maranao oral traditions. The Maranao, or 'people of the lake' are from the western highlands of Mindanao, a Muslim-majority state in the south.

🔲 **Pakaradia-An** (Tao Music, Philippines).

The album reflects its title, 'entertainment', in this compilation of lullabies, instrumentals, children's and religious songs. Some songs are connected with the epic tale, "Darangan", which Banisil sings in special vocal styles that feature classical language and texts from the Koran.

The Erasureheads

Four friends from the University of the Philippines toiled for four years before unleashing the album that broke 'alternative' music into the mainstream pop market.

🔘 **Ultraelectromagneticpop!** (BMG Pilipinas, Philippines).

Guitars and great hooks feature in crafty tunes that reflect the pulse of young Manila. Includes the hit love song, "Pare Ko".

Inang Laya

Inang Laya are an acoustic duo comprising Karina David and Becky Abraham. Karina pens the songs, sometimes with other artists like Joey Ayala ("Macliing Dulag") and Lester Demetillo ("Kasama Sa Kalsada"). One of the most respected of the folk-rock Pinoy bands, known for songs with street cred.

🔲 **Atsay Ng Mundo (Helper of the World)** (Dypro, Philippines).

Straight-up Pinoy folk-rock. Some impassioned singing, lots of guitars and more modern production than the older folk-rock recommendations here.

Jun Lopito

Generally regarded as the best guitarist in Manila, Jun Lopito has played with everyone from Pepe Smith to Grace Nono, and from reggae legends Cocojam to 'alternative' rockers the Jerks.

🔲 **Bodhisatvas** (Musico/BMG Pilipinas, Philippines).

Eight years in the making, this album compiles various songs from Lopito's career, with help from a who's who of top musicians and stars, a bunch Lopito refers to as *bodhisatvas* (literally, Buddhist saints). Quality Filipino rock.

Grace Nono

Nono (b 1964) grew up in Mindanao where she started to play guitar and sing in folkhouses. She studied anthropology at university and became the lead singer of cult cover band, The Blank. After living with the Manobo people in Mindanao, she began a solo career, using their music in her work.

🔲 **Tao Music** (Record Plant/BMG Pilipinas, Philippines).

The debut album that launched Nono's career. Nono's soaring voice is a revelation and the music is a surprising mix of folk and rock, with guitars and native instruments (lutes, zithers, gongs and bamboo and skin percussion). Includes her trademark song, "Salidumay", which is based on a lullaby from the Sierra Madre Cordillera. Recommended.

🔘 **Sang Buhay [One Life]** (Record Plant/BMG Pilipinas, Philippines).

Nono's latest album has a more assured, rock-oriented sound. The outstanding title track is an atmospheric acoustic song about 'this bittersweet fruit called life'. Other songs range from catchy, chanted courtship songs to tales of rites of passage.

Pinikpikan

Freestyle percussion workouts at arts events, festivals and parties are a permanent feature of Filipino cultural life. The annual Baguio Arts Festival was a key meeting place for a rough assembled bunch of artists, musicians and anyone who could bang a rock. This gathering of performers takes its name from a tribal province.

🔲 **Metronomad** (Tao Music, Philippines).

The recordings of the Baguio Festival sessions form the basis of this album and the participants thought the result similar to rhythms of the mountain-dwelling Igorots, who live in Pinikpian province. As 'an art interactive through musical rhythms' it works well, though some may find it too New Age.

Put3Ska

An eight-piece band playing ska with tagalog and English lyrics, and lots of attitude. The band built on the foundations of earlier ska bands like Skavengers and Skalawags and takes its name from the tagalog slang for 'son of a bitch', putriskaa.

🔘 **Put3Ska** (OctoArts/EMI, Philippines).

Their self-titled first album caught the public's attention with songs like "Manila Girl", as did livewire lead singer Myra Ruaro.

🔘 **Manila's Finest** (OctoArts/EMI, Philippines).

Their latest includes the upbeat "Birthday Holiday" and the almost Latino instrumental hit "Bang Tumba Ka!".

Polynesia

the real music of paradise

Polynesia is the largest geographical area covered in this book, but in terms of population and musical profile it is one of the smallest. Its musical reputation in Western circles rests on one of those occasional World Music hit recordings in the form of the Tahitian Choir – otherwise few people get to hear much else, beyond the bland, grass-skirted sound of tourist shows. **Ad Linkels**, who has spent years researching and recording the music, describes the real music of the 'happy isles'.

For more on Hawaiian music (which shares Polynesian roots), see p.56

The Polynesian triangle stretches from New Zealand in the south to Hawaii in the north and Easter Island (Rapanui) in the east. There are many types of music in this vast area of thirty million square kilometres, ranging from pre-conquest music and Christian church singing to rock bands and protest songs. The inhabitants of both areas, however, are thought to have arrived from southeast Asia some 3500 years ago, and share the same cultural roots.

Polynesian life and music was utterly disrupted by the coming of the Europeans. There are still some strongholds of 'pre-contact' music – in Tonga, for instance, where ancient dances such as the *me'etu'upaki*, *ula* and *'otuhaka* are still kept alive – but most music nowadays has merged with imported styles. This is not all bad, though: think of Hawaii and its exuberant music for ukeleles, based on the Portuguese *braguinha* guitar. And the same is true of other areas, where Polynesians have adopted Western genres. The results, they would maintain, are just as Polynesian as the older traditions.

Songs and Action

The main traditional element in Polynesian music is actually still very much alive: **the song text**. Melody, harmony, rhythm and dance movements are seen by Polynesians simply as the means to convey the words, which is why musical changes are not felt to be so great. For the natives of these islands, a song text sung to a Beatles' melody is no less Polynesian than the same lyrics with a traditional melody. The Maori words to the Beatles' "Something" (on the cassette *Toia*), for instance, are a tribute to the local Ratana Church. And on the same cassette,

Mungo Jerry's "In the Summertime" has been transformed into "Ko Ihu", an action-song pronouncing that Jesus Christ is the way, the truth and the life.

Singing and dancing are almost inseparable all over Polynesia, hence the importance of so-called **action-songs**. In these, dance is a stylised visual accompaniment to the sung lyrics – the dancer is a sort of storyteller illustrating or decorating the sung story through movements of the arms, hands and fingers. Sometimes a dance is even performed in a seated position, moving only the hands, fingers and head. Modern dances often have a more explicitly narrative form in which the dancers actually dramatise the story (instead of alluding to specific words in the text). Not all dances are performed to sung lyrics, however. Vigorous male dances are often performed to percussion music played on slit drums, rolled mats, empty tins or skin drums, and there is no song at all.

New songs and dances are composed on a regular basis for any important occasion – for example the visit of the King (in Tonga), or the opening of a new church building. And the more important the event, the more people participate. Traditionally, dancing and singing for an audience was not a one-way spectacle, and a song or dance-in-reply by another group was called for.

At **fiafia** nights in Samoa and Tokelau, this is still the custom, with each group responding to the other and trying to outdo them to increase their status. On more Westernised island groups like Hawaii and Tahiti, there are large, commercial dance contests with winners and prizes. While these are no longer traditional, they stimulate the revival of indigenous art and music.

Church Music

Protestant and catholic missionaries first arrived in Polynesia in the 1790s and, over time, they succeeded in converting almost all the inhabitants – with a devastating effect on traditional culture. Native music was considered pagan and had to be eliminated and replaced by **Christian hymns**. Pre-Christian images were burned and the old ceremonies, songs and dances forbidden. In certain places, however, aspects of the traditional forms were kept alive, as in Hawaii where the *hula* went underground, guarded by devoted specialists.

Christian hymns changed the musical ear of the Polynesians and new hybrid forms of religious music evolved based on imported church music mixed with the remnants of traditional polyphonic singing. Congregations, dispersed and isolated from each other across Polynesia, developed their own types of hymn singing. Today, Christian church singing is one of the chief activities of Polynesian life – and also a great attraction for Western visitors. As Sunday really is a day of rest and prayer, especially in the western Polynesian countries like Samoa, Tuvalu and Tonga, going to church to hear the beautiful singing of hundreds of voices is one of the few things that can be done on this sacred day.

In **Tonga**, the deep sound of the large wooden **lali** (slit drum) is the heartbeat of the country on Sunday, as daily life comes to a standstill. People go to church at least once, if not twice, to pray, sing in the choir or join in the community singing. The rhythmic drones of the lali summoning the congregation can be heard everywhere and each church has its own distinguishing lali rhythm. Church bells and cheaper alternatives such as empty gas cylinders suspended from a tree are more recent developments.

The choral singing style differs from island group to island group, but it's always impressive. One of the highlights of church music can be found in Tonga (especially in the more conservative Church of Tonga and Free Church of Tonga), where the members of the congregation still sing their **hiva usu**, unaccompanied hymns

based on remnants of the old tradition with singing in several voice-parts. Most of these are sung with loud, fervent voices by the entire church congregation, but the lead singer who adds vocal ornamentation to the main melody is at the centre.

A more refined and controlled Western style of singing has become very popular in the Methodist churches, especially the Free Wesleyan Church of Tonga. This is completely different to

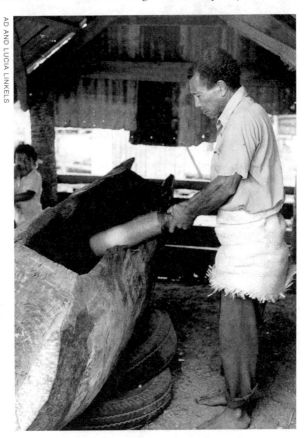

AD AND LUCIA LINKELS

Lali beating, Church of Tonga, Ha'apai, Tonga

the old style, and many of these Western-style services are accompanied by a brass band. Imported hymns (*himi*) are given Tongan lyrics, and more complex choral anthems (*anitema*), particularly the works of Bach and Handel, are also popular. A vast Tongan choir's rendition of the "Hallelujah Chorus" from Handel's *Messiah* was the first sound of the world's millennium celebrations.

The unaccompanied church choirs of the **Cook Islands** (singing *imene tuki* and *imene metua*) and **Tahiti** (*himene tarava*) are perhaps the most joyful

The Tahitian Gospel Choir tell it like it is

and powerful in Polynesia. It was this type of choir, on the island of Rapa Iti, a thousand miles south of Tahiti, that achieved international success when it was recorded by the French musicologist Pascal Nabet-Meyer in 1992 under the name of **The Tahitian Choir**. What really makes it special is the way the pitch drops at the end of the phrases – as if the tape recorder is slowing down or the choir is singing flat. Of course, it's neither of these, but it is a strange and unique sound, created by up to six independent voice parts in a dense mixture of fixed and improvised material. There is also a steady pulse, occasionally emphasised by male rhythmic grunting. Known as **tuki** in the Cook Islands, this is a succession of staccato sounds, usually *hi*, *ha* or *he*. While the main song continues, some or all of the men perform the tuki parts, creating a powerful, throbbing beat.

Traditional Instruments

The most important instrument in Polynesia is the **voice**, while hand-clapping and body-slapping transform the whole body into a percussion instrument. Other instruments are limited by the scarcity of natural resources – there isn't the variety of flora and fauna found in the larger, richer islands of Melanesia. Within Polynesia, the low coral atolls have even fewer instruments than the higher volcanic islands such as Samoa.

Traditional instruments, like the **conch** shell (*pu*), and the many types of wooden and bamboo **slit drums** (*lali*, *logo*, *pate*, *nafa*), are made of natural materials. All these are generally used as signalling devices, to call people to church, to school, or to announce a meeting. Slit drums are also used to accompany dances. The woven **pandanus** sitting mat is both the principal furnishing in a traditional Polynesian house and a percussion instrument. In Samoa the mat is rolled up, filled with lengths of bamboo (or empty bottles), and beaten with two sticks. In Rotuma a pile of folded mats is beaten by a group of singers. There are many types of slit and skin drums, with some of the most exciting music coming from the large ensembles of the Cook Islands. Other percussion instruments include coconut shells, sticks, stones and empty biscuit tins.

Nose-flutes were once common on several islands, but nowadays are only played in Tonga and, to a lesser extent, Hawaii. They were used both to lull the nobility and royalty to sleep and, conversely, to rouse them – making sure the chiefs, who had absolute power of life and death, would wake in a good mood. Tonga's most celebrated nose-flute player, **Honourable Ve'ehala** was himself a nobleman, as well as a one-man archive of traditional Tongan culture. He died in 1986, but Radio Tonga still begins its day's broadcasting with one of his recordings.

The **ukulele** and **guitar** were introduced from Europe, and are now the main instruments in contemporary pop all over Polynesia.

Western Polynesia

There are important cultural differences between the island groups of western Polynesia, such as Samoa and Tonga, and the eastern island groups. The hip movements of Hawaii, Tahiti and the Cook Islands, for instance, are considered improper in western Polynesia.

Samoa

Western Polynesia is often described as the 'heart of Polynesia', a region where the old traditions hold fast. This is especially true of **Western Samoa**, with its *fa'a-Samoa* (Samoan way of life) of which people are fiercely proud. Samoa is famous for its huge choirs and dancing groups. Seated dances are popular, such as the traditional **ma'ulu'ulu** (nowadays also performed standing), in which poetry is illustrated through melody, harmony, rhythm and movements. Modern action-songs are also based on this older dance form.

The **sasa** is another seated dance, performed to a fast and fierce rhythm played on a rolled pandanus mat, slit drums, empty tins or skin drums. Many non-Polynesians find it difficult to acclimatise to these seated dances and hardly consider it dancing when people do not move their feet as we do in the Western world. The **fa'ataupati** dance, performed standing, usually has no accompaniment – the dancers themselves provide the rhythm by slapping the bare parts of their bodies, giving rise to its nickname the 'mosquito dance'.

But the highlight of a Samoan evening is the **siva Samoa**, an individual, non-choreographed dance style which gives dancers the opportunity for personal expression, while also confirming the social order. The dance reflects the metaphorical roles of the *ali'i* (Chief) and the *tulafale* (Talking Chief) within the Samoan hierarchy of titles, ranks and social status. The tulafale is a sort of spokesman for the chief as well as being a poet versed in family and island history. The ali'i represents and personifies self-control, discipline, refinement and dignity. The tulafale is something rougher: characterised by aggression, raw energy and unpredictability. When a siva Samoa is performed, one person dances the ali'i role while the other dancers represent the tulafale. The more clownish or vigorous the movements of the tulafale, the more dignified and aloof the dance of the ali'i, thus displaying the latter's superiority.

Tonga

Tonga is the treasury of Polynesian music and dance. As the last remaining kingdom in Polynesia, it has visibly nourished the will to keep many traditions and ceremonies alive. Enormous groups practise and perform lengthy songs and dances to celebrate anything from the opening of a new church to a visit from His Majesty Taufa'ahau Tupou IV, the King of Tonga.

For such events, some of the pre-contact dances are occasionally revived, but new dances in the modern tradition are also composed. The more important the occasion, the bigger the groups are. A seated dance, for example (known as ma'ulu'ulu, as in Samoa), was performed by more than 1600 secondary school students on the main island to mark one hundred years of Catholic education in the country. Also impressive is the **lakalaka**, a standing dance in which the dancers sing a cappella, backed by a supporting group of singers. A group of four hundred singing dancers is not exceptional.

Tuvalu

The tiny nation of **Tuvalu**, consisting of nine small coral atolls with a population of only nine thousand, might be described as a musical microcosm of Polynesia, where contemporary and older styles co-exist. Some of the older people remember remnants of pre-European traditions in which poems were performed in a sort of heightened speech, or monotonal recitation.

The dances of the new tradition, on the other hand, the **fatele**, clearly show the influences of European melody and harmony. But the lyrics are still important and the inseparable link between singing and dancing exists in Tuvalu as elsewhere. Seated around the percussion box or box drum, the older men start to sing the song, which is repeated over and over. They beat the rhythm on the box or mat with their hands and each time a verse is repeated it gets slightly louder and faster. The other singers seated around the men in the middle join in and clap their hands. At the back, one or more rows of dancers illustrate the sung story and, after a while the accompaniment grows so loud that the singers have to sing at the top of their voices. Finally, when they've all reached maximum volume, the song ends. This type of music also exists in the neighbouring islands of Tokelau.

Fiji

The islands of **Fiji** are on the transitional zone between Polynesia and Melanesia. Although it is officially a part of Melanesia, and the indigenous Fijians bear a physical resemblance to the other Melanesians, Fijian and Polynesian culture share hereditary chiefs, patrilineal descent and a love of elaborate ceremonies. Music and dance are closely related to the western Polynesian varieties. **Meke** is the generic term for dance and the most important types are: *meke wesi* (spear dance for men), *meke i wau* (club dance for men), *meke iri* (fan dance), *vakamalolo* (sitting dance) and *seasea* (standing dance for women). The dances are accompanied by a choir singing in parts, as well as slit-drums and bamboo stamping tubes (*derua*).

Stroll along a street in Nadi on the main island of Fiji and you are assailed by the smell of **Indian** food, the sound of Indian music and vendors trying to lure you into their shops. Nearly half of the population is of Indian origin, dating back to the importation of labour for the sugar plantations by the British colonial government. But the indigenous Fijians still live and work separately from the Fijian Indians and the two traditions seldom come together in music.

Eastern Polynesia

Two island groups from Eastern Polynesia have particularly contributed to the romantic image of Polynesia in the Western world: Hawaii (see p.56) and Tahiti, with its surrounding islands in French Polynesia. Less well known is the music of Rapanui (Easter Island), while New Zealand (Aotearoa), although geographically separate, has a significant Maori population with many cultural links to Eastern Polynesia.

French Polynesia and the Cook Islands

The Tahitian music most people know consists of romantic songs about love, nature or the beauty of the islands. In Tahiti these songs are illustrated by dancers with symbolic hand gestures. The music of this **'aparima** dance type has strong Western influences and the songs are accompanied on guitars, ukulele and drums.

More exciting are the exuberant **percussion ensembles** of Tahiti and the Cook Islands, especially when backing the **'ote'a** dance (Tahiti), with its rapid hip movements from the women and knee-slapping from the men. These ensembles consist of a number of wooden (sometimes bamboo) slit drums

Skin drum and slit drums during a drum competition in Avarua, Rarotonga, the Cook Islands

Micronesia

Micronesia is a group of numerous small islands and island groups east of the Philippines and north of Melanesia; among the better known are Kiribati, the Marshall Islands, the Federated States of Micronesia, Guam, Nauru and the northern Marianas. Culturally, Micronesia has a lot in common with Polynesia. Vocal music is prominent and lyrics are the most important element of a song. There is both heightened speech-singing as well as polyphonic choral music and hymn singing, and song and dance are almost inseparable, just as in Polynesia.

Particularly interesting are the **ancient stick dances**, performed standing and sitting. Performers recount the history of their people, genealogies and the pattern of the stars. Some of the most remarkable chants

in Micronesia recount historical or legendary voyages, often with specific navigational details. The songs, however, are in mostly forgotten languages and people only understand a few words of them. Generally speaking, Micronesian dance movements do not illustrate or interpret poetry as in Polynesia, but decorate it.

There are even fewer musical instruments than in Polynesia and vocal music is much more important than instrumental. The Micronesians use whatever nature offers them – shells, conches, coconut wood and leaves – to make simple flutes and a jew's harp, and body percussion. On some of the atolls there are no instruments at all, but since European contact, guitars, ukuleles and harmonicas have become widespread in the Micronesian traditions.

Satawal stick dancers doing one of their sitting numbers

and two skin drums – one large, double-skinned bass drum and a smaller one with a single skin. The bass drum governs the hip and leg motions of the dancers while one of the slit drums directs the body and hand movements. The other drums take on supporting roles and together they produce a complicated pattern of interwoven rhythms.

On the more remote islands there are different styles. In the Marquesas Islands is the unique pig dance called **haka puaka** (or *mahohe*). The dancers make pig sounds while they mime actions of daily life such as husking coconuts, bathing or acting as a pig itself (in the northern islands). Four sounds, *hm*, *hah*, *ho* and *hay*, are performed rhythmically as strong, husky grunts.

Easter Island

Rapanui (Easter Island) is famous for its monumental statues. There have been many studies of these ancient *moai*, but little has been written about the people who now live here, and less still about their music and dance. This mystical island has always been isolated from the other Polynesian countries, not only because of the distances involved, but also because it is the only Polynesian country to be politically part of a Spanish-speaking country – Chile, in which the people of Rapanui are an ethnic minority.

Remnants of pre-Christian music can still be found, but there are some modern combinations

Upaupa (accordions), played during Carnaval Rapanui on Easter Island

life-style is more vigorous, as are the dances. The Maori say 'ma te tinana e korero' (let the body speak) and the traditional male 'posture dances' called **haka**, are characterised by stamping, quivering of the hand and forearm, and all sorts of facial gestures: rolling eyes, grimaces and sticking out the tongue.

The All Blacks rugby team has made one type of Maori haka famous by performing it on the pitch at the start of a game. But contrary to popular belief, the haka isn't always a war dance, but can also express welcome and farewell. Accompanying chants are performed in a sort of heightened speech somewhere between speaking and singing. Generally, Maori chants are characterised by the excited shouting of a rhythmical text, starting high and descending to the end of the phrase. In contrast to these vigorous male dances the Maori repertoire includes **poi** dances, performed by women using balls (*poi*) attached to a string, which are swung in intricate patterns by the dancers. These songs are accompanied by guitars and also performed as action-songs.

The Modern World

Most Polynesians (outside New Zealand) still live in villages and maintain a subsistence economy fishing and working the land. But all islands have at least one – usually small – city or township, where many of the traditional village ideas and values have been lost, and from where Western-style popular music spreads to rural areas. Although there are regional variations, two forms of pop music in particular can be found all over Polynesia – the music of brass and string bands. Both use instruments adopted from the West, but the way they are used is typically Polynesian.

In Samoa and Tonga, **brass bands** play at all kind of occasions, providing the national anthem at official ceremonies and the music for church services and balls. Most songs even have a middle section which is designed to be played by a brass band alone, with the other band members singing.

The **string band** is the quintessential South Pacific sound. Lazy, relaxed and peaceful – with soft singing in falsetto voices, accompanied by guitars, ukulele and other stringed instruments – this music has become a cliché of Polynesia. But there are also regional peculiarities. In Tonga, for instance, a banjo is common in the bands, but you won't find one in Samoa. The **ukulele**, of course, is played everywhere, but especially in eastern Polynesia, where it comes in different forms – one of

of South American and Polynesian styles peculiar to Rapanui. **Tango Rapanui**, for example, is characterised by relaxed guitar playing rather than intense bandoneon. The melody and rhythm differ greatly from Argentinian tango, but in the dance itself there are postures and movements that clearly resemble the Argentinian form, not least the very fact that it is performed by a couple who hold each other tightly – uncommon in Polynesian dancing. There's also dance music reminiscent of Mexican *corrido*, although the basic framework is the action-song found all over French Polynesia.

The ukulele and guitar can be found everywhere, while the **upaupa** (accordion) has been popular for a while, but is now only played by some older folks. The traditions of clapping stones together and playing the **kauaha** (the jaw bone of a horse), are maintained by some older people hanging on to the traditions, and by younger people trying to revive the past.

New Zealand

The traditional culture of the **New Zealand** (Aotearoa) **Maori** differs from that of the tropical islanders, perhaps because of the harsher natural surroundings and cooler climate. The traditional

Kava and Bush Beer

One of the most important and popular pastimes for men in Tonga is the drinking of **kava**. An informal *faikava* – the Tongan term for kava party – can last all night. It's typically a male activity, although the drink is usually prepared and distributed by a woman or girl. Kava is a non-alcoholic, but slightly intoxicating, beverage made from the root of the pepper plant *Piper Methysticum*.

During a faikava, which might be at home or in a special club, the men drink kava, talk and sing. And the singing is some of the most beautiful music to be heard – enhanced by the relaxed atmosphere of togetherness. Gradually, speech becomes slurred as the kava takes effect, and as the conversation dies down the men start to sing in small groups seated around their own bowl. The most common songs nowadays are the **hiva kakala** (fragrant songs). These are a kind of love song using the symbolism of flowers and natural beauty, and were originally sung unaccompanied, although modern versions are often sung with guitars and other stringed instruments.

It is hard to predict how long the faikava and its singing will survive. Many youngsters prefer *kava papalangi*, kava of the whites – that is to say beer or other alcoholic drinks – and frequent bars and discotheques rather than kava clubs. Compared to the tranquillising kava, beer has a very different effect and does not result in singing

Kava music from the Fungà Veimumuni Group, Tonga

hiva kakala, at least not in tune or in the faikava style.

You can hear this effect on the Cook Islands, particularly on Atiu, where the men gather in the early evening to drink **bush beer**. The missionaries forbade kava drinking and, unlike in Tonga, the custom disappeared. But in the mid-nineteenth century the making of home-brew from oranges was introduced from Tahiti, where people had learned it from the Europeans. As a result of attempts to ban it, Atiu bush beer went underground into *tumunu* – bush beer schools. Men still go to them to make and drink their beer, talk about village affairs and sing songs – more vociferously than at a Tongan faikava – accompanied on ukulele, guitar, and sometimes a percussion instrument like a plastic keg, beaten with two sticks.

---

them made out of half a coconut. String bands can be heard everywhere: at village balls where there is still no electricity supply, at more modern dances, at *kava* drinking gatherings (see box above), and at any other social event.

Wherever there's power, **electric bands** have sprung up, leading to the emergence of South Pacific pop. Some of the bands are electrified versions of the acoustic string bands while others are imitations of Western groups. Only a few incorporate traditional elements.

Tonga and Samoa have small **cassette industries** which release local songs or cover versions of inter-national hits with new lyrics in the local language. Similar tapes are found in the Cooks, French Polynesia and even on Rapanui. The sound quality of Fijian cassettes was widely held to be a cut above the rest, and in the 1980s a number of singers were successful all over western Polynesia. Some of the best-known Fijian stars are **Sakiusa Bulicokocoko**, **Saimone Vuatalevu**, **Lagani Rabukawaqa** and **Laisa Vulakoro**. **Tahiti**'s popular music is best described as cheap French Euro-pop. Like many tourist souvenirs, it doesn't travel well.

New Zealand, and particularly the North Island, is nowadays a multicultural, urban society. Native

AD AND LUCIA LINKELS

Brass band accompanying Samoan dances, Apia, Western Samoa

Maoris, European immigrants, migrants from Asia and a huge number of Pacific Islanders gather in Auckland in search of a better future – the city has the greatest concentration of Polynesians anywhere in the world. Based in New Zealand, the best, and internationally most successful, of all modern Polynesian bands is **Te Vaka** (The Canoe). They are a ten-piece multi-cultural group led by **Opetaia Foa'i** (born in Samoa, with a Tuvaluan mother and Tokelauan father), and number several different Polynesian nationalities, as well as whites. The group blends influences from all over the Pacific mixed with elements of Western rock and pop. A funky rhythm section of bass and drum kit is extended with a range of log and skin drums, plus electric and acoustic guitars.

In 1999 the Maori female vocalist **Hinewehi Mohi** and the album **Oceania** attracted a great deal of attention by fusing Maori chants with Western pop. The brainchild of Jaz Coleman (of the British post-punk band Killing Joke), the album had broad appeal, even if it turned out to be more of a pop record with exotic flavours than the new direction in Maori music the publicity claimed it to be. Not that Oceania were the first to mix Maori words and non-traditional music – as elsewhere, Bob Marley's rhythms and attitudes struck a chord with Maori youth. Indigenous **reggae** bands such

as The Herbs, Dread Beat & Blood, and Aotearoa successfully fused the music with important elements of Maori culture.

In the 1990s, the prevailing sound became **hip-hop**. An exciting new breed of bands – Upper Hutt Posse, Moana & the Moahunters, Dam Native and Wai – emerged with their own brand of music and politics. The resulting sound, often based in South Auckland, has created a vibrant local music culture along with stars such as the OMC, Moana and Annie Crummer (the latter a soulful ex-session singer who incorporates elements of her Rarotongan heritage). The question is not so much whether there will be an explosion of Polynesian pop – there has been – but when the rest of the world will take note.

Issues

As in traditional music, words are the most important element of Polynesian pop, although the allusive style has been lost and purists claim that lyrics have become banal and superficial. As the Tongan writer Epeli Hau'ofa says, "Our contemporary songs increasingly lack references to the beauty of nature and deal with bare emotions. They are mostly pathetic songs about sad and broken hearts. Our elders complain that our young composers are not as good as those of the recent past, because they are too direct. But is it their fault when there is less and less in our surroundings to inspire them into lyrical eloquence. If the sand on our beaches is replaced by broken bottles and empty cans, as is already happening; if our woods and trees are destroyed and our landscape scarred by gaping stone quarries, what will be left for our poets and songwriters to eulogise?"

In 1983, New Zealand band The Herbs wrote "French Letter", a song pleading for a nuclear free Pacific. "Stop the bomb", they sang, while a French-sounding accordion wailed in the background. A year later they sang "Nuclear Waste", but the French government were oddly oblivious, and started a new series of nuclear tests on Moruroa in 1995. Another piece of paradise was lost.

On the whole, however, this sort of protest song is rare. Although Polynesian songs chronicle island history, they usually do it in a neutrally descriptive way, leavened with humour and without expressing overt protest or criticism. Most songs are carefree and light-hearted, and it's usually the smaller things in life that crop up, such as the high price of food, or the difference between their own cocoa and the imported variety, as in the song "Koko Samoa".

I'm still not used to European cocoa
There is not a bit of cocoa to chew on
Just one cup is quite enough
So I just go on drinking Samoan cocoa

The aroma of Samoan cocoa is great
When it's made by a real Samoan
Pour the beans out onto the tin sheet
Stir with the mid-rib of a coconut frond
Watch carefully to make sure there's no grit

Polynesian Festivals

Festivals are the easiest way to see and hear what's happening in Polynesian music, and most islands have at least one annual event. You can hear it all together at the **Festival of Pacific Arts**, held every four years in a different location in the South Pacific. The 1992 Festival took place on Rarotonga in the Cook Islands, and in 1996 Western Samoa were hosts. In 2000 it will be held in Nouméa (New Caledonia). Almost all Pacific countries attend and send their best groups to perform. The purpose of the Festival is to excite Polynesians' interest in their own culture and it is not designed for tourists, although everybody is welcome.

You can experience the fastest moving hips, best drum orchestras and action-songs of French Polynesia at the Fête Tiurai, held in **Tahiti**'s capital city, Papeete, in July. The Tapati Rapanui, held on **Easter Island** in late Jan-

uary or early February has all kinds of activities, including traditional and modern dancing and singing, while the Heilala Festival takes place during the first week of July and coincides with the King's birthday. Agricultural shows are held on all the island groups of **Tonga** during September and October, with the King in attendance. April 17 is **American Samoa**'s Flag Day, and song and dance competitions are held in Fagatogo.

In **Western Samoa** independence is celebrated on the first three days of June with singing and dancing. The second Sunday in October is White Sunday, a religious festival in which children dressed in new white clothes walk to church. After the service, which might last for three hours or more, they take the place of honour at a family feast. October 1 and October 2 are **Tuvalu**'s National Days, and resound to the noise of the fatele.

With thanks to Phil Wilson
for additional material

 discography

A substantial number of Polynesian music discs are bland grass-skirt collections of poor-quality material. The selection below is more ethnographic, but it's the real thing. Many come from the Anthology of Pacific Music on the Dutch label, Pan, recorded by Ad and Lucia Linkels, which includes detailed notes and photographs.

General Compilations

Exotic Voices and Rhythms of the South Seas (ARC, UK).

The cover and title make this disc look like a collection of bland tourist pap. It's actually a very well-chosen and accessible collection of David Fanshawe's recordings from several Polynesian islands as well as music of Melanesia and Micronesia.

Spirit of Micronesia (Saydisc, UK).

Recorded by David Fanshawe between 1978 and 1984. The best introduction to the varieties of Micronesian music. Navigational chants, the Jebua Stick Dance from the Marshall Islands, hymn tunes plus ships, canoes and the rolling sea.

 Spirit of Polynesia (Saydisc, UK).

An excellent collection of recordings by David Fanshawe from almost all Polynesian countries. Includes the Tahitian choir from Rapa Iti, a Tongan faikava song, atmospheric recordings from Easter Island, spectacular drum dances from the Cook Islands, the Marquesas Pig Dance, a Fijian meke dance and Honourable Ve'ehala, the celebrated flautist from Tonga.

Western Polynesia

Compilations

Afo 'o e 'ofa – Strings of Love:
Tongan String-band Music (Pan, Netherlands).

The best and most authentic example of modern Polynesian music, trying to find a balance between the old Tongan way

of life and imported elements from overseas. Recordings from kava parties, village balls, hotel floorshows and pop bands. Lovely harmonies.

Fa'a-Samoa: The Samoan Way ... between conch shell and disco (Pan, Netherlands).

A musical portrait of Western Samoa at the end of the twentieth century. Massive choirs, action-songs and ma'ulu'ulu, plus string bands and police brass bands.

Faikava: The Tongan kava Circle (Pan, Netherlands).

Like kava itself, it's worth acquiring the taste for this. Intimate and genuine performances of strangely beautiful singing as you might hear it on an exceptional night down the kava club. Mostly a cappella, but a few tracks have string band accompaniment.

Ifi Palasa: Tongan Brass (Pan, Netherlands).

A wide variety of Tongan bands plus some indigenous wind instruments – conches and nose-flutes. Includes Tchaikovsky's 1812 Overture played by a college band with live fireworks and church bells.

Ko E Temipale Tapu: the Holy Temple (Pan, Netherlands).

The beating of lali (wooden slit drums) introduces a wonderful collection of church choirs. Ancient Tongan hymns performed in the old style as well as Wesleyan-style church hymns, some with a brass band.

Malie! Beautiful!: Dance music of Tonga (Pan, Netherlands).

Traditional dance music, but not a relic of the past. Ranges from pre-Christian dances to contemporary ones. Mostly voices and percussion with occasional guitars and banjo.

Tonga - Sounds of Change (Pan, Netherlands).

An overview of the music of the only remaining kingdom in Polynesia: the national anthem, kava songs, string bands, rhythmic *tapa* (cloth) beating, church music, brass bands and contemporary sounds.

Tuvalu: A Polynesian Atoll Society (Pan, Netherlands).

A microcosm of Polynesian music from Tuvalu. Ancient music, church music, fatele, and a couple of contemporary songs, including one about AIDS.

Viti Levu – The Multicultural Heart of Fiji (Pan, Netherlands).

Songs and dances from the indigenous Fijians as well as examples of Indian music in Fiji.

Eastern Polynesia

Compilations

Heiva i Tahiti, Festival of Life (ARC, UK).

David Fanshawe's atmospheric live recordings from the Tahiti July fêtes in 1982 and 1986. 'Ote'a, drum dances, 'aparima, action-songs and religious and secular himene are featured, but they work better live than on disc.

He Toa Takatini, A Selection of authentic Maori Songs and Chants (Ode, New Zealand).

Includes traditional chants, contemporary action-songs, and songs for poi dances.

Himene: Polynesian Polyphonies (Buda/Musique du Monde, France).

Protestant church choirs singing himene – the peculiarly Polynesian fusion of ancient chant and European hymns. Recorded in Tahiti and several eastern Polynesian island groups, it's good for comparing different styles, although the recordings are not as vivid as the Triloka and Shanachie discs opposite.

Imene Tapu and other choral music of the Cook Islands (Pan, Netherlands).

Traditional church choirs contrasted with contemporary secular choral music.

Once Were Warriors (Milan, France).

A good film and an impressive album. Old types of music and musical instruments such as the purerehua bullroarer, the koauau flute and paatere chant are mixed with rock music to create a dynamic blend of traditional and contemporary sounds.

Te Kuki 'Airani. The Cook Islands: Songs, Rhythms and Dances (Pan, Netherlands).

A must for drumming fans. Spectacular drum-dances, action-songs, chants and choral music, plus string band and brass band tracks. Recorded on the islands of Rarotonga and Atiu.

Te Pito O Te Henua – End of the world: Easter Island Songs and Dances (Pan, Netherlands).

A great collection, opening with the atmospheric sound of conch shells by the ocean. It includes songs accompanied by clapped stones, a rain-inducing song accompanied by a downpour, church songs, upaupa accordion music, a tango Rapanui and more.

Artists

Oceania

New, mainstream Maori band featuring vocalist Hinwehi Mohi.

Oceania (Point Music, US).

Produced by Jaz Coleman, this debut album has some good haka singing and Maori instruments – thanks to Hirini Melbourne who has been responsible for the revival of Maori flute playing. There are certainly some catchy numbers, but on the whole it's suited for the MOR and dance market.

The Tahitian Choir

The first Polynesian World Music success; discovered on the island of Rapa Iti in 1992.

 The Tahitian Choir: Rapa Iti (Triloka, US).

Hugely successful recording by Pascal Nabet-Meyer of the most extraordinary choral music. Inexplicably stirring.

Te Vaka

The most interesting of contemporary Polynesian bands, led by Opetaia Foa'i. Ten musicians and dancers with diverse Polynesian roots.

 Ki Mua (Warm Earth, New Zealand).

Te Vaka

Te Vaka's latest outing displays a healthy Pacific political consciousness. One of the best tracks, "Vaka Atua", is a song about the destructive effect of missionaries; others deal with global warming and the problems of immigration to New Zealand. Musically, there's an exciting mix of traditional and Western elements.

Te Vaka – The Canoe: Original, Contemporary Pacific Music (ARC, UK).

Fierce percussion music on slit and skin drums contrasts with ballad-like tracks backed by electric guitar, bass and kit-drum, plus some traditional instruments. An effective album about the experiences of a contemporary Polynesian in a big city away from home.

Tubai Choir

Another talented choral group from the relatively unspoilt island of Tubai.

Tubai Choir: Polynesian Odyssey (Shanachie, US).

An album of (mostly) Christian choral music, once again recorded by Pascal Nabet-Meyer.

Wai

Maori musicians Mina Ripéa (vocals) and Maaka McGregor (drums) formed Wai (Water) in 1999. An electrifying group with up to a dozen guest vocalists, dedicated to presenting the rich and dramatic culture of their people.

 100% (Jayrem, New Zealand)

Traditional vocal patterns (sung in the Maori language) are laced with natural sounds (breaths, insects and birds), indigenous percussion (poi) and action sounds (body slaps, foot stamping) and complemented with funk, hip-hop and drum 'n' bass grooves. A very strong debut.

POLYNESIA

Sri Lanka

sounds of serendipity

The composer and writer Paul Bowles, who in the 1950s owned an islet off the Sri Lankan coast, described the Sinhalese – Sri Lanka's majority population – as the only people he had ever come across who seemed completely tone-deaf. Not so asserts **Lalith Ganhewa**, who tells the musical history of the island formerly known as Ceylon (and before that Serendib – the fortunate), and its attempts to maintain a music industry distinct from India, just a short boat ride to the north.

Sri Lanka (known as Ceylon during the years of Portuguese, Dutch and British colonisation) has a population of around eighteen million. The (70 percent) majority are Buddhist **Sinhalese**, but in the north, where a guerilla war for Independence has been waged since the 1980s, there is a substantial population of Hindu and Christian **Tamils**. There are also significant groups of **Muslims** (many of whom speak Tamil), and small numbers of **Burghers** (descendants of the Dutch and Portuguese settlers). In addition, it was only in the 1920s that the island absorbed the last of its forest-dwelling aboriginal people, the **Veddas** – a people who believed and prayed to mountains, trees and even thunderstorms, and used drum rituals to placate the spirits.

Roots – and the Baila

Sri Lanka's mix of peoples, its position on trade routes between Asia and the Arab World, and its history of colonisation have ensured a diversity in its music and culture. However, by far the most significant influence is **Buddhism**. The Lord Buddha visited the island in 300 BC and Buddhism took deep root among the Sinhalese, a fact that has helped the Sinhalese to maintain a quite independent identity from south India. Buddhism also, of course, informs the sacred and ritual music of much of the island. On a more **folk level**, the music is essentially **agricultural** – songs for day to day work, in paddy fields during harvesting or transporting goods on bullock carts.

An enduring outside influence on the music came from the **Portuguese**, who colonised the island in the sixteenth century, bringing with them a tradition of ballads – *cantigas* – along with instruments such as the guitar and *banderinha* (ukelele). They also brought African slaves, introducing an African element to the island's musical mix. The songs of the Portuguese workers and slaves was known as *kaffirinha* (after the Sinhalese term for the slaves – *kafre*), and over time it gradually developed into a Ceylonese dance music called **baila**, acquiring Sinhalese words along the way.

Four centuries on, baila remains very much at the heart of Sri Lankan popular music, although the old acoustic forms (often no more than voice, guitar and handclaps or improvised percussion) have largely given way to combos with electric guitars, drums and synthesizers. Still, no party, wedding or other function would be complete without the band breaking into a baila such as "Hai Hui Babi Achchi", "Biuva Neda Wadakaha Sudiya" or "Chuda Maanikee". And baila has provided Sri Lanka with many of its leading music stars of the late twentieth century – singers such as the late **Voli Bastian, Anton Jones, M.S. Fernando, Paul Fernando** and **Walter Fernando**, and the acknowledged 'King of Baila' over the past three decades, **Desmond de Silva**.

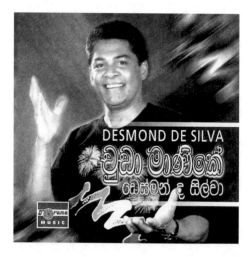

Stage Sounds

Theatrical music is another important strand. Buddhist Sri Lanka had a traditional, open-air song and drama culture – known as **Kolam** or **Sokari** or **Nadagam** – and even in the towns, up until recent decades, theatre was the only real entertainment media.

In the eighteenth century, the local theatre seems to have begun drawing on South Indian themes and music. In the nineteenth, after the ancient kingdom of Kandy fell in to the hands of the British, trade between India and Ceylon grew more intense and the new contacts brought with them Hindustani music from north India. Around 1870 a prominent drama group called **Elphinstone**, led by **K.M. Balivala**, came to Ceylon and performed in the capital, Colombo. They were hugely popular and theatre music became predominantly Hindustani in style thereafter, becoming known as **Nurthi**.

Important figures in this movement included **C. Don Bastian Jayaweera Bandara**, who adopted and improvised Indian music in his stage plays, and the producers **Charles Dias** and **John de Silva**. De Silva, by profession a lawyer, produced a number of Ceylonese folk stories at the Tower Hall theatre, hiring the Hindustani musician **Vishvanath Laugi** to compose the music. This mix of Hindustani music and Sinhalese songs became very popular, and "Danno Budunge" from De Silva's play *Sirisangabo* remains the best known 'evergreen' in Sri Lankan popular music.

Gramophones reached Ceylon in 1901 and by 1903 records were available in Sinhala – the first being a stage song called "Nurthi". In these early years of recording, a number of Sinhalese singers became established stars, recording songs largely from the Tower Hall productions. They reached even more people after the establishment of Radio Ceylon in 1925, a state-run station which was to enjoy a monopoly until private radio stations were set up in the 1990s.

Songwriter Club

With the emergence of Indian cinema, **Hindi film music** began to make big waves in Sri Lanka. Indian melodies were often re-arranged in Sinhala texts. By the beginning of the 1960s, Hindi Film music

had pretty much conquered the island and was a staple of Radio Ceylon (which developed a larger audience in India than at home and sold airtime to Indian producers).

In Sri Lanka, however, Sinhalese singers like **Sunil Shantha**, **Surya Shankar Molligoda** and **Ananda Samarakoon** developed just as much of a following – and set a new trend with songs of everyday life, told in simple narrative. This set off a kind of movement, in which lyrics played the chief role, known as 'songwriter club', the giant of which was the writer **Mahagama Sekara**. All his songs had very simple ideas but they packed in a deeply Sinhala poeticism. The singers Ananda Samarakoon and Sunil Shantha also composed their own music, the former later composing Sri Lanka's national anthem – alleged-

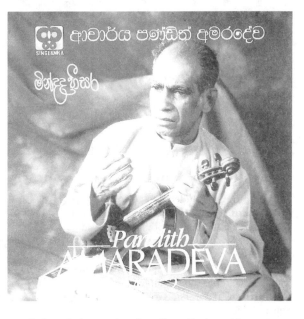

ly in two days flat, after a Ceylon athlete won an unexpected medal in the first Olympics after Independence.

Sri Lanka also produced its own movies and film music. Initially, these were little different from Indian themes, except for the language, but in the 1950s the composer **Mohammed Gauss** began creating uniquely Sri Lankan compositions. His lead was followed by a number of composers, most notably **Premasiri Kemadasa**, a self-taught musician who made a conscious effort to create a 'Native Style of Music', and the musical giant of today's Sri Lankan music scene, **W. D. Amaradeva**, who began his career as a violinist in Gauss's orchestra.

The Moonstones

In the mid-1960s, dozens of groups were formed around the island, playing guitar and other acoustic instruments, and singing **calypso-style baila**. Oddly, they often took Mexican-style names – the result, apparently, of a Mexican group brought over to play in a resort hotel – and they even played a few Mexican songs.

1. කඳ සුරිදුනි	*Kanda Surinduni*
2. හිරුගේ ලොවෙදී	*Hiruge Lowedee*
3. ගැමන් ලියුමක්	*Gamen Liyumak*
4. අඳුර ඉරා	*Andura Ira*
5. මෑණියනි	*Maniyanee*
6. මලට බඹරකු සේ	*Malata Bambaraku Se*
7. දුව මා වගේ *	*Duwa Ma Wage*
8. සිහින ලොවක්	*Sihinia Lowak*
9. ඇත එපිට	*Etha Epita*
10. සෙවණැලි වාගේ	*Sewanali Wage*
11. කිරි මුහුද	*Kiri Muluda*
12. හද විලේ	*Hada Vile*
13. සඳක් බැස ගියා	*Sandak Basa Giya*
14. රන් සමනලයින්	*Ran Samanalayin*
15. රන්දුනුකේ මලසේ	*Randunuke Malase*
16. සුදු මැණිකේ	*Sudu Manike*

Early groups included **Las Bambas**, **Los Muchachos** and the **Humming Birds**. Their soft baila songs became so popular that Radio-Ceylon (or Sri Lanka Broadcasting Company – SLBC – as it became after the island was renamed in 1972) devoted special programmes to it. More groups soon followed, notably **The Moonstones** (later The Golden Chimes and Super Golden Chimes), led by **Clarence Wijewardane** and **Annesly Malewana**. If Sri Lanka can be said to have had a Lennon and McCartney, these were the men, shaping a generation of pop music.

Inspired by Wijewardane and Malawana, Sri Lankan groups had quite a blossoming in the late-1960s and early-1970s, with a string of successful releases on the Sooriya Records label. But with the explosion of the South Indian movie industry and music scene in the late-1970s Sri Lanka became flooded with Hindi records, and local pop took a back seat.

To its credit, the SLBC took action in order to preserve a Sri Lankan music industry. The new chairman, Ridgway Thilakarathne, issued guidelines to prioritise songs of *Deshabimane Gee* (National Feeling) by 'graded artists'. The system had an effect, infuencing the arrangers to be more ethnically oriented, which led to a revival of folk instruments as well as local singers and record labels. The cream of today's musicians – names such as **W.D. Amaradeva**, **Sanath Nandasiri**, **T.M. Jayarathne**, **Neela Wickramasinghe** and **Nanda Malini** (who has more recently become known for her social and political protest songs with lyricist **Sunil Ariyarathne**) – came to prominence in these 'Ridgway Years'.

So too did the influential singer **Victor Ratnayake**, who held the country's first ever one-man concert. His set – which he called 'SA' (the first musical note of scale in Sinhala) has become a classic, performed more than 650 times in the 1980s and 1990s.

Another achievement of SLBC in this period came through the more or less single-handed efforts of the ethnologist **C de S Kulathilakethese**, who researched and recorded the traditional folk cultures of Sri Lanka's various ethnic groups.

Western-style Pop

Alongside Hindi and Sinhala pop, Sri Lanka's sophisticated population has long listened to – and played – Western music, including Classical, Light Classical (a strong local tradition), and pop. The country has had Western-style pop groups since the mid-1960s, when the charts were often headed by outfits like **Minon & the Jet Liners** and **Gabo & the Breakaways**.

The explosion in Western-style pop and semi-classical music, however, came when Sri Lanka opened its doors to an open economy in 1977. This led to the formation of two influential record companies – **Tharanga**, run by former journalist Vijaya Ramanayake, and **Singlanka**, run by Ananda Ganegoda. Ramanayake introduced tape cassettes to Sri Lanka and within no time these dominated a greatly-enlarged music market. He also produced a number of outstanding local artists including **Vijaya**

Kumarathunge (late husband of the nation's current president, Chandrika Kumarathunge), **Milton Perera** and **Neela Wickramasinghe**. Singlanka, meantime, nurtured artists such as the much-respected Sanath Nandasiri and crooner **Milton Mallawarachchi**.

In the 1990s Sri Lanka opened up further to both Indian and Western music, licensing **private radio** and relieving SLBC of its monopoly. By the end of the decade there were over a dozen stations in operation and as broadcasting quality increased, so too did the quality of studio recordings, with **Torana Records**, notably, meeting the challenge from foreign competition in style.

The Western-oriented pop radio stations have inevitably changed the style of local pop, with producers following international chart trends. There are all too many pastiche imitators, singing along to cheap synth and drum machine backing tracks. But impressive acts to emerge in recent years include **Namal Udugama**, **Samitha & Athula Adikari**, **Nirosha Virajini**, and the undisputed prince, **Rookantha Gunathilake**. Two young composers, **Harsh Makalanda** and **Diliup Gabadamudalige** (whom critics have dubbed 'Sri Lanka's Elton John'), have also done interesting work, bridge-building between Western and Sri Lankan music.

discography

Although CDs have arrived in Sri Lanka, they are still a luxury item for many Sri Lankans and sales (and choice of recordings) are dwarfed by cassettes. If you visit, you won't need to look far to find a cassette bar, though beware that many sell poor quality pirate tapes. It is hard to recommend individual cassette titles as pressings are rarely repeated, being replaced by a new tape with a new cover and a few changes in the selection of songs. To explore these, just ask by artist.

Compilations

 Best 16 Calypso Hits of Sri Lanka
(Torana Music, Sri Lanka).

An enjoyable collection of calypso-style baila songs from the 1960s and 1970s, re-recorded in 1999 by Stanley Peris with both new and original artists.

 Sanara Gee 16 – Tharu Arundathi
(Torana Music, Sri Lanka).

Sixteen beautiful light classical Sinhala songs from a role call of top artists – W.D. Amaradeva, Victor Ratnayake, Sanath Nandasiri, Edward Jayakody, Nirosha Virajini and Dayarathne Ranathunge. The second song on the album "Thala Mala Peedii" is a dual-language song in Sinhala and Tamil, sung by Victor and Nirosha, of a tale of two lovers facing the racial problem of Sri Lanka.

⊚ **Sri Lanka: Cantigas do Ceilão** (Tradisom, Portugal).

Field recordings of cantigas – the prototype of bailas – from the Portuguese Burger community of Batticaloa. A bit specialist for most tastes.

Artists

Pandith W.D. Amaradeva

Born Albert Perera in Koralawelle, Amaradeva began his career as a violin player in Mohammed Gauss's orchestra, but soon made his mark as a singer. He is the towering figure of Sri Lankan light music and a veteran of more than 3000 song recordings.

⊚ **Pandith Amaradeva Vol 2: Mindada Heesare** (Singlanka Racords, Sri Lanka).

Sixteen classic Sri Lankan songs, performed by the master. All have a fine poetry, matched by Amaradeva to soft light orchestral arrangements.

Herbert Dayaseela

Herbert Dayaseela is a fourth-generation folk musician, and an orchestra member of the SLBC. He holds international workshops on Sri Lankan drumming and folk music.

▦ **Sihala Gee – Folk Songs of Sri Lanka** (local cassette, Sri Lanka).

This private release is usually available in Sri Lankan cassette bars and provides a good overview of Sri Lankan folk song traditions.

Sunil Edirisinghe

Sunil Edirisinghe, from a family prominent in the Sri Lankan arts scene, forged his musical career singing the theme song "Sandakada Pahanaka" in the film *Mathara*

Aachchii, directed by his brother Sathischandra. He has subsequently released eight best-selling cassettes.

⊙ **Rosa Kusuma** (Singlanka, Sri Lanka).

This is probably the best of Sunil's CD releases with meaningful songs, richly arranged and performed.

Diliup Gabadamudalige

Composer, pianist and vocalist Gabadamudalige has been compared by local critics to Elton John. His compositions are an interesting fusion of Sri Lankan melodies and Western forms.

⊙ **New Frontier**
(Sound Lanka International Records, Germany).

Diliup's debut album fuses Western pop, jazz, Classical and Eastern music, blending traditional Sri Lankan melodies with Western classical arrangements.

Rookantha Gunathilake

The Prince of Sri Lankan pop, Rookantha was born in Kagalle and rose to fame as a film singer, debuting with the hit song "Bambara Pahase" in the film Sapthakanya.

⊙ **Charuka** (Torana Music, Sri Lanka).

This recent album, recorded after an extended visit to the US, shows Gunathilake clearly assimilating American influences. It was a huge-seller in Sri Lanka, notching up sales (as have all of his titles) of more than 100,000 cassettes.

Premasiri Kemadasa

A self-taught composer and conductor, Kemadasa created a 'Native Style' in his film music. He is one of the very few musicians in Sri Lanka brave enough to make revolu-

tionary experiments in both his music and lyrics (which often feature strident social criticism).

⊙ **Landmarks in the History of Singhala Film Music** (Musings, Sri Lanka).

An excellent compilation of Kemadasa's (genuinely landmark) film soundtracks, which are widely considered masterpieces in Sri Lanka.

Nanda Malini

Nanda Malini started out as a film singer, recording the duet "Galana Gangaki Jeevithee", with Narada Disasekara, for Sri Lanka's first colour film. But it is her collaboration with lyricist Sunil Ariyarathne, one of Sri Lanka's great talents and a living library of Sinhala poetry, that has been most memorable. Together they have forged a reputation for protest songs, and Nanda was also the first Sinhala singer to release an album in Tamil.

⊙ **Nilabare** (Singlanka Records, Sri Lanka).

This late-1990s album shows Nanda keeping up with trends, using a group of young composers and even trying a Sinhalese song in ragga style.

Sanath Nandasiri

Nandasiri received his music visharad in India and works as a lecturer of music at the University of Colombo. He is a superb tabla player, as well as an all-round musician and composer.

⊙ **Ma Hada Asapuwa** (Singlanka, Sri Lanka).

A good CD compilation of Nandasiri's songs, which has sold more than 80,000 copies as a cassette.

Victor Ratnayake

Victor Ratnayake was the first singer in Sri Lanka to hold a live one man concert – a set of mainly love songs that he called 'SA', and which has been hugely popular in performance since the 1980s.

⊙ **SA** (Sooriya Records, Sri Lanka).

A live recording of the legendary concert, featuring Ratnayake's finest songs.

Clarence Wijewardane and Annesly Malewana

Clarence Wijewardane and Annesly Malewana formed the seminal 1960s group, Moonstones, which later became the Golden Chimes and Super Golden Chimes, changing the whole Sri Lankan pop scene as they went. After huge success, they went their separate ways. Clarence died a few years back.

⊙ **Unforgettable Memories of Clarence**
⊙ **Annesley Malawana** (Torana Music, Sri Lanka).

These two CDs contain the very best hits of both artists. Although originally they sang many of them together, Torana re-recorded all of the songs in order to bring them out as individual albums.

Taiwan

from innocence to funny rap

The 'Made in Taiwan' image suggests plastic, mass-produced imitations, a tiger economy founded on factories, pollution and urban sprawl. But the other side of Taiwan – its mountains, gorges and sub-tropical forests – are what led it to be called Formosa ('Beautiful') by Portuguese mariners in the sixteenth century. At that time, before the many waves of Chinese immigration, the whole island was inhabited by indigenous groups whose music is part of a current revival of interest in Taiwanese identity. Writing from Taipei, **Wang Ying-fen** unwraps the musical layers.

The island of Taiwan, 160km off the southeast coast of mainland China, is one of the most densely populated areas in the world. The overwhelming majority is Han Chinese, migrants from many regions of China over the centuries. The **Holo** (about two thirds of the population), whose language is referred to as Taiwanese, are descendants of southern Fujianese that migrated to Taiwan from the seventeenth century; the **Hakka** (about 17 percent) migrated from eastern Guangdong province a little later than the Fujianese; and the '**Mainlanders**' (about 12 percent) are those that followed Chiang Kai-shek and the Nationalist government to Taiwan around 1949. '**Aboriginal**' groups, of Malayo-Polynesian origin, make up less than two percent of the population. The music of the mainlanders is covered in the article on Chinese Han Traditional music, on p.33.

During the period of Chinese rule (1662–1895) and the Japanese colonial period (1895–1945), the Taiwanese, the Hakka, and the aborigines were able to maintain much of the languages, dialects and musical culture of their ancestors. After the Nationalist government came to Taiwan in 1949, however, martial law was implemented to defend Taiwan from invasion by mainland Chinese Communists. Mandarin was strongly promoted as Taiwan's official language and local languages were suppressed. As a result, many non-mainlanders grew up unable to speak their mother tongues fluently. This, of course, hugely affected the transmission of the traditional culture of each ethnic group, and not least its music.

Since the lifting of martial law in 1987, the people of Taiwan have become highly conscious of their own ethnic identity as well as of the island's cultural and political outlook. Many efforts have been made to revive traditional music and to make it fit into modern Taiwanese society. Meantime, contemporary popular music has become an important means to make political statements, to bridge ethnic boundaries, and to enhance 'Taiwan consciousness'.

Holo Traditional Music

The Holo have inherited a large variety of the musical styles that their Fujianese ancestors brought to Taiwan, including folk songs, instrumental music and operas. Folk songs are learned informally, while the instrumental and operatic genres have been transmitted in amateur music clubs known as *quguan*. Such music clubs are voluntary associations where villagers or urban community members gather to learn, and their main function is to provide music troupes to perform for temple festivals or for weddings and funerals. Even today, in cities or in villages, temple festivals remain the best showcases of traditional music and opera.

In the southernmost tip of Taiwan, on the isolated **Hengchun Peninsula**, one can still hear folk singers, often accompanied by **moon guitar** (*yueqin*), a simple plucked lute with only two strings. There are just five tunes in the Hengchun yueqin repertoire but they are varied to fit the seven linguistic tones of the Taiwanese dialect, thus creating an endless number of songs. The most famous singer is the legendary **Chen Da** (1905–1981) whose recordings have touched many souls in Taiwan. In other parts of Taiwan, ballad singers such as the acclaimed **Yang Xiuqing** (a blind female singer), use different tunes from those of the Hengchun singers.

Among the instrumental styles, *nanguan* and *beiguan* are the most important. **Nanguan** is a vocal

Nanguan singer Tsai Hsiao Yüeh with ensemble

and instrumental ensemble form that originated in Quanzhou area in Fujian province (China). An ensemble generally consists of four silk-and-bamboo instruments (see p.37) and one wooden clapper. Plucked lutes (the *pipa* and *sanxian*) play a skeletal melody, while the flute (*dongxiao*), fiddle (*erxian*) and the singer perform ornamented versions of it. Quiet, elegant, and meditative, the music has an unmistakably ancient feeling. The songs are in Quanzhou dialect, with each word carefully enunciated and sung to a melismatic melody. The doyen of the art of nanguan singing is **Tsai Hsiao Yüeh**.

A good place to hear the music in its original context is at the Longshan Temple in Lugang city, an old historical town in central Taiwan. About a dozen traditional nanguan music clubs are still active, mostly hidden in city corners. Recently some new clubs have been conducting innovative experiments to bring nanguan closer to a modern audience. Successful examples include the group **Hantang Yuefu**, which has made several tours abroad since the late 1980s, and the new **Gang-a-tsui** nanguan troupe.

In contrast to nanguan, a **beiguan** instrumental ensemble is loud and noisy, with several double-reed *suona* playing together with percussion instruments. Even today in Taipei, you can often hear the wailing sounds of the suonas as they are played in parades for temple festivals or funerals.

Two operatic genres remain active and popular: the *budaixi* hand-puppet theatre and the *gezaixi* opera (known as *gua-a-hi* in Taiwanese). Several traditional **budaixi** troupes still survive, such as **Yiwanran** and **Xiao Xiyuan**, but the so-called **jinguang** (literally 'gold-light') hand-puppet theatre troupes are gaining popularity, with their larger puppets, flashy staging, special effects and hybrid music that combines traditional music with popular songs, both native and Western. In 1970s the first gold-light hand-puppet theatre, created by the innovative Huang Junxiong, was broadcast as a television series and became an instant success, creating several hand-puppet superstars. Now a cable television station named Pili is totally devoted to such shows, and their plots have even become hot topics on Internet discussion groups.

Gezaixi opera is commonly held to be the only genre that is truly native to Taiwan. Still relatively young, gezaixi is constantly absorbing new elements in order to adapt itself to the rapidly changing Taiwanese society. Nowadays, it can be seen on television, on makeshift outdoor stages in front of temples, and even on modern concert stages.

Each context requires something different. Television gezaixi is more like a soap opera, and has produced several superstars, such as **Yang Lihua**. Makeshift outdoor stages often feature the so-called o-pe-ra-hi (inherited from the Japanese occupation period), in which popular songs, modern costumes, and Japanese *chambala*-style fighting are mingled with traditional style performance. Keyboards and drum kit are added to the traditional accompaniment of percussion, string, and wind instruments. Modern concert stages feature the so-called 'refined' gezaixi, in which scripts are set rather than improvised, and large Chinese orchestras added. **Ming Hua Yuan** has been the most successful gezaixi troupe in recent years. With five sub-troupes performing all over Taiwan and an opera school of its own, it continues to demonstrate how a family business can become a major cultural enterprise.

Hakka Traditional Music

Gezaixi is not only popular among the Taiwanese but also among the Hakka. This explains why the Hakka **tea-picking opera** has now become gezaixi-like, although the music contains Hakka tunes. Besides the opera, the Hakka people are best known for their **shan'ge** or mountain songs. Similar to the Hengchun folk songs, the Hakka use only three tunes to fit the six linguistic tones of the Hakka dialect. Experienced singers are good at improvising song texts – often used as a means to test each other's wits. Nowadays, mountain songs are taught in many places, and contests are often held.

Hakka instrumental music known as **bayin** (eight sounds) is still practised in some music clubs, and often features the double-reed suona. The **Chen Family Bayin Troupe** of Miaoli County, led by Zheng Rongxing, is currently the best-known ensemble of this genre.

Taiwan Aborigines

The aborigines in Taiwan are generally classified into plains tribes and mountain tribes, each with its own language and culture. The plains tribes have long been assimilated by the Han Chinese, while the mountain tribes, although also facing assimilation, still retain many of their traditions. Of the ten mountain tribes, the Amis, Bunun, Tsou, Paiwan and Rukai are particularly famed for their **polyphonic singing**.

Aboriginal music is primarily vocal, and each group has its own distinctive style which soon becomes apparent even to an untrained ear. The **Amis**, with a population of around 120,000 in the eastern part of the island, are the largest indigenous group and their songs have beautiful, wideranging, yodelling-type melodies in counterpoint. There are about 35,000 **Bunun** in the central mountains and their music is richly chordal. Famed for their woodcarving, the **Paiwan** and **Rukai**, numbering around 67,000, live in the south and sing with a strong drone oscillating between two adjacent notes. Singing accompanies almost every aspect of tribal life, from daily chores to religious rites – shamanism is an important element. Instruments such as the jew's harp are sometimes used, and a nose flute features in courtship music.

Today there are several ways to witness aboriginal music-making. The best way to experience the music in its original context is to attend aboriginal rituals and **festivals**, many of which have now become open to outsiders thanks to governmental promotion. Among the more famous are the annual Harvest Festival of the Amis tribe, held around July and August on the eastern coast, and the three-day Pastaai ceremony (Ceremony of the Dwarfs) of the Saisiat tribe held every other year in the tenth lunar month. There are also two aboriginal **tourist parks** where performances are held regularly. One is the privately-run Formosan Aboriginal Cultural Village, in Nantou County in central Taiwan, and the other is the government-run Taiwan Aboriginal Cultural Park, in Pintung County in the south.

In recent years, efforts have been made by the aborigines, as well as by the Han people and the government, to preserve and revive aboriginal cultures. One important development was the formation of the **Formosa Aboriginal Dance Troupe** in 1991, which consists of young members from various tribes. Under the direction of Han scholars, they study closely with elderly tribe members, and aim to represent aboriginal music and dance as authentically as possible. The group have performed widely and successfully both at home and abroad.

Despite all these efforts, however, what really made aboriginal music famous in Taiwan was the use of the song **"Return to Innocence"** as the theme of the 1996 Olympic Games. Recorded by the German pop group Enigma, the track samples a song sung by an old Amis couple (Guo Yingnan – aboriginal name Difang Duana, and his wife Guo Xiuzhu), and was on Billboard's Top 100 chart for 22 consecutive weeks. The Guos themselves knew nothing of the use of their music until a friend heard the song on the radio. Unable to take it to court themselves, the case was taken up by a Taiwanese lawyer who eventually found an American attorney to file the suit. Supporters of the Guos estimate that the music has sold over eight million copies worldwide and point out that fifty percent of "Return to Innocence" includes portions of the aboriginal song. The case was settled out of court in 1999, and the Guos paid an undisclosed sum. The incident has drawn attention to the legal questions involved in sampling, a growing phenomenon, and helped to heighten Taiwan's awareness of its precious legacy of aboriginal music and culture – the Guos were demanding proper acknowledgment and respect for their copyright as well as for Amis heritage. They are now establishing a foundation to preserve Amis culture and music.

Stars of the "Return to Innocence" lawsuit, Guo Yingnan (right) and his wife Guo Xiuzhu

Pop and Rock

The lifting of martial law in 1987 was a turning point for Taiwan's pop music scene. Up until then, music fell into two major categories – Taiwanese and Mandarin pop songs. Strongly influenced by Japanese *enka* (see p.148), **Taiwanese pop** was sung in local dialect, mostly with enka-style vocalisation, and was popular mainly among the working class and the older generation. **Mandarin pop**, by contrast – helped along by the government's promotion of Mandarin as the official language – had a broader and younger appeal.

Amongst **Mandarin** singers, Taiwan-born **Teresa Teng** (1953–1995) was a star throughout the Chinese world. Her father arrived from the mainland with the Nationalist troops around 1949, and to help her struggling family she began to sing at a young age. Taking Shanghai pop singers of the 1920s and 1930s as her model, Teresa Teng's singing style and voice quality represents for many the quintessential Chinese singing style. Teng believed passionately in the 'Big China' idea, in which all Chinese form one culture, no matter where they live, which is perhaps why she had so many fans all over the world. Even today, many mainland Chinese pop singers openly acknowledge her as their model.

The lifting of martial law enabled the majority Holo population to finally embrace their own identity and their own Taiwanese dialect, a development that brought major changes to the content and the social status of **Taiwanese pop songs**. In 1989, Rock Records, the most important Mandarin record company, issued an experimental Taiwanese album entitled *Song of Madness* by a group of musicians named **Blacklist Studio**. Instead of singing about lovesickness and homesickness – the age-old themes of traditional Taiwanese songs – the album focused on the lives of ordinary people: on politics, the craziness and hardship of life, taxi drivers and festivals. Combining rap, rock, lyrical ballads and some Taiwanese traditional music, the project anticipated several major styles that followed.

In 1990, Rock issued a Taiwanese album by **Lin Qiang**, who combines rock with Taiwanese lyrics to sing about ordinary Taiwanese life. This album was an instant hit and marked the real beginning of so-called **New Taiwanese Song**, a blend of rock, rap and ballad styles, which quickly became part of the mainstream market. Many Mandarin vocalists have begun to sing in the new style, rather than the old enka manner, and Hakka dialect even appears in the songs of the hit group, **New Formosa Band**, led by Chen Sheng and Huang Lianyu (who is a Hakka himself).

Among the New Taiwanese Song musicians, **Wu Bai** (literally Five Hundred) is an excellent rock guitarist and has also been a leading figure in mainstream Taiwanese rock. But the most interesting figure is surely **Jutoupi**, who has created a unique style of his own. His three *Funny Rap* albums skillfully mingle Taiwanese dialect with Mandarin (spoken with different accents reflecting the various ethnic groups in Taiwan) to make sarcastic comments on many sensitive issues such

as vote brokers, sex, the ambiguity of Taiwan's identity as a nation and so on. Musically these albums sample a wide variety of the musics that exist (or once existed) on the island, ranging from traditional folk songs to Western pop and rock.

Jutoupi's fourth album, *Hexie de Yewan OAA*, released in 1996 after the Enigma copyright incident, was a dance album created entirely from samplings of aboriginal songs and music, with each song featuring a different tribe. This was the first time aboriginal music appeared on a mainstream record – albeit rather transformed. In the same year, **Zhang Huimei**, an aboriginal girl from the east coast of Taiwan, became an overnight superstar. Although she sings Mandarin pop songs, one of her songs, "Sister", clearly states her aboriginal identity through its use of Amis language and melody. Both Jutoupi's fourth album and the success of Zhang Huimei seem to imply that aboriginal music and musicians are gaining more popularity in the mainstream market. With some popular Hakka songs and other aboriginal groups filtering into the mainstream market, Taiwan's multi-ethnic society is now being reflected in its popular music.

discography

Taiwanese Traditional Music

Artists

Chen Da

Chen Da (1905–1981) was the best-known singer of the Hengchun Peninsula. He was 'discovered' by ethnomusicologists in the 1960s when he was already old and half

blind, but still able to improvise long ballads telling stories and teaching morals. His simple and straightforward voice and lyrics are deeply moving and he has inspired a whole host of musicians and music lovers in Taiwan.

Heng-Chun Narrative Singing
(Chinese Folk Arts Foundation, Taiwan).

Accompanying himself on the moon guitar, Chen Da sings a sad 'Prodigal Son' story. The song falls into four sections, each based on one of the traditional Hengchun tunes.

Qiu Huorong, Pan Yujiao & Sanchung Nanyishe Beiguan Club

Qiu Huorong and Pan Yujiao are the two most active exponents of beiguan music and opera, winning several awards and teaching many young students. Sanchung Nanyishe Beiguan Club is one of the few traditional beiguan music clubs that has remained active.

Tianguan Sifu (Heavenly Officials Bestowing Good Fortune) (Crystal Records, Taiwan).

In this album, the beginning of track 1 and the whole of track 4 give good examples of the music of the beiguan ensemble, with the double-reed suona playing the lead melody. This music is often heard during temple festivals in Taiwan. Other parts include samples of ritual operas presented at the beginning of a performance to pray for good fortune.

Tsai Hsiao Yüeh & Tainan Nanshengshe Nanguan Club

Tsai Hsiao-Yüeh began studying nanguan at the age of fourteen and recorded two LPs at the age of sixteen. Celebrated for the quality of her voice, she is a member of the Tainan Nanshengshe Nanguan Club, one of the oldest in Taiwan and the first group to tour Europe (in 1982).

Nan-kouan: Musique et chant courtois de la Chine du Sud Vol 1 (Ocora, France).

This is the first of six CDs covering Tsai's entire repertoire, recorded in France in 1982 when her voice was still at its best. The five songs demonstrate her singing style, full of subtle nuances and ornaments. Producer Kristofer Schipper supplies excellent liner notes.

Hakka and Aboriginal Music

Compilations

The Inner Voices of the Hakkas in Taiwan (Wind Records, Taiwan).

This four-CD set features the music of the southern-most of the two groups of Hakkas. There are two CDs of mountain songs and two CDs of bayin instrumental ensemble. Wind Records also publish an extensive catalogue of aboriginal recordings.

Polyphonies vocales des Aborigenes de Taiwan (Inédit, France).

Featuring music from the Amis, Bunun, Paiwan and Rukai tribes, this is a good introduction to aboriginal singing. Includes archive recordings from the 1960s and a concert recorded in Paris in 1988. Enigma obviously enjoyed it: "Return to Innocence" samples the first track.

Taiwan: Music of the Aboriginal Tribes (Jecklin Discs, Switzerland).

Recorded in the field by Swiss scholar Wolfgang Laade in the late 1980s, this CD provides the best sample of the various musical styles of seven mountain tribes and even one plains tribe (most plains tribes have been almost completely assimilated by the Han people). Accompanied by an excellent eighty-page booklet.

Pop Music

Artists

Blacklist Studio

Blacklist Studio are a group of musicians who came together to record this CD of Taiwan consciousness. Of particular note is Chen Minzhang who, taking Chen Da as his model, accompanied himself on the guitar (rather like Chen Da's moon guitar) and is the only popular musician to make special efforts to incorporate elements of Taiwanese traditional music (beiguan, gezaixi tunes) into his own.

Song of Madness (Rock Records, Taiwan).

Marks the first attempt by popular musicians to use Taiwanese language and to comment on Taiwanese society. Combines rock and rap, with some lyrical songs accompanied by a single guitar. These three forms became the main styles of New Taiwanese Song.

Jutoupi

Zhu Yuexin began as the 'Bob Dylan of Taiwan' (yes every country has one), accompanying himself on guitar and taking part in social and political movements. But after joining Rock Records, he changed his style completely, adopting the confrontational name Jutoupi (Pighead), and producing an intriguing punk/rock style, fused with a whole range of Taiwanese and Western styles, on a series of Funny Rap albums. It was too much for many of his old fans but his impact is probably greater than ever.

Funny Rap I: You Sick Suck Nutz Psycho Mania Crazy Taipei City (Rock Records/Mandala Works, Taiwan).

There are three *Funny Rap* albums, all remarkable for taking up political issues, sex, and other difficult topics. Many people in Taiwan often mix Mandarin with Taiwanese and even English in their daily speech, and this mixture of languages and dialects is a key element in these albums. In short they encapsulate Taiwanese society, its ethnic diversity, and its political situation. This first album, from 1994, was followed by **Happy New Year** (Mandala Works, Taiwan) and **ROC on Taiwan** (Magic Stone, Taiwan).

Hexie de Yewan O A A
(Rock Records/Magic Stone, Taiwan).

A big stylistic jump from rap to house, and a change in theme from Taiwanese society to the aborigines. Each song features samples of the music of one tribe over dance music. The liner notes give careful documentation of the sources of the music sampled and acknowledge the artists involved. The first mainstream album in Taiwan featuring aboriginal music.

Lin Qiang

When Lin Qiang's song "Marching Forward" swept Taiwan in 1990, he instantly became the model for many young people, not only because he created a new style of Taiwanese pop songs but also because he represented an image of a typical Taiwanese guy that young people could identify with. Unhappy with superstardom, however, he followed a more experimental path and recently he has been producing electronic and film music.

Marching Forward (Rock Records, Taiwan).

This 1990 album stands as an important landmark in Taiwan's pop history. In contrast with the old enka-style pop songs enjoyed by the previous generation, New Taiwanese Songs combine rock with Taiwanese dialect and have a youthful appeal. The album's hugely successful title track "Marching Forward" generates an optimism seldom found in the old Taiwanese pop songs.

Thailand

songs for living

Music is everywhere in Thailand. When you get up in Bangkok, the sounds of *pluk jai* (patriotic songs), sandwiched either side of the national anthem at eight o'clock, blare out from the radio. You walk to the local market and the petrol station en route is pumping out *string*, a Japanese-influenced bubblegum pop song. Next door a cassette vendor cranks up some *pleng pua cheewit* (songs for life), a type of folk-rock. And at the market the distinctive rhythms and rapping vocals of *mor lam* (Laotian traditional music) vie with the sweet sadness of Thai country music, *luk thung*. **John Clewley**, resident in Bangkok, introduces one of the most dynamic music scenes in Southeast Asia.

Thailand, a nation of over sixty million people, is handily placed at the confluence of Asia's two major cultural forces – India and China. The Thais are less Indian than the Malays or Indonesians and less Chinese than the Vietnamese. They retain discernible influences from both civilisations but, canny assimilators that they are, traits from other neighbouring groups have been absorbed as well, including Mon, Malay, Khmer, Lao, Burmese and Indonesian. Everything gets put through the Thai blender, including Western influences (although Thailand was one of the few countries in Asia never to be colonised by Europeans).

Music is a fundamental part of Thai life. It features in Buddhist and Brahmin ceremonies, animist rituals and court and dance dramas. There is also a wide range of popular song styles. Two indigenous styles, *luk thung* and *mor lam*, are incredibly popular and should not be missed on a visit, although tourists tend to be steered towards classical ensembles, the strange and eerie sounds made by *pii klong* musicians at Thai boxing matches, and the popular jazz compositions of saxophone-playing King Bumiphol Aduladej.

Consider the ethnic diversity of Thailand – there are some eighty languages and dialects at the last count – and you'll understand why there is so much music. In the north are the graceful *fon* paired dances; in the central region, rap-like jousting of *lam tad* and *pleng choi*; in the northeast, the thrilling vocals and verbal tricks of mor lam and the bubbling rhythms of *bong lang*; and in the south, the music that accompanies shadow plays, *nang taloong*. Visit a Thai village or a local festival, where the real heart of Thailand beats, and you may find *pleng phun bahn* (songs of rural folk).

Other ethnic groups, collectively known in Thai as **chao khao** (mountain people), still celebrate

JOHN CLEWLEY

Bong lang music, with cute young potbanger to front the band

their own New Year festivities and other important events with dance and music. These traditions are particularly strong in the northwest, among the Lahu, Lisu, Akha, Mien, Karen, Hmong and Lawa. Elsewhere, the relentless march of modernism has threatened or swallowed up local folk styles, but there are still many performers and, in these financially-troubled times, pride in all things indigenous is helping create a revival.

Historical Roots

Indian musical instruments had been in use in Thailand since the seventh century but a more specifically Thai identity emerged when the first Thai kingdom of **Sukhothai** was created, in 1257. A flowering of culture led to the creation of the Thai alphabet and court documents suggest that music was a key part of life – Sukhothai Thais played wind, string and percussion instruments and enjoyed singing. By the start of the **Ayuthaya** period (1354–1376), the **classical** Thai ensembles – *piphat*, *khrung sai* and *mahori* – were in evidence, and dance-dramas popular. Music-making got so out of hand, apparently, that King Rama I banned the playing of music on rivers – Ayuthaya was a city built on water – or near Royal buildings.

Following the establishment of a new capital in Bangkok in 1782, **court music** was again encouraged, and during the reigns of King Rama II (1809–1824) and Rama IV (1851–1868) many new styles and compositions were introduced. Western **military bands** first played in Thailand during this period, adapting Thai traditional music for the new form, and Thai royalty started to study in Europe. As a result, during the reigns of both Rama V (1868–1910) and Rama VI (1910–1925), court and classical styles were influenced by ideas from the West.

The Modern Era

By the time constitutional monarchy was introduced, in 1932, changes that would have far-

Thai Classical and Court Music

Thai **classical and court music** sounds strange and entrancing at first hearing, with metal gongs, eerie pipes, fiddles and zithers improvising around the slow, floating, melancholic melodies. The earliest type of ensemble, the **piphat**, dates back at least seven hundred years to the Sukhothai period, and historians believe the first ensembles had one woodwind and four percussion instruments, which suggests the music was rhythmic in character. It was initially developed to accompany classical dance-drama (*khon* or *lakorn*) and shadow puppet theatre (*nang*).

Classical **instruments** – some indigenous and others derived from neighbouring countries – can be divided into four categories: woodwind (the oboe-like *pi* and the *klui*, a bamboo flute), stringed (zithers like the *jakay*), melodic percussion (for example, the *ranat*, a boat-shaped wooden xylophone, and gong circles like the *khlong wong yai*) and rhythmic percussion (drums like the *tapone* and *ching* temple bells). There are three kinds of **ensemble**: the piphat consists of woodwind (especially the pi) plus melodic and rhythmic percussion; the *khruang sai* has strings, woodwind (klui) and rhythmic percussion; and the *mahori* combines all four categories of instruments.

The sound seems strange to Western ears, perhaps because Thai music uses a different tuning system in which the octave is divided into seven equal notes rather than the mixture of tones and semitones used in the West. In this way, four out of the seven notes are quite 'out of tune' with anything in Western music. In many pieces one or two of the notes are omitted, or only touched on in passing, which gives the music a pentatonic feel. All the instruments improvise around the lead melody, which is usually performed by the *khong wong yai* (gong circle). The *ranat ek* (a xylophone) may split each beat with some trilling and rolling, while the *pi nai* (a type of shawm) will embellish the melody with variations. Other instruments will insert slurs, glissando and syncopation at the same time.

Classical musicians have absorbed influences from other cultures, especially Cambodian traditions. A feature of some songs is the playing of Lao, Mon, Cambodian or Laotian styles in an impressionistic way. "Khamien Sai-Yok", composed in 1877, was based on a Cambodian lullaby, and describes musically the sound of a waterfall, birds singing and so on. In other borrowings, each part is given a Lao or Cambodian lilt, instantly recognisable by Thai listeners.

In the early part of the twentieth century, classical music could be heard on the streets of Bangkok as musicians practised around Phra Arthit road, just across from the Khao San road travellers' area. Sadly, the street musicians are long gone but the country's oldest classical band, **Duriyapraneet**, can still be found in the same area. It celebrated its centenary in 1998, and family members still perform at the Phiman Thai restaurant, on Sukhumvit Soi 49.

Classical music is widely taught in schools and at universities and as a result, many Thais can play one or two instruments. A revival has been underway for some time, aided by royal patronage from the classical-playing Crown Princess Maha Chakri Srindhorn.

reaching consequences for Thai popular music were already underway. Court musicians were transferred to the Fine Arts Department and Western sounds were all the rage. Thai musicians were starting to play Western classical, music from the movies, and dance craze music like tango and jazz.

Violinist Khru Uea (Teacher Uea) Sunthornsanan established Thailand's first jazz band in the 1930s, and later set up the hugely influential **Suntharaporn** band. The music he helped create was known as **pleng Thai sakorn**, the Thai take on Western music, and incorporated Thai melodies and airs. This style later developed into smaltzy romantic music, **luk grung**, which translates as child of the city and is usually associated with the upper classes of Bangkok. Khru Uea left a legacy of ballads and compositions like "Khaun Don", "Khuanchai Chula", and "Sawasdee Pimai" that

are still played today. Interestingly, he later started to blend his Suntharaporn jazz style with music from his classical band, **Duriyapraneet**, thus creating Thai traditional music with a Western flavour, a forerunner of the cross–cultural sound of modern bands like Fong Naam.

New influences from the West dragged Thai music into the rock'n'roll era during the 1960s. The popularity of Western stars like Cliff Richard and the Shadows encouraged Thais to mimic the new sounds. A new term was coined, *wong shadow* (wong means group, and shadow came from Cliff's band). The term would shift again in the 1980s when Thai forms of Western pop were labelled 'string'. In the early 1970s, musicians like the late Rewat Buddhinan, one of the founders of the Thai entertainment giant Grammy, started to develop Thai-language rock. This movement paralleled the activities of Japanese rockers like Hosono

There are many world-class musicians attached to the Fine Arts department and teaching in arts faculties. The problem for many musicians is not that there isn't a new generation coming through, but rather that there is a dearth of places to play and gain exposure.

Much media attention has been made of the new wave of classical bands like Fong Naam and Kangsadan, which have tried to modernise the tradition by combining the music with Western forms like jazz. **Fong Naam**, led by American Bruce Gaston and renat player Boonyong Ketkhong, has been the pioneer over the past fifteen years, recording both reinterpretations of classics and new compositions.

Although the band is best-known abroad for its classical repertoire, it has a more experimental reputation at home. **Kangsadan** and **Boy Thai**, which combine classical instruments with a modern percussion combo, have followed Fong Naam's footsteps, with Boy Thai adopting reggae and samba styles and attracting a teen audience. The result of these fusions has not always been successful. But in 1995, Kangsadan leader **Chaiyoot Tosa-ngan**, a ranat master, successfully performed his "Ranat Ek Concerto" with a Western symphony orchestra. His work offers another way forward for a 700-year-old tradition.

Fong Naam in action with Bruce Gaston fourth from left

ROBIN BROADBANK/NIMBUS

THAILAND

Haruomi and Shoukichi Kina. Protest rock, *pleng phua cheewit*, also took off, reflecting increasing activism for democracy in the kingdom.

Songs for Life

Starting as a form of progressive protest rock in the early 1970s, **pleng phua cheewit** (songs for life) came about as dramatic social changes were taking place in Thai society (the first democratic government was elected in 1973; sadly it lasted just three years before a military coup). **Caravan** was the pioneering band, blending Thai folk songs with Western folk-rock, and its members were at the forefront of resistance to the then military rulers.

On October 6, 1976, rightwing activists, police and military brutally suppressed students at Thammasat university, leaving many dead. Caravan, like many others, took to the jungle and mountains, joining clandestine Communist groups. The band continued to perform for farmers, creating some memorable songs like "Nok See Luang" (Yellow Bird), "Berp Khow" (Every Handful of Rice) and the most famous Caravan song of all, "Khon Gap Kwai" (Man and Buffalo). The term 'songs for life' comes from a poem by Thailand's best-known Marxist intellectual, the late Jit Poumisak. He was the lyricist behind several of Caravan's songs, including "Berp Khow":

> With every handful of rice you eat:
> That is my sweat you eat,
> As you grow to be a man.
> This rice tastes good
> To people of every class,
> But such suffering is behind it,
> Such deep-rooted bitterness!

An amnesty eventually returned student activists to mainstream society. Caravan disbanded, though it regularly reforms for Japanese tours, and individual members all have successful solo careers.

In the 1980s, **Carabou** emerged as the most potent songs for life band, especially with nationalistic hits like the three million seller "Made in Thailand" and "Ameri-Koi". Led by outspoken Ad Carabou (Yuenyong Ophakul), the band was one of the first rock outfits to tour nationally. One of their most famous songs, written in 1988, was "Thap Lang" (The Lintel). It recalled an incident in the 1960s, when a twelfth-century lintel was stolen from the khmer temple sanctuary of Phanom Rung; the Narai lintel, with its fine carving of a reclining Vishnu, was subsequently displayed in the Art Institute of Chicago. The lyrics ran: "The

Statue of Liberty stands pointlessly, has closed her eyes to the fact that the Narai was stolen from the Thai people ... take back your Michael Jackson, give us back our Narai Lintel." The song triggered a feverish wave of nationalism before the object was returned to its rightful place in the temple. Carabou recorded fifteen albums in all, but the band has now broken up. Ad and other Carabou members were prominent, musically and politically, during the bloody democracy demonstrations of 1992.

Currently, the top singer in the genre is fresh-faced **Pongsit Kamphee**. But the protest rock style is suffering from the release of too many average albums, and from the fact that the music, still rooted in Western styles of folk-rock, has changed little in twenty-five years. In 1998, the leaders of Caravan, Carabou and Pongsit Kamphee – three generations of the songs for life movement – joined together with the state-run Bangkok Symphony Orchestra for a concert to mark the twenty-fifth anniversary of the Democracy Revolution of 1973. No one seemed to see any irony in this.

Thai Pop Today

Despite the Asian economic meltdown of the late 1990s, the Thai music scene still bubbles away. The music industry developed exponentially on the back of the economic miracle and, with sales of more than US$171 million in 1997, Thailand is the second biggest market in southeast Asia after Indonesia. In Grammy, which has captured at least half of the Thai market, it has one of the top twenty record companies in the world.

The growth of **string bands** (small pop combos) during the 1980s was helped by the rapid development of the Thai media industries. Styles range from the bubblegum pop of mega-stars **Tata Young** (a multi-million seller and heir to aging superstar Thongchai 'Bird' Macintyre's throne) and **Patiparn 'Mos' Pattavikan**, to easy listening standards (pleng sakorn), dance, rock, reggae, ska, Thai rap and so on. Whatever is big in the US and Britain is reassembled with Thai lyrics. The most talented of all the current string outfits is the soft rock of brothers **Asanee & Wasan**.

The brightest pop development has been with so-called **alternative music**, inspired by British bands like Oasis and the Manic Street Preachers. One band with genuine class has emerged, **Modern Dog**. From the moment the four Chulalongkorn university graduates won the Coke Music Awards in 1992, the band has been the hottest rock act in town, revered for simple songs, catchy lyrics and an irreverent stage act – Thailand is a conservative society. Frontman Pod is one of the most charismatic band leaders to emerge in years. Dog's first album stayed in the charts for years, and their latest release, *Café*, is riding high.

Thai Country Music

When reigning queen **Pompuang Duangjan** died in 1992 at the tender age of 31, many thought it was the end of an era for **pleng luk thung** (Thai 'country music'). Her cremation, in her home

The late Pompuang Duangjan

town of Suphanburi, was attended by thousands, ranging from royalty to her legions of supporters among the rural and urban poor. Go to a temple fair (see box overleaf), either in Bangkok or upcountry, and you'll be guaranteed to hear one of Asia's great popular musics. Luk thung shows feature bright lights and glitz, large orchestras, up to fifty dancers (who go through many costume changes – from Marie Antoinette to a farmer, from Superman to a giant water-melon), comedians, a string of support singers, and the star.

The term was first coined in 1964, by television producer Jamnong Rangsitkuhn for a programme on regional music. The undisputed king of luk thung, the late **Suraphon Sombatjalern** had

already made his debut by then with the hugely successful "Nam Da Sow Viane" (Tears of the Laotian Girl) in 1952, and the songs of Toon Tongchai were also popular. Suraphon was at his peak in the 1960s, singing and composing a bagful of hits, many of which remain popular today. With female singer **Ponsri Woranut**, he developed the style into a mature form.

The name luk thung, which translates as 'child of the fields', neatly reveals the music's origins among the poor, and its lyrics are concerned with the harsh realities of life for poor struggling migrant workers. (Luk grung, on the other hand, is associated with Bangkok's ruling elite, and deals with romantic and idealistic issues.) DJ and luk thung historian, Jenpope Jobkrabunwan, says that the initial sound was folk-based but this changed in the 1950s due to external influences as diverse as Malay strings, Latin brass and rhythms (tours by Latin bandleader Xavier Cugat influenced many Asian pop styles), Hollywood movie music and 'yodelling' country and western vocal styles from the likes of Gene Autry and Hank Williams. Local entertainment styles like *likay* (travelling popular theatre) also influenced the skits and comedy breaks that are a key part of a luk thung show.

Suraphon Sombatjalern

There are strong musical affinities with other regional pop styles like Japanese *enka* and Indonesian *dangdut* but what is distinctively Thai – quite apart from the spectacular and glitzy live shows – are the singing styles and the content of lyrics. Wavering grace notes, glissandos and wailing ornamentation feature in the vocal styles and the singer must have a wide vocal range. Megastar **Pompuang** once said that because the music is so emotional the singer must be able to create a strongly charged atmosphere. Since Pompuang's death, **Sunaree Ratchasima** has replaced her at the top.

Pompuang had the finest voice ever to grace the luk thung stage. Powerful and full of emotional colour, it raises goosebumps even on those who don't understand Thai. She rose to fame at the end of the 1970s, joining stalwarts like **Sayan Sanya** and **Yodlak Salakjai**, before political troubles temporarily pushed the form into the background. In 1971, the most successful musical film ever released in Thailand, *Mon Rak Luk Thung* (Love Country Style), featured a number of well-known singers, and between 1970 and 1972 many luk thung films were produced. And as a national road network was constructed and rural development accelerated, luk thungs stars took their massive travelling shows to all corners of the country.

Like Pompuang, many singers came from the central region town of Suphanburi, and they added their own unique accent to the style. Many of them came from the rural peasantry: Pompuang was an illiterate flower-seller and daughter of a farm labourer, and Sayan was a rice farmer. They could therefore identify directly with the themes and stories that their audiences related to. Pompuang's experiences – denied education, exploited as a child, forced to work for a pittance and encouraged to migrate to the city for a life in the slums – mirrored those of many among her audience.

Typical luk thung songs narrate mini-novellas, based around characters like truck drivers, peasant lads or girls, poor farmers, maids, migrant workers and prostitutes; and themes centred around leaving home and going to the big city, dreaming of being a luk thung star, infidelity, grief, tragedy and sexual pleasure. The song titles tell it like it is: "Namta Sip-lor" (Tears of the Truck Driver); "Namta Sao Serp" (Tears of the Waitress), "Mai Tai Klap Ma Taeng" (If I Survive I'll Return and Marry You); "Klin Khlone Sap Khwai" (The Smell of Mud and Buffaloes); "Men Sap Khon Jon" (The

Thai temple fairs

Fifty years ago, **Ngan Wat**, the Thai temple fair, was a focal point for the community. Today, some of these colourful events have been displaced by other (Westernised) forms of entertainment, but if you visit Thailand at the right time, you'll find a temple fair somewhere. The season marks the conclusion of the Buddhist 'Lent', Awk Pansa, around October, at the end of the rainy season.

A typical fair lasts between seven and ten days, before everyone packs up and moves on to the next temple. A huge, brightly-lit ferris wheel dominates the scene, towering over the shooting galleries, water-dip lotteries and little car races, and even drawing the crowds away from the fortune tellers and strange freak shows offering the sight of the 'two-headed woman' or the 'wolf-boy'. Smaller stalls sell cheap toys, clothes, books and tasty speciality foods. But the main reason to visit is the entertainment at the temple site itself: an evening luk thung or mor lam show. In the old days, one of the famous Bangkok temple fairs like the Wat Samut Chedi (Golden Mount Temple) fair would be the place where a luk thung singer made his or her debut; these days it's more likely to be a talent show.

The fair at **Wat Plapachai**, in Chinatown, usually held every January, is typical. Working people, many of them migrant workers from the north and northeast, flock to the fair, and as there is also a Chinese temple in the grounds, a new Chinese theatre performance is thrown in every night. A different major luk thung or mor lam star performs in the temple school grounds, and a gig costs just 50 baht – just over a dollar. A modern development is the town fair, usually held in the grounds in front of the offices of the municipal authorities. All the rides and food from a temple fair are there but since the site is much bigger, there's more of everything. Each town will have its own special features. The **Buriram** fair (February), for example, has two main music sites: one for major luk thung and mor lam stars; the other the venue for a kantrum battle-of-the-bands. In a country where Westernisation is rapidly replacing traditional ways, the temple fair is one of the few places where you can still experience what is left of Thailand's traditional popular culture.

Poor Are Smelly). Risqué lyrics are banned but a sexual charge can be carried by the singing and presentation alone – some commentators have suggested that they are one of the few public spaces where sexual pleasure can be discussed.

As Pompuang charged into the 1980s, luk thung started to face a stiff challenge from string combos and the rise in popularity of Thai pop. In response, she adapted her technique to a more dancefloor-oriented sound which she called **electronic luk thung**. Very few singers had the range to follow her and her fame increased enormously. She even became the first luk thung singer to perform at a *hi-so* (high society) concert.

Bangkokians often look down their noses at luk thung as music for country bumpkins. This conflict between the city and the village, a direct result of rapid industrialisation, is neatly contrasted in her song "Sao AM" (AM Girl), which contrasted a village girl and her AM-band radio with a rich city boy and his FM radio:

> In the village we wear a sarong,
> Carry a big basket on our shoulders out to
>   the paddy field,
> Speak just simple Thai words,
> And listen to AM radio all the time.
> The radio set cost only 100 baht...
> You are a city man, you will lure me in vain.
> We are not compatible. You listen to FM
>   radio!!
> You think you can fool me because I'm a
>   country bumpkin...
> As a city guy, you are suitable for a city girl.
> You only want my youth
> You would drop me like a stone for a city girl.

> (Translation: Pasuk Pongpaichit and Chris Baker)

Those who gleefully predicted luk thung's demise after Pompuang's death got a real shock when the nation's first 24-hour luk thung station, **Luk Thung FM**, went on air in August, 1997. It has proved to be wildly popular, confirming that a luk thung revival is in full swing. Get into any taxi in Bangkok and the station will be blaring out. Perhaps tired of formulaic pop, listeners have been snapping up collections of luk thung classics, buying cassettes from a rising new generation of singers like Monsit Kamsoi, Yingyong Yodbuangarm, Dao Mayuree and Got Chakraband Arbkornburi, and attending their gigs in droves. It's even hip for the middle-class to like luk thung these days.

The current revival comes after several veterans have relaunched their careers; it started with Sornpet Sornsupan and, later, Sodsai Rungphothong,

who had a monster two million seller with his album *Rak Nong Porn*. Major label Grammy then released a **Dnu Hantrakul** remake of Surachai Sombatjalern's old hit, "Ai Num Pom Yao" (He is the Son of Suraphon). From 1989, **Jenpope Jobkrabunwan** assisted, with his revival of huge luk thung concerts featuring veteran performers, as did the revival of the "Mon Rak Luk Thung" television show, which brought classics to a young audience. And finally, the move by some teeny-bopper stars like **Got Chakraband** away from pop to full-time luk thung has brought many younger listeners to the style. There is now a debate about whether some of these new stars are just pretty faces, manufactured just like pop and rock, with little of the vocal expertise required to sing luk thung.

DJ Jenpope says that luk thung has never really lost its popularity. Just check out a provincial cassette store, he says, and you'll see two thirds of the stock is luk thung.

Mor Lam

Ask a Thai in Bangkok about **Isan** (the Thai name for the Lao-dominated northeastern region) and they'll come up with the usual images: it's poor, hot and arid, the people eat *som tam* (fiery hot, green papaya salad) and they speak Laotian. They might add there are fine boxers and great comedians, and, if they like luk thung, they may even mention **mor lam**, the traditional music of the Laotians, dominated by the sound of the bamboo mouth organ, the *khaen*.

Folk forms usually fade as pop music gains in popularity – and as a developing country shifts from a rural to an urban society – but in Isan the traditional forms of mor lam coexist with modern forms. The big shows by major stars like **Jintara Poonlarp**, **Pornsak Songsaeng** and **Chalermphol Malaikham** are very similar in style to luk thung events, and most mor lam singers can sing in both styles. In fact, over the past ten or fifteen years, mor lam stars have been challenging their luk thung counterparts. The subject matter of the two styles is similar, and there are some musical similarities in terms of presentation. But the rhythms of mor lam are funkier, the melodies a little different and the rapid-fire, rap-like vocals are delievered in Laotian. And while luk thung is a syncretistic form, created from a range of modern styles, contemporary mor lam is a direct descendant of the ancient folk music of the Laotians.

At its most basic, mor lam is formed around the *mor lam* (master of singing the lam style) and a *mor*

Music to box to – Mor Lam

khaen (khaen player). Singers narrate stories and epics, rush into courting jousts or tell the news, varying their delivery from sad to joyous, while wailing, whooping and compelling the audience to listen and dance. All the while, the music is driven by the punchy tones of the khaen (a mouth-organ complete with drone), as the mor khaen vamps around the singer or sets off on a solo. The effect is mesmerising and a performance can last all night.

Traditional mor lam comes in as many as fifteen different forms, according to National Artist **Ken Dalao**. These range from solo singing or khaen playing (*lam pun* and *mor lam dio*) to several genres with two or three singers who compete, backed by khaen (*mor lam glawn*, the best known trad style). Other forms are Buddhist sermons narrated and sung in lam style (*tet lae*), while many theatrical genres involve troupes of performers (*mor lam mu* and *mor lam ploen*), and there is a special ceremony to cure people afflicted by bad spirits, which is performed by elderly women (*mor lam pee fah*).

Dalao performs with his wife, **Bunpheng Faiphewchai**, and the first and only female mor lam National Artist, **Chaweewan Damnoen**. Unlike mor khaen, who are largely self-taught, he studied with his uncle for a year, mainly learning texts, and started singing at sixteen. He has been at it for fifty years: "You must be literate to

learn texts about history, religion and folk tales, you must know *dhamma* (Buddhist teachings) and the arts generally. After all that, you can start learning to sing and how to be a mor lam performer".

A performance by this trio is scintillating. Before they start, the mor lam perform a *wai khru* ritual, praising the teacher. In a quiet room, Dalao makes a *wai* (prays) on his knees to a tray that contains *kai* (articles of worship), usually from the mor lam's teacher: five pairs of candles and flowers in banana leaves, a pair of large candles, a bottle of rice wine, a comb, some hair and a one baht coin. He does this before every performance.

On a simple stage with a couple of hanging microphones, the three mor lam and a mor khaen kick off the show with a loud '*Oh la naw!*' (Oh Fortune!) and in turn each singer runs through a few words of respect for their teachers, a greeting to the assembled villagers, and a description of the event being celebrated, which could be a funeral or the completion of a new house. Then the real music begins as the mor lams take turns in verbal jousting. They sing, then move off to dance while another takes the mike, before returning to savage the others with their wit and virtuosity. They move through the slow mor lam rhythm (*lam tan san*) and on to the choppy rhythms of *lam tan yao* before hitting the danceable *lam toei*. The gig ends at daybreak with the conclusion, *sarup*, in a plaintive style.

Recently, a new turbo-charged, electrified version of mor lam glawn has developed. This style, called **mor lam sing**, has partly arisen as a reaction to the popularity of string and pop groups, and also because the younger generation likes the faster rhythms, and the chorus girls in very, very short skirts. Small, exciting gigs by groups from the urban centres of Khoen Kaen and Ubon Ratchathani take place all over Isan.

Traditional mor lam performer Chaweewan is disgusted by what she calls this vulgarisation of mor lam. She says the young performers aren't trained properly and have no understanding of the mor lam's role. "It's about money," she says, "and it is debasing our culture." Videos of pretty, scantily-clad mor lam singers are available and there are even how-to videos available for would-be stars. Ken Dalao is more philosophical, however. "It won't last, it's just a fashion. Mor lam glawn has been going for hundreds of years; it'll still be going in a hundred years, too."

Mor Lam pin-up, Jintara Poonlarp

Both have a point. Mor lam has survived because it is adaptable, still a relevant part of people's lives, in both its traditional and modern forms. When central-Thai *likay* started to make in-roads into Isan, the Isan counterpart *mor lam mu* developed to challenge the Siamese invader. And when luk thung did the same, mor lam changed again to *lam ploen* (the basic large show format for troupes of mor lam), incorporating elements of both styles but in a Laotian context. The point is that much *mor lam sing* is fun and exciting. It still features the

khaen and not the synthesizer, and it is what the younger generation wants.

You can easily find mor lam and mor lam sing at temple fairs in Isan or around Bangkok, and at festivals, especially at New Year in April. For more on mor lam, see also the article on Laos, on p.170.

Kantrum

Most visitors to the lower northeastern towns of Surin and Buriram are attracted by the elephant races in Surin or the kite festival in Buriram. Others go for the majestic Khmer temple ruins of Khao Phanom Rung (as in Carabou's Lintel Song) and Muang Tam. Most miss out on lower Isan's best kept secret – **kantrum**.

While mor lam is the music of the Laotians in Isan, kantrum is the music of the Thai-Cambodians who live near the Cambodian border. This fast-action dance style developed alongside local forms of traditional Cambodian music like *jariang* (folk narratives) and *ruem-trosh* (old New Year dances). *Cho-kantrum*, the traditional form, incorporates a pair of singers, two kantrum drums, *ching* (temple bells), *krab* (wooden sticks) and the *tro*, a two-string fiddle. The fiddle operates like the khaen in mor lam, supporting and vamping lines around the singers. About fifteen years ago, musicians in Surin started to electrify the sound, adding an electric bass, drum kit, electric *phin* (a lute with between two and four strings) and a chorus of cute dancers. Modern kantrum was born.

For years, few outside the Thai-Cambodian community knew of the undisputed king of kantrum, **Darkie**. He exploded onto the scene in the late 1980s with his classic "Kantrum Rock" series. Since then, he's starred in a movie, seen luk thung stars try their hand at luk thung with kantrum rhythms and made some funky albums. In 1997 he topped it all with the first kantrum crossover album to have success in the mainstream pop market: *Darkie Rock II: Buk Jah.*

Shunning the synthesizer preferred by competitors like Khong Khoi, Oh-Yot and Ai Num

Muang Surin, Darkie put the wailing fiddle center stage, cranked up the rhythms (kantrum has a harder beat than even mor lam) and set off with his deep, distinctive voice. Like another Thai-Cambodian, mor lam star **Chalermphol Malaikham**, Darkie is able to handle all the three main roots styles and his album features kantrum songs along with mor lam and luk thung sung in Cambodian. Chalermphol is known mainly for his mor lam, so his challenge to Darkie is minimal. After a decade at the top, Darkie proves there's still only one king.

The music industry groups all three roots styles together as part of the luk thung market, and it seems that the sound will adopt more of a pop style. Elements of each will sometimes be combined into one song – Darkie is already doing it in fine style.

discography

The albums below include a number of European/US label CDs, however much Thai music (especially pop) is available only in the country. Bangkok's Tower Records and the Imagine chain have good stocks (though not much luk thung), and the Bangkok Music Company stores do fabulous reissues of Thai pop with hand-painted black and white covers. 'Greatest Hits' cassettes of luk thung, mor lam and kantrum can be found near railway and bus stations, and markets. For classical music, luk thung and folk music, Suksapan stores – a government-run books and stationery chain – is worth a look, especially the store on Ratchdamnoen Avenue in Bangkok, just around the corner from Khao San Road, is particularly good.

Classical

Compilations

 Music of Chiang Mai (Auvidis/Unesco, France).

Three well-recorded tracks of different ensembles. A piphat orchestra playing music for the likay theatre; Chinese influenced ritual music with lutes, two-string fiddle, flute, drum and percussion; and an 'old Thai instrumental ensemble' with two-string fiddles, zither, flute and drum.

Artists

Boy Thai

An attempt to create popular music by fusing Thai classical onto a Western base. Led by some of Kangsadan's members, but with more of an emphasis on drums and popular tunes.

Siamese Samba (Pisces Music, Thailand).

Kangsadan's leader Chaiyut Tosa-nga nods towards popular music – reggae with khlui bamboo flute and the ranat sounding like a steel drum. When it doesn't work, which is about half the time, it sounds like easy listening.

Fong Naam

Led by Bruce Gaston and virtuoso renat player Boonyong Ketkhong, this is one of the most interesting classical ensembles playing traditional and contemporary music.

Ancient Contemporary Music from Thailand (Celestial Harmonies, US).

A double album showing off a wide range of Fong Naam's artistry, from schmaltzy lounge numbers to Laotian folk and spectacular classical pieces for piphat and string ensembles. Comes with thorough notes on the structure of Thai music and how to listen.

The Hang Hong Suite (Nimbus, UK).

This excellent disc features spectacular and uplifting funeral music as well as parodies of the music of neighbouring cultures. Their other Nimbus disc, **The Sleeping Angel** (Nimbus, UK) includes piphat and mahori music as well as a splendid renat solo. Both discs are currently out of print, but are likely to be repackaged by Nimbus before long.

Siamese Classical Music Vols 1–5 (Marco Polo, Hong Kong).

For those with a particular interest in the development of Thai classical music, these albums introduce the main historical styles and different ensembles. Vol 1: *The Piphat Ensemble before 1400 AD*; Vol 2: *The Piphat Ensemble 1351–1767*; Vol 3: *The String Ensemble* (two-stringed fiddles, zither and percussion); Vol 4: *The Piphat Sepha* (music from the last two centuries); Vol 5: *The Mahori Orchestra* (including flute, strings, tuned and untuned percussion).

Kangsadan

A band set up in the late 1980s by Pisces Music to develop new interpretations of Thai classical music. Initially, the group depended on masters like the late flute player Khru Jamnien and jazz sax player Tewan Sapsanyakorn. Also included were youngsters like the Tosa-nga brothers who have since come to the fore.

The Golden Jubilee Overture (Pisces Music, Thailand).

In 1995, ranat expert Chaiyut Tosa-nga composed the Golden Jubilee Overture, performed here with other pieces for King Bhumibol Adulyadej's fiftieth year on the throne.

The Prasit Thawon Ensemble

Leading classical ensemble founded in 1958. It is based in Bangkok and named after celebrated musician and composer Master Prasit Thawon.

Thai Classical Music (Nimbus, UK).

Brilliant playing from some of Thailand's best performers, mainly of piphat style. Includes the overture "Homrong Sornthong" and, on the track "Cherd Chin", some scintillating dialogues between different instruments. The best example of piphat on CD, and superbly recorded.

Tribal Music

Compilations

Karenni: Music from the border areas of Thailand and Burma (Pan, Netherlands).

The Karen are the largest of the Thai hilltribes, and this is the most accessible of the recordings listed here. Exciting gong

Music from the border areas of Thailand and Burma

music, drums, and a whole range of instruments – xylophone, zithers, flutes and percussion – from the Karen's bamboo world.

◉ Lanna Thai: Instrumental Music of northwest Thailand (Pan, Netherlands).

Lanna Thai is the northwestern part of Thailand, around the city of Chang Mai. An excellent collection of music from the various hill-tribes – Hmong, Lahu, Lisu, Kayah, Chinese. Some of the music is rather hard-going, but there are some fine ensembles, processions and a great recording of a kayah tubular zither accompanied by clucking chickens – and people trying to hush them.

Luk Thung

Compilations

◉ Mon Rak Luk Thung (Love Country Style) (RS, Thailand).

Features the stars of a 1990s television series based on the most successful Thai musical film ever made. An admirable effort at capturing the golden sounds of the seventies with strings and soft vocals. Hankies ready for the sad songs.

Artists

Got Chakrapand Arbkornburi

The rumour goes that the late Grammy founder Rewat Buddhinan, observing Got's middling rock career, told the singer to try his hand at luk thung. That was more than ten major luk thung releases ago, and Got is now the biggest name in the business. His looks and sweet voice make him a firm favourite, and his pop and rock sound has even brought youngsters back to luk thung.

◉ Rak Khun Yinkhwa Kry (I Love You More Than Another) (MGA/Grammy, Thailand).

This mega-selling album features a catchy monster hit, "Setthakit Han Sorn", about the effects of the economic crisis on the Thai people. Got doesn't have the emotional power of Monsit but the modern, flawless production on this album makes up for some of these deficiencies, and he moves with ease between ballads and dance numbers. The upbeat sound of the new generation.

Pompuang Duangjan

When Pompuang died in 1994, some 200,000 people attended her royally-sponsored cremation at Wat Thep Kradan in Suphanburi, and a nation mourned the loss of its greatest singer. No one could sing luk thung with her range and emotional power. Her career stretched from the end of the golden period, when she sang with Sayan Sanya, to the development of dancefloor-oriented electronic luk thung.

◉ Pompuang Li Bor Sor (Pompuang – Many Years) (Topline, Thailand).

An essential two-CD or cassette set (each can be bought separately) that covers most of Pompuang's greatest hits. The classics on Vol 1, *Pleng Wan* (Sweet Songs), like "Chao Na Sang Friend" (Rice Farmer Without a Partner) and "Kwam Rak Mun Ya Comb" (Love is Like a Bitter Medicine) have never been bettered. Vol 2, *Pleng Man* (Exciting Songs) collects up-tempo dance tracks like "Noo Mai Lu" (I Don't Know) and "Uh Uh Raw, Jang" (Hmm, He's Really Handsome).

Monsit Khamsoi

A northeasterner who failed at every talent contest, considered too ugly to make it, Khamsoi captured the hearts of the entire nation with his humility and his fabulously soft, emotive voice. His rise to fame coincided with the late 1990s revival in luk thung.

◉ Khai Kwai Chuay Mae (Selling the Buffalo To Help Mum) (Sure, Thailand).

This cassette, along with **◉ Sang Nang** (Sure, Thailand), established Monsit as one of the biggest stars in luk thung in the 1990s. Simple arrangements and sweet melodies provide the perfect backdrop for Monsit's high-pitched, haunting voice, as he sings soulful reinterpretations of the classics.

Boontone Khon–Num

Boontone is firmly in the pop style of wacky threesome Samtone, a band which mixed up luk thung, with a nod to mor lam, in a comic pop style. Cheeky lyrics and catch phrases that fit the turbulent times have propelled Boontone to stardom.

◉ Wah Laiti (M Star, Thailand).

During the economic crisis, Boontone brought comic relief with his song "Bai Tam IMF", in which he sings sarcastically that if you want to know where the money in your pocket will come from for all these government-sponsored 'Buy Thai' or 'Visit Thai' campaigns then just 'go and ask the IMF'.

Arpaporn Nakornsawan

Another fast-rising star from the northeast, Arpaporn is part of the new wave of stars who sing a more pop-oriented style, with flashy costumes, racy shows and lots of chat. She moves between luk thung and mor lam. Traditionalists hate her but the kids like the excitement.

◉ Lerk Leow, Kha (We've Split Up, Thanks) (Boxing Sound, Thailand).

When Arpaporn put the song "Laerk leow, kha" on everyone's lips in 1997, she started a craze: many other singers, including Boontone Khon-num, replied to her hookline with "Long Lerk Du Si" (Just Split Up and See What Happens). The humourous, street savvy side of luk thung.

Sunaree Ratchasima

The gap left in luk thung by the death of Pompuang Duangjan was filled by Sunaree Ratchasima. Sunaree's pure voice has always been a favourite of those who like their luk thung mellow and melancholic. She is a master of the ballad, and smart enough to stick with what she does best.

 Sip-See Pleng Wan (14 Sweet Songs) Vols 1–4 (Sure, Thailand).

Four volumes representing Sunaree's career so far, with all the major hits. Vol 1 features "Muh Ter Mai Fie Na" (Microphone and Spotlight), Vol 2 "Tang Sai Mai" (New Way), Vol 3 "Friend Chan Mai Dawng Raw" (My Boyfriend Doesn't Have to be Handsome) and Vol 4 "Glap Bai Tam Mia Du Gorn" (Go Back to See The Wife).

Sodsai Rungphothong

Sodsai Rungphothong is a veteran luk thung singer from the central region. Never one of the biggest stars, he toiled for years before deciding to re-record a song he had written years before. The song, "Rak Nong Porn" caught everyone's attention just as luk thung began its present revival.

Rak Nong Porn (I Love Nong Porn) (Topline, Thailand).

The killer comeback by veteran Sodsai, with the title track generating two million in sales. From the opening single guitar line and Sodsai's wailing, pitiful "Oh! Nong Porn" you know this is an instant classic. Old-style luk thung – jangling temple bells and brass blaring, and Sodsai wailing over it all, breaking with emotion. Stirring stuff.

Sayan Sanya

A poor rice farmer from the central heartland around Suphanburi with a long jaw, nose and a funny mole on his chin, Sayan paid his dues singing wherever he could before he rose to stardom in the 1970s. He has the most mellifluous voice in the business and recorded with Pompuang Duangjan.

Sayan: Dao Thong (Sayan: Golden Star) (CA Studio, Thailand).

The sad solo trumpet on the opening track sets the moody tone for the modern master to reveal his honeyed voice on this superb greatest hits collection. This is classic 1970s luk thung from the era of big shows and massive chorus lines; the brass – before keyboards and Casiotones made everything bland – echoes and swirls around these sad tales.

Suraphon Sombatjalern

Born and bred in Supanburi, the heartland of luk thung, the style grew up with Suraphon's career.

 **Luk Thung Talap Thong** (Onpa, Thailand).

The definitive collection of greatest hits from the greatest of them all. Great voice, great songs, great backing. Includes songs that really set the style's future direction, "Na Da Sao Vienne" (Tears of the Laotian Girl) and "Sip-hok Pi Hen Kwam Lang" (Sixteen years of Memories). Siamese soul.

Mor Lam and Laotian Music

Compilations

Instrumental Music of Northeast Thailand (King, Japan).

One of the best collections of traditional Laotian instrumental styles on CD. Many styles are played: *soeng* (group mor lam),

southern Laotian tunes and styles, khaen solos and some particularly fine bong lang. The khaen playing by acknowledged master Thongkham Thaika is outstanding.

Mo Lam Singing of Northeast Thailand (King, Japan).

Chaweewan Damnoen headlines this fine collection of many *lam* (singing) styles, including *wai khru* (paying respects to teacher), lam glawn, lam ploen and songs from Laos. Includes rarely heard *lam phi fah*, for a musical ceremony to drive out bad spirits from someone possessed. Thongkham Thaika is the excellent khaen player.

Artists

Jintara Poonlarp

Now on her twenty-fifth release, Jintara Poonlarp has been the undisputed Queen of Mor Lam for much of the decade. The northeasterner's earthy, smokey voice is powerful and compelling – forget those pretty-faced singers, this is the real thing.

Luam Hit Baet Pi (Master Tape, Thailand).

Her biggest hits in two volumes. Vol 1 features slow, plaintive mor lam, the closest Thailand has to the blues, with a few luk thung songs. Vol 2 showcases mor lam dance songs with the hits "Pi Ja Jeap Dong Nai?" (Where Do You Hurt?) and "Chao Bao Hai" (The Groom's Gone).

Isan Slété

A six-piece group put together by academic and multi-instrumentalist Dr. Jareonchai Chonpairot and led by Saman Hongsa. Saman's wife, Sri-ubon Hongsa, is the female vocalist and the khaen player is Thawee Sridamanee. The Hongsas have an electronics shop and most of the musicians have day jobs.

Songs and Music from Northeast Thailand (GlobeStyle, UK).

A wide cross-section of Laotian mor lam styles from the verbal jousting of "Lam Toei Thammada" to all-action lam ploen. Also featured is the ancient instrumental style, *bong lang,* named after a wooden xylophone tied to a tree, and it includes the *woad,* a set of bamboo panpipes.

The Flower of Isan/Isan Slété Songs and Music from North-East Thailand

Pornsak Songsaeng

Though his star has dimmed of late, as he faces the rising popularity of younger, more handsome mor lam singers, Pornsak has been at the top for over ten years. His sharp voice is instantly recognisable, at home moaning and wailing, or delivering the trademark rap-like mor lam. He usually has some of the best backing musicians in his band, and releases high quality recordings.

 Hot: Volumes 1 & 2 (JKC, Thailand).

A two-disc collection (discs can be bought separately) covering the biggest hits from the past decade. Jangling temple bells, driving electric phin (Laotian lute), the khaen and Pornsak's inimitable powerful voice.

Kantrum

Artists

Darkie

For more than a decade Darkie has been pumping out his fast-paced Thai-Cambodian dance music, kantrum, in the lower northeast. Driven by the funky fiddle and drums, kantrum is now popular outside the region. Darkie is head and shoulders above everyone else, a result of his powerful voice and commitment to using a real fiddle instead of keyboards.

Darkie, Rock II: Buk Jah (Movie Music, Thailand).

The first ever kantrum crossover: a hit album nationwide. Kantrum features alongside mor lam and luk thung sung in Cambodian. Darkie's booming voice moves from rap-like delivery to sobs and wails, shadowed closely by the fiddle and some funky rhythms. Unmissable.

Kantrum Rocks I & II (M&M, Thailand).

These seminal late 1980s recordings are still available from vendors. Raw-edged and full of hard beats, Darkie's rise to fame started with these albums.

Khong Khoi

Khong Khoi has emerged as Darkie's main challenger in recent years. His strong voice and good looks have made him popular with the younger generation.

Siaow Woy (PR Sound, Thailand).

An up-country recording with a roughness that Khong Khoi usually smoothes over in his Bangkok releases, but the smooth delivery and pop-oriented sound remains, with synths replacing the fiddle.

String and Songs for Life

Compilations

12 Khon, 12 Baep (Twelve People, Twelve Styles) (KC, Thailand).

A good compilation including most of the big names of the songs for life movement: Caravan, Pongsit Kampee and Carabou. Released for the twenty-fifth anniversary celebrations of the Democracy Movement, in October 1998.

Artists

Carabou

Ad Carabou (Yuenyong Ophakul) spent part of his youth in Manila, where he avidly watched Freddie Aguilar's shows. His six-member outfit debuted in 1981 and over the next fifteen albums went on to massive fame. Influential lyrics about social problems made them very popular as supporters of underdogs, but sadly, the music remains mired in the rock clichés and Dylanesque acoustics.

Made in Thailand (Krabue, Thailand).

Dating from the height of Carabou's popularity in the mid-1980s, *Made in Thailand*, their fifth album, was right in tune with the times and targeted social problems like consumerism, the sex trade and a failing education system. **Ameri-koi** (Krabue, Thailand) is even more nationalistic than the previous one – it's title means Greedy America – but it also hits out at Thai migrant workers exploited by labour brokers. Ad's voice is quite unique, though some find it grating.

Modern Dog

Four ugly students from Chulalongkorn University win a talent contest and search for a record deal. They ignore the major companies and go with up-and-coming indie label Bakery Music. Singlehandedly they have kicked off the alternative rock craze of the 1990s.

Modern Dog (Bakery Music, Bangkok).

An important release for Thai rock music. Modern Dog turned the rock world upside down with this album of self-penned alternative songs. The catchy love song, "Korn" (Before), stayed at the top of local charts for weeks due to singer Pod's unique singing style and witty lyrics.

THAILAND

Tibet

raising the roof

Tibet, the 'Roof of the World', long held a fascination for travellers from the West (the first Europeans penetrated Lhasa only in the early years of this century), and it continues to exert a strong hold on the imagination. Films like Seven Years in Tibet and Kundun evoke a 'lost kingdom' permeated by an esoteric form of Buddhism and by ritual and meditation: aspects to which the music certainly provides a soundtrack – 'New Age' before the term was invented. But the tragic story of a culture suppressed and a leader in exile brings other powerful resonances. **Mark Trewin** reports.

Tibetan civilisation, with all its cultural and religious heritage, came close to complete destruction following the invasion by Communist China in 1950. In the darkest days of the Cultural Revolution, all but a few of Tibet's six thousand monasteries – the main centres of culture and learning – were destroyed. During the last decade or so, however, political reforms in China have led to a controlled revival: selected monastic centres have been re-opened, and the cultural noose has been loosened to the extent that traditional classical and folk songs are broadcast by the state-run organisations in Lhasa. Meantime, across the countryside, visitors can encounter a rich and largely neglected world of popular music-making.

There are large Tibetan populations in Kham (the Chinese provinces of Sichuan and Yunnan) and Amdo (Qinghai and Gansu), but it is in the peripheral Himalayan regions – in Bhutan, Nepal, Sikkim and Ladakh – and among the exile communities throughout the world that the Tibetan people have most conspicuously preserved their shattered cultural heritage. It is largely from outside Tibet itself, therefore, that archival and commercial recordings have become readily available in the Western marketplace.

Ritual Music

Tibet is justly famous for its ancient and unique **Buddhist traditions**, in which music forms an essential part of ritual. Behind the stereotyped images of rows of seated monks chanting in the diffused glow of butter-lamps, there is a complex realm of sensory experience involving extraordinary musical phenomena quite unknown in any other part of the world. Just as Tibetan Buddhism was a unique development of the Mahayana form of Buddhism originating in India, its vocal and instrumental traditions have become distinctly Tibetan in character, and rank supreme among the country's various cultural expressions.

Generally speaking, music is used by monks as a vehicle for the recitation of sacred texts: the *sutras* (basic teachings of the Buddha) and the *tantras* (secret commentaries). The exact form the music takes, however, varies considerably according to the function and importance of the ritual, with the more impressive and dramatic musical forces employed to heighten and emphasise particular parts of the liturgy, especially at certain occasions of the ritual calendar.

Annual **festivals** are thus elaborate affairs which, in part at least, may take the form of outdoor public spectacles involving *cham* (masked dance-

DAVID LEWISTON/ELLIPSIS ARTS

Ritual orchestra in Khampagar Monastery, India

dramas), oracles, the exhibition of huge *thangkas* (Buddhist images) and large-scale exorcism rites. Festivals were revived at many Tibetan monasteries in the 1980s, and some of the most spectacular take place at the principal monasteries of central Ladakh, a relatively accessible district of Indian Kashmir.

On a routine basis, all monks learn the fundamental **chant** styles which accompany daily rituals, including unaccompanied recitations of principal texts and beautiful choral hymns used to deliver special poetic verses. Often these chants are quietly accompanied by the principal musical instruments – the cymbals (*bübchal*) and large frame-drums (*nga*) – which outline the metrical structure of the melodic formulae prescribed for each text. By contrast, in a more specialised, profound chanting style known as *yang*, all metrical sense disappears as the booming resonances of every drum-stroke mark the initiation of individually-intoned syllables, each of which is sustained in a low register, and subjected to subtle tonal inflections and embellishments.

These powerfully moving chant styles are a special feature of the more esoteric **Tantric rituals**, in which the participants come into ecstatic contact with the nature of the invoked deities. Such higher-status rituals typically call for the use of special instruments, depending on their symbolic associations as well as their specific sound qualities.

Ever-present are the cymbals and drums which lead the ensemble, but the purely instrumental interludes present a dramatic contrast to the chanted sections of a ritual performance, and the **instruments** are now played in different ways, and much more loudly. The drums are thunderous, while the cymbals, in particular, prove to be a remarkably versatile instrument, rendering a wide range of sonorities ranging from loud resonant clashes to tightly-controlled rolls. Additional instruments may include the haunting calls of the conch-trumpet (*dungkar*) or thighbone trumpet (*kangling*), the incisive rattle of the pellet-drum (*damaru*) and the brilliant jangle of the hand-bell (*drilbu*). Lines of several long metal trumpets (*dungchen*) – a favourite of monks and Western listeners alike – occasionally contribute rousing blasts in a deep growl, as if coming from the mountains themselves. The only melodic instrument, also played in pairs, is the oboe (*rgyaling*). Its penetrating nasal sound, sustained by circular breathing, projects a soaring melody above the rich, sonorous textures of the rest of the ensemble. The effect is a powerful, majestic and scintillating wall of sound.

In the case of these more specialised musical styles and techniques, variety is also to be found among the four main monastic schools, the Nyingmapa, Sakyapa, Kagyupa and Gelugpa, and in the Bonpo tradition. Differences are also evident between their various sub-divisions, since

SIMON BROUGHTON

Ceremonial trumpets at Tashilhunpo Monastery, Shigatse, Tibet

Tibet

A giant thangka is displayed annually in the summer, with an attendant festival, in Drepung Monastery (Lhasa) and twice a year (winter and summer) in Drepung (Central Tibet). Thangka displays or cham festivals and dances also take place in Shigatse, Tsurphu, Reting, Mindroling, Samye, Sakya and Shalu, all major monastic centres in Tibet.

Ladakh

The main monastic festivals are Hemis (around late June) and Phyiang (end July/early August). Stok and Matho follow one another in early March. The Ladakh Festival, which lasts two weeks from the begining of September, is tourist-oriented but includes plenty of music and dancing. The tourist office in Leh should have exact dates. Tel: (91) 1982 52094.

many aspects of the performing style are transmitted orally rather than notated (the sung texts, which do not vary widely, only include a few musical elements). Thus distinctions can even be made between individual monasteries, as well as between various geographical regions where a particular tradition may dominate.

In terms of stylistic differences, the clearest contrast is between the **Nyingmapa**, which has been described as 'romantic' in style, and the **Gelugpa**, which is more 'classical'. The former is rhythmically more dramatic and melodically elaborate, and tends to make more of a feature of special instrumental styles. The latter is more restrained, even austere, and instruments are used less extensively.

However, within the Gelugpa tradition, which dominated Central Tibet under the ruling Dalai Lamas, some exceptional vocal techniques were developed. These included a particular type of yang chanting known as *dzoke* (the voice of the hybrid yak) or **gyü-ke** (tantric voice), which is produced by forcing the voice into an exceptionally low register unusually rich in overtones. This produces a multiphonic – or chordal – texture where the subtle modifications of the vowel-sounds of successive syllables in the secret text, itself now disguised, are heard as sweeping timbres in the upper register – a sort of overtone singing. Gyüke still survives in Central Tibet and is so well-maintained that the chanting masters of exiled monasteries like Shechen in Kathmandu are recent arrivals from Tibet. This extraordinary style is particularly associated with the two Tantric colleges of **Gyüme** and **Gyütö** in Lhasa and the eastern district of Kham. The Gyütö tradition is among the most remarkable of the sacred Tibetan styles, and being maintained in exile in India, has achieved much attention in the West through field recordings and, more recently, concert performances.

Secular Music

Tibet may, musically speaking, be best-known for its distinctive ritual styles, but its secular heritage is also rich and varied. While in sacred music only wind and percussion instruments are used, strings are common in the secular tradition. Singing is the most prevalent form of music, often unaccompanied, or with traditional lute, violin, flute or percussion.

Although **secular music** has fared rather better under Chinese rule than the monastic music in Tibet itself – the official Lhasa-based performing arts institute has even toured in the West – Tibet's traditional musical styles of all kinds have also been actively promoted and conserved by the Tibetan exile community. It is only relatively recently, however, that the wide range of Tibetan musical forms associated with entertainment and everyday life has started to become more widely heard and appreciated. The principal guardian of this rich heritage outside Tibet is the **Tibetan Institute of Performing Arts**, founded by the Dalai Lama's government-in-exile shortly after he fled to India in 1959.

TIPA started life principally as a troupe of musicians, singers and actors specialising in **lhamo** (or *ache-lhamo*), a kind of opera from Central Tibet accompanied by cymbals and drum. Based on classical narratives with Buddhist themes, these music dramas are nevertheless secular in orientation and were designed (rather like medieval mystery plays) to educate people in and attract people to Buddhist belief. The sung texts are interspersed by improvised and typically comical episodes, as well as dramatic instrumental effects. This enchanting and lively genre provides a fascinating insight into the nature of Buddhist experience in Tibetan culture. A new phenomenon in Tibet itself is modernised lhamo, with added Tibetan, Chinese and Western instruments.

Other genres, once supported by Tibet's wealthy families, are also enjoying a revival. **Nangma** and **töshe**, generally performed alternately, are very similar in style (although they differ in their melodic structure) and consist of suites of songs, usually beginning in a slow tempo and speeding up to the finish. They are sung (or played) in an elegant style, accompanied by the restrained sounds of the Tibetan lute (*dramnyen*), dulcimer (*gyümang*), two-string fiddle (*piwang*) and flute (*lingbu*), and followed by a lively dance where foot-stamping adds a percussive, syncopated element. The singing, dancing and instrumental rhythms all follow different patterns which makes it particularly difficult for the dramnyen player who may be expected to do all three at the same time. The singers (who are also the dancers) and instrumental players are usually different people. There are quite a few nangma karaoke-style clubs in Lhasa these days (see overleaf).

Gar, another 'classical' form (which includes specific songs and nangma-style pieces) also features outdoor ceremonial music, performed by loud shawms and kettledrums in honour of the Dalai Lama and other dignitaries; similar instru-

MARK TREWIN

Gar-style ceremonial ensemble in Leh, Ladakh

ments may also be heard in the ceremonial and social music of Ladakh and other Himalayan regions.

The Tibetans are great singers and there's a great variety of **folksong** styles – work songs, courting songs, wedding songs, pilgrimage songs and even thieves' songs. Particularly celebrated are the long, unaccompanied **lu** songs, sung without prescribed rhythm in a high voice with glottal vibrations. Their difficult and archaic technique makes them

much appreciated when performed by buskers in Lhasa's main square or in government-sponsored concerts.

Another important element of Tibet's musical legacy is the sung epic of **Gesar**, Tibet's hero protector and avenger, which harks back to the mighty empire of the eighth century. The bards, alternating narration and singing, often claim to be directly inspired by Gesar in a trance, although there are few epic bards left in Tibet today.

New Directions, New Sounds

Officially sanctioned groups such as TIPA, which present a solid pan-Tibetan identity, exist to preserve traditional culture (albeit in a rather 'conservatoire' style) and have been cautious about experimenting with modern idioms. But musical life in exile is not just about preservation. In fact many young Tibetans show a creative versatility and eclecticism which often shocks Western traditionalists more than their own elders. Nor is this just a recent phenomenon. The seeds of change were already taking place in pre-Communist Tibet where, by the 1940s, recordings of popular music from India, China and the West were freely available – including, according to Heinrich Harrer (of *Seven Years in Tibet* fame), the latest hits of Bing Crosby.

It was nevertheless the young refugees newly arriving in the Himalayan regions during the 1960s who started to embrace Western music more actively. Being fiercely anti-Chinese, and remaining stateless in India, they rejected musical influences from these countries, turning instead to the West for both musical and political inspiration and support. With the growth of grassroots bands such as **Rangzen Shönu** (Freedom Youths) during the 1980s, American country, rock and protest music became important influences in creating a new form of Tibetan folk music that could provide a way of expressing the political hopes and frustrations of young exiles.

This home-grown music, foreshadowing the more mature and polished fusions of the 1990s, was made possible by the availability of cheap cassette technology in North India. Here, among other Tibetan groups native to the Himalaya,

TIBET

different forms of new music have also emerged during the last two decades. Even in isolated Bhutan, local versions of **Indian popular music** hold an immense appeal for young people, posing a threat to the survival of indigenous music sufficient in scale, it seems, to be of concern to more than just the tradition-conscious authorities in that country. Indian film music, especially in the popular *ghazal* form, is also the major influence on new music in Ladakh. Local stars such as **Phunsok Ladakhi** have accordingly blended modern Indian and Western influences with indigenous styles.

All these innovations were initially developed by, and for, an increasingly active Tibetan-speaking youth culture in exile. In Tibet itself, the Chinese authorities countered the influence of this music – often smuggled across the Himalaya – with the production of sanitised, censored cover versions. But with the partial easing of restrictions in the 1980s, a new Tibetan pop music emerged on the High Plateau. It is of two different kinds, each of them having to negotiate political restrictions. For example, reference to religion and lamas (especially the Dalai Lama) is forbidden. Some songs, like "Chörten Karpo", get round this by using metaphoric language: *chörten karpo*, the 'white stupa [a type of Buddhist monument] that we will always carry in our hearts', is understood to refer to the Buddhist faith, or even the Dalai Lama himself.

One very popular strand of new music, **Tibetan pop**, is heavily influenced by the worst Chinese equivalent (electric organ with synthetic beats and easy melodies). This music is played all over Tibet in public places and in the innumerable karaoke bars in urban centres (most of which play mainly Chinese pop). The leading figures are the Kham singer **Yatong**, and the Lhasa singers **Dadön**, now exiled in the US, and **Jampa Tsering**.

Another kind of new Tibetan music, however, grafts new lyrics, often with moralistic, if not covertly political, tones, onto traditional melodic and instrumental themes. It is sung with the dramnyen (lute) in the Central Tibetan style, or with the mandolin in the Amdo (northeast Tibet) style. There is a wealth of new musicians, most of them peasants who busk round the country to beg during the winter months. As they are neither rich nor part of any established infrastructure there are very few tapes available, but most Lhasans are able to sing the most famous of these songs.

Another important feature of Lhasa's music is the opening of traditional **nangma music bars**, a sort of Tibetan version of the karaoke bar, where customers jump up on stage to sing and dance classical nangma and töshe songs. Opened for the first time in 1998, they are currently seriously threatened by the government, partly because they challenge the Chinese businesses of karaoke bars, and partly because they advocate, by their very existence, a traditional music heritage instead of a modern one.

There are also some Chinese musicians who seem to have a more sincere curiosity and interest in Tibetan music. The group **Nomad** plays an unremarkable kind of Tibetan-influenced New Age music, and Chinese pop star **Dadawa** (see p.53) has gained enough popularity – or notoriety – to attract the attention of the outside world, though her music is unremarkable and the Chinese perspective on Tibetan idioms which it presents raises uncomfortable moral questions.

Tibet in the West

Rather different is the Western perspective on Tibetan music and culture which has largely driven developments outside Tibet. Long before the arrival of Tibetans in the Western world there was a fascination with the rich and mysterious sonorities of Tibetan ritual music, especially among students of Tibetan Buddhism and 'serious' composers, among whom a tradition of **experimental composition** can be traced back to the pioneering creations of the American composer Henry Eichheim in the 1920s, through Karlheinz Stockhausen to the most recent music of minimalist composer Philip Glass, who wrote the soundtrack to *Kundun* (1997).

In a not entirely unrelated vein, more popular manifestations of this Western interest emerged with the evocative soundscapes of **New Age music** in the 1970s, whose influence on present-day meditation and peace music is evident. American Buddhists **Henry Wolff and Nancy Hennings**, for example, were pioneers in this field with their first album of *Tibetan Bells* in 1971, leading to a further series of recordings in the 1980s in collaboration with The Grateful Dead's drummer and World Music promoter, **Mickey Hart**. This venture in turn inspired **Philip Glass**'s soundtrack to his earlier film, *Koyaanisqatsi*. In 1981, the French musician **Alain Presencer** produced *The Singing Bowls of Tibet* (Saydisc), a remarkable album of compositions and arrangements based around the enchantingly ethereal sounds of these unusual instruments used for meditational and other religious purposes.

The West's attraction to the more pacific and meditational aspects of Tibetan music has result-

Yungchen Lhamo

Yungchen Lhamo

Singer **Yungchen Llamo** fled Tibet in 1989 and has forged a career for herself as one of Tibet's most powerful voices in exile. "I am determined to make a path as a solo vocalist", she says. "My childhood was one of such despair and poverty. Since I escaped, by foot over the Himalaya like so many other Tibetans, I have been able to find freedom in the West. Part of the Chinese rationale for the occupation of Tibet is that the Tibetan people are backward and inferior. By forging a path for Tibetan artists, I am showing what we really can do if we have freedom. Tibet has many young, courageous and talented people working to keep our culture dynamic and alive. Tibetan culture will not die, nor remain static. We will grow as part of the modern world as long as we have a chance of freedom – something most Tibetans unfortunately do not have."

ed in new music which is highly variable in style and, it must be said, quality. Some of the more recent developments, however, are ravishing and it's well worth checking out the range of CDs which have been appearing on the market during the 1990s. Thankfully gone (almost), are the gloomy synthesizer textures and poor production quality which dominated much early material.

The growth of dharma centres in the West, serving Western Buddhist converts as well as an increasing number of Tibetan exiles, has created a growing market for meditation music intended primarily as aids to religious practice. There are now a number of CDs featuring individual Tibetan monks, either solo or in creative collaboration with Western artists, and some releases such as those of the Belgian resident teacher **Lama Karta** (Milan) are finding a niche among wider audiences. So too has the teaming up between the ubiquitous Mickey Hart and the now strangely famous **Gyütö Monks**, whose second album, *Freedom Chants*, included a live performance by Hart with Japanese-American music-guru **Kitaro** and Philip Glass in their honour, and heralded the monks' exposure to wider audiences in Glass's music for the film *Kundun*.

Kitaro, with the help of Richard Gere, also collaborated with Tibetan musician **Nawang Khechog**, enabling him to become one of the first Tibetan artists to achieve widespread acclaim in their own right. Another recent – and again apparently incongruous – collaboration was that between the Tibetan Buddhist nun **Choying Drolma** and the American progressive guitarist **Steve Tibbetts**, exhibiting a new move towards a sensitivity and equality in the partnership.

The most remarkable recent success, however, has been that of the singer **Yungchen Lhamo** (see feature box) who has performed at WOMAD and recorded on the RealWorld label. Her sheer musicality and personal vision transcend both the topical fascination with things Tibetan and the psychological scars of the Tibetans themselves. The sense of longing which is evident in her music is not just for a free Tibet, but for a world in which all people can experience peace.

With thanks to Isabelle Henrion and Stephen Jones.

discography

Ritual and Folk

Compilations

Achelhamo/Celestial Female: Parts from Tibetan Opera (Pan, Netherlands).

Featuring Achelhamo and Amdo operatic styles, this disc is for confirmed devotees of Tibetan opera, but is worth listing as one of the few recordings featuring music from inside Tibet itself. Recorded by Chinese scholar Tian Liantao in Lhasa and

Gansu.

 Amdo: The Tibetan Monastery of Labrang
(Ocora, France).

The Labrang monastery has been a major centre for the painful reconstruction of Buddhism in the Tibetan region of Amdo. Apart from the haunting vocal liturgy punctuated by cymbals and trumpets, this disc also features the monks adaptation of Chinese *shen-guan* music, as well as lively Amdo opera.

Dama Suna
(Erato/Detour, France).

Performed by the Tibetan Institute of Performing Arts, the cultural flagship of the Dalai Lama's government in exile based in Dharamsala, India. An unusually broad selection of mostly secular Tibetan music, and a useful and informative first-time buy. Contains nineteen tracks, including regional folksongs, nangma, gar, lhamo, as well as three atmospheric examples of ritual chant by the Gyütö monks. Good notes and lyric translations.

The Diamond Path: Rituals of Tibetan Buddhism
(Shanachie, US).

A vivid and colourful 1994 recording by David Lewiston of the Yamantaka Trochu rite from Khampagar Monastery, in the foothills of India's Western Himalayas. With a magnificent-sounding ritual orchestra including some thunderous dungchen trumpets, the ceremony gives 'the energy to dispel fear and to manifest infinite compassion'. It comes in one continuous track lasting over an hour.

Jigme Drukpa: Endless Songs from Bhutan
(Grappa, Norway).

Bhutanese and Tibetan-style folksongs sung by Jigme Drukpa, who also plays the Bhutanese bamboo flute, *yangchin* (hammer dulcimer) and dranyen (lute), seen as the national instrument of Bhutan. The disc, recorded when Jigme was on tour in Norway in 1998, claims to be the first Bhutanese folk music on CD. Song translations and synopses included.

Ladakh: Musique de monastère et de village
(Chant du Monde, France).

A nicely balanced package of field recordings of Ladakh's ritual and secular musical heritage. Part of a monastic service from Phyiang (Dregung Kagyupa) monastery exhibits contrasting chant styles, including the sustained yang style, and impressive instrumental interludes. The village folk music comes with lively oboes and kettledrums. Good notes, with some extraordinary chant notation.

The Music of Tibetan Buddhism (Rounder, US).

Three discs covering the four main Tibetan monastic orders recorded by Peter Crossley-Holland in 1961. There are impressive instrumental extracts from the first two sects and some extraordinary chant and overtone singing from the Gelugpa monks. With informative notes, this is a good introduction to ritual music.

Tibet Anthology (Wind Records, Taiwan).

The only current survey of music in Tibet itself, recorded in 1993–4 by Chinese scholar Mao Jizeng on six CDs. Sacred music is rather under-represented with just one disc, but there are good examples of lesser known forms of court music, ballads, folk songs and dance. Vol 1: *The Opera Music of Tibet*; Vol 2: *The Religious Music of Tibet*; Vol 3: *Tibetan Song and Dance Music*; Vol 4: *Tibetan Folk Songs*; Vol 5: *Tibetan Court Music and Instrumental Music*; Vol 6: *Tibetan Ballad Singing and Minorities' Music in Tibet*.

Tibet: Heart of Dharma
(Ellipsis Arts, US).

Recent field recordings of high quality by David Lewiston,

featuring ritual music from two contrasting traditions maintained in India: the Loseling college of Drepung monastery (Gelugpa), which specialises in the extraordinary dzoke multiphonic chant style more usually associated with the Gyütö college; and Khampagar monastery (Drukpa Kagyupa), which features dramatic instrumental styles. The 64-page booklet is an excellent introduction.

Tibet: Monks of the Sera Jé Monastery
(Amiata, Italy).

The Sera Monastery is still one of the principal monastic foundations in Lhasa, where it was rebuilt after the Chinese invasion and where rituals are continued to a limited extent. But like many monastic communities, it has also sprung up in exile – in the south Indian state of Karnataka. This CD presents instrumental ensembles and prayers (with some specialised chant styles) from the Gelugpa monastic ritual. It is by no means easy listening, but the colourful accompanying book helps.

Tibet: Musiques sacrée (Ocora, Frace).

Very listenable and atmospheric recordings made in monasteries in Nepal. Illustrates the contrasting styles of the Nyingmapa order (Tengboche monastery), with powerful instrumental episodes, and the more restrained chants (notably the sustained yang style) of the Gelugpa order (Thami monastery).

Tibetan Buddhist Rites from the Monasteries of Bhutan Vols 1–4 (Lyrichord, US).

A unique four-volume collection of field recordings from Bhutan made by John Levy in 1973. Available in a specially priced set or individually. Trumpets blast and cymbals crash with a real sense of presence. The excellent recordings feature monastic rituals of the Drukpa Kargyupa (dominant in Bhutan), but the Nyingmapa tradition is also represented. The fourth volume is a rare and fascinating compilation of Tibetan and Bhutanese folk music, featuring the enchanting music of the dramnyen lute.

Contemporary

Artists

Choying Drolma

Choying Drolma, born in Kathmandu in 1971 to Tibetan exiles, is a Buddhist nun from the Nagi Gompa nunnery in Boudhanath, Nepal.

TIBET

Chö (Rykodisc, US).

An unusual album resulting from an unlikely, but strangely successful, collaboration with US guitarist Steve Tibbetts. Combines yogic meditational songs with mainly acoustic Western instruments, achieving a lightness and clarity of sound texture which will appeal to those frustrated by the more heavy-handed synthetic crossovers.

Gyütö Monks

Originally a Tantric college in Lhasa, the Gyütö monastery, now relocated in India, trains monks in a unique style of yang chanting made famous in the West through concert tours since the mid-1980s, and latterly as a feature of Philip Glass' soundtrack to the film Kundun.

Freedom Chants (Rykodisc, US).

Produced by Mickey Hart, this album was recorded during their US tour in 1988, and exhibits their extraordinary chanting style.

Tibetan Buddhism: Tantras of Gyütö
(Nonesuch Explorer, US).

Reissue of two excellent 1973 field recordings from the monks' less dislocated setting of Dalhousie, North India, featuring extensive excerpts from the Mahakala and Sangwa Düpa Tantric rituals. Recorded by David Lewiston. Esoteric listening.

Nawang Khechog

After many years spent in India as a Buddhist monk, Tibetan flautist Nawang Khechog took up the didgeridoo whilst living in Australia, where he produced three albums before teaming-up with New Age/spiritual musician Kitaro in the US, where he now lives.

Karuna (Domo, US).

Produced by Kitaro, this imaginative album features Khechog's own style of experimental music, blending ambient sounds with the primal sounds of ancient cultures, including echoes of his native Eastern Tibet.

Yungchen Lhamo

The aptly-named 'Divine Songstress', from Tibet via Australia, has captivated live audiences worldwide with her haunting vocal style, and currently reigns supreme in the world of contemporary Tibetan music.

Coming Home (RealWorld, UK).

Fans of her first album, *Tibet, Tibet* are unlikely to be disappointed by this, her second. While the first concentrated on simple unaccompanied songs, the second, produced by Hector Zazou, is appealing to a wider audience with electronic and Western instruments. Although verging on a New Age sensibility, the accompaniments are generally inspiring and sensitive, and do not detract from her ever-soulful voice.

Vietnam

VIETNAM

ancient rock music

Vietnam, a long thin country winding along the shores of the South China Sea, was for far too long branded by its brutal jungle war. At last, with the end of the Cold War, its image has changed and the country has become a popular travel destination in southeast Asia. Yet who would guess that Vietnam boasts the oldest-known instrument in the world, the only percussion instrument that you don't touch, and a single-string instrument whose players rival guitarists in their virtuosity? **Philip Blackburn** reveals the secrets of Vietnam's extraordinary sounds.

China, France and America occupied Vietnam for one thousand, one hundred and ten years respectively, and their influences on art, architecture, food, fashion and music are roughly proportional. But the country has always had a knack for digesting ideas and making them its own: Taoist temples, chic berets and The Carpenters co-exist quite happily. Even India gets a look in, making Vietnam one of the few places where Indian and Chinese music meet. The Chinese influence is evident in operatic theatre and stringed instruments, while India bestowed rhythms, modal improvisations and several types of drum. Much later, during the nineteenth century, elements of European theatre and music were co-opted, and in recent decades most Vietnamese musicians received a classical, Western training based on the works of Eastern-bloc composers such as Prokofiev and Tchaikovsky.

While there are many imported ingredients that go to make up the musical soup, there are also some home-grown ones, notably the musical treasures of the fifty-odd hill tribes: people whose languages, costumes, music and traditions are quite distinct from that of the ethnic Vietnamese lowlanders. Music is the binding element in all Vietnam's traditional performing arts, particularly singing (*hat*), which is a natural extension to an already musical language.

Theatrical Music

Vietnam's traditional theatre, with its strong Chinese influence, is more akin to opera than pure spoken drama. The plots and characters are traditional and musical accompaniment – including a well-known repertoire of songs – forms an integral part of the performance. But nowadays the

Cai Luong - Vietnamese opera

JOHN CLEWLEY

two oldest forms, **cheo** and **tuong**, are struggling to survive, while even the more contemporary **cai luong** is losing out to television and the video recorder. Other traditional arts have seen something of a revival, however, most notably **water**

puppetry and folk-song performances. The stimulus came largely from tourism, but renewed interest in the trance music of *chau van* and the complexities of *tai tu* chamber music (see below) has been very much home-grown.

Vietnam's oldest surviving stage art, **hat cheo**, or folk opera, has its roots in the Red River Delta where it's believed to have existed since at least the eleventh century. Popular legends and stories of everyday events are performed, often with a biting satirical edge. The music, as with other forms of traditional Vietnamese theatre, is not composed for each play, but drawn from a common fund of music which has evolved over the years.

The cheo orchestra generally consists of flute, plucked and bowed strings, gongs and drums. Though the movements have become highly stylised over the centuries, cheo's free form allows the actors considerable room for interpretation; the audience demonstrates its approval, or otherwise, by beating a drum. cheo has the reputation of being anti-establishment, especially in its buffoon character who comments freely on the action, the audience and current events. So incensed were the kings of the fifteenth-century Le dynasty that cheo was banned from the court, while artists and their descendants were excluded from public office. Nowadays, the few cheo ensembles that still exist in northern Vietnam rely on scenes from unrelated libretti.

Hat tuong (known in southern Vietnam as *hat boi*) evolved from classical Chinese opera, which was probably introduced around the thirteenth century. It was originally performed for royal entertainment, before being adopted by travelling troupes. Its story lines are usually historical epics dealing with such Confucian principles as filial piety and relations between the monarch and his subjects. Tuong, like cheo, is governed by rigorous rules in which the characters are rendered instantly recognisable by their make-up and costume. Setting and atmosphere are conjured not by props and scenery but through nuances of gesture and musical conventions with which the audience are completely familiar – and which they won't hesitate to criticise if badly executed.

While performances of cheo and tuong are rare events these days, **hat cai luong**, or 'renovated theatre', is the most popular form of music drama in Vietnam today. If you see a large building with peanut and candy sellers outside, the chances are that there's a performance going on

inside. Cai luong originated in southern Vietnam in the early twentieth century, influenced by French theatre in its spoken parts, short scenes and relatively elaborate sets. The action is a tangle of historical drama and racy contemporary themes from the street, such as murder, drug deals and revenge. Its music is a similar hodgepodge: eighteenth-century chamber music played on amplified traditional instruments for the set pieces; electric guitar, keyboards and drums during the scene changes. Cai luong's use of contemporary vernacular has made it highly adaptable and enabled it to keep pace with Vietnam's social changes.

The traditional music accompanying cai luong theatre originated in eighteenth-century Hué. Played as pure chamber music, without the voice, it is known as **nhac tai tu**, or 'skilled chamber music of amateurs'. This is one of the most delightful and tricky of all Vietnamese genres: the players have a great degree of improvisational latitude over a fundamental melodic skeleton. They must think and respond quickly, as in a game, and the resulting independently funky rhythms can be wild. Although modern conservatoire training fails to prepare students for this most satisfying of all styles, there is now a resurgence of interest by young players in learning the demands of tai tu.

Water puppetry (*roi nuoc*) is an art unique to Vietnam. The Thang Long National Puppet Theatre, with its singers and instrumentalists from Hanoi, has taken its colourful show around the world. Roi Nuoc's origins are obscure, beyond

Water puppet musicians

that it developed in the murky rice paddies of the Red River Delta and usually took place in spring when there was less farm work to be done. The earliest record of a performance dates from 1121

AD, which suggests that by this date water puppetry was already a feature of the royal court.

Obscured behind a split-bamboo screen, puppeteers standing waist-deep in water manipulate the wooden puppets, some of which weigh over 10kg, using long poles hidden beneath the surface. Dragons, ducks, lions, unicorns, phoenixes and frogs spout fire and smoke, throw balls and generally cavort – miraculously avoiding tangling the poles. Brief scenes of rural life, such as water-buffalo fights, fishing or rice-planting take place alongside lion and dragon dances, legendary exploits and a watery promenade of fairy-like immortals. Even fireworks emerge to dance upon the water, which itself takes on different characters, from soft-focus shimmering red and gold to seething and furious during naval battles.

The art of water puppetry was traditionally a jealously guarded secret handed down from father to son; women were not permitted to learn the techniques in case they revealed them to their husbands' families. This contributed to its decline until the art seemed in danger of dying out altogether. Happily a French organisation, *Maison des Cultures du Monde*, intervened and, since 1984, Vietnam's

water puppet troupes have played to great acclaim. The newly carved puppets, revamped programme and elaborate staging can be seen nightly in Hanoi and Ho Chi Minh City. Where before gongs and drums alone were used for scene-setting and building atmosphere, today's national troupes often maintain a larger ensemble, similar to hat cheo, including zithers and flutes. The songs are also borrowed from the cheo repertoire, particularly declamatory styles and popular folk tunes, and the show often includes a short recital of traditional music before the puppets emerge.

Traditional Music

One of Vietnam's oldest song traditions is that of **quan ho**, or 'alternate singing', a form which thrives in the Red River Delta, particularly Ha Bac Province, and has parallels among the north's ethnic minorities. These unaccompanied songs are usually heard in spring, performed by young men and women bandying improvised lyrics back and forth. Quan ho traditionally played a part in the courtship ritual and performers are applauded for their skill in complimenting or teasing their part-

Vietnamese Classical: the Imperial Music of Hué

The city of **Hué**, situated on the Perfume River in the centre of the country, was the last capital of the old Vietnamese kingdom, presiding from 1802 to 1945. The remains of the palace were devastated in the 1968 Tet Offensive, but UNESCO declared the complex to be a World Heritage Site in 1993, since when an extensive restoration process has been under way.

The city has a long heritage of dance and ceremonial music. From the early seventeenth century, 120 courtly dancers and musicians were trained at special conservatoires associated with the palace. The emperors required dignified instrumental music for their rituals and audiences, as well as the intimate chamber music (**ca Hué**) enjoyed by their refined people. These styles of ritual and chamber music might be called Vietnam's classical music tradition.

From the fall of the Republic of Vietnam in 1975 until 1993 there was no court music in Hué, although like the city itself, this too is being resurrected. Nowadays,

the court band, Nhac Cung Dinh, waits in costume every day in a side room of the palace to troop out to play when visitors appear. Some musicians are in their eighties, and because these genres do not allow for a

Hué band Doàn ca Hué

great deal of variation or free improvisation, little has changed since they performed for the emperor himself. They are now teaching the younger generations.

ner, earning delighted approval as the exchange becomes increasingly bawdy.

Hat chau van is an ancient, sacred ritual music used to invoke the spirits during trance possession ceremonies. Statues of a pantheon of goddesses are placed in shrines to the Mother Goddess, Thanh Mau, found in both Buddhist pagodas and village temples. During the performance of hypnotically rhythmic music (the performers may be one or many, male or female) a medium enters a trance state and is possessed by a chosen deity. Because of the anti-religious stance of the Vietnamese government until 1986, the style was practised in secret, though some pieces were adapted for inclusion in state-sponsored cheo theatre. **Pham Van Ty** is one of the leading musicians of this style. Chau van is currently being revived by older practitioners in its original religious setting, promoted by a class of nouveau riche keen for the goddesses to intercede and protect their business interests.

Although the song tradition known as **ca tru**, or *hat a dao*, dates back centuries, it became all the rage in the fifteenth century when the Vietnamese regained their independence from China. According to legend, a beautiful young songstress, A Dao, charmed the enemy with her songs of the verdant countryside and the way of life in the villages. Fascinated by her voice, the soldiers were encouraged to drink until they became incapacitated and could be pushed into the river and drowned. The lyrics of ca tru are often taken from famous poems and are traditionally sung by a woman. The singer also plays a bamboo percussion instrument, and is accompanied by a three-string lute (*dan day*) and drum. She has to master a whole range of singing styles, each differentiated by its particular rhythm, such as *hat noi* (similar to speech) and *gui thu* (a more formal style, akin to a written letter).

In the latter part of the twentieth century ca tru was little performed. It was not encouraged by the Communist government because of its past associations with the elite classes and, when it was performed in singing bars, with prostitution. In the last decade there has been a revival of interest, however, and a Hanoi ca tru ensemble, led by Nguyen Van Mui, was established. Ca tru is closely related to the song tradition of Hué, **Ca Hué**, which is now performed for tourists on sampans on the Perfume River.

Traditional Instruments

A visiting US politician, Hubert H. Humphrey, once stepped off a plane with the intention of smoothing relations by attempting a little Vietnamese – a tonal language. But instead of 'I am honoured to be here', listeners heard 'the sunburnt duck lies sleeping'. The voice and its inherent melodic information are behind all Vietnamese music, and most instruments are, to some extent, made to do what voices do: delicate pitch bends, ornaments and subtle slides.

According to classical Confucian theory, instruments fall into eight **categories of sound**: silk, stone, skin, clay, metal, air, wood and bamboo. Although few people play by the rules these days, classical theory also relates five occasions when it is forbidden to perform: at sunset, during a storm, when the preparations have not been made seriously, with improper costumes and when the audience is not paying attention.

Many instruments whose strings are now made of steel, gut or nylon originally had **silk** strings; silk is now out of fashion, more for acoustic than ecological reasons. The most famous of these, and unique to Vietnam, is the single-stringed **dan bau** (or *dan doc huyen*), an ingenious invention perfectly suited to its job of mimicking vocal inflections. Its one string, originally silk, is stretched over a long amplified sounding box, fixed at one end. The other end is attached to a buffalo-horn 'whammy bar' (tremolo arm) which can be flexed to stretch or relax the string's tension. Meanwhile, the string is plucked with a plectrum at its harmonic nodes to produce overtones that swoop and glide and quiver over a range of three octaves. Nowadays, the instrument is often used with a small electric amplifier so that its delicate, but extraordinary sound can be heard alongside other instruments. It is now generally played as a wild single-stringed electric guitar.

Other important 'silk' instruments include the *dan nguyet* (moon lute), which is frequently used in traditional singing and theatre and has a beautiful circular body from which it gets its name; the *dan day*, a three-stringed lute with a long fingerboard used in ca tru and unique to Vietnam; the *dan ty ba*, a four-stringed lute like a Chinese *pipa*; the *dan tranh*, a sixteen-string zither; the *dan nhi*, a two-string fiddle of Chinese origin with the bow running between the strings; and the *dan luc huyen cam*, a regular guitar with a fingerboard scalloped to allow for wider pitch bends.

In the **stone** category, a pile of rocks lies in the corner of the Research Institute in Ho Chi Minh City. This six thousand-year-old stone marimba, a **dan da**, is the world's second-oldest instrument, the oldest being an identical set now in Paris. Played with heavy wooden mallets, it sounds just as it sounded long ago with six ringing tones (D-

T'rung player with support

F-G-A-C-D) – a perfectly tuned pentatonic scale. The instrument originated from a particular slate quarry in the central highlands where the stones, formed from petrified wood, sing like nowhere else.

Amongst the **skins**, various kinds of drums (*trong*) are used, played with acrobatic use of the sticks in the air and on the sides. Some originated in China, while others were introduced from India via the Cham people. One example is the double-headed 'rice drum' (*trong com*), which was developed from the Indian *mridangam*; the name derives from thin patches of cooked rice paste stuck on each membrane.

Representing **clay**, four thimble-size teacups are held in the fingers and often played as percussion instruments for Hué chamber music. Representing **metal**, the *sinh tien*, **coin clappers**, are another invention unique to Vietnam, combining in one unit a rasping scraper, wooden clapper and a sistrum rattle made from old coins. Bronze **gongs** are occasionally found in minority music (such as that of the E-De tribe of the central highlands), but Vietnam is the only country in southeast Asia where tuned gamelan-type gong-chimes are not used.

Air, **wood** and **bamboo** furnish a whole range of wind instruments, such as the many side- and end-blown flutes used for folk songs and to accompany poetry recitals. The *ken*, a double-reed oboe, is played in funeral processions and other outdoor ceremonies. Five thin bones often dangle from the ken player's mouthpiece to suggest the delicate fingers of a young woman, while disguising the hideous grin necessary to play the instrument. The *song lang* is a slit drum, played by the foot, used to count the measures in tai tu chamber music, while the *k'longput*, a rack of horizontal tuned bamboo pipes, is the only percussion instrument you don't actually touch: instead, players clap their hands to produce deep resonances. It is native to the Bahnar people of the central highlands, who are said to have created it after hearing the wind blowing into the openings of bamboo in the forest. Similarly, the *t'rung* is a suspended ladder of tuned bamboo pipes sounding rather like a high xylophone and popular for its ability to imitate the sound of water.

Vietnamese music often imitates or evokes natural sounds, animals and birds. Many of the conservatoire-style pieces have descriptive titles and the various types of flute in Vietnamese music can manage very passable bird imitations. More imaginatively, there are small, carved wooden frogs with ridgey backs. When these are rasped with a wooden stick they emit spookily realistic froggy croaks and grunts.

New Folk

Turn on the television during the Tet Lunar New Year festivities and you can't miss the public face of Vietnamese traditional music: ethnic-costumed dancers, musicians and singers smilingly portraying the happy life of the worker. Great arrangements of well-known tunes from all over the country, including some token minorities' music, are spiced up with fancy hats and bamboo pianos. This choreographed entertainment known as **nhac dan toc cai bien**, or modernised folk music, has only been 'traditional' since 1956, when the Hanoi Conservatoire of Music was founded and the teaching of folk music was deliberately 'improved'.

For the first time, music was learned from written Western notation (leading to the neglect of improvisational skills while opening the way for huge orchestras), and conductors were employed. Tunings of the traditional eight modes were tempered to accommodate Western-style harmonies, while bizarre new instruments were invented to play bass and to fill out chords in the enlarged bands. Schools, with the mandate of preserving traditional music through 'inheritance development', took over from the families and professional apprenticeships which had formerly passed on the oral tradition.

Not surprisingly, a new hybrid was born out of all this. Trained conservatoire graduates have spread throughout the country, promoted through competitions and state-sponsored ensembles on TV, radio, and even in the lobbies of classier hotels. The new corpus of music and song arrangements has become an emblem of national pride and scientific improvement. Folk songs, melodies from the ethnic minorities, Mozart and Chinese tunes are all ripe fodder for the arranger's pen. Much to the chagrin of the few remaining traditional musicians outside this system, this is now the predominant folk-based music generally heard in public. Local tribal musicians in the central highlands were asked how they felt about their music being 'improved'. At first they replied what an honour it was for their music to be considered by city people, but after the official interview they privately confessed their horror.

Music for new folk is entertaining and accessible, albeit risking tawdriness. At its best, though, it can be an astonishing display of a lively new artform. One family of six brothers (and one sister-in-law), led by Duc Loi, formed a percussion group in Ho Chi Minh City under the name **Phu Dong**, the name of a legendary weakling baby who, on hearing that his country was being invaded by the Chinese, grew to hulking proportions and sent them packing. The family members studied in Hanoi but spent time in the highlands learning the instruments of several minorities, and since 1981 they have played together and developed an infectious musical personality. Circular breathing and lightning-speed virtuosity are just some of the dazzling features of a performance, and their collection of instru-

ments is like a zoo of mutant bamboo. Most striking, though, is their use of the lithophone dan da, a replica of the original rock marimba. The effect of awakening this ancient voice, whatever changes in performance practice there may have been over the last six millennia, is shattering.

Vietnamese Pop

While there is no shortage of pop aficionados in Vietnam – witness the karaoke boom – the star-making industry is less than efficient and the public usually recognises the songwriter before the performer. Paris-trained **Pham Trong Cau**, jungle-trained **Diep Minh Tuyen** and **Thanh Tung**, a business mogul who doubles as the best-known writer of film scores, are all famous songwriters, but since the death in 1995 of **Van Cao**, musical hero and composer of the national anthem, **Trinh Cong Son** is the undisputed number one. Joan Baez was not far off when she dubbed him 'the Vietnamese Bob Dylan': the tunes are catchy and the lyrics right on. His first songs were written while in hiding from the military draft, and in 1969, when his album *Lullaby* sold over two million copies in Japan, Son's works were banned by the south Vietnamese government, who considered the lyrics too demoralising. Even the new government sent him to work as a peasant in the fields, but since 1979 he has lived in Ho Chi Minh City, drinking and painting, writing apolitical love songs and celebrating Vietnam's natural wonders, with over six hundred songs to his credit.

The standard band consists of a singer (who may perform a few modest gyrations), bass guitar and one or two electronic keyboards, hailed throughout the country as the greatest labour-saving device. Indeed, in rural areas where there is no electricity, these portable keyboards run happily on batteries, and all the rhythm buttons that are so rarely used elsewhere – rumba, tango, bossa nova and surf-rock – are employed liberally. The ubiquitous slap-echo on the singer's microphone is intentional; without it, they say, it sounds unprofessional. Each evening, when the traffic noise dies down, you can hear the mournful laments of neighbouring karaoke bars mingling together.

In the fickle galaxy of Vietnamese pop, the stars are ever changing. You can see the pop singers of Ho Chi Minh City pedalling from gig to gig or, if they are famous, sitting side-saddle on a Honda Dream. One by one they come on stage, sing a song (two, if they are well known – one slow, one fast) before hopping down the road to repeat the routine. Usually dominated by southerners, mostly male, for the first time three women from the north have entered the field and captured the public's hearts. **Hong Nhung** (Trinh Cong Son's protégée), **Thanh Lam** and **My Linh** run their own shows as a new breed of family business and have developed a higher level of sophistication in the song arrangements (especially those by Duong Thu) as a result of more international styles being heard in Vietnam. The big new name outside Vietnam is **Nhu Quynh**, who, after a career as darling of the Communist Youth movement, has ended up in California, adored for peddling corny songs.

With thanks to Jan Dodd.

discography

Traditional, New Folk and Tribal Music

Compilations

Echoes of Ancestral voices: Traditional Music of Vietnam (Move, Australia).

Music performed by husband and wife duo Dang Kim Hien and Le Tuan Hung. No flashy displays, just a fragile, uncompromising intensity. Hien's unearthly lullabies and elegant nhac tai tu duos using delicious microtones make this one of the most worthwhile discs of the traditional repertoire.

Music from Vietnam Vols 1 & 3 (Caprice, Sweden).

Volume 1 makes a good introduction (in conservatoire style) to traditional music, featuring quan ho folksongs, cai luong and hat cheo theatre, hat chau van possession ritual and new folk. Featured instruments include the dan bau, moon fiddle and k'longput. The excellent and accessible Volume 3 focuses on the astonishing musical traditions of the cultures residing in the central and northern mountains, kicking off with the E-de people and a beautiful 'free-reed' cow horn solo followed up by clattering polyrhythmic gong patterns. There's also music from the Nung, Muong and Hmong, with wonderful pipes, flutes, mouth-organs and songs. The second volume, listed below, features the 'classical' music of the City of Hué.

The Music of Vietnam (Celestial Harmonies, US).

An adventurous three-disc set. The first two discs feature diverse pieces in conservatoire-style. Through a compelling series of pieces, new and old, these form an entertaining overview of the full range of Vietnam's range of instruments from the dan bau to the k'longput and t'rung. The third disc, listed below, presents the ceremonial music of Hué.

The Music of Vietnam (Rounder, US).

Double CD on Rounder's reissued Anthology of World Music collection. The first disc covers court theatrical and ritual music, while the second really hots up with drumming and chamber music – a welcome antidote to today's conservatoire dominated times. While more recent releases outdo this set in terms of sound quality, these early seventies' recordings preserve the subtlest nuances of phrasing.

Musiques des Montagnards (Chant du Monde, France).

Two CDs of extraordinary archival and modern recordings from the central and northern highlands. Fourteen ethnic groups are covered and excellently described in the copious booklet.

Northern Vietnam: Music and Songs of the Minorities (Buda/Musique du Monde, France).

A selection of tracks including the Giay, Muang, Nung, Tay, Dao, Thai, Hmong and Kinh groups. Features a love song, courting tunes, wedding music, funeral music and the extraordinary hmong khen.

Stilling Time: Traditional Musics of Vietnam (Innova, US).

A sampler of field recordings from all over Vietnam, including songs and gong music of the ethnic minorities, as well as nhac tai tu and the only Phu Dong recordings to be found on CD. An introduction to the many surprises in store for the musical traveller.

Artists

Khac Chi Ensemble

Ho Khac Chi (b 1950) is a virtuoso of the dan bau. Educated in the Vietnam Conservatoire, he started the Khac Chi Ensemble in 1982 and moved to Canada ten years later. The group now includes his wife Hoang Ngoc Bich, Le To Quyen (vocals) and Nguyen Hoai Chau (percussion).

Moonlight in Vietnam (Rounder/Henry Street, US).

New music, expertly played on Vietnam's most extraordinary musical instruments, including the dan bau, k'longput, t'rung and a stick fiddle with a resonating disc held in the player's mouth. A spectacular stereo recording of astonishing sounds, including several vocal numbers.

Theatre, Song and Classical Music

Compilations

Court Theatre Music: Hat Boi (Audivis/Unesco, France).

Often confused with Chinese opera, hat boi (known as hat tuong in northern Vietnam) shares many conventions: vocal styles, costumes and gestures especially. But Vietnam's essence can be felt in the details: spirited ken (oboe) wailing and invigorating use of the (trong chien) battle drum. Much is lost by not watching a performance, but the music, the thorough liner notes, and the general air of antiquity help the imagination along.

Vietnamese Folk Theatre: Hat Cheo (King, Japan).

A generous quantity of cheo theatre, expertly played by the Quy Bon family and recorded in Hanoi. Features a chau van possession ritual and the famous story of the cross-dressing Thi Mau going to a temple.

Vietnam: Traditions of the South (Audivis/Unesco, France).

Southern ritual music from the eclectic Cao Dai, Buddhist, and indigenous spirit-possession religions, as well as a good helping of traditional cai luong theatre music. The liner notes and recording quality are dry but the music is very lively.

Ca Tru and Quan Ho (Audivis/Unesco, France).

Ca tru was barely clinging on in 1976 when this recording was made in Hanoi by noted scholar Tran Van Khe. Now there is a small revival of these somewhat arcane women's songs. The flagship of Vietnamese folk music, the quan ho songs included here, are also more than relics.

Music from Vietnam 2: The City of Hué
(Caprice, Sweden).

Three local instrumental and vocal groups give the enticing flavour of this city, and the disc features the sprightly aged Nguyen Manh Cam, former drummer to the emperor. Features ceremonial music with shawms, drums and a big gong, a military ensemble and a great court orchestra as well as more intimate chamber groups of singers with dan bau, moon fiddle, two-string fiddle and zither.

The Music of Vietnam, Vol2
(Celestial Harmonies, US).

Imperial court music recorded in Hué. This unique album includes the predominantly solemn ceremonial music that the emperor would have enjoyed. Excellent notes gives a comprehensive history and description of the forms.

Vietnam: Buddhist Music from Hué
(Inédit, France).

An atmospheric recording, full of ceremonial presence. It begins with sonorous drums and bells before two oboes enter for music marking the ascent to the 'Esplanade of Heaven'. Features the complete ceremony of Khai Kinh, 'Opening the Sacred Texts', recorded in the Kim Tien Pagoda in Hué. This sort of religious music does not make for easy listening on CD, but is nevertheless impressive, with rich vocals, drums, bells and strings.

Vietnam: Poésies et Chants (Ocora, France).

Master musician Tran Van Khe and friends chanting poetry and ravishing the zither and moon lute in the nhac tai tu repertory. Intimate performances backed up by excellent notes and translations. A companion disc, **Le Dan Tranh** (Ocora, France), is equally affecting.

Artists

Kim Sinh

Veteran blind singer and guitarist, with something of a cult international following (including Ry Cooder). His venerable musical personality is more affecting than many of the commercial cai luong releases available.

The Art of Kim Sinh
(King, Japan).

This recording has influenced a whole generation of young Californian guitarists and one struggles not to draw comparisons with the blues. The Vietnamese guitar (the six-stringed dan luc huyen cam) is like a regular Spanish style instrument with the fretboard hollowed out.

Pop

In a world of cheap, self-produced albums by karaoke addicts, look for anything by these artists to ensure quality: Khanh Ha (Vietnam's answer to Barbra Streisand), Y Lan (a raunchy, occasionally scandalous, performer) or Tuan Ngoc (a star of yesteryear). Any song by Trinh Cong Son, Van Cao or Pham Duy is also worth hearing. These recordings are sold primarily through Asian grocery stores, where the shop assistants will happily make recommendations.

Compilations

Hò! Roady Music from Vietnam
(Trinkont, Germany).

A brilliant idea – crass, funky street music from Vietnam taken from popular cassettes and recorded in situ with mopeds and car horns in the soundscape. It opens in cracking style with a plucked dan bau playing "Riders in the Sky" with what sounds like fireworks as backing. There's a wild funeral brass band (a touch of India here) and all sorts of surprises.

Artists

Thu Hien

Along with ca Hué singer Ai Hué, Thu Hien is never far away from any visitor in Hué who shows an interest in local music – and a performance in your hotel or boat can easily be delivered.

Ai Ra Xu Hue (Hué, Vietnam).

The mellowest Hué pop music, featuring the perfumed voice of Thu Hien.

Don Ho

Not to be confused with any other glamourous Don Hos, this one is often seen on the 'Paris-By-Night'-type concert circuit.

Ru Em (Thuy Nga, US).

Heart-throb lullabies from one of California's hottest singers.

Nguyen Thanh Van

San Francisco-based Van has produced six CDs, and has now entered the music video world singing tender Vietnamese pop songs – with an occasional Schubert or Bernstein classic thrown in for good measure.

Beo Giat May Troi (Diem Xua, US).

Passion and pathos from one of the up-and-coming stars of the Vietnamese pop world.

TWO

The Americas

USA · Greenland · Iceland · Canada · USA · PACIFIC OCEAN · ATLANTIC OCEAN · Maui · Hawaii (see Asia and Pacifc) · Mexico · Cuba · Bahamas · Dominican Republic · Jamaica · Belize · Puerto Rico · Honduras · Haiti · Guatemala · El Salvador · Nicaragua · Costa Rica · Panama · Venezuela · Trinidad & Tobago · Guyana · Surinam · French Guiana · Colombia · Galápagos Islands · Ecuador · THE ANDES · Peru · Brazil · Bolivia · Chile · Paraguay · Argentina · Uruguay · Falkland Islands

Inset map: Bahamas · ATLANTIC OCEAN · Cuba · Dominican Republic · Puerto Rico · Jamaica · St Kitts-Nevis · Haiti · Antigua & Barbuda · Guadeloupe (French Antilles) · Dominica · Martinique (French Antilles) · CARIBBEAN SEA · DUTCH ANTILLES · St. Lucia · St. Vincent · Barbados · Grenada · Margarita · Tobago · Colombia · Venezuela · Trinidad · LESSER ANTILLES

This map is drawn on the Peter's projection which shows the correct relative size of countries

Andean music

beyond the ponchos

Latin America's oldest musical traditions are those of the Amerindians of the Andes, the indigenous population spread across the modern states of Ecuador, Peru, Bolivia, northern Argentina and northern Chile. Their music is best known outside these countries through the characteristic panpipes of poncho-clad folklore groups. However, there's a multitude of rhythms and popular musics found in these countries which deserve a lot more recognition. Below **Jan Fairley** details some of the rich sounds to be found in the region, incuding Huayno and Chicha, still relatively unknown abroad, as well as the distinct coastal tradition of Afro-Peruvian music, rooted in black slaves brought to work in the mines.

For most people the charactersitic sound of the Andes is that of bamboo panpipes and *quena* flutes. These instruments have been used to create music in the Andean mountains, which stretch more than 4500 miles from Venezuela to southern Chile, since before the time of the Incas. Indeed, pre-conquest Andean instruments – conch shell trumpets, shakers which used nuts for rattles, ocarinas, wind instruments and drums – are ever present in museum collections, and the influence of the Inca empire means that Andean music traditions extend far beyond the mountains themselves. They can be defined partly through ethnicity, partly through language. **Quechua** (currently spoken by over six million people) and **Aymara** are still commonly spoken alongside Spanish and other Amerindian languages.

The dominant areas of Andean culture are **Peru**, **Ecuador** and **Bolivia**, the countries with the largest indigenous Amerindian populations in South America. Here, in rural areas, highly traditional Andean music, probably little different from pre-Inca times, still thrives today at every kind of celebration and ritual. But beyond this is a huge diversity of music, differing widely even between individual communities. Andean people tend to identify themselves by the specific place they come from: in music, the villages have different ways of making and tuning instruments and composing tunes, in the same way as they have distinctive

weaving designs, ways of dressing or wearing their hats. Use of different scales involving four, five, six and seven notes and different singing styles are also found from place to place, tied to specific ritual occasions and the music which goes with them.

Andean music can, however, be divided into three main types. Firstly, that which is of **indigenous origin**, found mostly amongst rural Amerindian peoples still living very much by the seasons with root Amerindian beliefs; secondly music of **European origin**; and thirdly **mestizo**

Local festival group at Tjio, Peruvian Andes, playing notched-end flutes

music, which continues to fuse the indigenous with European in a whole host of ways. In general, Quechua people have more vocal music than the Aymara.

CLAUDIO ROHRHIRSCH/SMITHSONIAN FOLKWAYS

Andean Traditions

Panpipes, known by the Aymara as *siku*, by the Quechua as *antara* and by the Spanish as *zampoña*, are ancient instruments and archaeologists have unearthed panpipes tuned to a variety of scales. While modern panpipes – played in the city or in groups with other instruments – may offer a complete scale allowing solo performance, traditional models are played in pairs, a tradition still as described by sixteenth-century chroniclers. The pipes share the melody, each with alternate notes of a whole scale so that two or more players are needed to pick out a single tune using a hocket technique. Usually one player leads and the other follows. While symbolically this demonstrates reciprocity within the community, practically it enables players to play for a long time without getting too 'high' from dizziness caused by over-breathing.

Played by blowing (or breathing out hard) across the top of a tube, panpipes come in various sizes, those with a deep bass having very long tubes. Several tubes made of bamboo reed of different length are bound together to produce a sound that can be jaunty, but also has a melancholic edge depending on tune and playing style. Many tunes have a minor, descending shape to them. Playing is often described as 'breathy' as overblowing is popular to produce harmonics. In general those who play panpipes love dense overlapping textures and often syncopated rhythms.

Simple **notched-end flutes**, or **quenas**, are another independent innovation of the Andean highlands found in both rural and urban areas. The most important pre-Hispanic instrument, they were traditionally made of fragile bamboo (though often these days from plumbers PVC water pipes) and played in the dry season, with **tarkas** (vertical flutes – like a shrill recorder) taking over in the wet. Quenas are played solo or in ritual groups and remain tremendously popular today, with many virtuoso techniques.

Large **marching bands of drums and panpipes** playing in the co-operative 'back-and-forth' leader/follower style captivated the Spanish in the 1500s, and they can still be seen and heard today. The drums are deep-sounding, double-headed instruments known as *bombos* or *wankaras*. These bands exist for parades at **life-cycle fiestas, weddings and dances** in the regions surrounding the **Peruvian–Bolivian frontier** and around **Lake Titicaca**. Apart from their use at fiestas, panpipes are played mainly in the dry season, from April to October.

There is nothing more amazing than being in a village and hearing the sound of a fifty-man panpipe band approaching, especially after they've been playing for a few hours and have had a few well-earned drinks. It is perfectly normal for a

Awatinas – the familiar face of Andean panpipe and poncho music

NARELLE AUTIO/HEARTBEAT

whole village to come together to play as an orchestra for important events and fiestas. Andean villages are usually composed of *ayllus* (extended families) whose land is often divided up so that everyone gets a share of various pastures, but with everyone working together at key times such as harvest and when caring for communal areas. Music is an integral part of all communal celebrations and symbolically represents that sharing and inter-dependence: drinks are drunk from communal glasses which everyone will empty in turn. The organisation and values of each community are reflected in the very instrument an individual plays, down to the position of players within circles and groups.

At fiestas, the most common object of Andean ritual is **Pachama** (Mother Earth), who is often fed coca leaves, dried potato and chicha corn beer in return for her gift of the earth and fertility. It is believed that if the earth is not fed, crops and animals will die. Similarly the sun (*Inti Raymi*) and moon are seen as deities, while the weather, including thunder and lightning, and geographical places such as mountains, rivers and lakes, all have special powers and deities which must be respected and propitiated.

Festivals take place in Peru, Bolivia and Ecuador at the times of summer and winter solstices and most of these have persisted since Inca and pre-Inca times. In Ecuador festivals of this nature with special dances of ancient lineage include shamanistic *Danza de la culebra* (Dance of the Snake) and celebrations for the Festival of Yuca, for San Juan (St. John), and many more for particular calendar dates, most of which are closely related to the agrarian cycle.

Folk music festivals to attract and entertain the tourist trade, encouraged by various Andean governments, are a quite different experience to music in the village context. While positively disseminating the music, they have introduced the notion of judging and the concept of best musicianship – ideas totally at odds with rural community values of diversity in musical repertoire, style and dress.

Andean Awakenings: the New Group

The political events of the 1950s and '60s are crucial to an understanding of Andean music. In **Bolivia**, the nationalist 1952 Revolution led to a period of social and economic reform which accorded more rights to the Bolivian 'Indian', introduced laws favouring Aymara and Quechua peasants, initiated agricultural reform, nationalised major mines and gave everyone the right to vote.

Such reforms brought new respect for the Amerindian and were enthusiastically supported by many Latin American intellectuals, some of whom began wearing woven ponchos (previously shunned as peasant wear) and taking a keen interest in Amerindian artefacts and culture. At the same time, rural people migrated to urban areas bringing their languages and traditions with them.

The new Bolivian administration created a division of folklore in the Ministry of Education, one of whose functions was the organisation and sponsorship of **traditional music festivals**. Radio stations started to broadcast in Aymara and Quechua and played the music of these communities, often with musicians performing live in the studio. Recordings followed.

Around 1965 an influential – and indeed definitive – musical model for the Andes emerged with **Los Jairas**, founded by **Edgar 'Yayo' Jofré**. He put the group together to play at the *Peña Naira* in La Paz – one of a string of new urban venues where people could hear *música folklorica*. The idea was to form a quartet of **charango** (Bolivian mandolin), **guitar**, **quena** and **bombo** (drum): instruments that had never been played together before, having had their own seasons in the mountain villages. The quartet arranged the music to show off each of the instruments' solo and group possibilities.

The original Los Jairas consisted of Edgar Jofré, singer and percussionist; **Julio Godoy** and **Ernesto Cavour** (both Bolivian) as guitarist and charango players, and quena player **Gilbert Favre** (a Swiss-French flautist); later they were joined by the guitarist and composer **Alfredo Dominguez**. Adapting Aymara and Quechua tunes into their repertoire, they forged a new melodic and rhythmic style, re-structuring Amerindian melodies to suit an urban and European aesthetic. Before Los Jairas, urban music in Bolivia was *música criolla*, which represented middle and mestizo classes with a repertoire of European-style dance songs, played on guitars, charangos, mandolins and occasionally the accordion – music which, for the most part, avoided Amerindian instruments and tunes.

In Chile, meanwhile, at almost the same time, **Angel and Isabel Parra** opened the Peña de los Parra in Santiago. The Parras, with their mother, seminal folklorist **Violeta Parra**, had performed Andean folk tunes in the night clubs of the Quartier Latin in Paris, where they had been close friends of **Gilbert Favre** (Violeta was for a time his lover). Favre learnt to play the quena in European style which, with its use of vibrato, dynamics and swooping glissandos, was completely contrary to Amerindian aesthetics. It is his style which has become standard for the urban folk music group.

Los K'jarkas

In Bolivia innumerable groups have followed the Los Jairas model. Among the more prominent – through tours or recordings – are **Los K'jarkas**, **Savia Andina**, **Khanata**, **Los Quipus**, **Wara**, **Los Yuras**, **Grupo Aymara** and **Paja Brava**. But there are exceptional musicians and groups to be found throughout the country, and they are taking Andean music in many directions. While some continue to deliver inspired arrangements of traditional tunes, others play foreign music on traditional instruments to demonstrate the instruments' virtuosity. There are also those who use both instrument and music as the basis for new composition, sometimes involving ideas and values from contemporary classical music. As a result the same 'tune' can appear in different guises under different titles in various styles.

Los K'jarkas, from the city of Cochabamba, were (and are) the country's most influential and successful group. Like many such bands, they formed around a family – the three Hermosa brothers, each bi-lingual in quechua and Spanish, and each composers. They have run a music school in Cochabamba for many years, contributing to a generation of musicians who have formed their own groups. In common with other Bolivian bands they exhibit a strong sense of national identity by wearing Amerindian peasant ponchos and using various emblems. The name 'K'jarkas' refers to the pre-Spanish fortresses while the group's logo – a stylised anthropomorphic condor and warriors carving from the archaeological site of Tiwanaku – appeals to a pre-Columbian past and millenary culture at the heart of the Andes.

Astute composition and arrangements, which take into account the multiple audiences within Bolivia, earned Los K'jarkas an enormous following. In 1992 when one of the brothers, Ulises, died, a procession of fifty thousand mourners paid their last respects as his remains were placed in a site reserved for the illustrious by the authorities of Cochabamba.

K'jarkas songs are largely sentimental, conjuring up a bucolic, rural vision of beautiful maidens, alongside evocations of Pachamama (Mother Earth). Where they score at home is in large part due to their incorporation of traditional urban dance forms. They use mainly the **huayno** dance form (for more on which see p.283) but at times

---

Llorando se fué

*She left weeping
and left me alone loveless
she's perhaps alone
remembering this love
that time cannot erase*

*I remember her today
there is no rancour in my breast
she's probably weeping
remembering this love
she did not look after.*

Gonzalo and Ulises Hermosa
translation: Gilka Wara Céspedes.

---

include the hugely popular **sayas** – a dance form that has African roots, from the slaves brought to Bolivia during the seventeenth and eighteenth centuries. Sayas are especially popular in Bolivia at carnival when they are most often performed in full regalia – the men in riding pants, boots with bells and big straw hats, the women in thigh-high boots, very short mini-skirts, lace edged petticoats, and decorated versions of the traditional Andean *campesino* bowler hat.

Sayas are popularly played by the brass bands beloved of Carnival as well as música folklorica groups. They are marked by a strong drum introduction and identifying musical signature. The K'jarkas song "Llorando se fué" is a classic example – and incredibly familiar. It was this rhythm, indeed this song, that mutated into the global **lambada** craze of the 1980s. The Hermosas, fortunately, had registered the song and won a sizable legal settlement from the Paris-based group who took it onto the international stage.

Canto Nuevo

The sound of Andean panpipes and quenas was at the heart of early **Chilean nueva canción** (see p.362), through groups like **Los Curacas**, **Inti Illimani** and **Quilapayún**. Influenced by Los Jairas and the work of the Parras, they adopted Andean instruments and music in the 1960s and '70s, adding extra Latin percussion, guitars and other instruments. The move neatly combined music and politics: the Andean roots asserting collective values and an unmistakable ancient Latin American identity.

In Bolivia nueva canción was reinterpreted in the 1980s as **canto nuevo**, whose top exponent is folk singer **Emma Junaro**. Her clear, lyrical

Panpipes and Ponchos in Europe

In the market square of any European town from Dublin to Budapest, in the summer months you're likely to find a band of musicians clad in ponchos or woven or embroidered waistcoats, often knitted hats, busking on bamboo quenas and panpipes and little charangos from Bolivia and Peru. Their music ranges from the mestizo traditions of the towns and the roots music of the villages to the more international Andean tunes.

Andean music in this popular form found its way to Europe sometime in the 1950s and by the mid-1960s it had its intellectual following in Paris through the work of groups like **Los Calchakis**. In Paris in the 1970s **Bolivia Manta**, a co-operative community of Andean migrants, kept the flame alive. In the 1980s and '90s the most familiar groups playing this highly professional, well-arranged and extremely beautiful music were Rumillajta (City of Stone in Quechua) and Awatiñas (Shepherds), members of the Condé family and friends. Both groups tour Europe, Japan and Australia.

Awatiñas were brought up as Aymara speakers and a good half of their performance is traditional Aymara music, including festive and circle dances that form part of the regular rituals associated with the land. This can be a challenge to Western ears. Awatiñas often appear with a banner saying "awatkipasipxananakasataki" (let our integrity shine) and are keen ambassadors of their culture. They compose much of their remaining repertoire themselves in the style of urban mestizo music and do charity work to raise funds in Europe for community and educational projects back home.

Rumillajta perform mainly mestizo songs in very beautiful arrangements, often on instruments they make themselves, although more recently they have included songs from other countries of the continent, including some nueva canción. Their album *Hoja de coca*

Rumillajta playing at home

(Coca Leaf) is a good example of the rich textures of their music with deep breathy pipes, both melodic and percussive, over a rippling strum. This is typical of overseas Andean groups – a playing developed to evoke the wind, rain and animals of the Andes – which you won't find in the music played back home.

voice interpreted songs with a political message, and she also covered the poetic-songs of Bolivian poet and key singer of criollo music, **Matilde Casazola**. (Again, see the nueva canción article – p.362 – for more).

Charangos and Mermaids

The **charango** is another key Andean instrument whose bright, zingy sounds are familiar worldwide. This small variant of the mandolin – with five pairs of strings – was created in Bolivia in imitation of early guitars and lutes brought by the Spanish colonisers, which indigenous musicians were taught to play in the churches. Its size was restricted by its traditional manufacture from armadillo shells (although these can sometimes be big enough for a full-blown mandolin), while its sound quality came from the indigenous aesthetic which has favoured high pitches from the pre-Columbian period through to the present.

In rural areas in southern **Peru**, particularly in the **Titicaca region** and province of **Canas**, the charango is the key instrument – used by young, single men to woo and court the female of their choice. In this area the tradition often involves the figure of a mermaid, *la sirena*, who offers supernatural aid to the young men embarking on a musical pursuit of their chosen one. The ethnomusicologist Tom Turino records that most towns and villages around Titicaca claim a sirena lives in a nearby spring, river, lake or waterfall, and notes that new charangos are often left overnight in such places – wrapped in a piece of woven cloth, along with gifts – to be tuned and played overnight by the sirena. Some villagers construct the sound box in the shape of a mermaid including her head and fish tail to invest their charango with supernatural power.

When young men go courting at the weekly markets in larger villages they will not only dress in their finest clothes, but get up their charangos in elaborate coloured ribbons. These represent the number of women their charango has supposedly conquered, thus demonstrating their manliness and the power of their instrument. At times a group of young people will get together for the ancient **circle dance** called the *Punchay kashwa* where the men form a half circle playing their charangos, facing a half circle of young women. Both groups dance and sing in bantering 'song duelling' fashion, participants using a set syllabic and rhyming pattern so that they can quickly improvise. "Let's go walking" one might call, to a riposte such as "A devil like you makes me suspicious", or an insult like "In the back of your house there are three rotten eggs".

In Peru as in Bolivia, the charango was until the 1960s regarded as an 'Indian' instrument of the rural, lower classes. Brought to towns and cities by rural migrants, it crossed over when Spanish-speaking middle-class musicians – who until then had only played European instruments such as guitars and mandolins – began to play it – and as a result of the cultural evaluation following the 1959 Revolution. The Peruvian ideological movement known as **Indigenismo**, active between 1910 and 1940, was also influential in the charango's re-appraisal. Indigenismo was a regionalistic and nationalistic movement which lauded indigenous culture as true Peruvian, rejecting criollo and Hispanic values. The movement was particularly strong in Cuzco, where charango performance by mestizos became part of its identity.

Song and Brass

Most **singing** in the Andes is done by women and the preferred style is very high-pitched – almost falsetto to European ears. There are songs for pota-

Charango styles

Charangos were originally made from the shell of an armadillo but as the animal has become rare and protected, today's instruments are generaly made of wood. There are many sizes and varieties: from those capable of deeper, richer, bass sounds with large round backs to flat backed instruments with more strident metal strings. There are also 'full size' Andean **mandolins** – about twice the size of a regular charango – which, confusingly, are sometimes made from (large) armadillo shells.

Tunings vary from place to place and from musician to musician with some preferring metal strings, others nylon, to suit a variety of strumming and plucking techniques. Nylon strings are often thought to produce deeper, clearer or sweeter sounds.

BOB HADDAD/MUSIC OF THE WORLD

In certain areas of Peru, for instance at the time of potato planting, a charango may play planting songs and dances in strumming style with a single line melody vibrating amongst open sounding strings. In contrast **mestizo styles** – used when playing creole musical forms such as *huaynos*, *marineras*, *yaravís* and *vals criollo* – may favour plucked melodic playing styles which can be very complex.

In Bolivia, **Don Mauro Nuñez**, who came from the town of Serrano outside the city of Sucre, had the biggest influence on charango techniques when some time in the early decades of the twentieth century he amplified the normal 'rasgueado' strumming motion of playing the charango and began to pluck strings in guitar fashion. In the late 1950s, when he was already old, he gained recognition in Peru and Argentina.

to growing, reaping barley, threshing wheat, marking cattle, sheep and goats, for building houses, for traditional dances and funerals and many other ceremonies.

The astonishing diversity of music, ensembles and occasions can be heard clearly on the superb *Smithsonian Folkways Traditional Music of Peru* series, documented and compiled by music ethnologist **Raúl Romero**. These recordings are mainly from the **Mantaro valley**, an area known for its saxophone and clarinet ensembles, and include women singing accompanied by the ancient *tinya* drum and violin and also the harp as well as clarinets and brass bands. There are so many festivities with music that the music profession is considered profitable and there are a great number of **brass bands** (first introduced in the 1920s as part of mandatory military service) as well as **orchestras** (*tipicas*) composed of saxophones, clarinets, violins and diatonic harp.

Romero notes that urbanisation, modernisation and migration, rather than undermining the need for traditional music, has led to its successful adaptation of new forms, and revival. He also notes the importance of mestizo (mixed Amerindian and European blood) and bi-lingual Spanish-Quechua culture in this process.

The context of the musical performance is still the determining factor in its style. Music which continues pre-Hispanic models is to be found within the context of closed community and ritual. Music which is mestizo, re-creating regional traditions, is dynamically driven by the fiesta system. New musical styles have evolved through migration to the capital Lima, with radio and record as their main vehicles of communication.

Music in Cuzco

Music explodes from every direction in the once Inca lands, but nowhere more so than in the Peruvian city of **Cuzco**, the old religious and political capital of the Inca state. For at least six hundred years people from all over the highlands have converged on the city, and if you're travelling in the region, it's a good first base for getting to grips with Andean music. Stay a week or two and you will hear just about every variety of Andean folk music that is still performed.

The streets are the best place to start. Most street musicians are highly talented performers and will play for hours on end. Around noon, you might see **Leandro Apaza** making his way down the great hill of Avenida Tullumayo. Carrying an Andean harp on his shoulder, he is led down the

street by a small boy because, like many accomplished regional musicians, he is blind. He will turn right onto Hatun Rumiyoq, the narrow alley that every visitor to Cuzco visits at some time to see the large stone perfectly fitted into place in the side wall of Inca Roca's palace. Leandro sets up his harp directly across from the great stone. **Benjamin Clara**, who sometimes accompanies him on mandolin, may already be there waiting. Benjamin cannot always meet Leandro downtown as he is lame as well as sightless and needs to be carried (see discography *Blind Street Musicians of Cuzco*).

The two are there to earn their living by playing the traditional music of the Quechua people. Their repertoire includes a host of styles, the most recognisable being the huayno, an unmistakable dance rhythm reminiscent of a hopped-up waltz, which once heard is not easily forgotten. It is musically cheerful, though the lyrics can be sorrowful, and sometimes full of double meaning, occasionally sexually explicit – a fact often not realised by those who cannot understand Quechua.

BOB HADDAD/MUSIC OF THE WORLD

Benjamin Clara (mandolin) and Leandro Apaza (harp)

Very few such musicians achieve any kind of media fame. If they do, it usually means the chance to perform in small clubs or restaurants for a meagre guaranteed wage plus whatever they receive in tips. One such individual is **Gabriel Aragón**. Another blind musician, he is a huge man, obviously mestizo, but possessed of a gentle voice and a soft touch on his harp. His fame means that he will often travel for an engagement, which may be a club date, a wedding or a traditional festival. At his restaurant gigs, he serves up some of the finest traditional folk melodies, ballads and dance tunes – a nostalgic repertoire greatly appreciated

The Andean harp: Don Antonio Sulca

In blind musician **Don Antonio Sulca**, of Ayacucho, Peru is one of the great masters of the Andean harp – one of the mountains' most characteristic instruments. This huge harp has a soundbox built like a boat and a mermaid's head decoration (like many charangos). Its form is thought to have evolved from the harp brought from Spain in the sixteenth century and the Celtic harp brought by the Jesuits to the Missions. It has 36 strings spanning five octaves and including resonant bass notes. In processions in the Andes, harpists often sling their instruments upside down across their shoulders, plucking with a remarkable backhanded technique.

Sulca plays solo or, more often, with his group **Ayllu Sulca**, composed of members of his *ayllu* (his extended family), on fiddles and mandolins. Their songs are mostly huaynos sung in Quechua. The most familiar of them, "Huerfano pajarillo" (Little Orphan Bird), about a bird which has strayed too far from home, is an allegory of the plight of the Amerindians forced to migrate

to earn a living. His stately style of playing *yaravis* – slow sad tunes – is unmatched. A pre-Hispanic form, they probably acquired thier doleful, introspective character during the early colonial period, when at least eighty percent of the Amerindian population perished. The yaravi composed at the death of the last member of the Inca royal family, Tupac Amaru, in 1781, became the best-known of all Peruvian tunes – **"El Condor Pasa" (Flight of the Condor)**.

Don Antonio Sulca also plays **dance music** from the early twentieth century, when forms like the foxtrot, waltz and tango were given the Inca touch to produce hybrid forms like the sublime waltz *incaico* "Nube Gris" (Grey Cloud). His version of his city's unofficial hymn, "Adíos pueblo Ayacucho" (Farewell, People of Ayacucho), celebrates emotional ties to the place where the Amerindians beat back the Spanish at the time of the conquest.

by older members of the community, who listen, drink, cry, sing, and dance the night away.

Conjuntos and Concerts

Cuzco's tavern scene, like that of any urban region, also plays host to young **cholo** and **mestizo groups**. They are constantly on the move throughout the evening, playing one set in each of the available venues in town during the tourist season. You can pick the club with your favourite ambience and settle in – most of the groups will pass through in the course of an evening, so you are almost bound to hear each of them at some point as the entertainment goes on all night long.

This kind of 'one-night tour' is limited only by the size of a city. In Lima, for example, a group of this type might confine itself to a specific area of town. The smaller mountain villages, by contrast, might have only one night spot – and if they are lucky a local band. In regions of heavy tourism, such as Cuzco or Ollantaytambo, there is usually a proliferation of groups. If you end up at one of these mini-fiestas, you may be egged on to dance, especially if you are a woman, and definitely be forced to join in a drink. Follow along, do your best, and don't mind being the butt of the odd joke. It will be worth it.

The ensembles typically consist of five to seven members. Their **instrumentation** includes one or two guitars, a charango, quenas, other flutes, panpipes and simple percussion. Harps, considered something of a dying art due to their size, weight, fragility and cost, are rarer these days. Most of the musicians are adept at more than one instrument and are likely to switch roles during their set. Their performing is a social event; their tour a rolling party as they are usually accompanied on their rounds by friends (you are welcome to join them).

As these musicians grow older many of them end up in the backup band of a veteran professional, rather than in a group of traditional musicians. This type of **conjunto** is most likely to be made up of urban middle-class musicians, usually serious students of music since early in life. They often have some type of classical training, may be able to compose and arrange, and, although emotionally tied to ancestral heritage, the bulk of their repertoire is newly composed using traditional idioms played on both modern and traditional instruments. They will also be able to play a variety of standards – classic pieces of traditional highland folk. These ensembles are usually quite well paid and do not normally move about throughout the evening. They play at the more elite nightclubs, hotel lounges and arts centres and sometimes if lucky tour abroad.

Although by the very nature of their own background and that of their audience these bands are not staunch traditionalists, they are promoted as such by those in charge of international cultural exchange. On tour abroad, they usually play well-known traditional pieces, and often accompany **folkloric dance groups**, while another part of their repertoire may be what is marketed as **Andean New Age** music, a blend of traditionalism with modern sounds. The vocal presentation of these groups is generally more accessible to foreign ears than the piercing falsetto tones of a traditional vocalist.

Peru's National Performers

Many performers have achieved mass appeal and recording contracts in Peru and can support themselves solely by their work as musicians. Nationally celebrated performers include **Florcita de Pisaq** (a huayno vocalist), **Pastorita Huaracina** (a singer of both cholo and mestizo varieties) and **Jaime Guardía** (a virtuoso of the charango).

These performers take pride in being bearers of tradition, play at most traditional festivals and hire themselves out to wealthier villages to provide music for those festive events that require it. Although they may hold little attraction for the wealthy urban population (who tend to deny their roots), they often appear at large venues in major urban areas. They appeal to the displaced campesinos and city migrants who live in the *pueblos jóvenes*, 'young towns' or squatter settlements that have sprung up on the outskirts of the large coastal cities.

These artists travel a circuit of major urban centres, including Cuzco, on concert tours. Recordings of them are generally only available locally, but they can sometimes be found in shops catering for Latin American immigrants. Occasionally, an artist will also end up on a Western-produced compilation CD.

Front Rooms and Festivals

There is a large contingent of non-professional musicians, and, in Peruvian cities, the middle class often perform in impromptu ensembles **at home** in their living rooms. They tend to play huaynos or *chicha* (see overleaf), styles accompanied by falsetto singing in Spanish or Quechua, and often a mixture of both.

The only way to hear a performance in someone's living room is, of course, to get yourself invited. Fortunately, this isn't difficult to do in the Andes, where only a committed sociopath could avoid making friends. To speed the process, bring alcohol with you, accept every drink offered, be sure to encourage others to drink from your bottle, eat everything served to you, and ask to learn the words and sing along. You'll quickly pick up the dance steps.

For the less gregarious, **festivals** are an equally rewarding source of traditional music. One of the best I've encountered takes place in January on the **Isla Amantaní** in Lake Titicaca, its exact date, as

is often the case in the Andean highlands, determined by astronomical events. This particular festival occurs during a period often called the 'time of protection' when the rainy season has finally begun. It is related to the cleansing of the pasturage and water sources; stone fences are repaired, walking paths repaved, and the stone effigies and crosses that guard the planting fields replaced or repaired. A single-file 'parade' of individuals covers the entire island, stopping to appease the deities and provide necessary maintenance at each site. At the front are local non-professional musicians, all male, playing drums and flutes of various types.

There are, too, festivals that are celebrated on a larger scale. On the day of the June solstice (midwinter in the Andes) the Inca would ceremonially tie the sun to a stone and coax it to return south, bringing warmer weather and the new planting season. **Inti Raymi**, the Festival of the Sun, is still observed in every nook and cranny in the Andean

Chicha

Once upon a time in the Andes, **chicha** meant the fermented maize beer made by people of Amerindian descent and drunk in great quantities on festive occasions. Nowadays, if you request chicha, Peruvians are more likely to point you towards a cassette stall, as the beer has given its name to a new and hugely popular brew of Andean tropical music – a fusion of urban cumbia (local versions of the original Colombian dance), traditional highland huayno, and rock.

The music's origins lie in the massive migration of Amerindians from the inner mountain areas to the shantytowns around cities such as Arequipa and Lima. Chicha emerged in Lima in the early 1960s and by the mid-80s had become the most widespread urban music in Peru. Most bands have lead and rhythm guitars, electric bass, electric organ, a timbales and conga player, one or more vocalists (who may play percussion) and, if they can, a synthesizer.

The first chicha hit, and the song from which the movement has taken its name, was "La Chichera" (The Chicha Seller) by **Los Demonios de Mantaro** (The Devils of Mantaro), who hailed from the central highlands of Junín. Another famous band are **Los Shapis**, another provincial group established by their 1981 hit "El aguajal" (The Swamp), a version of a traditional huayno. **Pastorita Huaracina** is one of the more well-known female singers. Another good band – and the first to get a Western CD release – are **Belem**, based in Lima.

While most lyrics are about love in all its aspects, nearly all songs actually reveal an aspect of the harshness of the Amerindian experience – displacement, hardship, loneliness and exploitation. Many songs relate to the great majority of people who have to make a living selling their labour and goods in the unofficial 'informal economy', ever threatened by the police. Los Shapis' "El ambulante" (The Street Seller) opens with a reference to the rainbow colours of the Inca flag and the colour of the ponchos the people use to keep warm and transport their wares. "My flag is of the colours and the stamp of the rainbow/For Peru and America/Watch out or the police will take your bundle off you!/Ay, ay, ay, how sad it is to live/How sad it is to dream/I'm a street seller, I'm a proletarian/Selling shoes, selling food, selling jackets/I support my home."

Chicha has effectively become a youth movement, an expression of social frustration for the mass of people suffering racial discrimination in Peruvian society.

Top chicha band, Belem

MO FINI/TUMI

republics, from the capital city to the most isolated hamlet. The celebration, following a solemn ritual which may include a llama sacrifice, is more of a carnival than anything else. Parades of musicians, both professional bands and thrown-together collages of amateurs, fill the streets. You will be expected to drink and dance until you drop, or hide in your room. This kind of party can run several days, so be prepared. Anyone spending more than two weeks in the Andes is almost bound to witness a festival of some sort.

Peruvian Huaynos and Orquestas Típicas

Europe may know the Andes through the sound of bamboo panpipes and quenas, but visit the Peruvian central sierra and you find a music as lively and energetic as the busy market towns it comes from – a music largely unknown outside the country. These songs and dances are **huaynos** one of the few musical forms that reaches back to pre-conquest times, although these days the **orquestas típicas** that play them, from sierra towns like Huancayo, Ayacucho and Pucará, include saxophones, clarinets and trumpets alongside traditional instruments like violins, charangos and the large Amerindian harp.

Orquestas típicas are spirited and infectious, the focus of their music gradually shifting from Inca past and a pan-Andean image to the contemporary cultures of regional departments. Because of the larger size of the provinciano colonies from Ancash, Junín and Ayacucho in Lima, the urban-country style primarily grew up around performers from these departments including **Pastorita Huaracina** (Ancash), **Hermanos Zevallos** (Junín), **Flor de Huancayo** (Junín), **Princesita de Yungay** (Ancash), **Paisanita Ancashina** (Ancash). Names such as Paisanita Ancashina ('little fellow countrywoman from Ancash') clearly evoke nostalgia of place and 'paisano' loyalty helping to ensure commercial success and bolster regional group unity and pride.

While some voices maintain the high-pitched dense quality of Andean singing, many major stars incorporate Western vibrato (absent in tradition-

al Andean singing) and a clear – from the diaphragm – vocal style. As musicians have become more professional, specialising in certain styles, technical performance on instruments has become cleaner and instrumental breaks hotter. Arrangements too have become tighter and follow other urban popular forms with vocal verses and instrumental solos.

The names of the singers express the passion of the people for the flora and fauna of their homeland – **Flor Pucariña** (The Flower of Pucará) and **Picaflor de los Andes** (Hummingbird of the Andes) are two of those singing in the 1960s represented on GlobeStyle's huayno compilation. Another CD of this music, on the Arhoolie label, features the most celebrated huayno singer of all time – **El Jilguero de Huascarán**. When he died in 1988 thousands of people packed the streets of Lima to attend his funeral, and recordings he made over thirty years ago are still sold on the streets.

Flor Pucariña and Picaflor de los Andes

The buoyant, swinging rhythms of huayno songs are deceptive, for the lyrics fuse joy and sorrow. The musical style is regionally marked with typical mestizo instrumental ensembles of the region represented and musical features, such as specific guitar runs, identifying musicians with, for example, Ayacucho or Ancash. Sung in a mixture of Spanish and Quechua, they tell of unhappy love and betrayal, celebrate passion, and often deliver home-spun philosophy. As Picaflor sings in "Un pasajero en tu camino": "On the road of romance, I'm only a passenger without a destination". At the same time, texts often allude to region of origin or specific towns, important hooks for local audiences.

As well as in their sierra home, huaynos can be heard in Lima and other coastal towns, where they were brought by Andean migrants in the 1950s. Before then the music of the coastal towns and cities was **música criolla**, heavily influenced by music from other parts of Latin America, Spain and Europe – a bourgeois music including everything from foxtrot to tango, which filtered down to the working class, often as hybrids called, for example, Inca-Fox. Migrants often found themselves living in desperate poverty in the shantytowns, scraping a living as maids, labourers or street-traders, but in the 1950s and 1960s would meet up at the Lima *coliseo* (a form of stadium) on a Sunday to dance to their music and assert identity and pride.

Between 1946 and 1949 there were thirty such centres for *espectaculos folkloricos* in Lima, but only two remained by the mid 1970s and there are none left today. A blend of resources from the two worlds, this music served as an aid to provincianos in the process of forging a new identity for themselves. But the coliseos began to lose their public as people began to demand more traditional performances of highland music and dance. In the 1960s and 70s regional-migrant clubs began to take control over the commercial entrepreneurs who

Susana Baca and Afro-Peruvian Music

Afro-Peruvian music has its roots in the communities of black slaves brought to work in the mines along the Peruvian coast. As such, it's a fair way from the Andes, culturally and geographically. However, as it developed, particularly in this century, it drew on Andean and Spanish, as well as African traditions, while its modern exponents also have affinities with Andean nueva canción. The music was little known even in Peru until the 1950s, when it was popularised by the seminal performer Nicomedes Santa Cruz, whose body of work was taken a step further in the '70s by the group Peru Negro. Internationally, it has had a recent airing through David Byrne's Luaka Bop label, issuing the compilation, *Peru-Negro*, and a solo album by Susana Baca.

Nicomedes Santa Cruz is the towering figure in the development of Afro-Peruvian muisc. A poet, musician and journalist, he was the first true musicologist to assert an Afro-Peruvian cultural identity through black music and dance, producing books and recordings of contemporary Black music and culture in Peru. In 1959, with his group **Conjunto Cumanana**, he recorded the album *Kumanana*, followed in 1960 by *Ingá* and *Décimas y poemas Afroperuanos*. In 1964 he recorded a four-album set *Cumanana*, now regarded as the bible of Afro-Peruvian music. Santa Cruz himself followed in the footsteps of **Porfirio Vasquez**, who came to Lima in 1920 and was an early pioneer of the movement to regain the lost cultural identity of Afro-Peruvians. A composer of décimas, singer, guitarist, *cajonero* (box player) and *zapateador* (dancer) he founded the Academia Folklorica in Lima in 1949. Through Santa Cruz's work and that of the group **Peru Negro** and the singer and composer **Chabuca Granda**, Latin America came to know Afro-Peruvian dances, the names of which were given to their songs such as "Toro mata", "Samba-malató", "El Alcatraz" and "Festejo".

The singer who looks like bringing the music international acclaim, beyond Latin America, is **Susana Baca**, who grew up in the black coastal neighbourhood of Chorrillos outside Lima. Interviewed at WOMAD in 1998, she recalled family traditions of getting together for a Sunday meal, and then making music with her father playing guitar, her mother, aunts, uncles and friends singing and dancing. By the time she was a teenager and first heard the recordings of Nicomedes Santa Cruz, she realised she had absorbed quite a repertoire of the traditional songs Black people had carried with them to Peru as slaves.

Susana Baca runs her own Instituto Negrocontinuo, with her husband Ricardo Pereira; its aim is to promote and increase the diffusion of Afro-Peruvian music, and to link together old and young musicians through a series of workshops on all aspects of the music and its culture. Her passion for this project first emerged at school and has increased steadily over the years. "We studied the culture of the Spanish and of the Incas which made the Andean girls proud, but we black girls didn't find our people in the history of Peru at all," recalls Baca. "Blacks came to Peru as servants of Spanish and Portuguese, as slaves to be bought and sold. As a child I was aware that we had our way of cooking, our music, dances, even our own traditional medicines – but it was only in the 1960s that this was first really asserted in public. A lot of people until then had been silenced, some ashamed of the whole history of slavery, of the sufferings of their great grandparents, rejecting their past. But then it began to take on a positive hue and people began to understand what it meant to be black."

One of the essential instruments of Afro-Peruvian music is the *cajón* – a box which the percussionist sits astride, leaning down to play. This is the same cajón that eventually made its way into Spanish flamenco –

had failed to reward the musicians well. Sunday performances switched to these new clubs which gave a share of the fee to the musicians and featured traditions specifically from their home regions.

Urban huaynos are performed and recorded by **orquestas típicas** and enjoy enormous popularity. In the rural areas the style is more rustic. Andean highland settlements are isolated by deep river valleys, making communication difficult in the past. Because of this, students of Quechua are tormented by the extreme variation in language sometimes found between two relatively close villages. One would expect a similar variation between song styles; this is sometimes the case, but the huayno beat is pan-Andean. Each district does add its own peculiar flavour, but as the saying goes, a huayno is a huayno, at least until you listen closely. During daylight hours, some forty Lima radio stations broadcast nothing but huaynos. Shortwave radio fans, or visitors to Peru, can tune in for a quick education.

Thanks to Thomas Turino and Raúl Romero in Peru, Gilka Wara Céspedes in Bolivia, Martin Morales at Tumi, Charles B. Wolff and Margaret Bullen.

through Paco de Lucía who, according to an apocryphal story, played in Lima in 1978 and first heard the cajón played at a party. Susana remembers, "It's true, I was there, I even sang and there was a great group of Peruvian musicians playing and of cajoneros, and Paco de Lucía liked it all so much they gave him a cajón. The instrument is so important because it carries the rhythm and the voice sings within that dialogue between guitar and cajón. My mother always said that it was the box of the people who carried fruit and worked in the ports. When they had a free moment they used them to play and sing and dance. Later they had a more special construction, different woods with a hole in one side that gives a more sophisticated sound, more reverberation. Cuba and Brazil also have similar traditions which also emerged amongst black musicians in ports."

Baca's own performing style is intimate and rooted in close contact with her band "Nothing is written down, the musicians improvise and invent, so we need to be able to see each other's eyes to make a good performance, to share and enjoy and release the power of the music. You can hear it in "La canción para el señor de los milagros" (The Song for the Lord of Miracles). It's a song of adoration for a Christ who is celebrated for two days in October in Lima. It's now one of the most important popular festivals – people follow the Christ figure in such numbers through the streets the city comes to a halt. It's wonderful. They asked me to sing that sacred song and I do."

Susana Baca

discography

Some Andean music can also be found in the discography for Chile (Nueva Canción) on p.369,

Andean music

Compilations

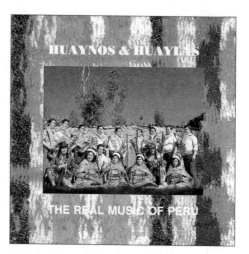

The Blind Street Musicians of Cusco: Peruvian Harp and Mandolin
(Music of the World, US).

Stirringly played marineras, huaynos, traditional tunes and instrumental solos exactly as heard on the streets of Cusco in 1984–5 from Leandro Apaza on thirty-three stringed harp; Benjamin Clara Quispé and Carmen Apaza Roca on armadillo-shelled mandolins; Fidel Villacorte Tejada on quena. Excellent ambience recorded in musicians' homes and *chichería* bars.

Bolivia Calendar Music of the Central Valley
(Chant du Monde, France).

Contemporary recordings of music which dates back to ancient times, music of the Quechua-speaking Amerindians played on panpipes, flutes and drums for rituals and ceremonies provides a feeling of real contact and movement from today to the pre-Colombian world: establishes tying of instruments to various seasons. Excellent notes.

Charangos et guitarillas du Norte Portosí
(VDE-Gallo/AIMP, Switzerland).

Compiled by a Bolivian, Florindo Alvis, these are spirited local recordings from Sucre and Cochabamba in Bolivia of songs in Quechua, often sung by a woman in high tones with a man lower second part accompanied by charango, vihuela, guitar or guitarilla. The intriguing notes explain special tunings for different times of the year and explain each piece, from potato planting songs to those for carnival.

Flutes and Strings of the Andes
(Music of the World, US).

The superbly atmospheric recordings of amateur musicians from Peru: harpists, charanguistas, fiddlers, flautists and percussionists, recorded in 1983–4 on the streets and at festivals, bring you as close to being there as you can get without strapping on your backpack and striding uphill.

From The Mountains to the Sea: Music of Peru, The 1960s (Arhoolie, US).

Brilliant window into the mix of indigenous, criollo, mestizo, Latin, tropical and European styles to be found in the capital including Peruvian rock, cumbias, valses, boleros, sanjuanitos, huaynos, tangos. Captures the spirit of many diferent groups, combinations of instruments and atmospheres.

Huaynos and Huaylas: The Real Music of Peru
(GlobeStyle, UK).

A tremendous selection of urban orquestas típicas, who replace traditional instruments with saxophones, clarinets and violins, this is a real eye- and ear-opener. The performers include the late Picaflor de los Andes, Flor Pucarina, with a host of songs expressing loss and love rooted in the Peruvian countryside.

Huayno Music of Peru Vols 1 and 2 (Arhoolie, US).

These excellent collections of huayno music from the 1950s to the 1980s focus on a slightly more local style than the GlobeStyle disc. Vol 1 includes songs from the master, Jilguero del Huascarán, while Vol 2 is drawn from the recordings of Discos Smith, a small label that released huayno and criolla music in the late 1950s and '60s.

Kingdom of the Sun (Nonesuch Explorer, US).

An atmospheric mix of Peru's Inca heritage and religious festivals recorded in Ayacucho, Chuschi and Paucartambo.

Mountain Music of Peru
(Smithsonian Folkways, US).

John Cohen's selection, including a song that went up in the Voyager spacecraft, brings together music from remote corners of the mountains where music is integral to daily life, and urban songs telling of tragedies at football matches. Good sleeve notes, too.

Música de Ecuador (Caprice, Sweden).

Superb 2-CD set of music from all over Ecuador including music from the Andean region, 'national music', village bands, music from the Chota-Mira river valley, from Esmeraldas province, and Amazonas. Includes wedding music, harp, village religious dances, panpipes, string bands, bomba music, marimbas, and more with Amazonian Amerindian vocal songs. Full booklet complete with pohtos and biographies of all groups.

 Peru – A mi patria
(World Network, Germany).

This wonderful disc covers a range of the mestizo traditions of Peru – revealing the fusion of Amerindian, Spanish and African musics. Opening with Carmen Flórez singing to a cajón (box) percussive backing, the album moves through tracks from guitar maestro Raúl García Zárate, Susana Baca's Afro-Peruvian song, the Quechua song (violin and falsetto voices) of Máximo Damián, and an enchanting brass band, Los Románticos de Sicay. Start right here!

Peru and Bolivia. The Sounds of Evolving Traditions. Central Andean Music and Festivals.
(Multicultural Media, US).

Lively, accessible introduction to today's sounds from both Peru and Bolivia, from Japanese aficionado Norio

Yamamoto's brilliant and diverse selection of recordings. Each piece in its natural context from people's homes to clubs to fiestas to streets with live local audiences. Harps, violins, drums, panpipes, and much more. Moving from Cuzco to Ayacucho, La Paz to Lima, Lake Titicaca and back to Marcapata village near Cuzco. Good notes.

 The Rough Guide to the Music of the Andes
(World Music Network, UK).

A vigorous and broad range of Andean music from contemporary urban based groups – including key 1960s musicians Los K'jarkas and Ernesto Cavou, and their 1980s European travelling bretheren Awatinas and Rumillajta; soloists Emma Junaro, Jenny Cardenas and Susana Baca; seminal Chilean group Inti Illimani and new song singer Victor Jara. Plus saxes and clarinets from Picaflor de los Andes . . .

 Traditional Music of Peru: Vol 1 Festivals of Cusco; Vol 2 The Mantaro Valley; Vol 3 Cajamarca and the Colca Valley; Vol 4 Lambayeque
(Smithsonian Folkways, US).

A definitive series of field recordings from the 1980s and 1990s of music from specific areas. Includes whole spectrum of music to be heard if you travelled around the whole of Peru. Excellent CD booklets. too.

Artists

Awatiñas

Awatiñas are one of the pioneering Aymara-speaking groups, including a number of members of the Conde Family, based half the year in La Paz, half in Europe. They have won success at home and abroad with their mixed repertoire of ritual music from their native village and urban mestizo styles arranged for concert performance.

 Kullakita (Awatinas Records, France).

Most tracks are new compositions in traditional style, arranged with this band's characteristic taste and skill.

Belem

Belem are one of the bands which has made Chicha – the music style named after the maize beer of the Amerindian peoples, a force to be reckoned with in urban Peru.

 Chicha (Tumi, UK).

A pioneering release of Peru's hot fusion music. Belem's mix of huayno, salsa, cumbia, and a touch of rock, deserves a listening. Andean pipe music, it ain't.

Arturo Zambo Cavero & Oscar Aviles

Arturo 'Zambo' Cavero is one of the great male voices of black Peruvian music, as well as being an accomplished cajón player. During the 1980s he teamed up with Oscar Aviles to become a celebrated partnership, their music seen as reflecting the suffering, patriotism and passion of the black people of Peru. As a key member of the group Los Morochucos, Oscar Aviles gained the reputation of being 'La Primera Guitarra del Peru' – Peru's leading Creole guitarist.

 Y siguen festejando juntos (IEMPSA, Peru).

Classic Afro-Peruvian music with the most representative voice and guitar musicians on the scene.

K'jarkas

Top Bolivian band which includes members of the Hermosa family, bi-lingual in Spanish and Quechua, who

have made the running for similar bands at home and abroad with their performances of their own compositions as well as traditional tunes. Their own music school has encouraged and trained a generation of new groups.

 Canto a la mujer de mi pueblo
(Tumi, UK).

While this tribute to Bolivian women in true male Latin fashion idealises women and their lives it contains superb examples of the genre with texts which blend the lives of women and nature. Also includes their own original song "Llorando se fue" which became the notorious Brazilian lambada.

Mallku de los Andes

Mallku de los Andes are Rumillajta founder Víctor Ferrell Torrico, and his talented Bolivian quartet.

 On the Wings of the Condor (Tumi, UK).

This is one of the most popular Andean albums ever, but none the worse for that: the engaging sound of the panpipes and charangos, smoothly and beautifully arranged.

Rumillajta

Rumillajta, whose name in Quechua means 'city of stone', have toured extensively in Europe, and are one of the most experienced Andean concert bands.

 Hoja de coca
(Tumi, UK).

This beautifully produced and arranged album of Bolivian music in its professional concert form has full range of styles delivered by a fine group of natural musicians playing many instruments made by their own hands.

Hermanos Santa Cruz

Hermanos Santa Cruz are family members of Nicomedes Santa Cruz.

 Afro Peru (Discos Hispanos, Peru).

Carrying on the tradition and heritage laid down by their forefathers, the Santa Cruz brothers present a 1990s version of Afro-Peruvian traditions.

Ayllu Sulca

Blind harpist Ayllu Sulca encapsulates everything that is mestizo music – the emergence of a hybrid blend between Amerindian and Spanish cultures. A virtuoso since early childhood, he plays as a soloist but mostly as part of his band – his 'ayllu' – which includes three of his sons.

 Music of the Incas (Lyrichord, US).

Accompanied by violin, mandolin and quenas, Sulca plays ancient Inca melodies and more recent waltzes with a pace and swing including rustic versions of salon music.

Afro-Peruvian music

Compilations

 **Afro-Peruvian Classics: The Soul of Black Peru** (Luaka Bop, US).

Music of the Black slaves brought to work in the mines of the coastal areas, which began to gain recognition in Peru in the 1940s. Popularised in the last twenty-five years, first by seminal musicologist and performer, Nicomedes Santa Cruz, then by Peru Negro, the group who got the music going in the 1970s; and the great Chabuca Granda; later Susana Baca and Cecilia Barraza continued the style. A unique blend of Spanish, Andean and African traditions, this is different to Caribbean and other Latin black cultures. This compilation includes the definitive dance song "Toro Mata", the first Afro-Peruvian success outside Peru covered by Queen of Salsa, Celia Cruz. A fine collection intended to introduce the music to a wider audience outside Peru, it does a great job.

Artists

Susana Baca

Susana Baca, one of the few Afro-Peruvian artists touring worldwide, grew up in the coastal barrio of Chorillos and learned traditional Afro-Peruvian songs from her family. Dedicated to recuperating and strengthening this past and making it relevant to the present she runs the Instituto Negrocontinuo (Black Continuum) in Lima and is as involved with the integral dance and other aspects of Afro-Peruvian culture as the music.

 Susana Baca
(Luaka Bop/Warner Bros).

Taking up the mantle of Chabuca Granda and Nicomedes Santa Cruz these are superb versions of Afro-Peruvian and criollo classics, sung with conscious emotion and passion, and with backing from a terrific Peruvian band.

Eco de Sombras Susana Baca
(Luaka Bop/Warner Bros, US).

Baca's new release for 2000 looks like crossing over to a broad international market, aided by US guest musicians John Medeski and Tom Waits veterans Marc Ribot on guitar and Greg Cohen on bass. Their contributions are powerful and sensitive, allowing the songs – stories of slave life and peasant struggles – to develop a richer palette.

Nicomedes Santa Cruz

The first true musicologist to assert Afro-Peruvian cultural identity through black music and dance.

Kumanana (Philips, Peru).
Socabon (Virrey, Peru).

Two albums showcasing Santa Cruz's majestic musicological studies of Afro-Peruvian music and culture.

Antilles

Zouk

dance-funk creole-style

French Antillean **Zouk** is one of the most significant World Musics: a blend of Caribbean pop, African guitar styles and American funk that – through its pioneering exponents, Kassav' – was the most copied global rhythm of the 1980s, until house music hit the scene. A couple of decades on, it just remains a significant force both at home and abroad: the most up-front and commercially successful music in the Creole Caribbean, huge at festival times on the islands of Guadeloupe and Martinique and their outlying colonies in Paris. **Charles de Ledesma** and **Gene Scaramuzzo** chart its course and take a sideways look at the **Kaseko** style of the neighbouring Dutch Antilles.

n the early to mid-1980s, zouk ruled supreme across the Caribbean and on a host of dance-floors from Paris to New York. Its impact at home was dramatic, as the French Antillean islands of **Guadeloupe** and **Martinique** – the heartland of zouk – became increasingly vibrant, energetic and creative places to live and visit. There was a definite sense of zouk having put the islands on the map, particularly in France, where the musicians had huge pop success, and the experience filtered through even to the smaller Antillian islands: Dominica, St Barts, St Lucia and St Martin all came on in leaps and bounds during the zouk years, hosting music and cultural festivals and contributing many of the growing, commercial, zouk sub-genres.

These days, zouk has faded from the European mainstream but remains a big business at home and in the Paris-based communities. The music divides into two main camps – the infectious, loping, faster and harder dance style known as **chire** or **beton**, and the seductive, ballad-like **zouk-love**. Both styles – and all the manifold sub-genres – have a commonality in the Creole language. Indeed, if there's a defining spirit in zouk it is the islands' unique take on patois, combining French, West African and Caribbean languages into a luscious melting pot of expression. Creole lends itself to the lilt, ambiance and texture of zouk perfectly.

Zouk was born largely in the studio and remains basically a recorded music with very few actual live performing acts. Its audience tends to identify strongly with the singers – there is a panoply of very big stars – leaving most of the instrumental players in the background. As with other Caribbean musics it keeps in sync with the low-budget musical trends of today with stripped down arrangements often utilising programmed instruments.

For live music lovers, *les vacances* (the French summer vacation months of July and August) and the pre-Lenten carnival season are the two times of the year to catch the best of the existing live scene.

JOHN CLEWLEY

Dance zouk: two legs good, three legs better!

Party Origins

Zouk traces its roots to West Africa, Europe and the Caribbean. Its immediate parents are Haitian *compas* and Antillean biguine (a European dance-hall craze in the 1920s), but there are strong influences from Pan-Caribbean *calypso* and indigenous rhythmic forms like **chouval bwa** from Martinique and the **gwo ka** tradition of Guadeloupe. More distant relatives include the drumming and singing carried by the slaves from West Africa, and to a lesser extent, French ballroom, classical styles like the mazurka, quadrille and waltz.

The word zouk is Creole for party – and by extension the sound systems employed. From the late 1950s through to the early 1980s – and the emergence of the Guadeloupian group **Kassav'** (the name is Creole for cassava) – the music heard at zouks became an amalgam of Caribbean styles, notably compas from Haiti and a French Antillean offshoot called **cadence**. Reggae and calypso (in those days still sometimes sung in Creole) and the occasional tropical beat from Puerto Rico and Venezuela, would be included in the mix as well. But by the 1980s, the predominant music of any hot zouk (party) was the sound of Kassav', and thus their music naturally became known as 'zouk music'.

Gwo Ka and Chouval Bwa

Zouk is a quintessentially modern music – a name to mention alongside salsa, samba and house. But it is only as rich and powerful as these genres because the past, the roots, are still there, if not always conspicuous. Its chief musical and spiritual origins are the *gwo ka* (drums) of Guadeloupe and the *tambour/ti bwa* (drum/bamboo percussion) ensembles of Martinique, with special fervour added by the carnival traditions of both islands.

There are seven basic rhythms to the **gwo ka** in Guadeloupe, and it's a live tradition – even young children can distinguish each of them. Two drums of different sizes make up the basic ensemble, the larger *boula* laying down the foundational rhythm for the second drum, the *markeur* (or *maké* in Creole), to interplay with dancers, singer or audience. In size the drums of the gwo ka range from the knee-high *ka markeur* to the waist-held *ka boule* which are made of local woods and carved with indigenous designs.

In their most traditional rural expression the drums are used in a communal experience called a *lewoz*. Still rooted in tradition, but moving a step towards the contemporary are the many *gwo ka moderne* groups of Guadeloupe. Ensembles like **Van Lévé**, **Poukoutan'n** and **Pakala Percussion** all stick to basic drumming/vocals but add touches like a conga or African *djembe* drum or store-bought percussion such as chimes, even an occasional electric bass guitar.

Moving (at times) further towards pop expression are artists like **Ti Celeste**, **Eric Cosaque** and **Marcel Magnat**, all of whom have released recordings featuring examples of both raw, unaccompanied gwo ka drumming and a more melodic expression utilising instruments and vocals. There have also been a few attempts at zoukified gwo ka – the best being by **Sartana**, **Anzala** and, back in the 1980s, an artist named **Gerard Hubert**.

Underneath the trappings, all of these artists play intricate improvisations around the seven basic rhythms. A fine example is Ti Celeste's "Ban Mwen" from the soundtrack to the film *Coeurs de Couleur*. While three boula and a markeur drummer set up fast, interlocking rhythms, two singers cut across the beat with a tense, beautiful melody. Another is **William Flessel**, who brought gwo ka to centre stage with his 1994 CD *Message Ka*. This is one of the greatest drum records in any tradition – nonstop, totally intoxicating Afro-Caribbean drumming and chanting, his troupe layering complex polyrhythms on hand drums, with call and response vocals alongside.

The vocal side of gwo ka is very unusual and not unlike the rural singing styles of Martinique, at times smooth and light, but most often grainy, guttural and nasal. This vocal form has survived from slavery days in the hills of Guadeloupe, where **Esnard Boisdur**, **Guy Konket** and **Eric Cosaque** are noted exponents of the style. Of course, experimentation is not beyond these artists either, as evidenced by Boisdur's rendition of "Devenn" in the film *Coeurs de Couleur*. Singing in Creole, his vocal texture and sense of phrasing sounds West African, while the uplifting melodies and complex harmonies are almost gospel.

At **carnival time on Guadeloupe,** dozens of gwo ka units tour the island, playing endless improvisations on a basic theme, much like the samba schools in Brazil. It is a participatory type of music with people grabbing any percussive instrument they can find and joining in. Also performed are dances of African origin such as the *calinda*, *laghia*, *bel-air*, *haut-taille* and the *grage*, mostly in remote villages. The most famous of the Guadeloupian carnival street bands, and the only one to have recorded albums, is **Akiyo**. Any of their albums (or their video) gives a quick and exciting lesson in the most popular carnival tradition, the **mas a St. Jean**, and the spirit of carnival in Guadeloupe.

The additional, year-around presence of carnival and gwo ka music on the radio and on discs – plus mega-concerts by Ti Celeste and others on the island, around the Latin world and in Paris – is largely due to **Kassav'**, who pulled gwo ka out of the hills and into the urban recording studios, thereby giving a new legitimacy to a tradition that had come to be considered unsophisticated. Wishing to include the traditions of Guadeloupe in their new music, Kassav' paid homage to Guadeloupe's legendary gwo ka drummer **Velo** on their early albums as well as including original songs that were propelled by the rhythms of the mas a St. Jean. While the band soon gave up on the gwo ka ensemble in their recordings (a move still lamented by many in Guadeloupe), the musical references to carnival were the key to the band's ultimate enormous success in the Antilles.

Martinique's carnival music, an uptempo version of the biguine called **biguine vide**, is also very much part of Kassav' zouk and is evident in the harder *chire* or *beton* styles of many other artists. The vocal interaction between zouk bands and their audience can be directly traced to the call and response involvement of carnival crowds (in both Martinique and Guadeloupe) and is one of the reasons for the total body and soul participation at zouk shows.

A growing phenomenon of the past decade and a half has been the emergence of large neighborhood **street bands** which hit the streets during carnival season playing drums, percussion and horns. The best of these bands – **Plastic System Band**, **Sasayesa**, **Tanbou Bo Kan'nal** and **Sissi Percussion** – have put out their own discs. But whether recorded or on the streets the preferred form of carnival music is long medleys of past carnival hits that allow everyone to join in. Every few years there surfaces a new song or two that captures everyone's fancy and becomes part of the canon of carnival hits for the medleys to come. Samples of these carnival medleys are most easily available on Ronald Rubinel's Multicolor albums, although carnival albums are produced yearly by many different artists.

The **tambour/ti bwa** ensemble of Martinique also fed into zouk, and indeed underpins the style – especially the chire and slower zouk-love varieties. This roots music ensemble (now mainly interpreted on a full drum kit or trapset) provided the original rhythm section for the biguine and is the foundation of another very exciting traditional music, strictly Martiniquan, called **chouval bwa**. A celebratory music, chouval bwa's origins are associated with carnivals and fairs when this galloping rhythm accompanied the *manege* or merry-go-round (chouval bwa is Creole for *cheval bois*, referring to the wooden horses of the merry-go-round).

The rhythmic centre of the chouval bwa orchestra is provided by the *tambour* drum (mounted like a horse with the player dampening the skin with the heel of the foot) and *ti bwa* (a piece of bamboo, three feet in length with a diameter of at least several inches and mounted horizontally then hit with sticks). In its most traditional form it also includes a bass drum-like tambour called the *bel-air*, accordion and *chacha* (a gourd or tin filled with stones). The players also sing chorus, responding to the calls of the leader, but the really defining aspect of the vocals is the percussive onomatopoeic phrasing that calls to mind the quadrille or square dance.

The one proponent of traditional chouval bwa still visible and recording is **Claude Germany**. Other players are forging new contemporary directions for the style. They incldue Martinique-based tambourist **Marce Pago** with his group **Tumpak** – who coined the term *zouk chouv'* on his 1987 album, a fine example of roots zouk packed with multi-rhythmic drumming and flute, accordion

Learning the Quadrille in Guadeloupe

Peter Culshaw had always fancied the idea of learning a dance like the Quadrille – and finally got his chance at the annual fete in the small town of Moule in Guadeloupe.

It is bizarre that a dance first made popular at the court of Napoleon I, and all but dead in Europe, thrives today, in an admittedly funkier way, thousands of miles away in Guadeloupe. The reason, inevitably, was sugar and slaves. According to the chronicler Père Labat, the French colonials encouraged their slaves to take up the fashionable European dances so that they would give up their heathen African ways. They also needed accompanists for their dances. But the slaves changed the Quadrille somewhat, and it became more rhythmic and considerably livelier than the dainty original.

The group I tracked down were called La Renaissance de Ste-Anne and featured accordion, clarinet, trumpet, violin, percussion – and triangle played by a Monsieur Etienne. The group had apparently once tried to play without him, but 'it just wasn't the same - it wasn't Quadrille'. Their one concession to modernity is an electric bass and a synthesiser playing the piano parts (it's more portable). They spice up their set with the occasional polka, waltz or beguine, but their true metier is the Quadrille.

The 'ball' to which I was invited was packed with a couple of hundred dancers. The atmosphere was a strange but attractive combination of the elegance of a French eighteenth century court and the wilder grace of Africa. The dancers' ages ranged widely, but even the octogenarians moved with extraordinary lightness and agility. The leader of La Renaissance is the formidable Monsieur Samson Marcellin, known to all as *Le Commandeur*, a tall, bespectacled figure who barks out the instructions for the Quadrille in French Creole over the music. *La Liman a goch tour main* means everyone has to move to the left while *Chaine Anglaise* means its time to change partners. More subtle instructions include *Coulice*, which translates more or less as 'to glide' and *Mannye ko'aw*, which is plea that the dancers should follow the beat more closely.

Monsieur Marcellin explained some of the finer points the next day. It seems there are seven figures in the Quadrille dance, including *le pantalon* (trousers), *la poule* (the hen), and *la pastourelle* (the shepherd girl). Some of these names reflect the origins of Quadrille in the *contre-danse* (country dance), which was imported by an English dance teacher into France in about 1710.

Quadrille, Monsieur Marcellin added, had become something of a local political football in Guadeloupe, with some black intellectuals keen to reject European colonial influences and to encourage indigenous music like the local drumming *gwo-ka*. But, if anything, there is increasing interest in the Quadrille, with at least thirty schools in Guadeloupe teaching it again. And respected *gwo-ka* drummer George Troupe told me that he thought that the opposition to Quadrille was misguided "We made the music our own and it's become as much Guadeloupean as anything else."

I was also told that if I wanted to learn the Mazurka I should really try neighbouring island Martinique ...

Peter Culshaw

---

and brass. Marce's more recent releases have mellowed a little but he remains an innovator, adding synthesiser, electric guitar and bass to enrich rather than abandon the original forms of chouval bwa.

The other top contemporary chouval bwa artist, **Dede Saint-Prix**, plays tambour and bamboo flute and has released albums that range from near tradition to techno extremes. More often than not, he has struck gold with his experimentations, and his residence in mainland France has given him an edge over Marce on international distribution.

Dede was also the founder of the percussive group **Pakatak** that continues to release occasional and interesting records heavy in chouval bwa under the guidance of its core membership of leader Krisyan Jesophe, Bago and Mario Masse. The group's *Chouval Bwa 87* album, an intriguing collage of Latin jazz and traditional percussion, features Kali on banjo, played as though it were a Cuban *tres*.

The Martiniquans Begin the Biguine

The **biguine**, the original pop music of the French Antilles, is a kind of folk-jazz. It evolved in Martinique as string band music, formed around guitar or banjo chords, with tambour and ti bwa percussion, and later clarinets and violins. Its popularity on the island, appearing mainly in shack-nightclubs, known as *paillotes*, brought it to mainland France in the 1920s.

The Paris biguine dances were a fusion of African style with French ballroom steps, launch-

Alexandre Stellio's biguine band

ing a biguine craze in Europe. These Creole tunes were the staple of the popular Parisian dancehall, Le Bal Negre, and the Martiniquan clarinettist **Alexandre Stellio** became a major international figure. Stellio's instrumental line-up closely paralleled traditional New Orleans jazz, although there is little apparent evidence of crossed influences. **The Orchestre Antillais**, led by Stellio and later by another clarinetist **Sam Castandet**, remained a presence on the Paris nightclub scene into the 1950s, playing biguines, boleros and tangos.

The biguine remains a significant music in Martinique and has encompassed many different styles through the century, as well as spawning the island's carnival music. It lost its pop dominance back in the 1950s when a generation began dancing to the new compas sound from Haiti but most early zouk artists were well-versed in its styles – and it received a new studio treatment in the 1990s through an incredibly successful series of Ethnikolor discs released by Ronald Rubinel.

You can still hear biguine played at live venues. Artists like **Max Ransay**, **Ralph Thamar**, **Michel Godzom** and **Kali** all play contemporary forms of biguine usually referred to as **biguine moderne**. Of these, Kali is the best known internationally. Part of the small but articulate community of Rastafarians in Martinique, Kali was a long-time member of the reggae band **Sixieme Continent** before picking up his grandfather's heirloom banjo and turning to biguine. Realising that the search for African roots espoused by the Rastas need extend no further than the culture of his hometown of Sainte Pierre, Kali began exploring his musical heritage of the past century. The result was a series of *Racines* (Roots) albums featuring banjo-dominated treatments of classic styles that are among the most pleasing discs to have been released in the past decade. His recent albums occa-

sionally incorporate his interest in roots reggae as well, creating a unique, successful blend.

The most accomplished clarinet player of biguine moderne, whose style can be directly traced to the early days of biguine, is **Michel Godzom**, one of the internationally unsung musical heroes of Martinique. He launched his career as a member of Martinique's most popular cadence-era bands **La Perfecta** and **Operation '78** but eventually retired from that scene to study the early style biguine as played by Alexandre Stellio. Since returning to the recording scene in the early 1980s he

Kali

has released nearly a dozen albums of biguine moderne. Like Kali, he has a highly distinctive approach. On his *Horizon* album, for example, his clarinet weaves and ducks through electronic bubblings, up-tempo biguine-vide and soft, sentimental passages. One of only a handful of regularly performing Martinique-based musicians, Godzom appears with his own band and has also been a member of several short-lived super groups like **Acoustic Zouk** and **Palavire**.

The Neo-Classicists: Malavoi

One intriguing Antillean offshoot is the group of classically trained musicians centred around the band **Malavoi**; they have radically reinterpreted the biguine, mazurka and waltz, giving them a spicy Latin feel. Their classic song, "Bona", for instance, starts with virtuoso violin and ends with a drum and vocal workout akin to Cuban rumba.

Malavoi and their string section, mid-1980s

Malavoi formed in the 1970s and had their heyday in the late '70s and '80s, when they created a sound mixing in Cuban charanga-style violins, horn sections, percussion from **Dede Saint-Prix**, and top-class singing from **Edith Lefel** and other guest Antillean vocalists. With each successive album of this era, they continued to re-invent their sound, combining traditional European dance forms with bossa nova, Haitian music, and rural melodies and home-grown chouval bwa rhythms. They seemed most assured, however, in their big-spirited string arrangements, where lead singer

Pipo Gertrude (who replaced Ralph Thamar in 1987) duetted with his guests.

In the 1990s, following the death of the group's leader Paulo Rosine, and subsequent departure of the original founder Mano Cesaire, Malavoi underwent a series of personnel changes. Their most recent releases, such as *She She*, show an uncertainty in direction yet indicate that the band are still capable of outstanding playing.

The Cadence Era

From the late 1950s through to the start of the 1980s, the Antilles pop scene was literally overwhelmed by Haitian music, starting with the big band styles of **Nemour Jean-Baptiste** (creator of compas direct) and **Weber Sicot** (creator of cadence rompas) and followed by the guitar-dominant **mini-jazz** style of the late 1960s.

Among the bands that formed in Guadeloupe and Martinique during the mini-jazz heyday were several future Antillean stars. **Les Leopards** featured Max Ransay and Michel Thimon, **Les Gentlemen** had Ralph Thamar (later of Malavoi), and **Les Vikings de Guadeloupe** gave an early start to Pierre-Edouard Decimus, Guy Jacquet and Gordon Henderson of Kassav'. These bands were well-versed in playing their homegrown biguine and Creole mazurka but their repertoires consisted mainly of the compas rhythm being played by the Haitian mini-jazz bands. It was this rhythm that became the foundation of today's zouk.

In playing Haitian mini-jazz, the Antillean musicians inevitably added their own idiosyncrasies, developing **cadence** forms as distinct from Haiti as they were from each other. And as if three different forms of music called cadence weren't enough, musicians from the island of Dominique also got in on the act. Due to a lack of local facilities, it was common for Dominican bands to travel to Guadeloupe to record. There they were encouraged by Antillean producers to include current cadence styles, inextricably adding the musics of Gramacks, the Bill-o-Men and Black Affairs into the mix. Most notably, Dominican **Gordon Henderson** who had started the 1970s playing in Les Vikings took Guadeloupian cadence and added calypso horns to it, creating a style he called cadence-lypso with his new band **Exile One**.

With the arrival of Exile One the guitar-dominated bands of both Haiti and the Antilles took on full horn sections, turning mini-jazz combos into big bands by the mid-1970s. This was the heyday of bands like **La Perfecta**, **Les Aiglons** (who scored the biggest ever pre-zouk Antillean hit with "Cuisse-La"), **Selecta**, **Operation '78**, **Experience 7**, an early non-string version of **Malavoi**, and more.

These bands recorded and played live, often as opening acts to visiting Haitian bands, until the late 1970s when the disco era's inexpensive sound system format brought the live music scene to a grinding halt in the Antilles – as elsewhere. Few bands were able to withstand the dearth of gigs and their record sales dropped off, too. However, members of two cadence bands, Les Vikings of Guadeloupe and La Perfecta of Martinique, were instrumental in the evolution of the islands' next musical phase . . .

The Super Group: Kassav'

When in 1995 the **Kassav'** anthology *Dife* was released, it was hailed as a reminder of the value

of singing in true, unadulterated Creole – lyric writers and singers in recent years had adulterated this essential element in zouk composition, no doubt to broaden their appeal to French listeners who didn't understand the patois.

The reason why this move by Kassav' was so important was that it reminded people of the early days, when their most famous song, "Zouk-La-Se Sel Medikaman Nou Ni" (Zouk is the Only Medicine We Have) ruled the French Caribbean airways, confirming that Kassav' were one of the biggest names in World Music while preaching that zouk music was the root to a liberated cultural identity separate from France, the island's erstwhile colonial rulers.

What was interesting was that Paris, France's capital, was the Kassav' base. Indeed the band had formed there, in a city which in the early 1970s was highly fertile territory for Pan-African and African-Caribbean musical fusions. Here Cameroonian *makossa* and Zairois and Congolese soukous were becoming stronger, harder and more confident styles, and zouk soon followed in the same direction. In turn, new hybrids like *maka-zouk* and *soukou-zouk* reflected the influence zouk musicians and producers like Kassav' and Ronald Rubinel

COLUMBIA, FRANCE

Kassav' live at the Zenith, Paris

would have on these hitherto more developed African styles. The Kassav' – and zouk – founders, **Jacob Desvarieux** and **Pierre-Edouard Decimus**, came out of this creative ferment.

Kassav' formed in 1978, Decimus and Desvarieux collecting around them the cream of the Paris resident French Antillean musicians. The original band line-up was all-Guadeloupian but before long they were joined by Martiniquans **Jean Claude Naimro**, **Claude Vamur**, **Jean-Philippe Marthely** (and Guadeloupian **Patrick Saint-Eloi**). Later the

member who would emerge as the band's star, **Jocelyne Beroard**, would crystallise the Creole vocal intonations which earlier vocalists Marthely and Saint Eloi hadn't fully embraced.

The first two Kassav' records displayed a rather wobbly balance of American funk with Creole vocals and cadence textures. But, crucially for zouk, they introduced an eleven-piece gwo ka drum unit. These percussive rhythms – the equivalent of Cuba's rumba and Brazil's samba – were usually only heard at carnival time in Guadeloupe.

Jocelyne Beroard

Undoubtedly the classiest woman of the Antilles music scene today is singer **Jocelyne Beroard**, one of the core members of the pioneering zouk group **Kassav'**. Her beautiful, powerful voice has enriched every Kassav' project since her debut performance on the band's second album in 1981, and over nearly twenty years she has been sought after for literally hundreds of other albums and musical projects encompassing both zouk and classic Antilles styles.

But what dramatically sets Jocelyne apart from all other singers on the scene is the fact that she is truly the embodiment of the group Kassav's original intent, echoed by Martiniquan filmmaker Euzhan Palcy in her classic Caribbean story *Simeon* – "to be a device for building positive self-esteem in a people who are embarrassingly rich in culture yet who have been brainwashed to think otherwise by the ills of slavery." In every aspect of her career she has used her high profile to legitimise and celebrate this viewpoint.

From her refusal to follow the past decade's trend of Antilles singers to soften their native Creole language, to her obvious pleasure in singing biguine and other classic Antilles musics, Jocelyne has gently, but firmly, made her position clear. Her appearance and demeanour in public have always been elegant, and her onstage interplay with Kassav' singers **Jean-Philippe Marthely** and **Patrick Saint-Eloi** has suggested a new direction for relations between men and women. The latter is in direct opposition to a long-standing lyrical tradition in the Antilles which typically addressed love and sex in a manner suggestive to the

Jocelyne Beroard

point of pornography. Lyrically, Jocelyne has yearned for the companionship of a man but not at the expense of her dignity, a perfect complement to Saint-Eloi, in particular, who has searched for a new level of sensitivity in his approach to women in his lyrics. Any who have witnessed live performances of duets like "Move Jou," "Pa Bisouin Pale" or "Kole Sere" know the fiery surges of emotion that passed between the singers.

Jocelyne launched her singing career in Paris, adding backing vocals to live performances and records by artists as diverse as Louisiana's Zachary Richard,  Cameroon's Manu Dibango and Jamaica's Lee Perry. Crossing paths with Kassav' was a match made in heaven in a multitude of ways, not the least of which was her fluency in English that has made her the band's spokesperson in the anglophone world. In addition to her countless compositions on Kassav' albums over the years, she also has two solo albums to her credit, *Siwo* from 1987 and *Milans* from 1991. Both were critically acclaimed and warmly received by zouk fans, and are still available, as is most of the Kassav' back catalogue. Work on an eagerly anticipated third solo album has been an intermittent affair, put on hold a number of times by various Kassav' projects.

Jocelyne can also be seen in performance on a number of videos including *Kassav' au Zenith*, *Grand Mechant Zouk* and Malavoi's *Matabis,* as well as in her acting role in Euzhan Palcyís *Simeon*.

Gene Scaramuzzo

Now they were being fused with rock guitar, cadence rhythms and hard, flattened, soca-esque horns. The mature Kassav' style – choppy and sparse but closely melodic – sounded like nothing that had come before, and put the Antillean once and for all on the Caribbean music map, as well as making the new sound popular on the blossoming Parisian nightclub scene.

If Kassav' were first more popular in their home city, Paris, than on the islands, that would soon change with their most famous song "Zouk-La-Se Sel Medikaman Nou Ni". Its explosive message found the hearts and minds of Guadeloupians in particular, as for the past century they had received second-class treatment from the French, who still partially governed both islands. If there was an indirect political message, however, that wasn't taken up by other zouk songwriters, and indeed Kassav' themselves shied away from discussing the issue of full independence from France.

Musically, through the 1980s, Kassav' went from strength to strength, acting as a reservoir for Antillean styles and absorbing elements like the chamber ensembles held over from the French *grand bals*. The swooping violins on songs like "Mwin Devue" bring a classical touch that sits with startling originality alongside Desvarieux's heavy metal guitar and JC Naimro's synthsizer-accordion. But for many it was the intensely funky, pumping bass, holding the elaborate music together like glue, which was at the core of their success. The traditonal drumming, gwo ka, was less in evidence than before but still put to ingenious use for links in medleys. Meantime the Kassav' singers would do wild things, like launching into Creole raps – a sound uncannily like the commands in French country dancing – which had been popular on the islands up until the 1950s.

Kassav' added West African guitar to the sooped-up cadence beat as well. This wasn't the first time contemporary African pop had found its way into French Caribbean music. The **Orchestra Rico Jazz** from Zaire had spent some years in the Antilles in the 1970s and had opened a few ears to polyphonic guitar playing. From then on, African guitar licks would creep into zouk, sounding as though they had always been there. After all, the two musics not only shared the same root, but zouk musicians living in Paris increasingly played and recorded with African musicians – throughout the 1980s influences travelled three ways, generating a wonderful musical triangle between West Africa, the Antilles and Paris.

The individual members of Kassav' then spread their wings on separate projects. There were brilliant songs on the band's album *Desvarieux and Decimus (GD)* but the group went off the boil in the early 1990s and the most exciting developments came with solo projects – particularly Jocelyne Beroard's *Siwo* which confirmed her position as the foremost singer in zouk. There were good things, too, from **Bizness**, a group formed by two Kassav' members, Patrick Saint-Eloi and Jean-Philippe Marthely, to perform when the mother band was resting. Meanwhile, **Kwak** and **Taxi Kreol** continued the large band tradition, applying razor-sharp production to melodic, mostly mid-tempo songs.

The 1995 release, *Dife*, restored Kassav' to their position as the top band in zouk with its sensitive exploration of all the elements which constitute zouk today, from emotive, but sometimes over-sweetened ballads, to rousing, dance-drenched, numbers. They enlisted new singers, like **Edith Lefel** and **Frederick Caracas**, and went back to playing live, too. There was even a tour of Africa, taking them home to the origins of the percussive music which has intermittently fired up their recordings and shows.

Through the 1990s, tropical artists from Brazil, Colombia and Dominican Republic have done zouk versions of Kassav' songs, while the group themselves have done things the other way, releasing a set of their top songs recorded in Spanish with a salsa beat. As a result, Kassav's popularity has now expanded through the Spanish Caribbean, Central and South America. They remain the brightest beacon in zouk, although other artists – the top names in the more commercial zouk-love and beton styles – sell more records today and are more popular on nightclub dance floors.

Contemporary Zouk

Despite the fact that the members of Kassav' have lived in Paris during the band's entire existence, their adherence to an Antillean identity has prevented their true adoption by the French as 'one of ours.' Success in mainland France has been reserved for only a handful of Antilles artists like **Zouk Machine**, **Joelle Ursull**, **Tanya Saint-val**, **Kali** and, most recently, the singer **Edith Lefel**.

Zouk Machine, which emerged from Guadeloupian Henri Debs' studio, led the way in this arena in the late 1980s with solid radio hits and frequent television variety show appearances. Estranged original Zouk Machine member **Joelle Ursull** then went on to make one of France's biggest selling pop records, "Black French", in 1990 by collaborating with French bad boy Serge

Gainsbourg. (It should come as no surprise that Kassav's Jocelyne Beroard likewise made her first real inroad into France's celebrity zone by singing a duet with French singing star Philippe Lavil). Ursull remains a big name on the Paris scene. She reduces the polyrhythmic complexities of zouk, blends in house rhythms and uses synthesizers to back her wonderful voice on French variety shows.

The influence of Kassav' is also heard in the work of **Edith Lefel** who lives in Paris and is likely to be the next to experience cross-over international success. Her biggest hits, "Poutch" and "La Vie Trop Kout", are perfectly crafted mid-tempo pop tunes where the taut textures of Kassav'-style zouk have made way for a less tense backdrop of synthesizers, horns and strong vocals. Her most beautiful song, "Yche Man Man", an

Combined Rhythm and Kaseko:
The Dutch West Indies

It comes as no surprise to discover that the music of the **Dutch Antillean islands** – Curacao, Aruba, Bonaire, St Eustatius and St Martin – is very much influenced by the dominant forms which surround it: zouk from the French Antilles, soca from Trinidad and merengue from the Dominican Republic. The popular style is mostly sung in *papiamento*, the patois of the larger settlements, Curacao and Aruba. It is known as Combined Rhythm, referring to the gelling of the local patois lyrics onto the merengue beats. There is a healthy scene on the islands with top bands **Gibu i su Orkesta**, **Expresando Rimto i Ambiente**, the **OK Band** and **Happy Peanuts** playing weekly and releasing occasional CDs.

The former Dutch colony of **Surinam** – on the northeastern coast of South America yet historically part of the Dutch Antilles – has a more individual style, known as **kaseko**, a music and dance developed by Surinamese Creoles – descendants of African slaves. Surinam's slaves (known as maroons) escaped their European captors earlier than any other enslaved colony, including Haiti, and created their own settlements. Kaseko seems to reflect this, in its vibrant, upbeat style, and its roots probably are close to African ritual dance – the name is thought to be a corruption of 'casser le corps' (break the body), an expression for the rural 'devil dance' in neighbouring French Guyana. Africa remains clearly apparent in the music's syncopated rhythms, based around the snare drum and a big indigenous drum called the *skratji* which drive the music along with kaseko's characteristic brass section (sax, trumpet and trombone), and in its lyrical delivery: the lead vocalist is regularly repeated and/or answered by the other singers, in a classic West African/Creole call and response way.

A vibrant, creative music, which has adapted easily to modern and electric instruments, kaseko has developed in recent years both in Surinam and in the Netherlands, where around a quarter of Surinamese now live. Their number include leading groups like those of **Carlo Jones**, **William Souvenir**, **Yakki Famiri** and **Zonnebloem** who have established a reputation there as excellent dance bands, very much like West African bands Somo Somo and Abdul T Jay did in London in the 1980s.

Kaseko also shows strong influences from the colonial-era military **marching bands** (still a live tradition in Surinam), New Orleans jazz, Cuban mambo, Haitian compas, and Caribbean calypso and merengue. And it reflects also the diverse ethnic mix of Surinam, whose population includes Amerindians and Indonesians, as well as Africans and indigenous groups.

island number one, shows the more forceful vocal approach to **zouk-love**, a gentler style that is often characterised by rather limpid vocals. It was recorded with the highly innovative guitarist **Dominique Gengoul** and singer **Jean-Luc Alger** of **Lazair**, who play in a particularly melodic, mid-tempo, funky way. Lefel's 1996 album *A L'Olympia* showed what a superstar she had become: a live (in Paris) album recorded before a massive ecstatic crowd, dancing in the aisles to her new blend of zouk, incorporating Latin, Pan-Caribbean and even Flamenco grooves.

Other big contemporary **zouk-love** acts include **Gilles Floro**, **JM Harmony** and **Tanya Saintval**. They make an attractive, but overtly comercial, music which has become almost the swing-beat, or the *salsa romantica*, of the Carribean. They have spawned hundreds of imitators, and alongside them critics who cry out that the soul of zouk has been replaced by a slick, nondescript sound. They have a point. Some new generation zouk bands have opted for a drum machine and keyboards that produce a kind of identikit sound – music for dancing which possesses neither thought or depth.

A further development has been to make a zouk which integrates a variety of other rhythms and styles, all ideally on the same album to maximise cross-over sales potential. **Jean Michel Rotin** is the current hot artist in this field mixing American commercial styles, like new jack (swing beat), funk and hip hop in with zouk. Then there's the zouk-funk of **Muriel Custos** and **Elza Bruta** and perhaps the biggest growth of all, **ragga-zouk** with artists who sound Jamaican: **RuffNeg**, **Lord Kossity** and **Karukeragga**.

Nearly twenty years after zouk's inception it seems that it has joined reggae and salsa as a Caribbean music with enduring and worldwide influence. There are zouk bands all over the Caribbean and Central America, in the Dominican Republic and on Colombia's Atlantic coast. The zouk craze has never abated. Moreover, through all the flotsam and jetsam that is zouk today – and that means 250 or so albums released for each summer Vacances – quality and class are still much in evidence. As one zouk fan wrote recently on the internet: "What I want is to hear great singers, guitars, keyboards, rhythm and maybe an accordion, a harmonica or a banjo and (please!) a blazing, boozy brass section to add spice!" Zouk will still serve that up, simply because its roots go so deep, the language is so evocative, and the rhythm and melodies so tantalising.

Above all, zouk will always be inextricably linked to a unified expression of French Antillean culture. As another, local fan noted on the zouk web site, it is a music that has helped the disparate peoples across the French and Dutch Caribbean see that they have much in common. "No matter where we are located, one thing for sure is that we have so much to share – language, music, food, culture, dance and even mentality – and yes, we speak Creole in some form or another."

discography

Zouk and Cadence

Compilations

Collection Prestige de la Musique Caribene (Hibiscus/Cocosound, Martinique).

Many of the greatest artists of Martinique, Dominique and Guadeloupe recorded on the Martiniquan 3A label during the 1970s cadence era. This essential collection features the original recordings of greatest hits by many of these performers, compiled in single discs devoted to artists including Gramacks, Vikings de la Guadeloupe, Malavoi, and Eugene.

 Dance Cadence (GlobeStyle, UK).

An inspired compilation which introduced pop-style cadence to the World Music market. Also highlighting some cracking early zòuk dance numbers.

Les Années du Zouk (Declic, France).

Four CDs in all, including tracks as recent as 1998. Strong on zouk-love style.

Maxi Zouk (Declic, France).

Another four-CD set, put together by Zouk arranger Eric Basset. Includes faster zouk styles and new zouk-love.

Zouk Attack (Rounder, US).

Inimitable selection of 1980s/90s zouk classics including Gazolin', Patrick Parole and Frederick Caracas, some of the most inventive arrangers of the genre.

Artists

Jocelyne Beroard

The lead vocalist with the group Kassav' and veritable Queen of zouk and Caribbean singing (see box profile).

Siwo (Declic, France).

This much-loved disc from Jocelyne is one of the great Kassav' offshoots – a fabulous set of rousing, passionate songs backed by brilliant Kassav'-orientated rhythms and musicianship.

Max Cilla

Martinique's Max Cilla, one of the great flautists of the Caribbean draws on classical music in his gentle, reflective approach to Antillean swing.

Des Flutes des Mornes (Hibiscus, Martinique).

Cilla blends Latin, African and Antillean rhythms and melodies in a magical, acoustic set.

Jacob Desvarieux

Desvarieux is Kassav's frontman and heavy guitarist, a superb musical mind and an attractive singer. On his solo outings, as with Kassav', he has blended folkloric roots with his experience as a session musician working in the Paris studios to create the fusion that brought zouk to world attention.

Yelele (GD, Guadeloupe).

One of the first solo releases from the Kassav' stable in 1984. A superb set showing the way forward for modern zouk with shortish tracks and bags of ideas.

Gilles Floro

A one-man orchestra capable of singing and performing every instrument, Guadeloupian Gilles Floro goes well beyond technical skill. Following a cadence-era career with the popular Les Aiglons, his discography of nearly a dozen solo releases since 1986 has put him on top as the star crooner of the Guadeloupian style of zouk-love.

Kristal (Sonodisc, France).

This recent release is typical Gilles Floro; beautiful vocals and direct, appealing arrangements.

Simon Jurad

This internationally unsung Martiniquan guitarist and songwriter was one of the key figures in the musical revolution that led to the zouk explosion. Jurad came to public notice as a member of Martinique's famed cadence-era band La Perfecta, splitting off to form Operation '78, spearhead of the subsequent zouk movement as it developed in Martinique. Despite frequent nightclub gigs and the release of a multitude of very popular solo albums, he remains somewhat on the sidelines.

Operation '96: Plein Tubes (Hibiscus, Martinique).

Jurad is shining here – on one of the best releases in a career spanning nearly two dozen. *Plein Tubes* is a star–studded affair inlcuding younger musicians performing alongside Jurad, profiling some of the biggest cadence-era hits of his career.

Kassav'

Without any doubt, Kassav' – the fathers of zouk – are the most important band to emerge from the French Antilles. They are also one of World Music's true supergroups, having found their voice by fusing the traditional *gwo ka* drum ensemble with rock guitar, a tough brass section and a sparse, melodically inventive style. At their peak in the 1980s the group were recording ten or more albums a year, under various names and permutations. Things calmed down but, as well as pursuing solo careers, the group still record and perform occasionally.

 Zouk Is The Only Medicine We Have (Greensleeves, UK).

This 1988 release compiled Kassav's greatest hits from the golden era, including their most famous number – the title track ("Zouk la sé sèl meedikaman nou ni") – and the lovely "Kaye Manman" by lead singer Jocelyne Béroard.

 Live au Zenith (Columbia, France).

The concert in question – at Paris's major venue – took place in 1986, so covers similar material to the disc above. It's one of the great live sets – non-stop stuff, showcasing singers and instrumentalists in turn, and a testament of just how hot the band could be on stage.

Un toque latino (Sony Tropical, France).

This 1999 outing doesn't quite reach the heights of Kassav's earlier work, but it remains beautifully produced, sumptious, modern World Music, absorbing influences from Brazil, Africa and notably Cuba (lots of piano rifs and brass solos) into the mix. The tunes are mostly new ones, though "Zouk la sé sèl meedikaman nou ni" gets dusted down for one more time.

Lazair

Top singer/guitarist production duo, with a great touch for melody and a funky beat.

Yche Man Man (Kadence, France).

With Edith Lefel, the title track is one of zouk's classics: beautiful, long and enchanting – a late-night party treat.

Edith Lefel

Top zouk singer, embracing most of the sides of traditional and modern zouk.

A L'Olympia (Rubikolor/Sonodisc, France).

Sensational live performance by Lefel, one of the founders of the softer, more commercial mid-tempo zouk-love. There is real energy, and a wide range of rhythms employed.

Malavoi

An ever-changing unit of musicians, Malavoi have been creating their own unique fusions since the 1970s, mixing French Antillean styles (biguine, waltz and mazurka) with zouk, Cuban charanga, and Western Classical modes. They have enjoyed success with a number of contrasting styles and line-ups, including a fine side project called Matebis in 1992 (a name subsequently adopted by onetime member Jean-Paul Soime). Another active offshoot is Palavire (see below).

 Live au Zenith (Blue Silver, France).

A sublime 1987 concert, featuring the group in its George Debs-era heyday, with Ralph Thamar on lead vocals A sublime 1987 concert featuring the group in its Georges Debs-era heyday with Ralph Thamar on lead vocals, bandleader Paulo Rosine on piano, and a wonderful violin section with Mano Cesaire, Jean-Paul Soime and Christian de Negri. Current singing sensation Edith Lefel was at the time of this live performance still merely a member of the chorus. The album captures the strong stage presence and the wonderful musicality of the group.

She She (Declic, France).

This 1996 album features great hand drumming, violins, piano and vocals on experimental interpretations of biguine, mazurka and zouk numbers.

MATEBIS

Matebis (BMG, France).

An invitee album in which the core of Malavoi plays some of their past hits as well as classic and newly penned songs by

Martiniquan stars like Marce Pago, Edith Lefel, Jocelyne Beroard, Ralph Thamar, Kali and others. The artists were clearly caught up in the spirit of the event and give exceptional performances.

Palavire

Formed by Malavoi founder Emmanuel 'Mano' Cesaire and his son Claude, Palavire cut a wider swath of Martinique's musical heritage, treating it to a sophisticated but funky interpretation. Their first album, Plezi, had a touch of Malavoi to it, with its violins; subsequent discs have moved toward a 'musique populaire' approach.

◉ **Plezi** (Hibiscus, Martinique).

One of the biggest successes of the summer of 1994, this Malavoi-infected funky zouk record is a very good example of young musicians taking chances and succeeding.

Tanya Saint-Val

The fifteen-year singing career of this talented Guadeloupian star has included six albums, each one showing a different side to her musical interests. She has created a string of hits ranging from hard chire to zouk-love, from American soul singing to rootsy collaborations with Guadeloupian carnival street band Akiyo.

◉ **Amethyste** (BMI, France).

The 1996 *Amethyste* album is her latest and most popular yet. For more, look for her 1994 **Akiyo** project, and **Mi** (Philips, France).

Sex Machine

As the name suggests, you can expect bold, big zouk dance treats from this trio.

◉ **Mwen Peche** (GD, France).

Golden period up-tempo zouk with keyboards sounding like West African kora, horns like the best soca and scorching vocals.

Soukoue Ko Ou

This was one of the early Kassav' side projects, when the lineup was still predominantly Guadeloupian, and saw the top band in a more lilting, folksy mold.

◉ **Ou Vacances** (NR, France).

This summer vacances release re-visited one of the Antilles favourite Haitian hits, Tabou Combo's "New York Ameliore," and a stunning tribute to Dede Saint-Prix, "Hommage a DD." Wonderful, rolling work-out, dance floor bliss!

Joelle Ursull

The former singer with the band Zouk Machine, Ursull has a cool, clear, yet powerfully erotic voice. She performs music that is a blend of House and zouk, heavy on percussion and synths.

◉ **Miyel** (CBS, US).

The best collection from this talented singer over a combination of zouk-love and faster rhythmic arrangements.

Les Vikings de Guadeloupe

Les Vikings de Guadeloupe, whose members included Kassav' founder Pierre-Eduard Decimus and Dominican singer Gordon Henderson, form a link between early cadence and zouk proper.

◉ **Les Precurseurs du Zouk** (Cocosound, France).

A great run through of some of the hits of this large band – really a Caribbean orchestra – with blazing horn, vocals, percussion, the works.

Volt Face

After leaving Kassav' in 1990, founding member Georges Decimus formed Volt with Dominican Gramacks legend Jeff Joseph, so far releasing a total of five albums.

◉ **Electrik** and **Live** (CNR Music, France).

Like early Kassav', this band is not afraid to venture into unknown musical territory, sometimes successfully, sometimes not. All recordings have been interesting. *Electrik* and *Live* are the most recent and thus the most easily available.

Zouk Machine

Female trio, particularly big on the creatively rich Paris scene of the late 1980s and early '90s.

◉ **Maldon** (Henri Debs, Guadeloupe).

The best album from ZM, featuring sizzling vocals and strong arrangements.

Zouk Time

Zouk Time is a Liso Studio project that began in Guadeloupe in the summer of 1987. An ever-changing aggregation of musicians, they have released nearly a dozen fine albums of swinging Guadeloupian zouk-love.

◉ **Guetho a Liso** (4M Production, France).

The first album by Zouk Time and it may very well be the best. A sweet set including the wonderful title track featuring Zairian soukous star Kanda Bongo Man.

Biguine

Compilations

◉ **Au Bal Antillais** (Folklyric, US).

A great collection of biguines, recorded into the 1930s in Paris, including some tracks from the great clarinettist Alexandre Stellio.

◉ **Collection Patrimoine**
(Sully Cally Music, Martinique).

An ambitious project by Martiniquan musician/ethnomusicologist Sully Cally that includes reissues of classic albums of Martiniquan artists in the traditional music styles of old biguine and belair, as well as the occasional release of new recordings by old bands playing classic material. Leona Gabriel, Al Lirvat, Honore Coppet and Ti Emile are among the artists featured.

Artists

Djo Dezormo

On an island where social commentary rarely finds its way into the popular music, one sterling exception is Djo Dezormo. For nearly three decades he has annually released a topical carnival record and he has struck the big time on many occasions.

Voici Les Loups (Hibiscus, Martinique).

A 1993 Carnival release, this album features all uptempo music in classic styles like mazurka and biguine, featuring the massive biguine-vide carnival hit "Voici les Loups."

25e Année Chanson and **Les Années d'Histoire** (JE Productions, Martinique).

These albums feature remakes of Dezormo's most popular carnival songs spanning 1973 through 1999. The hits are spread out over both discs, and either (or both) give a good overview of the uptempo sounds of Martinique carnival.

Michel Godzom

One of only a handful of steady live performers in Martinique, clarinettist/saxophonist Godzom performs a variety of classic styles from biguine to quadrille. On record he delivers everything from reproductions of his live sets to adventurous experiment utilizing horns, strings, guitars and percussion.

Hotel Diamont des Bains (Georges Debs, Guadeloupe).

One of the best contemporary biguine sets, strong on ideas and adept on musical innovation within the genre's tight framework.

Alexandre Stellio

One of Martinique's first international stars, clarinettist Stellio was a fixture and an innovator first on the island and then in the Paris nightclub scene of the early-twentieth century. His sound is still at the root of most Antillean players of classic musics like biguine and mazurka.

Et Son Orchestre Creole (CBS, France).

Biguine tunes from the 1920s and '30s – short, sweet, wonderfully melodic and classically danceable.

Chouval Bwa and Gwo Ka

Compilations

Coeurs de Couleur (Atoll Music, France).

Movie soundtrack featuring gwo ka singing from the hills of Guadeloupe by Esnard Boisdur and drumming from Ti Celeste.

Guadeloupe: Gwo ka, Soiree Lewoz a Jabrun (Ocora, France).

Live recording from a session in the Guadeloupian hills. Drum and voices only – stirring stuff.

Artists

Akiyo

The 30-member Akiyo has revived a Guadeloupian street carnival tradition called mas a St. Jean that was one of the original roots of the music of Kassav'. The mas consists of distinct rhythms but goes far beyond that to include costuming and a generally rebellious ambiance – and at carnival time a massive second line of revellers numbering as many as five thousand.

Memoires (Remix) (Declic, France).

This most recent release is a remix of their first album which, besides including the typical exciting melange of carnival,

tambours and traditional gwo ka heard on each of the subsequent albums, distinguishes itself from the others for the catchy melodies provided by a keyboard synthesizer.

William Flessel

Flessel is a brilliant gwo ka drummer who creates exciting tapestries of pecussive sound.

Message ka (Sonodisc, France).

Ringing, richly potent call and response percussion and chant with its roots firmly in the Afro-Caribbean world. Master drummer Klessel leads the drumming and chanting.

Kali

Kali, from the Martiniquan town of Ste-Pierre, began his career playing reggae but in the past decade has established himself playing island roots music. A superb multi-instrumentalist, and specifically, banjo player, he is an expert in the classic sounds of Martinique, the biguine and belair styles, and he is a wonderful singer and melodist, to boot.

 Debranche (Declic, France).

1995 set from Kali expands his penchant for beautiful and simple compositions with his trademark banjo. A great talent for haunting melodies and the most evocative of Caribbean rhythms.

Marcé et Tumpak

With his band Tumpak, drummer/singer/composer Marcé Pago is one of Martinique's main proponents of a rural classic drumming style called chouval bwa. His albums range from traditional work-outs to glorious, haunting, percussive masterpieces that feature tinges of biguine, African rhythms, zouk and jazz.

Zouk Chouv' (GlobeStyle, UK).

Grand fusion of the percussive styles of the islands' interior with bright electric instrumentation. A folk-jazz dance World Music classic.

Eugene Mona

An innovative Martiniquan drummer/singer/songwriter , Eugene Mona was instrumental in breathing new life into the belair and other traditional musics of the island. He died, tragically, shortly after the huge success of his album Blan Manje, an electric masterpiece that pushed zouk to new frontiers.

Volumes 1 & 2 (Hibiscus, Gaudaloupe).

This exquisite two-CD set of flute, drum and vocal tracks represens the best of Mona's output from the 1970s, music released alongside the then-burgeoning cadence scene.

Blan Manje (Hibiscus, Gaudaloupe).

Mona's last release, this award-winning album features a percussive, tradition-rooted zouk that rarely surfaces amidst the genre's largely formulaic releases.

Dede Saint-Prix

Martiniquan Dede Saint-Prix, alongside Marcé Pago, stands as the major chouval bwa star of Martinique. This dynamo of energy has released a multitude of records since the 1970s under a variety of group names, exploring musical territory from Malavoi's charanga to traditional chouval bwa to ragga. Be assured that any record with his name on it is sure to be percussive-driven.

 Chouval Bwa Sans Frontieres (Declic, France).

This star of tambour and bamboo flute is in his element here, with brilliant rhythm experimentation, superb catchy songwriting and a surprising range of singing. All of which make this particular album a classic that should be heard by anyone interested in percussive, pretty music.

 Mi Se Sa (Mango, UK).

Luscious fusion of flute and chouval-bwa creating a tightly rhythmic cadence/zouk sound.

Ti Celeste

Although Guadeloupian Ti Celeste is best known as a traditionalist, weaving intricate percussion improvisations around a basic groove, he has not been reluctant to adapt some of zouk's innovations to his own purposes.

 Ses Plus Grands Succes (Henri Debs, Guadeloupe).

A wonderful overview of many of Ti Celeste's biggest hits, dating back to the late-1970s. Plenty of mesmeric roots drumming.

Dutch Antilles

Compilations

 Switi – Hot! Kaseko Music (MW Records, Netherlands).

An excellent introduction to kaseko which includes sizzling dance numbers from Yakki Famiri, Master Blaster and Zonnebloem, as well as more traditonal acoustic tracks from Carlo Jones and the Surinam Troubadours.

Artists

Cedric Dandaré

Netherlands-based Dandaré is a guitarist and arranger who mixes Dutch Antillean rhtyhms (and traditional instruments) with jazz and Latin music.

Rhythmical nature (Sony, Netherlands).

A 1996 album recorded with Dandaré's fourteen-piece orchestra, featuring Antillean and Dutch musicians.

Carlo Jones & the Surinam Troubadors

Surinam-born saxophonist Carlo Jones has played music since childhood, graduating through police and military brass bands at home. Now settled in the Netherlands, he leads the Surinam Kaseko Troubadors, a highly seductive big band, whose line-up includes alto sax, sousaphone, trumpet, trombone, banjo and marching drums.

 Carlo Jones and the Surinam Kaseko Troubadors (MW Records, Netherlands).

A compulsive initiation into the kaseko sound, this highly recommended album has a real humour and bounce that owes a good deal to New Orleans jazz. Carlo takes the lead with squealing sax, but there are wonderfully agile and punchy sousaphone riffs from André Jones, and it's all powered on by the marching drums.

William Souvenir

Souvenir was born of Aucan and Saramaccan parents, in the Paramaribo area of Surinam. A self-taught guitarist, he has played in kaseko and calypso groups, and is much influenced by Haitian music. He moved to the Netherlands in 1970 and has worked with Mighty Botai, Surinam's foremost calypso singer.

A tin télé (MW Records, Netherlands).

A 1990 retrospective of Souvenir's varied but always highly danceable sounds, including zouk, merengue, kaseko and calypso. The songs – mostly love songs, but also addressing environmental concerns – are in Sranang Togo dialects.

Yakki Famirie

Yakki Famirie are a young ten-piece kaseko band, based in Surinam, led by saxophonist Theo Swanenberg. They fuse styles from the Maroon communities of Surinam with a wide range of Caribbean styles.

Gowtu (World Connection, Netherlands).

A very danceable set which stresses the Cuban and Calypso ingredients in the music rather than the traditional marching band kaseko. Includes cover of Gloria Estefan's "Oyé Mi Canto" (in English and Spanish) and Miguel Matamoros's "Son De La Loma". Strong brass and Cuban keyboards.

Argentina   Tango

vertical expression of horizontal desire

It's been said that Argentina has two national anthems – the official hymn and the tango. Forget the mannered ballroom dacing image, tango is a real roots music: sometimes sleazy, sometimes elegant, but always sensuous, rhythmic and passionate – 'the vertical expression of a horizontal desire.' **Teddy Peiro** and **Jan Fairley** succumb to its charms.

The great Argentinian writer Jorge Luis Borges was a tango enthusiast and something of a historian of the music. "My informants all agree on one fact", he wrote, "the Tango was born in the brothels." Borges's informants were a little presumptuous, perhaps, for nobody can exactly pinpoint tango's birthplace, but it certainly developed amongst the *porteños* – the people of the port area of Buenos Aires – and its bordellos and bars. It was a definitively urban music: a product of the melting pot of European immigrants, Criollos, blacks and natives, drawn together when the city became the capital of Argentina in 1880. Tango was thus forged from a range of musical influences that included Andalucían flamenco, southern Italian melodies, Cuban habanera, African *candombé* and percussion, European polkas and mazurkas, Spanish contradanse, and, closer to home, the *milónga* – the rural song of the Argentine *gaucho*. It was a music imbued with immigrant history.

In this early form, tango became associated with the bohemian life of bordello brawls and *compadrítos* – knife-wielding, womanising thugs. By 1914 there were over 100,000 more men than women in Buenos Aires, thus the high incidence of prostitution and the strong culture of bar-brothels. Machismo and violence were part of the culture and men would dance together in the low-life cafés and corner bars practising new steps and keeping in shape while waiting for their women, the *minas* of the bordellos. Their dances tended to have a showy yet threatening, predatory quality, often revolving around a possessive relationship between two men and one woman. In such a culture, the *compadríto* danced the tango into existence.

The original **tango ensembles** were trios of violin, guitar and flute, but around the end of the nineteenth century the **bandoneón**, the tango accordion, arrived from Germany, and the classic tango orchestra was born. The box-shaped button accordion, which is now inextricably linked with

Argentine tango, was invented around 1860 in Germany to play religious music in organless churches. One Heinrich Band reworked an older portable instrument nicknamed the 'asthmatic worm', which was used for funeral processions as well as lively regional dances, and gave his new instrument the name 'Band-Union', a combination of his and his company's names. Mispronounced as it travelled the world, it became the bandoneón.

In Argentina, an early pioneer of the instrument was **Eduardo Arólas** – a man remembered as the 'Tiger of the Bandoneón'. He recognised its immediate affinity with the tango – indeed, he claimed it was an instrument made to play tango, with its deep melancholy feeling which suited the immigrants who enjoyed a sentimental tinge in their hard lives. It is not, however, an easy instrument, demanding a great deal of skill, with its seventy-odd buttons each producing one of two notes depending on whether the bellows are being compressed or expanded.

Vicente Gréco (1888–1924) is credited as the first bandleader to standardise the form of a tango group, with his **Orquesta Típica Criolla** of two violins and two bandoneóns. There were some larger bands but basically the instrumentation remained virtually unchanged until the 1940s.

El Chóclo (The Ear of Corn)

This cheeky, blustery tango
Gave wings to the ambitions
Of the streets where I grew up.
The tango was born with this tango,
And like a shrieking sound
It fled the stench and scum
In search of the sky.
Strange alchemy, love in cadence,
It opened up new roads
With only hope as a guide.
A mixture of rage, sorrow, faith, absence,
Lamenting with the innocence
of a catchy rhythm.

And in a flash the tarts and chicks were here,
The moon in puddles, hips rolling,
And loving with savage longing ...

When I recall you, beloved tango,
I feel the earth moving under our feet
As we danced, and hear the rumbling of the
*   past.*
Mother is no longer here now
But when your song begins on the ban-
*   doneón*
I hear her creep in on tip toe to kiss me.

Enrique Sántos Discépolo

First Tango in Paris

Before long the tango was an intrinsic part of the popular culture of Buenos Aires, played on the streets by organ grinders and fairground carousels, and danced in tenement courtyards. Its association with the whorehouse and low-down porteño lifestyle, plus its saucy, sometimes obscene and deeply fatalistic lyrics, didn't endear it to the aristocratic families of Buenos Aires, who did their best to protect their children from the corrupting new dance, but, like rock'n'roll in America, it was a losing battle.

A number of rich, upper-class playboys, such as poet and writer **Ricardo Guïraldes**, enjoyed mixing with the compadrítos and emulating their lifestyle from a 'debonair' distance. It was Guïraldes who, on a European grand tour in 1910, was as responsible for the spread of the dance to Europe. In 1911 he wrote a famous homage, a poem called "Tango" in honour of the dance: "... hats tilted over sardonic sneers. The all-absorbing love of a tyrant, jealously guarding his dominion, over women who have surrended submissively, like obedient beasts ... ".

The following year Guïraldes gave an influential impromptu performance in a Paris salon to a fashionable audience for whom tango's risqué sexuality ('the vertical expression of horizontal desire' as one wag dubbed it) was deeply attractive. Despite the local archbishop's admonition that Christians should not in good conscience tango, they did, and in very large numbers. Tango was thus the first of the many Latin dance crazes to conquer Europe. And once it had been embraced in the salons of France its credibility back home greatly increased. Back in Argentina, from bordello to ballroom, everyone was dancing the tango.

And then came **Rudolph Valentino**. The tango fitted his image to a T and Hollywood wasted no time in capitalising on the charisma of the superstar, the magnetism of the tango and the attraction they both had on a huge public. Valentino and Tango! Tango and Valentino! The combination was irresistible to the moguls, who swiftly added a tango scene to the latest Valentino film, *The Four Horsemen of the Apocalypse* (1926). The fact that in the film Valentino was playing a *gaucho* (Argentinian cowboy) son of a rancher – and gauchos don't dance the tango – didn't deter them for a moment. Valentino was a special gaucho and this gaucho could dance the tango. And why not? The scene really was incredible: Valentino, dressed in the wide trousers and leather chaps of a gaucho in the middle of the pampa, holding a carnation

Rudolph Valentino in 'The Four Horsemen of the Apocalypse'

between his lips, and a whip in his hand; his partner, a Spanish señorita, kitted out with headscarf and hair comb plus the strongest pair of heels this side of the Río de la Plata.

Predictably enough, the tango scene was the hit of the film and, travesty though it was, it meant the dance was now known all over the world. Tango classes and competitions were held in Paris, and tango teas in England, with young devotees togged up as Argentine gauchos. Even the greatest tango singer of all time, **Carlos Gardél**, when he became the darling of Parisian society, and later starred in films in Hollywood, was forced to perform his tangos dressed as a gaucho. And yet – GAUCHOS NEVER DANCED THE TANGO!

Gardél and Tango's Golden Age

Back in Argentina, in the 1920s, the tango moved out of the cantinas and bordellos into cabarets and theatres and entered a classic era under bandleaders like **Roberto Fírpo**, **Julio de Cáro** and **Francisco Canaro**. With their *orquestas tipicas* they took the old line-up of Vicente Greco (two bandoneóns, two violins, a piano and flute) and substituted a double bass for the flute. This gave added sonority and depth, a combination which was to continue for the next twenty years, even in the larger ensembles common after the mid-1930s. It was during this period that some of the most famous of all tangos were written, including Uruguayan **Gerárdo Hernán Matos Rodríguez**'s "La Cumparsíta" in 1917 – the most famous tango of all time. He took it to Fírpo who was performing with his band in a Montevideo café: the rest as they say is history!

The first **tango-canción** (tango songs) used the language of the ghetto and celebrated the life of ruffians and pimps. **Angel Villoldo** and **Pascual Contursi** introduced the classic tango lyric of a male perspective, placing the blame for heartache firmly on the shoulders of a fickle woman, with Contursi putting lyrics to Samuel Castriota's "Lita": "Woman who left me, in the prime of my life, wounding my soul, and driving thorns into my heart ... Nothing can console me now, so I am drowning my sorrows, to try to forget your love ...". Typical of tango songs, male behaviour itself was beyond reproach, the man victim of women's capriciousness.

In its **dance**, tango consolidated its contradictory mix of earthy sensuality and middle class kitsch. It depends on an almost violent and dangerous friction of bodies, colliding often in a passion which seems controlled by the dance itself. A glittering respectability hid darker undercurrents in the obvious macho domination of the male over the female in a series of intricate steps and in the close embraces, which were highly suggestive of the sexual act. The cut and thrust of intricate and interlacing fast leg movements between a couple imitated the movement of blades in a knife fight.

Carlos Gardél

The extraordinary figure of **Carlos Gardél** (1887–1935) was – and still is – a legend in Argentina, and he was a huge influence in spreading the popularity of tango round the world. He was actually born in Toulouse, France, but taken to Buenos Aires at the age of four by his single mother. He came to be seen as an icon of Arrabal

culture, and a symbol of the fulfilment of the dreams of the poor *porteño* workers.

In Argentina, it was Gardél above all who transformed tango from an essentially low-down dance form to a song style popular among Argentines of widely differing social classes. His career coincided with the first period of tango's Golden Age and the development of *tango-canción* (tango song) in the 1920s and '30s. The advent of radio, recording and film all helped his career, but nothing helped him more than his own voice – a voice that was born to sing tango and which became the model for all future singers of the genre.

In the 1920s, like most tango singers, Gardél sang to guitar rather than orchestral accompaniment. Everything about Gardél, his voice, his image, his suavity, his posture, his arrogance and his natural machismo spelled tango. Interestingly enough he started out as a variety act singing traditional folk and country music in a duo with José Razzano. They enjoyed great success but Gardél's

recording of Contursi's "Mi noche triste" (My Sorrowful Night) in 1917 was to change the course of his future.

During his career, Gardél recorded some nine hundred songs and starred in numerous films, notably *The Tango on Broadway* in 1934. He was tragically killed in an aircrash in Colombia at the height of his fame, and his legendary status was confirmed. His image is still everywhere in Buenos Aires, on plaques and huge murals, and in record store windows, while admirers pay homage to his life-sized, bronze statue in the Chacarita cemetery, placing a lighted cigarette between his fingers or a red carnation in his buttonhole.

After Gardél the split between the **traditionalists** such as **Filibérto** and **D'Arienzo**, later **Biagi** and **De Angelis**, and those musicians called the **evolutionists**, such as **De Cáro**, **Di Sarli**, **Troilo** and **Puglíese** became more pronounced. Bands, as elsewhere in the world during this period, became larger, in the mode of small orchestras, and a mass following for tango was enjoyed through dance-halls, radio and recordings until the end of the Golden Age around 1950.

Tango Politics

As an expression of the working classes, the fortunes of the tango have inevitably been linked with social and political developments in Argentina and the social classes they empowered. The music declined a little in the 1930s as the army took power and suppressed what was seen as a potentially subversive force. Even so, the figure of **Juan D'Arienzo**, violinist and bandleader, looms large from the 1930s on. With a sharp, staccato rhythm, and prominent piano, the Juan D'Arienzo orchestra was the flavour of those years. His recording of "La cumparsíta" at the end of 1937 is a classic and considered one of the greatest of all time.

Tango fortunes revived again in the 1940s when a certain political freedom returned, and the music enjoyed a second golden age with the rise of Perón in 1946 and his emphasis on nationalism and popular culture to win mass support. This was the era of a new generation of bandleaders. At the top, alongside Juan D'Arienzo were **Osváldo Puglíese**, **Hector Varela** and the innovative **Aníbal Troilo**. Of all bandoneón players, it was Troilo who expressed most vividly, deeply and powerfully, and so tenderly, the nostalgic sound of what is now regarded as a noble instrument. When he died a few years ago half a million people followed his funeral procession to the cemetery.

Aníbal Troilo – The Fat Man – testing the first Argentine-produced bandoneón with manufacturer Luis Mariani (far left) and bandleader Francisco Canaro (far right)

Buenos Aires in the late 1940s was a city of five or six million and each barrio would have ten or fifteen amateur tango orchestras, while the established orchestras would play in the cabarets and nightclubs in the centre of the city. Somehow in this era, however, tango began to move away from working class to middle class and intellectual milieus. Tango became a sort of collective reminiscence of a world that no longer existed – essentially nostalgia. As a popular lyric, "Tango de otros tiempos" (Tango of Other Times), put it:

Tango, you were the king
In one word, a friend
Blossoming from the bandoneón music
of Arólas
Tango, the rot set in
When you became sophisticated
And with your airs and graces
You quit the suburbs where you were born
Tango, it saddens me to see
How you've deserted the mean dirt-streets
For a carpeted drawing-room
In my soul I carry a small piece
Of that happy past!

But the good old times are over
In Paris you've become Frenchified
And today, thinking of what's happened
A tear mars your song.

In the 1950s, with the end of Peronism and the coming of rock'n'roll, tango slipped into the shadows once again.

Astor Piazzolla and Tango Nuevo

Astor Piazzolla (see box opposite) dominates the recent history of tango, much as Carlos Gardél was the key figure of its classic era. Born in Mar de Plata in 1921, Piazzolla spent his childhood in the Bronx, New York, where he was hired at age thirteen by Carlos Gardél to play in the film *El día que me quieras* and booked for his Latin American tour. Luckily for Piazzolla he hadn't taken up the offer when the fatal aircrash in which Gardél died occurred. Back in Argentina, from 1937, Piazzolla played second bandoneón in the orchestra of Aníbal Troilo, where he developed his feel for arrangements. (While the first bandoneón takes

Astor Piazzolla

Astor Piazzolla (1921–1992) brought the tango a long way from when it was first danced in Buenos Aires a century ago by two pimps on a street corner. In his hands this backstreet dance acquired a modernist 'art music' gloss.

Born in Mar de Plata, yet spending his childhood in New York, Piazzolla's controversial innovation came from his classical music studies in Paris with **Nadia Boulanger**, who thought his classical compositions lacked feeling – but upon hearing his tango "Triunfal" apparently caught him by the hands and said, "Don't ever abandon this. This is your music. This is Piazzolla."

Piazzolla returned to Mar de Plata in 1937, moving to Buenos Aires two years later, where he joined the seminal orchestra of **Aníbal Troilo** as bandoneónista and arranger. In 1946 he formed his own first group and in 1960 his influential **Quinteto Nuevo Tango**. With this group, he experimented audaciously, turning tango inside out, introducing unexpected chords, chromatic harmony, differently emphasised rhythms, a sense of dissonance and openness. Traditional tango captures the dislocation of the immigrant, the disillusionment with the dream of a new life, transmuting these deep and raw emotions onto a personal plane of betrayal and triangular relationships. Piazzolla's genius comes from the fact that, within the many layers and changing moods and pace of his pieces, he never betrays this essence of tango – its sense of fate, its core of hopeless misery, its desperate sense of loss.

Piazzolla translated the philosophy expounded by tango poets like Enrique Sántos Discépelo – who, in "El cambalache" (The Junkshop) concludes that the 20th-century world is an insolent display of blatant wickedness – onto the musical plane. A Piazzolla piece can shift from the personal to the epic so that a seeming cry from a violin or cello becomes a wailing city siren as if following a shift in landscape from personal misery and nostalgia to a larger, more menacing urban canvas.

In Piazzolla's tangos, passion and sensuality still walk side by side with sadness, but emotions, often drawn out to a level of almost unbearable intensity, are suddenly subsumed in a disquieting sense of inevitability. If you close your eyes while listening to his work, you can exploit the filmic dimension of the music: create your own movie,

walk Buenos Aires alone at Zero Hour, visit clubs and bars, pass through empty streets shadowed by the ghosts of a turbulent history. Piazzolla always said that he composed for the new generations of porteños, offering a music that allowed them to live an often dark and difficult present while absorbing their past.

Piazzolla's own ensembles turned tango into concert music. "For me," he said, "tango was always for the ear rather than the feet." This process escalated in the 1960s, when he started to work with poet **Horacio Ferrer**. Their first major work was a little opera called "María de Buenos Aires" (1967) but it was the seminal "Balada por un loco" (Ballad For A Madman) which pushed the borders of tango lyrics far from those of thwarted romance and broken dreams of traditional tango song. Surreal and witty, the ballad's lyrics reveal the tortured mental state and condition of a half-dancing, half-flying bowler-hatted apparition which appears on the streets of Buenos Aires. While it appalled traditional tangueros, the song inspired new aficionados at home and abroad, particularly among musicians.

Elected 'Distinguished Citizen of Buenos Aires' in 1985, Piazzolla's commitment to tango and its future was unequivocal. A prolific composer of over 750 works, including concertos, theatre and film scores, he created some atmospheric 'classical' pieces, including a 1979 concerto for bandoneón and orchestra, which combines the flavour of tango with a homage to

Bach, and, in 1989, "Five Tango Sensations", a series of moody pieces for bandoneón and string quartet, commissioned by the Kronos Quartet. These are thrilling pieces, as indeed are all of his last 1980s concert performances released posthumously on CD.

the melody, it is the second bandoneón that gives the music its particular harmony and flavour.)

Troilo left Piazzolla his bandoneón when he died and Piazzolla went on to ensure that tango would never be the same again. In the 1950s he won a government scholarship to study with Nadia Boulanger in Paris (one of the most celebrated teachers of composition, who included Aaron Copland among her pupils). It was Boulanger who encouraged Piazzolla to develop the popular music of his heritage.

Piazzolla's idea was that tango could be a serious music to listen to, not just for dancing, and for many of the old guard it was a step too far. As he explained: "Musicians hated me. I was taking the old tango away from them. The old tango, the one they loved, was dying. And they hated me, they threatened my life hundreds of times. They waited for me outside my house, two or three of them, and gave me a good beating. They even put a gun at my head once. I was in a radio station doing an interview, and all of a sudden the door opens and in comes this tango singer with a gun. That's how it was."

In the 1970s Piazzolla was out of favour with Argentina's military regime and he and his family moved to Paris for their own safety, returning to Argentina only after the fall of the junta. His influence, however, had spread, and his experiments – and international success – opened the way for other radical transformations.

Chief among these, in 1970s Buenos Aires, was the fusion of **tango-rockéro** – tango rock. This replaced the flexible combination of bandoneón,

Where to find tango in Buenos Aires

Buenos Aires has been enjoying something of a tango revival in recent years. There are several dozen **clubs**, and a national radio station, **FM Tango** (95.6m), which transmits 24-hour tango. There are even tango courses, theory and practice, taught today in the university. When you arrive in the city, check listings in the tabloid *Clarín*, which devotes two pages every Tuesday to tango clubs and tango revues at the theatres.

Leading clubs include **El Viejo Almacén** (Av Independéncia & Balcárce), a large salon oriented towards tourists but also popular with Argentines, where chances are the Sexteto Mayór will be playing if they are in town. For a more authentic experience – and a great spectator sport if you don't feel up to dancing – try the **Salon La Argentina** (c/Rodríguez Pena 345), a cavernous dancehall, packed at weekends; the tiny **La Cumparsíta** on Balcárce, where you can hear tearful songs from the street; or the large and fashionable **Paladium**, on c/Reconquista near c/Paraguay, where the weekend dances comcomplete with old newsreels of Carlos Gardél flashed onto the walls!

To get a flavour of the arrabal districts where tango was born, try the Caminíto blocks down by the port in the neighbourhood of La Bóca. **Caminíto** was named after the famous tango of the same name written by Juan de Dios Filibérto, who was born here around the turn of the century. The painted houses with balconies retain the air of the old tango districts, with bars and restaurants frequented by Italian immigrants.

Tango aficionados might also want to visit the **Casa de Tango**, Guardia Viéja 4049, a cultural centre dedicated to tango. Its president, until his death in 1995, was Osváldo Pugliese, one of the last remaining tango giants. And if you want to know everything there is to know about tango, you should call the **Academia Porteña del Lunfárdo** (Academy of Buenos Aires Slang; Estados Unidos 1379, 1101 Buenos Aires; ☎383 2393) and arrange an appointment to meet José Gobéllo, its founder. If there is a man who knows about the tango, it is José Gobéllo. He can tell you who wrote what, the date, the place, the kind of manuscript – the lot. His *Crónica generál del tango* is the most comprehensive work on the tango and its history and to hear him go poems is entertaining and thrilling.

The best **bandoneóns** are still made in Germany, but Buenos Aires has one high-quality artesan, Duilio Maríni, an Argentine of Italian descent. Each instrument takes nine months. "It's like delivering a baby, he says, and each time I cry!" He has a waiting list of three years.

bass and no drums, as favoured by Piazzolla, with a rock-style rhythm section, electric guitars and synthesizers. It was pioneered by **Litto Nébbia**, whose own album, *Homage to Gardél and Le Péra*, is one of the most successful products of this fusion, retaining the melancholy of the traditional form in a rock format. Tango moved across to jazz, too, through groups such as the trio **Siglo XX** – Osvaldo Belmónte on piano, Narciso Saúl on guitars and Néstor Tomasini on saxophone, clarinet and percussion.

Meantime, the old guard had kept traditional tango alive, two key figures being Roberto Goyeneche and Osvaldo Pugliese. **Roberto 'Polaco' Goyeneche**, born in 1926, had been vocalist for many orquestas tipicas before he followed in the footsteps of key singers Rivero and Fiorentino by singing with Troilo between 1955–64. He then became a soloist working with various bands including **Hector Stamponi**'s quartet, remaining a key interpreter until his death in 1994. He made more than one hundred records over his forty-year career. Pianist **Osvaldo Pugliese** remained one of the major tango musicians until his death in 1995 with many younger talented musicians serving their apprenticeships with him.

These days in Argentina, the tango scene is a pretty broad one, with rock and jazz important elements, along with the more traditional sound of acoustic groups. There is no shortage of good *tangueros* and they know each other well and jam together often. Nobody would think they had not been playing together in a band every night for years.

The big tango orchestras, however, are a thing of the past, and economic considerations mean that tango bands have returned to their roots, to an intimate era of trios, quartets and quintets, even a sextet is already serious business. Two of the best sextets, the **Sexteto Mayór** and **Sexteto Berlingieri**, joined together in the 1980s to play for the show "Tango Argentino", and subsequent shows which revived an interest in tango across Europe and the USA, with each group going its own way in Buenos Aires. The Sexteto Mayór, founded in 1973 and starring the virtuoso *bandoneónistas* **José Libertélla** and **Luís Stázo**, is one of the best tango ensembles playing in Argentina today. They can be seen periodically at El Viejo Almacén, Casa Blanca, and other tango places in Buenos Aires, when they are not on tour.

In a more modern idiom, singers like **Susana Rinaldi** and **Adriana Varela**, working with Litto Nébbia, are successfully renovating and re-creating tango, both at home and abroad, Varela particularly in Spain. They are names to look out for along with bandoneónistas **Osváldo Piro**, **Carlos**

Vintage virtuosos, Sexteto Mayór

Buono and **Walter Ríos** (Ríos is also working with the great 'new song' singer Mercedes Sosa); violinist **Antonio Agr**i who worked with Piazzolla and more recently with Paco de Lucía; bandoneónista, arranger and film-score composer **Nestór Marconi**; singer **José Angel Trelles**; pianist and composer **Gustavo Fedel**; and **Grupo Volpe Tango Contemporaneo**, led by Antonio Volpe.

Latterly tango is enjoying an upsurge of popularity in Argentina and other parts of the world – particularly Europe, where couple dancing seems right back in fashion. While there may be little discrepancy between the numbers of men and women looking for romance, flirtation and sex, moern pressures seem to prevent many people finding an ideal companion, making tango dancing – with its physical and emotional intensity, moments of courtship, male bravura and female agression – a way of making contact and something of a wish-fulfillment.

According to choreographer Juan Carlos Copes, tango has responded to the viscitudes of contemporary gender values: "The tango is man and woman in search of each other. It is the search of an embrace, a way to be together, when the man feels that he is male and the woman feels that she is female, without machismo. She likes to be led; he likes to lead. The music arouses and torments, the dance is the coupling of two people defenceless against the world and powerless to change things."*

*Quoted in the definitive and beautifully illustrated book ¡Tango! by Simon Collier (Thames and Hudson, 1995).

discography

Compilations

Buenos Aires by Night (EMI, UK).

Here are twenty tracks by some of the all-time tango greats: Carlos Gardél, Hectór Varela, Aníbal Troilo, Osváldo Puglíese and more.

Nuevo Tango Argentino (Nuevos Medios, Spain).

Tango from a fine group of 1980s and '90s innovators – such as Nestór Marconi – and soloists – including Adriana Varela, one of the leading voices of the present revival. Produced by Litto Nébbia whose track record in popular music, rock and tango ensures a special contemporary vision.

The Rough Guide to Tango (World Music Network, UK).

The Rough Guide has tracks from 20 of the greatest Tango musicians, from the classics – Carlos Gardél, Aníbal Troilo, Hector Varela, Virgilio Expósito – through Astor Piazzolla, to contemporary artists such as Adriana Varela and Litto Nebbia. Every one a winner.

THE ROUGH GUIDE

Tango

The Story of Tango (EMI Hemisphere, UK).

The Story follows Tango's development from pianist Jos Basso and bandleader Aníbal Troilo, through Carlos Gardél, to a wonderful *tango-milonga* from Francisco Canaro, to the first 'modernist' Osvaldo Pugliese, to Sexteto Mayór. Undoubtedly a key disc.

The Story of Tango – Volume 2 (EMI Hemisphere, UK).

This focuses on a number of key tango orchestras recorded from 1949 to 1954, almost all playing instrumental versions of classics, revealing that Piazzolla's new tango was not inspired solely by European, classical influences. Virtuoso instrumentalists in this startlingly rich orchestral tradition include Hectór Varela and many others.

Tango Ladies: El Tango Hecho Carne (Harlequin, UK).

These gems of tango-canciónes, performed by key women singers of the pre-war period such as Ada Falcón and Azucena Maizani. Many of the singers were involved in the movie industry which embraced tango and their music throws a different light on tango during its Golden Age.

Women of Tango (EMI Hemisphere, UK).

There were, and are, many great women tango singers – and one of their staples is celebrating the moment of individual disintegration when a lover realises they have been forsaken. The rich intonation of singers like Tita Merella on this disc, almost conversational in style, is an ear-opener, declaimed with the unexploded anger of the wronged.

ARGENTINA

Artists

Haydee Alba

Singer Haydee Alba is known as a tango-canción singer - for listening rather than dancing – and uses the intimate tones of her velvety, smoky voice to express the tragically conflicting emotions of tango.

 Borges: Milongas y al tango (Playasound, France).

Alba's tribute to Borges features 15 tangos and milongas – three of which he particularly loved, the others his lyrics set by composers from Anibal Troilo to Astor Piazzolla. She is backed by a tight ensemble of paino, double bass, guitar and bandoneón.

Carlos Gardél

Like many Argentine immigrants Carlos Gardél came from Europe but went on to become a symbol of the culture of the new country and its quintessential music, tango. His voice, image and attitude made him a huge star, both in recordings and films, the greatest of the first generation of tango singers and the model for generations to come. His death in a plane crash at the height of his career turned him into a legend, and enduring icon.

The Best of Carlos Gardél (EMI Hemisphere, UK).

The best album for the beginner, with twenty classic tracks, all recorded 1933–35 just before he died. From "Mi Buenos Aires Querido" to "Lejana Tierra Mia", this is a true celebration of both the great man and tango.

Carlos Gardél: Su Obra Integral (20 volumes) (El Bandoneon, Switzerland).

The complete works of Gardél on twenty or so individual CDs. Good choices include *Bandoneo Arrabeler*, with songs reminiscing about the community which played a key part in tango's early development, and *El Gaucho*, which pays tribute to the *milongas* and folk songs of the rural gaucho.

Roberto 'Polaco' Goyeneche

Singer Goyeneche followed Gardél in style, and worked with many of the great orchestras (including Anibal Troilo's and Hector Stamponi's) from the 1940s until his death in 1994. He made more than a hundred discs.

La Última Curda (Nuevos Medios, Spain).

The last recording of the great baritone singer – romantic, melodious, and with his timing as perfect as ever.

Litto Nébbia

Litto Nébbia has had an international musical career recording and touring for over 30 years – and composing over 900 songs. With a range of experience spanning nueva canción and rock nacional as well as tango, he is a key figure in today's Argentine music scene, and a leading producer. His own singing is neatly understated, with an occasional echo of 'new song' characteristics.

Homage to Gardél and Le Péra (Melopea, Argentina).

Nébbia has helped bring tango to a generation wich grew up with rock: this album, a tribute to Gardél and Le Péra, brings together tango's melancholy with a broad musical sensibility and a fine ear for instrumental arrangement.

Astor Piazzolla

Bandoneón master Astor Piazzolla brought tango into the territory of the avant-garde. Frustrated with it as simply dance and song, he revolutionised it as a musical form, bringing it to a new concert public through compositions which introduced modernist harmonies and melodic ideas inspired by contemporary new European music and jazz. Undoubtedly the most important figure in post-war tango, Piazzolla is arguably one of the most significant musicians of the second half of the twentieth century.

Zero Hour (Nonesuch, US).

Piazzolla himself thought this set, recorded in 1986, was the finest he ever made, with its evocative fusion of moments, emotions, situations distilled into moving form, charting the urban life of the individual in the city at Zero Hour, the time between midnight and dawn.

Muerte del Angel (Live with the Quinteto, 1973) (BMG/Milan, US).

With the quinteto Piazzolla experimented with a chamber attitude to tango – moving from tango's orchestral focus and his prior *orquesta tipica* line up. Recorded on a cold July night in Buenos Aires, this is a fine exploration of his sound.

Luna (EMI Hemisphere, UK).

This was the final concert of Piazzolla's 'new tango' Sextet, recorded in Amsterdam in June 1989. The Sexteto was Piazzolla's last line-up, existing for only a year, with violin replaced by cello, and took the experiment with timbre and texture as far as it would go. The disc functions almost as a Requiem for the great man.

Osváldo Pugliese

Bandleader Osváldo Pugliese was one of the greatest tango pianista of the Perón era.

Osváldo Pugliese y su Orquesta Tipica (El Bandoneon, Switzerland).

This re-issue of a 1949 recording sees Pugliese accompanied by three superb violins, five punching bandoneóns and vocalist Jorge Vidal.

Sexteto Mayór

Currently Argentina's premiere tango ensemble in the traditional style, the Sexteto Mayór is a shifting collection of
virtuosi led by the two hugely experienced bandoneón
players José Libertélla and Luís Stázo, who started their
vintage group in the early 1970s.

Trottoirs de Buenos Aires
(World Network, Germany).

This largely instrumental album of classic tangos is entirely
thrilling, with Adriana Varela unleashing her deep, husky-
toned voice on four songs. Unashamedly emotional, and
utterly convincing.

WITH SEXTETO BERLINGIERI

Tango Argentino (Atlantic, US).

The two veteran sextets on the soundtrack of the highly successful musical. An excellent introduction to the history of
tango, on CD as on stage.

Aníbal Troilo

Aníbal Troilo was one of the most inventive of bandoneón
players and his orchestra was hugely influential in the
1940s. During this period, Piazzolla was playing second
bandoneón and arranging – one of the many who
learned from the great maestro.

El Inmortal "Pichuco" (El Bandoneon, Switzerland).

A fine album featuring some of Troilo's classic era recordings,
dating from 1941.

Adriana Varela

Adriana Varela has become *the* voice of modern tango
and her concerts in Buenos Aires are immediate sell-outs.
She includes Latin pop, as well as tango, in her repertoire,
sung in her ambiguously-gendered, deep husky-toned
manner without a trace of melodrama or vibrato.

Corazones perversos (Nuevos Medios, Spain).

Passionate songs, as the title (perverse hearts) promises, and
fine arrangements and production from Litto Nebbia.

Argentina   Chamamé, cuarteto and folk

dancing cheek to cheek . . .

Tango aside, Argentine music is mostly rooted in the rural dance traditions of the countryside, an amalgam of Spanish and immigrant Central European styles with indigenous musics. Many of these dances – rancheras, milóngas, *chacareras* and more – are shared with the neighbouring countries of Chile, Peru and Bolivia – while others, like chamamé are particularly Argentinian. **Jan Fairley** reports on these roots musics.

This short article focuses on the urban musics of chamamé and cuarteto, and on rural folk music. Argentina, however, also has Amerindian roots, a music explored from the 1930s on by Atahualpa Yupanqui, which grew new shoots in the politicised **nueva canción** (new song) movement. Argentina's contribution to this music – and in particular that of singer **Mercedes Sosa** – is explored in the Nueva canción article on p.362. The country also has a thriving **rock nacional** scene, outside the orbit of this book. During the Junta years, with artists such as **Charly García** and **Litto Nébbia**, Argentine rock was a force for defiance; these days, in easier times, the leading bands are **Los Enanitos Verdes** and **Los Fabulosos Cadillacs**.

Chamamé

Chamamé is probably Argentina's most popular roots music. It has its origins in the rural culture of Corrientes in the northeast – an Amerindian area which attracted nineteenth century settlers from Czechoslovakia, Poland, Austria and Germany, including many Jews. These immigrants brought with them middle-European waltzes, mazurkas and polkas which over time merged with music from the local Guaraní Amerindian traditions, and African rhythms from the music of the region's slaves. Thus emerged chamamé, a music of poor rural *mestizos*, many of whom looked more Indian or than European, and whose songs used both Spanish and the Indian Guaraní languages.

Chamamé's melodies have a touch of the melancholy attributed to the Guaraní, while its history charts the social, cultural and political relationships of *mestizo* migrants in a new environment. Until the 1950s, it was largely confined to its Corrientes home, but during that decade many rural migrants were moving into Buenos Aires to work in new

industries, bringing their music and dances with them to local dance halls and cultural centres. Chamamé began to attract wider attention – in part, perhaps, because it was a rare folk dance in which people dance in cheek-to-cheek embrace.

The essential sound of chamamé comes from its key instrument – the large piano accordion (on occasion the bandoneón). It sweeps through tunes which marry contrasting rhythms, giving the music an immediate swing. Its African influences may have contributed to the music's accented weak beats so that bars blend and swing together. The distinctive percussive rhythms to the haunting, evocative melodies are the unique, compelling feature of this music.

Argentina's reigning King of Chamamé is **Raúl Barboza**, an artist who has had particular success in Europe in the 1990s. He followed in the footsteps of his Corrientes-born father Adolfo, who founded his first group in 1956. Barboza's conjunto features a typical chamamé line-up of one

Chamamé king Raúl Barboza

or two accordions, a guitar (occasionally two gui-tars whose main job is to mark the rhythm) and *guitarrón* (bass guitar).

Cuarteto

The Argentine dance style known as **cuarteto** first became popular in the 1940s. Named after the original **Cuarteto Leo** who played it, its line-up involved a solo singer, piano, accordion and vio-lin, and its dance consisted of a huge circle, mov-ing anti-clockwise, to a rhythm called *tunga-tunga*. In the 1980s it underwent a resurgence of inter-est in the working-class 'tropical' dance-halls of Buenos Aires, where it was adopted alongside Colombian *guarachas*, Dominican *merengue* and Latin salsa. It slowly climbed up the social ladder to reach a middle-class market, notching up big record sales. The most famous contemporary singer of cuarteto is **Carlos 'La Mona' Jiménez**.

Folklorica

In a movement aligned to nueva canción, dozens of *folklorica* singers and groups emerged in the 1960s and 1970s – their music characterised by tight arrangements and four-part harmonies. Alongside nueva canción star **Mercedes Sosa** (see p.364), leading artists of these decades included the groups **Los Chalchaleros**, **Los Fronterizos** and **Los Hermanos Abalos**; and guitarists **Eduardo Falú**, **Ramón Ayala**, **Ariel Ramírez** (notable for his zambas and his Creole Mass), **Suma Paz** and **Jorge Cafrune**.

The 1980s saw the emergence of new folk com-posers including **Antonio Tarragó Ros** and **Peteco Carabajal**, while in more recent years groups have come through experimenting and re-evaluating the folk dance traditions of *zamba*, *chacar-eras*, *cuecas*, and the like, with a poetic emphasis. Among this new wave are **Los Trovadores**, **Los Huanca Hua**, **Cuarteto Zupuy**, **El Grupo Vocal Argentino** and **Opus 4**.

The best place to see folklorica music is at the annual **Cosquin national folklore festival**, which has been a fixture since the 1960s.

discography

Compilations

 Argentine: Musical Patrimony of the North-West Territories (Playasound, France).

A chance to hear the country music of this vast area: from *bagualas* to carnival dances.

 Before The Tango: Argentina's Folk Tradition 1905–1936 (Harlequin, UK).

A fascinating collection of recordings which map the folk music of the country from the beginning of the century. It moves from improvising verses of payadores, through blind harpists to pasodobles, to *cuecas* and a Galician *muineras*: music from the interior of the country brought by immigrants from Spain, Italy and other parts of the world.

Before the Tango

Argentina's Folk Tradition

HQ CD 114

 Chamamé (Iris Musique, France).

A compilation featuring a number of small bands playing chamamé instrumentals and songs or poetic texts. Includes Los Zorzales del Litoral, Hector Ballario, Grupo Convicción and pick of the bunch, singer and accordionist Favio Salvagiot in a band with two dynamic accordions. However, none of the performances are equal to the two chamamé discs recommended below.

Artists

Raúl Barboza

Born in Buenos Aires but absorbing the musical influ-ences of his father's Corrientes background, Barboza is known as the King of Chamamé – a popular, deeply nos-talgic music with percussive melodies. Barboza won the endorsement of Astor Piazzolla: "He's a fighter who deserves my respect and admiration."

Raúl Barboza (La Lichere, France).

With guitar, bass, harp percussion and second accordion, Barboza leads a compelling concert set of quintessential chamamé: typical rasguido dobles and polkas that sound like nothing you've ever heard in Europe.

Rudy and Nini Flores

The Flores are two young brothers from Corrientes Province playing instrumental chamamé: Rudy (born 1961) on guitar and Nini (born 1966) on accordion.

 Chamamé – Musique du Paraná (Ocora, France).

A superb, intimate disc of great artistry. A sharp, poignant and mischievous accordion sound that sustains the interest in nineteen chamamé duos.

The Bahamas

junkanoo and sloop john b.

Bahamian music has a tough time maintaining its identity. This Caribbean collection of islands and cays lies squarely in the economic shadow of the US, and the musical shadow of rock and reggae. But it has a cult-star in the late, great guitarist Joseph Spence, and, as **Jeff Kaliss** discovers, an enduring sparkle of distinctive genres with roots in Protestant church music, community festivities and even African rhythms and rituals.

The place to start looking for music in the Bahamas is the Edem Music Store in Nassau. It's located on a dusty thoroughfare in a modest neighbourhood known as Over the Hill. Edem's proprietor, sexagenarian Duke Strachan ('Straw-en'), is one of the few suppliers of musical instruments and sheet music in The Bahamas. He also runs a limousine service, acts as director of The Bahamas National Youth Orchestra, and is unofficial guardian of the island nation's little-known musical traditions – a role with more than its fair share of challenges.

"There's been a tremendous change, and it's not to my likeness," laments Strachan, with unintentional wordplay. "The islands lost a great heritage when we changed our type of cultural sound, and the older ones who created the flavour of The Bahamas are just about gone. There are some people now trying to capture things Bahamian again, but all of a sudden they are right back to soca and reggae, coming out of Jamaica and Trinidad, which are much bigger here than anything else. Bahamians most of the time find that everything that is foreign is better . . . and not only music."

It's a familiar syndrome dating back to The Bahamas' colonial past, and in this case sustained by the islands' proximity to the southeast coast of Florida – the forty westernmost inhabited islands and cays are located less than a hundred miles from the coast – close enough to tune into American radio and TV. Many millions of tourists from the US, Europe, Japan, and elsewhere swarm here each year for long white beaches toasted by hot sun. In the evening, wandering through the moist, perfumed air, they wash down deep-fried conch or grouper with tropical drinks to a backdrop of familiar, uninspiring pop-Caribbean music, or to hotel-ensemble favourites like the "Banana Boat Song" (aka "Day-O") and "Island In the Sun" (both writ-

ten by Barbadian-American Irving Burgie and popularised by Jamaican-American Harry Belafonte).

You have to dig pretty deep to hear more home-cooked sounds – but there's a tradition here, and it's still breathing. And to World Music enthusiasts, the island has a genuine superstar in the late **Joseph Spence**, who lived out his later years close

GUY PROUSSART

Joseph Spence with his sister, Edith Pinder, Nassau, 1978

to Strachan's music shop. Spence was known locally as an eccentric street-corner performer, but he was also one of the most innovative and expressive guitar players of any genre anywhere, and an idol for guitarists like John Renbourn and Henry Kaiser.

Spence has been the subject of several revered US recordings, along with the **Pinder family** (his in-laws). Their music was based on **Baptist and Anglican hymns and spirituals**, many of them antique and rarely found elsewhere, and on the local *ant'ems* of **sponge fishers** – songs like "Sloop John B" (made famous by The Beach Boys).

Baptist Roots

The Bahamas' **British and Protestant traditions** date back to the mid-seventeenth century, when a group of English Puritans set up a colony on the north coast of Eleuthera Island. The islands' indigenous inhabitants – the 'Indians' whom Columbus encountered on his first landfall in 1492, later identified as **Arawak**, a people from South America – had been decimated by enslavement and disease, and were replaced by slaves from Africa.

By the 1700s, The Bahamas were a centre of expanding commerce and piracy, but by mid-century the British had establish a colonial government in Nassau and the islands attracted Loyalists (and their slaves) forced to flee the newly-created United States because of their allegiance to the Crown. After slavery was outlawed in British possessions – in 1807 – and emancipation declared – in 1834 – The Bahamas became a popular destination for blacks escaping the institutionalised slavery of the American South, including many from the Carolina and Georgia Sea Islands. These great waves of immigrants, who continued to arrive until the end of the American Civil War, were mainly Baptist Protestants. They brought with them a tradition of hymns and spirituals, which had melodies, rhythms, rituals and celebrations stretching much further back, to roots in West Africa shared with several other Caribbean neighbours.

Junkanoo and Goombay

In recent decades the annual **Junkanoo** in the capital city of Nassau has become the strongest, albeit abstracted, link to African traditions in The Bahamas, attracting as it does the financial and hands-on support of middle-class professional Bahamians who compete for prizes, as well as hordes of tourists. Junkanoo parades assemble on Boxing Day and New Year's Day, rather than on the pre-Lenten date of the carnaval/carnival celebrations in Brazil and elsewhere in the Caribbean. The costumes, as bright as those of Rio, have changed through the centuries, parodying the formal clothing of the colonialists, emulating West African ceremonial garb, and today focusing on group themes.

Junkanoo's origins remain tantalisingly obscure, despite comprehensive research by the late Bahamian ethnologist E. Clement Bethel and subsequent members of his family. One of the theories examined by the Bethels suggests that the festival, restricted to the time of year when colonial masters felt particularly benign (Christmas), was intended to commemorate John Connu, an eighteenth-century headman in West Africa. Another theory centres on the 'junk' used to create costumes and instruments in earlier times, including the **goombay drum**, whose name is derived from an instrument associated with West African fertility dances and chants, the precursors of the ring-dance and ring-play still heard in outlying parts of the Bahamian archipelago.

As described by the Bethels, "the goombay drum of Junkanoo is constructed from a wooden or metal barrel, originally the container of food, rum or oil, and has a single membrane of sheep or goat skin stretched and nailed over one end . . . the other important Junkanoo instrument is the cowbell. . . usually played in pairs." Later, whistles and other kinds of hand-held bells and scraped handsaws enhanced the cacophony of the annual parade.

Since the eighteenth century, varieties of Junkanoo (and of the goombay drum) have surfaced throughout the northern Caribbean and in North Carolina, but outside of The Bahamas only Belize seems to have retained the Junkanoo festival. Even in Nassau, its vitality has been controlled over the years by extreme fluctuations of the Bahamian economy, by periodic tightenings of colonial repression, and by changes in the political climate.

After (black) majority rule was achieved in 1968 and independence granted from the British Commonwealth five years later, the 'rushing' of Nassau's Junkanoo paraders down Bay Street fell under more rigid control as the educated black upper middle class came to dominate the festival. Fervent competition between themed groups for lucrative prizes emerged as a result, manifesting itself in elaborate and fantastic costuming, as well as an expanded musical section incorporating brass instruments alongside the conventional drums and bells. While not involving as broad a diversity of

Blind Blake (centre) and the Royal Victoria Hotel Calypso Orchestra, Nassua, 1952

Bahamians as it used to, the festival now adds up to a better show for foreigners. In fact, several of the major hotels feature mock Junkanoo parades as part of their nighttime floor shows throughout the year, inviting tourists to join a sort of conga behind costumed entertainers beating goombay drums.

'Goombay' is also a term applied to a jumpy rhythm, somewhere between calypso and soca, once common in Nassau's nightspots, community halls and in the few older hotels like the British Colonial, where Duke Strachan performed in the 1960s. At that time, the most 'visible' goombay practitioner may have been **Blind Blake**, who provided a musical greeting, fortified with calypso and vaudeville rag hits, at Nassau's airport, and who also recorded several albums now available on cassette.

The Baha Men

The rhythms associated with goombay and Junkanoo are pretty flexible and today's younger black Bahamian performers deploy both, along-side borrowings from calypso, reggae and rock, and electric instruments. The most successful among them are **The Baha Men**, who come in for fairly positive words from Duke Strachan – "they're good, they're trying to keep some Bahamian music alive . . . but in my opinion, not enough."

I ran into a crowded record release party sponsored by Bacardi at the 601 Club on Bay Street for the Baha Men's fourth album, which confirmed their popularity on the home front and the beginnings of a reputation abroad. (They are big in Japan and have a distribution deal with Mercury Records). The group formed as teenagers in the lat 1970s, as High Voltage, and initially played mostly American light-rock to Nassau hotel and club audiences. But they gradually built more of a national identity and sound, changing name to Baha Men in 1991.

On stage at the 601, beneath a wall of Junkanoo feathered masks, the Baha Men had a line up of electric guitars, keyboards and bass, plus a couple of traditionally-garbed goombay drummers (doubling on whistles and timbales). Lead vocalist

Nehemiah Hield, with bleached hair and a moving singing voice a little like Stevie Wonder, relayed to the audience their mission "to take Junkanoo music to the rest of the world, so they know that there is a Bahamian music." Ironically, the announcement was followed by a spirited medley of KC & The Sunshine Band disco hits. But there was plenty of material grown closer to home, including the intoxicatingly bubbly "Island Life", with goombay's characteristic tricky skip on the second beat, high, chattering guitar work, and a tale of a youth's awakening to the responsibilities and joys of Bahamian manhood.

Backstage between sets, guitarist, keyboardist, and songwriter Herschel Small discussed the group's influences and its allegiance to the Bahamian sound. Their first album, he explained, was an attempt to put young people in touch with the "old stuff", but in a way that a 1990s audience could appreciate. "The market is always looking for something new", he said, "and this Junkanoo sound is definitely different from anything out there, different instruments playing different rhythms . . . I would hate to think that the folk stuff would die, because it's a very sweet, soulful music, the old stuff that Joseph Spence played, and some of Blind Blake's singing-rapping."

Spurred on by the number of visiting Americans who buy their music, the group is now keen to take it to a wider US audience. It's no surprise, then, that the further the band's music strays from Bay Street, the more R&B, rock, and soul share set lists and album tracks with goombay and Junkanoo.

K.B.: In the Air Everywhere

The tug between home pride and expanding markets has also challenged **Kirkland Bodie**, a multi-talented guitarist, singer, songwriter, and producer better known in the music business as K.B. Seated at the poolside bar of the British Colonial (now owned by Best Western), the slender, handsome performer is warmed by an afternoon breeze and the sounds of one of his own hits, "Play By Ma'Sef," bubbling from the outdoor speakers. "This is soca, with Junkanoo mixed in," he explained. "I marry both into it. They are festive sounds; you can't talk about depressing stuff while the rhythm is like that."

Still, he remembers his frustration as leader of a rock cover band in the early 1980s. It wasn't until the band managed to create a first Junkanoo song – "it was rock, but the goombay element got it

across" – that Bahamian radio and audiences began to pay attention. It helped that K.B. had developed a particular talent for serving up salacious lyrics ripe with innuendo, in the tradition of both goombay and calypso.

By the time the group's members went their separate ways in the late 1980s, they'd been able to abandon their day jobs, "and in this market that's hard to do, unless you work in the hotels", K.B. points out. He was more in the mood to tour than to cater to tourists in the Nassau area and on the back of his new group's hit, "Juicy Susie", began to travel around the islands of The Bahamas using Freeport (on Grand Bahama island) as a home base. He now has an American manager and plays 'deck parties' in New Jersey and New England, as well as throughout the Bahamas.

KIRKLAND BODIE

K.B. – Kirkland Bodie

In Nassau and Freeport, K.B. continues to play larger venues, sometimes opening for the islands' musical statesman, **Ronnie Butler**. Described as "godlike" by K.B., Butler has been a star in the Bahamas since he started out singing calypso in the 1940s. A singer and guitarist, he has an incredibly charming, virile baritone voice, and is best-known for his version of the classic Bahamian calypso "Burma Road."

Riddim & Rhyme – Joseph Spence

To hear the recorded legacy of the late **Joseph Spence** is to get a glimpse of the raw joy of music. It's a gift which prompts even Bahamian pop star K.B. to take a break from the celebrations of dance and romance on his "Conch Juice" album and pay a soulful tribute to Spence's great talent:

> U were so gifted, your brothers couldn't see,
> But my heart u lifted, your music set me free,
> With just a simple smile
> and the magic in your hands,
> Shows us proof of God, working through a man.

K.B. begins this track, "Riddim & Rhyme", with a sample of Spence picking and singing "Victory Is Coming", one of many songs Spence extracted from the "shape note hymnals" popular in The Bahamas. The melody is simple enough, but Spence had a trademark way of arranging his material. As Lenny Carlson wrote in his introduction to a book of transcriptions, "[Spence] usually harmonizes melody notes using 6ths, [and] his harmonic output is more like Baroque counterpoint than simple melody against static chords. The different voices are continually moving." This was partly a result of Spence's multiphrenic picking virtuosity, and it was oddly juxtaposed with Spence's preference to use his instrument "out of tune, with his own well-defined sense of intonation."

Joseph Spence was born on Andros, the largest of the Bahamian islands, in 1910. He absorbed the joyous sounds of the Baptist church, where his father was a pastor, and played dances with his great-uncle, the popular Tony Spence, but most of his meagre income in the 1930s came from sponge fishing, a trade replete with song. Later in the decade, Spence relocated to Nassau and married Louise Wilson from Cat Island, who introduced him to more formal, hymnal-based religious music. They remained on New Providence, Spence working as a mason and carpenter, except for several extended stays in the 1940s and '50s picking crops in the American South. Spence picked up other sacred and popular songs while in the States, and his recorded repertoire came to include material from all these sources.

Following up on notes from the great American folk music recordist Alan Lomax, who'd visited Andros in the 1930s, blues scholar **Sam Charters** and his fiancée happened to arrive on the island in 1958 at the same time as Spence, and were entranced to overhear what Charters thought to be two musicians involved in "some of the most exuberant, spontaneous, and uninhibited guitar playing we had ever encountered." It was Spence, of course, then aged 47, and Charters proceeded to capture what would become Folkways' seminal album, *Music of The Bahamas, Vol 1.*

Peter Siegel and **Jody Stecher**, two young New York musicians, made their own recording trip to Nassau seven years later, and bolstered the Spence Stateside legend further with *The Real Bahamas* on the Nonesuch label. There followed invitations for Spence to play concerts and record in the US, and meetings with guitarist fans such as Ry Cooder and Taj Mahal. Even The Grateful Dead adopted Spence and the Pinders' "I Bid You Goodnight" as a blissful closer for their own riotous performances.

But as K.B.'s lyric suggests, Spence's American legend didn't translate into star status or big money in his own country. "You know him better than I do," laughs the Ministry of Tourism's Roney Ambrister. "But I've heard that he would sit down under a tree or on the corners or around the barber shops [in Nassau] and play, just he and friends. . . It reminded you of the folks on the [outer] islands, when somebody dies and they have a settin'-up." Even when dealing with somber lyric themes, Spence's immense and unpredictable good humour and delight, infectious among those who knew him in Nassau, are audible in his recorded legacy.

Spence himself was laid to rest in 1984. His indelible sound is preserved in his own recordings, and his spirit in the hearts of many American and a few Bahamian fans, as well as on a Green Linnet tribute album that assembles Taj Mahal, Henry Kaiser, Jody Stecher, Dave Grisman, Martin Carthy, Madagascar's Rossy, 3Mustapha3, and a host of other musicians peforming Spence's music. But there's no evidence of a living Bahamaian continuation of his tradition to survive him. Maybe he was truly one of a kind, and the ability to produce that sound had to go with its maker.

Rake-and-Scrape

One Bahamian tradition that K.B. pays tribute to, using samples in his music, is called **rake-and-scrape**. This gets its name from the use of a saw. The player stands with the handle secured against his thigh, bending the saw with one hand and scraping it with a screwdriver or other metal object in the other hand.

Rake-and-scrape bands come from the Family Islands, where they continue to accompany *quadrille* dances. These derivatives of European waltzes, polkas, and mazurkas – performed during community functions and without the vocals, brass, and noisemakers of Junkanoo – co-existed with other older musics until the government began extending electrical service throughout the archipelago in recent decades. They are in decline now, but still performed by a handful of older ensembles.

A group of mainly old-timers gathers Sundays at *The Same Old Place* in the centre of New Providence, to dance to the **Lassie Doo Boys**, one of the best and most popular of current rake-and-scrape bands. Edmund Rahming, who works a day job as a garage mechanic across the street from Duke Strachan's music store, is one of the group's two guitarists, and his brother Wellington their manager. The saw functions as a rhythm instrument, alongside drums and maracas; it is also made melodic by varying the tension on the blade, while a different timbre is achieved by occasionally scraping the top of the saw, rather than the teeth.

When the Lassie Doo Boys get inside a chugging Bahamian hybrid of calypso or soca, it's an easy groove to sweat and sway to, and when they adopt an American hit like Lloyd Price's "Stagger Lee" (recorded in a similar and locally successful version by Bahamian pop star Eugene Davis), they make it their own, independent of its origin. On slower covers like Kris Kristofferson's "Help Me Make It Through the Night", the effect may seem somewhat comical. But Edmund Rahming and his buddy Duke Strachan proudly recall a visit decades ago from the late American soul/rock singer Brook Benton. "The way we did his song, 'Endlessly'", beams Duke, "he fell in love with that."

Rhyming, Religion and Recording

The **spiritual-based music** embraced by performers such as **Joseph Spence**, the **Pinders** and the **McQueens** is distinct in several ways from other Bahamian forms. Thanks primarily to recordings by Sam Charters, Jody Stecher, and Peter Siegel, the music had an earlier and wider exposure in the US than any other from The Bahamas. The recordings resulted in paid concerts in the US for Spence and a few others (unique before the current era of the Baha Men and K.B.), but unlike goombay, the sound was never considered commercial in its native country, and was associated instead with work (especially sponge fishing), worship, wakes, and informal community gatherings.

The roots of such music may be traced to regions of The Bahamas far from Nassau, including Spence's native island of Andros, and to the relative absence there of US-based pop forms like R&B and rock – unique elements which, alas, resulted in the almost total disappearance of the form by the 1990s, when most of the practitioners celebrated in the Folkways and Nonesuch recordings had died.

The American South shared some of the spirituals heard in these recordings, and some of the close harmonising (especially by Sam and Bruce Green and colleagues) evokes early American gospel groups as the Mitchell Singers. But what seems unique is the technique known as the **rhyming spiritual**, where a lead singer – **the rhymer** – maintains a spirited, highly syncopated and often improvisational line on a Biblical or topical theme against a repeated foundation of other voices, usually a cappella.

The songs, referred to as *ant'ems*, were shared, alongside topical ballads (sea shanties, in effect), by **sponge fishermen**, whose ensemble rhyming was perfected on their boats. The song forms continued on an occasional basis after that trade was virtually extinguished by a blight in the late 1930s.

Jody Stecher describes rhyming as "the combination of the traditions of singing sermons and African drum and bell rhythms," and the most inspiring on record are those he and Peter Siegel captured for Nonesuch, led by the reedy, ethereal, almost rap-like vocals of **Frederick McQueen**. Taking the vocal lead for the **Pinder Family** was Joseph Spence's sister, **Edith Spence Pinder**. She was possessed of a feisty alto, set tantalisingly between the bass of her brother or that of her husband, Raymond Pinder, and the high treble harmony of her daughter, Geneva, with Joseph's guitar often working the sole, wily instrumental accompaniment. On his solo recordings, Spence and his guitar perform the uncanny task of filling in for the other missing voices.

While this harmonisation has a home in the Protestant church, the rhythms, the role of the rhymer, and the spirit of these performances seem related, even if distantly, to group forms passed down from West African ancestors. Some Bahamian songs convey topical stories of launchings, shipwrecks, and such, alongside the stories with a Christian moral message. In all cases, the content is highly emotive.

Another Bahamian tradition with West African roots is that of **Obeah** – a form of witchcraft practised on the islands as an alternative to Christian spiritualism. This found a musical embodiment in the songs of Tony McKay, aka **Exuma**, the Obeah Man, who passed away in 1996. "You could put him in line with a Spence," says Roney Ambrister. "He was a jubil fellow, very happy, he would grab his guitar, kick off, and the rest of the band would follow him". Ambrister is also keen to point out that "there was no such thing as 'Obeah music'" – the spiritual charge lay instead in McKay's fantastic clothing, artwork, and mystical lyrics: "His time is short, his time is long/Exuma ain't right and Exuma ain't wrong."

Like Spence, McKay recorded several albums for Siegel and Stecher and others, which have been rereleased in recent years. These albums seem to attract little attention from either natives or tourists in The Bahamas, though, and the rhyming spiritual is little heard, except at wakes.

discography

Compilations

🔘 **The Bahamas: Islands of Song**
(Smithsonian Folkways, US).

The wide-ranging cast of Bahamian musicians on this CD participated in the Smithsonian's 1994 Festival of American Folklife in Washington, D.C. and were recorded in the following year at a Nassau club. The Bahamas have spawned better guitarists and rake-and-scrape groups than those presented here, but there's much of interest: a hand-clapping Ring-play session of West African origin, reworkings of old English folksongs, and a couple of male a cappella groups working in close harmony. And the historical notes by the Bahamian government's Gail Saunders and Kayla Olubumni Lockhart Edwards are invaluable.

🔘 **The Real Bahamas, Vols I & II**
(Nonesuch Explorer, US).

Siegel and Stecher's historic 1965 recording sessions featuring Jospeh Spence placed him in the merry and melodious midst of his sister's family, the Pinders. And there are different, intriguing contributions of rhyming spirituals, a cappella harmonisation, and topical story songs from Frederick

McQueen and Sam and Bruce Green, all now gone. Stecher's updated liner notes and Guy Droussart's luminous photographic portraits further illuminate an inspiring yet totally natural musical monument.

Artists

Baha Men

A modern roots band, the Baha Men were created in 1991 by Nehemiah Hield, former singer of High Voltage, with electrified instrumentalisits and enthnic percussionists. They have gained worldwide distribution . . . and are big in Japan.

🔘 **Here We Go Again** (Raging Bull, US).

The polished production values and synthesis of American Light Rock conventions don't sabotage this would-be worldclass band's island roots, though you have to pick through the tracks to find where they flourish best. That's on the goombay-socas "Island Life" and "Le' Ma Go", but there's also an affecting soul ballad ("Mother Moon, Father Sun") and a well-harmonised cover of the surf-rock classic "Beach Baby". A good and different choice for your next outdoor or indoor beach party.

Blind Blake

Back in the 1940s and '50s, the late Alphonse 'Blind Blake' Higgs brought smiles to the countenance of the resident Duke of Windsor with "Love Alone" – a calypso about the royal's loss of this throne to love – as well as amusing decades of incoming tourists with his impromptu performances at Nassau airport.

📟 **Experience Blind Blake** (G.B.I., The Bahamas).

Blind Blake recordings are available mainly on cassettes of questionable quality and with much material extraneous to the home culture. This collection, issued as "A Quincentennial Item" in 1992 (commemorating the 500-year anniversary of the landing in The Bahamas of Columbus, "the first tourist"), includes goombay favourites such as "Pig & Goat" and "Comin' Tonight" alongside Blake's humorous ragtime frolics and his classic calypso "Love Alone".

K.B.

K.B. – Kirkland Bodie – grew up mostly in Florida but returned to his roots in The Bahamas, taking along his musical emulation of black American rock and R&B stars. Unable to succeed with bands restricted to imported covers, Bodie found his career flourishing when he began drawing his sound from his roots. He now also produces young, like-minded Bahamian artists.

🔘 **Conch Juice** (Stars, The Bahamas/US).

This musical bouillabaise of homemade (but electronically enhanced) goombay and rake-and-scrape with imported soca and reggae is delightfully upbeat and danceable; one taste and you'll understand why you hear this kind of thing blasting from transitor radios on every jitney and tour bus you take and in all the hotel bars along Cable Beach and the stores on Bay Street. But don't overlook "Riddim & Rhyme", K.B.'s heart-felt tribute to Spence. Recorded at one of Nassau and Freeport's handful of studios.

Ronnie & The Ramblers

Ronnie Butler was one of the first artists – in the 1950s and '60s – to widen the embrace of foreign musics while maintaining a stance in The Bahamas. He is now the elder statesman among the islands' pop performers, heavily booked for regattas and seasonal festivals.

🔘 **Burma Road** (Ronnie Records, The Bahamas).

Guitarist and vocalist Ronnie Butler has been declared "god-like" by younger musician K.B., and Butler's baritone voice, as smooth and heady as a glass of Goombay Punch, is indeed divine, whether he's delivering an original jump-up goombay tale ("Native Woman") or a wave-rocked calypso take on Harry Nilsson's "Everybody's Talkin" (here uncredited and retitled, "Echoes of my Mind"). Butler also takes credit for the extremely popular title tune, although its origins reportedly date back to a 1940s demonstration by Bahamian labour against exploitation by foreign developers (an ongoing problem). In any case, Butler enhances the lyric with verses from Bahamian folk songs and an extended comic 'rap' about the pleasures of native cuisine and the foolishness of aping foreign fashions.

Joseph Spence

Best-known outside his homeland, the late Spence developed intricate guitar techniques with which he arranged and accompanied spiritual Protestant and topical Bahamian material.

🔘 **The Complete Folkways Recordings – 1958** (Smithsonian Folkways, US).

In its original form as two LPs recorded by Samuel Charters, this was the means by which the wonder of solo Spence was first exported to the rest of the world, revealing the Bahamian master's entertaining approach to guitar and voice, as eccentric and brilliant as Thelonious Monk's to the piano. Serious students of the guitar should also purchase Lenny Carlson's painstaking transcriptions, published by Smithsonian Folkways and Mel Bay, of the album's nine tunes.

Belize

drum'n'flute legacies

For such a tiny country, Belize enjoys an exceptional range of musical styles and traditions, from the ethereal harp melodies of the Maya or the up-tempo punta of the Garifuna, to marimba, brukdown, soca or steelpan. And it's loud! Some visitors complain about the noise of Belizean society and the sheer volume at which music is played, but if you get into the music at a street jump-up, a late night party or a local fiesta, as our guide **Ronnie Graham** has done, it's one of the quickest ways to the heart of Belizeans and their culture.

Before the arrival of the Spanish, the indigenous **Maya** of the Central American highlands played a range of traditional instruments – drums, trumpets, flutes, bells, shells and whistles. Most music was ritual in character, involving up to eight hundred dancers for major state occasions, though smaller ensembles were more common.

After the civilisation collapsed, a new music developed among the **Mestizo** people – the 'mixed' offspring of Spanish conquistadores and Maya communities. This music combined elements of its two constituent cultures: Maya ceremonial musical occasions, vocal inflexions and stringed and blow instruments, and from Spain, recreational music, the guitar and violin. Catholicism, which swiftly displaced Maya religion, also had an impact, providing a new set of cultural reference points, as well as organised church singing, while a new tradition of brass band music derived from the military garrisons which enforced the new Pax Hispanica.

Modern Mestizo Music

Modern **Mestizo music**, in the west and north of Belize, offers a delightful variety of neo-traditional styles, generally less frenetic and more mellow than the music elsewhere. Out west, in San Ignacio and Benque (and over into Guatemala), and probably owing more to Tikal than Madrid, the **marimba** is king. A Central American relative of the African xylophone, this is a massive, multi-keyed wooden instrument often played by two musicians at once.

Marimba ensembles such as **Alma Belicena** and **Los Angeles Marimba Band** are large musical groups, usually incorporating double bass and trap drums, and will often be found playing in the

Cayo and Orange Walk Districts at public events and private functions. The tradition is very much alive with younger, usually family musicians taking the place of veterans.

From the Spanish side of the same tradition and appearing frequently in the Orange Walk and Corozal areas are itinerant **mariachi bands** who appear in Belize from over the border in Mexico to entertain Belizeans during public holidays, fiestas and weddings.

Marching band, San Pedro, 1928

British, Africans and Creoles

While the Spanish influence in Belize clearly pre-dates the first appearance of the British in any organised way, it was predominantly the **British** who, in the sixteenth and seventeenth centuries, carved out the colony. As well as their church and military music, they brought their dances – the schottische, quadrille, polka and waltz – and, over the next three centuries, introduced much of the hardware and software for playing music – Western musical instruments and sheet music, record players and discs, and, in more recent decades, massive sound systems.

A perhaps stronger musical influence arrived in Belize via the slave trade during the eighteenth century. The colony's slaves came mainly from Rivers State, Efiks and Calabaris in southeast Nigeria – via Jamaica and Barbados – and brought with them **West African** and Caribbean rhythms and melodies. In the logging camps of the interior, their music met with Western instrumentation to create a specifically Belizean Creole musical tradition known as **brukdown**.

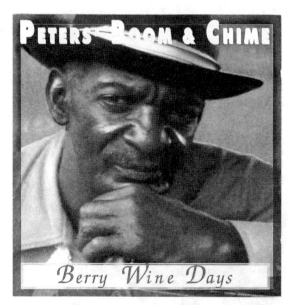

This survives today, played by groups featuring guitar, banjo, accordion, drums, the dingaling (a kind of bell), and the jawbone of an ass (played by rattling a stick up and down the teeth!). In Belize City, a group known as **Mr. Peters' Boom and Chime** perform professionally on special occasions. Otherwise brukdown is a recreational rural music, best enjoyed in the Creole villages of Hat-

tieville, Gracie Rock, Boom, Bermudian Landing and Isabella Bank.

There is also a **Creole folk-song** tradition, which **Brad Patico**, an accomplished guitarist, does his best to keep alive from his base in Burell Boom. He collects old material, some of which is incorporated into his all too infrequent public performances, which often turn into inspired singa-longs as audiences recall past airs and melodies.

Originating in the same cultural patrimony is **Brudda David Obi and his Cungo Beat.** David is a product of a Creole, black nationalism which found its political expression in the black power movement of the late 1960s and its written expression in Evan X Hyde's weekly *Amandala* newspaper. An accomplished musician and songwriter, he plays regularly in Belize City and has made a number of cassettes and CDs, including a collaboration with Mr. Peters.

The Garifuna: Paranda and Punta

The **Garifuna** – or, more correctly, Garinagu – reflect their triple cultural heritage with direct and vibrant traditions drawn from three continents. Drumming and social organisation clearly originate in Nigeria; their main language and family names are Spanish; whilst their agriculture, language and more obscure musical traditions draw on their **Carib forbears** in **St. Vincent** (*Alliouana* in Carib).

The Garifuna were enslaved in West Africa during the seventeenth and eighteenth centuries, before being sold into the sugar and cotton plantations of St. Vincent. But fired by a spirit of independence and human dignity, they escaped to the interior of the island with what owners could only view as alarming regularity. Throughout the eighteenth century a unique intermingling occurred as escaped slaves intermarried with indigenous Caribs to produce the so-called black Caribs of St. Vincent.

The black Caribs continued to provide a thorn in the flesh of the nascent colonial slave society and, with their land wanted for plantations, in 1797 the entire community of four thousand was shipped across the Caribbean to the large island of **Roatan**, several hundred kilometres off the coast of Central America, many of them dying in the voyage. Finally left to their own devices, the survivors, using Roatan as a springboard, established a number of coastal communities on the Central American mainland, arriving and settling in Belize (British Honduras) in 1802.

During the nineteenth century and most of the twentieth century, in their new homes at Dangriga, Barranco, Hopkins and Punta Gorda, the Garifuna steadfastly refused to participate in any way in the colonial system, marginalising themselves from the mainstream development of Belizean national culture and in the process refining the Garifuna culture with its twin mother tongues of Garifuna and Spanish and its material foundation in fishing and farming.

Musically, traditional African rhythms – vocals and percussion – were enriched through the close ties binding the Garifuna in Belize with those who had settled further south in Honduras and Nicaragua. This led to a potent cross-fertilisation of African and Latin cultures, which was to explode to national prominence as *punta rock* in the 1970s, as Belize moved towards independence. In its earlier stages, the meeting of African and Latin music led to a style called **paranda** – a music of great charm, played on acoustic instruments – drums, scrapers, shakers and guitar (see box).

There were many master musicians and cultural nationalists who pushed the culture forward

Paranda: the forgotten music

"There used to be dozens of us *paranda* players in every town when I was young," remembered Paul Nabor, the master of this seductive acoustic Afro-Caribbean music. The short 72-year-old sat in front of his small wooden thatch home, strumming his guitar, and reminiscing about an era gone by. "It dates back to the 1800s," he explained in a raspy voice, "but there aren't many people still playing it, maybe one person per village." Nabor himself is the last living *parandero* in the southern Belizean coastal village of Punta Gorda.

Paranda is both a Garifuna rhythm and a genre of music. The basic rhythm can be heard in Garifuna traditional drumming styles that date all the way back to St. Vincent and West Africa. The music seems to have developed shortly after the Garifuna arrived in Honduras, where they first encountered Spanish music, and adopted the acoustic guitar. It has changed little in the past hundred or so years, retaining a purely acoustic instrumentation, backing the guitar and voice with percussion from large wooden Garifuna drums, shakers, scrapers and turtle shell percussion. Imagine African percussion, Cuban son, American Blues, and West African Guitars all wrapped into one. That is the sound of Paranda.

Africa in Central America

The music has only very recently been heard outside of its home communities. In the summer of 1995, when producer Ivan Duran (of Belize's Stonetree Records) was recording the Punta Rock album, *Keimoun* with Andy Palacio, Andy played Duran a tape of Paul Nabor, recorded at Punta Gorda. Duran was overwhelmed and the following year, he, along with co-producer Gil Abarbanel began what came to be known as the Paranda Project.

This took the pair to dozens of Garifuna villages throughout Central America, looking for remaining Paranderos. They found only a handful, most of them elderly – Gabaga Williams (83), Junie Arranda (59), Paul Nabor (72), Jursino Ceytano (62) – and a sole younger generation singer, Aurelio Martinez (29). Duran brought them together in Belize City for a historic session, together with Lugua Centeno, the greatest Garufuna percussionist.

The subject matter of Paranda songs is as diverse as Central America's terrain. Junie Arranda says that many of his Paranda songs (like much of Garifuna music in general) are a way of 'getting back' at people. He has songs about people in town who owe him money, past girlfriends, and former employers. He also sings of the devastating Hurricane Hattie of 1961, which wrought destruction upon much of Dangriga, killing hundreds.

Following the 2000 release of the first Paranda album, producer Ivan Duran has plans for solo albums with Paul Nabor and Aurelio Martinez. Maybe this almost forgotten music form will take its place alongside Cuba's son and Brazil's samba as one of the most infectious styles of African music in the Americas.

Dan Rosenberg

during the twentieth century, but pride of place must surely go to **Isabel Flores**, master drummer and drum-maker, and the enigmatic **Pen Cayetano**, extraordinary guitarist and artist. More than anyone else, Pen pioneered popular garifuna music, inventing **punta rock** in the late 1970s by adding guitars to a traditional drum rhythm and sparking a new cultural assertiveness which saw dozens of younger musicians take up the challenge. **Roy** and **Phylis Cayetano,** along with **Joe Palacio,** provided the intellectual underpinning for this cultural renaissance in an influential series of

books and articles, while the community gave practical support to the **Waribagabaga Drum and Dance Troupe**, representing a more roots approach to Garifuna performance culture.

Pen Cayetano's **Turtle Shell Band** initially set the standard for punta, with a rough and ready sound which hypnotised audiences, but within a few years they were joined by dozens of singers and bands, such as **Sounds Incorporated**, **Children of the Most High**, **Black Coral**, **Titiman Flores**, **Mohobob**, **Jeff Zuniga**, and – most notably – **Andy Palacio** (see box).

Andy Palacio and Sunrise Studios

For more than a decade **Andy Palacio** has dominated Belizean music – indeed, he is the country's only truly professional star. He seems to appeal to just about everyone in the country, from teens to oldsters, and has brilliantly incorporated a diversity of national and regional styles into his unique popular sound. He has also been instrumental in developing a recording scene.

Born in Barranco, the southernmost Garifuna village, a short boat ride from Livingstone in neighbouring Honduras, Andy grew up amid the rural mix of garifuna, Maya and mestizo communities, speaking English, Garifuna and Spanish. As a teenager in the 1970s, he experienced at first hand the new Belizean cultural nationalism of the PUP (People's United Party), which brought the country to independence, introducing a broader ideological dimension to his cultural affinity with the Garifuna musical tradition.

After leaving school, Andy trained as a teacher but already his skills on the guitar, combined with a penchant for a neat lyric and a compelling voice had marked him out for a very different kind of career. The significant and decisive break came in 1987 when he accepted the offer of an exchange visit to Hackney, North London, courtesy of Cultural Partnerships. It turned out to be a year well spent as Andy picked up the latest recording techniques and honed his musical and compositional skills. A year later he returned to Belize with enough equipment to open a studio and run a small band.

He also brought several London recordings of the songs that would become huge hits back home, transforming the music scene and laying the first foundations of the new national sound. The first was "Bikini Panti", an English-Garifuna, punta-rock satire on Belize's burgeoning tourist business. Palacio had

IVAN DURAN

Punta Rockin' with Andy Palacio

composed the song a few years before but with the enhanced London production, augmented by guitarist Lenny Hadaway (Arrow's right-hand man) and Louis O'Neill (Scotz keyboard genius) it set a new

These groups consolidated the popularity of punta, digging into other traditional rhythms and modernising everything that they could find. By the mid-1980s, the musicians of Dangriga had succeeded not only in updating traditional Garifuna culture, but had made punta into the embryonic national style.

Belize gained its **independence** in 1981 and while the country had previously enjoyed a high level of ethnic integration and tolerance, the new political dispensation led to a conscious effort to promote the strength and diversity of the new nation's constituent cultures. Belizean music benefited, as the Bliss Institute, the Arts Council and Radio Belize all received a new lease of life as means for building the nation, and the Garifuna, at ease in English and Spanish, and enjoying their own cultural renaissance, were seen as an integral part of the process.

The key musical event for their music – Punta – was the 1987 release of *Punta Rockers* on the Sunrise label, a compilation that brought together **Pen Cayetano**, **Andy Palacio**, **Sounds Incorporated**, and the L.A. based Garifuna group **Chatuye**. Dur-

musical standard for Belize – and it was a dance-floor killer. Another London recording, "Me Goin Back", meantime, provided an expression of new national confidence, with is calypsonian lyrics ("Now check this one from Belize, because it's hard like Caribbean breeze . . .").

With these two hits to his credit, Andy helped to set up the **Sunrise Recording Studio**, and brought in the pioneers of punta rock to record the compilation *Punta Rockers*. Featuring Garifuna musicians from Belize and the US, this was a revelation, selling several thousand cassettes, and confirming punta's position as Belize's pre-eminent party music, and Andy's status as a pivotal figure in the production and distribution system. Previously, the country – with its tiny 100,000 population – had not seemed able to support a recording industsy of its own, beyond the odd calypso or brukdown party single.

Over the next few years, however, Sunrise moved to make up for lost time, with a string of cassette releases. **Alma Belicena** and the **Los Angeles Marimba bands** both released beautiful marimba recordings; **Florencio Mes** covered traditional Maya melodies (recorded on home-made stringed instruments in a barn in Toledo), while the **Children of the Most High** and **Waribagabaga** chipped in with impressive punta roots rhythms. Other sessions produced the first recording of **Brad Patico** and his Creole-brukdown-folk songs; the **Belize Police Band** and the **All-Star Steel Band**, as well as Andy's own first cassette release, *Come Mek We Dance*.

This activity established a new platform for music in Belize and provided Andy Palacio with a springboard for the US market. He began making trips to Belizean strongholds in Los Angeles, Chicago and New York, performing punta hits for appreciative and homesick audiences. But punta's breakthrough into wider markets, ironically, came through a hitherto obscure Honduran outfit, who in 1989 covered "Bikini Panti" and pushed it to global dance floor success.

By the early 1990s, with Sunrise incorporated into the Belize Broadcasting Corporation, Andy moved to consolidate his career. He tried for a while, without great success, to make it in the US, before returning to make the CD *Khalfa* (1994) and doubling up with top rapper Poopa Curly for a 1995 single on the Sea Breeze label. The same year his new single, "Samudi Ganou" (Saturday Night) took Belize by storm.

The next stage in the Palacio career began in 1995 when he joined **Stonetree Records** – a new venture set up by Ivan Duran in the western Belizean town of Benque. The result was the stunning *Keimoun (Beat On)*, recorded in Belize, finished in Cuba and mastered in Mexico. Its hard driving, Caribbean-Latin rhythms demonstrated Palacio's confidence in his multi-cultural musical skills, grafting a diverse collection of Cuban and Belizean musicians onto the basic punta rhythm.

On his next release, *Til Da Mawnin* (1997) Palacio reversed the process, laying down the basic tracks and vocals in Cuba and mixing in punta percussion back in Belize. Produced by Alejandro Colinas (of *Africando* fame) this saw Andy break more new ground, reinforcing the cultural association between the Garifina of Belize and their roots in the Carib communities of St. Vincent, and celebrating the mixed musical patrimony and regional cultural diversity in "Viva El Caribe":

African music in the festival,
Spicy Caribbean flavour in the festival
Oh lord ! what a fete
Everybody soaking wet

Salsa, Soca, Reggae, Cumbia and Merengue
Punta rock, they goin on bad
Calypso from Trinidad
Zouk and Vallenato
Cadence and Guauanco

There's no better introduction to Belize.

ing the years which followed, individual stars went on to establish national and regional reputations before the concept was picked up again by Stonetree Records in the mid-1990s with the release of startling CDs by **Lugua and the Larubeya Drummers**, the **Parranda Greats** compilation, **Garifuna Women**, the

Titiman Flores on the road

Turtle Shell Band, as well as a new Punta rockers series led by **Titiman Flores** and **Mohobuob**.

The punta rock produced by these groups through the 1990s was a genuinely new sound, melodic and emotive, yet deeply, danceably percussive, underpinned by African rhythms, and punctuated by major league guitar riffs. It was a little like Antillean zouk in its energy and its burst towards popularity, yet it has a melodic lilt which resembles in some ways merengue from the Dominican Republic.

Caribbean and African American influences

Over the past two decades, other African, Caribbean and US elements found themselves incorporated into the Belizean musical mix – reggae, merengue, steel pan, soca, zouk and rap all struck a resonance with the largely Creole culture. The music of black America was particularly influential on popular listening tastes, as a model that stood apart from the old colonial sphere of Britain, and Belize these days has a pretty good **rap** artist of its own in **Poopa Curly**.

Soca's (and some might say rap's) predecessor, **calypso**, had formerly made some impression in

Belize, though mainly through the efforts of **Lord Rhaburn**, an artist who stood out as the 'voice of Belize' from the 1960s to the '80s, with songs about the struggle for independence and other topical issues, scoring annual hits for major occasions like the Bliss Holiday, National Day and later, Independence Day.

The keynote to modern Belizean music, however, is its inclusiveness, bringing together Creole and mestizo, garifuna and European. Bands like **Santino's Messengers**, **Youth Connection**, **Gilharry Seven** and **Brudda David Obi** each have musicians drawn from all the major ethnic groups – and draw on each tradition.

These groups (and their offshoots) perform at weekend clubs and hotels in Belize City, Orange Walk and Dangriga, starting late and getting hotter as the night develops into endless rounds of cold *Belikin* (Belizean beer) and rum'n'-coke. Promising venues include *Lindberg's Landing*, *Big Apple*, *Fort George*, *Lumba Yard*, *Riverside*, *Orange Walk Hotel* and *The Bellevue*.

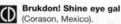

discography

You'll need to hunt around gift shops in Belize for the Sunrise cassettes of the 1980s – even the classic Punta Rockers has not had a re-release. But with the appearance of Stonetree Records, Belize has at last a range of internationally available CDs.

Artists

Brukdon! Shine eye gal
(Corason, Mexico).

A great survey of bands playing Belize's distinctive calypso. Mini-Musical Female Duet and Brad Pattico emphasise the British 'white' style, while The Tigers, The Mahogany Chips and Wilfred Peter's wonderful Belizean Boom 'n Chime Band are much more African. Tracks range from trios of voice and guitar to the large and raucous boom and chime bands.

Music from Guatemala Vol. 2: Garifuna
(Caprice, Sweden).

As well as in Belize, Garifuna communities are found in Guatemala, Honduras and Nicaragua. This disc presents three contrasting Garifuna groups: the old-style Grupo Ugandani (who begin with a lovely acoustic *paranda* song), the very African-sounding percussion group Suamen, and The Garifuna Boys, playing Punta Rock including Garifuna drums. This disc is the second and best of a pair exploring the music of Guatemala. **Vol 1** is for marimba fans only.

 Paranda: Africa in Central America (Erato/Detour, France).

While Punta Rock is the best-known music of the Garifuna communities of Belize, *paranda* is its most charming. It's a hybrid mix of African and Latin with acoustic instruments including large drums, shakers and scrapers plus guitar. Sadly it's a genre that has almost disappeared, forsaken for more modern styles. This marvellous disc captures some of the last remaining paranderos including Paul Nabor, Gabaga Williams and Garifuna drummer Lugua Centeno Petio. Andy Palacio also pays homage on one track.

Artists

Bredda David & Tribal Vibes

Brother David, originator of Kungo Music, has for the last twenty years occupied a unique niche in the Belizean scene with his Creole/African/black American fusions. Underpinned by the occasional punta or reggae rhythm, Kungo music adds electrifying guitar and positive cultural messages to create a statement of Belizean nationality.

Raw! (Stonetree, Belize).

Rock guitars overlaid on the new generic Belizean rhythm, and sharpened by David's inclusive lyrical wit, come together to produce a satisfying run around the Kungo kingdom. Decidedly danceable and eminently entertaining. *Raw* is the strongest statement yet of David's musical vision.

Lugua and the Larubeya Drummers

Evangelisto 'Lugua' Centeno pounds out his ferocious punta rhythms with a sound that cuts across all boundaries. With powerful female background vocals and a variety of punta rhythms, this is roots Africa in Belize.

Bumari (Stonetree, Belize).

Roots Punta at its strongest, Lugua and his merry men open a new chapter in the distinguished history of garifuna percussion with this inspired foray into the soul of a people. Brooding, spiritual and inspirational.

The Original Turtle Shell Band

Formed in the Dangriga cultural heartland in the late 1970s by guitarist Pen Cayetano, The Original Turtle Shell Band were pioneers of the punta phenomenon, and a bridge between traditional and modern electric punta.

Serewe (Stonetree, Belize).

This recent recording shows the band at full maturity, incorporating paranda and hungu hungu rhythms to augment the more familiar punta. Whether you kick back and get high, or simply dance and smile, *Serewe* will remain a state-of-the-art recording for years to come.

Andy Palacio

Andy Palacio (see box feature) has been Belize's main musical export for the best part of a decade. His current association with Stonetree Records has resulted in a string of superb recordings.

 Keimoun (beat on) and **Til Da Mawnin** (Stonetree, Belize).

On these two recent releases, Andy displays his mastery of punta and widens his scope to incorporate Cuban and Anglophone Caribbean influences. Recorded in Belize and Cuba, pressed in Mexico and available globally, these recordings set the standard for Belizean tropical music, combining the swing and sophistication of the Cuban tradition with lyrical flair and down to earth rhythms. *Keimoun* just about has the edge for a first choice.

Mr Peters and his Boom & Chime

Wilfred Peters is the undisputed king of brukdown and brings a driving accordion to his musical journeys through Creole history. He seldom performs these days but remains a seminal figure in Belizean music.

Berry Wine Days (Stonetree, Belize).

Crudely classy, this recording, delivered in thick Creole accent and with unique phrasing is a landmark in Caribbean music. The group's accordions are supplemented by unorthodox yet irresistible percussion.

Brazil

meu brasil brasileiro

Brazilian music is a whole world of its own. It may be best known for samba – the irrepressible rhythm of carnival – but that's only a fraction of a story that takes in everything from the drum groups of Bahia (where Paul Simon got his inspiration for *Rhythms of the Saints*), to forró, an accordion-led dance music that's a little like zydeco. **David Cleary** gets down to the roots and ramifications.

Meu Brasil brasileiro – My Brazilian Brazil, a line from an Ary Barroso song, "Aquarela do Brasil", sums up the way Brazilian music has long since burst its national boundaries while remaining true to its roots. In the 1940s it was translated into English and sung by Carmen Miranda in one of her first Hollywood films; in the 1980s it gave Terry Gilliam the idea for the film *Brazil*, where it served as the basis for the soundtrack. Words that were once Portuguese – samba, bossa nova, lambada – have entered the international vocabulary. Brazilian music is World Music in its most literal sense, played across the world, recognised globally, its influence noticeable in the musical output of many other countries from the US to Nigeria.

"Who hasn't been influenced by Brazil?" said Sérgio Mendes, when asked about Brazil's impact on American jazz. The top Brazilian stars, like Milton Nascimento and Gilberto Gil, sell out Montreux or Madison Square Gardens as easily as the Canecão in Rio, while luminaries like Paul Simon and David Byrne – and an entire generation of American jazz musicians before them – have made musical pilgrimages to Brazil. And yet, funnily enough, Brazilian music on the World Music scene is like an iceberg: a highly visible tip but with an enormous mass of music and musicians lurking beneath the surface, unknown for the most part abroad.

Carmen Miranda

A National Genius

The same rich ethnic cocktail that formed Brazilian society from African, European and Indian ingredients underlies a national genius for music, and a bewildering variety of rhythms, melodies and regional genres. Everyone's seen clips of the orgiastic music-making of Carnaval (along with other forms of orgiastic activity), but music is an all-year backdrop to life in Brazil.

Hop into a taxi in any Brazilian city and you weave your way through the traffic to the sound of distorted but foot-tapping music pounding through tattered speakers – the beat will be different, depending on the city. Walk into a bar at the weekend, or head for the beach, and you'll run into ordinary Brazilians making often extraordinary music.

Instruments help but aren't essential: match-boxes shake to a syncopated beat, forks tap against glasses, and palms slap on thighs or table-tops – and that's all that's required. This is a country that has had a significant recording industry since the 1920s, where musicians are called *artistas* and draw audiences from the whole population rather than mainly the young, and where some of the most innovative writing in the language occurs in song lyrics: **Caetano Veloso** and **Chico Buarque** are known throughout the Portuguese-speaking world as great writers as well as musicians.

Some MPB Geography

Música popular brasileira, habitually shortened to **MPB**, is the catch-all term Brazilians use for Brazilian music in general. It first cropped up in the 1930s, when the growth of a national radio network made it possible for musicians to build up a national audience, and it still refers to the elite corps of nationally – and often internationally – famous *artistas* whose records are available everywhere. But underlying modern MPB, as it has done ever since the term was coined, is a rich tradition of **regional music-making**, and it's in these regional centres that musicians cut their teeth and start to experiment with other musical influences, from elsewhere in Brazil and abroad. It's the regional variety of Brazilian music that explains its remarkable capacity to produce exciting new sounds, since there are so many genres to pick and mix with outside influences that the permutations are almost endless.

On any musical map of Brazil, **Rio** figures large, especially historically: it was here that **choro**, the precursor to **samba**, developed in the nineteenth century, and in the city's favela slums that samba began to develop around the time of World War I. But viewed from inside Brazil, Rio is only one of a number of musical centres. The city of **Salvador de Bahia**, six hundred kilometres north, has produced as many MPB stars as Rio, and with its unique blend of African and Brazilian influences – not to mention the most musically inventive Carnaval of any Brazilian city – it now has a strong claim to be the music capital of the country. Then there is **Recife**, which lies at the centre of another hotbed of genres that Brazilians lump together under the heading of **música nordestina**, northeastern music.

Further north and you hit **eastern Amazonia**, famous for burning rain forests but also – and not a lot of people know this – for **lambada**, which started out as a souped-up variant of **carimbó**, the dance music of Belém, a city with its own regional genres but also strongly influenced by the Guyanese and French Guianan rhythms available on the radio dial. Go deeper into Amazonia and you hit the heartland of **boi**, a once obscure brand of folk music from central Amazonia recently popularised by an astutely marketed annual festival in the river town of Parintins, and now a national craze. Even **São Paulo**, long derided by non-Paulistanos as a musical desert, has in recent years become home to a thriving rock and punk scene.

But, as for most tourists, any guide to Brazilian music has to start in Rio . . .

Aquarela do Brasil (Watercolour of Brazil)

Brazil, my Brazilian Brazil
My courtly mulatto, I will sing you in these
    verses
Oh the samba it makes, the sinuous dances
The Brazil I love, land of Our Father
Brazil for me, for me, for me.

Ah, open the curtain on our past
Sing praises to the cerrado
Put the Recôncavo in the congado
Brazil for me
Let me sing again about the glory of the
    moonlight
Every song my love song
I want to see this Lady walking proud
Sweeping her lace dresses through the ball-
    rooms
Brazil for me, for me, for me.

Ah, this palm which gives us coconuts
Where I string up my hammock
In the clear moonlit nights
Brazil for me
And where there are murmuring fountains
Where I quench my thirst
And where the moon comes to play
Ah, this Brazil, so lovely, so richly favoured
And my Brazilian Brazil
Land of samba and tambourines
Brazil for me, for me, for me . . .

Ary Barroso

(Recôncavo – Salvador hinterland; cerrado –
tablelands; congado – Afro-Brazilian dance).

Rio Roots

It was in a downtown Rio *bairro* known as 'Little Africa' that **samba** began in the early years of this century. This was a quarter where ex-slaves and the few black bourgeois lived from the eighteenth century on, their numbers steadily reinforced by contingents from the hillside *favelas* that were already a feature of Rio's landscape. Samba, here, started as Carnaval music and horrified Rio's established (and white) society: it was lewd, loud, the drums were too African, and so the police regularly raided the area to arrest *sambistas*.

There's nothing of the *bairro* left today: it was swept away by the docks and warehouses of Rio's port as it was expanded in the 1920s. The beaches from where poor blacks set out on Sundays for day trips to the islands in Guanabara Bay are long since filled in: where the wharfs stand is where Carnaval as we know it today began, as the returning day-trippers, well-oiled, danced and sang and formed the embryonic, informal music groups that a couple of decades later would evolve into *Escolas de samba* (samba schools), the highly organised neighbourhood associations that parade in the modern Carnaval.

Why schools? Before he died in 1975, **Ismael Silva**, a great sambista who was born at the same time as samba, explained: "The sambistas used to rehearse in an empty lot near a teachers' college, and people always said, that's where the professors come from. But nobody knew more about samba than us. People started joking, no, *this* is where the professors come from. That's how the idea of a samba school came about."

Choro

Even before samba there was **choro**, literally 'crying, sobbing'. The original Carnaval music, it still survives today as live music, not just on dusty records, some 120 years after it surfaced. It is mainly instrumental, played by a small combo that might include a flute, a guitar, a cavaquinho – a miniature guitar introduced to Brazil by the Portuguese – and a clarinet.

With its roots in European salon music and Portuguese *fado*, choro is generally through-composed with little space for improvisation in its original form. Probably the most influential composer of choros was **Pixinguinha**, (1898–1973), whose classic "Lamento" is still played. Choro was also one of the primary inspirations of the great Brazilian classical music composer **Heitor Villa-Lobos** (1887–1959), who spent his formative years playing cello and guitar in choro bands in Rio's cafés, on street corners and at parties.

Choro is in some ways the opposite of samba, as quiet and private as samba is loud and public. You come across it most often these days as background music in stylish bars in the big cities of southern Brazil. It is currently undergoing something of a revival after decades of neglect, largely thanks to the well-known sambista **Paulinho da Viola**, who has been arguing for a return to Brazilian roots and including a choro or two on all his recent records, most notably the self-explanatory "Chorando". Several choro bars have sprung up in recent years in Lapa, one of the oldest and most traditional nightlife areas in central Rio, as choro recolonises its old haunts. One of the best choro groups, **Os Ingênuos** from Salvador de Bahia,

recorded in the mid-1990s by Nimbus, gives a good introduction to the choro style and its diverse solo instruments: the seven-string guitar (an extra bass string brings out the highly mobile bass lines), cavaquinho, trumpet, trombone and soprano sax.

The basic rhythms of choro come from the dances favoured by European immigrants in the last century, especially polkas and waltzes, but overlaid by Afro-Brazilian syncopation to produce a jazzy Brazilian sound, like tropical Dixieland played on string and wind instruments rather than brass. With the clarinet wailing and cavaquinho notes sliding all over the place, you can hear how choro got its name.

Samba

It was this choro syncopation that carried over into **samba**, a versatile rhythm that can assume many different forms. Heated up, with a shouted call-and-response verse backed by literally thousands of samba-school drums on parade, it becomes *samba de enredo*, the mass Carnaval music famous the world over. Quite apart from the spectacle, a *desfile* – the formal parade of samba schools that is the centrepiece of Rio's Carnaval – is the loudest music you will ever hear: the drums up close are a physical force as much as music, enveloping and vibrating every part of your body – transfixing, but not the sort of thing that makes the transition to record very effectively.

Slowed down and broken up a little, the samba becomes **samba-canção**, literally 'song samba', where a lead singer is backed by a group that varies in size but is always built around guitar and percussion. Samba-canção is the staple of Rio's clubs and *dancetarías*, and itself breaks down into sever-

al varieties, ranging from the quiet, delicate plucking of a single guitar to frenetic dance numbers played by a large combo. These samba styles include *samba breque*, 'break samba', a choppy, almost reggae rhythm, and *samba do pagode*, a good-time soaring dance rhythm exemplified by artistas like **Agepê**, **Clara Nunes** and **Alcione**, and bands like **Raça Negra**, which swept Rio and the country from north to south and first hooked David Byrne, like many others, on Brazilian music.

Closely related, if more downmarket, is the current national craze, **samba da garrafa**, literally 'bottle samba'. Basically an uptempo brand of pagode, it originated as an accompaniment to an outrageous Carnaval dance, where a solo dancer, man or woman, gyrates their hips and pelvis above an empty beer bottle. Its most famous exponent is not a musician at all but a dancer, **Carla Perez** (aka *A Bunda Nacional*, which translates as the National Arse), who is only slightly less famous

A Carnaval!

In Brazil, somehow, **Carnaval** got out of control. All countries colonised at some stage by Catholics have festivities in the days leading up to Ash Wednesday, but in Brazil it goes further – in every sense – than any-

Carnaval in Rio

And Carnaval wouldn't be Carnaval without music: it still plays the crucial role in the development of Brazilian music that it did a century ago, when black revellers in Rio started adding rhythm to European melodies and gave birth to samba. One of the driving forces of Brazilian music is that each year the Carnaval songs have to be new, so the runup to Carnaval sees an outpouring of new music on radio and TV, as musicians compete to supply Carnaval hits. A Carnaval hit – determined by what people start singing on the streets, which is then picked up by radio and TV – is a direct route to national exposure, and every year Carnaval breaks new acts to a national audience.

Carnaval comes in different shapes and sizes; all cities and towns have one, but there are three major events that attract hundreds of thousands of participants from out of town as well. **Rio**'s is the best known, revolving around samba and the parade of the samba schools in a spectacle beyond even Cecil B de Mille. But the idea of having the public in the grandstands watching is utterly foreign to the other two great Brazilian Carnavals in **Salvador** and **Olinda**. There the idea is to not have any spectators at all, only participants. Salvador's entire population jams itself into the colonial streets of the centre and gets down to the best Carnaval music in the country, dancing to trios elétricos, bands playing precariously balanced on top of lorries with speakers bolted on, or with the afoxés, Salvador's Africanised answer to Rio's samba schools. It's different again in Olinda, the

where else. From the Friday the country shuts down for five days, and practically the whole population gets down to the most serious partying in the world.

beautiful colonial district of Recife, where the Carnaval beat is frevo, faster even than samba and even more impossible for foreigners to dance to.

than Pele at the moment. For Brazil's urban poor, samba is, like football, an obsession and, for the lucky ones, a route to international celebrity.

Bossa Nova

Rio's other great contribution to World Music was **bossa nova** (new wave), which began in the chic beach neighbourhood of Ipanema by day, and moved to the Copacabana clubs by night, before being discovered by American jazz musicians and going on to become an international craze in the early 1960s. Outside Brazil it often sank under the massed strings and tuxedos of foreign record producers, leaving most people with the misleading impression that bossa nova is muzak best-suited to elevators and airports. **Tom (Antonio Carlos) Jobim**, the man who penned "A Garota de Ipanema" (The Girl from Ipanema), would later talk of being haunted by innumerable cover versions murdering what in its original form is still one of the most beautiful Brazilian songs ever recorded.

Bossa nova is one of the few brands of popular music that was invented single-handed: the rhythm was devised by Jobim, a classically trained conservatory musician given to hanging out in bars at night, but first sung by Bahian **João Gilberto**, who in July 1957 released the first bossa nova record, a Jobim number ironically titled "Desafi-

On the ball – new bossa star, Vinicius Cantuária

Tom Jobim

nado" (Out of Tune). It was an instant smash in Brazil, where bossa nova, gently crooned to the accompaniment of a single guitar, always had a much more delicate, individual touch than in its later North American distortions.

For a couple of glorious years Jobim, Gilberto, and a small group of other musicians, notably **Vinícius de Morães**, were able to mount a serious challenge to samba's dominance within Rio's music scene, and in 1959 bossa nova took off abroad as well: **Astrud Gilberto**'s quavering English version of "The Girl from Ipanema" became Brazil's biggest ever international hit.

There were several reasons behind this success. One was the increasing development of the Brazilian record industry, which by now was exporting to the US and allowing bossa nova to come to the attention of influential jazz musicians like Stan Getz and Charlie Byrd. But underlying that was the large market for a sleek, sophisticated urban sound (bossa nova is lounge-bar rather than dance floor music) among the burgeoning middle classes in Rio, who found Jobim's slowing down and breaking up of what was still a samba rhythm an exciting departure.

Although the bossa craze abroad was eclipsed by the arrival of The Beatles, at home the music survived in its natural habitats of Ipanema and the middle-class areas of the Zona Sul, while Jobim went on to become one of the elder statesmen of MPB until his tragic death from cancer in 1996, still only in his fifties. The form has also had a recent revival in **New York**, through the collaboration of the Brazilian-born musician and producer **Arto Lindsay** with **Vinicius Cantuária**, a singer and guitarist who ironically had found himself straitjacketed in Brazil as a rock/pop singer, and reinvented himself playing bossa – mixed in with drum'n'bass and contemporary rhythms by Lindsay – in the US.

Bahia: Dancing to a Different Drum

Salvador, capital of the huge northeastern state of Bahia, is like no other city in Brazil. Almost everyone you see on the streets is black, and **African** influences are everywhere. You can taste it in the food, with sauces based on palm oil, peanuts and coconut milk, you can see it in the hundreds of cult houses of *candomblé* and *umbanda*, the Afro-Brazilian religions with millions of devotees across Brazil, and most of all you can hear it in the music.

An outrageously high proportion of the major **MPB** stars comes from Salvador and around: a very partial list includes Caetano Veloso, Gilberto Gil, Gal Costa, Maria Bethânia, Dorival Caymmi, Belô Velloso, Carlinhos Brown, Vinícius de Morães, and – among the newer stars of the firmament – Virginia Rodrigues and Silvia Torres.

What makes Salvador's music special is its rhythm, reflected in the importance of drumming and percussion, which in Salvador reaches a peak unmatched elsewhere. No other Brazilian city, not even Rio, can boast such a range of cosmopolitan influences on its local music, with rhythms from the Caribbean, Africa and North America finding their way to the city, being absorbed somewhere in the bewildering range of local genres, and resurfacing as something new and very Brazilian.

The 1980s were an especially good decade for Salvador, building on the achievements of the 1970s, when a wave of black consciousness partly inspired by American soul music transformed the city's Carnaval. A number of new black **Carnaval groups** were set up, playing African-influenced music with heavier, more complicated

rhythms than the frenetic Carnaval styles popular elsewhere in the northeast. In the 1980s reggae was absorbed into the city's music in a similar way, and the result was a new Salvador sound that by the late 1980s was vying with samba and MPB for national attention. It mixed up reggae, salsa and samba, added percussion and lyrics that often had an African theme, and came up with a highly danceable style called *fricote*, or *deboche*.

· Underlying this success was a thriving network of independent labels and studios based in the city, and the fact that every Carnaval seemed to break a new Bahian singer or group nationally. The new generation of young stars from the city, joining the old MPB veterans, include singers like **Margareth Menezes**, **Daniela Mercury**, **Luiz Caldas** and **Abel Duere**, and groups like **Banda Mel**, **Reflexu's**, **Ara Ketú** and **Olodum**. As a result, through the 1990s, Salvador mounted a serious challenge to Rio as the dominant city in Brazilian musical culture.

It was **Olodum** who Paul Simon heard playing on the streets, while on a trip with singer Milton Nascimento, and went on to record as the inspired base for much of his album *Rhythms of the Saints*. The band began life as part of the rising black consciousness movement, reflected in a rootsy, back-to-Africa sound based entirely around drumming and chanted lyrics about Africa, slavery and racism. **Reflexu's** are in a similar vein, though they have lightened the percussion with synthesizers and a honeyed female voice. Both are excellent in their own way, and especially good live – they were spawned by Carnaval; political correctness can rarely have been more enjoyable.

A trio of women singers from Salvador have made it big in the 1990s. The best-known abroad is **Margareth Menezes**, spotted by David Byrne and plucked from the Salvador club scene to support him on tour in the US, where, as Byrne happily admits in the sleeve notes to her album *Illegib*™, she often blew him off the stage. She has a beautiful voice and is electrifying when singing native Bahian rhythms. Unfortunately, like many young Brazilian stars who make it big, she insists on cluttering up her discs and live act with thrash-rock that would have sounded outdated in 1975.

Less well-known abroad, but a major star inside Brazil, is **Daniela Mercury**. She has everything – a fantastic voice, writes her own music, sticks to Bahian sounds, is remarkably beautiful and, to cap it all, is a quite superb dancer even by Brazilian standards. A more recent Bahian MPB sensation is **Virginia Rodrigues**, a woman of Nigerian-Brazilian descent, who sings what she calls 'Brazilian gospel' in a dramatic chorister-like voice. Caetano Veloso discovered her singing a cappella in a street theatre group and was bowled over, took her under his wing, and produced her stunning albums, *Sol Negro* and *Nos*.

Margareth Menezes

Another Bahian strand in the 1990s came with fusing the heavy percussion sound of Bahia with rock-funk elements. The masters of this are **Timbalada**, led by **Carlinhos Brown**, and sometimes involving up to sixty musicians, hammering out their rhythms with percussion, horns, electric guitars and electronic beats. Brown himself, incidentally, is an eclectic talent, rated perhaps Brazil's top current producer. He has been responsible for the rise of two key women singers in recent years – **Marisa Monte** and **Silvia Torres**.

Forró and Nordestina

Northeastern Brazil has a deceptive coastline, lush green with coconut palms framing the best beaches in Brazil, fertile soils and large plantations. But drive directly inland, and in most places it takes less than an hour before you hit the *sertão*, the rocky, arid hinterland where droughts can last for years and periodic waves of migrants – *flagelados*, 'the scourged' – give up the unequal struggle with the land and head for the coastal cities. It looks unpromising, but music seems to flourish here, even if little else does.

One reason is the peculiar delight the region takes in wordplay and poetry: most markets have stalls selling *literatura de cordel*, 'string literature', printed ballads by regional poets, and in music this poetic tradition is reflected by **repentismo**, where balladeers pair off against each other with guitar in hand, and improvise verses in a variety of complicated metres on themes shouted out by the audience. A historical impulse was the popularity of dances as social gatherings, especially in rural areas, where prospective marriage partners could look each other over. Since slaves were imported mainly to work on the coastal plantations, most black nordestinos now live in the coastal strip. The main influence on the music of the sertão was Portugal: old Portuguese folk melodies lurk beneath the surface of much música nordestina.

Música nordestina has many different forms, but all are instantly recognisable as northeastern: the rhythms are very strong but slower than in other parts of the country, the beat often comes from accordion and/or guitar rather than percussion, and the lyrics are sung in a gravelly, nasal nordestino accent, which you can tell apart even if you don't speak a word of Portuguese.

The varieties of nordestino music include *frevo*, Recife's Carnaval beat; *maracatú*, a blend of African rhythms with Portuguese melodies, most popular among blacks around Recife; and *baião*, a thumping dance style built around a trio of accordion, bass drum and triangle. However, by far the most popular form is a jaunty, danceable style called **forró** – a word that's allegedly a corruption of the English 'for all', the name of the dances British companies laid on for their employees in nineteenth-century Recife.

Forró can be played fast, slow or somewhere in between, but whichever it's one of the most enjoyable – and danceable – forms of Brazilian music. Like Louisiana zydeco, the music is accordion-led with a robust and frenetic sound. In its traditional form, forró is played by a trio of *sanfona* (accordion), triangle and drum, with a singer crooning out over the strongest, most foot-tapping rhythm Brazil has to offer. Only danced by couples, it's from forró that the more athletic dances associated with lambada developed. Essentially, the couple swivel round the dance floor, joined only at the pelvis, and nobody in Brazil looks twice at a display that would clear the dance floor most places in the First World.

The accordionist and singer **Luiz Gonzaga** (1912–89) is considered the first big name of forró, popularising the music – and other nordestino styles – outside his native region and becoming an idol among the northeastern migrants in São Paulo and Rio. He moved to Rio in the 1940s and had an enormous hit with a simple but very moving song about a farmer forced to migrate; called "Asa Branca" (White Wing), after a bird traditionally said to be the last to leave the sertão in a drought, it

became a regional anthem and one of the best-loved of all Brazilian tunes, a national standard.

Gonzaga blazed a trail for a number of other northeastern musicians, who became major MPB stars from the 1960s onwards without ever abandoning their regional roots. They included Gonzaga's son, **Gonzaguinho**, tragically killed in a car crash in 1991; **Elba Ramalho**, who looks uncannily like Bette Midler and has a remarkable voice to match; accordionist/singer **Dominguinhos**; **Morães Moreira**; **Alceu Valença**; **Geraldo Azevedo**; and **Fagner**. Most of these musicians bring in additional instruments – including electric guitar and brass – while keeping the accordion to the fore.

Amazonia: Lambada and Boi

Eastern Amazonia is yet another distinctive musical region: it has its own rhythms and dances, most notably carimbó, a lilting, enjoyable dance style that was electrified in the 1960s and became the basis of Belém's nightlife. From the mid-1970s, Belém's DJs and musicians started playing around with carimbó rhythms, adding elements of the merengue, salsa and reggae constantly played on the radio stations of the Guianas only a few hundred kilometres north, and produced a new dance music they started to call **lambada**.

Lambada made its way to Salvador in the 1980s, where it was absorbed and transformed like so many other musical imports, and by the mid-1980s a Bahian version, lighter, even boppier and based around synthesizers, was hitting local radio stations. There, so the Brazilian story goes, it was heard by French record producers on holiday, who were equally interested in the spectacular dance

---

Danado de Bom (Damn Good)

*It's damn good, it's damn good
My friend, it's damn good
Pretty, kicking, delicious forró music
It's damn good*

*Check out Camilla on the bass drum
Joe Cupid on the triangle
And Mariano on the bell
There's my brother on the guitar
My nephew on the strings
And Chippy in the middle of the mess
Check out the kids on the spoons
There's more than enough juice
There's enough drunks to irk you
Guys are sticking to their partners like fleas
Girls are winking
And asking me to dance*

*What a first-class gig!
The place is already packed
And folks just keep on coming
From the kitchen to the backyard
The accordion player and drummer
Back and forth
Damian, my good friend
You can put out the lamp
Because it's almost dawn
Hang tough on your squeezebox, chief
Because a forró like this
Can go on forever.*

Luiz Gonzaga and João Silva

that Bahia developed to go with it: they signed up Bahian lambada dancers and musicians, took them back to Paris in 1988 and the rest, as they say, is history. (Although music history being what it is, there is another parallel version, which is that the basic lambada melody came from a song by Bolivan Andean group K'jarkas – see p.276).

The Belém musicians who had played such a critical role in the development of lambada hastily put out records with titles like "The Original Lambada" but it was too late: the Bahians had sewn up the market, and added insult to injury by rushing out all kinds of Bahian pop, labelling it lambada, and selling it in Europe, where the market was more interested in dancing than musical roots. Hence the fact that lambada as known internationally refers more to a dance than a style of music. The word had become a marketing category first and foremost, and no longer bore any relation to the original music or the region it came from.

Still, in the long run, the Amazonians got their own back. The most recent musical craze to have come out of northern Brazil is **boi**: a rhythmical percussive style of music that is most characteristic of Maranhão state, just to the east of Amazonia proper, where the annual *bumba-meu-boi* festival, with groups performing the characteristic dance that goes with the music, is a bigger deal than Carnaval. It also exists as rootsy folk music in the Amazonian interior, carried by generations of Maranhense migrants, and there it might well have stayed had it not been for the town of **Parintins**, which holds an annual Carnaval in June consciously modelled on Rio, but using Amazonian imagery: Indians, jaguars, and so forth. In the 1990s this festival began to be astutely marketed as a summer Carnaval holiday, and began to attract tourists to Parintins from all over. Amazonian musicians were commissioned to jazz up the old boi styles, and came up with a poppy, electrified dance music which soon burst its regional boundaries and is now heard as often in São Paulo as in Amazonas. The Parintins festival has gone from strength to strength on the back of the craze.

MPB and the Military

Modern MPB, like so much else, really began in the 1960s. The impulse was the military coup of 1964, which initiated over twenty years of military rule. In a backhanded tribute to the special importance of music in Brazil, one of the regime's first acts was to impose direct censorship of song lyrics and radio and TV playlists, which they followed up by persecuting musicians thought to be

critical of the military; most of the MPB stars of the 1960s spent a year or two in exile in the 1970s.

These strict controls on musical output, which were not relaxed until 1985, had the opposite effect to that intended: they proved a creative spur, forcing musicians to use oblique, subtle images that could make it past the censor, and at the same time gave MPB a coherence it would not otherwise have managed, uniting practically all serious musicians against the military and compelling them to deal with politics as well as the eternal preoccupations of sex and drugs and rock'n'roll. You can get an idea of the depth this gave MPB by listening to a song like **Chico Buarque**'s "Tanto Mar" (So Much Sea), which is ostensibly about a party although all Brazilians of the time – 1973 – recognised it as a salute to the Portuguese Revolution of that year, "The Revolution of the Carnations" as it's known in Portuguese.

It was a fine party
I had a great time
I've kept an old carnation to remind me
And even though the party's over
They're certain to have overlooked a seed
In some corner of the garden
So much sea between us,
So much sea between us.

The first sign that the military would find it impossible to keep the musical lid on things was **tropicalismo**, a musical movement that erupted in the late 1960s and marked the arrival of a new and extravagantly talented generation of musicians who are still among the leading lights of MPB, most notably **Caetano Veloso** (see box feature) and **Gilberto Gil**. Tropicalismo was the most controversial twist MPB ever came up with, since it consisted of mixing a large number of regional genres together, stirring in rock influences like electric guitars and elaborate studio production, and topping everything off with extraordinarily dense, oblique lyrics.

Caetano and Gil were booed off stage and violently attacked in the press at first, accused of being unpatriotic for turning to foreign rock for inspiration and for using electric instruments – a stupid criticism, since música nordestina was as important an influence on tropicalismo as rock. However, the young, thoroughly alienated as Brazil lurched into dictatorship, loved tropicalismo's iconoclasm and rejection of convention.

At its worst tropicalismo reproduced the self-importance and studio excesses of much North American and British rock of the period, but at its best, as in Caetano's song "Tropicália", which became the movement's anthem, it was the most successful blend to date of Brazilian musical imagination with rock music. Although tropicalismo only lasted a couple of years, and

Tropicalismo founder Gilberto Gil

more or less ended when Caetano and Gil were forced into exile in London in 1971, it left a lasting mark – not least because it inspired many more far less successful attempts to blend rock from abroad with elements of MPB.

Both the founders of tropicalismo went on to greater fame, Gil as the leading Salvador artista and an increasingly successful politician, and Caetano to become, along with Chico Buarque, the most admired and productive MPB star, now in his fourth decade of recording and if anything getting better with age.

Chico, Milton and Elis

The 1960s also saw the emergence of two stars who were never part of the tropicalismo wave but who have remained at the forefront of MPB ever since. Chico Buarque and Milton Nascimento remained within Brazilian musical styles for the most part, but took them to new heights.

Chico Buarque shot to stardom in the 1960s first as a sambista, singing beautifully crafted sambas alone with only his guitar. What marks him out is the superb quality of his lyrics; excerpts do him little justice, since his trademark is the intricate building up of themes over the course of a song. At first there was little love lost between Chico and the tropicalistas, who suspected that the conservatism of his music reflected his politics as

well, but Chico soon earned his political street-cred by writing what became the most famous anti-military songs, "Apesar de Você" (In Spite of You) and "Vai Passar" (It Will Pass), and spending a year in exile. His dense lyrics and haunting tunes are still flowing, and along with Caetano, who has similar lyrical gifts and is equally in love with the Portuguese language, Chico has become one of the select band of MPB figures with whom the entire country is on first-name terms.

Another is **Milton Nascimento**, who came up at the same time and via the same route as Chico, but is musically poles apart. Where Chico was comfortable with what lay musically to hand in his native Rio, Milton's music has returned again and again to the reflective, spiritual music of his native state of Minas Gerais, to the north of Rio, whose people have a reputation for introversion and whose music is heavily influenced by the Catholic church. When you add to this Milton's extraordinary, soaring voice, and his songwriting genius, the result is a dense, compelling sound that has made Milton one of the best-known Brazilian

---

Chiclete com Banana
(Chewing Gum with Banana)

I'll only put be-bop in my samba
When Uncle Sam grabs the drum
When he grabs the tambourine and the
*   zabumba*
When he understands that samba isn't
*   rumba.*
Then I'll mix Miami with Copacabana
Chewing gum with banana
And that's how my samba will go.
I want to see it all mixed together
Samba-rock, brother
But, on the other hand
I want to see the boogie-woogie played
On tambourine and guitar
I want to see Uncle Sam cooling out
In a Brazilian drumming session.

Gilberto Gil

Caetano Veloso – Tropicalismo Man

Since he burst onto the national music scene in the early 1960s **Caetano Veloso** has been at the centre of Brazilian music - so much at the centre, in fact, that he sometimes seems a kind of Leonardo da Vinci of Brazilian popular culture. His books of poetry and his song lyrics have made him, along with Chico Buarque, into one of the most respected poets in the Portuguese-speaking world. He paints, directs innovative videos for his own songs, and, at just over fifty, he is still making great records.

In the mid-1960s Brazilian music split down the middle between the eclectic, innovative tropicalismo style pioneered mainly by Caetano, and the more musically conservative brilliance of Chico Buarque. Of all the singers of that time, Caetano was best able to absorb all the influences of the 1960s and blend them with his Bahian roots, and several of his songs sum up the period for a generation of Brazilians in the same way as The Beatles or Tamla Motown did elsewhere.

One of his most popular songs from that period, "Alegria, Alegria", has had a second life. It was used as the theme tune to a smash-hit TV series in 1992 called Años Rebeldes (The Rebel Years). The series followed a group of students who graduated in 1964, the year of the military coup, through the military years as they joined guerrilla groups, became hippies, got shot, sold out, fell in and out of love with each other, etc. It served as a rediscovery of the period for a new generation of Brazilian youth born after the worst of the military years were over. The series happened to be shown as a corruption scandal involving President

Collor gathered pace and "Alegria, Alegria" became the theme tune of the enormous – and successful – demonstrations calling for his impeachment. Tens and then hundreds of thousands of people were clapping and singing along with the song, culminating in the line "Porqué não, porqué não?" (Why not?): ie why not throw the rascal out?

Today, when Caetano could easily be resting on his laurels, he continues to produce the most innovative and challenging Brazilian music. His records in recent years have the same volatile mixture of Brazilian and foreign influences (notably in collaboration with New York noise merchant, **Arto Lindsay**) that characterised tropicalismo, but have acquired a new maturity and depth in both music and lyrics. And, to top it off, one is beginning to have to speak not just of Caetano, but of his family as well. His sister, **Maria Bethânia**, has long been one of the most important female singers in MPB. And in the 1990s his niece, **Belô Veloso**, emerged as one of the best of the new generation of MPB singers.

Caetano, meantime, seems on the top of his form. His 1999 live album, *Prenda Minha*, sold an unprecedented million copies in Brazil, after one of its songs was adopted as the theme for the country's leading TV soap. He then followed up with a European hit, a homage to the film music of Federico Fellini. And he has also been instrumental in the career of **Virginia Rodrigues**, one of the most significant new talents in recent years.

All in all, a wonderful talent.

Brazil's new voice – Virginia Rodrigues, flanked by Milton Nascimento (left) and Caetano Veloso

musicians abroad, especially in North America. Since he speaks little English, he is less known abroad for his politics, but he has become the most prominent public spokesperson for black Brazilians and involved himself in the struggle for Indian land rights years before it became fashionable.

Were she still alive, a third star in this MPB trinity would be **Elis Regina**, whom few would argue is the woman who has made the greatest contribution to Brazilian musical history. Elis burst onto the music scene after winning a nationally televised song competition in 1965, when she was only eighteen, and it was immediately obvious that she had the finest voice of her time. She went on to release a series of records that made her the undisputed queen of MPB. Her voice was a unique blend of technique and soul: she could put an extraordinary depth of emotion into a song, keeping perfect control at the same time. Tragically, she became something of an Edith Piaf figure: she struggled with drugs and alcohol for most of her career, and died alone in 1982, when she was at the height of her powers, from an overdose that may or may not have been suicide.

Looking Ahead

Brazil, like most places, is full of people eager to argue that things aren't what they used to be, and while they have a point when talking about modern Brazilian football, they're on less sure ground when they express the argument – surprisingly common within Brazil – that Brazilian music is in decline. That's not to say there aren't justified criticisms to be made. The most obvious is that no one of similar stature has come up in MPB to replace the towering figures of the 1960s, most of whom are still producing very high-quality music. But they are also all in their late fifties by now, and they don't have a direct line to Brazilian youth the way they did. While some very high quality singers have emerged in the 1990s, such as **Marisa Monte** and **Daniela Mercury**, a depressingly high proportion of Brazilian youth, especially in the urban centres of the south, have been sucked (or suckered) into the global market for FM blandness, and US and British rock dinosaurs still manage to fill Brazilian stadiums.

There's also the problem of the relationship between Brazilian music and the international music scene. This has a positive side, as David Byrne's repeated trips to Brazil have shown, but it has a downside as well. Many Brazilian musicians have tried to blend rock with Brazilian music; tropicalismo did it with some success, but most attempts to do so since have been embarrassing failures. A rare exception were the mid-1990s experiments of **Chico Science**, who created a dynamic fusion of samba with rock and rap; however, Science died, untimely, in 1997. The Rio-based singer **Daude** has also had some success fusing Brazilian rhythms (notably from her Bahia home) with hip hop and Western dance music.

The basic problem for most artists is musical incompatibility: Brazilian music is built around complicated melodies and rhythms and the Brazilian musical imagination is versatile and subtle – not the ideal cultural recipe for good rock'n'roll, in other words. There is a Brazilian rock scene, centred around São Paulo, but it's very tame and derivative compared to that of London or New

JAK KILBY

Marisa Monte

York. Brazil has been much more successful in absorbing non-rock influences from abroad, as the music scene in Salvador shows, and we can look forward to more productive plundering of Caribbean and African music in the years to come (a traffic that goes both ways, as people like King Sunny Ade will tell you).

All the same, it is easy to exaggerate the negative side. For all that people say Brazilian music isn't what it was, a foreigner finds it difficult to understand what they're worried about. Long-established genres like samba are still breaking up into new variants, and new music, like the Salvador sound, is being produced at a more than healthy rate. There are more studios and independent labels now than ever before, and the regional music that is the bed rock of MPB is doing as well as ever. If there were a World Cup for music, *meu Brasil brasileiro* could still give anyone a game.

discography

MPB, Samba, Choro, Bahia

Compilations

 Beleza Tropical: Brazil Classics 1 (Luaka Bop-WEA, US).

The first of David Byrne's excellent Brazilian compilations concentrates on a selection of top MPB (the catch-all term for Brazil's national pop music) stars, including Jorge Ben, Gilberto Gil, Caetano Veloso, Chico Buarque, Milton Nascimento and Maria Bethânia (Caetano's sister). A fine introduction.

Compilations

 Brazil Now (EMI Hemisphere, UK).

A fine round-up of Brazilian voices of the 1990s – Carlinhos Brown, Clara Nunes, Gilberto Gil, Maria Bethânia, among them – with a look back to "Brazil Then" with tracks from Djavan, Elis Regina, Paulinho da Viola, and more.

 Brazil Roots Samba (Rounder, US).

The rootsy side of samba from the *favelas* of Mangueira and Portela, featuring old guard artists Monarco, Wilson Moreira and Nelson Sargento.

Casa de Mãe Joana (Blue Jackal, US).

Named after a bar in Rio (Rua São Cristovão 73), this is a wonderful collection of lyrical *samba-canção* (song-samba) with a typical backing band of cavaquinho and violão guitars, bass and gentle percussion and flute. The singers aren't international names, but the performances are warm and bittersweet, with the female vocalists Helô and Dorina standing out. Listen to the latter sing "Meu Amigo Violão" and revel in the consolation of her guitar.

O Samba: Brazil Classics 2 (Luaka Bop-WEA, US).

This David Byrne compilation is music to die for: one of the all-time great compilation albums, perfectly paced, and packed with gorgeous tracks from Clara Nunes, Agepê, Alcione (including the stunning "Sufoco"), Martinho da Vila and others. A true feast of samba.

Velha Guarda da Mangueira (Nikita, Brazil).

This is a kind of Brazilian *Buena Vista Social Club*, bringing together veterans of Rio's oldest samba school, Mangueira. With standards by luminaries such as Cartola and Nelson Sargento, it is a refreshing look back at the spontaneous and intimate style of the 1950s before all the glitz and commercialisation of samba took over, and features guest appearance from big names Beth Carvalho and Fernanda Abreu. Not a weak track in sight ...

 Yelé Brazil (EMI Hemisphere, UK).

A compilation that focuses on the more African side of Brazil's musical heritage – particularly strong in Bahia – with plenty of samba and the hybrid samba-reggae as well as massed drumming and noisy, invigorating grooves.

Artists

Agepê

Agepê is a singer from the northeast, and an important figure in the romantic-sounding samba joião movement.

 Os Grandes Sucessos de Agepê (Philips, Brazil).

Great samba-canção by one of the kings of the Brazilian dance floor.

Alcione

Alcione has one of the great voices of samba with an astonishing breadth of command over different styles of samba. She also plays clarinet and trumpet, and trails a constellation of gold and platinum records behind her.

 Romántica (Philips, Brazil).

Another utterly seductive album of samba-canção.

Jorge Ben

São Paulo-based Jorge Ben is undoubtedly one of the more important artists in the development of MPB, and was the first to blend rock, soul and especially funk into samba – rhythm'n'samba or *suingue* (swing) as it has been called – bringing him huge success. He has called himself Jorge Ben Jor since 1989 after finding that some of his royalties had gone to George Benson!

Personalidade (Polygram, Brazil).

A fine 'best of' collection – including his song "Taj Mahal", which was later horribly transmuted into Rod Stewart's "Do You Think I'm Sexy?" (Ben sued Stewart for royalties).

Maria Bethânia

A magnetic performer, Bahia's Maria Bethânia (sister of Caetano Veloso) was nicknamed Brazil's Greta Garbo during an early career as an actress. She subsequently turned to music, forming a hugely influential tropicalismo group with Caetano, Gilberto Gil and Gal Costa. She is known chiefly for her renditions of romantic ballads.

Alibi (Polygram, Brazil).

A terrific album of ballads by Barque, Gil, and of course Caetano Veloso, delivered with Maria's senuous contralto tones. Released in 1978, the disc remains the biggest selling MPB album ever, with a million-plus sales.

Carlinhos Brown

Producer and percussionist Carlinhos Brown has become ubiquitous in Brazil these last few years, with credits on every record from Marisa Monte to Sergio Mendes and rock group Sepultura. His own direction lies in taking the Afro-Brazilian percussion of Bahia and adapting it to various pop forms, both on solo outings with a variety of guest stars and with the percussion bloco Timbalada.

CARLINHOS BROWN

Omelette Man (Virgin, France).

Brown's most recent solo outing has his long-term collaborator Marisa Monte taking vocal duties, while Brown himself lets loose on all manner of rhythmic things, using brass as percussion, and, not least, singing his own percussion lines. Fascinating stuff.

TIMBALADA

Cada cabeça ee um mundo (Polygram, Brazil).

Brown's *Afro-blocó* have been playing carnaval since 1993 and recording a sequence of amazing albums, cranking up the percussion with brass, electric guitars, and electronica. This was their second release, in 1994, and remains probably the most gripping.

Chico Buarque

Since he appeared on the scene in the 1960s, Chico Buarque has made his name as a singer, guitarist and writer of some of the most elegantly crafted lyrics in the whole field of modern popular music. In addition, his fine melodic gift has ensured him a myriad of fans without a word of Portuguese.

Vida (Philips, Brazil).

Chico Buarque on top form: dense, haunting songs picking apart life, love and politics.

Gal Costa

Salvador de Bahia's Gal Costa has one of the finest voices in the history of MPB. She was part of the tropicalismo group featuring Gilberto Gil and her schoolmates Caetano Veloso and Maria Bethânia in the 1970s, and has had a string of solo hits ever since, often recording songs by Caetano Veloso.

Acustico (BMG, Brazil).

This is a wonderful reprise of Costa's greatest hits, in a purely acoustic setting, from an MTV-Brazil *Unplugged* session.

Aquarela do Brasil (Polygram, US).

Gal Costa sings the songs of Ary Barroso – an inspired combination.

Martinho da Vila

Martinho da Vila, with his distinctive deep smoky voice, has a great fondness for the persuasive rhythms of Partido Alto. One of the great sambistas.

O Canto das Lavaderias (RCA-Victor, Brazil).

If you've heard Vila's tracks on Luaka Bop's *O Samba* then you'll almost certainly want more. This is the one to go for.

Paulinho da Viola

Paulinho da Viola, arguably the greatest living sambista, has as great an interest in exploring the roots of samba as he does in pushing forward the boundaries.

 Eu Canto Samba (Columbia, Brazil).

This rich stew of jazzy, laid-back sambas – with a couple of emollient choros on the side – is proof that samba can be quiet and intimate as well as loud and electrifying.

Fred Dantas and Ailton Reiner

Fred Dantas and Ailton Reiner, respectively trombonist and bandolim player with choro group Os Igênuos (see over), are also talented arrangers and leaders in their own right. Reiner in particular has a remarkable knowledge of the classic repetoire for one only in his twenties.

 Choros from Bahia (Nimbus, UK).

A triumph of delicacy and communication among musicians: the aesthetic of this wonderful group blends lines, rhythms and harmonies into one intricate whole. A masterpiece. Now reissued in a budget 4CD set Dance Music from Brazil.

Djavan

Djavan (Caetano Viana) is part of the classic 1970s MPB generation and his love songs – they are always love songs – have been covered by Gal Costa, Caetano Veloso, and others. His own voice is subtle and he has recorded often in the US with such guests as Stevie Wonder.

Djavan (Columbia, Brazil).

A 1989 outing that is perhaps Djavan's best – though be sure to get the Brazilian version; he also recorded it in English and Spanish, which don't work so well.

Levada do Pelô

The Pelô is Salvador de Bahia's old slave market, and now the home of Levada de Pelô, a huge group of up to a hundred drummers under the leadership of Walter Cruz.

Bahia Brasil (Seven Gates, Brazil).

You thought Phil Spector had something to do with a wall of sound? Try this.

Gilberto Gil

The extravagantly talented Gilberto Gil, who spent the early 1970s in exile in London owing to his opposition to Brazil's military regime, was one of the founders of tropicalismo, a blend of various regional musics with rock, while his later songs show the influence of reggae more strongly. He is one of Brazil's most individual and best loved voices.

 Personalidade (Polygram, Brazil).

This selection of Gil's acoustic hits is a fine introduction to the beautiful tunes and seductive voice of one of MPB's most internationally successful stars.

Quanta – Ao Vivo (Mesa, US).

A wonderful 1997 Grammy Ward winning album that deals among other matters with atomic physics, death, natural healing and the insidious and everpresent Internet, marking an imaginative leap and a return to form for this most expansive of Brazil's songwriters. Gil has (after several trials) managed to reconcile the demands of the global (and particularly US) market for slick production values with the earthy force of Samba de Roda and the sounds of the northeast with great success.

WITH CAETANO VELOSO

Tropicalia 2 (Nonseuch, US).
A terrific 1994 reunion album from two of the tropicalismo originals, thirty years on from their forging of the movement.

Os Ingênuos

Choro, in some ways the parlour version of samba, is far less known outside Brazil than its brasher cousin. Os Ingênuos are a tuneful group from Bahia whose instruments include seven-string guitar, cavaquinho and soprano sax, and they demonstrate that the 120-year-old tradition remains in safe hands.

Choros from Brazil (Nimbus, UK).

This was the first recording of choro readily available outside Brazil; it's quite delightful, and ought to stir up a clamour for more to be available. Now reissued in a budget 4CD set Dance Music from Brazil.

Margareth Menezes

Margareth Menezes, a young singer from Salvador de Bahia, came to international attention when she supported David Byrne on tour in the US in 1989. She has an electrifying voice and tremendous panache . . . and an unfortunate tendency to mix great Brazilian material with awful 1980s rock-outs.

Ellegibo (Polydor, US).

This 1990 album is a mixed set (too much antique thrash-metal guitar) but brilliant in parts, and with the bonus of a poppy duet with soca star David Rudder.

Daniela Mercury

Daniela Mercury, from Salvador de Bahia, is one of Brazil's brightest talents, with a fantastic voice, a gift for song-writing and a gift for dance remarkable even by Brazilian standards. She has made her reputation with the

Bahian drum-based *axe* sound – and live or on disc the beat never lets up.

O Canto da Cidade (Columbia, Brazil).

Strong tunes, Bahian rhythms perfectly blended with reggae, salsa and a dash of rock, topped by Daniela's soaring voice made this 1993 debut an instant classic.

Feijão Com Arroz (Sony, Brazil).

Most fans rate this 1997 disc even higher – the influences are similar – the arrangements slicker – and the variety stunning as Daniela moves through a different style on each song.

Carmen Miranda

Carmen Miranda (1909–55) was Brazil's original star – a singer, dancer and actress, immortalised as "The Lady in the Tutti Frutti Hat" in the 1943 American musical, *The Gang's All Here*. But don't let the fruit and frills make you forget that she had a damned fine voice, and she knew how to use it.

Carmen Miranda, 1930–45 (Harlequin, UK).

All you could hope for in a Miranda compilation: 25 original sambas, choros and marchas, backed by a restrained combo.

Marisa Monte

Marisa Monte is as good a voice as any at the end of the 1990s, equally sublime when singing MPB standards, samba, or a song like Lou Reed's "Pale Blue Eyes". She has been well produced by Arto Lindsay and has worked with others on the New York scene such as Laurie Anderson and Ryuichi Sakamoto.

Rose and Charcoal (EMI Metro Blue, US).

This is a drop-dead-gorgeous acoustic set, produced by Lindsay, with material ranging through Paulinho da Viola to the above mentioned Lou Reed. Irresistible.

Os Mutantes

'The Mutants' were a late 1960s creation – a pop-MPB band who mixed with the Tropicalismo crew before veering off into their own increasingly bizarre, self-mocking and psychedelic experiments. They lasted through a dozen albums, and various incarnations, into the 1980s,

 Everything is Possible – Best of Os Mutantes (Luaka Bop, US).

A compilation on David Byrne's album is the perfect way to sample Os Mutantes. The jokes don't all stand up, the music can seem just as dated as its UK/US equivalents, and yet … nothing else sounds quite like the Mutants.

Milton Nascimento

Another great singer – and songwriter – Milton Nascimento's songs are gentler, jazzier and more reflective than much of MPB, suffused as it is with the bustle of Rio. Once again, the sound of his voice and the compelling strength of his melodies make a knowledge of Portuguese a plus, not an essential.

 The Art of Milton Nascimento (Verve, US).

A generous 20-track compilation of Milton, live and in the studio, solo and alongside Veloso, Costa and others.

 Milton (A&M, US).

Milton's voice is beautifully matched here by arrangments featuring jazz players Wayne Shorter and Herbie Hancock. The opening track, in particular, is a stunner.

Clara Nunes

Clara Nunes, the queen of samba, was tragically killed in 1989, but is immortal in every other sense. She was one of the first to use candomble and Afro-Brazilian rhythms in samba, and the first female Brazilian to have a gold record in the US.

 The Best of Clara Nunes (EMI Hemisphere, UK; World Pacific, US).

Certainly the greatest hits, and very probably the best of this fine singer.

Olodum

Olodum, whose name is allegedly derived from the Yoruban word for God, came to international attention through their work for Paul Simon. One of the great Bahian 'Afro-Blocs', they create a great wall of polyrhythmic percussion. Their lyrics frequently reflect a consciousness of their African origins.

 Os Filhos do Sol (World Circuit, UK; Continental, US).

A relatively commercial album that adds to the drums and chanting a far more varied orchestration involving guitar, brass and a stronger vocal presence.

Reflexu's

Reflexu's are in a similar vein to Olodum, but a little less drum heavy, lightening the sound by the use of synthesiser and female voice.

 Da Mãe África (Mango, US).

A record with an eye to the main commercial chance, but magical all the same, from the Salvador group that shot to national stardom with their cover version of Olodum's "Egito-Madagascar".

Elis Regina

Elis Regina (1945–82) was one of Brazil's biggest-ever stars, virtually unrivalled as a woman singer through the 1960s and 1970s. Her rough-edged voice perfectly blended emotion and technical assurance and she was sought by all of the finest MPB songwriters. She died from a drugs and alcohol overdose – a Janis Joplin-like figure, still much loved and lamented.

 Fascination: THe Best of Elis Regina (Verve, US).

An excellent compilation of twenty songs, with Elis interpreting key MPB and bossa nova composers including Gilberto Gil, Tom Joobim and Baden Powell.

Virginia Rodrigues

Virginia Rodrigues, born in 1965, of Nigerian-Brazilian descent, is Brazil's new diva – a woman with a stunning, soaring contralto of operatic quality. She was discovered by Caetano Veloso singing a cappella in a street theatre group in Bahia and has gone on to record under his direction, to universal amazement and respect. Like millions of black Brazilians, she is an adherent of the 'neo-African' Yoruba Candomblé religion.

 Nós (Hannibal/Ryko, UK/US).

Rodrigues's debut album, **Sol negro** (Hanibal/Ryko, UK/US) was a startling disc, introducing her voice to the world in what, after a couple of listens, seemed just a little inappropriately novel forms – uptempo samba for example. *Nós* (Us), by contrast, does everything right. Produced by Caetano Veloso's longstanding arranger Jaques Morelenbaum, it presents Rodrigues largely within her Afro-Brazilian heritage, adapting the songs of Bahia's *Afro-blocós*, pairing down the percussion to frame the voice. There is a lovely duet with Caetano, too. In a word – essential.

Chico Science & Nação Zumbi

Chico Science founded the band Nação Zumbi (Zumbi Nation) in order to explore the potential of fusing Recife's thunderous *maracatú* rhythm with the techno and hip-hop sounds, and laid out the ground rules for the new *mangue* (swamp) beat. His death in a road accident deprived both Brazil and the rest of the world of a great talent.

⊕ Da Lama ao Chaos
(Columbia, Brazil).

This debut record was a stunner – hard, techno-driven sounds, with moments of expansive vocal and rhythmic beauty. In another time, it could have been a vast global hit.

Simone

Simone Bettancourt is another MPB star who just needs the one name. She has one of the sultriest voices in the business and has made classic recordings of songs by, in particular, Chico Buarque.

⊕ Simone: The EMI Years (EMI Hemisphere, UK).

A gorgeous 17-song anthology, including songs by Buarque, Nascimento and Gilberto Gil.

Silvia Torres

Silvia Torres began her career in the 1980s singing with the Bahian group Mar Revolto, who regularly opened for Gilberto Gil. She went solo in 1989 and has released a series of ever more interesting discs, rootsy and jazzy by turn, and looking to the sertaõ (interior) rather than to the African heritage of the tropical coast.

⊕ Silvia Torres (Mélodie, France).

This 1999 album from Torres is her best to date, produced by the inspired Carlinhos Brown, and ranging through many settings, from simple guitar and cavaquinho to marcha to reggae and percussive, avant garde jazz. The vocals are superb throughout.

Caetano Veloso

The multi-talented figure of Caetano Veloso – musician, poet and artist – has been at the centre of MPB since the early 1960s, and is still producing some of the most complex, challenging and musically vital sounds around.

⊕ The Best of Caetano Veloso: Without Handkerchief Without Document (Polygram, Brazil).

A lot of Veloso's early classics (up to the mid-1980s) are here – "Alegria, Alegria", Soy Loco Por Ti, America", "Tropicália" and surely his most beautiful love song "Você é Linda". Dating from before Veloso teamed up with Jaques Morelenbaum as arranger, they also show how that partnership has deepened his music.

⊕ Estrangeiro
(Elektra, US; Island, UK).

It might seem strange to highlight a Spanish language disc from Brazil's most enduring star, but this 1994 set of songs from South America and the Caribbean is one of the most beautiful things Veloso has ever done. The title track dates from mid-1950s Peru and there are sublime versions of "Pecado" (Argentina) and "Maria Bonita" (Mexico) – all with fantastic arrangements from Jaques Morelenbaum.

⊕ Omaggio a Federico e Giulietta (Emarcy, Italy).

Veloso's tribute to Fellini and his wife, this was recorded live in San Marino in 1997. It is as mellow as he gets, largely acoustic, and ranging through old classics, movie songs (including a wonderful take on "Let's Face the Music and Dance"), and a perfect rendition of the beautiful bossa nova song, "Chega de saudade".

Tom Zé

Tom Zé, along with Gil and Veloso, was one of the original tropicalismo stars, but his subsequent career lapsed into obscurity, due in part, perhaps, to his relentless experimentation, which can err on the side of the wilfully

bizarre. But all the same, he's an important and often interesting singer.

⊕ Return of Tom Zé: Brazil Classics 5
(Luaka Bop-WEA, US).

The wild man is superbly reassessed in a compilation by David Byrne and the Luaka Bop crew.

Bossa Nova

Compilations

⊕ Bossa Nova (Nascente, UK).

A good trawl through classic songs with most of the top names including Djavan, Vinícius de Morães, Jorge Ben, Maria Bethania, Chico Buarque and others (Tom Jobim being the one notable absentee).

⊕ The Story of Bossa Nova (EMI Hemisphere, UK).

The artists here are on the whole lesser names but this is nonetheless a fine, 20-track bossa primer, kicking off with a lovely take on "Chega de saudade" by Leila Pinheiro, moving on to the ding-a-ding skat of "A Rã" from João Donato, and staying just the right side of cheesy MOR.

⊕ BossaCucaNova and **Brasil 2mil: The Soul of Bass-o-Nova** (Crammed Discs, Belgium).

New life for old bossa on these discs. *BossaCucaNova* has classic songs remixed by leading Rio DJ/producers. Bass-o-Nova features modern bossa from Vinícius Cantuária, Chico Science, Arto Lindsay, Virgínia Rodrigues, and others.

Artists

Luiz Bonfa

Bossa Nova pioneer Luiz Bonfa (born 1922) was responsible for many standards, as a singer and composer, sometimes in collaboration with Jobim. He was co-composer of the film Black Orpheus (and of its theme "Manhã de Carnaval"), and was crucial in fusing bossa nova with American jazz, working and recording with Stan Getz.

⊕ Bonfa Magic (Milestone, US).

A 1991 recording of Bonfa's bossa classics, including, of course "Manhã de Carnaval".

Vinicius Cantuária

Cantuária has had two careers – the first in Brazil, where he wrote Caetano Veloso's biggest 1990s hit, and played a mix of MPB and rock'n'roll. He then moved to New York, met up with Arto Lindsay and Ryuichi Sakamoto and, with them, rediscovered bossa nova, adding electronic textures that let the music breathe anew.

VINICIUS CANTUÁRIA

⊕ Tucumã (Verve, US).

Bossa nova for the late-90s – and it has rarely sounded so good. This is Cantuaria's second US disc, recorded with a cutting edge crew of New Yorkers including Bill Frisell, Laurie Anderson and Sean Lennon.

ARTO LINDSAY

⊕ O Corpo Subtil (Ryko, US).

This is the first and most sublime of a trio of bossa-inspired albums from the New York (but Brazil born) avant-rock musician, Arto Lindsay. Lindsay sings partly in English, partly Brazilian. Cantuária co-composes and plays guitar.

Astrud Gilberto

Many lovers of Brazilian music have, shall we say, an equivocal view of Astrud Gilberto, with her breathy vocals and big, big hit. Make up your own mind.

 Verve Jazz Masters 9 (Verve, US).

There are dozens of Astrud compilations, almost all featuring "The Girl from Ipanema". This one leads the pack by some way, featuring her finest live and studio performances from the mid-1960s.

João Gilberto

João Gilberto is arguably the voice of Brazil. At the start of his career he was told he couldn't sing, but he went on to become the most influential interpreter in almost every aspect of modern Brazilian music, recording such classics as "Desafinado" and "Insensatez". A famous recluse, his bossa nova style has influenced the whole field of Brazilian vocals.

 João Gilberto (Polygram, US).

An immaculate compilation of classic bossa, with useful notes from Arto Lindsay.

Tom (Antonio Carlos) Jobim

Tom Jobim, a classically trained musician from the conservatory with a taste for the nightlife of the Rio bars, was the inventor of the bossa nova rhythm, and exerted great influence on its sophisticated harmonic language as well. His death in 1996 seemed to bring an era to its close.

The Art of Tom Jobim (Polygram, US).

Classic songs from the inventor of bossa nova. You may not understand the words of "Desafinado" or "Isaura", but you'll certainly recognise the melodies.

Forró/Nordestina

Compilations

Code: Brasil; Target: Recife (MELT 2000, UK).

Four local percussion, flute and ritual bands selected by Brazilian percussionist Airto Moreira who took them into a theatre in Recife and laid down these tracks. Lo-tech, hi-energy music ranging through the richly-toned harmonica playing of 74-year-old José Tavares da Silva to a frenetic pipes and drums band.

Forró, etc – Music of the Brazilian Northeast: Brazil Classics 3 (Luaka Bop-WEA, US).

A great compilation of nordestina music – one of Brazil's most infectious sounds – including tracks from the old master Luiz Gonzaga, and most of the bigger, more commercial artists.

Music for Maids and Taxi Drivers (GlobeStyle, UK; Rounder, US).

Another superb compilation, with inspired music to match its inspired title. It's a little more rootsy than the Brazil Classics selection and maybe has even more energy.

Artists

Luiz Gonzaga

Luis Gonzaga was the grand old man of forró, the vibrant accordion-led music of Brazil's sertão, the great arid rock-strewn plains of the north-east. An accordionist and singer, he was the first to bring it to an audience outside his native region, becoming a hero to the migrants forced into the big cities by drought and poverty in the process.

Asa Branca (RCA, Brazil).

Gonzaga's greatest hits. The title song is a national standard, one of the best-loved of all Brazilian tunes.

Gonzaguinho

The promising career of Gonzaguinho, son of the great forró artist Luis Gonzaga, was cut tragically short by his death in a car crash in 1991. He had forged a reputation as a singer and composer, mainly in an MPB-samba vein, and with superb lyrics on love, politics and the concerns of Brazil's underclass.

Luizinho de Gonzaga (Tropical, US).

A funky forró tribute by Gonzaguinha to his father, with a sad sense of loss underlying it.

Oficina de Cordas

Oficina de Cordas are a seven-piece string band including guitar, bandolim, cavaquinho, viola nordestina. They take a classical approach with refined arrangements.

Pernambuco's Music (Nimbus, UK).

While the northeast is best known for its heavy percussion bands or the rough and ready sound of forró, this is music that is elegant, infectious and ebullient. Mostly by popular composers of the first half of the 20th century. Now reissued in a budget 4CD set Dance Music from Brazil.

Pé de Serra Forró Band

The Pé de Serra Forró Band is a rather more downhome band of five rocking musicians.

Pé de Serra Forró Band (Schott Wergo, Germany).

This complements the other available recordings of forró music, with its atmosphere of a well-lubricated party. English lyrics included.

Canada

no more solitudes

While Canada hasn't made the greatest waves on the World Music scene, it's home to some rich musical traditions – notably those of the indigenous Inuit, the French settlers in Québec, and the Scottish and Irish population on the east coast. The first boasts the unique singing games of katajjaq, the second the exuberant band La Bottine Souriante and the third, currently enjoying a surge of energy, the wild Cape Breton fiddlers Ashley MacIsaac and Natalie MacMaster. **Charles Foran** traces the history and the new developments.

As a culture, Canada is neither here nor there. It is everywhere: at times it seems to be just about everyone. First off, the country is as wide as the continent it sits atop. Musicians in St. John's, Newfoundland, have to endure a longer flight to make a gig in Vancouver, British Columbia, than if they travelled to London, England. Between Newfoundland and England lies the Atlantic Ocean; between St. John's and Vancouver lies southern Canada. Size doesn't simply encourage regional cultures: until the rise of technology, it virtually precluded a national one. If televisions, VCRs and CDs have brought the 'old' tri-part Canada – English, French, and Native – culturally closer (debatable in itself), it has also helped produce the successive global seismic shifts that now make the country home to people from every other nation on the planet. If Canada was once a series of solitudes – as our favourite metaphor argues – it is now a mishmash, a cacophony. In such a state, some art forms, restricted by language or convention, suffer. Not music, though.

Inuits Old and New

Before Europeans 'found' their New World, North America was already an old one. In the expanse that was to become Canada, dozens of native communities lived and died – and made music. Our written knowledge of the music begins only with seventeenth century observations, mostly by French missionaries. Two hundred years later musicologists began to note down native traditions and compositions. Technology has made the historical record easier to chart; it has also changed that history. The radio and recording studio have allowed traditional forms to become 'fixed' and

rebroadcast over wide areas. Even the other key historical development – the introduction of fiddles and accordions into native repertoires – is related to the march of time and technology, in this case whaling ships crossing the Atlantic to ply the Arctic seas.

Today, some 25,000 **Inuit people** consider the vast northern spheres of Canada home. Their instrument has always been the **drum**, used either solo or in a group for dancing. **Throat singing**, where women produce a range of sounds from deep in the throat, is an equally ancient musical form. At its purest, melodies matter less than exchanges between singers intent on matching wild tones and high-octave reaches, usually until one dissolves into giggles (see Katajjaq box).

Until recently, native music tended to be functional rather than for entertainment. For instance, drum dance songs described a hunt, or requested good weather or luck in gambling. One early commentator on Eskimo repertoires noted the absence of such world traditional music staples as love or work songs. Even lullabies were often simply crooned versions of drum melodies. But for more than a century now the Inuit have been incorporating influences from the outside. At first it was visitors to the North – sailors from Scotland and Ireland – who provided the input. Of late it's been records and radio, most notably **country music** picked up on short-wave and at occasional concerts. The result is a unique mix of indigenous, Irish and Scottish, Appalachian and country sounds.

In recent decades, Inuit music has been enthusiastically recorded by the Canadian Broadcasting Corporation. The CBC Northern Service set up their first station in Iqaluit, Northwest Territories, in 1961. Among important early recordings were those by button-accordion legend **Charlie**

Katajjaq and Inuit singing games

Two women stand nose to nose holding each other's arms and utter a typesetter's nightmare of guttural sounds, grunts, inhalations, exhalations and more, until one can keep a straight face no longer and collapses into a fit of giggles. This is **katajjaq** – one of world music's most curious spectacles – and the best-known of Inuit singing games, thanks to some good recordings and, even better, the singers going on tour.

Games are an important part of Inuit culture and are sung by women. They are a way of educating children, but also showing everyone the relationships between members of the community. Some are real games – hide and seek, juggling, string games – accompanied by songs, and others are vocal exercises. In hide and seek the 'seeker' sings a song instead of counting while the others hide and, while juggling, the juggler sings as long and as fast as possible without dropping the ball.

katajjaq is played amongst the Inuit of **Northern Québec** and on **Baffin island**. An important part of the game is the illusion – the listener can't distinguish who is doing what because the players do not sing the syllables or breathe simultaneously. They follow each other so one voice has its strong accent on the weak one of the other. The superimposition of these strong and weak accents is part of the art as well as producing beautiful sounds, full of invention. A katajjaq ends

when the voices do become simultaneous or when one of the players can't keep going because she's out of breath or just lost in the imaginative vocal patterns of her rival. It's a game of endurance, but being fun it dissolves into laughter when they can't keep on. There's no winner as such, the idea is to have fun and share something exhiliarating with a good partner.

The vocal sounds are made out of a word, or part of a word, or meaningless vocables to imitate natural sounds or moods. Inspiration might be found in the cries of geese, screeches of sledges, the cooking of seal flippers, the hisses of the Northern Lights or the cries of caribou. The Canadian Inuit are people of the caribou and have certainly learned to mimic their deep guttural sounds. Living in the tundra, they evoke in their chants all the animals and birds around them, as well as the terrifying cracking of the ice-field and searing blow of the North Wind.

katajjaq singers usually form close partnerships (it's difficult to sing spontaneously with a new partner). The old women are, of course, the best singers, but they are passing on the art and some of the young ones are already very good. The young duo **Tudjaat** are incorporating katajjaq into modern pop songs.

Etienne Bours

Mary Iqaluk and Nellie Echalook from Inukjuak

Panigoniak. His relaxed, cheerful sound set the tone for subsequent generations. **Simeonie Keenainik**, an Eastern Arctic aboriginal, is perhaps the finest accordion player today, and though his array of jigs, reels and polkas may sound part Newfoundland, part Québec, it has become unmistakably Inuit.

Susan Aglukark's music is harder to fix in the tradition. This young Central Arctic singer has come to bear the burden of her culture's aspirations. Her pleasant pop songs, sung in Inuktitut but arranged like those of any other commercial singer, divide critics. (She does address serious issues in her lyrics, though, including sexual abuse.) Whatever its value, her music has given Inuit culture a boost.

There are, too, plenty of **pow wows** – traditional drumming festivals – in the sub-Arctic regions of the country and one can always hear excellent traditional singing. The **Stoney Park Singers**, from Alberta, have won numerous international awards, and the two-woman group **Tudjaat** are bringing the hair-raising intensity of throat-singing to a wider audience. The fiddling traditions of the **Métis** of **Manitoba** – themselves part-aboriginal, part of European descent – and Québec's **Northern Cree** are also firmly in the roots camp. A 1970s National Film Board of Canada documentary showed Cree fiddlers playing with an astonished group of Scottish musicians. The Cree, it turned out, had a style uncannily similar to that of nineteenth-century Scottish fiddlers – a legacy of interactions between natives and whalers generations ago. The Métis style – no surprise for a province where American country music is so popular – has a lift and bounce openly indebted to the Grand Old Opry.

Again and again, it has been the ability of native musicians to incorporate other traditions that has kept the music vital. Hailing from a reserve in Saskatchewan, **Buffy Sainte-Marie** (although now resident in Hawaii) has been a World Music fixture for decades. Her charisma is matched by that of the group **Kashtin**. Two Innu men, Florent Vollant and Claude McKenzie, from a remote reserve in northern Québec, may sing in a language spoken by fewer than 10,000 people, but their passionate, roots-rock music quickly found an enthusiastic audience. *Akua Tuta*, their 1994 recording, went platinum in Canada.

Finally, though he is justly famous as the frontman of the seminal group The Band, **Robbie Robertson**, a part-Mohawk from near Kingston, Ontario, has in recent years returned to his own roots – notably on his albums *Contact from the Underworld of Redboy* (Capitol) and *Music for the Native Americans* (Capitol), which features some Canadian artists, including Kashtin.

For more on Buffy Sainte-Marie and Robbie Robertson, and these traditions, see the Native America article (p.593).

Three Waves, Two Traditions

The early European settlers (French, Celtic and English) created three distinct regions but only two genuine musical cultures. New France became **Québec**, a nation first within an English colony and then, after the 1867 Act of Confederation, a province within the country of Canada. Be it Québec the province, or Québec the country, the place has long nurtured and cherished its artists, including musicians. Politics played a part in its musical revival of the 1970s, and the lures of global pop culture are now challenging the commitment of the Québecois to a genuine local tradition.

Likewise, the provinces of Newfoundland, New Brunswick, Prince Edward Island and Nova Scotia, guarded their **Scottish and Irish ancestries** with tenacity over the centuries. Their commitment has paid off unexpectedly with the current explosion of **East Coast music** – the 'hottest' scene in the country.

Interestingly, of the original emigrant paths, the one that ventured furthest up the St. Lawrence Seaway, to what is now the province of **Ontario**, formed the economic and political power base for the country without ever producing much music. Until Toronto's rebirth as a multicultural Mecca – beginning in the 1960s – with its ever more remarkable musical marriages, a largely WASP (White Anglo-Saxon Protestant) heritage had left the city, and the culture of Southern Ontario, bereft. (Gordon Lightfoot, the popular folk balladier, is a rare name from the province.)

Québec – Les Chansonnieres

They came mostly from northern France and they brought along songs and melodies, fiddles and spoons. For generations the good people of **Québec** played music in kitchens and halls in villages and towns throughout the province, rarely to the delight of their censorious parish priests. They also sang songs. In 1865 Canada's first important collector, Ernest Gagnon, published a book of 100 traditional folk songs, claiming the actual body of material was 'incalculable.' That figure only multiplied until, ironically, radio and then television granted the music a wider audience, but diminished its creation at a roots level. Thanks once again to Radio-Canada (the French arm of the CBC), this history has been preserved, and in 1967 a massive project, The Centennial Collection of Canadian Folk Songs, put on disc this fragile history, much of it Québecois. Whether it is **Jacques Labrecque** singing "Un canadien errant," a song beloved by generations of French Canadians, **Yves Albert** offering a local version of the ancient European love song "À la claire fontaine", or the great Acadien **Edith Butler** performing a ballad from New Brunswick, the anthology makes a lie of the notion, popular among the post-nation state crowd, that Canada never had a past to denigrate or, worse, ignore.

Two great singers helped bring to an end the province's *grande noirceur* – the 'great darkness' of a church-dominated state in which the majority of citizens lived in subservience to various masters. Both **Gilles Vigneault** (b. 1916) and **Felix Leclerc** (1912–1983) drew heavily on the songs they heard as children. In Vigneault's case, that childhood was spent in remote Natashquan in the north; Leclerc's upbringing occurred on the magnificent Île d'Orleans downstream from Québec City. Forging unique, highly expressive styles in the tradition of French chansonniers like Leo Ferré and Jacques Brel, and penning lyrics of passionate, often nationalist poetry – both men were also accomplished poets – Leclerc and Vigneault recorded songs of profound impact. For many Québecers, for example, the first public airing of Vigneault's "Mon pays," sung by Monique Leyrac at a song festival in 1965, marked a watershed in their own political thinking. "Mon pays c'est pas mon pays", Vigneault wrote, "c'est l'hiver" (My country is not my country: it is winter). The songwriter was speaking metaphorically – virtually every major Québecois artist supported sovereignty, and still does – but the association works on a literal level, as anyone who has endured one of Montreal's six-month winters can attest.

Another 'moment' in Québec's coming of age saw the 'lion' (Leclerc), the 'wolf' (Vigneault), and the 'fox' (young rocker **Robert Charlebois**) on stage together in the summer of 1974. The setting – the Plains of Abraham, site of the 1759 battle that lost New France to the British – was apt. A new battle for the province's destiny was underway, and the union of Québec's musical patriarchs, along with the charismatic Charlebois – credited with legitimising the use of local dialect called *joual* in popular music – seemed to portend victory.

On the roots front, 1970s bands like **Le Rêve du Diable** (The Devil's Dream) and **La Bottine Souriante** (The Smiling Boot) took the old tunes and call-and-response songs – often ribald tales of antics in the back-beyond – and pumped them with youthful vigour and just the right irreverence. Purists applauded the integrity, critics noted the innovation, while everyone else, outdoors on St-Jean Baptiste day in Québec City, or huddled in a *boîte chanson* in Old Montreal on a frigid winter eve, simply picked up the good-time vibe. La Bottine Souriante started out with the local musical traditions of the Lanaudière region, one of Québec's richest musical areas, then widened their reach by exploring connections between French and Celtic dance traditions, all powered by **Michel Bordeleau**'s extraordinary *accords de pieds* – the foot percussion that is an essential part of both French and Scottish Canadian music and is one of this band's party pieces. They've gone on to embrace other global sounds, but always keep their Québecois identity and joi de vivre.

In Québec, as elsewhere, the revival manifested itself more commercially with folk. Seminal recordings seemed to appear fortnightly: **Gilles Valiquette**'s "Chanson pour un café", the early records of brother and sister duo **Richard and Marie-Claire Seguin**, **Beau Dommage**'s anthemic ballad "La complainte du phoque en Alaska," written by Michel Rivard, plus the eponymous debut by the hugely popular band **Harmonium**.

Also worth noting were the first recordings of Montrealers **Kate and Anna McGarrigle**. Though their roots explorations tended to focus on American influences, a song like "Chanson

Kate and Anna McGarrigle

La Mistrine
La Bottine Souriante

pour la Sainte-Catherine", with its whimsical chorus "Il y a longtemps qu'on fait de la politique/Cent ans de guerre contre les moustiques" (It's been ages since we were political/A century of fighting the mosquitos) locates them firmly in their native Québec.

If the decade produced a masterpiece, it may well be *La tête en gigue* by **Jim Corcoran** and **Bertrand Gosselin**. The record, whose English title might work best as 'Light-Headed', is a seamless amalgam of folk and traditional sounds that captured the sunny spirit of the times. **Paul Piche**'s ardent, often sinfully catchy protest songs and the laconic wit of **Plume La Traverse** also helped define the era. Québecois roots and folk music could only soar, seemingly, and the province's political aspirations – René Lévesque's Parti Québecois held power provincially – looked ready to be realised in a 1980 referendum on sovereignty.

The glow, however, faded. In keeping with the ebb of nationalist fervour, roots music in the 1980s saw its audience shrink back to the faithful. Bands broke up, sales declined, and major artists failed to even land recording contracts. Québec may have held a second referendum in 1995 – another victory for the federalists, this time by the narrowest of margins – but separatist fervour sought no musical inspiration in the 90s, fearing perhaps the taint of old-style parochial nationalism and baby boomer agendas.

The best, though, have hung tough. Now in their third decade as a band, **La Bottine Souriante** continue to astonish, lately going 'world'

with jazz, Cajun and salsa inflections. The group has even added a full horn section to the batch of fiddle, accordion and guitar, and their concerts are as rowdy and spirited as ever. Without question, they are French Canada's most successful musical export and recently signed to EMI Hemisphere.

In addition, at least three new major artists have emerged in recent years, even if to the sound of one-hand clapping. Hailing from the northerly Abitibi region along the border with Ontario, **Richard Dejardins**' lean style – long narrative songs accompanied only by piano or guitar – and fiery intensity recall Felix Leclerc or, for that matter, early Bob Dylan. Québec's leading newspaper, *Le Devoir*, once gave over the front page of its arts section to print the lyrics to an epic Dejardins song on native history. His "Tu m'aimes-tu?" (Do you Love Me?) is a recording for the ages, and his hilarious, sad road song, "Et j'ai couché dans mon char," (And I slept in my Car) speaks more from the heart about the experiences and expectations of ordinary Québecers than does the entire ouvre of global Québec superstar Celine Dion.

Danielle Martineau's sophisticated music is a joy, with a style reminiscent of Zachary Richard. An accordionist and singer, she shifts from straight pulsating Cajun to delicate original compositions, at once loyal to tradition and open to new sounds. The same can be said of **Michel Faubert**. A fine storyteller as well as a singer and musician, Faubert has produced two exceptional recordings – the aptly-named *Maudite Mémoire* (1992) and 1995's

J'ai couché dans mon Char	I Slept in My Car
J'ai roulé 400 miles sous un ciel fâché aux limites de la ville mon coeur a clenché	I drove 400 miles Under a furious sky When I hit town My frozen heart cried
Les gros flashes aparaîssent dans mon âme égarée les fantômes se dressent à chaque pouce carré	Flashes of light Illuminate my lost soul Ghosts appear At every road toll
Revenir d'exil comporte des risques comme rentrer une aiguille dans un vieux disque	To return from exile Has its risks Like sticking a needle In an old disc
Y a eu ben du progrès ben d'asphalte, ainsi d'suite j'me demande qui je s'rais si j'tais resté icitte	There's plenty of progress, Lots of pavement, and so on I wonder who I'd be If I'd never gone.

excerpt from "J'ai couché dans mon Char" by Richard Dejardins; translation, Charlie Foran

Careme et Mardi Gras. He may be a roots musician, but he is a cunning, alert one: his juxtapositions of old melodies with raw guitar lines are purposeful, and he uses the studio – as well as his high, winsome voice – to haunting effect.

The East Coast – Kitchen Music Unbound

The Maritime provinces of Canada were primarily settled by Irish and Scottish communities fleeing famine or economic hardship at home. On **Cape Breton island**, for instance, there was a huge influx of Scottish settlers in the late eighteenth and early nineteenth centuries due to the Highland Clearances. To this day, the descendants of those immigrants show a pride in their Scottish heritage. Musically, this is reflected in a **Scottish fiddle style** – generally accompanied by piano - much more rootsy and dance-like than the classical veneer that's developed in the British Isles. Many musicians from Scotland, in fact, repeat their ancestors' immigrant journey, albeit for shorter periods, in order to re-discover their own traditions as preserved on craggy Cape Breton.

All that activity aside, the revival in East Coast music was hard to foresee. Just two decades ago it was still necessary to seek out East Coast music in the kitchens of Newfoundland fishing villages or the church halls of Cape Breton. Poverty, isolation and the lack of interest in Celtic music left the Maritimes feeling that their traditions and passions were at best quaint, at worst embarrassing.

Typical of this era is the story of fiddler **Rufus Guinchard** (1899–1991). Though Guinchard played at dances in his hometown of Daniel's Harbour from the age of fourteen onwards, he was fully seventy-two before The Breakwater Boys, a group of younger Newfoundland musicians keen to explore the old music, sought him out. Guinchard played and recorded with that band, and others, and he toured Canada, Europe and even Japan until well into his eighties. By the eve of his ninetieth birthday – celebrated with parties all over Newfoundland – Rufus Guinchard had been awarded the Order of Canada and became spiritual mentor for a generation.

It was the band **Figgy Duff**, however, that finally brought the music off 'The Rock', as Newfoundland is fondly called. From the late-1970s until their demise a decade later, the group played powerful traditional music. Pamela Morgan's singing was ethereal, whether on a sealing song like "The Greenland Disaster" or the French ballad "Quand j'etais fille a l'age quinze ans", and the band, driven by accordion and drums, punched out the jigs and reels. After a long silence, Morgan has recently begun a solo career, while Dave

Fanting, another former member of the band currently plays in the roots-rock outfit Rawlings Cross.

Two Cape Breton families, the **Rankins** and the **Barra MacNeils**, formed popular groups in the late 1980s. Until the recent explosion, if Canadians knew any younger East Coast musicians it was likely these genial, media-friendly musical families. Both groups play first-class traditional music, though some may find their misty Celtic songs bland. But even the rise of the Rankins and Barra MacNeils, reminders of the kitchen music cultures of the island, where extended families – and multi-generations – of musicians still rule the scene, couldn't prepare the world for the phenomenon that is **Ashley MacIsaac** (see box) and friends.

Is it really only five years since Cape Breton's child fiddler prodigy opened his first adult album with the words (and title): "Hi! How are you today?" Madman, enfant terrible, doting musical son – the gifted MacIsaac, now all of twenty-four

Natalie MacMaster

ADASTRA

has, through the originality of his recordings and his mesmerising, often unbuttoned live performances, granted East Coast music the lofty status of being fashionable, even cool. Make no mistake, though, MacIsaac may strut about like a kilted punker and his videos may feature regularly on Canada's rock video network, but he comes from

a long line of fiddlers, and his music is first and foremost traditional, played with fire and abandon but never disrespect.

Equally gifted, if less possessed, is MacIsaac's childhood neighbour **Natalie MacMaster**. She, too, is the child of Cape Breton fiddling royalty. Her great uncle, Charlie MacMaster, is a legend, while her uncle, Buddy MacMaster, has been celebrated in print by no less than Ashley MacIsaac himself. MacIsaac's poetry may be rough, but his sentiments are amusing:

With God inside, and Heaven's vindication
Sound came out our saviour's fingers and
*   there began creation*
There began creation on Cape Breton island
And his name was Buddy MacMaster.

The 'saviour's' niece, Natalie, has long been acclaimed for her pure technical skill, not to mention her ability to fiddle while executing the high leg kicks of traditional dance. MacMaster tours with some of the finest East Coast musicians – including the virtuoso guitarist, **Dave MacIsaac** – in her band.

If Ashley MacIsaac's impact was instant, the long-term legacy of **Mary Jane Lamond** may yet be incalculable. In many ways the opposite of the mercurial fiddler, this Cape Bretoner spent years learning Gaelic and traditional singing. Her approach was almost scholarly but the result, the record *Suas e!* is a wondrous testament to a living tradition. Sung entirely in Gaelic, the album moves effortlessly from hip-hop melodies to a sampling of old women performing *waulking* songs, old Scottish cloth-working songs. Her 1999 follow-up, *Lon Duic*, continued in this bold vein.

Lamond's producer, **Laurel MacDonald**, is an equally original artist. Her solo albums *Kiss Closed my Eyes* and *Chroma* are truly global music, combining elements of Celtic, Middle-Eastern and choral singing. Each of them are lovely, under-appreciated works, and MacDonald's musical blendings are typical of the 'new' Cape Breton sound – rooted in the past but looking outward, confidently.

Down the road from the island, meanwhile, Nova Scotia's capital, **Halifax**, has also been host to major musical developments. **Scott Macmillian**'s ambitious *Celtic Mass for the Sea*, a symphonic work for voice and orchestra, is but one example of the growing spirit of adventure that has seized the Maritimes. Macmillian also plays guitar in **Puirt a Baroque**, a trio committed to exploring the links between traditional and classical music. Whatever your views on the thesis of their album *Bach*

Ashley MacIsaac – Devil in the Kitchen

Has **Ashley MacIsaac** come to praise the music or to bury it? Critics are still divided. Much is made of his on-stage manner and off-stage madness. His kilt flies during a televised high kick, flashing the family jewels; he pub-crawls gay bars when in Manhattan and roller

PETER LEON

Ashley MacIsaac

skates in Shanghai. At age seventeen – 'discovered' by prominent Americans who summer on Cape Breton island – he finds himself performing Philip Glass's music in New York; later, he jams with Paul Simon and ex-Talking Head David Byrne.

All of which impacts on how Ashley MacIsaac is perceived, both within the East Coast music community and by Canadians in general. Safe to say, MacIsaac enjoys being outrageous. He seems a genuine free-spirit; he doesn't bother attempting to look or talk or, for that matter, play like anyone else. Why would he? Musically, his strong rhythmic style, with its full stroke and emphasis on the 'dig' at the start of a note, is decidedly rough and, yes, prone to producing his trademark frizzled bow hairs and resin-peppered fiddle.

Members of the Cape Breton Fiddlers' Association may denounce MacIsaac for playing too fast and wild, but they're either forgetting that the music is designed to be 'dirty' – i.e. for dances, often without amplification – or else they are plain deaf. When he wants to, as on "MacDougall's Pride" from *Hi, How are you Today?*, his tone can be as sweet as bird song. He just happens not to want to play that way much.

Attend a MacIsaac performance and you soon realise that he isn't playing the music so much as the music is playing him. In one of his head-bobbing, eyes-closed frenzies, the fiddler deconstructs the tune, repeating certain lines and dropping others without missing a beat or losing time. MacIsaac is so deep inside the melodic structure he is able to rearrange it as he goes.

No doubt this is in part because MacIsaac, who made a flawless record before he was old enough to drive, knows the stuff in his sleep. This mastery helps explain why he seems to be having such a ball and appears, on occasion, to treat the business with irreverence. The thought hasn't crossed Ashley MacIsaac's mind that what he does is related to dusty archives or the serious task of preserving the past. When MacIsaac plays Cape Breton music, he is just being himself.

meets Cape Breton (the title gives it away), it is superb music. Mention should also be made of Halifax's large and deep-rooted **Afro-Canadian** population. The city produces some excellent gospel music, most notably **The Gospel Heirs**,

a group happy to counter a traditional song with dance music rhythms and downtown R&B.

A concert featuring musicians from Nova Scotia or Newfoundland generally includes plenty of laughs that belie the precision of the playing – a spirit nurtured at the **Lunarberg Folk Festival** outside Halifax. **Big Wide Sea** and **Fanting's Rawlins Cross** are two of the leading Newfoundland bands straddling **roots and rock music** – a fusion not to all tastes – but their concerts are energising, always getting a crowd dancing.

Meantime out in the East Coast's other provinces, French **Acadien** music is undergoing a revival in New Brunswick and tiny Prince Edward Island, led by the effervescent **Barachois**. They are the leading exponents of Acadien music – the sort that was kicked out by the British in 1755 and became the basis of Cajun music in Louisiana. Barashois' musical roots are in French songs infused with the local Scottish and Irish fiddling styles, and this four-piece band led by **Albert Arsenault** features fiddle, piano, guitar and tuba plus various kitchen percussion – knives, forks and pots. Acadien Canada boasts two great fiddling families, the **Arsenaults** (of which Barachois is one incarnation) and the **Gallants**, and the singer **Edith Butler** still graces the occasional stage.

Celtic music outside the East Coast has one international star, **Loreena McKennitt**, from Stratford, Ontario, and one emerging phenomenon, the **Lahey fiddling family** from the

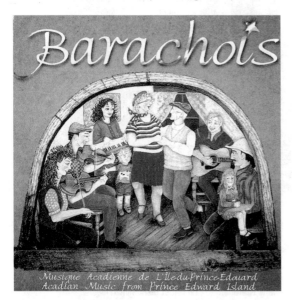

Musique Acadienne de L'Île-du-Prince-Edouard
Acadian Music from Prince Edward Island

central part of the province. McKennitt established herself as a refined practitioner of New Age Celticism with her 1992 record *The Visit*. Since then, she has begun to take in more world influences, often to great effect, though her lyrics, when she strays from traditional texts or well-known poems, still tend towards the fuzzy.

The Stew

Canada is one of the most multicultural nations on earth. If we can boast three distinct old-style musical traditions, we're lucky. Everywhere else – i.e. in the big cities – ethnic lines are dissolving and 'pure' traditions are becoming infected with strains of otherness.

In **Montréal**, for example, the fiesty independent label Oliver Sudden produces albums of Chinese, Vietnamese and Indian music, all drawn from local talent, while the Christmas concert to attend is one given by the **Montréal Jubilation Choir**. Equally, there is no better North American city in which to hear South African music, if **Lorraine Klaasen** is in town. Or check out the band **Zekuhl** which includes a Québecer raised in Cameroon, another of Mexican parentage with a background in samba, and a Chilean guitarist.

Each year the organisation **Musique Multi-Montréal** organises a performance of local World Music, mixed in with roots music from Québec. The events are hosted by one of the city's musical bright lights – the polyphonic Karen Young, Jim Corcoran, or Eval Manigat from Haiti. These gatherings shift from classy flamenco to hypnotic ragga to pulsating gumboots from South Africa. Musicians gather at the end to perform together: the city in a nutshell.

In **Toronto** there are some excellent **Balkan and Turkish bands** like **Staro Selo** and the **Altin Yildiz Orkestar**, and a world-class Klezmer group, **The Flying Bulgar Klezmer Band** (see p.585 for more on them and klezmer). There are also many intersections and crossbreedings. **Punjabi by Nature** takes the fusion of rock and bhangra that emerged in England in the 1980s and throws in the dancehall reggae rap favoured by local musicians like **Snow and Dream Warriors**. Until the death of founder Tarig Abubakar Ahmed, the **Afro-Nubians** featured musicians from Sudan and Canada, Germany and Sweden. Ahmed's band had no problem crashing Zairian soukous into reggae and even Afro-Arab sounds. Oliver Schroer, meanwhile, fronts the whimsical **Stewed Tomatoes**, an unhinged fiddle band as likely to groove on Frank Zappa as Ashley MacIsaac. Just about everything goes in Toronto's World Music scene, and if there is a motto it is this: the richer the stew the better the taste.

Travelling west, there are **Winnipeg**'s klezmer whizzes **Finjan**; in **Vancouver**, not surprisingly, one finds plenty of groups like **Uzume Taiko**, composed of **Japanese-Canadian** youth into everything from jazz to Indonesian gamelan. Many fine **Chinese** musicians also work out of that city, including the talented **Silk Road Music** ensemble. The list goes on and on, and will only lengthen. If Canada's musical past is relatively easy to summarise, its future – in the hands of these ever more diverse, ecumenical groupings – may prove a challenge to describe. All to the good.

discography

Inuit/Native Traditions

Compilations

Canada: Inuit Games and Songs (Auvidis/Unesco, France).

A fine introduction to katajjaq singing games, which could easily be mistaken for an album of energetic sex ... Good recordings with notes by Jean-Jacques Nattiez, the French Canadian musicologist who has done extensive research on the subject.

Canada: Jeux vocaux des Inuit (Ocora, France).

Other types of singing games from Caribou, Netsilik and Igloolik Eskimos once again recorded by Jean-Jacques Nettiez.

Music of the Inuit. The Copper Eskimo Tradition (Auvidis/Unesco, France).

Mainly drum songs from the Copper Eskimos who live on the banks of the Coppermine river in Canada's Northwest territories. Drum songs are hard listening, but there are helpful notes explaining their significance.

Waastuuskun/ Northern Lights (CBC North, Canada).

Compilation of northern Québec Cree music recorded in a community where Inuit, Cree, English and French live side by side. Includes Cyrille Fontaine's haunting "Shaman, Tell me Why", and superb fiddling. A strong example of the Native adoption of European traditions.

Artists

Kashtin

The name of this duo – Innu men, Florent Vollant and Claude McKenzie (guitars and vocals) – means 'Tornado'.

Akua Tuta (Sony, Canada).

Traditional values meet roots rock – the album title is Innu for 'Creation'. Crisp song-writing, passionate vocals, all in a little-known native language.

Stoney Park Singers

Eleven singers and drummers of the Nakoda tribe, Westley Band in Alberta.

Aude's Journey (Sweet Grass Records, Canada).

Simple arrangements, heartbeat drumming, fierce vocals. Puts you at a prarie pow wow.

Tudjaat

A pair of katajjaq singers, Madeline Allakariallak and Phoebe Atagotaalak, who are the first to take it into a into World Music fusion.

Tudjaat (Sony, Canada).

Different throat singing styles used as a sort of accompaniment in an ensemble of guitars, keyboards, bass and drums. Not the best introduction to katajjaq (they even do a version of "You Are My Sunshine"), but an interesting example of katajjaq fusion.

Quebec

Compilations

The Centennial Collection of Canadian Folk Songs (Radio Canada International, Canada).

Five CDs of classic songs from Québec and the Maritimes. The linear notes alone make the compilation invaluable.

Musical Travelogue: Québec (Auvidis/Silex, France).

A musical journey through traditional Québecois music – folksongs, reels and other dances on fiddle and accordion with old-time singers and players including Edith Butler and Gilles Vigneault.

Artists

La Bottine Souriante

Founded in 1976 by lead vocalist Yves Lambert, La Bottine Souriante (The Smiling Boot) have existed in several incarnations drawing on ever wider musical influences. They have over ten albums to their credit and a reputation as one of the most exciting roots bands anywhere. They are currently a nine-piece band including fiddles, accordion, piano, sax, brass and bass and the breathtaking foot percussion (an old French Canadian tradition) of Michel Bordeleau.

Les épousailles (Gamma, Canada).

This 1980 album was the band's first attempt at down-the-line Québecois revival music. Wonderful raw and raucous playing.

 La Mistrine (Musicor, Canada; EMI Hemisphere, UK).

In this 1994 album there's the added horn section and the hit song "Le rap à ti-pétang" about a woman who loses her husband in the bedding because he's so small and then sets light to the bed straw and roasts him alive. Punchy brass and wailing sax, plus those feet.

Rock & Reel (EMI Hemisphere, UK)

This 1999 outing shows the band still consistently inventive and packed with bravado.

Jim Corcoran and Bertrand Gosselin

Popular duo of young American folksinger with Québecois multi-instrumentalist.

"La tête en gigue" (Kebec-Disc, Canada).

It took an outsider like Corcoran, ironically, to capture the sweet sensibility of the Québec folk revival. A fluid, graceful recording that mixes tragic ballads like "Ce matin, sans hésiter" with the genial pop sounds of "Bye bye nuage, welcome soleil."

Richard Dejardins

Much travalled pianist and singer from the Abitibi region of Quebec.

 Tu m'aimes tu?
(Fukinic, Canada).

Bittersweet and tender, outspoken and strident: the chansonnier tradition lives on in Dejardins.

Henri Landry

The Landry family left France in the seventeenth century. Henry Landry was born in Pontbriand near Québec in 1923, learned the fiddle at an early age and spent a lifetime playing for weekly dances and weddings. Most of his repertoire was learned from Fortunat Vachon, a fiddler slightly older than Landry famed in the region, and consisted of Irish style jigs and reels as well as waltzes, the 'blues of Québec'.

Ⓜ **Henri Landry: Fiddler from the Eastern Townships** (Buda/Musique du Monde, France).

This collection recorded in 1975 kicks off with a cracking reel on the solo fiddle with *accords de pieds* (dance-like foot taps). It also features tunes with piano and guitar accompaniment. Homely old time music-making.

Felix Leclerc

Giant of Québec's musical and literary culture, whose music is still sung in pubs and poems taught in classrooms around the province.

Ⓜ **L'encan** (Polygram, Canada).

A combination of greatest hits and obscure live recordings including "Le tour de l'ile" and a cover of Michel Rivard's "La complainte du phoque en Alaska".

Kate and Anna McGarrigle

Bilingual Montreal sister duo, famed for lovely songs and haunting harmonies.

Ⓜ **Kate and Anna McGarrigle** (Warner, Canada).

The brilliant first recording, including "Heart Like a Wheel" made popular by Linda Rondstadt. Their French-language album, *French Record* (Polygram, Canada) is also a must – a collection of French songs more rootsy than most of their English material.

East Coast/Celtic

Compilations

 Fire in the Kitchen (BMG/Wicklow, US).

On a new label from The Chieftain's Paddy Maloney, this disc features an East Coast dream team of fiddlers Ashley MacIsaac and Natalie Macmaster and vocalists Mary Jane Lamond and Laura Smith.

Ⓜ **Traditional Music from Cape Breton Island** (Nimbus, UK).

An excellent collection recorded live at a 1993 festival in Cork, Ireland. It features Natalie MacMaster and her Uncle

Buddy MacMaster, John Morris Rankin, Carl MacKenzie and others in playing strathspeys, reels and jigs.

Artists

Barachois

The leading band playing French Acadien music. A four-piece combo led by Albert Arsenault with fiddles, guitars, percussion and step-dancing. Traditional French repertoire with influence of the Celtic Maritimes.

Ⓜ **Barachois** (Barachois, Canada; Iona, UK).

Great 1997 debut album that lives up to their energetic live performances, showing that the ancestors of the Cajuns still know how to 'let the good times roll'.

Figgy Duff

This groundbreaking Newfoundland group of the late 1970s and '80s, led by the late Noel Dinn, elicited comparisons with The Chieftains.

Ⓜ **Figgy Duff** (Posterim Records, Canada).

Even the use of a drum-kit – not an endearing fusion idea – works on this great debut album. Pamela Morgan's voice was a revelation.

Ⓜ **Restrospective 1974–93** (Amber/EMI, US).

As you'd imagine, a good cross-section of their output.

Mary Jane Lamond

Despite beginnings in the Montreal punk scene, Mary Jane Lamond has emerged as leading Scottish Gaelic singer and musicologist. She works often with Ashley MacIsaac.

 **Suas e!**
(BMG/Wicklow, US).

A miracle of scholarship, daring, and stubborn delight at making forgotten music in a vanishing tongue as infectious and – yes – danceable as any pop chart hit. The title means 'Get on Down!'

Suas e!

Ashley MacIsaac

Cape Breton's boy genius fiddler, now a young man of mission (see box feature, p.357).

Hi, How Are You Today? (A&M, Canada).

The past and the future, hand in hand. A fearsome thrash of the Cape Breton standard "Devil in the Kitchen" sets the tone for a superbly accomplished album.

Fine, Thank You Very Much (BMG/Wicklow, US).

For those who find the above a bit too much, the pure traditional follow-up, just to prove he can do it all.

Helter's Celtic (Loggerhood Records, Canada).

This 1999 outing had Ashley back in frantic form, keeping everyone guessing his intentions.

Natalie MacMaster

Now in her early twenties, Natalie was brought up in a musical family in Cape Breton and started playing aged nine. She was strongly influenced by her uncle Buddy MacMaster, a celebrated Cape Breton fiddler. Natalie is noted for her step-dancing as well as her masterly fiddle-playing.

My Roots Are Showing (Warners, Canada; Rounder, US; Greentrax, UK).

The traditional side of Natalie's art – strathspeys, reels and jigs with piano and guitar accompaniment plus footstamps!

No Boundaries (Warners, Canada; Rounder, US; Greentrax, UK).

Natalie's mildly experimental album with influences from ragtime and country music, but verging on MOR roots fiddle.

Loreena McKennitt

A superb harpist who started out exploring Celtic music, but has ventured into wider world sounds.

The Mirror and the Mask (Warner Music, Canada).

The voice, as ever, is ethereal and the playing, as always, is stellar. In stepping away from her Celtic roots, McKennitt makes a musical voyage from Morocco to Chile to Spain. A long way round, but worthwhile!

Stan Rogers

Rogers was a baritone Nova Scotian (1950–1984) who penned some classics and won a huge following before an aeroplane crash cut short a brilliant career.

Fogarty's Cove (Barn Swallow Records, Canada).

Fans will object to having to choose only one recording. Still, Rogers' voice never sounded as powerful as on this 1977 outing including "Fogerty's Pirateers", his best-known song. Nor was his song-writing ever so heartfelt, or so strong.

Multicultural

Compilations

Balkan Journeys Close To Home (Golden Horn Productions, US).

A lively collection of Baltic and Turkish dance music from four Toronto-based bands: Staro Selo, Neda Voda, Mastika and the Altin Yildiz Orkestar. Get on down to some complex beats.

Artists

Afro Nubians

Multi-cultural group led by the late Tarig Abubakar Ahmed from Sudan, plus musicians from Germany and Sweden fusing African, Middle Eastern and reggae sounds.

Tour to Africa (Stern's Records, UK).

With the death of Tariq Abubakar, this record becomes a danceable memorial to a great talent, and a fine group.

Zekuhl

Founded in 1991 and led by Cameroonian vocalist/guitarist Manu Njock, Zekuhl also includes Chilean guitarist Rodrigo Bustamante, Cameroonian bassist Guy Lange and German drummer Bertil Schulrabe.

Zekuhl (Tacca Musique, Canada).

World rhythms and textures all bound up in one young Montreal band.

Chile/Latin America　　Nueva canción

an uncompromising song

Nueva canción (new song) developed in the 1960s in **Chile, Argentina and Uruguay**, and also Cuba where it is known as *nueva trova* (see p.408). A music rooted in the guitar traditions of the troubadour, the songs could be love lyric or chronicle, lament or call to action, and, as such, they have played a part in Latin America's political and cultural struggles. In Chile, the great singer-songwriter Victor Jara was murdered for his art by Pinochet's thugs, while groups like Inti Illimani were forced into exile. In Argentina, too, the singers Atahualpa Yupanqui and Mercedes Sosa both suffered arrest by military governments. **Jan Fairley** looks at the history and legacy of this music of 'guitar as gun'.

Latin America's revolutionary politics have found expression in many of the continent's musics, but never more directly than in **nueva canción**. This 'new song' emerged at the end of the 1960s in Argentina and Chile, and over the next three decades it fulfilled

Quilapayún poster from 'the longest tour in history' (see p.367)

an important role in countries from Uruguay to Nicaragua, and (in a different relationship to government) across the Caribbean in Cuba. It was brought to international attention, above all, through the lyrical songs of Chilean theatre director and singer-songwriter **Víctor Jara**, who was murdered by the military in Chile during the 1973 coup d'etat.

Pity the Singer . . .

Pity the singer who doesn't risk his guitar and himself ... who never knew that we were the seed that today is life.

Cuban **Pablo Milanés** "Pobre del cantor"

Nueva canción spans a period of over thirty years, from the early 1960s, when Latin singers and song-writers became part of the political struggle to bring about change and reform. As a result of their activities, many of their number were arrested or forced into exile by dictatorships which through murder, torture and disappearance wiped out so much of a generation. The sense of a movement grew as the musicians involved met one another at festivals in Cuba, Nicaragua, Peru, Mexico, Argentina and Brazil, visited each other's countries, and occasionally sang each other's songs.

The 1960s was a time of politics and idealism in South America – far more so than in Europe or North America. There was a stark challenge presented by the continent's obvious inequalities, its inherited power and wealth, its corrupt regimes, and by the denial of literacy and education to much of the population. It is within this context that nueva canción singers and writers must be understood. With voice and guitar, they composed songs of their own hopes and experiences in places where many of those involved in struggles for change regularly met and socialised.

It is a music that is now, in some ways, out of time: the revolutionary past, the 1960s rhetoric of guitar as gun and song as bullet. Yet the songs – poems written to be performed – are classic expressions of the years of hope and struggle for change, and their beauty and truth nurtured those suffering under dictatorship or forced into exile. They are still known by heart by audiences throughout the continent and its exile communities.

Nueva canción was an expression of politics in its widest sense. It was not 'protest song' as such. The musicians involved were not card-carrying members of any international organisation and were often independent of political parties, although in the early 1970s the Chilean musicians were closely linked with the Popular Unity government of Salvador Allende – the first socialist president and government to be legitimately elected through the ballot box.

What linked these and other musicians of the movement was an ethical stance – a commitment to improve conditions for the majority of people in Latin America. To that end they sang not only in concerts and clubs but in factories, in shanty towns, community centres and at political meetings and street demonstrations. People in protest the world over have echoed the Chilean street anthems "El Pueblo Unido Jamás Sera Vencido" (The People United Will Never Be Defeated) and "Venceremos" (We Will Win).

Atahualpa Yupanqui and Violeta Parra

The roots of the nueva canción movement lie in the work of two key figures, whose music bridged rural and urban life and culture in the 1940s and 50s: the Argentine **Atahualpa Yupanqui** (1908–1992) and the Chilean **Violeta Parra** (1917–1967). Each had a passionate interest in their nation's rural musical traditions, which shared an Iberian and Amerindian sensibility. Their work was also in some respects paralleled by the Cuban Carlos Puebla, for more on whom see the Cuba article (p.386).

Atahualpa Yupanqui, born Hector Roberto Chavero, adopted as a political statement the name of one of the last Incas. He spent much of his early life travelling around Argentina, collecting popular songs from itinerant *payadores* (improvising poets) and folk singers in rural areas. He wrote his

first song, "Caminito del indio"' (The Path of the Indian), in 1926, and during a long career introduced a new integrity – and a distinguished playing style – to Argentine folk music (see p.315). He also introduced an assertive political outlook – his most famous song is "¡Basta ya!" (Enough Already! – that the Yankee tells us what to do) – and was forced into exile in 1932 and 1949, and again in 1967, at which point he moved permanently to Paris.

CHANT DU MONDE/HARMONIA MUNDI

Atahualpa Yupanqui

It was Paris that had welcomed Yupanqui before, in 1950, when he played in Left Bank clubs and, with his stark, intense style, won the admiration of Edith Piaf. In Paris, too, he met and shared stages with **Violeta Parra**, whose own career in Chile had mirrored his own. Like Yupanqui, Parra travelled extensively, singing with and collecting songs from old *payadores* – rural, popular poets – and preserved and popularised them through radio broadcasts and records. She also composed new material based on these rural song traditions, creating a model and repertoire for what became nueva canción. Her songs celebrated the rural and regional, the music of the peasant, the land-worker and the marginalised migrant.

Musically, Parra was a pioneer in the use of **Andean or Amerindian instruments** – the armadillo-shelled *charango*, the *quena* (bamboo flute) and panpipes (see Andean Music, p.273), and in her enthusiasm for the **French chanson** tradition.

She spent time in Paris in the 1960s with her children Angel and Isabel, where they met Yupanqui, Piaf and the flautist Gilbert Favre, who was to found the influential Andean band, **Los Jairas** (see Andean music, p.275), and with whom Violeta fell in love. Returning to Buenos Aires, she performed in a tent in the district of La Reina, which came to be called the Carpa de La Reina (The Queen's Tent). However, with a long history of depression, she committed suicide in 1967.

Parra left behind a legacy of exquisite songs, many of them with a wry sense of humour, including the unparalleled "Gracias a la vida" (Thanks to life), later covered by Joan Baez and a host of others. Even her love songs seem informed by an awareness of poverty and injustice, while direct pieces like "¿Que dira el Santo Padre?" (What does the Sainted Pope Say?) highlighted the Church's responsibility to take action. As Parra wrote (in the décima form she often used in her songs) in her autobiography:

I sing to the Chilean people
if I have something to say
I don't take up the guitar
to win applause
I sing of the difference there is
between what is certain
and what is false
otherwise I don't sing.

Mercedes Sosa – the interpreter

Mercedes Sosa is not a songwriter but has won a huge international reputation by interpreting the songs of others. She shows an uncanny ability to choose songs of the moment, drawing material from diverse sources for their emotion, poetry and melody, and singing them for "mi gente, mi pueblo" (my people, my country).

Her infectious singing style ranges from the gentle to the formidable. It can be joyful and caressing, as in Perteco Carabajal's "Las manos de mi madre" (The hands of my mother ... are like birds in the air), which paints a picture of mothers kneading bread on the verandah, just as they knead life. It can voice the epic, as in Petrocelli's "Cuando tengo la tierra" (When I have the Land) with her wild declamation of the lines "Campesino, when you have the land ... you will have the moon in your pocket." It can portray outrage, too, as in her astonishing version of rock singer Leon Gieco's "Sólo le pido a Dios": "I only ask God not to make me indifferent to war. It is a great monster that tramples on the poor innocence of the people."

Sosa was exiled from Argentina in 1978 after the military arrested both her and much of her audience at a concert. In exile, her voice was a constant of political commitment, particularly during the 'dirty war' fought by the military, and again during the Malvinas/Falklands war. Allowed to return in 1982, she began to include in her repertoire *rock nacional* songs, which challenged the regime, working with Charly Garciá and others, as well as folk singers Víctor Heredia and León Gieco. Once again, Sosa had crossed over between different genres and publics in her inimitable way, bringing musics and peoples together.

Sosa's views embody both strength and tenderness: "An artist isn't political in the party political sense

JAN FAIRLEY

– they have a constituency which is their public – it is the poetry which matters most of all." Reportedly fighting illness for a time in the 1990s, she rose like a phoenix in September 1998 to give a series of concerts at the legendary Luna Park, Buenos Aires, and was back in superlative form.

The Movement Takes Off

Nueva canción emerged as a real force in the mid-1960s when various governments on the continent were trying to effect democratic social change. The search for a Latin American cultural identity became a spontaneous part of this wider struggle for self-determination, and music was a part of the process.

The first crystallisation of a nueva canción ideal emerged in Argentina in 1962 at a meeting of the Journalists' Circle, where singers and poets, among them the Argentinian **Mercedes Sosa**, unveiled the 'nuevo canciónero' – a musical manifesto which aimed to respond to "new agreements and chords in the air", to re-evaluate indigenous song forms and to be the voice of poor and marginal Argentineans. Sosa (see box) was a key singer for the movement. Unusually, she was not a writer, but instead a superb interpreter of canción from across the continent. Her coverage of the songs of other great Latin musicians brought the work of singers such as Violeta Parra, the Cuban Silvio Rodríguez, and the Brazilian Milton Nascimento to a new public.

At the same time as Sosa was establishing a canción movement in Buenos Aires, a crucial folk club was opening in Chile. This was the legendary (and now re-opened) crucible of nueva canción, the **Peña de los Parra**, which **Angel and Isabel Parra**, inspired by the Paris *chanson* nightclubs, opened in downtown Santiago in 1965. Among the regular singer-songwriters performing here were **Víctor Jara** and **Patricio Manns**. Their

audiences, in the politically charged and optimistic period prior to the election of Allende's government, were enthusiastic activists and fellow musicians.

Victor Jara

The great singer-songwriter and theatre director **Víctor Jara** took nueva canción onto a world stage. His songs – and his life – continue to reverberate, and his work has been recorded by rock

singers like Sting, Bruce Springsteen, Peter Gabriel and Jackson Brown, and (memorably) by the British singer Robert Wyatt. All have been moved by Jara's story and inspired by his example.

Jara was born into a rural family who came to live in a shanty-town on the barren outskirts of Santiago when Víctor's father died; he was just eleven. His mother sang as a *cantora* for births, marriages and deaths, keeping her family alive by running a food-stall in the main Santiago market. It was from his mother and her work that Jara gained his intuitive knowledge of Chilean guitar and singing styles.

He began performing his songs in the early 1960s and from the beginning caused a furore. During the government of Eduardo Frei, for example, his playful version of a traditional piece, "La Beata" – a send-up of the desires of a nun – was banned, as was his accusatory "Preguntas por Puerto Montt" (You ask for Puerto Montt), which accused the Minister of the Interior of the massacre of poor landless peasants in the South of Chile. Working with Isabel Parra and the group

CHILE
A *B*

Plegaria a un labrador
(Prayer to a Labourer)

Stand up and look at the mountain
From where the wind comes, the sun and the
    water
You who direct the courses of the rivers
You who have sown the flight of your soul
Stand up and look at your hands
So as to grow
Clasp your brother's, in your own
Together we will move united by blood
Today is the time that can become tomorrow

Deliver us from the one who dominates us
through misery
Bring to us your reign of justice and equality
blow like the wind the flower of the canyon
Clean like fire the barrel of my gun

Let your will at last come about here on earth
Give to us your strength and valour so as to
    fight
Blow like the wind the flower of the canyon
Clean like fire the barrel of my gun

Stand up and look at your hands
So as to grow
Clasp your brother's, in your own
Together we will move united by blood
Now and in the hour of our death
Amen.

                                    Víctor Jara

Huamari, Jara went on to create a sequence of songs called "La Población", based on the history and life of Santiago's shanty-town communities. His great gift was a deceptively simple and direct style applied to whatever he did.

One of his best-loved songs, "Te recuerdo Amanda" (I remember you Amanda), is a good example of the simplicity of his craft. A hauntingly understated love song, it tells the story of a girl who goes to meet her man Manuel at the factory gates; he never appears because of an 'accident' and Amanda waits in vain. In many of his songs, Jara subtly interwove allusions to his own life with the experiences of other ordinary people – Amanda and Manuel were the names of his parents.

Jara's influence was immense, both on nueva canción singers and the Andean-oriented groups like **Inti Illimani** and **Quilapayún** (see opposite), whom he worked with often, encouraging them to forge their own new performance styles. Enormously popular and fun-loving, he was nev-

ertheless clear about his role as a singer: "The authentic revolutionary should be behind the guitar, so that the guitar becomes an instrument of struggle, so that it can also shoot like a gun." As he sang in 1972 in his song "Manifiesto", a tender serenade which with hindsight has been seen as his testimony, "I don't sing just for love of singing, but for the statements made by my guitar, honest, its heart of earth, like the dove it goes flying ... Song sung by a man who will die singing, truthfully singing his song."

Like many Chilean musicians, Jara was deeply involved with the Popular Unity government of Salvador Allende, who following his election in 1970 had appeared on an open-air stage in Santiago surrounded by musicians under a banner saying "There can be no revolution without song". Three years later, on September 11, 1973 – along with hundreds of others who had legitimately supported the government – Jara was arrested by the military and taken to the same downtown stadium in which he had won the First Festival of New Chilean Song. Tortured, his hands and wrists broken, riddled with machine-gun bullets, his body was dumped with five others alongside a wall of the Metropolitan Cemetery; his face was later recognised amongst a pile of unidentified bodies in one of the Santiago mortuaries by a worker.

Jara left behind him a song composed during the final hours of his life, written down and remembered by those who were with him at the end, called as a poem of testimony "Estadio Chile" (Chile Stadium). It was later set a cappella to music as "Ay canto, que mal me sales", by his friend and colleague Isabel Parra.

Exiles and Andean Sounds

After Pinochet's coup d'etat anything remotely associated with the Allende government and its values came under censorship, including books and records, whose possession could be cause for arrest. The junta issued warnings to musicians and folklorists that it would be unwise for them to play nueva canción, or indeed any of the Andean instruments associated with its sound – *charangas*, panpipes and *quenas*.

It was not exactly a banning but was menacing enough to force the scene well underground – and abroad, where many Chilean musicians lived out the junta years in exile. Their numbers included the groups Inti Illimani and Quilapayún and later Illapu (see below), Sergio Ortega, Patricio Manns, Isabel and Angel Parra, and Patricio Castillo. They were not the only Latin Americans forced from their country. Other **musician exiles** of the 1970s included Brazilian MPB singers Chico Buarque, Caetano Veloso and Gilberto Gil; Uruguay's nueva canción singer Daniel Viglietti; and Argentina's Mercedes Sosa.

Inti Illimani

In Chile, the first acts of musical defiance took place behind church walls, where a group of musicians who called themselves **Barroco Andino** started to play Baroque music with Andean instruments within months of the coup.

It was a brave act, for the use of Andean or Amerindian instruments and culture was instinctively linked with the nueva canción movement. Chilean groups like **Quilapayún** and **Inti Illimani** wore the traditional ponchos of the peasant and played Andean instruments such as panpipes, bamboo flutes and the charango, and the maracas and shakers of Central America and the Caribbean. That these were the instruments of the communities who had managed somehow to survive slavery, resist colonialism and its aftermath had a powerful symbolism. Both 'los Intis' and 'los Quilas', as they became familiarly known, worked closely with Víctor Jara and also with popular classical composers Sergio Ortega and Luís Advis.

In 1973 the two groups travelled to Europe as official cultural ambassadors of the Allende government, actively seeking support from governments in Europe at a time when the country was beseiged economically by a US blockade, and undermined by CIA activity. On September 11, when General Pinochet led the coup d'etat in which Salvador Allende died, the Intis were in

Daniel Viglietti: Uruguay's *cancionista*

One of the first Latin-American 'new songs' to have an impact outside its own country was "Canción para mi América" (Song for my America) by **Uruguayan** singer-songwriter **Daniel Viglietti**. Its lyrics – "Give your hand to the Indian, it will do you good; he will show you the roads to follow, and where the blood must be spilled" – set the tone for the nueva canción movement, which at times linked musicians from practically every country in Latin America, and from Spain, too, which was still enduring the oppression and censorship of the Franco dictatorship.

Viglietti went on to write a series of classic songs, including the "Milonga de andar lejos" (Milonga from far away), with its lines "I want to break life, how I want to change it". In 1969 his song "A desalambrar" (Take the fences down), which called for the redistribution of land to those who worked it, was banned by the authorities. In 1972 the military dictatorship in Uruguay objected to a performance of his and he was imprisoned. Worldwide protest, including a telegram signed by leading figures and the French intellectuals Jean Paul Sartre and Simone de Beauvoir, eventually helped secure his release.

Brothers in Arms

The **Cuban experience** which produced the nueva trova songs of **Pablo Milanés** and **Silvio Rodríguez** (see p.408), and which offered support to many nueva canción artists, was unique in the Americas, forging a new tradition of reflection and an expression of self-doubt, emotional experience, hopes and beliefs. Elsewhere on the continent, nueva canción at times played a much more direct and oppositional propaganda role.

In **Nicaragua**, before the Sandinistas' 1979 victory over the Somoza dictatorship, brothers **Carlos** and **Luís Enrique Mejía Godoy** composed "Carabina – M1" and other instructional songs. Broadcast on clandestine guerrilla radio, they cheerfully gave instructions to a scattered population, many of them illiterate, on how to clean and assemble their weapons and participate in the armed uprising. Their songs were important as much for their direct advice on how to make Molotov cocktails, as for the feeling of contact and solidarity they gave to isolated groups of fighters.

During the Sandinistas' period of power, the 'Volcan-to' (a fusion of 'volcano' and 'song') movement was launched to bring musicians together. Song was involved in much needed literacy campaigns and even in encouraging people to eat maize products when the North American embargo caused a wheat shortage. In fact, the whole story of the Nicaraguan Revolution – from the guerrillas fighting behind the lines to the Sandinistas in power and their defeat at the ballot box – is tracked in the work of Luís Enrique, who has more recently turned his attention to working with indigenous Amerindian motifs.

Nueva canción was used in a similar revolutionary fashion by the **Yolocamba I'ta** in **El Salvador**, and in any number of cultural movements up and down the continent in the 1970s and early '80s, before the longed-for collapse of so many of the dictatorships. In **Mexico**, in particular, the work of **Amparo Ochoa**, and the *folkloristas* **Gabina Palomares** and **Judith Reyes** was essential and influential.

Forward ever: Sandinistas carrying the 'guitar as gun' concept into the battlefield

Italy and the Quilas in France. For the Intis the tour ("the longest in history", as the Intis joke) turned into a fifteen-year and fifty-four days European exile for the group, an exile which put nueva canción and Amerindian music firmly on Europe's agenda of Latin American music.

The Intis and Quilas were the heart and soul of a worldwide Chilean (and Latin American) solidarity movement, performing almost daily for the first ten years. Both groups also recorded albums of new songs, the Intis becoming increasingly influenced by their many years in Italy, creating such beautiful songs of exile as "Vuelvo", with key singer-songwriter and musician **Patricio Manns**.

The impact of their high profile campaigning against the military meant that the Intis were turned back on the airport tarmac long after politicians and trade union leaders were repatriated. They eventually returned on 18 September, 1988, Chile's National Day, the day of one of the biggest meetings of supporters of the 'No' vote to the plebicite called by Pinochet to determine whether he should stay in office. Going straight from the airport to sing on a huge open-air stage and to dance the traditional *cueca* (Chile's National Day dance), the group's homecoming was an emotional and timely one. In 1998, after ten years of re-building their lives, making music and supporting various projects, including the Víctor Jara Foundation, the group's personnel, almost unchanged since 1967, is now adapting to the amicable departure of Max Berrú and Jose Séves to pursue other projects.

The Andean instruments and rhythms used by Quilapayún (who disbanded in the 1980s) and Inti Illimani have been skilfully used by many other groups whose music is equally interesting – groups like **Illapu**, who remained popular throughout the 1980s (with a number of years in forced exile) and into the 1990s.

Future and Legacy

Times have changed in Chile and in Latin America generally, with revolutionary governments no longer in power, and democracy restored after dictatorships throughout most of the continent. The nueva canción movement, tied to an era of ideals and struggle, and the years of survival under dictatorship, might seem to have lost its relevance.

Its musicians have for the most part moved on to more individual concerns in their (always poetic) songwriting. But the nueva canción form, the inspiration of the song as message, and the rediscovery of Andean music and instruments, continues to have resonance and influence. Among a new generations of singers inspired by the history of new song are **Carlos Varela** in Cuba (see p.408) and the Bolivian singer, **Emma Junaro**.

In the 1980s and '90s, Junaro reinvented nueva canción as **canto nuevo**, with a light, jazzy feel to the music, and a clear, lyrical voice. She has, notably, covered the songs of Bolivian poet and criollo singer, Matilde Casazola. These weave Amerindian beliefs into a musical framework resonant of the sounds of southern Bolivia, using tunes associated with the country music of the *gau-cho* and migrant communities. Junaro is usually accompanied by Uruguayan guitarist **Fernando Cabrera** whose sensibility evokes both the pioneering work of earlier Argentinian musician Atahualpa Yupanqui, as well as classical and jazz tones.

And there will be others. For Latin America, nueva canción is not only music but history.

Emma Junaro

discography

Nueva canción has had a raw deal on CD – it peaked in the decades before shiny discs and for many classics, you'll need to search secondhand stores for vinyl. If you travel to Chile, you can also obtain **songbooks** for Victor Jara (the Fundación Víctor Jara publish his complete works), while most other songs of the period are featured in Clasicos de la Musica Popular Chilena Vol 11 1960–1973 (Ediciones Universidad Catolica de Chile).

This discography includes a round-up of nueva canción discs from territories beyond Chile. Related artists from Cuba and Mexico, however, or more specifically 'Andean' groups are covered in those discographies.

Chile

Compilations

Music of the Andes (EMI Hemisphere, UK).

Despite the title, this is essentially a nueva canción disc, with key Chilean groups Inti Illimani, Quilapayun and Illapu to the fore. There is also an instrumental recording of "Tinku" attributed to Victor Jara.

Artists

Illapu

Illapu, with a track record stretching back over twenty-five years, and a big following in Chile, play Andean instruments – panpipes, quenas and charangos – along with saxophones, electric bass and Caribbean percussion. Their music is rooted in the north of the country where most of the band hail from.

⊙ **Sereno** (EMI, UK).

This enjoyable collection gives a pretty good idea of what Illapu have got up to over the years and includes strongly folkloric material, as well as dance pieces influenced by salsa, romantic ballads and the earlier styles of vocal harmony.

Inti Illimani

The foremost Chilean new song group who began as students in 1967, bringing the Andean sound to Europe through their thousands of concerts in exile, and taking European influences back home again in the late 1980s. The original band, together for 30 years, featured the glorious-voiced José Séves.

⊙ **Leyenda** (CBS Sony, US).

'Legend' is a pretty fair summary of the Intis' influence – both as title and in the content of this 1990 concert recording, joined by guest guitarists Paco Peña and John Williams.

⊙ **Arriesgaré la piel** (Xenophile, US).

This was the final album from the (more or less) original line-up – a celebration of the music the Intis grew up with, from creole-style tunes to Chilean cuecas.

Víctor Jara

The leading singer-songwriter of his generation, Víctor Jara was murdered in his prime by Pinochet's forces in September 1973. His legacy is an extraordinary song-book, which can be heard in his original versions, as well as a host of Latin and Western covers.

 Manifesto
(Castle, UK).

Re-issued to mark the 25th anniversary of his death, this is a key disc of nueva canción, with "Te recuerdo Amanda", "Canto libre", "La Plegaria a un labrador" and "Ay canto", the final poem written in the Estadio Chile, before his death. Includes Spanish lyrics and English translations.

⊙ **Vientos del Pueblo** (Monitor, US).

A generous 22-song compilation that includes most of the Jara milestones, including "Te recuerdo Amanda" and "Preguntas por Puerto Montt", plus the wonderful revolutionary romp of "A Cochabamba me voy". Quilapayún provide backing on half the album.

⊙ **Víctor Jara Complete** (Pläne, Germany).

This 4-CD box is the definitive Jara, featuring material from eight original LPs. Pläne have also released an excellent single disc selection of highlights.

Violeta Parra

One of South America's most significant folklorists and composers, Violeta Parra collected fragments of folklore from singers, teaching them to the next generation and influencing them with her own superb compositions. Parra's songs have also been superbly recorded by Mercedes Sosa (see Argentina, opposite).

⊙ **Canto a mi America** (Auvidis, France).

An excellent introduction to Parra's semial songs.

⊙ **Las últimas composiciones** (Alerce, Chile).

A re-issue of Parra's 1965 release which turned out to be her last as well as latest songs ('últimas' means both in Spanish).

Quilapayún

This key Chilean new-song group worked closely in their early years with Víctor Jara and in 1973 – the year before the coup – they split into multiple groups in order to get their message across on as many stages as possible. They co-authored, with Sergio Ortega, the street anthem "El Pueblo Unido Jamás Sera Vencido" (the People United Will Never Be Defeated). Although they disbanded in the late '90s, their influence lives on.

⊙ **Santa María de Iquique** (Dom Disque, France).

Chilean composer Luis Advis's groundbreaking Cantata, composed for Quilapayún, tells the emblematic and heroic tale of the murder of unarmed nitrate workers and their families in 1971.

Argentina

Artists

Mercedes Sosa

Sosa's rich voice and broad international choice of songs from Cuba to Brazil, as well as her diverse Argentine repertoire and her profoundly human view of politics, established her as one of the leading and most powerful women singers of Latin America.

 30 Años
(Polygram, Argentina).

There are a lot of indifferent Mercedes compilations around, but this 1993 disc is the business. It includes essential numbers like "Gracias a la Vida", "Todo Cambia", "Maria Va" and a beautiful version of Silvio Rodriguez's "Unicornio", tying her into the nueva canción circuit.

Gracias a la vida (Phillips, Spain).

Sosa's tribute to Chilean Violeta Parra, with inspired arrangements for guitar, piano and drum that employ a range of Argentine regional rhythms.

Atahualpa Yupanqui

The guitar styles of nueva canción would be nothing without this man and his pioneering work – collecting from all over his native land and composing his own potent, focused pieces which inspired the next generation.

30 ans de chansons (Chant du Monde, France).

A fine retrospective released after Yupanqui's death in May 1992, featuring the best of his repertoire, including the classic "Basta ya" ("Enough of the Yankee telling us what to do").

 Magia de Atahualpa Yupanqui (Toshiba, EMI, Japan).

Eight CDs – the definitive set of Atahualpa songs, heard by most nueva canción singers as they grew up. From Argentine rural melodies collected from old singers to his own compositions. Glorious.

Others

Some discs from nueva canción artists from Nicaragua, Costa Rica, Uruguay and Venezuela which have no other home in this book.

Compilations

April in Managua (Varagram, Netherlands).

The line-up for this peace concert, held at a time when the energies of the US military were focused on Nicaragua, is extraordinary: Uruguay's Viglietti, Mexico's Amparo Ochoa and the Gabino Palomares, Cuba's Rodríguez, Brazil's Chico Buarque, Argentina's Mercedes Sosa, as well as Nicaragua's own Luis Enrique and Carlos Mejía Godoy.

Live from El Salvador (Redwood Records, US).

A great concert to help the people of El Salvador, recorded on home territory around 1990. Includes Mexico's Amparo Ochoa, Costa Rica's Adrian Goizueta, Holy Near from the US and Cutumay Camones and others from El Salvador.

Nicaragua Presente!: Music from Nicaragua Libre (Rounder, US).

The 'new song' of the ordinary people of Nicaragua from the early 1990s – tailors and janitors, housewives, soldiers and children. Amazingly rich and varied music from such a small country, from the northeastern Miskito traditions to the marimbas of the Monimbo.

Artists

Luis Enrique & Carlos Mejía Godoy

The leading figures of volcanto in 1980s Nicaragua, the Godoy brothers' music mapped the Sandinista struggle both as troubadours and as performers using country music styles.

Guitarra Armada: Music of the Sandinista Guerillas (Rounder, US).

A historic album, still available on cassette, of songs of armed struggle, notable for advice on how to make Molotov cocktails and assemble an M1 carbine.

Adrian Goizueta y el Grupo Experimental

This Costa Rican group were one of the few to bring a classical edge to the new song genre.

Vienen llegando: New Song from Costa Rica (Aural Tradition Records, Canada).

A new, more classical approach to new song for the early 1990s, with a feeling for its more intellectual edge fused with a Costa Rican poetic sensibitlity.

Emma Junaro

Junaro is a fine contemporary singer who has been called the Bolivian Joan Baez, although this gives no indication of the sonorous, emotional range of her voice.

Canta a Matilde Casazola – mi corazón en la ciudad (Riverboat, UK).

Whether interpreting the poetry of Criollo legend Matilde Casazola, or singing songs about the disappearance of Maria Pilar's husband, Junaro brings fine nuances to arrangements by Uruguayan Fernando Cabrera. Cabrera's own classically influenced creole guitar work is reminiscent of seminal guitarist Atahualpa Yupanqui and its jazz feel and subtle acoustic sounds creates an extraordinary emotional ambience.

Lilia Vera and Pablo Milanés

A sublime partnership: Venezuela's key 'new song' singer and the great Cuban star of nueva trova (see p.408).

Lilia Vera y Pablo Milanés (Areito, Cuba).

Venezuelan singer Vera and Milanés exchange songs with a breathtaking rapport. An enchanting disc filled with love songs and compelling rhythms.

Daniel Viglietti

The Uruguayan singer was one of the key figures in the early years of the new song movement in Latin America. Viglietti, with his characteristic, unadorned, direct voice and strong guitar rarely records these days, so it's worth searching out early albums.

Esdrujúlo (Discomedia, Spain).

Dedicated to his mother, this is vintage Viglietti, with his passionate tones of supressed anger. The album includes a lovely air for solo guitar written around 1960 for Yupanqui.

Colombia

el sonido dorado

Colombia is one of the powerhouses of Latin music, with its highly influential national music, cumbia – one of the great Latin rhythms – and a major role in the salsa world. But its riches don't stop there. Travel around the roads (or cassette racks) of this huge, chaotic nation and you'll find everything from Andean music to a techno-style merengue. **Kim Burton** checks in.

Colombia stretches almost 2000 km north to south and over 1000 km east to west – and encompasses a tropical coast, rolling savannah, icy Andean highlands, and, on the Pacific coast, dense rain forest. In the veins of its people runs the blood of native Indians, Spanish settlers, African slaves and English freebooters. All have left their mark on the tapestry of music that fills the streets, buses, bars and cafés - a tapestry as varied as any on the South American continent.

In the mountainous interior, for instance, you find a mellow Andean style called **bambuco**; along the northwestern Atlantic coast there's accordion-led **vallenato**; and then there's **llanera**, led by harps, on the plains, and the rootsy **champeta** and **currulao** on the Pacific coast. **Cumbia**, meanwhile, has spread from its local origins in the Atlantic regions to acquire a national - and international - presence.

Colombia also has a strong showing of the music often called **'international Latin'**: boleros, senti-mental ballads and Spanish language pop music, of which the most capable and interesting exponent is the sentimental **Charlie Zaa**. And, of course, the country has also produced several highly successful and innovative **salsa** groups, with **Joe Arroyo** an international superstar, rivalled only by Vallenato magician **Carlos Vives**. Meanwhile, as elsewhere in Latin America, **techno–merengue** and **salsa remixes** are currently sweeping the dancefloors.

Roots of Cumbia

If there is one type of music that can stand as 'Colombian' it is the **cumbia** – a typically Latin mixture of solidly grounded and complex layered rhythm with an airily syncopated melody. This has grown from its birthplace on the Atlantic coast to acquire the status of a national music – indeed, the song "La Pollera Colora" is an unofficial national anthem. And although there is one specific cumbia dance with an associated rhythmic template (a drum pattern emphasising the offbeat and a similarly marked rhythm from the shakers or ride cymbal), 'cumbia bands' will play a whole host of dances and songs from the regions – such as *puya*, *paseito* and *porro*.

Traditional **cumbia ensembles** consisted of percussion and vocals only, but they have developed into much larger bands boasting trumpets, trombones and saxophones, electric keyboards and other modern refinements. Conventionally cited as a musical form growing out of the interactions of the Indian population and the African slaves (some say that the dance represents the courtship of an Indian woman by an African man), cumbia's distinctive shuffling steps are reputedly survivals from the days when the black slaves in their barracks would attempt to dance while restrained by their fetters and leg-irons. Some, believing that the African contribution is greatest derive the name

Dancing in the street, cumbia style

Las Cosquillitas*

My love . . .
I would like you to . . .
If you wanted to . . .
If you could . . .
Wow! That's something I like!
But, it's that I . . . I . . . I . . . aaagh!

What do you want darling?
What do you like?
What do you want?

That you kiss me and hug me
That you spoil me
That you please me
Every time I ask!
That whenever I need you
Don't let me down for a moment
If you don't please me
I will die (of emotion)

That you whisper in my ear
Sweet and pretty nonsense
That you squeeze me hard
And kiss my sweet lips
That you kiss me wherever you will
From head to toe
But what I ask the most
Is that you give me cosquillitas

And do you like it here? Yes gently!
And over here? Yes, like that!
And over there too? Yes, that's good!
Carry on, go on, don't stop, it's too good.
Meliyara and her orchestra invite you all to
    dance!

Lucho Campillo, La Sonora Meliyara.
[*las cosquillitas means teasing or foreplay]

The drums and marimbula are African in origin and in the part they play within the ensemble, while the indigenous Indian population contributed the maracas and *guache*, gourds or metal tubes filled with seeds, which drive on the rhythm above the beat of the drums. The European part of Colombia's heritage is heard in the shape of the melodies and the forms of the verses, which often follow the rules of medieval Spanish poetry, while two rather more unusual instruments reflect further

JAK KILBY

Toto la Momposina

Indian. These are a wild-sounding folk clarinet called the **flauto de millo** – a piece of cane with a tongue cut in one end to act as a reed, and four finger holes – and a long flute with a deep and rounded tone, the **gaita**.

Many of these instruments are used by the singer Toto La Momposina and her troupe of percussionists, singers and dancers. This touring group presents cumbia and related music – mapal, puya and merengue – in a partly theatrical display of Colombian roots music. Toto, who performs widely at home and abroad, as well as recording for both US and European companies, is also involved in a project dedicated to preserving, researching and teaching the fast-disappearing old music, which is feeling the pressure from the new, commercially more attractive versions that are taking its place. Those interested in the more traditional version of the dance can see it during carnaval in Barranquilla, where long troupes of cumbiambas wind their way through the streets of the town, the dancers dressed in traditional costume. The more modern version can be seen at any club where Colombians congregate.

cumbia from the Guinean *cumbe* dance, whereas others believe that its origin may be in the *areitos*, funeral ceremonies that are common to several Caribbean tribes.

Some of the Atlantic region's folkloric groups still play a roots cumbia using a **drum choir**. A deep *bombo*, played with sticks, calls the other instruments at the start of the song: the conga-like *tambor macho*, which holds down the basic groove with its strong offbeat, and the *tambor hembra*, which is the lead drum, improvising freely and responding to the inventions of the singer. Sometimes a bass line is provided by the *marimbula*, a large low-pitched thumb-piano.

Cumbia Hits Town

It was in the 1940s that cumbia started to leave the countryside and become a dance of the urban middle and upper classes, where its interpretation changed radically. It was in this period that cumbia's regular **four-square rhythm**, with a distinctive loping beat, likened to riding a horse at a trot, became established.

The first bandleader to begin this process, influenced by North American big-band music and Cuban-American mambo, as well as the local tradition of the *porro* brass bands (see below) was the clarinettist **Lucho Bermudez**, from the town of Carmen de Bolívar. Bermudez's style of cumbia abandoned some of the polyrhythmic complexities of the original cumbia beat for more urbane arrangements. However, the songs stayed close to the old folkloric melodies, albeit smoothed out for the more refined salons and dance-halls of the cities.

La Sonora Dinamita – a mover la colita

Some of the bands that followed stayed closer to the original spirit of the cumbia, more rural in sound, and often featuring clarinet solos influenced by the rough tone and melodic idiosyncrasies of the flauto de millo.

The **Cuban influence**, spread by means of radio broadcasts and recordings, continued to make itself felt and contributed to the sound of what has been dubbed the **'Golden Age' of cumbia**, the 1950s and early 1960s. It was this period that saw the founding of **Discos Fuentes**, the most important of the country's record companies who for a time had a huge share of the mar-

ket and a paramount influence that was unrivalled until the advent (or rather renaissance) of Sonolux records, a company which now releases the work of most of the country's younger idols.

One name umbilically linked with Discos Fuentes is that of Julio Ernesto Estrada, nicknamed **Fruko** and known as the 'Godfather of Salsa' from his involvement in the introduction of that music to the Colombian market in the 1970s. He not only played in many important bands, but oversaw the creation of many of the Discos Fuentes projects; some of these were short-lived, but others have survived for decades with a shifting personnel and fronted by a succession of different singers.

One of the best of the orchestras to appear in the early 1960s was not actually a Discos Fuentes initiative, although that company soon snapped them up. **Peregoyo** (Enrique Urbano) **y su Combo Vacana** played compositions based around the folk music of the Buenaventura area on the Pacific coast, as well as slightly distorted versions of Cuban son, and had great and continuous success until they eventually split up in the mid-70s. Part of their unusual charm came from their use of guitar instead of the more common piano, their mildly out of tune brass section, and their rough and ready sound.

La Sonora Dinamita, also formed in 1960, by composer/singer **Lucho Argain** and the ubiquitous Fruko, also met with immediate success, particularly in Mexico – where cumbia has become an important strand in popular music. They disbanded after a few years but reformed (with a different line-up) in the 1970s. Their unashamedly popular style, mixing cumbia with elements of Central American, Mexican and Caribbean music, and a strong salsa influence, made them huge stars with a long list of hits like "A mover la colita" "Café con ron", "La Bamba"and "Tu Cucu" – the last a Colombian version of Rockin' Sidney's zydeco hit, "My Toot Toot", to which it pays tribute with an occasional blast of New Orleans style horns. The band can be heard on an extensive Fuentes reissue series, numbering at last count 19 CDs.

ALEJANDRO VELASQUEZ/SONOLUX

La India Meliyara

introduction of *montuno* sections and the use of piano *guajeos* (repeated syncopated patterns outlining the harmony) instead of the traditional off-beat chords of earlier times. Both **La Sonora de Baru** and **La Sonora Dinamita** – two of the best modern cumbia bands – make frequent use of this technique. Later on actual salsa rhythms were introduced – Rodolfo's hit tune "La Colegiala" (familiar to many in Europe from its use in coffee commercials) changes rhythm from cumbia to salsa for its chorus, a commonly used device.

Cumbia remains a lively and developing style of music, and every year sees a new star appear – sometimes to fade as rapidly – and these days the resources of the contemporary recording studio and the computer are all drawn into the mix. The currently succesful **Ivan y sus Bam Band** represent another twist, with a rock'n'roll image and a slick stage show heavily reliant on a corps of four female dancers, a brass section and a cumbia or tropical feel laid out over a heavy drum machine back beat. The combination, plus a spot of the techno-merengue which threatens to become the lingua franca of of every Latin dance club in the world, has brought them a strong following among young Colombians.

Vallenato

The sweet, hot accordion-led music called **vallenato** takes its name from its origins in Valledupar on the Atlantic coast. Originally a purely regional music, during the 1980s and 1990s it spread throughout the country to acquire the status of a national music second only to cumbia. Although its origins are obscure, it was supposedly invented by the legendary **Francisco el Hombre**, a shadowy figure based on the historical figure of accordionist Francisco Moscote Guerra (see the 'Accordionist from Hell' box, p.377).

Whatever the origin – and the contribution of the Indian population has undoubtedly been paramount – it shades into cumbia. It uses the same rhythms – *paseo*, *puya*, *merengue* (a fast six-eight beat unrelated to the Dominican merengue) – and there has been a great deal of cross-fertilisation between the two genres. However, vallenato has its own specific melodic patterns, sound and favourite songs, and in its classic form uses a single drum and a scraper instead of the complex layers of the drum ensemble. Although the accordion is sometimes thought of as synonomous with vallenato, it is not entirely necessary – and of course, not every appearance of the instrument in Colombian music makes the song a vallenato.

One of the first singers with the 'new' Dinamita was Melida Yara Yanguma, better known as **La India Meliyara**. She now heads her own group, **La Sonora Meliyara**, with which she has had some success in updating cumbia with distinctive new songs. In many of these she put a woman's twist on the typical macho traditions of cumbia – in particular the sexual boasting of the *parrandero*, the party-going man.

Yet another of Discos Fuentes' early 1960s alumni was **Los Corraleros de Majagual**. A big band with a large brass section, percussion and accordion, they forged a middle way between cumbia and vallenato (see below), proving both a successful unit in their own right and a training ground for a string of talented cumbia and vallenato musicians, including **Lisandro Meza**, **Calixto Ochoa**, **Armando Hernandez**, **Alfredo Gutierrez**, and Fruko himself, who joined as *timbalero*. The number of hits Los Corraleros have produced over their thirty years of recording is prodigious. Perhaps the most famous of them all was "Caballo Viejo" (Old Horse), composed by their Venezuelan guitarist **Simon Diaz** in the 1960s. A decade on it was given the Cuban charanga treatment by Roberto Torres, which was in turn revamped by France's Gipsy Kings into **"Bamboleo"** – one of the biggest hits of the 1980s.

From the 1970s on, a new influence hit big band cumbia in the form of **salsa**, most obviously in the

The **accordion** appeared in Colombia's coastal regions at the end of the last century (one story, seemingly apocryphal alas, is that a shipment was washed ashore from the wreck of a German freighter), and had firmly established itself on the region's music by the 1920s, taking over in songs that previously used simple percussion and a pair of gaita or *carrizo* flutes. Something approaching this original sound can be heard from younger revivalist groups such as **Patakore**, although they are careful not to call their music vallenato.

In its simplest form a **vallenato conjunto** needs only three musicians. The accordionist (normally playing a three-row button model) is usually the singer and bandleader, while the other essential instruments are the **guacharaca scraper** and the caja vallenata (vallenato box). This last is a small, fairly high-pitched single-headed drum, originally covered with goatskin, although X-ray film, more reliable in the heat and humidity, is more common today. The three instruments, with their origins in the three continents of Europe, Africa and America, conveniently suggest the confluence of idioms that make up the vallenato whole; the Iberian, the black African and the native Indian.

There are plenty of classic vallenato trios today, and it was with such a conjunto that the great **Alejo Duran**, 'El Rey Negro del Vallenato', started his lengthy career, first as a caja player, but soon moving to the accordion. Although he spent most of his life working as a cowboy, and only began his recording career in 1950, he was crowned 'Rey Vallenato' at the first *Fiesta de Vallenato*, held in Valledupar in 1968. (This event, part festival and part competition, is held in the city in April or May each year, and is one of the best opportunities to hear the current stars of the music).

As well as being a fine accordionist and singer, Duran also wrote and recorded a collection of songs that became instant classics. He died in 1989 at the age of 71, having played the accordion for over sixty of those years.

Most of the contemporary vallenato bands such as those of **Lisandro Meza** or the brilliant virtuoso **Alfredo Gutierrez** (a highly entertaining musician whose party trick is to play the accordion with his toes) add an electric bass, and maybe extra percussion in the shape of conga and cowbell, to the original trio, while the use of a brass section is not unknown.

Vallenato accordions are German-made but are specially adjusted before export to provide the warm yet penetratingly reedy sound that Colombian performers favour. It's in the tuneful energy of the music and the virtuosity of the performers that the appeal of vallenato lies. In this, the outstanding feature is the role of the accordion, play-

POLAR MUSIC INT.

Singer and soap star Carlos Vives

ing virtuoso introductions and interludes, making sly comment between the lines of the verses, improvising melodic solos and pumping out vigorous riffs to heighten the excitement. Idiosyncratic bass lines notch up the tension still further. The whole gains much of its appeal from the interplay of African-derived rhythms with sweet, wide-ranging melody.

Energetically syncopated, tumbling bass is one of the great glories of modern vallenato. It is said to have been introduced in the mid-1960s by the bass player **Caliya** in his work with **Los Corraleros de Majagual**. Rhythmically, it is far freer than the functional, rather four-square bass parts of the cumbia bands and earlier vallenato, and occasionally sounds as if it's on the verge of entirely uprooting the music altogether.

Vallenato lyrics are rarely of much interest, dealing with love in usual sentimental fashion (torment and false promises), sometimes throwing in a line in praise of a wealthy man in the hope of some financial return. In earlier times the songs would sometimes reflect more everyday life, and these days the writers occasionally approach serious subjects. There is actually a sub genre, *vallenato-protesta*, though this hasn't gained much of a hold with popular audiences.

Among the best vallenato musicians working today in the traditional mould or close to it are **Lisandro Meza** and **Alfredo Gutierrez**, **Diomedes Díaz and Nicolas 'Colacho' Men-doza** (who sometimes work as a duo, El Binmio de Oro), and **Calixto Ochoa**.

Vallenato also has a US-based stepchild in the form of the **charanga vallenata**, invented by Cuban exile **Roberto Torres**. His innovation was to add to the vallenato accordion a charanga-style ensemble of flute, violins and percussion. The result was a totally fresh and highly successful approach to vallenato classics, which has, so far, filled three albums. Others followed his lead, notably New York Cuban **Jorge Cabrera**, who added slick brass arrangements. Although it's never really taken root in Colombia itself, charanga vallenata is now a distinct strand in the web of Latin music.

However, the most momentous change in vallenato came in 1993, with the release of the **Carlos Vives** album, *Clasicos de la Provincia*. This was nothing short of a sea-change for the music. Vives is a star of soap operas (Latin America's wildly popular tele-novelas), as well as a singer and guitarist, and he had earlier played the role of vallenato's most distinguished composer **Rafael Escalona** in a TV series, leading to the release of a couple of albums of vallenato tunes, But it was *Clasicos de la Provincia* that made him a superstar. Its modern

The Accordionist from Hell

Once upon a time Francisco el Hombre was travelling through Alta Guajira when strange news met his ears. Some villagers came to tell him that an extraordinary new accordionist had arrived in the area, a musician so fine that he outclassed even Francisco himself! Intrigued and perhaps a little worried by the news, Francisco set off to find the stranger.

One day, mounted on his faithful burro, he found himself in a barren and lonely region. Suddenly he heard, far off in the distance, the sound of an accordion – but somehow he could not tell what direction the music was coming from. The music grew louder and louder until it seemed to fill the air around him and in the midst of his astonishment he saw an elegantly dressed man mounted on a black horse, who seemed to have sprung from nowhere. "I am your rival", said the horseman, and he began to play all the dances of vallenato with such skill and finesse that Francisco was left open-mouthed with awe.

Then, of course, he suddenly realised that such perfection could not be attained by a creature of this world and that the horseman must be a creature of the other world – none other than the Devil himself! Muttering a prayer to himself, he strapped on his own accordion and, taking advantage of a moment's silence as the stranger ended one of his tunes, began to play the melody of the Creed – in reverse. As the first notes filled the air, the stranger was seized with panic and disappeared, leaving behind a huge cloud of smoke and the reek of sulphur.

Francisco's victory over the Devil, soon known throughout the villages of la Guajira, is still talked of even today, and confirmed for all time the fame of the greatest accordionist who ever lived, the only man to outplay the Prince of Hell – Francisco el Hombre.

Colombian *salsero* Joe Arroyo with adoring fans

production techniques, precise arrangements and a talented band – **La Provincia** – coupled with Vives's fine voice and charismatic stage presence turned vallenato into a modern pop music.

Vives displays an immaculate flair for combining traditional elements – accordion, gaitas, caja – with rock – pumping basslines, driving drums and guitar – that manages to avoid coarsening the original sense of the songs. *Clasicos* perhaps leant a little too heavily on the rock side of things for some, but his two following releases *Tierra del Olvido* and *Tengo Fe* have put greater trust in the original feel, and at the same time become more adventurous in mixing non-Colombian elements into the music. The latter is a departure, in that it includes examples of Vives's original song writing.

Following in the footsteps of Vives (or with hopes of doing so), there has been a troupe of younger muscians and singers. Among the more successful was the teenage **Adriana Lucia**, who with her 14-year-old accordionist Gustavo Babilonia Jr forged a smooth and sweet poppy sound. Equally pleasant, and again without much depth, is the singer **Tulio**, another actor who has moved into music.

Vives's own backing group have also been forging a path of their own, going under the name **Bloque**, blending cumbia, guajiras and champeta with rap and rock. They have recently signed a contract with David Byrne's Luaka Bop album.

Salsa

The development of Cuban music into **salsa**, a rhythm forged in the barrios of Puerto Rico and New York, has been an important thread in Colombian music over the last three decades. Although the influence of Cuban son and mambo, spread by radio and recordings and by the physical presence of Cuban musicians and bandleaders was present well before that, and is clearly heard in the *descargas*, *sones* and rumbas of bands like Peregoyo y su Combo Vacana, the wholesale imitation of a foreign model did not really occur until salsa had attained its own fully-fledged and individual style.

The earliest Colombian attempt at salsa was predictably a Discos Fuentes initiative and, equally predictable, spearheaded by Fruko, who put together the country's first salsa band after a visit to New York in 1970. Although the strongest influences on **Fruko y sus Tesos** were the contemporary New York and Puerto Rican bands, the sound and spirit of Fruko's Colombian band was recognisably different. Like many of the earlier examples of Colombian salsa, their songs were often dark-hued, with a fondness for predominantly minor keys, and low voicings in the brass section. A strain of melancholy runs through much Colombian music and even Fruko's greatest salsa hit, "El Preso" (The Prisoner) reflects this: "For me there is no sky, or moon or stars, for me the sun does not shine... Ay, ay ay, how dark my fate is... I have lost all hope...". Gloomy, in its way, though the swing, as ever, is relentless.

Fruko was also involved in a group called **The Latin Brothers**, who had a string of hits in the mid-1970s. Like most of the Discos Fuentes projects there was something faintly old-fashioned about their trombone-led sound, but over the decades they have acted as a school for some of the greatest of Colombia's salsa and tropical musicians, both instrumentalists and singers. Among their number was **Joe Arroyo**, the biggest Colombian figure in salsa, and inventor of the purely Colombian phenomenon called **musica tropical**, a salsa based music that incorporates the native rhythms of the coast.

A masterful singer who merges cumbia, salsa, merengue, compas, soca and other Caribbean musics seamlessly into his 'Joe-son' mix, Joe Arroyo's early life followed the well-trodden path of many Colombian singers; he started singing professionally at the age of eight, and by seventeen had joined Fruko y sus Tesos. After a period with the Latin Brothers, he formed his own group **La Verdad** in 1981. His effective mixture of Colombian and general Caribbean rhythms presented in an exhilarating and colourful stage show has brought him to the forefront of those Latin musicians whose appeal is not limited to one country, but stretches across the continent and beyond.

Colombia also has a more straightforward salsa style, closer to the Nuyorican and Puerto Rican

Discos Fuentes

The **Discos Fuentes** label, originally based in Cartagena but now in the industrial centre of Medellín, has been central to the development of the music industry in Colombia.

The company was started by electrical engineer Don Antonio Fuentes in 1934, after he'd set up Cartagena's first radio station and found a lack of local music to programme. The earliest recordings were financed by the Tropical Oil Company, whose jingles featured on the records. For the first decade the discs were pressed in North America, an expensive and time-consuming operation, but in 1945 Fuentes built his own pressing and production plant in Colombia.

After that, Fuentes did everything in-house – the recording, the pressing, cassette manufacturing, printing and distribution. This has given them a distinct identity, style and sound. They are the oldest and still the biggest label in Colombia, with a catalogue of over 1800 titles covering the whole history of Colombian music. They have also bought up some smaller independent labels like Tropical and Folklor, thereby adding to their comprehensive list. They work their back catalogue hard and consider it the backbone of the company, releasing and re-releasing various compilations and combinations all the time. Over the last ten or so years a series of agreements with various foreign record companies has made their products much more easily available outside Colombia.

One of the leading lights of the Fuentes stable is the ubiquitous Fruko, who came to work at Discos Fuentes when aged twelve. While serving his apprenticeship in the Fuentes studios he played timbales with Los Corraleros de Majagual and formed his own band, Fruko y sus Tesos, who are still in the top league of Colombian salsa. He is now Fuentes' leading arranger and producer, handling his own band, the salsa Latin Brothers, and cumbia's La Sonora Dinamita. Another important arranger is the somewhat younger Alberto Barros, who leads and plays trombone in modern salsa group Los Titanes.

But the importance of the founder, Don Antonio Fuentes, cannot be overstated. He has been directly involved in the formation of all the major groups on the label and deeply involved in the creation of cumbia as we know it today. Fuentes' patriarchal style, and that of his company director Isaac Villanueva, has created an empire that truly represents all facets of Colombian music.

bands. The leading band of this type is probably Cali's **Grupo Niche**, led by arranger and producer **Jairo Varela**, whose sophisticated and inventive arrangements have brought them international success. **Grupo Galé**, **Orquesta Guayacan** and **La Misma Gente** are other significant bands in this field. Their polished, high-octane sound contrasts with the down-home feeling of their predecessors, and for the most part they eschew local rhythms and colours for a more mainstream approach; but their patriotism is not in doubt, as Niche's smash hit homage to their home town, "Cali Pachanguero", goes to show. More recently formed are **Alkimia**, who although sharing the slick arrangements and tight ensemble playing of the purer salsa bands, are more eclectic in their approach to rhythms, and verge on the 'tropical' movement. They also have an interest in the revival and re-arrangement of older tunes. Another eclectic group is **Los Titanes** (formed 1982), whose strongly grounded salsa style is leavened by influences as diverse as vallenato, flamenco and recently, rap, while **Los Nemus del Pacifico** although generally slavishly following the small band conjunto style, also draw on the black music of the Pacific coast on occasion.

Country Sounds

Representatives of a lively rural tradition – and one which has contributed a great deal to the cumbia sound – are the **porros**, village fiesta bands from the provinces of Savanna de Bolivar, Cordoba and Sucre. Porro is the name both of the bands and of the rhythm they most often play, although most will throw in other local dances. Their chief characteristic is a wild enthusiasm and festive spirit, perhaps best summed up by an apocryphal tale of an orchestra hired by a well-to-do young man to serenade his girlfriend. The lover suggested a fee of fifty pesos and two bottles of rum to be shared by the band members while they were playing. After a huddled discussion the leaders returned with a counter-proposition: the band would prefer two pesos and fifty bottles of rum . . .

Porros are normally brass bands with a clarinet lead, saxophone, trumpet, tuba (or sousaphone), a euphonium-like bombardino, and a three-man rhythm section of bass drum, snare drum and a pair of cymbals. Such a line-up derives from the European-style military bands that were introduced early into Latin America and whose descendants are also found in Guatemala and Mexico (where they're known as *bandas*).

Most porros have only a local reputation, although a few with greater ambitions have achieved wider renown, and recorded for the larger companies. One such is the **Banda de 11 Enero**, typical in its homegrown arrangements of favourite tunes and rickety goodtime feel. The record companies tend to favour groups closer in sound to the regular cumbia big bands, like **Pedro Laza y sus Pelayeros** and the **Orquesta Climaco Sarmiento** (led by a one time clarinet player with Lucho Bermudez). These retain the typical orchestration, with plenty of brass, collective improvisation (or arrangements that approximate it) and squealing close harmony clarinets, but they are still infinitely smoother than the rural versions. **La Sonora Cienaguera** (as heard on World Circuit's collection *Cumbia Cumbia 2*) has the correct headlong feeling, but still sound as though they have tucked their shirts into their underpants compared to the no holds barred racket of a village band in full cry. There is an annual **festival of Porros bands** in the village of San Pelayo, near Montera.

Plain Tales from the Plains

Both vallenato and cumbia come from the coastal area of the country, on the Caribbean shore. **Los Llanos**, the vast plains of savannah and scrub that stretch across much of Colombia and into Venezuela, with an agricultural economy and a population that prides itself on its skill in breeding and training horses, have their own **musica llanera**. This is a music with tremendous drive and swing, rhythmic and bouncy for the most part, yet with a big sentimental streak.

Since both the plains and their music are bounded by physical rather than political geography, nearly everything that can be said about Colombian llanera music is also true of its Venezuelan equivalent. To gringo ears the most unexpected member of the ensemble is the one that leads it - **the harp**. It seems that the instrument was first brought to the continent during the eighteenth century, intended for use in church, although at first sight a harp seems as out of place by an altar as tied to the saddle of a horse. However, it is relatively portable and adaptable, and is actually to be found in one form or another in most of the countries of Latin America. In llanera music, it is supported by a small group from the guitar family: the *cuatro*, the mandolin-like *bandola* and its larger sibling the *bandolin*, and the small *tiple*. Above their pounding cross-rhythms *capachos* (maracas) rattle away, while some of the more countrified bands might include a rather scrappily played violin or an accordion.

As in all Colombian music, there is a rich variety of rhythms, harmonic patterns and traditional melodic shapes, each with its own name and associated dance. Often the word **joropo**, originally describing a dance performed during the celebration of birthdays, baptisms or saints' days, is used as a blanket term for llanera dance music (usually songs), while *coplas*, romances and *tonadas* are sung to be listened to rather than danced to. The words are usually accounts of local life and habits and often speak of the charms and delights of one particular town or province, even those well outside the Llanos themselves.

Although the majority of lyrics are less than inspired, there is one type where verbal skill and wit are highly prized. This is the **contrapunteo**, an improvised verbal duel between two contestants striving to outdo one another in their treatment of a prearranged subject. The music and the verse metre, as well as the melody, are fixed by tradition in a form well-adapted to its purpose, as it gives the singer the option of repeating a couplet while awaiting inspiration, and to pause a little for thought during the instrumental interludes. The shape of the melody itself assists the singer: beginning with a sustained high note, it descends

TODO EL SABOR DEL LLANO

en la voz de

LUIS ARIEL REY

via a short intonation on one note, leading to a sudden low swoop at the end, helping him (rarely her) excite laughter and applause with a telling final phrase. There is a tremendous number of musicians who play such music, mostly little known outside their own area.

One of the earliest Colombian llanera singers to record was the late **Luis Ariel Rey**, who remains one of the music's towering figures. Although his first recordings in 1950 were without harp, using a small group of string instruments, by the end of the decade he had formed a group whose line up set the model mostly followed today. Other names to watch out for on disc are harpist **Carlos Rojas** (also a well-known composer), singer and cuatro player **Orlando Valdemarra**, and the conjuntos **Sabor Llanero** and **Alma Llanera**, as well as the all star group **Cimarron**, a collection of virtusosi which has toured abroad. The harpist **Alfredo Ronaldo Ortiz** also deserves a mention: Cuban born and raised in Venezuela and Colombia where he studied medicine, he is a concert recitalist rather than a roots player, but he includes llanero among other Colombian and South American styles in his concerts and recordings.

The Heart of the Country

The Colombian Andes still hold a large Indian population, and the music of the area, usually referred to by Colombians as **musica de la interior**, shares some characteristics with the better-known Andean music of Peru and Bolivia.

Generally, though, it is gentler and mellower in sound, with a harmonic content more typical of the rest of Colombia, and attention given to melodic rather than rhythmic complexity – although the frequent simultaneous use of 6/8 and 3/4 times can disconcert the unwary.

The typical Andean group is a trio of tiple bandola and guitar, although harp, violin and clarinet also make appearances. The movement of the bass lines, played by the guitarist on the lower strings of the instrument, is far freer than in any of the tropical musics and is given to bursting into delightfully complicated runs and arpeggios that complement the melancholy movement of the melodies and dances.

The best known of these dance melodies is **bambuco**, a term that is often used in place of *musica del interior*. Although the question of its origin is unsettled, it is most popular in the cafetera region of the central cordillera, and appears to flow mainly from native and Spanish roots. At the turn of the century it was though of as the 'national' music par excellence, and by the middle of the 1920s bambucos and pasillos made up a large proportion of the discs being produced. In the late 1930s that bambuco ceded its place to cumbia, and these days it is more a music for listening than dancing.

The **Morales Pino Trio** are the finest representatives of bambuco at a very traditional level, led through its tricky melodies by Oriol Rangel. The popular **Estudiantina** is a larger band that is more contemporary in its approach. They feature the organist **Jaime Llano González**, whose smooth salon approach is reminiscent of that of **Alfredo Ronaldo Ortiz**, with whom he has collaborated on record.

As with several other areas of Colombian music the last ten years have seen an increase in the number of younger groups dedicated to performing the music, linked with a sense of their local and national identity and pride, while in Bogota the Academy named after the distinguished composer of *musica del interior*, **Francisco Cristancho**, is devoted to preserving this and other forms of *musica popular*.

Black Colombian Music

The vast majority of Colombian musical styles reflect the nation's intermingling of peoples and cultures. In cumbia or vallenato, for example, Indian, African and European elements have met and interacted to form an entirely new, purely Colombian music from which the separate strands can no longer be disentangled; whereas in llanera music the African influence is mimimal compared to the European and Indian contribution. Yet there are

some styles which exhibit an almost pure **African ancestry**.

On the **Pacific coast**, in the area known as El Choco, where there is a large black population, African music survives in something close to its original form, with instrumental groups containing drums, marimbas and shakers. The vast majority of this music is connected in one way or another with the syncretic rites and rituals fusing African spirit cults with Catholicism that are found throughout the New World.

A group of musicians and singers performing a *currulao* from this area sounds quite astonishingly West African. The loping beat of the drums, the interlocking patterns of the marimbas and complex layering of vocals: all could as easily be traditional music from Mali, the country from which the majority of slaves on the Pacific coast were brought. In the area's secular or semi-religious music, sung at fiestas and other holiday gatherings, the Spanish tinge is stronger, and traces of Iberian folk melody peep out now and again. The area has also, oddly, preserved several elements of European dance in the shape of the mazurka, polka and contradanza. The music has not spread out very widely from its base, even within Colombia, but in the area around Buenaventura a small-scale local recording industry serves the immediate neighbourhood.

The coastal city of **Cartagena** has another specifically black music: **champeta** – an extraordinary grab bag of influences drawn from Caribbean and African popular music. Unlike the tropical style represented by Joe Arroyo (who is himself from Cartagena), it pays less attention to the indigenous Latin sound, but draws chiefly on central African soukous, along with Haitian compas and Jamaican ragga. Inclined to the repetitive/hypnotic, the music grew under the influence of African bands visiting the country, and African records played in the streets by the sound systems known as *picos*. Taking their name from the English word 'pick-up', these resemble outdoor discos on wheels, providing music for street parties and celebrations. At present the bands and singers are in a rather immature stage, rather like the earliest attempts at Colombian salsa, but of the more strongly soukous influenced bands and singers **Boogaloo**, **El Pupy** (Miguel Herrera) and **Luis Towers** are worth checking out, while lovers of raggamuffin style reggae will probably take to **Elio Boom**.

Lastly, away from the mainland, the island of **Providence** has a mainly black population descended from plantation workers who were brought from the British Caribbean islands. They retain customs and food from home and sing and play a kind of music with a strong resemblance to traditional Jamaican mento.

Thanks to Sandra Alayon-Stanton.

discography

General compilations

 Afro-Hispanic Music from Colombia and Ecuador (Smithsonian Folkways, US).

This is a very well-chosen introduction to the African sounds of El Choco on the Pacific coast.

 La Ceiba (Aspic, France).

An excellent collection of the more traditional side of Colombia's music, this includes examples of cumbia, vallenato, llanera, bambuco, the music of the Pacific coast and the wild sounding calls of cattle herders.

 Colombia y su musica – Vol 2 (Philips, Colombia).

This five-CD, 100-track box set features older recordings of many traditional Colombian songs and showcases some of the lesser known regional styles such as bambuco from the Andean regions, music llanera from Los Llanos & mapale from the coast.

 Musique Tropique (Sonodisc, France).

A perfect introduction to more contemporary Colombian sounds, Musique Tropique takes in popular-oriented cumbia, vallenato and porro from such leading groups and artists as Los Corraleros de Majagual, La Sonora Dinamita, and Lisandro Meza.

Salsa and Tropical

Compilations

 Salsa Colombiana (World Network, Germany).

This extensive collection of salsa (and some tropical) tracks features dancefloor favourites alongside less well known but still electrifying cuts, with tracks from Joe Arroyo, Los Nemus del Pacifico, Fruko and others.

 El Vacile Efectivo de la Champeta Criolla (Palenque Records, France).

Champeta, the deeply African music of Cartagena, is still the little known stepchild of Colombian music in global terms. This selection of some of its best exponents should turn you on (or off) forever. Powerful local pop music, it is raucous, rocking and has attitude a-plenty.

Artists

Joe Arroyo

A genuine master with a rich voice and an ecletic approach, Joe Arroyo is one of the few bona fide international superstars that Colombia has produced.

 La Noche (World Music Network, UK).

There are a number of compilations of Joe Arroyo's hits on local and international labels alike. Frankly, the quality of his work is such that any of them would be a safe bet, but this collection of tracks that have filled dancefloors from Baranquilla to Bournemouth has to be awarded the palm.

Grupo Niche

Grupo Niche have been responsible for some of the most striking examples of modern, high octane Colombian salsa, and unlike some of their predecessors, have met with notable success in the United States and further afield. They have dozens of cassettes and CDs available, with variable line-ups, so pick with some care: they range from wonderful to pretty average.

 Grandes Hits (Globo, Colombia).

Great hits indeed, in a NY/PR style, but with just enough of a flavour of Colombia's folklore to make them special.

Fruko y sus Tesos

Julio Estrada, aka 'Fruko', is undoubtedly the most important figure in the story of Colombian salsa - founder of countless bands, indefatigable talent scout and forceful entrepreneur.

 Todos Bailan Salsa (World Music Network, UK).

The range of Fruko's talents is displayed on this fine selection of favourites. There's no escaping the fact that many of the tracks sound a little old fashioned, but then, they are quite old – and much of the music was itself often based on models that had been around for a time.

Grupo Galé

Led by percussionist and composer Digo Galé, this is perhaps the most exciting and hard-driving of the bands following Grupo Niche's Nuyorican path.

 Greatest Hits (Codiscos, Colombia).

Since the band shows few signs of letting up, perhaps 'Greatest Hits So Far' would be a better title, but hits they are indeed, and very fiery ones too.

The McClean Brothers Rhythm

The McLean brothers are from the island of Providencia, whose population are decended from the British Caribbean, and whose music reflects that history.

 Calipsos y Mentos en La Isla de Providencia (McLean Brothers Rhythm, Colombia).

In this recording Orlando & Hernando McLean perform samples of a tradition that owes much to the early sounds of Jamaica.

Cumbia, Vallenato and Llanera

Compilations

 Cumbia Cumbia and **Cumbia Cumbia 2** (World Circuit, UK).

This splendid pair of selections of hits from the Discos Fuentes stable contain in *Volume 1* the cumbia that everyone knows, "La Colegiala", and several more that everyone ought to know. *Volume 2* is more adventurous, focusing on the hits of the 1960s, and is possibly more rewarding.

 cumbias de oro de Colombia

 Fiesta Vallenata (GlobeStyle, UK).

A great compilation of the more local-sounding vallenata bands. Listen to the typically wild bass on Julio de la Ossa's 'Puno Molio', and marvel.

The Rough Guide to Cumbia (World Music Network, UK).

A beginners' guide to Colombia's infectious national rhythm featuring Cumbias from the 1940s to today. Includes the classics "Yo me llamo Cumbia" (Leonor Gonzalez Mina), "La Polera Colora" (Los Black Stars) and "La Piragua" (Wilson Choperena).

Artists

El Binómio de Oro

The Binómio de Oro, who have just celebrated their twentieth anniversary, are one of Colombia's favourite vallenato combinations, strangely under-appreciated abroad.

 A su gusto (Codiscos, Colombia).

This perfect example of the reason why people listen to vallenato, with its combination of pumping accordion, throbbing bass and passionately sentimental vocals, could surely convert the hardest heart.

Bloque

Bloque are the backing musicians behind Colombian superstar Carlos Vives but they are making waves of their own with a mix of rock and rap and Colombian rhythms.

 Bloque (Luaka Bop, US).

A hugely promising debut release, underpinned by some of the tightest Latin percussion you could hope to hear. That sets it all in good stead as the Colombian roots music flows into shouting rock guitar solos and snarling raps.

Los Corraleros de Majagual

Los Corraleros were one of the country's most important cumbia/vallenato bands, with an important role in the development of vallenato into a nationwide popular music.

 14 Exitos (Discos Fuentes, Colombia).

A small selection of their many hits, showing just how they achieved their prominence.

Diomedes Díaz & Nicolas Mendoza

Vocalist Diomedes Díaz and accordionist Nicolas 'Colacho' Mendoza both had highly succesful solo careers, but their collaboration is world-beating.

¡Cantando! (GlobeStyle, UK).

This is one of the great vallenato records. Sweeter and fuller-sounding than is usual, it places the emphasis on limpid melodies and rich harmonies above the jogging vallenato rhythm section. All in all, a sublime introduction.

Alfredo Gutierrez

Alfredo Gutierrez began his career thirty years ago with Los Corraleros, and is one of the great instrumental virtuosos of vallenato.

 El Palito (Tumi, UK).

This mix of cumbia and merengue gives a good introduction to the style of this veteran accordionist.

Pedro Laza y sus Pelayeros

Pedro Laza represents a cleaned-up version of porro, but his extensive track record requires attention.

 Porros Vols 1 & 2 (Discos Fuentes, Colombia).

This is a far more polished sound than most of the village-based porro outfits, but hot and danceable stuff from an old master nonetheless.

Lisandro Meza

Accordionist and singer Lisandro Meza combines a unique sound and powerful gifts as both composer and performer. Justly, he's a major star.

 Cumbias Colombianas (Tumi, UK).

This is a fine selction from the many hits that made Lisandro Meza one of the reigning stars of vallenato. When this compilation was released by a Latin American label, it turned out to be his biggest selling album.

Alfredo Rolando Ortiz

Ortiz leads a classic *llanera* – plains' country music – band with traditional repertoire and line-up (harp, cuatro and maracas).

 Clasicas de la Cancion Llanera (Codiscos, Colombia).

A beautifully recorded, all-instrumental collection of many of the best known llanera songs, including the great "Ay Si Si" by Luís Ariel Rey.

Peregoyo y su Combo Vacana

Founded in the early 1960s, introducing electric guitar and bass to the traditional sounds of Buenaventura, the Combo Vacana was a training ground for many later succesful musicians and a huge influence on bandleaders and party-goers alike.

◎ **Tropicalismo** (World Circuit, UK).

These recordings from the mid-1970s are rough but rocking, and show a side of Colombian musical taste that has more recently been overtaken by the more glossy US influenced salsa dura.

La Sonora Dinamita

La Sonora Dinamita – The Dynamite Combo – are one of Colombia's most successful dance bands. Originally formed in the early 1960s, they reformed in the 1970s after a fourteen-year lay off, and have had an incalculable influence on the development of Colombian salsa.

◎ **A mover la colita** (World Music Network, UK).

There are plenty of dancefloor favourites to be found here, from "A mover la colita" (Move Your Bum) to "Yo la vi", and if the sometimes dark flavour of Colombian music is to your taste, you should find this indispensable – providing you can brave the seemingly endless procession of double entendres and sexual bravado in the lyrics.

Toto La Momposina

The first lady of Cumbia, now dividing her time between the UK and Colombia, is active in the preservation of the traditional music of her area, as well as pushing forward in new directions with the incorporation of Cuban and popular African styles in her music.

⦿ **Pacanto**
(Nuevos Medios, Spain; MTM, Colombia).

Her latest, and by far her best disc to date, this excellent collection of traditional and original songs covers the cumbia spectrum and beyond, with tracks for drum and voices only interspersed with others featuring a red hot horn section (with some great trombone solos) and joyous Congolese guitar.

Carlos Vives

One-time soap star Carlos Vives, with his confiding vocal style and an electrifying stage presence backed up by an amazingly tight band, redefined the vallenato style for the nineties, and looks set fair to command the beginning of the new millennium as well.

◎ **Tierra de Olvido** (Sonolux, Colombia).

Arguments over which album so far shows Vives at his best are still raging, but this showcase for his transformations of the tradition is one of the main contenders, with fabulous accordion riding above complex percussion grooves, avoiding the excessive sentimentality that sometimes threatens to undermine the emotional impact of the music.

Alfonso 'Poncho' Zuleta

Alfonso Zuleta is a member of one of the most important vallenato dynasties. Together with his brother Emiliano, he leads Los Hermanos Zuletas, who gained official favour recently when invited to play at the presidential birthday party.

◎ **Grandes Exitos** (CBS, Colombia).

One of the very best recordings of vallenato music. Among the hits included is the top-selling "Mi Hermano Y Yo" (Me and My Brother).

Cuba

Son and Afro-Cuban music

¡que rico bailo yo! how well I dance

Cuba is beyond question the most important source of music in Latin America. Its root rhythms – rumba and *son* – created the pan-Latin music of salsa, and in their older forms they continue to provide abundant riches, recognised (again) at last in the global success of the Buena Vista Social Club projects. But Cuban musical success and influence is by no means new. Its *danzón* groups helped to shape jazz in the early decades of the twentieth century and continued at the forefront of the music through to the 1950s, unleashing mambo and chachachá crazes throughout Europe and the US, and providing the template for much modern African music, in particular Congolese soukous. And while the West backed off from post-revolutionary Cuba – with the US enforcing its ongoing 40-year blockade, and American jazz (and rock) sidelining 'Latin jazz' dance music – the island continued to evolve its son in various forms, as well as developing an influential nueva trova style of political song (covered in a separate article on p.408). **Jan Fairley** explores the roots and riches.

ué rico bailo yo!" – "How well I dance!" is the title of a classic song by Orquesta Ritmo Oriental that epitomises the confidence and spirit of Cuban music. For this is the island that has given the world the habanera, rumba, the mambo, the danzón, the

chachachá – dance music that has travelled all over the New World, the Old World, and gone back to its roots in Africa. And at home it is a music that feels inseparable from Cuba's daily life and history, whether drawing on its African (slave) roots and

rituals, commenting on topical issues, or just creating a celebration of rhythm and sensuality.

The great Cuban folklorist Fernando Ortíz explains the development of the island's music as the interplay between **sugar and tobacco**. Cuba's African slaves were settled on the great sugar estates and created their religious and secular music from root African traditions. The Spanish, particularly Canary Island *guajiros* – farmers who settled small land holdings – grew tobacco, and they brought with them the tradition of **décima** improved verse (ten-line verses, with a rhyming scheme established by the first line), and couple dancing. Most popular music forms – and not only in Cuba – have developed from the fusion of these two cultures.

African Roots

The Spanish imported African slaves to Cuba from 1522 until the 1880s – long after the trade was illegal elsewhere. There are Cubans alive today whose *grandparents* were slaves, and all the older people in the rural areas can recall the feudal plantations that endured right up to the 1950s. Little surprise, then, that Cuban music has deep and evident roots in **African ritual and rhythm**, which fused with songs and dances brought by the Spanish colonists and European settlers. By contrast, there is almost no detectable influence from the pre-Hispanic tribes, beyond the use of maracas (shakers); Cuba's Indian culture was effectively obliterated by Spanish colonisation.

Cuba's slaves, by the 1840s, constituted nearly half of the population. They had been brought mostly from the West African coast – Nigeria, Ghana, Togo, Cameroon, Benin and Congo – and asserted their distinct cultural identities through the cult religions of Lucumí, Abakúa, Congo and Arara. Each of these cults developed in Cuba its own music, rhythms and rituals, which were preserved in mutual aid associations called *cabildos*. In Cuba today a fair section of the Black population maintains a faith based on **Santería**, a religion which drew on a spread of cults, and reveres a panoply of African deities or *orishas*, which are paired with Catholic saints.

Santería is expressed publicly in regular **bembé** sessions performed in honour of the various orishas. These are often attended by whole communities in suburban streets. Musically, they involve three congas or bata drums which pattern the rhythms for participants to sing out the calls for the various orishas and their particular dances. Each orisha, identified by its emblematic colour, has specific attributes and a source element. Changó (red and white) is the spirit of war and fire, passion and lust, and is twinned with Santa Barbara. Ochún (gold), the flirtatious goddess of love and rivers, protects children and marriage, and is twinned with the Virgen de la Caridad del Cobre, Cuba's patron saint. Each deity has its own call and response, and each follower of Santería identifies with their own deity and its characteristic **toques** (drum patterns) and chants.

These complex rhythms are at the heartbeat of Cuban popular music, working away beneath the Latin layers. In the mid-twentieth century the batá drums and *chekere* (rattles) of the ceremonies began to crop up in bands, and much of the physical and emotional intensity of Cuban music emanates from the power and participation of the African ritual it has incorporated.

Afro-Cuban Rumba

Forget the glitzy ballroom-dancing image of **rumba**. The genuine article, heard in Cuba itself, is informal and spontaneous – a pure Afro-Cuban music for voices and percussion. Performed in neighbourhood bars or tenement patios, or on street corners, it becomes the collective expression of all who take part.

Rumba has roots in Afro-Cuban religion but it consolidated as a form in the docks of Havana and Matanzas, with workers in their spare moments singing and dancing and playing rhythms on cargo boxes. Its modern repertoire is secular and divides into three main dances: the **guaguancó**, **yambú** and **columbia**. The guaguancó is a couple dance in which a symbolic game of sexual flirtation is initiated; at its climax the man executes a pelvic thrust or *vacunao*, which the woman may, through her own dance, accept or reject. The yambú is also a couple dance, with slower, more stately steps (and no vacunao), popular with older people. In contrast, the columbia is a fast, furious and highly acrobatic solo male dance.

The music of rumba consists of percussion and vocal parts. The typical percussion includes one or two **tumbadores** (low-pitched conga-drums), a high-pitched conga drum called a **quinto** (which is usually the 'lead' drum) and a pair of **palitos** – sticks beaten against the wooden body of one of the drums. The vocal sections involve a leader (solo voice and quinto) and responder (chorus, low congas and palitos). Guaguancó and yambu also include a short defining, vocal introduction called the *diana*.

Both rumba and Cuban son have key rhythms called the **clave** or 'key' – in the sense of a key to a code, to which all other rhythms relate. This is often played by a pair of round wooden sticks (*claves*), which are held in a cupped hand and struck against each other, but the clave may be played by other percussion, or just in the heads of the musicians. Around the clave, interlocking cross rhythms are created by instruments such as the *guagua* (a wooden tube played with sticks), the *maruga* (an iron shaker), and the ubiquitous *cajón* (originally a wooden packing-case). For religious occasions, batá drums might be added.

The basic **pattern of rumba** informs much Afro-Cuban music. A long lyrical vocal melody unfolds above the patterns of the drums, allowing the lead singer to state the main theme. Then on a pre-arranged cue the rhythm tightens up, the chorus joins in, and the **call and response** section begins, allowing the singer to improvise (*inspiraciones*) and express heightened emotions, while the quinto drum trades rhythms with the other percussion. This section, when the band gets going and the dancing starts to heat up, is known as the **montuno**. Fused with the rhythms of son, it created *son montuno* – the basis of salsa.

Rumba texts deal with a wide variety of concerns – sad, humorous or everyday topics – and are generally sung in Spanish, although the columbia often interjects chants from Santería and other Afro-Cuban cults. Rumbas may be improvised through repetition of just a few phrases.

Roots-style rumba can be heard easily enough around the island. Good events and places to check out in **Havana** are the *Sabados de Rumba* (Rumba

LUCY DURAN

Rumba band Los Muñequitos de Matanzas

Saturdays), organised by the Conjunto Folklorico Nacional, and the *Callejon Hamel* (in Centro Habana), which painter Salvador González has set up with the spirited young group **Clave y Guaguancó**. In the town of **Matanzas**, you should visit the local Casa de la Trova where the stunning **Los Muñequitos de Matanzas** (Little Dolls of Matanzas) perform. The group have been going for near on fifty years, their members now embracing three generations.

Danzón, Charanga and the Chachachá

While rumba and son represent the essential Afro-Cuban tradition, **danzón** is the chief musical strain from Cuba's European settlers. Played by *orquesta tipicas*, this sedate and dignified dance evolved from European country dances to become Cuba's own original dance music export, establishing itself notably in Mexico.

The **orquesta tipica** developed as a recreational version of the military marching band, its sound coming from the lead of violins and brass, with a pair of *timpani* (round-bottomed marching drums). Played in the ballrooms of colonial houses, these dances (and the orquestas) were gradually African-ised as they were adoped by African and mulatto domestic servants, and later by urban Cubans, until they took shape as the **habanera**.

Cuban band eader **Miguel Failde** is said to have been responsible for establishing the habanera form

in the late 1880s, when he slowed down the old country danzón, divided it into sections and added a provocative pause and syncopated rhythm. The latter came from the *contredanse* brought in the 1800s by the French who had fled to the Santiago area from the nearby island of Saint Domingue (Haiti/Dominican Republic) after a slave uprising. Listen carefully to danzón, and you'll hear, too, that insistent, Afro-Cuban percussion rhythm, just to remind you where you are.

Other danzón pioneers, who developed the music at a similar time and along a similar course to New Orleans jazz, include **Antonio María Romeu**, **José Urfe** and **Enrique Jorrín**, all of whom were active in Havana in the early decades of the twentieth century. Later, in the 1930s, a key contribution was made by the orchestra of **Arcano y sus Maravillos** who incorporated congas and introduced a final *montuno* section (as in son), thus paving the way for danzón and son to cross fertilise. This new style caught on like wildfire.

In the early twentieth century, the danzón orchestras had also created an offshoot known as **charanga** or *charanga francesa* in which ensembles replaced brass instruments with violins, flute, double bass and piano. The 'francesa' tag had a double source: the absorption of the classic French trio of flute, piano and violin; and the music's popularity with the *francesas*, the madames who ran the high-class brothels in turn-of-the-century Havana. The charanga ensembles thrived for decades, adopting many Cuban musics into their repertoire, especially in their glory years between the 1930s and 1950s. Great charangas of this age included **Orquesta Aragón**, **Orquesta Riverside** and **Orquesta America**.

Orquesta America, founded by the violinist Enrique Jorrín, are acknowledged as the creators of **chachachá**, the most popular ever Cuban dance, which swept across Europe and America in the 1950s. Jorrin apparently composed the first chachachá, "La Engañadora", after watching Americans struggle with the complex Cuban dance rhythms. In New York, chachachá, with its straightforward 1-2-3 footwork, was popularised by top Cuban-led big bands such as those of **Machito**, **Perez Prado**, **Tito Puente** and **Tito Rodríguez**, until it was pre-empted by the mambo, a development that came more from the tradition of son conjuntos (see below).

In Havana, several of the leading charangas are still going, half a century after their creation, often with musicians who played with the founders. The most notable is Orquesta Aragon, who have flourished for years under the guidance of virtuoso flautist **Ricard Egües**. Among younger generation charangas, **Candido Fabré y su Banda** and **Charanga Habanera** carry on the music's tradition of adopting and mutating styles, the latter playing the salsa-like style known as **timba**, forged in the late 1990s and drawing on Cuban rumba and American hip hop.

The thread that links these earlier Cuban styles of danzón and charanga to son and salsa is what music writer Peter Manuel has called the 'anticipated bass' – a bass line pattern in which the final note of a bar anticipates the harmony of the following bar. This characteristic evolved from the **habanera**, with its suave, romantic melodies and recurring rhythm, and from its offshoot, the **bolero**. It is this Cuban rhythm pattern that underpins the whole basis of Latin music, from salsa to Colombian *cumbia* to Dominican *merengue*.

The Sound of Son

Son is the predominant musical force in Cuba and is regarded almost as a symbol of the island, unifying its European and black culture. These days it takes many forms, from simple, rustic bands to the brassy arrangements of New York salsa and hard-edged Cuban timba.

However, sones have a common form. Structurally (and lyrically) they comprise two parts: an opening verse or a developing set of verses, followed by a **montuno** section in which the improvising *sonero* (singer) is answered by a chorus who sing the refrain (often one of the verses previously established). It is the voice of the sonero, above all, that audiences respond to. Musically, sones (like rumba) are centred upon a clave rhythm. As bongos, maracas and *guiro* (scraper) improvise rhythmic counterpoints to the clave, the bass plucks the 'anticipated' movement described above, and on top comes a 'Latin' layer of harmonic and melodic elements – notably from the Cuban guitar known as the **tres** (so-called for its triple sets of strings).

As one of the most famous early *soneros*, Miguel Matamoros, told it: "No one knows exactly where son is from. It is from the Oriente countryside, the mountains, but not from any one place. They say it is from Baracoa but anywhere in the mountains there someone would bring a *tres* guitar and right away a song was created. The old *sones* were made of nothing more than two or three words, which when I was young old black men could sing repeatedly for the whole night. Like that son which goes 'Alligator, alligator, alligator, where is the alligator?'"

In the late nineteenth century, **Oriente** province had a very mixed population that included thousands of refugees – black and white – from Haiti's revolutionary wars. As francophone immigrants, they brought new elements to Cuba's African and Spanish mix, lending the extra ingredient to the forging of son, in the 1880s, by black and mulatto musicians. Son reached Havana around 1909, notably through the **Trio Oriental** – who during the following decade created the classic sextet format. Renamed the **Sexteto Habanero**, they featured tres, guitar, bongo, string bass and a pair of vocalists (who also played claves and maracas). It was the sonero voice, above all, which insinuated the son melody into people's hearts.

American companies began recording groups like the Sexteto Habanero and **Sexteto Boloña** as early as 1912 but it was the advent of Cuban radio in 1922 and the regular broadcasting of live bands that consolidated the success of son. In 1920 the singer and bandleader Miguel Matamoros copyrighted a son for the first time – "El Son de La Loma", one of the most popular ever written.

In the late 1920s, with the addition of a trumpet, the *sexteto* became a **septeto** and the son began to swing. One of the most significant septetos, **Septeto Nacional** (another group still going strong) came into being in 1927 under the leadership of the great **Ignacio Piñeiro**. Piñeiro was the composer of the acclaimed and enduring "Echalé salsita" (Throw Some Sauce In It), whose opening theme was adapted by George Gershwin for his Cuban Overture, after he had become a

Sexteto Habanera in the early 1920s

friend of Piñeiro on a trip to Havana. (The song is also a possible origin of the term 'salsa' in Latin music.) During a long career, Piñeiro composed *guajira-son*, *bolero-son* and *guaracha-son*, a fusing of genres typical of Cuban popular music.

Another classic son, "El Manicero" (The Peanut Vendor), emerged in 1928. Written by Moises Simon for **Rita Montaner**, it was a huge hit for her in Paris, breaking Cuban music in Europe for the first time. In 1930 **Don Aspiazu's Havana Orchestra**, with their singer **Antonio Machín**, took the song to New York. Machín sang it to a slow rumba rhythm, with dancers performing choreographed rumbas on stage, and it became the top selling record in the US in 1931 – the first Cuban music to chart in America. Machín subsequently had a long career, mainly in Spain, as a singer of romantic son-boleros.

Two leading instrumentalists and bandleaders furthered the son sound in the mid-years of the century: the blind tres player **Arsenio Rodríguez** and trumpeter **Félix Chappotín**. Rodríguez is considered the father of modern Afro-Cuban sound. His musical roots lay in the Congolese rituals of his

family, instilled in him by his grandfather who was a slave, and it is said that he brought many of the toques used to address deities into son. He was a prodigious composer – his sones remain dominant in the repertoire – and his group, which he expanded with first congas and later an extra trumpet, more percussion and piano, became the most influential of the 1940s. Rodríguez also changed the structure of son, expanding the montuno with a descarga section of improvised solos. In 1951 he moved to New York, turning his group over to Chappotín, whose most significant innovation was to add the tight horn arrangements favoured by American swing bands of the period. *Buena Vista* star Rúben González was just one of the great Cuban musicians who passed through these bands.

A perhaps even more seminal bandleader – and one of Cuba's greatest ever soneros – was **Beny Moré**, the 'Barbarian of Rhythm'. Moré began his career singing with Miguel Matamoros and then with the highly influential jazz-oriented band of Cuban ex-pat Pérez Prado in Mexico City. When he returned to Cuba in 1953, he formed a trailblazing band which he led with characterisitc virtuosity and showmanship, singing, dancing and conducting. He was a brilliant arranger, too, drawing on a whole spectrum of styles, including son and guaracha rhythms, slower, romantic boleros, and the mambo that he had evolved with Prado. After the revolution, he stayed put in Cuba, and kept the party going until his death, hastened by alcohol, in 1963. Just 43, he was already a legend; 100,000 Cubans attended his funeral, and he continues to be cited by modern son musicians as the greatest of them all.

Cuban son, in the broader sense, was in the 1940s and 1950s very much a part of mainstream popular music, in North and South America as well as the Caribbean. The big US crazes were for chachachá and up-tempo mambo, while all other variants tended to be called rumba (or rhumba) when most were in fact son; indeed rumba came to be a US catch-all for anything Latin. In New York, mixed in with mambo, the Latin rhythms of Puerto Rico, Colombia and Dominican Republic, and an injection of hi-tech instrumentation and rhythm, son was eventually to transmute into salsa (for more on which, see p.488).

TUMBAO

Beny Moré

Music and the Revolution

It's impossible to understand developments in Cuban music without accounting the **politics of the island**. Havana, during the 1920s and 1930s, became the favourite nightclub playground for American tourists evading the prohibition laws, and, post-war, developed as a major centre for gambling and prostitution. While this gained Havana an undesirable reputation as a 'whorehouse of the Caribbean' with Mafia connections – and the population at large was desperately poor and largely illiterate – it meant good money for entertainment and music. In addition, the close links with New York gave rise to stylish, inventive and cutting-edge big bands.

After **Castro's 1959 revolution**, the island's music business was, like everything else, transformed. Radio stations and record companies became state institutions. The mob pulled out with dictator Batista, while US-owned property was appropriated for workers. As hotels and nightclubs remained empty, many musicians joined those Cubans leaving the country for exile in Miami or New York. Among their number were **Celia Cruz** and her band **Sonoro Matancera**, who applied for US residency after securing a residency at the Hollywood Palladium. Cruz, in the decades since, became the unrivalled 'Queen of Salsa' (see p.493), while identifying herself strongly with the anti-Castro/Cuban boycott movement.

For Cubans who remained, the US boycott meant an endemic and often desperate struggle for economic survival amid chronic shortages of basic goods. For musicians, at least until the liberalising of the economy in the late-1990s, opportunities to record and sell records, or to tour abroad, were severely limited and it is only in the past few years that Cuban music, as played in Cuba, has re-entered the international mainstream.

On the island, the post-revolution music scene shifted from the glamour of nightclubs and big orchestras to more local music-making centred on **casas de la trova** (see box) and to a system of state-employed musicians. From the 1960s onwards, promising young players were given a Conservatoire training – a university musical education drawing on both classical and popular island traditions – and when they graduated, they joined the ranks of full-time musicians categorised as *profesionales* to draw a state salary from the Ministry of Culture (which in turn took 90% of their earnings).

With few opportunities to travel, musicians were forced back on their roots, playing continually to local audiences. It was frustrating especially for younger musicians who found it tough and often impossible to get equipment to form bands, or to make their own records. **Egrem**, Cuba's state-

Soneros, Lyrics and Boleros

Cuba has a roll-call of great soneros, starting with the great **Miguel Matamoros** in the 1920s, moving through **Beny Moré** in the 1940s and '50s, to the US-exiled **Celia Cruz**, the acknowledged queen of son and salsa for the past forty years. Their voices differ but in general a high-pitched, somewhat nasal voice has been favoured. The other essential quality of soneros is a

Don Aspiazu's Havana Orchestra

total awareness of what every instrument is doing in order to exploit and improvise their vocals.

The most popular themes in son, trova and bolero **lyrics** are fickle love and romance. Cuban musicians are besotted with their island and its women, composing romantic serenades to each, often interlinked. In song the island is often referred to as a woman, just as the revolution and commitment to it are often described in mother/lover terms. Songs about women tend to apply all the stereotypes to their subjects – beauty, seduction, faithlessness, betrayal, rejection, and so on. The language, usually very witty, often has a double meaning, on a second, deeply sexual level, which can be both chauvinistic (pretty endemic in Cuba) and very funny.

The **bolero**, which evolved in the early twentieth century as a popular slow-dance song with lyrics in European *bel canto* style, unashamedly illustrates this sentimental and romantic tradition, celebrating eternal love, wallowing in the sweet pangs of unrequited longing or lamenting the fickleness of faithless women. It became popular as a voice and guitar idiom throughout much of Latin America by the 1920s. Although heavily influenced by Italian song, the bolero also accommodates subdued Afro-Cuban rhythms and sometimes segues into a montuno section, creating a bolero-son or even bolero-cha.

owned (and only) recording company, had to function in an economy which had higher priorities than importing vinyl, or even paper for record sleeves. Popular albums sold out instantly on release and the shortage of vinyl meant no re-pressing.

Artists who managed to tour abroad – which in the 1980s included Irakere and other 'new Cuban jazz' musicians – could record for foreign labels. But life wasn't so easy for them, either, and the defection of Irakere musicians **Arturo Sandoval** and **Paquito D'Rivera**, both at one time ardent supporters of the revolution, brought into sharp focus the pressures on the music industry under Castro's government. And for musicians who didn't made it on to international tours, the US blockade continued to frustrate any direct contact with the Latin fusions developing in places like New York.

The changes in the mid-1990s, forced upon Cuba by the collapse of the Soviet Union, its Cold War backer, have brought much welcome change, with musicians particularly affected by the eco-nomic liberalisation and legalisation of the dollar. These days musicians are still nominally organised through Institutes of Music but they can work freely inside and outside the country, contract to recording companies, negotiate their own rates, and pay only a small percentage of hard currency earnings to the government. As a result, the most successful musicians are among the best-paid professionals on the island.

Egrem, meanwhile, has been licensing its priceless archive to a host of companies around the world and renting out their old studio in Havana to producers and bands from outside Cuba. They have built a new up-to-date recording studio in Miramar on the proceeds. Meanwhile the singer Silvio Rodríguez helped find private investors to pay for the state-of-the-art Abdala Studios, which are a match for any in the world. And both Rodríguez and Pablo Milanés have created small home studios which are used by many Cuban groups for free.

Such changes maybe reflect a belated realisation by the government of Cuba's musical resources. In the 1980s, it was reported that musicians travelling abroad brought in the economy's largest hard currency earnings after sugar, fruit and tobacco. And that figure must have soared in the last years of the century, spurred by the vastly successful *Buena Vista Social Club* recordings, produced by US guitarist Ry Cooder, Cuban arranger Juan de Marcos González and the London-based World Circuit label (see feature box overleaf).

Casas de la Trova

One of the best places to hear music in Cuba is at a **Casa de la Trova**. Most towns have at least one of these clubs, which are an old Cuban institution – places where *trovas* or ballads were traditionally sung by *trovadores*. Nowadays the performances are more diverse and often completely spontaneous, with people joining in and getting up to play whenever they feel like it. You can hear anything from a single trovador with a guitar to a traditional Cuban sexteto or septeto. Entry is open to all-comers for usually a very modest charge.

The casas range from grand old colonial buildings with courtyards and palm trees to small, impromptu performing spaces with a few chairs off the street. In practice they are like informal clubs or bars (although often there are no drinks on offer) where musicians gather to play, people gather to listen and everybody exchanges opinions and reminiscences.

The most celebrated Casa de la Trova is in **Santiago**, on Calle Heredia, and there is music here afternoons and evenings every day of the week. The casa consists of just a patio (used for late night shows) and a single room with wide windows open onto the street and a small platform at the end for the performers. Further up Calle Heredia are other venues like the *Peña del Tango* and the *Museo de Carnival*, which often have more organised musical performances.

In **Havana** there are two Casas de la Trova, the *Cerro* (c/Panchito Gómez 265 & c/Perfecto Lacoste y Néstor Sardiñas) and the *10 de Octubre* (Calzada de Luyanó & c/Reforma y Guanabacoa). The latter is a little out of the way, in the Lujana area, but worth finding: a small local hall in a line of severely peeling colonial terraces, it possesses all the charm of old Havana, and appropriately enough features regular performances by the historic Sexteto Habanero.

There are other good Casas de la Trova in **Baracoa**, **Sancti Spiritus**, **Matanzas**, **Trinidad**, **Pinar del Río** and **Guanabacoa**.

Also worth checking out for concerts are the **Casas de Cultura** around the island, another revolutionary Cuban institution.

Saturday night at the Santiago Casa de la Trova

Son Veterans: The Buena Vista Social Club

"This is the best thing I was ever involved in," said **Ry Cooder** without hesitation upon the release of *Buena Vista Social Club*, the album of acoustic Cuban rhythms he recorded in Havana."It's the peak, a music that takes care of you and nurtures you. I felt that I had trained all my life for this experience and it was a blessed thing," he declared in a profound fit of musical ecstasy.

Since then *Buena Vista* has sold more than two million copies, won a Grammy award and become a live show capable of selling out New York's Carnegie Hall. Yet Cooder is the first to admit that *Buena Vista* is not really his album at all and that it belongs primarily to the arranger **Juan de Marcos González** and the legendary Cuban veterans whom he rescued from obscurity and retirement and assembled in Havana's Egrem studio to record the album over seven days in March 1996.

"These are the greatest musicians alive on the planet today, hot-shot players and classic people," says Cooder. "In my experience Cuban musicians are unique. The organisation of the musical group is perfectly understood, there is no ego, no jockeying for position so they have evolved the perfect ensemble concept."

Compay Segundo

The role of **Compay Segundo**, the composer and guitarist who Cooder describes simply as "the last of the best" was central to the project. "As soon as he walked into the studio it all kicked in. He was the leader, the fulcrum, the pivot. He knew the best songs and how to do them because he's been doing them since World War One", says Cooder. Nick Gold described the way they worked together during the recording of Buena Vista: "Ry would ask Compay to play his songs and record him on a small tape recorder. He'd listen to the tape overnight and then tell Compay which tunes he wanted to use."

The grandson of Ma Regina, a freed slave who lived to be one hundred and fifteen years old, Segundo was born Máximo Francísco Repilado Muñoz in Siboney in eastern Cuba in 1907. His family moved to Santiago in 1915 and as an adolescent Segundo worked in the tobacco fields by day but headed for the local bars at night to play. Initially a clarinettist he had soon invented his own seven-stringed guitar, known as the armonico, a unique instrument with a double G string which he still plays and which gives his music its unique resonance. In the late 1920s he played with the great **Nico Saquito** before moving to Havana where he formed a duo with Lorenzo Hierrezuelo and earned the nickname by which he is still known. In 1950 he formed **Compay Segundo y su Grupo**, which included the singer **Pio Leyva**. Yet by the following decade he had virtually

retired from music, working as a tobacconist for seventeen years, during which time he proudly boasts that he never missed a day.

Cooder says: "I once asked Compay his theory of life and he said "I make love, I dance, I sing." So much energy. He's the happiest individual I've ever met, but he's a sly old rounder too. He's got this foxy Cuban thing in a very beautiful way."

A visit to Segundo's modest apartment in Havana proved the description to be entirely accurate. A spry, dapper man, looking two decades younger than what his birth certificate says, Segundo cradled his armonico, using it to illustrate musical points and breaking into song at regular intervals. He explained his dislike of modern salsa and contemporary Cuban dance styles – "I prefer to dance close to a woman, to feel her body rhythmically swaying against the hips" – and then he played a tape of the American salsa star Willie Colon singing one of his compositions. "I haven't ever had a cent for that. Because of the blockade the Americans will not pay me for my own song," he said in sadness rather than anger. I asked him if he had ever thought of leaving Cuba. He seemed surprised that anyone

Compay Segundo and Ry Cooder

should even ask the question. "What for? Here there is tranquillity. I have everything I need. Why would I want to go anywhere else?"

Why indeed? At the age of eighty-seven Segundo signed a new recording deal in Spain, where he has since become a household name after his song "Chan Chan", which opens Buena Vista, was adopted as the theme of a Spanish soap.

Rúben González

Rúben González is described by Cooder as "the greatest piano soloist I have ever heard in my life, a cross between Theolonius Monk and Felix the Cat." Born in 1918 González is a quietly-spoken, modest man who together with Líli Martínez and Peruchín in the 1940s forged the style of modern Cuban piano playing. He first recorded with Arsenío Rodríguez and later joined Enrique Jorrín's orchestra, staying

Rúben González

with the band leader for 25 years, travelling widely through Latin America. In the 1980s he briefly took over the band when Jorrín died but retired soon afterwards.

When invited to play on Buena Vista, González did not even own a piano. He also suffers from arthritis but his touch swiftly returned during the sessions and he would be the first to turn up each morning, waiting at the studio door before it was unlocked. "I knew Rúben's music but I didn't even know if he was still alive," says Cooder. "Yet there he was and he wouldn't stop playing. He'd play twenty things in the morning before anyone else had drunk their coffee. So I left a cassette machine by the piano. It was a scramble to know what was happening. You ask what was that one and he's already played another five things. So I'd play him back the tape and say I want that."

In the two days following the recording of Buena Vista, Gold suggested to Rúben González that he made a solo album. He chose some classic Cuban songs and hand-picked a few friends to accompany him. The album was recorded live with no overdubs, deeply rooted in Cuban tradition but possessing a remarkable freshness and spontaneity. Since its release, González has toured Europe and recorded a second solo album in London.

Ibrahim Ferrer

Other key members of the Buena Vista club included **Omara Portuondo**, the bolero singer known as 'the Cuban Edith Piaf', **Eliades Ochoa**, the singer and guitarist from Santiago who leads **Cuarteto Patria**, and the sonero **Ibrahim Ferrer** (born in 1927), whose solo album Cooder produced on a return visit to Havana.

Cooder described his first encounter with Ferrer during the Buena Vista sessions: "He walked in looking like a big old cat. He is on a different level from the rest of us. He stepped up to the microphone and opened his mouth and this pure sound came out."

Ferrer's album is in effect the follow-up to Buena Vista. Recorded, like its predecessor, at Egrem Studio in Havana, it features many of the same personnel, including Rúben González, bass player Cachao Lopez, Omara Portuondo and the arranger and conductor Juan de Marcos González. In addition, Gold and Cooder unearthed further forgotten stars of Cuban music, including the guitarist **Manuel Galvan** from the 1960s Cuban doo-wop group Los Zafiros who was found languishing in obscurity and had not played in several years and **Henros Jiminéz**, an eighty-year-old arranger who worked with Beny Moré in the 1950s. The album also features the a cappella girl group Gema 4 and a 26-piece brass ensemble on several tracks.

The Ferrer recordings were also filmed by **Wim Wenders**, the German film director who Cooder worked with on the soundtrack of Paris, Texas. In addition to three weeks spent filming in Cuba, Wenders' full-length documentary feature included archive footage of Segundo and González and live material from the Buena Vista concerts in Amsterdam and New York during the summer of 1998. Wenders says: "Ry talked to me about the experience he had in Cuba with these amazing musicians. When I heard he was going back, I knew I had to make a film about it."

Nigel Williamson

The Son Goes On

With the exception of the 'singer-songwriter' Nueva Trova artists (of whom more in the article following), all of the best-known contemporary Cuban bands and musicians – both on the island and abroad – have evolved from the son tradition. They include traditionalists, revivalists and a good number of groups re-booting the tradition, or fusing it with other forms.

Among the traditional groups, leaders include **Septeto Nacional**, originally founded by Ignacio Piñeiro and re-established in 1985 to perform classic son, and the the wonderful, unfeasibly long-established **Orquesta Aragón** (see p.389), with their even more old-fashioned charanga. **Orquesta Ritmo Oriental**, with a traditional flute and violin charanga line-up, play a mix of son, chaganga and música campesina (country music), while **Orquesta Original de Manzanillo** have also imaginatively adapted the charanga sound.

Juan de Marcos González (left) with Pío Leyva

An excellent revival band, following the classic sexteto traditions, is **Sierra Maestra**, who remain firmly Cuban-based but tour frequently in Latin America and Europe. One of the group's founders was tres player and arranger **Juan de Marcos González**, the mastermind behind the startlingly successful **Buena Vista Social Club** and **Afro-Cuban All Stars** albums (see box). While these projects are rooted in the revival of classic, pre-Revolutionary son (and bolero), the Afro-Cuban All Stars also incorporate de Marcos's own compositions and his arrangements give more than a

nod to contemporary styles. And the groups have brought together old and new generation players – something Cuba has always been good at.

Two important musics which have fed into (and taken from) son are the rural **música campesina** and **changüí**. Música campesina (literally 'country music') is characterised by Cuban punto (local versions of the Spanish decima and verso song forms), often wittily improvised, with classic use of vocal harmonies and an upbeat, swingy guitar and percussion backing. Its top exponent, who has created a music all her own, with doses of Afro-Cuban rumba and son, is **Celina González** (see feature box, p.398).

The key player in changüí, over the past decades, was the late **Elio Revé**, whose **Orquesta Revé** provided opportunities for a string of young players. The potency of Revé's music came from the fusion of its strong regional form with urban son and the use of batá drums from Santería ceremonies. His lyrics were imaginative, too, reflecting popular opinions on social and political issues. A charismatic personality, his death in a car accident in 1997 was a major loss. His sound lives on, in a rather more salsa-driven form, in **Dan Den**, a band formed by his long-time cohort Juan Carlos Alfonso.

An earlier partner in Revé's band – and arguably the most significant figure in late-twentieth-century son – was Juan Formell, who in 1969 formed his own group, **Los Van Van**. At root a very tight charanga band – flute, violin, piano, percussion – Formell invented new changes in rhythm and timbre, introducing Afro-Cuban elements and, like band leaders before him, duplicating percussion parts to other instruments, notably strings. Adding a trombone, synthesiser and drum, Van Van developed a variant of son called **songo**. They remain a band at the innovative edge of Cuban dance music, producing infectious hit songs, like "Titimani" and "Muevete", whose topical lyrics capture the ironic edge of daily life in the capital. And even now, Formell's interaction with his audience really has to be seen.

A more jazz-oriented direction was taken by the group **Irakere**, formed in 1973 by composer-pianist Jesus 'Chucho' Valdés, Paquito D'Rivera and Arturo Sandoval. Irakere were the first big contemporary Cuban jazz group, combining son and Afro-Cuban music with modern jazz. Their name and their music emphasised their African inheritance – Irakere is Yoruba for "forest" – and their arrival heralded a new age in Cuban and Latin jazz. Irakere's line-up has changed often over the years, with members going on to found their own groups, though its most notable transformation came in the late 1980s when D'Rivera and Sandoval both defected from the island to follow careers abroad.

During the same period, Adalberto Alvarez and his band **Son 14** took son further, demonstrating a challenging awareness of salsa developments outside the island, and creating a wealth of compositions which have had huge hit coverage abroad.

As to a new generation, perhaps the future was indicated at the beginning of the 1990s by the band whose name implies just that: **NG La Banda** (New Generation The Band – pronounced 'Eney-ghey La Banda'). Founded in 1988 by ex-Van Van and Irakere flautist José Luis Cortes, they set out to 'search for the Cuban music of the future', establishing a more aggressive, street-based contact with their public – on one level an ironic

Cuban counterpart to heavy US rappers with their chanted slogan "The Band That's In Command!". They carried out their own aggressive marketing and promotion of their first record *Abriendo el siglo* (Opening the Century) which put them in a central position on the musical map, a position they really established with their great 1993 hit, "Echale limon" – 'Put a Lemon in it' – the Cuban slang for when things go wrong.

A decade on, NG remain hugely popular and innovative, mixing in elements of rap and jazz, along with complex arrangements by *los metales de terror* – the horns of terror! NG's lead in bringing aspects of rap and hip-hop into son provided the main thrust of the 1990s, and as the influence of black US musical styles grows a number of groups are gaining attention, among them **Las Orishas**, who recorded their first album in Paris in 1999, rapping above son and rumba riffs.

Another 1990s phenomenon was the emergence of high profile soloists from the previous decade's great bands – notably **Paulito F.G.** (Fernández Gallo), previously singer with Adalberto Alvarez y Su Son, and **Isaac Delgado** and **Manolín 'El**

Elio Revé (right) gets on down

Celina González and Cuban Country Music

With its layers of pulsating African percussion and Latin melodies on guitar and tres there's no mistaking Cuban country music for its American namesake. **Música campesina** is a kind of roots salsa and its own undisputed queen is **Celina González**. Her music ranges from a sparse combination of voice, percussion and guitar, to more of a big-band sound with punchy brass and strings. But whatever the line-up, her style is rooted in the music of the Cuban countryside – various types of son as performed by rural bands fusing Afro-Cuban rhythmic patterns and Spanish verse forms and melodies.

Celina González was born 16 March, 1929 in Jovellanos, a small town in Matanzas province, east of Havana. This region is at the heart of the old sugar plantations where rural traditions have remained the strongest – and with them the African religious and musical elements brought by the slaves. When young, Celina moved to Santiago de Cuba at the eastern tip of the island, another powerhouse of Cuban music. There, as a sixteen-year-old, she met **Reutilio Domínguez**, who became her singing partner and husband – a collaboration that began in 1948 with the legendary trovador Nico Saquito, and ended only with Reutilio's death in 1971.

Before the revolution Celina and Reutilio made a name for themselves performing with the basic resources of a guitar, bongos and powerful vocal harmony. "We had a radio programme in Santiago," Celina recalls of the time, "where we used to sing songs denouncing the government and praising the Cuban people, and this caused us a lot of problems. But we were lucky to get a contract with Saurito, one of our most famous radio stations in Havana, and since then I've worked regularly on radio and TV." Celina has worked, too, with a huge range of Cuban musicians, singing as easily with a full orchestra as with a small acoustic group.

She is a staunch supporter of the Cuban revolution and continues to live in a suburb of Havana. In her house is a large statue – almost an altar, decorated with fairy

LUCY DURAN

lights and plastic flowers – of Santa Barbara, the saint for whom she wrote her first and most famous song. Her early songs were in fact largely religious, reflecting her interest and belief in Santería; despite being white herself, the Afro-Cuban religion had been part of her upbringing. The Santa Barbara song expresses devotion to the Catholic saint and at the same time is a song for the Yoruba god Changó, mirroring the way the two deities are twinned in the Santería pantheon. Beneath it runs a pulsating dance rhythm.

In the 1970s, after the death of her husband, their son Reutilio Junior joined Celina as her singing partner, and, with the band **Campo Alegre**, helped update the music by incorporating the trumpet, bass, congas and marimba from the urban septetos of Havana. Although for top artists in Cuba the music business is often frustrating, Celina has done all right. Her kind of music was looked down on and discriminated against before the revolution, but these days every single Cuban radio station has at least one daily programme devoted to música campesina, while Celina has her own daily programme on Radio Taino.

Abroad, Celina and Reutilio gained a reputation in the early 1950s, singing with Beny Moré in New York, and touring the Caribbean. The years of Cuban isolation meant a long break from the international scene but over the past decade Celina has again toured extensively outside the island, attracting huge crowds at music festivals in Latin America – she is a huge star in Colombia and Venezuela – and playing, too, in Europe and North America, where compilations of her hits have gained a new audience.

In 1998, her fiftieth anniversary as a performer, Celina recorded a new album of her own as well as another with the classic charanga **Orquesta America** – her startling bright, swingy tones singing witty guarachas. Having won numerous awards and now being sought after by Cubans living outside the island, her popularity shows no sign of waning.

Médico de la Salsa' (The Salsa Doctor – a real doctor, in fact, who realised there was a great deal more money to be made in music) from N.G. La Banda. These are all key figures in **timba** – Cuba's increasingly dominant contemporary son – with its hip-hop and salsa influences. Another major

new name is **David Calzado** and **Charanga Habanera**, who became one of the most talked about bands in late 1990s Cuba, mixing rap rhythms inside a very aggressive, polyrhythmic salsa with a heavy timba-rumba edge, and appearing with extremely provocative dancers.

EMI/HEMISPHERE

NG La Banda

Unfortunately, the **salsa dance clubs** these groups fronted in Havana became closely tied up with Cuba's developing prostitution scene. Songs like NG La Banda's "La Bruja" (The Witch) told the tale, alas from a stereotypical male chauvinist view point. Bad publicity abroad concerning sex tourism resulted in the closure of many of the clubs, and this, combined with easier travel, resulted in top groups looking for work abroad, moving in and out of the country to play for new markets in the US, Latin America and Spain.

In March 1999 a project called **'Music Bridges'** brought together a large number of top Cuban musicians to work for a week with counterparts from the US and Europe. This had numerous spin-offs, including a stunning **Edesio Alejandro** recording with Gladys Knight ("Vasilon – Feeling Good"). The same year Alejandro, a Cuban film and TV composer, had a remix of his song "Blen-Blen" in the Ibiza dance charts all summer with a video full of Santería images on regular cycle on MTV Europe. His latest album, *Black Angel*, was produced by Bon Jovi's Obie O'Brien: quite some sign of the times.

As the first 2000-decade gets under way the Cuban music scene is now more open than at any time since the 1950s, with the US and Europe seen as a natural market. In the US, however, a crucial question continues to be posed by the government boycott and its constant highlighting through the actions of Cuban 'exile' musicians like Celia Cruz – who left the island in the early 1960s and refus-

es to appear alongside Cuban-resident musicians. *Buena Vista* may have captured the hearts of millions of Americans and Europeans, but the Miami Cubans still want none of it.

discography

There has been a vast output of Cuban discs in recent years, spurred in large part by the astounding success of the Buena Vista album. That's good news – for all the quantity, there is scarcely a duff disc among them – and many of them are stunners. The discography below, by neccessity, is more selective than most in this book. If you want to explore further, an invaluable source is the Brooklyn, New York-based Latin music store Descarga (www.descarga.com), whose online and printed catalog covers possibly the majority of recordings of Cuban music released at home and abroad.

General compilations

Cuba, I Am Time
(Blue Jackal Entertainment, US).

This magnificent 4-CD compilation, released in 1997, is worth its weight in gold. It features more than 50 artists and includes pretty much the best of each genre/style: Vol 1 *Invocations* covers the Afro-Cuban roots; Vol 2 *Cantar en Cuba* strolls through the great vocalists; Vol 3 *Bailar con Cuba* does the same for instrumentals; and Vol 4 *Cubano Jazz* showcases such Cuban jazz as Gonzalo Rubalcaba.

From Afro-Cuban Music to Salsa
(Piranha, Germany).

A superb roots package, this CD of roots rather than big name artists scores both for its music and for a brilliantly produced booklet, written accessibly (and in English) by Cuba's foremost musicologist and illustrated with stunning photos of musicians and instruments.

◉ **Oriente de Cuba** (Nimbus, UK).

A budget five CD set of music from Oriente province. Includes rumba, trova, the rare estudiantina tradition like a mixture of danzón and son and the rural son of the Familia Valera Miranda which has enormous atmospheric charm.

Vintage Bands

Recent years have seen some terrific re-releases of classic (1920s–50s) Cuban and Cuban-American bands. Discs below include son, chachachá, mambo and charanga.

Compilations

◉ **Hot Cuban Dance Music 1909–37** (Harlequin, UK) and ◉ **The Cuban Danzón – 1906–29** (Arhoolie, US)

These discs feature son in its earliest acoustic form from the sextets and septets who laid the foundations, at a similar time to original New Orleans jazz. The music – a transition between formal dance tunes and jazz – is timeless and appealing and the recordings suprisingly good; the Harlequin release is especially recommended with sleeve notes (including lyrics) perfectly evoking the era.

◉ **The Roots Of Salsa** and **Sextetos Cubanos** (Arhoolie, US).

Another fine pair of vintage discs that move the story on to (respectively) the 1920s and '30s and the by now developed son of the Havana sextetos. The *Roots* disc features the Habanero and Boloña; *Sextetos* has Matancero and Nacional. Tracks are rough and ready and utterly charming.

◉ **Cuban Counterpoint: History of the Son Montuno** (Rounder, US).

A key disc to understanding the African roots of son, this is an academic collection that could send you to the dance floor. Its intent is to track the way in which Hispano-Cuban son interacted with African forms to give rise to the hybrid montuno-son. Tracks range through rural beginnings to the popular mainstream, including early rustic gems, through the Sextetos Habanero, Boloña, the Septeto Nacional, Arsenio Rodríguez to Celia Cruz and Beny Moré.

Artists

Felix Chappotín

Felix Chappotín has a status in Cuban music on a level with Louis Armstrong in American jazz. A great trumpeter, he was unfailingly inventive and had a huge sound that stretched way up into the stratosphere. Whether leading his own band or in collaboration with Arsenio Rodríguez, he created an enormously rich and exciting sound.

CONJUNTO CHAPPOTÍN Y SUS ESTRELLAS

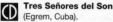 **Tres Señores del Son** (Egrem, Cuba).

The three gentlemen in question are Chappotín, singer Miguel Cuní and the brilliant pianist Luís Martínez (Lili), who were among the great figures of the 1940s and '50s. This fabulous collection showcases all three, with the extra treat of deep-throated old-style coros, and driving percussion.

Conjunto Matamoros

The Conjunto Matamoros were a typical old-style combo with congo, bongo, piano and trumpet; they produced a string of hits in the 1940s and '50s.

◉ **Bailaré tu Son** (Tumbao, Spain).

This is an entrancing selection of classic-era son, with sparkling piano and hugely enjoyable vocals.

Machito and his Afro-Cubans

Machito (Frank Grillo) and his brother-in-law Mario Bauza took the powerful riffing and layered textures of big swing jazz bands and brought them into Cuban dance music to majestic effect with his Afro-Cuban Orchestra. Their recordings include rumba, mambo, boleros, and perhaps most seductively of all, chachachá.

 Cha Cha Cha at the Palladium (Tio, US).

This album, recorded live at the Palladium Club in New York, catches Machito and band at their all time best – and at long last it has been re-released on CD. Chachachá never sounded better than on the opening "Oyeme mama".

◉ **Kenya** (Tumbao, US).

A close rival for the ultimate Machito album, *Kenya* (released at the time of Kenyan independence) features the great Patato Valdes on percussion, and soloing from jazz blowers Cannonball Adderley, Doc Cheatham and Joe Newman.

Beny Moré

Beny Moré (1919–63) – 'El Barbaro del Ritmo' – the Wild Man of Rhythm – is widely regarded as Cuba's greatest ever sonero, a charismatic bandleader with a unique vocal style, sweeping from croon to falsetto. He recorded first in the 1940s, with Conjunto Matamoros, forged mambo with Perez Prado, and led *the* Cuban big band of the 1950s, Orquesta Gigante. He lived, drank and partied hard, and died tragically young.

◉ **La Colección Cubana: Beny Moré** (Nascente, UK).

A budget introduction to the master, compiled mainly from RCA recordings of the 1950s.

◉ **The Very Best of Beny Moré – Vol. 1** and **Vol. 2** (BMG, US).

If you know you want more Beny Moré in your collection, then these are a better and broader investment.

Orquesta Aragón

Orquesta Aragón, founded in 1939, became the seminal charanga and chachachá band. They took Cuban music to Paris in the 1960s, back to Africa in the 1970s and led by Rafael Lay Jnr., son of the founder violinist, are still the cream of the crop. With their trademark sweeping strings and trilling flute, there are few sweeter sounds in Cuban or indeeed Latin music.

 Riverside Years (RCA International, US).

Aragón are featured here at the peak of their powers and popularity in the 1950s, with the golden voice of Beny Moré and stunning piano solos from Perez Prado.

◉ **La charanga eterna** (Lusafrica, France).

The group's 60th anniversary album – with guests Omara Portuondo, Brazil's Cheo Feliciano, and Africa's Papa Wemba – this shows Aragón to be still one of the very best Cuban bands in existence.

Perez Prado

Prado (1916–89) was the original Mambo King – the man who invented the style with his Mexico-based Cuban orchestra in the late 1940s, and who wrote and recorded the huge 1955 (and much reprised) hit "Cherry Pink and Apple Blossom White" – the apogée of America's mambo craze. Jazzers see him as a pop lightweight but he was a seminal figure in the emerging Latin jazz sound.

ORQUESTA CASINO DE LA PLAYA

◉ **Memories of Cuba 1937–44** (Tumbao, Spain).

Pre-mambo classics from Prado's first band, which included a trio of great vocalists – Cascarito, Miguelito Valdés, and Antonio de la Cruz.

PEREZ PRADO AND HIS ORCHESTRA

◉ **Havana 3am/Mambo Mania** (Bear Family, Germany; also appears on other labels).

Havana 3am was Prado's great studio album and includes "Cherry Pink ...". It is neatly paired on this two-for-one disc with an album of no-holds-barred mambo.

Arsenio Rodríguez

Arsenio Rodríguez (1911–70), blind from age eight (he was kicked by a horse), was a superb tres player and one of Cuba's all-time great bandleaders and son composers. In Cuba, he wrought a revolution in son, adding piano, trumpets and congas to the classic septet, and in many ways laid the roots of salsa. He lived mainly in New York from the 1950s, where he recorded with Machito and others.

◉ **Dundunbanza** (Tumbao, Spain).

This is irresistible Cuban-era Arsenio, featuring tracks recorded in Havana from 1946–51 with a horn section led by the masterful Felix Chappotín.

Sexteto Habanero

Sexteto Habanero were the group who brought son to Habana – and created its group format, having begun in Oriente province as a trio. They were not just pioneers but one of the most seductive of all Cuban groups recorded, in their 1920s heyday featuring vocalist Abelardo Barroso and the bongo playing of Agustin Gutierrez. The group has been revived and still plays classic son today, almost a century after its formation.

◉ **Sexteto y Septeto Habanero: Grabaciones Completas 1925-1931** (Tumbao, Spain).

If you're a fan of vintage son, then this 4-CD box of the Habanero sextet and septet recordings is hard to beat. It has all 98 tracks recorded by the original group and comes with an informative and luxuriously illustrated booklet. ◉ **Las Raices del Son** (Tumbao, Spain) is a single-CD edited selection, for the less committed.

La Sonora Matancera

La Sonora Matancera, who chose to leave the island soon after the 1959 revolution, are best known for their association with the great Celia Cruz (see Salsa article, p.488). But they worked with many of the other great singers of the 1940s and '50s, as well as providing one of the most important models for the New York salsa boom of the 1960s and '70s.

◉ **La Sonora Matancera and Guests: 65th Anniversary** (TH-Rodven, US).

An historic record of the band, featuring 1950s recordings with Celia Cruz, Bobby Capo and Ismael Rivera, the great voices of Cuba, the Dominican Republic and Puerto Rico.

'Modern' Son and Related Styles

'Modern' is maybe stretching things here a little but there is a discernible change in Cuban music post-Revolution, when many of the big bands and singers left for the US to forge jazz and salsa directions. 'Son' is also used at its most sweeping, as discs below include charanga, changui (rural son), campesina (country), and much that is essentially salsa.

Compilations

◉ **Ahora Si! Here Comes Changui** (Corason, Mexico).

A superb set of changui from Grupo Changui de Guantánamo, Familia Valera Miranda and Grupo Estrellas de Campesinas.

◉ **Casa de la Trova** (Corason, Mexico).

One of the great musical experiences of Cuba is a visit to the Casa de la Trova in Santiago – an experience nicely rendered on this authentic and atmospheric 1994 disc featuring ten of the regular bands from the venue, playing bolero, son and guaracha.

◉ **Cuba Caribe** (EMI Hemisphere, UK).

This fine 1999 selection of contemporary bands exhibits an unashamed salsa orientation, including hot tracks from Adalberto Alvarez, Juan Formell, Tamayo, and a salsa-rock creation from José Luis Cortés and NG La Banda.

◉ **Cuba Classics 2: Dancing with the Enemy** and **Cuba Classics 3: ¡Diablo al Infierno!** (Luaka Bop/Warner, US).

These two volumes (see Silvio Rodríguez for *Vol. 1*) from David Byrne's label are fabulous compilations, perfectly paced, and mixing the big names with some truly obscure bands and recordings. *Vol 2* covers the 'typical' Cuban sound of the 1960s and '70s; *Vol 3* delves into the more eclectic 1980s and '90s, with salsa, charanga, and even an outing for Cuban ska.

◉ **Cuba Fully Charged** and **¡Sabroso!** (Sterns/Earthworks, UK).

Two more lively, mid-1990s compilations featuring many of the best dance bands now playing in Cuba, including NG La Banda, Sierra Maestra, Irakere, Los Van Van and Orquesta Revé. *Fully Charged* is basically a son collection while *¡Sabroso!* tilts more towards salsa.

◉ **Cuban Gold: Que se sepa ¡Yo soy de La Habana!** (Qbadisc, US).

New York-based Qbadisc, run by Ned Sublette, have had an ear to the ground in Havana since the 1980s, and this was a seminal compilation of contemporary Cuban bands on its release in 1994. Featured bands include Los Van Van and Irakere, along with less well-known names like Grupo Manguare and Orquesta Original de Manzanilla.

◉ **Cuba Música Campesina** (Auvidis/Silex, France).

This is the best campesina anthology – a collection of rural bands capturing the country style in all its freshness. It even has a decent version of the most popular of Cuban songs, "Guantanamera".

Cuba Now (EMI Hemisphere, UK).

A showcase of key songs from four leading salsa/son groups of the late 1990s: El Médico de la Salsa, NG La Banda, Los Van Van, and Adalberto Alvarez. It's worth a listen for Van Van's gorgeous "Ese pone la cabeza mala" alone.

 Cubanisimo (Piranha, Germany).

One of the best live sets recorded outside the island in recent years – at the 1997 Berlin *Heimatklange Summer Festival* – featuring superb songs from Estudiantina Invasora, Afro-Cuban All Stars, Cubanismo, Candido Fabre, Bamboleo, Los Muñequitos de Matanazas, and Vocal Sampling – the latter creating every percussive and vocal sound imaginable.

 ¡Pinareño! (Piranha, Germany).

An album devoted to ensembles from Pinar del Río in the west of Cuba, including sones, canciónes, and the famous Grupo el Organo Pinareño, who accompany a huge mechanical organ with live percussion.

 The Story of Cuba (EMI Hemisphere, UK).

A fine disc covering some of the best bands of the past twenty-odd years, from the Irazú Big Band Cuba with their stately danzón to Cuban country sounds, superb Latin Jazz, rumba and chachachá.

Artists

Adalberto Alvarez y Su Son

Pianist, singer and guiro supremo Adalberto Alvarez founded the group Son 14, then in the late-1990s created a more individual style as Adalberto Alvarez y Su Son – currently one of the hot properties on the Cuban scene.

 La Salsa Caliente (Sonido/Vogue, France).

This is a good example of Alvarez's highly commercial sound – making the odd nod to son – that goes down a storm on his regular festival tours.

Buena Vista Social Club/ Afro–Cuban All Stars

The Buena Vista Social Club and Afro-Cuban All Stars were brought together by arranger Juan de Marcos González (of Sierra Maestra), Ry Cooder, and Nick Gold of the World Circuit label. Their idea was to record Cuba's elder statesmen of son and mambo – notably the singers Ibrahím Ferrer and Pio Leyva, and pianist Rubén González – alongside leading contemporary players. The results are big band son of the old style, with historic songs imaginatively and seductively updated. Grammy award-winning, with sales of over two million, these are the discs which have won back a worldwide audience for Cuban music. (See also entries for Ibrahím Ferrer, Rúben González and Compay Segundo).

BUENA VISTA SOCIAL CLUB

Buena Vista Social Club
(World Circuit, UK).

Ry Cooder steps into the hallowed Egrem studio and gently assures Cuban's legendary elder statesmen that the way they have always been making music is the best. The album includes exquisite versions of classics like "Chan-Chan", "La Bayamesa", "Años" and brilliant examples of son improvisation such as "De camino a la vereda". Cooder's own contribution lies in the production, utilising the mellowness of Egrem's old wooden studio acoustic, recording each song in one take, to ensure a natural sound and unhurried pace.

AFRO-CUBAN ALL STARS

A Todo Cuba Le Gusta
(World Circuit, UK).

An equally wonderful record, with irresistible swing, formidable singing, and great arrangements. Maestro pianist Rubén González is on top form here, the trumpet solos are as sweet as honey, and there is an impeccable rapport between the soneros and the whole. **Distinto, Diferente** (World Circuit, UK), the combo's 1999 follow-up, has some great tracks, too, with gorgeous arrangments and fine sentiments – notably De Marcos's olive branch to the Cuban-US diaspora, "Reconciliación".

AND BEFORE ...

 The Stars of Buena Vista (Tumi, UK).

A nice compilation of material performed by the *Buena Vista* artists in various groups, before their sudden ascendance. The recordings range from the 1950s to the mid-1990s.

Conjunto Céspedes

Deeply Cuban, although based in Oakland, California, the Céspedes family group have a vivid repertoire of roots Cuban music, with convincing compositions by group members and fine vocals from Gladys 'Bobi' Céspedes.

 Vivito y Coleando (Xenophile, US).

Released in 1995, this is Céspedes' best set to date, ranging from a traditional Lucumi prayer to a cover of Pablo Milanés's "Buenos dias America" (Good Morning America), with some wonderful rumba and son in between.

Cubanismo

Trumpeter Jesús Alemañy, another some-time member of Sierra Mestra, has been re-working the classic Cuban trumpet sound over the past few years to stunning effect with his 15-piece group, Cubanismo.

 Cubanismo! (Hannibal/Ryko, UK).

This was the first and most sparkling of a trio of fine albums produced by Joe Boyd in which Alemañy and his hot band bring a contemporary edge to the classic son. The follow-ups, **Malembe** and **Reincarnación** (Hannibal/Ryko, UK), won't disappoint, if you're hooked.

¡CUBANISMO!

Dan Den

Trombone-heavy dance band Dan Den, founded by Juan Carlos Alfonso from Orquesta Revé, hit a peak of popularity in the mid-1990s with their funky mix of contemporary Cuban dance grooves.

Viejo Lazaro y otros exitos (Qbadisc, US).

A feast of great dance tunes and rhythms – along with some very funny lyrics, printed in Spanish and English in the CD booklet.

Issac Delgado

One-time singer with NG La Banda, Issac Delgado has developed a more salsa feel in his solo work, with an urgent groove characteristic of modern Cuban fusions.

Con Ganas (EMI, Colombia).

Recorded in Venezuela and released in Colombia, this intoxicating album of sparse textures and tightly performed arrangements spawned several hits. It remains the best introduction to Delgado.

Estrellas de Areito

The 'Stars of Areito' (Cuba's state-owned label) got together for a legendary five-day recording session in 1979 to produce a Cuban rival to the then-dominant New York salsa band, Fania All Stars. Producer Juan Pablo Torres put together a dream band covering three generations of players that included veterans Féliz Chappotín, Enrique Jorrin, Pio Leyva and Rubén González; second generation stars Paquito D'Rivera (sax) and Arturo Sandoval (trumpet); and the more youthful Amadito Valdes (these days, the outstanding timbales player of Buena Vista/Afro Cuban All Stars).

Los Heroes (World Circuit, UK).

This groundbreaking 2-CD set sounds in many ways a *Buena Vista* precursor – not surprising, given the participants and the idea of mixing generations. The sound ranges through classic conjunto son, danzón and chachachá (with some gorgeous flute from Orquesta Aragón's Rafael Lay), and into more jazz-oriented *descargas* (jams). Needless to say, it's a treat, and a key disc of modern Cuban music.

Familia Valera Miranda

Familia Valera Miranda are an amateur son group – unusually with women as well as men – based in Oriente province, where they sing for local celebrations. Their rural take on the music has a real charm. They have toured in Europe occasionally in recent years.

Music from Oriente de Cuba: Son (Nimbus, UK).

There are very few discs available of rural, local son, so this atmospheric recording, with throaty bass, and rustic renditions of such classics as "Para ti nengón" is all the more welcome. Now re-released in five CD set on p.400.

Ibrahim Ferrer

If you've seen Wim Wenders' *Buena Vista* movie, you'll surely have lost your heart to the singer Ibrahim Ferrer as he duets with Omara Portuondo on the beautiful bolero "Dos gardenias" and gently wipes her tears as they sing, or as he clowns around atop the Empire State Building. Projected to fame by Buena Vista – he had largely background duties in his career as a singer with Beny Moré and others – he was a natural choice to follow Rúben González into solo recording.

Buena Vista Social Club Presents Ibrahim Ferrer (World Circuit, UK).

After Rúben González, this 1999 album is *Buena Vista*'s most successful offshoot to date. Ferrer sings mainly romantic boleros – notably in duets with Pío Leyva and Omara Portuondo – but shows he can mambo with the best on "Que bueno baila usted". Backing is tremendous, from Ry Cooder (more effective here than on *Buena Vista*), Los Zafiros guitarist Manuel Galbán, and female vocal quartet Gema Cuatro. Iif you want to hear how Ferrer sounded the best part of forty years ago, check out **Mi Oriente** (Tumbao, Spain), recorded with Orquesta Oriental Chepin in 1962.

David Calzado y la Charanga Habanera

Calzado is one of the most outspoken of Cuba's new generation of musicians – an ostentatious figure, driving a sports car around Havana, yet still rehearsing in the barrio he grew up in. His band, La Charanga Habanera, are the island's current pacesetters, responsible for a heavily rap-influenced sound and an acrobatic dance culture.

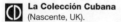 **Tremendo Delirio** (Magic Music, Mexico).

The sound of now: tight salsa arrangments mix with rap and romance. The lyrics are pure street and pretty impenetrable for anyone not actually living in Havana.

Celina González

Celina González is the Queen of Cuban country music – música campesina – and continues the tradition of country son, guajira and guaracha, keeping abreast of the times without over-arranging the music.

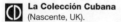 **Fiesta Guajira** (World Circuit, UK).

An excellent compilation drawn from Celina's 1980s albums on the Havana-based Egrem label. The songs here show the singer at her very best.

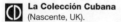 **Celina González with Orquesta America** (Tumi, UK).

An outstanding collaboration between the founders of chachachá and the Queen of Country Music.

Rubén González

Pianist Rubén González was born in 1920 and his career credits date back to 1943 when he played with the legendary Arsenio Rodriguez orchestra. He subsequently had a 25-year stint with Enrique Jorrín before easing into retirement in the 1970s. And then came Buena Vista Social Club and – as World Circuit had studio time remaining – his first ever solo album, titled a little on the ironic side.

Introducing Rubén González (World Circuit, UK).

What can you say about a solo debut at age 78? Well, it's utterly wonderful – a series of son/jazz improvisations, with elegant, restrained backing from the Buena Vista crew. Co-producer Ry Cooder was moved to compare González to Thelonius Monk in his originality and musicianship (he has a percussive – yet always lyrical – style distinguished by all his fingers landing on the keys at exactly the same moment). There are few more heartening successes.

Irakere/Chucho Valdes

Irakere, formed in 1973 by innovative pianist Chucho Valdes, Arturo Sandovál and Paquito D'Rivera, were pioneers of new Cuban jazz, welding chromatic harmonies and intricate arrangements onto a solid base of Afro-Cuban rhythms. They have been hugely influential over the past thirty years and if these days they are essentially a vehicle for Valdes, that's a major attraction in itself.

IRAKERE

La Colección Cubana (Nascente, UK).

This budget-priced and generously long 1998 compilation is as fine an introduction as you could hope for, exhbiting the band's tradition of combining virtuoso musicianship and sophisticated improvisation with a profound appreciation of their African roots.

CHUCHO VALDES

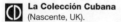 **Bele Bele en la Habana** (Blue Note, US).

Valdes shows he is still in superlative form on this 1998 outing, presenting his own brand of jazz, based on son, rumba and improvisations.

Jóvenes Clásicos del Son

The Jóvenes Clásicos are a new young band, steeped in the son tradition, but intent on revisiting it with a sensibility drawn from rap, funk, soul, salsa. merengue, pop and jazz. Their producer is Sergio Rodriguez, formerly of the a cappella group, Vocal Sampling.

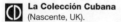 **Fruta bomba** (Tumi, UK).

An impressive 1999 debut, experimenting with rhythmic choral harmonies and introducing a clean modern feel to son with wonderfully playful lyrics immersed in the preoccupations of today's young Cubans.

Klimax

This contemporary band are led by drummer/arranger Giraldo Piloto, another alumnus of NG La Banda (see below). Their smooth, salsa-influenced approach is as 'poppy' as anything to be heard in Cuba today.

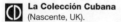 **Juego de mano** (Egrem, Cuba).

Poppy for sure – but also novel. Flashy horn-lines combine with dramatic breaks and sudden 'breakdown' sections where the band drops out to leave the singers supported by drums alone – a feature of modern Cuban salsa.

NG La Banda

NG (Nueva Generación) La Banda formed in Havana in 1988 – a group of conservatory graduates – and swiftly gained a reputation as the Young Turks of Cuban dance, Their timba style, combining son, salsa, jazz and funk, is frenetic, with explicit, funny street lyrics. Critics suggest their arrangements are over-complex and self-regardingly acrobatic, but they are undeniably among the greats of modern Cuban music and they have unleashed numerous solo careers, notably Issac Delgado and Cuba's current heart-throb Manolín 'El Medico de la Salsa'.

En la Calle (Qbadisc, US).

The band's 1992 debut – a disc of flat out performances with the gas pedal firmly to the floor, innovative arrangements and virtuoso performances.

The Best of NG La Banda (EMI Hemisphere, UK).

If you're new to NG, this is a good starting point: a budget-priced compilation of their 1990s albums. Bandleader José Luis 'Tosco' Cortés has honed his arrangments on these discs, allowing the vocals to breathe a little more, especially those of newcomer Jeny Valdés who joined the group for 1997's *Veneno* album.

Eliades Ochoa y Cuarteto Patria

Cuarteto Patria emerged in 1940 in Santiago de Cuba and the group is still going strong, performing their *guajira* (country) son with immaculate pace and balance. They have been led since 1978 by Eliades Ochoa – one of the younger Buena Vista figures, with his trademark outsize cowboy hat – and have a long association with the famous Casa de la Trova in Santiago, Oriente.

Sublime Illusion
(Virgin, UK).

This 1999 outing is one of the best 'individual' post-*Buena Vista* sets – an enchanting collection of son, bolero and guaracha tracks from the cowboy of Oriente province and his band, distinguished by Ochoa's warm heartfelt voice and tres-like customised guitar. A couple of tracks have horns added to the delicate guitar sound, and there are guest appearances from Ry Cooder, accordionist Charlie Musslewhite and Los Lobos' David Hidalgo, but the disc maintains a real guajiro feel.

Cubafrica (Melodie, France).

Camaroonian saxophonist Manu Dibango joins Ochoa and the cuarteto in this exuberant collaboration between Cuba and West Africa. Dibango's classic "Soul Makossa" becomes "Rumba Makossa", but for the most part it's Cuban music that forms the basis here. Mellow and uplifting.

Orishas

Rap is big right now among young Cuban bands and audiences, and Orishas, a group of four Havana rappers, are one of the most promising arrivals on the scene.

A Lo Cubano (EMI, France).

An inspired mix of traditional son and rumba riffs and instrumentation, over which rap deliveries mix with the soulful voice of a sonero. Recorded partly in Havana, partly in Paris.

Orquesta Revé

The death in 1997 of veteran timbales player Elio Revé – Orquesta Revé's founder – robbed Cuban music of one of its great innovators, a bandleader who had melded changui with son and other variants. Under his leadership, Orquesta Revé served as a training ground for many of Cuba's finest musicans, while providing some of the hottest dance floor grooves around.

La Explosión del Momento (RealWorld, UK).

This is Afro-Cuban changui-son at its best, played by its creators: dance music a-go-go, quirky, rhythmic and infectious with classic, sassy contemporary lyrics. If you want to sample, check out the exhilarating "Ruñidera".

Orquesta Ritmo Oriental

The Orquesta Ritmo Oriental, founded over thirty years ago, retain the line-up of a traditional charanga band but their arrangements and style of playing reflect the sharper, more punchy sound of modern Cuban dance music.

Historia de la Ritmo Vol 1 and **Vol 2** (Qbadisc, US).

Violins, wooden flute, piano, bass, singers and percussion are to the fore in these great charanga selections, recorded mainly in the 1970s.

Omara Portuondo

Born in 1930, Omara Portuondo has been one of Cuba's top bolero singers for half a century. She was a key member of the female quartet Los Daida in the 1950s, is a veteran of Havana's 'Tropicana Night', and is a frequent guest with Orquesta Aragón. She sings as well today as ever and it was little surprise that she won over everyone in Wim Wenders' *Buena Vista* film.

Buena Vista Social Club Presents Omara Portuondo (World Circuit, UK).

Songs of unrequited love with *Buena Vista* veterans as the backing band. The flow of songs is smooth and seductive, the musicianship of the highest order. Varied arrangements from spirited Big-Band to lush string quartet. Smooching material par excellence!

OMARA PORTUONDO & CHUCHO VALDES

Desafios (NubeNegra, Spain).

There is a sublime rapport between Portuondo and Irakere pianist Valdes on this virtually unrehearsed and 'live' disc, recorded at Sylvio Rodriguez's Ojala! studios in Havana. As the title suggests, each took the other's musical 'challenges' and leads on a cluster of classics, moving from son through blues, and full of improvisatory moments.

Compay Segundo

Singer and guitarist Compay Segundo (Francisco Repilado) was one of the chief artists of *Buena Vista* – and one of the oldest in the project, with a career stretching back to the 1930s, including a long spell with Orquesta Riverside. He has always written prolifically: strong melodies with tight rhythm, perfect harmonies and a killer chorus. He is still on good form in his 90s.

Compay Segundo y su grupo, 1956–57 (Tumbao, Spain).

In the wake of *Buena Vista* (and Segundo's own rather disappointing 1999 outing, *Calle Salud*) there have been many reissues of Segundo albums. This one is a winner, with his group on good form, and he and Buena Vista sidekick Pío Leyva having a whole lot of fun with the songs.

Septeto Nacional de Ignacio Piñeiro

The Septeto Nacional is another historic group – founded in 1927 by sonero, singer and composer Ignacio Piñeiro, who became a friend of (and influence upon) Gershwin. They have been through many incarnations over the decades but continue to play Piñeiro compositions and other classic mambo, chachachá, descargas and salsa.

Mas Cuba Libres
(World Network, Germany).

This joyous and sensual recording celebrating the Septeto's 70th anniversary brought in some very special guests, including *Buena Vista* singer Pío Leyva and the great danzón pianist (and some time Afro-Cuban All Star) Guillermo Rubalcaba (the father of jazz pianist Gonzalo Rubalcaba), whom some enthusiasts would put on a par with Rubén González.

Sierra Maestra

Formed in 1976 by (the future Buena Vista arranger) Juan de Marcos González, Sierra Maestra are arguably the best contemporary son band on the island, infusing traditional material with new energy. Heirs of Piñeiro, they fuse sensual rhythms with witty lyrics and a wonderful, caressing mellowness.

⊚ **Dundunbanza** (World Circuit, UK).

A superb 1994 disc with just the right pace to let the songs reveal their qualities. They include some wonderful reworkings of Arsenio Rodríguez numbers as well as a compellingly beautiful title track, which itself is well on its way to achieving classic status.

⊚ **Tibiri Tabara** (World Circuit, UK).

A 1998 release, celebrating their twenty-first anniversary with classic son and other related genres, including changui and sucu-sucu.

Son 14

Founded in 1977 by Adalberto Alvarez and sonero Eduardo Morales, Son 14 brought a joyous new energy to Cuban dance music, introducing the headlong rhythmic urgency that is a feature of the current sound. They have become erratic on disc since Alvarez left but live they still put on one of the best shows in Latin music.

⊚ **Son 14 with Adalberto Alvarez** (Tumi, UK).

An unerring selection of the very best from the group's eleven albums, beginning with the trademark "A Bayamo en coche", finishing with a brilliant guaguancó dedicated to conguero Chano Pozo, "Fue el rey de la rumba".

Los Van Van

Los Van Van (The Go Gos) are the creation of singer, bassist and arranger Juan Formell, who cut his teeth in Orquesta Revé, whose changui sound he revolutionised with electric guitars and bass. He left Revé to form Los Van Van in 1969 to create an entirely new sound – *songo* – by grafting danceable elements of Afro-Cuban, rock and jazz to a charanga line-up. It worked brilliantly and created the root of all new Cuban music for the next three decades. Formell still leads the band, who are stunning live, and still innovative on disc.

⊚ **Los Van Van: La Colección Cubana**
(Nascente, UK).

All that you could ask for: a budget-priced, sixty-minute selection of Los Van Van's finest 1980s and '90s tracks, featuring Formell's energetic arrangements and strident lyrics ("La Habana no aguanta mas"), and the virtuoso piano and percussion of long-time members Cesar Pedroso and Jose Luis 'Changuito' Quintana.

JUAN FORMELL Y LOS VAN VAN

⊚ **Te pone la cabeza mala** (Caribe/EMI, Spain).

The latest songs from the kings of Cuban salsa-songo. Put on their metal by new groups and soloists emerging in the late 1990s, Van Van merely turned out another challenging set, incorporating rap influences, with witty, ironic, finger-on-the-pulse lyrics.

Vieja Trova Santiaguera

This leading group of veterans, with a combined age of several millennia if you are to believe their publicity, support wondrously rough-voiced harmony vocals with tres, guitar, bass and hand percussion.

⊚ **Hotel Asturias** (NubeNegra, Spain).

The unique Cuban mixture of passion, sweetness and relaxation is heard at its best on this latest release from the indefatigable quintet.

Vocal Sampling

Here's something wonderful and bizarre: six singers who produce a full-on salsa sound purely with voice. They are perhaps best (indeed, astonishing) in concert but are by no means just a novelty act.

⊚ **Live in Berlin** (Ashé, Belgium).

Son and bolero as you will never hear them elsewhere – warm and affectionate and even danceable.

Los Zafiros

Los Zafiros (The Sapphires), founded in 1962, were a leading Cuban pop quartet through the decade, applying a Platters-like 'doo-wop' vocal harmony style to son. They were innovative musicians, whose crazy lifestyles burnt them out. A key member was bassist and arranger Manuel Galbán, now a lynchpin of Vieja Trova Santiaguera as well as a Buena Vista guest.

⊚ **Bossa Cubana** (World Circuit, UK; Nonesuch, US).

A disc quite unlike any other Cuban material around, Bossa Cubana is a seductive doo-wop take on son, bolero, calypso and bossa nova, with a gorgeous backing sound of twangy electric guitar pop.

Rumba and Afro-Cuban Music

Recordings below feature traditional Afro-Cuban music, mainly religious in nature, including the roots traditon of rumba as well as its dance music offshoots.

Compilations

⊚ **Africa in America** (Corason, Mexico).

Cuba is central to this comprehensive 3-CD set, though it goes way beyond the island, tracing developments of Afro-

American music in nineteen countries around the Caribbean and Central America. It is a superbly compiled resource, full of material you will never hear elsewhere.

◉ **Afro-Cuba: A Musical Anthology** (Rounder, US).

A useful selection of field and studio recordings from the main Santería cults.

◉ **Tumi Cuba Classics Volume 3: Rumba** (Tumi, UK).

Originally released by the Egrem label, this is probably the best compilation of rumba available, mostly Guaguancó, but with examples of Columbia, Yambú and others from Los Muñequitos, Los Papines, singer Celeste Mendoza and the Conjunto de Clave y Guaguancó.

Artists

Clave y Guaguancó

This is contemporary street corner rumba with an edge: a group who are stirring things up by integrating the old tradition of boxes, batá and congas – each player sits on the first, has the second by his side and the third on his lap, creating an extraordinarily rich timbre and pitch.

◉ **Dejalá en la Puntica** (Egrem, Cuba).

Racing drums underpin richly textured coros and dramatic solo singers on this fine record. One quite outstanding track, "Iyawo", is a recording of an orisha song, which combines sacred and secular patterns to tremendous effect.

Grupo Afrocuba de Matanzas

Formed some twenty years ago, Grupo Afrocuba de Matanzas are an ensemble of percussionists and singers specialising in performances of music from untouched folkloric tradition. They have also pioneered use of the sacred batá drums in secular rumba.

◉ **Rituales Afrocubanos** (Egrem, Cuba).

Packed full of ritual music, this recording includes not only the usual songs of praise from the Lucumí religion, but also Arara and Bantu music from alternative African roots.

Los Muñequitos de Matanzas

Cuba's top rumba ensemble and first professional group, Los Muñequitos de Matanzas have honed their style to mature perfection over forty-five years.

◉ **Rumba Caliente** (Qbadisc, US).

This is classic Cuban rumba – rich in African elements, using percussion and vocals only, and brilliantly melodic. This Qbadisc release combines two Cuban albums, recorded eleven years apart.

Lazaro Ros

Lázaro Ros, who began his connection with the ritual music of Santería in 1938 at the age of thirteen, is the best known Cuban singer of religious music. He preserves the roots side of Afro-Cuban songs and chants with his Grupo Olórun, and has also adapted the music in rock versions with the band Sintesis.

◉ **Olorun** (Green Linnet/Xenophile, US).

Eleven toques for eleven orishas, with beautiful singing from Ros and Grupo Olórun, backed only by drumming.

Mercedita Valdes

Mercedita Valdes, a Santería priestess of the Yoruba tradition, is one of Cuba's finest singers of religious music.

◉ **Tumi Cuba Classics Vol 2: Afro Cuban** (Tumi, UK).

Cult music performed by initiate experts is presented here as unadulterated performance.

Yoruba Andabo

Although founded as long ago as 1961, this group of rumberos is an adventurous outfit, reaching back into the tradition to revive the use of the cajón box, and at the same time integrating batá into the classical conga choir.

◉ **El Callejón de los Rumberos** (PM, Spain).

This is accessible, exciting and attention-grabbing roots rumba: passionate singing above well-recorded drumming of startling polyrhythmic complexity.

CUBA

Cuba

Trova and Nueva trova

troubadours old and new

Post-revolution Cuba has produced one great musical style – **Nueva trova** (new song) – that stands somewhat outside the mainstream of *son*, and has close links with the South American developments of *Nueva canción* (see the article on Chile, p.362). **Jan Fairley** delves into the music's troubadour roots and contemporary developments, and talks to one of its guiding spirits, Silvio Rodríguez.

N ueva trova – like Nueva canción – emerged in the 1960s and 1970s, the years of protest throughout Latin America, when Cuba was seen by many as a beacon against the oppression of the continent's dictators. Cuba's new song, like its Chilean and Argentinian counterparts, miraculously instilled a political sensibility into achingly beautiful songs of love and personal exploration, songs which made its key singers **Silvio Rodríguez** and **Pablo Milanés** hugely respected throughout the Spanish-speaking world. As the Dominican Republic's merengue superstar Juan Luís Guerra, put it, "Rodríguez and Milanés are the master songwriters – they have influenced everyone."

Nueva trova (and canción) are often thought of as 'protest songs' – though they rarely have any direct message. However, by singing of everyday life and beliefs – and in Cuba that meant the shap-

ing, everyday influence of the Revolution – the songs had an intrinsic political aspect. To Cubans, trova – old and new – is characterised above all by poetic language and metaphor, by an ambiguity and questioning tone. Latterly, the questioning has grown more critical in tone, with island-based artists like **Carlos Varela** engaging with the problems of an island that has given no power to a younger generation, and US-based exiles like **Juan-Carlos Formell** addressing similar concerns from a diaspora persepctive.

Despite the pan-Latin popularity of Silvio Rodríguez and Pablo Milanés, Cuban trova tends to be an uncommerical part of the music scene at home. It is very much a living tradition, with new trovadores emerging each year. However, not much gets recorded and to hear new trova you really need to visit the island and spend a few evenings at the local *casas de la trova* (see p.393).

Troubadour Roots

Cuba's original *trovadores* were true troubadours, who roved the island in the early decades of the twentieth century, accompanying themselves on guitar while singing country songs, *sones* and boleros. Their songs were typically concerned with love and patriotism, often with Cuba itself personified as a woman.

One of Cuba's most popular singers of all time was the diminutive **Sindo Garay**, from Santiago de Cuba, the creator of the unforgettable bolero "La Bayamesa" (Girl from Bayamo), written in 1909 and still a part of the trova repertoire. The town of Bayamo was the cradle of the independence movement and the 'girl' in question was thus the love of all Cuban patriots. Garay was a leading trova singer during the Machado dictatorship in the 1930s and 1940s and was a fixture at the *Bodeguita del Medio*, a bar near the cathedral in old Havana which was to play a key role in the run-up to the revolution, as a meeting place of intellectuals and critics of Batista.

Other major figures of the early trova world included **Joseíto Fernández**, who wrote the rustic "Guantanamera" (a tribute to the women of Guantanamó, with various versions including lines from Cuba's national poet, José Martí), one of the most covered songs of all time, and regarded as a kind of national hymn; **Nico Saquito** from Santiago de Cuba, who composed over five hundred songs in the trova tradition (and who, incidentally, worked with both the young Celina González and Compay Segundo); and **Carlos Puebla**, whose quartet sang witty songs of the revolution's achievements, including such classics as "Y en eso llegó Fidel" (And Then Fidel Arrived) and "El son de la alfebetización" (The Son of Literacy).

A regular at the *Bodeguita del Medio*, Carlos Puebla's strength – bolstered by his *cuarteto típico*, the Tradicionales – lay in his lilting, poetic subversion of country guajira and guaracha forms, singing in duo with his right-hand man and with key use of the marimbula. Nicknamed 'the voice of the revolution', he was Cuba's only notable political singer until the nueva trova movement of the early 1970s. In common with those later singers, however, political songs amounted to only a small portion of his output, and he also performed covers of sones by Matamoros and others.

New Songs

The **Nueva trova** movement had clear links with the *nueva canción* (new song) composers appearing in this period throughout Latin America, but its emergence was entirely independent. Created by those who were reaching adolescence at the time of the revolution – for whom Fidel's maxim of 'Within the revolution, everything; outside the revolution, nothing' seemed only logical given the experiences of their childhood – great emphasis was placed on lyrics, replacing the love and nationalism of the old trova with an exploration of personal experience and desires, relating the contradictions and anxieties of life from within the context of a revolutionary society.

The new music drew on Cuban folk guitar traditions and those from the wider Spanish-speaking world (which in turn were influenced by French chanson). Its singers became known as *canto-autores* (singer-songwriters) and while their philosophy and perspective was Cuban, it had something in common with their European and North American counterparts, notably singers such as Joan Manuel Serrat and Lluis Llach who were struggling to maintain their Catalonian identity under Franco's dictatorship, and with the nueva canción singers of Chile, Uruguay and Argentina.

Key developments in nueva trova occured when a group of young musicians came together at Havana's ICAIC film school, under the direction of Cuba's leading composer and guitarist, **Leo Brouwer**. Among a group which included Vicente Feliú, Noel Nicola and Sara González were **Pablo Milanés** and **Silvio Rodríguez**, who were to become arguably the most influential singers of their generation in the Spanish-speaking world.

They had by no means an easy start. With their attitude, dress and music, these new trovadores were regarded as suspect at a time of dogmatic Communist cultural values. Milanés was actually sent for eighteen months on 'special military service' – a euphemism for the camps where bohemians and gays were sent for hard-labour, cutting cane in the fields.

Milanés and Rodríguez

In their long and prolific careers, Pablo Milanés and Silvio Rodríguez have composed a huge body of work, including bitter-sweet love songs that capture a mood absent in other Cuban musics. Their root ingredients are those of the classic troubadour – vocals and solo acoustic guitar – though both have led bands of varying size, their music easily adapting itself to big arrangements.

A hallmark of their songs is a sense of metaphysical emotion of joy and loss, an existential

**El breve espacio en que tú no estás
(The Brief Space Where You Are Not)**

*A trace of dampness still remains
Your perfume fills my solitude
In the bed your outline remains like a promise
To fill the brief space where you are not.*

*I still don't know if she'll come back
No one knows what the next day will bring
She breaks all my preconceptions
She never admits sadness
She asks for nothing in return for what she
    gives
She's often violent and tender
And never speaks of unions for life
And yet gives herself
As if there were only one day to love*

*She won't share a meeting
Yet she likes the songs
That capture what she thinks
Still I didn't ask: will you stay?
I feared her answer might be – never!
I would rather share
Than live my life without her
She's not perfect
But it's close to what, till now,
I had only dreamed about.*

Pablo Milanés

questioning, particularly of the viscitudes of personal relationships, a pervasive use of metaphor and indirect subject, a sense of reflection and vulnerability and a non-gendered approach to the complex and uneven experience of love. They are part of a generation which re-defined the subject matter of Cuban song, changing its parameters and opening it up, while demonstrating innovative use of popular music forms.

The Cuban experience is pre-eminent in the lyrics of both composers. Indeed, in the early 1990s, after a key tour to celebrate the achievements of the revolution – singing from a huge repertoire of songs on every aspect of island life – Silvio Rodríguez seemed to have followed in the steps of José Martí and taken on the mantle of national poet in the eyes of his public and the Cuban press.

Between 1992 and 1996 Rodríguez produced a triptych of albums (titled *Sylvio*, *Rodriguez* and *Dominguez*), paring down his big band to solo vocals and guitar. Harkening back to the ICAIC days, the feel of the discs was unequivocally

unplugged, consciously 'amateur', with Rodríguez multi-tracking to duet with himself – keeping nuanced stumbles and asides, as if he had just sat down, picked up any old guitar and started to sing in somebody's living room. Each of the albums included a reflective sequence of powerful and on occasion bleak songs, rooted in cameos of individual lives, the disillusions and breaking points. The whole process was a political statement in itself, a wooing of small audiences back to basics.

In 1997 Rodríguez gave concerts in a limited number of South American cities to celebrate the life of Argentine-Cuban Ernesto 'Ché' Guevara, whose anniversary year it was. He was joined by singer-songwriter friends such as the Parras in Chile and the Brazilian Chico Buarque who performed with him in Argentina. Milanés, too, began a tour of South American cities in 1998 visiting many cities in Chile. Both musicians have also made important recordings with a host of other musicians in the Spanish speaking world, most recently with musicians from mainland Spain.

Another Generation

In the early 1990s, a new and more critical generation found a voice in the highly articulate songwriter **Carlos Varela**. His lyrics expressed the troubles of Cuban society and the frustrations of the island's youth, without much recourse to metaphor. The song "Guillermo Tell" (William Tell), for example, had a direct warning to the old generation of politicians: "William Tell, your son has grown up/And now he wants to shoot the arrow/It's his turn now to prove his valour/Using your very own bow!"

Carlos Varela

¡Ojalá! – Silvio Rodríguez

¡Ojalá! – Let's hope! – is the name given to the recording studios **Silvio Rodríguez** built in Havana in the mid-1990s, and seems to epitomise a man who was arguably the most significant singer-songwriter of his generation in the world. As one of those responsible for creating nueva trova, Rodríguez, like his close friend and fellow singer Pablo Milanés, has moved on from being openly regarded as suspicious in his tastes in

Silvio Rodríguez

the early 1960s, to one of the revolution's major supporters and, for a time, one of its major wage earners. As well as building the studios where the Ojalá label records everything from Cuban rap to new, young trovadores, Rodríguez has recently been involved in directing the building of a large complex of state-owned studios in Havana, one of which can accommodate an entire symphony orchestra.

"In the beginning people didn't understand us," Rodríguez recalls. "Our songs were self-critical and there was no tradition of that, but they were songs full of commitment. The 1960s were the hot soup of what was happening – new things – and there was a moment

when the nueva trova was in the front line of the ideological fight. Now we see clearly that it was and it is a privilege that before us no other generation of trovadores could be real protagonists."

While his actions have rarely cast a shadow on his steadfast relationship with the state – which he explores in the classics "te doy una canción" (I Offer You A Song) and "Vamos andar" (Let's Walk) – Rodríguez's undogmatic, metaphoric songs, many with a broad, international perspective, are very far from being a mouthpiece for the revolution. Despite his membership of the Cuban parliament since 1992 (he is now in his second term) his songs have never explained policy (as Carlos Puebla's did). "I have never tried to be the voice of the Revolution – that is Fidel. It doesn't appeal to me to be something official because there hasn't been anything more anti-official than my songs, which are critical a lot of the time, show contradictions, doubts and reservations. But yes, I am someone who feels for the revolution, who believes in it, who believes in Fidel. I feel it is necessary to have a sense of unity in terms of feelings for the country and the will to overcome all the problems we have. Even though I think it will always be like this, there will always be things to overcome and we are going to be in disagreement with a whole lot of things because that is life. One does things for human reasons not for ideological ones.

"I think that one of the things that most motivates me is the inaccessible, what you cannot do, what you aspire to and desire. This is a constant presence in my songs: it's a little like the line of the horizon. It seems there is always a place further away and the hope of finding that place is, I think, the desire of all human beings."

Musically, like other contemporary trovadores, Varela fluctuates between the old-style acoustic treatment of Milanés and Rodríguez and a rock (often heavy rock) backing. He has recorded in Spain, and now regularly tours Spain and North America.

In April 1999, Silvio Rodríguez organised an important free concert in Havana, celebrating the *Casa de las Americas*, where many of his generation

of trovadores had first performed, under the banner 'Remember – The Revolution! – Now!'. Rodríguez played a number of songs with Varela, who sang his poignant "Robinson, solo, en una isla" (Robinson, alone, on an island). But it was **Gerardo Alfonso** – with his flowing rasta-style locks – who really stole the show. Alfonso had forged a reputation in the 1990s with key songs at key moments – notably "Sabanas blancas" (White

Sheets) in 1992, when so many Cubans left the island, and "Son los sueños todavia" (They Remain Our Dreams), composed in 1996 after Ché Guevara's remains were found in Bolivia and shipped 'home' to Cuba for burial.

Alfonso, Varela and others seem sure to ensure the trova tradition remains an integral part of Cuban music. Meantime in the US, **Juan–Carlos Formell**, the son of Los Van Van's founder, Juan Formell, has been adapting the genre, with a strong jazz element, to his own songs, reflecting on his Cuban childhood and the stifling aspect of the Castro regime. Maybe before long, the two strands will meet.

discography

Compilations

 Antologia de la Nueva Trova – various volumes (Egrem, Cuba).

Egrem, the Cuban state label, has digitally re-mastered many of its original recordings and has been putting out a series of anthologies of the trovadores singing today. There are many volumes. Volume 3 is a good starting-point for contemporary trova, including Alfonso's "Sabanas blancas" and Varela's "Jalisco Park".

Artists

Daniel Castillo

Born in 1907 in Santiago de Cuba, Castillo is one of the oldest soneros and bolero singers, with a true rustic troubadour spirit and style. Able to turn professional with the revolution he was the founder in 1962 of the Cuarteto Oriente. Since 1998 he has been surrounded by several younger generations of musicians including his grandson Gustavo Reve.

 La Trova (Corason, Mexico).

A classic repertoire of romantic trova, with Castillo singing second voice (harmonically embellishing while the first voice provides the melody), accompanied by two guitars, bass, bongos, original style spoons, and flute.

Juan–Carlos Formell

Juan Carlos Formell, the son of Los Van Van leader Juan Formell, has been resident in New York since the early 1990s: as he puts it, "part of the exodus of young Cuban musicians who had no place in their country because the moment had been cut off". His band, Cubalibre, became a resident fixture at the Zinc Club, and allowed him to hone his songwriting for his first album (Songs...), nominated in the 'Tropical' sections of the Grammy Awards.

 Songs from a little blue house (BMG Wicklow, US).

This is a beautiful, accessible album of singer-songwriter exile compositions, based around Formell's childhood memories of his grandmother's home in Cuba's Oriente province. The music and lyrics are quintessentially Cuban,

imbued with references to the Afro-Cuban Santeria religion and to Cuban musical history. The gentle passion of Formell's singing is matched by inspired arrangements, rooted in nueva trova-style guitar supported by Latin percussion, bass and brass.

Pablo Milanés

One of Cuba's great composers of nueva trova, Milanés is, with Silvio Rodríguez, a kind of national poet of Cuba. Developing as a singer of negro spiritiuals, boleros, son and 'filin', he is a superb songwriter, guitarist and singer, with jazzy yet clear tones, and diverse musical influences. He has recently gained a mainstream popularity through the use of his songs in a number of Latin soaps.

 Cancionero (World Pacific, US).

A marvellous 1993 anthology of Milanés, compiled by Qbadisc maestro Ned Sublette.

 Vengo naciendo (Universal, Mexico).

A recent album that shows the soaps haven't got to Milanés, leaving his poetic sense and comment on the ambivalence of love and life firmly intact. Included is a superb version of the show-stopping "Yolanda", one of his most popular songs.

WITH SILVIO RODRÍGUEZ

 Silvio Rodríguez y Pablo Milanés en vivo en Argentina (Cubartista, Argentina).

A remarkable record of a remarkable occasion – a concert in Argentina to celebrate the end of dictatorship in that country, which brought together the two Cubans with Argentine musicians who had sustained the spirit of freedom through the dark times.

Carlos Puebla

The grand old man of Cuban trova and revolutionary song, Carlos Puebla composed country music, guarachas and guajiras as well as seminal songs about the Revolution's triumph and its early radical policies. His quartet, Los Tradicionales, were the house musicians of the Bodeguita del medio, the legendary bohemian bar in old Havana.

 La Bodeguita del medio (Milestone/Riverside, US).

A priceless piece of Cuban history, this is a 1957 recording from the *Bodeguita* itself, with the Tradicionales in early trio form (guitars, vocals, percussion) gently serenading with songs about love, Cuban history and the Bodeguita itself. Full of ambience, the disc makes you feel they are right there beside you.

 Carlos Puebla y sus Tradicionales (Egrem-Artex, Canada).

This anthology presents some of Puebla's great songs – political and otherwise – with his classic quartet of guitar, marimbula, close harmonies and percussion.

Silvio Rodríguez

Silvio (as everyone knows him) is Cuba's foremost singer-songwriter – a key musician of the 1970s and '80s whose songs were known by heart by a generation – not just in Cuba but throughout the Latin world. A highly prolific songwriter, he has always been deeply engaged with the personal experience of Cuba's revolutionary period. Or as the Cuban press has said of his songs: "Here we have the great epic poems of our days." He has worked with many musicians, including Pablo Milanés (see above), and, most recently, Classical guitarist Rey Guerra.

 Cuban Classics 1: Canciones Urgentes (Luaka Bop/Warner, US).

This compilation on David Byrne's Cuban Classics series shows the man at his very best – check the live recording of "Unicornio" in particular.

Silvio Rodríguez en Chile (Fonomusic, Spain).

2-CD set of a historic 1990 concert in newly democratic Chile, with a tremendous sequence of Rodríguez classics given a jazzy feel by Chuko Valdés and Irakere. This was almost the same concert which he took to every nook and cranny of Cuba during his 1989 tour for the thirtieth anniversary of the revolution.

Silvio (Alerce, Chile/Spain), **Rodríguez**, **Dominguez** (Fonomusic, Spain).

Silvio's 'unplugged' trilogy, recorded between 1992 and 1996 and getting back to basics with home recording. The first disc, Silvio, is perhaps most essential, featuring the extraordinary apocalyptic song "El necio" and the haunting insturmental "Crisis".

Carlos Varela

Carlos Varela is a younger singer, whose articulate, sarcastic lyrics dealing with Cuba's current problems and the frustrations of living there have won him wide popularity – as well as some political trouble – on the island.

Monedas al Aire (Qbadisc, US).

Varela's revelatory first album, rocking up the familiar guitar with less metaphoric, more direct lyrics than nueva canción (sleeve notes in Spanish and English).

Como los peces (Ariola, Germany; BMG, US).

A more rock-oriented album – and perhaps the first notable rock album to come out of Cuba – finds Varela in assertive lyrical mode, for all his Guevara-bereted image.

Dominican Republic

merengue attacks

On its home turf of the Dominican Republic, merengue is ubiquitous. It pours out of passing cars, thrums from boom boxes, blares from apartments and, in the countless rural taverns and high-tech dance clubs that dot the island, it is the main item on every menu. No wonder then that merengue's explosion across the globe is a source of intense pride for all Dominicans. **Sean Harvey** and **Sue Steward** report on the soundtrack to a nation.

Dominican pride in merengue is almost synonymous with the sense of statehood: to love merengue is to love the island itself and the people who inhabit it. And merengue musicians are major league celebrities. **Johnny Ventura**, icon of the 1970s, returned home from the US to become a major political figure with presidential ambitions. Multi-platinum Latin superstar **Juan Luis Guerra**'s conquest of the world, topping even the sales of crooner Julio Iglesias, is an unparalleled national success story.

Nevertheless, there may be some who have yet to catch the fever. Perhaps your first experience went like this. One insomniac night you sought to unwind while TV-surfing across the Dracula time slots. Eventually you arrived at the Spanish-language channel to find some talentless beefcake shaking his stuff, miming the vocals a half-second late behind a chorus of three bikini-clad ladies and a band enrobed in garish, frilly velvet. Above their heads beamed the strobing neon sign: '¡Merengue!' If that happened to you, take comfort: for every shining beacon of a Beatle lies the underbelly of a Spice Girl, and you have merely experienced the worst. And the best is spectacularly good.

Johnny Ventura (on timbales) with his band

Roll Call

As with all Afro-Caribbean genres, merengue is easily identified by its **beat pattern**. Compared to salsa or calypso, the merengue pattern seems aggressively unsyncopated, its souped-up military rat-a-tat landing squarely on 1 and 3. But one of several interlocking patterns rattles through the rhythm section over this signature on-the-beat thump – the way a city seethes around its neatly numbered grid.

Merengue refined itself for centuries across the dusty pueblos and sugarcane fields of the Dominican Republic – and parts of Haiti, the other half of the island of Hispaniola. The instrumentation was originally acoustic – an accordion leading, with backing from a box bass, a *guayo* (metal scraper) and a two-ended *tambora* drum.

The music can still be heard in this basic form – notably in recordings by virtuoso accordionists like **Francisco Ulloa** and **Angel Viloria** – but these days **merengue instrumentation** is a blend of traditional rural orchestration with contemporary electronics and salsa-influenced horn sections. Saxophones and trumpets are always present in contemporary bands, with a trombone occasionally added. The main purpose of the horns is to fire off a series of crisp, pyrotechnic riffs. The bass never strays far from thumbing out the underlying groove. The piano underlines the harmony with arpeggios and syncopated chord movement and is often electric. The accordion is no longer at the core of the music, though it still pops up in bands.

The **percussion section** is the backbone. The congas slap out a series of African beats that provide the primary fire and groove, along with the *tambora* (which is anchored by a hand at one end and rapped with a stick at the other). Often a bass drum is used, an innovation that began as Dominican performers incorporated disco elements during the 1970s – an attempt to stave off bankruptcy in the face of the Bee Gees. And always beneath its more ostentatious neighbours is the incessant scrape of the *guira* – traditionally fashioned from a kitchen utensil – sole cultural inheritance of the exterminated *Tainos* who inhabited the island before Columbus, its tireless hoarse rasping like that of a dying man begging to be remembered.

But those who skim the cream off this rich cross-cultural blend are the **singers**. The most traditional merengue voice is a reedy, nasal style that occasionally manages to be haunting amid the up-tempos. **Juan Luis Guerra** is the principal exponent today. But the more richly sonorous Latin tradition is evident as well, notably in the work of **Johnny Ventura**, the Dominican answer to Elvis.

Choruses tend to come in threes, engaging in extended **call-and-response sections** with the lead voice, which is swapped among them when there is no superstar. Meanwhile, they engage in virtuoso floor shows, dancing in split-second formations like The Temptations in fast forward, and maintaining an impossibly fast hand-jive. Bandleaders engage in the proceedings to varying degrees. Ventura's hip-swivelling histrionics are on a par with the legendary James Brown, while trumpet great **Wilfrido Vargas** maintains a dignified distance from his chorus's erotic foreplay.

Francisco Ulloa (with accordion) and his conjunto

Double and triple entendres involving sexuality and politics are standard procedure in the **lyrics**, while direct polemics are eschewed in favour of irony. "Dominicans have a wry sense of humor",

DAVE PEABODY

says Guerra. "Irony works better than heavy messages and it's more fun!" In his writing, a first-rate poetry emerges using surrealistic images culled from *campesino* life. More often, though, merengue is the language of escapism, and its lyrics seek to banish the exhausting outside world.

The Immaculate Conception

There are many stories regarding the **origins of merengue**, most of them patently apocryphal. One tale dates its inception to the Dominican Revolution against Haiti in the early nineteenth century. A soldier named Tomas Torres abandoned his post during a critical battle which the Dominicans later won, and the first merengue song was composed by the victors to mock poor Tomas's glaringly unpatriotic survival instinct.

The main purpose of this fabrication is to shield Dominican society from the unsavoury fact that their national music was probably transported from Haiti, and owes a debt to the traditions of Africa as well as Europe. Dominicans tend to look down their noses at the Haitians, and Dominican high society is extremely reluctant to acknowledge the African elements of their culture.

Nevertheless, a musical form called **mereng** with an alarmingly similar rhythmic structure developed in **Haiti** (then St. Domingue) during the eighteenth century among the landed mulatto classes. Until the colony's last years, Europeans and Africans were allowed to intermarry, permitting some people of African heritage to attain a level of power and wealth, even while others were subjected to the worst plantation slavery system of them all. The Europeans brought with them an abiding love of **contra dance** – the primary ballroom genre throughout the Colonial Caribbean. Mereng was a *danza* form infused with African rhythm – and, now known as *méringue*, it is still current in Haiti, in a slower, lilting form.

Merengue infiltrated the then Spanish colony of Santo Domingo through the pueblos, via Haitian invaders and former French gentry fleeing the machete after the revolution across the border. From there it made its way to elite urban ballrooms., where it encountered resistance from local society due to its 'African-ness'. Victims of the latest dance craze were likened to virgins who had soiled their good names. Taboo in the ballrooms, merengue was left to the auspices of rural Dominican folk. Perhaps because it was easy to dance to, perhaps because the lyrics were so irreverent and lewd, it took a huge hold amid the vast agricul-

tural stretches of the **Cibao valley**, and its main city, Santiago.

One final touch was needed for merengue to achieve classic form, and it came, oddly enough, via **Germany**. The country was an important business partner for the Dominican Republic during the nineteenth century, buying a great deal of the tobacco grown in the Cibao plantations. Many German exporters made a side business out of selling **accordions**, which quickly made inroads into the merengue ensemble, replacing the older string instruments. This changed the sound considerably, for the first imported accordions played only in one major key, banishing all minor-key merengues for a time to the dustbin of memory.

Merengue entered something of a 'golden age' during the dictatorship of **Rafael Trujillo**, who held power from the 1930s until his assassination in 1961. Trujillo was from peasant roots – and a poor dancer with two left feet – and he promoted the music as a populist symbol of national expression. He constrained its traditional role as a music of social commentary but provided a forum for musicians in the dancehalls. Larger **merengue orchestras** were developed, with piano and brass to cater for the new urban audiences.

Trujillo himself used merengue at the slightest excuse. A top-notch big-band group would follow him around on campaign stops, and state radio stations blasted favourite tunes between edicts. The entrenched antipathy of the urban elite began to melt as 'El Jefe' started to frequent their salons, a pistol in his pocket and a song in his heart, causing a stately ballroom merengue to re-emerge.

For this and other offences, Trujillo was eventually assassinated. But once merengue was dusted off and out of the closet, there was no stopping it, both at home and in immigrant communities in the US. Trujillo's fall, and the end of his isolationist policies, sparked a wave of migration to the major cities of North America, where Dominicans joined Puerto Ricans, Cubans and others in the vast urban barrios that served as the cultural cauldrons from which modern Latin music fomented. (One teenage Dominican immigrant to New York was **Johnny Pacheco** – a man who went on to virtually create salsa as the founder of the Fania Record label; see p.489).

New Influences

Back home, the key figure in the development of a modern merengue sound and image was **Johnny Ventura**, who in the 1970s set about marketing his music to compete with the US imports. Ventura was the first of the *merengueros* to fashion a pop icon status, using large-scale advertising, trademark floor shows and a sound more closely aligned with that of the US record industry. Merengue acquired a sharp, stuttering momentum that the old style only hinted at.

Emigration continued on an even greater scale in the 1980s, due to a major recession, and an increased Dominican presence in **New York** and **Miami** meant a much higher profile for the music. **Wilfrido Vargas** was the top star of this new era, pushing the music into uncharted harmonic and rhythmic territory. Vargas and his band started out playing bossa novas and rock'n'roll because he thought it was the best way to make a buck, and for a time he even featured disco covers. When it became financially viable for him to focus solely on merengue, he was much more open to outside elements than artists of the past, incorporating elements of salsa, compa, zouk and reggae – and recently house music and rap – into the idiom.

Vargas's experiments met with a certain amount of resistance from the purists, but his expansion of the vocabulary is now considered orthodoxy. Other big stars have followed suit, notably singing great **Cuco Valoy**, whose passion is Cuban music and calypso given a political slant.

Juan Luis Guerra – and Bachata

The towering figure in modern merengue, **Juan Luis Guerra** emerged on the scene in 1984, with his group **4:40** (the 'perfect note') and a completely new concept. His innovation was to slow down the merengue, softening it with harmonies inspired by Manhattan Transfer and The Beatles, adding a light, jazzy touch, and also a poetic sensibility – in the manner of *nueva canción* songwriters like the Cuban Silvio Rodríguez. This had never been seen before in the music and it proved hugely appealing to audiences both at home and in the US and Latin America.

Guerra drew on a whole range of Western music influences – he had studied at Boston's Berklee School of Music – and took a fresh look also at Dominican roots, bringing into the music a back country rhythm known as **bachata**. This was a bolero-type song, traditionally associated with soldiers, sailors and dockyards, and which (like early tango) displayed a darker, more melancholy view of the universe than mainstream music allowed. Even in its home country it was pulled out only at three or four in the morning amid communal

inebriated stupors. Guerra turned bachata around on his seminal *Bachata Rosa* album (1990), giving it a slick, commercial production along with his trademark lyrics, addressing the concerns of his people. The disc was a huge success, propelling Guerra to the top of the *Billboard* Latin charts. Indeed, at one stage in 1991, his albums stood at #1 and #2.

The song lyrics on each of Guerra's landmark albums are an important element – and they must rank among the most beautiful ever conceived. Guerra studied literature before music and, as he puts it, "the lyrics reflect my enthusiasm for poets like Neruda and Vallejo." Many of them – such as "I Hope it Rains Coffee in the Fields" – betray an affinity with magical realism: "[That] comes from a poem I found in the village of Santiago de los Caballeros. It's probably the work of a *campesino* – a peasant – and it was such a beautiful metaphor, I had to develop it."

Ojala que lluva café

Ojala que lluva café en el campo
que caiga un aguacero de yuca y té
del cielo una jarina de queso blanco
y al sur, un montaña
de berro y miel
oh, oh, oh, oh
Ojala que llueva café

I hope it rains coffee in the fields
that there falls a shower
of yuca and tea
from the sky a tub of white cheese
and to the south, a mountain
of butter and honey
oh, oh, oh, oh
I hope it rains coffee in the fields

from the album *Ojalá que llueva café*

The poetry of Guerra's lyrics constantly has its focus on Dominican images and issues: "Cost of Living", for example, addresses long term economic stagnation, while "Guavaberry" is about an indigenous fruit that causes the skin to itch upon contact. For it is Guerra's urgent life's work to produce a populist music to which the people back home can relate. "I certainly write for a home audience. [At one point] the band decided to shift back toward our roots – toward merengue. We felt in a way we were playing a music that seemed elite, and we wanted to play a music that appealed to everyone at home, a music that seemed more natural and intuitive."

ARISTA

Juan Luís Guerra

These remixes work surprisingly well – merengue's regular beat structures lend themselves easily to house adaptations – although they're not, inevitably, to everyone's taste. If you don't like house, you're unlikely to consider meren-house a desirable development, and the older audiences don't go for house. Still, those who grew up with the music can take comfort that the old forms lie embedded in the new like geological strata. Contemporary merenhouse band **Fulanito**, for example, pays homage to the history of their music by large-scale sampling of the accordion and other traditional instruments, whispering in the background behind the industrial urban noise like a ghost memory.

Major New York **merenhouse groups** like Fulanito, **Proyecto Uno** and the upstart **Illegales** – along with merenhouse-influenced salsa rap giant **Dark Latin Groove** – have achieved Latin star statuses that prevent them from playing any but the most major venues. But in Washington Heights, the overwhelmingly Dominican *barrio* that produced them, hundreds of imitators are cropping up, performing live street shows, subway revues and house parties in the hopes of being discovered by the recording industry – which is hot right now for Latin house. The music of this generation is a potentially quite new animal, with one ear on the *perico ripao* grooves of their parents and the other on the multi-layered industrial urban noise of young African-America.

Nonetheless, nobody has introduced a richer vein of world influences into a local roots music. "You look in Juan Luis's bag," says one collaborator, "and you see West African tapes, South African tapes, Indian music – he's listening to a whole different thing". The foreign musical colours he has adapted in recent years include Congolese soukous (working with guitarist Dibbo Dibbala), South African choral music, Cuban son, and, of course, salsa. On his 1998 album, *Ni es lo mismo ni es igual*, he was revisiting bachata and acoustic merengue, as well as giving a nod to new styles with a merengue-rap (a characteristic social number on health care on the island).

Merenhouse

Juan Luis Guerra had something of a lay-off in the mid-1990s, while the merengue scene moved off in new directions, picking up (like much Latin music) on influences from **hip hop** and **house**. The hottest name to emerge in this so-called **merenhouse** style is **Elvis Crespo**, who has fused US-style house music with a relatively traditional mainstream pop merengue style. Others have followed, notably in New York, where all the big merengue stars have released remixes of their hits for the new dance-fixated audiences.

Merengue Live

Santo Domingo's Malecon, a three-mile stretch of boardwalk with the Caribbean on one side and wall-to-wall night spots on the other, is alive with the very best that merengue has to offer, year round, all night long. However, for the very best merengue experience, the time to visit the island is the last two weeks of July, for the annual **Merengue Festival** in **Santo Domingo**. Bands both from the island and the US play the festival and for the duration the Dominican capital becomes one massive, pulsating outdoor discotheque.

The US economic upswing of the 1990s has had a profound effect on **New York**'s Dominican barrio of Washington Heights -- eradicating a murder rate that was once the highest in the nation and sending droves of New Yorkers from all walks to the newly hot merenrap clubs in this once uninviting neighbourhood. The current hot spots are *Studio 84*, the *Warehouse* and the *Copacabana*. Meantime, you can hear old-style merengue at venerable Latin nightclubs like Dyckman Street's *Las Vegas* and *Casa Quisqueya* in Brooklyn.

discography

Compilations

 Aqui Esta Merengue (Karen, US).

A roundup of Dominican merengue featuring Wilfrido Vargas, creator of the 1980s merengue-fusions with zouk and soca; his former protegé, Sergio Vargas, one of the sweetest voices in Latin music today; plus all-woman orchestra Las Chicas del Can and more.

 Essential Merengue: Stripping the Parrots (Corason, Mexico).

Five local bands demonstrate the rootsy sound of country merengue – accordion, tambora and guayo, the metal scraper that drives the band and dancers onwards. Hypnotic call-and-response vocals are interrupted by startling accordion riffs, while the groove never sleeps.

 Haiti Cherie Merengue (Corason, Mexico).

A compilation of Haitian street bands playing their slower, more lyrical and tattered-at-the-edges rendition.

Merengue: Dominican Music and Dominican Identity (Smithsonian Folkways, US).

A fascinating historical panorama of merengue from the early years of the 20th century to rural bands in the 1990s. It's good on Rafael Trujillo's promotion of merengue and national identity and includes rare historic recordings, rural bands, stately salon-merengue and the first all-women merengue orchestra led by Belkis Concepción.

Merengue Mania (Nascente, UK).

The material on this budget-priced CD goes back to the 1960s when legendary merengueros such as Luis Kalaff, Trio Reynoso ruled the roost. Heavy on the accordion and sax, these classic dance tunes sound as raw and raunchy today as when the merengue craze first swept across the Caribbean.

Revolucion En La Casa (Nascente, UK).

This high-energy 'Essential Latin Hose Collection' features New York Dominican *meren-house* group Fulanito and *meren-bachata* innovators Monchy y Alexandra, alongside a host of Puerto Ricans and others creating the new, hugely popular Latin house.

Artists

Fulanito

Fulantio is the foundational merenrap band that has led the way. The wild success of their smoothly layered Spanish rap over sampled old-style merengue grooves with accordion has forced every other band in the field to become imitators.

El Hombre Mas Famoso de la Tierra (Cutting Edge, US).

Fulanito's first, and still by far their best, album, featuring jerkily sampled accordion, tambora and guira over rap lyrics and hip hop grooves that oscillate wildly between exuberant and broody.

Juan Luís Guerra

Juan Luís Guerra and his band 4:40 have cut a swathe through the field of Latin American popular music with their brand of jazz-inflected merengue fused with discreetly erotic or magical realist lyrics and mildly critical socio-political themes. Although the basis of the band's music is merengue and bachata, Guerra and his band also draw on salsa, South African choral music, Congolese guitar and Western pop (the spirit, if not the sound, of The Beatles is ever present). A blend of energy and romance that sweeps all before it.

Bachata Rosa (Karen, US).

The album title means 'Pink Trash' – about as ironic as you could contrive for the best-selling Dominican album of all time, on which Guerra gave a whole new sublime life to the country bachata style.

Areito (RCA, US; Arista, UK).

For some fans, *Areito* just has the edge over Bachata Rosa, with Guerra's melodic and lyrical invention firing on all cylinders and the band – especially the horns – on top form.

Fogarate (Karen/Polygram Latino, US).

Guerra's 1995 outing was fascinating, introducing *soukous* style merengue through the presence of Congolese guitarist Diblo Dibala, along with forays into Cuban son and salsa.

Ni es lo mismo ni es igual
(Karen/Polygram Latino, US).

The long-awaited 1998 comeback album: not quite a classic but hugely enjoyable and diverting nonetheless. Tracks range from acoustic ballads to bachata, and there's a poppy number about computers ("Mi PC") and even a merengue-rap.

Los Hermanos Rosario

The Rosario brothers have led one of the most popular merengue bands on the island and abroad since the mid-1980s.

Los Mundialmente Famoso Hermanos Rosario
(Karen, US).

Featuring "Morena Ven", the band's greatest, well-deserved hit, this is another slice of speedy, mocking and immaculately played merengue.

Los Sabrosos del Merengue

Los Sabrosos del Merengue, led by pianist Carmelo Marrero, are one of the best examples of the (non-house) merengue sound of today – energetic and drilled to absolute precision, with tumbling piano, jaunty singing and hard-driving tambora.

Haciendo Historia
(MP, US).

A perfect example of early 1990s big band dance merengue, this disc spawned an energetic clutch of hits.

New York Band

Dominican trombone legend Franklin Rivers' first and most popular band featured a line-up of the top Dominican horn players of the 1980s.

Mama No Quiere Que Yo Cole (Karen, US).

Probably the best album to come out of the 1980s global explosion. The title is a double entendre – Mama Doesn't Want me to Gatecrash.

Pochy y Su Coco Band

Pochy (sometimes spelled Pochi) and his Coco Band are a great example of the sly, light-hearted and sometimes almost tongue in cheek aspect of merengue. Outrageously speedy and complicated arrangements race away behind the singer, whose singing suggests that he has one eyebrow permanently and quizzically raised.

Pochi y su Coco Band
(Kubaney, Dominican Republic).

One of the band's earliest recordings, this is infused with youthful high spirits and an optimistic glow. Things got a bit crazier later on, but this is a good place to begin.

Francisco Ulloa

Ulloa is a master accordionist, playing traditional-style acoustic merengue – but if that sounds rootsy and sedate just wait till you hear his frantic arpeggios, echoed by sax and triple-time bass and a driving throb from the tambora.

¡Merengue! (GlobeStyle, UK); ¡Ultramerengue! (GlobeStyle, UK).

Wild music from a man who must have more than the natural compliment of fingers to bring it off. On some tracks he adds African marimba (thumb piano) to the mix, for even more percussive invention.

Cuco Valoy

Although Cuco Valoy – known as 'El Brujo', the wizard – is from the Dominican Republic, he is as likely to perform Cuban-style *son* as merengue. He and his band Los Virtuosos are equally convincing in both styles.

Salsa con Couco (Discolor, US).

This collection of some of Couco's greatest hits is well worth acquiring, not least because it contains perhaps his most famous song "Juliana", and the typically loopy "La Muerte de Don Marcos".

Wilfrido Vargas

Legendary merengue innovator and dignified elder statesman, Vargas brought the influence of a dozen different World Music forms into the family, along with an expansion of the harmonic vocabulary comparable to the achievement of Charlie Parker.

Abusadura
(Karen, US).

One of his most striking and popular recordings, with influences from around the world, as well as merengue versions of a couple of classic bachatas.

Sergio Vargas

Former protegé of Wilfrido Vargas, singer Serio Vargas struck out on his own and found great success with a smooth and sophisticated approach to merengue.

Sergio Vargas (Sony, US).

This is the disc with his biggest hit, "La Ventanita", and a good example of the current sound, more sweet than sweat.

Johnny Ventura

The Dominican Elvis, Johnny Ventura did a lot to update merengue, and was the first merenguero to fashion himself an image as a pop icon. The old timer has recently gone into politics as a means of escaping the State Fair tour circuit.

Guataco (Kubaney, US).

A classic Ventura album with many of his hits and some great singing. The old-time saxophone sound mimics the accordion with its mile-wide, furious vibrato, even as the influence of disco begins to creep in.

Angel Viloria

Accordionist Viloria's recordings are the best recorded examples of pure merengue tipico cibaeno. Played with only an accordion, a tambora and a guira, it manages to swing as hard as the best of the big bands. Also features classic old-style saxophone on some cuts.

Merengues, Vol 1 and Vol 2 (Ansonia, US).

Together these two albums form the canon of classic old-style merengue. It's hard to believe that a band consisting of one drum, a modified cheese scraper and an instrument usually reserved for use with lederhosen can really rock this hard.

Haiti

compas points

Haiti shares the island of Hispañola with the Dominican Republic, but it takes a brave soul to visit, given the current crisis levels of violence and street crime. But the music is there, if you can make it, with the local compas beat every bit as irresistible as its better-known neighbour, merengue. **Sue Steward** and **Sean Harvey** trace dance, carnival and voodoo in this unique mix of African and French Caribbean culture.

aiti's most immediate associations are voodoo, violence and the brutal regimes of Papa and Baby Doc Duvalier. The Duvaliers presided over the country's decline to the poorest, least-developed territory in the Western Hemisphere. Their loyal thugs, the Tontons Macoutes, terrorised the entire populace, co-opting the voodoo traditions of the secret Bizango societies (brought from Africa and intend-

ed to protect the community). Since the end of the regime, Haiti has slid uneasily between democracy, military rule, and gridlock. Development aid has not been forthcoming, poverty remains abject, and US-style gangs have taken over the streets.

And yet there is no starker contrast between Haiti's parlous social and economic situation, and the joyful, melodic dance music that has existed here since the 1950s. Haiti then, like Cuba, was a

STEVE WINTER

Haitian dancers

magnet for American tourists with Port-au-Prince, its capital city, rivalling Havana in its nightclubs, where some of the greatest musicians of the day were employed. This scene collapsed during Papa Doc's reign of terror, though there were respites under the Baby Doc regime at the end of the 1970s, when the island became a hip resort for rock aristocrats like Mick Jagger and Iggy Pop, and again at the end of the 1980s, when film-maker Jonathan Demme put together *Konbit*, a fine compilation of Haitian music.

Haiti's music, based on the wonderful rhythms of **compas**, is as rich as any in the Caribbean, and would be ripe for exploration on its home ground if things weren't quite so dangerous. But as the US Travel Advisory puts it: 'there is no safe area in Haiti'. Meantime, there's a reasonable chance of catching Haitian bands on tour, and great discs are still coming out of the island.

Africa, Creole and Voodoo

Like all Caribbean islands, Haiti's character, and the character of its music, has been shaped by its colonial history. The French pacified the anarchic western part of Spanish Hispañola in 1640, and at the height of French colonisation Haiti was the richest colony in the world, the 'Pearl of the Antilles', exporting more sugar, coffee and tobacco than the other islands put together. These industries were sustained by **African slaves**, who by 1800 numbered over half a million: eight times as many as the whites and mulattos, a ratio that precipitated the country's liberation and shaped the island's strong African identity.

Haiti's strong African character is still obvious today: in the food, the Creole language, the voodoo and the music. Despite continuing disdain from the educated mulatto elite, **Creole** (*Kreyo'l*), a phonetic fusion of various African languages and French, remains the nation's mother tongue. Created as a way for African slaves to communicate with their French overseers, it became the primary means of communication among the slaves who were segregated from their countrymen without a common language, and the vehicle through which a national identity was cemented. A recent campaign for Creole pride has been endorsed by a number of popular dance bands, including the radical **Boukman Eksperyans**, who sing mainly in Creole. Their catchy hit, "Se Kreyo'l Nou Ye" (We Speak Creole), on the album *Vodou Adje*, has become something of an anthem for the young generation.

The word **voodoo** (more commonly *vodou* in Haiti) is originally Dahomeyan, from West Africa, and means 'spirituality'. Voodoo practices united the many African religions brought by the slaves with Catholicism, European folk belief and even freemasonry, effectively bonding Africans with different languages and cultures. Drummers – still an integral part of the worship service – conveyed coded messages and gave psychological and spiritual sustenance to the slaves. Voodoo still has that function in the stricken island today: there's an old saying that 'Haitians are eighty percent Catholic and a hundred percent Voodoo'.

In voodoo, music is the vehicle of transport between the physical and spiritual realms. In a voodoo ceremony, held at outdoor temples called *hounforts*, the *houngan* (priest) prepares the congregation with drumming and chanting, calling the gods (*loas*) down to inhabit a chosen living being or inanimate object. The loas, who speak through the possessed person, are identified with particular Catholic saints.

Persistent (and respectful) visitors to Haiti can get to see one of the secret ceremonies in a hounfort, or failing that, join a voodoo evening with drumming, dancing and chanting at the legendary Hotel Olaffson in Port-au-Prince. The roots renaissance of the past decade has also revived the rhythms of the Haitian countryside, as can be heard on the breathtaking field compilations *Angels in the Mirror* and *Rhythms of Rapture*, and in the neo-traditional acoustic drum-and-voice ensemble **Troupe Mackandal**.

That Dirty Compas Beat

Compas, the popular music of Haiti, has little in common with voodoo and owes more to colonial dance rhythms. Typically, it is played by a big band, or **orchestre**, and is divided into sections that change abruptly in mood, texture and key. The overall sound is sweet and smooth and the melodies are carried on flowing guitar lines, regulated by a characteristic rocking beat that pivots between the hi-hat and a bass drum on the floor.

Like most Caribbean music, compas is a mix of styles, with a base in traditional rhythms like **méringue** – a slower, Haitian variant of the Dominican merengue, retaining the guitar that has been supplanted over the border by the accordion. In the most rural parts of the country, there is still a thriving tradition of European court dances played over Caribbean drum rhythms. A good example is the *menwat*, a Haitian variant of the

Nemours Jean-Baptiste

played an important part in shaping the local sound, and vice versa. Dominican merengue originated as a colonial dance of the Haitian mulatto classes, and Cuban dance bands from the 1930s onwards have imported the most popular music of the day: boleros, rumbas and mambos. **Calypso** too has left a permanent mark in the form of the huge orchestras like **Septentrional** and **Tropicana d'Haiti**, both of whom still release regular *Anniversaire* albums, swinging with the sensuous lilt of old-style calypso.

The foundations of modern compas were laid early in the century. With the US occupation of the island (1915–1934) came **Swing Band** music, and suddenly the horn sections of the sedate orchestras playing Cuban or European dance styles 'swung'. The most influential was **Les Jazz des Jeunes**, founded in the early 1940s by René St-Aude, a saxophonist who now runs a record shop and label in Brooklyn. Les Jazz des Jeune's blend of Afro-Cuban and Afro-Haitian music with swing dominated the scene until the arrival of a pair of flamboyant young saxophonists who, in the 1960s, created two new strands of popular music.

These men were **Nemours Jean Baptiste**, who invented **compas direct**, the basis of today's compas sound, a big-band mix of mambo and compas with a steady bass drum and cowbell beat, and **Webert Sicot**, who came up with **cadence rampa**, which stuck closer to the Cuban line. For nearly a decade the two were bitter rivals, taunting each other's fans with confrontational lyrics,

minuet, a holdover from the days when virtuoso slave violinists played in colonial opera houses. Compas also absorbed many other Caribbean influences, especially salsa, soca and zouk, and later took in jazz, funk and rap from North America. A further strain was Central African **soukous**, whose intricate guitar patterns were imported by Haitian teachers who went to work in Zaire (Congo) after that country's independence.

Haiti's proximity to Cuba, just fifty miles away, and to Puerto Rico and the adjoining Dominican Republic, has meant that **Latin music** has always

Carnival in Port-au-Prince

The **carnival** in Port-au-Prince represents a route of six to eight kilometres through the city. Groups, mounted on trucks disguised as floats, covered with loudspeakers and microphones, move forward at a tortuous pace in the middle of a veritable human sea that sweats, dances and pushes. Throughout the entire trajectory, lasting from six to seven hours, each group plays only a single composition, and when they arrive back at the Place de l' Hotel de Ville for the popular dance (which lasts another two hours) they continue playing the same piece! Perhaps the director of the orchestra has also contracted for a nightclub engagement on the same evening, where they have to play from midnight until three o'clock in the morning, taking care to open and close the dance with a long version of that same carnival *méringe*.

After three days of these bachanals, one can deduce that the compas musicians have played intermittently for nearly fifty hours, under appalling conditions, while consuming a good amount of alcohol and an overdose of decibels. Moreover, the musical core of their repertoire is a hit of energy, designed to excite the crowd, and its execution at an exaggeratedly quick tempo requires superhuman quantities of energy. So, they have to hold their rhythm for three days, under the sun, and three nights in insufferable heat, even when they can't hear what they're playing. The golden rule is: Never Fade. On the hundred and one stops of this competitive route, they have to win one-on-one on the applause meter before being able to stake a claim as heroes of the evening.

From **Ralph Boncy**'s *La Chanson d'Haiti: 1965–85*, translated by Gage Averill for *The Beat* magazine.

until Sicot wrote the truce song "Polemic Fini" in 1965, proclaiming in its chorus, "Oh yes, the polemic is over".

Truce or not, rivalry (often of a pretty vicious nature) is a perennial feature on the Haitian music scene. It encompasses the big established orchestras, Septentrional and Tropicana, and seeps into relationships at home and among the exiles in New York, Miami and Montréal.

Mini-Jazz, Zouk and American Fusions

The 1960s were in all respects a critical decade in Haiti as Papa Doc installed his oppressive state machinery, prompting the flight of hundreds of thousands of Haitians to the United States and Canada. For the musicians at home, or in these new communities, influences came from beyond the Caribbean, as The Beatles and American and French pop singers spawned a generation of **'mini-jazz' bands** who performed at house and school parties. With electric guitar, bass, saxophone, drums and percussion they played covers of imported pop and Haitian classics, and original teen-oriented songs. Their ranks included the groups Ibo Combo, Les Freres de Jean, Les Fantasistes de Carrefour, Shleu Shleu and Los Incognitos de Petionville, many of whom provided a start for today's influential musicians.

Most of the mini-jazz bands mutated into larger formations and moved to the US in the early 1970s. Los Incognitos metamorphosed into the most famous of all Haitian bands, **Tabou Combo**, who put **compas** on the international map. Profoundly influenced by American funk, their 1969 debut album, *Haiti*, launched a new era for the music, while *8eme Sacrement*, recorded in 1984, after their move to New York, sold millions and reached number one in Paris. The latter includes the group's big performance song, "New York City", a high-speed swirl of funfair accordion, electric guitars and sizzling hi-hats, amid which the singer switches from French to Spanish to English. It sounds as fresh and modern as anything produced today and still sends audiences into ecstasy.

In recent years, compas has undergone radical changes, especially among Haitians living in the US. In New York – Brooklyn has the largest

mini all stars

EARTHWORKS
Fanatiques Compas
Glorious celebration of the music of Nemours Jean-Baptiste, the originator of Haitian compas

Haitian community after Haiti's capital, Port-au-Prince – and Miami, access to hi-tech equipment and to other musical styles has made changes inevitable. Throughout the 1970s, influences filtered into compas, above all from salsa. The group **Skah Shah**, for instance, employed a salsa-style backing section of trumpets and trombones to create a delicious new combination with the compas rhythm section and shifting guitars.

From the mid-1980s, French Antillean **zouk** was another major force in the Caribbean, and a three-way trade developed between merengue, zouk and compas, with their respective bands producing a rush of sparkling covers of each other's songs. The song "Vacances" captivated Haiti in the early 1970s, on its release by merengue and compas bands Les Fantasistes de Carrefour and Shleu Shleu, and then re-emerged as a monster zouk hit for the Guadeloupian band Kassav in the 1980s. Kassav and the other disco-oriented zouk bands continue to be hugely popular in Haiti.

Many of Haiti's so-called **Nouvel Jenerayshun** (New Generation) came through at home and abroad during the 1980s. They have the typically bright, electronic sound associated with both merengue and zouk bands. Exponents like **Sakad** – a funk-based outfit – featured sharp synthesizers, themes borrowed from American dance music, the intricate horn arrangements of merengue, and breathy female choruses (women singers were a radical step for the Haitian pop industry, though they've been a vital part of voodoo music for centuries).

System Band is among the pioneers of the new generation, combining jazz-oriented horn lines – with the section performing synchronised kung fu moves between riffs – and what they refer to in one song as 'that dirty compas beat' with synthesizers and a variety of electronic devices. They have spawned notable imitators like **The Phantoms**, a rival group whose horn lines are harmonically simpler and more along the lines of a staccato Latin aesthetic. Even more radically, bands like **Zin** in New York and Miami's **Top Vice** have introduced **rapping** over a compas backing. Another recent arrival is a spate of female bands, most notably **Karesse** and **Risque**, a new generation of women who attach loosely feminist lyrics to the compas beat.

Haiti in the US

New York

New York's largest Haitian community is centred around **Nostrand Avenue, Brooklyn**: a street where every other storefront is a church, and there are more record stores and barber shops than tropical food outlets. Here **JD's Records**, run by record producer Jerome Donfred, sells the entire history of Haitian music. There are racks of classics from big orchestras like Septentrional, the whole range of Tabou Combo, local zouk and rap-influenced bands like Zin, and political records like Fedia Laguerre's "Operashun Dechoukaj" (Operation Uprooting – a reference to the uprooting of the Tonton Macoutes after the Duvaliers left), which can't be sold in Haiti. Around the shop are Haitian newspapers, such as *Haiti Culture* and the music magazine *Nouvelaute*, and fliers for local clubs like *Le rendez-vous* and *Château d'Or*. Other record stores at the centre of the scene include **Nou-vel Jenerayshun** on Flatbush Avenue and **Mark Records** on Rutland Avenue in Queens.

Miami

Miami's Little Haiti is closer geographically, and also in look, to Port-au-Prince, with its Creole shop signs and graffiti, although the restaurants and record shops indicate a higher standard of living than can be had on the island. Elegant nightclubs like *Le Limekey* and *Obsession* heave with couples dancing cheek-to-cheek in their finest silks until dawn. This is an uneasy bicultural ghetto, with regular run-ins with both the police and the neighbouring Afro-Americans of Liberty City – the favourite local Haitian band of the moment is called Top Vice. But here, as in New York, the population pulses with a vitality and optimism that is impossible to conceive of back home.

Tabou Combo's catalogue parallels the recent history of compas, from the accordion and guitar drive of the New York City era, to its 1980s electronic, zouk-influenced entry into the rap age. Their live album, *Aux Antilles*, reveals how they've adapted compas to the synthesised format and reworked their own history through new versions of earlier hits. Their offshoot, **New York Superstars**, has moved into straight rap delivered over a compas beat: the sound of late 1990s Brooklyn.

In 1996 Tabou Combo's abandonment of compas orthodoxy was taken a step further by the incredibly successful US-Haitian 'soft hip hop' group **The Fugees**, a trio (featuring superstar singer **Lauryn Hill**) whose compas and zouk roots are apparent alongside those of soul, reggae and funk. The group's key musician and arranger, **Wyclef Jean**, is the son of a Haitian Baptist minister and emerged out of the US-Haitian gospel scene where travelling choirs, accompanied by funk-reggae bands and sophisticated floor shows,

Tabou Combo

electrify Pentecostal congregations in New York and New Jersey.

At home in Haiti, **Pentecostal music** consists of hauntingly beautiful a cappella hymns (akin to voodoo music but minus the 'pernicious' drum accompaniment), but enormous audiences on the island have latched onto The Fugees' secularised gospel sound and incorporated it into their repertoire of cultural influences and styles.

Ra-Ra: Talking Nasty with the Gods

Back on Haiti, with no chance of access to hi-tech zouk gear, many Port-au-Prince bands and musicians have turned to the island's roots, particularly voodoo and the Easter carnival music, **ra-ra**, for inspiration.

Ra-ra is traditionally played at carnival street parades by devotees possessed by a particularly mischievous brand of loa called the *Gedes*. This possession gives them both supernatural stamina and the right to castigate anyone along the route for past misdeeds, in language that Haitians would otherwise consider extremely offensive. The music is

Boukman Eksperyans

made up of short, interlocking rhythmic figures played on keyless metal trumpets and bamboo tubes, accompanied by a variety of percussion instruments and occasionally saxophones and trumpets. The larger the ensemble, the more multi-layered and beautiful its sound. You can hear it in its raw form on *Caribbean Revels*, a Smithsonian Folkways CD recorded in situ in Haiti and among

Haitian cane cutters in the Dominican Republic.

The ra-ra beat is also a trademark of the band **Boukman Eksperyans**, who have pioneered a blend of Afro-Haitian religious music, sung in Creole. They feature prolonged percussion workouts on a set of traditional instruments, while weaving in rock guitar, funk and reggae bass lines. In "Nou pap sa bliye" (We're Not Going to Forget This) the band chants out the African and voodoo sources of the rhythms they use: "Petro, Congo, Rada, Ibo, Nago: our ancestors were there." The two female singers dip and swoop, mimicking the street dancers in the ra-ra processions; Haitian audiences go wild in recognition of their street culture in this context. Lolo Beaubrun, the group's leader, explains their use of voodoo elements as "an attempt to reinstate our culture, which had been despised and rejected for years. Even Boukman himself was written out of history because he was a voodoo priest."

While Boukman Eksperyans pioneered this style and still maintain it now, their career has been punctuated by periods of silence in the face of threats and danger. Their 1992 carnival entry, "Kalfou Denjere", for example, was banned in the wake of the military coup as 'too violent', and the authorities also prohibited broadcast of their 1990 anthem "Kèm Pa Sote", with its chorus "My heart doesn't leap; you don't scare me." Other ra-ra bands, like **Boukan Ginen**, were forced to leave Haiti altogether for the safety of New York.

The artist considered most subversive – and thus the most persecuted musician on Haiti – is singer-songwriter **Manno Charlemagne**. He sings guardedly metaphorical lyrics backed by a big band that employs the traditional tall upright drums. Seen as a kind of Haitian Bob Marley, and drawing vast crowds in concert, he openly opposed both Duvalier and the 1991 coup leaders, giving very public backing to the deposed President Aristide. He remains a key figure of the Haitian music scene, and has now returned to the island after spending a year in asylum in the Venezuelan embassy in Port-au-Prince, followed by two more years in exile in Miami.

Other current island-based bands include **Sanba-Yo**, who occupy a similar rock-roots territory to Boukman Eksperyans, with a ra-ra beat and other rural rhythms and choruses, and **Coupé Cloué**, led on electric guitar by grandmaster Gesner Henry, which still plays true compas. One of the few surviving mini-jazz bands, Coupé Cloué have an ambivalent reputation on Haiti, having played at Tontons Macoutes parties (not that bands can exactly refuse to play for the Macoutes, if invited). Their music has updated itself over the years but still bears the sensual languor of the tropics rather than the brash speed of the new US-based sounds.

Younger bands on the island include **Mizik** and **Tropicana**, both of whom play a safe, old-fashioned line; **Foula**, who have developed a voodoo-jazz-funk sound with a range of traditional rhythms; and **RAM**, led by Richard Morse, who contributed a track to the soundtrack of Hollywood's first AIDS movie, *Philadelphia*. Morse is the owner of the Olaffson Hotel, centre of the Port-au-Prince music scene. Once a home away from home to a clutch of rock legends (for a little extra you can spend the night in the Mick Jagger Bungalow), it offers workshop space to musicians, dancers and artists in outhouses behind the hotel.

The international acclaim that has greeted groups like RAM and Boukman Eksperyans' pop interpretations of traditional **voodoo music** has led in the past few years to a re-examination, both in Haiti and in the United States, of the music in its more orthodox form. Just as it has been for the past four centuries, voodoo music is still alive and well throughout the countryside. **Boukan Ginen** and **Troupe Mackandal** these days perform to sell-out concert audiences in the US and Europe, while at home, acoustic voodoo music from bands like **Djakata** is now being played to packed nightclub audiences in Port-au-Prince.

discography

Compilations

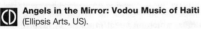

Angels in the Mirror: Vodou Music of Haiti (Ellipsis Arts, US).

This astonishing release acts as a virtual tour of the Haitian countryside and the diversity of its hard-grooving voodoo-influenced music. It includes Haiti's major African drum patterns, each of which has produced a music as rhythmically compelling and distinct as salsa or calypso, rural adaptations of colonial music such as menwat (Haitian minuet), and a dance ensemble that has been in continuous existence since its stint as a seventeenth-century French military band. The

CD comes with a 64-page introduction to Haitian music and voodoo, including background on each track, folktales, recipes and sixty beautiful color photographs.

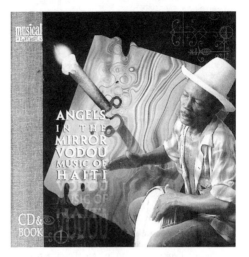

 Caribbean Revels (Smithsonian Folkways, US).

A remarkable disc capturing the rough and ready sound of authentic ra-ra, recorded in cemeteries and streets in Haiti in the late 1970s.

Haiti Cherie (Corason, Mexico; Rounder, US).

Méringue, very unlike the fast and furious merengue from the neighbouring Dominican Republic, is a gentle, almost dreamy guitar-based music. This selection of the work of four of the street orchestras known as *ti* bands.

Konbit: Burning Rhythms of Haiti (A&M, US).

This superb compilation by film-maker Jonathan Demme was made with the collaboration of compas fans The Neville Brothers, who play on a couple of tracks, and it perfectly

illustrates the trends of the past forty years. Opening with Nemours Jean Baptiste and compas direct, the selection then moves through mini-jazz units, big-band synth-era sounds and ra-ra beat from Sanba-Yo before it finally bows out with the funk of Sakad.

 Rhythms of Rapture: Sacred Musics of Haitian Vodou (Smithsonian Folkways, US).

This is the best introduction to the roots movement that has reclaimed Haitian folk music. It includes a dozen field recordings of the music in its traditional form, from *menwat* bands to voodoo ceremonies and women singing in the street as they walk to the market. Interspersed are acoustic roots selections from popular bands like Ra-Ra Machine and Troupe Mackandal along with electronic voodoo music from RAM, Boukan Ginen and Boukman Eksperyans. Of special historic significance is the first-ever recording of music from a super-secret Bizango society rite. The booklet insert features a series of terrific essays on Haitian musical styles.

Artists

Toto Bissainthe

Haiti's great, late Creole diva, Toto Bissainthe spent long years in exile in Paris before her death in 1994. She had a big, theatrical voice and sung to acoustic ra-ra rhythms created often by just bass and percussion.

 Haiti Chant (Chant du Monde, France).

In this live performance dating from the early 1980s, the 'Queen Minstrel' takes an experimental approach to her island's traditional drum and vocal music, creating an exhilarating and sometimes startling mix of relentless groove and moving ballads.

Boukan Ginen

Roots band Boukan Ginen were formed by ex-members of Boukman Eksperyans in 1990 and, like the mother-lode band, they sing in Creole against a thunderous backdrop of rhythms. Latterly they have added reggae and Cuban influences into their mix.

 Jou a Rive (Xenophile, US).

The band's 1995 debut remains their strongest disc, with some great vocal harmonies and no-holds bass and drums.

Boukman Eksperyans

Formed in 1979, and named after a Voodoo priest who was in the vanguard of the 1804 uprising against the French, Boukman Eksperyans are notable both for their fearless musical experimentation and the brave political edge to their lyrics – their 1990 carnival song "Ke'm Pa Sote" (I'm Not Afraid) was an anthem in the protests that led to the collapse of dictator Prosper Avril. They are still based in Port-au-Prince, a big band led by 'Lôlo' Beaubrun, and veterans of many global tours. Catch them live if you possibly can.

 Libeté (Pan Pou Pran'l) (Mango, UK).

Libeté (Freedom – Let's Take it) reflects the political turmoil of the time of its creation with its urgent, thrilling sound. Along with **Vodou Adjè** and **Kalfou Danjeré** (Mango, UK), it demonstrates Boukman's direction of the 1980s and early 1990s, when they spurned compas for other rhythms, especially ra-ra music. There are strong influences from the US in the guitar parts, and from neighbouring Jamaica in the bass lines. All three albums are highly recommended.

 Revolution (Tuff Gong/WEA, US).

This 1998 offering from Boukman continues along their intriguing path of mingling political comment, ancestral African roots music and danceable rhythms.

Ti-Coca

Ti-Coca (David Mettelus) is one of the best singers in Haiti today, creating an old-time compas music backed by his accordion-led acoustic quintet, Ouanga Negues.

Haiti: Ti-Coca, Toto Bissainthes (World Network, Germany).

A gorgeous compilation from the Network label. Ti-Coca is featured on ten songs, which show elements of merengue and Cuban bolero creeping into the compas mix, and a gentle lilt from both voice and accordion. As a bonus, the CD rounds off with three songs from Toto Bissainthe (see above).

Coupé Cloué

Coupé Cloué was the nickname of professional football player Jean Gesner Henri (1925–98), and became the name of his *compas*-direct dance orchestra. This thrived for decades, up until his death, with a sound enriched by his soukous-derived guitar style.

 Maximum Compas from Haiti (Stern's/Earthworks, UK).

A fine album that epitomises Coupé Cloué's lush, languorous, guitar-led style and long Creole addresses. There is a strong Cuban influence detectable in several of the tracks.

Ensemble Nemours Jean Baptiste

Saxophonist Nemours Jean Baptiste (born in Port-au-Prince, 1918) was a creator of modern compas and Haiti's most influential bandleader. His heyday was in the 1950s and 1960s, which he spent in a kind of feud with his Antillean 'rival', cadence-originator Webert Sicot.

Musical Tour of Haiti (Ansonia Records, US).

This great collection of tracks showcases Baptiste's punchy, rhythmic band of the 1960s, featuring saxophone, accordion and a brass section that swaggers its way across the beat of a pumping bass drum and driving cowbell.

THE MINI ALL STARS

◉ Mini All Stars: Fanatiques Compas
(Stern's/Earthworks, UK).

An addictively swinging tribute to Nemours Jean-Baptiste, with new, but faithful arrangements of classic Nemours hits, memorably performed by former colleagues and worthy heirs.

Wyclef Jean

One third of The Fugees – the mega-selling Haitian-Americans – Wyclef Jean was born in Haiti in 1970, as he makes reference to even in the name of his band (from Refugees). Following the success of The Fugees' soulful hip hop album The Score (1996), he has popped up all over the US music scene, producing, writing and remixing for everyone from Santana to the Neville Brothers, and has also toured his own Haitian-inflected solo material.

◉ Wyclef Jean Presents the Carnival Featuring Refugee Allstars (Ruffhouse/Columbia, US).

This is basically a hip hop album but it is also a distinctly Haitian one, with raps in Creole as well as English. There is also a guest spot from Cuban exile Celia Cruz on the Cuban classic a cappella number, "Guantanamera".

Orchestre Septentrional

Before Nemours Jean Baptiste came along, Orchestre Septentrional and their longstanding rivals Orchestre Tropicana d'Haiti defined the sound of big band dance music on the island.

 La Boule de Feu Internationale '40th Anniversaire' (Marc Records, Haiti).

A wonderful recording that retains the sound of the 1940s and 1950s, with duelling trumpets and saxophones, wild guitar and masses of swing.

Orchestre Tropicana d'Haiti

Tropicana d'Haiti were the great rival of Orchestre Septentrional (see above) through the 1940s and 1950s.

◉ La Fusée d'Or (Geronimo, US).

This disc pointedly claims (in its sleeve notes) to represent 'for fifteen years the only big Haitian orchestra of an international quality'. Traditional Haitian rivalry aside, the vocals are sublime and the rhythm the usual mixture of local grooves, calypso and mambo with a higher than usual proportion of roots elements.

Ra-Ra Machine

Port-au-Prince-based Ra-Ra Machine, led by singer and percussionist Clifford Sylvain, feature a fusion of Haitian countryside's populist voodoo music with rap and Latin grooves. At times they move away from electronics and play some of the best acoustic roots music going.

◉ Vodou Nou (Shanachie, US).

A series of transformations performed on traditional Haitian roots music, including electronics, Latin grooves and some rap. Other cuts are pure acoustic voodoo music with a cappella choruses reminiscent of South Africa's Ladysmith.

Shleu Shleu

Shleu Shleu were one of the products of Haiti's beat boom – the 1960s mini-jazz era.

◉ Haiti mon pays (Ibo Records, Haiti).

A record that is the epitome of the beat boom era, with its 'uptown Port-au-Prince' sound, featuring topical songs about Haiti, baseball, fishing and girls.

Skah Shah

Profoundly influential, Skah Shah was one of the very first bands to create a fusion of compas with Latin music and funk. They're still one of the most popular bands working in New York's Haitian community.

◉ Forever (Mini Records, US).

One of the best products of New York's 1970s cultural fusions, mixing the typical guitar-based sound of compas with a spicy salsa-inspired brass section.

System Band

The best Haitian group working in New York today, with a more authentic Haitian compas sound than the funk fusions of their competitors.

 Averge (Louis Productions, Haiti/US).

The classic System Band album with muscly, jazz-influenced horn lines over classic compas rhythms.

◉ System Live (Louis Productions, Haiti/US).

A brilliant concert album that provides some of the fire of live Haitian performance that can't quite be replicated in the recording studio.

Tabou Combo

The Fugees aside, Brooklyn-based Tabou Combo are probably the best known of all Haitian bands. They have, incredibly, been at the forefront of Haitian music for more than thrity years – since their 1969 debut album, 8ème Sacrement – and have moved from straightforward compas into fusions with first zouk and latterly rap.

◉ 8ème Sacrement (Mini Records, US).
◉ Zap! (Mini Records, US).

These two discs drop compas into Brooklyn's Caribbean cauldron and fish it out again to discover how famously meandering accordion and Cuban-style conga can get along.

Zèklè

Zèklè, one of the bands at the heart of the 1980s Nouvel Jenerayshun scene, made a welcome return in 1994 with their album San Mele.

◉ San Mele (Nouvel Jenerayson Records, US).

Sharp songs from Ralph Boncy and Joël Widmaier, and a neat pop sensibility that is enhanced by the bright electric sound typical of the era. A gem.

Zin

A Nouvel Jenerayshun band from New York, Zin were one of the first to introduce rap to the compas beat.

◉ Lage'M (Zin, US).

A blend of zouk, compas and soul fired up by the urban beat of the street.

Jamaica

the loudest island in the world

Jamaican music has been a global force for the last thirty years – a remarkable feat, considering the island's tiny size and population – yet many of its diverse strands are hardly known. **Gregory Mthembu-Salter** and **Peter Dalton** dig up the island's musical roots – maroon, religious and carnival music, mento, ska and rock steady – to find the sources of the great Caribbean powerhouse that is reggae music.

This article also reports on reggae in the **US** (p.448) and in **Africa** (p.442), while the story of **Jamaican music in the UK** is covered in the article following, on p.457.

Jamaica is a serious contender for the title 'loudest island in the world'. On any night, and especially at weekends, it shakes to the musical vibrations of thousands of sound systems, revival sessions, grounations, Maroon and Kumina possession ceremonies, and old-time *mento* dances. Tens of thousands of radios, cranked up to full volume, add to the hubbub. Inevitably, the sounds with the most wattage grab the limelight, but other musical styles have proved enduring. Some have been around on the island for four hundred years.

Tell it to the Maroons

In 1492, the history books tell us, Jamaica was discovered by Christopher Columbus. "Christopher Columbus was a dyam liar," reply Jamaicans, "The Arawaks was here first." And so they were. The Spanish who followed Columbus, however, saw fit to carry out the genocide of the island's original population and by the time Oliver Cromwell's navy wrested the island from the Spanish in 1670, they had been wiped out. In their place were small numbers of African slaves, mostly from Ghana,

JAK KILBY

Original roots group, Maroons and Ettu

who had been armed by the Spaniards and instructed to defend the island from the British while they themselves escaped.

Most took to the hills instead, to remote parts with names like Me No Sen, You No Come, where their descendants, the **Maroons**, live in their own secluded communities to this day. They forged a percussive style of music, still played today at possession ceremonies – religious rituals in which the musicians and dancers get increasingly frenzied as they become possessed by whichever type of spirit, ancestor or god they have invited to the occasion. The music is available on a couple of well-annotated discs (see discography), which point to the roots that nourished reggae.

With colonisation came **plantations**, which were thrown into turmoil by the Abolition of Slavery in 1838. Despite prolonged advance warnings, few plantation owners had bothered to restructure their operations, and more slaves continued to die than be born on their estates. Faced with a diminishing workforce, planters resorted to devious devices. A number of Angolans were brought over in ensuing decades under the guise of 'indentured servants'. These people seem to have been the main constituents of the **Bongo Nation**, who are responsible for the religion and music known as **Kumina**. The music, again available on a couple of ethnographic recordings, takes a similar form to Maroon music.

Maroons and the Bongo Nation make up a tiny proportion of Jamaica's population. Few others were able to preserve their African cultural identities in such an undisturbed fashion. But although the repressive system severely curtailed music-making, an extremely rich **folk tradition** emerged on the island, and one drawn from an amazing range of creative sources. In the enormous canon of Jamaican folk music, there are traces of African, British, Irish and Spanish musical traditions, and heavy doses of Nonconformist hymns and singing styles. Each of these influences is blended with characteristic Jamaican wit, irreverence and creativity. There are songs for courting, marrying, digging, drinking, playing ring games, burying – and just for singing, too. One of the classics is "Hill and Gully Rider", a timeless ode to transport on an island strong on hills and weak on roads.

Unfortunately, few of the available recordings of this folk music are of much value. Most seem to have been made by earnest ethnomusicologists in the 1950s, recording people plainly embarrassed to have a huge microphone put in front of them. When in Jamaica, however, you can hear examples of it, particularly in the country areas, and it has reg-ularly emerged as an element in the stark, minimalist modern **dancehall music**. As DJ Admiral Bailey says, "Old time someting come back again".

Gimme that Old-Time Religion

As well as being extremely loud, Jamaica is also extremely religious. If you get up early on a Sunday morning, and walk from town into the ghettos, or into the hills, you pass by an incredible variety of **religious ceremonies**, each with its own music. From the graceful plantation-era buildings of the Anglican Church come the thin, reedy voices of middle-class Jamaica, struggling with turgid Victorian hymns. From smaller churches further along emanate the more boisterous melodies of the Nonconformist churches, and, further still, the tambourine-shaking sounds of the Pentecostal denominations. But up in the hills – and down in the ghettos – can be found the jumping sounds of **Pocomania** and **Revival Zion**.

Both these Churches date from the early 1860s, when a great religious revival swept through Jamaica. Both draw on Christian and African traditions, with more Christianity in Revival Zion, and more Africa in Pocomania. As in the Pentecostal churches, both types of service feature much Bible-reading, tambourine-rattling and foot-stamping, but unlike the Pentecostal churches, they also use persistent and hypnotic percussion, and **trumping**. Trumping is the process that leads to possession, and involves moving in a circle, often around a symbolic object, like a glass of rum, and breathing very deeply. Worshippers grunt as they rotate, faster and faster as the spirit possesses them. The combination of trumping and drumming is unforgettable and recordings – though available – don't do it justice. However, the Poco sound, with its powerful, rolling side-drum patterns, has, like Jamaican folk, turned up in a dancehall mode.

Most Jamaicans are Christians. As is well known, however, a sizeable minority are not, including, most notably (at least in musical circles), the Rastafarians – of whom more below. Often ignored are Jamaica's **Hindus** – people of Indian origin who, like the Angolans of the Bongo Nation, were 'indentured' to the plantations after Abolition. Though most intermarried, there is still a distinctive Jamaican Indian culture and associated music, though not on the scale of Trinidad, where Indians settled in far greater numbers. Again, Jamaican roots discs include intriguing examples of their **baccra** music – Hindustan compositions often referred to by Jamaicans as 'coolie music'.

Rastafari for I and I

Rastafarians make up only around thirteen percent of the island's population but their influence on Jamaican music is out of all proportion. And Bob Marley is only the tip of the iceberg.

Rastafari is non-doctrinal, in the sense that it holds that no one church is powerful enough to impose its version of religious purity, and that one person's version of it is as valid as another's, as long as he or she is possessed of the Spirit of Jah (God). Certain themes, however, do recur, among them the belief that Jah is a living force on earth. Jah enables otherwise disparate humanity to unite. To embody this in speech, Rastas refer to each other as 'I'. Thus I am I, you are I, and we are I and I. Such is the Rasta emphasis on the importance of the spoken word that many other words are similarly altered: 'Unity' becomes 'Inity', 'Brethren' becomes 'Idren', and so on. Unity, or Inity, is essential if Rastas are to stand strong against the wicked forces of Babylon – the oppressive (or downpressive) system.

Marcus Garvey, a forceful campaigner for black unity, pan-Africanism and a return to Africa, is of great importance to many Rastas, who revere him as a prophet. In one of his pamphlets, published in the 1920s, he urged Africans of the New World to look to Africa for a Prince to emerge. This was taken by many to mean the Emperor of Ethiopia, **Haile Selassie I**, who claimed descent from Solomon. Selassie's battles in 1937 against Mussolini – or the 'wicked forces of Rome'– were taken as fulfilling the prophecies of the Book of Revelation, and he was worshipped as the reincarnate Christ. Selassie was deposed in 1974 and died a few years later, although to Rastas 'Selassie cyaan dead' and is living still. Rastas believe that they are awaiting repatriation to Africa – Zion – and regard themselves, and all New World black people, as living 'slavery days' in bondage.

From time to time Rastas hold reasoning sessions, in which matters religious, social, political and livital (about life) are discussed collectively. Larger and more protracted reasonings are called **grounations**. Like their Revival Zion and poco-maniac counterparts, grounations feature Bible-reading, hymns, foot-stamping and drumming. Rasta drumming (usually called *nyahbingi* or *burru* drumming), though, is much slower, with a beat more or less the speed of a human pulse. Other differences include the reasoning itself and the copious consumption of *ganja* – Jamaican colly weed, or marijuana. Most Rastas adore ganja and lovingly cultivate it, cure it, smoke it, brew it (non-

alcoholically), use it for medicines of all sorts, and, above all, talk about it. For this, Babylon brutalises them no end, but to little avail. As Jah Lion sings, "When the Dread flash him locks, a colly seed drops."

Grounations occur quite frequently in Jamaica and are generally well advertised and easy to find. There are some good recordings of them, too, though inevitably they fail to capture the atmosphere and significance. By far the best Rasta music on disc are the extraordinary 'Grounation' sessions, performed by **Count Ossie and his Mystic Revelation of Rastafari**. The late Count Ossie was a master Rasta 'repeater' drummer from the Kingston ghetto. In the early 1960s a number of very talented musicians came under his influence, including members of the subsequently legendary Skatalites. Listen to the sessions, which also feature the great sax and flute player Cedric Brooks, and you will find astonishing Rasta drumming and chanting, bebop and cool jazz horn lines, and apocalyptic poems.

The Party Line: Mento

Religious music has left Jamaican Sundays fairly well covered, but Saturday nights have a very different sound. Most plantation owners conceded Saturday nights to their slaves, as well as the various feast days: crop-over, the yam festival, Christmas and the New Year. Plantation owners' diaries abound with complaints of splitting headaches in the middle of the night, and even references to what seem like the forerunners of today's sound systems. One eighteenth-century plantation owner wrote: "I am just informed that at the dance last night the Eboes obtained a decided triumph, for they roared and thumped their drums with so much effect that the Creoles were obliged to leave off singing altogether."

The main surviving elements from all of this are mento, which draws from several of Jamaica's folk music styles, and the Christmas carnival sounds of **jonkonnu**. The latter, like all the carnivals of the Americas, is a time of display, finery and revelry. Its music is traditionally played on fife and drums,

and can still be heard in that form today, though calypso and mento, and whatever reggae sounds are in vogue, regularly slip in too.

Mento was recorded in the 1950s, largely by the businessman Stanley Motta, in response to the international popularity of Trinidadian calypso, which it superficially resembles. Motta recorded performers like Count Lasher, George Moxey and Lord Composer in his small Hanover Street studio in Kingston, then pressed the results in London and shipped the 78 rpm discs back for sale in

Touch Me Tomato – The Jolly Boys

When Bob Marley's mother, Cedella, was asked in a BBC TV documentary about his musical beginnings, she burst into a lilting, saucy song, "Touch me Tomato", with which the young Bob had entertained the neighbourhood.

> Please mister don't you touch me tommy at all
> Please don't touch me tommy at all
> Touch me on my pumpkin potato
> For goodness sake don't touch me tommy at all
> Touch me this, touch me that
> Touch me everything I've got
> Touch me plum and apples too
> But here's one thing you must not do...

The song was mento: a music as sweet as sugar cane, as rude as a bunch of bananas and, surprising as it may seem, the principal root of reggae. Hugely popular in the 1930s and '40s until it was swamped by the new styles of ska and reggae, it has now been rediscovered with the revival of interest in roots music.

The **Jolly Boys** have been playing the music regardless of fashion at the Trident Hotel, Port Antonio, Jamaica, for years. There are four of them, although only one, Moses, is a founder member of the group and remembers the good old days, when they played for Hollywood parties at Errol Flynn's villa in Port Antonio. Moses plays banjo and sings, Allan Swymmer sings lead and plays the bongos, Noel Howard fills out the texture and rhythm on guitar, and Joseph Bennett plays the *kalimba*, a large thumb piano that provides the bass. It's a beautifully balanced acoustic sound, perfectly in keeping with a languorous life in the sun.

"We sing what the old people used to sing," says Moses. "A lot of them dead and gone. The younger generation don't know the old-time songs. They take some of the sound and make reggae. Reggae come right down from there." The music is relaxed and unmistakably good-time with an infectious lilt like Trinidadi-

an calypso. It's underpinned by rhythmic patterns on the bongos and interspersed with instrumental solos on the banjo. The lyrics are rarely deep, and often bawdy: at least half the songs are about sex. But they have the richness of colour, rhythm and dialect that marks out the best of Caribbean poetry.

The Jolly Boys see themselves as a living archive of Jamaica's roots music. "What you don't use, you surely lose. It's part of our heritage so you don't want to throw it to one side. Someone's got to be there to present it to the new world. It's good to have a museum and I think we're one!"

JAK KILBY

Joseph Bennett on kalimba

Jamaica. Recent tours by and CDs of the **Jolly Boys** from Portland have extended awareness of mento, which was previously almost exclusively rural Jamaican. The music contains many of the elements that have made its relative, reggae, so successful. It is witty, topical, rebellious and unafraid to 'wind and grind'. Actually, most mentos seem to come round to the subject of sex sooner or later – usually sooner. Musically, mento contains that essential shuffling strum – the 'kerchanga, ker-changa' – that marked out reggae from its more metronomic predecessor, rock steady.

Mento was the popular sound of rural Jamaica until the late 1940s (big swing bands were dominant in urban areas), when radios finally became both affordable and available to many Jamaicans. The new radio owners soon discovered that US stations were a good deal more lively than the stuffy local ones and before long a whole generation was going crazy over **American R&B**. People started flying over to the US, scouring record shops for exclusive pressings, rushing back and playing them through homemade box speakers at parties in people's yards. Thus were sound systems born.

Sound Systems

Sound systems – essentially mobile discos – were a crucial development in Jamaican music and were to reverberate right through the next five decades, giving rise to the Jamaican record industry – the first local discs were produced for the sound sys-tems. As early as the 1950s, the sound-system DJs would talk over the records they played, attracting custom, and the technique slowly developed into the tradition of toasting or chatting, of which more later. The earliest sound systems played the hard-edged US jump blues of such artists as Wynonie Harris and Rosco Gordon (along with balladeers like Johnny Ace), and the best known of these sounds was 'Tom the Great Sebastian', with the legendary Count Machuki as MC.

Another key event was the emergence of the handful of sound-system chiefs who were to become the chief record producers in Kingston. They struggled for supremacy in the open-air dancehalls amid an atmosphere of intense, often violent competition that was to become permanently associated with the Jamaican music scene. Three men soon dominated: **Vincent 'King' Edwards**, **Clement 'Sir Coxsone' Dodd** and **Arthur 'Duke' Reid** – their titles perhaps an ironic tilt at the old plantation chiefs, and certainly a nod in the direction of admired US band leaders like Duke Ellington and Count Basie. At the end of the 1950s, they were joined by another contender – **Cecil 'Prince Buster' Campbell**, with his Sound Of the People sound system.

Stanley Motta had already made the island's first recordings with mento artists, while future prime minister **Edward Seaga** set up **WIRL** (West Indies Records Ltd), mostly to press US R&B tunes. From the mid-1950s, the studios were also being used to record local R&B, at first to

Duke Reid crowned "King of Sounds and Blues", Success Club, Kingston, late 1950s

make exclusive recordings for particular sound systems. Beginning with sessions in 1958–59, the first local R&B discs for public sale started to appear. Employing Ken Richards & his Comets as the session band, Edward Seaga recorded one of the classics from these early sessions – Higgs & Wilson's "Manny Oh". **Joe Higgs** went on to become one of Jamaican music's foundation figures, recording a string of hits (both solo and with his partner Roy Wilson) and tutoring many younger performers in Trench Town – most notably both the teenage Wailers and the Wailing Souls.

Seaga was one of the few early producers who did not own a sound system; another was the man who would eventually make Bob Marley a global name, **Chris Blackwell**. The wealthy, Harrow-educated Blackwell launched his R&B and Island labels at the close of the 1950s, soon scoring a major local hit with Laurel Aitken's "Boogie In My Bones", a classic example of Jamaican jump blues. In 1962, Blackwell moved to London, where he kicked off the UK version of his **Island** imprint with the apposite choice of Lord Creator's beautiful "Independent Jamaica".

The early Island label was to meet the tastes of Jamaican émigrés in the UK with releases from almost every top producer working in Kingston, including Duke Reid, Leslie Kong, King Edwards and Clement Dodd. Before long, hipper young whites in the UK were dancing to a distinctly Jamaican afterbeat, and in 1964 Blackwell had the guitarist Ernest Ranglin arrange **Millie Small**'s "My Boy Lollipop", the international pop-ska hit.

Ska

By the mid-1960s, Jamaica's musicians, notably the innovatory Skatalites, had established something distinctly Jamaican. Using fast R&B as their music's basis, they cut out half the shuffle, leaving an abrupt series of off-beats. They called it **ska**, and it quickly took off in the dancehalls of Jamaica and Britain, where Jamaicans had begun to settle in significant numbers (see p.457). Ska bands employed much the same line-up as R&B groups, with a piano, electric guitar, stand-up bass, drums

and a couple or more brass instruments. Most of the musicians came from a jazz background – swing bands were popular in wartime Jamaica – and they were world-class soloists and improvisers.

From this point on, the availability of Jamaican music improves dramatically: there were masses of ska records. The **Skatalites** were the masters, especially when their phenomenal trombonist Don Drummond was still alive. They were also incredibly prolific – their entire output, amounting to hundreds of records, was recorded in just fourteen months, which was the entire lifespan of the original band. Nonetheless, radio stations gave more time to the blander sounds of bands like **Byron Lee and the Dragonnaires**, who were patronised by Edward Seaga's studio.

Ska is primarily instrumental, perfect for dancing, but its rhythms can be difficult to sing over. Some artists did so successfully, especially the Wail-

Skatalites at Studio One, with Mittoo on piano, McCook standing with sax, and Don Drummond (inset)

ers, the Maytals, Justin Hinds & the Dominoes, Stranger Cole and future movie star and crossover act Jimmy Cliff. But the sound-system operators still needed something extra to spice up their dances. Many brought in **DJs** to do just that, developing the old act of talking over records into an art of its own. The greatest of the early DJs were Count Matchuki, King Stitt and Sir Lord Comic. Sadly, they were rarely recorded in this period, though Sir Lord Comic made an impact with "Ska-ing West" and "The Great Wuga Wuga".

Jamaica became independent in 1962 and for a period the whole of society seemed infected by euphoria. You can hear it in ska's joyous tempos, even if the horn solos often expressed a contrasting melancholy. People were flocking into Kingston every day, seeking work, money, and a better life. Some found it, but thousands never did, and settled in fast-growing shantytowns like Dungle, and badly built housing schemes, like Trench Town, Riverton City and, later on, Tivoli Gardens. From this community of the underemployed and the abused, those whom Jamaicans call 'sufferers', came the infamous rudeboys.

Rudeboys were young men who gave voice to their disaffection, establishing a reputation for ruthlessly defending their corner and hustling their way to their next meal or dance entrance fee. The island's two main political parties, the Jamaican Labour Party (JLP) and People's National Party (PNP), soon recognised their vote-garnering value. Both parties began distributing weapons, patronage and, if in government, inviolable protection to their 'dons', in return for bringing in the votes at election time. It was a recipe for the violence that has plagued every election to date, particularly those of 1976 and 1980.

Rock Steady

Although the last years of ska reflected the mood of the rudeboys, it was **rock steady**, ska's successor, that became their sound. Over the rock-steady beat, rudeboys sang of their problems, their fears, and their 'rude' attitude. Typical was the song "Dreader than Dread," by Honeyboy Martin and the Voices: if you were foolish enough not to believe them, "you'll wind up in the cemetery, because you'll be dead".

The youthful **Wailers** had already enjoyed their first Jamaican hit with warnings to the rudies, "Simmer Down" and "Rude Boy", and their main rivals, the **Clarendonians**, told of how "Rudeboy Gone To Jail". But the most enduring rudeboy disc was the one that first brought word about the rudie phenomenon to the wider world: **Desmond Dekker**'s "007", which charted in both the UK and the US. Musically, ska's jazzy horn lines faded from prominence, while the bass, by now an electric one, grew more important and

Alton Ellis, the godfather of rocksteady

the rhythm guitar played a steady off-beat – a style that was to develop into reggae.

The slower pace of rock steady provided the perfect opportunity to express tender emotions, too. Vast numbers of love songs poured out of the studios, often with sensuous American soul tunes for their inspiration, and close harmony execution influenced by US groups like the Impressions, the Temptations and the Tams. Duke Reid's Treasure Isle studio led the field for rock steady, with Sir Coxsone's Studio One a close second.

The leading session bands of the period were Tommy McCook's **Supersonics** and Lynn Tait's **Jets**, with the Roland Alphonso-led **Soul Vendors** holding their own at Studio One. Besides Alphonso, the Soul Vendors also inherited another former Skatalite – the keyboard player **Jackie Mittoo**, arguably the most influential musician in Jamaican music's entire history. Augustus Pablo's early self productions, many of the Channel One and Joe Gibbs hits of the mid–late 1970s and much of the dancehall explosion of the 1980s were based on the music created by Mittoo in the rock steady, or early reggae years, and a decade after his death from cancer, the rhythms he helped build are still regularly refashioned or sampled.

Rock steady produced a string of wonderful **vocal-harmony groups**: the **Paragons**, the **Techniques** (at first with the great Slim Smith as lead singer, and then Pat Kelly), the **Gaylads**, the **Heptones** (featuring Leroy Sibbles, who also played many of the classic Studio One bass lines), the **Melodians**, the **Silvertones**, and the greatest harmonisers of them all, **Carlton & his Shoes**. The Leonard Dillon-led **Ethiopians** were less typical in that they showed little soul influence in their harmonising, which was rooted in a more traditional Jamaican country style; nevertheless, they had several major hits during this period, particularly with songs about trains, such as the great "Train To Skaville" (despite the title, a rock-steady tune) and "Engine 54".

Then there was the man who gave rock steady its name with one of his many Treasure Isle hits – the incomparable **Alton Ellis**. Alton had started his career as half of the popular Alton & Eddie duo, performing doo-wop ballads, and then led the Flames, a trio who scored with several warnings to the rudeboys. By the close of the decade he had gone solo and was concentrating on affairs of the heart. He was rivalled only by a handful of singers – stars such as **Delroy Wilson**, **Slim Smith** (who had sung with both the Techniques and the Uniques), **John Holt** (formerly of the Paragons) and **Ken Boothe** (originally Stranger Cole's singing partner). And proving as important a songwriter as soulful singer was **Bob Andy**, another major talent who has yet to receive the recognition he deserves.

> There is a greater output of recorded music in Jamaica than in any other country in the world. This is because right from the beginning the different manufacturing and distribution companies in Jamaica opened their facilities for individual producers. So anybody who has enough money to go into a studio and make a record and then go to a pressing plant and order five hundred records to be pressed can start a label. So a lot of people have tried their luck.
>
> **Chris Blackwell**, founder of Island Records.

Tougher than Tough: Reggae Takes Over

As the 1970s beckoned, Jamaican music changed once more when a new, lolloping rhythm called **reggae** hit Kingston. Producers and musicians had searched around for a new beat and hit upon the idea of incorporating the old-time mento shuffle with rock steady, thus bringing Jamaican pop that much closer to its roots. The other, perhaps more important factor in this new development involved the continuing influence of Afro-American music, and the increasing popularity of the hard-edged funk of James Brown.

This purely musical shift would have meant little, however, had it not been for other, more profound shifts that were taking place in society. Politically, there was a growing mistrust on the part of the 'sufferers' of the ability of the system to provide for them – and the size of their communities was growing fast. The visit of the Ethiopian **Emperor Haile Selassie** to Jamaica in 1966 had also encouraged a huge growth in **Rastafari**, which dismissed politics as 'politricks', and looked instead for the return to Africa, when the captives would be set free. Rastafarian singers and musicians were increasingly asserting their right to preach their message, and to be heard.

Despite considerable misgivings, ex-policeman Duke Reid and Coxsone Dodd, the studio chiefs, had little option but to oblige. For one thing, there was the first real competition to their and Prince Buster's cosy triumvirate. **Producers** who had

'I Play the Fool Catchwise': Lee Perry

Lee Perry, otherwise known as 'Scratch', or 'The Upsetter', has played a critical role in the development of Jamaican music since the late 1950s. Though he is a distinctive vocalist, he is best known as an innovative producer. His career began in 1959, when he worked as a bouncer with Prince Buster for Sir Coxsone Dodd's mighty Downbeat sound system. Within a short time, both of them were producing records, usually uncredited, at Dodd's Studio One. Perry left Dodd in 1967, worked briefly for Joe Gibbs, then established his famous Upsetter label in 1968.

Even in his early releases, like the classic "People Funny Boy", Perry showed a genius for the use of the bizarre sound effect – in this case, glass breaking and a baby crying – and for scathing personal attacks against the many he deems to have crossed him. It was in this early period that he concocted many of his best rhythms, to which he returned again and again: "Return of Django" (a British hit), "French Connection", "Cold Sweat", and many others.

The late 1960s also saw Perry in an immensely fruitful partnership with the **Wailers**. Of all the producers they worked with, he alone seemed best to have understood the sparse arrangements that offset so perfectly their quavering harmonies – and Marley's vocals improved to an incredible extent under his supervision. Perry was also one of the first producers, in the early seventies, to recognise and encourage the phenomenal talents of dub maestro **King Tubby**. Perry excelled with dub, and, though many Jamaican producers have released great dub music, few have touched the eccentric, ganja-soaked brilliance of the Upsetter's Black Ark offerings. (The Black Ark was Perry's studio – until he burned it down in 1980 – and a true mecca for dub fiends from all over the world.)

Though some of the major singers and DJs of the 1970s, like Max Romeo, Junior Byles, U-Roy, Prince

Lee Perry

ADRIAN BOOT

Jazzbo and the Heptones recorded at Black Ark, it was never the hits factory that some studios became. Perry did score a huge and deserved hit with **Junior Murvin**'s "Police & Thieves" in 1976, but, for the most part, his releases were steady, low-key sellers that were better received outside Jamaica. In 1978, Island Records, who had been releasing some classic Black Art material in the UK, rejected both Perry's solo *Roast Fish, Collie Weed & Cornbread* and, more amazingly, what remains the most fully accomplished set recorded at the Black Art, the Congos' *Heart Of The Congos*.

Though Perry has been involved in every important Jamaican musical development from the late 1950s to the late 1970s, and has in many cases pioneered them, it is the quirky and unique nature of his output that makes him memorable. He has frequently been accused of madness, and tales abound of his peculiar habits: planting records in his garden, performing whirling dervish dances at the mixing desk, declining interviews but granting outerviews and, of course, burning his studio, since when the increasingly impenetrable mysticism and silliness of his records do seem to be the acts of a madman. Some of his recent releases are worth checking out, but Perry has contributed little to the dancehall and ragga styles that dominate reggae today, and shows little interest in doing so.

already made something of a mark, such as Derrick Harriott, Sonia Pottinger and Bunny Lee, built on their rock steady successes to become major players. In the same period, a genuine golden era for Jamaican music, the likes of Clancy Eccles (who had been a popular singer in the late 1950s), Winston 'Niney' Holness, Harry Mudie, Joe Gibbs, Winston Riley (a founder member of the Techniques), and the legendary **Lee Perry** (see box opposite), all emerged as producers.

The list of notable artists, already lengthy, expands hugely at this point. Those who started out at this time, and are still famous, include **Burning Spear**, the late **Dennis Brown**, **Gregory Isaacs** and **Horace Andy**; in addition, several who made their recording debuts in the ska/rock steady years were making some of their best music, including **Delroy Wilson**, **Larry Marshall**, the **Maytals**, the **Wailers** and Jamaica's greatest love balladeer, **John Holt**.

Wailing and Groaning

The Wailers – Bob Marley, Peter Tosh and Bunny Wailer – started life as one of many ska groups competing for attention in the mid-1960s. It was producer Lee Perry, the 'Phil Spector of the Caribbean', who recognised their potential, putting them together with the unrivalled drum and bass duo of Carlton and Aston 'Family Man' Barrett from his studio band, The Upsetters. Together, they recorded a marvellous sequence of songs, which were later collected on the albums *Soul Rebels* and *African Herbsman*.

Musically, Marley matured fast in this period, and he already had an incredible songbook, including classics like "Lively up Yourself", "Trench Town Rock" and "Kaya", which were to resurface in later years under Island Records, to which the band signed in 1972. Island relaunched the group in 1974 as **Bob Marley and the Wailers** (see box overleaf), with Peter Tosh and Bunny Wailer leaving to pursue successful solo careers. Marley, meanwhile, went from strength to strength. Purists might argue that his new female backing singers, the **I-Threes**, were a poor substitute for the beautiful close harmonies of the original Wailers, and that the arrangements of his Island records conceded too much

to the unsubtle demands of rock, but no one could deny the power of his lyrics, nor the magnetism of his performances.

No one could deny the phenomenon of his success, either, which placed reggae and Jamaica on the world map. Thanks to his powerful persona, and some shrewd marketing, Marley became a symbol of rebellion all over the world. This brought him enormous fame abroad – especially in Africa, where he had superstar status from Casablanca to Cape Town – and a very high profile at home. In such a politicised society as Jamaica, it also made him a target, and sure enough, he was nearly assassinated in the violent election year of 1976. Bravely, Marley decided to try to use his prominence to encourage peace on the island, bringing together the two party leaders at the famous One Love Concert in 1978.

Marley died of cancer in 1981. Peter Tosh was shot dead six years later in circumstances that have yet to

The original Wailers: Bunny Wailer, Bob Marley and Peter Tosh

Robert Nesta Marley was born in Nine Miles, Jamaica, in 1945. His mother, Cedella, was nineteen and black, and his father, whom he hardly met, was fifty-one and white, an ex-British army officer from Liverpool. Bob Marley spent his youth in the tough Trench Town ghetto of West Kingston, which he immortalised in his rudeboy songs, but his up-country roots in Nine Miles, where he listened to mento (Jamaican pop) and his mother's gospel songs, were also significant. Nine Miles was also, appropriately enough, in the heart of so-called 'ganja parish'; in mid-career, Marley was said to smoke a pound of the herb each week.

In Kingston Marley joined up with childhood friends Peter Tosh and Bunny Wailer to form the Wailers, and their first song, "Simmer Down", a reaction to the street violence of rival gangs, was a big hit in 1964. The rudeboy image of the Trench Town ghetto was central to their early Jamaican hits and the ghetto experience remained a crucial part of the Marley songbook.

Bob Marley, late 1970s

ADRIAN BOOT

From 1972, when the Wailers were signed up by Chris Blackwell of Island Records, Marley began to move onto the world stage. His messages of strength and social unity were potent and the time was ripe. By the mid-seventies rock had lost its sense of rebellion and Marley's was the revolutionary voice to shock the complacency of Anglo-American music. With Tosh and Wailer, he recorded the wonderful *Catch A Fire* and *Burnin* albums – the first reggae records conceived as albums rather than a collection of songs – though his commercial breakthrough in the UK came in 1975 with *Natty Dread*, which included the first cut of "No Woman No Cry" – a song that was to give him one of his biggest international hits when a live cut was released as a 45 the following year. Bob Marley was finally up there with the big-name rock stars in Britain and repeated the trick in the US with the *Rastaman Vibration* album. Around the world, and especially in Africa, his was the biggest name of all.

In 1976 Marley won the dubious distinction of being the first international music star subject to an assassination attempt. Seven armed men broke into his home at 56 Hope Road, Kingston, on the eve of an electioneering concert organised by Prime Minister Michael Manley and the ruling PNP party. He sang at the concert all the same, with a bandaged arm, and then left for the safety of Miami for a while. As Jamaica headed for civil war, Marley returned for a historic performance in 1978 that symbolically linked the arms of opposing leaders Manley and Edward Seaga on stage in the song "**One Love**", a hymn to peace and brotherhood.

Marley's Rastafarian belief was central to his music and his message: the "One Love" concert was to commemorate the visit of Haile Selassie to Jamaica twelve years earlier. The Selassie myth and the idea of the promised land in Africa had reverberations, too, on Marley's second most famous concert, celebrating the independence of Zimbabwe in 1980. The new Zimbabwean flag shared the Rasta colours – yellow, red, green and black, representing the sunshine, the bloodshed, the jungle and the people. Marley gave the performance of his life at the celebrations to mark the new nation's freedom.

Just thirteen months after this triumphal concert Marley died of cancer. His funeral brought ten thousand people onto the streets and Jamaica to a standstill for two days. His body now lies in a mausoleum (and Ethiopian Orthodox shrine) in Nine Miles, his home village, attended by dreadlocked guards.

Jamiacan reggae, in the twenty years since (and, arguably, also for a few years before) Bob Marley's death has moved on in a multitude of directions. Indeed, there are many who would suggest his influence on the music is no greater than a dozen other seminal musicians. But globally, there is no doubt that Bob Marley is the most significant of all **World Music** artists. When reggae is played in Africa, or Latin America, or Asia – and it is huge in many areas of the world – it is Marley who is the musical model. He is the idealised icon, too, particularly in Africa, where his message – of struggle and pride – remains enormously potent.

ADRIAN BOOT

Toots Hibbert – Reggae Got Soul

a central role in the origins of both: the popular sound system owner and master engineer, Osbourne Ruddock, aka **King Tubby**.

The jive talk of DJs had been adding to the excitement at dances from the late 1950s, when Coxsone had urged Count Machuki to shout his own catch phrases over discs (rather than simply introduce them). Tubby's experiments in stripping vocal discs to their instrumental basics gave the man with the microphone the space to say a lot more than the occasional line or two.

Despite their following in the dancehalls, it was some time before the flamboyant characters at the mike made much of an impact in the studio. **King Stitt** – known as 'the Ugly One', because of a facial disfigurement – was the first DJ to consistently score on record, most notably with a series of early reggae hits for Clancy Eccles, such as "Fire Corner" and "Vigerton 2". Yet these were still primarily instrumentals, featuring Eccles' session band, the Dynamites, with occasional (but very effective) interjections from Stitt.

be properly explained, after a turbulent career that had earned him many enemies, thanks to his uncompromising stances, particularly on the issue of ganja. Only the mystic man, Bunny Wailer, survives. He has been seen around more frequently lately, castigating young people for abandoning their roots and their principles, and receiving precious little respect for doing so.

After Marley, the other key singer in bringing the reggae sound to an international audience was **Toots Hibbert**, who joined Nathaniel Mathias and Henry Gordon to form Jamaica's top vocal group of the 1960s, the **Maytals**, becoming the internationally known Toots & the Maytals in the next decade. Toots' mother was a Revival Zion preacher, and he inherited from her his legendary impassioned groaning, which is clearly derived from Revival's trumping tradition. Otis Redding and American soul also influenced Toot's style. He missed the rock steady era while jailed for possession of herb (a stay immortalised in his classic "54-46 Was my Number"), but upon his release, the reunited trio blasted into reggae, with Leslie Kong-produced classics like "Pressure Drop", "Bla Bla" and "Sweet & Dandy".

DJs, Dub and Singers

By the close of 1973, Jamaican music's two most radical and influential elements were established: the mixed-down dub form and DJ 'toasting' on record. Not surprisingly, both innovations grew out of the two institutions that have always been at the heart of reggae's development: the recording studio and the dancehall. And one man played

ADRIAN BOOT

Osborne Ruddock, aka King Tubby

DJs only took centre stage when, significantly enough, the main man on Tubby's Home Town Hi Fi began talking on record. Ewart Beckford, better known as **U-Roy**, made his first forays into the recording studio with interesting enough sides for Keith Hudson, Bunny Lee, Lee Perry and Lloyd 'Matador' Daley, but the hits only came when he tackled the (then) recent rock steady hits at Treasure Isle.

Rapidly following U-Roy's phenomenal success – he held the top three places in the Jamaican charts for three months in 1970 – were a flood of records from other gifted DJs. His main rival was the equally distinctive **Dennis Alcapone**, though memorable discs were forthcoming from men like Big Joe, Charlie Ace, Winston Scotland, Lizzy, and Scotty, as well as DJs who were to become major names for the rest of the decade – **I-Roy**, **Prince Jazzbo**, **Dr. Alimantado** (under a variety of names) and **Dillinger**.

It was U-Roy's style that continued to rule, however, at least until the rise to stardom of a dreadlocked DJ from the Lord Tippertone sound system. The man who called himself **Big Youth** employed a new chanting style and Rasta-inspired lyrics. And it was this approach that was to influence the next generation of DJs, including Trinity, Prince Far I, Clint Eastwood and Jah Lloyd. The dominance of Big Youth and his disciples was then to continue until the dawn of the 'dancehall' era at the close of the decade, when the likes of General Echo, Lone Ranger and Ranking Joe reinstated the U-Roy style.

Dub music also developed in its own right. Its spacey, trance-like nature attracts the mystic, and

Reggae in Africa

Reggae is everywhere in Africa. Hotel bands all over the continent can manage "One Love" and other cover versions and a number of local styles are evolving, most notably in West Africa. Nigeria's **Sonny Okusuns** produced some intriguing efforts in the 1970s, while in the 1980s and '90s the mantle was transferred to **The Mandators**, a fine and enduring band, and to **Majek Fashek**, their former lead guitarist.

Somewhat better known in the West, however, are the most confident releases of **Alpha Blondy**, from the Ivory Coast. His *Apartheid is Nazism* album was a rich blend of reggae and West-African rhythms, while his follow-up, *Jerusalem*, recorded in Kingston with Jamaican musicians, showed he could do orthodox roots reggae with the best of them. Moving south, Zimbabwe is also very into reggae, with memories of Bob Marley's 1980 Independence concert still fresh for many. **John Chibadura** has recorded some brilliant reggae tunes, although jit remains his staple.

A more committed reggae voice is that of South Africa's **Lucky Dube** – Africa's most phenomenal reggae artist – who proved his worth by triumphing at the Jamaican Sunsplash in front of the most critical audience in the world. He began singing Zulu *mbaqanga* music at the end of the 1970s but switched to reggae in 1984, adopting a style modelled closely on his hero, Peter Tosh. *Slave* and *Prisoner*, his most prominent releases, have each sold over half a million copies in South Africa alone, making him the country's most successful ever recording artist. He has toured worldwide,

to ecstatic response, perfecting his performance choreography in the process, and frequently unleashing a Smokey Robinson-style falsetto.

Ragga music has been making inroads into Africa recently, too. Shabba Ranks toured Nigeria, Ghana, Zimbabwe and South Africa in 1994, and received adulation everywhere he went. It won't be long therefore before African ragga emerges. Indeed, there are signs that it is already doing so. Johannesburg's **Umkhonte keShaka** combines Zulu and ragga sounds to great effect, though he is yet to tour outside the country.

few were more mystical than **Augustus Pablo**, famous both for his production and his eerie melodica playing. His relationship with King Tubby (who mixed his early self-productions) was particularly fruitful. When Island UK released "King Tubby Meets Rockers Uptown" – the ver-

Winston Rodney – Burning Spear

sion of a Jacob Miller vocal – it introduced many outside the reggae world to dub. The album of the same name became a milestone, and remains perhaps the greatest dub set ever released.

Also important in dub developments were **Errol Thompson** and **Sylvan Morris**, as well as Tubby's apprentices, **Scientist** and **King Jammy** (later to be a major producer). Dub and DJ art added a further branch with the 'dub poetry' of Briton **Linton Kwesi Johnson** and Jamaicans **Mutabaruka** and **Mikey Smith**. Smith, a wonderful

and radical artist, was another casualty of political violence, murdered by JLP gunmen in 1982.

In the mid-1970s, the music changed once more. At the forefront of this evolution was the **Channel One** studio, whose house band were the **Revolutionaries**, built around the powerhouse of drummer Sly Dunbar and bassist Robbie Shakespeare. Together, **Sly and Robbie** developed the **rockers** sound, initiated by Augustus Pablo, giving classic rock-steady rhythms a new, militant feel to great and popular effect. Their creative and innovative spirit is still very much alive, and they have been players and producers on many of the top reggae hits of the last thirty years.

The rockers sound gave a fresh lease of life to the vocal trio, an enduring feature of Jamaican music that had been a perfect vehicle in the rock-steady and early reggae periods. Groups such as the **Mighty Diamonds**, the **Wailing Souls** and the **Gladiators** scored a number of hits employing rockers rhythms – as did former rock-steady star and then member of Marley's I-Threes, **Marcia Griffiths**. Chris Blackwell even sent the London-based (though Jamaican born) **Ijahman Levi** to Kingston to place his reflective songs over rhythms from the musicians associated with the rockers style – including both Sly Dunbar and Robbie Shakespeare.

The producer **Joe Gibbs** and his engineer **Errol Thompson** (the 'Mighty Two'), produced their own, less subtle variation of the rockers sound, and were particularly successful with records from Joseph Hill's **Culture** and the golden-voiced **Dennis Brown**, as well as the DJs **Trinity**, **Prince Far I** and one hit wonders, **Althea & Donna**.

Among the singers of this period, **Burning Spear** (Winston Rodney) stood head and dread above the competition. Originally from the Studio One stable, he achieved roots prominence in 1976 with two astonishing albums, *Marcus Garvey* and *Man in the Hills*. At a time when Bob Marley was gathering an international rock audience, Spear's rootsier sound gained a massive following. His performances, too, were stunning, whirling away into trance-like heights. A staunch advocate of Rastafari, he is still particularly vocal about Marcus Garvey and the necessity of repatriation.

Equally committed to his own variation of Rastafarianism (which involves a central role for Jesus instead of Selassie) is **Yabby You** (Vivian Jackson). An impressive producer and vocalist, he took his name from the chorus of his initial Jamaican hit, the powerful "Conquering Lion". No one was more 'dread' or patently sincere in his faith than Jackson, and both his and Spear's work are required listening for anyone harbouring doubts about the positive influence of Rastafarianism on reggae of the 1970s. So too are the albums of the finest harmony group of the era, the **Abbysinians**. This trio of committed Rastafarians represented a different tradition from the Mighty Diamonds, who were direct descendants of the soul-influenced rock-steady harmonisers. The Abyssinians developed a far 'dreader', more African sounding style apposite for their messages of repatriation and faith in Jah.

Jamaica has maintained few self-contained bands, encompassing both musicians and singers, but after Island's signing of the Wailers, a few such units emerged. One that Island signed up was **Third World** – a group made up of the sons of solidly middle-class Jamaicans, far removed from the backgrounds of most struggling performers at Channel One. Nevertheless, there was no disputing their musicianship, and they could be as roostsy as anyone when they chose to.

As the 'roots' era drew to its close, another group stepped forward to take centre stage. **Black Uhuru** had already been through a couple of different line-ups when they added an American woman, **Puma Jones**, who perfectly offset the masculine tones and image of the group's founder Ducky Simpson and lead singer Michael Rose. Produced by Sly & Robbie, they were widely tipped for international stardom, and to a degree achieved this, without ever filling the position left vacant by Marley.

Dancehall and Slackness

Throughout the period of Jamaican music when roots and culture were dominant, the centre of action and innovation remained the **dancehall**. This was where the hottest tunes could be heard on 'dubplates' (acetates) prior to their official release, and where new DJs made a name for themselves. Competition among the sound-system operators ensured constant musical change.

In essence, all Jamaican popular music has been meant for play in the dancehall. But the use of the word 'dancehall' to describe a specific style came about in the late 1970s, associated at first with producer **Henry 'Junjo' Lawes**, who began his rise

Dancehall vocalist Frankie Paul

to the top by recording a brilliant teenage singer **Barrington Levy**, over raw rhythms from what was to be the dominant session band of the new era, the **Roots Radics**. Lawes (who was shot dead in London in 1999) was to go on to produce practically every major name of the early 1980s, including the man who combined the techniques of singer and DJ, **Eek-A-Mouse**, and the top chatters like the albino **Yellowman** (whose Jamaican popularity was on a par with Marley's), **Ranking Toyan** and **Josie Wales**.

Lawes didn't launch his own Volcano Hi Power sound system until 1983, but among the exciting sounds that had come to rock the dancehalls were Gemini Disco, Aces International, Metro Media, Killimanjaro, Virgo Hi Fi and Black Scorpio, alongside veterans like U-Roy's Stur-Gav Hi Fi, Prince Jammy's High Power and Ray Symbolic. Each had its own young DJs and singers, and exclusive dubplates. The former African Brother and Studio One singer, Lincoln **'Sugar' Minott** was producing himself by this time, and the Youth Promotion sound he set up drew on the burgeoning youth talent of the Kingston ghettos to become another major player.

By 1980, more records by DJs than singers were being released in Jamaica. Led by the outrageous Yellowman and **General Echo**, many made their name on the 'slackness' (obscenity) of their lyrics – a far cry from the spirituality of Marley and Burning Spear. Dub-poet Linton Kwesi Johnson saw the change as "a reflection of the serious decline in the moral standards of Jamaica...and in itself a reflection of the decline in the economic welfare of Jamaicans, and the whole dog-eat-dog ethos of the prevailing ruling party."

Certainly, the programme of IMF-sponsored monetarism espoused by the JLP (Jamaican Labour Party), which won the election in 1980, was much harsher than the non-aligned socialism of the previous incumbents, the PNP (People's National Party), and recession hit Jamaica hard in the 1980s. But not everyone chatted slackness. Rasta DJs, like **Charlie Chaplin**, Josie Wales and the very influential **Brigadier Jerry**, were a prominent part of the scene, as was the locks-wearing crooner **Cocoa Tea**, whose voice was as sweet as his name. The most prolific Jamaican vocalist of the 1980s, **Frankie Paul**, observed things with just as sharp an eye as the

DJs, and commented on love, culture and the dancehall itself, as did his main rivals in the dancehall, Johnny Osbourne, Half Pint, Barrington Levy and Little John.

The most original vocal stylist of the period, **Ini Kamoze**, bypassed the usual sound-system circuit, making a classic album with Sly & Robbie in 1984. However, it wasn't until a decade later that he had a massive and much-deserved US pop hit with his reworking of the song "Hot Stepper".

Ragga

Jamaican music is a faddish beast, and before long things changed again. As had happened so often before, the initial changes were technological. Digital technology meant you could make tunes with only a couple of musicians – usually a bass player and a drummer. New rhythm tracks then became much cheaper to build, and production costs were further reduced by the extension of an established trend – that of the version.

Versions are reworkings of an original tune, sometimes from a different producer and set of musicians, and at other times employing the same rhythm track as the original hit, but with new mixes and

fresh DJs (or singers). The first digital record was a **King Jammy** production, Wayne Smith's "Under Me Sleng Teng", produced in 1985. The rhythm – loosely based on Eddie Cochran's "Something Else" – has been used endlessly since, and is as much a dancehall staple as the Studio One chestnuts. After this groundbreaking tune, Jammy's sound was the dominant one of the 1980s, with DJs like **Chaka Demus**, **Admiral Bailey** and **Lieutenant Stitchie** – as well as the singers **Pinchers**, **Nitty Gritty** and **King Kong** – available and on call. Interestingly enough, the DJ who became ragga's first international icon, **Shabba Ranks**, had his first Jamaican hits for Jammy's incredibly successful label, but only fulfilled his true potential for other producers.

Many of the early digital tunes now sound very thin, but some producers used the new technology to make some very serious tunes indeed. Foremost among them was, of course, Prince/King Jammy, but there was also **Augustus 'Gussie' Clarke**, who set a new standard with his production of Gregory Isaacs' "Rumours" in 1988. Equally crucial sounds came from Jammy's former employer, **King Tubby** (who went from mixing other producers' tracks to launching his own Firehouse and Waterhouse labels), Bobby Digital, Winston Riley, Hugh 'Redman' James, Mikey Bennett, Steelie & Cleevie (a bassist and drummer who also played on most of their rivals' productions) and the Penthouse Studio maestro Donovan Germain. Their new music was generally up-tempo, with heavy, rumbling bass lines that were admirably catered for by the vast bass speakers sported by the modern sound system.

The digital DJ of the eighties was characteristically **ragga** – ragamuffin in style and attitude. Ragamuffin was to the digital age what rudeboy was to the late 1960s – the essence of a bad, street attitude whose proudest boast is that "we run tings, and tings nuh run we". Hot lyrical themes were crack cocaine and guns, a reflection of the state of Kingston at the time. In contrast to the braggadocio of the rough and tough DJs were gentle love songs – often covers of US soul hits – from sweet-voiced singers like **Thriller U**, **Wayne Wonder** and **Sanchez**. These were firmly in the tradition of late 1960s rock steady, and form a side of the ragga revolution that's generally been ignored by outside commentators.

Sex – one of the mainstays of ragga tunes – also received some radical treatment as women DJs like **Lady Saw** answered male slackness on its own raunchy terms. Another gifted woman at the mike, **Lady G**, concentrated mainly on cultural material, often from a refreshing woman's perspective. It was a surprising shift considering how curtailed women's roles had been in the Jamaican scene. There has only ever been one female producer, **Sonia Pottinger**, who had her heyday in the rock steady era, and female singers have either sung love songs – lovers' rock, dominated by UK reggae singers – or, like Bob Marley's I-Threes, sturdy Rasta lyrics.

These days, however, women assert themselves on the dancefloors. No dance is complete without a women's posse dressed to kill (the current style is bare-as-you-dare plus platinum-blonde wig), winding and grinding with whoever dares take them on. There is even a dancehall queen, and numerous princesses who often have day jobs as models and who have become as much in

PAUL COOTE

Lady Saw – radical slackness

demand as DJs themselves. Male fashion remains more cautious, but behaviour from both sexes on the dancefloor is ever more extrovert. People started out carrying lighters to the dance, flashing them for any particularly wicked selection. Now some use gas canisters, igniting the spray to produce six-foot jets of flame in time to the beat.

Reggae's internationalism has resulted in huge global influence for Jamaican music. **Versions**, **remixes** and **raps** – staples of the modern music industry – all stem from Jamaica. American **hip-hop** and **rap** have had some reverse influence, too, showing up in tunes like the Sly and Robbie production "Murder She Wrote" deejayed/sung by **Chaka Demus and Pliers**. Artists such as these and **Shaggy** also experimented with R&B, scoring international hits with tunes like the former's "She Don't Let Nobody" (based on a Curtis Mayfield sample) and the latter's "Oh Carolina".

Return to Consciousness

By the 1990s a further shift had taken place in the dancehall, away from the slackness and guntalk that had made ragga notorious. During the last half of the previous decade, only Yami Bolo, Admiral Tibet and Junior Reid were regularly making records concerned with 'truth and rights', but this gradually changed. Two influential figures in this return to 'conscious' themes were a DJ and a singer from the Destiny Outernational sound system, **Tony Rebel** and **Garnett Silk**.

Chatting 'cultural' lyrics long before rasta values returned to fashion, Rebel also produced modern roots singers like Ras Shiloh, Uton Green and Everton Blender on his Flames label. His friend, the late Garnett Silk cut strong conscious tunes for leading Jamaican labels, and was signed to the US

major Atlantic Records before his accidental death in a gas canister explosion in 1994. He left behind an inspiring body of work which can be heard most clearly in the styles of singers like Ras Shiloh and Peter Morgan of the vocal-harmony group **Morgan Heritage**.

The move away from lyrics glorifying gunplay received a further impetus after the violent death of the promising young DJ Pan Head in 1993. This inspired two incisive commentaries from fellow mikemen: **Buju Banton**'s "Murderer" and **Beenie Man**'s "No Mama No Cry". Buju has continued in a largely conscious vein ever since, particularly impressing with his masterful *Til Shiloh* album. Two of the DJ stars who were most associated with slackness, **Shabba Ranks** and **Capleton**, turned in a similar direction. Indeed, the latter has even taken to wearing the turban of the strict Bobo dread culture of Prince Emanuel Edwards, while a new wave of similarly committed chanters have followed in their footsteps, including **Anthony B** and the very popular **Sizzla**.

Among the singers most successfully expressing the 'new' Rasta vision of the world have been **Luciano**, who has made two impressive albums for Island, **Jah Mali**, former London-resident **Mikey General**, **Bushman** and **Everton Blender**. Outstanding records from the rejuvenated **Michael Rose** (particularly with Sly &

Roots Messenger – Luciano

Reggae in the US

The roots of American reggae are found in the Jamaican communities of cities like New York and Miami, where its initial development was influenced by a variety of music scenes – jazz, soul, funk – which offered ways for émigré musicians to earn their living. By the late 1970s, however, New York – the epicentre of US reggae activity – had at least one important studio devoted to the music. Situated in the Bronx, this was owned by Lloyd Barnes, a singer who had recorded for Prince Buster. With his session band the Reckless Bread, Barnes produced visiting Jamaicans, including Horace Andy and Sugar Minott, as well as locals like Noel Delahaye and Wayne Jarrett. Under-appreciated at the time, the music that appeared on Barnes' labels has since gained international recognition, with the impressive series of dub albums particularly appreciated in Germany.

While Barnes succeeded in creating his own roots sound, US reggae only registered in Jamaica itself with the next stage of the music's development. During the **dancehall** period of the early 1980s, several new studios/labels were launched. These included Hyman Wright and Percy Chin's **Jah Life** in New York, Phillip Smart's **HC&F** on Long Island, and Delroy Wright's **Live and Learn** in Washington. Jamaican singers like **Michael Prophet** and **Barrington Levy** made strong discs in the US and the period saw some gifted performers emerge from the New York scene, including the oddly-named **Scion Sashay Success**, who was popular in both the Kingston and London dancehalls.

The next stage in US reggae came with the shift to **ragga**. As the entire reggae world adjusted to computerised rhythms, new producers set up operations in the US. These included Don Moodie's **Don One** in Brooklyn, which was successful in the late 1990s with the singer **Glen Washington**, and Kenneth Black's **Skengdon** in Miami. The latter came up with one of the most popular dancehall rhythms of the 1980s, **Chaka Demus**'s "Young Gal Business", a massive hit in Jamaica. But the New York performer who made the greatest impact in this period was the UK-born **Shinehead**. An amazingly versatile artist, Shinehead sang sweetly, deejayed and rapped to match the toughest competition from West Kingston – or anywhere else. Coming up through the highly-rated African Love sound system, his debut album was a masterpiece, with his interpretation of Michael Jackson's "Billie Jean" becoming a standard that can still rock any dance today.

Shinehead has still to achieve the crossover success he deserves, but true international stardom has certainly come the way of **Shaggy**, who followed in his footsteps with a similarly eclectic approach. His inspired reworking of the Folkes Brothers' "Oh Carolina" standard might have seemed like another of those one-off reggae hits that strike a chord with a broader public, but he showed his genuinely wide appeal again with the even more popular "Boombastic", which topped both the US and UK pop charts. Produced by the forward-looking **Robert Livingstone**, Shaggy's music has drawn from the latest trends in Kingston ragga and from US hip-hop culture, and it is this fusion that has

Shinehead: a man ahead of his time

informed most of the interesting US reggae of the 1990s. Top Jamaican artists like Shabba Ranks, Bounty Killer and Capleton have recorded with US hip-hop acts, while US-based artists such as **Louis Ranking**, **Born Jamericans** and the singularly uncompromising **Red Fox** have balanced the two cultures in some striking and imaginative ways.

Robbie) and **Cocoa Tea** have also contributed to the roots revival. The vocal harmony group also made a comeback with the Brooklyn, New York group **Morgan Heritage** – the five children of the singer Delroy Morgan – who first set foot in a Jamaican studio on a visit in 1995, and have recorded outstanding material ever since.

In terms of **rhythm**, there were two contrasting trends in the last half of the 1990s. Producer **Dave Kelly**'s "Pepper Seed" of 1995 initiated a fashion for minimal, incredibly infectious and strictly **digital tracks**, many of the strongest being built by a visitor from London, Paul 'Jazwad' Yebauh. Appearing on labels such as Mad House, Shocking Vibes, Xtra Large and 2 Bad, these are meant for maximum excitement in the dancehall, particularly when voiced by popular DJs like **Bounty Killer, Merciless, Buccaneer, General Degree** and **Spragga Benz**, or young pretenders **Lexxus** and the **Ward 21** collective (who not only rap but build their own hardcore rhythms).

In contrast to the gruff, 'badboy' tones of many of the top men at the mike, there has also been the phenomenon of **Red Rat** and **Goofy**, both bringing a fresh adolescent sensibility to dancehall runnings. The new cultural performers sometimes voice the same hot dancehall rhythms, though more often favouring the alternate style on offer – fuller-sounding reworkings of vintage hits.

No DJ has enjoyed greater success over hardcore ragga rhythms during the last couple of years, however, than Moses Davis, aka **Beenie Man** (though arch rival Bounty Killer has run him a close second). Cutting his first record when only eight years old ('Beenie' means small), he has since developed into an artist of real stature, even entering the UK pop charts in 1998 with the catchy "Who Am I".

The traditional love balladeer hasn't been left out of the picture, either. Under the guidance of Donovan Germain, the soulful **Beres Hammond** – whose career dates back to the Zap Pow band of the 1970s – found favour with new audiences. Germain saw the potential of placing Beres's warm, emotive tones over modern dancehall rhythms, and scored massively with the hit 45, "Tempted To Touch" in 1990. Hammond hasn't looked back since, with a trailer-load of further hits.

The singing sensation of the last years of the Millennium, though, was **Mr Vegas**. This new boy on the block created the sort of pure dancehall excitement once associated with Barrington Levy and Little John. Whether he will develop

into a lasting talent remains to be seen, but no one is hotter at present, which means he has the pick of every producer's best rhythms. This alone will keep the momentum running, at least until the next hot new name appears.

Keeping Up

Jamaican music is totally **singles oriented** (with a few notable exceptions, the best albums are compilations) and the output is phenomenal. Most singles are pressed on seven-inch once, and then deleted. Hits usually make it to twelve-inch, and last longer, but even then you have to move fast. The only way to follow it is to go to the dances, listen to pirate radio, or buy reggae magazines (*Echoes* is the best in Britain; *The Beat* has good coverage in the US). If none of those is available, your best bets are the quarterly Jet Star *Reggae Hits* series or the Greensleeves Samplers.

Alternatively, go to Jamaica. Ideally, you should time a visit for the four-day **Reggae Sumfest** which takes place every year in the first week of August at Montego Bay. This has taken over from the old Reggae Sunsplash (now more or less obsolete) and with virtually all the stars appearing, it's a big event – fun and unitimidating. In addition, any time of year, try exploring Jamaica's many **record shacks** – there's a whole host around Orange Street and up around Half-Way Tree in Kingston.

discography

Since Jamaican music is singles oriented, most of the best albums are compilations. Good specialists for these are the UK label Blood & Fire, with Steve Barrow's impeccably researched, selected and presented albums, and the US label Heartbeat who are currently releasing vintage Studio One material.

Two notes: First, US-based reggae artists are included in this discography, UK ones appear on p.461, and African reggae artists are covered (by country) in Volume One of this guide. Second, since reggae has such a huge catalogue (and a full-size Rough Guide book of its own), this discography has (more or less!) limited selections to one CD per artist.

General Compilations

 Tougher than Tough:
The Story of Jamaican Music (Island, UK).

This four-CD set is quite an investment but it would be hard to imagine a better compilation of Jamaican music. The discs cover just about every phase of the story from 1958 to 1993, beginning with a superb selection of pre-ska R&B, then moving through the ska and rock-steady hits of the 1960s to an overview of reggae's manifold styles and sub-genres. The songs are gathered from a wide variety of labels – not just from the Island catalogue – and there are superb, virtually book-sized sleeve notes from Steve Barrow.

Folk and Mento

Compilations

Drums of Defiance (Smithsonian Folkways, US)
The Roots of Reggae (Lyrichord, US).

These two well-annotated anthologies cover the deepest roots music of Jamaica from the Maroon communities.

O From The Grass Roots Of Jamaica
(Dynamic, Jamaica).

A variety of Jamaican folk styles, including jonkanoo, ring play and kumina. The only drawback is that the tracks aren't identified according to their styles on the sleeve.

From Kongo to Zion and **Churchical Chants of the Nyabinghi** (Heartbeat, US).

Traditional rasta music from nyabinghi ceremonies is to be found on both these collections.

Roots: Bongo, Baccra and Coolie, Volumes 1 & 2 (Smithsonian Folkways, US).

The first volume includes some of the small amount of Kumina music found on record, plus Hindu baccra music; the second features Revival Zion and carnival music.

Artists

Count Ossie and his Mystic Revelation of Rastafari

Count Ossie (Williams) was a Rastafarian drummer from Kingston who teamed up with sax/flute player Cedric Brooks's musicians to form the Mystic Revelation of Rastafari.

Grounation (MRR, Jamaica).

An extraordinary mixture of traditional Rasta drumming accompanied by bebop and cool jazz horn lines, apocalyptic poems, and much chanting. The definitive set of pure rasta music.

The Jolly Boys

The Jolly Boys have been playing mento on banjo, bongo, guitar and kalimba since its heyday in the 1930s, and are unquestionably the finest exponents around.

Pop'n' Mento
(Cooking Vinyl, UK; First Warning, US).

Sunny and lewd, this is classic good-time mento from the veterans.

Ska and Rock Steady

Compilations

 Duke Reid's Treasure Chest
(Heartbeat, US).

Once opened, the treasure chest reveals forty-one gems from the producer who ruled during the late 1960s. Includes both the expected classics and obscurities.

Ska Bonanza: The Studio One Ska Years
(Heartbeat, US).

A beautifully-packaged two-disc set that takes in Jamaican R&B, as well as the full-blown ska of the Skatalites, the Maytals, the Wailers and many more.

Ska Boogie: Jamaican R&B, the Dawn of Ska
(Sequel, UK).

One of the few compilations of Jamaican shuffles and boogies. Highlights include Owen Gray's tribute to Coxsone, playing "On the Beach", and the original cut of "Oh Carolina" from the Folkes Brothers.

Artists

Bob Andy

An original member of the Paragons, Bob Andy's subsequent solo work for Studio One, Rupie Edwards, Harry J and Sonia Pottinger is incomparable. His UK pop hits with Marcia Griffiths (as Bob & Marcia) only hinted at his true greatness.

Song Book (Studio One, Jamaica).

A fitting title: this features many of the best songs from Jamaica's finest songwriter, and they were never sung more soulfully, or over such memorable rhythms.

Carlton & His Shoes

Carlton Manning has been elevating the love song to a spiritual level since the late rock steady days. His music is simply the most beautiful and ethereal the island has ever produced.

O Love Me Forever (Studio One, Jamaica).

The ultimate album for original Jamaican love songs, with the most sublime harmonies imaginable.

Desmond Dekker & Aces

Dekker's golden age was during the rock steady and early reggae years, when producer Leslie Kong provided the perfect settings for his distinctive tenor.

Action! (Beverley's, France).
Intensified (Beverley's, France).

Very welcome CD releases (with extra tracks) of Dekker's greatest albums – both produced by Leslie Kong.

Alton Ellis

Alton Ellis epitomised the cool sound of rock steady, and popularised the name with his song of that title.

Cry Tough (Heartbeat, US).

This is a good introduction to rock steady in general, and to Alton Ellis in particular. Most of his major Treasure Isle hits are found here.

The Ethiopians

The Ethiopians, led by Leonard Dillon, began as a ska band, moved over to rock steady, and hardly altered their 'country'-style vocals for any of the music's subsequent developments.

Original Reggae Hit Sound (Trojan, UK).

This covers the Ethiopians' golden period from 1966 to the early seventies, and includes anthems like "Train To Skaville", "The Whip" and "The Selah".

The Heptones

While Duke Reid grabbed most of the top vocal trios of the late 1960s, Dodd had the Heptones – led by Leroy Sibbles, an important bass player as well as songwriter and singer.

On Top (Studio One, US).

All of the trio's Studio One albums are worth picking up, but this mixture of outstanding love and 'reality' tracks is the one to begin with.

Jackie Mittoo

No single musician contributed more to reggae's development than the late keyboards player Jackie Mittoo. He played on countless sessions, while the instrumentals released under his own name form one of the music's cornerstones.

 Tribute To Jackie Mittoo (Heartbeat, US).

A glorious thirty-one track compilation that covers both the rock steady and reggae periods, and includes previously unreleased tracks as well as the acknowledged classics.

The Skatalites

Featuring the trombonist Don Drummond, the Skatalites had an all-star musical cast, and produced simply the greatest ska sounds.

Ska-Boo-Da-Ba (Westside, UK).

The definitive album of hot ska instrumentals. Produced by Justin and Philip Yap, who paid their musicians more than others and were rewarded with something extra in return. If you want more of the Skatalites, try any of their Studio One albums.

King Stitt

DJ pioneer King Stitt, known as 'The Ugly One', had his time on record in the late 1960s with producer Clancy Eccles. For over a decade before, he had helped shape Coxsone's dances.

 Dance Hall '63 (Studio One, US).

This is not in fact a 1963 recording but a recent attempt to recreate the atmosphere of a dance of that era with Stitt adding introductions and interjections to some classic Jamaican R&B and ska.

The Techniques

The Techniques were one of the few quartets in an age of vocal trios, and produced some of the greatest harmonies of the rock steady era.

 Run Come Celebrate (Heartbeat, US).

A good example of classic rock steady vocalising, over some of Duke Reid's greatest (and most versioned) rhythms.

The Uniques

Keith 'Slim' Smith was one of Jamaica's most expressive ever singers, and had a run of great records with Llolyd 'charmers' Tyrell and Jimmy Riley in this vocal trio.

 Watch That Sound (Pressure Sounds, UK).

There have been several compilations of the Uniques' rock-steady/early reggae classics, some packaged as Smith albums. But this fine. well packaged selection looks near definitive. Jamaica has never been more soulful.

Reggae

Compilations

 If Deejay Was Your Trade: The Dreads at King Tubby's 1974–77 (Blood & Fire, UK).

Bunny Lee produced these sixteen dynamite tracks from Kingston's premier DJs of the 1970s – U-Roy, Dr Alimantado, Dillinger, Tapper Zukie and others.

Artists

The Abyssinians

The Abyssinians brought heavenly harmonies to Rasta-inspired roots music, although their output was limited.

 Satta Massagana (Heartbeat, US).

The legendary debut album from the trio that defined close-harmony singing for the roots era. The CD adds four extra tracks of the same stunning quality.

Big Youth

It was Big Youth who made deejaying dread during the 1970s, and even his singing tracks have panache.

 Everyday Skank: The Best Of Big Youth (Trojan, UK).

Cultural toasting at its dreadlocked best. Arresting self-productions are slotted alongside equally impressive work from the likes of Gussie Clarke, Joe Gibbs and Keith Hudson.

Black Uhuru

Black Uhuru, for all of Island's hopes, were perhaps too militant to take Marley's place on the world stage.

 Showcase (Heartbeat, US).
 Stalk of Sensemilla (Island, UK).

The first of these Sly & Robbie-produced sets collects several of their initial Jamaican hits (complete with dubs); the second showed just how unformulaic roots reggae could be.

Dennis Brown

Known as the Crown Prince of reggae in the 1970s, Dennis Brown, whose death in 1999 was the biggest shock to the reggae world since the loss of Bob Marley at the start of the decade, was equally at home with romantic or cultural offerings. Only Gregory Isaacs rivalled his popularity in the Jamaican reggae world.

ⓘ **Visions** (Joe Gibbs, Jamaica).

The 1997 album that sold like a 45 hit, and took both the singer and his producer, Joe Gibbs, into the premier league.

Burning Spear

Burning Spear was one of the few Jamaican performers to actually improve on his early work at Studio One – with both Jack Ruby and the best of his self-productions.

ⓘ **Marcus Garvey** (Mango, UK).
ⓘ **Social Living** (Blood & Fire, UK).

Spear's 1975 Marcus Garvey tribute, produced by Jack Ruby, was full of exquisite vocals and horns. The self-produced *Social Living*, marked by a smokier ambience, came closest to being its equal.

Jimmy Cliff

Cliff seemed to lose direction after his move to the UK in the mid-1960s, but his credibility was restored with his staring role in The Harder They Come, and its excellent soundtrack.

ⓘ **The Harder They Come** (Mango, UK).

No reggae collection is complete without this 1972 soundtrack, combining early reggae standards from the Maytals, Desmond Dekker and the Melodians with Cliff songs like the title track and "Many Rivers to Cross".

Culture

Culture were one of several reggae acts to benefit from Marley's international success. Their work for both Joe Gibbs and Sonia Pottinger summed up much of what was finest about late 1970s roots reggae.

ⓘ **Two Sevens Clash** (Shanachie, US).

The trio's appealing (and best selling) debut, with its gorgeous vocals, great rhythms and inspired mixes.

Marcia Griffiths

Marcia Griffiths, a third of Bob Marley's backing trio, the I-Threes, has been Jamaica's top woman singer for three decades.

❍ **Naturally** (High Note, Jamaica).
❍ **Steppin'** (High Note, Jamaica).

Naturally has recuts of Marcia's Studio One hits, plus great interpretations of Marley, Bunny Wailer and Bob Andy material. *Steppin'* is built around her major hits of the late 1970s – "Hurtin' Inside", "Peaceful Woman" and "Stepping Out Of Babylon".

Joe Higgs

Well known as the original Wailers' mentor, Joe Higgs was one of Jamaica's earliest singing stars. Incredibly, his first album only appeared in 1975.

ⓘ **Life Of Contradiction** (Micron, Jamaica).

A reflective, very serious debut set, and one that was totally outside the reggae mainstream of the time. Stands as a genuine masterpiece.

John Holt

One of the top half-dozen voices of Jamaican music, the former lead singer of the Paragons was overlooked by reggae's 1970s crossover audience, who found love songs not 'dread' enough.

ⓘ **Time Is the Master** (Moodisc, US).

The only reggae producer to get away with strings was Harry Mudie, and no voice was more suited to them than John Holt's mellifluous tenor.

Ijahman Levi

Jamaican-born Ijahman Levi was living in London when he made his initial impact. Island Records then took him back to Jamaica for an album they hoped would sell to the rock audience.

ⓘ **Haile I Hymn** (Mango, UK).

Levi's unique, soulful, meditative brand of reggae at its best, in 1978. The album brought accusations of pretentiousness at its release, as there were only four extended tracks. Now, it sounds a classic.

I-Roy

I-Roy died homeless in 1999, an end made even more tragic when you consider what a debonair figure the DJ cut when at the peak of his powers in the 1970s. As a witty, sophisticated lyricist, none could touch him.

ⓘ **Don't Check Me With No Lightweight Stuff** (Blood & Fire, UK).

16 groundbreaking tracks that cover the great DJ's most prolific and successful period. Like all Jamaican performers on a roll, he was given only the hottest rhythms around, including those that had supported hits from Augustus Pablo, Errol Dunkley, the Paragons, and Bob Marley.

Gregory Isaacs

He has the reputation of a real-life 'bad boy'; but it has been Gregory Isaacs's talent, as well as attitude, that's kept him at the top in the tough reggae world.

❍ **Soon Forward** (African Museum, Jamaica).

The second set he recorded for Virgin, and the finest of his self-productions.

Prince Jammy

Before he launched computerised ragga in 1985, Prince Jammy produced some fine roots tunes, and drawing from youth talent local to his West Kingston studio, played an important role in fostering the 'Waterhouse' style of urgent, slightly off-key vocalising.

ⓘ **Crowning of Prince Jammy** (Pressure Sounds, UK).

A couple of heavyweight dubs here recall Jammy's apprenticeship with King Dubby, and there are serious vocals from, among others, the Waterhouse wailers, Junior Reid, and dancehall stars Sugar Minott and Half Pint.

Bob Marley and the Wailers

Bob Marley (1945–81) and the Wailers were the only reggae unit to make the crossover into big-time international stardom, fuelled by Marley's effective voice, unique melodic gift and unerring ear for a commercial sound. It's no less than astonishing that he was able to achieve such world-wide success without compromising the quality of his music in the least. For more on the man, see p.440.

see p.440.

 Songs of Freedom
(Tuff Gong/Island, UK).

The four-CD collection *Songs of Freedom* has 78 songs, dating from 1962 to Marley's death in 1980. Including virtually all the classics, plus lots of rare treasures, it is the definitive Bob Marley collection. If you want just a single disc of highlights, then ⊚ **Legend** (Island, UK) is a near-faultless selection.

⊚ **Burnin'** (Tuff Gong/Island, UK).

You want original Wailers albums, rather than compilatons? Well, this 1973 album one was a classic from day one, with sparse roots rhythms and harmonies employed to startling effect on such songs as "I Shot The Sherriff", "Small Axe" and "Duppy Conqueror". Fame – and vocal backing from the I-Threes – still lay ahead of the group.

⊚ **Exodus** (Tuff Gong/Island, UK).

Released at the height of his popularity, 1977's *Exodus* was Marley's ultimate crossover album, packed with great songs ("One Love", "jamming", "Three Little Birds"), rolling rhythms, and sparkling harmonies. The world listened and a thousand reggae bands, from Johannesburg to Jakarta, set to work to imitate the Wailers' delivery.

The Mighty Diamonds

The rise in the mid-1970s of one of reggae's greatest vocal-harmony trios will always be associated with that of Channel One as the top studio of the era.

⊚ **Right Time** (Channel One, US).

A fine selection of sweetly harmonised vocals, militant 'rockers' rhythms and Garveyite lyrics.

Mutabaruka

Mutabaruka's dub poetry was always in a class of its own, and he delivered his invectives over some genuinely hard rhythms.

⊚ **Check It** (Alligator, US).

Guitarist Earl 'Chinna' Smith's rootsy production, employing the High Times Band, helped make Mutabaruka's debut set the best dub poetry album of them all.

Augustus Pablo/King Tubby

It was a youthful Augustus Pablo who made people take the melodica seriously, while King Tubby's radical dub mixing perfectly complemented his eerie playing. Pablo died in 1999, a huge loss to the music.

⊚ **King Tubby Meets Rockers Uptown**
⊚ **Original Rockers** (both Greensleeves, UK).

The first of these essential sets has the raw dubs of Pablo's early self-productions; the second collects many of the most exceptional instrumental 'A' sides (plus Dillinger's "Brace A Boy" toast).

Lee Perry

The diminutive singer and producer Lee 'Scratch' Perry made his initial impact at Studio One in the ska era, before producing the early Wailers discs. His glory days, however, came at his own Black Ark studio in the 1970s, where he produced a huge volume of music, notably with Max Romeo and Junior Murvin ("Police and Thieves"), and as himself – The Upsetters.

 Arkology
(Island Jamaica, UK).

Even the faintest interest in Lee Perry's productions merits the purchase of this three-disc set, with its string of riches, from Scratch himself, as well as Junior Murvin, Max Romeo, Augustus Pablo and the Heptones. If you're hooked, then ⊚ **Produced & Directed by The Upsetter** (Pressure Sounds, UK) fills in the gaps with equally awe-inspiring examples of Black Art alchemy.

Third World

Third World have always been one of the best self-contained Jamaican bands and, for all their international appeal, far more than a slick crossover act.

⊚ **Reggae Ambassadors** (Mango, US).

A two-disc compilation that stretches from their debut set of 1976 to a 'combination' outing with ragga DJ Terror Fabulous. "Roots With Quality" as one track has it – and only reggae snobs could find fault with that.

Toots and the Maytals

Though they made great ska, the gospel-influenced trio's finest period came a few years later, with Leslie Kong, still the most under-rated of Jamaica's great producers.

⊚ **Sweet & Dandy** (Beverley's, France).

Tracks of the calibre of "Pressure Drop", "Monkey Man" and "54-46 That's My Number" make this the best of Toots and the Maytals' albums.

Peter Tosh

Peter Tosh, always the angriest of the Wailers, released a stunning series of singles under his own name for Scratch, Joe Gibbs and his own Intel Diplo label. He left the group in 1973, and was shot dead in mysterious circumstances fourteen years later.

⊚ **Honorary Citizen** (Columbia, US).

A wonderfully packaged three-disc set. The first collects much of Tosh's best material from rare Jamaican 45s; the second comprises live recordings; and the third has variable album cuts (the earlier ones are the best). Worth buying for the marvellous first disc.

U-Roy

The DJ from King Tubby's sound was not the first to jive-talk on record, but it was U-Roy's hits for Treasure Isle in 1970 that established the phenomenon still with us today – in both its original Jamaican form and as US rap.

 Version of Wisdom
(Virgin Frontline Classics, UK).

U-Roy's *Version Galore* was the first DJ album ever, and it has never been bettered. It is joined here by the rest of his groundbreaking output for Duke Reid.

Bunny Wailer

Bunny was the best singer of the original Wailers, and the first to mature as a songwriter. His most compelling solo work appeared shortly after he left the group and formed his own label.

⊚ **Blackheart Man** (Island, UK).

Arguably the greatest 'solo' album recorded from any of the original Wailers. Most of Bunny Wailer's finest songs are

JAMAICA

found here, and the performances, arrangements and rhythms are sublime.

The Wailing Souls

One of the most enduring of Jamaican vocal groups, the Winston Matthews-led Wailing Souls have successfully adapted to every stage of the music – from 1970s Studio One rhythms to King Jammy's digital approach.

◉ **Wild Suspense** (Mango Reggae Refreshers, UK).

The self-produced album that was at least the equal of their classic Studio One debut. Immaculate roots harmonising and wicked Channel One rhythms.

Yabby You

Many singers and DJs voiced Rasta sentiments in the 1970s, because that was what was selling. But there was never any doubting Yabby You's commitment, or his talent as a singer and producer.

◉ **Jesus Dread** (Blood & Fire, UK).

Definitive roots and culture spread over two discs. One is built around his classic Conquering Lion set, with extra versions; the second collects subsequent tracks of the same 'dread' order from the likes of Wayne Wade, Trinity and Michael Rose, as well as Yabby himself.

Dancehall

Compilations

◉ **Forward:
A Selection Of Greensleeves Top Singles 1977–82** (Greensleeves, UK).

Covers the period when roots reggae became dancehall; particularly valuable for collecting many of Henry 'Junjo' Lawes's most popular productions.

◉ **A Dee-jay Explosion In a Dance hall Style** (Heartbeat, US).

Live dancehall albums were a popular, if short-lived, trend of the early 1980s. Capturing Gemini Disco in session, this remains one of the strongest, with such artists as Eek-A-Mouse, Sister Nancy and Ranking Toyan on top form.

Artists

Eek-a-Mouse

Beginning as a straight roots vocalist, Ripton Hilton became Eek-a-Mouse, not quite a deejay or a singer, but the first 'singjay' artist.

◉ **Wa Do Dem** (Greensleeves, UK; Shanachie, US).

One of the wittiest, most imitated examples of the singjay style. The title track was the record that started it all.

Half Pint

The sheer joy of being in a recording studio was always evident in Half Pint's best discs, and made up for all the young singer's melodies sounding much the same.

◉ **Money Man Skank** (Jammy's, Jamaica).

The dancehall singer's most satisfying album, not least because of the brash, infectious High Times Band rhythms produced by Prince Jammy.

Ini Kamoze

The most original vocal stylist to emerge in the early 1980s, and Sly & Robbie's greatest discovery. Ini Kamoze has been far from prolific, but his creativity has yet to diminish.

◉ **Ini Kamoze** (Island, Jamaica).

Kamoze's unique voice and songs over some of Sly & Robbie's most progressive rhythms of the 1980s.

Barrington Levy

The young Barrington Levy was one of the few singers who held his own against DJ dominance in the early 1980s. His debut, *Bounty Hunter*, has a strong claim to being the first dancehall album.

◉ **Collection** (Time One, UK).

A strong selection of Levy's hits, mainly for Henry 'Junjo' Lawes and Jah Screw. Covers his career from initial, groundbreaking tunes to his triumph of the 1990s with "Too Experienced".

Sugar Minott

Sugar Minott's voice is sweet as his name, and for the first half of the 1980s he could do no wrong.

◉ **Black Roots** (Black Roots, Jamaica).

After graduating from Mr. Dodd's academy, Sugar formed his own label and released this masterpiece. Includes the popular 45s "River Jordan" and "Hard Time Pressure".

Frankie Paul

The prolific Frankie Paul was the Jamaican singer of the 1980s who most deserved crossover success. A great talent who still makes outstanding records.

◉ **Twenty Massive Hits** (Sonic Sounds, UK).

This is one of the best of innumerable Frankie Paul compilations. Check, too, his albums for Henry 'Junjo' Lawes, Winston Riley, George Phang and King Jammy (for starters!).

Yellowman & Josie Wales

Yellowman was the biggest DJ of the first half of the 1980s and his best records show plenty of originality, humour and style. The gruff-voiced Josie Wales was his main rival.

◉ **Two Giants Clash** (Greensleeves, UK).

Tackling rough Roots Radics rhythms, both chatters seem evenly matched here.

Ragga

Compilations

◉ **Conscious Ragga Volumes 1 & 2** (Greensleeves, UK).

Drawing from a wide range of performers and production camps, these excellent selections concentrate on the return to 'culture' in the 1990s.

◉ **Reggae Hits** (Jet Star, UK).

Currently numbering 25 volumes, this is an invaluable series offering a convenient and economic way of catching up with what has happened in the modern reggae world.

Ragga, Ragga, Ragga (Greensleeves, UK).

Just as recommended is this series (now up to 13 vols) from Greensleeves – especially if you want a greater concentration on hardcore rhythms and DJs.

Artists

Buju Banton

The homophobic sentiments of his "Boom Bye Bye" did not do Buju Banton any favours with the international media. A pity, as this detracted from the DJ's very real talent, and the inoffensive nature of most of his lyrics.

'Til Shiloh
(Loose Cannon, UK).

Buju's masterpiece marks the point where ragga became thoughtful. His furious response to Pan Head's death, "Murderer" is here, but even more memorable are the reflective "Till I'm Laid To Rest" and "Untold Stories".

Beenie Man

The most popular ragga DJ in the world: Beenie Man is amazingly imaginative and his prolific output still regularly surprises.

The Many Moods Of Moses (Greensleeves, UK).

The marvellous UK pop hit "Tell Me" is included, along with the Sly & Robbie produced "Foundation", which is just as strong.

Bounty Killer

Rockstone DJ voices have been something of a tradition in Jamaican music, but none has been gruffer and rougher than Bounty Killer's.

My Experience (VP, US).

Guest appearances from compatible hip-hoppers helped sell this to the wider world, while a generous selection of Bounty Killer's Jamaican hits kept his dancehall followers happy.

Capleton

Few DJs were slacker than the early Capleton. But then came a remarkable shift to uncompromising 'reality' tunes like "Almshouse", "Prophet" and the phenomenal "Tour".

Prophecy (DefJam, US).

Cultural ragga, complete with nyahbingi drumming on a couple of tracks. The hip-hop remixes, including one of "Tour", work well too.

Cocoa Tea

Cocoa Tea's lyrics have developed since his first hits of 1983, and he is now just as assured with songs about culture as romance.

Love Me (VP, US).

The sweetness of Cocoa Tea's voice is offset by the roughhouse tones of the DJs Shabba Ranks, Josie Wales and Buccaneer on what is largely a collection of the singer's hits for Bobby Digital.

Chaka Demus & Pliers

Both the DJ Chaka Demus and the singer Pliers had moderately successful solo careers before joining voices to become international stars.

Tease Me (Mango, UK).

Mid-1990s ragga, produced by the ever-inventive Sly & Robbie, and mixing in Curtis Mayfield soul, ska, hip-hop and, the most original touch of all, bhangra rhythms.

Beres Hammond

The soulful Beres Hammond represents a return to traditional values – melody and emotion – and is possibly the greatest singer in contemporary Jamaican music.

A Love Affair (Penthouse, US).

The classic Donovan Germain-produced set that established Beres as the major Jamaican vocalist of modern times.

Luciano

Luciano, with his records for producer Philip 'Fatis' Burrell, led the 1990s cultural renaissance. He is now freelancing in typical Jamaican fashion and easily keeping up standards. One of the key current artists.

Where There Is Life
(Island, Jamaica).

"It's Me Again Jah" topped the Jamaican charts, and its relaxed, dignified feel carries over to the rest of this exceptionally well-crafted cultural set.

Mr Vegas

Mr Vegas has already gone past the six-month spell at the top that critics assigned him when he first appeared in 1998. The average age of his fans is probably 14 but he has brought something genuinely fresh and exciting to the music. He entered the UK pop charts with the catchy "Heads High".

Heads High (Greensleeves, UK).

Mr Vegas's brash approach stands up well over the course of this debut album, kicking off with his chart success and moving on to tunes like "Latest news" and "Big Things A Gwan" that established him in the dancehall.

Shabba Ranks

Shabba Ranks was the first important DJ star of the ragga age, and for all his crossover success, he still releases 45s aimed squarely at the Jamaican market.

○ **Golden Touch** (Greensleeves, UK).

Appearing just prior to his signing with Epic (and international stardom), this Mikey Bennett production remains his most consistent album – and there's not a single slack line.

Garnett Silk

Starting as a DJ, the late Garnett Silk spearheaded the new 'consciousness' movement in Jamaican reggae when he turned to singing and made a stunning series of heart-felt cultural discs for producers such as Bobby Digital.

○ **Gold** (Charm, UK).

Drawing from a variety of production camps, this twenty-track set gives the best overview of Silk's important cultural output.

Sizzla

Among the new strictly-cultural DJs wearing turbans and chanting down Babylon, the youth known as Sizzla has made the greatest impact.

○ **Praise Ye Jah** (Xterminator/Jet Star, UK).
○ **Black Woman & Child** (Greensleeves, UK).

Serious bobo-dread chanting over the pick of the rhythms from, respectively, Philip 'Fatis' Burrell and Bobby Digital.

US Reggae artists

Artists

Wayne Jarrett

A singer in the Horace Andy vein, Wayne Jarrett cut the outstanding "Saturday Night Jambaree" for Jah Life and "Youth Man" for Glen Brown, as well as tracks of a comparable calibre for Wackies.

○ **Bubble Up** (Wackies, UK).

This presents six vocal tracks that reach the standard of his model, Horace Andy, along with their dubs. An ideal set with which to sample the Wackies' approach.

Red Fox

Red Fox has recorded in both Kingston and New York studios to stunning effect. The most exciting Big Apple reggae talent since Shinehead.

○ **As a Matter of Fox** (Elektra, US).

A fourteen-track assault, this is a contender for the hardest reggae album ever to emerge from New York.

Shaggy

Produced by the innovative Rober Livingstone, Shaggy has been one of the great, and entirely deserved, crossover success stories of the ragga age. And his hits work just as well in the dancehall as on pop radio.

○ **Boombastic** (Greensleeves, UK).

None of his albums quite match the brilliance of his 45s, but this comes the nearest.

Shinehead

He can croon a soul ballad, rap, deejay and even whistle. Perhaps his fusion of styles was ahead of its time; he certainly paved the way for Shaggy's global success.

 Rough and Rugged (African Love Music, US).

The most scintillating, inspired and fully accomplished US reggae album ever. Listen to the range of styles and prepare to be suitably awed.

Jamaica

Reggae in the UK

lovers and poets – babylon sounds

To complete the story of Jamaican music, **Gregory Mthembu-Salter** and **Peter Dalton** set their course east across the Atlantic to the UK, where Jamaican – or 'West Indian' – culture has been laying down roots for over fifty years. Ska, dub and bands like Aswad and UB40 have long had crossover acceptance to white British audiences, and almost from the outset British-Jamaican reggae artists have been ploughing an independent furrow, developing new forms such as dub poetry and lover's rock.

Anywhere you find two or more Jamaicans, any country, on a Saturday night, you must have a blues dance. This handy maxim, from Prince Lincoln of the **Royal Rasses**, has been true of Britain since the middle of the last century. For 1948, with the arrival of arrival of 492 Jamaicans on the Empire Windrush, saw the beginning of a process of large-scale economic migration from the English-speaking Caribbean to the UK that was to last twenty years.

Today, Britain has a West-Indian community of around 700,000 people, most of whom were born in Britain. Their predominant experience is one of neglect by the system, which once used them as a labour pool, but when the work dried up cast them as a scapegoat for all urban ills. The community, however, has been vocal in its rejection of these roles, and in its articulation of its own evolving identity. This articulation has come in every form, but perhaps most powerfully in music. As the King-David style dub warrior, South London reggae maestro **Jah Shaka**, has said, "We've had to do our speaking on sound systems."

Starting Out

It wasn't long after the first Jamaicans arrived that **record labels** to cater for them established themselves in the UK. The names of these pioneers are the stuff of the many obsessively collated lists that aficionados exchange joyfully whenever they come together – Melodisc, Blue Beat, R&B, Planetone and, the longer-lasting Island and Trojan. The sheer newness of what was going on lends a kind of epic quality to the many stories that surround the Jamaican music scene in the early 1960s: Daddy Peckings of West London getting fresh releases of pure, wicked ska straight from Sir Coxsone's backyard and passing them on to Duke Vin for use on

his sound system in Ladbroke Grove; Mod posses scouring small record shops for copies of Prince Buster's "Madness", the latest killer of a music they called bluebeat, after the label; homemade speakers mashing it at the dance, disturbing the midnight peace in the inner-city badlands of the UK.

Some artists came from Jamaica to stay, notably the singers Jackie Edwards, Owen Gray, Laurel Aitken, Alton Ellis, Dandy Livingstone, Errol Dunkley and Desmond Dekker. The island's top guitarist, **Ernest Ranglin**, was another early arrival, playing mostly jazz, but finding time to arrange **Millie Small**'s pop-ska hit, "My Boy Lollipop", which sold over seven million copies around the world. Occasionally, too, Jamaican hits made the UK charts: there were hot ska tunes like Prince Buster's "Al Capone" and the Skatalites' "Guns Of Naverone"; early reggae killers like Desmond Dekker's "Israelites"; instrumentals like

ADRIAN BOOT ARCHIVE

Lollipop girl Millie Small

Lee Perry's "Return of Django"; reggae with strings added in London like Bob & Marcia's "Young, Gifted and Black" (mainly from Trojan); and, later, Marley anthems like "One Love".

But generally reggae was ignored by mainstream **radio**, and on the whole, still is – with the shining exceptions of DJs Chris Goldfinger, Ranking Miss P and David Rodigan – which explains why reggae pirate stations have done so well. The first prominent pirate, DBC, the Dread Broadcasting Corporation, whose slogan was "Tune In If Yu Rankin", began broadcasting in London in 1981. Most major British cities now host at least one pirate, in between government-enforced breaks in transmission.

Bands of the 1970s

British-based reggae did not develop as a force on a par with the Jamaican original until the mid-1970s, though Jamaican émigrés like Laurel Aitken and Dandy Livingstone produced records that sold well to the skinhead audience of 1969–70. The first major band were the **Cimarons**, which included Winston Reedy, who was later to become a major 'lovers' rock' star (see p.459). The Cimarons were formed in 1967, though they didn't come into their own until the next decade, when they even scored a Jamaican number one with their version of Marley's "Talking Blues". Their records lacked consistency, however, and a far more reliable group, once they found their mature style, was **Matumbi**, founded in 1972 by **Dennis Bovell**. Matumbi drew upon soul as well as reggae for its inspiration, and even Glen Miller for the arrangement of their UK chart entry "Point Of View".

Most of the other stalwarts, who came together a little later, adopted a less eclectic but heavier

style that epitomised their status as conscious urban dreads. The prime example is Ladbroke Grove's **Aswad**, which formed in 1975 and released a succession of brilliant records, loved by a reggae audience but not quite making it among pop/rock listeners. In the 1980s, however, they began (sometimes embarrassing) attempts at crossover and finally got what they wanted in 1988, when their song "Don't Turn Around" reached number one in the UK charts – a first for a British reggae band.

ADRIAN BOOT

Steel Pulse displaying heavy-duty dreadlocks, led by David Hinds (centre)

The late 1970s was a vibrant time for British reggae and spawned a succession of bands in London, Birmingham, Bristol, and other West-Indian strongholds. **Steel Pulse**, from Handsworth, Birmingham, were the strongest, releasing the classic *Handsworth Revolution*, an album that caused a stir with its stark proclamation that 'Babylon is falling' – a prediction that seemed to come true when riots took over the streets of St Paul's, Toxteth, Moss Side, Handsworth and Brixton. Other

JAMAICA

notables included London's Black Slate, Reggae Regular and Misty in Roots, Bristol's Black Roots and Talisman, and the Naturalites from Nottingham. Singers of the era included **Gene Rondo** (whose "Rebel Woman" is still a 'revive' favourite today), the **Blackstones** (one of the few examples of the Jamaican vocal-harmony trio in the UK) and the under-rated **Delroy Washington**. In the early 1980s, these were joined by **Pablo Gad**, who sang and toasted about "Hard Times", and **Bim Sherman**. After a strong series of self-produced records in Jamaica, the latter had settled in London where he was often to be heard on the **On-U** sound.

The alliance of reggae and **punk** at the end of the 1970s came about as part of the 'Rock against Racism' movement, which also produced a number of multiracial pop-reggae bands. **The Specials**, **The Beat** and **The Selecter** were all formed in the Midlands in the late 1970s by young black and white men – and one white woman, Pauline Black, lead singer of the Selecter. **Two-tone**, as their music was known, borrowed heavily from ska and rock steady, and particularly from Prince Buster, with the encouragement of two vintage Jamaican trombonists **Rico Rodriguez** and **Vin Gordon**. Two-tone added its own lyrical concerns, displaying a vigorous anti-racist commitment. The pop group **Madness** also started out as two-toners, with a highly marketable brand of 'nuttiness'. At much the same time, Birmingham's **UB40** showcased a new kind of pop-reggae which proved to be very successful for a time. Like Aswad, both bands have had considerable success in the national mainstream charts.

Producers and Poets

A significant event in reggae's development in the UK was the emergence of British producers with distinctive sounds that were a great deal more sophisticated than pioneers like Aitken and Livingstone. **Dennis Bovell** was one of the best, impressing fans with both lovers' rock and roots 45s on a bewildering variety of small labels, as well as two albums dominated by dub techniques that appeared on Rama – *Ah Fe Wi* and *Ah Who Seh? Go Deh*. Another important British-based producer is the **Mad Professor**. After working on sound systems for most of the 1970s, he established his Ariwa label in 1979. Inspired by King Tubby, Joe Gibbs and, of course, Lee Perry (with whom he has worked), he has produced some of Britain's finest dub, most notably with his "Dub Me Crazy" series, currently up to part eleven. He has also developed what many see as the definitive British lovers' rock sound (see below).

Two producers who have remained uninterested in lovers' rock are Jah Shaka and Adrian Sherwood. **Jah Shaka** is predominantly a sound system man, specialising in extraordinarily heavy dub, with the strictly spiritual intent of giving praise to the Creator, Jah Rastafari. Besides the special dubplates produced directly for his sound, he produces many of his own dub albums, in the form of 'The Commandments of Dub' series. Though they lose something when not blaring out through ten-foot speakers, they can transform any living room into a place of dread. **Adrian Sherwood** is also a Lee Perry fan, and produces the kind of heavy dub scratch perfected in the mid-1970s. He has often worked with **Gary Clail** on the **On-U** and **Tackhead** sound systems, and the pair have released a number of albums.

One of UK reggae's innovations were the **dub poets**, who delivered rhythmic readings of their charged and usually political verse over dub tracks. There are a number of these poets scattered throughout the country, but the ones to have gained most prominence are **Sister Netifa**, **Benjamin Zephaniah** and, especially, **Linton Kwesi Johnson**. Johnson, an astute commentator on the West-Indian experience in Britain, invented the dub poetry term, by which he referred to DJs generally. In collaboration with the ubiquitous Dennis Bovell, he has produced a number of fine albums.

Lovers' Rock

While such groups received considerable coverage in the mainstream music press, Britain's other unique, and far longer-lasting reggae innovation, **lovers' rock**, was virtually ignored outside the black music papers. Lovers' rock was more or less invented by the sound-system owner **Lloydie Coxsone**, who made a reggae version of Robert Parker's soul tune "Caught You In A Lie", with Louisa Marks, then fourteen years old. There was nothing revolutionary about that – Jamaicans had been covering US soul hits since rock steady – but what was different was the style, which had enough female sensuality, and enough of the modern soul sound for it to appeal to those wanting an alternative to heavy roots.

Providing the glorious rhythm for Louisa's hit was **Matumbi**, and Dennis Bovell and his band were to play a major role in the genre's subsequent development (their interpretation of Bob Dylan's "Man In Me" remains a classic). But it was the husband and wife team of **Dennis** and **Eve Harris** who actually gave the style its name when they launched their legendary Lovers' Rock label. They held talent shows every Sunday at a South London record store, and went on to produce discoveries like **Brown Sugar** (featuring Caron Wheeler, later to find fame with Soul II Soul).

Many of the stars recorded on the Mad Professor's **Ariwa** imprint were (and are) characterised by a heavier bass sound, a more rootsy feel, and, at times, rare social comment. South London's **Fashion Records** also updated the lovers' rock genre for the 1990s. Launched in 1980 with Dee Sharp's sublime "Let's Dub It Up", Chris Lane and John McGillivray's label employed facilities at both Forest Hill's A-Class studio and Penthouse in Kingston to stunning effect. Though covering every facet of modern reggae, this (now sadly defunct) label scored particularly well with some of the most sophisticated lovers' rock to date. Tuneful and heartfelt records by singers like Winsome, Nerious Joseph, John McClean, Janet Lee Davis, Barry Boom and Peter Hunnigale.

Lovers' rock has an almost entirely black market, remaining under-celebrated beyond that constituency. Nonetheless, the hits still continually top the UK reggae charts, and have thus found their way onto Jet Star's *Reggae Hits* series, along with several compilations devoted solely to the genre. And the genre has one major crossover star in **Maxi Priest**, who mixes lovers' rock with contemporary R&B and roots, and has enjoyed consistent success, even making the US charts.

Contemporary Sounds

Although bands have played a more central role in the development of British than Jamaican reggae, its bedrock was the same: the **sound system**. In recent years, there has no longer been anything like the number of reggae sounds that once flourished in the UK, and even Jah Shaka now mainly appeals to young white followers (some of whom have formed their own sound

systems and make records based on the spiritual warrior's approach). But in the 1970s there were literally hundreds of sound systems rocking Town Halls, community centres and private houses in inner city areas. The most famous were **Sir Coxsone Outernational** (one of several which took its name from a Jamaican sound), **Fat Man Hi Fi** and **Jah Shaka**. And commanding equally dedicated followings in their areas were Jah Sufferer, D'Nunes, Java, Sofrano B, Quaker City, Sir Jessus, Moa Ambessa and Jah Tubby.

In the dancehall era of the 1980s, a sound from Wood Green in north London, **Saxon**, came to a position of pre-eminence, and was particularly renowned for its DJs, or MCs, as they preferred to be known by then. These included **Peter King**, who played a key role in developing the renowned 'fast talk' style associated with the period, the equally talented Asher Senator, and no less than three chatters who enjoyed success beyond the UK reggae chart. **Smiley Culture** had a best seller in the specialist market in 1984 with his "Cockney Translator", which runs smoothly between Yardie and Cockney slang, and entered the pop charts the following year with "Police Officer". **Tippa Irie** also made the UK pop charts with "Hello Darling" in 1986. And while Philip 'Papa' Levy never reached the national Top 30 in the UK, his "Mi God Mi King" did have the honour of topping the Jamaican charts - the first British DJ record to do so.

Another highly original DJ who emerged in the 1980s was **Macka B**, a Rastafarian from Birmingham who toasted on the Wassifa sound and teamed up with the Mad Professor. The latter relates the partnership thus: "He just phoned me up out of the blue, 'Ah Professor, me name Macka B, an me have some lyrics.' He sent a tape, I liked it, and we did the album *Sign of the Times* right off in two days." Since then Macka B has made his name with some of the most articulate, witty and conscious lyrics around.

The 1990s saw a new wave of inventive DJs. These have included the gravel-voiced Sweetie Irie, the cultural Starky Banton, Chukki Starr and Nico Junior, and two very distinctive chatters who

UK producer-dubmaster Dennis Bovell

MORE CUT

have also clicked with the jungle audience, **Top Cat** and **General Levy**. The modern UK chatter to have achieved the best reception in Jamaica, however, has been the teenage **Glamma Kid** from Tottenham. His debut disc, "Fashion Magazine", was a massive hit, and he has since recorded in Kingston.

Almost inevitably, there were attempts at crossovers between **hip-hop** and reggae. Linton Kwesi Johnson saw this as part of a historical process of black musical fusion: "Jamaican DJs were originally influenced by American jive talkers. Hip-hop appropriated the studio techniques of Jamaican dub, so it's entirely natural". First off were the **London Posse**, whose seriously militant songs can be found on Mango's two Ragga Hip-Hop compilations along with a number of other fusion artists. Perhaps a more surprising crossover came from ragga's **Apache Indian**, based in Birmingham, who raps on issues including the Indian caste system and AIDS, and has topped both the British reggae and bhangra charts.

A major innovation of recent years has been **jungle** – a hardcore reggae-techno fusion outside the scope of this book (but see *The Rough Guide to Drum'n'Bass* for the full story) – which has established itself as a mainstay of large sections of the club scene. A new generation of black Britons, for obvious reasons, finds it easier to relate to a homegrown development like jungle than the music from Jamaica that sustained their parents. Nevertheless, as the West Indian community moves forward into its second half century, fresh talent still emerges in the ragga, lovers' and roots fields in the UK. And it is certain that reggae will continue to be a dynamic, if undervalued, part of Britain's cultural heritage, castigating the oppressors and nicing up the dance.

discography

Reggae and Ragga

Artists

Aswad

The band that defined UK roots reggae in the mid-1970s, and for over a decade were the toughest in the land – on record and in their stunning live appearances.

 Roots Rocking: The Island Anthology (Island Jamaica, US).

This two-disc Island collection charts the band's career from the rootsy mid-1970s through live tracks recorded at the 1983 Notting Hill Carnival, and on to smoother lovers' hits. All that's missing is any of their CBS material, which makes ⓪ **New Chapter** (CBS, UK) indispensable as the strongest single Aswad album.

Starky Banton

Starky Banton made an impact when he amusingly dismissed the jungle phenomenon with his "Jungle Bungle" – "One bag a noise and a whole heap a sample/That's something my ear holes can't handle!" His work since has been in a serious cultural mode.

⓪ **Powers Youth** (Fashion, UK).

Militant cultural deejaying delivered with total conviction and complemented by wicked dubs.

Linton Kwesi Johnson

Linton Kwesi Johnson was one of dub poetry's pioneers, and had the taste to employ Dennis Bovell for the dub part of the equation.

⓪ **Forces of Victory** (Island, UK).

An album of highly charged political poems, brilliantly supported by Dennis Bovell's dub-heavy arrangements.

General Levy

The defection of black youth in the UK from reggae to its off-shoot jungle hasn't prevented exciting new DJs from appearing, and some, like the talented General, have successfully catered for both markets.

⓪ **Wickedness Increase** (Ffrr, UK).

UK ragga that's as hardcore as anything from West Kingston – and as witty and inventive.

The Mad Professor

From his south London base, Neil Fraser has consistently met the divergent demands of both the lovers' rock audience and the (mainly white) followers of the dub experiments that earned him his sobriquet.

⓪ **Dub Me Crazy Volumes 1–10** (Ariwa, UK).

The Mad Professor's series is into double figures now. The most innovative British dub on record.

Misty In Roots

Southall's Misty In Roots gained a large white following through Rock Against Racism gigs, along with numerous appearances on John Peel's radio show.

Live At the Counter Eurovision (People Unite, UK).

A band that made their name with live performances, and fittingly released one for their debut set.

Steel Pulse

Formed in the Handsworth district of Birmingham, Steel Pulse were the most successful of all the UK reggae bands that emerged in the 1970s, and still have a large following in the US.

 Handsworth Revolution (Island, UK).

This tough, original 1978 debut album was one of the strongest British reggae albums of the decade.

UB40

Named after the card issued to those receiving unemployment benefit, UB40's hits have all been a little retro, although their latest project took them to Jamaica to record with cutting-edge ragga DJs.

 Signing Off (Graduate, UK).
 Present Arms (DEP, UK).

UB40 cracked the crossover market with their earliest and best recordings, featured on this first pair of albums, and they haven't looked back since.

Lovers' Rock

Compilations

 Pure Lovers Volumes 1–11 (Jet Star, UK).

Includes a fair potion of the major lovers' rock hits of recent years, covering both the Jamaican and UK varieties, and established and new names. Currently there are eleven volumes, with a new one appearing every few months.

Artists

Janet Lee Davis

Though vocal techniques were sometimes a little shaky in the early days of the genre, by the 1990s lovers' rock was producing singers as accomplished as Janet Lee Davis.

Missing You
(Fashion, UK).

Quite possibly the ultimate Fashion-produced album to date. It includes successful 45s like the title track, "Do You Remember" and her marvellous duet with Peter Hunnigale, "We Can Work It Out", along with much more material of a similar calibre.

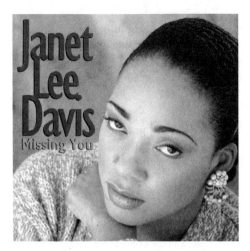

Peter Hunnigale

While early lovers' rock was largely the preserve of young women singers, several important male talents have since emerged. Peter Hunnigale is one of the most gifted singers in the UK – in any genre.

 Reggae Max (Jet Star, UK).

Don't be put off by the cheap packaging: this is the easiest way of catching up with twenty massive hits in the reggae market that should have been world-wide smashes.

Louisa Marks

Louisa Marks was still a schoolgirl when she kick-started a new genre with the plaintive "Caught You In A Lie". Every lovers' rock singer since has owed her something.

 Breakout (Bushranger, UK).

Classic and stylish lovers' rock, including "Caught You In A Lie", "Six Sixth Street" and "Moving Target" from the 1970s.

Maxi Priest

Maxi Priest sang alongside Saxon's DJs during the early 1980s. A few years later his mixture of lovers' rock, soul and roots allowed him to make the leap to international stardom.

 Bonefide (Ten, UK).

Employing an eclectic approach, and the cream of musicians from London and Kingston, this is pop-reggae at its best. Includes the hit that established him in the US, "How Can We Ease the Pain?".

Mexico

much more than mariachi

Mariachis – those extravagantly passionate bands with their sly rhythms, natty hats and silver buttons – have been shorthand symbols for Mexico in a thousand low-budget films and television episodes. But their conspicuousness may have blinded the English-speaking world to the less obvious traditions of a country rich in musical culture. **Mary Farquharson** puts on her sunglasses and goes in search of *bandas*, *cumbia Mexicana*, *norteño* ballads and *huapango*.

The international boom in Mexican music began in the 1940s, at the same time as **Cuban music** exploded onto the world scene. Classic songs like "Besame Mucho" and "Cielito Lindo" crooned out from cinema screens and radios and were played by 'Latin' orchestras all over the world. By the 1960s, however, the so-called Golden Age had ended, and Mexican cinema and the music associated with it retreated to within the country's borders. While Mexican music is yet to see an international resurgence on the scale of Cuba's, its live music – from romantic trios to twenty-piece dance orchestras – continues to thrive

at home, feeding eager audiences that love to dance and to sing whatever the problems they face – and Mexicans have seen plenty of those.

At the same time as Buñuel was making movie history in Mexico City, **Celia Cruz** came from Cuba to seek her fortune, along with Beny Moré, Bienvenido Granda and **Pérez Prado**, the last of whom developed the *mambo* rhythm between shifts as a session pianist at the Churrubusco film studios. These musicians were attracted by the bright lights of a city that didn't sleep, and from Mexico they moved on up to the even brighter and more sleepless New York City. But they usually returned, and salsa queen Celia Cruz continues to do so today –

Mariachi Coculense "Rodriguez", 1935

both she and the US-Panamanian salsero **Willie Colón** have double careers in Mexico as dance-hall stars and as actors in Mexican soap opera.

Cosmopolitan and bohemian Mexico City has long welcomed musicians from all over Latin America and taken their styles of music to heart. **Danzón** came from Cuba and **cumbia** from Colombia and Mexico is now the international capital of both styles. Go to the *Salon Los Angeles* in the old centre of Mexico City on a Tuesday evening and you will find seven hundred couples dancing. Sunday is the big night, however, when the enormous wooden floors carry the scent of shoe-polish and perfume, and three different fourteen-piece orchestras play *danzones* old and new.

Son

As in Cuba it is a traditional form called *son* that stands at the heart of Mexican music. **Mexican son** grew out of the encounter between Spanish, indigenous and African cultures in the eighteenth century. This was the same encounter that produced Cuban son and other Latin American styles like the Venezuelan *joropo*, but Mexican son now sounds very different from the Cuban variety.

Mexican son describes eight or nine different styles – including *mariachi* – all of them rooted in rural forms that rely on the participation of their public to add counter-rhythms through *zapateado* (foot-stamp dancing). They are incredibly creative. A son musician has to be able to make up lyrics on the spot in order to respond to a comment from the dance floor, and the lead musician has to be able to create new flights on his violin or guitar that will satisfy a public that demands nothing less than inspiration. Son is almost always played by string bands with lyrics, sung in four line *coplas*, that are witty, sexual, poetic and proud.

The best-known forms are **sones jaliscienses** (*sones* from Jalisco) which formed the original repertoire of the **mariachi bands**. Mariachis became nationally and internationally popular following the cinema boom, when regional music was being recorded by major labels, notably by RCA (see feature box). Sadly, few of the commercial mariachi bands now play *jaliscienses* or its more developed *ranchera* form, preferring the more simple ballads and cumbias their public all know from the radio and TV.

Over on the Gulf coast, the **sones jarochos** from Veracruz have a discernible African influence. The style has received a lot of attention, not least because of the international hit, "La Bamba".

Old jarocho musicians like **Andres Huesca**, **Nicolás Sosa** and **Lino Chávez** had tasted the big time in Mexico City before, and today there is a new interest in the form. The first lady of this style is without doubt **Graciana Silva**, 'La Negra Graciana', who for years offered her sones for ten pesos a piece in Veracruz's square. One day, however, her audience included record producer Eduardo Llerenas who invited her to record for his staunchly independent label, Discos Corason. The release generated great interest and a series of major concerts in Europe.

In the south of Veracruz state the indigenous presence is much stronger and the harp is rarely played. Instead, the line-up consists exclusively of *requinto* and *jarana* guitars of different sizes and tunings. The sones are played more slowly and with a more melancholy feel. A number of young bands are curently experimenting with fusion and composing new songs. They gather every February for the spectacular **Fiesta de la Candelaria**, held in the river town of Tlacotalpan, where a stage is set up and band after band invited to play. Several of

the better-known have invited the older musicians of the region to join them, and the voices of the old soneros are a welcome contribution to their sound. Leading this generation of Jarocho musicians is **Gilberto Gutiérrez** and his band, **Mono Blanco**.

Perhaps most vibrant of all the forms today is **son huasteco**, the Huastecan style, in which a virtuoso violin is accompanied by a *huapanguera* and a *jarana* (both types of guitar), the two guitarists singing falsetto vocals between the flights of the violin. Each song is reinvented every time it is played: the singers compose new verses and the

The Mariachi Tradition

Son jalisciense, the traditional music of **Jalisco**, became internationally famous through its **mariachi bands**, which became popular at wedding ceremonies in Jalisco around the turn of the century (some say the name is a corruption of the French word *mariage*). One version of mariachi history tells how, in 1907, Mexico's last dictator, General Porfirio Díaz, organised a garden party for a visiting US secretary of state. Since he wanted to include Mexican music, a quartet from Jalisco were contracted – and told to change their white cotton trousers for the *charro* suits worn by the men who owned the haciendas where they worked as servants. A quartet, even in their fancy dress, still seemed too poor for the occasion, so eight musicians and two dancers were contracted. The Jaliscan son was never the same again, and mariachi, along with its costume, was born.

The **early mariachis** played violins, guitars, a harp and the enormous *guitarrón*, an acoustic bass guitar; trumpets were added later while the harp has generally been dropped. From the 1920s, when the legendary – and still flourishing – *Cantina Tenampa* opened with a resident group in Mexico City, mariachi bands have played mainly in taverns. They are employed today all over Mexico, as well as across the border, where they make better money playing to homesick field workers.

Since most bands are paid by the song, the leader will identify likely customers in a Texas or California workers' bar. The trumpeter grabs a seat at their table, launching himself into a classic piece from the badly-missed home country. As the drinkers indulge their sadness, the singer utters the cry, the violins wail and the trumpeter prepares to slide straight into the next song so that, by the end of the evening, a week's wages can easily have been spent on music. Although mariachis began with a repertoire of *sones* from Jalisco, today they also play cumbias, polkas, waltzes, ballads and an incredible range of popular songs on request. "With only two hundred songs, you might as well stay at home in the village", says a mariachi leader. Like most of his colleagues, he can play around fifteen hundred pieces on demand.

The **golden age** of mariachi was in the 1950s, when the *ranchera* (country) music they played accompanied a series of Hollywood films, with Mexican matinee idols serenading their lovers. Many of the greatest films featured **Mariachi Vargas**, a group that was founded in the 1930s and is still considered to be the best in Mexico. Virtually all the original members have died but the band replaces old stars with the pick of the younger generations and they remain very hot. It was Mariachi Vargas, notably, who **Linda Ronstadt** chose as backing on her *Canciones* album of ranchera classics.

Linda Ronstadt and Daniel Valdez of Mariachi Vargas

BOB BLAKEMAN/ASYLUM RECORDS

Most of the mariachi songs are old-established classics, although some of the more adventurous and technically accomplished bands will perform songs by the remarkable **Juan Gabriel**. Gabriel is a rare phenomenon in Mexico, an enormously talented composer, arranger, singer and TV star with an excellent understanding of Mexican regional music. He writes and performs *canciones norteñas* and sones as well as commercial ballads and soft rock. He plays with mariachis and a symphony orchestra, and his concert seasons all over the country sell out months in advance. For years he was excluded from radio and television on account of being gay – but his talent eventually won through.

If you want to hear the bands who still master the original repertoire, it's better to keep away from Mexico City's infamous Garibaldi Square and head off to southern Jalisco, where incredible twelve- or fourteen-piece mariachis like **Los Reyes del Aserradero** and **Mariachi Tamazula** offer spectacular violins, plenty of trumpet and vocal harmonies in a sophisticated version of the country sones that were orignally played on a harp and three guitars.

MEXICO

violinist creates new flourishes in response to the calls of a public which won't accept imitations. There are literally hundreds of Huastecan son trios; the most outstanding being **Los Camperos de Valle**, **Trio Tamazunchale** and the youngsters, **Dinastía Hidalguense**. Less-known bands play in cantinas and country fiestas throughout the region. In the cafés of Mexico City's Coyocan *barrio*, trios sell their sones by the piece, offering impressive versions of "La huasanga", "El llorar" and "El fandanguito", amongst others, which are technically very demanding.

Seldom heard in the city, but enormously popular back home in the villages of the Sierra Gorda mountains, is the **arribeño** style, the most poetic form of son, performed by **trovadores** – country poets, often with no formal education, who compose verses about local heroes, the planets, the earth and the continuing struggle for land. The way this works is that two trovadores, each playing the huapanguera and each accompanied by two violins and the small *vihuela* guitar, confront each other on tall bamboo platforms erected on the sides of a village square. According to an estab-

A New Year's Huapango Duel

'¡Xichu!' shouted the boy, and the old school bus revved up – our only chance of getting to the small village fiesta where we had heard there would be a huapango duel. Squeezed aboard with the other revellers, we wound our way through the mountains, heading for an isolated spot more or less at the meeting place of the states of Guanajuato, Queretaro and San Luis Potosi, in central Mexico.

We arrived to find the small plaza packed out, and red-lipped carnival figures announcing that the fiesta was about to begin. It was New Year's Eve. The guests of honour, seemingly just a few old men, sat in a line on a temporary wooden stage. They were troubadours: reporters, analysts, prophets, historians and gossips who have kept this isolated region in touch with the world for hundreds of years. To do so they use music – the **huapango arribeño**, which, up here, still gets an airing at weddings, baptisms and saints' days – in tandem with local pop groups.

The fiesta we had come to, however, was a special occasion in the huapango calendar: a duel and test of talent. Through the night, two bands and two singers

Los Leones de Xichu stirring up the dance

lished structure, they enter into musical combat, improvising verses which are interspersed with zapateado dancing.

Each year on December 31, **Guillermo Velázquez**, probably the greatest living arribeño trovador, organises a festival in his village which pays homage to the old musicians before starting an all-night *topada* musical combat (see feature box, 'A New Year's Huapango Duel').

In the Mexican west – the hotlands of the Balsas River Basin – there is another son traditon, **sones calentanos** which are known for their complex melodies on violin. The star of this form is a legendary violinist called **Juan Reynoso**. A winner of the prestigious National Prize for Arts and Science (the only country musician to be so honoured), and nicknamed 'The Paganini of the Hotlands', Reynoso is an extraordinary violinist whose flights take unexpected turns that his fellow musicians struggle constantly to follow.

Further west, in a region where the heat is so intense that it is known as 'Hell's Waiting Room' you find **sones de arpa grande** (sones of the big

would hurl improvised verse at each other in turn, showing off their skills. Shortly before dawn, the public would decide the winner. There was no prize other than prestige – and of course future party bookings.

Guillermo Velazquez who, with his younger brother Eliazar, had organised this annual tribute to the old troubadours, was first to climb up onto the platform that stood, like scaffolding, on one side of the square. In the crowd, his rival, **Cándido Martinéz**, feigned confidence, greeting the friends and acquaintances who would judge him with applause or derision when it was time for him to mount the scaffolding on the other side of the square.

Guillermo opened with a familiar verse, introducing himself and his pedigree:

I'm Guillermo Velazquez
and I've never lost my roots
I was born in Xichu, Guanajuato
And there I will go to rest one day

He then launched into the **vallena**, a verse improvised to suit the occasion. It had been a troubled year, and Guillermo began with an analysis of world events. In *décima* verse – each line with eight syllables organised in an intimidating rhythmic structure – he prepared an argument that would be developed over the coming hours. When he recited, the public stood and listened. When he paused, closing his eyes for inspiration, the crowd danced, the *zapateado* of their feet tapping out a counter rhythm to the instrumental *estribillo* led by two violins.

Guillermo is recognised as the most talented troubadour in the region but the more experienced Cándido knew his weak points. After reciting his own greetings to the crowd, he paid profound respects to Guillermo as a man and a poet and then accused him of losing touch with is *campesino* (peasant) roots. According to Cándido's improvisation, Guillermo's interest in international politics was not shared by the crowd at the fiesta. Guillermo has travelled, he has

taken the huapango arribeño to Africa and Europe; Cándido accused him of having fallen for the seduction of another world.

Cándido represented an older generation of troubadours, whose role was to inform rather than analyse. Tonight he was filling heads with technical information about the year that was about to end. In rhyming verse, he counted the days, hours and seconds that were slipping past; it was a lesson in arithmetic from a carpenter who had never gone to school.

Although by midnight a few drunks had collapsed under the scaffolding and babies were asleep under their grandmothers' shawls, the square was still crowded with men and women dancing: a sea of cowboy hats, brims almost touching, feet stamping on wooden boards laid specially for the purpose. A group recently returned from the fields of California held up their ghetto-blasters in front of the platform, recording the festival for their return to the North.

The concert was now entering the **bravata**; the tone becoming less serious as the two musicians began to make personal digs at each other. Guillermo, who as a child was selected to study in an American seminary, was accused by his rival of having been expelled for stealing the silver chalice. He replied that, had he been expelled, it would have been for stealing Cándido's daughter. As dawn approached, the troubadours moved on to *sones* or *jarabes*, which give more of a leading role to the music and the dancers, or at least those with the energy to show off complicated footwork.

Cándido and Guillermo refused to give up. At ten in the morning they were still playing and the crowd still danced between verses. The sun was shining but no one wanted to go home. Finally, Cándido admitted defeat. The home crowd cheered. Both groups of musicians climbed unsteadily down from the scaffolding, greeted each other warmly and wandered towards Guillermo's house, where mutton had been cooking all night. While Guillermo drank black coffee, Cándido caught the eye of a woman and began to serenade her. It was New Year's Day; he was down, but definitely not out.

harps). These bands – comprising a big harp, one or two violins and two guitars – don't thrive as they used to, but it is still possible to track down masters such as **Juan Pérez Morfín**, who plays with another great violionist, **Beto Pineda**. The style involves the sound boxes of the big harps being beaten in counter-rhythm by one of the musicians of the band, or by a local fan who pays for the privilege. The harpist, meanwhile, must hold on to the melody – and his harp – delivering a vocal line that can sound something like a shout from the soul.

This style of son used to thrive at country fairs, and urban brothels, but today, the audience are the locals who organise parties on the small farms far from the city, or wealthy stable-owners who pride themselves on their dancing horses. The horses will apparently only dance to the big harp music and they do so on wooden platforms, beating out rhythm and counter-rhythm with their hooves.

Although son is basically *mestizo* (mixed blood) music, several indigenous cultures play instrumental sones to accompany their ritual dances and two indigenous cultures, Purépecha and Zapotec Indi-

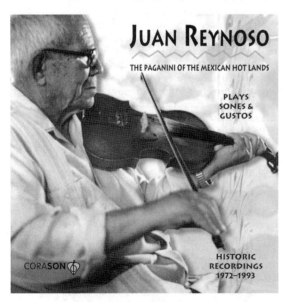

JUAN REYNOSO

THE PAGANINI OF THE MEXICAN HOT LANDS

PLAYS SONES & GUSTOS

CORASON

HISTORIC RECORDINGS 1972–1993

ans, have composed a large repertoire of sones for weddings and other parties.

Sones abajeños are the frenetic party music of the **Purépecha** Indians of Michoacán, played on guitars, violins and a double bass. Between abajeños, the same musicians sing the hauntingly beautiful Purepécha love songs, *pirekuas*, which are composed in honour of a girlfriend or of some local event. Outstanding Purépecha son bands include **Atardecer** (Sunset) from the lake-village of Jarácuaro and **Erandi** (Dawn).

In the southern state of Oaxaca, the vibrant **Zapotec** culture has produced some of the country's great love songs, and inspired mainstream Mexican romantic singers along the way. Sung in both Zapotec and Spanish, the **sones istmeños**, as they are known, are played to a slower 3/4 rhythm and are more melancholy that the mestizo sones. They boast some great solo passages on the requinto guitar and uniquely Zapotecan vocals, creating a very beautiful repertoire that has tempted some of Mexico's greatest urban vocalists to learn the Zapotecan lyrics and perform them in big-city venues. **Lila Downs**, half-Mixtecan Indian, half-American, is among the most successful and, typically, her repertoire also includes rancheras, boleros and jazz.

Ranchera

The great **divas** of Mexican music, of which there is a long tradition, are currently turning to Mexican traditional and country music to develop their own repertoire. Singer-songwriters like **Eugenia León**, **Tania Libertad** and **Betsy Pecanins**, who had enormous popularity in the 1980s with their *nueva cancion* (new song), are now singing their own versions of norteñas, mariachi music, sones istmeños and Mexican boleros. Outstanding amongst this illustrious company is **Eugenia León** whose vocal range and passion embraces a broad range of musical styles.

This diva tradition has a direct line back to the early days of **ranchera** music, an urban style that emerged alongside the new towns and cities in the early decades of the century and which became massively popular with the growth of film and radio. 'Ranchera' comes from the word *rancho* (farm), although the music was composed in the towns and cities for a public that wanted to remember how it used to be. The wit and freshness of the original son lyrics were replaced by bitter words about loss and betrayal, while musically the intensity shifted from the complex melody and rhythms of son to the melodramatic style that has come to characterise ranchera.

The first great diva of ranchera music was **Lucha Reyes**, whose emotionally charged voice hinted at her own inner turmoil. She died tragically, but her songs have been resuscitated by the great Mexican cabaret singer **Astrid Hadad**, who offered a post-modern take on Reyes for the early 1990s, carried off very successfully because of her particular blend of humour with a very fine voice.

Astrid Hadad

Although Astrid now includes a breadth of Latin cabaret music in her repertoire, her great moments were captured in her first CD of ranchera songs called, quite simply, *¡Ay!*

Of the classic ranchera singers, the divas are now few and far between since the death of **Amalia Mendoza** and, more recently of the great **Lola Beltrán** and of **María de Lourdes**. Today, fame and fortune has passed to a younger generation of male singers and, in particular, to **Alejandro Fernández**, a superstar who has left his father, the ranchera star Vicente Fernández, in the shade. Although musically there is not too much of the original ranchera left in Alejandro's repertoire, the melodrama and the association with ranch culture still exists. The mariachi trousers and sombrero hat are still in place but Alejandro represents a different generation with his sultry, slightly unwashed, good looks – more in the style of rock idols.

Norteño – the Roots of Tex-Mex

After ranchera, the style that has most popularity throughout Mexico is **norteño**. Known north of the border as **Tex-Mex**, norteño has its roots in the *corrido* ballads that retold the battles between Anglos and Meskins in the early nineteenth century. The war turned out badly for Mexico, which lost half its territory, and Mexicans living in what are now California, Arizona, New Mexico and Texas found themselves with a new nationality (see p.604 for Tex-Mex music in the US).

The late 1920s was the Golden Age of the corrido, when songs of the recent revolution were recorded in the hotels of San Antonio, Texas, and distributed on both sides of the border. The **accordion**, which had arrived with Bohemian immigrants who came to work in the mines in the late nineteenth century, was introduced into the originally guitar-based groups by **Narciso Martínez** and **Santiago Jimenez** (father of the famous Flaco) in the 1930s, and the sound that they developed became the essence of corrido ensembles on both sides of the border.

When the accordion appeared, it brought the polka with it, and by the 1950s this had blended with the traditional duet singing of northern Mexico and with salon dances like the waltz, mazurka and the *chotis* (the central-European schottische that travelled to Spain and France before arriving in northern Mexico) to produce the definitive norteño style. The accordion had already pepped up the songs with lead runs and flourishes between the verses, but the conjuntos norteños needed to round out their sound to keep up with the big bands and so added bass and rolling drums – the basis of today's **conjuntos**.

Cruce el Rio Grande

I crossed the Rio Grande
Swimming, not giving a damn
The Border Patrol threw me back
I disguised myself as a gringo
And tinted my hair blonde
But since I didn't know English
Back I go again

Popular norteño ballad

Unlike most other regional styles, norteño is popular throughout the country. At a party in an isolated mountain community in central Mexico, the host may well take out his accordion and play norteño corridos until the dawn breaks. In an ice-cream parlour on the Pacific coast, the piped music is likely to be a norteño waltz. And waiting for darkness to cross the border at Tijuana, norteños form the soundtrack.

This country-wide popularity is most likely due to the **lyrics**. Norteño songs speak to people in more realistic and gripping ways than in the cosy pseudo-sophistication of Mexican pop music. The ballads tell of anti-heroes: small-time drug runners, illegal 'wet-back' immigrants, a small-time thief with one

Los Tigres del Norte in serenading mode

blond eyebrow who defied the law. Norteño reflects the mood of a country that generally considers the government to be big-time thieves and hence has a certain respect for everyday people with the courage to stand up to a crooked system.

Groups like **Los Tigres del Norte** and **Los Cadetes del Norte** take stories from the local papers and convert them into ballads that usually begin "Voy a cantarles un corrido" (I'm going to sing you a corrido) before launching into a gruesome tale sung in a deadpan style as if it were nothing to go to a local dance and get yourself killed. One of the most famous corridos, "Rosita Alvírez", tells the story of a young girl who struck lucky: only one of the three bullets fired by her boyfriend hit and killed her.

Los Tigres are by far the most successful of all norteño groups – superstars, in fact – having won a Grammy and subsequently been adopted by Televisa. They now record in both the US and Mexico, having achieved superstardom on both sides of the border. Quite early in their career, the band modified the traditional style by adding a sax and mixing the familiar rhythms with cumbias; however, their nasal singing style and the combination of instruments identifies the music very clearly as norteño.

The Banda Boom

The enormous success of Los Tigres del Norte and their updated norteño sound resulted in a phenomenon that changed the face of Mexican music in the 1990s: **banda music**. This was a fusion of the norteño style with the brass bands that have played at village fiestas all over the country for the last century. There are now hundreds of bandas in Mexico – ranging in size from four to twenty musicians – and all playing brass and percussion, with just an occasional guitar. Their repertoire includes norteño polkas, ranchera ballads, cumbia, merengue and salsa – all arranged for brass.

The most exciting of these groups is a fiery orchestra from Mazatlán, **Banda del Recodo**. This is not a new band, indeed its former leader, **Don Cruz Lizárraga**, had been in the business for half a century, starting out in a traditional *tambora* marching band (the tambora is the huge, portable side drum) that played a straight repertoire of brass-band numbers. However, Don Cruz had always had an eye for musical fashions, adapting his mate-

Banda del Recodo

rial to merengue, ranchera or whatever anyone wanted to hear. His great banda hit was a version of Cuban bandleader Beny Moré's classic "La Culebra".

The banda boom currently dominates television music programmes, and is heard in most places across the country other than the capital, where cumbia and salsa stay top of the bill. Elsewhere, it is the bandas that fill the stadiums and village halls, and it's their names you'll see painted in enormous multicoloured letters on any patch of white wall along the roads. The craze has brought with it a series of new dances, too, including the *quebradita* – a gymnastic combination of lambada, polka, rock'n'roll, rap and cumbia, which is danced with particular skill anywhere north of Guadalajara.

In 1996, during a successful two-month tour of Europe, the band's founder Cruz Lizárraga died, and the Banda del Recodo passed into the hands of two of his musician sons: Germán, now in his late fifties, and the younger Alfonso. Changes were afoot. The band left the independent label where they had made some one hundred records and signed to the Televisa media empire. Several of the older musicians have been replaced with younger ones, and the original sound has suffered, although record sales have never been better.

Cumbia

Although the banda line-up dates back to the village band tradition and the tambora music of northwest Mexico, today's bandas rely heavily on **cumbia** for their repertoire – the simple dance music that came originally from Colombia but has taken deep root across Mexico.

Cumbia, now more popular in Mexico than in its native Colombia, has become simpler in its new home, more direct and danceable. For a long time, a national radio station used to call out '¡Tropi...Q!' – the last letter a 'cooooooh' that could unblock traffic jams – and then launch into the latest cumbia hit, which was played without reprieve for a month and then forgotten. A song about cellular telephones replaced "No te metes con mi cucu" (Don't Mess With My Toot Toot), which in turn had taken over from a song about fried chicken and chips – a thinly disguised treatise on how a macho likes his bird.

The flirtatious, addictive cumbia was the most popular music in Mexico in the 1980s, until bandas came along, and it remains a force throughout the country. Outside the capital, it tends to take on a more mellow, romantic tone, a sound closely associated with the band **Los Bukis**, who, before splitting up in the mid-1990s, made several albums, among them *Me volví a acordar de tí*, which sold 1.5 million legal copies and an estimated four million more in bootleg cassettes.

In the same line, an insipid mixture of cumbia, norteño and ranchera, which is sometimes known as **grupera** (or *onda grupera*), emerged in the late 1980s and continues to be enormously popular in small towns and villages – village populations have been known to swell four or five times over when a band like the **Yonics**, **Banda Machos** or the (now defunct) **Bronco** come to play. These musicians, like the bandas who share the same audience, arrive in a fleet of well-equipped coaches – one for them, one for the generator, one for lights and equipment and lavish leather suits and, quite often, one for their families.

This music was despised by the media executives who, for many years, thought it common and continued to plug the familiar pretty faces of the pop idols that they manufactured. But since the 1990s, the phenomenal commercial success of the self-made grupera, banda and norteña musicians has forced the entertainment business to think again. Groups like **Limite**, currently at the top of the lucrative country dance scene, are now regularly featured on TV shows and are invited to play in the hallowed halls of México's Auditorio Nacional, once the stronghold of protest singers and foreign ballet companies.

Mexican Rock

Despite its history as a melting pot of Latin music, Mexico was virtually closed to **rock music** until the late 1980s, when a change in import rules, and in political policies specifically banning rock concerts, resulted in a flood of music from north of the border and from Europe. The result has been the emergence of **Mexican rock bands**, arguably the most important musical phenomenon of the last decade.

The boom began with middle-class rockers like **Los Caifanes** playing to middle-class audiences who knew about the outside scene because they, or their parents, travelled regularly to Europe and the States. (Ironically, the Caifanes' massive hit was a cover of a traditional Cuban son, "La Negra Tomasa", which appealed to a public that understood son and salsa better than rock.)

However, in the 1990s **Café Tacuba** and **Maldita Vecindad** began to reach bigger audiences. Both were interested, to some extent, in exploring Mexican roots, reinterpreting Mexican son in their own way just as Los Lobos had done so successfully in Texas a decade earlier. The fusion

of rock with salsa and son created by newcomers **Los de Abajo** caught the attention of David Byrne, who released their first album in late 1998.

With the arrival of **Maná**, from Mexico's second city, Guadalajara, Mexican rock entered the superstar level, albeit with a style that hovers rather too close to the pop ballads that are promoted by the enormous Televisa media giant. Most recently, the emergence of a rap-band called **Molotov** has challenged the polite pulp of Televisa and they have become controversial cult heroes as a result of their first CD, which sold a million copies in Mexico alone. Rock, in its different guises, is booming and new bands like **Plastelina Mosh**, **Control Machete** and **El Gran Silencio** are finding a home in the *barrios* (neighbourhoods) of the world's biggest city.

discography

Mexican recordings are widely available in the US – less so in Europe. Arhoolie have an extensive series of historic re-issues of mariachi and other bands, some of which are included below. But the label to look out for is Corason, based in Mexico City, which is recording and releasing consistently excellent CDs of traditional music from around Mexico and the Caribbean.

Sones and Mariachi

Compilations

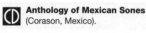 **Anthology of Mexican Sones** (Corason, Mexico).

This three-CD set is the definitive survey of traditional Mexican sones featuring wonderful recordings of rural bands and giving a good idea of regional styles. Excellent accompanying notes, photographs and lyrics in Spanish and English.

El Caimán: Sones Huastecos (Corason, Mexico).

Each disc in the Masters of Mexican Son series takes its title from an animal that is also the title of one of the sones. Whether el Caimán (the alligator), can be thought to characterise the Huasteca style with its fiery fiddles, guitars and falsetto voices is up to the listener. Ten bands recorded between 1976 and 1996 – the most vital and intense of Mexican country music.

La Iguana: Sones Jarochos (Corason, Mexico).

The iguana focuses on sones jarochos from Veracruz, featuring the penetrating vocals, syncopated rhythms, brilliant solos on harp and furious percussive guitars that characterise the style. Son jarocho was made internationally famous by "La Bamba", which appears in a rustic version played by the Conjunto de Santiago Tuxtla. The disc features half a dozen other groups recorded over twenty years.

El Ratón: Sones de arpa grande (Corason, Mexico).

The mouse is used to characterise some of the wildest and least-known music in Mexico. The sound boxes of the big harps become drums that are beaten by other musicians or by passers-by who pay for the privilege. Two violins and guitars complete the line up of this dust-raising music from the Mexican west.

 La Tortuga: Sones Istmeños (Corason, Mexico).

The tortoise comes from the Tehuantepec isthmus in southern Mexico, revealing the debt that Mexico's bolero singers and composers owe to the Zapotecan Indian soneros. This disc features soulful love songs sung mostly in the Zapotec language, accompanied by guitars played by musicians sophisticated and rustic.

 Pure Purépecha (Corason, Mexico).

A gem that brings together three duets of Purépecha Indians from Michoacán, singing sweet pirecua love songs, and some rowdy abajeño sones from Conjunto Atardecer.

Pirekuas, the Purepecha Indian love songs and Abajeño dance music

Artists

Conjunto Alma de Apatzingan

The prize-winning Conjunto Alma de Apatzingan, from Michocoan in southwestern Mexico, are one of the most respected ensembles in the region, and have flourished for over twenty years.

 Arriba! Tierra Caliente (Arhoolie, US).

One of a series of releases of Mexican regional music from Arhoolie, this combination of jaunty guitars, violin and harp with tearful singing is extremely approachable and enjoyable.

Los Camperos de Valle

Los Camperos de Valle, from the state of San Luis Potosi, are a trio playing violin, guitar and the small jarana guitar. They are masters of Huasteco son, considered by many to be the most beautiful music in Mexico.

 El Triunfo: Sones de la Huasteca (Corason, Mexico).

A great place for an introduction to this idiosyncratic but thrilling music. Harmonised vocals, rowdy guitar and furious fiddling from Heliodoro Copado. **The Muse** (Corason, Mexico) is a fine follow up.

Conjunto Alma Jarocha

The Conjunto Alma Jarocha are a typical small group from the Veracruz area, with harp and *jaranguita* guitar.

 Sones Jarochos (Arhoolie, US).

A fine disc, the first in Arhoolie's Mexican series, with the typical sound of the Veracruz son – instantly familiar to anyone who has heard "La Bamba". Features some of the most danceable harp playing you are ever likely to hear.

Dinastía Hidalguense

This young trio, the fiery violin and falsetto vocals soaring above two percusssive guitars, are the stars of dances all over the Mexican Huasteca.

 Sones huastecos (Corason, Mexico).

The band feature on a couple of tracks of the El Cáimán compilation, but this disc is worth it for the seemingly effortless falsetto leaps which come at the end of the vocal lines – an extraordinary sound.

Mariachi Coculense de Cirilo Marmolejo

Cirilo Marmolejo was the leader of the seminal mariachi band – one of the first to be recorded.

 Mexico's Pioneer Mariachis Vol 1 (Arhoolie, US).

This set of wonderful archive recordings from the 1920s and '30s is given extra value by its inclusion of what is claimed to be the first ever mariachi recording, from 1908.

Mariachi Reyes del Aserradero

The Reyes del Aserradero are an excellent mariachi band from Jalisco state.

Sones from Jalisco (Corason, Mexico).

Contemporary mariachi from the heartland of the music, minus the cheese. A sizeable band with four violins, a couple of trumpets and guitars.

Mariachi Tapati de Jos Marmolejo

The Mariachi Tapati de Jos Marmolejo was yet another pioneer mariachi band.

 Mariachi Recordings: 1906–36 (Arhoolie, US).

These archive recordings feature the playing of the great trumpeter Jess Salazar.

Mariachi Vargas

Silvestre Vargas, the leader of this mariachi, has managed to stay at the top of his field for over fifty years. Always flexible, his band released one disastrous album of mariachi-rock but have otherwise had hits all the way. They work in the US for much of the year.

 20 exitos (Orfeon, Mexico).

Big-band style mariachi from the most famous group in Mexico. Twenty tracks, twenty hits.

La Negra Graciana

Graciana Silva, 'La Negra', started playing the harp aged ten and from that time played for a living in parks and on the streets with her father on jarana guitar and her brother on violin. Now over sixty years old, she still occasionally plays solo on the streets, or sings with family members.

 Sones Jarochos (Corason, Mexico).

An intimate recording of La Negra with brother Pino Silva on jarana guitar and her sister-in-law on second harp. Delicate arpeggio flourishes and a web of textures from the two harps, plus fierce guitar and playful lyrics sung between Graciana and her brother. The old Veracruz favourite "La Bamba" appears in a charming version.

Los Pregoneros del Puerto

Los Pregoneros del Puerto, from the Veracruz coast where harp and jarana guitars still dominate, are one of the finest of the bands from the area.

 Music of Veracruz: Sones Jarochos (Rounder, US).

An enchanting album of rippling sones jarochos, this delightful collection will make you rethink your ideas about the harp.

Juan Reynoso

Born in 1912 (or perhaps 1914), Reynoso is the greatest surviving old-time fiddler in Mexico.

 The Paganini of the Mexican Hotlands (Corason, Mexico).

The title is well-deserved. The earliest recording on this disc was made in 1972, the last in 1993 – when Reynoso was eighty years old. He plays with a gritty swagger and rhythmic drive, throwing in the odd pizzicato between energetically bowed phrases. Backed by family and friends on vocals, guitars and drum.

Ranchera and Norteño

Compilations

 15 Regional Classics of Mexico (Rounder, US).

With its emphasis on the popular bands like Los Pingüinos del Norte and Los Caimanes, this budget-priced collection of rancheras, corridos, polkas and other forms makes a good place to start when exploring commercially recorded Mexican music.

 Conjuntos Norteños (Arhoolie, US).

A great pairing of Mex and Tex, two excellent bands from either side of the border, comparing and contrasting Mexican norteño music and Texas conjunto. From Mexico, Los Pingüinos Del Norte (The Penguins of the North) are a rural-style band with accordion, guitar and bass singing nasal corrido ballads. Recorded live in a real cantina in 1970. From Texas, The Trio San Antonio. Good notes and song translations.

 Corridos & Tragedias de la Frontera (Arhoolie, US).

A two-CD compilation of some of the first recordings of corrido ballads from 1928–1937. These are newspapers in song, performed by the significant artists of the day, including Pedro Rocha and Lupe Martínez. But the point of this music is not the individual artists, but the message – movingly delivered across the decades. Superly packaged.

 The Mexican Revolution (Arhoolie, US).

In Russia, South Africa, even Cuba, there's nothing like this four-CD set to give the musical context for a moment in history. Here are songs and corridos about the events of the Mexican revolution spanning seventy years, from 1904 to 1974. The four discs are titled *Outlaws and Revolutionaries*, *The Francisco Villa Cycle* (named after Pancho Villa, the most celebrated outlaw of the revolution) *Local Revolutionary Figures* and *Post Revolutionary Corridos and Narratives*. The interest is more historical than musical, but there are some real treasures here made accessible by fantastic notes, translations and photographs.

Artists

Flaco Jiménez

Accordionist Leonardo 'Flaco' Jiménez, the son of the great Santiago Jiménez, started playing in conjuntos and dances in the early 1950s. He is a huge name in the Tex-Mex world north of the border. For more details, see Tex-Mex article).

 Ay te dejo en San Antonio (Arhoolie, US).

The best of Flaco's many recordings. For Tex-Mex listings, including the excellent **Buena Suerte, Senorita** (Arista/Texas, US), see p.613.

MEXICO

Jos Alfredo Jiménez

Jos Alfredo Jiménez was the king of ranchera and embodied the best and worst of Mexican machismo. As he predicted in one of his songs, everyone in Mexico missed him when he died.

ⓘ **Homenaje a Jos Alfredo Jimenez**
(Sony Discos, US).

This collection of the man's greatest hits is absolutely typical of the emotionally charged pride of ranchera music.

Linda Ronstadt

Linda Ronstadt is well known as a figure in North American pop music, but she has also a great interest in ranchera music, stemming from her Mexican roots.

ⓘ **Canciones de mi Padre** and
ⓘ **Más Canciones** (Asylum, US).

These ranchera classics are sung very convincingly by the Mexican-American rocker, accompanied by Mariachi Vargas.

Los Tigres del Norte

Los Tigres del Norte, one of the best norteño groups in the business, have had tremendous success throughut Mexico and abroad with their supercharged mixture of norteño and cumbia, adding sax for extra punch.

ⓘ **Corridos Prohibidos** (Fonovisa, US).

A great sampling of corridos about Mexican low-life and heroism which would grace any collection.

Cumbia, Banda, Canción and Folk

Compilations

ⓘ **Mexico: Fiestas of Chiapas and Oaxaca**
(Nonesuch Explorer, US).

Atmospheric recordings from village festivities in southern Mexico. Marimba conjuntos, brass bands, some eccentric ensembles and great fireworks on the opening track. The next best thing to being there.

Mexico
Fiestas of
Chiapas & Oaxaca

Recorded by David Lewiston

ⓘ **Mexico: Raíz Viva** (World Network, Germany).

A slightly unfocused selection of contrasting music. Seven tracks from folk revival group Los Folkloristas including Gabino Palomares' powerful "La maldición de Malinche" (Malinche's Curse), one of the significant songs of the nueva canción movement. Three songs from Amparo Ochoa, the voice of Mexican nueva canción until her death in 1994 and Tlen Huicani and Los Camperos de Valles playing sones from Veracruz and Huasteca respectively.

ⓘ **Mexique: Fêtes de San Miguel Tzinacapan**
(Ocora, France).

Small bands of native flute and drum, plus ensembles using the immigrant guitar and violin. Performed by Indian musicians accompanying religious festivities.

ⓘ **Mexique: Musiques Traditionnelles**
(Ocora, France).

For the more folklorically inclined, music from the many little-known indigenous communities of Mexico.

ⓘ **New Mexico: Hispanic Traditions**
(Smithsonian Folkways, US).

A good ethnographic recording from the Mexican diaspora in the US. Dances, songs, corridos and religious music performed in rustic style.

Artists

Banda del Recodo

The Banda del Recodo, the godfathers of the 'banda' sound that swept Mexico in the early 1990s, were founded by Don Cruz Lizgarra in the 1950s, and have shown themselves masters of adaptation. They began with fairly straightforward, if cheerful, renditions of traditional tunes, then branched out into mambo and eventually ended up as a massively funky dance band.

ⓘ **Tengo una ilusion** (Fonovisa, Mexico).

Driven by astonishing brass playing, this is a great example of the way in which norteño music, heated up and played on the brass bands that have been around playing for village fiestas for over a century, has taken over the Mexican scene.

Los Bukis

Los Bukis, a band from Michocoan in central Mexico, were instrumental in the move away from the Colombian style of Cumbia to a more mellow, romantic approach, much loved in Mexico and amongst the emigrant communities north of the border.

ⓘ **Me volvi a acordar de ti** (Melody, Mexico).

This is the sound of soft cumbia – and the most popular Mexican record ever.

Los Folkloristas

Mexico's seminal folklorico group, with over thirty albums to their credit, Las Folkloristas revive traditional Mexican songs and add their own. There have been shifts in personnel over the years: one of the early stars was 'El Negro' Ojeda, later followed by the supreme voice of Amparo Ochoa.

◉ **El canciónero popular: Amparo Ochoa con la colaboracion del grupo Los Folkloristas**
(Discos Puebla, Mexico).

One of the definitive discs of early nueva canción. Includes the seminal version of Gabino Palomares' powerful "La maldición de Maliinche" (Malinche's Curse), arguably one of 'new song's' most significant singles, as well as others by Salvador 'Chava' Flores and Peru's Nicomedes Santa Cruz.

◉ **Mexico! Las Folkoristas** (Flying Fish, US).

Folk singers in true lively style, with swinging voices and inspired Latin arrangements – mostly of Mexican sones from all over the country.

Agustin Lara

Agustin Lara, a legendary crooner, was known as a man who idolised prostitutes and married for love twelve times. He was also one of Mexico's greatest composers of popular music, specialising in bolero ballads and music from Veracruz. His most famous song is "María Bonita".

◉ **Agustin Lara** (Orfeon, Mexico).

Lara tugs at the heartstrings with all the conviction that eleven divorces can bring. It is all utterly romantic, utterly convincing.

Rocanrol

Café Tacuba

Café Tacuba, formed in Mexico City in 1990, set out to create an authentically Mexican rock music, drawing on the country's roots music traditions. They have been hugely successful in Mexico and, recently, with an album embracing a panoply of Latin and American styles, have begun to get coverage on US alternative rock stations.

◉ **Re** (WEA Latina, Mexico).

A largely acoustic 1994 outing from the Tacuba boys, exploring and rock-interpreting a range of Mexican roots music.

Caifanes

Mexico's pionering rock band, Caifanes (1985–95) were pivots of the 'Rock en Español' movement. Frontman Saul Hernandez moved on to create his own band, Jaguares, in similar vein.

◉ **El mervio del volcan** (BMG, US).

The last Caifanes album was perhaps the best, hugely confident – and, rightly so, for it was another platinum seller.

Los de Abajo

Formed as a ska-rock band, with a committed political agenda, in Mexico City in 1992, Los de Abajo (Those from Below) are an oddball bunch – a kind of Mexican Chumbawumba. After two self-produced cassettes, they landed a deal with David Byrne's Luaka Bop label.

◉ **Los de Abajo** (Orfeon, Mexico).

The group's 1998 Luaka debut showed no temptation to compromise: strong lyrics, danceable tunes, lots of energy, slices of funk, rock, reggae, mambo, cumbia, even polka.

Panama

dancing between the oceans

Mention Panama and only a few stereotyped images tend to come up – hats, the Canal, flags of convenience, Noriega. But music? Salsa fans will know Rubén Blades, of course, but he is as much an American as a Panamanian star. And there it stops. Panama's music is the 'forgotten' music of Central America – though maybe 'forgotten' is the wrong word here, since the rest of the world has yet to discover it. Travelling in the interior, to the coasts, or in Panama city you would be amazed at the vitality and lived-in quality of the music encountered. **Nigel Gallop** and **Robin Broadbank** ink in the blanks on the map.

You can drive across Panama, from the Pacific to the Caribbean, in little over an hour. It's a small country with a population of less than three million, mostly *mestizo* but with an important black minority. Amerindian tribes enjoy a degree of autonomy unusual in this part of the world and have their own quite separate musical identity. To the east the country shades off into the jungle region bordering Colombia, of which Panama was a province until independence in 1903. To the west are the cultural heartlands of the Azuero peninsula, and it is there, above all, that Panama's richest folk music and dance traditions are to be found.

Anyone who gets to the numerous fiestas in the **Azuero region** is in for a real treat, as long as they can handle the cane liquor that fuels these events. Almost all towns have their patron saints' day and, of course, they all celebrate Holy Week, Corpus Cristi and Carnival. Panama's folk and traditional musics are under threat from the salsa industry, and from the 'colombianisation' of its own distinctive *cumbia panameña*, but Panama-

nians remain intensely proud of their own musical traditions.

Basically, the music has Spanish roots with a strong African percussive and vocal element. Some researchers hold that the black input into the mainstream dates back to the beginning of colonisation in the sixteenth century, via Sevillians of African origin who sailed from Spain, and early inter-racial marriage, so that the music has been Afro-Hispanic from this early period. It's not only rhythmically and melodically attractive, but also has its own distinctive singing style.

Esther Nieto and Los de Azuero recording for the Nimbus 'Music of Panama' CD

La Mejorana

One of the most significant words in Panamanian folk music is **la mejorana**, the name of the quintessential local folk instrument – a small, five-stringed guitar similar to the Colombian *tiple* and Venezuelan *cuatro*. But the word has wider significance too, being applied to the songs and dances that the guitar accompanies, as well as the tunes and accompaniments that are played on it.

These various tunes may be referred to as *puntos*, *toques*, *tonos*, or, most commonly, **torrentes** – and there are a great number of them, some for dancing to, some for singing. Among the dances are the *cumbias*, *socavones* and *llaneros*, while the song forms include *llantos*, *valdiviesos* and *mesanos*. Rhythmic foot-stamping (*zapateado*) may accompany both songs and dances.

As a **dance**, the mejorana originated in the two towns of Ocú and Los Santos, the former developing a somewhat rustic form and the latter a more refined version. In both cases, however, it is a double line dance. Singing to the mejorana is a strictly male preserve and the players – the *mejoraneros* – are also male. The songs invariably start off with a **saloma**, which sounds very similar to the *ay, ay, ay* of Andalucian *cante jondo* (the Flamenco 'deep song'). This introduction can take the form of a complete melody in a falsetto voice, yodelling or mere shouts and interjections expressing personal emotion and encouragement to others of the group. The male singers use the **décima**, a ten-line verse form which stems directly from the poetry of sixteenth-century Spain.

Like the saloma, the **llanto**, a sad, tragic genre, has a very strong flamenco feel. The **gallina** or gallino, on the other hand, is used for romantic verses. The singing style tends to the same upper register, often skipping over into a falsetto.

Tamborito, Congo and Calypso

A number of beautiful dances are at the heart of Panamanian music, of which the most important is the **tamborito** – regarded by Panamanians as their national dance. It is rendered even more attractive by its accompanying costumes. The woman wears a *pollera panamena*, with billowing white lace and cotton skirts, colourful embroidery and accompanying *tembleque* jewellery, which is set in the wearer's hair, and trembles as she dances. The man wears a sober, white, cotton shirt outside his dark trousers, with a small bag at his side and the typical straw hat worn at a jaunty angle.

An essential element of the music is the female lead singer known as the **cantalante**, backed by a female chorus clapping and singing the four-line stanzas of the *copla*. Like the male décima verse form, the copla harks back to traditional Spanish poetry. Dancing begins in the centre of the room, as a series of couples step out, one after another. The steps are small, smooth and flowing as the man pursues and the woman withdraws. The tamborito is accompanied by three drums. Two of them – the *pujador* and *repicador* – are upright and are played by hand, while the third – a small *caja* or *tambora* – is played with sticks.

The Spanish-speaking black communities on the Caribbean coast have their own version of the tamborito known as the **congo** – also with upright drums and female call-and-response chorus. The congo, however, is very different, encompassing elements of burlesque, ridicule and sexual suggestion, as the men make acrobatic and lascivious approaches to the women who fend them off with their voluminous skirts while writhing at the same time to the sensual rhythms. The congo dance forms part of a whole system of social and religious ritual, and is related to the traditons of Cuban Santería, Haitian Voodoo and Brazilian Candomblé.

Similarly distinct are the **Isthmus**, English-speaking immigrants of Jamaican origin. Situated on the Caribbean coast, they form a very important minority, having brought their **calypso** and **mento** traditions from their island home.

Cumbia and Punto

Almost as popular as the tamborito is the **cumbia panameña**, a variant of the better-known Colombian cumbia, and with a common origin in the eighteenth century dance called the *bunde*.

The cumbia panameña can be danced either *suelta* or *amanojá* – with couples either holding each other, or detached – though the latter is more traditional. The men and women each form a circle with the women taking the outside and, of course, both sexes facing each other – the women holding a bunch of candles in one hand.

The *amanojá* style, also known as the *pindín*, is gradually ousting the more traditional suelta. Violin, accordion and even harmonica are usually the main instruments accompanying the dance, backed by drums, flute, maracas, a scraper (here called a *churuca*), triangle and guitar. The *atravesao* is a more vigorous version, combining the rhythms of the cumbia with the fast steps of the creation of the composer **Ricardo Fábrega**. Containing elements of both the tamborito and cumbia, it actually derives from the Cuban *danzón*, which has gradually acquired acceptance as a folk dance.

Another very characteristic dance from the folk repertoire is the slow, stately and elegant **punto**, clearly of Spanish origin, traditionally accompanied on violin, guitar, flute and drums, although here again the accordion has been making heavy inroads. The four movements of this most attractive dance are the *paseo*, *zapateo*, *escobillado* and *seguidilla* – all clearly Spanish in origin. In the same vein are the so-called **salon dances** – the *pasillo* (in waltz time, also very popular in Colombia and Ecuador), *danza* and *contradanza* – all of them immigrants from European ballrooms.

Pageants and Festivals

The **tuna** – dear to the hearts of all Panamanians – is a musical procession that is a typical feature of carnival, saints' days and even political events. An ad hoc group, largely made up of women, surges through the streets, clapping their hands and singing in the saloma style. The tail of the procession is often formed by a brass band on a lorry. The tunas are perhaps best seen in Los Santos, Azuero, where they accompany the allegorical floats of the two rival beauty queens of Calle Arriba and Calle Abajo, representing the two parts of the town that meet in the central plaza – a custom stemming

Los Juglares del Dexas

Los Juglares del Dexas, the folk-music group of Panama University, was founded in 1971 to maintain the Panamanian folk tradition in the face of changes pushed by the commercial record industry. Rejecting modern trends such as the virtual eclipse of the violin by the accordion and the abandonment of the mejorana in favour of the Spanish guitar, the group hopes to bear the standard for 'authentic' Panamanian folk.

Originally inspired and co-ordinated by the celebrated *mejoranero* **Juan Andrés Castillo**, the group has represented Panama in a number of overseas music festivals, most recently at the Festival des Jeux Santons in France in 1995. Among the founders were the well-known violinists Miguel Leguizamo Senior and Escolastico 'Colaco' Cortes, although the line-up has changed since their deaths to include the violinist Miguel Leguizamo Junior, mejoranero 'Tonito' Rudas, singer and *churuquero* Raul Vital, accordionist Aceves Nunez and percussionists Ricaurte Villarreal and Victor Ruiz.

Mejorana player Juan Andrés Castillo

from colonial times which has now spread to other places in the region.

There are various **folklore festivals**, of which the most spectacular are the *Festival de la Pollere* at Los Santos on July 21, the *Festival del Manito* at Ocú in mid-August and the *Festival de la Mejorana* in Guararé on September 24. Los Santos is a great place to be at Corpus Cristi, if only to see the spectacular traditional dances of the **grandiablo**, in which the *diablicos limpios* (clean little devils) dance to the sound of *caja* (drum) and fife, while the *diablicos sucios* (dirty little devils) sway to the sound of the guitar accompanied by castanets and foot-stamping. As always, the devil gets the best tunes.

With thanks to Dr. Dora P. de Zárate.

discography

See the Salsa discography (p.503) for Rubén Blades.

Compilations

 Musica Folklorica Panamena Vol 2
(Discos Nacional, Puerto Rico).

Only obtainable in Panama. Originally recorded on acetate, the accordion predominates as an instrument, and there are good background salomas to songs by La Alondra Interiorana. A reasonable introduction to the music, but fails to demonstrate the full variety.

Los de Azuero – Traditional Music from Panama (Nimbus, UK).

Recorded in Panama City in 1998, this features top-flight traditional musicians, with compelling instrumentals and vocals in all the main styles. Good notes including full song texts with translations.

Panama, tamboritos y mejoranas (Musica Tradicional, Mexico).

Recordings of mainly non-professional performers and small groups in Panama city and the Azuero region by Eduardo Lleranas and Enrique de Arellano (whose 'Música Tradicionál' label preceded their existing 'Corazón' series). This is easily the best recording available outside Panama – expertly recorded and with excellent and authoritative sleeve notes in English and Spanish.

Street Music of Panama (Original Music, US).

Recorded by the Frenchman Michel Blaise, and orginally released on vinyl, this CD collects some good and varied material, including a track of gritos.

Artists

Conjunto Folklorico 'Tonosí'

A well known folk group, led by accordionist Uruguay Nelson, who have recorded a number of albums.

Musica folklorica Panameña Vol 1 and Vol 2 (Discos Nacional, Puerto Rico).

The accordion dominates these discs, which capture some of the excitement and atmosphere of tamboritos and cumbias. The recording is local and a bit uneven.

Danzas Panama

Recorded under the title of 'Danzas Panama', this is essentially a disc from leading cantalante Lucy Jaen.

Instrumental Folk Music of Panama (JVC, Japan/US).

A good introduction to Panama's folk music – this is, at present, the only CD readily available outside the country. It is, however, somewhat pedestrian and under-represents Panamanian song.

Luis Noriel Sanchez & Gustavo Sanchez

Two brothers from Coclé in Azuero who sing décima verses to guitar accompaniment.

Encuentro de dos grandes de la décima (Blue Moon, Panama).

Imitates the style of a mejorana quite skilfully, but the real instrument would have been a lot better. Nonetheless, a reasonable example of some of the many torrentes. A local recording without notes.

Puerto Rico

not quite the 52nd state

If Cuba is the key creative source of Latin Caribbean music, Puerto Rico is its equal as a supplier of performers – and it was the great Puerto Rican immigrant community in New York (the Nuyoricans) that was largely responsible for turning Cuban *son* into salsa. Meantime, Puerto Rico's own national style, the *plena*, provides a bracing upbeat alternative to salsa and merengue in the Latin dance clubs. **Philip Sweeney** stows away on a cruise ship to report from old San Juan.

Puerto Rico is a much smaller island than Cuba or the Dominican Republic, and its lack of big plantations meant that it had a relatively small slave population. Its music, as a result, has much stronger Hispanic elements than African ones, with the Cuban *son* and *guaracha* to the fore. The other core influence is the US. Puerto Rico has since 1952 been a US Overseas Commonwealth Territory, and it only narrowly voted against statehood in 1999. This status has led to a constant flow of immigrants to the US, where its musicians (rather than those of isolated Cuba) were central to the creation of salsa.

Puerto Rican musicians – whether born on the island or in the USA – have long moved between the music scenes at home and in New York and Miami. This article focuses, as much as makes sense, on the local island scene. For more on the development (and current state) of salsa, see the Salsa article following (p.488).

Danza and Plena

Like Cuba, Puerto Rico possesses its own versions of various Afro-Hispanic musics. The oldest established is **danza** – an equivalent of the Cuban *danzon*, adapted at aristocratic dances in the nineteenth century from European waltzes and mazurkas. Also Hispanic in origin is the **seis**, a song form based, as with much Cuban music, on the *décima* (ten-line) tradition of rhyming improvised verse. The **plena**, by contrast, is more of a Caribbean form – a colloquial, narrative song, reminiscent of calypso, accompanying a couple dance.

Although danzas are still quite common – "La Borinqueña", the island's anthem, is one – it is the plena that is the core local element of Puerto Rican popular music. Plenas featured prominently in the repertoire of the **jíbaro** (country) artists of the 1930s and 1940s, played by ensembles using *pandereta* (tambourine), congas, bongos, *güiro* (scraper), guitar and the little four double-string guitar called a *cuatro*, similar to Cuba's *tres*.

The most famous performers of this era were the bands of **Rafael Hernandez**, whose **Trio Borinquen** made its name in New York's growing Puerto Rican community, and the great **'Canario'** (Manuel Jiménez). A merchant seaman and part-time musician, Canario had a prolific recording career that included his own classic compositions such as "La nieve de los años" (Snow of the Years) and "Por primera vez" (For the first time). He was also the first bandleader to augment the traditional Puerto Rican ensemble with piano, bass and brass. This led to two separate strands for the music, with a modern, New York-inclined, brass-scored music, and a simple string-based jíbaro sound, purveyed through the same period by artists such as **'La Calandria'** (Ernestina Reyes), **'Ramito'** (Morales Ramos), and, later, **Pedro Padilla**.

The modernisation of the plena started by Canario was continued in the 1940s and 1950s by **Cesar Concepción**, with his slick nightclub sound, by top pan-Latin popular crooners **Bobby Capó** and **Daniel Santos**, and by **Mon Rivera**, who was the last artist to have a US #1 hit record with a plena – in 1964. The big brass-sound plena was also central to the music of **Rafael Cortijo** – a key Puerto Rican figure in the development of salsa, of whom more below.

With the passing of Cortijo, the most vital and roots-based of the modern *pleneros*, the genre faded from the commercial mainstream, although traditional groups such as **Los Pleneros del Quinto Olivo** kept the flag flying, while in New York expatriates such as **Los Pleneros de la 21** (named after a bus-stop in the San Juan music *barrio* of Santurce) fulfilled the same role.

Then in the 1990s came a plena resurgence spearheaded by **Plena Libre**, a 12-piece band led by the classically trained bassist and arranger, Gary Nuñez. Plena Libre combined traditional elements with a more dynamic salsa-influenced brass and staging, and by 1999 they were popular enough to headline at the Roberto Clemente Stadium with star *salsero* Andy Montanez. Other artists in this revival include the group **Plenealo**, and the singers **Fe Cortijo** (daughter of the great bandleader) and **José Nogueras**, and, most recently, **Truko y Zaperoko**, a conglomerate formed of the traditional group **Los Pleneros del Truko**, and the progressive outfit **Zaperoko**. In New York, **Willie Colón**, faithful to his family tradition, has revamped several plena classics during his career, including "Volo" by Rafael Hernandez, complete with Andrews Sisters-type female chorus.

Plena may be dwarfed in commercial terms by salsa and merengue, but the genre is still of considerable importance to patriotic Puerto-Ricans: even the pop star **Ricky Martin** (who is now probably the most famous Puerto Rican ever) included a plena finale, with a group of *pleneros* from New York, in the series of mega-concerts with which he started the millennium.

Bomba

Puerto Rico has another core musical form called **bomba** – a distinctly African, heavily percussion-based music similar to Cuban rumba. It is to be heard in the towns of **Loiza Aldea**, close to San Juan, and **Ponce** in the south of the island – two former sugar refining centres that have retained large populations of slave-descendants. The music accompanies a couple dance in which the man moves separately from the woman, interacting with the improvisation of the *requinto* drummer.

Bomba's chief exponents in Loiza Aldea are the Cepeda family, led for years by their patriarch **Rafael Cepeda**. Since his death, the group has been run by Modesto and William Cepeda (the latter also leads the group **Afro Boricua**), who perform and lead workshops in plena and bomba dance and percussion. The Ponce-based group **Paracumbé** also play superb bomba, in a southern style in which women (rather than

men who form the chorus in the north) handle the call-and-response vocals. This style was shaped by that of Haiti, which historically was easier to get to from Ponce than San Juan, over the mountains.

In New York, Manny Oquendo's Puerto Rican salsa-jazz band, **Orquesta Libre**, always pays homage to its ancestry in funky mobilising bombas, driven by the upright double bass of Andy Gonzalez. Bomba also made a surprise, if heavily disguised, reappearance in the 1990s as an ingredient of Puerto Rican merengue (see below).

The Big Combos

In the 1940s and 1950s urban Puerto Rican bands entered the New York pan-Latin melting pot which, dominated by Cuban bandleaders, gave rise to big-band Latin jazz, rumba, mambo and chachachá. Early Puerto Rican stars in this scene were the Morales brothers, especially bandleader and composer **Noro Morales**, and the great mambo interpreter **Tito Rodríguez**.

Born in San Juan, Tito Rodríguez moved to New York in the 1930s to work as a singer and percussionist with his brother Johnny's Conjunto Siboney. He moved on through the Cuban Xavier Cugat's orchestra before founding his own Mambo Devils during the Perez Prado-led mambo craze. With **Tito Puente** (also Puerto Rican born) and Machito, he was one of the star trio of New York bandleaders, 'The Mambo Kings', during the heyday of the *Palladium* dancehall on Broadway in the 1950s. He later became best known for singing boleros, a kind of Latin Nat King Cole. He died in 1973, having returned home to the island.

While Rodríguez was Puerto Rico's biggest tropical star of the era, the musician who did most to preserve Puerto Rican flavour was bandleader and percussionist **Rafael Cortijo**. Cortijo brought the plena back into fashion – performing both the classic songs of El Canario and new ones of his own – and also adapted the bomba, for which he augmented his brass-led band with traditional drums. His sound was an eclectic mix of rootsy, black feeling, with dinstinctively Puerto Rican (as opposed to Cuban) touches – for example, female voices rather than male in the chorus. He was a pioneer, too, of rock-style guitar solos, which he more or less introduced to Latin music. His most outstanding work featured the brilliant, husky-voiced *sonero* **Ismael Rivera**, and his band served as a training ground for young Puerto Rican musicians. He died in New York in 1983.

In 1962, Cortijo's pianist **Rafael Ithier** formed with six fellow band musicians **El Gran Combo**,

Willie Rosario

with the aim of creating a slicker dance music, based on the soulful Cortijo sound. Their new style met some resistance before securing a huge island hit with the song "Akangana". They went on to develop a rich, tight swing sound, influenced by Cuban jazz rhythms, featuring a trombone-boosted brass section playing over Ithier's rolling keyboard. Fronting the group were a tightly choreographed trio of singer-dancers, starring, until his departure in 1977, the soaring voice of the great *salsero* **Andy Montanez**.

El Gran Combo were the island's top band of the 1970s and 1980s, and they are still going strong, a national institution alongside their long-term swing rivals, **La Sonora Ponceña**, from the southern town of Ponce. Formed in the 1950s by

Enrique 'Quique' Lucca – and led since the 1970s by his son, multi-instrumentalist, piano star and virtuoso arranger 'Papo' – the Ponceña's trademark is a front line of four impeccable singers who interact with stunning timing with a rich four-trumpet brass section.

Puerto Rico has two other artists of almost equal longevity and popularity – singer **Cheo Feliciano** and bandleader Willie Rosario. Feliciano started his career in New York, where he performed with everyone from Tito Rodríguez to Eddie Palmieri, and carved himself a considerable reputation as a warm-voiced romantic singer of bolero and salsa.

Willie Rosario worked as a journalist and newsreader in New York before deciding, under the influence of Tito Rodríguez's performances at the *Palladium* dancehall that he must take up music. Based in Puerto Rico since 1972, Rosario's salsa band, featuring a four-trumpet and baritone sax brass section, and himself on timbales, has acted as a launching pad for a succession of young singers including **Gilberto Santa Rosa** and **Tony Vega**.

Everybody Salsa

Puerto Rican artistes were prominent in the New York-based creation of **salsa** in the 1970s, when the pan-Latin mix was given a rock flavouring and again began to appeal to a crossover audience, and the island itself was a crucial stop on the salsa trail, featuring on tours by all the major artists and proving an important market for record sales.

Among key Puerto Ricans in the development of salsa were Sonoro Ponceña's **Papo Lucca**, who guested with the original Fania All Stars, and **Bobby Valentin**, a bass-player, trumpeter and bandleader who had played with Charlie Palmieri in New York in the 1960s. In the 1970s Valentin recorded a string of salsa hits, including the 1973 classic "Soy Boricua' (I Am A Puerto Rican), and also founded the highly influential salsa record label, Bronco, in Puerto Rico in 1974. Another big name of the 1970s was **Roberto Roena**, a top bongo player and noted dancer, who emerged from El Gran Combo to create his own **Apollo**

Sound, exploring jazz and mambo rhythms, before joining up with Fania.

Other Puerto Ricans who established their reputations in this classic or 'hard' salsa era include **Luis 'Perico' Ortiz**, a virtuoso trumpeter and eclectic, experimental, arranger responsible for dozens of top collaborations and recordings of his own; **Tommy Olivencia**, another trumpeter and producer whose tutelage has helped the careers of Frankie Ruiz and Eddie Santiago (see below), the young *salsa romantica* stars; **Yomo Toro**, a *cuatro* player whose mastery of an instrument uncommon in 1970s New York made him a much sought-after session player and led to a solo contract with Island Records; and the songwriter **Tito Curet Alonso**, currently one of the top producers of salsa standards.

The most famous Puerto Rican salsa star of all, however, during the 1970s and 1980s, was the charismatic and brilliant singer **Hector Lavoe**. He had played in the young Willie Colón's first ever band and became a leading light of the Fania All Stars, adored for his emotional, ghetto-attuned lyrics and high, fluid improvisatory singing. Problems with drugs and illness, the murder of his son, and a suicide attempt that left him temporarily paralysed, led to an intermittent career, but one punctuated by outstanding songs. He died in 1997, a salsa legend whose life became the subject of a successful stage musical, *Quien Mato A Hector Lavoe*, which played in New York and San Juan.

In the 1980s, Puerto Rican artistes were central to salsa developments, with the creation of the new **salsa-romantica** tyle. Salsa romantica – or *salsa erotica*, depending on the strength of its lyrics – brought to the fore young romantic singers, crooning over a more relaxed 'soft' salsa backing. The style's early Puerto Rican stars included New Jersey-based **Frankie Ruiz** (who died in 1998 after years of alcohol and drug abuse), and **Lalo Rodríguez**, the singer of perhaps the biggest pan-Latin hit of the 1980s, "Ven, devórame otra vez" (Come and Devour Me Again). By the 1990s, however, the top star was **Eddie Santiago**, whose band introduced a smooth four-trombone sound (he avoided trumpets so as not to drown his rather quiet voice). He has had a string of hits, alternating between a lyrically explicit style ("Insaciable"), and a purely romantic mode ("Lluvia" – Rain).

Along with Santiago, Puerto Rico's top selling salseros at the beginning of the zero-years are the highly-polished singer **Gilberto Santa Rosa** and newcomer, **Victor Manuelle**, who made his name at a concert by Santa Rosa in his home town of Isabela, when friends dared him to get up on stage and trade *son* improvisation with the star. He was swiftly signed up for chorus singing, and, taken up by Sergio George, the musical director of New York salsa entrepreneur, Ralph Mercado, launched a solo career. Among new generation *salseros*, he is rivalled only by Marc Anthony.

Latin Pop, Canción Merengue and Rap

Puerto Rico has long maintained a thriving pop scene, with local artists adopting and adapting international trends. This trend began in the 1960s, when **Lucecita** dominated the charts with her Latin covers of Beatles and Dusty Springfield songs. Puerto Rico's international pop star of the same period was the blind singer and guitarist **José Feliciano**, who had a massive hit crooning The Doors' "Light My Fire", and has gone on to record more than forty gold and platinum records.

Both Feliciano (long based in Miami) and Lucecita are still working and popular today, while their modern equivalents, **Ricky Martin** and **Chayanne**, are at the peak of their success. Both these singers emerged from the Latin 'boys bands' of the 1980s. Martin, born in San Juan in 1971, was a member of Menudo, a hugely successful teen heart-throb ensemble, before leaving to forge a second career as a TV soap star in Mexico. He became a world pop hit-maker in 1997 with "Un, dos, tres, Maria" and hasn't looked back since. In February 2000, his return to play the giant Hiram Bithorn Stadium in San Juan was treated in the media like a Presidential visit.

La Vida Musical de ... EDDIE SANTIAGO

Another imported style that Puerto Ricans gave their own gloss was **Nueva canción**, the 'new song' of the early 1970s, popularised by politicised singer-songwriters such as the Chilean Victor Jara (p.365) and Cuban Silvio Rodríguez (see p.409). In Puerto Rico, the music was given *jibaro* style backing. It was and remains popular, although not especially commercial, being cold-shouldered by the conservative (often Cuban-exile) management of the media. Two names have dominated the field saince the outset: **Andres Jimenez 'El Jibaro'**, whose songs outspokenly espouse Puerto Rican independence, and **Antonio Cabán 'El Topo'**, whose *danza* "Verde Luz" (Green Light) was an anthem of the semi-clandestine independence movement throughout the 1970s and 1980s.

In the 1980s, **merengue** from the Dominican Republic (see p.414) swamped the US Latin or 'Tropical' market, and Puerto Rico followed suit. Soon, however, the island began to produce its own *merengueros*, and then to export them, and for the past few years many of the top pan-Latin merengue acts – **Olga Tañon**, **Grupo Manía**, and the superstar **Elvis Crespo** – were Puerto Rican, not Dominican. Puerto Rican groups began to beef up the galloping saxophone-led merengue rhythm with a thudding insistent bass beat which was widely ascribed to bomba input: thus the term *merengue-bomba* was born. More recently, many of the groups, as in salsa, have grafted on a **house** (as in the Western dance music) component. They include **Grupo Heavy** and **3-2 Get Funky**.

Puerto Rico was also a prime centre when **Latin rap** was born in the 1980s. Its most talented and popular exponent is the San Juan-born Luis Armando Lozada, better known as **Vico C**, author of a string of hits such as "Dulce, Sexy, Sensual" before becoming reborn as a Christian in 1999. **Christian music**, as throughout the Latin world, is a substantial genre in Puerto Rico and there exist a number of Christian plena groups.

discography

This discography should be read alongside that for salsa (following), which features many of the New York and Miami-based Puerto Rican artists.

Compilations

 The Music of Puerto Rico 1929–47
(Harlequin, UK).

A selection of plenas, jibaro and música típica culled from the era of guitar trios, imported from Puerto Rico into New York: sweet, high voices straight from the countryside and the nostalgic Spanish flavour of the island with wry comment on everyday life in the new home, Nueva York. Some tremendously emotive voices, including the fabulous Canario.

 Puerto Rican Plenas
(Disco Hit, Puerto Rico/US).

An excellent collection, including simple trio pieces (Los Antares, Trio Vegabajena), bigger ensemble numbers (some with accordions, including Canario's "El Perro de San Geronimo"), and full dance bands (extending to an early Sonora Ponceña item).

🄌 **Tributo a Roberto Clemente** (RykoLatino, US).

A team of musicians drawn from the hard core of Fania's early line-ups with local Puerto Rican baseballers-cum-musicians, most notably singer Andy Montanez, under the leadership of Fania pianist Larry Harlow. A huge superstar line-up crammed into the studio and paying homage in these gorgeous songs and stirring solos to the island's most important sportsman and role model, Clemente.

Artists

Canario y su Grupo

El Canario (Manuel Jimenez) was a bandleader and some time merchant seaman, who stood traditional Puerto Rican music on its head in the 1940s, adding piano, bass and brass to the traditional string-based plena/jibaro sound, charting a course that led ultimately to salsa. He was a great songwriter, arranger and singer.

🄌 **Plenas** (Ansonia, US).

As Ned Sublette writes in the Descarga catalogue: 'If you care about Puerto Rican music, you care about the plena, and if you care about the plena, you have this'. Quite so.

Rafael Cepeda

The patriarch of the premier bomba family of Loiza Aldea, Rafael Cepeda is known as El Roble Mayor – the Old Oak. He has passed on his Afro-Puerto-Rican lore and rhythm bank to a sizeable family, who work in a variety of musical modes, from anthropological to avant-garde.

🄌 **El Roble Mayor** (Bombalele, Puerto Rico/US).

A *paseo* through the sacred and profane songs of the bomba canon, complete with spoken introduction, led by the

EL ROBLE MAYOR
RAFAEL CEPEDA
ACOMPAÑADO · GRUPO FOLK EXPERIMENTAL · BOMBA LE LE DE LOS · HERMANO CEPEDA

eponymous oak tree (who is also self-described on the liner notes as a 'Living historic monument').

Cesar Concepción

It was the bandleader Cesar Concepción who, between the still folksy Canario, and the tough proto-salsero Cortijo, brought plena to the smart hotel ballrooms of San Juan and New York in the 1940s and 1950s.

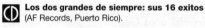 **Cesar Concepción, Vol.1** (Harlequin, UK).

A typically well-produced piece of musicology by the Harlequin label, presenting a selection of high-swing plenas and mellifluous boleros from the band's post-war heyday.

Rafael Cortijo and Ismael Rivera

Rafael Cortijo was Puerto Rico's most influential bandleader of the 1950s and 1960s, reworking the island's plena and bomba rhythms into a seductive mix. His work with the singer Ismael Rivera was a marriage made in heaven, the percussion-heavy arrangements of Cortijo combining with Rivera's husky, brilliant improvisations.

Los dos grandes de siempre: sus 16 exitos (AF Records, Puerto Rico).

A chance to hear for yourself the chemistry between these two friends in some of their greatest songs, recorded in their tragically short careers.

El Gran Combo

Oringally a breakaway group from Rafael Cortijo's band, El Gran Combo have been a national institution in Puerto Rico for over four decades – they can still fill any town square on the island during the summertime festival season. At their heart are leader Rafael Ithier's understated but elaborate piano playing and, out front, the adored trio of singer-dancers.

35 Years around the World (Combo, US).

A swathe of perfect songs covering the career of Ithier's band, which is synonymous with Puerto Rico. Its star vocalists are the principle attraction with their loud, almost raucous delivery.

Grupo Afro Boricua

Afro Boricua is a roots project of composer William Cepeda (son of the bomba artist Rafael Cepeda – above).

 Bombazo (Blue Jackal, US).

This 1999 disc is both enjoyable and fascinating: Cepeda takes classic Puerto Rican songs and 're-Africanises' them, with bomba percussion rhythms.

Grupo Manía

The island's top bomba-merengue outfit, Grupo Manía are a set of boy-band cuties with the viscera of Santo Domingo rhythm devils.

Masters of the Stage: 2000 veces Manía (Sony, US).

You shouldn't expect an awful lot of variety from a Grupo Manía disc – but what you get here (as on the rest of their releases) is straight-down, fun music.

Hector Lavoe

Salsero Hector Lavoe was a Puerto Rican legend, even before his death in 1997. His career was beset by tragedy,

drugs and illness, and his voice and songs show it all. He started out playing with Willie Colón, singing of raw barrio life, and together they created some of the great salsa tracks of the early 1970s before Colón moved on to a new partnership with Rubén Blades.

La comedia (Fania, US).

Lavoe's wonderful 1978 album, featuring his greatest hi "El cantante" (The SInger).

Victor Manuelle

Puerto Rico's latest contribution to the global salsa fest, Manuelle is a tremendous young singer who rose through the ranks from local bands to solo success in the 1990s. His style presents a counterbalance to the Latin rappers – high-energy salsa and romantic ballads.

A pesar de todo (Sony Tropical, US).

Victor Manuelle's voice here reveals a tribute to Rubén Blades in his clipped pronunciation, and to the smoothy balladeers who fill the charts. A voice which will carry salsa into the next century.

Andy Montanez

A long-established star, Andy Montanez was for years the lead singer with El Gran Combo, and he is now one of the venerable gentlemen of Puerto Rican salsa. His passion for Cuban son led him to visit the island – which incurred the wrath of the Miami Cubans who banned him for a year from attending their Little Havana Carnival.

El Swing (TH-Rodven, Venezuela).

Montanéz's almost operatic singing style soars through this, and every collection of his recordings.

Paracumbé

Paracumbé are Puerto Rico's top folklórico group – but if that suggests sanitised music and costumed dancing, think again. This group, with its powerful women's chorus, play the best roots plena and bomba on the island.

 Tambó (Ashé Records, US).

This is the most seductive disc of plena and bomba that you'll find – living, historic Africa in Puerto Rico, flawlessly recorded. Highlights are the beautiful call-and-response bomba songs of the women chorus (a southern tradition – men tend to sing bomba in the north of the island), and the plena vocals of Nelie Lebron Robles, set against accordions, drums and scrapers.

Plena Libre

The group Plena Libre led the plena revival of the 1990s, thanks to the determination of leader Gary Nuñez, who published their first two records and led the twelve members on five years of assiduous touring the discos, fiestas and private parties of the island.

Juntos y Revueltos (RykoLatino, US).

The band's second internationally-distributed CD displayed their trademark mix of traditional percussion, modern bass and trombones, voices both classic (the veteran plenero Victor Muniz) and romantically modern (Giovanni Lugo), and even a female conga player.

Los Pleneros del Truko y Zaperoko

Los Pleneros and Zaperoko are plena groups, established in the 1980s; the Pleneros are essentially traditional, while Zaperoko fuse plena with Cuban and jazz influences. They came together to record in 1999.

 Fusión Caribeña
(RykoLatino, US).

A really delightful roots record, featuring new takes on classic plena alongside original compositions by both groups, and a very Puerto Rican version of the Cuban son "El cuarto de Tula", sounding quite differnent to its appearance on Buena Vista Social Club. Throughout, the arrangements are splendid – both interesting and danceable.

Puerto Rican All Stars

The All Stars are a gang of great singers – ranging from salsa godfather Andy Montanez to the latest superstar Victor Manuelle – backed by a forceful orchestra with generous-sized trumpet, trombone and sax sections.

◉ **De Regresso** (RMM, US).

A flawless showcase for Puerto Rican salsa, which serves as a good primer for the various styles of the singers. As well as Andy Montanez and Victor Manuelle, the new generation are represented by Hernandez's talented daughter Liza, and by Primi Cruz and Darvel Garcia.

Tito Rodríguez

Tito Rodríguez (1923–73) was born in San Juan's music district of Santurce, moving to New York as a teenager, where he sang with the Cuban/Latin orchestras of Xavier Cugat and Noro Morales. He was a great all-rounder – a sonero and ballad-singer, percussionist and bandleader – and carried the flag for the island as one of the stars of Broadway's pre-salsa Latin big bands.

◉ **Mambo mona** (Tumbao, Spain).

A well-presented and annotated selection from Rodríguez's mambo heyday, including the eponymous number, which later changed its title to become the artist's signature hit, "Mama Guela".

Willie Rosario

Veteran bandleader and timbal-player Willie Rosario is back in vogue more than ever, thanks to his unbending espousal of classic hard salsa values.

 Back to the Future
(J&N/Sony Discos, US).

The album that put Rosario and hard salsa back at the top. It

is replete with star guests – Bobby Valentín and Louie Ramirez arranging, Gilberto Santa Rosa and Tony Vega singing.

Gilberto Santarosa

The slickest singer in Puerto Rican salsa – and that says a lot – Santarosa rose to fame as co-lead singer with Willie Rosario's band. He has managed to captivate the young generation with his catchy melodies.

◉ **Nace aqui** (Sony Tropical, US).

One for lovers of the softer face of salsa.

La Sonora Ponceña

With El Gran Combo, La Sonora Ponceña are the island's most beloved band – formed in 1956 and led by jazz-influenced pianist Papo Lucca since 1975. Their smooth salsa arrangements, four swirling interlocking trumpets and darting harmonising vocalists are instantly recognisable. No one approaches them.

 La Sonora Ponceña of Puerto Rico
(Charly, UK).

A compilation of greatest hits from vintage 1970s to early 1990s and including their jumpy *saoco* rhythm launched in the early 1990s. A showcase for Lucca's classy, smoothest arrangements, with plenty of limpid piano solos and the occasional appearance of the gritty-voiced Yolanda Rivera.

Yomo Toro

A virtuoso of the cuatro (small Puerto Rican guitar), Yomo Toro brought the flavour of the Puerto Rican countryside into New York salsa in the Fania records of the 1970s and in his own later solo work. He is based in New York these days, where he appears with the Latin Legends band.

◉ **Funky Jibaro** (Island, US).

This 1998 album is Toro's most traditionally-based recording, revisiting the jibaro (country music) forms.

Vico C

Vico C is the leader of probably the best Latin rap act to emerge in the past few years. He became a reborn Christian in 1999 and it remains to be seen what effect this will have on the music.

◉ **Greatest Hits** (BMG, US).

A cross-section of classic work from Vico's B.C. period.

Salsa

Latin/Caribbean/US

cubans, nuyoricans and the global sound

Salsa was born out of the encounter of Cuban and Puerto Rican music with big-band jazz in the Latin barrios of New York. Today it is a global music, massively popular across the Caribbean, Latin and the US, and with established outposts, too, in Europe, Japan, and Hong Kong. **Sue Steward** charts the stations of the salsa world, along with the music's roots and transformations – from hard to soft, *romantica* to *classica*, and rock to merengue.

Further coverage of salsa, its offshoots and relations is to be found in the individual articles (and discographies) for Colombia, Cuba, Dominican Republic, Puerto Rico and Venezuela.

Salsa is a word with vivid associations but no absolute definitions, a tag that encompasses a rainbow assortment of Latin rhythms and styles, taking on a different hue wherever you stand in the Spanish-speaking world. In her own definition, the acknowledged Queen of Salsa, Afro-Cuban singer Celia Cruz, says: "Salsa is Cuban music with another name. It's mambo, chachachá, rumba, son . . . all the Cuban rhythms under one name." To which a Puerto Rican might add plena and jibaro, a Columbian cumbia, a Dominican merengue, and so it goes.

Literally the word salsa means 'sauce' and in Latin American musical circles it takes its origins from a cry of appreciation for a particularly piquant or flashy solo. It was first used to describe a style of music in the mid-1970s, when a group of New York-based Latin musicians began overhauling the classic Cuban big-band arrangements popular since the mambo era of the 1940s and '50s. They set about reworking these songs and rhythms into something tougher and more appropriate to their modern bicultural lifestyles, adding influences from rock, funk and a range of Latin Tropical music. The salsa tag was coined by a Venezuelan radio DJ, so legend has it, and it caught on. Big time.

Tapping the Roots

Like so much Latin music, salsa has dual roots – in the Spanish music of the colonisers and in the African traditions of slave communities. The balance between these influences varies considerably from one territory to another in Latin America and the Caribbean, and salsa reflects that.

On **Puerto Rico**, for example, relatively few slaves were brought in, and the island's music bears a greater Spanish flavour. This is most evident in the high, plaintive singing style of the hill farmers, backed by the *cuatro* and other guitars – a style epitomised by the venerated 1930s and '40s singers like El Canario. The pure, high, nasal voice is still essential for singers from Puerto Rico and the island has been responsible for giving salsa a seemingly endless procession of *salseros* whose plaintive tone recalls the Caribbean's Spanish history.

The influence of Spanish (Andalucian) music also endured on **Cuba**, although accompanied by strong African traditions. The island's dominant style of **son** – salsa's direct ancestor – coalesced the dual ancestry in the African rhythms and the call-and-response relationship of its vocalists, and in the unmistakeably Spanish flavour of the guitar. Son soared to popularity in the 1930s, when the great original *sextetos* and *septetos* were formed, and the songs of that age, timelessly sweet and lyrical, like "Mama Ines", "Suavecito" and "Loma de Belen", have been endlessly updated and revamped in modern salsa recordings.

The son bands were the basis of modern salsa groups. By the late 1940s, the Havana sextets had given way to larger, more powerful bands, with guitars almost entirely replaced by piano – better suited to the scale of the casinos and dance halls – as the core instrument. The immediate forerunners of today's salsa bands were the great Cuban mambo and charanga orchestras of the 1940s and '50s – orchestras like **Aragon**, **Riverside** and those led by trumpeter **Felix Chappotín** and **Arsenio Rodríguez**, who played in Havana to free-spending Americans as well as local audiences.

Meanwhile, over in **New York**, at the mecca of the mambo, the **Palladium Dancehall**, and in **Mexico City**, where Latin players went to work in the buregoning film industry, energetic new musical arrangements were being built around the Cuban model by bands led by the likes of **Perez Prado**, **Machito**, and the Puerto Ricans **Tito Rodríguez** and **Tito Puente**.

This was the era of razor-sharp arrangements, swinging horn sections based on the great swing bands of the day (Kenton, Basie, Miller), and a line-up of formidably inventive percussionists. Accompanying them were a roomful of dancers, riveting acrobatic soloists whose moves were imitated all around the USA. As bandleader Tito Puente put it – "Everyone was an exhibitionist at the Palladium". In the 1940s and 1950s, Latin dance music was the mainstream musical current across the US and Europe, with mambo, chachachá and rumba reigning supreme.

Mambo veteran Tito Puente on timbales

However in the 1960s, Latin music lost the plot in the US as first rock'n'roll, doo-wop, R&B, and then The Beatles and pop music took over the young Anglo market. The Palladium lost its drinks license in 1966 and closed down, and the Cuban crisis suddenly stopped the flow of Cuban musicians and even Cuban sheet music to the US. Latin music in the US, through the 1960s, emerged from its own scene only through occasional youth crazes – such as the tongue-twisting songs known as **boogaloo**, a fusion of soul and mambo, epitomised by Joe Cuba's 1967 hit "Bang! Bang!". Meantime, serious Latin players retreated into jazz and charanga.

Fania Draws Up the Template

The powerhouse for the revival of Latin music and the emergence of salsa in the 1970s was New York's **Fania Records**, with its Manhattan studios under the direction of musician-producer **Johnny Pacheco**.

Pacheco was originally from Dominican Republic and had been playing flute and arranging New York Latin bands since the late-1950s, notably with pianist Charlie Palmieri. Pacheco set up Fania Records in 1964 with an Italian-American lawyer and Cuban music fan, Jerry Masucci, and his earliest signings included a Brooklyn teenager, **Willie Colón**, and a young Puerto Rican singer, **Hector Lavoe**. Their 1967 debut record, *El malo* (Bad Guy), had a new, raw inner-city edge that pointed a direction for the label and its artists.

The Fania team – Pacheco, Puerto Rican bassist **Bobby Valentin**, Jewish-American arranger **Larry Harlow**, and Latin percussion maestro **Louie Ramírez** – put out a stream of records in the late 1960s and early 1970s, taking the old Cuban *son* templates and occasionally introducing classic Puerto Rican numbers, which endeared them to the vast numbers of 'Nuyoricans' and other exiles in the US. In 1971 they created the **Fania All Stars**, playing shows around the city to huge acclaim, while their MC (and cover artist), a Puerto Rican New Yorker called Izzy Sanabria, drove them on, yelling "Salsa!" as

The Sound of Salsa

The basic salsa unit remains much the same as it was in the mambo era, with big bands or **orquestas** divided into horn and rhythm sections, plus piano and bass, which act as a bridge between the two. They are fronted by one or more **soneros** or *salseros* (lead vocalists) while the all-important **coro**, the chorus that answers the sonero's vocal improvisations, is usually sung by band members.

The crucial **percussion section** regulates a complex mesh of rhythms and powers along the music, while the other sections are ranged around it. Of paramount influence on the individual sound of a salsa (or mambo) band is the taste and skill of the **arranger**, who choreographs the sections and gives the band its feel. Salsa sections work with and against each other, in a way that draws on 1940s big-band riffing as much as African call-and-response.

The **sound** of salsa is determined particularly by the balance between the horns and the rhythm section, and by the choice of lead instruments. The latter is affected strongly by fashion: in the 1950s and 1960s, when **charanga** bands were all the rage, their sweet flute-and-violins combination was essential; shortly after came **conjuntos** – trumpet-led groups with a hard, steely edge. The Puerto Rican band **La Sonora Ponceña**, with its original line-up of five trumpets and no saxophones, has consolidated this sound.

In the 1960s, **Eddie Palmieri** sparked a craze for trombones, which continues today in the bands led by **Oscar D'Leon** and the younger, jazz-influenced **Jimmy Bosch**, while in Cuba, **Ritmo Oriental** and **Los Van Van** broke all the rules by pitting three violins (as employed by charanga groups) against three trombones, creating an exquisite rough-tough-sweet effect. The rich, deep tones of a single baritone saxophone, epitomised by **José Alberto**'s band were a new flavouring in the late 1980s, and into the 1990s.

Synthesizers and synthesised percussion came into the story in the 1980s, particularly with the merengue bands (from Dominican Republic), and it was a short step from big band traditional merengue with a synthesizer to 1990s **techno-merengue** groups powered by electronic instruments and samples, aided by a token *guiro* (scraper). **Rubén Blades** had actually broken with big band tradition in the late 1980s, with his sextet, **Seis de Solar**, whose first album, *Buscando America*, featured a synthesizer player performing the horn parts, and a kit drummer. The shock was as great for some salsa purists as when Bob Dylan went electric, but the band's compactness enabled Blades to tour his politicised songs more cheaply and easily, which contributed to his enormous international crossover success.

Willie Colón (on trombone) and band

Fania co-founder Johnny Pacheco (left) with Pete 'Conde' Rodriguez and Alberto Valdes

he introduced the soloists. By 1973 the All Stars were big enough to sell out the Yankee Stadium. Salsa had arrived.

The Fania bandleaders, playing in a host of permutations, went from strength to strength, with Willie Colón, in particular keeping developments moving, introducing **Yomo Toro**'s *cuatro* guitar (from Puerto Rican country music) and adding Brazilian songs to the repertoire. Harlow, meantime, took the revolutionary step of moving to electric piano, further modernising the sound. In 1974, the ultimate Cuban *sonera*, **Celia Cruz**, made her first appearance with the Fania crew, unleashing one of her greatest ever recordings, "Químbara", with its virtuoso rhythmic vocal.

Fania soon had its rivals and copyists in New York, Miami, Puerto Rico, and right across Latin America and the Caribbean, as salsa shaped the whole gamut of Latin music. But the 1970s really belonged to Fania and its roster of artists, who included Willie Colón's new partner, **Rubén Blades**, the Puerto Rican star singers **Héctor Lavoe** and **Cheo Feliciano**, maverick pianist **Eddie Palmieri**, conga master **Ray Barretto**, and the pioneering young bands **Tipica 73** (which spawned **Jose Alberto** and **Alfredo de la Fé**) and **Conjunto Clasico** (the launch pad for singer **Tito Nieves**).

In the 1980s, Fania's star waned, as competition hotted up from two notable labels, TH-Rodven, a Dutch-Venezuelan business, and Ralph Mercado's **RMM**, which became the dominant force in New York. The RMM label has, since then, carried the salsa flag through increasing stages of integration with other American music and has been instrumental in closing the decades-long gap between salsa-Americana and salsa-Cubana.

Romantica and Fusions: the 1980s

The 1970s, in retrospect, was a classic era of 'hard' salsa, with tight rhythms and taut phrasing. In the 1980s a new softer strain appeared, known as **salsa romantica**, or *salsa erotica* when the lyrics were charged up. Latin music, of course, had a long tradition of romantic balladry but the combination of smoochy boleros with upbeat salsa and charanga orchestration was a new one, originated by the Fania producer **Louie Ramírez** with vocalist **José Alberto** on the 1984 bestselling album, *Noches calientes* (Hot Nights).

The romantic style was swiftly imitated, notably by Puerto Rican singers. But the arrangers also had a hand with musical innovations, slowing down

Willie Colón and Rubén Blades

Trombonist and singer **Willie Colón** has been demolishing salsa's clichés ever since he had his first hit, "El Malo", at the age of sixteen: a song he recorded with a lean two-trombone octet that blasted forth the tough sound of teenage Brooklyn's salsa-jazz-bugalú.

Colón was responsible for more innovations in New York's salsa heyday than any other producer. He incorporated Brazilian music and he paid tribute to Puerto Rican styles. His lavish brass arrangements backed the era's greatest singers, including Celia Cruz, the evocative appealing voice of Hector Lavoe, and the provocative poetry of Rubén Blades. As an introduction, the compilation *Exitos de Willie Colón* (Fania) illustrates that breadth and variety and showcases the great vocalists for whom he worked his musical magic.

Colón's potent, late 1970s, socio-political vignettes with Rubén Blades are still best-sellers. Blades became a mouthpiece for oppressed Latin America and Colón's own political contributions are sometimes overlooked, but his songs like "Era Nuclear" and "El General" (from the 1984 album *Criollo*), and "Legal Alien" (from the mid-'90s), are no less significant. And the partnership was hugely successful: their 1978 album *Siembra* was, at the time, the most successful Latin album ever.

What he called his "Latin-Jazzbo" single, "Set Fire to Me", a kind of jazzy house tune with a fiery piano solo from Charlie Palmieri and thunderous timbales solo from Tito Puente, brought Colón unexpected crossover dance chart success in 1986. But every Willie Colón album contains surprises; starting with the rich musical cultures on his Latin American doorstep, he moves ever outwards. He is a skillful magpie who draws in new ideas from all kinds of music and a supreme musician and composer. Regardless of the latest innovation, his trombone is always a solo feature set against his love for the power of the contorting arrangements of a "bone section" which have always been a delight in his songs. Jerky, angular phrases drawn from his 1970s hit with Hector Lavoe "La Murga" are still a Colón

JOHN CLEWLEY

Rubén Blades

trademark some twenty years after he first adapted it from a Panamanian folk song.

The Panama-born **Rubén Blades** who has been called a 'Latin Bruce Springsteen', is one of the few salsa stars to give his music a political edge, addressing the realities of life in Latin America. He ascribes his success to having widened the audience for the music, breaking the stereotypes of most salsa lyrics. "My criticism of salsa is that its songs are stuck physically and mentally in a ghetto. Instead of just looking at the street corner for my subjects, I looked down the neighbouring street, then at the city and the whole world. Suddenly the sales jumped. The middle classes that didn't feel any connection with salsa before were suddenly hearing stories that affected them as part of the city and they started buying the records."

Blades trained in Panama City as a lawyer before moving to New York to pursue his passion for music. After the years with Willie Colón, he set up his own sextet, **Seis de Solar** and released what remains perhaps his best album, *Buscando America* (Searching for America), in 1984. Themes to those songs included the murder of El Salvadorean priest Oscar Romero, and the 'disappeared' victims of Latin American dictatorships. As part of Blades' proselytising mission, the song lyrics were printed on the sleeve in both Spanish and English.

Following excursions into film and two unsuccessful attempts at standing for president of Panama, Blades returned to music in the 1990s, teaming up again with Willie Colón for a tropical album, *Tras la tormenta* (1995) and with Paul Simon in a controversial Broadway musical, *The Capeman* in which he played a Puerto Rican New Yorker, jailed for murder. With a full salsa orchestra, the music was exceptional but for various political reasons, the show was a failure. Undeterred, Blades joined a new Latin rock label based in California and appeared on stage in Miami alongside three Panamanian crossover bands – looking for all the world like their school teacher on an end-of-term concert, but sounding as strong as ever.

the songs, allowing the melody to dominate the rhythm, and making great use of rhythm 'breaks' and chord changes – not hitherto a feature of salsa. The dancing changed, too: slower songs allowed closer, more sensual dancing. So far, so good – salsa needed change. However, all too much of the new romantica was formulaic nonsense, and others were little more than X-rated and often misogynistic *erotica* lyrics. Not that these were all so bad: former Eddie Palmieri singer **Lalo Rodríguez** had the biggest salsa hit of the decade with the catchy "Ven, devórame otra vez" (Come and Devour Me Again).

As the 1980s progressed, salsa became fused with all kinds of influences, notably **Latin rap and hip-hop**, while the mainstream, whether salsa classica

Celia Cruz: Queen of Salsa

They call **Celia Cruz** the Queen of Salsa, the greatest female singer to emerge from Cuba, and a living legend. Her rich contralto voice has thrilled audiences for over half a century, first as the toast of 1950s Havana, then in a series of Mexican-produced films, and more recently in the 1984 movie of Oscar Hijuelos's book, *The Mambo Kings Play Songs of Love*, in which she performed with her regular touring partner Tito Puente – the King of Mambo. As witnessed by this film, and

Celia Cruz

her duet with David Byrne, "Loco de Amor", in the movie, *Something Wild*, she is one of the few Latin stars to have acquired an all-American audience.

Celia left Cuba after the 1959 revolution, on the same plane as her backing band, the popular La Sonora Matancera. Since that date, she has recorded with every Latin artist of note – with the exception of those Cubans who remain based on the island. She is a subtle critic of Castro and a staunch supporter of the US boycott.

The salsa song "La Dicha Mia" (My Luck), written for Cruz by Johnny Pacheco, documents her musical career, with a few wry asides about her singing partners. "I left Cuba and headed for New York, looking for another atmosphere and recorded with the great Tito Puente", she sings. Next comes the great Dominican, Johnny Pacheco ("We caused a sensation"), then collaborations with Willie Colón, Papo Lucca and his Sonora Ponceña, and the singer Pete 'El Conde' Rodrìguez. The chorus chants, "It's the luck of the Great Lady", to which she responds: "I thank God and the saints every day for my luck."

The greatness of Celia Cruz is immediately apparent in her performances. On stage, even over seventy, she still possesses dazzling energy, sensuality and rapport with the audience, chatting and joking with them, dancing throughout a two-hour set, and ad-libbing with extraordinary style and speed. When Johnny Pacheco first worked with Cruz, he was amazed by her reaction to the song "Caramelo", in which she needed to improvise a few lines about fruit: "It was like watching a computer: she listed every tropical fruit you can imagine at a speed I couldn't believe."

RICARDO BETANCOURT/RMM

SALSA

or salsa romantica, hit a rut. The problems were not entirely of their own making, however, for in 1988 recession in the Dominican Republic had led to upwards of half a million Dominicans moving to New York. They brought a passion for **merengue** and more or less took over the city's salsa-oriented Latin clubs.

The man credited with reviving salsa's fortunes at this juncture was pianist and producer **Sergio George**, who joined RMM after a spell working in Colombia with Discos Fuentes producer **Fruko**. He created a new trombone-heavy sound, looking back to mambo roots and melodies. Oddly, his first #1 hit was an album by all-Japanese group **Orquesta de la Luz**, who produced a punchy, word-perfect salsa despite their lead vocalist speaking no Spanish. But further success came, as he devloped an in-house RMM orchestra, with José Alberto, Celia Cruz and Tito Puente, and with two young singers, **Marc Anthony**, **Victor Manuelle** and **La India**, of whom more below.

Timba – Cuba Steps Up

No one, no matter how anti-communist their stance (and stances don't get more anti-communist than those of the Cuban exiles in Miami), would deny that salsa is essentially Cuban music. Even the Cuban state media acknowledge the fact these days, having tactically abandoned their original line that the term was an American imperialist cover-up for poaching their music. In fact, during the 1990s Cuban and American salsa came closer together, with initiatives coming from both directions, in particular from Cuban **timba** – salsa, by any other name, but with an innovative jumped-up rhythm and phat, funky bass.

Timba was developed chiefly by two Cuban bands, **Los Van Van** and **NG La Banda**, growing out of the complex twisting *songo* rhythms pioneered by Los Van Van's Juan Formell in the 1980s. As Cuba became less and less isolated in the 1990s, Cuban bands made regular 'educational' visits to the US, and these gradually turned into fully commercial trips. The salsa that had been brewing on the island was no longer a secret as Cuban musicians such as **Isaac Delgado**, **Juan Carlos Alfonso** (of the group Dan Den) and **Paulito F.G.** revealed the influence of New York and Puerto Rico's smooth arrangements in their songs. In 1998, Isaac Delgado's sublime vocals could be heard on a New York produced album, and he even played an underground club in Miami – the first concert in the city by a Cuban national since Castro took control of the island.

At the same time, Miami's new star of the 1990s was a recent arrival from Cuba – **Albita Rodríguez**, an androgynous guitarist, singer-songwriter and bandleader, whose music was an updated take of the Cuban country style called guajira, with a nod to the classic mambo and showmanship of Beny Moré. She arrived in Miami in 1993, having walked across the Mexican border with her group, after a long period playing in Colombia. Championed by Madonna, Albita recorded a fine album, *Una mujer como yo*, for Emilio and Gloria Estefan's Crescent Moon label. Ironically, it was Grammy-nominated – but pipped by the *Buena Vista Social Club* veterans. Still, the reintegration of the music of the two Cubas was surely underway.

New Moves

Cuba's reappearance on the US Latin/salsa scene is not just a question of its artists getting to play or record in New York, or the revival of the historic rhythms of the *Buena Vista Social Club*. The island's music – and above all the **songo** rhythm that powers timba – has been feeding into cutting edge New York salsa and Latin hip hop. And in reverse, Cuban artists like Paulito F.G and NG La Banda have been catching onto hip hop, and the group Dan Den has been adapting its timba to a more polished sound shaped by New York salsa.

Once again, the major innovative force in the US in all of this is RMM producer **Sergio George**, who became hooked on *songo*. He took the rhythm as a base for his production for a young rap-based trio called **Dark Latin Groove** (DLG), who breathed the fire of *songo* rhythms and the energy of rap and soul into salsa. Their records inspired countless singers who added rap verses

Salsa **singers**, like their son and mambo predecessors, are traditionally expected to be improvisers, ad-libbing during verses and sometimes over the instrumental solos, chatting and scatting to the rhythms, darting in and out with their back-up chorus (usually two or three singers). Reputations used to hang on that skill: the great Cuban soneros **Ignacio Piñero** and **Beny Moré** all developed formidable technique, never missing a beat. And today, to see Celia Cruz racing through the complexities of a song is a startling experience.

In the 1980s, with the formulaic salsa romantica, improvisation ceased to be desirable, until a new wave of soneros, particularly **José Alberto** and the Colombian **Joe Arroyo**, spurned a reliance on sexually explicit lyrics as a route to success, and returned to free form. Sadly, the new wave of singers in the 1990s, with their rock star need to abandon the back-up chorus and front the band alone also frequently did away with the improvisations and the ad-libbed montuno slot.

Most salsa songs are pure escapism, with the same function as the soap operas that fill Latin American TV channels, musing on love and sex, dance and romance, and scornful of commenting on the awful realities of everyday life. However, a few salseros make social or even political comment. The most notable is lawyer, performer, actor and movie star, **Rubén Blades** (see p.492), who for three decades has been a spokesperson for North American Hispanics, and in 1994 and 1998 contested elections for president of Panama. Blades' parables and allegories resist the nationalism that pervades salsa and divides its audiences. On stage he reinforces his songs with short speeches, telling his audiences, "We are all Americans – Latin Americans". Almost uniquely, he sees his audience as stretching beyond the traditional Latin market and has actively sought crossovers with American and British rock musicians. In the 1980s, for example, he recorded an album called *Nothing but the Truth*, featuring songs in English by Lou Reed, Elvis Costello and Sting.

A handful of other songwriters, including Willie Colón (who also translates his lyrics into English on the sleeves), fellow Panamanian **Omar Alfanno**, Dominican salsero **Cuco Valoy**, Colombian singer Joe Arroyo, and veteran Puerto Rican legend, **Tito Curet Alonso**, also deal with issues. In Cuba, **Los Van Van**'s songs have functioned like samizdats for decades, airing local issues which were otherwise whispered about and passing comments in lyrics which became catchphrases.

into their salsa songs, and others who went all the way into salsa-hip-hop fusions.

Scores of other young Latinos, meantime, reared in the US and Puerto Rico on rap and house music, MTV and reggae, have jumped in behind DLG, creating new dance-mutations. Merengue was the most adaptable to the electronic pulses, and hybrids like **mereng-house**, **salsa-merengue** accompanied Latin rap into the charts, alongside a newly toughened **salsa gorda** (fat salsa). Groups like the Dominican Republic's **Los Illegales** included rap and electronic beats in their salsa and merengue tracks as naturally as they dropped in English catchphrases.

As the zero-decade opens, the names to watch in salsa – as distinct from the **Ricky Martin** brand of salsified pop – are the trio of RMM/Sergio George artists, Victor Manuelle, Marc Anthony Muñiz and Linda 'La India' Caballero. **Victor Manuelle** is simply the most talented Puerto Rican singer of his generation, while **La India** is charting a course to diva-hood and is as much at home producing Latin hip hop or soul-boogaoo as salsa. **Marc Anthony**, in similar vein, is carving out a new path for salsa that takes rock as a given influence and transmutes it into a string of hits. He has a stunning, soulful voice, records both in Spanish and English, and has a burgeoning movie career.

Reassuringly, the old guard are still playing and recording, too. Latin music doesn't throw away

MarcAnthony

SALSA

its star musicians like the US, and with Buena Vista, veterans are right in fashion. The Cuban-born but long-term Miami-resident bassist and composer **Cachao** is still running a band in his eighties, and plenty of old time mambo/salsa players are active in the US jazz and Latin jazz scene. Salsa classica remains a force.

Salsa Stations

Leaving aside Brazil – whose traditions are very much its own – virtually every major Latin and North American city has its own individual salsa scene, as do the European cities with significant Latin communities. Artists around these far-flung salsa stations often add traditional instruments and musical forms to the core rhythms, creating a local sabor or flavour. The Colombian Joe Arroyo, for example, will drop in a winding clarinet tune – a memory jolt to the traditional lead instrument of the cumbia. Following is a round-up of the most interesting scenes, appearing from A–Z: Colombia, Cuba, Miami, New York, Puerto Rico and Venezuela.

Salsa's celebrities have the status in Latin America of football players in England or the US, and salsa lyrics unite exiles and generations. They also contain subtle clues to identity. Targeting the older exiled Cubans, the regal Celia Cruz goes straight to the heart in songs like the epic "Bemba Colo-ra" (thick red lips), which closes all her shows, singing yearningly of beauty spots in the Cuban countryside. For Colombians in Miami, New York or London, a song like Grupo Niche's "Cali Pachanguero" (about a party-animal from Cali) will always bring the house down. For Puerto Ricans everywhere, the mention of the word 'Borinquen' (the Indian name for the island) will be greeted with shouts, cheers and flag-waving. Similarly for the Dominican crowd, the buzz word 'Quisqueya' is liberally dropped into songs.

One unifying theme in salsa throughout the region is its reference to **Afro-Catholic religions**. Afro-Cuban Santería (see p.387) has equivalents throughout Latin America, some involving the same saints and deities and others having local variations. When the Cuban singers Celina González and Celia Cruz sing to Santa Barbara, they are also hailing the deity Changó, god of thunder, fire and fighting, whose red and white colours are highly favoured in González's outfits. Even though Cruz isn't a *santera* herself, she grew up around the religion and in performance often drops her voice even lower and cries "Yemaya", invoking the goddess of the seas and maternal love, a deity with special significance for island and coastal people. When she swoops and turns on stage, waving a blue and white scarf (Yemaya's colours), everyone knows she is dancing with the saints. Such links are unspoken but acknowledged by most of the people watching, even if only through the blue and white or red and white bracelet on their wrist.

JAK KILBY

Alfredo de la Fe (with violin) and group

Joe Arroyo

Colombia's music scene is exceptionally rich, but one artist shines above all others – the singer, composer and bandleader **Alvaro José Arroyo Gonzalez**, the country's most popular singer and most exalted salsa export. Colombian salsa is flavoured heavily by *cumbia*, the national music (see p.372), as well as Cuban *son*, and to this mix Joe Arroyo has welded a myriad Caribbean influences: the rocking rhythms of Haitian *compas*, the dazzling Dominican *merengue*, splashes of reggae and Trinidadian *soca*. The emergent style is unique – as its name, *Joe-son*, infers – and influenced salsa everywhere in the 1980s and '90s. Miraculously, although it draws on just about every style going, and appeals to audiences across Latin America and the Caribbean, it does not have a hint of homogenisation.

Arroyo started singing professionally at the age of eight, in a strip joint in the port of Cartagena, and

Colombian legend Joe Arroyo

joined the illustrious band of **Fruko y sus Tesos** at sixteen. His distinctively abrasive tenor voice, darting and leaping around the rhythms and melodies, has been part of Colombia's soundscape ever since.

He founded his own group, **La Verdad** (The Truth), in 1981, with whom he sings songs of praise to his country and its cities ("En Baranquilla me quedo" – I'm sticking around Baranquilla) and of historical events that unite the people. The band had their first international break a couple of years later at the New York Labor Day Fiesta, and from there they went from strength to strength – despite a drugs overdose that nearly killed Arroyo in the early 1980s.

These days, La Verdad's live stage show, with their split-second precision playing, and Arroyo's magnetic voice and inimitable dancing style, remains one of the most exhilarating in all Latin music.

Colombia

Salsa has been immensely popular in Colombia since the 1970s. As in many other Latin American countries the local bands began by copying what they heard on the radio and records, but very soon started to incorporate elements of local music. The national **cumbia** rhythm was orchestrated to fit the salsa model, and many bands also worked with the accordion-led **vallenato** sound, and other local dance rhythms from the Caribbean coast.

One of the earliest Colombian groups to carry out such experiments was **Peregoyo y su Combo Vacano**, who had begun in the 1960s playing cumbia mixed with Cuban *son*. However, it was **Joe Arroyo** and his band **La Verdad** (see box) that really put Colombian salsa on the international map. Arroyo is a true salsa superstar and one who ranges further than most in his 'tropical', drawing on merengue, zouk and calypso which pour from the islands (Trinidad, Martinique) into the coastal Colombian towns where he lives. **Clan Caribe**, too, have had massive success

throughout the continent, adding elements of soca and reggae to the mix.

Joe Arroyo got his break working with the record label **Discos Fuentes** (for more on which, see p.379) whose king is the bassplayer, singer, composer and producer Ernesto Estrada, better known as **Fruko**. Fruko is himself a key player on the Colombian salsa scene, with his long-established band **Los Tesos**, but it is as an arranger that he is best known, consistently producing the catchiest and freshest in tropical music for a set of long-lasting bands, including the **Latin Brothers**, **La Sonora Dinamita**, and **Los Nemus del Pacifico**. He has been called, aptly, the 'Quincy Jones of Latin music'.

Other big names in Colombian salsa include Diego and Jaime Galé and their band **Grupo Galé**, from Medellin, and the Cuban-born violinist **Alfredo de la Fé**, who lived in the same town for several years. There are also a clutch of bands based in the old sugar town of Cali, which has an independent recording and club scene. Cali's progeny include **Orquesta Guayacan** and the long-established **Grupo Niche**, who both specialise in the most seductively catchy tunes.

While bands like La Sonora Dinamita stayed loyal to the compulsive 2/4 beat of the cumbia, another strand developed around the vallenato line. What began as a country folk dance in the towns and villages dotted along the wide river plains of the northeast, has become a national passion. Accordionists such as **Lizandro Meza** and **Alfredo Gutierrez** are now national heroes, and a new generation – sons of those men – have brought teenaged audiences to **vallenato-salsa**.

In 1996, a young TV soap star, **Carlos Vives** put together a band and landed straight in the charts with a modernised, salsified, rock-influenced form of vallenato. His records launched a brief craze for vallenato which was picked up in Miami by **Gloria Estefan** (in one of her most musically successful albums, *Abriendo Puertas*) and by **Albita** (*Una mujer como yo*). Even Julio Iglesias inserted a couple of accordion songs into his repertoire.

Vives's band has also gone out on its own as **Bloque**, playing an **rock-salsa** fusion, and has recorded for David Byrne's Luaka Bop label.

Cuba

In **Cuba**, the cauldron of salsa, the years after the revolution were spent re-evaluating and rebuilding the music scene. Many bands, particularly **Irakere**, **Orquesta Reve** and **Los Van Van** spun heavily on the Afro-Cuban traditions in creating a distinctive new sound, and with the island effectively sealed off from the world by the US boycott, it was left to develop in a virtual musical vacuum until Castro's 1981 expulsion of 125,000 Cubans to the US. This, the so-called Mariel Exodus, resulted in the arrival in New York of a number of musicians including the magnificent conga player **Daniel Ponce**. Along with defectors such as sax player **Paquito D'Rivera** and trumpeter **Arturo Sandoval** (the co-founders of new Cuban jazz group Irakere), they injected a crucial new vitality into Latin jazz and salsa, and introduced for the first time the **timba** and **songo** rhythms which had been brewing in post-revolutionary Cuba.

By the 1990s, **Cuban influences** had begun to flood into salsa again with increased access via Europe's music festivals and touring schedules for the bands. Many US and Puerto Rican artists covered the hits of Cuban singers – Willie Chirino in Miami and La Sonora Ponceña and Roberto Roena in Puerto Rico all had hits with tunes written by Los Van Van and **Son 14**.

On the other side of the divide, Cuban bands like **Paulito F.G.** and **Dan Den** adopted many ideas from salsa, especially its honey-smooth orchestrations. The singer **Isaac Delgado** even managed to join Ralph Mercado's RMM label and performed in Madison Square Gardens on the same bill as Celia Cruz – although she declined to speak or sing with him.

The late 1990s have seen an explosion of Cuban groups, heavily infuenced by what they see on MTV and on the CDs which arrive via family in the US. **Rap** and **rock** began to infiltrate the salsa, and the groups **Bamboleo** (whose stunningly beautiful members have shaven heads and a very personal rap-inspired style) and David Calzado's **Charanga Habanera** both fell for a rehash of 1950s-style a cappella harmony vocals and fast-chanted Spanish raps in amongst the **songo-salsa**. With the new accessibility, Cuba's musical future is more unpredictable than any other part of Latin America.

Miami

Miami sits like a lighthouse, just ninety miles from Cuba, radiating and receiving music from the Caribbean and Latin America. It is a rich city, where sponsorship still pays, music is the greatest lure, and summer festivals and street parties fill the weekends with music. America's biggest street party plugs Little Havana's main street, Calle Ocho, every March as the Cuban Carnival draws over a million people to fifty stages hosting the best music in Latin America.

Miami was known as Old Cubans' Town until the early 1980s, when the drugs trade brought in the first wave of **Colombians**, and a double-edged economic miracle transformed the city. The Cuban Mariel Exodus in 1981 changed the population again, while subsequent events in Central America brought in substantial numbers of Nicaraguans and Salvadoreans. There are scatterings of Puerto Ricans and Dominicans, too, each maintaining their own separate, exile-music scene.

Miami is home to a league of Cuban legends, whose youthful, glamorous images you'll find on record sleeves in the nostalgia stores of Little Havana, and whose deep-lined faces pop up at special nights in the city's hotels and nightclubs, and at outdoor gigs. The ubiquitous Cuban singer **Roberto Torres**, who created his own Cuban-Colombian hybrid, **charanga-vallenata**, in the 1980s, is a local hero, singing crisp and clear behind radio ads, opening shows in the hotel nightclubs, and running the **Guajiro label,** dedicated to keeping the pre-revolution tradition alive, and local musicians in work. If you visit, try to track down concerts by the Celia Cruz contemporaries, **La India de Oriente**, **Charanga de la 4** or any gig featuring the leading Latin flautist, virtuoso dynamo, **Nestor Torres**.

Miami's Cuban 40-somethings who arrived in the city as children, have opted for styles at all positions along the Latin music spectrum. They include the original Latin pop pioneer, **Miami Sound Machine**'s **Emilio Estefan**, **Joe Galdo** (ex-MSM drummer and now a dance music producer with a heavy Latin bias at Chris Blackwell's South Beach Studios), **Carlos Oliva** (of Los Sobrinos del Juez)

who pioneered salsa-rock in the 1970s, **Willie Chirino**, the salsa bass player who dreamed of being a member of the Beatles and who is a backbone member of the city's salsa scene, and **Hansel y Raul**, two harmony singers with a preference for the sweetened charanga style.

This Beatles-and-salsa generation created what is known as the **Miami Sound**, the variable blend of salsa with rock and pop. Chirino favours a vibrant percussion section, a salsa-Caribbean base and rock fantasies, while **Emilio and Gloria Estefan** – the most successful Latin artists in mainstream American – have trawled through many types of Latin and Spanish music during their successful career. They hit the salsa groove head on with 1970s hits "Doctor Beat" and "Conga" which took them into Europe's clubs, while Gloria's 1990s albums *Mi Tierra* (son) and *Abriendo Puertas* (merengue) took her into the salsa/tropical music charts, as did her millennial release, Alma Caribeña (Caribbean Soul), a fusion of Dominican bachatas, Cuban son and boleros, with a very classy, big-band production. None of these records sold as much as her English-language rock albums, though she sounds far more at ease with her own language and rhythms and they stand proudly in amongst conventional salsa recordings.

Husband Emilio meanwhile runs his own **Crescent Moon** label for Sony, to record local Miami Latin artists. His successes include the Cuban exile diva **Albita**, who performs every weekend to a passionate home crowd and a handful of tourists at *YUCA's* (Young, Upward Cuban Americans) club. Emilio Estefan also paid homage to the veteran mambo bass player **Cachao**, in a couple of tremendous albums co-produced with film actor Andy Garcia.

New York

New York is central to the story of salsa and its developments are tracked in the main article, preceding. What follows is a guide to what and who you can hear in the city, and where. The neighbourhoods divide fairly neatly into nationalities, each with

PAUL BERGEN/REDFERNS

Miami voice, Gloria Estefan

SALSA

their own musical identities, and if you do some homework, checking the Friday edition of *El Diário* or the music magazine *NY Latino*, you will be directed to some fabulous mixed salsa bills in the night-clubs, and occasional all-star extravaganzas at the stadiums. Summer is the peak time for street parties and salsa concerts in Central Park and particulary at Orchard Beach in the Bronx.

High up in Manhattan, **Washington Heights** is about 80-percent Dominican. The heavy merengue (and ubiquitous meren-house) beat rumbles through clubs where the island's top bands play alongside New York's even more frenetic local outfits – like **Victor Roque's band** and **The New York Band** – and couples blur in a spin, their hips matching the impossibly fast scraped 2/4 pulse of the metal grater-like guiro, essential for hissing out the propulsive rhythm or the synthesised beats. On the streets, shockwaves radiate from massive speakers in the back of cruising cars, leaving saxophone jags and guiro scratches in their wake.

Over in Queens, the flavour switches: the **Jackson Heights** neighbourhood is overwhelmingly Colombian, known as 'Little Medellin'. Inside clubs like *La Discotueqa*, *Illusiones* or *Juan Pachanga*, Afro-Cuban salsa is overshadowed by the light, bright cumbias and accordion-led vallenatos, and couples kick their heels and dance facing each other with arms outstretched.

In the mirrored glitz of *Latin Quarter* on 96th Street and Broadway, just a few blocks from **Spanish Harlem**, the crowd is predominantly rooted in **Puerto Rico**, but the bands represent the whole spectrum, usually tied to the RMM label, as the club is owned by label boss Ralph Mercado. Puerto Rican bands El Gran Combo, Andy Montanez, Gilberto Santarosa and Sonora Ponceña all frequently jet in; José 'El Canario' Alberto is a regular; merengue acts also play there. It is a perfect opportunity to see the different dance styles matching the music – the restrained and subtly sexy technique of the older Puerto Rican crowd compared to the twirling younger dancers.

Downtown, Americans and Latins mingle at *SOB's*, one of the most loyal enterprises for promoting salsa outside of the community. The bills are always interesting, perfect ways to catch up with some of the top new bands, as well as offering themed nights and Latin jazz. The magnificent salsa-jazz pianist Eddie Palmieri is a regular – his knack for discovering the new young talent on trips to Puerto Rico continues to reinvigorate his band, and guarantees a thunderous set, almost too musically riveting to dance to.

Latin-Jazz was a growing feature through the 1990s, running a parallel and overlapping story with salsa. New York has been its capital ever since Mario Bauza and Machito coined the concept of Afro-Cuban Jazz and Tito Puente picked up the baton. Today's musicians have mostly trained in classical music and salsa. Mainstream jazz has been transformed by the presence of the new breed of rhythm-based players, particularly the pianists **Hilton Ruiz**, **Michel Camilo**, **Chucho Valdes**, **Gonzalo Rubalcaba** and the saxophonist **David Sanchez**, who have transformed the style with their rhythmic often danceable creations. **Paquito D'Rivera**, formerly of Cuba's big band Irakere, and now a New Jersey-ite, pops up in many settings around the city. His presence since the early 1980s has invigorated the Latin jazz scene which is centred in the city.

The **Lower East Side** has had a tradition of radical Puerto Rican arts and music, ever since the formation of the *New Rican Poets Café* in the 1960s. Leave off the spandex and high heels for a visit to this Latin bohemia where poets, politicians and Latin-jazz types jam with each other in open-ended *descarga* sessions. From the NuYorican Poets came the concept of **NuYorican Soul** – a loose pool of young singers, musicians and poets who worked in Latin, jazz and soul music, and grew up performing rap and hip-hop and new jazz. Their albums *Nu Yorica 2* and *Nuyorican Soul* both reveal the non-commercial, non-salsa face of the Latin sound, and include the top female singer India as well as soul diva Jocelyn Brown, jazz vibes player Roy Ayers, and guitar guru George Benson alongside some of the greatest innovators in Latin jazz (Tito Puente, Hilton Ruiz, Dave Valentin, David Sanchez, Steve Turre).

Finally, the annual **Labor Day Salsa Fiesta** is a summer stadium jamboree and a perfect way to catch up with the top Latin and tropical acts. The tradition was founded by Fania records in the 1980s, when it showcased their mighty rosta; today it is an RMM night, when the full range of salsa, rap, tropical, jazz, and ballad singers are paraded to perform in front of the **RMM Orchestra**. Differences in nationality, age and musical styles are forgotten for a night as 20,000 New York Latinos sing and dance and edge their way to delirium.

Puerto Rico

Puerto Ricans were integral to salsa's development and the island and New York communities have between them produced a roll-call of great salseros. The list includes **Daniel Santos**, **Ismael Rivera**,

Cheo Feliciano, Andy Montanez, Gilberto Santa Rosa, the albino Cano Estremera, *salsa-erotica* pioneer Eddie Santiago, Frankie Ruiz and Marvin Santiago.

The island's home-based salsa has a characteristically smooth, sweet sound, with polished arrangements and languorous pace. It is less syncopated and African than the Cuban variety, and danced in a glide rather than in the angular, funky Cuban style. The local scene has been dominated by two great bands for over thirty years: El Gran Combo and La Sonora Ponceña. Their longevity has created an unrivalled cohesion and a repertoire of songs that every islander can recite. Both are driven from the keyboards, El Gran Combo by Rafael Ithier, whose style is florid and bright, and Sonora Ponceña's four-trumpet line-up by the jazz-influenced maestro, Papo Lucca.

A visit to the Puerto Rican capital, San Juan, can be musically disappointing: there is little club scene to speak of and the hotels tend to provide everything else but salsa, from country to rock. But visit the island in July, when every sizeable town celebrates its Saint's Day, and you can take in a spree of *fiestas patronales*, with all-night dancing and music provided by the island's great and small salsa bands on stages in every town square.

Venezuela

For Venezuela, salsa is almost a national music, and in its capital, Caracas, a city in a bowl between mountains, a city where cars never stop, horns puncture the hazy air and salsa explodes from every street corner. Venezuela's proximity to Brazil has resulted in a strong samba and bossa nova influence, evident in the smooth, sweet, apparently effortless sound of bands like Daiquiri. There are some very long-established bands, too, such as Billo y su Caracas Boys and Los Melodicos, both of which seem to get ever better with age, and have proved launching pads for most of the leading singers, like the hugely popular José Luís Rodríguez, aka El Puma.

In global terms, the big name, of course, is Oscar D'Leon, these days to be seen as often in New York or Miami as in his home country. His brand of salsa is in fact rooted in Cuban rather than Venezuelan sounds, and he is heavily influenced by the Cuban swing bands with their horn phrasing and son-rhythm piano solos. His singing, too, which leaps from croon to falsetto, owes much to the Cubans, and, above all, his idol Beny Moré. He maintains a spectacular 19-piece orchestra, a showcase for incredibly tight musicianship, while

he dances, sings and duets with his teenage sons, sometimes lugging his trademark white baby-upright bass across stage. This is one of the most exciting shows in salsa today.

Other Venezuelan bands, such as Nelson Pueblo and Un Solo Pueblo, play salsa mixed in with *llanera* – the country's national music (for more on which, see p.624).

discography

A salsa discography could fill this whole book, so the selections below are much more selective than usual. There are further recommendations (including different, more 'local' discs by the same artists) in the individual discographies for Colombia, Cuba, Puerto Rico and Venezuela. Those disographies also include recommendations of salsa's precursors (Cuban son, mambo, etc) and relations (Dominican merengue, Colombian cumbia, Puerto Rican plena, etc).

Compilations

🎵 **Combinacion Perfecta** (RMM, US).

The 1993 launch debut of new young stars La India and Marc Anthony with the 'Senior Voices' of the RMM label, including Celia Cruz, José Alberto, Cheo Feliciano and Pete 'El Conde' Rodriguez – a classic batch of New York salsa hits.

 Demasiado Caliente – Hot! (Coco, US).

Top-grade 1960s Latin jazz in all its permutations: Machito and Mario Bauzá, founders of Afro-Cuban jazz; pianists Eddie and Charlie Palmieri; bomba-jazz from Puerto Rico's Cortijo; and Tito Puente in his prime.

 Mambo Mania: The Kings and Queens of Mambo (Rhino, US).

Want to try one mambo disc to explore the roots of salsa? This will do nicely, featuring tracks from Celia Cruz with her Cuban band La Sonora Matancera, Pérez Prado, Beny Moré, Tito Puente, Machito – all the suspects, in fact, and even Desi Arnaz (Mr Lucille Ball) for good measure. Once you're hooked, check the Cuba discography for more.

 ¡Oye Listen! (GlobeStyle, UK).

An irresistible collection of songs by island- and American-based Cubans, Colombians and Panamanians: salsa with splashes of son, cumbia, mambo and rumba.

🎵 **Revolucion En La Casa** (Nascente, UK).

This high-energy 'Essential Latin Hose Collection' features New York and Miami Cubans, Dominicans and Puerto Ricans from the salsa-house and meren-house scenes. Stirring stuff that shows where salsa went in the late 1990s.

🎵 **The Rough Guide to Salsa Dance** (World Music Network, UK).

This is a far more compelling selection than the (confusingly titled) *Rough Guide to Salsa* on the same label. Treats in store include José Alberto El Canario, Celia Cruz, La Sonora Ponceña, Occar D'Leon, Charlie Palmieri and Willie Colón. And there's even a creditable slab of salsa from the Afro-Cuban All Stars.

Salsa Moderna (Nascente, UK).

A 1998 album of London DJ John Armstrong selections from the *salsa romantica* riches of Miami-based MP records. It includes a good selection of new voices, like Mimi Ibarra, Maelo and Conjunto Chaney, alongside more familiar names such as Tito Gomez and Willie Rosario.

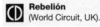 **Viva Salsa!**
(Fania, US; Charly, UK).

A four-CD anthology featuring the Fania team – lots of Ray Barretto and Johnny Pacheco – along with a whole disc of Tito Puente. Also includes a booklet on the label's history.

Artists

Africando

The Africando project was conceived when Malian flautist Boncana Maiga, a Malian flautist who toured with Fania All Stars in the early 1980s, convinced the leading Senegalese producer Ibrahim Sylla to record an album of salsa classics with some of Senegal's top singers and a Latin rhythm section. After all, West African popular music had developed from the same 1940s and '50s Cuban roots. There have been four albums to date, the first three featuring the late, great Papa Seck.

🎧 **Africando** (Stern's, UK).

The four *Africando* CDs change as they broaden the terrain and bring more guests on board, but underlying each one is a rhythm base of 1940s and '50s Afro-Cuban music topped with the soaring vocals from the plains of West Africa. This first disc, fresh and entirely original, was perhaps the best.

José Alberto 'El Canario'

Dominican Republic singer José Alberto chose the Cuban route into music rather than merengue and emerged from the 1970s charanga, Tipica 73, to settle into leading his own band. Since the late 1980s his trademark of slick and polished salsa romantica and driving dance music has produced a string of hit albums for the RMM label. His role as the Cuban musician, Casanova, in the movie The Mambo Kings prompted a sophisticated set of thematic videos to accompany the hits.

Back to the Mambo: Tribute to Machito (RMM, US).

This collection of songs to (and some by) the great Latin jazz pioneer and dance-floor mover Machito features some tasty piano solos from producer Isidro Infante and breathless parade of swinging horns. El Canario's intitially gimmicky whistling flute imitations are now part of his live act, and display an awesome technique and sense of rhythm, in the duet here with 'real' flautist Dave Valentin. A bonus feature is Tito Puente's cracking percussion.

Albita

It clearly does a career no harm when you get invited to play at Madonna's birthday party, and you are introduced with the words 'If I come back to this world, I want to come back as Albita'. Still, the Cuban Albita Rodríguez and her band had played their dues, working for three years in Colombia before walking across the Mexican border to the US. Settled in Miami, they play a salsa-fied version of Cuban country music, guajiro.

🎧 **No se parece a nada** (Crescent Moon, US).

This was Albita's US debut and the Estefans pulled out all the stops, enlisting Cachao Lopez on bass and Robert Blades (Rubén's brother) on several of the arrangements. It's a deeply seductive set, as was its Grammy-nominated follow-up, 🎧 **Una mujer como yo** (Crescent Moon, US).

Adalberto Alvarez

Alvarez was the lead singer with Cuban band Son 14, who contributed to the creation of the island's modern conversion of the Afro-Cuban son. He is one of Cuba's hottest current properties, with a highly commerical sound.

🎧 **La Salsa Caliente** (Sonido/Vogue, France).

These songs still make the odd nod to son and go down a storm on his regular festival tours.

Marc Anthony

Salsa's heart throb of the moment, Marc Anthony could just be the man to break down the remaining barriers between the music of the Americas, a process that Ricky Martin has done such a good job in getting underway. Like his female equivalent, La India, he is a graduate of New York's Latin hip-hop scene who has turned back to his roots. He sang alongside Rubén Blades in the Paul Simon musical The Capeman in 1997.

Contra la Corriente (RMM, US).

Anthony brings to the salsa scene bilingual salsa rap and ballads, a cool, preppy fashion mag image, and sharp RMM orchestra to suit audiences everywhere.

Joe Arroyo y La Verdad

Arroyo is a Colombian individualist whose instantly recognisable, often strangely pitched voice has been one of the leading forces of Colombian salsa since his early days as lead singer with Fruko y sus Tesos (see p.504). He is a pioneer of the 'Tropical' sound which draws the music of the surrounding Caribbean into the salsa format.

Rebelión (World Circuit, UK).

Rebelión is a compilation showcasing Arroyo's flawless arrangements, impassioned singing, and infectious fusion of styles and idioms. It's a perfect introduction. If you want more

SALSA

(and you will), move on to his 1991 album **Fire in My Mind** (Mango, UK) which features some wonderful Afro-Caribbean tracks.

Rubén Blades

Salsa's most articulate and politically committed artist, Blades (born Panama, 1948) made his mark through the 1970s partnership with the trombonist Willie Colón. As a solo artist, with his small 'rock combo' Seis del Solar, his songs became anthems all over Latin America. His 1997/8 performance in Paul Simon's The Capeman musical was a commercial disaster and a musical triumph.

 Buscando America (Electra, US).

Blades' wonderfully accomplished and eclectic 'salsa concept album' draws on rock, reggae and doowop – and gets away with it.

WITH WILLIE COLÓN

Siembra (Fania, US).

A stunningly original collection of songs by Blades and Colón, this 1978 album was Latin music's best-seller for nearly twenty years. Blades' stirring poetry and persuasive singing with the solid Fania rhythm and horns behind them endeared him to all of Latin America.

 Tras la tormenta (Sony Tropical, US).

The powerful partnership between Colón and Blades was rekindled on this 1995 outing, exploring a range of tropical, pan-Caribbean sounds with a heavy nod to soca. Includes the hit tune "Talento de television".

Cachao

Cachao (Israel Lopez) was born in Havana in 1918 and played bass in the group Arcaño y Sus Maravillas, helping to develop mambo. He moved to New York in the 1950s and worked with just about everybody, including Tito Rodríguez and the Palmieri brothers before heading south to settle in Miami. He has played on literally hundreds of sessions, and is, simply, a virtuoso.

Master Sessions Vol. 1 and **Vol. 2** (Crescent Moon, US).

Cachao at last got to do a solo album – and a film, too – at the ripe old age of 76. The result is enchanting, as Cachao rolls out a masterclass in improvised Afro-Cuban rhythms. The sidemen are pretty good, too – Paquito D'Rivera, Jimmy Bosch and the great mambo trumpeter Chocolaté Armenteros.

Willie Chirino

Miami's favourite salsa rocker and bass player, Chirino always favoured black jeans and leathers when all around him wore pastel suits. His songs represent that strand of Miami Sound which hugged the coast of Cuba more closely than the Estefan model.

 Amandote (CBS, US).

Chirino's salsa is tropically flavoured with several splashes of Beatles. Guest saxophonist Paquito D'Rivera toughens one track while Chirino's Cuban drum corps keeps the ancestral flame alight.

Willie Colón

New York salsa's original bad boy from the late-1960s Fania stable has matured into one of Latin music's most significant composers and performers. His infinitely catholic repertoire never stayed locked into the old Cuban format and every record presents new surprises.

 Grandes Exitos (Fania, US).

Colón's trombone passion infuses every track on this fine selection of his eclectic repertoire, including songs with Celia Cruz and, in particular, showcasing his original lead singer and fellow bad boy, Hector Lavoe.

Celia Cruz

Salsa's undisputed queen, Celia Cruz has been in demand throughout a half century of transformations of the Cuban son. She began with La Sonora Matancera, with whom she left Cuba for the US after Castro took power, and in the US has sung for several decades in bands led by Tito Puente, as well as with Johnny Pacheco's Fania line-ups. She never misses a beat.

The Best of Celia Cruz (Charly, UK).

As good a Greatest Hits collection as any (and there are lots of Cruz compilations), including the sublime "Cucala" and, of course, the extended, hypnotic groove of "Bemba Colorá".

 Duets (RMM, US).

This set of 1997 tribute duets sees Cruz alongside the Miami-Cuban salsa-rocker Willie Chirino, her sometime producer and raspy-voiced Willie Colón, and the youthful challenger of the crown, La India, as well as her perfect musical partner and band leader, Tito Puente.

Oscar D'Leon

D'Leon comes from Venezuela but was born with a Cuban soul. His career is built on adaptation of Cuban son – in some cases jazzed up and jumpy with a recognisably Colombian tropical flavour, in others closer to the model set by his lifelong idol, the Cuban giant, Bene Moré.

 El Sonero del Mundo (RMM, US).

Straightahead, irresistibly danceable New York salsa led by D'Leon's unmistakably rich voice, joined on the hit duet, "Hasme el Amor" by new salsa-pop icon, La India.

DLG

Huey, James and Fragrancia – Dark Latin Groove – the three coolest dudes in Latin New York – transformed salsa in only three albums and then split up. Their brilliance is largely due to their mentor and producer Sergio George's revolutionary productions.

 Swing On
(Sir George/Sony Tropical, US).

The guest line-up of some of salsa's leading soloists proves how seriously DLG are taken. The Dominican heavyweight salsero, Cuco Valoy, drops a wonderfully dramatic falsetto around the trio's reggaefied raps in a marvellous reworking of his hit "Juliana"; merengues and salsa are interrupted by Spanish raps and English lyrics but never interrupt the salsa beat, the *phat* Cuban bassline ... or the dark Latin grooves.

Alfredo de la Fé

In the 1970s, as a young Cuban violin virtuoso, Alfredo de la Fé provided some of the lead lines in the classic New York fiddle-led conjunto, Tipica 73. Something of a global traveller since the 1980s, he has experimented voraciously with the classic Cuban charanga model and is an avid pioneer of electronic effects.

¡Salsa! (Discos Fuentes, Colombia; Mango, UK).

A collection of updated charanga made in Medellin, featuring a wealth of long, stirring, rhythmic solos on De La Fé's customised, computerised five-string violin.

Fania All Stars

The Fania label basically created salsa, from its core Cuban and Latin ingredients, under the direction of Johnny Pacheco and a team of producer-arrangers including Larry Harlow, Louie Ramirez, Luis 'Perico' Ortiz, and Willie Colón. In the 1970s just about everyone of significance in the salsa world passed through their studios and, although eclipsed in the 1980s by RMM and others, their legacy is unrivalled. Many of their classic albums – from Celia Cruz, Rubén Blades, Ray Barretto, Eddie Palmieri and others – have appeared on the Charly label, while the magical era is vividly recreated in the video Celia Cruz and the Fania All Stars Live in Kinshasa, Zaire (BMG, 1974), which features every illustrious Fania soloist performing to a rapturous African crowd.

FANIA ALL STARS

 Live at Yankee Stadium Vols I and **II**
(Fania, US).

Classic numbers and the greatest names in 1970s New York salsa. The Fania All Star concerts included *cuatro* guitarist Yomo Toro, Latin jazz legends Mongo Santamaria and Ray Barretto and Cameroonian saxophonist Manu Dibango.

VARIOUS ARTISTS

Tributo a Roberto Clemente (RykoLatino, UK).

This 1999 tribute to the Puerto Rican baseball legend assembled a huge superstar line-up drawn from the hard core of Fania's early line-ups, under the leadership of Larry Harlow. Star Puerto Rican singer Andy Montanez also put in a winning performance.

Fruko y sus Tesos

Bass-player Fruko's reputation in Colombian music is unparalleled: for nearly four decades he has produced a string of hits from the leading bands working the Medellin studios of Discos Fuentes.

The Godfather of Salsa
(Discos Fuentes, Columbia; Mango, UK).

Here with his own band Los Tesos, Fruko stays close to the Cuban son style as his basis, and works outwards from there. Closer to the North-American sound than Joe Arroyo's music. Good stuff all the same.

El Gran Combo

Originally a breakaway group from Rafael Cortijo's Combo, El Gran Combo have been a national institution in Puerto Rico for over four decades – they can still fill any town square on the island during the summertime festival season. At their heart are leader Rafael Ithier's understated but elaborate piano solos and, out front, the adored trio of singer-dancers.

 35 Years around the World
(Combo, US).

A swathe of perfect songs covering the career of Ithier's band, which is synonymous with Puerto Rico. Its star vocalists are the principle attraction with their loud, almost raucous delivery.

Grupo Galé

Colombian percussionist, composer and producer Diego Galé is a leading arranger and all-rounder who often plays every percussion instrument on his records. His immensely popular line-up presents neat, smooth salsa in similar vein to Grupo Niche (below), with whom he has recorded.

Listo Medellin (Codiscos, Colombia).

The album which helped tear young Colombians away from the mighty Grupo Niche, presenintg a collection of smooth new classics.

Grupo Niche

One of Colombia's most adored bands since 1979, Niche are the home team for the coastal city of Cali, Colombia's 'Capital of Salsa'. Their sumptuous melodies and perfect arrangements are closer to Puerto Rican salsa than many flamboyant, tropical styles associated with Colombia.

SALSA

Grandes Exitos
(Globo, US).

The 'Greatest Hits' include Niche's great, rhythmically stunning anthem, "Cali Pachanguero", about a hard-living guy from Cali. These perfected arrangements are possible when the leader, Jairo Varela, can afford to spend limitless time in his own studio, getting every instrument right. And it shows.

La India

Former Latin hip-hop singer La India broke through at the end of the 1990s to become potentially a key salsa star on the strength of collaborations with Tito Puente (on a re-mix of "Ran Kan Kan" which stormed the dance charts) and pianist Eddie Palmieri. To have Palmieri on your first album is some responsibility but La India handled it with typical aplomb.

 Llego La India
(RMM, US).

La India's high-pitched girlish voice is still finding its natural scope but any restrictions in technique are more than compensated for in the tremendous enthusiasm which pours from every song plus, of course, the state-of-the-art salsa backing she has from Palmieri on this disc. The title track is an all-time crossover classic, adorned with a wild Palmieri solo.

◉ **Sobre El Fuego** (RMM, US).

Produced by the new top producer, Isidro Infante, this was a Grammy-nominee, whose high point is the duet "La Voz de la Experiencia" with Celia Cruz.

Hector Lavoe

Salsero Hector Lavoe was a Puerto Rican legend, even before his death in 1997. His career was beset by tragedy, drugs and illness, and his voice and songs show it all. He started out playing with Willie Colón, singing of raw barrio life, and together they created some of the great salsa tracks of the early 1970s before Colón moved on to a new partnership with Rubén Blades.

 La Comedia
(Fania, US).

Lavoe's wonderful 1978 album, featuring his greatest hit "El cantante" (The SInger).

Victor Manuelle

Puerto Rico's latest contribution to the global salsa fest, Manuelle is a tremendous young singer who rose through the ranks from local bands to solo success in the 1990s. His style presents a counterbalance to the Latin rappers – high-energy salsa and romantic ballads.

◉ **A pesar de todo** (Sony Tropical, US).

Victor Manuelle's voice here reveals a tribute to Rubén Blades in his clipped pronunciation, and to the smoothy balladeers who fill the charts. A voice which will carry salsa into the next decade.

Tito Nieves

Tito Nieves, 'The Pavarotti of Salsa' is a chubby tenor who has paid his dues in several New York salsa bands since the 1970s, particularly the classic Conjunto Clasico. But it was his English-language cover of 1960s hit "I Like It Like That" which carried him to the US charts.

◉ **Dale cara la Vida** (RMM, US).

If you want to relive Nieves' classic 1970s salsa tones, then this is the album to track down.

◉ **I Like It Like That** (RMM, US).

Nieves' irresistibly catchy cover of the 1960s Johnny Rodrigues boogaloo took him into the US charts, out of the Latin ghetto, and set a trend for English-language lyrics with Latin beats. The ensuing album ploughed deeper into salsa-house.

Orquesta de la Luz

The late 1980s phenomenon of a Japanese band who sing phonetically and play by rote was more than a gimmick. Orquesta de la Luz proved that you don't have to be born within the sound of the conga drums of Havana to play salsa, and producer Sergio George convinced the salsa audiences with a series of hit records.

◉ **La Aventura** (BMG Ariola, Japan).

Slot this into your CD drive, close your eyes, and you really won't believe you're listening to a Japanese band. By the time they completed this album Orquesta de la Luz could improvise as well as many true salseros and fall back on a rock-solid salsa foundation. Contemporary salsa, 1980s style, still sounding good two decades later.

Orquesta Guayacán

Guayacán are one of the newer generation of Colombian salsa outfits and like Grupo Niche are specialists in sublime melodies.

◉ **14 Exitos** (Sony/Sonolux, Venezuela).

Any record by this band containing the hit song "Oiga, mira y ven" is worth grabbing – its tune eats into your brain, its rhythm would make Lazurus walk.

Eddie Palmieri

Piano stylist Eddie Plamieri is one of New York salsa's treasures. His musical experiments and passion for the Afro-Cuban religious music of santeria have drawn fans to his erratic and highly entertaining concerts since the 1950s. His startling technique was heavily influenced by jazz modalists like McCoy Tyner, but his music also reveals his lifelong passions for both trombones and the Afro-Cuban santeria religious music.

 History of Eddie Palmieri
(Tico, Venezuela).

No Latin music collection is complete without at least one Palmieri LP (Charlie and Eddie, that is). This one is essential, if only for perhaps the most sensual track of all time, "El Café", a slow Cuban guajira that just creeps upon you.

◉ **El Rumbero del Piano** (RMM, US; Verve, UK).

A gorgeous 1998 album which turns back to Eddie's roots in Puerto Rico and is his most straighahead collection in years.

Roberto Pla's Latin Jazz Ensemble

Colombian percussionist Pla was the original 'token' Latino in London's salsa scene, always handy to drop in those authentic beats to any pop single but he has gone on to mould a remarkably successful big band from local gringos passionate about salsa.

◉ **Right on Time** (Tumi, UK).

Pla's full-size twelve-piece big band in action. The disc includes Pla's tribute to his wife – the salsa DJ Dominque ('Cumbia Dominique') whose club nights at HQ and Bar Rumba hugely contributed to the expansion of London's live salsa scene.

SALSA

Puerto Rico All Stars

The All Stars are a gang of great singers – ranging from salsa godfather Andy Montanez to the laterst superstar Victor Manuelle – backed by a forceful orchestra with generous-sized trumpet, trombone and sax sections.

◉ **De Regreso** (RMM, US).

A flawless showcase for Puerto Rican salsa, which serves as a good primer for the various styles of the singers. As well as Andy Montanez and Victor Manuelle, the new generation are represented by Hernandez's talented daughter Liza, and by Primi Cruz and Darvel Garcia.

Tito Rodríguez

Tito Rodríguez (1923–73) was born in San Juan's music district of Santurce, moving to New York as a teenager, where he sang with the Cuban/Latin orchestras of Xavier Cugat and Noro Morales. He was a great all-rounder – a sonero and ballad-singer, percussionist and bandleader – and carried the flag for the island as one of the stars of Broadway's pre-salsa Latin big bands.

◉ **Mambo mona** (Tumbao, Spain).

A well-presented and annotated selection from Rodríguez's mambo heyday, including the eponymous number, which later changed its title to become the artist's signature hit, "Mama Guela".

Willie Rosario

Veteran bandleader and timbal-player Willie Rosario is back in vogue more than ever, thanks to his unbending espousal of classic hard salsa values.

◉ **Back to the Future**
(J&N/Sony Discos, US).

The album that put Rosario and hard salsa back at the top. It is replete with star guests – Bobby Valentín and Louie Ramirez arranging, Gilberto Santa Rosa and Tony Vega singing.

Gilberto Santa Rosa

The slickest singer in Puerto Rican salsa – and that says a lot – Santa Rosa rose to fame as co-lead singer with Willie Rosario's band. He has managed to captivate the young generation with his catchy melodies.

◉ **Nace aqui** (Sony Tropical, US).

One for lovers of the softer face of salsa.

La Sonora Ponceña

With El Gran Combo, La Sonora Ponceña are Puerto Rico's most beloved band – formed in 1956 and led by jazz-influenced pianist Papo Lucca since 1975. Their smooth salsa arrangements, four swirling interlocking trumpets and darting harmonising vocalists are instantly recognisable. No one approaches them.

◉ **La Sonora Ponceña of Puerto Rico** (Charly, UK).

A compilation of greatest hits from vintage 1970s to early 1990s and including their jumpy *saoco* rhythm launched in the early 1990s. A showcase for Lucca's classy, smoothest arrangements, with plenty of limpid piano solos and the occasional appearance of the gritty-voiced Yolanda Rivera.

Yomo Toro

A virtuoso of the cuatro (small Puerto Rican guitar), Yomo Toro brought the flavour of the Puerto Rican countryside into New York salsa in the Fania records of the 1970s, in his own later solo work, and on countless sessions. He has been based in New York since the 1950s, where he appears with the Latin Legends band.

◉ **Funky Jibaro** (Island, US).

This 1998 album is Toro's most traditionally-based recording, revisiting the jibaro (country music) forms.

Carlos Vives

Former Colombian TV soap star, Vives, pulled together a band of multi-instrumentalists and captured the dance floors all over the country, dispersing the hit bands on all sides with adaptations of the traditional accordion-led vallenato style. After this album, the band split to form a neo-punk-pan-Latin outfit, Bloqué, which signed to David Byrne's Luaka Bop label.

◉ **Classicos de la Privincia** (Sonolux, Venezuela).

Vives' traditional accordions are dropped into a modern Latin night-club terrain, and emerge even more appealing, if a little less raucous.

Thanks to Gerry Lyseight, Radio DJ for BBC's London Live, and to Fabian Cardona at Mr Bongo's salsa record store, London, for their assistance with this shopping list.

SALSA

Trinidad

Calypso/Soca

put water in the brandy?

Developed in Trinidad in the nineteenth century, **calypso** is one of the great popular musics – lyrically intricate as well as hugely danceable – and was one of the earliest Caribbean forms to have internatonal success, having crossed over to mainstream markets in the US and UK in the 1930s, through immigrants from the islands. Although in the shadows of reggae and salsa, these days, it is still going strong at Carnival time on its home base of Trinidad and neighbouring islands, both in its traditional form and in its modern, funked-up, hi-tech variant of **soca** (*soul-calypso.* **Charles de Ledesma** and **Georgia Popplewell** get down to the *mas'.*

Calypso is that rare thing: a music that stands and falls on its lyrics. Its tunes, of course, are crucial, and there is always that irresistible airborne spring to its rhythms – quite different to reggae's earthy bass beat. But it is really the words that matter most, rooted as they are in social and political comment, and peppered with patois and slang. It is a music that comes to the fore at the Trinidad and Tobago Carnivals and at these party times calypsonians can get away with the most slanderous, satritical comment: controversy, or *bacchanal* as people call it, is the music's lifeblood.

In its most traditional form, this bachanal is expressed in *extempo* or **picong** – a Carnival tent ritual in which two calypsonians trade verses laced with innuendo and barbed commentaries. Verses are sung to the same traditional melody, each stanza ending with the patois refrain *sans humanité* (no pity) – the singers' attitude to each other and to the public figures they pillory.

Soca, which emerged in the 1970s, drawing on US soul music and a range of Caribbean rhythms, in its funkier, more dance-based sound, put much less emphasis on the lyrics. Its jump to pan-Caribbean and international markets, in particu-

TRINIDAD & TOBAGO
Land of Calypso

Aldwyn Roberts Kitchener **50**c

lar, created a dilemma for many calypsonians – as the veteran Chalkdust, put it: "Are we to put water in the brandy, singing just two or three words you can understand and dance to? Or are we to keep to the traditions of calypso and tell the story?"

That dilemmas was solved to some degree by a trend for calypso/soca artists to mix material, including on their annual releases both 'jump up' dance numbers and more traditional 'message' calypsos. The advent of the **rapso** (rap-calypso) with its oral virtuosity, has also helped to shore up calypso's lyrical tendencies.

Other new genres, too, have been added to the calypso/soca mix. The rhythms and instruments of Trinidad's (Asian) Indian population led to a creative infusion – **chutney** (which is covered in a separate article on p.527) – with Indian artists like Drupatee and Rikki Jai, and crossover artists like Brother Marvin regaling audiences with their inventive combination of Asian folk melodies, soca beats and calypso-laced versification.

And then there are the **other islands in the West Indies**. These had long-established calypso scenes of their own and over the years calypsonians like St Vincent's Beckett and Antigua's King Short Shirt scored regional hits. However, it was

Arrow from **Montserrat**, who broke the scene wide open with his 1983 hit "Hot! Hot! Hot!" (still the top-selling soca disc ever). Following his lead, a succession of bands broke through in the 1990s, particularly from **Barbados**, where groups like krosfyah and Square One and singers like John King have become prolific practitioners of a stylish, melodious, high-quality sound.

Calypso Origins

The great calypsonian Roaring Lion compared his art to that of the jongleurs and troubadours who travelled medieval Europe telling stories and spreading news. Traditionally, calypsonians have been commentators on contemporary life and current events, and as Lion observed: "The whole history of Trinidad is in calypso voices." It is scarcely an exaggeration.

Musically, **calypso roots** are a mix of African (slave) and European (planter and colonial) influences. The more direct include *gayap*, a type of communal work song, and Afro-creole drum dances such as the *calenda* (stick-fighting dance). European guitar and song forms brought by the French creole and Spanish planters also fed into the mix.

The most significant, however, was the **gayap**, which has a typical African call-and-response form, and often took as its subject a competition or event. The slaves sang the first part to celebrate victory, then the second to pour scorn on the losers. On the plantations each work group was led by a **chantwell**, a lead singer or master of ceremonies, who would sing one line which the others would answer in chorus as they worked. Chantwells such as the legendary **Elephant** (so called because of his thunderous voice) could be said to be the forerunners of today's calypsonians, and were sometimes called upon to entertain the masters during their parties and revels. After Emancipation, chantwells continued to serve a similar function at Carnival and other celebrations.

According to commentator John Cowley, the word calypso was first used in Trinidad in 1883, by a local cleric who described an "abominable dance [which was the] cause of perversion of young men and girls." The word is thought to be a corruption of the West African word **'kaiso'** – a cry of encouragement akin to 'olé' or 'bravo'. It is still occasionally used in this sense; at a performance, enthusiasts might shout 'Kaiso! Kaiso!' in praise of a finely crafted calypso. Some purists even refer to the whole calypso genre as kaiso, viewing the very word calypso as an adulteration. (Most recently,

rapso poet **Brother Resistance** contributed to the re-popularisation of the term by highlighting it in his poems-over-rhythms).

Veteran calypsonian Chalkdust sees calypso as a peculiar hybrid springing from African roots: "The origins, the melodic patterns and rhythmic structure, are African. But culture changes and we have pulled from the French – in the *mas* (Carnival masquerade); we have pulled from the English – we speak English; we have pulled from the Spanish – in the melodies; and we have pulled from jazz and the Americans. They have all influenced calypso."

This mix reflects Trinidad's particular **colonial history**. Originally settled by the Spanish in 1532, a policy introduced in 1783 to encourage immigration of Roman Catholics resulted in the influx of many **French-speaking immigrants**, particularly after the French Revolution. Other French settlers came from St Lucia and Dominica after these islands fell under British rule in 1784; with African slaves from the French Caribbean after slavery there was abolished; and from Saint Domingue (Dominican Republic) after the Haitian Revolution. Trinidad therefore found itself in the peculiar situation of being a colony of Spain, with a population consisting mainly of French creoles and African slaves, with French as the predominant language. Then in 1802, along with its sister island, Tobago, Trinidad became a British colony.

The French planters brought with them the Catholic tradition of celebrating the pre-Lenten season with **Carnival masquerade balls** and processions. While the African slaves could not take part, they set up alternative **canboulay** processions (the word coming from the French *cannes brulées*, referring to the practice of burning the sugar canefields before harvesting). With emancipation in 1834 these two forms of Carnival merged.

The calypso thus emerged in the context of a complex relationship between coloniser and colonised, with the result that satire, parody, innuendo and political comment became features of both the music and of the Carnival masquerade.

Carnival

Calypso is inseparable from the idea of **Carnival**. Carnival and its canboulay forerunner was the time for letting off steam and featured bands of drummers and stick-fighters, with chantwells egging them into action. Both the African drumming and stick-fights were banned by the British after the Canboulay Riots in 1880, and the Sunday-night canboulay procession was replaced by the **Kalenda March and Dance** on Monday morning. But the music remained and developed.

Today, the **Carnival season** in Trinidad and Tobago begins just after New Year and culminates in a two-day street party on the Monday and Tuesday preceding Ash Wednesday. Throughout this

Denyse Plummer stating her case in the Calypso Monarch Finals

vives in the in **Extempo Competition**, one of several official competitions held each year. The other two traditional prizes are for the **Calypso Monarch**, awarded to the performer of the year's best calypso, and the **Road March**, the calypso played most often on the road. These have existed since the early days, and are open only to citizens of Trinidad and Tobago. During the 1980s, however, as corporate sponsorship raised the festival's profile, other prizes were created for all-comers, notably the **International Soca Monarch**, **Chutney-Soca Monarch**, **Calypso Queen**, **Young Kings** and **Ragga Soca Monarch**. A Schools' Calypso competition also encourages young performers. Competitions aside, the tents serve as vital ground for apprentice singers – and there is never a shortage of them – as well as bands, and it is here, almost without exception, that calypsonians first establish their reputations.

The other big Carnival prize is the **Panorama** competition, awarded to the best *pan* orchestra. Steel drums, known as **pans**, are one of the most evocative sounds of Carnival, and like calypso, their roots go back to popular forms of protest. After stick-fighting and African drums were banned, *tamboo-bamboo* bands would beat bamboo sticks together as an accompaniment to Carnival songs. These too were eventually banned, but reappeared, again transformed, in 1937, when a Carnival band performed with an orchestra of frying pans, dustbin lids and oil drums. After the war, this makeshift battery was replaced by a carefully tempered orchestra of oil drums, finely tuned by beating with a hammer and chisel (see box overleaf).

period calypso and calypsonians are everywhere. In the run-up, the year's calypsos are rehearsed and aired in **calypso tents**, originally bamboo tents, but now halls or cinemas, often capable of holding an audience of thousands.

In the old days the tents were an arena for chantwells to engage in contests where they traded insults with their rivals – a tradition that sur-

Alongside calypso, steel orchestras are the dominant musical and rhythmic influences in the lead up to the Carnival celebrations. An orchestra can

The Steel Pan

Steel pans begin life as forty-five-gallon oil drums. All of them, except for the large bass, must be cut to size, and a five-pound sledgehammer is used to sink the unopened end into a convex shape – deeper for the higher drums and shallower for the cello and bass pans. The position of the notes (around the perimeter and in the centre) is outlined with compasses and chalk and then beaten out with a hammer, fire and water. A coating of chrome may be added to produce a better surface. The final tuning is carried out using a small hammer and rubber-tipped playing stick – a painstaking and specialised process, made a little easier these days by electronic gizmos.

In a steel orchestra the **melodies** are usually played on the tenor pans, and at that pitch a complete range of notes can be fitted onto one drum. A double tenor is a lower melody instrument and has the notes distributed over two drums. A double second is a pair of drums for accompanying chords, and a treble guitar a trio of pans for lower harmonies. The lower the note required, the more space it takes up on the drum, so the bass might need a range of four or six pans with just a few notes on each.

The steelbands really got going after 1941, when the US Navy had bases on the island. Although Carnival was officially suspended for the duration of the war, it was celebrated secretly in the poorer districts of Port of Spain, and the players (*panmen*) acquired a dangerous and disreputable reputation, their name synonymous with trouble. That continued after the war and during the 1956 Carnival, two steelbands, Tokyo and the Invaders, had a street battle which lasted for hours.

AMOCO RENEGADES

Jit Samaroo, steel pan arranger for Amoco Renegades

Today, steel orchestras have become respectable and play a classical repertoire as well as pop selections (called *bomb tunes*) in concerts around the world. But nothing can beat the sensation of hearing a band on the streets – you can sense its history in the physical thrill of those hammers on steel.

The sight of a steelband, assembling, rehearsing, and ultimately rolling the pans on metal racks on their way to compete in the Panorama competition, is absorbing and thrilling. Indeed, the Panorama competition, whose preliminaries, semi-finals and final stages are held in the weeks before Carnival, is arguably the single most exciting single event of the whole proceedings. It is wonderfuly described by the novelist Earl Lovelace in his evocation of Carnival, *The Dragon Can't Dance* (Longman, UK):

'Panmen troop off street corners, desert their battlefield and territory, and turn up the hill to the steelband tent to assemble the drums... The tent becomes a cathedral, and these young men priests. They will draw from back pockets those rubber-tipped sticks, which they had carried around all year, as the one link to the music that is their life, their soul, and touch them to the cracked faces of the drums.

Hours, days; hours, days; for weeks they beat these drums, beat these drums, hammering out from them a cry, the cry, the sound, stroking them more gently than they will ever caress a woman; and then they have it. At last they have it. They have the tune that will sing their person and their pose, that will soar over the hill, ring over the valley of shacks, and laugh the hard tears of their living when, for Carnival, they enter Port of Spain'.

comprise up to two hundred players (most of whom don't read music). Its sound is stunning in the hands of arrangers like **Len 'Boogsie' Sharpe** and **Jit Samaroo**, and bands such as **Exodus**, the **Amoco Renegades**, **WITCO Desperadoes** and **Phase 2 Pan Groove**, who create phenomenal melodic and percussive tapestries out of the season's calypsoes.

Visiting the panyards, the arenas where steel orchestras practise in the weeks leading up to Carnival, is a feast for ears and eyes, and a popular pastime for both locals and Carnival visitors.

Oratorical Calypso

From abolition to ninety-eight
Calypso was still sung in its crude state
From French to English it was then translated
By Norman Le Blanc who became celebrated
Then it was rendered grammatically
In oration, poetry and history.

The lines above, from a song by Lord Invader, provide a potted history of calypso's progression and its role in recording the events of the island. It is a story whose records begin in the late nineteenth century, when chantwells with names such as Hannibal and Boadicea entertained at Carnival time and launched tirades against the repressive policies of the colonial government. **Norman Le Blanc** made his name in 1898 singing about the British threat to abolish the Port of Spain City Council, and he and other early bards regularly lampooned the colonial government and their rival calypsonians. They forged out of African communal song a distinctive style that drew on Cuban melodies, Spanish guitar and patois words from everyday usage. The first recordings of these early calypsoes took place in 1914.

By the 1930s, calypso was entering a golden age of popularity and creativity, its singers improvising with great wit and dexterity on current issues. The stars of this era adopted sobriquets – 'Lord', 'King', 'Mighty' and so on – in reference to the music's competitive roots. They included **Lord Executor**, considered calypso's greatest extemporiser, **Lord Invader**, **Mighty Destroyer**, **Atilla the Hun** and the young **Roaring Lion** (who remained a key figure on the scene right up to his death in 1999). Their songs began to find an audience abroad as well as on the islands. In the pre-war years, Roaring Lion and Atilla the Hun travelled to the US to record, and the (white) singer **Paul Whiteman** had a US hit with his calypso "Sly Mongoose".

This early heyday co-incided with movements against British colonial rule, and as the government censored the media, so-called **oratorical calypso** took on a news-sheet role, expressing popular discontent. Calypsonians often ran into trouble with the police over songs that were considered politically unsuitable or obscene, and for a while in the 1930s the government attempted to license their songs. Calypsonians

ROARING LION

The young Roaring Lion (centre)

were required to submit their compositions for inspection before public performance, and officers stationed in the Carnival tents ensured that the songs met with approval. The calypsonians were unimpressed, or as Atilla the Hun put it, in song:

To say these songs are sacrilegious, obscene or profane
Is only a lie and a dirty shame
If the calypso is indecent, then I must insist
So is Shakespeare's Venus and Adonis
Boccaccio's tales, Voltaire's Candide
The Martyrdom of Man by Winwood Reid
Yet over these authors they make no fuss
But they want to take advantage of us.

The idea proved unworkable and unpopular and it was soon dropped.

TRINIDAD

Postwar Calypso: Kitchener and Sparrow

World War II and the arrival of American troops at the Chaguaramas base in Trinidad brought about a new wave of political calypso. Musicians like the **Saga Boys** and the **Mighty Sparrow** – the island's rising star – camouflaged their invective against US influence, as usual, in song. Invader famously wrote "Rum and Coca-Cola" (a song based on the Cuban "Son de la Loma") about local girls whisked away by the Yankee dollar. Adopted by **The Andrews Sisters**, it became an enormous hit in the US – and gave rise to a copyright suit. The Andrews' plundering of the song (which was about prostitution) gave the words an added irony:

> Rum and Coca-Cola
> Go down Point Cumana
> Both mother and daughter
> Working for the Yankee dollar.

Lawsuits notwithstanding, though, the post-war American recording industry took due note of this calypso success, and RCA-Victor (Elvis Presley's label) signed up **Sparrow**, as well as the Jamaican-born American singer **Harry Belafonte**. In the 1950s Belafonte had worldwide success with his album *Calypso*, the first ever LP to sell a million copies. Singing in American English with little of the Trinidadian linguistic inventiveness or political message, he was hardly the real McCoy. However, Belafonte's songs – the best of which were written by **Lord Melody** – put calypso on the world map, and primed an American audience for calypso's greatest postwar stars, Lord Kitchener and Mighty Sparrow, singing in patois.

Lord Kitchener (born Aldwyn Roberts, 1922) represented a new generation of calypsonians dubbed the **Young Brigade** – the name of the renegade calypso tent he and fellow calypsonian **Killer** formed at the 1947 Carnival. The Young Brigade singers took the lyrical innovations of Lord Invader a step further, leaving aside topical events to create humorous fictional narratives, and introducing a more dance sensibility to the music.

Kitchener travelled extensively, living for a while in London, where he is remembered for leading a group of calypsonians on to the pitch at Lord's cricket ground in 1950, after the West Indies's first victory against England. Back home he notched up a record eleven Road March victories at Port of Spain Carnival. These triumphs stretched from 1946 to 1976, when 'Kitch' retired from competition, devoting most of his musical energies to composing for steelbands; technically accomplished, he also delved into jazz territory. He proved an adaptable calypsonian, too, recording a worldwide soca hit, "Sugar Bum Bum", in 1978, and as recently as 1997 his "Guitar Pan" tune was on everyone's lips, its bounce and harmonic elegance proving irresistible for many of the pan orchestras competing in Panorama. He died in February 2000, mourned by the whole island.

Although born in Grenada, **Mighty Sparrow** (born Slinger Francisco, 1935) moved to Trinidad as a child and the island claims him as its own. A brilliant singer and arranger, he is (and was, even before Kitchener's death) the dominant figure of postwar calypso, both in Trinidad and Tobago and in the US, where in the 1960s and '70s he would often fill New York's Madison Square Gardens. He chose the name Sparrow, he says, because whereas other calypsonians got their message across by standing on the spot and pointing at the audience, he hopped around on stage. The story goes that he used the sobriquet 'Little Sparrow' on his Carnival debut but his rapid success led competitors to deride this upstart diminutive bird – a Sparrow, after all, hardly ranks with a Lion, Tiger or Executor. So Sparrow added the prefix Mighty as a form of damage limitation and promptly gained his first Calypso King title (in 1956) with the endearing "Jean and Dinah". (To demonstrate how quickly things move in

REDFERNS

Mighty Sparrow

TRINIDAD

the calypso world, Sparrow's performance was broadcast on Carnival Monday morning and by afternoon "Jean and Dinah" had become the Road March, with masqueraders word perfect in its unusually long chorus).

Sparrow's musical success brought political influence, which he lent, enthusiastically, to Dr. Eric Williams' People's National Movement, which was elected to power in 1956. Sparrow wrote a string of calypsos in their support:

> Praise little Eric, rejoice and be glad
> We have a better future here in Trinidad
> P.N.M. it ain't got nobody like them
> For they have a champion leader
> William the Conqueror.

For many Trinidadians, particularly those from the poorer communities, this nationalist government came as a breath of fresh air, though disillusionment with Williams and his party set in soon after

Independence in the mid-1960s. Sparrow articulated this mood as well, in the song "Get To Hell Outa Here". And he continued doing it. "If you really know the true role of the calypsonian," he has explained, "then you should understand that somewhere along the line you gonna be treading on the corns of the people in power."

The third key figure in post-war (and also, in his case, pre-war) calypso was **Roaring Lion** (born Hubert Rafael de Leon, 1909), a traditionalist calypsonian who never disguised his contempt for what he perceived to be soca's lack of wit and narrative lyrics. As he put it: "Fellows just yelling 'Party! Party!' all the time; where's the story in

that?" Sparrow, however, in some ways opened the way for soca, with his musical energy and stepped up stage performance.

Kitchener, Sparrow and Lion were all masters of calypso's trademark **sexual innuendo**. In early days, calypsos would often mask their obscenity and get round radio bans by use of double-entendres (up until the 1970s calypsos were banned altogether from radio during the Lenten season), but they gradually became explicit. One of the commonest themes is the calypsonian's sexual prowess. Sparrow's "Village Ram" is a typical example:

> Not a woman ever complain yet with me
> I ain't boasting but I got durability
> And if a woman ever tell you that I
> Ever left her dissatisfy
> She lie, she lie, I say she lie.

Kitchener's own best-known contribution to the genre was the good-natured "Gee Me The Ting (What The Doctor order Me)", an international soca hit in 1983.

Women Calypsonians

As the lyric above might suggest, calypso can be shockingly sexist – and, although one of the most famous nineteenth-century chantwells, **Boadicea**, was a woman – it has been very male-dominated over the years. But in the past twenty years, things have changed somewhat as a generation of women calypsonians have made their mark, and a new slant on sexual politics has appeared in the songs.

Up until the 1980s, calypso and soca songs about sex and relationships took for granted a double standard, allowing men total sexual freedom while requiring women to be faithful and obedient. But these days, male calypsonians tend to downplay their sexual capacities and often cast themselves as the victims of women, whom they accuse of cuckoldry or voracious sexual appetites. In the 2000 hit "Market Vendor", for example, calypsonian Preacher is intimidated by the contents of his wife's shopping list, which includes "two sapodillas and a nine-inch banana."

The first modern women calypsonian to break onto the scene was **Calypso Rose** (McArtha Lewis), who was a singing partner of Kitchener in the late 1960s. In 1978 she was the first woman to win the title of Calypso King (prompting the organisers to change the title to Calypso Monarch), with the aptly-themed calypso "Do Dem Back" (i.e. retaliate).

In the last twenty years calypsonians like **Singing Francine** and **Denyse Plummer** have

Singing Sandra (right) and the United Sisters in a calypso tent

written and sung thoughtfully on sexual politics and women's concerns. Francine advises women to leave men who mistreat them in her hit song "Run Away":

Cat does run away, dog does run away
Fowl does run away when you treating them bad
What happen to you?
Woman, you can run away too.

The island's reigning queen, **Singing Sandra**, has also hit out with forthright material, particularly on her "Voices from the Ghetto," which won her the Monarch title in 1999. The same year, the Road March title was won by a woman for the first time – **Sanell Dempster**.

The 1990s saw the rise of a new generation of female performers who flaunt their sexuality much more openly. Singing Sandra has been part of a powerhouse female collective called the **United Sisters**, whose repertoire includes numbers like "Four Women To One Man". **Denise Belfon** is known both for songs such as "Ka-Ka-Lay-Lay" and for mesmerising dancehall gyrations. Many of the female singers in the soca bands have also modelled their choreographies on Jamaican dancehall styles. One of the most accomplished women performers to have emerged in recent years is **Allison Hinds**, front woman for the highly successful Barbadian band **Square One**.

Hot! Hot! Hot! – Soca Takes Hold

In the early 1970s calypso began to evolve under the influence of American **soul and dance** music, and **new technology**. Calypsonians and bands were increasingly recording in Brooklyn, New York rather than Trinidad. Arrangers began shaping the sound to fit a dance formula, introducing drum machines and funky bass patterns. The vocal style was changing too, becoming more expressive and influenced by the fuller, more upbeat rhythmic structure. In the 1970s **disco and funk** culture was at its peak in New York, and there was money to be made from a sound that satisfied the dance floor's craving for grooves closer to James Brown, Isaac Hayes and the Motown sound.

One of the earliest recordings in this new vein was **Lord Shorty**'s *Soul of Calypso*, a 1974 album that led directly to the coinage of the new term **soca**. The term is commonly seen as an abbreviation of the two first syllables of soul and calypso, though Lord Shorty himself saw it as an easier spelling of *sokah* – a combination of soul and the word *kah*, first letter of the Hindi alphabet. Shorty was keen to bring the music of Trinidad's Indian community into the wider body of calypso. But Shorty's vision was short-lived, as soca sidelined any Indian traits in favour of a soulful bass hook and a disco drum beat, creating a ground-

Calypso in London

Bill Rogers will stay
As a resident in the UK
Tell them how I am living so fine
Nothing at all to disturb my mind
Tell them I give lung to you
Blasting out mission, too.

Bill Rogers "Sightseeing in the UK".

Bill Rogers from Guyana was one of thousands of emigrants from the Caribbean who settled in Britain after World War II and made London a second capital of calypso. Others included **Lord Kitchener** and **Lord Beginner**, two of Trinidad's greatest calypsonians, who disembarked from the *Empire Windrush* at Tilbury on June 21, 1948 and by 1950 were recording sessions for EMI. **Lord Invader**, too, the composer of "Rum and Coca-Cola", spent part of the 1950s in Britain.

A valuable selection of this British West Indian music was released on the UK Charly label in the 1980s as *Port Of Spain Shuffle* and *Caribbean Connections*: they're no longer on catalogue but well worth tracking down. As well as tracks from Kitchener and Beginner, there are some great numbers from **Roaring Lion**, who came to London to play at the 1951 Festival of Britain and stayed on through most of the decade, running a cosmetics company and an immigrants' accommodation agency, as well as singing calypsos.

In their new environment, the calypsonians combined the roles of cultural ambassadors for Trinidadian music and nostalgists for life back home. But they also brought their tradition of calypso as social observation to the immigrants' experience of Britain. Beginner, for example, wrote a calypso about waiting for the results of the 1950 General Election to be posted on the lights in Piccadilly Circus:

Names went up in rotation
Some said we'll get more employment
Others said better house rent
Balloon went up too
I saw red and blue
For Attlee supporters roar
And for Churchill who won the war

One of the most popular records of the 1950s, as much with British as Caribbean audiences, was **Lord Melody**'s "Cricket, Lovely Cricket", which celebrated the West Indies' first victory over England on British soil. Roaring Lion's calypsos were more concerned with island culture, though he had something of an obsession with the Royal Family, as well as a name for sauciness. A classic example was his "Tick! Tick! (The Story of the Lost Watch)", a double-entendre number about a girl who steals a watch and hides it in her vagina – the police can hear it ticking but can't find it. There are still Roaring Lion records in the BBC library with old stickers saying 'Do not play this track!'.

Half a century on, calypso retains a presence in London through the annual **Notting Hill Carnival** – the biggest Carnival in Europe – which features steelbands and road march calypso on floats and on stage. This has helped a number of artists emerge, the best known being **Tiger**. Starting his singing career in Trinidad he moved to London in the early 1970s, and became Notting Hill's first Calypso King – a title he has won eight times since. He is still singing calypso, but a large part of his time is taken up with the Association of British Calypsonians, an organisation set up to improve the status of calypso in the UK.

breaking mixture of funk, mid-tempo ska and calypso.

In a sense, Shorty's free co-optation of these forms was a Trinidadian equivalent of the way Toots Hibbert (of Toots and the Maytals) shifted Jamaican music from a countrified insularity into the dangerous world of rock guitars and soulful vocals. On the downside, soca lost some of the unique vocal inflections that had characterised calypso, substituting them with a flatter, less distinctive soul-soaked purr. The rhythm rather than the voice led the songs, which clearly addressed the body rather than the mind, with lyrics – "Paartiee tonite, paartiee all nite!" – often barely audible and trivial in content.

These new developments weren't due only to international influence – Trinidad itself was enjoying new-found oil wealth and the atmosphere was one of celebration. And calypso's role as a music of controversy and social comment was not entirely abandoned. In 1986, for instance, when a drop in oil prices triggered a financial crisis, **Gypsy**'s "The Sinking Ship" caught the mood of the nation. Gypsy reinforced the tradition of sustaining a satirical metaphor over numerous verses:

The Trinidad, a luxury liner
Is sailing the Caribbean sea
With an old captain named Eric Williams
For years sailed smooth and free.

But sadly Eric Williams passed away
The ship hit rough water that day
And someone turned the bridge over
To a captain named Chambers
Made blood crawl, things start to fall
Hold me head when a sailor fall.
Captain, the ship is sinking,
Captain, the seas are rough.
Shall we abandon ship?
Or shall we stay on it
And perish slow? We don't know
Captain, you tell me what to do.

1986 was an election year and the song was credited with striking the final blow which removed the People's National Movement from power after thirty years. Gypsy has kept a social observation in soca since, notably in "Little Black Boy" which won him the 1997 Calypso Monarch title. The issue of racism is a touchy subject in Trinidad and Tobago, and he bravely took it on it in his modern calypso classic about a child's hard life.

Another significant musician who has crossed between calypso and soca, notably maintaining the tradition of calypso as comment is the Mighty Chalkdust (Hollis Liverpool – the name derives from his profession as a schoolteacher). He won the Calypso Monarch prize twice in the 1970s, but in 1983 put on his soca hat and produced the

Long ago, when you hear kaiso,
it was protest and commentary
The things the government
didn't want you to know
They were sung in the tent likely, you see?
But today, when the kaiso play,
all the lyrics describing fête
And the philosophy of yesterday
has suffered a musical death.
Man used to live in poverty
so he liked social commentary
But now my pockets have money,
man want to fête and scream
Man want to kaiso tell,
to hear about government
But now he have finance,
man want to dance.
No more protesting song,
sarcasm and picong
Lyrics don't stand a chance,
man want to dance.

Chalkdust "Man Want to Dance".

magnificent album *Kaiso with Dignity*, which included the funk-soca "Drunk Monk" with a cracking dance break. He was was back on the front lines a decade later when he penned the masterpiece, "Kaiso in Hospital" – a lament on the all-pervasive tendency of soca singers to merely 'jam and wine' and not comment on society.

Given the complex cultural legacy with which any Trinidadian musician of a certain generation must contend, it was perhaps no surprise that a non-Trinidadian would have been the first to have a major worldwide soca hit. Montserratian calypsonian **Arrow**'s "Hot! Hot! Hot!", first released in 1983, was a huge seller around the world, providing a Carnival and party soundtrack for years to follow.

As well as writing soca with pure party content, Arrow introduced radical musical innovations, adding salsa and merengue to the mix years before Trinidadian artists looked at these forms. His stage repertoire runs through straight soca ("Bills"), zouk-soca ("Zouk-Me"), and Latin-tinged soca ("Limbo Calypso"). He believes in intermingling Caribbean music styles, bringing together cultures, and he has undeniably done much to introduce soca to a wider audience with his superbly adept backing band, **The International Force**.

Following on from Arrow's musical fusions, interesting developments came from the Trinidadian **Lord Nelson**, who created a **soca-funk** fusion, and Tobago-born **Shadow**, who introduced a deep bass sound and swooping Tobago-style violin melodies – heard to breathtaking effect, with his quavering baritone vocals, on his classic "De Hardis". Arrow broke further new ground with a soukous-like rolling drum beat, while **Superblue** (Austin Lyons, then performing under the name Blue Boy), another multiple Road March winner, drew on the **African spiritual** tradition with his early hit, "Soca Baptist". Meanwhile, Lord Shorty, soca's originator, retired to the country to become a spiritual visionary, changing his name to **Ras Shorty I** and forming his large family into a **gospel-soca** band, the **Love Circle**.

These innovations were at their peak during the late 1970s and early 1980s, by which time calypso constraints had more or less gone out the window. Some of the best late-generation Kitchener and Sparrow songs also emerged in these years, when **producer-arrangers** like **Art de Coteau, Eddie Quarless, Pelham Goddard, Carl 'Beaver' Henderson, Clive Bradley, Ed Watson** and **Leston Paul** ruled the roost and exercised a tremendous influence on the soca sound. Many of these arrangers are still in demand today,

Montserratian calypsonian Arrow, whose "Hot! Hot! Hot!" is the best-selling soca single of all time, spoke to Simon Broughton about the transition from calypso to soca – and the loss of the old traditions.

In the past calypso has been strongly political in its lyrics. You placed the emphasis on dance. Do you feel any need to address issues in your songs and reflect the history of the music?

A lot of my earlier music up to 1979 was message-oriented, because I was trying to be Calypso King of Montserrat and Calypso King of the Caribbean, and even my new material touches on issues. But of course, my primary goal is dance music, and to unite through my music all people, all races – to have everyone singing and dancing together. I leave it more to the news media to tell the people of the problems of the world. I'm taking the message of hope and happiness.

There's something about soca music which gives you the feeling that you want to get up and dance. Forget whatever problems you have, let's take you into some temporary utopia, let's forget the bills and just enjoy yourself! Even people who have never heard the music before, after one or two songs everybody is into the rhythm and the beat.

You've been accused of being the man responsible for destroying the old calypso. How do you feel about that?

I think I might be guilty of that, but for good results. I've been able to put a more commercial appeal onto soca and calypso. I think that the calypsonian or soca artist of the Caribbean can no longer be burdened with being the mouthpiece of the people. We are now in an age when Caribbean people are a lot more outspoken and we have opposition parties. It's no longer one-party rule and as musicians we should do what we have to do – make people happy.

Trinidad calypso was good, but now it's a new age and we need to move on. We need to take this music beyond the people of the Caribbean and show that the world can dance to it. This is what soca music has done.

JAK KILBY

TRINIDAD

and have been joined by a new crop of movers and shakers, including **Kenny Phillips**, **Graham Wilson**, **Martin 'Mice' Raymond**, **Shel Shok**, **Kirk Mitchell**, **Richard Ayoung**, and **Nicholas Brancker** from Barbados.

Songwriters, too, have been critical elements in the mix. **Winsford Devine** has penned lyrics for Sparrow and especially **Baron**, the hugely popular, sweet-voiced exponent of 1990s **lovers' soca**, while **GB** (Gregory Ballantyne) has written hits for David Rudder and others. There are an infinite number of ways of re-configuring the basic 'jam and wine' lyric pattern of soca, but often the standout number has that bit extra, with a helping of wit and social awareness from the calypso.

Brass and Bands

Brass has long been an integral feature of the calypso sound and the calypso tents have resident bands to back the competing singers. While steelbands ruled the streets, it was the brass ensembles who took centre stage in the fêtes and dancehalls. Today brass bands dominate the streets as well, providing music for the masquerade bands, and the **Caribbean Brass Festival**, established in 1991, is one of the Carnival season's largest public events.

The leading brass bands of the 1970s and '80s – **Gemini Brass**, **Blue Ventures**, **Charlie's Roots**, **Shandileer**, **Roy Cape Kaiso All Stars** and **Sound Revolution** – eagerly embraced soca, adapting with ease to the music's faster pace. While covers of the season's hits formed (and form) the core of their repertoire, original band songs became an increasingly important part of the soca scene as charismatic lead singers imposed themselves as soca stars in their own right.

Early stars included **David Rudder** and **Chris 'Tambu' Herbert**, who led Charlie's Roots, and Shandileer's **Carl and Carol Jacobs** and notably **Ronnie McIntosh**, who had huge party hits like "Ent". **Colleen Ella** and **Colin Lucas** developed successful numbers such as the hugely-enduring "Dollar Wine" with the backing of the band **Taxi**.

Many of the young solo artists of recent times, including **Ghetto Flex**, **Nigel and Marvin Lewis**, **Kurt Allen**, **Destra**, **Lisa Romany**, **Nicole Graves** and **Candy Hoyte**, have also sung, or still sing, with bands. **Sanell Dempster**, who won the Road March title with 1999's "River", is lead singer for **Blue Ventures**.

Rudder and Stalin: Soca Does Message

Of all the musicians who have come through the bands, the most consistently interesting is **David Rudder**, an artist rooted in the calypso tradition but wide open to new ideas and fusions, and a campaigner for soca's international dimension. "Calypso was very insular at one time," says Rudder. "It was what was happening on the block. I see the music going beyond the boundary of our island-ness. I see it as a world statement, not an island statement."

A long-time lead singer with Charlie's Roots, Rudder came on the scene as a solo calypsonian in 1986, with two massive songs. "The Hammer" revelled in the sound of the steelband in tribute to the great pan player and tuner Rudolph Charles ('the man with the hammer', who had died the previous year), while "Bahia Girl" used the theme of cross-cultural sexual attraction as a metaphor for the cultural and musical linkages between Trinidad and Brazil. Rudder made a clean sweep of the competitions that year, taking the Calypso Monarch, Road March and Young King titles.

Rudder reappeared the following year with "Calypso Music", a lyrically inventive, melodious anthem on the origins of calypso, which was immediately acknowledged as a one of the finest calypsos ever written (rare is the Trinidadian who cannot sing you at least a couple of verses.) He also withdrew from competition that year, on the grounds that he preferred making music to winning prizes. It was a revolutionary and contentious gesture in a musical culture that all too often sticks to well-known formulas rather then attempting to evolve or develop.

Since then Rudder has continued to produce some of Trinidad's most original and thought-provoking compositions. In an overtly political vein, the title track on his *1990* album played on the initials IMF as meaning 'Islands Must Fail':

ADRIAN BOOT

David Rudder

classic old school calypso. "High Mas", the big tune on his 1997 album, *Beloved*, controversially addressed the role of religion in the lives of Trinidadians, using the Lord's Prayer as its lyrical model. On his 2000 album, *Zero*, Rudder also looked to a broader set of musical influences, weaving in elements such as Algerian rai and bhangra.

Another soca-calypsonian who never fails to deliver a message in his songs is **Black Stalin** (Leroy Calliste). A Rasta who won the Calypso King of the World title in 1999, Stalin is known for his electrifying stage performances. Sometimes he acts the true oratorical calypsonian, standing and wagging his finger confrontationally at the audience – he did his apprenticeship in Kitchener's Carnival tent – and other times leaps around, dreadlocks swinging wildly, to make the point. Perhaps his most memorable song of all was the 1986 "Bun Dem" which begged Saint Peter to be prepared to cast into the fire world leaders like Thatcher, Reagan and Botha.

Soca Fusions

Since Blue Boy's "Soca Baptist" took the Road March title in 1980, soca has become the music of choice among a nation of hardened fêters – although, mysteriously, it often takes a back seat after Carnival is over. Still, there are around four hundred new releases each year, an increasing number of them released outside Trinidad and Tobago, in other Caribbean islands and in the US. The new Trinidad-style Carnivals cropping up yearly in other Caribbean islands and in cities in North America and Europe, have furnished a ready market for recordings and live performances, and most soca artists leave Trinidad after the Carnival season and tour non-stop until late in the year.

In 1994 the soca-calypso dichotomy was officially recognised when a separate **Soca Monarch** competition was established. Since then, the most frequent winners have been **Superblue**, who won the Monarch prize five times, and **Chris 'Tambu' Herbert**, formerly David Rudder's singing partner in Charlie's Roots, who won the Road March three years in succession, from 1988 to 1990 (when he recorded the soca anthem par excellence, "No, No, We Eh Going Home"). Other consistent contenders have included **Ronnie McIntosh**, **Iwer George** and the younger groups **Machel Montano and Xtatik** and **Blue Ventures**. These artists have developed the knack of making surefire soca dance hits which combine wit and parody with sexual teasing and strong call-and-respone hooks – a formula that always goes down well with partygoers and masqueraders on the streets at Carnival time.

A growing youth market has exerted a strong influence upon soca: waving their rags (usually towels or bandanas) and flags, the crews and posses of young Trinidad and Tobago dominate revels such as the Caribbean Brass Festival. The youth market has fuelled the emergence of a crop of young performers who, perhaps not unlike Kitchener's Young Brigade, have flown in the face of convention and re-made soca in their own image. The new music is often criticised by the older generation for its lack of lyrical content, for its preoccupation with partying and sex (or perhaps its refusal to mask such through the use of subtlety and innuendo), its fast pace and its easy co-optation of other musical styles, most controversially those from that musical powerhouse in the northern Caribbean – Jamaica.

The influence of **reggae and dancehall** on soca has been huge, and not surprisingly so, since Jamaican music has long been the most popular sound among Trinidad and Tobago's youth. A key figure in the meeting of soca and reggae has been the Jamaican bandleader and entrepreneur **Byron Lee**. Since 1974, Lee and his band the **Dragonaires** have based themselves in Trinidad during the Carnival season, playing the fête circuit and feeding off the energies of the local brass bands. Post-Carnival, they take the season's hits on a whirlwind tour of the Caribbean and North America, and, perhaps more importantly, record an album of cover versions which, thanks to good distribution, usually outsells most Trinidad soca releases. By the mid-1980s the band (which features Trinidadian singers and musicians) was producing original soca numbers and in the 1990s they introduced the now-ubiquitous Jamaican flavour of **ragga-soca**, of which more below.

Other Trinidad soca/calypso fusions include a tradition of **choirs**, many of whom perform a calypso and folk repertoire. Then there is the unclassifiable veteran singer-guitarist **André Tanker**, whose music straddles folk, jazz and calypso. And sitarist **Mungal Patasar** has developed a fusion of classical and Indian folk music and calyspo with his group Pantar.

Ragga-soca

Ragga-soca worked brilliantly – soca lending itself to the Jamaican-style half-rap, half-sung lyrics – and it has become such a strong part of the Carnival scene that a Ragga-Soca Monarch prize was added. The genre also provided Trinidad with one of its biggest international hits of the 1990s, "Joe Le Taxi", recorded by the soca/chutney singer **Sharlene Boodram**.

Arrangers such as **Kirk Mitchell** and **$hel Shok** have co-opted the Jamaican dancehall formula of building several tracks over the same rhythm (or riddim): "Pigtail" and "Y2K" being notable rhythms developed in Trinidad in recent times. Influential deejays like **Chinese Laundry** and **Third Bass** have also parlayed their knowledge of bass lines and rhythm tracks into part-time careers as recording artists and performers. Young artists like **Bunji Garlin**, **KMC** and **Magadan** have borrowed not only Jamaican rhythms and vocal styles, but at times also the Jamaican language and accent. This controversial (and as yet unnamed) new hybrid combining dancehall, soca and urban hip-hop has occasioned long public debates about music and national identity.

Foremost among Trinidad's new wave of ragga-soca bands is **Machel Montano and Xtatik**, who mix soca and calypso, reggae, dancehall, hip-hop, techno, rock and even country-and-western if the occasion requires it. Even more striking are the band's live stage performances, which feature pyrotechnics, acrobatic dance moves and displays of sexuality daring even by Carnival standards. Front man Montano has been a soca star since the age of ten, when he sang "Too Young To Soca," and became the youngest ever winner of the Road March title in 1997, with the hit "Big Truck."

Rapso

Soca and calypso are the dominant sounds of the Carnival season and certainly the trademark musical genres of Trinidad and Tobago. Yet after the bacchanal, the scene shifts abruptly. Apart from a few post-Carnival fêtes and concerts featuring the season's winners, the nation largely gives up soca and calypso. Jamaican-inflected ragga-soca from artists like Bunji Garlin and groups like Xtatik still get airtime, but reggae, dancehall, American pop,

R&B and hip-hop become the styles most often heard on the radio and in minibus taxis.

One new trini hybrid that has carved out a space at Carnival yet remains current throughout the year is **rapso**, a politically conscious fusion of rap and calypso (though it scarcely sounds like either). This has its origins in the 1970s, when singer **Lancelot Layne** created a kind of roots music, inspired by the Midnight Robber, a traditional Carnival masquerade character famous for his bombastic speeches, and taking inspiration from the old chartwells. His poetic, drum-driven chants were developed in the following decade by artists such as **Brother Resistance and the Network Riddum Band** and **Karega Mandela** into a kind of Trini 'conscious' reggae, with lyrics extolling ghetto resistance to oppression, backed by Jamaican-influenced rhythms, driven by drum and bass, and brass.

In the 1990s a new kind of rapso emerged, spearheaded by young bands such as **3 Canal**, **Ataklan** and **Kindred**. They widened the range of themes, combining political and spiritual concerns with more personal preoccupations, and introducing instrumentation and vocal styles gleaned from soul and reggae.

The upsurge in rapso has also prompted a return to the traditions that underpin the music and the music has become associated with **J'Ouvert**, the early-morning introduction to Carnival Monday, when the **'rhythm sections'** – groups of percussionists beating rhythms out of anything from bits of iron to dustbin covers to glass bottles – take to the streets alongside masqueraders wearing rags, mud and black grease. **3 Canal** has been a major populariser of J'Ouvert rapso, producing tuneful, often political songs for the occasion. Other bands that produce interesting J'Ouvert selections include **The Laventille Rhythm Section** and **Black Lyrics**.

Rapso also opened the door for actors, comedians, **spoken-word performers** such as **Nikki Crosby**, **Rhoma Spencer** and **Sprangalang** (Dennis Hall) to seek a slice of the soca pie with novelty hits like Crosby's "I'll Learn to Wine".

Caribbean Currents: Bajan Soca

Since the 1980s, Trinidad's neighbouring islands have played an increasing role in the Carnival music scene. **Arrow** from **Montserrat** broke the scene wide open in the 1980s and soca has come of age on the smaller islands. Each year Trinidad and Tobago's Carnival can expect contributions

RITUALS

3 Canal

from singers and bands from **Antigua**, **Barbados**, **Grenada**, **St Vincent** (notably with soca singer **Beckett**) and even **St Martin**. Jamaica is a dominant if ambivalent influence, too, and a two-way one – in 1990, Byron Lee introduced Carnival to Jamaica with the founding of the Trinidad-style **Byron Lee Jamaica Carnival**.

Antigua has a vibrant Carnival culture, and it was the threat of Road March victory by an Antiguan calypso – **King Short Shirt**'s 1977 hit "Tourist Leggo" – which caused the Road March competition to be closed from that time onward to non-citizens of Trinidad and Tobago. The fast pace of the music from Antiguans like Short Shirt and **Swallow** also set the tone for an increase in the tempo of Trinidadian soca. Antigua's **Burning Flames**, whose founding members were once part of Arrow's band, continue in that vein today, having broken onto the wider scene in 1990 with "Workey Workey". Now regulars at the Trinidad Carnival, Burning Flames collaborated with fellow Trinidadian hyperactives Xtatik on 1999's "Showdown".

By far the largest contributor, however, and the greatest influence, has been **Barbados**. Barbados' summer Carnival, the **Crop Over**, has grown steadily, and Bajan (Barbadian) singers like **Gabby**, **Grynner**, **Ras Iley**, **Red Plastic Bag**, and bands like **Spice,** were turning out fast-paced, melodic soca by the mid-1980s; Spice's "De Congaline" was much covered in Trinidad. Gabby, interestingly, wrote some of the most political calypsos of the 1980s. One of his biggest hits, "Jack", was a critique of the tourist hotel industry on Barbados, which was barring locals from access to the island's beaches. The song caught the attention of

Guyanese singer/producer **Eddy Grant**, who subsequently became Gabby's producer, introducing another vein of sound and turning Gabby into a Caribbean-wide star. Another notable Bajan singer-composer is **John King**.

By the 1990s Bajan soca had matured fully, producing the highly successful soca bands **krosfyah** and **Square One**. Krosfyah's sound is energetic and fresh, often carrying positive, conscious messages. Trinidadian partygoers surrendered themselves to the infectious rhythms of their hit "Pump Me Up" during the 'Bajan invasion' of 1996, the year Barbados announced itself with great fanfare as a musical force to be reckoned with. Krosfyah is yet to repeat that level of success in Trinidad, though they have been concentrating mainly on the US market. Their lead singer **Edwin Yearwood** is highly respected in Trinidad and in 1997 came third in the Soca Monarch competition, the highest ever ranking for a Bajan singer. His songs such as "All Aboard' have also become hits for Trinidadian artists such as Tony Prescott.

Square One has enjoyed great popularity in Trinidad and Tobago since the late 1990s with a string of hits by various band members, including frontwoman, Allison Hinds, one of soca's most accomplished performers, whose adaptation of a Surinamese folk song, "Faluma", was a hit of the 1999 Carnival.

Bajan soca has exerted a strong influence on Trinidad bands, many of whom have adopted krosfyah-like elements such as the chorus of male voices, as well as **Ring Bang**, a rhythm developed (and subsequently copyrighted) by **Eddy Grant**, which is one of the signature features of the Bajan sound. Barbadian arrangers such as **Nicholas Brancker**

KALINAGO

Square One singer Allison Hinds

have also developed substantial working relationships with Trinidadian artists.

Like the younger generation of Trinidadian artists, 'up-the-islands' bands have been open to new musical influences. **Red Plastic Bag** incorporated Spanish guitar on their hit "Sweet Rosita," while **Positive Vibes** have blended soca with *spouge*, the up-country folk music of Barbados, played on guitars, mandolins and hand drums.

discography

Over 400 singles are produced each year for the Carnival season in Trinidad and Tobago. To keep up, you'll need to check out the annual CD compilations of hits issued by various local labels:

- Carnival Party Rhythms (Rituals, Trinidad).
- J'Ouvert (Rituals, Trinidad).
- Soca Colours (Chinese Laundry, Trinidad).
- Soca Gold (Hot Vinyl/Smokey Joe's, Trinidad).
- Soca Switch (Chinese Laundry, Trinidad).

- Soca Stampede (Rituals, Trinidad).
- Island Jamz (Jo-Go, Trinidad; Jam Down, US).
- Strictly Soca (JW Productions, US).

As these are issued each year, and not always reissued once sold out, individual volumes are not included below.

Vintage Compilations

Calypso At Midnight and **Calypso After Midnight** (Rounder, US).

These two CDs capture an historic moment in the history of the calypso – a concert organised and recorded by ethnomusicologist Alan Lomax (see p.533) at the New York Town Hall in December 1946. Featured artists include Lord Invader (writer of "Rum and Coca Cola" – Trini's first US hit), and there are also sections of Spiritual Baptist singing and traditional unaccompanied drumming.

Calypso Breakaway 1927–41 (Rounder, US).

A classic collection from the golden era, featuring songs by King Radio, The Lion, Lord Beginner and Attila the Hun.

Calypso War: Black Music in Britain 1956–58 (Sequel, UK).

A fine collection of calypsos including Lord Invader, The Mighty Terror, Lord Ivanhoe and Jamaica-born Ben Bowers.

Kings of Calypso (Castle Communications, UK).

Good compilation including Mighty Terror, Lord Invader and newer artists like Noel Anthony.

Trinidad Loves To Play Carnival 1914–1939 (Matchbox, UK).

A wonderful archive jaunt through the history of street marches and early Carnival calypsos, with highly informative sleeve notes including all the lyrics.

West Indies: An Island Carnival (Nonesuch Explorer, US).

Fascinating anthology of rustic groups from various islands of the Lesser Antilles – Trinidad, St Lucia, St Vincent, etc. In addition to calypso, there are examples of religious music: Hindu, Muslim and Afro-Trinidadian Shango.

Modern Compilations

Panorama 99: Steelbands of Trinidad and Tobago (Sanch, Trinidad; Delos, US).

Recorded live at Panorama, the Trinidad Carnival's steel pan competition, this two-CD selection showcases fourteen of Trinidad and Tobagos top bands from 1999. Most of the bands number nearly a hundred players and perform renditions of popular calypsos (by Lord Kitchener for example) as well as specially written Carnival composition.

Ragga Soca (JW Productions, US).

A strong current trend in soca is to mix the beats up with dancehall. Here the talented bands Atlantik and Xtatik show why they have emerged as the top exponents.

The Rough Guide to Calypso and Soca (World Music Network, UK).

An excellent single-CD introduction to the music, this ranges through classic calypso from Lord Pretender and Kitchener, through tracks from Tambu and David Rudder, to new stars like 3 Canal, Square One ... and ends up with Sharlene Boodram's irresistible "Joe Le Taxi".

Calypso & Soca

THE ROUGH GUIDE

Say What? Double Entendre Soca from Trinidad (Rounder, US).

A selection of soca songs, mainly from the 1980s, showing that the new music kept its bite – most of the double entendres here being political rather than sexual. Danceable too.

Soca Music From Trinidad (Rounder, US).

A soca compilation in two volumes that puts the emphasis on lyrical content. Thoroughbred wit from top calypsonians Chalkdust, Plainclothes, Shadow and Rio.

This Is Soca (Nascente, UK).

A 1998 soca anthology including Superblue, Tambu, Rudder and Chutney star Marcia Miranda.

2000 Calypso Compilation: A Tribute to Pan (JW Productions, US).

Calypsos written especially for steel orchestras usually appear as minor tracks on annual compilations. *A Tribute to Pan* gathers together the 2000 season's most popular pan calypsos as rendered by their original singers. Veteran De Fosto, long destined heir to Lord Kitchener, is represented, as well as Super Blue, Oba, Denyse Plummer, Hollis Wright, Sparrow, and others.

Wind Your Waist (Shanachie, US).

To wind in this context is to dance in the erotic, rhythmic way the music of Trinidad unashamedly makes you do. Skilled or not, you can hardly avoid dancing to these tunes from Arrow, Shadow, Burning Flames, Drupatee (Chutney soca) and Spice (from Barbados).

Artists

Ataklan

Trinidad's answer to Beck? Ataklan is certainly the biggest new rapso talent around – a fiercely independent songwriter and singer – and arguably the most original artist to have emerged on the island since David Rudder.

Atamorphosis (Taj Records, Trinidad).

A self-produced album that offers a good 20-track sampling of Ataklan's quirky, zestful style.

Atlantik

Atlantik are one of the cornerstones of the band scene in Trinidad and Tobago.

Hard As Steel (JW Productions, US).

Atlantik borrows the familiar hooks and beats of the 1990s and re-weaves them into a stylish product, using the formula that successful soca bands have followed for the past few years – building individual tracks around a stable of singers and their particular styles and talents.

Baron

One of the sweetest voices in soca, Baron is an absolute master of the slow, sexy 'lovers' ballad.

Tears of Gold (JW, US).

1997 classic from the master of lovers' soca; his high, persuasive voice rising above solidly crafted soca beats.

Black Stalin

One of calypso's most flexible, thoughtful and principled contestants, Black Stalin is as much at ease in the high-powered soca dancehall as in the calypso tents.

Rebellion (Ice, UK).

A fine introduction to Stalin's style and content, featuring his massive hit "One Tune Pan Man", with high-tech production from Ice label chief Eddy Grant.

Roots Rock Soca (Rounder, US).

A selection of Stalin hits from the 1970s and '80s, including much of his greatest soca disc, *Caribbean Man*.

Burning Flames

Antigua's Burning Flames are the undisputed kings of the soca scene in the Leeward islands. Known for their catchy tunes and energetic vibes, they are one of the new breed of Caribbean bands who are at ease playing ragga, zouk or soca – even Latin, if required.

 Dig (Mango, UK).

Reggae meets soca in this release from the Flames; includes their Pan-Caribbean hit, "Workey Workey", (originally covered by Byron Lee).

Hokuspokus/Magical Music (Arrow Music, Trinidad).

Soul, kadans, reggae and other influences combine in one of the Flames' best albums to date. Includes "Showdown" – their 1999 collaboration with fellow hyperactives Xtatik from Trinidad.

Calypso Rose

Hailing from Trinidad's sister island, Tobago, Rose (McCartha Lewis) is definitely calypso music's leading woman singer. Not only has she put female calypsonians on the map, winning the Calypso Monarch in 1978, but she's made a mark for her native Tobago, too.

Soca Diva (Ice, UK).

Cracking numbers with vicious wit and winning melody with Rose's trademark soul-soaked husky purr everpresent and wonderful.

TRINIDAD

Chalkdust

Chalkdust is one of the greatest living calypso writers in Trinidad – hilarious, clever (sometimes a little too much so) and a social commentator second to none. He's probably the most famous school teacher in the Caribbean.

 Port of Spain Gone Insane (Ebony Records, UK).

A tuneful, danceable album including "Too Much Quacks" and "Man Want To Dance", about the decline of calypso standards. Chalkie's precise and colourful vocal style remains thoroughly entertaining and informative.

Crazy

Crazy is an explosive performer and singer, though you'll need to have lived in Trini a while to understand his very street patois. Unimpressed by the airs and graces of other front rank singers, he remains a man of the people and one of Trinidad's most popular characters.

⊙ **Leh We Jump** (DY, US).

A good set which captures Crazy's versatility well – he's as at home on mid-tempo, witty songs as much as on the more 'jump 'n wine' style of soca.

Gabby

A calypsonian who has emerged during the soca years, Gabby is equally at home on big, fast soca productions as on his witty, slower, lyric-centred calypsos.

⊙ **Soca Trinity with Grynner and Bert "Panta" Brown** (Ice, UK).

A lively, humorous set from leading satirical calypsonians; includes Grynner's most famous song, "Best Brown".

Gypsy

Gypsy has a haunting voice and a knack for penning superb calypso anthems, including, notably, 1986's "The Sinking Ship" and 1997s "Little Black Boy".

⊙ **Natural High** (Hot Vinyl, UK).

The essential Gypsy selection, including "The Sinking Ship" and "Party and Fire Jump". Gypsy

Natural High Gypsy

Lord Kitchener

Lord Kitchener (Aldwyn Roberts, 1922–2000) was, with Mighty Sparrow, the acknowledged father of modern calypso – and he alone was the king of 'jump up' soca. A man of acerbic and slack wit, Kitch was a formidable claypsonian and writer, a larger than life character who was a crucial figure on the Trinidad music, Carnival and steel pan scene for more than half a century.

 Klassic Kitchener Volume One (Ice, UK; RAS, US).

The first of these *Klassic Kitchener* volumes is perhaps most classic and enjoyable of all, featuring some calypsos dating back to the 1940s. There are two further volumes in the series – both full of treats.

⊙ **Longevity** (JW Productions, US).

A superb 1993 release, with Kitch's handling of up tempo soca rhythms second to none. Big, brassy, confident music for Carnivals the world over.

⊙ **Classic Kitch** (JW Productions, US).

This final recording of the Grand Master is as good a sampling as any of the veteran calypsonian's impressive range. The nine tracks include a remix of old evergreens such as "Gimme The Ting".

KMC

One of the young turks of the Trinidad and Tobago scene, Ken Marlon Charles' sound incorporates reggae, dancehall, and hip-hop into a mix that still sounds deeply Trinidadian.

⊙ **2000 Pieces of KMC** (VP Records, Trinidad).

KMC broke onto the scene in 1998 with the rollicking hits "Soca Bashment" and "Bashment to Carnival". He continues the trend on *2000 Pieces*, with his unique blend of reggae/dancehall-inflected soca and growling voice.

Krosfyah

This nine-piece band from Barbados, with lead vocalist Edwin Yearwood, are spearheading the so-called 'Bajan Invasion' of Soca. They took Trinidad Carnival by storm in 1996 and have gone from strength to strength, with strong lyrics, a distinctive sound and consistently excellent production.

Hot Zone (Kalinago, US).

One of krosfyahs successes has been the seamless blending of Caribbean styles, from vintage calypso to reggae and zouk into a melodic and danceable sound. This 1999 release includes a blues-styled ballad, a tribute to Bajan freedom fighter "Sarah" and the useful Soca fare such as "Too Sexy" and "Hotty Hotty Gal".

Machel Montano

Born in 1975, Montano is already a veteran, having made his calypso debut at age 10, and carrying off his first big hit, "Too Young to Soca" two years later. His experience shows in his remarkable grasp of what it takes to bridge the gap between soca and other styles and come up with a product that is undeniably Trinidadian and still appeals to the young, dancehall-crazed masses.

⊙ **Heavy Duty** (Xtatik, Trinidad).

The Prince of Soca set out his store as a mature artist on this 1997 album, featuring his Road March hit "Big Truck".

2000 Young to Soca (JW Productions, Trinidad).

Machel's latest outing is soca, yes, but seasoned with hip-hop, R&B, reggae, chutney, rock and jazz – the result is a rich, funky tapestry.

The Mighty Sparrow

Only the late Lord Kitchener rivalled The Mighty Sparrow (born Slinger Francisco in Grenada, 1935) in the calypso world. A giant of a personality, known and loved throughout the Caribbean, Sparrow has recorded well over one hundred albums and it is a testament that almost any one of them will provide a good insight into his wit and observation, haunting vocal style and patois phrasing.

WITH LORD KITCHENER

 Mighty Sparrow and Lord Kitchener's Carnival Hits (Ice, UK).

Sixteen hits from the two veterans – as fine an introduction as anyone could hope for.

Party Classics Vols 1 & 2 (Charlie, UK).

A collection of Sparrow's great hits from the 1950s on.

Red Plastic Bag

Red Plastic Bag is a Barbados singer leading the assault on Trinidad hegemony. He has great songs, adventurous arrangements and excellent use of pan-Caribbean and other Latin influences.

Red Alert (Rohit, US).

Includes one of the best Latin/soca fusions ever, "Sweet Rosita". Here, flamenco guitar joins an infectious beat and winning, hilarious lyrics.

Roaring Lion

A mainstay of twentieth century calypso with Sparrow and Kitch, the late, great Roaring Lion (Rafael de Lion, 1909–99) never embraced the soca idiom as much as the others. But he remained a hugely popular, elegant, opinionated and incisive lyricist and singer.

 Standing Proud (Ice, UK).

An essential anthology of octogenarian Lion's finest work, including his best-known song, "Never Make a Pretty Woman your Wife (Always Marry a Woman Uglier than You)".

Rootsman

Rootsman is a charismatic dreadlocked singer, slightly less prolific now than in the 1980s, but still a fine lyricist, and a tunesmith up there with the best of them.

The Best of Rootsman with Bally (JW Productions, US).

An enormously enjoyable album from these leading soca artists, including Rootsman's irresistible "Soca In De Palace".

David Rudder

David Rudder (born Port of Spain, 1961) has been the most important talent in Trinidad since his Carnival debut in 1986 fronting Tambu's band, Charlie's Roots. He is an original, provocative artist whose visionary music, infused with a love and knowledge of soul, zouk and jazz, is uniquely his own, and combined with top-notch lyricism.

The Hammer (Lypsoland, Trinidad; London Records, UK).

The pivotal Rudder set from 1986, including the Road March and Monarch prizes, "The Hammer" and "Bahia Girl".

 The Gilded Collection, Volumes 1 and 2 (JW Productions, Trinidad).

These late-1990s compilations include consistently strong material from Rudder and Charlie's Roots.

Zero (Lypsoland, Trinidad; JW Productions, US).

Rudder's current range of musical influences are in evidence on this recent album, featuring tracks such as "Shake Down Time", which incorporates rai and bhangra riffs.

Shadow

Shadow (born Winston Bailey, 1942, Tobago) was the Year 2000 Calypso Monarch – the first time he had won the title, despite a string of soca hits. He is a singer, bassist and bandleader.

The Best of Shadow, Vol. 1 (Straker's, Trinidad).

Released in 1995, this rounds up 20-odd years of Shadow's funky output, including his 1974 Road March winning tune and hugely influential rhythm, "Bassman".

Shorty

Shorty's work is seminal to the development of modern soca: he is usually credited as one of the originators of both the term and the form. He moved from soca to rural roots Rasta music, refashioning himself as Ras Shorty I.

Greatest Hits (Charlie's, Trinidad).

Almost all the classics, presented in their original versions, are here – and they show how much Shorty was ahead of his time. "Shanti Om" (which was covered by Bombay duo Babla and Kanchan) preceded the chutney-soca onslaught by more than a decade; "Who God Bless" and "Higher World" foreshadow Shorty's eventual revoking of urban pleasures.

Singing Francine

There still aren't enough women singers making an impact in the soca music industry but Francine's offerings are always valuable. She has a great voice and is a thoughtful lyricist.

This is Singing Francine (Red Bullet, Netherlands).

Excellent introduction to Francine, with a good selection of up-tempo soca tracks with fine lyrics.

Square One

One of the leading Barbadian bands, Sqaure One are ably fronted by dynamic singer Allison Hinds.

In Full Bloom (I-Man/Gator Records, Trinidad).

With this album, which includes the hits "Faluma" and "Kitty Cat", Square One cemented their status as a force to reckon with across the Caribbean.

Fast Forward (I-Man/Gator Records, Trinidad).

The group's 1999 offering, including memorable songs "Iron Bazodee" and "Togetherness".

Superblue

The Road March King of Port of Spain, Superblue is the wunderkind of the soca classic. His deep, cannon of a voice booms brilliantly over the heaviest of soca beats: horns wailing, rhythm thumping and backing vocals ululating in unison.

⊙ **Flag Party** (Ice, UK).

1993 classic from a man who keeps the soca saucy and full.

⊙ **Hooray** (SJP, Trinidad).

A collection of Superblue's greatest hits of the late 1990s, including "Jab Jab" and "Barbara".

Tambu (Chris Herbert)

Tambu (Chris Herbert) leads the group Charlie's Roots, along with David Rudder, and is the main Carnival presence. He had one of the biggest hits ever with 1987's "This Party It Is", and has kept the songs and anthems coming, with excellent, poetic material.

⊙ **Culture** (Lypsoland, Trinidad).

One of the classic Carnival records, including the great Road March winner, "This Party It Is".

3 Canal

This three-man collective have taken the rapso form and added a funky World Music sensibility, while maintaining rapso's emphasis on strong lyrics and messages. They are at their very best at J'Ouvert – the pre-dawn revels that usher in Carnival.

⊙ **The Fire Next Time** (Rituals, Trinidad).

The Carnival traditions remain at the core of 3 Canal's sound and lyrics, but on this album they incorporate a fusion of Caribbean and transnational sounds (techno, drum'n'bass, R&B, funk) into the Rapso matrix.

Xtatik

Fronted by Machel Montano, Xtatik are one of the big Soca success stories of the past few years – an energetic young band bursting with ideas and unafraid to blend Latin, rap, swing, zouk and dancehall into the soca mix.

⊙ **Here comes the Band** (JW Productions, Trinidad).

This heady brew of 22 numbers by Xtatik and the Mad Bull crew is a mixed bag – but the 10 or so tracks that really work are great. Xtatik's impish naughtiness and infectious sense of fun is in full effect, complete with musical hooks purloined from far and wide and remade in the band's image.

TRINIDAD

526 *Calypso/Soca*

Trinidad

Chutney

the caribbean's hot hindi sound

Trinidad has a substantial Indian population – recruited as labourers by the British in the nineteenth century – which has maintained folk traditions from the motherland. The community has also produced a unique pop music – chutney – mixing Indian rhythms and instrumentation with calpyso, soca and other strands. It emerged onto the public stage in the 1970s and swiftly become popular enough to have its own Carnival prize – the Chutney Soca Monarch. **Tina K. Ramnarine** reports.

Chutney is no misnomer for Trinidad's Indian pop music. Ask around the island how the name came about and the answer is always the same – it is, simply, a hot music. Its hotness lies in the singers' use of double entendres and, more importantly, in the music's fast and repetitive rhythms, which are played on *tassa* and *dholak* drums and the *dhantal* (an iron rod struck by a horse-shoe shaped beater). These rhythms are intended to drive audiences to dance.

The Ingredients

Chutney has developed mainly in Trinidad, although the music has outposts in Guyana and Surinam, and other parts of the Caribbean. It has only recently entered the mainstream of Caribbean musical life but the story of its development as a popular genre begins with the **arrival of Indians in the Caribbean** in 1838.

Following the emancipation of slaves in the British Caribbean, labourers were recruited from other parts of the Empire to maintain the sugar plantations. These included nearly half a million Indians who were taken to the Caribbean as indentured (contracted) labourers between 1838 and 1917 – and by the time indentureship was abolished, most had come to regard the Caribbean as home. They came from different regions and spoke different languages and dialects, but there was a

Chutney ensemble playing dholak, harmonium and dhantal

majority leaning to the northern provinces of Uttar Pradesh and Bihar.

The Trinidad Indians maintained their own culture, traditions and folk music. Among its forms were the 'private' folk songs performed by women for family and friends on special occasions – notably weddings and births. These songs stand as one of the chief roots of chutney.

On Display

The first public chutney shows took place in Trinidad in the mid-1970s, pioneered by the singer, **Sundar Popo**. Its rise was swift and dramatic. By the end of the 1980s, chutney was an established style, with a booming cassette culture, and fans in all sectors of the community; by 1995 it had an official role at Carnival with a Chutney Soca Monarch competition and its own Carnival **chutney tents**.

Developing at this time, when calypso was being energised into soca and fusing with all kinds of Caribbean influences, it is little surprise chutney took on a panoply of influences. These included calypso, soca, reggae and rap, and from further afield, folk, devotional and film songs from India. In her song "Indian Soca" (1989), **Drupatee** sings:

Indian soca, sounding sweeter,
hotter than a chulha (stove),
Rhythm from Africa and India,
blend together in a perfect mixture.

But the title of Drupatee's song gives a somewhat misleading picture, for chutney is more than just the 'Indian' version of soca. Chutney singers place great importance on the music's origins in Indian folk and ritual traditions.

There has been one major change in chutney's transformation, however, in the increasing role of men, as singers and especially musicians, both in the commerical music and its folk or celebratory occasions. In contemporary chutney the dholak, dhantal and harmonium continue to be an essential part of the musical texture but guitars, keyboards and drum machines tend to dominate.

Some of the women's folk songs were quite bawdy, and since they were often performed as part of wedding ceremonies they dealt with themes of love and marriage. Many current chutney songs deal with the same kinds of **themes**. The 1995 Chutney Monarch, **Sonny Mann**, for example, gained his title with "Lotay La", a song full of innu-

endo about a woman who is rolling drunk and dancing. Performed in the Hindi dialect, Bhojpuri, the song wasn't understood by everyone, even in the Indian community, and as its meaning became more generally known it sparked controversy – just as the early calypsos had done.

As in calypso, chutney singers began to address **topical, social and political issues**. Sundar Popo wrote a song for the celebration of Indian Arrival Day in Trinidad in which he narrated an account of Indian migration to the island:

The Fatel Rozack came from India
with me nanee and me nana ...
in the boat they came,
singing and playing their tabla.
Remember 1845, the 13th of May,
225 immigrants who landed on that day.

At the last elections in Trinidad (in 1995), Jairam Dindial recorded a song proclaiming: "We're voting UNC – Basdeo Panday, Basdeo Panday our next Prime Minister." He got his wish.

Chutney Soca

While there is a debt to Indian traditions, chutney is a distinctly Caribbean music. Its lyrics deal with issues that concern people in the Caribbean, and its musical style is closer to calypso than to any Indian music. Indeed, leading chutney singers such

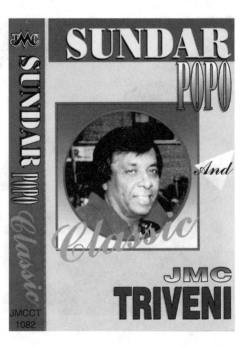

as **Terry Gajraj**, **Drupatee**, **Rikki Jai** and **Chris Garcia** are also soca/calypsonians who have sung in the Carnival calypso tents, and chutney is sometimes called **chutney-soca** in recognition of the soca dance element.

Just as calypsonians spar and compete with each other through their song texts (that famous Trinidadian *picong*), so too do the chutney singers. Sonny Mann's song was controversial because he described the drunk, dancing woman as "bhowjie", meaning a sister-in-law or an older female relative. This seemed to indicate a lack of respect for the social and gender relations observed by Indian-Caribbeans. **Sundar Popo** released a song, "Cold Water", in response, admonishing: "Sonny Mann cool yourself with cold water, you lotaying your bhowjie and not your brother."

While chutney has been much influenced by calypso, the process has not been entirely one way. The ever-popular **Mighty Sparrow** used Indian themes and Hindi words in "Maharajin" (1992), a love song to an Indian girl: "I will tell you true, the way I feel for you, I'll do anything to make you happy. So if you think it's best to change me style of dress, I will wear a *caphra* or a *dhoti*." The dhantal, dholak and harmonium featured in the instrumental accompaniment. **Mighty Trini**, **Ajala** and **Ras Shorty I** have also produced popular songs with Indian themes, respectively "Curry Tabanca" (which has become part of the steel band repertoire), "Sohani" (which features a sitar), and "Shanti Om". This last song became popular not only in Trinidad but also in **India**, where chutney has been making some inroads of late, largely through the efforts of the Indian musicians **Babla** and **Kanchan**.

In Trinidad, meantime, chutney is becoming as national a form as calypso, with all sectors of the population participating in its performance. In 1997 the young chutney singer **Sharlene Boodram** reached the top of the Trinidad charts (and had a global hit) with the song "Joe Le Taxi", singing with the ragga singer General Grant. **Sonny Mann** also collaborated with grant, as well as the soca star Denise Belfon, on a variant of his hit "Lotay La". Chutney has also gone mainstream in its adoption by the mainstream Trinidad labels, such as Rituals, and it is no longer to be found only on small runs of cassettes.

Chutney, like soca, has also been fusing like crazy over the past few years, with crossover strains including **ragga chutney** (Apache Waria and Terry Gajraj), **chutney-bhangra**, **chutney-hip-hop**, **soca-bhangra** and **bhangra-wine**. Chut-

Sharlene Boodram

ney singers, these days, sing about the 'ragga dulahin' (ragga bride) who is 'plenty fun and knows how to party' (Double D's "Ragga Dulahin"). It's come a long way from the wedding party.

discography

Like soca and calypso, chutney has a song and Carnival bias and the latest hits are easiest found on compilations. There are a number of series, such as Chutney Gold (JMC, US) becoming established.

Compilations

 **Chutney Gold, Volumes 1 and 2** (JMC, US).

A good budget series, featuring the annual hits by most of the major names.

Chutney Party: Various Artists (Rituals, Trinidad).

A good introductory volume featuring hits by Heeralal Rampartap, Cecil Fonrose, Sarah and Sally Sagram, and Sonny Mann.

Hot Chutney Flavours (M.C. Records, Trinidad).

This compilation includes less familiar names like Ramdeen Maharaj, Michael Duham, Asha Kamachie and others. Rajkumar Kariah sings "Everybody Singing D Chutney" and he's right! There's a proliferation of chutney recordings in the local market at the moment.

Hot & Spicy Chutney (Nascente, UK).

This is an excellent and accessible introduction to various types of chutney. It includes classics like Sundar Popo's "Scorpion Gyal" and some of the latest fusion developments such as Double D's "Ragga Dulahin".

Artists

Sharlene Boodram

Sharlene Boodram started off her singing career at the age of eight with calypsos. Now approaching 20, she has won prizes across the Caribbean and notched up an international hit with the ragga crossover song "Joe Le Taxi".

⊙ **Colours of Unity** (Rituals, Trinidad).

This is as good an example as any of ragga-chutney. In a male-dominated market, Sharlene Boodram is one of the few really successful chutney female singers.

Jairam Dindial

Dindial is a singer following a family tradition. He is from a well-known family of musicians.

📼 **Jairam Dindial: Classical and Chutney**
(Praimsingh, Trinidad).

Dindial sings some traditional songs on this cassette recording as well as chutney. A good example of a politically-motivated campaign song is included.

Chris Garcia

Better known as a soca artist, Chris Garcia has played on some Indian-Caribbean connections to establish a niche for himself amongst chutney audiences.

⊙ **Chutney Bacchanal** (JMC Records, US).

The title track is more soca than chutney but it was another hit song. Maybe this could be seen as a further example of fusion? In 1996, large numbers of school children had memorised the nonsense words to the chorus of the title track, intended to sound like Hindi.

Sundar Popo

Sundar Popo is one of the central singers in the history of chutney, credited with introducing this genre into a public performance space. He is still an active performer.

⊙ **Sundar Popo and JMC Triveni** (JMC Records, US).

Popo sings some of his hit songs with one of Trinidad's most well-known backing bands.

⊙ **Cool Yourself with Cold Water**
(JMC Records, US).

Includes songs composed to celebrate one hundred and fifty years of Indian presence in Trinidad and Popo's reply to Sonny Mann's "Lotay La".

Anand Yankaran

Anand Yankaran is one of the most popular chutney singers. While he sings updated chutney songs he also comes from a family of established singers.

⊙ **Party Time**
(JMC Records, US).

These recordings include club mixes of songs like "If your Mammy like ah Sadine".

USA

filling the map with music

In May 1998 veteran singer and folk activist Pete Seeger led a concert at New York's Carnegie Hall to celebrate the fiftieth birthday of **Folkways** – one of America's crucial record companies. It's thanks to this label – now known as Smithsonian Folkways – that much of America's roots music was ever recorded and made available, an achievement which played an important part in fuelling the dynamic folk revival. Pete's son, **Tony Seeger**, heir to the huge Folkways archive at the Smithsonian Institution, tells the story of the label, while **Richie Unterburger** profiles the USA's other great folk music pioneer archivists, **Harry Smith** and **Alan Lomax**. ·

A merican popular music – blues, country and folk, most directly, but even rock-'n'roll – owe a considerable debt to the roots music of the states, as it developed in the last part of the nineteenth century and the early decades of the twentieth. Indeed, when it was re-released on CD, many greeted Harry Smith's *Anthology of American Folk Music* as the great missing link, the root history, of music in the USA. That recording is perhaps the single most important in the Folkways archive, but it is just one aspect of an extraordinary label and story.

SMITHSONIAN FOLKWAYS

Moses Asch, founder of Folkways Records

Moses Asch and the Folkways Story

The enthusiast and visionary **Moses Asch** (1905–1986) founded Folkways Records with **Marian Distler** on Labour Day 1948. Their aim was straightforward, if immodest – to create a public archive of all the sounds in the world. Asch chose the name 'Folkways' because he considered all music to be 'folk' – Beethoven as much as South American Indian singers. In the forty years that he ran the label, Asch issued albums ranging from the music of remote Amazonian villages to New York avant-garde poetry, from unaccompanied ballad singers to bluegrass, from ancient Greek literature to modern Soviet poetry. He documented not only music, but the raw sounds of the struggles for liberation and justice in Africa, Ireland, Poland, the United States and elsewhere.

Folkways' success was due to Moses Asch's dedication to his ideal and to the work and enthusiasm of a large number of compilers who travelled around the world recording music and writing notes, often for a pittance of money. Mike Seeger

was given a hundred dollars to make the banjo music recordings released as the remarkable compilation *American Banjo, Three Finger and Scruggs Style*; he travelled around for months with a carry-all and a heavy portable recorder, sleeping in his car and occasionally stopping in motels for showers. Equally enthusiastic artists often sold Asch their recordings outright and made do with minimal royalties, while he struggled to keep the company afloat.

By the time of Asch's death, the Folkways catalogue numbered getting on for 2000 recordings, ranging through every US regional tradition, jazz and blues, poetry and political speeches, traditional music from almost every country in the world, and the sounds of anything from frogs and trains

USA

to junkyards and car races. And alongside the performances, many releases contained extensive notes, often including song texts and analysis.

The **Smithsonian Institution** acquired the rights to the archive from the Asch family on the understanding that the recordings would be preserved and made available to the public for the foreseeable future. Almost unique in the record industry, no Folkways recording was ever deleted and if you couldn't find a copy in the record store, you could order directly from Folkways. All titles are still available from the Smithsonian Institution, released on high-quality cassette or, increasingly, on CD.

The Institute have added to the catalogue themselves, issuing new releases like the awesome 20-volume *Music of Indonesia* series, and Smithsonian Folkways discs feature prominently in discographies throughout this book. But the label is especially crucial to the music of the US, which runs to fifteen pages of the current catalogue. Field recordings from Texas to Maine capture and preserve the variety and beauty of speech and song throughout the nation, alongside historic gems of old-time, bluegrass and Native American music. The jewel, however, remains the legendary **Anthology of American Folk Music**, edited by Harry Smith. This capricious compilation of archive recordings changed the course of American folk music and fuelled the 1960s revival. "I'd match the *Anthology* up against any other single compendium of important information ever published", says guitarist John Fahey. "The Dead Sea Scrolls? Nah. I'll take the *Anthology*."

Harry Smith

Harry Smith (1923–1991) was physically small – stunted by rickets – but as if to make up for it, had a personality larger than life. He created a good many myths about his life, but we know for certain he was born in Portland, Oregon and spent his latter years in New York City. He began studying and recording 'peyote songs' of the Kiowa Indians and then became a painter, filmmaker, collector of Ukrainian Easter eggs, occultist, friend of Alan Ginsberg, and professional eccentric.

Smith's 84-track *Anthology*, now a boxed set of six CDs, was first released in 1952 as three double LPs – their volumes devoted to *Ballads*, *Social Music* and *Songs*. It was Smith's vision, as well as his extraordinary personality, comments and artwork (included on CD-ROM in the re-issue) that give the *Anthology* its character. The original booklet was set out like an old-fashioned mail order catalogue with pictures and headlines sum-

Harry Smith

ming up the lyrics, alongside quotations 'useful to the editor'.

In his selections, Smith deliberately ignored field recordings and the Library of Congress Archives in favour of commercial releases by labels such as Brunswick, Victor, Columbia and Okeh. He wanted music that people had been prepared to pay good money for. This was the first collection to treat folk, hillbilly, and blues recordings of the 1920s and '30s as valuable; during World War II they had often been melted for war efforts.

The *Anthology* revealed a forgotten world of American music to a new generation. Listening to the high, lonesome vocals of **Clarence Ashley**, the bird-quill playing of **Henry Thomas**, the swinging violin of **Eck Robertson** or the one-time best-selling blues singer, guitarist and wrestler **Blind Lemon Jefferson** was (and is) like hearing a distant culture. At the same time, they are unmistakably American and became a crucial ingredient in the US folk revival.

Following its release, surviving musicians like Clarence Ashley, Eck Robertson, Dock Boggs and

Mississippi John Hurt were tracked down and fêted at folk festivals, and songs from the *Anthology* resonated through the work of the **New Lost City Ramblers**, **Mike and Pete Seeger**, **Bill Monroe**, **Joan Baez** and **Bob Dylan**, as well as among artists not readily associated with the folk revival such as **James Brown** and the **Grateful Dead**. There's a memorable version of Clarence Ashley's "The Coo Coo Bird" by **Big Brother and the Holding Company**, with Janis Joplin on vocals.

There are now countless re-issues of 1920s recordings and whole retrospectives of several of the artists featured in Harry Smith's distinctive LPs. But the *Anthology* remains an unmatched collection reflecting an astonishing period of American music when local performers were celebrated enough to record commercially, but still close enough to their roots and communities to retain an unfakeable down-home feeling.

Alan Lomax

The third key figure in the history of American folk music is **Alan Lomax** (born 1915). A more scholarly figure, Lomax was an astonishingly prolific collector of music at a crucial moment – just before local traditions became subsumed into homogonised culture. As Brian Eno has written: 'Alan Lomax is a completely central figure in

twentieth century culture. Without him it's possible that there would have been no blues explosion, no R&B movement, no Beatles and no Stones and no Velvet Underground... he was the conduit, mainlining the uniqueness and richness and passion of African-American music into the fertile early beginnings of Western pop music.'

Lomax hit the road in the 1930s, as a teenager, helping his father, John, make field recordings for the Library of Congress, lugging a 350-pound portable celluloid and aluminum-disc recorder. Black folk singer and guitarist **Leadbelly**, found languishing in a Texas jail during the depression, was the most famous of their discoveries, yet the Lomaxes sought out numerous other folk musicians throughout the country. Alan was responsible for compiling a lengthy oral history from early jazz legend **Jelly Roll Morton** for the Library of Congress, at a time when such music was considered frivolous, and African-Americans rarely considered to have stories worth documenting. In the early 1940s Lomax recorded country bluesman **Muddy Waters** on a Mississippi plantation, several years before Waters packed up for Chicago where he became the city's greatest electric blues musician.

Lomax spent much of the 1950s travelling, recording an incredible assortment of music in Britain, Italy and Spain, but he is most renowned

PETER FIGLESTAHLER/ROUNDER

Alan Lomax, originator of the Global Jukebox

for the extensive series of projects he undertook in the **American South** upon his return to the US at the end of the decade. The bulky machines of the 1930s had long since been replaced by smaller portable tape recorders that enhanced both mobility and fidelity. Sometimes accompanied by a young **Shirley Collins** – who in the 1960s would become one of Britain's greatest folk singers – Lomax recorded Ozark mountain ballads, black and white spirituals, hymns, gospel choirs, hair-raising prison ballads and Delta blues, all with equal respect and enthusiasm.

One of the performers he discovered, **Mississippi Fred McDowell**, would became a star of sorts in the 1960s blues revival. However, most of the musicians Lomax found never intended to make a career out of music, ensuring a spontaneous, sincere quality that remains captivating on his discs. Listing to Lomax's recordings reissued on Atlantic's four-CD set *Songs of the South*, or the 13-volume *Southern Journey* series on Rounder, you keep being surprised by how downright entertaining and moving much of the material is. Lomax knew that the very act of recording the musicians was changing their art to some degree; the performers had almost without exception never heard themselves on tape before. The thrill of being able to hear their own music perhaps spurred many to deliver their best.

Like Harry Smith's *Anthology*, Lomax's recordings were treasured by musicians of the American 1960s folk revival, although Lomax himself did not entirely welcome the metamorphosis of the movement into folk-rock. He actually came to blows with Bob Dylan's manager, Albert Grossman, at the 1965 Newport Folk Festival – famous as the event at which Dylan went electric.

Lomax remained busy with recording and anthropological work into the 1990s, publishing the acclaimed study *The Land Where the Blues Began*, and developing a multimedia interactive database, **The Global Jukebox**, to illustrate relationships between dance, song, and social structure. Serious strokes reduced his professional activities, but he was able to assist in the planning of Rounder's *Alan Lomax Collection*. Drawn from around four thousand tapes in the Library of Congress, this was launched in 1997 and is expected to total about 150 CDs. "A kind of vaccination against cultural boredom", remarked rock musician David Byrne (a great compiler himself at Luaka Bop). "The sheer variety of music that Lomax has recorded explodes any notion that there is one way of making music or appreciating it." The Lomax archive was recently sampled by Moby on his bestselling *Play* album.

discography

Compilers

Alan Lomax

The vast archives of Alan Lomax (born 1915) are gradually being issued in their entirety by the Rounder label. The following are just a few of the American essentials ...

The Alan Lomax Collection: Sampler (Rounder, US).

This 38-track sampler disc isn't perhaps the most satisfying among this vast and still expanding collection, but it nicely illustrates the extent of Lomax's work and features recordings from all the separate Rounder collections, including *Deep River of Song* (recordings by black artists in Appalachia, Texas and the Caribbean from 1933–46); *Southern Journey* (the rural south); the legendary *Prison Songs*; and a vast number of discs from around the world.

Prison Songs Vol. 1: Murderous Home (Rounder, US).

Prison work-songs were among the first sounds that John and Alan Lomax documented from 1933. They felt that the segregated world of the southern penitentiaries were the closest modern equivalent to the conditions of slavery. Although they found few songs that dated back to that era, they discovered a hitherto unknown repertoire encapsulating the feelings of the inmates at work in brutal conditions under the burning sun.

Southern Journey Vol. 5: Bad Man Ballads – Songs of Outlaws and Desperadoes (Rounder, US).

The violence, protest and rebellion in American folk music as depicted in scorching recordings of mountain balladeers, Virginia quartets and Mississippi prisoners.

Harry Smith

The eccentric Harry Smith (1923–91) remains synonymous with his great Anthology, originally issued in 1952, which fuelled the whole American folk revival.

Anthology of American Folk Music (Smithsonian Folkways, US).

Harry Smith's *Anthology* is one of the most important releases in the history of American folk music. The recordings from the 1920s and '30s sound like music from another world, but still have an enduring power and fascination. This reissued set of 6 CDs is beautifully produced and includes excellent notes and a reproduction of Smith's original eccentric commentaries.

Other US Compilations

Smithsonian Folkways

The two compilations below cover a range of styles; many others are detailed in the individual style discographies following.

Crossroads Southern Routes: Music of the American South (Smithsonian Folkways, US).

A good 1990s anthology of music from the Southern States including Gospel, Cajun, Tex-Mex, Appalachian, Bluegrass as well as Blues, New Orleans jazz and more. The enhanced CD includes pictures and info on the performers and styles of music.

River of Song: A Musical Journey Down the Mississippi (Smithsonian Folkways, US).

An aural sampling from the great north–south artery, the Mississippi River, which passes through some of the most musically-resonant cities in the US: Minneapolis, St. Louis, Memphis and New Orleans. Starting with Native American group Chippewa Nation performing at the annual powwow in Minnesota and ending with Canary Island settlers where the river flows into the Gulf of Mexico, the discs include specially recorded music from well-known groups and local performers in traditional and contemporary styles from gospel, blues, Bluegrass and country to New Orleans jazz, R&B, Cajun and Zydeco – with Swedish and Lao surprises too. A rich and atmospheric tapestry.

Artists

Woody Guthrie

Guthrie (1912–1967) is one of the legendary figures of American folkmusic, both for his songs of social protest and as an inspirational figure for subsequent generations of singers. Guthrie was on the road in his early teens, playing harmonica and guitar across Oklahoma and Texas, and his songs of the 1930s are unmatched in their evocation of the effect of the depression on America's poor. Guthrie recorded for Alan Lomax at the Library of Congress in the late 1930s and for Moses Asch at Folkways in 1944. He was closely connected to leading American folk artists like Leadbelly, Pete Seeger and Cisco Houston and has influenced contemporary musicians like Bob Dylan, Bruce Springsteen and Billy Bragg.

This Land is Your Land: The Asch Recordings Volume 1 (Smithsonian Folkways, US).

Many of Guthrie's essential songs are found here, in atmospheric recordings including several versions of the title track, considered by many to be America's alternative national anthem. Also in the series: **Volume 2, Muleskinner Blues** includes performances of standards and older folksongs; **Volume 3, Hard Travelin'** features topical and union songs; and **Volume 4, Buffalo Skinners** collects cowboy and outlaw songs with Cisco Houston on backing vocals and guitar on many songs.

WITH LEADBELLY

The Original Vision (Smithsonian Folkways, US).

An unmatched collection featuring Woody Guthrie and Leadbelly, two of America's most powerful folksingers.

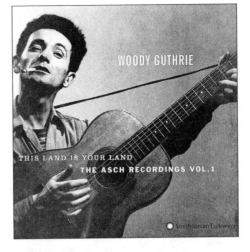

WOODY GUTHRIE

THIS LAND IS YOUR LAND
THE ASCH RECORDINGS VOL.1

Smithsonian Folkways

Pete Seeger

Born in New York City in 1919, Seeger learned to play banjo and ukelele and developed an interest in American folk music. He travelled the country learning songs from farmers and workers, met and performed with Woody Guthrie and maintained a successful solo career, despite being blacklisted by the House of Un-American Activities Committee. His songs include "Little Boxes", "Where Have All the Flowers Gone" and "We Shall Overcome".

Sing-A-Long Live at Sanders Theatre (Smithsonian Folkways, US).

A 2-CD set capturing the exhilaration of Seeger on stage at Harvard, in 1980.

Where Have All the Flowers Gone: The Songs of Pete Seeger (Smithsonian Folkways, US).

A stellar line-up of singers demonstrating the importance of Seeger for American folk and popular music. 2 CDs include Bruce Springsteen in "We Shall Overcome", Jackson Browne and Bonnie Raitt, Bruce Cockburn, John Trudell, Sweet Honey in the Rock, Peter, Paul and Mary, Billy Bragg, Dick Gaughan and more. Seeger concludes characteristically with a 1996 number audibly influenced by Indian music, "And I'm Still Searching".

USA

high an' lonesome

Hillbilly, or **Old-time music**, shares much the same roots as the blues – except that it was the music of the white poor of the Appalachian mountains, rather than the black poor of the south. It has long been associated with traditional, rural America, and it was from these fiddle and banjo tunes that country music developed. **Nick Barraclough** and **Kurt Wolff** unearth the old-time roots and chart the growth of their more commercial offshoots, **bluegrass** and **newgrass**.

Old-time mountain music was seeded in the southeastern United States, a region stretching as far north as the Ohio River and as far west as Arkansas and even Texas, but it grew especially rich in the **Appalachian mountains** of Virginia, West Virginia, Kentucky, Tennessee, and North Carolina. Less than a century ago, in the years before World War II, this was a world without electricity and instant entertainment, where music was nurtured by the pain of poverty and isolation.

When these poor white country folk came from the hills to search for work in the cities, they were derisively labelled **hillbillies** – the term that came to be adopted for their folk music, a tradition of songs that had been handed down from family to family. Biographies of country singers often begin with a reference to hearing pa or grandpa playing the fiddle while mother or sister played the piano or organ ... and all of them sang. It was invariably the men, however, who came to the forefront, as in the interwar years it was not seen as fitting for a woman to be an entertainer.

The hillbillies were Protestants and, although not devoted churchgoers, had deeply held beliefs in salvation, hell and damnation, all of which were reflected in the music. They included numbers of **Old Regular Baptists**, who sang unaccompanied and unharmonised, and strongly disapproved of musical instruments, as well as followers of **Holiness Pentecostal** churches who had 'happy clappy' services with guitars and banjos in church.

Unknown Appalachian musicians in the 1890s

First Recordings

Although recordings had been made in the US since the 1890s, only in the 1920s did the recording industry take an interest in rural music from Appalachia and the South. When they did, however, it took off fast, and the best regional performers suddenly found themselves in show business. Record companies sent agents into southern cities large and small to record regional fiddlers, balladeers and string bands. The most famous of these early recording sessions was held in 1927 in the Tennessee/Virginia border town of Bristol, conducted by **Ralph Peer**, a pioneering talent scout who did work for Okeh, Victor, and other labels. Two of country music's most influential acts were 'discovered' during this two-week session: the Carter Family and Jimmie Rodgers.

The Carters were the archetypal, old-time family band – the line-up numbered Alvin Pleasant 'A.P.' Carter, his wife Sara, and his brother's wife Maybelle. What caught Peer's ear was that, unlike other hillbilly bands whose instruments thrashed around and all but drowned out the singing, the Carters combined clear vocals with complementary instrumentation. They made famous many of the classic old-time songs such as "Will the Circle Be Unbroken", "Bury Me Beneath the Willow" and "Keep On the Sunny Side", and set a standard for future instrumentalists with Maybelle's considered and confident pick/strum guitar style and Sara's autoharp, a zither-like instrument with felted wooden bars that formed chords.

Jimmie Rodgers was country music's first star. Whether singing with a band or just his own guitar, he brought a showman's sophistication and panache to hillbilly music by incorporating Tin Pan Alley, blues, and western influences into his huge repertoire of original songs. In turn, he influenced the worlds of rock, pop, country, and swing. There was a lot of blues in Rodgers' songs, many

of which followed the twelve-bar format, though with a two-to-the-bar feel. He sang about his life on the railroad, lost loves and tuberculosis – the disease that hampered his life. By 1933 he had sold upward of twenty million records. The story goes that farmers all across the US would visit the general store and order 'a loaf of bread, a pound of butter and the latest Jimmie Rodgers record'.

The success of Jimmie Rodgers and the Carter Family encouraged others to make more of what

COUNTRY MUSIC FOUNDATION/FOUNDER RECORDS

Old-time legends, The Carter Family

had been just a way of entertaining the folks at home. Eventually, musicians were endorsing products from tonics to laxatives, on stage and on air.

The popular musical base was expanding, too: **fiddles** and **banjos** were ubiquitous and the **guitar** was coming into fashion. The Carter Family brought great popularity to the **autoharp**, too, an instrument that could be played with relative ease – as long as you could get it in tune. Other newly available instruments, including the **mandolin** and **Hawaiian steel guitar**, were also much in demand.

USA

Hard Livin', Hard Dyin'

The themes of the original hillbilly songs ranged within fairly limited boundaries: pathos, disappointment, tragedy – and train imitations. Not a lot of fun, you could be forgiven for thinking, and indeed much of it was pretty maudlin. But there was a joyously raucous side, too, especially in the music of Gid Tanner and the Skillet Lickers and Charlie Poole and the North Carolina Ramblers.

Gid Tanner and the Skillet Lickers were one of several North Georgia hard-driving bands with a riotous style that came largely through Tanner's own antics: he sang in a falsetto, played an unrestrained hoe-down fiddle style and generally assumed the part of a rustic fool, often to the chagrin of the other band members. It was quite a band. The revered blind guitarist Doc Watson said his first influence was the Skillet Lickers' own blind guitarist **George Riley Puckett**, famous for his adventurous guitar runs. The band also featured banjoist Fate Norris and seminal fiddler **Clayton McMichen**, whose formidable skill allowed him to play in many other styles as well as simple old-time music.

The Skillet Lickers deliberately projected an image of hard-drinking, rough-living young men whose business was to make and drink whisky, and who played a bit of music on the side. **Charlie Poole and the North Carolina Ramblers** were only slightly more ordered. Indeed Poole was one of the first examples of the Hank Williams syndrome – a hard-living country singer doomed to burn himself out at an early age – he was killed by a heart attack at the age of 39. The music he'd made was a joy, however: good-time and irresistibly infectious. Songs like "Moving Day", "Goodbye Little Liza Jane" and "Don't Let Your Deal Go Down" owed as much to vaudeville and ragtime as they did to the mountains. And the sound was equally distinctive: the trio featured Charlie playing fingerstyle banjo with a bluesy fiddle lead backed up by long, flowing melodic guitar runs.

Brother Duets

Hillbilly music achieved a level of purity and simplicity with the development of brother duets. It was generally held that those of the same blood would naturally empathise musically. The effect was close to the later recording technique of double tracking, where the same voice is recorded twice singing the same part or a harmony. The best of the early brother duets were the **Blue Sky Boys**, **Bill and Earl Bolick**, the **Delmore Brothers** and the **Monroe Brothers**. Where much hillbilly music was considered to be coarse, vulgar and badly presented, brother duets were more acceptably clean and precise. The singing was high-pitched, with one voice carrying the melody and the other harmonising a third or a fifth above. Instrumentation was a strummed guitar and a mandolin playing rhythm on the off-beat, with the occasional punctuating riff or 'turnaround'.

The finest and most commercially successful of the brother duets were the **Louvin Brothers**, Ira and Charlie. Many of the songs they wrote and recorded during the 1940s and 1950s, such as "I Don't Believe You've Met My Baby" and "When I Stop Dreaming", became big country hits and part of the repertoires of singers such as Emmylou Harris and Gram Parsons two decades later.

The brother duet form went on to influence the way popular music was to develop. Ricky Skaggs claims that the Monroe Brothers, Charlie and Bill (Bill who was to become the 'father of bluegrass'), had "the greatest influence on twentieth-century music". This bold statement starts to hold some water when he goes on to explain: "The Monroe Brothers influenced the Louvin Brothers, The Louvin Brothers influenced the Everly Brothers, the Everly Brothers influenced John Lennon and Paul McCartney..."

Hillbilly Turns Old-Time

Had it not been for the folk boom of the late 1950s and early 1960s, old-time music might well have died out as it evolved into bluegrass, honky tonk and rock'n'roll, but the tradition was kept alive, mainly by **The New Lost City Ramblers**, a group formed by **Mike Seeger**, brother of the folk singer, Pete. Ironically the music so closely identified with southeastern hillbillies was now being played by an urban-born and educated set. Mike Seeger was a New Yorker who came from a family of musicologists; **John Cohen** was a photographer also from New York; and **Tom Paley** was a Yale doctor of Mathematics.

The Ramblers, however, played with absolute, studied fidelity to the original mountain sound, with the explicit intention of performing American folk music as it had been before radio and TV had begun to homogenise the regional sounds. They gleaned their material from recordings reissued from the Library of Congress by John Lomax and also from Harry Smith's *Anthology of American Folk Music*, a highly influential collection first issued

New Lost City Ramblers John Cohen and Tom Paley with Jody Stecher (right)

with a travelling show in the early years of the century and recorded several 78s for Columbia and Victor in the 1930s. Ashley came back out of retirement and onto the circuit, where he played, notably, with Arthel 'Doc' Watson.

'Doc' Watson, a blind guitarist and singer, was the real star of this old-time revival. He was himself 'discovered' by bluegrass musician and folklorist **Ralph Rinzler**, who was introduced to him in Deep Gap, North Carolina, by Ashley. The breadth and quality of Watson's repertoire and his ability as a banjoist and harmonica player impressed Rinzler enormously, but his outstanding feature was his guitar style. Using a flat-pick he could play the most complicated fiddle tunes with absolute accuracy and at quite a pace, and he would also sing upbeat country songs such as "The Tennessee Stud", punctuating each line with a flurry of notes.

Rinzler got Doc and most of his family together for recording sessions, where they sang a mix of ballads, church songs, instrumentals learnt from other family members, and commercial releases. Their vibrant recordings (on Smithsonian Folkways) represent a good cross section of the local, family-centred music played in small communities throughout the region.

Watson's career took off in earnest at the 1961 Newport Folk Festival and continues today with a

in 1952 (see p.532). They sought to reproduce these diverse sounds on stage, requiring large numbers of instruments and long pauses for retuning. Though occasionally they missed some of the fun side of old-time music, they brought the tradition to a large number of young Americans who were dipping into folk music for the first time.

With the Ramblers' success came confusion over how to describe their music. The folksong magazine *Sing Out* called it **bluegrass**, but their readers soon corrected them. Finally **'old-time'** or 'old timey' was settled on. 'Old-time music was the old-time name for real mountain-type folk music', wrote Mike Seeger in a 1997 *Bluegrass Unlimited* article. It differed from folk – a term which mutated in the 1950s to include contemporary singer-songwriters – in that old-timers played songs from the turn of the century or earlier that had been passed down by hand through sometimes several generations.

Touring widely, the Ramblers inspired many other musicians to turn to old-time music. They also sought out the real old-time boys. Two of the most important to be 'rediscovered' had been featured in the *Anthology of American Folk Music* – Virginia banjoist **Dock Boggs** and **Clarence Ashley**, a singer and banjo picker, who had toured the southern Appalachians

Doc Watson, Clarence Ashley and Gaither Carlton, Deep Gap, NC, 1960

Hard lives: Roscoe Holcomb (left), on the porch

repertoire that has broadened from the folk songs of the mountains like "Matty Groves" to encompass more modern country and blues songs such as "Sitting On Top of the World". He is quick to acknowledge his influences – Riley Puckett, Merle Travis and Don Reno – "I don't think there's one guitarist with a good lick I didn't profit by". In his turn, Watson has influenced just about every young guitarist coming onto the old-time and bluegrass scene, and his version of "Black Mountain Rag" is a classic that every self-respecting player has to master.

One of the most extraordinary musicians Cohen 'discovered' in his travels was singer and banjo player **Roscoe Holcomb**. It was to describe his vocals that Cohen coined the phrase 'high lonesome sound', an expression now widely-used to describe old-time American music. Holcomb's life and music belonged to another era – he had worked in the mines, broken his back in a lumber mill and cracked his hands from pouring concrete. His jagged voice bent and elongated the notes he accompanied with his idiosyncratic 'rapid-fire' banjo. On hearing him for the first time, Cohen wrote 'I was deeply moved, for I knew this was what I had been searching for – something that went right to my inner being, speaking directly to me'. For many, including Bob Dylan, who heard Holcomb on tour, listening to his music was a searing and intense experience.

Bluegrass

It goes against every instinct held by a folklorist to assert that a music has been 'invented', but bluegrass comes the closest. In 1938 **Bill Monroe** (see box) split with his brother Charlie and formed a group of musicians which he named the **Blue Grass Boys**. Monroe was born in Kentucky, the Blue Grass State – hence the name of the band.

It's tempting to go on about a natural coalescence of musical styles from all over the world converging in this one band (there are obvious traces of Scottish and Shetland fiddle, east European polkas, Irish folk music, blues, jazz and gospel), but as far as Monroe was concerned, he just took what was available: an old-time fiddle player, a fingerstyle banjo player, a rhythm guitar player, himself playing the mandolin, and, when he could get one, a double bass player. The difference was that instead of the easy-going, shambolic, ragged-but-right sound any other band of that line-up would have had at that time, Monroe injected a discipline of tempo and a fire born of competition among the players.

The old-time influence was still strong, especially in the song repertoire, but in a short space of time the music had evolved dramatically, as had the presentation. Bill Monroe dressed his band in shirts and ties, eschewing the hillbilly image, and he made them play in keys no old-timer would have ventured into, B flat or even B – the higher the better. Vocal harmonies began to follow a formula – the melody, baritone (below the melody) and tenor (above), strictly in thirds and fifths, invariably moving in synchronised parallel.

Monroe had four roles in his band: leader, mandolin player, songwriter and singer. He often preferred to take the tenor part in a piercing falsetto that swooped and soared, often overshadowing the lead singer. He did more with the mandolin than had ever been done before, playing it fast and hard, driving the band along with a percussive off-beat and taking solos with flashy runs at breakneck speed. Monroe's songwriting was also prolific. His work ranges from instrumental tunes such as "Roanoake" and "Wheelhoss" to songs of his young life like "Uncle Pen", written about his fiddle-playing uncle Pendleton Vandiver, and "Blue Moon of Kentucky", which was to be one of Elvis Presley's first recordings in 1954.

Bill Monroe

Never one to play down the significance of his music, Bill Monroe (1911–1996) described it thus: "It's got a hard drive to it. It's Scotch bagpipes and old-time fiddling. It's Methodist and Holiness and Baptist. It's blues and jazz and it has a high, lonesome sound. It's plain music that tells a good story. It's played from my heart to your heart and it will touch you."

Even though he asserted that he 'never copied any man', Monroe's influences were clear. Born in Rosine, Kentucky, his mother Melissan and **Uncle Pendleton Vandiver** were both fine fiddle players. Bill was given the mandolin to play because his older siblings had taken up the more popular fiddle and guitar. Bill was intrigued not only by the old-time mountain music around him, but also the blues and gospel he heard played by local black musicians. He began playing seriously with brothers Charlie (guitar) and Birch (fiddle), and during the mid- to late 1920s, Bill and Charlie,

JOHN COHEN/DEBORAH BELL PHOTOGRAPHS

Bill Monroe, Luray, Virginia, 1960

as the **Monroe Brothers**, gained quite a following with songs such as "Bringin' In the Georgia Mail" and "New River Train". They had their first hit in 1930 with an instrumental called the "Kentucky Waltz". In 1938 the brothers parted, Charlie forming the **Kentucky Partners** and Bill forming the first incarnation of the **Blue Grass Boys**.

Some of the greatest musicians in American folk and country music played in the band: Flatt and Scruggs, who went on to achieve even greater commercial success than Monroe: Jimmy Martin, Don Remo, Carter Stanley, Bill Keith, Vassar Clements and Del McCoury were all Blue Grass Boys early in their careers. As a bandleader Monroe was notorious. On one famous occasion when the Blue Grass Boys had stopped for a break on a long journey across Tennessee, the guitarist had his thumb badly crushed when the boot lid was slammed shut. While the other band members commiserated, Monroe wandered over to see what the problem was, declared 'Well you can't play with your thumb all mashed up' and left him there with his bag at the side of the road. The pay was poor, the conditions rough and when band members weren't on the road they were expected to help out on the Monroe farm. But the kudos they took away from having played with the band was considerable.

The late 1950s and early 1960s saw Bill Monroe in great demand as the folk boom spread across the States and in the 1960s and 1970s he was booked to appear in Japan, Europe and Canada. The 1970s also saw his creation of the annual **Bean Blossom Bluegrass Festival** in Indiana, which led to two fine albums. In 1982, MCA had no fewer than twenty-four Bill Monroe albums available and one estimate has him selling a total of more than fifty million copies. He went on touring and appearing regularly at the Grand Ole Opry (a 'barn-dance show' and Nashville institution) up to his death in 1996.

USA

Sixty years of rules set down by Bill Monroe are adhered to by the latest generation of bluegrass musicians, as the music finds itself alongside and, to a great degree incorporated into, the huge commercial success of new country music.

Monroe's Boys

Over the last five or six decades, Monroe's band has been a training ground for young bluegrass musicians and an impressive number of greats passed through it. The most distinguished of Monroe's alumni were **Lester Flatt** and **Earl Scruggs**, the Blue Grass Boys' guitarist and banjoist respectively from 1944 to 1948. Flatt had a strong baritone voice and solid guitar style, but the star was Scruggs, whose three-finger banjo style revolutionised the instrument and became the distinguishing sound of bluegrass.

Flatt and Scruggs left Monroe in 1948 to form the **Foggy Mountain Boys**, which became the most successful commercial bluegrass band. Flatt's voice was more appealing to a wider audience than Monroe's because it was a little deeper and more resonant. Songs like "Jimmy Brown the Newsboy" and "Let Those Brown Eyes Smile at Me" almost crossed over with mainstream country. But the song that brought most fame to Flatt and Scruggs was a rather poor composition called "The Ballad of Jed Clampett", written for the TV series The Beverly Hillbillies. Regular nationwide exposure meant that for the first time bluegrass became recognisable all across the United States.

A decade later came the use of banjo (Flatt and Scruggs' instrumental "Foggy Mountain Breakdown") as aural backing to a fast car chase in the 1967 film Bonnie and Clyde. For many second- and third-generation bluegrass musicians, the Beverly Hillbillies theme and "Foggy Mountain Breakdown" were their introduction to the music. Banjoists had hitherto played in a variety of styles: 'frailing', a combination of downstrokes where the fingernails brush the strings and up-picking by the thumb and first finger; and the 'clawhammer', using the thumb to lay down a rhythm and picking out notes with the first and second fingers – more like a guitar style. Instead Scruggs rolled. His secret was never to play the same string with the same finger twice consecutively. He constructed a set of licks (or brief formulaic phrases) that he could play at speed with unerring accuracy.

The other big commercial boost given to bluegrass was the use of "Dueling Banjos" in the 1972 film Deliverance, where city man on an adventure holiday meets a banjo-playing hillbilly. They play an apparently improvised duet on guitar and banjo. The tune in fact goes back to a 1955 duet, "Feuding Banjoes", by Don Reno (one of the era's finest banjo pickers) and Arthur 'Guitar Boogie' Smith; it was also popularised to some extent by the West Coast bluegrass band the Dillards.

The proliferation of bluegrass through the 1950s was slow, but there was one other band who stood alongside the Blue Grass Boys and the Foggy Mountain Boys: the **Stanley Brothers**. Where Flatt and Scruggs had readily embraced opportunities presented by TV, radio and cinema, and were travelling all over the US, the Stanley Brothers in many ways never moved out of the mountains. Their sound is still bluegrass at its purest, with Carter Stanley's mournful baritone and Ralph's clear, rasping tenor. The brothers played guitar and banjo respectively. Ralph's banjo-playing, though simpler than Scruggs', was as hard-driving and clear as his voice. When Carter died of a liver ailment in 1966, the band polarised to Ralph's uncompromising style, and as with the Blue Grass Boys, it became a training ground for future stars such as **Ricky Skaggs**, **Larry Sparks** and **Keith Whitley**. The legacy of their songs is considerable, too: "How Mountain Girls Can Love", "Little Maggie" and "I am a Man of Constant Sorrow" have all become classics.

For many, the best lead singer Bill Monroe ever used was **Jimmy Martin**, a high, reedy singer with a strong rhythm guitar style. Just as uncompromising as Monroe, he could be very abrasive with his own band, the **Sunny Mountain Boys**. He insisted that his musicians played virtually flat-out, up against the microphones; one of his banjo players, Mark Pruett, once said Martin would pinch his backside if he ever drifted away from the mike. The Jimmy Martin sound was at its best when banjoist **J.D. Crowe** was in the band. The definitive driving, clear, fluffless style of his playing perfectly complemented Martin's more commercial bluegrass songs, such as "On the Sunny Side of the Mountain" and "You Don't Know My Mind".

Jimmy Martin left Bill Monroe in 1954, and teamed up with the **Osborne Brothers**, Sonny and Bobby, who played mandolin and banjo. They later struck out on their own and achieved a good deal of commercial success but they were viewed as heretics by many bluegrass purists because they broke the rules: every now and again they used electric instruments, even drums. Their extraordinary vocal harmonies, often with the lead part at the top and the two other parts below, would move in parallel, then, at the end of a phrase, swoop around and exchange parts. They were just as controversial in their selection of material. Though they cut straight bluegrass material like "Ruby", they eventually included Nashville-type country songs as well such as "Hey Joe" and "Rocky Top", which became their theme song and one of the genre's best-known tunes.

Bluegrass and the Folk Revival

With the folk revival of the late 1950s and '60s, bluegrass took off across the US, initially with concerts and college gigs, then the beginnings of the festival circuit that now fills any bluegrass band's calendar from April to September each year. Not only was bluegrass heard in all of the states of the US, but the southeastern bands were now recruiting players from as far afield as upstate New York, New England and California. The hillbilly stigma, though it lives on to this day, was receding. College kids, new to the music, brought a fresh approach in terms of worldliness and more academic techniques. The work of banjoist **Bill Keith**, fiddle player **Richard Green**, mandolinist **David Grisman**, and guitarists like **Clarence White** and **Tony Rice**, was, through the 1960s and 1970s, to give bluegrass more sophistication, versatility and credibility.

DAVE PEABODY

The Dillards

The band that broke through in terms of sheer entertainment was the **Dillards**. Their pivotal figure was Doug Dillard, a banjo player from Salem, Missouri. The Dillards went to California to seek their fortune in 1962 and for once it worked. Within a couple of weeks they had secured a

recording contract with Elektra, residencies in the best clubs and regular appearances on the Andy Griffith TV show. Their appeal stemmed from an ability not only to play and sing brilliantly, but also to entertain. Where most other bluegrass bands of the time, and many since, had an almost taciturn stage presentation, the Dillards included comedy in a slick, almost cabaret-style show. **Mitch Jayne** fronted the band and, as can be heard on their excellent *Live-Almost* album, begins the show by saying "We're the Dillards and we're hillbillies. Thought I'd better tell you that in case you thought we were the Budapest String Quartet!". The band eventually progressed from their first bluegrass line-up, and material like "The Old Home-Place" and "Never See My Home Again", to include drums and electric instruments in the late 1960s.

One of the clubs in Los Angeles where the Dillards made their name was the **Ash Grove**. Another Californian band to establish their reputation there was the **Three Little Country Boys**, who eventually became the **Kentucky Colonels**, featuring guitarist Clarence White and his brother Roland on mandolin. Their distinguishing feature was Clarence's guitar playing – it was the first time that the guitar was regularly used as a lead instrument. His style was influenced by Doc Watson – it was fast and flowing and set a challenging standard for other guitarists to come. The Kentucky Colonels were hardly a driving band, but typified the laid-back, Californian approach to bluegrass. Clarence went on to join the Byrds and was about to form his own band when he was killed by a drunk driver in July 1973.

A much more authentic or 'rootsy' sounding band of the time was based in Washington, D.C. **The Country Gentlemen** – Charlie Waller, John Duffey, Eddie Adcock and Jim Cox – were so called because their roots were more in folk, although they developed gradually into a bluegrass band. They adopted a studious approach to the music, with carefully constructed vocal harmonies, using instrumentation to complement the song as opposed to the Jimmy Martin hell-for-leather

USA

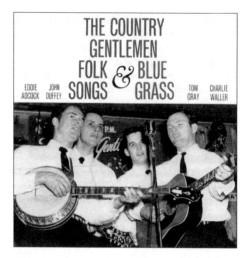

approach. This was the first band to sell a song lyrically as well as melodically, a good example being the sensitivity with which they performed songs like "Bringing Mary Home" and compositions from contemporary writers like Gordon Lightfoot, Dylan and Manfred Mann.

After he left The Country Gentlemen in 1969, **John Duffey** formed **Seldom Scene**, a prime example of how bluegrass had been taken on by a new social culture: Ben Eldridge (banjo, guitar) was a mathematician, Tom Gray (bass) a cartographer, Mike Auldridge (dobro) a commercial artist, and John Starling (guitar) a surgeon. The music was as precise as the muscians' backgrounds would suggest. Duffey stressed that he was 'very choosy' about the songs the band recorded, claiming they only ever recorded two songs with which he was unhappy. The band picked up a large, educated, middle-class following, including some rising country stars, notably Emmylou Harris, who became a great bluegrass fan, and Linda Ronstadt. Their material ranged wide – from "The Muleskinner Blues" to Steve Goodman's "City of New Orleans" – but was always played with sensitivity, dynamism and flashes of brilliance.

Newgrass

Bands like The Country Gentlemen, Dillards and Seldom Scene were the pioneers of what's become known as **'progressive bluegrass'** or **'newgrass'**, a genre which emerged to serve the large urban audience that bluegrass was beginning to attract. And, of course, towards the end of the 1960s, the lure of fame and fortune offered by rock'n'roll proved too much for many young bluegrass musicians. As highly skilled singers and instrumental-

ists, they were much in demand, though since few could write particularly well, long-term success generally eluded them and they found themselves drifting back to bluegrass.

One such bunch of musicians was **Muleskinner**, formed after Bill Monroe failed to make it to a recording for a TV show in New England. The rest of the band, pulled together for the occasion, decided to carry on without him. The band – **Peter Rowan** (lead singer, guitar), **Clarence White** (guitar), **Bill Keith** (banjo), **Richard Green** (fiddle) and **David Grisman** (mandolin) – were one of bluegrass's first supergroups.

Peter Rowan had been one of Bill Monroe's favourite lead singers and Richard Green one of his most innovative fiddle players. These two had left bluegrass in the late 1960s for the world of rock and played in the moderately successful Seatrain. Bill Keith, another ex-Blue Grass Boy, had breathed new life into the banjo by his introduction of a melodic flowing style, often called 'chromatic'. Instead of the old Scruggs technique of stringing together a series of licks, Keith could play complete tunes by a complicated system that involved rarely playing two consecutive notes on the same string or with the same finger, instead crossing alternately from string to string, often playing a higher note on a lower string. David Grisman did as much for the mandolin as Keith had for the banjo. As influenced by swing and jazz as he was by bluegrass, the performance of his composition "Opus 57" showed the way he was set to go later, in the 1970s, with his own quartet.

Muleskinner only made one album, but the inclusion of songs like "Muleskinner Blues", which featured drums, and Clarence on electric guitar, and the more traditional "Dark Hollow", showed that even though they were a generation on from the original bluegrass bands and some of the edges had been rounded off, the passion was still there.

Old And In The Way was another supergroup that involved Rowan and Grisman, but this time included the eccentric banjoist **Jerry Garcia**, better known as the Grateful Dead's guitarist, and **Vassar Clements** from Florida, an inspired bluesy player who had performed in Monroe's band as a teenager. Their live album, *Old And In The Way*, pulled away from many of the traditions of bluegrass. The band was scruffy and long-haired, mistakes were made – and left in – and although they played hoary old hillbilly favourites like "Pig In a Pen", they also included Rowan's personal tribute to marijuana in "Panama Red".

Where these bluegrass musicians' excursions into rock were invariably ill-fated, more success was to come as they jumped on and, to a great extent, built the new country bandwagon of the early 1980s. The best-known of these musicians was **Ricky Skaggs**, a prodigious mandolin player, fiddler and guitarist, who cut his teeth as a member of Ralph Stanley's band. He went on to join ex-Sunny Mountain Boys banjoist J.D. Crowe in **The New South**, where he met **Jerry Douglas**, the player who has done more for the **dobro** than anyone since Mike Auldridge of The Country Gentlemen.

Skaggs and Douglas went on to form **Boone Creek**. Whereas a lot of progressive bluegrass in the late 1960s and early 1970s was coming out of California and the northern states, this was a band of young players all from the southeast. As a result

they sounded more like the real thing, although they broke the rules by including drums and piano on their recordings. Skaggs left Boone Creek when bluegrass aficionado **Emmylou Harris** invited him to join her Hot Band. His career subsequently blossomed when he formed his own band and became a driving force in country music's neo-traditionalist renaissance. He took and used many elements of bluegrass in his music, and inspired other new country artists to do the same.

While Skaggs left bluegrass and became part of new country, **New Grass Revival** came closest to making bluegrass itself a mainstream, commercially viable music, rather than a sub-culture. The main figure in this band was always **Sam Bush** from Bowling Green, Kentucky. He formed the

Bluegrass and Old-time Festivals

Festivals are an integral part of the bluegrass and old-time music scenes. Oddly enough, they owe some of their success to Henry Ford, the pioneer of the American automobile industry. Ford was a big fan of Appalachian music, and he was also deeply worried that jazz and ragtime music were eroding the country's moral fibre. As a result he often donated prize money for old-time fiddle contests.

Fiddle contests have been held in American since at least the eighteenth century, the earliest on record being in 1736. Eck Robertson, who in 1922 became the first commercial country recording artist, earned his musical reputation at fiddle contests throughout Texas. Contests and festivals became a big attraction again among folk revivalists during the 1950s and 1960s. The first multiday all-bluegrass festival was held in Roanoke, Virginia in 1965, and since then festivals have blossomed all over the country. Most feature a mix of traditional and progressive bluegrass acts and old-time performers.

Leading festivals include:

Arkansas Folk Festival Mountain View (April)
Mountain View was established during the 1960s by singer Jimmie Driftwood. Its home, the Ozark Folk Center, also hosts annual guitar, autoharp, and dulcimer festivals, as well as other music events.

MerleFest (April/May)
Doc Watson conceived this Wilkesboro, North Carolina, festival in honor of his late son Merle, who accompanied him for twenty years until he died in 1985.

Memorial Day Bluegrass Festival (May)
Banjoist and bandleader Ralph Stanley began holding this annual Memorial Day weekend bluegrass festival at his family's 'Old Home Place' (the Hills of Home Park between Coeburn and McClure, Virginia) after the 1966 death of his brother Carter, his partner in the Stanley Brothers.

Bean Blossom (June)
Bean Blossom, as it's popularly known after the name of its site in Indiana, was set up by Bill Monroe and maintained as the Bill Monroe Memorial Bluegrass Festival.

Telluride Bluegrass Festival (June)
A well-established festival that takes place at Telluride, high in the Rocky Mountains of Colorado.

Old Fiddlers Convention (August)
A fine fiddlers' gathering in Galax, Virginia – a region that's famous for its old-time music heritage.

IBMA Bluegrass Fan Fest (October)
Run by the International Bluegrass Music Association, the Fan Fest is held in Louisville, Kentucky, in conjunction with a trade show and the annual International Bluegrass Music Awards. It is *the* bluegrass event of the year, with dozens of top bluegrass performers either booked to perform or simply hanging around listening.

The US magazines *Bluegrass Unlimited* and *Dirty Linen* publish comprehensive lists of festivals each year. For information on the Internet, including links to all the festival sites, check *Bluegrass News* (*Bluegrass-news.com*) or the impressive, Estonia(!)-based *Blue Grass Roots* site (*BGR.ee/links*).

USA

group in 1972 and despite many personnel changes it survived until the end of the 1980s. They were progressive from the outset: their debut album featured a breakneck version of "Great Balls Of Fire", which went on to become a bluegrass standard for other bands. The band's sound was made even more distinctive when they were joined by **John Cowan** on bass. Cowan knew virtually nothing of bluegrass, being a pop and rock fan, but he soon became a convert and New Grass Revival subsequently developed a sound tinged with rock, particularly in their vocal style, which appealed to a younger audience. In their 1980s recordings, after they had been joined by a phenomenal New York banjoist, **Béla Fleck**, they signed major record deals and songs like "Hold On to a Dream" and "Can't Stop Now" looked at one point like becoming the first real bluegrass hits since "Rocky Top" and "The Ballad of Jed Clampett".

The Scene Today

The scene today is thriving, and it anticipates even wider popularity. One of the early indicators of the new optimism was the establishment in 1985 of the **International Bluegrass Music Association** (IBMA). Based in Owensboro, Kentucky, the IBMA holds a hugely popular awards cere-

DAVE PEABODY

Alison Krauss

mony, trade show and music festival each autumn, and has also established the Bluegrass Hall of Honor, located inside the International Bluegrass Music Museum in Owensboro. The first inductee, in 1991, was, of course, Bill Monroe.

Bluegrass has always been participatory music. At the many festivals held all over the United States

each year, the campsites are filled with musicians of all abilities meeting for the first time or reuniting to play standards from the enormous repertoire of bluegrass songs that has been amassed over the years. The atmosphere at these festivals is casual but curious – not unlike a county fair. The acts on the main stages can be enticing, but the real action happens in-between and all around: word will get around that there's a brilliant young mandolin player in one particular session on the far side of the parking lot, and folks will head that way to check him or her out. And unlike the worlds of rock or even, these days, country, the current stars of bluegrass are still accessible to their fans, often seen jamming along with the campers.

Coming directly from the heart of the American South, traditional bluegrass has always existed in a fairly conservative climate. **Women players**, for instance, were quite scarce for decades; the only female musicians you would see would be the wives, girlfriends, or sisters of one or another of the players. Accordionist Wilene 'Sally Ann' Forrester, wife of fiddler Howdy Forrester, was a female Blue Grass Boy in the early 1940s. During the 1960s and 1970s, however, as the music widened its audience, the climate began to change and players like **Roni Stoneman**, **Ginger Boatwright**, **Hazel Dickens**, **Laurie Lewis**, and **Delia Bell** brought greater recognition to female bluegrass and old-time musicians.

Ironically, by the 1990s, the tables had turned altogether, when singer, fiddler, and bandleader **Alison Krauss** hit the scene. A child prodigy, she was signed to Rounder Records when only fourteen, won her first Grammy several years later, and was the first bluegrass artist to join the Grand Ole Opry in almost thirty years. She has become the top-selling bluegrass artist of all time, with country music videos and platinum albums to her credit. Though some of her music does take inspiration from country and pop, through all this success she and her band, **Union Station**, have kept in line with the traditional Monroe style.

During the 1980s, as newgrass evolved into 'supergrass' and 'spacegrass', a resurgence of traditional bluegrass music was built around acoustic instruments, high lonesome harmonies, and tight arrangements – quite unlike the long electrified jams and solos favoured by many newgrass outfits. Groups like the **Johnson Mountain Boys** and bandleaders like **Del McCoury** showed just how powerful the 'old' style of bluegrass could sound in the hands of musicians who knew how to speak its language. Today McCoury is one of the undisputed masters of bluegrass. Another leading act is the **Nashville Bluegrass Band**, led by banjoist Alan O'Bryant and guitarist Pat Enright and including onetime Kentucky Colonel, mandolinist Roland White. These artists and others such as James King, Lynn Morris, and Doyle Lawson – not to mention stalwarts like Ralph Stanley, Mac Wiseman, and Jimmy Martin, who still frequent the festivals – are keeping the scene rich, vibrant, and very much alive and well. It may not be like it was in the golden era of the 1950s, when bluegrass was a brand-new phenomenon and artists who sang about "My Little Cabin Home on the Hill" really had grown up in those rural and primitive surroundings, but given all that's changed in the worlds of bluegrass and country music since Monroe's debut over half a century ago, the fundamental energy of the music is still amazingly intact and bright.

discography

Old Time

Some amazing collections of early hillbilly and old-time music have appeared recently, including field recordings cut on front porches, and commercial 78s originally released by labels such as Brunswick and Victor. Sound quality isn't always ideal: pre-1940s material, for instance, was recorded onto discs or cylinders; and postwar tape recordings were often made with primitive field equipment. Still, on the CDs listed below the down-home quality of the music shines through beautifully.

Compilations

Anglo-American Ballads Vol 1 (Rounder, US).

First issued in 1942 by the Archive of Folk Song in the Library of Congress, which had been collecting rural folk songs since 1928. Includes Woody Guthrie's "The Gypsy Davy", Pete Steele's "Pretty Polly" and versions of "The House Carpenter" and "Barbara Allen".

Black & White Hillbilly Music: Early Harmonica Recordings from the 1920s & 30s (Trikont, Germany).

A fascinating glimpse into the harmonica in Appalachian music (and beyond) through early commercial recordings. As the first mass-produced musical instrument, the harmonica was used extensively by both black and white musicians and

demonstrates the common ground in their music. Includes a great harmonica duet (by unknown musicians) from 1927 called "Cackling Hen Blues". Good notes in German with an English summary.

The Bristol Sessions (Country Music Foundation, US).

1991 collection of thirty five tracks Ralph Peer recorded in 1927 during his legendary recording session in the Tennessee/Virginia border town of Bristol. The singers are some of the early greats: the Carter Family and Jimmie Rodgers, of course, but also Ernest Stoneman, Blind Alfred Reed, and gospel singers Ernest Phipps and Alfred G. Karnes. An excellent collection that shows the wide range of 1920s hillbilly music.

Close To Home: Old Time Music from Mike Seeger's Collection 1952–1967 (Smithsonian Folkways, US).

It's hardly surprising that Mike Seeger, member of the New Lost City Ramblers and tireless collector of the old stuff from the 1950s, amassed a great collection of recordings of veteran players of fiddle, banjo and guitar, and unaccompanied ballad singers. Tracks by Sara and Maybelle Carter, Elizabeth Cotten, Snuffy Jenkins, Eck Robertson and Dock Boggs, as well as many lesser-known artists.

Mountain Music of Kentucky (Smithsonian Folkways, US).

A double CD of field recordings made in 1959 by John Cohen of the New Lost City Ramblers. The tunes of Roscoe Holcomb, Marion Sumner, George Davis, Mr & Mrs Sams and others from this musically rich state are about as earthy and honest as folk music gets. Also includes Old Baptist and Holiness church music.

Old-Time Mountain Guitar (County, US).

Eighteen mostly instrumental recordings from between 1926 and 1931 of early guitarists like Roy Harvey, Sam McGee, John Dilleshaw, and slide whiz Frank Hutchison.

Old Time Music on the Air: Vols 1–2 (Rounder, US).

These two separate volumes are a decent representation of old-time music as played by longtime stalwarts and newcomers alike. Artists include Hazel Dickens, Jody Stecher and Kate Brislin, Benton Flippen, Cathy Fink, and Mac Benford and the Woodshed Allstars.

**Southern Journey Vol 2:
Ballads and Breakdowns** (Rounder, US).

Alan Lomax recorded these raw, beautiful vocal and dance tunes in the Blue Ridge Mountains of Virginia in 1959. Part of the massive Alan Lomax Collection of folk recordings reissued by Rounder.

Times Ain't Like They Used to Be, Vols 1–4
(Shanachie/Yazoo, US).

Four excellent collections (available seperately) of commercial hillbilly and blues from the 1920s and 1930s. Includes the same sort of material (and some of the same artists) as Harry Smith's *Anthology* (see p.532), but these are much higher-quality transfers painstakingly re-mastered from the original (and very rare) 78s. The songs jump with life and warmth.

Artists

Clarence Ashley

Clarence 'Tom' Ashley (1895–1967) was born in Bristol, Tennessee and learned songs and banjo from his aunts. He played with various bands, notably the Carolina Tar Heels, but stopped in the mid-1940s after a hand injury. He was brought out of retirement in the 1960s thanks to Ralph Rinzler's enthusiasm for his recordings in the Harry Smith Anthology. Doc Watson was also rediscovered at the same time and the two enjoyed a late-flowering second career.

**The Original Folkways Recordings of
Doc Watson and Clarence Ashley**
(Smithsonian Folkways, US).

Sessions recorded between 1960 and 1962 which demonstrate the impact of the real old-time music on the new urban enthusiasts. These were previously released as *Old Time Music at Clarence Ashley's*, but appear on this double CD with twenty previously unreleased tracks. Includes a 1962 version of Clarence's classic "The Coo-Coo Bird" and many other downhome Appalachian classics from Clarence, Watson and several supporting singers and musicians. Excellent photos and notes.

Dock Boggs

With a voice just a few steps away from primitive, and a banjo he picked like a guitar instead of strumming or flailing, as was the common practice, Dock Boggs's music was as chilling, raw, and thoroughly mesmerising as nearly anything that emerged from Appalachia in the 1920s. He is said to bridge the worlds of black blues and white folk music.

Country Blues (Revenant, US).

A superb collection that does Boggs's music (and his heritage) justice. The tracks include his twelve original 1920s recordings, five previously unreleased alternate takes and four bonus tracks by Bill and Hayes Shepard, contemporaries of Boggs.

His Folkways Years, 1963–68
(Smithsonian Folkways, US).

Two discs featuring fifty songs and tunes that offer a comprehensive survey of Appalachian music. Mountain style singing and that distinctive finger-picking banjo style.

Carter Family

Simple, haunting, and gorgeous, the Carter Family's rich repertoire of traditional melodies are among country music's most crucial foundations. Sara, Maybelle and A.P. have also been a major inspiration for their strong harmony vocals, which were the focus of their music as opposed to fiddles and the other string-band instruments that were standard at the time.

**The Carter Family: Their Complete Victor
Recordings** (Rounder, US).

The Carters' entire Victor catalogue has finally been reissued, and the results are superb – raw in spirit but smooth in tone, haunting yet entirely beautiful. It's hard to go wrong with any of the nine CDs in this series (which is organised in chronological order), but the earlier collections are packed with classic songs and make a great starting point. Volume 2, *My Clinch Mountain Home, 1928–1929*, includes the classic "I'm Thinking Tonight of My Blue Eyes", and Volume 3, *When the Roses Bloom in Dixieland, 1929–1930*, includes the songs "Jimmy Brown the Newsboy" and "Wabash Cannonball".

The Carter Family on Border Radio (Arhoolie, US).

You could argue that today's pop music started on the Tex-Mex border in the late 1930s. In those days the huge 'border blaster' radio stations by-passed US legislation by setting up their transmitters just across the Rio Grande in Mexico. The strength of the signal took their programmes right across the US and could even be picked up in Europe. The Carter Family were border radio favourites. So who was listening at the time? The young Elvis, Carl Perkins, Johnny Cash, Chuck Berry... Carter classics on one CD.

Darby & Tarlton

The vocal harmonies and shimmering steel guitar make the music of Tom Darby and Jimmie Tarlton stunning but surreal. A strange blend of blues, folk, Hawaiian, and western influences, it's like something from another planet – yet at the same time grounded in Southern soil. Darby and Tarlton recorded together between 1927 and 1933, and two of their earliest songs, "Columbus Stockade Blues" and "Birmingham Jail" are country standards.

On the Banks of a Lonely River (County, US).

This excellent 1994 CD collects songs the pair recorded for Columbia in the late 1920s. Tarlton's steel playing is some of the era's greatest, and if his falsetto doesn't give you chills, nothing will.

Delmore Brothers

Alton and Raybon Delmore were one of the great brother acts that rose to prominence in the 1930s. Using beautiful, precise harmonies and lively acoustic arrangements, they wrote and recorded classics like "Gonna Lay Down My Old Guitar", "Browns Ferry Blues" and "Blues Stay Away from Me." During the forties and fifties they brought in electric instruments and cut equally excellent boogie-woogie material such as "Freight Train Boogie" and "Hillbilly Boogie".

Brown's Ferry Blues (County, US).

A superb collection of the Delmores' earlier acoustic recordings. Not to be missed.

Hazel Dickens

While most of her folk-music peers of the 1960s and 1970s were raised and educated in urban areas, Hazel Dickens hailed from deep in West Virginia's coal-mining territory. Her rural roots are reflected in her earthy voice and heartstopping original songs like "Black Lung"; "Will Jesus Wash the Bloodstains from Your Hands" and "Mama's Hand". Whether singing alone, with duet partner

Alice Gerrard or with groups like the Strange Creek Singers, her music is outstanding.

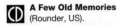 **A Few Old Memories**
(Rounder, US).

Compiles songs from several of Hazel's 1980s albums, all of which are excellent. A mix of old-time and country songs with original material.

Laurie Lewis

Laurie Lewis has strong roots in bluegrass, but this singer, songwriter, fiddler, and bandleader has proven herself equally adept at writing and playing country, folk, old-time and even Cajun music. With Kathy Kallick she formed the Good Ol' Persons, an all-female old-time group, before moving on to lead her own string band, Grant Street.

 The Oak and the Laurel (Rounder, US).

Lewis duets with Tom Rozum, a mandolinist who joined Grant Street in 1987. It's a great collection of old-time songs that are among Lewis' rootsiest to date.

Louvin Brothers

These two Alabama boys could harmonise like no other singers in country music. The Louvin Brothers represent the epitome of a heritage of close-harmony brother groups that included the Blue Sky Boys, the Delmore Brothers and the Monroe Brothers. Like their predecessors, the Louvins played stripped-down, acoustic-based music that emphasised their singing; the results were otherworldly and absolutely gorgeous. Their career lasted from the 1940s through the mid-1960s, when Ira was killed in an automobile accident.

 When I Stop Dreaming:
The Best of the Louvin Brothers (Razor & Tie, US).

A great single-CD collection of both secular and gospel material from throughout the brothers' career.

New Lost City Ramblers

From their first recordings in the 1950s, this group of eager young musicians played a huge part in reviving interest in older folk and hillbilly music styles, helping define 'old-time' music for future generations of folkies. The initial lineup of John Cohen, Mike Seeger, and Tom Paley was modified when Tracy Schwarz replaced Paley in the 1960s. The group has continued working on and off to the present day.

 The Early Years 1958–1962
(Smithsonian Folkways, US).

Highlights the group's first dozen albums, featuring the original lineup of Cohen, Seeger, and Paley.

Charlie Poole

Banjoist Charlie Poole and his group the North Carolina Ramblers were one of the most exciting string bands of the hillbilly era. Overall, Poole's music had a rough energy that matched the hard textile-mill lifestyle he grew up amidst, though at the same time it was brimming with humor and charm. Poole's three-finger banjo picking style, prevalent around the Piedmont region of North Carolina where he grew up, was influential.

 Charlie Poole and the North Carolina Ramblers
Vols 1–3 (County, US).

These three individual CDs compile Poole's Columbia recordings from the mid-1920s through 1930, and it's some of the most visceral yet well-crafted string band music of the era.

Jimmie Rodgers

It's a good bet that no single artist before or since has had more impact on country music's development than Jimmie Rodgers. A white Texan who could play the blues as deftly as western numbers and popular songs, he mingled song styles with seemingly effortless showmanship. He died young, due to tuberculosis, but during his six-year career Rodgers gave the genre new energy, and pointed the industry toward its future.

 First Sessions, 1927–1928 (Rounder, US).

This is the initial volume of an excellent eight-CD series covering Rodgers' entire recording career in chronological order. His music is a vital part of country music's foundation, and many decades later it is still solid and full of life.

Mike Seeger

A founding member of the New Lost City Ramblers, Mike Seeger is a skilled multi-instrumentalist, a fine singer, and one of the foremost authorities on old-time music. During the fifties and sixties he sought out traditional hand-me-down songs and helped 'rediscover' artists like Dock Boggs. He continues to give older music new life in his own numerous recordings.

 Solo – Oldtime Country Music (Rounder, US).

The instruments Seeger plays and the songs he covers come from all over the map, but he is always true to their roots. Scholarly, but absolutely enjoyable.

 Southern Banjo Sounds (Smithsonian Folkways, US).

A great collection of solo banjo songs, each showcasing a different Southern style from the nineteenth and early twentieth centuries, played on 23 mostly vintage banjos.

The Skillet Lickers

Wild and kooky in spirit, the Atlanta, Georgia-based Skillet Lickers were the quintessential old-time hillbilly string band. The group centered around Gid Tanner who played fiddle, banjo, and guitar, and was also a skilled showman. The other central musicians were influential singer/guitarist Riley Puckett, fiddlers Clayton McMichen and Lowe Stokes, and banjoist Fate Norris. Between 1926 and 1931 they made more than eighty recordings.

 Old-Time Fiddle Tunes and Songs from North Georgia (County, US).

Sixteen raucous songs that virtually define the dance-oriented string-band sound of the 1920s.

Jody Stetcher and Kate Brislin

Jody and Kate have been musical partners for decades, playing a mix of old-time, blues, country, and other assorted acoustic musical styles. Their recordings are highlighted by Kate's clear, strong voice and Jody's incredible skill on mandolin, guitar, banjo and other instruments.

 Heart Songs: The Old Time Country Songs of Utah Phillips (Rounder, US).

The songs of singer, storyteller and rambling man Utah Phillips are beautifully rendered in this low-key, acoustic gem of an album.

Doc Watson

The discovery of Doc Watson (b 1923) was a result of the folk revival sweeping the US during the fifties and sixties, and Watson's highly accessible and entirely enjoyable music went on to help bridge the gap between older Appalachian traditions and contemporary folk and country audiences. Watson's influence has been large: he is a superb vocalist, has a huge repertoire of songs and is one of the best flatpicking guitarists of his day. His son Merle accompanied him on guitar for two decades until killed in a tractor accident in 1985.

 The Watson Family
(Smithsonian Folkways, US).

Collects recordings Ralph Rinzler, Eugene Earle, Archie Green, and Peter Seigel made of Doc Watson and his family during the early 1960s. They're Watson's most traditional, and they're utterly beautiful.

THE WATSON FAMILY

Bluegrass

Compilations

 The Best of Bluegrass, Vol 1: Standards
(Mercury, US).

This excellent survey features pretty much all the classic bluegrass players (except for Monroe, who didn't record for Mercury) with cuts from the Stanley Brothers, Flatt and Scruggs, Carl Story, the Osborne Brothers, The Country Gentlemen, and others.

◉ **Hand-Picked: 25 Years of Bluegrass on Rounder Records** (Rounder, US).

A great double-CD collection highlighted by top-notch artists like Joe Val, Del McCoury, the Johnson Mountain Boys, Lynn Morris, Alison Krauss and James King.

◉ **Live Again! WCYB Bristol Farm and Fun Time** (Rebel, US).

A great collection of radio transcriptions from the forties and fifties featuring the Stanley Brothers, Mac Wiseman, the Sauceman Brothers, Flatt and Scruggs, and Curly King. Brings the music to life.

 Mountain Music Bluegrass Style
(Smithsonian Folkways, US).

The fiddle playing by Tex Logan that opens this disc saws and swoops, and it continues in cracking style. A Folkways classic from 1959, featuring various local bluegrass bands recorded in living rooms and kitchens.

◉ **Out of the Mountains – The Essential Bluegrass Collection** (Nascente, UK).

A selective collection of more recent bluegrass from the eighties and nineties. Includes covers of "Duelling Banjos" and "Foggy Mountain Breakdown" from Carl Jackson, plus an inspired version of Jimi Hendrix's "Third Stone from the Sun" by a group called Psychograss.

◉ **Top of the Hill Bluegrass** (Sugar Hill, US).

This twenty-track compilation of Sugar Hill bluegrass acts includes artists like the Nashville Bluegrass Band, Lonesome Standard Time, Peter Rowan, Hot Rize and Doyle Lawson.

Artists

The Country Gentlemen

Progressive bluegrass got its full-fledged start with The Country Gentlemen, the first major band to kick off with a mix of bluegrass, folk, country and rock material. Guitarist and singer Charlie Waller is the only founding member who has stuck with the band through its many incarnations.

◉ **Country Songs Old and New**
(Smithsonian Folkways, US).

Precise, no-nonsense recordings that, when first released in 1960, appealed to folk revivalists and traditional stalwarts alike.

Flatt and Scruggs

Bill Monroe may be the father of bluegrass, but Flatt and Scruggs did more to popularise the music than anyone else. Flatt's guitar picking and strong lead voice, coupled with the mighty banjo playing of Earl Scruggs, have become defining characteristics of bluegrass. They began as members of Monroe's Blue Grass Boys in the mid-1940s before pairing up for more than two decades.

◉ **The Essential Flatt and Scruggs** (Sony Legacy, US).

A double-CD collection of the pair's Columbia material from the fifties and sixties. Classic stuff.

Johnson Mountain Boys

One of the great neo-traditional bluegrass bands, the Johnson Mountain Boys formed in 1978 when 'newgrass' was at its peak and the music was, in the opinion of many loyal bluegrass fans, too hippie, too pop, and/or too forgetful of its roots. It was time to get back to basics. The Johnson Mountain Boys gave traditional bluegrass a fresh new spirit.

 Blue Diamond
(Rounder, US).

A 1993 recording of some of the most exciting bluegrass music to have been put on disc in the last few decades. The playing alternates between beautifully understated and all-out raging.

Alison Krauss

Alison Krauss is a gifted singer, instrumentalist and bandleader from Illinois who has almost single-handedly

USA

brought bluegrass back within sight of mainstream country fans. Traditional bluegrass is a rich part of her music, but over the years she has – both as a solo artist and with her band Union Station – blended contemporary folk, country and even hints of rock and pop into her acoustic-based repertoire. Her high, strong voice rings with the spirit of Bill Monroe but also brings to mind singers like Dolly Parton and Emmylou Harris.

 Now That I've Found You: A Collection (Rounder, US).

Not quite a greatest hits album, this 1995 CD gathers several of Krauss and her bandmembers' personal favourites from previous albums, along with a few new songs and unreleased takes.

Longview

Formed in 1995, this contemporary bluegrass supergroup features the Johnson Mountain Boys' Dudley Connell, Lonesome Standard Time's Glen Duncan, James King, Joe Mullins, Don Rigsby and Marshall Wilborn.

◎ **Longview** (Rounder, US).

The music on Longview's debut has a sharp and lively edge yet never loses sight of its roots. Superb solo, duo and trio vocals highlight one of the finest bluegrass albums in years.

Del McCoury

With a pure, mountain-flavoured tenor that practically defines 'high lonesome', Del McCoury has become one of the most highly regarded singers and bandleaders of late twentieth-century bluegrass. When he really lets go the hair stands up on the back of your neck; yet at the same time there's so much joy in the music that you can almost hear McCoury smiling. His band includes his sons Ronnie and Rob, also excellent players, and he has recently had a huge success with 'new country' star Steve Eare.

◎ **The Cold Hard Facts** (Rounder, US).

McCoury's voice gets stronger and his band tighter with each new album. The material, the arrangements, the playing and the singing on this album are extraordinarily powerful.

 The Mountain (Grapevine, US).

Nashville singer and guitarist Steve Earle teams up with Del McCoury and his band for a cracking disc which looks back

to the wellsprings of bluegrass tradition – with great mandolin, banjo and fiddle duets (Stuart Duncan and Jason Carter) – as well as forward into a bright future for the music.

Bill Monroe

Bill Monroe (1911–1996) is the source of bluegrass. The inventive, hard-driven mandolin player didn't set out to forge a new musical genre when he and his brother Charlie parted ways in the 1930s, but that is exactly what happened. His shadow hangs over every bluegrass song to this day – in the high-lonesome vocals, intricate instrumental work, driving rhythms and mournful songs of rural life.

 16 Gems (Columbia, US).

No exaggeration in the title – these recordings from the mid-1940s are among Monroe's most classic. They include cuts by the Blue Grass Boys line-up featuring Flatt and Scruggs that marked the pinnacle of traditional bluegrass.

◎ **The Essential Bill Monroe and the Monroe Brothers** (RCA, US).

Compiles Monroe's earliest bluegrass recordings, cut before Flatt and Scruggs joined the band, as well as nine excellent Monroe Brothers duets from the 1930s.

Larry Sparks

Ohio-born Larry Sparks alternates between fired-up bluegrass numbers and slow-burning, mountain-tinged country ballads that are deeply lonesome and blue. His voice is organic, rich, and decidedly rural; he couldn't sing any other way if he tried. He sang alongside Ralph Stanley in the 1960s before embarking on a productive solo career.

◎ **Classic Bluegrass** (Rebel, US).

An excellent compilation of material Sparks recorded during the seventies and eighties. "John Deere Tractor", later covered by the Judds, is a high point of his career.

Stanley Brothers

The Stanleys were the first group to record in the style of Bill Monroe's Blue Grass Boys, and over three decades they gave the genre new depth. Their music is marked by strong vocal harmonies backed by Ralph's energetic banjo and Carter's steady guitar playing. Carter, the lead vocalist, was also one of the strongest songwriters the genre has yet seen, speaking openly of loneliness, lost love, and death while at the same time echoing the pastoral beauty of his rural upbringing in Virginia's Clinch Mountains.

◎ **Angel Band: The Classic Mercury Recordings** (Mercury, US).

On these mid-1950s sides, the duo's harmonies are tight, fully developed and gorgeous.

Ralph Stanley

After Carter Stanley's death in 1966, Ralph regrouped the Clinch Mountain Boys and persevered on his own. Ralph's hazy, haunting tenor has since grown into one of the most distinct voices in bluegrass.

◎ **Clinch Mountain Country** (Rebel, US).

This thirty six-song, double-CD collection pairs Ralph with the likes of Dwight Yoakam, Gillian Welch, Porter Wagoner, Alison Krauss and even Bob Dylan. Great fun. It's a sequel to his earlier and equally fine duets collection, ◎ **Saturday Night & Sunday Morning** (Freeland, US).

USA

Cajun and Zydeco

music is the glue

Head out of New Orleans a couple of hours along Highway 10 to Lafayette – a mess of gas stations and advertising hoardings – and you find yourself in the heart of Cajun and Zydeco country. The music tends to be sold with images of alligators, swamps and spreading cypress trees draped with Spanish moss, but its home is not so much the bayous as the flat Louisiana prairies where farmers grow rice and cotton and farm crawfish. **Simon Broughton** and **Jeff Kaliss** let the good times roll on some of the most thriving regional music in the United States: **Cajun**, **zydeco**, **la-la** and **swamp pop**.

Louisiana, the poorest State in the Union, is renowned for the hardness of its life and the spiciness of its cuisine. Its music shares both charactersitics, with high, searing vocals backed by accordion, violin, and guitar, and waltzes and two-steps that in turn sparkle with a determined gaiety or convey bleakness and tragedy.

Despite long periods of repression and neglect, **Cajun**, the 'French music' of Louisiana's whites, has been enjoying enormous popularity at home and around the world in recent years. Paul Simon recognised the potential early, enlisting the supercharged backing of Rockin' Dopsie on his *Graceland* album, and Hollywood likewise spiced the soundtracks of *Belizaire the Cajun* and *The Big Easy* with Cajun performers.

Zydeco, the music of Louisiana's black population, is – in Rockin' Dopsie's definition – "a little jazz, a little blues, a little French and a little rhythm'n'blues, all mixed together". It shares its Afro-American origins with blues, jazz, and rock, and as a result, has easily assimilated these 'black' styles. Attempts to integrate them with the more European-based Cajun melodies and rhythms, haven't always been so successful.

Cajun Music

The French ancestors of the Cajuns were settled at the far end of North America, in rural Acadie, a region the colonising British renamed Nova Scotia after they forced the French out at gunpoint in

Joseph and Cleoma Falcon: the first ever Cajun recording artists

1755. Some Acadiens were repatriated to France, others made their way to the French West Indies, but many of them, after years of wandering down the Mississippi River, found their way to Louisiana, where they established themselves as the dominant clique among the other European and Afro-Caribbean groups in the region. The culture of the **Louisiana Acadiens** – a name which was eventually corrupted to become 'Cajuns' – arose out of this multicultural gumbo. Many of the old Cajun folk songs have French equivalents, while others are based on European contradanses or incorporate elements from Anglo-American or Caribbean traditions.

Whatever its roots, music has always been a release for Cajun communities. After a week of hard work, the tradition was *laisser les bons temps rouler* – and today they still 'let the good times roll' in bars, dancehalls and restaurants to the sound of those merry or melancholy waltzes and driving two-steps. "The people are not interested in music for the sake of music", says the leading accordion player Marc Savoy. "They're interested in the atmosphere this music creates, so that they can socialise, so they can drink and relate to one another. Music is the glue that holds the whole culture and society together."

Language plays a part, too. Although many of the more commercial Cajun (and zydeco) bands sing in English, some perform partly or wholly in the Cajun French dialect which was banned or marginalised for decades. While inevitably it now incorporates a good many English words and pronunciations, the language is central to the success of one of the few regions to have stubbornly resisted assimilation into the American mainstream.

Fiddles and Accordions

Before the accordion took over, it was the fiddle that was played at Louisiana *bals de maison* – house parties and dances. **Cajun fiddlers**, like some of their Celtic and later country compatriots, adopted a double-string bowing technique, playing a drone beneath the melody to be better heard over the dancing feet. Some performed in pairs, playing a lead and rhythmic backing – a style continued by the famous duo of **Dennis McGee** and **Sady Courville** until McGee's death, aged 96, in 1989. McGee was really the last of the old-time Cajun fiddlers, with a repertoire and style established in the days before the accordion fully took over the role of lead instrument. His wonderful fiddle recordings are a win-

> ### Jolie Blonde
>
> *Pretty blond girl, look what you've done*
> *You've left me to go away*
> *To go away with another than me*
> *What hope and what future can I possibly*
> *   have?*
> *Pretty blond girl, you've left me all alone*
> *To go back to your family*
> *If you had not listened*
> *to the advice of everyone else*
> *You'd be here with me today*
> *Pretty blond girl, you thought you were*
> *the only one*
> *You aren't the only one in the world*
> *for me to love*
> *If I can only find one other pretty blond girl*
> *Lord knows, I'll have it all.*

dow on another era, as are those of Varise Connor and Wade Frugé.

What we now think of as the typical **Cajun ensemble** has its beginnings in the 1920s, when the fiddle began to share solos with the accordion, with guitar and triangle for rhythmic backing. In part, the accordion owed its rise to its durability in the hot and humid Louisiana climate, but it could also play both melody and accompaniment, and its volume was a great asset in the packed and noisy dancehalls. With this new instrument came a new style of Cajun music, since the accordion wasn't appropriate for the old-style fiddle tunes with their idiosyncratic intonation and ornaments.

The first Cajun recordings were made at around the same time, by accordionist **Joseph Falcon** and his guitarist wife **Cleoma**. Their first record, "Allons à Lafayette", was recorded in a hotel room in New Orleans in 1928 and released as a Columbia 78, with "La valse qui ma portin de ma fose" (The Waltz That Carried Me To My Grave) on the B-side. It sold thousands in Louisiana, Texas, and across the USA. Soon after, Cleoma's brother **Amédée Breaux** recorded the most famous Cajun song of all time, "Jolie Blonde" – often described as the Cajun national anthem and believed to have been composed by Cleoma about her brother's first wife. Many of the songs from this period are classics that have retained a place in the popular repertoire for over sixty years.

The other key musician in these early recordings was **Amédée Ardoin** (1896-1941), a black accordionist. (He is often quoted as the first black musician to record 'French Music', but Douglas Bellard beat him to it). It was rare in those days for a black musician to play at white gigs – it's not common

Amédé Ardoin
Pioneer of Louisiana French Blues 1930-34
"I'm Never Comin' Back"
The Roots of Zydeco

even today – but Amédée was respected and hugely popular at house parties and dancehalls. He could make $2.50 playing with a band at a white dance, whereas at black dances his groups would have to pass a hat around. Amédée was renowned not only for his accordion style but for his immense vocal power and range and his ability to perform for hours on end. The recordings he made with his white partner, Dennis McGee, on fiddle were to be an inspiration to the next generations of accordionists

like Iry LeJeune, Nathan Abshire, and Marc Savoy. Amédée died tragically in 1941 after what seems to have been a racial attack. He was savagely beaten by two white men after accepting a white woman's loan of a handkerchief to wipe his face during a dance. Ironically what his music embodies is the common roots of white Cajun and black zydeco music (of which more below), and their rich cross-fertilisation over the years.

From Repression to Revival

Early in the twentieth century, oil was discovered in Louisiana and its coastal waters, and the effects were soon felt with an influx of new money and Anglo-American labour from out-of-state. The French, having already fled from the English in Nova Scotia, were subjected to further repression by 'Anglos' after the Louisiana Purchase in the nineteenth century. Their language was banned in the new schools and by the early 1930s the younger generation of upwardly mobile Cajuns were regarding French culture as backward and embarrassing. They yearned for 'acculturation' into the English-dominated U.S.A.

Musically, this resulted in the new-style Cajun sound of the thirties: string bands influenced by

Hackberry Ramblers

hillbilly music and western swing, sounds which were increasingly heard on radio and record. **The Hackberry Ramblers** were the leaders of the new trend (incredibly, they're still going, and play regularly in Lake Charles). Their fiddler, **Luderin Darbone**, had learned to play fiddle from a correspondence course and by listening to hillbilly fiddlers in Texas. Along with lilting versions of Cajun classics, the Ramblers recorded new songs like "Une piastre ici, une piastre là-bas"(A Dollar Here, a Dollar There), which reflected life in recession-torn America.

The Hackberrys and other new bands were fiddle- and guitar-led, and boasted drum kits and electric steel guitars. With such amplification, the fiddlers could be heard in the noisiest dancehalls and they adopted a smoother, lighter touch, abandoning the soulful intensity of the earlier styles. The most popular Cajun fiddler of this period was **Harry Choates**, of "Port Arthur Blues" fame, who brought English lyrics into the Cajun gumbo and recorded western swing standards. Other notables were Leo Soileau and J.B. Fuselier.

Probably the greatest Cajun accordionist of all time, **Iry LeJeune** is recognised as the musician who brought the accordion and the soul back into Cajun music with his piercing vocals and poignant playing style. LeJeune was the son of a tenant farmer. Being almost blind he couldn't help out in the fields, and spent his time practising the accordion instead. Inspired by the old recordings of Amédée Ardoin, he eventually went out to play his rustic-sounding music, carrying his accordion in a flour-sack.

The release of his "La valse du pont d'amour" (The Love Bridge Waltz) in 1948 was a seminal date in the history of Cajun music. Along with other LeJeune recordings, it has earned Eddie Shuler's Goldband Records a distinguished place in Cajun history. Quite why these records were so popular after years of slick Americanised music is unclear – perhaps people craved the security of homegrown culture in the aftermath of World War II – but Iry LeJeune certainly gave Cajun cul-

ture a much-needed boost. He died at the height of his career, hit by a car on October 8, 1955. LeJeune's work was continued, fortunately, by his son Eddie, and Iry's old recordings, despite their poor quality, are still enjoyed by new generations.

The other great accordionist of this period was **Nathan Abshire**, whose "Pinegrove Blues" has become a Cajun classic. His style was much more exuberant and bluesy than LeJeune's, and he lived long enough to enjoy the international interest that Cajun music began to receive from the 1960s onward. Abshire created some of the greatest Cajun music and, though poor and illiterate, he remained one of the most celebrated representatives of Cajun culture until his death in 1981.

While this old-style revival was in progress, popular music in America contened to develop apace and Cajun musicians like Laurence Walker and **Doug Kershaw** recorded songs in English, embracing the new sounds of rock'n'roll and

Iry LeJeune taking a cigarette break with Wilson Granger (fiddle) and Alfred 'Duckhead' Cormier (guitar)

Nashville. Such music is considered a dilution of the Cajun patrimony by purists, but it was merely the start of a tradition which broadened out into the range of voices in evidence today. The 1960s Cajun rock'n'roll recordings of **Laurence Walker** and **Aldus Roger** have these days achieved quite a revered status, in recognition of the distinctive hybrid form.

In the early 1960s, the growth of the national folk revival movement drew attention to less assimilated cultures of the United States, and from 1964 Cajun musicians were regularly invited to play at the internationally recognised **Newport Folk**

Festival in Rhode Island. Their rapturous reception meant that musicians like the Balfa Brothers, Nathan Abshire, Canray Fontenot and Clifton Chenier began to enjoy a global reputation along with increased respect at home, and more Louisianans were encouraged to develop their own acts. Then, in 1968, the Council for the Development of French in Louisiana (**CoDoFiL**) was created, helping to counter the official governmental policy, and French-language education was established at all levels. The Council has since been responsible for promoting French musical culture through events like the annual **Festivals Acadiens** in Lafayette and the **Zydeco Festival** in Plaisance, the largest annual Cajun and zydeco music gatherings.

D. L. Menard and Eddie LeJeune

D.L. Menard

D. L. **Menard**'s house in Erath is like everybody's dream of rural living in Louisiana – a spacious front and back porch furnished with the rockers he makes in his rocking-chair workshop next door. When he sings, D.L. has a nasal voice evoking the inspiration of the country legend whose portrait hangs on the wall: "everybody calls me the Cajun Hank Williams, but I know better that there was only one Hank Williams and nobody will replace him. But I have a lot of Hank Williams' style and every time I write a song it's not pure Cajun – there's that country flavour in it."

D.L. started playing the guitar and singing in the late 1940s, when country music was in vogue, and his most distinctive songs with the **Louisiana Aces** have a country feel to them, with accordion, violin and steel guitar. "I bought me my first guitar when I was sixteen and a half years old. I found it in the Montgomery Ward catalogue and I had to pay eleven dollars for it. That was a mail order guitar and it came to the post office in Erath. At seventeen I played my first dance and I've been playing ever since."

He wrote his most popular song, "The Back Door", in 1961 and it has become the second Cajun anthem, alongside "Jolie Blonde". 'When I wrote that song I had no idea it was going to be a hit, but every time I picked up my guitar my kids asked me to sing that song. I recorded it mainly so that the kids would have a souvenir of the song after I'd passed away. I had to pay for recording it because we were an unknown group. But it made a hit and still every Cajun band is playing it.'

Eddie LeJeune

As the son of Iry LeJeune, the greatest Cajun accordionist of all time, **Eddie LeJeune**, had an awful lot to live up to. However, he is without doubt the most honest and soulful accordionist and singer in Cajun music today. "Pure and traditional Cajun music is not only performing on stage, but anywhere you perform – at a house dance or a party. Your feelings and the expression you give out must come straight from the heart, not just from the lyrics. And your feelings are expressed also in the way you play your instrument."

"The way I am playing and recording today with just three instruments – an accordion, fiddle and guitar – is the way my father played and people even before my father. When you have more people in a band it takes out your personal feelings in the music. When you're playing three musicians you can control the music and just go for it as the mood takes you and express your-

Eddie LeJeune and D. L. Menard hanging out by the back door

self better. I feel very proud when I play my father's songs because although I'll never be the musician my father was, at least I have the ability to carry on good, clean, pure, traditional Cajun music. And there are times when I have gotten into it so much that I don't even see the crowd in front of me, because when I sing I close my eyes and this true feeling comes from my heart and the audience captures it as well. These feelings are very emotional and it does penetrate."

Cajun Ambassadors and Purists

One group that long represented the quintessential Cajun sound was the **Balfa Brothers**. The sons of a sharecropper in Grand Louis, brothers Will and Dewey played the fiddle and Rodney the guitar, alongside accordionists like Hadley Fontenot and Nathan Abshire. Their repertoire was a glossary of Cajun's all-time greats, played in a pure acoustic style renowned for its intense vocals and wonderful fiddle duets.

The Balfa Brothers were Cajun music's greatest ambassadors, playing at festivals throughout the US and abroad. At home, Will's regular job was driving a bulldozer and Dewey's the school bus. Both were killed in a road accident in 1979, but Dewey continued to play, making an appearance with Marc Savoy among a bunch of threatening bayou musicians in Walter Hill's film *Southern Comfort*. Highly regarded as a teacher, Dewey successfully pushed for Cajun music to be introduced into the school curriculum and was considered the grand old man of the art up to his death in 1992.

Dewey's daughters Nelda and Christine have preserved their father's love of tradition in the **Balfa Toujours** band, while two of today's best Cajun musicians, accordionist **Marc Savoy** (see box below) and fiddler **Michael Doucet**, were part of the close circle around Balfa. Savoy runs

Marc and Ann Savoy

A direct descendant from the French who were expelled by the English from Nova Scotia, **Marc Savoy** maintains his own fortresses against cultural invasion in the form of a sturdy sprawling farmhouse some seven miles outside Eunice and the Savoy Music Center a little closer to town. Every Saturday morning he summons accordion, fiddle, guitar and triangle players for traditional Cajun music jams, served up with fresh boudin from Eunice washed down with beer. This musical militia has included the late fiddlers Dennis McGee, once a tenant farmer for Savoy's grandfather, and Dewey Balfa, with whom Savoy performed, as well as younger Cajun modernist Steve Riley and Savoy's guitarist and archivist wife, **Ann Savoy**.

It's a merry, melodious scene, but Savoy is fiercely serious about defending the roots from which those melodies spring. The Anglos who repressed the French language and music and later tried to co-opt them "did not have anything that was as good to replace what they were trying to destroy", Savoy believes. Actually, he's less apt to put down what non-Cajuns like than what other musical styles and the rush to make money have done to Cajun music. "All the bands here are trying to be very slick and polished and professional", Savoy complains. "What sells these bands are not the distinctive differences in the music, but the assimilation into mainstream American music...Of course, music must change, but when you add coconuts to gumbo it stops being gumbo." The steady march of local traditionalists and adoring visitors to the Center convinces Savoy that "what makes Cajun music appealing to the real Cajuns, and to some out-of-state people, is that it's not polished, it's not rehearsed, it's not arranged; it's warm, it's real, it's raw".

He and Ann record and tour with fiddler Michael Doucet as the Savoy-Doucet Cajun band, and Ann has published the first of an invaluable multi-volume work, *Cajun Music – A Reflection of a People* (Bluebird Press), collecting song transcriptions, lyrics, and interviews with some of the best Cajun, Creole, and zydeco musicians. The couple has also helped spread Cajun culture and the Savoy myth through their appearance in several delightful and tuneful documentaries by **Les Blank**, filmed with the advice and assistance of Arhoolie label founder and Cajun devotee Chris Strachwitz.

Cajun purists Michael Doucet, Marc and Ann Savoy

DAVE PEABODY

the Savoy Music Center in Eunice, where he makes Acadian accordions that are considered the finest in the business.

Prominent in the Cajun renaissance alongside Marc Savoy are **Barry Ancelet**, folklorist with the Center for Lousiana Studies of the University of Southwestern Louisiana and special projects coordinator for CoDoFiL, and fiddler **Michael Doucet**, whose own group **Beausoleil** has gone through various configurations – with drums, electric guitars and even saxophone in the line-up – but now concentrates on high-quality traditional Cajun music with a repertoire that goes well beyond the standards. The group takes its name from the Acadian resistance leader Joseph Brous-sard, aka Beausoleil, who founded the town in Louisiana that bears his name.

While Savoy, Ancelet, and Doucet may be the intellectual leaders of the tradtional Cajun revival, the accordionist **Eddie LeJeune**, a worthy heir to his father Iry's legacy, and songwriter and guitarist **D.L. Menard**, author of the all-time favourite "La porte en arrière" (The Back Door), are two of the tradition's most instinctive proponents (see box on p.556).

One Foot in the Bayou

At the other end of the scale from Savoy and the purists, there are many commercially successful

Swamp Pop

The local record companies of south Louisiana produce another sort of music, known as **swamp pop**. In its 1960s heyday, this sold much greater quantities than either Cajun or zydeco, with cover versions of popular rock'n'roll hits, reshaped in Louisana fashion for the local market.

Actually, to describe swamp pop as a covers' music is seriously to understate the music's charm and energy. "Swamp pop is just our old south Louisiana sound", says Floyd Soileau of leading label, Swallow Records, searching for a definition. "Sometimes it's bluesy, sometimes it's country and sometimes it has a heavy Cajun accent. It's that gumbo, that mixture of all those influences", he adds, falling back on the usual analogy. "When you hear something that was cut down here, you'll always be able to say 'Aha, that was cut in south Louisiana!' If you're after a slick sound, you're not going to come down here to cut it! Just as we have an accent, our music will also have that little accent." Swamp pop discs issued today still sound as if they were made thirty years ago. An accordion often features in the mix, and they can be guaranteed to end with a steep, inelegant fade.

Back in the 1960s, a surprising number of swamp pop releases climbed into the US national *Billboard* Top 100 in the 1960s and **Tommy McLain**'s rendition

of "Sweet Dreams" even made the Top 10 in 1966, giving it the bizarre distinction of being the biggest hit to come out of Ville Platte, site of Soileau's recording studio and store. But it's not their once-in-a-blue-moon national success that makes these records interesting, but their characteristic local eccentricity. Floyd Soileau recalls as one of his studio's proudest moments the recording of Johnnie Allan's "Promised Land". This cover of Chuck Berry's song, reinforced with driving accordion breaks, has become the swamp pop anthem. "I was working with Johnny on the song and he thought we should throw a little seasoning in and get **Belton Richard** to do the accordion. He came in, heard it through and just put the accordion in on the first take. The rest is history!"

In lounges and studios across south Louisiana, swamp pop is still being played and recorded. One of the best releases of the 1990s was the **Charles Mann** version of Dire Straits' "Walk of Life", supercharged with accordion, which was recorded in the 'studio' (a converted bar) of Lanor Records in Church Point. Charles Mann can be seen performing in dancehalls across the region, though much of the rest of his repertoire is cloyingly sentimental. Should you need any persuading, the best way to hear the current swamp pop hits is to frequent the Louisana drinking establishments and feed the jukeboxes.

groups and musicians who have fused Cajun music with blues, rock and country.

But at what point does music stop being Cajun? What Marc Savoy might see as coconut-tainted Cajun is served up by accordionist **Zachary Richard**, who plays a rock-inspired hybrid of Cajun and zydeco which is popular in New Orleans and out-of-state. **Filé**, who released the classic "One Foot in the Bayou" (see the lyric below), stick much closer to mainstream rock-'n'roll while keeping the accordion centre-stage.

Jo-El Sonnier's music has a distinct country feel, and apart from *Cajun Life* (Rounder), an album of laid-back Cajun classics, he has recorded most of his songs in English. **Wayne Toups** and Zydecajun probably set the Balfas spinning in their graves and threaten to send Marc Savoy to an early one. **Paul Daigle**, an accordion prodigy of the 1970s, grew up to became a Louisiana favorite in the company of former pop singer Robert Elkins and their band, **Cajun Gold**. True to his roots, however, he still maintains his auto body shop near Church Point and doesn't perform as much as the world deserves.

The best of the bunch, perhaps, are **Steve Riley and the Mamou Playboys**, whose line-up of accordion, fiddle, guitar, drums and triangle is pretty traditional. Their mission is to 'perpetuate the styles and repertoires' of their mentors while 'recharging the songs of the past with the vitality of the present'.

Diamond Rings, limousines
Down home girl, uptown dreams
Penthouse suites, Broadway shows
Just don't move her like the zydeco
She done gone up to the city
Now she don't know what to do
She got one foot in New York City
And one foot in the bayou

Lyrics by David Egan, on Filé's *La Vie Marron*

The Creole Sound: La-La and Zydeco

Cajun country was never a major slave region, and **Louisiana's black population** tended to come from other parts of America or the Caribbean to work as tenant farmers – even before the arrival of the Acadians from Canada. These Louisiana blacks, and their mixed-race neighbours, came to be known as Creoles, and the term is still applied to that population and its pre-zydeco music.

La-La Roots

The earliest **Creole** music was made in the fields, without instruments, the singing backed up by clapping and stomping. Even outside of work, the music was sparse, few Creoles having enough money to buy instruments, though there were formidable players among the few that did.

The old-style dance music these guys played – and in some cases still do – is known as **La-La**, or old-style Creole. Less prettily melodic than Cajun music, its sound was a combination of accordion and fiddle, backed up by washboard, with a definite spring in the rhythm that would later link it to R&B. Blended with blues, rock and other popular forms, it developed into **zydeco**, a corruption of *les haricots* – French for runner beans. Taken from the old Creole song "Les haricots sont pas salés" (The Beans Aren't Salted), recorded and popularised by Clifton Chenier as "Zydeco sont pas salé", the term somehow came to represent the musical style, though the lyric was actually a reference to the poverty of the Creole diet.

Foremost among the old-style Creole accordionists were **Amédée Ardoin**, **Sidney Babineaux** and **Adam Fontenot**. A huge influence on Cajun music, Ardoin's recordings in the 1930s and 1940s reveal that black and white music had much in common at that time; indeed, Ardoin's best-known collaborator was white fiddler Dennis McGee.

One of the latest and greatest of old-style Creole musicians was Adam Fontenot's son, fiddler **Canray Fontenot** (1922-1995). At the age of

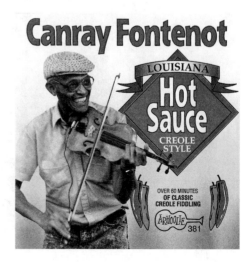

nine he made his first fiddle, out of a wooden cigar-box strung with wire, and played it for two years until his uncle bought him a real violin. Canray's songs are highly personal, reflecting the hardships and joys of his life, and in his last years he received due recognition, making dozens of recordings and appearing at festivals around the world. His most celebrated partnership was with accordionist **Alphonse 'Bois Sec' Ardoin** (Amedée's cousin) and the pair of them are responsible for some of the best la-la recordings around. They performed at a club run by Bois Sec's son, Lawrence, next to the Ardoin family house in Duralde.

The family tradition has been passed on and updated by Bois Sec's accordionist grandson, **Chris Ardoin**, who helped his grandfather take the music as far afield as Carnegie Hall. Practically the only other group still playing the old-style la-la repertoire are the **Lawtell Playboys**, featuring the renowned fiddler Calvin Carrière, who perform around the Opelousas area.

Clifton Chenier's Zydeco

Contemporary-style **zydeco** music dates from the post-war years and its development and popularity can largely be credited to **Clifton Chenier** (1925–1987). Born on a farm near Opelousas –

still the centre of zydeco territory – Chenier grew up working in the fields of cotton, rice, sugar and corn. It wasn't until the late 1940s, when he was employed at the oil refinery in Lake Charles, that he picked up the accordion and began playing at dances. Signed up by Speciality Records, an R&B label, in 1955, he went on to record over a hundred albums in the thirty years.

Over his long career, Clifton's repertoire included everything from simple rustic zydeco to major hits with the **Red Hot Louisiana Band**. Nobody questions his title as King of Zydeco: Chenier transformed the old-style la-la music into the bluesy and rock-based zydeco sound of today, which is led by the accordion and backed by heavy drums, guitar, electric bass and sometimes saxophone or brass. Adding its unmistakable rasp to the sound is the *frottoir*, the old washboard reincarnated as a more versatile corrugated steel vest, played with spoons or bottle openers.

Frottoir playing was developed into a real art form by Clifton's brother, **Cleveland Chenier**, who played with blues singer Lightnin' Hopkins as well as in his brother's band. In common with many zydeco musicians, Clifton favoured the triple-row or piano-key accordions, with their wider range of chromatic, bluesy notes than the simpler double-row button accordions preferred by Cajun musicians.

Zydeco godfather Clifton Chenier

Zydeco Today

The zydeco sound begun by Clifton Chenier has gone from strength to strength, and nowadays over a weekend in Lafayette, or at *Richard's* or *Slim's Y-Ki-Ki*, two famous zydeco clubs near Opelousas, it's a virtual guarantee that you'll hear some top-class players. Despite the number of recordings now available, zydeco is really a music that demands to be heard live – to feel that relentless beat on the floor of the dancehall, to hear the wild accordion and get swept up in the action and the sweat of the dance.

The elder statesman of zydeco today is **Boozoo Chavis**, a contemporary of Clifton Chenier, who had his first big hit, "Paper in My Shoe", on Eddie Shuler's Goldband Records in 1954. Several unsatisfactory takes of the song were recorded over three days, until Shuler struck on the idea of loosening up the band with whisky. The story goes that at the end of the take that was finally released, Boozoo fell out of his chair but carried on playing nonetheless – Shuler had to fade the track out (a technique that was new at the time) to hide the crash. After a brief career in the 1950s, Boozoo retired to concentrate on breeding racehorses, only to make an acclaimed comeback in the mid-1980s. He has played gigs right across the US – although he's still best heard on his home territory.

After Clifton Chenier's death, the King of Zydeco title had fallen to **Rockin' Dopsie**, who was crowned in 1988 by the Mayor of Lafayette. He died in 1993, however, and the crown is again up for grabs. Contenders among today's leading lights must include Boozoo Chavis, and **Rockin' Sidney**, author of zydeco's biggest hit, "My Toot Toot". Meanwhile, the undisputed Queen of Zydeco is **Queen Ida**, a singer and accordion player with a modern rootsy sound who is now based in her adopted home – a centre of transplanted Louisiana music – the San Francisco Bay Area.

Without doubt, today's most successful group is **Buckwheat Zydeco**, led by Stanley Dural Jnr, who played for two and a half years in Clifton Chenier's Red Hot Louisiana Band. The band are signed to Island – one of the few zydeco acts on a major label – and were featured in the Hollywood film *The Big Easy*. **John Delafose and the Eunice Playboys** played highly rhythmic zydeco with an Afro-Caribbean flavour until Delafose's death in 1994; his sons Geno and Tony joined

Queen Ida giving it some wellie

John on "Père et Garçon," one of the best zydeco releases of the 1990s. It contains dances deeply rooted in Louisiana tradition from the likes of Amédée Ardoin and Clifton Chenier, as well as the Delafoses' own material.

Another musical family to look out for are **Roy** and **'Chubby' Carrier**, a pair of terrific accordion players based at the delightfully out-of-the-way Offshore Lounge in Lawtell. Family, says Chubby, is the key ingredient in traditional zydeco music. "Families is what's happening. We played zydeco music; it wasn't played nowhere else but in our homes. We keep ourselves together. When we come back from mass on Sundays, we have cookouts – then we have our music. Mom would actually move her coffee table – that was our dancefloor, in our living room."

C.J. Chenier, son of Clifton, can be found at a variety of jazz festivals in fantastic garb and accessories that evoke the image of funkadelic master Bootsy Collins, but he has clearly embraced the accordion and zydeco career of his late father, and is quick to note that zydeco continues to evolve.

"Even when you listen to Clifton, he doesn't limit himself to zydeco, he's blues and boogie", says the younger Chenier. "It's a different age now, and even if I play his song, it's gonna sound different."

A more radical approach was taken by **Beau Jocque** (born Andrus Espre), who died in 1999. He had played horns in high school and was a fan of ZZ Top and James Brown before he ever approached his father's zydeco-chugging accordion. He ended up by merging the styles, and got even more modern with echos of urban hip-hop

Festivals, Dancehalls and Radio Stations

The best way to hear both Cajun and zydeco is live and in situ, and there are any number of clubs in and around Lafayette to choose from, as well as two great festivals. Beware, though, that the region's predominantly Catholic faith means that dances often stop for Lent – after the big Mardi Gras celebration everything quietens down till Easter.

Festivals
Festivals Acadiens, Lafayette (☎318/232-3808). A celebration of regional music, food and crafts in the third week of September. Girard Park hosts the music festival on Saturday and Sunday and there's an expanded Downtown Alive! dance in Jefferson St on Friday night.
Zydeco Festival, Plaisance (☎18/942-2392). Louisiana's main zydeco festival is held on the Saturday before Labor Day (the first Mon in Sept) in Plaisance, between Opelousas and Ville Platte, with music from 11am to midnight.

Dancehalls
Borque's, Lewisburg (☎318/948-9904). The most picturesque of dancehalls, nine miles south of Opelousas. Saturday and Sunday evenings.
Dup's Lounge, Rt 13 N, Eunice (☎318/457-9162). Four miles north of Eunice, Dup's is a run-down cabin with sawdust on the floor – perfect. The Saturday afternoon dance makes it the ideal stop after Fred's Lounge.
El Sido's, 1523 Martin Luther King Drive, Lafayette (☎318/235-0647). Large dancefloor with zydeco dances on Friday and Saturday nights. Nathan and the zydeco Cha-Chas are regulars.
Fred's Lounge, Sixth St, Mamou (☎318/468-5411). The Saturday morning live radio broadcast has made this a place of pilgrimage for Cajun music fans. The current band is Don Thibodeaux and Cajun Fever.
Gilton's Lounge, US-190 E and Rt 95, Eunice (☎318/457-1241). Cavernous zydeco dancehall that

sees some of the big names – and was immortalised in song by Boozoo Chavis.
Grant Street Dancehall, 1113 W Grant St, Lafayette (☎318/237-8513). Premier Lafayette nightclub for Cajun, zydeco and other bands.
Hamilton's, 1808 Verot School Rd, Lafayette (☎318/984-5583). Wooden-frame zydeco dancehall on the southern fringe of Lafayette.
Mulate's, 325 Mills Av (Rt 94), Breaux Bridge (☎318/332-4648). The world's most famous Cajun restaurant with live Cajun music, generally of superior quality.
Offshore Lounge, off US-190, Lawtell (☎318/543-9996). Set back behind the railtracks in Lawtell, next to some fine wooden houses – a landmark you'll need – this is a fine zydeco dancehall run by accordionist Roy Carrier.
Papa Paul's, Poinciana (Rt 1160) and 2nd St, Mamou (☎318/468-5538). A first-rate old-style zydeco dancehall with dances virtually every weekend.
Rainbeaux Club, 1373 Rt 182 W, New Iberia (☎318/367-6731). Large old-fashioned dancehall with Saturday night Cajun dances.
Richard's Club, US-190 W, Lawtell (☎318/543-6596). A premier zydeco venue in the Opelousas area. Weekend dances in a wooden building with a homely atmosphere.
Slim's Y-Ki-Ki, Rt 167 N, Opelousas (☎318/942-9980). One of Louisiana's top zydeco dancehalls since 1947. Hot, crowded and highly recommended.

Radio Stations
Indicative of Louisiana's hard-working agricultural life are the early-morning Cajun music programmes, scheduled to give a quick blast of accordion before a day in the rice fields. Several of these are recorded before live audiences – and attending can be a lot of fun.

The most famous show is the weekly live broadcast from **Fred's Lounge** in Mamou on **KVPI**, a station that

and rap, while vocalising in a corrugated blues wail. Jocque's sound is sometimes referred to as 'nouveau zydeco' and in many ways he personified the competitive nature of modern zydeco players in general and accordionists in particular. He was renowned for his onstage instrumental 'battles' with Boozoo Chavis, and his verbal jousts with **Keith Frank**, a Chavis admirer full of fun and clever accordion riffs who is much beloved of dance crowds in Acadiana. Where Frank has stuck to halls, festivals, and record labels close to home,

Jocque has moved on to national tours and the Massachusetts-based Rounder label.

Hot on Jocque's trail to the same label and some of the same national venues is **Geno Delafose**, now touring with his own **French Rockin' Boogie** band, named for one of his early hits. There's much about his album, *La Chanson Perdue,* that certifies his eclectic yet traditionalist approach. "I like the music I grew up with, and I don't want to see it just slip away", says Geno. "In Louisiana, there's not many of the younger Zydeco musicians who

Saturday morning at Fred's Lounge, Mamou

has been broadcasting French music since 1957. At 9am on Saturday morning *Fred's Lounge*, an ugly brick building, is packed to bursting with Cajun revellers swigging beer, waltzing and two-stepping within the ropes that mark the dancefloor. Illuminated beer signs share the walls with stern notices from Fred – 'Please do not stand on the tables, chairs, cigarette machine, booths, jukebox and chairs' and 'This is not a dance hall. If you get hurt dancing we are not responsible' – which make letting the good times roll seem rather perilous. The radio show is MC'd by Martel Ardoin, his basic broadcasting gear set up on a wooden table, who reads ads in French for local feed mills, a filling station and Jack Miller's Barbecue Sauce.

The **stations and shows** include:

KVPI 1050 AM (Ville Platte; ☎318/363-2124). Cajun Mon–Fri 4–5pm, Sat 9.15–11am live from *Fred's Lounge*; Sat 11–12pm, Sun 4–5pm. Zydeco Sun noon–1pm.

KEUN 1490 AM (Eunice; ☎318/457-3041). Cajun Mon–Fri 5–7am, Sat 7am–midnight (6–8pm live from the Liberty Theater, Eunice, hosted by Cajun scholar Barry Ancelet); 8–10pm live from *Michot's Main St Lounge*, Basile). Sun: Zydeco 9am-12 Noon, Cajun from 1pm.

KXZZ 1580 AM (Lake Charles; 318/439-3300). Zydeco daily 6:30-8pm.

KRVS 88.7 FM (Lafayette; 90.5 FM in Lake Charles; ☎318/231-5668). Cajun Mon–Fri 5–7am, Sat 6–8pm (recorded the previous week in the Liberty Theater, Eunice), Sun 6am–5pm. Zydeco Sat 6am–noon.

KJCB 770 AM (Lafayette; ☎318/233-4262). Zydeco Mon & Thurs 7–9pm, Sat 9–12am, Sun noon–3pm.

KROF 960 AM (Abbeville; ☎318/893-2531). Cajun and zydeco Mon–Fri 6am–12pm, Sat & Sun 6am–6pm.

keep the traditional style going. The nouveau zydeco started out with Beau Jocque, who really added a lot of bass and funked and pumped it up, and with Keith Frank doing the same thing and Chris Ardoin. They're really doing a good job of keeping it going, but it's a lot different from what I play. Mine is plain and simple. A lot of my music is singing in French, and I do a lot more waltzes. I guess you could say it's more rootsy."

discography

Cajun/Zydeco compilations

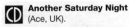
Allons en Louisiane
(Rounder, US).

A CD-ROM and audio CD package giving a lively insight into South Louisiana culture and music. The audio CD is compiled from Rounder's excellent Cajun and Zydeco catalogue including Steve Riley, Chris Ardoin, D.L. Menard, Eddie LeJeune, Geno Delafose, Beau Jocque and Boozoo Chavis. The CD-ROM includes interviews, recipes, dance-club descriptions and dance instruction!

[] **Cajun and Creole Masters** (Music of the World, US).

The great fiddlers recorded in 1986 – Canray Fontenot with Bois Sec Ardoin, Dennis McGee and Sady Courville – plus a storming duet ("Merci Mondieu") with Courville on violin and Michael Doucet on guitar.

[] **Folksongs of the Louisiana Acadians**
(Arhoolie, US).

Songs of diverse origins sung in traditional combinations of fiddle, accordion and guitar. Some relate to the Appalachian repertoire and others much further back to eighteenth-century France. Real old-time music, several tracks featuring wonderful fiddler Wallace 'Cheese' Reed.

[] **J'ai été au bal Volume 1** and **Volume 2**
(Arhoolie, US).

These two CDs are the most comprehensive introduction to Cajun and Zydeco music, although the emphasis is more on

Cajun. From early recordings of Joseph Falcon, Amédée Ardoin and Dennis McGee, through the Hackberry Ramblers, Harry Choates and Iry LeJeune to Clifton Chenier, Boozoo Chavis, Michael Doucet and Wayne Toups. Essential.

[] **Kings of Cajun** (Music Club, UK).

This is the first volume of a number of good Cajun compilations. Includes Nathan Abshire, Balfa Brothers, Austin Pitre, Boozoo Chavis and others.

[] **The Rough Guide to Cajun and Zydeco**
(World Music Network, UK).

A well-compiled selection that for the most part concentrates on the current names, including traditionalists like Eddie LeJeune, D.L. Menard and the Savoy-Doucet Cajun Band, and young-bloods Buckwheat Zydeco, Jo-El Sonnier and Bruce Daigrepont. However, there are also a few classic tracks from Clifton Chenier, Nathan Abshire and Wallace 'Cheese' Read.

[] **Zydeco – The Early Years** (Arhoolie, US).

Live recordings of small Zydeco bands in the early 1960s including Clifton Chenier's first cuts.

Swamp pop compilations

[] **Allons Cajun Rock 'n' Roll** (Ace, UK).

Swamp pop tracks, dating mainly from the 1960s, from Aldus Roger and Lawrence Walker, plus some more recent releases, all from the La Louisianne label. Close your eyes and imagine the jukebox.

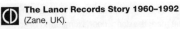
Another Saturday Night
(Ace, UK).

As the cover states, these are 'Classic Recordings from the Louisiana Bayous'. Includes some of the swamp pop classics like Tommy McLain's "Before I Grow Too Old", Vin Bruce's "Jolie Blon", Johnnie Allan's "Promised Land" and Belton Richard's "Another Saturday Night". There are a couple of excellent sequels, [] **Louisiana Saturday Night** (Ace) and [] **Lafayette Saturday Night** (Ace).

[] **Eddie's House of Hits:**
The Story of Goldband Records (Ace, UK).

Some of the idiosyncratic highlights from Eddie Shuler's Lake Charles-based Goldband Records. Includes Cleveland Crochet's "Sugar Bee" and early Rockin' Sidney and Dolly Parton, plus swamp pop stars Cookie and the Cupcakes' "Blue Bayou Shuffle".

[] **The Lanor Records Story 1960–1992**
(Zane, UK).

A great retrospective of Lanor productions, including swamp pop classics such as "The Walk of Life", "Chewing Gum" and tracks by Roy Carrier, Shirley Bergeron and Beau Jocque.

Cajun artists

Nathan Abshire

Nathan Abshire (1915–1981) was born into a poor, accordion-playing family and started playing at house dances from the age of eight. As a youth he is said to have filled during breaks for legendary creole accordionist Amédée Ardoin. After World War II he played with his most celebrated group, the Pine Grove Boys, and was a key figure in the revival of the accordion after the thirties swing craze. In the sixties and seventies he enjoyed a celebrated partnership with the Balfa

Brothers, but increasingly suffered from heavy drinking. His accordion case displayed the message 'The Good Times Are Killing Me'.

 The Best of Nathan Abshire (Swallow, US).

Just what it says: recordings from the peak of his career, with the Balfa Brothers. Created from two LPs: *Pine Grove Blues* and *The Good Times Are Killing Me*. Includes the classic "Pine Grove Blues".

The Balfa Brothers

The classic Cajun band, led by fiddler Dewey Balfa, with Will on second fiddle and Rodney on guitar. They won international attention at the Newport Folk Festival and spearheaded the Cajun revival in Louisiana.

 The Balfa Brothers Play Traditional Cajun Music (Swallow, US; Ace, UK).

Two albums on one CD containing some of the all-time great Cajun songs, including "Lacassine Special", "Parlez nous a boire", "'Tit galop pour Mamou" and "Les flammes d'enfer". Definitive performances, with Marc Savoy on some tracks.

Balfa Toujours

An acoustic band featuring Dewey Balfa's daughters, Christine and Nelda. The band's line-up includes accordion, fiddle, guitar and drums.

 La Pointe (Rounder, US).

Recorded at the site of the original eighteenth-century Acadian settlement in Canada, La Pointe brings it all home with songs by and about the extended Balfa Family as well as several Creole and Cajun classics, performed with tangible respect and joy.

Beausoleil and Michel Doucet

One of the leaders of the current Cajun revival, Doucet (b 1951) is a very fine fiddler and a good vocalist. He learnt from veteran fiddlers Dennis McGee, Dewey Balfa and Canray Fontenot, but has also taken Cajun music into various fusions with his band Beausoleil. One of the most popular bands on the circuit, Beausoleil began as a small acoustic ensemble, but has expanded at times to include sax, bass and drums.

 Beau solo (Arhoolie, US).

An outstanding solo disc on which Doucet sings, and plays the accordion and fiddle, with his brother David on guitar. Some old favourites and some more unusual choices.

 Vintage Beausoleil (Music of the World, US).

A live concert in New York city in 1986, one of the band's best periods. Includes the wonderful creole fiddler Canray Fontenot as guest.

Hackberry Ramblers

The Hackberry Ramblers made a hit with their swing version of "Jolie Blonde" in 1935 and were the quintessential string band of the thirties. Instrumentation included fiddle, guitars, steel guitar, piano and electric bass. Luderin Darbone and Edwin Duhon, now in their eighties, are still playing today.

 Jolie Blonde (Arhoolie, US).

Two excellent covers of the 1935 classic "Jolie Blonde" are on this collection of tracks that helped re-launch the Ramblers in the sixties.

Eddie LeJeune

Son of famed accordionist Iry LeJeune, Eddie (born 1951) is a worthy successor. He has the piercing vocals, the button accordion technique and prefers the traditional acoustic line-up of accordion, fiddle and guitar.

 Cajun Soul
(Rounder, US; Hannibal, UK).

One of the very best of recent Cajun albums. Eddie includes a few of his father's classic songs, with D. L. Menard on guitar and Ken Smith on fiddle. The "Lacassine Special" is storming.

Iry LeJeune

LeJeune (1928–1955) was one of the great Cajun accordionists, whose "Love Bridge Waltz" of 1948 brought the accordion back into favour. His soulful, poignant and sometimes bleak music, influenced by Amédée Ardoin, stands as one of the authentic sounds of Cajun music.

 Cajun's Greatest (Goldband, US; Ace, UK).

Twenty five songs including the classic "Love Bridge Waltz" and several reworkings of Ardoin numbers. Not hi-fi recordings, but comes with excellent notes by Ann Savoy. Listen out for LeJeune's dog on the "Duraldo Waltz".

Dennis McGee

The last great Cajun fiddler with a link to the pre-accordion past, McGee (1893–1989) is an important influence on today's musicians like Marc Savoy and Michael Doucet. He recorded in two celebrated partnerships, with accordionist Amédée Ardoin and fellow fiddler Sady Courville.

 The Complete Early Recordings (Shanachie/Yazoo, US).

In the twenties and thirties, accompanied by Ernest Frugé and Sady Courville, McGee wailed what would become Cajun classics, and models for generations of fiddlers to come. Vital and daring music.

The complete early recordings of

DENNIS McGEE
1928-1930

"The foundation on which Cajun music is based ... the heart of our music." MICHAEL L. DOUCET

Newly remastered from original recordings.

with Ernest Frugé and Sady Courville
EARLY AMERICAN CAJUN CLASSICS

D.L. Menard

Guitarist D.L. Menard, (b 1932) is known as the 'Cajun Hank Williams' with his country tinged tunes and nasal singing voice. He played with the band the Louisiana Aces.

The Swallow Recordings (Swallow, US; Ace,UK).

A first-class compilation of two of Louisiana's greatest – singer, songwriter and guitarist D. L. and wild accordionist Austin Pitre. Popular Cajun honky-tonk from the 1960s, including D.L.'s classic, "La Porte en Arrière" (The Back Door).

Wallace 'Cheese' Read

Born in Eunice, fiddle player Wallace Read (1924–81) didn't have a professional musical career, but grew cotton and played for local dances and parties.

Cajun House Party (Arhoolie, US).

A real cracker of down-home music with Cheese on fiddle and vocal duty and Marc Savoy on accordion. Mainly from sessions in 1979.

Steve Riley and the Mamou Playboys

The best of the young Cajun bands. Riley was born in 1969 in Mamou and is one of the progressive figures in Cajun music, revitalising old tunes and fusing them with zydeco, while usually keeping to the spirit of the music.

La Toussaint (Rounder, US).

This 1995 album was their first of largely original material, but it keeps a traditional feel, with a strong backbeat on drums, wailing vocals and an element of homage to Canray Fontenot, Marc Savoy and Clifton Chenier.

Savoy-Doucet Cajun Band

One of the best traditional set ups around, as fiddler and vocalist Michael Doucet joins up with accordionist Marc Savoy and guitarist and vocalist Ann Savoy.

Two-Step d'Amédé (Arhoolie, US).

The album takes its title from an instrumental number by Marc Savoy based on an Amédée Ardoin tune. Other highlights include "Diggu Liggy Lo", "Les flammes d'enfer" and the eerie "Kaplan Waltz".

Wayne Toups

Accordionist Wayne Toups is one of the popular Cajun modernists blending Cajun and creole styles with his band Zydecajun. Once dubbed the 'Cajun Springsteen', he's about as 'rocky' as Cajun music gets. His album, Blast from the Bayou, was the first to hit the Billboard pop charts.

Back to the Bayou (Swallow, US; Iona, UK).

This 1995 release sounds pretty much like a mainstream rock release with Cajun flavouring. Most songs are in English, but there's a rather sprightly version in French of D.L. Menard's "The Back Door".

Zydeco artists

Amedée Ardoin

Amedée Ardoin (1896–1941) was the most celebrated and popular early black recording artist, renowned for his strong voice and ability to perform for hours on end. He enjoyed a celebrated partnership with fiddler Dennis McGee, but died in a mental asylum after a racial attack. He only made 34 recordings but his influence was huge.

I'm Never Comin' Back (Arhoolie, US).

The early heart of creole music with a solo session from 1934 and several tracks with Dennis McGee. Legendary recordings in the history of Cajun and zydeco music.

Buckwheat Zydeco

Buckwheat Zydeco, led by Stanley Dural Jr (b 1947), is contemporary zydeco's most popular international band. Dural, on piano accordion, produces some strong blues influenced music, but a lot of mediocre commercial music as well.

Buckwheat's Zydeco Party (Rounder, US).

The best compilation of Dural's hits with his full band sound. Compiled from two Grammy-nominated recordings of the early 1980s.

Boozoo Chavis

The current elder statesman of zydeco, Chavis (b 1930) grew up playing the button accordion at dances around Lake Charles. In 1954 he had a huge hit with "Paper in My Shoe", his version of a nineteenth century creole song, which became a standard. After years out of the music business he returned to zydeco in the 1980s, and is still a powerful live performer.

Live! At the Habibi Temple, Lake Charles, Louisiana (Rounder, US).

This includes a stonking version of "Paper in My Shoe" and plenty other characterful tracks. Recorded live in 1993.

Clifton Chenier

The undisputed King of Zydeco, Clifton Chenier (1925–1987) created modern zydeco by blending rock and R&B with his piano accordion and old-style creole music. He rose to popularity in the seventies with the Red Hot Louisiana Band.

Zydeco Dynamite: The Clifton Chenier Anthology (Rhino, US).

A two-CD collection ranging from 1954 to 1984 – right across Clifton's career. All the important songs are here, accompanied by a great booklet with photos. For a single CD choice, try ▣ 60 Minutes with the King of Zydeco (Arhoolie, US), which is also a superb compilation.

Geno Delafose

Brought up in one of the great zydeco families of the region, Geno started out in his father's band, the Eunice Playboys. Since Delafose senior's death in 1994, Geno has firmly stepped into his shoes, maintaining the traditional artistry of zydeco music within a contemporary context.

La Chanson Perdue (Rounder, US).

In this excellent 1998 release, Geno joins hands with Cajun musical brothers and sisters – Balfa Toujours players Christine Balfa and Dirk Powell – and fellow Mamou High School alumnus, fiddler Steve Riley. Solid zydeco and Cajun spiced sounds plus a refry of the rock classic "Save the Last Dance for Me".

Père et garçon (Rounder, US).

1992 album featuring father and son – Delafose senior moving onto washboard for his son's tracks. Two generations of first-class zydeco musicians playing really danceable music.

Rockin' Dopsie

Rockin' Dopsie (1932–1993) was born into a sharecropping family near Lafayette. His father played button accordion at local dances and Dopsie (pronounced Doopsie) followed in his footsteps, always keeping an authentic rawness in his playing. He became friendly with Paul Simon, who asked him to play on the *Graceland* album, which introduced the sound of zydeco to millions of listeners. An Atlantic records contract followed.

 Louisiana Music (Atlantic, US).

Some driving dance tunes and slower bluesy numbers capture the essence of Dopsie's style.

Canray Fontenot

Fontenot (1922–1995) was the last of the great creole fiddlers, and had a wonderful, smiling personality. He played in a celebrated partnership with accordionist Alphonse 'Bois Sec' Ardoin for half a century, although Fontenot worked principally as a rice farmer and labourer.

 Louisiana Hot Sauce, Creole Style (Arhoolie, US).

Twenty-seven wonderful tracks of an old man putting all his astonishing vivacity and life into songs recorded between the 1970s and the 1990s. Raw and impassioned playing.

 La Musique Creole (Arhoolie, US).

The memorable pairing of Fontenot and Bois Sec, recorded in 1966 and the early 1970s.

Beau Jocque

Beau Jocque (1957–99), with his band the Zydeco Hi-Rollers, was the funkiest of 1990s zydeco artists, combining his music with funk, R&B, and latterly hip-hop. He recorded eight albums for Rounder and his sudden heart attack aged only 43 deprived zydeco of one of its most flamboyant stars.

 Git It, Beau Jocque! (Rounder, US).

All Beau Jocque's albums are intense, but this 1994 live outing captures the excitement and high energy of his gigs in

Harry's Lounge in Breaux Bridge and Slim's Y-Ki-Ki in Opelousas. The set includes his signature number "Give Him Cornbread".

 Pick Up On This (Rounder, US).

Raw, funky zydeco without too much of the rock and rap influences. The characteristic shrieks and deep bass growl are heavily present, as is the heavy, blues-tinged accordion.

Rockin' Sidney

Rockin' Sydney (b 1938) is famous for zydeco's first international hit "My Toot Toot", released in 1985. He started out playing guitar and singing R&B before learning the accordion and turning to zydeco in the early eighties.

 My Toot Toot (Ace, UK).

A great cross-section of Sidney's output from the early sixties and mid-eighties, including, of course "My Toot Toot", his most successful cut.

USA

Gospel

devil stole the beat

Gospel music, with its roots in the so-called negro spiritual, has influenced most other streams of American popular music, and many of its teenage prodigies – most notably Sam Cooke, Aretha Franklin, Al Green and Elvis Presley – crossed over to become soul or rock'n'roll stars. Meantime the mainstream of gospel remains vibrant in countless churches and radio stations across the US, keeping its roots nourished and re-importing a little funk from soul and R&B along the way. **Viv Broughton** and **James Attlee** put on their Sunday best.

C ountless thousands sing in gospel choirs, both well-known and obscure. They simply stand up on a Sunday and pour all the faith, the frustration, the anguish and the defiant hope that make up their daily lives into a sound that invariably brings an ecstatic response of 'Amens' and 'Hallelujahs' from the rest of the congregation. To experience the raw power of gospel at its purest, be adventurous – go find a pew. It's the churches that are the grass-roots of

the folk art of American gospel music, and even the multi-million-dollar industry at the top has never lost touch with its constituency. For every crossover act that tops the R&B or soul charts there are hundreds of more traditional artists working the gospel circuit, thrilling primarily black church audiences with a musical style that has changed little in three decades.

Gospel singers have a saying that has been passed down from generation to generation. 'The devil

Blind Willie Johnson taking gospel to the streets, 1920s

stole the beat,' they will tell you, meaning that far from Satan having all the best tunes, much of the so-called 'devil's music' has borrowed its style from the black church. There's some truth to this. Many of **rock'n'roll**'s characteristics, from rhythms to vocal styles, from dance steps to stage-diving, were first conceived on the gospel circuit – and it's perhaps no surprise that it started early, with **Elvis Presley**, **Little Richard** and **Jerry Lee Lewis** – among many other American singers – learning at the feet of gospel's own legends.

On the **soul** and **R&B** front, black music, from the earliest days of recording to the present, has had two roughly parallel streams: the sacred and the secular, each feeding, and feeding off, the other. Some performers, even superstars like **Al Green** and **Aretha Franklin**, switch camp in both directions, braving the disapproval and misunderstanding of their peers. And for all the mutual mistrust, one genre would certainly be the poorer without the other.

Spiritual Roots

The style of music most people know as gospel was born only around seventy years ago – in Chicago, in the depths of the Depression. Its seminal figure was a piano player and ex-blues musician by the name of **Thomas A. Dorsey** (1899–1993), who began composing songs based on familiar spirituals and hymns fused to blues and jazz rhythms. He called them 'Gospel Songs' and began hawking them around the churches of America, bringing a much-needed message of hope in hard times.

Singers like **Sallie Martin** and the young **Mahalia Jackson** travelled the length and breadth of the country with Dorsey, familiarising audiences with the new songs like "Peace in the Valley" and "Take My Hand, Precious Lord". They articulated the faith and troubles of ordinary people in a language they could identify with. Other important early Gospel songwriters were **Charles Albert Tindley** (1851–1933), who worked in Philadelphia, and **Lucie Eddie Campbell** (1885–1963) out of Memphis.

Of course gospel's roots are planted far deeper in history. Two centuries before Dorsey was knocking on church doors with his briefcase full of tunes, America was in the grip of a religious revival – the Great Awakening. Fiery preachers drew huge crowds to open-air gatherings in the woods, termed 'camp meetings', where new hymns and 'camp songs' were sung with abandon into the small hours. At the fringes of these meetings, African slaves listened to the music and were enthralled, music being an integral part of the tribal religions banned by slavemasters in the New World. Slaves who converted to Christianity gave new life to the English hymns and religious songs with a transfusion of West African rhythms and vocal styles, producing an entirely new song form which came to be known by white America as the **negro spiritual**.

The spiritual survived and continued to mature well into the twentieth century and, as the form developed and new songs were composed, it became a vehicle for political as well as religious sentiment. Certain songs, such as "Go Down

Gospel Train

The gospel train is a-coming,
* I hear it just at hand*
I hear them car-wheels rumbling,
* and rolling through the land*

Get on board, chillen,
* get on board, chillen,*
Get on board, chillen,
* there's room for many a-more*

I hear the bell and the whistle,
* they're coming round the curve*
She's playing all the steaming parts,
* straining every nerve*

No signal for another train
* to follow on that line*
Oh, sinner you're forever lost
* if once you're left behind*

This is the Christian banner,
* the motto's new and old*
Salvation and repentance
* are burned there in gold*

She's nearing now the station,
* oh, sinner don't be vain*
But come and get your ticket,
* and be ready for that train*

The fare is cheap and all can go,
* the rich and poor are there*
No second-class aboard this train,
* no difference in the fare*

"Gospel Train" is a classic 'negro spiritual' of the sort popularised by the Fisk Jubilee Singers in the 1870s.

From *Wade in the Water*, Vol 1
(Smithsonian Folkways).

Moses" and "Let My People Go", were coded demands for freedom couched in biblical allegory while others, like "Steal Away to Jesus", served on occasion as messages of impending escape.

In a sanitised and expurgated form, the spiritual became a drawing-room favourite in white American and European homes. A black university singing group called **The Fisk Jubilee Singers** appeared before the crowned heads of Europe and were reputed to have brought tears to the eyes of Queen Victoria on the visit they made to Britain in 1871. The subsequent all-male 'jubilee groups' condensed the style and brought into being one of the great cornerstones of gospel music: the gospel quartet.

Jubilee Quartets and Singing Preachers

In the 1920s and 1930s, companies like Capitol and Paramount scoured the south for religious artists. The recordings on these 'race records' – the industry euphemism for black music – fell into three main categories: Jubilee quartets, so-called 'jackleg' preachers, and singing preachers.

Jubilee quartets such as the **Golden Gate Quartet** and **Norfolk Jubilee Quartet** were among the first black recording stars, their sophisticated vocal stylings and close harmony arrangements of old spirituals selling 78s in their thousands.

Jackleg preachers – itinerant evangelists like Blind Willie Johnson and Washington Phillips – were the next unlikely stars of the genre. Used to playing for dimes on the street, the immensely influential **Blind Willie Johnson**, whose unique slide-guitar style and acerbic vocals made his records eagerly sought after by jazz and blues collectors, received little more in royalties than he had as a busker. He died in poverty in 1949 from pneumonia, having been refused entry to hospital because he was blind. **Washington Phillips**, who made a handful of exquisite recordings, had an achingly beautiful sound, accompanying himself on songs like "I Had a Good Father and Mother" with an obscure and hauntingly melodious string instrument, the dulceola.

The most successful of all these early religious artists were the **singing preachers**. These fervent reverends, guaranteed to turn a sinner's knees to jelly at fifty paces, regularly outsold the major blues stars of their day. Leader of the pack was the **Reverend J.M. Gates**, whose hair-raising warnings about the consequences of a life of infamy had colourful titles like "God's Wrath in the St Louis Cyclone", "Hitler and Hell", "Death's Black Train is Coming" and "Will Death be your Santa Claus?"

The end of World War II ushered in an era generally acknowledged to be a golden age for gospel music. Over the next twenty years, thousands of gospel artists packed churches and concert halls across America, often selling records in huge quantities. The first stars of the gospel boom were the quartets. Stylistically, **quartet singing** had taken a quantum leap: the smooth harmony of the jubilee groups was now being joined by one or two lead voices who were not afraid to make use of all the range and histrionic emotion at their disposal.

Powerhouse singing was coupled with stage performances that left audiences in a pandemonium of excitement. One of the most hysteria-raising quartets of all time was the **Five Blind Boys of Mississippi** – their blind lead singer, **Archie Brownlee**, was known on occasion to jump off the balcony of auditoriums during performances. The group had such a reputation for laying out their audience that the City of New Orleans once required them to pay out special insurance because they were sending so many people to hospital in comas. Generating this sort of hysteria, known as 'wrecking the house', was something the quartets did on a regular basis throughout the era.

The quartets produced many of the greatest voices in soul music – **Sam Cooke** cut his teeth in the **Soul Stirrers** and **Wilson Pickett** in the **Violinaires**. **Johnny Taylor** followed in Cooke's footsteps, both in the Soul Stirrers and later into soul stardom. The influence of the quartets extended beyond the singers who actually

Columbia
Viva-tonal *Recording*
ELECTRICAL PROCESS
Vocal Novelty accomp.
WHAT ARE THEY DOING IN HEAVEN TODAY
WASHINGTON PHILLIPS
14404-D
(147575)
MADE AND PAT'D IN U.S.A. JAN. 21, '13 AND RE 16589 NEW YORK, U.S.A. COLUMBIA PHONOGRAPH COMPANY, INC., N.Y.

crossed over, however. Many of the vocal stylings and stage antics of soul and rock artists of the past three or four decades originated in the frenetic performances of these pioneers.

Of all the frontmen in quartet music, the lead voices of the **Reverend Claude Jeter** of The Swan Silvertones and **Julius Cheeks** of the Sensational Nightingales have been the most influential. Claude Jeter's falsetto was the template for generations of singers up to and beyond Al Green: the tearing, pleading soul voice sound can be traced to Julius Cheeks' bravura performances. The hard men of 1960s soul like **James Brown** and **Wilson Pickett** would never have torn it up the way they did if it hadn't been for the Nightingales.

Not that all the great voices of the golden age were male. Many female groups travelled the gospel highway through this period, including the **Roberta Martin Singers**, the **Clara Ward Singers**, **The Caravans** and **The Davis Sisters**, to name but a few.

The Staple Singers, a Chicago family group based around Roebuck 'Pop' Staples, his two daughters and a son, began recording in the mid-1950s and had a series of hits in the gospel, R&B and soul charts over the next three decades. Their sound was the most bluesy that gospel ever got – built as it was around the heavily tremeloed guitar of 'Pop', originally a Delta bluesman, and backed by session men on bass and drums.

Big Time Gospel

Mahalia Jackson, who had cut her teeth in the Thomas Dorsey roadshow in the 1930s, was the first gospel artist to cross over to an international audience when in 1946 she recorded "Move On Up a Little Higher" for Apollo Records. It was gospel music's first million-seller. The receipt of a prestigious French award in the early 1950s propelled Mahalia into a new phase of her career and she embarked on the first of many tours of Europe, gaining a rapturous reception from a new, non-gospel audience. Back in the States she made the decision to switch to a mainstream label, signing to Columbia in 1954. Inevitably, as her success with white audiences grew, she lost touch with her grass-roots gospel following. But much of the fortune she earned was put to good use in the com-

White Gospel

Soul and R&B are not the only musical forms to bear the stamp of gospel. The white churches of the rural south shared hymns, spirituals and rhythms with their African American counterparts. They too often knew about grinding poverty, and they too longed for a better deal on the other side of Jordan – and expressed their longing in song.

Many future luminaries of country music cut their teeth on gospel. For white rural Baptists and Pentecostalists anything else was the devil's music, and the church was often the only place for a country boy to learn the trade of a musician. By the 1930s, vocal groups were touring church halls and radio stations in the south with a slightly sanitised version of the music that was laying out black audiences. Some made it to

Nashville and country stardom and many of these, finding redemption at the bottom of the bottle, later returned to the fold, cutting gospel albums after they had made it big in the country or bluegrass worlds.

Hank Williams, **The Carter Family**, **Bill Monroe**, **Boz Scaggs** and **Tennessee Ernie Ford** have all sung gospel, and it was this music that Elvis Presley sang when he was relaxing with his friends. Even the wildest country rocker of them all, **Jerry Lee Lewis**, was prone to bouts of remorse and periodic returns to church. Today, southern (white) gospel is now a fully fledged sub-genre within country music, with its own charts and award ceremonies. While much of it strays a little too near the white fundamentalism of the TV preachers for most tastes, the best recordings run gospel a close second.

Mahalia Jackson

Cissy's daughter **Whitney Houston**, schooled in the twin arts of gospel and soul singing, would go on to join another generation of singers from within the black church to find pop success. Other notable female gospel singers to crossover into soul, R&B and jazz success have included **Dionne Warwick**, who started out singing with the **Drinkard Singers**, and 'Queen of Rhythm and Blues' **Dinah Washington**, who began her career as Ruth Jones in the **Sallie Martin Singers**.

Heavenly Voices: the Gospel Choirs

The emergence of choirs as major performing and recording artists in gospel is mainly a post-war phenomenon and owes much to the man they called the 'Godfather of Gospel', **Reverend James Cleveland**. An early signing to Savoy Records, Cleveland generated unprecedented excitement when his hoarse holler was combined with the red-hot harmonies of **The Angelic Choir of Nutley**, New Jersey. Their album, *Peace Be Still*, sold an astounding one million copies.

Cleveland went on to record literally hundreds of albums, but his greatest contribution was probably the founding of the annual **Gospel Music Workshop of America** in 1968. These workshops have spawned choirs across the nation and beyond – notably in South Africa and Britain – and have inspired countless singers down the years. Today every US state has its Mass Choir and every city from New York to London its own Community Choir. Similarly, The Church of God in Christ (**COGIC**), a large Pentecostal movement, pioneered gospel workshops and conventions and has been a driving force behind the growth in gospel choirs.

There's nothing quite like a gospel choir in action – it's something to do with the tension between the choir's practised split-second timing and the breathtaking improvisations of the soloists, often urged on by shouts of encouragement from the ranks. Among the current hot choirs, The Tri-City Singers, The New Jersey Mass Choir, The Thompson Community Singers and The Mississippi Mass Choir are always worth seeing, while The West Angeles Church Of God In Christ is the leading COGIC choir in the country. And still active on the circuit is Edwin Hawkins, who introduced much of the world to the gospel choir in 1968, when the **Edward Hawkins Singers** had an international hit with "Oh Happy Day".

Most radical of the modern choirs must be the thirty-member **Sounds of Blackness** from Minnesota. Their debut cross-over album *The Evo-*

munity, particularly in support of her friend Martin Luther King's Civil Rights Movement, and she was a mother figure and an inspiration to a generation of singers who followed in her footsteps.

Among those influenced by Mahalia was the young **Aretha Franklin**. A preacher's daughter from Detroit, Aretha grew up in a house where gospel stars like Mahalia, Clara Ward, Sam Cooke and James Cleveland would regularly drop in and hold all-night singing sessions. She made her debut at the age of twelve at her father's New Bethel Baptist Church, and gained experience travelling the country with the family roadshow – her father was a star in the style of the recording preachers of the twenties and thirties. Her first recording was made live at New Bethel when she was a mere fifteen years old; it's hard to believe her age, listening to her powerful, moving rendition of the old Dorsey standard "Precious Lord".

By the time Aretha was eighteen she felt ready to follow her friend Sam Cooke into the pop arena. After a false start at Columbia, she finally made it at Atlantic Records. Producer Jerry Wexler 'took her to church', letting her sit down at a piano and be herself. Her first record to take off was "I Never Loved a Man the Way I Loved You", and it sold a million within a matter of weeks. The gospel-soaked backing vocals on those early hits were provided by a group of singers known as **The Sweet Inspirations**, directed by Cissy Houston, herself a gospel artist and choir director, as well as a soul singer in her own right.

lution of Gospel, co-produced by the mega-platinum team of Jimmy Jam and Terry Lewis, was a massive hit on both sides of the Atlantic. Work songs, spirituals and African choral interludes are all included in the choir's powerfully theatrical live set, which combines the scorching lead vocals of **Ann Bennett-Nesby** with some of the hardest dance rhythms around.

The great urban gospel phenomenon of recent times, however, has been **new traditionalists**, young ministers like **Hezekiah Walker**, **John P. Kee** and especially **Kirk Franklin** (see box overleaf). A dynamic young preacher, pianist and singer from Texas, Kirk Franklin has astounded every-

Rev James Cleveland

one with a shrewd mix of tough R&B backing, choreographed choir moves and uncompromising lyrics. His debut album, released in 1995, sold nearly two million copies and he shows no sign of slowing down, even launching highly successful sub-groups like God's Property.

The Detroit Sound

Gospel music today is crossing over as it has never done before, mainly thanks to a crop of musicians who have combined the gospel-singing prowess of their parents' generation with today's urban R&B. Various cities have taken their turn under the spotlight in gospel's development, but the 1980s and early 1990s belonged to the one-time heartland of black music in the US, the former-Motown power-base of Detroit.

The premier exponents of gospel's 'Detroit Sound' come from two families of great renown: the Winans and the Clarks. **Delores and David Winans** brought up their ten children in strict, traditional Pentecostal fashion; no secular music was even allowed in the house. But it was the Winans's children who brokered gospel's move into the mainstream of contemporary music. The four eldest offspring, twins Marvin and Carvin along with brothers Michael and Ronald, made their debut in the early 1980s with *Introducing The Winans*, which was produced by Andrae Crouch, contemporary gospel's pioneering songwriter.

The Winans had their first big hit with "Let My People Go", from the 1986 album of the same name. The song struck a chord in the black community and beyond by comparing black South Africans caught in the apartheid system with the Children of Israel imprisoned by Pharaoh in ancient Egypt. They were doing what the composers of spirituals like "Go Down Moses" had done a century or so earlier, when they used the tribulations of the Israelites as a metaphor for slavery.

Since then, The Winans have remained firmly plugged into the pulse of contemporary music, regularly hitting the top of the R&B as well as gospel charts. They've also earned their share of flak from within the gospel community for collaborations with a variety of non-gospel artists: they sang on Michael Jackson's *Bad* album, and subsequent releases featured guests like Michael McDonald, Stevie Wonder, Kenny Loggins and rapper and swingbeat supremo Teddy Riley.

Other of the Winans family have followed in their siblings' footsteps. Surpassing the group's success in the contemporary field have been seventh son **BeBe** and sister **CeCe Winans**, whose breakthrough came with their third album, *Heaven*, in 1988. The single "Celebrate" crossed over into R&B and pop formats and received heavy club and radio play, eventually earning Grammy, Dove and Soul Train awards. Following her divergence from BeBe in the mid-1990s, CeCe became probably the most successful of the contemporary gospel divas with her hit duet with Whitney Houston.

Her brother **Daniel Winans**'s career has remained more rooted in the church tradition and his periodic releases are fiery choir albums. Not to be outdone, the youngest siblings record as **Angie and Debbie** and even the previous generation have a stake in the industry in their own right, recording as Mom and Pops Winans – which just leaves the family dog unsigned.

The other familial dynasty on the Detroit scene are **The Clark Sisters**, who had a dance-crossover hit with "You Bring the Sunshine" in 1983. The Clarks are the supremely soulful daughters of the late **Mattie Moss Clark**, the hugely influential International Music Director of COGIC and a formidable singer and choir director in her own right. Her expert advice and tutelage has encouraged generations of aspiring singers – not least her four daughters Jackie, Dorinda, Karen and Twinkie. These days they rarely tour

as a group but individual performances, especially by Karen and Twinkie are experiences not to be missed.

Vanessa Bell Armstrong, who attended McKenzie High School with both the Winans and the Clarks, grew up singing in front of the mirror, pretending to be another long-time Detroit resident, Aretha Franklin. Although she recorded with choirs in her teens, Vanessa didn't release her first solo album, *Peace Be Still*, until she had raised five kids. She has since dropped the traditional material that caused many to compare her to her childhood idol, in favour of an 'inspirational' style that has seen her duetting with soul star Jonathan But-

Kirk Franklin

DAVID REDFERN/REDFERNS

The biggest star to emerge on the gospel firmament in the nineties, funky, joyful, controversial **Kirk Franklin** – who hails from Texas – started playing the piano when he was four. At seven, he started to dabble in songwriting, penning 'sacred' lyrics to Elton John's "Benny & The Jets", and at eleven he was leading the adult choir at the Dallas/Fort Worth Mt. Rose Baptist Church.

Franklin and his seventeen-member ensemble **The Family** first came to prominence in 1991, and have enjoyed huge success with their urban-flavoured gospel sound. However, it was his collaboration with the Californian youth choir **God's Property** in 1997 that made him a household name in the US. Their single "Stomp" – co-written by George Clinton and featuring rapper 'Salt' – topped the American R&B charts, earning multiple Grammy and various other award nominations in the process. It attracted equal amounts of praise and

scorn from the gospel fraternity, and secured Franklin a deal for a television sitcom.

The 'church boy', as he likes to call himself, has straightforward views about recording and notoriety. "What I was trying to do [with "Stomp"] was to take a sample of music that was popular from an era that was not so crazy as today. We brought Salt in on it; she's been a friend of mine for a couple of years now. She's got a good heart, a good spirit, loves God... once you get to know people who do secular music, you find that there are probably more people doing secular music that have bigger hearts than those of us doing gospel sometimes! A lot of times, it ain't about the talk; it's about the walk."

Franklin sang on the soundtrack of Spike Lee's movie, *Get On The Bus* – which didn't go down too well with the church. But Franklin was relaxed. "Well, the church gives me hell for everything I do – but it's cool, though. I enjoy it. Controversy gives you a platform and a voice. And we know that Jesus was controversial; he healed folk on the Sabbath and the Establishment weren't having that. I want for society to hear the word 'Christians' and not think that all we do is kill each other, blow up abortion clinics and set farms on fire in Waco. We're not a bunch of lunatics and fanatics. And I think people need to see that because nobody wants to be part of anything that they can't relate to."

The Nu Nation Project, Franklin's fourth album, entered the Billboard album chart at No. 7 on its release in November 1998. As a back-handed riposte to critics who had accused his music of being 'too worldly', the album opened with a spoof court trial in which he was in the dock 'for trying to take the gospel to the world'.

George Luke

ler and being cited by Luther Vandross as his favourite singer.

Outside Detroit too, gospel has expanded into the dance market, and gospel artists regularly show up on the playlists of urban radio stations across the US – and in Britain, too. Queens of the gospel-disco scene include **Mavis Staples** (from The Staple Singers) and **Gloria Gaynor** (yes, she who will survive). Another direction has been taken by the extremely popular **Amy Grant**, who has recorded gospel with a soft rock-tinged sound – with country inflections.

Old-time Gospel

Not all the best-selling gospel artists of recent years have given their music a contemporary twist. There is still a massive market in the US for traditional-style gospel performers among a black church audience that has little interest in the latest club sounds. Some gospel-watchers claim that a reaction against the crossover acts is underway, which could certainly be the case given the huge sales some of the more traditional artists are achieving.

Tramaine Hawkins, who attracted much criticism from her gospel peers for the crossover dancefloor hit "Fall Down" in 1985, has returned to her roots with a vengeance. Her 1990 traditional-style album, *Tramaine – Live*, became one of the hottest movers in gospel. Though Tramaine first tasted the big time when she sang on the Edwin Hawkins Singers' hit "Oh Happy Day", she remains a relative newcomer compared to the veterans of the circuit.

The undisputed Queen of Gospel is still **Shirley Caesar**, who began her recording career at the age of ten and rose to stardom during her time with The Caravans in the fifties and sixties. A dynamic and much-loved performer, her *Live in Chicago* choir album, released in 1988, sold over a quarter of a million copies. Shirley is not the only link back to that era, indeed many of her contemporaries are still on the gospel highway, and Dorothy Norwood, Inez Andrews and Albertina Walker from The Caravans have all recorded in recent years. A new generation of performers, too – like John P. Kee and Hezekiah Walker – are mixing traditional fiery performance styles with modern studio techniques for an audience who prefer their gospel uncut with secularism.

Some of the great quartets from the golden age of gospel are still out there performing, too, albeit

The Five Blind Boys of Alabama – still a thriving quartet

If you have some time to travel around, you can get to hear an astonishing variety of gospel music at festivals, conventions and workshops across the United States, as well as in churches and, of course, on the radio. The listings below are just a very brief selection. For more pointers, and up-to-the-minute gospel news and reviews, check the **Black Gospel Music Clef** website (*www.blackgospel.com*).

Chicago Gospel Festival

Sponsored by the City of Chicago, this is the premier showcase for gospel acts. It takes place each year on the second weekend in June, when around 70,000 gospel fans gather at the Petrillo Music Shell in Grant Park, downtown. Acts range across the board from traditional choirs and quartets to the most modern contemporary sounds. The music programme runs on both days from noon to 10pm – and it's all free. For information, phone the Festival Office on ☎312 744 3315.

COGIC

Conventions play a vital part in the life of the black church and they inevitably feature performances by both well-known and undiscovered artists. The largest, attracting up to 100,000 people, is the annual COGIC Convention, held at the Cook's Convention Center, Memphis, at the beginning of November. Delegations travel from as far afield as Africa, Haiti and London, and the United Choir is often several thousand strong. Much of the music happens during the night at 'midnight musicals', which often last until dawn and can develop into thrilling contests as singers from all over America and beyond vie with each other for ovations. Needless to say, gospel record company A&R peo-

ple are always in attendance, on the lookout for new talent.

Non-COGIC visitors will find themselves welcome at these events – the only real problem is finding accommodation, as reasonably priced rooms tend to be booked up months in advance. For further information, contact The Church Of God In Christ, 272 S Main St, Memphis, TN 38101 ☎901.527.1422. They have a useful Website at *www.cogic.com*

Workshops

Gospel workshops also have a major role in American gospel. At these gatherings, often attended by thousands, aspiring singers can sign up for tuition from top artists and at the end of the workshop give a public performance in front of a large audience.

The biggest event of the year is the Gospel Music Workshop of America, founded by James Cleveland, which is held for a week every August at a different location around the US. On payment of a flat fee visitors can wander around the workshops all week – an unforgettable musical experience. For information, contact The Gospel Music Workshop of America, PO Box 34635, Detroit, MI 48234 ☎313.898.2340.

Churches

Searching out gospel at grass-roots level in the churches is obviously a hit-and-miss affair, but much of the music's power and excitement lies in its spontaneity. Gospel performers often try to re-create that excitement in concert, exhorting their audience 'come on people – let's have CHURCH tonight!'.

The hospitality of the gospel community is proverbial. However, beyond church walls, the realities of urban

with a touch less frenzied power than in their youth. **The Mighty Clouds of Joy** made their debut in 1959 and have been on the road ever since, appearing at gospel shows, jazz festivals and rock concerts all over the world. Lead singer **Joe Ligon** is often cited as the greatest living male gospel singer and when audience's hear him scream they don't doubt it. Slick they may be, but after over thirty years of performing The Mighty Clouds of Joy are still an unmissable live experience. Young new groups in the Clouds' mould are out there too – catch **The Christianaires** if you can.

The original a cappella style of quartet gospel singing is undergoing something of a revival too. One group in particular, **Take 6** from New York,

are enjoying great success with material that infuses the harmonies of groups like The Golden Gates with a modern sensibility, drawing on elements of jazz, soul and hip-hop. Meanwhile their success has brought some of the earliest quartets out of retirement.

The Fairfield Four, whose heyday was in the forties and fifties, started out in 1921 as a jubilee group. Today they still make occasional appearances around their hometown of Nashville, and they have begun appearing on international festival stages. Another quartet, **The Five Blind Boys of Alabama**, whose first hit was in 1949 and who were once rivals to the Mississippi Blind Boys, are still touring the gospel circuit as well as branching

Rev Al Green, pastor of Memphis, doing the day job

America remain. Church buildings are sometimes in the poorer parts of town and it goes without saying that such areas are not the safest place for non-streetwise visitors to wander. It would probably pay to give the church office a call beforehand to say that you are planning to attend and to ask directions – someone may even offer to meet you. Listed below are some suggested churches to visit; check local phone books for addresses and numbers.

Berkeley, CA
Ephesians Church Of God In Christ. The pastor is Tramaine Hawkins' grandfather, Bishop E.E. Cleveland.

Chicago, IL
Christ Tabernacle Baptist Church. The venue for recording sessions with Reverend Milton Brunson and Reverend Maceo Woods.

Cleveland, OH
Christian Tabernacle Evangelistic Church.

Detroit, MI
The Perfecting Church (pastor Marvin Winans); Mount Everett Church Of God In Christ (where the pastor is Vanessa Bell Armstrong's father); New Bethel Baptist Church (attended by Aretha Franklin).

Houston, TX
Church Of Jesus Christ. The pastor is the Reverend George Foreman, former heavyweight boxing champion.

Jackson, MS
Blair Metropolitan A.M.E. Church. Powerbase of the Mississippi Mass Choir.

Los Angeles, CA
Faith United Methodist Church; Testimonial Cathedral Church Of God In Christ; West Angeles Church Of God In Christ.

Memphis, TN
Full Gospel Tabernacle (where the pastor is the legendary soul and gospel artist, Al Green); Church Of God In Christ (the headquarters of COGIC).

Nashville, TN
The Born Again Church. The local church for many gospel artists resident in or visiting Music City.

New York, NY
Brooklyn Tabernacle. Home of the excellent Brooklyn Tabernacle Choir.

out to win new converts at World Music and rock events. Probably the best-known female group is currently **Sweet Honey in the Rock**, founded in 1973 by composer and gospel historian Bernice Johnson Reagon. The group's repertoire includes many of the gospel classics, but also blues and American folksongs – like the Grammy winning version of Leadbelly's "Grey Goose". On their latest album, *25*, they even covered Bob Marley songs, and explored the roots of African American music in West Africa.

In all its manifestations, from a cappella to R&B and dancefloor, Gospel has come a long long way from the simple folk spirituals of a hundred years ago but the lineage of the music is intact and continues to thrive despite, or perhaps because of, its stubborn refusal to be subsumed in the mainstream swamp of American popular music.

discography

Gospel music recordings outnumber blues and country music combined, stretching across styles and sub-genres from turn-of-the-century a cappella spirituals to the toughest urban rapping. It must be said, there's a mountain of CDs out there of interest to few but the artists and their mothers – but the best of them are simply the best music in the business, featuring the world's greatest voices and most soulful performances.

Compilations

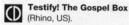

Jubilation! Great Gospel Performances Vols 1 and 2 (Rhino, US).

One of the best and most comprehensive collections currently available. Drawn mostly from the golden age, these 36 gems have been astutely chosen to represent key tracks from the career of every key gospel artist of the period. Vol 1 includes Mahalia, Golden Gate Jubilee Quartet, Soul Stirrers, Swan Silvertones, Aretha, Shirley Caesar and others. Vol 2 adds the Harmonizing Four, the Staple Singers, the Five Blind Boys of Mississippi, the Original Gospel Harmonettes and several more in that class.

Sacred Steel: Traditional Sacred African-American Steel Guitar Music in Florida (Arhoolie, US).

One of the curious regional traditions of gospel music is the use of Haiwaiian-style steel guitars to accompany the congregations in the Keith Dominion and Jewel Dominion sects in Florida. This disc, which features recordings from the 1990s, introduces some of the veterans, including Willie Eason (b 1921), one of the first to play gospel on the electric steel guitar, and Henry Nelson.

Wade in the Water: African American Sacred Music Traditions (Smithsonian Folkways, US).

This four CD collection (available separately or as a box set) is an excellent historic survey of US gospel music. **Volume 1** features classic spirituals sung by college campus groups including The Fisk Jubilee Singers and a community choir. **Volume 2** concentrates on congregational singing from six old-style groups. **Volume 3** highlights the work of the 'Pioneering Composers', as recorded by diverse musicians from community performers to internationally-known names like Sweet Honey in the Rock. **Volume 4** presents 'Community Gospel' from a range of groups in Alabama in 1992 and 93. Each disc comes with good notes and lyrics.

AFRICAN AMERICAN GOSPEL: THE PIONEERING COMPOSERS

WADE IN THE WATER VOLUME III

The Great Gospel Men (Shanachie, US).

Twenty-seven tracks of awesome vocals. Apart from Rev. James Cleveland and a couple of others, the vast majority are unfamiliar names, but they're none the worse for it.

The Great Gospel Women (Shanachie, US).

Most of the celebrated gospel singers are women, and among the thirty-one tracks here are well-known names like

Mahalia Jackson, Marion Williams and Dorothy Love Coates, as well as plenty of lesser-known artists.

Testify! The Gospel Box (Rhino, US).

A very impressive 3-CD survey of spiritual gospel songs from the early 1940s to the end of the 1990s. Includes the Golden Gate Jubilee Quartet, Dorothy Love Coates, the Original Five Blind Boys, Mahalia Jackson, Aretha Franklin with Rev. James Cleveland, the Caravans, Shirley Caesar, Take 6, The Winans and Sounds of Blackness – to pick just a few.

Artists

Vanessa Bell Armstrong

Armstrong (b 1953) grew up among the important names of the Detroit sound. She is a powerful R&B singer moving between traditional and contemporary styles.

Greatest Hits (Malaco, US).

A compilation of her mid-1980s material, preferable to her later crossover gospel style.

Shirley Caeser

Caeser (b 1938) started out with one of the greatest women's gospel groups, the Caravans, which also included Albertina Walker, Inez Andrews and Rev. James Cleveland on piano. She went solo in the mid sixties and has remained one of the more traditional of leading gospel artists.

Live in Chicago (Word, US).

Recorded with the Thompson Community Singers and Rev. Milton Brunson, this is gospel in action, ranging through singing, testifying and storytelling. Powerful stuff.

Her Very Best (Word, US).

A 1991 collection from four of her excellent Word albums, including "Jesus, I Love Calling Your Name" and "Sailing on the Sea of Your Love" with Al Green.

Karen Clark-Sheard

Detroit has produced some of gospel's most distinctive voices, including the fabulous Clark Sisters, in which Karen Clark-Sheard dazzled audiences with her technically astounding voice and breathtaking performances. The sometimes explosive dynamics within the Clark family kept Karen in the background until she stepped out and made Finally Karen, her first album, which many consider to be one of *the* gospel releases of the 1990s.

Finally Karen (Island, US).

Contemporary gospel music that confidently straddles the various traditions, and showcases Karen's exquisite vocal prowess. Several guests – Donald Lawrence, Faith Evans and the other Clark Sisters – contribute. A convincing slice of modern gospel to confound sceptics who would chain the music to the past.

Rev. James Cleveland

Cleveland (1932–1991), the 'Godfather of Gospel', was born in Chicago but most famously worked with the Angelic Choir of New Jersey and the Southern California Community Choir. A hollering vocalist and pianist, he pioneered the big gospel choirs that grew up in the 1950s, played with the Caravans and founded the Gospel Music Workshop of America.

Peace Be Still (Savoy, US).

A classic gospel album from the early sixties recorded live with the Angelic Choir of Nutley, New Jersey. This album kicked off the massed gospel choir sound.

Dorothy Love Coates

Holding her own against the hard men of gospel quartet, Dorothy Love Coates scorched her way round the gospel circuit throughout the sixties and seventies. Still an uncompromising and combative figure in her home town of Birmingham, Alabama, she never achieved the fame or fortune of lesser talents.

The Best of Dorothy Love Coates and the Original Gospel Harmonettes
(Fantasy/Specialty, US).

These are the choice recordings Dorothy and her singers made for Art Rupe during her time with Specialty. Her fervour and sincerity shine through. "Get Away Jordan" is as perfect an example of committed gospel music as any.

Sam Cooke

In 1957 – and before it was dubbed as such – soul music found its first male superstar. But after quitting gospel music for the glamour of mainstream pop and cabaret, Sam Cooke turned out to be too challenging a talent for the innately racist showbusiness of fifties' America. Instead, he crafted the great gems of the era: "You Send Me", "Another Saturday Night" and the bitter riposte to supremacists, "A Change Is Gonna Come".

Sam Cooke with The Soul Stirrers
(Fantasy/Specialty, US).

If you think Sam's later pop recordings were special, treat yourself to these. By common consent, Sam Cooke was on world-beating form during the sessions, and there can be few better examples of the quartet style of gospel than in this classic line-up of the mighty Stirrers.

The Fairfield Four

The original Fairfield Four, with Nashville's Rev. Sam McCrary, is long departed, but the present line-up, rediscovered by festival audiences and lionised in recent years by the likes of Elvis Costello, preserves the early pre-war quartet tradition beautifully.

Standing In The Safety Zone
(Warners/WEA, US).

The album that relaunched this quartet in 1992, a mere seventy years on from its inception. Choice tracks include "Roll Jordan Roll", "Keep Me Near The Cross" and the title cut. The stunning, subtle harmonies seem as instinctive as breathing.

Five Blind Boys of Mississippi

One of the most celebrated quartets of gospel, and one of the most long-lived, through several changes of name and personnel. They began in the 1930s as a quartet, led by Archie Brownlee, and added a fifth singer a decade later, after which they became superstars as the Five Blind Boys. Brownlee died in 1960, but the group continues.

 Best of the Five Blind Boys of Mississippi Vol 1 (MCA, US).

Just what it says: classic tracks of the greatest 'quartet' ever, featuring the screams and yells of Archie Brownlee.

Aretha Franklin

As the shy but prodigious daughter of a famous gospel preacher, Aretha Franklin made her first appearances in her father's Detroit church at the age of twelve. Following her friend Sam Cooke's example, she launched into a secular career, signing first to Columbia and then to Atlantic, where she recorded a string of sublime hit records including "Respect", "I Never Loved A Man The Way That I Loved You" and "Dr Feelgood".

RHINO RECORDS

Aretha Franklin

 Amazing Grace
(WEA/Atlantic, US).

In 1972, the Queen of Soul went back to church and delivered one of her greatest-ever performances. Still under the brooding tutelage of her father, Baptist Minister C.L. Franklin, she joined another of her mentors, Rev. James Cleveland and his Southern California Community Choir to rework the traditional gospel songs and spirituals of her Detroit childhood. This double album is the best of Aretha's three church recordings, combining excellent sound quality, a searing live performance and one of the greatest female voices on record.

Kirk Franklin

A young minister and singer from Texas who has taken gospel by storm in the past few years, outselling absolutely everybody. His brand of urbanised gospel music takes in hip-hop and 'street-soul'.

 Kirk Franklin & Family
(Uni/Gospocentric, US).

Stylistically, about as far from Blind Willie Johnson as you could get, but if you like your beats raw, this is the record to go for.

Al Green

Al Green, the peerless superstar of seventies soul, has long been revered for his delicate Memphis falsetto. As the Reverend Al Green, preacher and gospel singer, he tends to be more impressive in person than on record, but no collection would be complete without a few cuts.

▣ **The Lord Will Make A Way** (Myrrh, US).

Recorded in 1980, this was the first of Al Green's full-out gospel albums, bolting vintage southern gospel onto a classic Willie Mitchell production style.

Mahalia Jackson

Mahalia (1911–1972) was the matriarch of gospel singers, possessed of the bluesiest of Southern voices that slid and growled like a bordello queen. Conventional, it is said that she lost her edge (and most of her black audience) when she signed to Columbia Records, so be wary of anything originally recorded for that label. While there are some great performances there's an awful lot of orchestrated studio slush as well.

 The Apollo Sessions 1946-1951
(Pair, US).

These two discs capture Halie at the peak of her powers. Twenty tracks include "In The Upper Room", "Didn't It Rain" and gospel's first million seller, "Move On Up A Little Higher"

Blind Willie Johnson

What Robert Johnson is to the blues, Willie Johnson (1900–1949) is to gospel. Blinded in childhood, Willie Johnson sang and played on the streets of Texas and Louisiana and recorded just thirty tracks for Columbia between 1927 and 1930. His gravelly-voiced recordings (covered by Eric Clapton, Ry Cooder and Bob Dylan among others) remain extraordinarily powerful today.

 The Complete Recordings of Blind Willie Johnson (Sony, US).

Johnson's ethereal bottleneck guitar and visceral vocal style – on "Dark Was The Night, Cold Was The Ground" for instance – evoke terror, beauty and faith in equal measure. Cheap, primitive recordings these may be, but this is unexpurgated religious art at its most emotive.

Washington Phillips

Washington Phillips was an itinerant African-American eccentric who performed gospel songs exclusively with a dulceola, a curious stringed instrument similar to a zither.

▣ **I Am Born To Preach The Gospel: The Complete Recordings ...** (Shanachie/Yazoo, US).

Phillips' fine recordings from Dallas in the 1920s are evocative and delicate readings of hymns, spirituals and early gospel songs. The dulceola's chiming arpeggios provide a dramatic counterpoint to his plaintive voice. The effect is hypnotic in the extreme and you may find yourself returning again and again to this record. A gem rather than a masterpiece.

The Staple Singers

In 1950, Roebuck 'Pop' Staples strapped on his sixty dollar pawnshop guitar and presented three of his children to the Mount Zion Baptist Church in Chicago. Thus began a fifty-year reign as the first family of gospel soul. During the mid-sixties they switched over to the mainstream and scored many huge and enduring hits including "Respect Yourself".

▣ **Uncloudy Day** (Charly, UK).

This classic album, originally recorded for Vee Jay, pre-dates the move away from pure gospel and is generally considered to be their finest. Mavis Staples' sinewy (not to say sexy) voice perfectly counterpoints daddy Roebuck's tremulous guitar.

Sweet Honey in the Rock

Doyenne of African-American cultural history Bernice Johnson Reagon has led this five-strong ensemble of women singers for twenty-five years. Only Minneapolis's Sounds of Blackness have straddled the sacred and secular traditions in anything like the same way as Sweet Honey, and they have a devoted following, initially among politicised blacks, but now encompassing a global audience. Sublime vocal harmonies and uncompromising messages.

 Sacred Ground
(Warners/WEA, US).

This album is perhaps the most overtly 'spiritual' of their recordings, re-visiting hymns and songs that rose out of slavery and the civil rights movement including "No More Auction Block", "Balm In Gilead" and "Jordan River". Rich, sweet and strong.

▣ **Give Your Hands To Struggle**
(Smithsonian Folkways, US).

A recording from 1975. With songs like "Freedom in the Air" and "We've Come a Long Way to Be Together", it's a glowing testimony to the long-standing relationship between the African American church and the Civil Rights movement.

Take 6

Innovative vocal sextet from New York who have brought a jazz-inflected, contemporary approach to the classic gospel quartet sound. Ray Charles and Stevie Wonder have joined as guests.

▣ **Take 6** (Reprise, US).

Golden Age gospel reborn. Their debut album from 1988.

The Winans

Four brothers from Detroit who developed a contemporary R&B style from their gospel roots.

▣ **Let My People Go** (Qwest, US).

The first album to take The Winans into the mainstream and win a worldwide audience, yet keeps enough of the real gospel ingredients.

USA

Klezmer

rhythm and jews

To call somebody a 'klezmer' used to be something of an insult, implying a poor folk musician who could barely read music. That has certainly changed in the past twenty years. Klezmer music, brought to America in the early twentieth century by Jewish immigrants from eastern Europe, has been enjoying a dynamic revival in the US, and has moved beyond Jewish audiences to a strong place in the World Music market. **Simon Broughton** traces the history and introduces the new generation.

As portrayed in *Fiddler on the Roof*, the itinerant klezmer musician, shlepping his way from shtetl to shtetl, is a distinctive image of pre-war Jewish life in the Ashkenazi communities of Eastern Europe. And with the mass emigrations of the twentieth century, the music became even more itinerant, resurfacing among the diaspora in America and throughout the world. It was a music that fed into American jazz in the 1920s – that melting-pot of a decade – but which went quiet in the post-war years until its revival in the 1970s and 1980s. Today, you can find a dozen ensembles in New York alone, and over a hundred across the US, ranging from the quaint and traditional to the experimental and ultra-hip.

Klezmer is also very popular in germany, where a number of groups are based, and there are others, too, around Europe (west and east) and a few in Israel.

Despite its historic and contemporary residence in the New World, klezmer remains rooted in the music of the Yiddish-speaking communities in Poland, Romania, Russia and Ukraine – even the most modern versions sound distinctively eastern European. However, it is not, and has never been, a static music, as it has always absorbed influences and tunes from local music, adding an expressive character that is quintessentially Jewish. The music today is also actively looking back at its own roots. Because the whole world of Jewish music in eastern Europe was annihilated in the Holocaust,

FOLK ROOTS ARCHIVE

Old-world klezmer band

klezmer musicians have had to reconstruct the past as well as invent the future.

A Kingdom Without Borders

In **pre-war eastern Europe**, Ashkenazi Jews were settled across a huge territory stretching from the Baltic to the Black Sea. They maintained communities in small country *shtetls* (villages) and in urban centres like Vilna, Minsk, Warsaw, Białystok, Łodz, Kraków, Kiev, Bucharest, Kishinev and Odessa. Across this diverse patchwork of groups was a unifying bond of customs and, in **Yiddish**, a common language.

The word 'klezmer' comes from two Hebrew words, *kley* and *zemer*, meaning 'instrument of song'. The name originally referred to the instruments themselves, then later to the men who played them. According to the klezmer revivalist Giora Feidman: "we are all born singers, this is a natural force. To express this natural force we need one instrument. We are the instrument of song. My father always tried to explain to me the role of what we call an artist or a musician in society.

Serve society. You are a channel for sound, for music, for love."

In eastern Europe, the *klezmorim* served their communities by playing at **Jewish weddings**, but, like the Gypsies, the other professional musicians of eastern Europe, they also performed at markets, fairs, taverns and Christian weddings, where they played the local peasant dance music, and at the houses of landowners and nobility, where waltzes, quadrilles and light classical pieces were required.

It was a rich repertoire, and was often passed on from father to son: the *kapelyes*, or ensembles, often came from dynasties of musical families. Traditionally, these groups were string ensembles with the violin as principal instrument – the popular 1936 Yiddish film about klezmorim, *Yidl mitn Fidl* (Yiddle with his Fiddle) has a group of two violins, clarinet and string bass. One of the simplest instrumentations was violin and *tsimbl* (hammer dulcimer or cimbalom). In the larger bands you might have found an accompanying violin, a cello or double bass and perhaps a flute.

During the nineteenth century, with the proliferation of military bands, the clarinet – which is today considered the essential klezmer instrument

Hassidic wedding in Brooklyn, 1980s

– began to take the place of the violin. Old photographs of klezmer ensembles from the early years of the twentieth century also show trumpets, trombones and tubas, which became popular once Jews were eligible to serve in the European armies. What the violin and the clarinet share, of course, is their fundamentally expressive quality, almost akin to the human voice, which is an essential part of klezmer music. As the Yiddish writer Sholom Aleichem said: "You can compare the heart in general and the Jewish heart in particular to a violin with several strings."

Although klezmer is essentially secular music, it flourished in a religious society, and it draws some of its distinctive quality from the particular ornamentation and expression of **cantorial chant**. The 'crying' and 'bending' of notes suggests the emotive style of the synagogue. It also recalls an older musical form that doesn't fit too comfortably into Western scale patterns, and the oriental-sounding augmented second that often crops up in klezmer melodies highlights links with the Turkish *makam* modes. The klezmer *Freygish* mode, Turkish *Hicaz* mode and the so-called Gypsy scale are the same. The more **'oriental' klezmer melodies** have much in common with early *rembétiko* music played in Asia Minor. Many klezmer musicians worked in Istanbul, and one of the common klezmer dance forms is called a *terkishe* – similar in rhythm to the Greek *syrto* with its tango-like beat.

Eastern European folk dances, rhythms and intonations were another influence, as certain of the dance names suggest. Among the most popular are the *freylekh* (literally 'happy') circle dance and the syncopated rhythms of the *bulgar* chain dance, which was originally a Bulgarian-style dance from Bessarabia (it later became hugely popular in New York). A trio of Romanian styles are also well-known – the *hora*, the *sírba*, and the slow, rhapsodic *doina*.

As well as the secular dance music, there's a slower, meditative klezmer repertoire based on the **Hassidic nigunim** – religious melodies (often for dancing) composed and sung by followers of Baal Shem Tov, the eighteenth-century leader of the Hassidic movement. Maintaining a philosophy in some ways akin to Sufism, these melodies are seen as a way to get nearer to God and are believed to have great power. One rabbi in the early years of this century fervently sang a nigun rather than take an anaesthetic while his leg was amputated. The slow-to-medium tempo *khosidl* is also based on a Hassidic dance style.

The New World

At the end of the nineteenth century the Jews of eastern Europe were suffering economic hardship, persecution and pogroms, and started to leave in large numbers. Between 1880 and 1924, around three million – a third of the then population – emigrated to the US. The legendary klezmer clarinettist **Dave Tarras** was one of those who came through Ellis Island in 1921. His bag was fumigated and his clarinet broken but, like many of the newly arrived immigrants, he wasn't expecting to make his living through music.

It wasn't too long, however, before US record companies saw the potential of releasing 78s for the Jewish market. The most popular styles amongst the immigrant community were cantorial music and popular songs, with instrumental music some way behind. But in 1917 violinist and bandleader **Abe Schwartz** was taken up by Columbia and the clarinettist **Harry Kandel** signed to Victor. Kandel's Orchestra became one of the most popular of all American klezmer bands and, while there were still violins in the band, it was Kandel's clarinet that led and established the American klezmer style. According to Henry

The young Dave Tarras with balalaika (and aunt)

Sapoznik – one of the leading lights of the American klezmer revival who has worked on the 78rpm archives of klezmer music – around seven hundred titles were released between 1895 and 1942.

The most celebrated players of this generation were **Naftule Brandwein** (1889–1963) and **Dave Tarras** (1897–1989). Brandwein, who was unable to read music, is remembered for the energy and fire of his playing and his eccentric performances. He was likely to turn up at Bar Mitzvahs dressed in a plug-in neon Uncle Sam suit and perform with his back to the audience so they couldn't learn his tricks. A 1924 press release gushed: "Here's speed for you! Observe the swiftness of this remarkable music, the clarity and ingeniousness of the melodies that come so rapidly from Naftule Brandwein's musicians, and you will be thrilled."

Dave Tarras, on the other hand, was a highly trained musician famed for his smooth and elegant style. In Sapoznik's memorable phrase, "Tarras glides and swoops where Brandwein rips and tears". Tarras lived long enough to witness the revival of interest in klezmer and pass on his expertise (and indeed his clarinet – to Andy Statman) to the new generation, but Brandwein's influence as an anarchic genius of the clarinet is unsurpassed.

The old 78 recordings of these early klezmer musicians have become the principal source material for the new generation: 'three-minute musical Rosetta Stones' as Henry Sapoznik calls them. The period of mass Jewish emigration to America coincided exactly with the development of the recording industry, and the 78s are snapshots of a tradition in transition, as it moved from a pre- to a post-industrial society.

Once established in the US, klezmer started to draw on the traditions that surrounded it. In New York, Jewish musicians were playing more foxtrots than freylekhs, although there were orchestras that specialised in a specifically Jewish-American sound. In the 1920s, Joseph Cherniavsky's **Yiddish American Jazz Band**, featuring players such as Brandwein and Tarras, performed in Yiddish theatres and on the vaudeville circuit.

Much has been made of Jewish elements in mainstream American jazz music – particularly in the work of composer **George Gershwin** and clarinettist **Benny Goodman**, both sons of Jewish immigrants from eastern Europe. The wailing glissando on the clarinet that opens Gershwin's "Rhapsody in Blue" is often cited, but Sapoznik points out that "the supposed 'Jewish' opening was in fact made up by reed virtuoso (and full-time Gentile) Ross Gorman during rehearsals of the

work." And if Benny Goodman performed Jewish tunes, notably "And the Angels Sing" (based on "Der Stiller Bulgar") and "Bay mir bistu sheyn" with trumpeter Ziggy Elman (Harry Finkleman), the predominant sound is less klezmer than swing. Once again the music of Jews and Gentiles was shared – black clarinettist Boyd Senter, for example, had a glissando sound that comes close to the Jewish players of the period. It's an issue still current today, when non-Jewish klezmer bands inevitably invite the question 'Do you have to be Jewish to play klezmer?'

Making it in America inevitably meant moving up and out of the ghetto, so Yiddish music learnt more than it taught. After World War II, the clarinettist and saxophonist **Sam Musiker**, who was from a klezmer family, as his name implies, led a band that achieved a real klezmer and jazz fusion. But most immigrants preferred to forget their life in the old country and were even ashamed of it. The demand for Jewish music dwindled to a few tunes trundled out at weddings. Meanwhile Hitler put an end to the Jewish communities of eastern Europe and their culture forever. Klezmer, it seemed, was a music of the archives.

The Klezmer Revival

One of the best-known klezmer musicians today is clarinettist **Giora Feidman**. His work predates the US klezmer revival scene but he is a singular, inspirational figure, who has revitalised the music through the sheer artistry and humanity of his playing. A fourth-generation klezmer born in Argentina, he became a member of the Israel Philharmonic Orchestra in the 1960s. Surprised to find almost no klezmer being played in Israel, he set out to play and popularise the music, eventually devoting himself entirely to it. He isn't a purist – he has played Gershwin and classical crossovers and his repertoire is as much Israeli as Yiddish, including many spiritual *nigunim* – but he has been hugely important in popularising the music. He is also simply one of the best clarinettists around, able to speak, laugh and cry through his instrument.

In the US, the revival of klezmer was set in motion in the mid-1970s by a group calling themselves **The Klezmorim** in Berkeley, California, by clarinettist **Andy Statman**, and **Henry Sapoznik**, who created an **Archive of Recorded Sound** at the **YIVO** (the Institute for Jewish Research) in New York. There, Sapoznik catalogued and re-issued the best old klezmer 78s on a series of compilations, which were picked up by an entirely new generation of Jewish (and some non-Jewish) musicians, with an interest in roots music. They set up revival groups to play klezmer, and it wasn't long before there was a festival, **KlezKamp**, in the Catskill Mountains, where classes, workshops and concerts brought young musicians together with the surviving old-timers.

The veteran stars at KlezKamp have been **Sid Beckerman**, **Howie Lees** and **Max Epstein**, all American-born and thus inheritors of both the European klezmer tradition and the American dance band experience. The revival has given them a new lease of life. "It's a wonderful thing," says Epstein, "I lived this music all my life practically and I've finally come into my own. Retirement is not for me, 'cause if I stop playing I'll die. So I'm sticking with it. I'm eighty years old, I've still got a few notes left and I'm going to peddle them off before I die." Alongside the old masters, the luminaries of the revival generation take masterclasses and workshops.

GIORA FEIDMAN & ENSEMBLE
YIDDISH SOUL

Andy Statman and **Henry Sapoznik**, the pioneering figures of new klezmer, both started out playing Appalachian music – Statman was a bluegrass mandolinist, and Sapoznik plays the banjo. Statman, also a jazz-saxophone player, became the disciple of Dave Tarras and inherited his clarinets. He has recently been exploring Hassidic nigunim and spiritual melodies, drawing on his experiences of jazz and contemporary musical styles. Sapoznik is leader of **Kapelye**, one of the veteran bands in the business, which has spent twenty years reviving the old-time Jewish music and theatre repertoire of the twenties and thirties.

Another key group is the **Klezmer Conservatory Band**, formed in 1980 in Boston. Listening to this large ensemble, led by saxophonist **Hankus Netsky** and which has featured over the years many top young klezmer players, you can hear how American big-band music has fed back into the Jewish repertoire.

New Directions

As the revival developed, two trends became established. A radical approach - taken by groups such as The Klezmatics, Brave Old World, the Flying Bulgar Klezmer Band, David Krakauer, the New Klezmer Trio, and Naftule's Dream – has continued to reinvent the music, bringing in all sorts of new influences and styles. Meantime, in Europe especially, a traditional wing is looking back to the music's folk roots, exploring the classic repertoire. Interestingly, these movements are not mutually exclusive and many of the leading figures in the klezmer world are both innovators and traditionalists. Many bands also feature Yiddish songs from outside the strict klezmer tradition: songs like "Rozhinkes mit mandlen" (Raisins and Almonds) and "Di Sapozhkelekh" (The Boots), or Jewish socialist anthems like "Alle Brider" (We're all Brothers).

Amongst the best of the innovative bands are **Brave Old World** featuring Michael Alpert on vocals and violin and Kurt Bjorling on clarinet. They mix strong traditional material with more classical arrangements and new compositions. As Alpert says, they are "striving to take klezmer music to its next stage: away from imitating the past and towards creating a living music for the future". Their own songs (in Yiddish) include the striking "Chernobyl", about the site of the nuclear disaster, which was once a thriving Hassidic shtetl.

The hippest band in klezmer is undoubtedly **The Klezmatics**. They are up to the minute, yet deeply rooted in the tradition. Their leader, the eclectic trumpeter **Frank London**, explains: "The Jewish music tradition has always been one of reacting to the place where they were living, whether they were in Odessa or Romania. The Klezmatics started playing the old tunes off 78 records, but we couldn't keep our own personal music history out of it, nor did we want to. Alicia Svigals, our violinist, who grew up listening to

Led Zeppelin records, would scream guitar licks, and I would bring in the experience of working with people like David Byrne and the Art Ensemble of Chicago. We can't help it. We're Jews. This is New York City. And this is our music!"

To see what London means, take a listen to the opening track of The Klezmatics' 1992 album *Rhythm and Jews*, a tune called "Fun Tashlikh" – an old number from Naftule Brandwein – which they yanked up to date with improvisatory bass clarinet, wailing brass, and an underpinning Nubian drum rhythm suggesting the old links between klezmer and Arabic music. It's a sensational sound, and the band is even better live.

Recently The Klezmatics have been working with Israeli singer **Chava Alberstein**, writing new songs to Yiddish poetry. Several members of the group have also branched out into their own more radical formations – trumpeter Frank London's **Hasidic New Wave**, clarinettist David Krakauer's **Klezmer Madness!**, and clarinettist Matt Dariau's **Paradox Trio**.

Another hugely significant figure in the 1990s was superstar violinist **Itzhak Perlman**, who produced a couple of excellent klezmer albums and concert tours. The key to these projects' success was that Perlman worked with four of the top revival bands – Brave Old World, The Klezmatics, The Andy Statman Klezmer Orchestra and the Klezmer Conservatory Band – and, as Alicia Svigals put it, "came to it believing that we had something to teach him. His ears are like sponges. He listened to our playing and filtered it through his own musical process. He doesn't just copy or parody, but he makes it virtuosic and this amazing sound comes out." Perlman's album, *In the Fiddler's House*, released by EMI in 1995, outsold any previous klezmer release by a factor of ten.

In Europe the Klezmer revival is booming and innovative klezmer groups include **Klezmer Groove**, based in the UK (with a good line in reggae fusion), **Klezmokum** and **Di Goim** in Holland and **Aufwind** in Germany. Further east, there's now an annual Klezmer festival in St. Petersburg and a trio of classically-trained musicians, **Kroke**, are based in Krakow, Poland, one of the former heartlands of Jewish music (the group is named after the Yiddish word for the city). With a clutch of recordings, and performances at WOMAD, they have shown themselves to be one of the best new progressive groups in European klezmer.

The New Old World

As the klezmer revival comes of age, the new generation no longer feels the stigma of immigration and the need to assimilate. On the contrary, many are actively reaching back into the past. Since the fall of the Berlin Wall it has become easier to travel to eastern Europe, and many Jews have gone to explore their roots. As the traces of Jewish music in post-war eastern Europe are faint, the **Gypsy bands** that still play for weddings and other celebrations in Romania and Ukraine are about as close to the traditional klezmorim as you can get.

This living tradition, combined with the influence of a parallel movement towards period 'authenticity' in classical music, has inspired fresh performing styles and the use of old or reproduction instruments. These 'old style' performances of klezmer have shed new light on the expressive details of the music such as phrasing and ornamentation, and avoid the shmaltz that can often turn the music into sentimental shtetl nostalgia.

Although many of these authentic revival bands are based in Europe, most of them are driven by Americans who have grown up in the klezmer revival. Clarinettist **Joel Rubin** – a former member of Brave Old World now based in Berlin – is one of the leading researchers into the history and development of klezmer and particularly the work of Russian collector **Moyshe Beregovski** (see box opposite). *Bessarabian Symphony*, Rubin's recording of duos with Joshua Horowitz on historical button accordion and tsimbl, drew on Beregovski archives, while *Beregovski's Khasene* recreated music from Ukraine in the first decades of the twentieth century. "Beregovski's archive", says Rubin, "gives us the clearest available picture of the musical traditions of the Ukrainian Jewish shtetl from the second half of the nineteenth century up to the outbreak of the Second World War."

These authentic revival bands often make use of **old-style instruments**. Rubin plays a **C-clarinet** (as used by Naftule Brandwein), which is more piercing and folk-like than the conventional B-flat and A instruments, and produces expressive irregularities of tone. His former musical partner, **Joshua Horowitz**, has actually named his own band, **Budowitz**, after Karl Budowitz, the maker of his nineteenth-century accordion. "It encourages certain bass figurations, lines and harmonies which a

modern accordion would not," says Horowitz. "And the melody side invites different fingerings and ornaments. These old instruments are small and soft, yet it takes much more physical energy to play them. Their inefficiency makes possible more nuance, because the lightly touched embellishment notes come out more firmly than on a modern accordion where they're too crudely audible." Horowitz's band also includes C-clarinet, violin and cello, as well as a tsimbl designed (and played) by Horowitz on the

The Lost Archive of Moyshe Beregovski

During the half century from 1898 to 1948, Russian and Soviet Jewish folklorists collected thousands of folk melodies which together form the largest archive of eastern European Jewish musical traditions. The most important and prolific collector was **Moyshe Beregovski** (1892–1961). Building upon his training as a cellist, choir director and music pedagogue, Beregovski began to collect Ukrainian-Jewish music in 1927. In 1949 the archive he had founded at the Ukrainian Academy of Sciences. was closed and he was arrested in the Stalinist anti-Jewish purges. Two years later he was sentenced to ten years and deported to Siberia for having studied Jewish music, which was seen as anti-Soviet. He remained in the Gulag for four years, but was released early due to illness.

Beregovski was the first collector of Jewish folk music to apply scholarly methodology to his work, which was distinguished for its attention to detail, and he was the first to have viewed the music within the larger context of a multi-ethnic Central and Eastern Europe. Beregovski's major work was *Jewish Musical Folklore*, a planned five-volume thesaurus of melodies culled from his archive, of which only the first volume was published. After his arrest, Beregovski was neglected in the Soviet Union, while he was largely ignored in the West due to his rhetoric, which was couched in Stalinist jargon.

The Jewish music archive at the Ukrainian Academy of Sciences comprised not only the melodies that Beregovski had collected, but also several earlier private and institutional collections that it had acquired, including those of the composer Joel Engel (1868–1927), folk song researcher Zusman Kisselgof

Moyshe Beregovski

(1876–1939), the St. Petersburg Society for Jewish Folk Music; as well as the Society for Jewish History and Ethnography, under whose auspices the folklorist and writer Shlomo Ansky (1863–1920) – author of *The Dybbuk* – had led the Jewish Ethnographic Expedition from 1911–14. The music in the collection consisted of field recordings, transcriptions made from those recordings, transcriptions written down by ear directly from singers and instrumentalists, as well as notations made by amateur and professional musicians and singers themselves.

This archive forms, in the words of Lord Yehudi Menuhin, "an inestimable treasure house of Jewish musical culture". Its incredible breadth is unequalled in the history of Jewish musicology – ranging from klezmer instrumentals to various types of Yiddish folk and popular songs, hassidic nigunim, music of the *purimshpiln* (Yiddish folk theatre), liturgical chants and cantorial singing, *zmires* (Sabbath table songs), as well as the voices of celebrities. The earliest items in the collection date from 1885, and the last piece was collected in December, 1948. By that time the collection included 1265 musical cylinders containing around 3000 musical items, plus many thousands of pages of musical notations and text transcriptions.

In 1949 the entire archive 'disappeared'. Many presumed it had been destroyed on Stalin's orders, but a large portion of it miraculously re-appeared in 1994 at the Vernadsky Library of the Ukrainian Academy of Sciences. It is hoped that the materials will eventually be made available to the public.

Joel Rubin

lines of old models. What distinguishes Budowitz and Joel Rubin's band are their irregular phrases and speeds, and their use of ornament, all of which were ironed out of more regular performance styles over the course of the twentieth century.

Both Rubin and Horowitz also include members of the flourishing **Hungarian folk scene** in their bands, musicians who know the ways of the related eastern European styles inside out. This brings a distinctive and appropriate rural style to the music that you don't get from American bands. Another group that includes Hungarian folk players is **Di Naye Kapelye** (The New Band), led by American Bob Cohen in Budapest. "The klezmer

stuff I heard in America wasn't funky enough for me and I always thought 'come-on, that's not what my grandfather listened to'. We are not a New York band so we don't have the swing and jazz influence. The aim is to put into practice my grandfather's aesthetics."

Cohen has spent a decade recording and collecting music from the few Jewish survivors in eastern Europe (including his grandfather's Moldavian stamping ground) and learning from old Gypsy musicians who played alongside Jews before the war. His researches have given Di Naye Kapelye a much more rootsy, village sound and a new repertoire that doesn't come from the old 78s that form the staples of the American bands. "The accepted style for playing second fiddle in klezmer is really busy. They would never have played like that in eastern Europe. The Gyp-

sies don't play like that and there's no way you could play twenty minutes for a dance if you did that. They simply developed that busy style of playing when they were making those little three-minute records in the States." So Cohen's band perform pieces with the typical line-up of a Moldavian village band – fiddle, *koboz* (lute) and drum. He played their recording to Itzik Schwartz, born in 1906 and one of their Jewish sources in Romanian Moldavia, who said – "Yes, that is what I remember!"

The group **Muzsikás**, based in Budapest, is not a klezmer band and its members are not Jewish. But as the leading Translvanian folk group, they have carried out research into the old Jewish repertoire of Transylvania through some of the Gypsy musicians who played with klezmorim before the war. They learned Jewish tunes from an old fiddler from Maramureş, Gheorghe 'Cioata' Covaci and from tsimbl player Árpád Toni. Most of these pieces sound nothing like the more familiar klezmer repertoire and much more like Hungarian or Romanian Transylvanian tunes. "That's because the conditions in Transylvania were unique in Europe," says Daniel Hamar of Muzsikás. "From the late sixteenth century, the principality of Transylvania enjoyed great religious tolerance. Jewish people could integrate into society more...and their music is a product of this shared culture. It is a hundred percent Jewish and a hundred percent Hungarian."

The most famous Hungarian Jewish song, "Szól a kakas már" (The Rooster is Crowing) has a very beautiful melody. The story goes that a rabbi heard this song sung by a Hungarian shepherd boy and paid him to teach it to him and then forget it. It has the melodic contours of an old Hungarian tune, yet also sounds very Jewish. In fact, in the west of Hungary, where the Jewish population was small, it is known as a Hungarian melody and in the east of Hungary, where a lot of Jews were settled, it is known as a Jewish religious song.

Klezmer in Israel

The klezmer scene in **Israel** is low-key. The State of Israel has always been uneasy about Yiddish culture, choosing to emphasise the Hebraic links with the Semitic culture of the Holy Land. So while the American klezmer revival is often nostalgic, the Israeli is mystical, bringing to the fore the music's roots in Hassidic nigunim or religious songs. Much of the Israeli repertoire incorporates Arabic and Druze elements and several of the Israeli groups have explored these connections.

There is an annual klezmer festival in **Safed**, in Galilee, but the town is better known for the **Lag Ba'omer**, a festival of thanksgiving celebrated by both Ashkenazi and Sephardic Jews on nearby Mount Meron. For hundreds of years, klezmorim have been invited to play here: in the evening a flame is lit over the tomb of the rabbi Shimon Bar-Yochai, and the musicians play specific Mount Meron tunes for the occasion.

Sulam, led by Israeli-born clarinettist Moshe Berlin, is perhaps the best-known klezmer band on the current Israeli scene. Their line-up includes a number of Soviet emigrés (a group which has contributed much to the klezmer revival), and they play a powerful mixture of eastern European nigunim and secular melodies. Much of the klezmer music performed in Israel, however, is the product of Hassidic and orthodox communities, which still forbid music in the city of Jerusalem, in mourning for the destruction of the Temple. And many of the best musicians are unknown to the general public, since they perform only for their own people on special occasions.

*With thanks to Henry Sapoznik
and Joel Rubin.*

discography

The best website for klezmer info and reviews is Klezmershack (www.klezmershack.com).

Compilations

◉ **Doyres (Generations): Traditional Klezmer Recordings 1979–1994** (Trikont, Germany).

A very good compilation of the important figures of the klezmer revival including The Klezmorim, Andy Statman and Zev Feldman, Dave Tarras, Kapelye, Joel Rubin and the Epstein Brothers, the Klezmer Conservatory Band plus Mosha Berlin from Israel and Muzsikás and a Ukrainian Brass band from eastern Europe. There's a companion volume ◉ **Shteygers (Ways)** with more contemporary arrangements.

◉ **The Jewish Alternative Movement: A Guide for the Perplexed** (Knitting Factory Records, US).

A sampler of the more extreme end of contemporary klezmer including Hasidic New Wave, Naftule's Dream, the Paradox Trio, Klezmer Madness and Hassidic performers Yosi and Avi Piamenta, and Neshama Carlebach.

◉ **Klezmer Music: A Marriage of Heaven and Earth** (Ellipsis Arts, US).

A great compilation of some of the best contemporary klezmer bands with a lavishly illustrated book and photographs. Includes Brave Old World, The Klezmatics, Andy Statman, The Flying Bulgar Klezmer Band, Naftule's Dream, Budowitz and others.

◉ **Klezmer Music: Early Yiddish Instrumental Music 1908–1927** (Arhoolie, US).

A classic collection of old 78 rpm recordings. Includes several eastern European tracks from Turkey and Poland, including the spectral Haneros Haluli from 1909 recreated by the Hungarian group Muzsikás. Also tracks from Abe Schwarz, Naftule Bredwein and Dave Tarras.

◉ **Klezmer Pioneers: 1905–52** (Rounder, US).

A broader compilation of old masters, including Abe Schwartz, Harry Kandel, Naftule Brandwein, Dave Tarras and Sam Musiker. Excellent notes.

◉ **Oytsres – Treasures: Klezmer Music 1908–1996** (Schott/Wergo, Germany).

The most recent of Joel Rubin's collections of archival recordings with excellent photographs and notes. Includes very rare material from pre-war eastern Europe and good examples of important names like Naftule Brandwein, Shloimke Beckerman, Cherniavsky's Yiddish-American Jazz Band and Dave Tarras. It's strange that the only contemporary example is Rubin himself.

◉ **Patterns of Jewish Life** (Schott/Wergo, Germany).

A two-CD set taken from a series of concerts of Traditional and Popular Jewish Music in Berlin in 1992. Includes klezmer and Yiddish songs from the Łódz Ghetto from Brave Old World, old time klezmer from the Epstein Brothers, plus Yiddish theatre music, Cantorial song, Sephardic music and Hassidic rock from the Piamenta Brothers.

◉ **The Rough Guide to Klezmer** (World Music Network, UK).

A good survey of the leading contemporary bands, including Brave Old World, The Klezmatics and The Flying Bulgar Klezmer Band, plus a sprinkling of archive tracks from Brandwein and others, neatly placed alongside the new versions that they inspired.

The Soul of Klezmer (World Network, Germany).

A two-CD compilation ranging through old archive recordings, pioneers of the revival like The Klezmorim, Andy Statman and Zev Feldman and Kapelye, plus the leading contemporary bands. A few surprising selections, but a good overview nonetheless.

 **Yikhes: Klezmer Recordings From 1911–1939** (Trikont, Germany).

The best compilation of remastered 78s, including a couple of 1911 tracks from Belf's Romanian Orchestra, one of the few European bands to have been recorded, plus tracks from violinist Abe Schwartz, accordionist Max Yankowitz, clarinettists Naftule Brandwein and others. Excellent notes in German and English.

Artists

Naftule Brandwein

Brandwein (1889–1963) was the universally acknowledged genius of the klezmer clarinet. He was born in the Polish Galician town of Przemysl and his father was a fiddler and *badkhn* (wedding poet). He left for the US in 1908 and started working for Yiddish theatre bands, calling himself the 'King of Jewish Music', a title which stuck. He died largely forgotten in 1963, but his recordings are now legendary for their spontaneity and fire.

King of the Klezmer Clarinet (Rounder, US).

The 25 tracks on this disc are the staples of every contemporary klezmer band – favourites like the "Hot Bulgar", "Naftule Plays for the Rabbi", "Oh Father It's Good" and the "Hot Tartar Dance". Recorded between 1923 and 1941 and now superbly cleaned-up. Good notes by Henry Sapoznik.

Brave Old World

An excellent four-piece ensemble featuring Michael Alpert (vocals and violin), Kurt Bjorling (clarinet), Alan Bern (accordion and keyboards) and Stuart Brotman (bass). Each of their three CDs to date includes some fine traditional numbers plus novel inventions.

Beyond the Pale (Pinorrekk, Germany).

Some cracking rural-style pieces learned from old Ukranian fiddler Leon Schwartz, reinterpretations of Tarras and

Brandwein, including a cool jazz version of his "Escorting the In-Laws Home" and an original Yiddish song about the ironies of performing in Berlin after the Wall came down.

Budowitz

Led by accordion and tsimbl player Joshua Horowitz, Budowitz play authentic old-style klezmer music. The band's current line up includes the excellent clarinettist Merlin Shepherd.

Mother Tongue: Music of the 19th Century Klezmorim (Koch Schwann, Austria).

Very fine ensemble playing of C-clarinet, violin, tsimbl, accordions and cello in subtly different combinations. A beautiful approach to the Old World sound. Repertoire from old recordings, plus archives and recent fieldwork. Very detailed notes about the repertoire and playing style.

Wedding Without a Bride (Buda/Musique du Monde, France).

An excellent new disc exploring the virtually uncharted wedding repertoire of southeastern Poland through the recollections of Majer Bogdanski, who was born in Poland in 1912 and now lives in London. This is one of the best recreations of Old World klezmer, with impeccable and poetic playing from Horowitz on the timbl and Merlin Shepherd on the clarinet, although some may find Bogdanski's vocals hard to get used to. Excellent notes.

The Epstein Brothers

Some of the last old time klezmer musicians working in America, clarinettist Max (b 1912), trumpeter Willie (b 1919) and drummer Julie (b 1926) have been playing together all their lives. Their life and music in Florida was the subject of the excellent film A Tickle in the Heart.

Zeydes un Eyniklekh (Grandfathers and Grandsons) (Schott/Wergo, Germany).

A splendid collection of tunes from the repertoire of Dave Tarras. The Epsteins are backed up on sax, piano, drums and Joel Rubin on C-clarinet. A meeting of generations and a celebration of the American-Jewish klezmer tradition. The companion disc, **Kings of Freylekh Land** (Schot/Wergo), features the Epsteins playing their own material.

Giora Feidman

Born in Buenos Aires, Feidman went to Israel as a young man to be principal clarinettist of the Israel Philharmonic. Surprised to find so little klezmer music in Israel, he led the revival there before moving to New York in the early 1970s. He is a magnificent clarinettist, with an amazing ability to speak through his instrument.

Yiddish Soul (World Network, Germany).

Live in concert in Germany, with guitar and double bass. The light acoustic trio shows off Feidman's extraordinary clarinet playing perfectly. A typical mixture of popular klezmer tunes and Israeli numbers.

The Flying Bulgar Klezmer Band

Based in Toronto and led by trumpeter David Buchbinder, the Flying Bulgars are one of the best of the mildly experimental groups.

Agada (Traditional Crossroads, US).

This 1993 album contains good original material and some wacky arrangements of classic numbers, notably "Sumkinda Hora" a lop-sided version of Brandwein's "Hot Tartar Dance".

Their latest release, **Tsirkus** (Traditional Crossroads, US), gets more experimental, with mainly new compositions.

Kapelye

Now around twenty years old, Kapelye has been one of the leading bands from the early days of the revival. Led by Henry Sapoznik, the band has concentrated on American style klezmer from the twenties and thirties.

 On the Air (Shanachie, US).

A wacky exploration of the world of 1920s-style Yiddish radio drawing on great tracks by Harry Kandel, Brandwein, Abe Ellstein and Dave Tarras, among others. The music is interspersed with typical commercials in Yiddish and English, and radio slots like "Jews in the News". Inimitable notes by Henry Sapoznik. Their earlier release **Chicken** (Shanachie, US) features a more standard repertoire including a good medley of wedding music.

Mickey Katz

Katz (1909–1985) was an LA-based clarinettist, bandleader, songwriter and comedian, and a curious figure in American-Jewish music. He played in comedy bands for Jewish parties and, after World War II, joined Spike Jones' band the City Slickers. While with the band he did a Yiddish take-off of "Home on the Range" and then extended the idea into a whole range of Yiddish American fusions – My Yiddishe Mambo, the Yiddish Square Dance, the Wedding Samba and so on.

 Music for Weddings, Bar Mitzvahs and Brisses (World Pacific, US).

An extraordinary album from the mid-fifties containing most of Katz's quirky Yiddish parodies – "Keneh Hora" is a "Hava Nagila" take-off and the "Wedding Samba" is a Latin version of "De Stiller Bulgar" and "As the Angels Sing". Fine playing from Katz and his brassy band, including trumpeters Ziggy Elman and Mannie Klein.

Khevrisa

Like kapelye, khevrisa is an old Yiddish word for a klezmer ensemble and this newly created US ensemble is dedicated to playing old-style European klezmer. Led by Steven Greenman (violin), formerly of Budowitz, and Zev Feldman (tsimbl), both long-time lights of the klezmer revival, Khevrisa also includes Alicia Svigals (second violin) of the Klezmatics and Michael Alpert (second violin) and Stuart Brossman (bass) from Brave Old World.

 European Klezmer Music (Smithsonian Folkways, US).

A superb new recording of old-style European klezmer. Feldman made a great pioneering recording of clarinet and tsimbl duos with Andy Statman in the late 1970s and this 2000 release draws on the considerable work he and the other members of the band have been doing in recent years. The music is delicate, supple and played with authority and love. An excellent accompanying booklet too.

The Klezmatics

A six-piece band led by trumpeter Frank London, with Alicia Svigals on violin, Lorin Sklamberg on vocals and strong contributions from clarinet, bass and drums. Klezmer's hippest New York band, combining a radical approach with a deep knowledge of the tradition.

 Rhythm & Jews (Piranha, Germany).

It's hard to pick between The Klezmatics' five albums to date: all are highly recommended. This one, from 1990, is still very fresh and can claim to be one of the greatest klezmer records ever made. Some great explorations of Brandwein tunes with "Bulgar a la Klezmatics" and "NY Psycho Freylekhs" being particular highlights. Try **Jews with Horns** (Piranha, Germany) next.

 The Well (Green Linnett, US).

In a rare New York/Israeli Yiddish collaboration, the Klezmatics perform with Israeli singer Chava Alberstein in a beautiful and moving collection of original songs composed to Yiddish poetic texts.

The Klezmer Conservatory Band

The klezmer big band, led by sax player Hankus Netsky, with Ilene Stahl on clarinet, Mirian Rabson on violin and Jeff Warschauer on mandolin and flute, plus cornet, trombone, piano, bass and percussion. Vocals from Judy Bressler.

 Dancing in the Aisles (Rounder, US).

A wide range of styles, including some Molly Picon songs from Yiddish musicals of the 1930s, a Meron mystical tune, an In Memoriam for Yitzhak Rabin, a classical medley and standard klezmer dance numbers.

David Krakauer

Long-term clarinettist with The Klezmatics, Krakauer has worked with the Kronos Quartet and has his own group – Klezmer Madness!

 Klezmer Madness (Tzadik, US).

Some very wild reworkings of Brandwein tunes, the best being the "Bogota Bulgar", written for the wedding of a Jew to a Colombian. Also includes a version of the Michael Alpert Chernobyl song and "Living with the H-Tune", the ubiquitous Israeli favourite "Hava Nagila".

Kroke

Kraków based trio of Tomasz Kukurba (violin/viola), Jerzy Bawol (accordion) and Tomasz Lato (string bass) mixing Jewish and Polish musicians. The band bring accomplished musicianship and an experimental and inventive approach to the music. Kroke have four discs to date. They are strong live and have performed at WOMAD.

 Live at the Pit (Oriente, Germany).

This atmospheric 1998 album kicks off with an exploration of the Harry Kandel tune "A Night in the Garden of Eden" which runs like a thread through their second album, *Eden*. This live recording includes a good balance of familiar tunes and inventive evocations – sometimes like a dream, sometimes like a nightmare – of Kraków's ancient Jewish legacy.

Frank London's Klezmer Brass All Stars

Trumpeter Frank London is best known as the leader of the Klezmatics (see above), but was a founding member of the Klezmer Conservatory Band (see above), the Les Misérables Brass Band and also plays in the radical group Hasidic New Wave. The Klezmer Brass Allstars is a new project featuring six brass and wind players from the best American ensembles plus percussion.

 Di Shikere Kapelye (Piranha, Germany).

The title means 'The Inebriebriated Orchestra', a mythical nineteenth-century east European band of illustrious neer'-do-wells always invited to perform but never welcome to stay in one place. Learning a lot from Balkan Gypsy bands like the Kocani

Ensemble, the All Stars bring a swirling earthy virtuosity to their music. It is punchy and powerful but also moving and subdued when necessary. Recorded in the Knitting Factory Bar in NYC.

Muzsikás

Hungary's premiere folk ensemble playing Hungarian and Transylvanian village music.

ⓘ Máramaros: The Lost Jewish Music of Transylvania (Ryko/Hannibal, UK).

A beautiful disc of Jewish dance tunes, laments and songs, recorded with old-time Transylvanian Gypsies. Great vocals from Márta Sebestyén.

Di Naye Kapelye

The name is Yiddish for 'The New Band'. The group, led by Bob Cohen, is based in Hungary and performs old time Yiddish music in rural eastern European style. Includes several members of the Budapest folk scene, with a line-up of violin, accordion, clarinet, bass and assorted folk instruments.

ⓒⒹ Di Naye Kapelye (Oriente, Germany).

Debut album from 1998 with a good mixture of klezmer standards plus a more unusual repertoire collected in eastern Europe. Some strong earthy dances and devotional, meditative music.

Itzhak Perlman

Itzhak Perlman grew up in Israel to Yiddish-speaking parents from Poland. He took up the violin at an early age and has become one of the leading classical violinists of his generation.

ⓒⒹ In the Fiddler's House (EMI, UK).

A wonderful collaboration with four leading contemporary klezmer bands – The Klezmatics, Brave Old World, the Andy Statman Klezmer Orchestra and the Klezmer Conservatory Band. Tracks include Reb Itzik's "Nigun", specially composed for Perlman; "Flatbush Waltz", one of Andy Statman's most successful pieces; a fine improvisational doina with clarinettist David Krakauer and a beautiful version of the Brandwein classic "Escorting the In-Laws Home". Perlman's playing, while not strictly idiomatic, is always good to listen to and the arrangements are strong. The follow-up live album, ⓘ **Live in the Fiddler's House**, is also great.

Joel Rubin

Joel Rubin, born in the US but currently living in Berlin, is one of the best of the revival clarinettists. He has worked closely with old-time klezmer musicians the Epstein Brothers.

ⓘ Beregovski's Khasene (Schott/Wergo, Germany).

A very fine recreation of "Forgotten Instrumental Treasures from the Ukraine" taken from the Beregovski collection. Idiomatically performed with (mainly) Hungarian musicians including celebrated Gypsy cimbalom player Kálmán Balogh. The title translates as Beregovski's Wedding.

ⓒⒹ Bessarabian Symphony: Early Jewish Instrumental Music (Schott/Wergo, Germany).

Gentle, intimate music matching the expertly-played C-clarinet with accordion and tsimbl. Recommended, with good notes.

Andy Statman

Mandolin and clarinet player Andy Statman has been an important figure in klezmer since his work with Dave Tarras in the late 1970s.

ⓘ Klezmer Suite (Shanachie, US).

A classic reworking of some of Tarras's tunes by Statman and an orchestra.

ⓘ Songs of our Fathers (Acoustic Disc, US).

Recently Statman has been moving from klezmer to devotional music. In this well-produced instrumental album with mandolinist David Grisman, he explores hymns, songs and melodies connected to the Hassidic repertoire.

Sulam

Israeli klezmer group led by clarinettist Moshe Berlin. Berlin started playing at a young age at the traditional Mt Meron klezmer gathering, but didn't record until this disc in 1990. Most of the musicians in the band are from the former Soviet Union – on violin, flute, piano and drums.

ⓘ Klezmer Music from Tel Aviv (Schott/Wergo, Germany).

Repertoire from the Mt Meron Lag Ba'omer festival, including nigunim and some eastern European dance tunes.

Alicia Svigals

US-born violinist with The Klezmatics and one of the best players of klezmer fiddle.

Alicia Svigals

ⓘ Fidl (Traditional Crossroads, US).

The violin is central to the traditional klezmer repertoire and this is a great demonstration of its power and versatility. Idiomatic playing, both solo and in small instrumental ensembles. Includes a couple of great duets with Joshua Horowitz on tsimbl.

Dave Tarras

Along with Naftule Brandwein, Tarras (1897–1989) was one of the greatest clarinettists playing Jewish music in America. He was born in a Ukrainian shtetl into a family of musicians and played in the family kapelye. He went to America in 1921 and played with the Abe Schwartz Orchestra and Cherniavsky's Yiddish-American Jazz Band, where he replaced the unreliable Naftule Brandwein as clarinettist. After a long career he was brought out of retirement for concerts and recordings in 1978 and 1979 and became an inspiration for the klezmer revival.

ⓘ Yiddish-American Klezmer Music 1925–1956 (Shanachie, US).

An amazing collection of popular Yiddish music, with Tarras playing with various bands for radio, theatre and commercials. Extensive notes by Henry Sapoznik.

USA

Native American

ha-ya-ya, weya ha-ya-ya!

In the early years of the twentieth century, North America's indigenous communities had little to sing about. Typically, their traditional music was banned or discouraged and they faced a depressing future. It looked as if their culture could either survive as museum fodder or be so thoroughly assimilated into the mainstream that its roots would be lost. But, as **Andrew Means** asserts, there has been a dramatic turnaround, with music very much out front.

Numbering around two million in the USA and a further half million in Canada, Native Americans form only a fraction of the North American population as a whole. But they are a significant minority, with a rich diversity of cultures (there are more than 500 tribes in the US alone), which is expressed, not least in music. While non-Native consumers might equate Native America mainly with **flute music** and its New Age hybrids, for Native communities it is **powwow music** and

regional styles like Arizona's **chicken scratch** that hold most meaning and appeal.

It's not hard to fathom why this division exists. Flute and drum form an appealing duality. Just listen to the flute's soaring treble and alto melodies contrasting with the deep, resonant pulse of the powwow drum. One is a voice of individual fancy, the other the heartbeat of a close-knit community. There is also an elemental balance at work here – between the wind and the earth. By contrast, much Native music is functional: the measured

Navajo Nation Fair Powwow

drum beat and falsetto voices of powwow music, for instance, are used purely to accompany dances. Out of context, without the colourful costumes, agile dancers, and ambiance, the repetitive character of powwow music, or the songs of the New Mexico and Arizona Pueblos, can be hard-going.

Part of the reason, perhaps, is because there are few melodic **instruments** in traditional Native music. The voice tends to carry both vocal and instrumental roles and many songs include **vocables** (sounds with no literal meaning) to express pure feeling. The only common traditional instruments are drums, shakers and flute. Less common is the **mouth bow** – whose string is plucked while the player's mouth is pressed against one end of the bow, thus amplifying the sound – while a beautiful rarity is is the **Apache fiddle**, carved from the hollow stalk of the agave plant, and with a thin, delicate tone.

Alongside traditionally-based music, there are sizeable Native American followings for (and performers of) **country**, **blues** , **rock**, **hip-hop** and **reggae**. Reservations, for instance, have long been on the touring itineraries of visiting Jamaican artists, whose message of deliverance from Babylon echoes the sentiments of the Ghost Dance – before its demise at the hands of the US Cavalry. Native America has also produced a handful of major artists in mainstream genres, notably folk singer **Buffy Sainte-Marie**, and **Robbie Robertson** (former singer of The Band), who has led the way in new fusions of traditional sounds and inspirations.

Powwow

Although the **powwow** is only one thread in a Native American tapestry of ceremonial dance music, as a phenomenon embracing many tribes, it has become a symbol of Native American cultural unity and strength. A big powwow, such as the annual **Gathering of Nations** held in Albuquerque, New Mexico (the subject of several recordings), attracts dancers and 'drums' (the word is applied to the group of performers who sit around the drum, singing as they beat time) from across the United States and Canada.

The word powwow is derived from an Algonquin Indian word, *pau wau*, referring to medicine men or spiritual leaders, but that is as far as its origins can be established. Some insist that in essence it goes back hundreds, maybe thousands of years; others that it was created as a tourist spectacle by traders and Indian agents around the turn of the century. The truth probably embraces part of each theory. Whatever, the ceremony, rooted in the

musical tradition of the **Plains tribes**, such as the Sioux, has become a popular intertribal event across the continent, where it often incorporates local dances. Some of the performers have also earned a reputation far beyond their own communities. The **Black Lodge Singers** of the Blackfoot tribe, for instance, augment the powwow circuit with occasional performances in concert halls. A broad geographic division dictates that northerners tend to sing at a higher pitch, and there are differences too in costume.

Wherever the powwow is held, the main events are the **men's traditional dances**, in which vividly clad dancers typically imitate a stalking warrior, and the **women's fancy** or **shawl dance** and **jingle dance**. In the shawl dance, the women act out the part of a butterfly, grieving over its dead mate. The jingle dance – the older of the two – is so named because the participants' costumes are covered with snuff-can lids that have been beaten into a bell-like shape, making a metallic rustling noise with every movement.

Proceedings usually begin with a grand entry into the arena, led by flag bearers. Then there may be a round dance or friendship dance in which everyone – spectators and costumed dancers – sidesteps around the arena in a big circle. **Stomp dances**, featuring a single-file of dancers and call-and-response singing may also be included, particularly in the southeast where they are associated with the Cherokee, Chocktaw and Chickasaw.

Experts say that the **powwow drum** evolved from European-style marching band bass drums turned on their sides. Around the end of the last century Plains tribes began to adopt these drums for their dances. Before then, Plains drums tended to be smaller frame drums, more suitable to the lifestyle of a nomadic people. Many drums used today are custom-made, being about the size of the bass drum but using wood and hides, and often octagonal in shape rather than a circular. Typically, between a half-dozen and dozen players sit around the instrument, each keeping time with one long drumstick and each contributing to the intense cascade of vocables. Powwows usually have several drums situated around the dance arena – or, in the case of traditional Southern-style powwows, one drum in the middle.

Drums undergo rituals before being played, starting with a blessing when they are first made. As Chris White, a member of the Oklahoma group Southern Thunder, explains: "As we set up, we will usually burn some sweetgrass or we'll have some tobacco – even if we just light up a cigarette and pray with that... A drum has a spirit of itself.

The Native American Flute

The revival of Native American flute-playing began in the early 1980s, and the instrument has since become something of a cultural icon. Its most widely-celebrated ambassador is **R. Carlos Nakai** – a Navajo-Ute from Arizona, whose first album, *Changes* (Canyon), was released in 1983. Since then Nakai has sold over two and a half million units through Canyon Records alone.

After setting out to be a classical trumpet-player, Nakai turned to the flute after a car accident left him with facial nerve damage which made him unable to form the embouchure necessary to play the trumpet. "When I found the instrument in the 1960s and began to get serious about it in the early 1970s", he says, "there were very few people who seemed to have any knowledge of – or pay any attention to – the tradition of flute playing."

Nakai was among the first to record the flute accompanied by ambient electronics and the sounds of nature – the classic **New Age** sound. *Cycles*, his first recording with synthesizer, was used by Martha Graham for her dance piece "Night Chant", which has been successful round the globe. In addition, Nakai has played with jazz combos and classical orchestras – a challenge in view of the Native flute's idiosyncratic tuning, which varies from instrument to instrument. Attempts have been made to produce diatonic flutes, but Nakai says that "such a hybrid seems to lose the intrinsic magical quality of sound that is common in the hand-crafted art".

The flute used by most players is the traditional end-blown instrument of the Plains tribes, which has five or six holes. It was usually made of cedarwood and was customarily used by a young man to serenade his loved one. Distinguishing the classic Plains instrument from other end-blown flutes is a wedge-shaped feature (called a bird, or saddle) positioned below the mouthpiece. This saddle is tied on top of two openings in the flute between the mouthpiece and the finger holes. Air blown into the mouthpiece comes out of the first of these holes, is split by a brass plate under the saddle and re-directed back into the flute through the second hole and along the air chamber. The result is a stronger, reedy tone.

A flute is often decorated to indicate its significance and power. The end and saddle may be carved into the shape of an animal or bird's head, and it may be tied with beads and feathers. Pitch and the intervals between notes depend on the preferences or abilities of the maker. "They're all like driving different cars", flautist and singer-songwriter **Bill Miller** explains. "Some of them are more difficult to play with the airflow and others have different wood. But I play how I feel. I play pretty much like nature. Like the birds will sing, and all of a sudden there will be a loud note or a short one or a long one."

As Miller's comments suggest, much of the flute repertoire is improvisational and often spiritual. And unlike much Native music, it tends to be personal. Very few people, however, are playing the old courting melodies, a fact which veteran flautist **Kevin Locke** regrets. He lives on the Lakota Standing Rock Reservation in South Dakota and looks out on the graves of

JAK KILBY

USA

Kevin Locke

Chief Gall and Sitting Bull, heroes of the Battle of Little Big Horn. "We had a lot of old time flute-players that I remember very well. But now there's really not very much of the traditional material played on the flute. Nobody's playing the original material, the love songs, which is a very distinctive genre. You can see hundreds of these flute recordings and none of it has anything to do with traditional flute music. People are improvising and making their own material. Most of it isn't based on Indian musical traditions at all."

It's alive. Those singers have to be able to bring that spirit out of that drum so it can touch those people and those dancers in the arena."

Traditionally **women** sit behind the men at the drum and contribute to the vocal harmonies. Only recently are female drummers and even all-women drums being heard. White accounts for this by pointing out that tribal cultures tend to separate male and female tasks. Some traditionalists see the relationship between drummers and the drum in terms of a mystical equivalent of sexual union in which female drummers would be inappropriate.

But like most forms of music, powwow is and always has been evolving. Much the same could be said of the **flute**, which has become an indisposable soundtrack for Native Americana (see box). Flutes, along with whistles made from eagle bones, frequently appear in TV portrayals of the mythical wild west. And **Kokopelli**, originally a flute-playing figure portrayed in ancient rock petroglyphs, is one of the most popular images on tourist souvenirs associated with the West.

Religious and Ceremonial Music

While powwow serves as an inter-tribal connection, there are numerous styles and genres peculiar to certain communities. These may be tribal in nature, such as the healing songs sung by Navajo shamans of the southwest or the communal ceremonial music of the Pueblos of New Mexico. They may be songs once used to celebrate victorious battles and raids, or songs rooted in an activity such as corn-grinding or hunting. Sometimes they can be an individual's song, received in the course of a vision or personal experience.

Perhaps the acme of vision-seeking is the **Sun Dance of the Plains** – a marathon event during which dancers have thongs tied to sticks piercing the skin of their shoulders or upper chests. Visions follow fasting and the physical exertion of the dancing as participants eventually break free of the thongs. In addition, there are still traces of the ill-fated **Ghost Dance**, which spread from the Paiutes of Nevada in the 1880s. This round dance, in which men and women join hands and sing while shuffling clockwise, was supposed to herald a new age in which whites would be destroyed and the Indian dead would return. What resulted instead was increased racial tension and the crushing of Lakota Sioux resistance at Wounded Knee, south Dakota, in 1890.

Context is crucial to the appreciation of ceremonial music, which can sound monotonous in

the extreme on a recording, but comes to life when experienced as part of a dance or religious event. There are often restrictions on outsiders at these events, however, ranging from an outright ban to limitations on cameras and recording equipment.

The twenty or so Pueblos of New Mexico and the Hopi of Arizona hold some of the best-known annual ceremonies. Most are weather or crop related, reflecting the communities' agricultural lifestyle. One that visitors can attend in part is the Zuni's **Shalako**, a creation myth re-enactment held in winter. Navajo rituals, in contrast, are renowned

for their focus on curing individuals. These ceremonies typically take several days, and involve chanting and construction of sandpaintings. The **Night Way** or Yeibichai is used to cure patients of insanity or bad nerves and takes place over nine days of singing, dancing and praying. It culminates in the appearance of masked dancers depicting supernatural beings, and an initiation rite.

A large number of Native Americans have, of course, adopted Christianity, and there is a strong tradition of **Native American gospel music**. Acting as a sort of synthesis between Native and Christian beliefs are the famous **Peyote Songs** of the Native American Church, hallucinogenic-inspired rituals which emphasise righteous living and the attainment of peyote-induced visions.

The peyote cactus – whose seedpods have hallucinogenic effects when chewed – arrived via the indigenous people of Mexico in the eighteenth century. Traditionally, participants sit in a tipi, forming a circle, and take turns to sing as the cactus pod kicks in, customarily performing four songs each. In the early twentieth century, the Native

Canyon Records

Canyon Records, based in Phoenix, Arizona, is the largest recorder, producer and distributor of traditional and modern Native American music. It began almost by accident in 1951, when **Ray Boley**, who had recently set up a studio, was asked by the Phoenix Little Theatre to record a few songs by Navajo singer **Ed Lee Natay** for use in a play. The singing and drum accompaniment so impressed Boley that he decided to put out an album: *Natay – Navajo Singer*. More than forty years later, that part-time hobby has become a major business, with over five hundred titles in the Canyon catalogue.

Canyon's principal market is among the Native American people themselves and the catalogue has expanded accordingly to include Indian country, gospel, chicken scratch and contemporary singers and musicians like R. Carlos Nakai. And while many Canyon recordings sell no more than five hundred copies, the extraordinary range and size of Boley's catalogue gives him an annual turnover of about 160,000 units. The philosophy of the company is organic and supportive, and the artists respond in kind. The big-selling Nakai, for example, despite offers from the majors, prefers to stick with a label that has Native American music at its heart.

Canyon Records founder Raymond Boley with Navajo singer Ed Lee Natay

American Church was founded, and peyote adopted as its sacrament, with singing accompanied by a rapidly beaten water drum and rattle. (According to modern US law, Native American Church members can use peyote in their ceremonies, but the cactus can be legally harvested only in the Rio Grande Valley of southwestern Texas, where it grows wild.)

A striking contemporary interpretation of the peyote musical genre has been developed by **Verdell Primeaux**, an Oglalla/Yankton Sioux, and **Johnny Mike**, a Navajo. On their album *Sacred Path*, they splice contrapuntal vocal parts with subdued electronic backwashes, creating meditative prayers that seem as timeless as they are beautiful. The gentle harmonies contrast with the rapid drum beats and insistent solo singing of classic peyote music.

Music with a Message

Native American music was the first 'ethnic music' to be recorded, carefully etched onto wax cylin-

ders in the 1890s, but apart from colourful presentations like Buffalo Bill's Wild West Show, outside interest in traditional music and dance was mainly scholarly. In recent decades, however, a renewed self-confidence in Native American culture has emerged. It stems, in part, from the political agitation of the late 1960s and early 1970s, when a new generation of Native Americans began calling for better political representation, better social and environmental conditions, and greater cultural recognition.

The pioneer Native American songwriter was Buffy Sainte-Marie, whose song, "Now that the Buffalo's Gone" remains a powerful expression of Native angst, and set a pattern of lyrical concern. Another leading outfit from the 1960s and early 1970s was the group **XIT**, from New Mexico, whose albums *Plight of the Redman* and *Silent Warrior* put a spotlight on Natives' struggles for fair treatment. **Floyd Westerman** of the Lakotas is another venerable singer-songwriter, and an actor too – he played Ten Bears in *Dances with Wolves*. He is a veteran agitator for Native American rights,

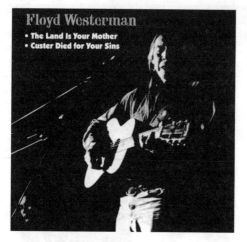

Floyd Westerman
• The Land Is Your Mother
• Custer Died for Your Sins

especially on environmental issues, as can be heard on his "B.I.A. [Bureau of Indian Affairs] Blues":

> B.I.A. don't you blame me for your problems,
> I'm not your Indian any more
> You belong to Whiteman, weya, ha-ya-ya
> B.I.A. you can't change me, don't you try
> We don't want your Whiteman rules no more
> We can live our own way,
>   ha-ya-ya, weya ha-ya-ya!

Closely aligned with lyrics as an expression of Native culture is the **spoken word**. Over the years a series of activists and poets have used music as a foundation for recitation. The pioneer was **John Trudell** (Santee Sioux), whose 1986 release, *Aka Grafitti Man* (The Peace Company), won the admiration of Bob Dylan among others. In the late 1990s, **Joy Harjo** and her band **Poetic Justice** continued in a related vein. Their album *Letter From The End Of The Twentieth Century* frames Harjo's sometimes mystifying verse with guitars, saxes, drums, assorted percussion and tribal singing.

Contemporary groups often employ flutes and powwow drums to give their music a Native character. Take, for instance, two bands based in Phoenix, Arizona – **Keith Secola and His Wild Band of Indians** and **Clan/destine**. Both employ powwow drumming and group vocables in a rock context. Secola's composition "NDN Cars" is an affectionate parody of the old beat-up cars beloved of large Indian families and is a good example of a song that reflects contemporary Native culture without the cryptic or didactic tones of some of the more political writers.

Native American culture has always relied heavily on the memory of its people for its historical and cultural records. Songs vividly reflect values

and experiences and the importance of women and families in Native communities is a recurring theme. It is reflected particularly in the work of two widely respected singers, **Sharon Burch** of the Navajo (Diné) tribe and **Joanne Shenandoah** of the Oneida-Six Nations Iroquois of upstate New York. These two have shown the appeal of their tribal repertoires while also building on them with evocative songs of their own.

Other notable contemporary women singers include **Sissy Goodhouse**, a Lakota from North Dakota, who made a significant contribution with her album *Tiwahé* (Makoché). With its traditional and powwow songs and family participation, *Tiwahe* underlines her sense of communal heritage. **Rita Coolidge** has been delving into her Cherokee background, and the resulting album, *Walela*, with her sister Priscilla and niece, Laura Satterfield, features smooth, lilting harmonies reminiscent of the tone that made Rita a pop star in the 1970s.

Not surprisingly, rap and hip-hop have had an impact on urban Natives eager to voice cultural grievances. Many groups use a backdrop of Indian drums and chanting. *Reservation Of Education* by Robby Bee And The Boyz From The Rez (SOAR) and *Are You Ready For W.O.R.* (Canyon), by the Oakland-based WithOut Rezervation are notable releases worth investigating for their blend of modern urban styles with lyrics about long-standing native social and political concerns.

Fusion

A significant factor in the renaissance of Native American music is the blending of old and new musical styles. This process took off in the 1960s, when the group **Redbone** spliced powwow chants with rock'n'roll. More recently, experiments in music have drawn from the New Age movement: Native American flutes and drums have provided the soundtrack for those who seek salvation – or just relaxation.

The leading figure in Native American fusion is **Robbie Robertson**, a part Mohawk, born in Canada, who was the singer with The Band, Bob Dylan's cohorts. His first musical exploration of his Native American heritage was a soundtrack for a Turner documentary series in 1994, which was released as *Music For The Native Americans*. This seminal album put indigenous styles into contemporary contexts and drew on collaborators from across the continent – the Kashtin pop duo, Claude McKenzie and Florent Vollant from Quebec's Innu tribe, and the part-Cherokee singer Rita Coolidge. The result was a rock-ambient tapestry that showed

Chicken scratch

Straddling the border of Arizona and Mexico is the homeland of the Tohono O'odham, or Papago people. A couple of centuries ago they developed a taste for the dance music they heard from the Spanish. Over time they absorbed influences from polka-playing German immigrants and Mexican *norteño* music, and the result today is a style of dance music known as **waila** (a distortion of the Spanish word for dance, baile).

The style is also called **chicken scratch**, because of the spectacle presented by dancers: foot-dragging is de rigueur, and the shuffling sound is as much a part of waila as the band onstage. The dance-steps are simple compared with, say, salsa legwork or some of the old-world partner dances with which the waila styles share names. The main dances are the waila itself (a two-step polka), the chotis (in 4/4), the mazurka (played as a fast waltz without the usual Polish end stop) and – most recently – the cumbia.

One basic characteristic of waila is that there are no vocals and no flashy instrumental solos – just the groove. The original bands used fiddles and acoustic guitars, a sound still represented by the **Gu-Achi Fiddlers** and the **San Xavier Fiddle Band**, but nowadays chicken scratch bands have graduated to the button accordions, saxophones, electric guitars and drumkits of current line-ups like **Southern Scratch**, the best-known band.

At a traditional church feast, or *piest*, the waila can last from sundown to sunrise, with the band playing in a shelter adjoining a dance area decorated with ribbons. In colder weather, coals are heaped under the surrounding benches so that both dancers and observers can stay warm on and off the dance floor. Nowadays however, many listeners are more likely to hear waila in a bar or dancehall adjoining O'odham country (tribal law prohibits liquor sales so there are no bars within the reservations).

But perhaps the best way to hear waila is at the O'odham reservation near Tucson, Arizona, which has hosted an annual **chicken scratch festival** every April since 1988. Several thousand people attend, mainly Tohono O'odham, but with local Tucson Anglos (and even a few curious out-of-towners) well in evidence. Contact: Angelo Joaquin Jr, Festival Director, PO Box 40531, Tucson, AZ 85717-0531 (☎520/881-0599; *tohono@azstarnet.com*).

Remarkably, no waila bands have ever played in Europe, and very few have even played outside the Tohono O'odham social circle. As yet, the high tide mark of chicken scratch in World Music probably remains a concert by the original chicken scratch band, the **Joaquin Brothers**, held in New York's Carnegie Hall in 1992.

Ben Mandelson and Andrew Means

AIMEE MADSEN

USA

Richard García of Southern Scratch

how vibrant and topical Native American sounds could become in modern studio treatments.

Robertson's 1998 album, *Contact: From The Underworld Of Redboy*, took the experiment further, fusing Native and computer/electronica rhythms. The album, a critical and commmerical success, drew much attention for the song "Sacrifice", which used the voice of Leonard Peltier, recorded in jail, to highlight his widely perceived wrongful imprisonment on ethnic grounds. "When I was making this record", Robertson said, "it struck me that this musicality from the Native community of North America has always lived in this very secretive, private, oppressed, sometimes illegal place... Native music has lived underground for so long, and now it is time to step forward. It's time to do what we can just to share this with peo-

Robbie Robertson *Contact* From The Underworld Of Redboy

ple." The album includes some of the big names of Native American music – **Joanne Shenandoah**, Inuit throat singers **Tudjaat**, and peyote singers **Primeaux & Mike**.

Robert Mirabal, from Taos, New Mexico, forged a similar musical path with his 1997 album *Mirabal*, in which flutes, rattles, drums and vocables mesh seamlessly with electric instruments in what Mirabal calls 'Alter-Native' music.

This cross pollination has become a staple among players of the wooden Plains-style flute, using various combinations of guitars, keyboards and studio electronics. It comes as no surprise these days to find a dyed-in-the-wool powwow group like the esteemed **Black Lodge Singers** teaming up with Navajo-Ute flutist **R. Carlos Nakai** and a symphony orchestra to record a work by an Arizona academic, James DeMars (*Two World Concerto*). Or, for that matter, when a New York jazz pianist like the late **Don Pullen** journeys to the Flathead Reservation of Montana to seek inspira-

tion from the **Chief Cliff Singers** (*Sacred Common Ground*, on Blue Note).

Complicating the issue, however, is simmering controversy about who exactly is entitled to be a Native American performer. There is a degree of hostility within indigenous communities to those regarded as New Age usurpers, and non-Natives have had to tread carefully. Many Native Americans, meantime, are experimenting with modern genres more boldly than ever before.

discography

To keep up to date on Native American music, check the Index of native American Resources on the Internet (*www.hanksville.org/NAresources*). This includes links to radio stations, record labels and CD stores.

Compilations

American Warrriors: Songs for Indian Veterans (Rykodisc, US).

In honour of Native American veterans and those who lost their lives in battle, this disc includes recordings made at a 1995 powwow marking the fifty-year anniversary of the end of WWII as well as archive recordings back to 1910. The traditional music and chants have their roots in War Dances and Victory Songs spanning battles from the Little Big Horn to Vietnam and Desert Storm. Several contributions from the Black Lodge Singers are included.

Creation's Journey: Native American Music (Smithsonian Folkways, US).

Traditional Native American music can be hard-going on disc, but for those who want to investigate this is a good introduction to songs, dances and ceremonial music from the various regions of the US plus Canada, Mexico and Bolivia. Good notes.

Gathering of Nations Powwow (SOAR, US).

These discs are annual releases of recordings from North America's biggest powwows, held in Albuquerque, New Mexico.

Heartbeat: Voices of First Nations Women (Smithsonian Folkways, US).

Highlighting the burgeoning role of women in Native American music, this album is the usual meticulous effort from Folkways. Participants include traditionalists as well as the notable contemporary voices of Joanne Shenandoah and Buffy Sainte-Marie.

Navajo Songs (Smithsonian Folkways, US).

Archive recordings of excellent quality made in 1933 and 1940 by Laura Boulton. Ritual, dance and game songs that give a fascinating picture of Native American culture more than half a century ago. Extensive notes.

Plains Chippewa & Metis Music from Turtle Mountain (Smithsonian Folkways, US).

Drum songs, fiddles, chansons, country and rock 'n' roll from two tribes of the Turtle Mountain reserve in north Dakota. The music reflects the cultural mix introduced by the fur trade, including ritual chants and drumming, fiddle reels and jigs, country and rock 'n' roll. Excellent notes.

The Rough Guide to Native American Music (World Network, UK).

A fine introductory survey ranging across the spectrum from traditional Zuni singer Chester Mahooty and the Garcia Brothers of the pueblos to rappers Without Rezervation and female trio Walela. It also includes the Blackstone Singers, the Black Lodge Singers, Southern Scratch, Primeaux & Mike, R. Carlos Nakai and balladeers Sharon Burch and Joanne Shenandoah.

Talking Spirits: Native American Music from the Hopi, Zuni and San Juan Pueblos (Music of the World, US).

The ceremonial chanting on this album sounds as if it could have been heard by the Spanish explorers of the sixteenth century as they encountered the stone and adobe (mud brick) villages of these singers' ancestors.

Tribal Fires: Contemporary Native American Music (EarthBeat!, US).

Part of a series – the others being *Tribal Voices* (songs) and *Tribal Winds* (flutes) – this is a good example of music incorporating traditional sounds, viewpoints and images in a contemporary context. Includes Robert Mirabel, Keith Secola and Joanne Shenandoah.

Under the Green Corn Moon: Native American Lullabies (Silver Wave, US).

A mixture of contemporary and traditional ditties from various tribes and regions sung by well-known (notably Robert Mirabel and Joanne Shenandoah) and not-so-well-known artists, sensitively accompanied by drums, rattles and other appropriate instruments.

Wood That Sings: Indian Fiddle Music Of The Americas (Smithsonian Folkways, US).

For a culture lacking in stringed instruments, this is a surprisingly good collection. The title comes from the Apache name *Tsii'edo'a'tl* (Wood that Sings) for the indigenous one-stringed violin. Other tracks include waila and other European-influenced styles plus material from Central and South America. Fascinating music and good sleeve notes.

Artists

Kevin Locke

Flautist, singer, hoop-dancer, storyteller and outstanding all-round entertainer, Kevin Locke (born 1954, South Dakota) employs the music and traditions of his Lakota heritage with a range of contemporary resources.

Open Circle (Makoché, US).

The sounds of nature and a multi-ethnic studio accompaniment here enhance Locke's dexterous playing of the Plains-style flute.

Keepers of the Dream (Earthbeat!, US).

An album of Locke's more traditional repertoire, including some elusive flute love songs.

Gu-Achi Fiddlers

The Gu-Achi Fiddlers are an old-time chicken scratch band of the Tohono O'odham (Desert People) of Southern Arizona. Their line-up includes two fiddles, guitar, side drum and bass drum.

O'odham Fiddle Music (Canyon, US).

The first ever commercial recording of raw Chicken Scratch, a step which followed the band's success at the first O'odham Fiddle Orchestra Contest in San Xavier in 1984. A typical collection of polkas, mazurkas and two-steps as re-incarnated in the New World.

Bill Miller

Singer-songwriter Bill Miller started out in a Mohican band in the Stockbridge-Munsee reservation of Wisconsin. He mixes indigenous styles with the country flavours of his adopted base of Nashville.

The Red Road (Warner Western, US).

Featuring Miller's contemplative compositions accompanied by guitar and the sounds of flute and powwow. This is a particularly good blend of ancient and modern influences.

Robert Mirabal

From the Taos Pueblo tribe of New Mexico, Robert Mirabal expresses himself in various types of Native American and pop culture. Besides being a flute player and maker, he is also a poet, short story-writer, playwright and painter.

Mirabal (Warner Western, US).

After several albums concentrating on the flute, Mirabal puts Native sounds and imaginative ideas into a pop/rock framework with this album. Both the songs and the arrangements show imagination, and suggest Mirabal could be a cultural bridgebuilder to watch.

R. Carlos Nakai

Born in 1946 in Flagstaff, Arizona, R. Carlos Nakai is steeped in Navajo culture but a great assimilator of influences. Growing up on the Navajo reservation and later studying classical trumpet, he became acquainted with the Plains-style flute in adulthood. Using his research and imagination, he has become the major catalyst in developing the instrument beyond its traditional parameters and has had huge success in the New Age market.

◎ Two World Concerto (Canyon, US).

Three strong compositions by James DeMars fusing Native American and symphonic traditions. The "Two World Concerto" and "Grey Hawks Rising" are for Native American flute and symphony orchestra, while "Native Drumming" is a piece for flute, powwow drums and singers and orchestra. The powwow performers are the Black Lodge Singers of the Blackfoot tribe of Washington state who have several albums of their own on Canyon Records.

NAKAI · BLACK LODGE
CANYON SYMPHONY ORCHESTRA

TWO WORLD CONCERTO
THE MUSIC OF JAMES DeMARS

◎ Inside Canyon de Chelly (Canyon, US).

Nakai and fellow flautist Paul Horn show how a natural setting can enhance the beauty of their instruments.

◎ Sundance Season (Celestial Harmonies, US).

The Sun Dance Ceremony of the Ute tribe took place over several days to ensure harmonious survival on Mother Earth. This disc features fine solo recordings of Nakai plus a finale with eagle-bone whistles.

Ed Lee Natay

The son of a Navajo leader, the late Ed Lee Natay was a traditional singer of material from the southwest.

◎ Navajo Singer (Canyon, US).

Originally released in 1951 and now on CD with additional songs, this album was the first record on the Canyon label. Not only does it give an idea of the rich Navajo repertoire, but also contains fascinating material from nearby Pueblos. Sung in a strong confident voice with rattle and drum accompaniments.

Cornel Pewewardy & The Alliance West Singers

Once designated as Indian Country, Oklahoma has a sizeable representation from several tribes. Cornel Pewewardy is a leading exponent of the Kiowa tradition from the southern Plains.

◎ Dancing Buffalo – Dances & Flute Songs from the Southern Plains (Music of the World, US).

Songs to accompany dances, but Pewewardy's flute solos make good listening in themselves. Best of all is a selection of Kiowa Christian hymns incorporating intriguing glissandos.

Primeaux & Mike

Verdell Primeaux, of the Oglala/Yankton Sioux, and Johnny Mike, who is Diné (Navajo), are singers in the Native American Church, and have recorded several albums of peyote songs and healing songs associated with that religion.

◎ Walk in Beauty (Canyon, US).

Used to enhance meditation and prayer, healing songs are unaccompanied – in contrast with the mesmerising drum and rattle of peyote songs. This duo embroiders healing songs with their own innovative style of gliding vocal harmonies. For more traditional peyote songs try this duo's **◎ Songs of the Native American Church** (Canyon, US).

Robbie Robertson & The Red Road Ensemble

Renowned as a member of The Band (Bob Dylan's one-time backing group) Robertson is partly Mohawk, and was raised on Canada's Six Nations Reservation. In recent years, he has been a catalyst for re-evaluating Native American culture and history. His 1998 album **◎ Contact From The Underworld Of Redboy** (Capitol, US) continues the process.

◎ Music for The Native Americans (Capitol, US).

Released in 1994, this was a seminal album in showing how Native American music could be created in the studio. It mixes allusions to Native myths and history with electronic effects as well as Robertson's electric guitar and the voices of Rita Coolidge and the urban New York group Pura Fe.

Buffy Sainte-Marie

Born in Saskatchewan, Canada of Cree descent, Buffy Sainte-Marie remains one of the most accomplished singer-songwriters to chronicle Native American woes. She was at the height of her influence in the 1970s, and won an Oscar in 1982 for her song "Up Where We Belong" from the film An Officer and a Gentleman.

◎ The Best Of Buffy Sainte-Marie (Ace/Vanguard, UK).

A double-CD for the price of one, featuring her best material from the 1960s and early 1970s. Includes "Universal Soldier", "My Country, Tis of Thy People You're Dying" and "Now That the Buffalo's Gone".

Joanne Shenandoah

A member of the Iroquois Confederacy, Oneida Nation, Joanne Shenandoah is one of the leading singers addressing Native American issues.

◎ Once in a Red Moon (Canyon, US).

Her strongest album, including "Mother Earth Speaks" and "Patterns of the Drum", which is dedicated to her grandfather who "struggled to maintain the pattern of the drum while trying to survive in the modern world. His spirit continues with me today".

Southern Scratch

Led by bass guitarist Ron Joaquin – part of a multi-generational musical family – this southern Arizonan group is the best-known exponent of waila.

◎ Em-we:hejed: For All Of You (Canyon, US).

A good example of the polka-based instrumental music popular on and around the Tohono O'odham reservation of southern Arizona. Line-up of sax, accordion, guitars, percussion and drums. For old-time, fiddle-based chicken scratch try the Gu-Achi Fiddlers on Canyon.

Floyd Westerman

Born in 1918 of Lakota stock, Floyd Westerman is a singer, poet and actor. Sung in a country ballad idiom, his songs rank as some of the most powerful statements ever made about the unjust treatment of the Native population and the destruction of the environment.

◉ **The Land is Your Mother** and **Custer Died for Your Sins** (Trikont, Germany).

Two of Westerman's best albums combined on one CD. Good music and strong lyrics.

Andrew Vasquez

A Kiowa-Apache, Vasquez comes to the flute by way of dance. He has been an accomplished powwow dancer, and toured internationally with the New York-based American Indian Dance Theater.

◉ **Wind River** (Makoché, US).

Named after Vasquez' wife's Shoshone homeland, this album is among the more contemporary flute recordings, featuring a blend of percussion, ambient sounds and even a little poetry.

XIT

Formed in Albuquerque, New Mexico, Xit was a pioneering Native American rock group, featuring guitars, drums, pointed lyrics and Native American vocables. They disbanded in 1981.

◉ **Plight of the Red Man** (SOAR, US).

This 1970 disc is a classic protest album with such songs as "The Coming of the Whiteman". It also features the enduring, beautiful love song "Niha Shil Hozho" (I am Happy About You).

accordion enchilada

Most of south Texas was part of Mexico until the US claimed it in the mid-nineteenth century, so it's hardly surprising that a strong Mexican tradition still dominates in the state. But Texan music has evolved in its own distinctive way, and its influence has even crossed back over the Río Grande to Mexico itself. Like Tex-Mex food, the music has won consumers all round the world, but it packs a bigger punch than your average tortilla or enchilada. **Ramiro Burr**, based in San Antonio, Texas, outlines the story of conjunto and Tejano music.

With its fusion of Mexican *rancheras*, boleros, and foot-stomping polkas, **conjunto** (pronounced con-hoon-toe) music has been part of the Texas heartland for almost one hundred years. And despite hard times when the music was neglected and relegated to second-class status, conjunto is enjoying a thriving renaissance in the new millennium.

The word *conjunto* is Spanish for 'group', but in south Texas it has come to mean specifically the indigenous, accordion-led dance music, which in the finest American tradition blends the best of several cultures. The music is similar to Mexican *música norteña* (see p.469), but the emphasis in conjunto is on the danceable 2/4 polka beat rather than the nasal singing of norteño ballads. In the late 1950s conjunto spawned **Tejano**, a more pop-oriented urban form relying on keyboards and synthesizer in place of the accordion, but these are still good times for conjunto.

An authentic conjunto is basically a four-man unit with a *bajo sexto* (twelve-string guitar), bass, drums, and – at its heart – the indispensable **button accordion**. Just as the fiddle might define Western swing, you can't have conjunto without the accordion. "The accordion is probably one of the most important instruments in Texas music", says Pat Jasper, resources director of the Texas

PHILIP GOULD/ARHOOLIE

Narciso Martinez, Conjunto's first star

Folklife Festival. "The accordion is popular in many communities, but there is not one single tradition more vibrant than conjunto."

For years conjunto was considered disreputable dance music, good only for the lower classes. But in recent decades it has been 'discovered' by new Anglo audiences, and 'rediscovered' by its own people. Artists like **Flaco Jiménez**, **Mingo Saldivar**, **Valerio Longoria**, and the **Texas Tornados** have helped spread the music to Europe and Japan on their annual tours. Jiménez, in particular, has been a whirlwind ambassador for the music, recording with Dwight Yoakam, the Mavericks, Ry Cooder, Peter Rowan and even the Rolling Stones. "There's no mystery to conjunto's appeal", says veteran DJ, Guero Polkas. "Conjunto music is American made. It may have German influence and Mexican roots, but it was forged here in Texas. The bajo sexto and accordion is *nuestra música folklorica*, our folk music. It is to us what zydeco is to blacks in Louisiana, or bluegrass in Kentucky."

Conjunto Roots

According to conjunto historian Manuel Peña, the embryonic conjunto form originated in **south Texas** in the late nineteenth century when German, Czech and Polish immigrants introduced the accordion into the region. It was incorporated by early string bands who appreciated the instrument's volume and versatility, being able to play both melody and bass. These bands mixed the storytelling folk traditions of Mexican *corridos*, rancheras and boleros with European dance forms such as the waltz and polka. But the music and the lyrics always retained a rootsy focus, reflecting the concerns of the rural, agrarian southwest in songs about hard work, class struggles and longing.

While still in their infancy, American labels like Victor, Columbia and Okeh were looking for regional and 'ethnic' music, and the first Texan tracks were laid down in the late 1920s. Blind accordionist **Bruno Villareal** is generally credited as being the first conjunto-style accordionist on record (for Okeh in 1930), but the late accordionist **Narciso Martínez** is considered the father of conjunto music. Born in 1911 in Reynosa, Tamaulipas, Mexico, Martínez lived in the Río Grande valley settlement of San Benito, following the migrant work-circuit by day and playing by night. Martínez rapidly earned a reputation as one of the most accomplished accordion players in Texas and was instrumental in establishing the basic conjunto unit, together with bajo sexto player Santiago Almeida. While Bruno Villareal's style was very traditional, with equal emphasis on melody and bass, Martínez emphasised the treble part and left the bass parts to his guitarist. This became the model for all the subsequent conjunto groups. Like most south Texan accordionists, he played a two-row button accordion – until the 1950s when three row models became widely available.

Nicknamed 'El Huracán del Valle', Martínez's career stretched from the early 1930s right through to his death in 1992. In the thirties and forties instrumental dance music was popular, until supplanted by norteño-style singers and singing duos after World War II. During this latter period Martínez was a leading accompanist to popular singers like Carmen y Laura and Lydia Mendoza. Neither the recordings (a flat thirty-dollar fee per album) nor the performances (often ten dollars for a *sol a sol*, sundown to sunup) were lucrative for Martínez, but he toured widely, playing dances and shows until sidelined by the new-style bands in the late 1950s. Out of his hundreds of recordings, perhaps the best-known are the polka "La Chicharonera", his historic first recording of 1936, and two of his personal favourites, "La Chulada" and "La Desvelada" from the 1950s. In 1983 he was given a US National Heritage Fellowship but

Conjunto Rhythms

The prominent rhythm in **Tejano conjunto** is the polka, with its duple *oom-pah, oom-pah* beat, which originated in Bavaria. Most of the other conjunto dance rhythms also originated in Europe, like the *vals* (French waltz), *shottis* (schottische) and mazurka. The *huapango* comes from Mexico and the *cumbia* from further afield, in Colombia. Most bands also interpret Mexican song forms: *boleros* (romantic, or sad love songs) *rancheras* (songs idealising hacienda and rural life) and *corridos* (ballads, often based on real incidents, about the historical US-American conflicts, criminals, smuggling, immigration or the general hardship of life). Alternatively, like rancheras, they may be lyrical songs about bad women, alcohol, lost love or other incidents reflecting the social conditions of the time.

he never chose to become an American citizen, stressing his allegiance to his Mexican heritage.

While Martínez came from a rural background, another great conjunto accordionist, the late **Don Santiago Jiménez**, came from the city of San Antonio. Known as 'El Flaco' (The Skinny One), Jiménez is noted by historians for his introduction of the *tololoche* (double bass) into the conjunto ensemble. Like Martínez, Jiménez also began recording in the mid-thirties. Among the dozens of Jiménez's recordings, his most notable works include "Viva Seguin" and "La Piedrera". His legacy, however, also includes the First Family of Conjunto, in the form of his two sons, the traditionalist Santiago Jiménez Jnr, and Leonardo 'Flaco' Jiménez, who has more progressive tendencies (see below).

Música Norteña

In a music heavily dominated by men, **Lydia Mendoza**, the First Queen of Tejano Music, stands out. She started singing and playing the mandolin in 1927 and her songs with mandolin or guitar are classics in the sentimental and melancholy style.

Armando Marroquín and Texas' most prolific local label, Ideal Records were behind the popularisation of female *duetos* after World War II. Marroquín's wife and sister-in-law Carmen y Laura (Hernandez) were Ideal's first recording act whose initial hit "Se Me Fue Mi Amor" lamented the absence of a woman's beloved, posted overseas on military service. These female duetos singing Mexican-style ranchera songs were accompanied by the standard conjunto accordion and bajo sexto backing and created a popular style peculiar to south Texas, **música norteña**.

The Mendoza family started their recording career in a San Antonio hotel room in 1928, and Lydia Mendoza made her first solo recordings in 1934. After the war, Lydia's sisters Juanita and María Mendoza became hugely popular on the jukeboxes as **Las Hermanas Mendoza**. Almost all the lyrics for these women were written from the male point of view, about women's faithlessness and suchlike, which audiences enjoyed hear-

ing sung by sweet female voices. A few of them, however, such as "Mal Hombre", recorded by Lydia Mendoza in 1934, broke the mould:

I was still a young girl
When, by chance, you found me
And with your worldly charm
You took away my innocence
It was then that you did to me

Lydia Mendoza in the 1930s

U.T. INSTITUTE OF TEXAN CULTURES/ARHOOLIE

What all of your kind do to women
So don't be surprised now
If I tell you to your face
What you really are
Cold-hearted man!
Your soul is so vile, it has no name
You are so despicable, you are evil
You are a cold-hearted man

Lydia Mendoza and Carmen y Laura were frequently accompanied by top notch conjunto bands like Narciso Martínez and Santiago Alameida, and by Paulino Bernal from the next generation of accordion virtuosi.

Another important female vocalist, who rose to fame during the 1950s, was **Chelo Silva**, the so-called 'Queen of the Bolero'. The bolero in question was of the Mexican variety, a romantic song, as opposed to the Spanish triple-time or Cuban duple-time dance. It was given a particularly expressive power by Silva's low, sultry voice. She worked with some fine conjunto acts (including Flaco Jiménez) and sax players, but also made several splendid recordings without accordion, using just guitar accompaniment. Her songs speak wistfully of love, betrayal and desire, often from a female point of view.

Post-War Conjunto Developments

Riding on the booming post-war years, one of the pioneers of the conjunto mainstream was **Valerio Longoria**, from San Antonio. His first button accordion cost ten dollars and he remembers, in the early years, being paid just four dollars for playing at an all-night street party. He is noted for introducing romantic Mexican bolero melodies to the accordion, and adding drums to the conjunto line-up. An excellent singer, he was one of the first to popularise the Mexican *canción ranchera* in conjunto music and he also introduced Colombian *cumbias* into Texas dancehalls, notably the catchy "El Canoero". Longoria received a National Heritage award in 1986.

The next important name in conjunto was **Tony de la Rosa**, who began his career in the late 1950s from his rural home in Sarita. Not only did he achieve phenomenal success, he also exerted a huge stylistic influence on the music. Like Longoria he was noted for his rancheras, but his most significant development was to transform the acoustic conjunto band into a big modern line-up with drum kit, amplified bajo sexto and electric bass. These changes, which arrived along with the fashion for soulful duets, slowed the music down from the frantic pace of the rural dances into a slower, more sophisticated idiom.

As an accomplished accordionist de La Rosa also emphasised the melodic side of the instrument and thrilled audiences with lengthy and intricate accordion runs in his choppy, staccato style. In the early 1960s he dominated the conjunto music scene, attracting packed houses wherever he played. Over the course of a lengthy career, he recorded more than 75 albums, his repertoire including many polka instrumentals and a number of tunes that have become standards: "La Periodista", "Palamo Negra", "El Circo", "El Sube y Baja" and his instrumental adaptation of "Atotonilco", an old Mexican favourite. Today de la Rosa is semi-retired, but he still makes occasional appearances.

A third great player, still active, who rose to fame in the 1960s, was **Esteban Jordan** (aka Steve Jordan), the most radical accordion player of them all. He started out playing relatively conventional conjunto with his brothers, with whom he recorded as Los Hermanos Jordan. However, as the decade rolled on, Jordan's accordion style grew ever wilder and he would improvise solos like a rock guitarist: no surprise then that his treatment of the accordion has been likened to that of Jerry Lee Lewis on piano or Jimi Hendrix on guitar. Again, he introduced a new sound to conjunto, one which was immortalised in a range of Hohner accordions designed by Jordan and marketed as the 'Steve Jordan Tex-Mex Rockordion'.

A key band of the 1960s and early 1970s was **El Conjunto Bernal** – led by Paulino Bernal and his brother Eloy – which also enjoyed great commercial success, selling thousands of records and filling dancehalls and ballrooms across the southwest. The brothers also introduced a new sound, one which featured faster, more upbeat polka rhythms and close two- and three-part harmonies. This art developed from their pivotal recording of "Mi Unico Camino" with Rubén Perez on lead vocals and the brothers Bernal providing the second and third part harmonies.

Tejano

By the 1950s, there were two popular genres in Mexican-American music, the conjuntos and the *orquestas Tejanas* (Texan big bands). The former were for the lower classes while the latter catered for ballroom dancing and the affluent. But in the mid-fifties conjunto spawned its modern urban cousin, **Tejano**, when bandleader **Isidro Lopez**

USA

IDEAL

Isidro Lopez

brought conjunto's defining feature, the accordion, into his big band. Just as modern country music evolved from rural folk, modern Tejano music grew out of its conjunto roots.

Lopez heavily influenced **Little Joe** but early rock'n'roll had an equally strong pull. When Little Joe first started, it was as Little Joe and the Latinaires with the band decked out in glittery costumes and performing choreographed dance steps. Gradually, the big band or orquesta Tejana style faded away and mainstream pop took over.

By the 1960s there were only two viable music movements: the earthy accordion-led, folksy conjunto and the big city sound of Sunny Ozuna, Little Joe, Augustine Ramirez and others. In the mid-sixties **Sunny Ozuna** scored with a couple of English-language hits, "Talk To Me" and "Smile Now, Cry Later". But by the end of the decade he had switched over to become a fully-fledged Tejano artist, knocking out a series of Tejano hits – "Mi Chulita", "Reina de mi Amor" and "Carinito". Bandleader **Freddie Martínez** made his move in the 1970s with the super hits "Te Traigo Estas Flores" and "Botoncito de Carino".

Ozuna and Martinez were typical of the new Tejano groups – small combos that utilised horn sections and keyboards. The emphasis though was on dance music: Tejano and covers of Top 40 hits.

In the mid-seventies Little Joe scored his biggest hit with the new Tejano anthem "Las Nubes", a rush of irresistibly danceable music with melancholy lyrics. The decade also saw the rise of the horn/accordion fusion outfit **Roberto Pulido y Los Clasicos** and the seminal **Latin Breed**, whose horn sections and jazzy arrangements recalled the orquestas Tejanas of the past.

Tejano artists reflected the **pop culture** of the time, from the long hair and bellbottoms look of the 1970s to the emphasis on keyboards and synthesizers of the 1980s. When MTV dawned, it strongly influenced Tejano artists like La Mafia and Mazz, who pioneered the concept of Tejano dance as a visual concert, complete with the big lights, sounds, dry ice and other arena rock theatrics. While the look had changed to reflect American mainstream rock, the emphasis was still on getting crowds to pack the dancefloor. By now Tejano groups played the latest disco hits of the day intermixed with their own foot-stomping Tejano tunes.

The 1980s were significant for both the big city Tejano and folksy conjunto. Two major pop culture successes set the stage for the resurgence of both genres – **Los Lobos'** grand success with the *La Bamba* movie and soundtrack, and the overwhelming sales of **Linda Ronstadt**'s roots ranchera album *Canciones de Mi Padre*. For many Mexican-

CAROLINE GREYSHOK/WARNER BROTHERS

Los Lobos: the wolves who took "La Bamba" to the world

Americans in the US who were often torn between being 'American' and assimilating fully (losing one's accent and mother tongue), and remaining 'Mexican' and losing job and social opportunities, the pop crossover success of Ronstadt and Los Lobos seemed to prove that one could have it both ways. You could hold on to your cultural roots and still enjoy success as a fully integrated American.

At the same time, census and economic reports indicated that Hispanic or Latinos in America were the fastest growing segments of the population. Their combined economic, cultural and political power would be something to be reckoned with in the 1990s. Meanwhile, there was a greater appreciation for roots music worldwide, a kind of backlash against technology and over-production in the music industry. It was against this powerful demographic backdrop that modern Tejano and roots conjunto enjoyed their biggest renaissance.

Flaco Jiménez

Accordion Revival

A worldwide interest in roots music, from African rhythms and Louisiana zydeco to Mexico boleros and conjunto polkas, was further fuelled when the **accordion** was 'discovered' by many contemporary rock, country, pop, jazz and Tex-Mex artists. Mainstream rock artists from John Cougar Mellencamp and Bruce Hornsby to Paul Simon and Tom Waits appreciated the accordion as a versatile, dynamic instrument that evoked a sense of humanity in a seemingly over-programmed, computerised world. For **Steve Jordan**, there was no comparison – the attraction of the accordion over electronic wizardry lay in its humanity and individuality: "There's way too much synthetic stuff being played right now. To me, it tells me they're being lazy with this programmed music machinery. There's nothing like the accordion man ... and it's hard to learn and hard to play."

Conjunto has had players like Steve Jordan who have incorporated new jazz and rock styles, and veterans like Valerio Longoria and Mingo Saldivar who have helped perpetuate the traditional form. But there had never been an artist who combined both styles, or who played with rock and country artists. Until that is, premiere conjunto accordionist **Flaco Jiménez** appeared on the scene. The son of Santiago Jiménez Sr – the most widely travelled ambassador of conjunto music in the world – Flaco learned to play by watching his father but soon learned to appreciate other styles such as jazz, rock and blues. He developed a faster, flashier style of his own and in 1974 appeared in the highly acclaimed documentary film *Chulas Fronteras*, pro-

duced by Les Blank and Arhoolie/Folklyric producer Chris Strachwitz. He went on to win his first Grammy in 1986 for best Mexican/American performance with his rendition of his father's "Ay Te Dejo en San Antonio".

Ay te dejo en San Antonio
(I'm leaving you here in San Antonio)

I don't even want to kiss you, or you to kiss me
Or to look at you or even hear your voice
Because I found out you have another lover
And in Laredo you already had two others

You like to dance very much
And you dance right to the beat
You'll go all the way to Laredo
And still want more and more

I'm a rancher, a gambler and a rambler
And now I'm leaving and never coming back
You left me without money and without a car
You've taken to running round the world on me

Now I'm going, I'm leaving you here in San Antonio
I can't take away your cheating ways
There's times you look just like the Devil
When you move your little waist to dance

Ranchera, written by Santiago Jimenez, Snr.

USA

In 1990, Flaco joined Augie Meyers, Doug Sahm (both formerly with Sir Douglas Quintet), and Tejano singer Freddie Fender as part of the new group **The Texas Tornados**, and later that year the band was awarded a Grammy for "Soy de San Luis", a tune also written by Don Santiago Jiménez Sr. A major part of this group's success is obviously their cross-generational and cross-cultural appeal. While Meyers and Sahm attracted fans of their late 1960s Tex-Mex rock (from their days as the Sir Douglas Quintet), Fender and Jiménez brought their Tejano and conjunto devotees. Sahm died in 1999.

Flaco has also teamed up with other well-known musicians to form a larger Tejano super group, **Los Super Seven**, comprising Los Lobos' David Hidalgo and Cesar Rosas, Freddy Fender

MARK GUERRA/REPRISE

USA

Tex-Mex supergroup, The Texas Tornados

and Flaco himself from the Texas Tornados, country singer Rick Trevino, Tejano/R&B singer Ruben Ramos and Texas rocker Joe Ely. Their eponymous debut CD of 1998 was a slick and stylish success.

The other player in the Jiménez legacy is **Santiago Jiménez Jr**. Unlike his brother Flaco, Santiago plays straight-ahead traditional conjunto. With an appreciation of his father's contributions and his interest in keeping the traditional style alive, Santiago has always played in a natural but beautiful style, free from any pop adornments or pretensions. Among his many hits, Santiago has made a point of rerecording his father's classics, including "La Piedrera", "Viva Segiun" and "Soy de San Luis".

Current Trends

Alongside the big names like Flaco and Santiago Jiménez Jr, modern conjunto has an impressive range of players: neo-traditionalists Los Palominos and Intocable; the more contemporary and rare phenomenon of female accordionist and bandleader Eva Ybarra; the Austin, Texas, Polish-Mexican band, Los Pinkys; and even a credible Japanese conjunto, Los Gatos.

Palominos and **Intocable** play classic conjunto with the standard four-man conjunto ensemble that includes accordion and bajo sexto. Palominos stand out for their perfect pitch two and three-part vocal harmonies, while Intocable front man Ricky Munoz sounds a lot like norteño legend Ramon Ayala, albeit thirty years ago. **Los Pinkys** are fronted by bajo sexto player Bradley Jaye Williams, a Polish-American from Michigan, and Austin native and accordionist Isidro Samilpa. Their debut record *Esta Pasion* (on the Rounder label) features a mix of polka stompers, brooding boleros and swinging cumbias.

Eva Ybarra was born into a musical family in San Antonio and started playing in cantinas and dance-halls at an early age, but she has had to fight for recognition as a female accordionist and bandleader. Ybarra is an accordionist, vocalist and composer and her classic conjunto band features two- and three-part harmony vocals with Gloria Abadia and Guadalupe Betancourt.

Los Gatos, formed by Japanese rock guitarist-turned-accordionist Kenji 'El Gato' Katsube, played the Tejano Conjunto Festival for the first time in 1993. They won such rave reviews that they've been back every year. In 1997, the group, which includes three other musicians from Osaka and Kyoto, have produced two CDs on the Corpus Christi-based Hacienda Record label, their latest produced by none other than Kenji's longtime hero, Tony de la Rosa. The CD even features a duet with de la Rosa and they sing in Spanish, English and Japanese.

In the 1990s, the most popular figure in Tex-Mex was, beyond any doubt, **Selena**. This late lamented Texan legend started singing as a child in her family's restaurant and although she grew up speaking English, her father insisted on Spanish for her career. She won her first Tejano music awards aged 15 and was signed by EMI Latin. With a raunchy stage show and best-selling discs like *Amor Prohibido* she firmly inhabited crossover territory, running a fashion boutique as an A-List celebrity. But it all came to a tragic end in 1995, when Selena, aged 23, was shot in the back by her former fan-club manager.

The current queen of Tex-Mex music (and a good deal more) is San Antonio-born **Tish Hinojosa**. The youngest of thirteen children in a Spanish-speaking family, she remembers: "There was always music in our house. My mother listened to Mexican radio in the kitchen and she loved the finer, romantic side of Mexican culture. My Dad was a mechanic in a cemetery and he loved the

fun accordion music and the conjunto tunes on the juke box. Of course, through my older sisters, I was also immersed in the jangly pop of the sixties – Aretha Franklin, the Byrds and the Beatles."

A Rough Guide to San Antonio – Where to Hear, Buy, and Dance to Conjunto

Not without justification is **San Antonio** recognised as the world capital of Tejano and conjunto music. There are no fewer than five radio stations that play Tejano either full- or part-time. There are a dozen major dance-halls or nightclubs in the area, with either great bands or pretty good DJs.

Radio Stations
KEDA-AM (1540) is the longtime conjunto authority in central Texas. The station celebrated its 32nd year in central Texas in 1998 and they still haven't changed the format – the latest in conjunto, Tejano and norteño groups, with a special emphasis on homegrown and regional acts.
KXTN-FM (107) is hardcore Tejano, but neo-traditional conjunto bands get regular play.
KLEY-FM (94.1) plays a regional/Mexican variety with norteño, ballads and some Tejano.
KCOR-AM (1350) and **KSAH-AM (720)** play a mix of contemporary hits, including a heavy dose of rancheras, grupo, banda, conjunto and norteño music.

San Antonio Dancehalls
Tejano Texas, Grissom and Timberpath. For years the king of Tejano dancehalls, the club has live music on Thursdays and Saturdays. With a capacity of 3000, there's lots of dancing and walking space.

Far West Rodeo, N.E Loop 410 at Interstate 35. Another monster club that does double duty: in the summer of 1998 it was booking live country and Tejano bands on alternative weeks.
Smaller Clubs include: Fiesta Club, 2035 Pleasanton; El Ranchito, 7167 Somerset; Lerma's Nite Club, 1602 N. Zarzamora; Randy's Ballroom, 1534 Bandera.

Festivals
The musical highpoint of the year is San Antonio's **Tejano Conjunto Festival** held in May. It features more than thirty groups playing five nights of outdoor concerts on a hilltop setting in the city's West Side. Young guns come to learn from the pros, pioneers are recognised, but above all, it's a time to dance. Contact: Guadalupe Cultural Arts Center, 1301 Guadalupe, San Antonio, Texas 78207-5519 (☎210/271-3151; fax 271 3480).

Record Shops
If you can't find what you need at the major *Blockbuster* or *Sam Goody* retail chains (which are usually pretty well stocked in the hottest titles), you can check out three good mom-and-pop stores: *Janie's Record Shop*, 129 Bandera; *El Norteno*, 6411 N.E. Loop 410, or *Del Bravo*, 554 Highway 90 West.

Drawing on all these sources, and particularly the Mexican corrida and conjunto repertoire, Hinojosa's soft, but focused voice and songwriting ability has made her a major star of the current Texan musical scene. Her albums, on the Watermelon and Rounder labels, feature her rootsier Spanish repertoire, while her crossover albums for Warner Brothers include a high percentage of English-language ballads.

discography

Virtually the whole history of Tex-Mex music exists on the Arhoolie label based in El Cerrito, California. Arhoolie boss Chris Strachwitz has had a long interest in the music and acquired Ideal Records when the company was sold. Alongside a large number of excellent Arhoolie recordings of leading artists, the company has released many historic recordings from the Ideal and other labels. The best are featured in the listing below, but all are worthwhile and come with comprehensive notes (many of which we've drawn on for this article), photographs and often translations of lyrics.

Compilations

 ¡Conjunto! Texas-Mexican Border Music
(Rounder, US).

There are three volumes of these excellent compilations of Texan conjuntos and similar Mexican conjuntos norteños. Vol 1 includes Tony de la Rosa, Steve Jordan, Flaco Jiménez, Los Cachorros de Juan Villareal, Ramon Ayala y Los Bravos Del Norte and others. Song translations included.

Conjuntos Norteños (Arhoolie, US).

A great pairing of Mex and Tex, two excellent bands from either side of the border. From Mexico, Los Pingüinos Del Norte (The Penguins of the North) are a rural-style band with accordion, guitar and bass, singing nasal corrido ballads live in a cantina in 1970. From Texas, The Trio San Antonio is led by accordionist Fred Zimmerle who played bajo sexto to Valerio Longoria for many years.

15 Early Tejano Classics (Arhoolie, US).

Music from the 1950s and the birth of Tejano, with its smoother big-band sound and prominent saxes. Includes Isidro Lopez, Carmen y Laura, Beto Villa, Tony de la Rosa, Freddie Fender, bolero queen Chelo Silva and others. Part of Arhoolie's budget American Master Series.

15 Tex-Mex Conjunto Classics (Arhoolie, US).

A great sampler from the Arhoolie catalogue of down-home conjunto. It includes all the essential names: Narciso Martínez, Lydia Mendoza, Flaco Jiménez, Santiago Jiménez (both father and son), Tony de la Rosa, Conjunto Bernal, Steve Jordan and more.

Norteño and Tejano Accordion Pioneers 1929–1939 (Arhoolie, US).

A great compilation charting the early history of the conjunto accordion, reissued from original 78rpm recordings. Includes Bruno Villareal, Narciso Martínez (and his first recording "La Chicharonera"), Don Santiago Jiménez and lesser-known names.

Tejano Roots
(Arhoolie, US).

A quick education in the big names of conjunto and Tejano music. Includes Narciso Martínez, Lydia Mendoza, Carmen y Laura, Chelo Silva, Valerio Longoria, Tony de la Rosa, Conjunto Bernal, Isidro Lopez and Freddy Fender. Great notes about the artists and the Texas recording industry.

Tejano Roots: The Women (Arhoolie, US).

The pioneering women of early Tex-Mex music, often accompanied by big-name conjunto musicians like Narciso Martínez and Conjunto Bernal. Includes Carmen y Laura, Hermanas Guerrero, bolero queen Chelo Silva and a couple of Lydia Mendoza tracks.

Artists

Conjunto Bernal

Premier conjunto ensemble, led by accordionist Paulino Bernal with his brother Eloy on bajo sexto. They pioneered an unforgettable musical trail in the late 1950s through the use of two accordions and two-and-three-part vocal harmonies.

Mi Unico Camino (Arhoolie, US).

Captured in their prime on the Ideal Records label. Achingly beautiful harmonies in tales of romantic encounters, failures and rediscoveries. The killer title track alone is worth the price of the CD.

Tish Hinojosa

Born in San Antonio, resident in Austin, Tish Hinojosa is currently the leading female vocalist of Tex-Mex music, with ten albums to her credit. She sings great roots music in the Mexican corrida and Texan conjunto tradition, plus crossover ballads in English on her Warner albums.

 Dreaming From the Labyrinth/ Sonar del Laberinto (Warner Bros, US).

Effortlessly switching from Spanish to English and back, in this 1996 album Hinojosa pours through a likeable set of original songs of hope ("Batalla de Hombre No Habra"), philosophy ("Sacrificios"), and dreams ("Orilla de un Sonar").

Frontejas (Rounder, US).

Hinojosa's best roots album with just one duff duet with Ray Benson in Spanish and English. Other guest artists include master accordionists Flaco Jiménez, Santiago Jiménez Jr and Eva Ybarra.

Flaco Jiménez

Accordionist Leonardo 'Flaco' Jiménez was born in 1939 into one of the great families of conjunto music and started playing dances in the early 1950s. Early on he developed a fast, flashy accordion style. He has played with musicians as diverse as Dwight Yoakam, Ry Cooder and the Rolling Stones. He is a member of the two Tex-Mex super-groups, The Texas Tornados and Los Super Seven.

 The Best of Flaco Jiménez (Arhoolie, US).

This is Flaco at his most traditional, with small acoustic line-ups put together for his sixtieth birthday in 1999. The disc kicks off with his father's classic ranchera "Ay te dejo en San Antonio", and the edgy "El Guero Polkas", accompanied by squeals of joy from either the guitarist or bass player in the trio, is splendid.

Buena Suerte, Senorita (Arista/Texas, US).

A 1997 album of pure joy that goes back to the traditional, raw conjunto sound. Features Jiménez ripping through touching ballads ("Mis Brazos Te Esperan"), rollicking polka stomps ("Mala Movida"), pulse-quickening rancheras ("Contigo Nomas") and instrumentals featuring his weaving accordion runs.

 Los Super Seven (RCA/BMG, US).

Flaco's typical Tejano/conjunto fusion in a seven-piece super-group, whose line-up includes David Hidalgo of Los Lobos and Freddy Fender of the Texan Tornados. Solid roots rancheras, brooding boleros and whip-sharp polka stomps are the chief item on the menu here, crisply delivered by a handful of old pros: Highlights include the infectious polka "Margarita", the reflective ballad "Mi Ranchito" and the pulse-quickening huapango "La Madrugada".

Don Santiago Jiménez

Along with Narciso Martínez, Santiago Jiménez (1913–1984) was one of the important and influential early figures in conjunto music. He recorded most extensively after the war in the late 1940s and 1950s. The family tradition continues with his sons Flaco and Santiago Jr.

 His First & Last Recordings (Arhoolie, US).

What the title says – two sessions from 1937 and 1979, the latter featuring Flaco on bajo sexto. Both recordings feature excellent trios of accordion, guitar and double bass – the typical Santiago Jiménez sound.

Santiago Jiménez Jr

Son of the fabled conjunto legend Santiago Jiménez, and brother of Flaco, Santiago Jr (born in 1944) has steadfastly played in his father's traditional style, bringing the classic conjunto sound to new audiences.

 Corridos de la Frontera (Watermelon, US).

A button accordion, bajo sexto (twelve-string guitar) and a bass is all Jiménez needs to recreate old-time conjunto magic. Listen to the corridos of "Valente Quintero" and "Jacinto Trevino" and hear tales of men facing hard times. In "Preso sin Delito" Jiménez sings about a man wrongly imprisoned, and in "La Carga Blanca" about ill-fated drug-smugglers.

Esteban (Steve) Jordan

The most interesting and unorthodox accordionist in Tex-Mex music, Jordan started recording in the late 1950s and is still active today. He sticks to traditional triple-row button accordions, but he sometimes adds electronics and his playing is innovative. He's often known as 'El Parche' for the patch over his right eye.

The Many Sounds of Steve Jordan (Arhoolie, US).

Beginning with raw conjunto from the early 1960s, the album continues with his most celebrated release from the 1980s: "El Corrido De Jhonny El Pachuco".

Los Lobos

Though big on the rock circuit, Los Lobos have never forsaken their Mexican roots. They've bridged both worlds in a cohesive mix of roots rock and folksy ballads.

 La Pistol y El Corazon (Slash, US).

Old Mexican roots music is brought to life with traditional instruments. Given the band's reputation for party rock grooves, there's a lot of restraint on this mostly acoustic disc.

Valerio Longoria

Born in 1924, Longoria got his first accordion aged seven and first recorded aged twenty-two. He was one of the seminal figures in the development of conjunto during the 1950s and remains an elder-statesman of the music today.

 Caballo Vieja (Arhoolie, US).

Absolutely first-class accordion playing in a quartet including his two sons Flavio (sax) and Valerio Jr (bajo sexto) and grandson Valerio (drums). Rancheras, cumbias, boleros and polkas, including some of Valerio's own compositions recorded in 1989.

Narciso Martínez

Known as the father of conjunto music, Martínez (1911–1992) established the conjunto style and his accordion playing influenced all that followed. He first recorded in 1936 and worked with bajo sexto player Santiago Almeida. He was the first artist to record for Ideal Records, in 1946, and accompanied singers Lydia

Mendoza and Carmen y Laura. In his latter days he worked as a zookeeper in Brownsville.

 Narciso Martinez:
Father of the Texas-Mexican Conjunto (Arhoolie, US).

This essential collection doesn't include Martínez's earliest material (this can be found on another Arhoolie disc), but a selection of his tracks recorded for Ideal between 1946 and 1961. Mainly instrumental (accordion and bajo sexto), but includes a few tracks with Lydia Mendoza, Carmen y Laura and Las Hermanas Mendoza.

Lydia Mendoza

Born in 1916 to Mexican immigrants who fled the chaos of the Mexican Revolution, Lydia was taught to play guitar and mandolin by her mother. The family performed in bars and restaurants and started recording in the late 1920s. Lydia's first big hit was "Mal Hombre" in 1934 which became her theme song. She went on to work with seminal musicians Narciso Martínez, Tony de la Rosa and Beto Villa, and recorded over a thousand songs.

Mal Hombre (Arhoolie, US).

The earliest recordings from 1928 and the 1930s, featuring "Mal Hombre" (vocals and guitar) and the family band.

Los Pinkys

Polish-American Bradley Jaye Williams, from Saginaw, Michigan, moved to Austin where he met up with conjunto accordionist Isidro Samilpa in 1993. Williams' mother was raised on Polish polkas and from an early age Williams loved a variety of styles from country to conjunto. Samilpa is an old conjunto hand who played the Sixth Street (the Austin equivalent of New Orleans' Bourbon Street) circuit for years.

Esta Pasion (Rounder, US).

The thumping electric bass lines and rippling accordion runs are all here in full force as Los Pinkys tear through a variety of standard rancheras ("Pa'Que Me Sirve la Vida" and "El Parrandero") and slow-burning ballads ("Angel de mis Anhelos").

Tony de la Rosa

Born in 1931, de la Rosa was one of the most important figures in conjunto music in the 1950s and 1960s. He was principally responsible for modernising and electrifying the traditional conjunto sound.

Atotonilco (Arhoolie, US).

A great cross-section of songs dating from 1953–1964 which chart de la Rosa's band as it developed from its rural roots to create the modern conjunto sound. Many old favourites, including "Palamo Negra", "El Circo" and the title track.

Selena

Selena (1971–1995) achieved a large popular following in a tragically short time. She started singing in her family's restaurant and then on the Tejano circuit of bars, clubs and regional fairs. Her music always remained something of a family business. Picked up by EMI Latin while she was still in her teens, she won a Grammy for Selena Live!. Aged 23, Selena was murdered by her business and fan-club manager, whose integrity had been called into question. Her life was the subject of the movie Selena! (1997).

Amor Prohibido (EMI Latin, US).

Much of Selena's output was in English, and much of that was soft-centred crossover, but this best-selling album captures her sex appeal and her most authentically Tejano sound.

Chelo Silva

The Queen of the Bolero, Silva (1922–1988) rose to fame singing on the radio in the early 1950s. With a low, expressive voice, she was signed to Columbia records and became very popular in Mexico, Latin America and Spain as well as the US. She continued singing until the 1980s.

La Reina Tejana del Bolero (Arhoolie, US).

For those who've had enough of all those jaunty polkas, this is a really beautiful collection of slower romantic boleros taken from her recordings for Ideal in the late fifties and early sixties, with some exquisite guitar, sax and accordion accompaniments. As an extraordinary extra there are a few numbers from a KCOR live radio broadcast (with Flaco Jiménez) recorded off-air from a car-radio in 1983.

Eva Ybarra

Eva Ybarra started playing the accordion aged four, and was performing in local restaurants by the time she was six. Celebrated as practically the only female conjunto accordionist and band leader, Ybarra 'La reina de acordeón' has established a reputation beyond her novelty value. She plays a light, punchy accordion and writes much of her own material.

A Mi San Antonio (Rounder, US).

A good collection of original ballads, polkas, rancheras and cumbias. Great chromatic accordion runs on Ybarra's wistful "Triste Adiós".

USA

try a little fairydust

The USA has embraced 'World Music' for almost as long as popular music has been around: tango, mambo, rhumba, calypso, polka, Tex-Mex, reggae, merengue – all of these have erupted as crazes and created enduring followings. American musicians, too, from Classical and especially jazz traditions, have long experimented with global sounds. But in recent years it has been a handful of American (and British) rock musicians that have been central to establishing the whole World Music genre, with key movers and shakers like Paul Simon, David Byrne and Ry Cooder (and in Britain, Peter Gabriel) spreading fairydust around the globe through their collaborations, and creating a new mainstream market for global sounds. **Nigel Williamson** and **Mark Ellingham** chart the action.

American **jazz players** took Latin rhythms for granted in their repertoire, pretty much from the outset, and as far back as the 1950s John Coltrane and others were exploring the time signatures and tones of Indian music (see East-West Fusions, p.109), and looking at the African roots of jazz. By the 1970s these musical adventures had led to a real world-jazz fusion in the work of trumpeter **Don Cherry**, who was influenced (like many others on the US jazz scene) by working with Dollar Brand, the exiled South African pianist who later took the name **Abdullah Ibrahim**. World Music also played a part in the 1960s phenomenon of **lounge music**, when **Martin Denny** took Hawaiian and Pacific sounds into records such as *Exotica* and **Les Baxter** presented Peruvian chanteuse **Yma Sumak** (*Voice of the Xtabay*).

But in the **American rock world** – which is the focus of this article – the roots of World Music fusion are to be found in a series of 1970s albums from those pioneering spirits Taj Mahal, Mickey Hart and Ry Cooder, and, building upon these, in the later work of David Byrne and Bill Laswell.

Pioneers and Samplers

Bluesman **Taj Mahal** was perhaps the most groundbreaking and committed world fusionist. His 1972 album *Happy Just To Be Like I Am* took as its theme the musical trade routes between black America and Africa, and two years later he turned to Caribbean influences on *Mo Roots*.

Mickey Hart, drummer with the Grateful Dead, put together one of the earliest rock-world fusion ensembles, the **Diga Rhythm Band**, with the tabla player **Zakir Hussain** (again, see East-West Fusions). **Ry Cooder**, meantime, took a first step towards World Music with his 1976 outing, *Chicken Skin Music*, featuring Tex-Mex and Hawaiian flavours, courtesy of the accordionist **Flaco Jiménez** and the slack-key guitar master **Gabby Pahinui**.

Another significant move came with experiments in sampling global sounds. **Joni Mitchell** used a backing track from **The Drummers of Burundi** on her *The Hissing of Summer Lawns* (1975), a move which was taken further in Britain by the producer **Simon Jeffes** (of seminal global-magpies Penguin Café Orchestra) who revived Adam Ant's pop career with the injection of Burundi rhythms, and in Germany by the group Can and their bassist and 'radio player' Holger Czukay (notably on the 1979 album, *Movies*). However the most interesting and influential world sampling album was **David Byrne** and **Brian Eno**'s *My Life In The Bush Of Ghosts* (1981), which presented a collage of African and Arabic vocals and fragments of radio recordings over hypnotic dance grooves. The record stands at the root of the whole 'Global Dance' movement, which went huge, especially in Britain, with the digital technology of the 1990s.

These early world fusion excursions co-incided with the emergence of a network of small, indepedent **record labels**, making available to US and European audiences music that, previously, could only be heard on locally issued vinyl or cassettes. In Britain, **Peter Gabriel** helped launch the crucial WOMAD festival in 1982, and toured with Senegalese star **Youssou N'Dour** – notably on the Amnesty International world tour with Bruce

Paul Simon on tour with Ladysmith Black Mambazo

Springsteen, Sting and Tracy Chapman in 1987. Meantime a bunch of record producers and music promoters had a meeting in a London pub and hit upon the tag 'World Music' for their wares.

However, for the mainstream music industry – and its mass markets – these developments made little impact until the appearance and huge commercial success of an album called *Graceland* (1986). Step on up, Paul Simon . . .

Amazing Graceland

The *Graceland* album could easily not have happened. When **Paul Simon** visited South Africa in 1984–85 to record with local artists such as the a cappella group **Ladysmith Black Mambazo** and zulu jivers **Mahlathini and the Mahotella Queens**, he was defying a UN ban on cultural links with South Africa (although there was no actual ban on recording there). Simon seems to have blundered into this situation without much thought, but the ends this time justified the means. Not only was Simon's flagging career revived, with stunning songs such as "Homeless", and a million-selling, Grammy-winning disc, but the album did enormous favours to the South African artists involved and to the whole profile of African and 'World' music.

Subsequently, Paul Simon paid his dues to Ladysmith, producing their successful (and Grammy winning) album, *Shaka Zulu*. Prompted by singer Milton Nascimento, he then turned his attentions

to Brazil on 1990's *The Rhythm of the Saints*, employing the Afro-style percussion of **Olodum** from Bahia. The album also picked up on other global rhythms, notably West African highlife style guitar from Cameroonian **Vincent Nguini**, and Puerto Rican bomba, recorded in New York. Simon next resurfaced in 1997 with a compelling, if flawed and ill-fated, Broadway musical, *Capeman*, featuring a Puerto Rican soundtrack and salsa stars **Rubén Blades** and **Marc Anthony**.

New York Fusions: Byrne and Luaka Bop

In 1989 Peter Gabriel, along with the WOMAD organisation, set up the **RealWorld** label in order to promote World Music artists. That same year, in New York, **David Byrne** created **Luaka Bop**, a label that began by putting out a series of superbly sequenced Brazilian compilations – essentially the tapes that Byrne had for years been making for his own enjoyment. The label was soon broadening its horizons, issuing in the 1990s Cuban, Indian *filmi*, and Afro-Peruvian music (notably from singer **Susana Baca**), along with a number of quirky, cutting edge Latin groups.

It is Brazilian and Latin music that has inspired many of David Byrne's own solo albums. His 1989 *Rei Momo* was heavily Brazilian-influenced, and when he discovered the brilliant **Margareth Menezes** singing in the clubs of Salvador, he took

Bill Laswell: How Does He Do It?

Like a wide-eyed child watching a magician, anyone contemplating the astounding career of bassist, producer and label boss **Bill Laswell** will no doubt feel compelled to ask "How does he do it?" Responsible for over 200 albums since 1982, Laswell has consistently broken down boundaries, redrawn musical frontiers and created some of the most innovative and successful stylistic hybrids to be heard anywhere. A heavily paired-down list of his production credits gives an impression of the incredible breath and versatility of his musical genius: Sly and Robbie, Africa Bambaata, Mick Jagger, Fela Kuti, PIL, Herbie Hancock, Bootsy Collins, Manu Dibango, Laurie Anderson, Toure Kunda, Peter Gabriel, The Last Poets.

Laswell's approach on his own discs, released under his own name, or those of any number of sidegroups and collaborators, is to seek out and engage what might be called 'master musicians' from a host of different cultures and fuse their talents together in the studio. Regular participants over the years have included such greats as P-Funk's **Bernie Worrell**, guitarists **Nick Skopelitis** and **Sonny Sharrock**, **Bootsy Collins**, **Sly Dunbar** and **Robbie Shakespeare**, **Ginger Baker**, **Herbie Hancock**, percussionists **Aiyb Dieng** from Senegal and **Daniel Ponce** from Cuba, drummer **Ronald Shannon Jackson**, Japanese composer **Ryuichi Sakamoto** and kora player **Foday Musa Suso**. The central tenet of his philosophy has always been: music knows no boundaries, only the music business does. This belief was also played out in the numerous groups which Laswell was involved in as bass-player and prime-mover; **Material**, **Deadline**, **Praxis** and **Last Exit**, to name but a few.

In 1990 Laswell formed the **Axiom label** as a permanent home for his creative vision. The label has produced some of the most imaginative fusions ever to come from Africa, Latin America and the Arab world. Amongst the 30-odd full-length CDs nestle rare groundbreaking gems like **Gnawa Music of Marrakesh** album *Night Spirit Masters*, a rootsy recording of Moroccan gnawa music; **Mandingo**'s *New World Power*, Laswell's collaboration with Foday Musa Suso on the theme of West Africa; **Bahia Black**'s *Ritual Beating System*, an exploration of Bahian samba rhythms with Wayne Shorter and Herbie Hancock; and **The Master Musi-cians of Jajouka**'s *Apocalypse Across The Sky*, Laswell's attempt to finish the work Brian Jones began back in the late 1960s.

Axiom engages itself in a continuous polemic which strives to promote passion, openness, experimentation and the search for the underlying soul of culturally distinct musical styles without hindrance, bashfulness or new age pussyfooting.

Andy Morgan

Bill Laswell

AXIOM

USA

---

her on tour as support, setting himself the tough task of following her explosive sambas. Byrne continued his Latin infatuation in the movie *Something Wild*, which found him duetting with the queen of salsa **Celia Cruz**, and on the soundtrack of *Blue In The Face*, on which he collaborated with the Tejano star **Selena** as well as the Indian film composer **Vijaya Anand**.

Byrne has worked on various projects with **Arto Lindsay**, a fellow New Yorker who spent his childhood in New York with missionary parents, and who can switch in song from English to Brazilian Portuguese. A veteran of New York's avant garde jazz and noise groups, Lindsay had pursued a parallel career in Brazilian music, producing and working with singers such as **Caetano Veloso** and **Marisa Monte**. In the 1990s, with Brazilian guitarist **Vinicius Cantuária**, he brought the two strands together, fusing the bossa nova form with dance rhythms and electronic sequencing on a stunning and innovative series of discs.

Maybe the most significant of all figures in New York World Music fusion, though, is the hyperactive bassist and producer **Bill Laswell** (see feature box), who since the early 1980s has added his own cutting-edge grooves to the work of artists from dozens of different cultures.

Meanwhile Over On the West Coast

America's West Coast – and California, in particular – has been another major ground for World Music fusions. The archetypal West Coast band, **The Grateful Dead**, were receptive global experimenters, and their drummer, Mickey Hart, has been key to the development of World Music in the US. Following his partnership with Zakir Hussain in the **Diga Rhythm Band**, Hart recorded with Brazilians Flora Purim and Airto Moreira, and went on to form **Planet Drum**, a 'global percussion ensemble' that includes players as diverse as **Giovanni Hidalgo** (who brought Latin swing to Dizzie Gillespie's band), Afro-beat pioneer **Sikiru Adepoju** and tabla king **Zakir Hussain**. With dynamic percussion and recorded samples

SUSANA MILLMAN/RYKO

Planet Drum front (l-r): T.H. 'Vikku' Vinayakram; Babatunde Olatunji; Giovanni Hidalgo; Sikiru Adepoju, back (l-r): Airto Moreira; Flora Purim; Zakir Hussain; Mickey Hart

they have created the sorts of sounds that clubbers have chilled out to from London to LA.

Mickey Hart also wears another hat as ethnic music producer. With fellow Grateful Dead member **Bill Kreutzmann**, he's been working at the vast US Library of Congress archives of recorded sound, helping to preserve recordings in danger of crumbling away and releasing the highlights on his **360° label** (linked to Rykodisc). Archives from West Africa, Brazil and Bali have been released in this way and Hart has also made new recordings – with the Gyuto Monks (Tibetan monks resettled in India), with Balinese gamelan ensembles (*The Bali Sessions*), a longtime love of Hart's, and *Voices of the Rainforest*, an environmental-ethnographical recording from the forest dwelling Kaluli people of Papua New Guinea. The latter was often played between sets at Grateful Dead concerts, and the audience went wild about it.

Another 1960s West Coast survivor is **David Lindley**, whose guitar-work graced albums by Jackson Browne and James Taylor. Together with fellow guitarist **Henry Kaiser**, he visited Madagascar in 1991 to record two fine albums, *World Out Of Time*, accompanying some of the island's greatest traditional musicians. The pair moved on to do the same trick with Scandinavian fiddle music on *The Sweet Sunny North*.

The guitarist **Bob Brozman** is another Californian who has made a series of collaborative albums. A one-time blues player, Brozman has become one of the world's leading exponents of the Hawaiian steel guitar. In the 1980s he rediscovered the veteran Hawaiian player **Tau Moe** and the album they recorded, *Remembering The Songs of Our Youth*, is an acclaimed masterpiece. Equally wonderful is his recent *Jin Jin/Firefly*, a duo recording with the Okinawan *sanshin* (banjo) player **Takashi Hirayasu**.

In the 1990s, **Taj Mahal** has also worked in a slack-key Hawaiian idiom – not surprisingly, given that he has made his home on the islands – on *Sacred Island* and *Hula Blues*. Looking further afield, he recorded a little indifferently with the sitarist **V.M. Bhatt** in 1995, and then quite superbly, with Malian kora player Toumani Diabaté on 1999's *Kulanjan*. Diabaté, who had already made the successful fusion albums Songhai with flamenco group Ketama, proved a perfect foil for the bluesman, and they were fortunate to have Songhai pro-

Kronos – String Fusions

Increasingly in the last few years World Music has been revivifying programming in the West's mainstream classical concert halls. And even before this, paralleling the fusions with jazz and rock, there has been a fertile area in the meeting of World and classical sounds. Without doubt, the leading pioneers have been the San Francisco-based **Kronos Quartet**, the first group to adopt a rock sensibility, discard tails and make the string quartet cool. Since their formation in 1973, Kronos has worked with a large number of artists featured in the two volumes of this book, among them the late master of new Tango, **Astor Piazzola**, kora maestro **Foday Musa Suso**, Armenian duduk player **Djivan Gasparyan**, Chinese pipa player **Wu Man**, and Tuvan throat-singers **Huun-Huur-Tu**.

The group's latest album, *Kronos Caravan* (Nonesuch, 2000), explores a loosely-defined Gypsy and Middle Eastern theme, with collaborations with the **Taraf de Haidouks** from Romania, kamancheh player **Kayhan Kalhor** from Iran and a Bollywood filmi tune recorded with **Zakir Hussain**. Kronos's leader, **David Harrington**, is irrepressibly excited about discovering new sounds. For him, World Music borders on a religion: "The world of music is a huge place and I am attracted to the different ways of making sounds and the role of music in different societies. When I listen to music I think of it as a way of praying."

It's obvious from the artists that Kronos work with that they are interested in musicians who are similarly open-minded in their own tradition. "It just seems to work out that way," says Harrington. "Those sorts of people are attracted to us and we are attracted to them. For us, it's about coming together from different places. The imagery of sounds and the worlds that they imply, must capture our imagination."

Kronos's groundbreaking World Music album (and their most successful in terms of sales) was *Pieces of Africa*, a collaboration with African musicians and composers which has sold over 250,000 copies since its release in 1992. "I remember the first time I heard African music," says Harrington, "I thought that's incredibly beautiful – and rooted in a sonic world that we wanted to explore. We are not simply trying to recreate African music for string quartet – that would be empty and pointless – we are making something more abstract. I think it was Rilke who said 'The further great art gets from its point of origin, the waves it produces get larger!'."

Simon Broughton

ducer **Joe Boyd** (who as founder of Hannibal Records deserves more than a footnote in World Music and fusion history) presiding.

Such achievements notwithstanding, by far the most influential Californian rock star turned world-music-guru, is **Ry Cooder**, dispenser of global fairydust par excellence ...

The Ry Phenomenon

In the 1960s **Ry Cooder** played with bluesman Taj Mahal, and with rock legends Captain Beefheart and the Rolling Stones (on the *Let It Bleed* sessions). He then went solo, recording movie sountracks, and exploring rockabilly, blues and folk roots on a number of mainly acoustic albums, before charting World Music terrain for the first time on 1976's *Chicken Skin Music*.

Unlike Paul Simon or Peter Gabriel, who despite their wider musical interests continue to work in a rock idiom, by the late 1980s Cooder had turned his back on rock music in something approaching disgust. "In America there is no long any social context to music, it is just business," he said. "The records I was making were meaningless because they weren't part of anything." Instead, he embarked on a series of global collaborators as far apart as India, Japan, Vietnam, Ireland, West Africa and Cuba, working with local musicians as equal partners and immersing himself in their tra-

ditions, regarding his own role as that of catalyst. "Paul Simon goes in there and takes what he wants but he is still essentially singing his own songs. My approach is to take the tradition and push it around a little," Cooder says. "You have to do that because you can't just make folkloric records of what people have always done in the same way they have always done it. You try to create a situation in which they are not just going into their pattern or their routine. It's a subtle thing because these are master musicians, but you try and twist it enough to give it fresh possibilities."

The integrity of this approach has won huge respect – and, latterly, sales. The first such venture, *A Meeting By The River* with the Indian musician **V.M. Bhatt** won a Grammy in 1994, and the following year he recorded – in just three days – the magnificent *Talking Timbuktu*, on which he duetted with the Malian guitarist **Ali Farka Touré**. It won another Grammy and topped World Music charts for months on end. Cooder also collaborated in the 1990s with Okinawa group **Nenes**, providing slide guitar that worked perfectly with the four women's chanted vocals.

Then in 1997, along with Nick Gold of World Circuit, Cooder headed for Havana, and produced the veteran **Buena Vista Social Club**, assembled by Cuban arranger Juan de Marcos González. The story of this magical and incredible three-million-selling disc, and that of its follow-ups – Cooder

Ry Cooder with Compay Segundo (centre), recording Buena Vista Social Club

also produced solo discs by pianist Rúben Gonzalez and the bolero singer Ibrahim Ferrer – is told in detail elsewhere in this book.

Current Cooder work-in-progress includes an album with the veteran Vietnamese guitarist **Kim Sing**, and in 1999 he told *Folk Roots* that he was interested in making a Malagasy record. Given his current track record, either are likely to provide gold dust for the collaborators.

Cooder, though, is acutely aware that over-commercialisation can easily destroy a music's creative impetus. He saw it happen with his first love, the blues, and fears the same fate may befall Cuban music. "Young pop musicians know there is a tremendous energy in Cuba so they are going to go and grab it because they understand rock'n'roll is basically dead." Even the success of Buena Vista he concedes could be a double-edged sword. "It's dangerously close to a theme park in some ways, which I don't favour. But on balance I'm not unhappy about it because of the opportunities that are being created."

Cooder's approach seems blameless. But of course, white rock stars working with indigenous musicians are always going to arouse suspicion and undoubtedly some have exploited the World Music scene for self-serving ends. Yet the Malian star Salif Keita, who has worked with Wayne Shorter and Carlos Santana, surely has the smart perspective on what has proved to be an overwhelmingly beneficial two-way cultural traffic. "It's not bad," he says with only a hint of cynicism. "White people get the inspiration and we get the popularity."

discography

This discography covers US World Music fusion albums and should be read alongside the India/East-West discography. British-based fusion artists, such as 3Mustapha3, and British Indian artists who have fused their traditions with dance music, are covered in Volume 1 of this book (see pp.75–81 and pp.83–90)

Compilations

🄐 **Planet Soup** (Ellipsis Arts, US).

This is a set of three CDs, charmingly, if irrelevantly, titled *Gazpacho* (cold, summer soup from Spain), *Tiga Nadje* (peanut soup from Mali) and *Mulligatawny* (hot, spicey soup from India). Each focuses on the meetings of musicians and bands from different traditions, and there are plenty of successes along the way, including, from a US perspective, the banjo/tabla partnership of Jim Bowie and Badal Roy, and a combo of Delta blues and Tuvan throat singing from Paul Pena and Kongar-ool Ondar. Other featured musicians include Astor Piazzolla, Värttinä (Finland) and Aisha Kandisha's Jarring Effects (Morocco).

Artists

Bob Brozman

Brozman (born California, 1954) is a far too little-known American guitarist and musicologist whose discovery of a pile of old 78s inspired him to a lifetime's study of the Hawaiian steel guitar.

WITH TAU AND ROSE MOE

🄐 **Remembering The Songs Of Our Youth**
(Rounder, US).

A landmark recreation of the Hawaiian music of the 1920s with veteran steel guitarist Tau Moe and his wife Rose.

WITH TAKASHI HIRAYASU

 Jin Jin/Firefly
(Riverboat Records, UK).

This is a delight – traditional children's melodies from the Japanese island of Okinawa reworked by Takashi Hirayasu, singer, guitarist and master of the sanshin (three stringed banjo) alongside Brozman's exemplary Hawaiian guitar.

David Byrne

New Yorker David Byrne (actually born in Scotland, 1952) came to fame with the Talking Heads, the most adventurous of rock bands in the late 1970s/early 1980s. But rock proved too limiting for Byrne's expanding cultural interests and collaborations with the likes of Brian Eno and Ryuichi Sakamoto led him into a solo career deeply influenced by Brasilian and Latin rhythms. In 1989, he set up the Luaka Bop label, which has since issued some of the quirkiest, cutting edge global sounds around.

DAVID BYRNE AND BRIAN ENO

 My Life In The Bush Of Ghosts (Sire/Warner, US).

This groundbreaking 1980 collaboration with Eno is where it all began for Byrne and World Music – and, looking back, it is years ahead in its sampling of global sounds (African music, Islamic chant, American evangelical preachers) to create new soundtracks.

DAVID BYRNE

 Rei Momo (Warners, US).

An inspired 1989 album of Brazilian- and Latin-tinged pop, picking up on salsa, samba and merengue, and including the song "Loco de Amor" which Byrne sang with Celia Cruz for the Jonathan Demme movie, *Something Wild*.

Ry Cooder

No one has worked with master musicians around the world with more empathic understanding than guitarist and producer Ry Cooder (born Los Angeles, 1947). All of his collaborations, from Mali to Okinawa, Texas to Cuba, have been characterised by an uncanny ability to bring something fresh out of those around him.

RY COODER

 **Chicken Skin Music** (Warners/Reprise, US).

Tex-Mex and Hawaiian flavours, courtesy of the accordionist Flaco Jiménez and the slack-key guitar master Gabby Pahinui, sit gloriously alongside Leadbelly and Ben E. King tunes on the first leg (1976 vintage) of Cooder's remarkable voyage around the musical globe

RY COODER AND VM BHATT

Meeting By The River (Water Lily Acoustics, US).

This 1993 disc stands as one of the most successful East-West recordings ever, with Bhatt and Cooder sure-footed vina/slide guitar partners on a disc that feels steeped in the Hindustani melody system. It rightly won a Grammy.

RY COODER AND ALI FARKA TOURÉ

Talking Timbuktu (World Circuit, UK).

Cooder's 1994 partnership, with Malian blues guitarist Ali Farka Touré, was another Grammy winner and an equally enduring seller. It is, simply, a great record, an entirely natural-sounding creation of shimmering guitar textures between Cooder's slide and Ali Farka Touré's deep African blues and acoustic ensemble.

NENES

 Koza Dabasa (Ki/oon Sony Records, Japan).

A superb album from the four women singers of this Okinawa (Japan) group. It was recorded partly in Los Angeles, with Ry Cooder, David Lindley, Jim Keltner and David Hidalgo (of Los Lobos).

BUENA VISTA SOCIAL CLUB

Buena Vista Social Club (World Circuit, UK).

Standing at 3m copies and rising, this 1997 recording is the best-selling World Music album of all time, a gold-plated classic with little (and perhaps extraneous) input from Cooder on guitar, but a production presence that inspired the Cuban veterans to previously unattained heights.

 Buena Vista Social Club Presents Ibrahim Ferrer (World Circuit, UK).

This 1999 follow-up to *Buena Vista* showcased the voice of the 72-year-old bolero singer Ibrahim Ferrer. Cooder again produced as well as contributing some wonderful guitar duets with Manuel Galban.

Mickey Hart and Planet Drum

Grateful Dead drummer Mickey Hart (born Long Island, NY, 1943) has long been active in promoting global percussion and the world's endangered cultures. His Planet Drum releases feature extraordinary line-ups of percussionists from all over the globe. (See also Indian/Western Fusion, p.109).

 Planet Drum (Rykodisc/360°, US).

A dream team of drummers including Nigerians Babatunde Olatunji and Sikiri Adepoju, Brazil's Airto Moreira, India's Zakir Hussain and Puerto Rico's Giovanni Hidalgo. An extraordinary feast of percussive virtuosity.

 Supralinga (Rykodisc/360°, US).

The double-CD follow up dilutes or enhances the idea, depending on your point of view, with added vocals from the Gyuto Monks and salsa singer Bobi Cespedes.

The Kronos Quartet

Formed in 1973 in San Francisco, the Kronos (string) Quartet were the first to make string quartet music hip and have been Classical music's foremost world fusionists. Since the early 1990s they have commissioned from and collaborated with a large number of World Music figures from all around the globe.

Pieces of Africa (Nonseuch, US).

Kronos leader David Harrington set out to 'make something new and more abstract' out of African music on this 1992 recording. The result was exciting and unique as the quartet, work together with kora, mbira and tar (drum) on pieces by Dumisani Maraire (Zimbabwe), Hassan Hakmoun (Morocco), Foday Musa Suso (Gambia), Justinian Tamusuza (Uganda), Hamza El Din (Sudan), Obo Addy (Ghana) and long-term Kronos collaborator, South African contemporary composer Kevin Volans. Quartet music has never been so danceable.

 Early Music (Nonesuch, US).

Travelling (back) through time as well as around a range of cultures, this album is a quiet, meditative counterpart to the energetic rhythms of *Pieces of Africa*. A more classical sensibility comes through on excellent contributions from Wu Man on Chinese lutes, overtone singers Huun-Huur-Tu and Olov Johansson on Swedish nykelharpa.

Bill Laswell

Bill Laswell (born Salem, IL, 1952) is almost unbelievably prolific – a producer, bassist, composer, and manager of several labels. He co-founded the ensemble Material which has seen a rolling roster of musicians including important collaborators such as L. Shankar, Simon Shaheen and Foday Musa Suso. His Axiom label is the home for his World Music projects, although he's also also been working recently with (Chieftain) Paddy Moloney's Wicklow label.

NICKY SKOPELITIS

 Ekstasis
(Axiom, US).

For many this 1993 outing is World Music fusion at its finest – and it certainly has absolutely right-on mainstream appeal. Laswell and a stellar host of fusion suspects – Foday Musa Suso, Simon Shaheen, Bachir Attar, Zakir Hussain – line up with his long-time collaborator, guitarist Nicky Skopelitis.

BILL LASWELL

Bahia Black: Ritual Beating System (Axiom, US).

Pure rhythm and its ability to entrance has always fascinated Laswell, and here he expresses this fascination in the context of Brazilian afro-bloc samba with colours added by three greats of modern US music, Wayne Shorter, Herbie Hancock and Henry Threadgill.

BILL LASWELL/SACRED SYSTEM

Imaginary Cuba: Deconstructing Havana (Wicklow, US).

A rather Eno-ish idea – how will Cuban music sound as the 21st Century unfolds? Laswell samples tracks from musicians including Frank Emilio Flynn and rumba group Clave y Guaganco and applies 'a mystical dub-tastic reconstruction' with studio electronics, keyboards and guitars.

Arto Lindsay

Arto Lindsay (born Brazil, 1950) is a veteran of the New York avant-jazz and noise scenes. But he had a parallel career as a producer of Brazilian musicians, including Caetano Veloso and Marisa Monte. In 1996 the two strands came together as he began a series of albums fusing bossa nova with drum'n'bass and other electronic dance forms.

 O Corpo Subtil
(Ryko, US).

This is the first and most sublime of Lindsay's bossa-inspired albums, sung partly in English, partly in Portuguese. Vinicius Cantuária co-composes and plays guitar. If you're hooked, keep going with the follow-ups, **Mundo Civilizado** (1997), **Noon Chill** (1998), and, perhaps best of the lot, **Prize** (1999).

Taj Mahal

One of the original World Music pioneers, guitarist Taj Mahal (born New York, 1942) started with the blues and traced the musical trade routes of his ancestors back from there. He has collaborated with dozens of global artists, including VM Bhatt and, most recently and successfully, with the Malian kora player, Toumani Diabate.

TAJ MAHAL

The Hula Blues (Tradition and Moderne, US).

Taj visited Hawaii to record this delightful crossover collection where Mississippi meets Maui. It is less traditional than Bob Brozman's approach.

TAJ MAHAL AND TOUMANI DIABATE

 Kulanjan
(Hannibal/Ryko, UK).

Here Taj traces the roots back to West Africa with top kora player Toumani Diabate in both Malian and American blues repertoire. Voted the best album of 1999 by *Folk Roots* readers, this stands as a dazzling African-American collaboration.

Paul Simon

Paul Simon (born Newark, NJ, 1941) was a seminal figure in 1960s folk-rock as half of Simon and Garfunkel, but by the mid-1980s his solo career had run out of steam. He revived it with the help of a few friends from around the globe and two of the best World-Pop crossover albums ever recorded. His most recent project was a fine but ill-fated Broadway musical, *Capeman* (1997), using Puerto Rican music and singers.

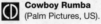 **Graceland**
(Warners, US).

Magnificent songs, irresistible rhythms and the first most people around the world heard of the joyous sounds of Ladysmith Black Mambazo and the zulu jive of Mahlathini and the Mahotella Queens.

Rhythm Of The Saints (Warners, US).

A less feted follow-up which found Simon working with Brazilian musicians on another brilliant collection of cleverly executed and melodic pop songs.

Ned Sublette

Ned Sublette is a New York-based Texan with a passion for Latin and Caribbean music (he set up the pioneering Cuban music label, Qbadisc). He is also a fine guitarist and country singer – attributes perfectly in tune with his recent salsa and merengue recordings.

Cowboy Rumba
(Palm Pictures, US).

Sublette really brings off this unlikely fusion of red-neck songs with merengue and Cuban son and salsa rhythms supplied by top-notch Cuba-based musicians like NG La Banda and Los Muñequitos de Matanzas, and the Puerto Rican cuatro player Yomo Toro. Quirky and delightful.

Venezuela

salsa con gasolina

Fuelled since the 1970s by its oil revenues, Venezuela has fostered an important recording scene and a good market for Latin music – especially salsa, which is hugely popular. Yet with the exception of star *salsero* Oscar D'Leon, its own music is not well known – and perhaps inevitably overshadowed by neighbouring Brazil, Colombia and, out to sea, Trinidad. **Philip Sweeney** and **Dan Rosenberg** delve into the rich folk traditions of *llanera* (plains music), Afro-Venezuelan music, *calipso*, and other forms.

L ike a miniature version of Brazil, Venezuela is a country of widely differing terrains, ranging through the Amazon-like jungle adjoining the southern Orinoco river, to the cattle-rearing expanses of the central grassland *llanos*, to the steaming Caribbean coastline, to the capital, Caracas, where the skyscrapers and mansions of the business elite are encircled by the hill slums of countless poor salsa-lovers.

Although professional music-making is limited pretty much to Caracas and dominated by pan-Latin salsa, merengue and pop, the country retains a great range of traditional and folk music, with many regional variants of harps, guitars, *cuatros* (small guitars), mandolins and drums. As elsewhere in the region, it has developed from a mixed base of Spanish, African and indigenous Indian elements, though the latter has been of marginal influence on mainstream popular music.

Llanera

The music that is widely identified as Venezuela's national style is **llanera** (from *llanos* – plains), or *musica criolla* (Creole), as it is sometimes called. It is played by ensembles of **plains harp** (with their pronounced bass strings), guitars, cuatros, mandolins, tambora double-headed drums, *charrasca* scrapers and *furruco* friction drums. Such groups accompany the **joropo** – a couple dance popular throughout the country – and can be heard in bars and dancehalls in the cattle towns of the interior, as well as country-themed restaurants in Caracas.

In its most refined form, represented by the work of the great harpist and composer **Juan-Vicente**

© 1999 · ℗ 1999 Made in the Czech Republic
Product of: Arquivos de Música Antiga/Portugal

INTERSTATE
℗Harlequin
HQ CD 140

Distributed by: Interstate Music Ltd, 20 Endwell Road,
Bexhill-on-Sea, East Sussex TN40 1EA, England

1941-1944

Veteran Venezuelans, Billo's Caracas Boys – they're still going strong

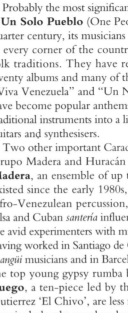

VENEZUELA: FREDY REYNA, LILIA VERA
SERENATA GUYANESA, TRÍO LLANERO

WORLD NETWORK

Lilia Vera

Torrealba, llanera music has the status of a light classical art music (recordings of Torrealba's work *Alma Llanera* have been made with symphony orchestras). In its modern popularised showbiz form, its status is similar to that of Country & Western. It is not a music for the young or hip, but top performers are extremely popular. One of the best known is **Simon Díaz**, a prolific singer and the composer of the song "Caballo Viejo", which was taken up first by the Cuban American salsa artiste Roberto Torres and then transformed, via the addition of a new chorus, into the Gipsy Kings' international hit "Bamboleo". (Diaz is said to have written "Caballo Viejo" – Old Horse – to a Miss Venezuela explaining why he couldn't have an affair with her.)

Other top Criollo singers who perform llanera music along with other regional styles include **Reynaldo Armas**, **Reyna Lucero**, **Luis Lozada**, **Freddy Salcedo**, **Armando Martinez**, **Lilia Vera**, **Fredy Reyna**, and the groups **Cimarron** and **Trio Llanera**. One artist who stands out from the pack, having modernised and tropicalised a basically llanera sound is **Nelson Blanco** and his group **Le Manga E'Coleo**. The cuatro virtuoso **Cheo Hurtado** also plays llanera, among other styles, with his various groups.

Afro-percussion and Folklorico Groups

Venezuela takes its music and traditional culture very seriously. There is a strong tradition of music research – fostered notably by the Caracas arts centre, Fundación Bigott – and several professional *folklorico* groups are active in reviving and adapting traditional forms, particularly within the rich area of traditional **African-origin percussion**.

Probably the most significant of all these groups is **Un Solo Pueblo** (One People). Over the past quarter century, its musicians travelled to virtually every corner of the country, researching local folk traditions. They have recorded more than twenty albums and many of their songs – notably "Viva Venezuela" and "Un Negro Como Yo" – have become popular anthems. They incorporate traditional instruments into a line-up based around guitars and synthesisers.

Two other important Caracas-based groups are Grupo Madera and Huracán del Fuego. **Grupo Madera**, an ensemble of up to 18 members, has existed since the early 1980s, playing a fusion of Afro-Venezulean percussion, Latin jazz, llanera, salsa and Cuban *santería* influenced music. Madera are avid experimenters with musical combinations, having worked in Santiago de Cuba with local *son-changüi* musicians and in Barcelona with **Ai Ai Ai**, the top young gypsy rumba band. **Huracán de Fuego**, a ten-piece led by the drummer Nestor Gutierrez 'El Chivo', are less fusionist – although they include salsa numbers by Joe Arroyo in their repertoire – and more research-oriented. Much of their work centres round the *cumaco* drums of Congolese origin, used in the syncretic cult of Saint Benito, prevalent in Gutierrez's home province of Maracaibo.

Lastly, there's the very active touring group **Los Vasallos del Sol**, formed at Fundación Bigott in

NUBE NEGRA

Huracán del Fuego drummer, 'El Chivo'

Africa in Venezuela

The slave trade touched virtually every corner of the Americas, but nowhere was its impact so profound as the Caribbean and Atlantic coasts. Today, up and down Venezuela's pristine northern **Caribbean shore** lie village after village that look, feel and sound remarkably African. From the huge five-foot-long wooden *mina* drums of Curiepe to the bamboo *quitiplas* of Barlovento to the *golpes de tambor* (drum beats) of the state of Aragua, the traditional music of this region is truly Africa in the Americas.

The Spanish slave trade existed in Venezeula for three centuries until it was abolished in 1834. Most of the African music in Venezuela seems to have arrived in the earliest years of slaving and what is played today is considered, compared with its musical cousins across the Atlantic, 'old African music', rhythms and styles dated from the fiteenth century, with touches of Indian, Spanish and Caribbean influences.

There are literally hundreds of variants – each village has its own instruments, its own rhythms – but researchers have found that large communities can trace their roots to the **Dahomey** region in West Africa, primarily Ewe-Fon and Araras-Geges. The huge **mina drums** found in Barlovento, Venezuela, are rooted in the Bantus of the 'Gold Coast' who originally called the instrument *Fantiashanti*, while the **celoepuya** (rounded wooden drums) are quite similar to those played in Senegal and Nigeria.

One Afro-Venezuelan style heard throughout Venezuela is **parranda**, though it varies greatly from state to state. A kind of troubadour music, it is per-formed by small groups of singers (*parranderos*) accompanying themselves on *cuatro* or guitar. It has origins – and still persists – in Christmas singing, when people set out from the churches singing joyous songs, going door to door asking for gifts, liquor, treats or food. A similar Christmas music can be heard in Trinidad and other Afro-Caribbean communities, such as those along the coast in Belize and Guatemala (see p.325).

The **Fulia** is rooted along Venezuela's central coast. It too varies by region but typically uses guitar, cuatro, and percussion. It is heard at most festival celebrations, notably the Cruz de Mayo – a harvest festival with both Catholic and indigenous roots – and the San Juan festival in June. The **Sangeo** is another rhythm closely associated with the San Juan, over in the state of Aragua (west of Caracas). *Sangeo* derives from the African word 'Sanga', which means to dance while walking slowly. For the San Juan festival, the drummers march into the streets, singing Sangeos, dancing with flags.

Another important form in northwestern Venezuela, near the border with Colombia, is the **Gaita**. This involves a variety of percussion instruments including the *furruco* – a cousin of the Brazilian cuica with its strange 'yelping' sound. A wooden drum with a 3-ft stick through the centre of the skin, it is played by a drummer who coats his hand with wax and rubs up and down the stick. The Gaitas of Zulia are part of a huge celebration on the 13th of December used to kick off the celebration of the Christmas season.

Dan Rosenberg

Mural showing mina drums and dancers

1990 by Jesus Rondon. Their name (Servants of the Sun) refers to the strong festival-base of traditional music in Venezuela around the summer and winter (Christmas) solstices. They have done extensive research into Afro-Venezuelan music, incorporating local village music into both their recordings and workshops at the Fundación. Over the past decade, they have performed all over Europe and Latin America.

Venezuelan Calipso

While the northern Caribbean coast is rich in Afro-percussion and salsa, the southern provinces round the towns of **El Callao** and **Cuidad Bolivar** have a tradition of Trinidadian percussion and **calipso** (as they spell it in Venezuela).

In the 1880s, thousands of immigrants from the eastern Caribbean came to this region in a South American gold rush. Today, their descendants sing a unique version of calipso. The lyrics are in a kind of part-Spanish, part English, the rhythms come from Trinidad, Guadeloupe and St. Kitts, while the chords are rooted in Spanish Andalucía. Like its cousin in Trinidad, Venezuelan calipso is an essential part of the Carnival celebrations every February, with huge floats, elaborate costumes, and song and dance all day and night in the days leading up to Lent.

Among the better known calipso bands from the region are **VH**, who had a national hit with the song "Woman del Callao", and a group with both Spanish and English names – **La Misma Gente** aka **The Same People**.

Pop and Dance Bands

Within the mainstream pop sphere, Venezuela possesses numerous **Latin rock** acts – current leaders being **Yordano**, **Ilan Chester** and the group **Daiquiri** – and several top salsa-ballad artistes, notably **José-Luis Rodriguez 'El Puma'**. There are also many **dance bands** playing salsa or a range of currently popular pan-Latin rhythms, particularly in recent years Dominican merengue. And then there are **Los Amigos Invisibles** – a hard-to-classify outfit who fuse rock with an assortment of tropical rhythms and retro-references and a tongue in cheek approach. Their album *The New Sound of the Venezuelan Gozadera* was taken up by David Byrne's Luaka Bop label.

The derogatory term **musica gallega** (immigrant music) is sometimes applied to the unintellectual, unpretentious music of traditional **dance bands**. These remain a popular part of the scene, led by three veteran bands – Billo's Caracas Boys, Los Melodicos and the Pofri Jimenez Orquesta – with a line-up of guitar, bass, percussionists, half a dozen brass and four or five singers.

Billo's Caracas Boys, the oldest of these ensembles, was formed in the 1940s by the Dominican bandleader Luis Maria 'Billo' Frómeta, who dominated the local scene in the 1950s and 1960s with his tight arrangements of mambos, cumbias, guarachas, plenas and boleros, featuring a succession of star singers, including the young 'El Puma'. Led since the death of Billo by his son Charlie, the Boys remain popular, if perhaps a little less so than their longstanding rivals.

Los Melodicos were founded in 1958 by Renato Capriles, who continues to run the large band (four saxophones, three trumpets, three trombones, twenty-two members at a minimum, transported around the country continually in its own Mercedes coaches) like a well-planned business, with pension schemes for the musicians, whose line-up in the 1990s included the glamorous young singer **Liz Lisbeth**.

Porfi Jimenez (second row, with bass trumpet) and his Orquesta, 1980s

The **Porfi Jimenez Orquesta** is led by another Dominican-born musician, Porfirio Jimenez, who arrived in Caracas as a trombonist with the Rafael Minaya Orquesta in 1953, founded his own band ten years later and took twenty hard-working years to move into the top rank. He had a string of hits in the 1980s, notably the huge seller "Culúcucú" in 1987. Jimenez still leads his band, unusually on bass trumpet, and features merengues, socas and whatever is in demand for dancing.

JAK KILBY

Salsa

Salsa is huge in Venezuela and, as you might expect with Brazil across the border, it has

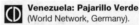
Oscar D'Leon marshalling the troops

a samba and bossa nova influence, evident in the favouring of a smooth, sweet, sound. The country also has a bona fide salsa star in bandleader **Oscar D'Leon**.

Leon was a leading figure in the international salsa boom of the 1970s, his trademark trick being to sing, dance and play his white upright baby bass at the same time – quite a feat. He formed his first successful band, **La Dimension Latina**, in 1973, charting with the hit "Pensando en Ti", before creating a new outfit, Salsa Mayor, and later, as Oscar D'Leon y su Orquesta, moving to New York. There he spent the 1990s as one of the stars of top salsa label RMM, duetting regularly with the US-domiciled queen of salsa, Celia Cruz.

On the departure of D'Leon, La Dimension Latina replaced him for a while with **Andy Montañez**, former star vocalist of the Puerto Rican Gran Combo, making Montañez, it was rumoured, the first 'salsa millionaire' with his transfer fee. Montañez has long moved on, too, but Dimension Latina are still major players, much in demand for their velvety four-trombone sound and smart presentation, under the musical directorship of Joséito Rodriguez.

Another salsa institution is **Guaco**, formed as a folkloric group in the town of Maracaibo in the 1960s, and for years one of the great tropical orchestras. They play salsa, often with a Cuban timba shading, but also incorporate elements of jazz, funk and traditional Venezuelan styles and instruments. Founded by Alfonso Aguado, Guaco has long been under the direction of his brother Gustavo, a composer, arranger and powerful singer. He runs the band with a backbone of veterans but pulls in promising young musicians and singers to keep the sound fresh and innovative.

A similar approach, focusing on a mixture of hard salsa, Latin jazz and traditional forms such as the *gaita de furro* of Maracaibo and the Caracas *merengue*, is taken by the percussionist **Orlando Poleo**, who after two decades of work in New York, Caracas and Paris formed his own top-name band in 1995.

discography

Compilations

Venezuela: Pajarillo Verde
(World Network, Germany).

A good cross-section of llanera and other regional folk styles by four well-established traditional artistes, Fredy Reyna, Lilia Vera, the Serenata Guyanesa and the Trio Llanero. Includes local waltzes and merengues, bamboleos, joropos, and even an English language callipso in an accent to baffle all but the most expert of ethno-linguists.

The Music of Venezuela (Zu-Zazz, UK).

The 15 tracks compiled here range across Venezuelan regions and styles, featuring local groups and folklorico ensembles playing mainly llanero and joropo songs, featuring harp and cuatros. There's also an oddball recording of country style merengue played on a single-string mouth bow.

Artists

Los Amigos Invisibles

As you'd expect of an act on David Byrne's label, the Caracas-based Los Amigos are hard to pin down – their music draws on Venezuelan roots (with lots of Afro-style percussion) but pulls in lashings of Latin jazz, bossa nova, and US funk and lounge music.

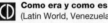 **The New Sound of the Venezuelan Gozadera** (Luaka Bop, US).

The group's international debut made quiet waves on the US and British lounge scene, with its quirky rather than kitsch dance work-outs and understated bossa novas.

LUAKA BOP

Los Amigos Invisibles

Billo's Caracas Boys

A Venezuelan institution, Billo's big band was founded when its leader arrived in Caracas in 1937 from his native Santo Domingo to take on a residency at the Roof Garden of the Hotel Madrid. Though Billo died in 1990, the band is still going strong.

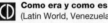 **Billo's Caracas Boys 1941-44** (Harlequin, UK).

An excellent selection from the band's early years, when its style was based on Cuban ensembles such as the Orquesta del Casino de la Playa. Replete with guarachas, boleros, merengues, joropos and period curiosities such as a cantering guasa and the opening son-swing.

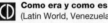 **Lo Mejor de Billo's Caracas Boys** (Velvet, USA/Venezuela).

A 'Best Of' compilation featuring sixteen of the band's dance favourites, including newer Colombian standards such as "Abusadora" and "A mover tu colita".

Oscar D'Leon

D'Leon comes from Venezuela but was born with a Cuban soul. His career is built on adaptation of Cuban son – in some cases jazzed up and jumpy with a recognisably Colombian tropical flavour, in others closer to the model set by his lifelong idol, the Cuban giant, Bene Moré.

 El Sonero del Mundo (RMM, US).

Straightahead, irresistibly danceable New York salsa led by D'Leon's unmistakably rich voice, joined on the hit duet, "Hasme el Amor" by current salsa-pop icon, La India.

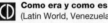 **La Formula Original** (RMM, USA).

D'Leon hasn't made a bad record in years, and his most recent, to end the millennium, is another classic, with high energy dance hits "Mi Mujer Es Una Bomba" and "Deja Que Te Quiera" and a cover title printed in Spanish, English, French and Japanese in recognition of his current audience.

Dimension Latina

D'Leon's old band, latterly proclaiming themselves 'Los Génerales de la Salsa', still put on a fine polished show, with impeccable co-ordinated uniform and dance steps, and three highly competent vocalists making up for the absence of their ex-boss and his star substitute, Andy Montañez.

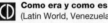 **Los dueños del Caribe** (Velvet, USA/Venezuela).

A good mid-period album of smooth old-school urban nightclub salsa.

Guaco

Formed in the 1960s as a Christmas festival percussion band, Guaco has grown into a dynamic, experimental and highly distinctive dance outfit. If Oscar D'Leon and the Dimension Latina fit into the Cuban-Puerto Rican tradition of classic son-based hard salsa, Guaco call more to mind a new wave Cuban model such as Los Van Van.

 Como era y como es (Latin World, Venezuela).

This 1999 outing is one of their strongest yet, a fizzing concoction of salsa, jazz, funk, joropo, gaita and touches of Brazilian and rock sounds.

Huracán de Fuego

One of the most active, skilled and insider-knowledgeable of Venezuela's Afro-percussion ensembles, Huracán are a kind of equivalent of the Cuban rumba group, Muñequitos de Matanzas.

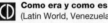 **Vamos a darle** (Nubenegra, Spain).

Studio recorded in Maracaibo and beautifully produced and packaged, with first-class liner notes (albeit in Spanish), this is an excellent introduction to the percussive richness of the country, and it isn't too ethnological to include a version of Joe Arroyo's hit "Rebelion".

Cheo Hurtado

Born in 1960, Cheo is the son of Venezuelan guitarist and composer Ramón Hurtado and is one of the country's leading cuatro players, making his own innovations to the instrument and its playing style. He has founded several groups playing traditional and pop music and teaches cuatro, guitar and mandolin.

 Cuatro arpas y un cuatro (Tropical Music, Germany).

An alternative to the punning title ('Four Harps and a Cuatro') might be 'The Best Cuatro Disc in the World . . . Ever'. The line-up is that of a typical country (llanera) ensemble – harp, cuatro, bass and maracas (rattles). Hurtado plays with four different harpists and the notes and rhythms fly so fast that it's often impossible to tell who's doing what. Traditional artistry and improvisation at its thrilling best.

Orlando Poleo

A polished and prolific conga, bongo and guiro player, Poleo works mainly out of Paris, and is anchored primarily in international Afro-Cuban jazz. Nonetheless he employs an interesting range of Venezuelan rhythms on his guest-star-studded albums.

⊚ **El Buen Camino** (Colombia, UK).

Recorded in Caracas in 1997, and featuring musicians of the calibre of Cuba's Chucho Valdez and 'Maraca' Valle, this is a sizzling collection, the percussion, flute and sax-driven jazz style harbouring curious rhythms such as the *gaita de furro* from Maracaibo, the Caracas merengue (decidedly not Elvis Crespo) and treats such as a *chachachá* in French.

Un Solo Pueblo

Un Solo Pueblo is Venezeula's most popular folk-pop band. Over the past quarter century, the group has recorded more than 20 albums. Many of their songs have become popular anthems.

⊚ **Caramba** (World Network, Germany).

This collection features the best of Un Solo Pueblo's 25-year history, spanning a broad range of Venezuelan musical forms, including gaitas, calipsos, parranda, and sangeo.

Los Vasallos del Sol

Under the leadership of musical director Jesus Rondón, Los Vasallos del Sol is a 26-member song and dance troupe specialising in Afro-Venezeulan music, primarily from along the Caribbean coast.

⊚ **Tibio Calor** (Ashe Records, US).

A landmark album of African music in the Americas, featuring six drummers and a dozen of the country's top vocalists.

THREE

Directories

Record Labels

Record Shops

Contributors

Record Labels | Directory

This Labels Guide covers specialists in American, Latin, Caribbean, Indian, Asian and Pacific music (and often a whole range of World Music). For further addresses and Web links, try the list maintained by American roots magazine *Dirty Linen* at *www.futuris.net/linen/88*

Ace Records

www.acerecords.co.uk

48–50 Steele Road, London, NW10 7AS, UK

Ace is the umbrella for a whole group of labels, including World Music imprint, GlobeStyle (see p.635). But it also releases a wide range of US regional music under its own name, including Cajun, swamp pop, zydeco, Tex-Mex, old-time and bluegrass.

Amiata

www.amiatamedia.com

Via Gabriele D'Annunzio 227, 50135 Firenze, Italy

Named after a volcanic mountain in Tuscany, Amiata leans towards spiritual and ambient music, mainly Asiatic, but its interesting *Secret World* and *Roots* series focus on cross-cultural and contemporary sounds.

Arc Music

www.arcmusic.co.uk

P.O. Box 111, East Grinstead, West Sussex RH19 4FZ, UK

World and folk music in all its forms, with a huge catalogue stretching from Australian didgeridoo music to Zimbabwean gospel. There are some gems among them, though many of the releases have a rather tacky tourist-brochure approach both to the artwork and the recordings.

Archives Internationales de Musiques Populaire (AIMP)

www.vdegallo.ch

Musée d'Ethnographie, 65-67 boulevard Carl-Vogt, CH 1205 Geneva, Switzerland

The World Music label of VDE-Gallo, this issues high quality ethnographic recordings from around the globe. Their discs are consistently good, although often of rather specialized appeal.

Arhoolie

www.arhoolie.com

10341 San Pablo Avenue, El Cerrito, CA 94530, USA

One of the great American roots labels, Chris Strachwitz's Arhoolie has been going since 1960 and has unrivalled releases of everything from the US (notably Tex-Mex, Cajun, country blues and other regional styles), Mexico, and more.

Arion

info@arion-music.com

36 Avenue Hoche, 75008 Paris, France

Although some of the large Arion catalogue tends towards the holiday souvenir end of things, they have some interesting things from the Andes, Indian subcontinent and Southeast Asia.

Ashé

www.rounder.com/rounder/catalog/bylabel/ashe

Distributed by Rounder

A classy Latin label forging a reputation for its Cuban, Puerto Rican and other Afro-Caribbean releases.

Auvidis Records

www.auvidis.com

47 avenue Paul Vaillant-Couturier, BP 21, F-94251 Gentilly cedex, France

Two labels here: Auvidis Ethnic covers all manner of music, both popular and obscure, some good, some not; the Auvidis/Unesco division documents traditional musical styles – discs that have recently been repackaged as a budget range. See also the related Inédit and Silex.

Axiom

www.hyperreal.org/music/labels/axiom/

400 Lafayette Street, 5th Floor, New York, NY10003, USA

Axiom was established in 1990 by prolific producer Bill Laswell (see p.617), a musician as at home with Bahian samba as American funk as Moroccan gnaoua rhythms. He has used the label to issue a stream of world fusion albums exploring his unique vision.

El Bandoneon

bandoneon@bluemoon.es

Camps y Fabrès 3–11, 08006 Barcelona, Spain

Bandoneon – as the name (the customized Argentine accordion) suggests – is devoted to tango, or more specifically to classic tango reissues. Their extensive catalogue includes more than twenty anthologies of Carlos Gardel alone, alongside a wealth of other crucial artists and orchestras from the 1920s to 1950s.

Blood and Fire

www.bloodandfire.co.uk

37 Ducie Street, Manchester M1 2JW, UK

A gem of a label, Blood and Fire is run by reggae archivist Steve Barrow, who releases well-conceived and superbly produced and packaged compilations of Jamaican music from the past three decades. All of his releases are critical and compelling.

Blue Flame

www.blueflame.com

Parlerstr. 6, D-70192, Stuttgart, Germany

A German label mainly featuring ambient and world fusion music, along with some choice Central Asia pop discs from Yulduz Usmanova and the Voice of Asia festival.

Blue Jackal

www.bluejackal.com

PO Box 87, Huntington, New York, NY 11743-0087, USA

This small label produces some fine contemporary Brazilian and Caribbean releases – such as the box set, *Cuba, I Am Time*.

Buda

www.budamusique.com

188 boulevard Voltaire, 75011 Paris, France

Wide ranging label run by Gilles Frucheaux. The *Musique du Monde* series is an extraordinary collection of mostly field recordings.

CAAMA Music

c.karpany@caama.com.au

101 Todd Street, Alice Springs, NT 8870, Australia

Based on Todd Street, in the middle of Alice Springs, the 'capital' of Australia's 'Red Centre', CAAMA is the leading label for Australian indigenous music.

Caiman

3110 NE Second Avenue, Miami, FL 33137, USA

Tel: 001 305 639 6660 Fax: 001 305 576 1842

A specialist Latin music label founded by Cayman-island based Dutch businessman, Raold Smeets (ambition: to become the Caribbean's Richard Branson), Caiman staked a claim with a debut CD by former Juan Luis Guerra percussionist, Chi-Chi Peralta, and has maintained a name with dance-beat variations on salsa.

Canyon

www.canyonrecords.com

4143 N 16th Street, Suite #6, Phoenix, AZ 85016, USA

Founded in 1951, Canyon pioneered recordings of Native American music. It has a diverse catalogue within the genre, though it is best known for Navajo-Ute flautist R. Carlos Nakai, who has given the label success in the New Age market.

Caprice

Caprice@srk.se

Nybrokajen 11, SE-111 48 Stockholm, Sweden

Caprice is owned by the Swedish Concert Institute and is partly funded by the Swedish government. The label boasts an impressive collection of traditional Swedish music, but also undertakes ambitious projects elsewhere in the world, with notable releases from East Africa, Vietnam and South America.

Celestial Harmonies

www.harmonies.com

PO Box 30122, Tucson, Arizona, AZ 85751, USA

A serious label with slightly New Age leanings – lots of Gregorian plainsong and Tibetan chant, as well as a comprehensive Music of Islam series and excellent Southeast Asian collections. All are pristine recordings with neat packaging from recycled paper.

Chanda Dhara

Schwilkenhofstr. 51A, D-70439 Stuttgart, Germany

Fax: 0049 711 804678

Top-notch concert recordings of Indian classical music with some outstanding Nikhil Bannerjee releases.

Le Chant du Monde

cdm@harmoniamundi.com

31–33 Rue Vandrezanne, 75013 Paris, France

Distributed by Harmonia Mundi (see p.636)

Quality field recordings made under the aegis of the Museé de l'Homme in Paris to archive the diversity of the world's music. They range from Alpine yodelling to Filipino tribal musics. Their anthologies *Voices of the World* and *Musical Instruments of the World* are fantastic, wide-ranging collections, with fat accompanying booklets.

Corasón

www.rounder.com/rounder/catalog/bylabel/cora

Distributed by Rounder

Corasón's heart lies with the village music of rural Mexico, and the sounds of its brothels and fiestas. But the catalogue is wide-ranging, with releases from around Central America and the Caribbean including some great contemporary Cuban, Dominican, Haitian and Panamanian discs.

Crammed Discs

www.crammed.be

43 rue Général Patton, 1050 Brussels, Belgium

With top acts like Zap Mama and the Taraf de Haidouks, the CramWorld series is particularly strong on soukous and the Balkans. Crammed's new Ziriguiboom series comprises full albums by new Brazilian acts, special compilations and reissues of rare and classic recordings.

Cutting Records

www.cuttingnyc.com

481 8th Avenue, New York, NY 10001, USA

The cutting-edge label created by former hip-hop DJ Aldo Marin, has contributed to a new genre of new-wave salsa and merengue crosses with house music. Their successes include Sancocho (with strong Puerto Rican folk elements woven through their songs) and Fulanito (with a Dominican merengue bias).

Dancing Cat Records

www.dancingcat.com

PO Box 639, Santa Cruz, CA 95061, USA

Founded by pianist-arranger George Winston, this is the undisputed king of Hawaiian slack key music. It is part of Windham Hill, which was recently folded into BMG. Hopefully it won't suffer.

Debs

170 rue du Faubourg Poissoniere, Paris 75010, France
Tel: 0033 42 81 17 42

Founded by musican/producer Henri Debs in 1974, the Debs catalogue includes titles ranging from the cadence era through to contemporary zouk, all recorded in Point-a-Pitre, Guadeloupe. However, limited pressings mean that generally only the newest titles are available.

Declic/Blue Silver

45 Rue St. Sebastien, 75011 Paris, France
Tel: 0033 49 23 77 70

This Paris-based endeavour, launched in 1986, records and distributes many major zouk stars as well as the majority of Antilles ragga artists. It dominates because of its international distribution system and willingness to keep most of its back catalogue available to buyers.

Discos Fuentes

www.DiscosFuentes.com
Cra. 51 No. 13-223, Apartado Aéreo 1960, Medellin, Colombia

Founded by Antonio Fuentes Lopez in 1934, Discos Fuentes is the leading label for Colombian music with over 1350 titles including cumbia, vallenato, salsa, merengue and Latin jazz. To the delight of some and the fury of others, many of the busty beach covers can double as garage pin-ups.

Ellipsis Arts

www.ellipsisarts.com
PO Box 305 ,Roslyn, NY 11576, USA

Ellipsis specialize in tall-format boxed compilations with superbly illustrated accompanying booklets (sometimes practically books). Highlight titles include *Planet Squeezebox* (Accordions), *Planet Soup* (global fusion) and *The Big Bang* (percussion). They also have a smaller-format series covering more esoteric themes, again with generous texts and illustrations.

EMI Hemisphere

www.hemisphere-records.com
64 Baker Street, London W1M 1DJ, UK

An enterprisingly un-corporate subdivision of EMI concentrating on reissues and compilations drawn from its extensive international back catalogues. They've recently started original recordings, too, with such groups as Canada's extraordinary La Bottine Souriante.

Erato/Detour

www.erato-detour.com
50 rue de Tournelles, 75003 Paris, France

Detour is the World Music arm of French classical label Erato. They have released some misconceived crossovers as well as excellent recordings like the

Tibetan disc *Dama Suna*, the Belizian *Paranda* compilation licensed from Stonetree (see p.641), and Mad Sheer Khan's fusion project *1001 Nights*.

Frémaux & Associés

20 rue Robert Girardineau, 94300 Vincennes, France
Distributed by Discovery (UK) Tel: 01672 563931

The backbone of this label is jazz and blues, but they also have a good line in gospel, old-timey, and a vintage French music-hall collection, plus an excellent series of remastered Antillean and Madagascan 78s.

GlobeStyle

www.acerecords.co.uk
48-50 Steele Road, London NW10 7AS, UK

Launched by Ben Mandelson and Roger Armstrong back in the 1980s, this was a pioneering World Music label, which introduced a host of African music, the Japanese group Nenes and South Indian maestros U. Srinivas and Kadri Gopalnath to Western audiences. Under the wing of the more R&B-oriented Ace Records, GlobeStyle was a bit hibernatory in the 1990s but it has recently shown signs of life.

Gramophone Company of India

www.saregama.com

The Gramophone Company of India, which made its first recording in 1902, is popularly known as HMV in the subcontinent, although it is now part of RPG, one of India's largest business enterprises. The company owns an unrivalled archive of Indian classical and playback music, and many of the most important recordings in Hindustani music's recent history are to be found on this label.

Grapevine

grape@iol.ie
5-6 Lombard Street East, Dublin 2, Ireland

As well as a longstanding range of Irish traditional releases, Grapevine has a burgeoning reputation for issuing high-quality new albums by the likes of Emmylou Harris and Canada's The Rankin Family.

Greensleeves Records

http://hosted.greensleeves.easynet.co.uk
Unit 14 Metro Centre, St Johns Road, Isleworth TW7 6NJ, UK

This leading British reggae label started out in 1975 with classics from Augustus Pablo and Barrington Levy. Since then, it has stayed on top of the developing reggae scene with British dub, dancehall, ragga and 'new roots' releases, as well as licensing material from leading Jamaican producers.

Greentrax

www.webzone1.co.uk/www/scotsweb/greentrx.htm
Cockenzie Business Centre, Edinburgh Road, Cockenzie, East Lothian EH32 0HL, Scotland

Essentially a label for Scottish traditional and contemporary roots music, but they also release Natalie McMaster and other American Celtic artists.

Guajiro/SAR

10441 NW 28th Street, Miami, Florida, FL 33172, USA
Tel: 001 305 592 1931 Fax: 001 305 592 1932

Cuban singer Roberto Torres' Miami-based label flew the flag for Cuban classics long before the *Buena Vista Social Club* was conceived. Drawing from the substantial pool of exiled veterans from Havana's heyday clubs (including Torres himself), alongside accomplished younger players, the recordings are wonderfully evocative, polished and with an unashamedly old-fashioned quality.

Hannibal

www.rykodisc.com
Shetland Park, 27 Congress Street, Salem, MA 01970, USA
P.O. Box 2401, London W2 5SF, UK

Hannibal was started in 1990 by record producer and World Music guru Joe Boyd, who'd previously produced discs by Pink Floyd, Nick Drake, Richard Thompson and Fairport Convention. The label's catalogue is eclectic but united by a concern for strong production values. With its parent, Ryko, the label is now part of Chris Blackwell's Palm Pictures stable.

Harlequin

See Interstate Music Ltd.

Harmonia Mundi

www.harmoniamundi.com
Mas de Vert, B.P. 150, 13631 Arles Cedex, France;
19/21 Nile Street, London N1 7LL, UK;

This French early classical music label also acts as a distributor for many of France's more ethnographic labels like Ocora, L'Institute du Monde Arabe and Chant du Monde.

Heartbeat, US

http://www.rounder.com/heartbeat
Distributed by Rounder

Heartbeat's catalogue encompasses all genres and eras of Jamaican music, from ska and rock steady to roots reggae, dub and dancehall. As well as contemporary issues, Heartbeat have rights to Studio One, the classic label of producer Clement 'Coxsone' Dodd, from which they have released some great compilations.

Hemisphere

See EMI Hemisphere Ltd.

Heritage

See Interstate Music Ltd.

Hibiscus/CocoSound

8, bd de Strasbourg, Paris 75010, France
Tel: 0033 42 06 03 04

Founded in the late 1980s, this Martinique-based label launched many current stars like Kali and Eric Virgal.

Its high-quality Martinique-based operations continue to make it a favourite for zouk and ragga artists, although it occasionally loses the biggest to the Paris studios and labels.

Hugo Production (HK)

www.hugocd.com
PO Box 764 Shatin, Central Post Office, NT, Hong Kong, China

Established in 1987, Hugo produces both Chinese and Western classical music CDs, distributing mainly in China, Hong Kong, Taiwan and Singapore. They have a multi-volume series of regional masters of the traditional qin and zheng zithers, as well as much 'easy-listening' conservatoire-style Chinese music.

Ice

www.bajan.com/ice
Bayley's Plantation, St Philip, Barbados

Founded by Bajan star Eddie Grant, Ice has an impressive catalogue of Trinidadian and other calypso and soca music including collections of the great artists like Black Stalin, Lord Kitchener, Mighty Sparrow and Roaring Lion.

India Archive Music

indarcmus@aol.com
2124 Broadway, Suite 343, New York, NY, USA

The name says it all. Specialists in archive Indian classical music.

Inédit

www.mcm.asso.fr
101 boulevard Raspail, 75006 Paris, France

Linked with the Maison des Cultures du Monde in Paris, Inédit releases traditional music recorded mostly in Paris when groups are on tour. Many of the discs are quite specialized, but the recordings are first class and include a variety of Asian music. Distributed by Auvidis.

Interstate Music Ltd.

20 Endwell Road, Bexhill on Sea, E Sussex TN40 1EA, UK
Tel/Fax: 01424 219847

Interstate specializes in remastered historic recordings from 78s and forms a huge resource for those interested in tracing the roots and history of World Music. The Harlequin label, run by Bruce Bastin, boasts a vast amount of Latin music, while the Heritage label features a diverse selection of historic fado, gospel and some West African releases.

Intuition Music

www.schott-music.com/intuition
PO Box 27 01 26, D-50508 Cologne, Germany

This Cologne-based label – part of the music publishers Schott – has done much to introduce a classic Cuban music, among other World releases.

Iona Records

www.lismor.co.uk/ionahome.html

27–29 Carnoustie Place, Scotland Street, Glasgow G5 8PH, UK

Basically a Scottish and Celtic roots label, Iona also feature major Cape Breton and other East Coast Canadian artists.

Irma Tropical

www.irma.it/

Via Fontarina 2, 40121 Bologna, Italy

Irma issue perfect party compilations of up-to-the-minute salsa releases, all segueing seamlessly (no pauses) and budget-priced. They're an excellent entry-point into the maze of releases from all corners of the salsa universe. Non-partisan, good quality recordings, detailed source information for getting original CDs.

Island

www.island.co.uk

825 8th Avenue, 24th Floor, New York, NY, USA

Chris Blackwell founded Island Records as a local Jamaican label in 1959, at the time of the emergence of ska. The label moved to London in 1962 but continued to release Jamaican titles, most notably albums from Bob Marley & The Wailers. Since being bought by Polydor, the catalogue reflects a more mainstream pop/rock focus, although its Mango subsidiary retains flagship African artists such as Baaba Maal, Salif Keita and Angelique Kidjo.

J & N Records

2190 NW 89th Place, Miami, FL 33171, USA

Tel: 001 305 717 5153 Fax: 001 305 717 5197

An exciting, young, US-based label specializing in salsa-derived dance music which warps the Cuban and Dominican beats in rap, hip-hop and dance music.

Jaro

www.jaro.de

Bismarckstr. 83, 28203 Bremen, Germany

Jaro have a strong line in innovative cultural fusions, for instance the Bulgarian Voices in collaboration with Tuvan throat singers Huun-Huur-Tu; also more classically oriented excursions into Islamic and Christian traditions.

Jayrem Records

www.Maorimusic.com

P.O. Box 38-558, Wellington Mail Centre, New Zealand

Founded in 1983, Jayrem is the leading label for and distributor of Maori music and has played a crucial role in its development from their first success with Upper Hutt Posse to current leading band, WAI.

JE Productions

30, avenue des Caraibes, 97200 Fort de France, Martinique

Tel: 63 75 15

Emmanuel Granier launched this label in the mid-1980s with JM Harmony and soon established the label as a leader in the formulaic but popular Martiniquan zouk-love scene. Only the more recent releases are available.

Jecklin

www.jecklin.ch

Musikhaus am Pfauen, Rämistrasse 30 + 42, 8024 Zürich 1, Switzerland

A serious classical label with its *Music of Man Archive*, specialized but high-quality ethnographic recordings.

JVC

JVC Victor Inc. 13–5, 1–Chome, Shibuya-ku, Tokyo 151, Japan

This bulging catalogue of CDs with distinctive red stripes features mainly Asian music. Many are studio recordings by musicians on tour in Japan.

Karen

karenrec@bellsouth.net

7060-7062 NW 50 Street, Miami, FL 33166, USA

This pioneering merengue label, originally based in Santo Domingo, was responsible for the most significant merengueros of the 1970s and 1980s, particularly Johnny Ventura, Wilfrido Vargas and his progeny (Las Chicas del Can, Los Hijos del Rey), and exploded into the world's Latin charts with Juan Luis Guerra's revolutionary late 1980s albums. They have been a bit quiet in recent years.

King Records

kokusai@kingrecords.co.jp

1-2-3, Otowa, Bunkyo-ku, Tokyo 112-0013, Japan

With its base in Japanese traditional music, King Records' catalogue ranges beyond the island to encompass Indonesian gamelan and other Asian folk and classical traditions.

Knitting Factory Records

www.knittingfactory.com/kfr/

74 Leonard Street, New York, NY 10013, USA

Small label attached to New York's best avant garde music venue, with lots of radical klezmer on the programme and in the catalogue.

Larrikin

larrikin@geko.net.au

PO Box 16, Pyimont, NSW 2009, Australia

Australian roots, contemporary and Aboriginal music.

Long Distance

35, rue Barbès, 93100 Montreuil, France

Tel: 0033 1 48 59 90 25

Under the editorship of Alain Weber and Armand Amar, a small but interesting series including Gypsy musicians, Sufi music and recordings from Ethiopia, Uzbekistan and the Indian subcontinent.

Luaka Bop

www.luakabop.com

Box 652, Cooper Station, New York, NY 10276, USA

David Byrne's Luaka Bop label is strongest on Brazil and Cuba but its catalogue includes other Latin American artists (notably Colombia's new wave salsa groups Aterciopelados and Bloque) and compilations (Black Peruvian music, for example), as well as some Indonesian and Indian music. Releases are consistently interesting and Byrne's own compilations superb.

Lusafrica

lusafrica@aol.com

16 quai de la Charente, 75019 Paris, France

Founded by producer Jose da Silva, this Paris label launched Cesaria Evora onto the international stage. They focus on Portuguese-African music but have also branched into zouk and Cuban music.

Lyrichord

www.lyrichord.com/world

141 Perry Street, New York, NY 10014, USA

One of the veteran companies in the business, Lyrichord's reputation has been built on its global ethnographic field recordings. Recent releases have been less solemn, if not less raw, and there are some fine recordings of contemporary traditional music performed on folk instruments.

Mango

See Island.

Manteca

www.manteca.co.uk

Union Square Music, Unit 2, Grand Union Office Park, Packet Boat Lane, Cowley UB8 2GH, UK

A new label exploiting the market for popular World Music compilations. First releases include contemporary bossa nova, salsa and tango for dance enthusiasts, plus traditional and contemporary Australian Aboriginal music, and a compilation of big name African voices.

Mélodie

www.melodie.fr

50, rue Stendhal, F-75020 Paris, France

A strong label and distributor, particularly for francophone music in Africa and elsewhere.

M.E.L.T. 2000

www.melt2000.com

6c Littlehampton Road, Worthing, W. Sussex, BN13 1QE, UK

This adventurous new label, 'Musical Energy & Loud Truth beyond 2000', concentrates on South African jazz/crossover but has also released some Cuban and Brazilian albums. They are owned by Robert Trunz, founder of B+W hi-fi and percussion enthusiast, whose influence perhaps shows in the consistently high production values.

Messidor

Kleine Bockenheimer Strasse, 10-12, D-60313, Frankfurt/Main, Germany

Tel: 0049 69 920088-0 Fax: 0049 69 920088-22

The German label established by Götz A. Wörner produced high-quality recordings with Cuban musicians in the late 1980s and early 1990s, when such things were still difficult to achieve. Particularly significant were debut records from N.G.La Banda, Cuba's leading salsa ghetto boys.

Moment Records

www.momentrecords.com

237 Crescent Road, San Anselmo, CA 94960, USA

Founded by tabla legend Zakir Hussain, Moment features Indian classical and fusion music. Their emphasis, they claim, is on the evocation of *rasa* (mood) – which simply means that most of their releases are recordings of live performances.

Multicultural Media

www.multiculturalmedia.com

RR3, Box 6655, Barre, VT 05641, USA

MM issue a *Music of the Earth* series – a variable but extensive collection of field recordings reissued from Victor in Japan.

Mushroom/White Records

www.mushroommusic.com.au/

9 Dundas Lane, Albert Park, VIC 3206, Australia

Australia's largest independent label, with a strong list of local singer-songwriters, rock and roots musicians.

Music of the World

www.musicoftheworld.com

P.O. Box 3620, Chapel Hill, NC 27515-3620, USA

Set up and run by Bob Haddad, Music of the World have a strong Indian and Asian roster, as well as good Latin American, Native American and Cajun collections. The label was recently bought by EMusic who should keep the CDs available as well as supplying the music through Internet downloads.

MW Records

www.musicwords

P.O. Box 1160, 3430 BD Nieuwegein, The Netherlands

MW have a slightly eccentric catalogue, but with some fine and unusual discs in their Folk Classics and World Roots series. Their Dutch/Surinam releases are particularly outstanding.

Nascente

www.vci.co.uk

MCI Ltd., 72–74 Dean Street, London W1V 5HA, UK

Nascente's budget-priced compilations started as cheap and cheerful but have matured in recent years with some very fine and at times pioneering discs covering salsa and Cuban artists in particular, but also lesser known genres such as Trinidadian chutney music.

Navras

www.navrasrecords.com

22 Sherwood Road, London NW4 1AD, UK

Navras has the largest collection of (mainly North) Indian classical music outside the subcontinent with excellent recordings of Nusrat Fateh Ali Khan, Hariprasad Chaurasia, Shivkumar Sharma, Bhimsen Joshi, etc. Most are live concert recordings.

Neelam

www.neelam.com

13003 Trina Drive, Philadelphia, PA 19116-1813, USA

Neelam has made a name for itself, principally in the mail-order market, as a specialist in Indian classical and Marathi (from Maharashtra) music and videos.

Nimbus Records

www.nimbus.ltd.uk

Wyastone Lees, Monmouth NP5 3SR, Wales

Through the 1980s and '90s, Nimbus released a series of World Music albums recorded by Robin Broadbank, with careful attention to sound quality and explanatory notes. The Indian classical releases were outstanding and there were significant recordings from Southeast Asia, Cuba and Brazil. Sadly, just as most classical record companies are waking up to the popularity of World Music, Nimbus has cut right back, limiting itself to repackaging its back catalogue at budget price.

Nonesuch

www.nonesuch.com

75 Rockefeller Plaza, 8th floor, New York, NY 10019, USA

The Nonesuch Explorer series (largely recorded by David Lewiston) was one of the first to make field recordings and World Music widely available. It includes high-quality recordings from all over the globe, many of which have reappeared on CD. The Nonesuch label itself (part of Warner Music) releases the Kronos Quartet, the Gipsy Kings and Caetano Veloso, among others, and licenses many World Circuit recordings in the US.

Nubenegra

www.nubenegra.com

Humilladero 8, 1o Iz., 28005 Madrid, Spain

Manuel Domínguez's quirky Nubenegra (Black Cloud) focuses on Spanish, West African and Latin releases, the latter concentrating on Cuba, Venezuela and Brazil and including artists of the stature of Chucho Valdés.

Nuevos Medios

nuemed@interbook.net

Ruiz de Alarcon 12, 28014 Madrid, Spain

A crucial Spanish label, Nuevos Medios has been responsible for most of the 'new flamenco' acts of the 1990s, and also issues 'new tango' recordings from Argentina.

Ocora

Maison de Radio France, 116 Av. du President Kennedy, 75786 Paris cedex 16, France (distributed by Harmonia Mundi)

Linked with Radio France, Ocora has for many years been the world's leading company releasing traditional folk and non-Western classical music from all round the globe. Their CDs are usually well recorded, researched and presented.

Oriente Musik

www.oriente.de

Augustastr. 20B, D-12203 Berlin, Germany

A small and eccentric catalogue ranging from the eastern province of Cuba to the Mongolian steppe with strong collections of oriental tango and klezmer (including Kroke and Di Naye Kapelye) en route.

Palenque Records

62 rue Doudeauville, 75018 Paris, France

Tel/Fax 0033 1 4262 5671

French label specializing in the Afro-Latin music of Colombia and the Caribbean, including champeta.

Palm Pictures

www.islandlife.com

8 Kensington Park Road, London W11 3BU, UK

Palm Pictures, Chris Blackwell's reinvention of the Island/Mango labels (which he sold to Polygram), has swiftly become a force, producing innovative, well-crafted releases. As well as its own name releases, the company owns the Rykodisc roster of labels, including World Music specialist Hannibal.

Pan

paradox@dataweb.nl

PO Box 155, 2300 AD, Leiden, Netherlands

A very wide catalogue of ethnographic field recordings particularly strong on Russia, the Caucasus and Central Asia, West Africa, China and Polynesia.

Piranha Musik

www.piranha.de

Carmerstraße 11, 10623 Berlin, Germany

A distinctive label founded by Borkovsky Akbar featuring contemporary roots music round the globe – highlights include Mozambique, Egypt, Brazil plus Mediterranean Sephardic music and top US klezmer ensemble, the Klezmatics.

Playasound

Playasound@wanadoo.fr

96 rue du Chateau, 92100 Boulogne, France

This French label used to produce tacky tourist-style music but of late seems to be realigning itself with some high-quality releases.

Putumayo World Music

www.putumayo.com

324 Lafayette Street, 7th Floor, New York, NY 10012, USA

Putumayo emerged from the Latin American-oriented gifts and clothing chain, set up by Dan Storper, who now runs it as a fully-fledged independent label with branches in the US and Europe. With naive and colourful covers, the discs are intended to introduce World Music to people who didn't know they liked it: for instance *Music from the Coffee Lands*, which has been creatively marketed in coffee shops. The catalogue includes country compilations, musical journeys and a few individual artist discs.

Raga Records

www.raga.com
PO Box 635, New York, NY 10014, USA

A specialist in North Indian classical music, Raga has a good catalogue of archival, concert and modern performances from artists such as Nikhil Banerjee, Vishwa Mohan Bhatt and Zia Mohiuddin Dagar.

Real Rhythm Records

www.codmusic.com
Müllheimerstr. 89, PO Box 147, 4007 Basel, Switzerland

A small label recording contemporary Cuban bands with a couple of maxims: the bands must have a history (no all-star bands) and be music by Cubans for Cubans (no export-oriented acts). Includes Conjunto Casino and Septeto Nacional Ignacio Piñeiro.

RealWorld

www.realworld.on.net
Mill Lane, Box, Corsham, Wiltshire SN13 8PL, UK

The RealWorld label was founded in 1989 by Peter Gabriel and has been based on a symbiotic relationship between the WOMAD festival and Gabriel's excellent studios at Box in Wiltshire. The catalogue includes artists from all round the globe with a strong emphasis on fusion experiments – Afro-Celts currently being a big seller. RealWorld were also largely responsible for bringing Nusrat Fateh Ali Khan to worldwide attention. The WOMAD Select series offers more or less live-take recordings of WOMAD festival artists, designed for the artists to sell at concerts.

Rhino

www.rhino.com
10635 Santa Monica Blvd, Los Angeles, CA 90025, USA

Rhino grew out of a secondhand record shop in LA in 1978 and has since become one of the largest enterprises that remasters and repackages collections and compilations of popular music. Their catalogue includes some gems of US regional music.

Rituals Music

www.ritualsmusic.com
5 Longden Street, Port of Spain, Trinidad

Rituals is a progressive new Caribbean label that initially specialized in crossover style Rapso artists such as 3 Canal, Brother Resistance & Kindred. In 2000, they entered the soca arena with a bang by signing megastar Superblue, and they plan to leave a mark on the World Music scene with chutney artist Mungal Patasar, who they recently licensed to Virgin Records.

RMM Records

www.rmmrecords.com
568 Broadway, Suite 806, New York, NY 10012, USA

Ralph Mercado managed many of Fania's artists and promoted shows for the label before creating his own label RMM (Ralph Mercado Management which became Ritmo Mundo Musical) in 1987. As the older company waned and folded, RMM became New York's leading Latin stable with the aristocrats of salsa, including Celia Cruz, Tito Puente, Eddie Palmieri, Oscar D'Leon, Jose Alberto, India and Marc Anthony, as well as the young generation of merengue and salsa-hip-hop/rap groups.

Rock Records

www.rock.com.tw
4F, #465, Chung-hsiao East Road Sec. 6, Taipei, Taiwan.

A leading label for Mandarin rock and pop based in Taiwan, although it also records and sells records in Hong Kong and throughout mainland China.

Rounder Records

www.rounder.com
1 Camp Street, Cambridge, MA 02140-1149, USA

Rounder is one of the largest and best independent record labels in the USA. Most of its music features home-grown US regional styles such as bluegrass, Hawaiian, Cajun and zydeco, but it has expanded to cover many areas of the world, as featured in the excellent Anthology of World Music series. Rounder are currently issuing on CD the vast Alan Lomax Collection (see p.534), and they also distribute a roster of independent world labels including Ashé, Corasón and Heartbeat.

Rykodisc

www.rykodisc.com
78 Stanley Gardens, London W3 7SZ, UK

As well as handling the Hannibal label (see p.636), Rykodisc have an interesting range of roots albums of their own, including 1960s folk/Celtic reissues and the Library of Congress Endangered Music Project produced by Mickey Hart. They also have a Latin label, RykoLatino, with strong releases of salsa and music from Puerto Rico.

Saydisc Records

Chipping Manor, The Chipping, Wotton-Under-Edge, Glos, GL12 7AD, UK

Saydisc boast a splendidly eccentric collection of recordings ranging from Victorian street organs and church bells to British traditional song and a rather haphazard selection of World Music, including a series of Pacific discs recorded by David Fanshawe.

Schott/Wergo

See Wergo.

Shanachie Records

www.shanachie.com
13 Laight Street, 6th Floor, New York, NY 10013, USA

A diverse catalogue of music from all over the globe – most specially recorded, although many are released under licence. Their Yazoo label presents good compilations of old 78 recordings.

Smithsonian Folkways

www.si.edu/folkways
955 L'Enfant Plaza, Suite 7300, MRC 953, Washington, DC 20560, USA

Folkways was founded in 1948 by Moses Asch who wanted to 'fill the map with music'. By his death in 1987 there were over 2000 titles – lots of US folk, music from all around the world, plus poetry, political speeches, frogs, trains and motor cars. The catalogue was acquired by the Smithsonian Institution and is now curated by Anthony Seeger. The entire catalogue is still available (on cassette) and Smithsonian Folkways has reissued many of the best titles on CD, as well as continuing to release expertly researched recordings from the US and all over the globe. There are important releases of regional and Native American music, as well as the excellent *Music of Indonesia* series. For more on the history of the label see the US Archives article on p.531.

Sono (formerly Sonodisc)

85 rue Foundary, 75015 Paris, France

Owned by Jacob Desvarieux of Kassav, Sono is the main source of francophone African and Caribbean music with a huge catalogue that contains hundreds of compilations of Congolese hits, in particular. Also has a distribution arm known as Musisoft.

Sound of America Records (SOAR)

www.soundofamerica.com
PO Box 8606, Albuquerque, NM 87198, USA

Contemporary and traditional Native American music.

Stonetree

www.stonetreerecords.com
35 Elizabeth Street, Benque Viejo del Carmen, Belize

Belize's pioneering label was founded by Ivan Duran in 1994, with a goal 'to promote the obscure musical styles whose appeal reaches far beyond the boundaries of this region.' Artists include Andy Palacio, Mr Peters and his Boom & Chime and excellent Paranda music.

Sugar Hill

www.sugarhillrecords.com
PO Box 55300, Durham, NC 227717, USA

An established label focusing on country, blues, bluegrass, folk and other Americana.

Traditional Crossroads

www.rootsworld.com/crossroads
PO Box 20320, Greeley Square Station, New York, NY 10001-9992, USA

Specialists in high-quality remastering of historic Turkish and Armenian recordings, plus fine modern recordings of klezmer.

Trikont

www.trikont.de
Kistlerstraße 1, Postfach 90 10 55, D-81510 München, Germany

Eccentric label run by Achim Bergmann with particular strengths in German and Alpine recordings – from archive 78rpm reissues to the Alpine new wave. Also excellent hillbilly, Cajun and klezmer discs.

Triple Earth

iain@triple-earth.co.uk
PO Box 240, Wembley HAO 4FX, UK

Iain Scott's Triple Earth catalogue is an individual's pick rather than a strategic marketing plan – and all the better for it. Najma Akhtar, Aster Aweke and Mose Fan Fan's marvellous Congo Acoustic are to be found here.

Tropical Music

www.tropical-music.com
POB 22 30, 35010 Marburg, Germany

Small German label which covers a fair spread of the continents in an eccentrically patchy way. The emphasis is on Brazil, Argentina, Trinidad and Japan.

Tumbao Cuban Classics

tumbao@bluemoon.es
Camps i Fabres 3–11, 08006 Barcelona, Spain

Tumbao is a superb archive label, researching and reissuing Cuban music from old 78s and master tapes. The collection ranges from tinny early *son* trios to the big sound of postwar salsa. All the releases cover a particular period of a group or artist and have exemplary sleevenotes.

Tumi

www.tumi.music.ndirect.co.uk
8/9 New Bond Street Place, Bath, UK

Latin American and Caribbean artists, both popular and obscure, feature on this UK label, as well as some trendy ethno-trance acts. Cuban, Andean, salsa and tropical sounds predominate.

VDE-Gallo

www.vdegallo.ch
Rue de l'Ale 31, case 945, 1000 Lausanne 9, Switzerland

VDE-Gallo (now known as Gall in the US) is the parent of AIMP (see p.633). Their *Peoples* collection covers mainly vocal and flute music from various tribes and traditions around the world.

Water Lily Acoustics

www.waterlilyacoustics.com
PO Box 91448, Santa Barbara, CA 93190, USA

Water Lily are a small, radical label committed to the music of minority cultures, both contemporary and traditional. They have issued some strong fusion releases, notably Western/Indian collaborations (including Ry Cooder's first fusion release).

WeltWunder Records

www.weltwunder.com
Gehrden 35, D 21635 Jork, Germany

WeltWunder started out with percussion – drum masters like Mustapha Tettey Addy from Ghana – and have expanded into salsa, tango, East German folk, and a series of single country compilations.

Wergo

www.schott-music.com
Postfach 36 40, D-55026 Mainz, Germany

A division of Schott, the German music publishers, Wergo's Weltmusik imprint releases an impressive catalogue of mainly traditional music. Excellent Pakistani Sufi discs, Indian classical recordings, klezmer, Brazilian and African music.

Wicklow

www.wicklowrecords.com
#200-1505 W 2nd Avenue, Vancouver, BC V6H 3Y4, Canada

Part of BMG Classics, Wicklow was founded by The Chieftain's Paddy Moloney and takes its name from the Irish county where he lives. 'I want to discover people who've been out there some time and promote them,' he says. The eclectic roster includes Värttinä, Ashley McIsaac, Juan Carlos Formell, Yat-Kha and fusionist Bill Laswell.

Wind Records

www.wind-records.com.tw
5F, no.14 Lane 130, Min Chuan Rd, Hsin tien, Taipei, Taiwan 231

Wind Records, founded in 1988 in Taiwan, distributes widely. 'Dedicated to bringing back some of the forgotten beauty of Chinese music and the unexplored wisdom of Chinese culture', the results are mainly New Age-type arrangements suitable for meditation or t'ai chi. Their Historical Recording Collections, however, contain important archive recordings from before the Cultural Revolution.

World Circuit

www.worldcircuit.co.uk
106 Cleveland Street, London W1P 5DP, UK

Nick Gold's World Circuit have been a consistently interesting and astute label since the early 1990s,

producing imaginative recordings of mainly African and Latin artists, and notably pairing Ali Farka Touré with Ry Cooder on the Grammy-winning *Talking Timbuktu*. They deservedly struck gold in 1998 with the three-million-selling *Buena Vista Social Club*.

World Connection

albert.nijmolen@capitolonline.nl
Schermerstraat 9 rd, 2013 EP Haarlem, Netherlands

A new Dutch label with releases from the Dutch East Indies, and from Peru, Africa and Eastern Europe.

World Music Network

www.worldmusic.net
6 Abbeville Mews, 88 Clapham Park Road, London SW4 7BX, UK

World Music Network produce the growing range of *Rough Guide* CD compilations, which are often visually tied in with the travel books, although the discs are independently produced. World Music Network also run the specialist Riverboat label.

World Network

www.NetworkMedien.com
Network Medien GmbH, Merianplatz 10, D-60316 Frankfurt am Main, Germany

This top-quality German label run by Jean Trouillet and Christian Scholze has drawn on the extensive Cologne radio archive as well as producing its own enterprising new recordings. There's an ongoing series showcasing representative artists from individual countries (now up to 49 discs) plus a growing series of handsomely-packaged double CD/booklet digipacks. Highlights include Hommage à Nusrat Fateh Ali Khan, Sufi Soul and some excellent Central Asian artists including Alim Qasimov.

World Up!

world-up@uksonymusic.com
10 Great Marlboroough Street, London W1V 2LP, UK

Word Up! is the World and Latin music division of Sony – as opposed to the pop arm which houses the Ricky Martin types or Epic which has Gloria Estefan and the Estefans' Crescent Moon Latin music label. World Up! releases include Venezuelan Orlando Poleo, salsero Ruben Blades, Algerian Rai Kum, French-gypsy clan, Tekameli, South African Jonas Gwangwa, and a huge *This is Cuba* mid-price series drawn from Cuba's EGREM archives.

Xenophile

www.greenlinnet.com
43 Beaver Brook Road Danbury, CT 06810, USA.

This, the non-Celtic arm of Green Linnet, has a well-chosen set of recordings covering Cuba, Finland, klezmer and Madagascar, among others.

Record Shops | Directory

This Shops Guide, like the preceding Labels directory, covers specialists in American, Latin, Caribbean, Indian, Asian and Pacific music – though many cover a wider range. Most offer Internet and mail-order sales. Online/mail-order only stores are listed at the end of the directory.

Australia

Birdland

birdland@birdland.com.au
3 Barrack Street, Sydney, NSW 2000
Tel: 0061 02 9299 8527. Fax: 0061 02 9299 6854

Sydney's best all-round World Music store.

Austria

Lotus Records

www.lotusrecords.at
Pfeifergasse 4, Salzburg 5020
Tel/Fax: 0043 662 84 91 28

Probably the largest selection of World Music in the country, with special strengths in Yiddish and klezmer, belly dance, Sufi, tango, flamenco. A stone's throw from Mozartplatz, too.

Suedwind - Weltmusik

www.suedwind.at
Mariahilferstrasse 8, Vienna 1070
Tel/Fax: 0043 1 522 3886

Suedwind was set up as a non-profit-making organization to inform people about north–south relations and the Third World. They offer traditional music from Africa, Latin America and Europe.

Belgium

Musica Nova

Galerie d'Ixelles 24–28, Burssels 1050
Tel: 00322 511 6694

Sited in the heart of 'Little Matonge', this specializes in Congolese releases, though Pierrot the proprietor also stocks US, Afro-Cuban and Italian imports.

England

Ada Music

36 Market Place, Beverley, E. Yorkshire HU17 9AG
Tel/Fax: 01482 868024

This specialist operation dedicates its energies to finding the best in Scandinavian and other European folk but they can also supply a wide range of World Music releases. Good mail-order service.

Decoy Records

30 Deansgate, Manchester M3 1RH
Tel: 0161 832 0183 Fax: 0161 839 1713

One of the leading World Music shops in the UK, Decoy offer all genres from traditional to modern, acoustic to electric, global and local. Mike Chadwick (World Music DJ on Jazz FM) works here and other members of staff also DJ in clubs and on radio. Their combined knowledge is immense and they're not shy about making recommendations.

HMV Oxford St

www.hmv.co.uk
363 Oxford Street, London W1R 2BJ
Tel: 020 7629 1240

HMV's flagship London megastore has an extensive World Music section in the basement offering as good a choice as any independent specialist.

Honest Jon's

276 & 278 Portobello Road, London W10 5TE
Tel: 020 8969 9822 Fax: 020 8969 5395

Honest Jon's has been selling reggae, jazz, house, R&B, funk, rap, African, etc, out of two shops in Portobello Market seven days a week for 25 years. The World section has recently been expanded. New and secondhand items; plus a mail-order service.

Intoxica!

www.intoxica.co.uk
231 Portobello Road, London W11 1LT
Tel: 020 7229 8010 Fax: 020 7792 9778

Intoxica! specializes in the secondhand kitsch, collectors, Latin-jazz and cult end of the Latin music spectrum. Ask to see their 7-inch singles box for some unexpected gems from salsa's past.

Listening Planet

www.listeningplanet.com
22 Hughenden Yard, Marlborough, Wiltshire SN8 1LT
Tel: 01672 511151 Fax: 01672 511737

A mail-order store that covers all styles of music and specializes in tracking down obscure records on small labels. Apparently they're a persistent lot.

Mr Bongo

www.mrbongo.com
44 Poland Street, London W1V 3DA
Tel: 020 7287 1887 Fax: 020 7439 1828

London's premier salsa emporium, Mr Bongo is also a meeting point for Latin DJs and fans to swap notes and pick up flyers for the myriad salsa clubs and dance classes around the capital.

Roots Music

www.roots-music.co.uk

9 Derwent Street, Sunderland, Tyne & Wear SR1 3NT

Tel: 0191 567 0196 Fax: 0191 567 2711

Roots stocks an extensive selection of African, Latin, Caribbean and many other roots genres. A catalogue is available on request and individual requirements are researched.

Sona Rupa

hemant@vpl-int.prestel.co.uk

103 Belgrave Road, Leicester LE4 6AS

Tel: 0116 266 8181 Fax: 0116 261 0336

Sona Rupa are the UK's largest stockists of music from the Indian subcontinent, with British and imported labels.

Stern's African Records Centre

www.sternsmusic.com

293 Euston Road, London NW1 3AD

Tel: 020 7387 5550 Fax: 020 7388 2756

London's premier African music store is also pretty strong on Latin music. They have years of expertise behind them and are the UK distributors for many Latin and World Music labels, which means most desirable items are kept in stock.

Tumi

8–9 New Bond Street Place, Bath BA1 1BH

Tel: 01225 446025 Fax: 01225 331360

The headquarters of the Tumi record label doubles up as a bazaar-like shop selling crafts, clothes and furniture alongside CDs and cassettes of music from all over Latin America. Tumi specialities are Mexican, Peruvian, Chilean and Cuban music.

Finland

Digelius Music

www.digelius.com

Lalvurinrinne 2, Helsinki 00120

Tel: 00358 9 666375 Fax: 00358 9 628950

The top World Music shop in Scandinavia, Digelius has been run by Philip Page and his team since the dawn of time and now offers more than 10,000 different titles on CD, cassette and vinyl. Videos and books are also available. The company's Website specializes exclusively in Baltic and Nordic music.

France

Afric Music

3 rue des Plantes, Paris 75014

Tel: 0033 1 45 42 43 52

Favoured by the capital's Antillean as well as African music DJs, this is a compact little shop with an air of devotion and enthusiasm – the helpful assistants spinning novelty after novelty. Limited stocks of vinyl are on offer as well as a good selection of CDs.

Disc Inter

2 rue des Rasselins, Paris 75020

Tel: 0033 1 43 73 63 48

One of the biggest, best-stocked World Music stores in Paris – which compensates for its distance from the centre. The weekly chart is a help if you're stumped by their vast choice of African and Antillean music.

FNAC Forum

Forum des Halles, Paris 75001

and numerous other branches

The huge FNAC shops (this is a big central example) are a combination of music, book, hi-fi, computer, camera and general leisure megastores. All the Parisian FNACs and many of the regional ones have excellent World Music departments with a large selection of well-laid-out CDs, and lots of listening posts.

Moradisc

51 Boulevard de Rochechouart, Paris 75009

Tel: 0033 1 42 81 14 89

A great place to stop at after the rigours of being a tourist on the Butte Montmartre. This small and friendly shop offers a wide range of Afro-Antillean music on CD with the emphasis on soukous and zouk.

Virgin Megastore

56–60 av des Champs-Élysées, Paris 8

Virgin's Paris megastore is a real treasure trove and has a vast amount of its stock digitized so that you can pick up a disc, wave its barcode at a listening post, and sample. The World Music sections are impressive.

Germany

Canzone

www.canzone.de

Savignypassage Bogen 583, Berlin 10623

Tel: 0049 30 312 4027 Fax: 0049 30 312 6527

This well-established World Music shop is nicely laid out and intelligently stocked. Emphasis is on the Berlinerish obsessions of Eastern European, Greek, Turkish and tango music. Staff are helpful and you can listen at will. Also runs the Oriente label.

Weltrecord

weltrecord@t-online.de

Eppendorfer Landstrasse 124, Hamburg 20251

Tel: 0049 40 480 7908

Music from all over the world with special emphasis on Africa and the Arab world. All styles are catered for but traditional music is strongest. Videos, books and mail-order also available.

Yalla Music

yalla_music@gmx.de www.yalla.de

Rathenauplatz 24, Cologne 50674

Tel: 0049 221 240 9333 Fax: 0049 221 240 9332

A neat and tidy little shop selling African, Latin, Brazilian and Spanish music in abundance.

India

The Music Shop

Khan Market, Near India Gate, South Delhi

The best place in the capital to get CDs, cassettes and videos of Indian music.

Music World

Spencer Plaza (1st Floor), Anna Salai, Chennai

The best shop for CDs and cassettes in Chennai (Madras).

Rhythm House

Subhash Chowk (next to the Jehangir Art Gallery), Mumbai

CDs and cassettes of all types of Indian music plus a fair choice of Western pop and jazz.

Ireland

Celtic Note

www.celticnote.ie

14-15 Nassau Street, Dublin 2

Tel: 00353 1 670 4157 Fax: 00353 1 670 4158

This spacious store near Trinity College is the best stop in all of Ireland for Celtic music but there are pretty credible shelves of other World Music releases, too. Also books and videos.

Claddagh Records

http://indigo.ie/~claddagh

2 Cecilia Street, Dublin 2

Tel 00353 1 677 0262.

A huge range of traditional and roots music from around the world is on offer at the Temple Bar outlet of this specialist Irish music label. Helpfully informative staff can handle virtually every query.

Israel

Jazz Ear

21 Sheinkin Street, Tel Aviv

Tel: 00972 3 525 2590 Fax: 00972 3 528 8989

World Music record shop and distributor.

Malaysia

Tower Records

Plaza Jln.Bukit Bintang, Kuala Lumpur

KL's biggest record store features local, traditional and Asian sounds alongside its Western stock.

Martinique

Rubicolor

19, rue Papin Dupont, 97200 Fort de France

Tel: 70 67 77

This zouk/Antilles retail outlet sells all the discs of producer Ronald Rubinel who has been responsible for many of the biggest hits in the past decade such as Ethnikolor, TaxiKolor, Multicolor, etccolor.

Netherlands

Mundial

mundial@mundial.nl www.mundial.nl

Schuitendiep 17-1b, Groningen 9712 KD

Tel: 0031 50 314 3860 Fax: 0031 50 549 1109

A shop and mail-order operation which concentrates completely on World Music and especially tango, Latin and reggae. With several years of experience and contacts with suppliers around the world the shop reckons it can lay its hands on just about anything.

Musiques Du Monde

Singel 281, Amsterdam

Tel: 0031 20 624 1354 Fax: 0031 20 625 3124

As the name suggests, World Music, both new and used. Listen before you buy.

Roots Mail Music

http://biz.inter.nl.net/roots.mail.music

Van Goorstraat 4, 4811 HJ Breda

Tel: 0031 76 522 2235 Fax: 0031 76 520 0201

All kinds of World roots music.

Xango World Music Records

Zadelstraat 14 Utrecht 3511 LT

Tel: 0031 30 232 8286 Fax: 0031 30 232 8059

Another good Dutch source.

New Zealand

Fisheye Discs

James Smiths Corner, Manners Street, Wellington

Tel: 0064 4 473 4088. Fax: 0064 4 473 4087

The widest selection of local roots and World Music sounds in New Zealand. Retail and mail order.

Portugal

Discantus/Mundo da Canção

www.discantus.pt

Rua Duque de Saldanha 97, Porto 4349 - 030

Tel: 00351 2 51 93 100 Fax: 00351 2 51 93 109

This promoter of roots and World Music events also distributes and retails CDs.

Scotland

Coda Records

www.codamusic.co.uk
12 Bank Street, Edinburgh EH1 2LN
Tel: 0131 622 7246 Fax: 0131 622 7245

Coda have four stores in Scotland, all of which stock quantities of Scottish, Celtic, folk and World Music.

Spain

FNAC – Madrid

c/Preciados 28, Madrid 28013
Tel: 0034 1 595 61 00

As with sister stores in France, this huge multimedia shopping haven has a broad World Music selection.

Sweden

Multi Kulti

multi.kulti@swipnet.se
Sankt Paulsgatan 3, Stockholm 11846
Tel/Fax: 0046 8 643 6129

Multi Kulti owner Steve Roney has been selling traditional and popular music from around the world since 1986 – his friend Don Cherry named the store. Under the motto 'Renewal and retrospective absorption', they are glad to guide all-comers.

Switzerland

BeBop

Spitalgasse 36, PO Box 5431, 3001 Bern
Tel: 0041 31 312 5771 Fax: 0041 31 311 6713

One of the nicest shops in the heart of the old town, offering the whole range of World Music, plus plenty of American roots music.

Disco Club

22 rue de Terreaux-du-Temple, 1201 Genève
Tel/fax: 0041 22 732 7366

Almost every country in the world is covered with a wide selection of World and jazz releases. Brazil and Cuban sections are particularly strong with direct imports.

El Cubanito Music Shop

www.cubanito.ch
PO Box 3460, Badenerstrasse 4, 8021 Zurich

Linked to Zurich's most successful Latin club, this small shop has a strong selection of Latin dance music, including salsa, cumbia, merengue, Latin house, etc.

Maracas

Rosshofgasse 5, 4051 Basel
Tel/fax: 0041 61 262 1160

A small shop, centrally located specializing in Latin and Caribbean sounds, and some African releases.

Swagata

Theaterstrasse 7, 4051 Basel
Tel/fax: 0041 61 271 1762

Music from 180 countries with a particularly strong Asian selection. The owner is a real authority in World Music and Indian sounds in particular and stocks numerous imports and rarities.

USA

In addition to the US specialists listed below, honourable mentions should go to most larger branches of Tower, Virgin and Borders, all of whom have been stocking serious amounts of roots and World Music in recent years.

African Record Center

1194 Nostrand Avenue, Brooklyn, New York, NY
Tel: 001 718 493 4500

African and Caribbean music aplenty.

Amoeba

2455 Telegraph Avenue, Berkeley, CA
Tel: 001 510 549 1125

This vast store covers all kinds of music – new and secondhand. World Music isn't a particular speciality but the sections still dwarf most normal stores and prices are extremely competitive.

Antone's

2928 Guadalupe Street, Austin, TX
Tel: 001 512 322 0660

Austin's best record store for local and roots styles.

Bate Records

www.latinmoves.com/baterecords.htm
140 Delancey Street, New York, NY 10002
Tel: 001 212 677 3180 Fax: 001 212 777 1466

A vast downtown salsa store stocking the current chart hits from all over Latin America, racks of collectors' items from the history of salsa, plus a whole department of current 12" hits from the salsa-rengue, salsa-rap dance fusionistas.

Casa Latina

www.casalatinamusic.com
151 East 116th Street, New York, NY
Tel: 001 212 427 6062 Fax: 001 212 289 6950

Spanish Harlem's leading record store and hangout, Casa Latina is filled with CDs, videos, books, T-shirts and music memorabilia, and behind the counter a pair of experts will advise. Expect to rub shoulders with top DJs and legendary musicians checking arrivals.

Casino Records

1208 SW 8th Street, Miami, FL
Tel: 001 305 856 6888

Large Latin music store with Cuban music, new and old, well represented.

County Records

www.countysales.com
PO Box 191, Floyd, VA 24091
Tel: 001 540 745 2001

The largest bluegrass and old timey stockist anywhere in the world, with a dizzying range of albums, and their own label, too.

Do-Re-Mi Music Center

1829 SW 8th Street, Miami, FL
Tel: 001 305 541 3374

A comprehensive stock of Latin sounds, run by enthusiastic proprietor Rolando Rivero.

Down Home Music

10341 San Pablo Avenue, El Cerrito, CA
Tel: 001 510 525 2129

Just a mile or two north of the Berkeley border in El Cerrito, Down Home stocks roots music almost exclusively – blues, country, folk, Celtic, early R&B, ethnic, Worldbeat. It is especially strong on obscure independent/import reissues.

Drumbeat Indian Arts AZ

4143 N 16th Street, Phoenix, AZ
Tel: 001 602 266 4823

Formerly linked to Canyon Records (see p.634), this store has a good selection of Native American releases and craft items.

Elderly Instruments

www.elderly.com
1100 N Washington, PO Box 14249, Lansing, MI 48901
Tel: 001 517 372 7890 Fax: 001 517 372 5155

Elderly Instruments is a store and mail-order service offering a huge stock of modern and traditional instruments and 1000s of hard to find CDs and cassettes. Their speciality is all forms of American and Celtic folk. Other World Music titles are also in evidence in their catalogue.

Floyd's Record Store

434 E Main Street, Ville Platte, LA
Tel: 001 318 363 2184

A Cajun institution run by Floyd Soileau of Swallow Records, one of the premier Louisiana labels. A great selection of Cajun, zydeco and swamp pop from his and many other companies alongside audio equipment and gardening hardware.

Hear Music

1809 Fourth Street, Berkeley, CA
Tel: 001 510 204 9595

Listen to any CD in the store with no obligation. Extensive selection of international music.

Hear's Music, Inc.

www.hearsmusic.com
2508 North Campbell Avenue, Tucson, AZ 85719-3303
Tel: 001 520 795 4494 Fax: 001 520 795 1875

Hear's Music, Inc. is a retail music store and global mail-order company. They offer all forms of music (access to 500,000+ titles) but when it comes to their passion for all forms of World Music they might be considered obsessed! All in all they reckon they can lay their hands on over 60,000 different World Music titles. They also carry secondhand CDs, World Music videos and books. Customer service is paramount and all enquiries, however weird and testing, are welcome.

House of Musical Traditions

www.hmtrad.com
7040 Carroll Avenue, Takoma Park, MD 20912
Tel: 001 301 270 9090

House of Musical Traditions has been up and running since 1972 offering records, books, videos and instruments relating to roots music from just about everywhere.

Janie's

129 Bandera Road, San Antonio, TX
Tel: 001 210 735 2070

A legendary shop for Tejano and Conjunto music.

J&R Music World

23 Park Row, New York, NY
Tel: 001 212 238 9000

Prices at this large downtown establishment tend to be lower than those at the chain megastores and there are extensive aisles of Latin, reggae and World Music.

Louisiana Music Factory

210 Decatur Street, New Orleans, LA
Tel: 001 504 586 1094

The best place for Louisiana Cajun, zydeco, swamp pop and blues. Extensive stocks of hard-to-find titles plus a small stage for in-store appearances.

Made in Puerto Rico

2127 Third Avenue, New York (Spanish Harlem), NY
Tel: 001 212 289 1368 Fax: 001 212 472 2652

A wonderful place to shop: a store devoted to products from Puerto Rico. CDs include folkloric and salsa, and local musicians' home-produce. Also, pick up imported coffee, cigars, crafts, magazines and books. The shop leads into the New York Salsa Museum, a frenzy of costumes, photos and momentos of great names and moments in the city's salsa history.

Mostly Music

www.jewish-music.com
4805 13th Avenue, Brooklyn, New York, NY 11218
Tel: 001 718 438 2766 Fax 001 718 438 3845

'The Heart of Jewish Music' the store and excellent

Web site proclaim. All aspects of Jewish music from the great cantors to klezmer; CDs, videos and books.

Round World Music

593 Guerrero Street, San Francisco, CA

Tel: 001 415 255 8411

The best specialist World Music store in San Francisco, this is a favourite of David Harrington of the Kronos Quartet.

Sikhulu's Record Shack

274 W 125th Street, New York, NY

A convenient spot in Manhattan to hunt down African, Caribbean, soul and gospel goodies. Especially hot on South African releases.

Stern's Records

www.sternsmusic.com

71 Warren Street New York, NY 10007

Tel: 001 212 964 5455 Fax: 001 212 964 5955

The offspring of Stern's African Record Centre in London, Stern's Records has been the leading importer and distributor of African recordings in North America since 1989. This shop has the best African selection in the Western Hemisphere, plus music from just about every country in the world, with particularly strong selections of Indian, Cuban and Brazilian music. You can also order CDs, books and videos by phone, fax, post and email.

Tower Records (New Orleans)

408–410 N Peters, New Orleans, LA

Tel: 001 504 529 4411

This New Orleans branch of the chain has a refreshingly regional approach with Louisiana roots music old and new plus jazz and blues.

Tower Records (NYC)

692 Broadway, New York, NY

Tel: 001 212 505 1500

Best of the many Towers dotted around New York with an excellent international section.

Tropical Music

www.tropicaldisc.com

Dolphin Plaza, 2395 S Kihei Road, Kihei, Maui, HI 96753

Tel: 001 808 874 3000

A good all-round record store with a strong Hawaiian music section and handmade ukeleles.

World Music Institute

www.HearTheWorld.org

49 West 27th Street, Suite 930, New York, NY 10001-6936

Tel: 001 212 545 7536

A leading US presenter of traditional World Music and dance, the Institute maintains a New York store and an informative mail-order catalogue of around 5000 recordings, videos and books.

Internet/Mail Order

As noted, many of the physical stores above offer mail order, often through the Internet. Listings below, however, are purely Internet/mail-order stores. All ship internationally, but note that the import of more than two CDs may be liable to tax.

Africassette

www.africassette.com

This specialist mail-order company was started in 1991 with the intention of making cassette releases imported from Africa available to the world. It has since added CDs, videos and books, and expanded its coverage to the Caribbean and South America.

Amazon.com

www.amazon.com

The Amazon.com search engine is awesome and will pull up pretty much any US or UK release, and much besides, often accompanied by audio samples and a string of reviews from customers. What is maybe even more interesting is that they will be posting reviews from this book alongside CDs, making the acquisition of a vast and wonderful collection dangerously easy.

Borders.com

www.borders.com

Borders is a nice, clean browseable site – very much like its terrestrial stores. There's a reasonably deep catalogue and array of sound samples in 'International'.

The Brazilian Sound

www.thebraziliansound.com

As so many Brazilian discs are not distributed in Europe or the US, this is a great resource for CDs, movies and books all on sale at discounted prices.

CD Universe

www.cduniverse.com

CD Universe are another of the big players, battling for supremacy. Their World Music department is well laid out with links into browseable country-by-country sections, and an excellent search engine that generates nicely organized returns from a deep catalogue.

cdnow.com

www.cdnow.com

At time of writing, cdnow offers a smaller World Music selection than its rivals but they are pretty good on Latin music – and they have keen prices, lots of sound samples, and some decent weekly features.

Descarga

www.descarga.com

328 Flatbush Avenue, Suite 180, Brooklyn, NY 11238, USA

Tel. 001 718 693 2966

This Brooklyn-based Latin mail-order specialist is an awesome store with a vast catalogue available in print form, as well as on its superbly designed Web site. The latter has a great search engine (it will direct you to 187 CDs featuring Celia Cruz, for instance), extensive track listings, reliable reviews, and includes the Descarga journal with features and interviews. A must for anyone into Latin music.

Far Side Music

paulfish@mx5.nisiq.net
205 Sun City Hikawadai, 4-40-10 Hikawadai, Nerima-Ku, Tokyo T179, Japan. Tel/fax: 0081 3 3936 9464

Paul Fisher's Far Side music offers mail-order sales of music from Japan, Indonesia and elsewhere in Southeast Asia as well as sound advice. There are online and mail-out catalogues.

Jewish Music Distribution

www.jmht.org/jmd
PO Box 67, Hailsham, E. Sussex, BN27 4VW, UK

A specialist UK mail-order supplier for Jewish music.

JewishMusic.com

www.jewishmusic.com

A site for buying all types of Jewish music online including klezmer.

Khazana

www.khazana.com/cd

Possibly the largest catalogue of (predominantly) Indian classical music online, with over 4000 CDs.

Lamusica.com

www.Lamusica.com

This New York-based site was established in the mid-1990s to provide online *chisme* (gossip), reviews and interviews with the top names in salsa and salsa-pop. It has expanded into a Latin music Internet store.

Multicultural Media

www.multiculturalmedia.com
RR3, Box 6655, Granger Road, Barre, VT 05641, USA
Tel: 001 802 223 1294 Fax: 001 802 229 1834

Specialists in educational and worldwide media, this Vermont company features the Smithsonian's video and full CD range in its catalogue, as well as selections from global labels and its own Music of the Earth series.

Saregama

www.saregama.com

This Indian music Web site, with US and UK branches, sells CDs from The Gramophone Company of India and a range of other Indian labels at bargain prices.

Scope Music

scopemusic@yahoo.com
71/2 Ithaca Road, Elizabeth Bay, Sydney, NSW 2011 Australia.

Specialist mail-order company for Australian, New Zealand and Pacific roots music.

Tejano Classics

www.tejanoclassics.com

Specializes in older, vintage material not found on today's record labels.

Tower.com

www.towerrecords.com
www.towereurope.com

Tower's US and European sites deliver impressive catalogue returns and they have sound samples for a huge amount of discs. There's little in the way of text or reviews, but if you know what you're looking for you've a very good chance of finding it.

Contributors | World Music Volume II

James Attlee is a contributor to *Songlines* and *Gramophone* magazines and works in art publishing.

Nick Barraclough is a musician, writer and broadcaster who specializes in American folk music – bluegrass, Cajun, old-time, blues and country.

Colin Bass is a musician and radio presenter living in Berlin. He frequently records in Indonesia.

Philip Blackburn is a composer, instrument-builder, singer and writer and has organized several projects promoting Vietnamese music. He is currently Program Director of the American Composers Forum and runs the Innova Recordings label.

Etienne Bours is a journalist based in Belgium and World Music buyer for Belgian record libraries.

Marcus Breen lived in Melbourne, Australia where he edited *Our Place, Our Music*, a collection of studies on Aboriginal music. He now teaches in Chapel Hill, North Carolina, USA.

Robin Broadbank is a freelance music recordist and producer. He was responsible for directing and recording the Nimbus World Music series.

Simon Broughton is a freelance film maker, writer, broadcaster, co-editor of this book, and editor of the World Music magazine *Songlines*.

Viv Broughton is a collector, researcher and producer of gospel music. He is the author of *Black Gospel* (Blandford Press) and *Too Close To Heaven: The Illustrated History of Gospel Music* (Midnight Books).

Ramiro Burr is music reporter for the *San Antonio Express-News* and a frequent contributor to *Billboard*. He is author of *The Billboard Guide to Tejano and Regional Mexican Music*.

Kim Burton is a pianist, accordion player and writer specializing in Latin and Balkan music. She has participated in various GlobeStyle recordings.

David Cleary is Amazon programme manager for the Nature Council, based in Brasilía. This is a front to enable him to pursue his twin obsessions of Brazilian music and football.

John Clewley is a writer and photographer based in Bangkok. He's been *Bangkok Post* music columnist since 1994 and contributes to *Billboard* and *Asia Inc*. His last photo exhibition was *Sounds Asia: New Perspectives on Asian Popular Music*.

Mike Cooper is a slide guitarist and composer resident in Rome.

Peter Culshaw is a freelance arts writer, broadcaster and musician. He has for several years master-minded the UK's annual 'Music Village' events.

Peter Dalton is a contributor to reggae magazines *Dub Catcher* and *Boom Skack A Lacka*, and co-author with Steve Barrow of the *Rough Guide To Reggae* and *Reggae: 100 Essential CDs*.

Charles De Ledesma can often be heard enthusing on African, Latin and fusion music during BBC London Live's *Robert Elms Show* and, in the US on NPR's *All Things Considered*. He recently presented a magazine programme on AOL Internet radio and writes on travel for *The Independent*.

Veronica Doubleday performs Afghan music and is a writer and lecturer at the University of Brighton. She is author of *Three Women of Herat*, about the life of women in Afghanistan.

Mark Ellingham is a co-editor of this book and its predecessor. He set up Rough Guides in 1981 and remains Series Editor.

Jan Fairley is a writer and broadcaster based in Edinburgh; she has particular interests in Latin and Spanish music.

Mary Farquharson co-founded World Circuit in the UK and Discos Corason in Mexico, where she now lives. She started as a freelance journalist and continues to write about music when time permits.

Steven Feld teaches in New York University's Anthropology department and has been visiting Papua New Guinea since 1976.

Paul Fisher is a journalist, radio presenter and record producer born in the UK but now resident in Tokyo where he runs Far Side Music selling Asian CDs by mail order.

Charles Foran is the author of five books, including the novels *Kitchen Music* and *Butterfly Lovers*. He lives outside Toronto, Canada.

Nigel Gallop has been involved with the music of Latin America since his childhood in Mexico in the 1940s. He writes virtually all the music and dance sections of the *Footprint Guides* to the region.

Lalith Ganhewa was born in Sri Lanka and is a broadcasting producer at SFB 4 Radio MultiKulti, the 24-hour World Music channel in Berlin, Germany. He is also a composer and musician.

Ronnie Graham is a Scottish historian who has worked in development – currently for the charity Sightsavers – in Africa and the Caribbean.

Jane Harvey teaches at the Rotterdam Conservatory in the Jazz, Pop and World Music Department.

Sean Harvey is a musician and writer whose credits include stints with a dozen different New York Latin bands as well as authoring *The Rough Guide to the Dominican Republic*.

Jenny Heaton studied gamelan in Bali and Java for two years, before teaching in the UK and Germany. She was artistic director of the South Bank Gamelan Players in London from 1991–94.

Ken Hunt is a freelance writer and translator, with particular interests in India and Germany.

Okon Hwang is Associate Professor of Music at Eastern Connecticut State University with research interests in Korean popular music and the Westernization of Korean culture.

Stephen Jones is author of *Folk Music of China* (Oxford UP) and researches Chinese folk music at the School of Oriental and African Studies in London. He is also a professional violinist.

Jeff Kaliss is based in the San Francisco Bay Area where he writes about music for a variety of US and British publications. He is also author of a children's book on World Music.

Andy Kershaw is a writer, broadcaster and BBC radio's best-known World Music DJ. He writes a regular column in *Songlines*.

Rolf Kilius has worked as a sound engineer, computer analyst and music researcher. He spent two years in musicians' communities in Kerala.

Joanna Lee trained at London's Royal College of Music as a concert pianist and Columbia University as a musicologist. She currently teaches at the University of Hong Kong.

Ad Linkels is based in Holland where he produces CDs, writes books on the cultures of Polynesia and organizes Pacific-related projects for schools.

George Luke is a London-based writer and all-round music fan.

Ben Mandelson is a musician, record producer and widely-respected mover and shaker in the World Music business.

Robert Maycock is a specialist in Indian music which he covers for *BBC Music Magazine*, *Songlines* and other publications.

Andrew Means was born in England but now works as a freelance journalist in Phoenix, Arizona. He has been writing about Native American music for nearly twenty years.

Andy Morgan has done most jobs in the World Music universe, including spells with RealWorld and FNAC. He runs the Bristol-based global dance label, Apartment 22.

Gregory Mthembu-Salter is a writer based in Cape Town, where he spends his time raising a family, writing about Central African politics, and DJing.

Dave Muddyman is a composer and musician with the band Loop Guru. He co-edited the first edition of this book.

Heidi Munan is a writer and researcher living in Sarawak, East Malaysia. Her deep interest in the ethnic cultures of Borneo provides the material for her books, articles and broadcasts.

Carole Pegg was vocalist and fiddler with folk-rock band Mr Fox before training as a social anthropologist and studying music and performance amongst Mongols and other Inner Asian nomadic peoples. She is in charge of non-Western musics for the New Grove Dictionary.

Teddy Peiro is a *tanguista* extraordinaire and London's resident bandoneon player.

Georgia Popplewell is a writer and television producer/director based in Trinidad and Tobago who writes on music, film and sport. She is a contributing editor at *Caribbean Beat* magazine.

Rob Provine is Professor of Music at the University of Durham and has been studying Korean music since 1967.

Tina K. Ramnarine is a musician (orchestral and folk fiddler). She teaches ethnomusicology at Queen's University, Belfast, has researched and written on Caribbean popular and Scandinavian folk musics, and runs the Belfast World Music in the Community Project.

Helen Rees is Assistant Professor of Ethnomusicology at the University of California, Los Angeles. Since 1989 she has spent long periods in Yunnan doing traditional music research.

Dan Rosenberg is host of the 'Café International', a World Music/travel radio show that airs on WCBN-FM Ann Arbor, and for which he has travelled worldwide recording music and hundreds of interviews.

Joel Rubin is a clarinetist and researcher into traditional klezmer music, based in Berlin. He has published numerous anthologies of klezmer music and co-authored *Klezmer-Musik* (Bärenreiter).

Gene Scaramuzzo has been involved with the music and culture of the Caribbean since the late 1970s as a writer, musician and radio programmer. He lives in New Orleans.

Anthony Seeger is an anthropologist, ethnomusicologist and musician as well as being curator of Smithsonian Folkways.

Jameela Siddiqi is a novelist, journalist and broadcaster. She writes for *Songlines* and presented the award-winning BBC World Service programme *Songs of the Sufi Mystics*.

Simon Steptoe spent two and a half years studying Javanese and Sundanese gamelan in Surakarta and currently works as Gamelan and Creative Projects Officer for the Halle Orchestra in Manchester.

Sue Steward writes on Latin and Caribbean music for *Straight No Chaser, Songlines, The Daily Telegraph* and *The Independent*, and presents occasional radio programmes. Her book, *Salsa! Musical Heartbeat of Latin America*, was published in 1999 by Thames & Hudson.

Razia Sultanova was born in Uzbekistan, studied in Tashkent and Moscow, and is now researching Central Asian music in London.

Philip Sweeney is a long-time World Music writer, for *The Independent* and other newspapers. He wrote (on his own!) the groundbreaking *Virgin Directory of World Music,* and is currently writing a *Rough Guide to Cuban Music.*

Carol Tingey is a teacher and ethnomusicologist.

Mark Trewin is a Lecturer in Ethnomusicology at Edinburgh University and has done fieldwork in Ladakh.

Richie Unterberger is a music and travel writer living in San Francisco. He is the author of various books, including *The Rough Guide to Music USA* and *Turn! Turn! Turn!: The 1960s Folk-Rock Revolution.* He is also a senior editor for the *All Music Guide.*

Wang Ying-fen is director of the Graduate Institute of Musicology at National Taiwan University. She specializes in nanguan music.

Nigel Williamson writes about World Music for *The Times, Mojo, Songlines* and other publications.

Kurt Wolff is a San Francisco-based freelance writer and author of *The Rough Guide to Country Music.* He didn't grow up listening to Bob Wills or Bill Monroe, but he did learn to drive on a tractor.

Zhang Xingrong is a professor at the Yunnan Art Institute in Kunming and has done extensive musical research in Yunnan province.

Index

Mor lam 170, 247–249, 252
Mor lam sing 171, 249
Morães, Vinicius de 336
Morales, Noro 482
Morales Pino Trio 382
Moré, Beny 390, 400, 495
Moreira, Moraes 339
Morfin, Juan Perez 468
Morgan Heritage 449
Mori, Shin'ichi 148
Morris, Sylvan 443
Morsing 81
Morton, Jelly Roll 533
Motta, Stanley 434
Mouth bow 594
MPB 333, 337, 340, 344–345
Mr Peters Boom & Chime 326, 331
M.P.N. Ponnuswamy 81
M.P.N. Sethuraman 81
Mr Vegas 449, 455
Mridangam 73, 81
Mugam 25, 30
Mughal empire 71
Mughal-e-Azam 74
Mui, Anita 49, 54
Mulate's 562
Muleskinner 544
Multan Local Dance Party 207
Muñequitos de Matanzas, Los 388, 407
Muqam 44, 48
Muria 99
Murli 207
Murray, Neil 15
Murvin, Junior 438
Music Bridges 399
Música campesina 396, 398
Musica gallega 627
Música nordestina 333, 338–339, 349
Música Norteña 606
Música Popular Brasileira (MPB) 333, 337, 340, 344–345
Musica tropical 379
Musiker, Sam 584
Musique Multi-Montréal 358
Muslumov, Mohled 25
Mustapha, Sabah Habas 140
Mutabaruka 443, 453
Mutantes, Os 346
Muzsikás 588, 592

N

Na Hun-a 164
Naat 206
Nação Zumbi 343, 347
Nadagam 231
Nadamuni Band 82
Naftule's Dream 585, 589
Nagama, Takao 154
Nagaswaram 79, 81
Naimro, Claude 296

Nakagawa, Takahashi 150, 158
Nakai, R. Carlos 595, 600, 601
Nakano, Ritsuko 155
Nakayama, Shimpei 148
Nakhichevan 26
Nakornsawan, Arpaporn 251
Nam Jin 164
Namchylak, Sainkho 195, 197
Namiki, Michiko 147
Nandasiri, Sanath 232, 233, 234
Nangma 257, 258
Nanguan 38, 235
Nano S 123, 135
Naramuru, Yoshida 147
Narantsogt 192
Narasirato 'Are'Are Pan Pipers 187
Narayan, Aruna 69
Narayan, Ram 72, 78
Narayanswamy, P.S. 89
Nascimento, Milton 341, 347
Nashville 571
Nashville Bluegrass Band, The 547
Nasida Ria 136
Nasir, M. 180, 182
Nasyid 180
Natarajan, A.K.C. 82
Natay, Ed Lee 597, 602
National Dance Company of Cambodia 23
Native American music 350–351, 359, 593–603
  Canadian 350–351, 359
  gospel music 596
  religious and ceremonial music 596
Native American Flute 593, 595, 601
Naturan, Diomedes 214
Nawahi, Bennie 57, 62
Naxi 44, 46
Naye Kapelye, Di 588, 592
Nazar 206
N'Dour, Youssou 615
Nébbia, Litto 311, 313, 315
Negra Graciana, La 473
Negro spirituals 569
Nemus del Pacifico, Los 380, 497
Nene Band 216
Nenes 154, 159, 620
Nepal 198–202
Netsky, Hankus 585
New Age music 258, 595
New Age, Native American 595
New Formosa Band 238
New Grass Revival 545
New Guinea 183, 187
New Klezmer Trio 585
New Lost City Ramblers, The 533, 538, 549
New South 545
New Taiwanese Song 238
New York
  merengue 417, 425
  salsa 337, 488, 496, 499–500, 501–506
New York Band 420, 500

New York Superstars 425
New Zealand 224, 225, 226, 228, 229
Newar New Year Festival 201
Newars 200
Newfoundland 358
Newgrass 544
Newport Folk Festival 555
NG La Banda 397, 404, 494
Ngan Wat 246
Nguini, Vincent 616
Nhac dan toc cai bien 267
Nhac tai tu 263
NHK 145
Nhung, Hong 268
Nicaragua 368, 371
Niciton 195, 196
Nieves, Tito 491, 505
Night Way 596
Nitty Gritty 446
Nizamuddin Auliya Dargah 205
No Fixed Address 12, 13
Nobat 175
Nogueras, Jose 482
Noh 144
Noi Vanneth 22
Noise 165
Nomad 258
Nongak 160, 163
Nono, Grace 145, 213, 216, 217
Noor, Kamariah 177
Norae Undong 165
Norae-rŭl ch'annŭn Saram-dŭl 165, 169
Norfolk Jubilee Quartet, The 570
Norovbanzad, Namdziliin 190, 191, 196
Norteño 469, 474
North Korea 160, 166, 167
North Tanami Band 9
Northern Cree 352
Northern Québec 351
Nose-flutes 220
Notched-end flutes 274
Notting Hill Carnival, London 515
Nouvel Jenerayshun 424, 425
Nova Scotia 356
Nueva canción 276, 362–371, 408–413
Nueva trova, Cuban 408–413
Nunes, Clara 335, 347
Nuñez, Don Mauro 278
Nurhaliza, Siti 180, 181
Nurjanah, Ikke 133
Nurthi 231
NuYorican Soul 500
Nyingmapa 256
Nyipa, Kesing 178

O

Obeah 323
Obi, Bredda David 326, 330, 331
Oceania 226, 228

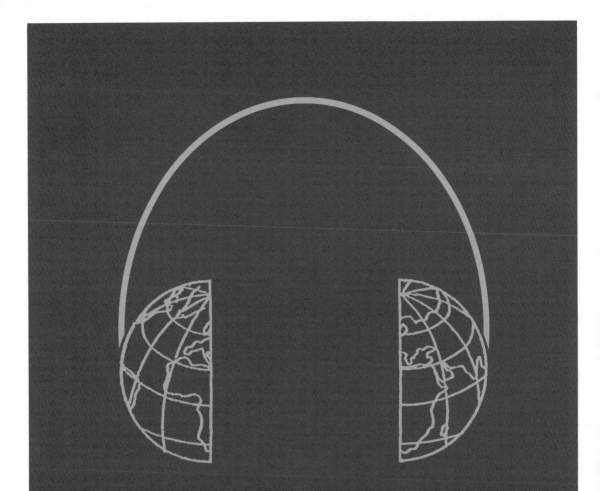

The World Through Your Ears

www.hemisphere-records.com

Utterly essential
Mojo

The Rough Guide to World Music
Volumes 1 and 2

The full range of Rough Guide music titles includes
Opera, Jazz, Rock, Reggae, Classical Music, House, Drum
n' Bass, Techno, Country Music and Music USA.

Forthcoming titles include Blues and Soul

They just improved the bible out of all recognition
Folk Roots